Introduction to Comparative Government

Introduction to Comparative Government

Third Edition

Michael Curtis
General Editor
Rutgers University

Jean Blondel
European University Institute

Bernard E. Brown
City University of New York

Donald P. Kommers
University of Notre Dame

Theodore McNelly
University of Maryland

Martin C. Needler
University of the Pacific

John S. Reshetar, Jr.
University of Washington

James D. Seymour
Columbia University

Stephen Wright
Northern Arizona University

 HarperCollins*CollegePublishers*

Executive Editor: Lauren Silverman
Developmental Editor: Richard Smith
Project Coordination and Text Design: Publication Services
Cover Design: Kay Petronio
Photo Researcher: Karen Koblik
Production/Manufacturing: Michael Weinstein/Paula Keller
Compositor: Publication Services
Printer and Binder: R. R. Donnelley & Sons Company
Cover Printer: The Lehigh Press, Inc.

INTRODUCTION TO COMPARATIVE GOVERNMENT, Third Edition

Library of Congress Cataloging-in-Publication Data

Introduction to comparative government / Michael Curtis, general
    editor ; Jean Blondel . . . [et al.]. – 3rd ed.
        p.   cm.
    Includes bibliographical references and index.
    ISBN 0-06-500552-X
    1. Comparative government.   I. Curtis, Michael, 1923– .
II. Blondel, Jean, 1929– .
JF51.I58   1993
320.3–dc20   92-27395
                                        CIP

94 95 9 8 7 6

Contents

5. The Government of Japan   255

THEODORE McNELLY

6. A Changing Europe   310

MICHAEL CURTIS

PART TWO   COMMUNIST AND
POST-COMMUNIST SYSTEMS   343

7. The Governments of the Former Soviet Union and the Successor States   345

JOHN S. RESHETAR, JR.

8. The Government of China   409

JAMES D. SEYMOUR

PART THREE   THIRD WORLD COUNTRIES   477

Preface

The third edition of this book provides an introduction to comparative government and politics by examining the politics of industrial democratic countries (Britain, France, Germany and Japan), Communist and post-Communist countries (the former Soviet Union and China), and three third world countries in different continents (India, Mexico, and Nigeria). Why have these nine countries been chosen to exemplify the politics, policies, and problems of democratic, changing Communist systems and third world countries? The reason is partly that these countries are of great historical or contemporary significance and have a wealth of political experience. The study of their political systems is interesting in itself and instructive for those wanting to understand the world in which we live. In addition, information about the politics of these countries often provides the main empirical data for the formulation of generalizations in comparative government. This third edition also includes a new chapter focusing on the dramatic changes taking place in both Western and Eastern Europe including the formation of the new European Community.

It should be understood that this book is not based on any narrow or rigid theoretical approach. Instead, the authors prefer that students should be exposed to alternative ways of comparing political systems. The first chapter, the Introduction, therefore proposes a number of alternative classifications of political systems and a general context that allows the nine systems to be compared in different ways.

Both individually and collectively, the nine authors of the book owe intellectual debts to many colleagues who have given valuable advice and also to our students at our different institutions. In particular, we would like to thank Mr. Jerome Maryon, a graduate student at King's College, University of London, for his assistance in preparing the chapter on Germany. We are especially grateful for his help in revising various subsections on the social economy and political parties. We also thank the various readers of earlier drafts of this manuscript, whose comments and suggestions improved the end result: John Wildgen, University of New Orleans; Jim Miller, University of Illinois, Urbana-Champaign; Tony Celso, University of Central Florida; Marguerite Bouraad-Nash, University of California, Santa Barbara; Ben Sanqiang Jian, Kent State University; Kris H. Lou, University of Oregon; Sunil Sahu, DePauw University; Joseph J. Zasloff, University of Pittsburgh. We particularly want to thank Lauren Silverman and Richard Smith, our editors at Harper-Collins, for helping to bring this third edition to fruition.

Michael Curtis

CHAPTER 1

Introduction

Michael Curtis

WHY STUDY COMPARATIVE POLITICS AND GOVERNMENT?

Why should we study the political systems, behavior, and values of other countries? Why should we try to make comparisons between countries? A simple answer is that an essential part of being educated today is knowing something about the politics of foreign countries. For many there is also a fascination and intellectual excitement in the study of foreign systems and in the discovery of political ways of life different from our own.

Study of foreign political systems, or comparative politics, is useful for additional reasons. We can better understand our own system if we can appreciate its similarities to and differences from other systems. We can see, for example, and try to understand why the United States Supreme Court can declare legislation unconstitutional while the highest court in Britain cannot. We can observe that the central authorities in the Soviet Union up to 1991 controlled the republics making up that country to a greater degree than the U.S. federal government controls the states. In both cases we are led to general conclusions about the nature of power in the United States as well as in the other countries. Knowledge of the politics of foreign countries allows us both as citizens and as students to discuss and evaluate more intelligently U.S. policy and attitudes to those countries.

Study of different systems lets us compare the ways in which governments face similar problems and respond to them and to the needs and demands of their citizens. All societies deal with crucial matters such as health, control over the economy, management of production, or changes caused by new technology and by modernization. Students will be interested in the distinctive ways in which different societies deal with problems of this kind. We can learn both positive and negative lessons from experiences such as the National Health Service in Britain, government proposals for economic planning in France, workers' participation in industrial management in Germany, the cooperation of the state and the industrial sector in the development of technology in Japan, the problems of modernization in Communist countries or countries influenced by communism, or from the efforts of a changing, diverse society such as India to maintain a democratic form of government.

An effective comparison of systems must accurately describe and satisfactorily explain the similarities and differences of the systems being compared. The first step in this process is to understand how individual systems, or parts of those systems, function. From the specific information and understanding of the political institutions and the political processes of different countries we may then pose questions of a more general nature. We can ask questions as to the extent and ways in which systems are democratic, their level of political development, their degree of stability or effectiveness in making decisions, or the manner in which political ideologies influence their policy.

To answer questions of this kind we need to decide on some criteria for analysis of the similarities and differences between countries. Such criteria, in turn, may often influence policy.

What criteria should be used to provide generalizations? Since Aristotle (384–322 B.C.) began the study of comparative politics, countless students have analyzed the nature and quality of political regimes. They have looked at the way the functions of government are performed and the relationship between rulers and ruled. Students have also examined the kinds of rules that exist and actions that are taken. They ask if the ruling groups are acting in their own interest or the interest of the whole community. They observe how much force and how much persuasion are being exercised.

The modern method of political science has sought to formulate general statements applicable to the large numbers of particular cases.[1] It argues that a necessary scientific approach means a search for generalizations, regularities of behavior, and—even more ambitiously—laws of the social and political process. The search for generalizations is necessary, and indeed essential, if comparative analysis is to be valuable, but it is not easy because of the multiplicity and diversity of human activities and because of the play of chance factors that affect the political process.[2]

In recent years two major additions have been made in the study of comparative politics. The area of interest was once largely limited to those few countries in Western Europe and the English-speaking world with highly developed institutions and a familiar history. These countries were the principal powers of the world; now there are over 170 nation-states. Students are therefore also interested in the politics of the newer nation-states, in which an increasing part of the world's population lives, and try to include these states within the scope of the generalizations about comparative politics. About 4 billion of the world's 5.3 billion population live in these states. More-

over, students are not content merely with descriptions of political institutions and constitutional arrangements; more attention is now paid to nongovernmental and social organizations and to the political behavior of individuals and groups.

This book takes these considerations into account. Each chapter deals with four essential aspects of the particular country in the following order:

1. *Factors that have helped shape political behavior.* Historical background, geography, economic and social conditions, ethnic and caste groups, religious beliefs and ideologies.
2. *The political process.* The ways in which rulers are chosen, the role of political parties and interest groups, the manner in which individual citizens participate in politics.
3. *The major political institutions.* The way they exercise power, the interrelationship between them, and the restraints on them.
4. *Public policy.* Certain basic functions performed by political institutions in all systems, such as maintaining internal order and external security, resolving the competitive demands of individuals and groups, raising expenditure to pay for services provided by government, regulating the behavior of citizens in differing ways.

The author of each of the country studies provides basic information about all these four aspects without the use of jargon or unhelpful methodologies so that the political system and its policies can be comprehensible.

With information and analysis of this kind we can formulate generalizations that are the heart of comparative politics. Our nine countries can be used for that purpose in a variety of ways that include the following:

1. The nine countries can be compared on the basis of the various political, social,

and economic problems they have encountered, and they can be compared according to their different paths to political development and modernity.

2. The three most important West European countries can be compared with the six non-Western countries. Questions can be raised about general differences in the nature and style of politics in Western and non-Western nations.

3. The two foremost past and present Communist countries—the Soviet Union and China—can be compared with the seven non-Communist countries and also with each other as differences and rivalries emerged between them.

4. The states created after World War II can be compared with the older states. India and Nigeria, two of the most important of the less developed countries, can illustrate the problems facing the newer nation-states in creating stable and effective political systems.

5. The liberal democratic countries can be compared with the nondemocratic countries. Thus, questions can be posed about why some countries are more likely to be democratic than others and what factors are likely to foster democratic systems.

6. The nine states illustrate different kinds of party systems—one, two, or multiparty—and the relations between those systems and governmental institutions and policy.

CLASSIFICATION OF SYSTEMS

Every political system is at once unique and different from all others and is in flux. Britain presents an interesting mixture of traditional and modern forms of organization and behavior. France, though an old state, has had its political continuity disrupted by frequent changes of system and internal divisions. The Soviet Union was the first Communist system to be established; its ruling party controlled not only its own system but also the policies of Communist parties in other countries for many years, until the collapse of its system in 1990–1991. In China, the most populous Communist state, the vast majority of the people are peasants, not proletarians as Marxist theory suggests. Germany and Japan are prosperous democracies that were rapidly successful after the devastation and collapse of their systems from defeat in World War II; Japan now has the highest gross national product per capita of any industrialized country. India is the most populous state, emerging from colonial rule after the war, that has remained essentially democratic in character. Nigeria, with a fifth of black Africans, has alternated between civilian and military rule.

Since political systems do not fit neatly in rigid categories, all classification is at best partial and temporary. Nevertheless, classification serves to illuminate some politically meaningful similarities and dissimilarities. Of the many ways to classify political systems, a few are discussed here.

The Number and Kinds of Rulers

Aristotle is usually regarded as the father of comparative political analysis. His classification (see Table 1.1) was based on the number of people who participated in governing (one, few, or many); on the ethical quality of their rule, depending on whether it was in the general interest or in their self-interest (A or B); and on their socioeconomic status (C). Those regimes that served the interests of the ruling group only were perversions of the true constitutional forms.

Aristotle clearly preferred the aristocratic form (2A) because the mean and moderate were most desirable. Other classical theorists in ancient Rome thought that simple and moderate forms of government would degenerate and that stability depended on the existence of a "mixed state" with all the social classes either participating or being represented to some degree.

Table 1.1   THE ARISTOTELIAN DIVISON

Number of rulers	A Rule in the general interest	B Self-interest rule	C Social group
1. One	Monarchy	Tyranny	King
2. Few	Aristocracy	Oligarchy	The wealthy
3. Many	Polity or democracy	Ochlocracy	The Poor

The Aristotelian theory has been useful in indicating the number and nature of the governing group. Modern democracies including the United States would be in category 3A. But in all systems a relatively small number of people either rule or dominate the political process. This group is sometimes termed the political *elite*. The elite may remain closeed to outsiders as in aristocratic systems or as in Communist or military-dominated systems. In such a case the system is likely to be *monolithic* in that only a single or a limited political point of view is allowed. In other systems the elite is open to the emergence of individuals from a diversity of backgrounds and with different views. The elite then consists not of members of one group but of a number of groups and individuals competing for political power. Systems of this kind, which allow for choice among competing elite groups, are known as *pluralistic* (see Figure 1.1).

Political Culture

Anthropologists have used the concept of culture to provide a total picture of the life, actions, and beliefs of a community. For comparative politics the concept of *political culture* has been used to clarify those community-held beliefs, feelings, and values that influence political behavior. In each community there are sets of attitudes toward the political system. They will depend on knowledge of the way in which the system operates, its personnel, and its policies. They will also depend on the ability of people to participate in the political process and on the degree to which the system is accepted as *legitimate* (the right of rulers to exercise power).

In all countries the political values, norms, and behavior patterns, or political culture, are transmitted to present and future citizens. This *political socialization* is produced by a variety of agencies such as the family, school system, religious bodies, mass media, popular literature and art, fable, heroes, and popular mythology. In developed systems, such as the United States, the family has been thought of as the dominant factor in the process of socialization, though this view has been qualified.[3] Socialization can take place either unconsciously, such as by membership in a caste in India, or more deliberately, as in the communes in China or the kibbutzim in Israel. The impact of all these agencies of socialization varies according to changes in population, and according to social relations, technological innovation, and political events.[4]

Political Development

Attempts to classify systems according to stages of political development have been stimulated by the creation, since 1945, of a large number of states, all trying to establish viable political systems and modernize their economies and societies. One influential early theory of political leadership types was formulated by Max Weber, who classified societies as follows:[5]

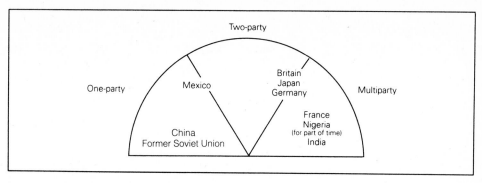

Figure 1.1 Party Systems

Traditional. Based on conformity of the people, rule on the basis of tradition or divine law by a monarch or aristocracy whose power is made legitimate by status or heredity.

Charismatic. Political leadership based on personal magnetism and devotion, and often exercised by a military leader or religious prophet.

Bureaucratic. A constitutional regime in which the legal rules are established and officials adhere to those rules and exercise authority according to known procedures.

Modernization is relatively easy to define, but it is more difficult to define political development. Many recent studies compare two "ideal types" of societies—*traditional* and *modern*—to help explain economic, social, and political differences.[6]

Some of the comparisons made are the following:

1. In traditional societies the vast majority of the population is engaged in agriculture, which accounts for a large part of the gross national product (GNP) of the country. In modern societies, such as that of the United States, only a small percentage of the population works in agriculture, which accounts for a small part of the GNP; in the United States it is now under 3 percent. Instead, the population works in industry and, to an even larger degree, in providing services, which in some countries now account for the majority of the work force.

2. In traditional societies the chief social relationships are the family, the tribe, or the clan, from which the dominant values derive. In modern societies there is a more complex and diverse set of relationships. Individuals belong to a variety of different groups, such as trade unions, business associations, religious faiths, and political and social organizations. The chief values come from a wide variety of sources. Science and technology are significant factors, though religious and traditional values may still remain to some extent.

3. In traditional countries the population is less literate, on average much poorer, shorter-lived, and more rural than in modern countries.

4. Politics in traditional countries have been less differentiated than in modern systems, where political functions are carried out by different categories of people and where political rule is justified by rational principles rather than by concepts like divine right or heredity.

The distinction between traditional and modern does not imply any judgment of inferiority or superiority regarding individuals or societies. Many traditional societies have produced significant cultures, elaborate political structures, and efficient administrative systems.

Factors such as greater industrialization, application of technology and science, economic growth leading to increases in gross national product and per capita income, more education for a larger part of the population, independence of women, increasing urbanization, improved transportation, and Western influence have disrupted traditional societies and changed the economic, social, and political structure in those countries as can be seen in Tables 1.2, 1.3, and 1.4.

Countries have taken different paths to modernity. In some cases the path has been Western-style democracy, in others fascism or communism, and in many of the newer countries different forms of nationalism and social change.

No exact correlation exists between economic and social change and political development. Earlier studies that tried to explain political development simply by trends in a society toward urbanization, industrialization, greater communication, and more education have now proved inadequate explanations of a complex process.

All states have differing mixtures of traditional and modern elements and are at different stages of political development. There is no single way in which the process of political development occurs or any one group that is crucial in that process. Change was fostered in Japan by the aristocratic oligarchy, in Western Europe by commercial traders and capitalists, in Latin America by strong leaders, in revolutionary countries by leaders of a political party or movement, in some countries such as Morocco by traditional authorities, in some African countries by bureaucratic-military elites, and in other new countries such as Nigeria by a variety of groups and institutions.

In all countries the process of political development leads to certain changes, of which some important ones are usually the following:

1. A complex governmental structure in which different institutions and people perform different functions, such as legislative, executive, judicial, and military actions.
2. Attempts to integrate the whole community to achieve a coherent and stable system.

Table 1.2   OUR NINE COUNTRIES AND THE UNITED STATES—POPULATION AND INCOME

	Land area (thousand km)	Population (million)		Urban pop. % 1990	Occupational Distribution, % 1985–88			GNP ($ bil.) 1988	GNP per capita ($)
		1960	1990		Agriculture	Industry	Services		
Britain	244	52.3	57.2	89	2.1	20.1	77.8	702	12,810
China	9,320	657.5	1,139.1	33	73.7	13.6	12.7	356	330
France	547	45.7	56.1	74	6.7	19.8	73.5	899	16,090
Germany	356	72.6	77.6	85	6.2	36.1	57.7	1,360	16,570
India	2973	442.3	853.1	27	62.6	10.8	26.6	271	340
Japan	371	94.1	123.5	77	8.0	23.6	68.4	2,577	21,020
Mexico	1,923	38.0	88.6	73	22.9	20.1	57.0	151	1,760
Nigeria	910	42.3	108.5	35	44.6	4.2	51.2	31	290
Soviet Union (former)	22,227	214.3	288.6	66	20.0	39.0	41.0	399 (GDP)	4,550
United States	9,166	180.7	249.2	75	3.0	19.0	78.0	4,863	19,840

Table 1.3 LABOR AND POPULATION

	Labor force, % of total population 1988–89	Women in labor force, % 1988–89	Occupational Distribution, % 1985–88			Population million 1990	Urban population, % of total 1990	Fertility rate 1990
			Agriculture	Industry	Services			
All developing countries	43.9	31.1	61.2	12.7	26.1	4,070	37	3.9
Least developed	38.8	27.7	73.1	7.0	19.9	440	20	6.1
Industrial countries	48.5	39.6	11.6	28.0	60.4	1,210	73	1.9
World	44.9	33.4	48.9	16.5	34.7	5,280	45	3.5

	Income	
	GNP ($ billion) 1988	GNP per capita ($) 1988
All developing countries	2,540	2,170
Least developed	80	720
Industrial countries	13,510	12,510
World	16,050	3,410

3. A claim to legitimacy of the ruling group based on a secular and more rational view of the right to rule.
4. A widening of political participation in some way to the whole population, which helps choose the ruling group.
5. The ability of government to manage tensions within the system and to implement policies.

One recent suggestion, proposed by the UN Development Program in 1990, is to compare systems using an index of human development rather than relying simply on statistics of productivity or income. The three key indicators would be life expectancy and a healthy life; degree of literacy and knowledge; and purchasing power of individuals. The index compares the quality and welfare of societies by taking

Table 1.4 HUMAN DEVELOPMENT INDEX RATINGS

	Life expectancy at birth 1990	Adult literacy %	Mean years of schooling 1980	Real GDP per capita ($)	HDI rating (1 is top)
Japan	78.6	99	10.4	13,650	0.99
France	76.4	99	9.4	13,590	0.97
Britain	75.7	99	10.8	13,060	0.96
Germany	75.2	99	8.8	13,388	0.95
Soviet Union	70.6	99	7.6	6,270	0.90
Mexico	69.7	84.7	4.0	5,320	0.83
China	70.1	68.2	4.8	2,470	0.61
India	59.1	44.1	2.2	870	0.30
Nigeria	51.5	42.7	1.0	1,030	0.24
U.S.	75.9	99.0	12.2	19,850	0.97

Source: Human Development Report, 1991

account of factors such as education, nutrition, social welfare, degree of inequality, cultural norms, social problems such as drugs, divorce, and homelessness, and extent of political participation and freedom.

Development is affected by many factors. These would include the different rates of economic growth, population increase (now about 2 percent in developing countries compared with 0.5 percent in industrial countries), degree of political stability, extent of ethnic or internal strife, the democratic or authoritarian nature of the political system, and the effect of world trade on a country.

In the developing countries as a whole, average life expectancy has increased by 16 years and adult literacy by 40 percent since 1960. Many of these countries have made striking gains in health and education, and have increased average income. Yet other developing countries have done poorly, and about one-quarter have actually suffered a fall in living standards. Poverty, especially in Africa, remains a serious problem for more than 1 billion people, one-fifth of the world's population,

many of whom lack primary health care and are illiterate. In the world as a whole, and in developing countries in particular, women still lag behind men in power, wealth, and opportunity, though there have been important changes in the lives of women over the last 20 years, as Table 1.5 and Feature 1.1 show.

Is there any correlation between human development and human freedom and civil liberties in societies? There does not appear to be an exact causal relation between the two, but it is clear that countries that rank high on the freedom index, based on compliance with international treaties and conventions of human rights (see Table 1.4 and Table 1.6), tend to rank high in human development. Comparison also shows that between 1985 and 1991 a number of countries became more democratic and enjoyed greater political freedom.

The Economic System

For some analysts the chief characteristic of political systems is the nature of the economic system. Many socialists hold this view, but it is

Table 1.5 WOMEN IN PAID OCCUPATIONS AND POLITICS (EXCLUDING UNPAID HOUSEWORK)

| | Women % of total workers | Occupation per 100 men | | | | Parliamentary Seats, % | | Year vote obtained | Senior and Junior Ministerial Positions 1987 | |
		Admin. management	Clerical sales service	Production transport laborers	Agr. forestry	1975	1987		No.	%
Britain	39	29	225	18	18	4.3	6.3	1918	7	7.9
China	43	12	71	55	88	22.6	21.2	1949	7	2.5
France	40	10	164	18	48	1.6	6.4	1944	4	9.8
Germany (West)	37	20	140	18	82	5.8	15.4	1919	6	8.3
India	25	2	11	15	31	4.3	8.3	1950	4	4.0
Japan	38	8	99	41	91	1.4	1.4	1945	0	0
Mexico	27	18	70	20	14	5.0	10.8	1953	1	1.4
Nigeria	35							1952(S) 1979(N)	4	4.3
Soviet Union	48					32.1	34.5	1917	8	1.0
United States	41	61	183	23	19	3.7	5.3	1920	27	11.7

Source: The World's Women, 1970–1990.

Feature 1.1 **Women in Society and Politics, 1970–1990**

Minority in world—2.63 million of world 5.3 billion; 55 percent of the world's women live in Asia

Live 4–6 years longer than men

Women under 15: 1/5 in developed areas, 45 percent in Africa

Many marry by age 18: 1/2 Africa, 40 percent Asia, 30 percent Latin America

Reduction in rates of childbearing and mortality

Head over 20 percent of all households

Illiterate women increased from 543 million in 1970 to 597 million in 1985 (352 million illiterate men)

Share in labor force: 40 percent East Asia; 39 percent developed countries; 17 percent North Africa and Middle East

Last to benefit from job expansion, and first to suffer from job contraction

Wages are much lower than men's wages, even in developed countries

Workplace generally segregated by sex; women are usually in less prestigious and lower paid jobs, in teaching, clerical, sales jobs

Lower proportion than men in senior positions of power, policy, and decision making, and in high status and high paying jobs

Hold 10 to 20 percent of managerial and administrative positions

Well represented in junior positions in public administration, political parties, unions, business

Less than 10 percent of members of parliament—highest consistent representation in the Nordic countries

Only 6 states in 1991 headed by women

Only 3.5 percent of world's political ministers (in 93 countries, no women ministers); most are in education, culture, social welfare, women's affairs (men largely control defense, economic policy, and political affairs)

Sizeable number (30 percent) of trade unionists and party members in Western Europe, but women hold few leadership positions

Considerably involved in nongovernmental and community-based organizations, in local representative bodies, and in environmental and educational movements

Source: The World's Women, 1970–1990.

---

particularly important for Marxists, who stress the nature of the production process and the social or class relationships that are bound up with particular historical phases of that process. The Marxist philosophy of history differentiates five broad successive types of social relationship. It sees history as propelled by the struggles between classes, the essential con-flict always being between those who own the means of production and those who do not. The state is seen as the reflection of the interests of the dominant economic class and the support of the interests of that class.

In contemporary capitalist systems, such as that of the United States, all organs of power would be seen mainly as organs of the capital-

Table 1.6 THE HUMAN FREEDOM INDEX

The goal of human development is to increase people's choices. But for people to exercise their choices, they must enjoy freedom—cultural, social, economic, and political.

The *World Human Rights Guide,* by Charles Humana, uses 40 indicators to measure freedom:

The right to

- travel in own country
- travel abroad
- peacefully associate and assemble
- teach ideas and receive information
- monitor human rights violations
- use ethnic language

The freedom from

- forced or child labor
- compulsory work permits
- extra-judicial killings or "disappearances"
- torture or coercion
- capital punishment
- corporal punishment
- unlawful detention
- compulsory party or organization membership

- compulsory religion or state ideology in schools
- arts control
- political censorship or press
- censorship of mail or telephone-tapping

The freedom for

- peaceful political opposition
- multiparty elections by secret and universal ballot
- political and legal equality for women
- social and economic equality for ethnic minorities
- independent newspapers
- independent book publishing
- independent radio and television networks
- independent courts
- independent trade unions

The legal right to

- a nationality
- a presumption of innocence until guilt is proven
- free legal aid when necessary and counsel of own choice

- open trial
- prompt trial
- freedom from police searches of home without a warrant
- freedom from arbitrary seizure of personal property

The personal right to

- interracial, interreligious, or civil marriage
- equality of sexes during marriage and for divorce proceedings
- homosexuality between consenting adults
- freedom of religion
- freedom to determine the number of one's children

Our Nine Countries, 1985
(Top is 40)

35	France	14	India
35	Germany	13	Nigeria
32	Britain	3	Soviet Union
32	Japan	2	China
15	Mexico	33	United States

---

ist class; opposing them would be Socialist or Communist systems.

There is an obvious connection among social relationships, the economic system, and political institutions. But there is no automatic correlation between an economic basis such as private ownership of property and political institutions or actions. Marxist theory has not taken account of the complexity and heterogeneity of modern societies and regimes in three main ways. First, nothing in Marxism effectively explains the considerable diversity of political forms that capitalist countries have taken, or the mixture of public and private enterprise in those countries. Second, even at

their zenith, Communist regimes were not a monolithic group (see p. 15). The acute disagreements and intermittent hostility between the Soviet and Chinese regimes reflected both ideological and tactical differences about communism as well as tension between two great rival powers. For almost 20 years China referred to the Soviet Union as *hegemonic,* interested in worldwide expansion. Similarly, the dispute between China and Vietnam, based on different geopolitical interests and historical enmity, led to hostilities in 1979. Third, conflict in politics has resulted from many factors other than class differences. The most important of these, which have often been more meaningful for a political system than class are as follows:

1. *Religion.* Catholics and Protestants in Northern Ireland; Muslims and Hindus in Asia; Muslims and Christians or Jews (see Figure 1.2).
2. *Race.* Blacks and whites in South Africa; blacks and Asians in Uganda.
3. *Language.* English and French-speaking populations in Canada; Flemish- and French-speaking populations in Belgium.
4. *Tribe.* Yorubas, Ibos, and Hausa-Fulanis in Nigeria.
5. *Caste.* The four major castes and thousands of subcastes in India.
6. *Nation.* Basques and Catalans in Spain; Serbs and Croats in Yugoslavia; Kurds in Turkey and Iraq.

Constitutional Democracies

Many contemporary systems describe themselves as democratic. Self-description however is not always accurate. The "people's democracies" of Eastern Europe or Yemen after World War II could more accurately be classified as forms of dictatorship.

Constitutional democracies such as the United States have certain characteristics. There are free elections with competing candidates and a political opposition that is free to criticize the government. The press and other media are free and censorship is rare. People are able to write and speak as they like and to practice any religion they choose. Personal and civil rights are usually respected. A wide variety of unofficial associations exists and no single group or element in society is dominant. The army does not intervene in politics, loyally upholds the regime, and is under the control of the political leaders. Political change takes place by a peaceful process. The rule of law ensures impartial justice for all.

In all constitutional democracies officials who make and enforce law are themselves sub-ject to the law. All government actions must be performed in a legal manner and can be controlled by appropriate authorities. These authorities may include the ordinary courts and the system of common law as in the United States and Britain, an elaborate code of law as in the German *Rechtsstaat*, or special administrative courts such as the Conseil d'État in France.

Constitutional democracies exist, with few exceptions, in the older and more developed political systems and in some countries influenced by them. Of the 5 billion people in the world, about 35 percent (in 48 countries) live under constitutional democracies, another 25 percent (in 54 countries) in partly constitutional systems, and 40 percent (in 56 countries) in nonconstitutional regimes.

Authoritarian Systems

Authoritarian systems or dictatorships may exist because a country has no traditional or standard of constitutional behavior, because there is no general consensus about the desirability of freedom, or because a limited and closed elite dominates the political process. Dictatorship may result from the instability or ineffectiveness of a democratic government, from the desire to put a particular ideology into effect, or from the reaction to economic changes and instability or to defeat in war.

In authoritarian regimes political activity is controlled, all the media are subject to censorship, liberty is restricted, there is no legally recognized opposition, public criticism is rare, and parliamentary institutions are absent or meaningless. Power is exercised by small groups such as military leaders, party officials, bureaucrats, or religious figures. But economic activities can usually be pursued with some independence, a certain degree of cultural freedom is allowed, and voluntary internal and external travel is possible. A large number of modern regimes embody similar characteristics. In many Latin American countries in the past political parties have been

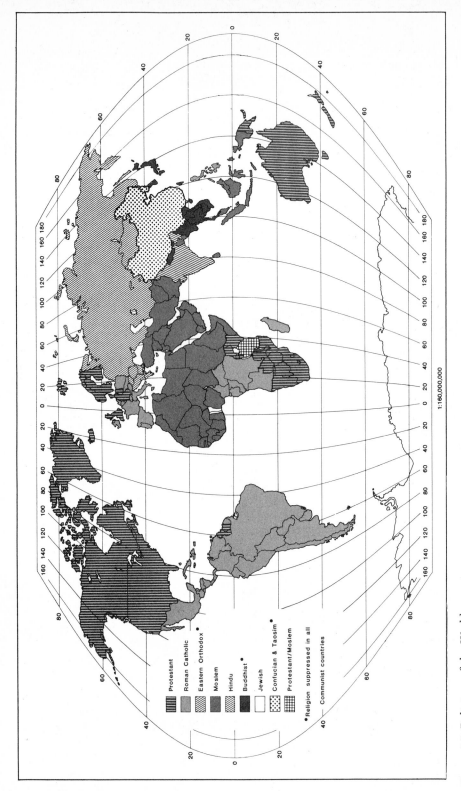

Figure 1.2 Religions of the World

Legend:
- Protestant
- Roman Catholic
- Eastern Orthodox
- Moslem
- Hindu
- Buddhist
- Jewish
- Confucian & Taosim
- Protestant/Moslem
- • Religion suppressed in all
- Communist countries

1:160,000,000

barred or suspended, the press has been censored, and opponents have been imprisoned arbitrarily.

Some authoritarian regimes are personal or party dictatorships supported by a considerable part of the population and interested in general social or economic reform. Such regimes may be based on a particular doctrine or may be more pragmatic and less doctrinaire, such as the Latin American populist systems that have been both nationalist and socially reformist.[7]

Of a different kind are the bureaucratic-authoritarian or authoritarian-corporativist regimes which appeared in Latin America in the 1960s.[8] They were dominated by technocrats, bureaucrats, and military personnel and were not based on labor political support. Often the economies of the countries ruled by these regimes were dependent on foreign capital.

Other authoritarian regimes are military dictatorships. Throughout history the military has interested itself in politics, in exercising power, or in influencing political decisions. In past Asian or Middle Eastern regimes there was little distinction between civil and military authority, the monarch was absolute ruler and controlled the army. The military has often intervened on behalf of politicians, usually those of a conservative disposition. Sometimes civilian political leaders themselves urge the intervention of the military or depend on the approval of the military, as in Turkey in 1908 and 1960. In some Latin American constitutions the military is given the task of guaranteeing the constitutional powers. Thirteen of the 19 Latin American countries were under some form of military rule in 1983. In 1991 there were none.

Sometimes the army leadership, regarding itself as the most honest, most efficient, and most advanced organization in a nation, may turn out the politicians or civilian rulers it believes to be corrupt, misguided, or inefficient. It may do so where political instability results from irreconcilable political divisions or continual political crises, or when the nation has been humiliated by defeat in war.

Totalitarian Systems

The existence of some similar important features in the Communist regime of the Soviet Union under Stalin, the Fascist regime of Italy, and the Nazi regime of Germany led some analysts to suggest a new concept of *totalitarianism*.[9] This concept implies the existence of a new twentieth-century type of system based on a dominant leader supported by a mass party acting on an aggressive ideology that explains and influences political actions.

According to this concept, a totalitarian system differs from an authoritarian regime in that it attempts to control behavior totally and subordinates all organizations and individuals to the ruling group. Whereas authoritarian regimes allow individuals and groups some independence of action, the central feature of totalitarian systems is that the state attempts to control the whole of society, minds as well as bodies, and to this end mobilizes the population, youth as well as adults.

As shown in Feature 1.2, the totalitarian system concentrates power in the hands of an individual or group. It eliminates all opposition parties, controls communication and the mass media, exercises control over the economy and over highly centralized planning, uses religion for its own purpose even though it is fundamentally irreligious, and makes deliberate use of terror as a controlling factor through the secret police, concentration or labor camps, and the completely amoral use of force. A single official ideology and a single party lead to the elimination of dissension, even within the one ruling party, and the refusal to allow any standard of morality other than that of the party or the leader.

The three regimes regarded as prime examples of the totalitarian model—Nazi Germany, Fascist Italy, and the Soviet Union under Stalin, if not after his death—did not embody all characteristics of the model to the same

---

Feature 1.2 Totalitarianism

Leadership by a single, dominant personality
One-party system
Comprehensive ideology based on class, race, or nation
State control over the economy
Monopoly control over the media
Censorship
Powerful secret police
Terror
Concentration camps

---

degree. Moreover, there was in reality less coherence and unity in decision making in these systems than is suggested in the model.[10] Nevertheless, despite the differences in ideology, purpose, and kind of support they obtained, these three regimes were similar in their ruthlessness and extreme dictatorial behavior, and they may be regarded as models of a particular kind of political system, which can be distinguished from authoritarian systems. Moreover, while authoritarian regimes have sometimes evolved into democracies as in the recent cases of Greece, Spain, and Portugal, no totalitarian system had done so until 1989.[11]

Communist and Non-Communist Systems

A classification of systems into Communist and non-Communist has been of great political significance in the making of U.S. foreign policy as well as for theoretical analysis. Communism today is purportedly based on the principles of Marxism-Leninism. From Karl Marx (1818–1883) is derived the belief, or ideology, that capitalism will be overthrown by a revolution of the proletariat, or working class, and be replaced by a classless Communist system after a transitional stage of socialism. In this system the guiding principle would be "from each according to his ability, to each according to his needs."

It was Lenin (1870–1924) who called for the creation of a highly centralized and disciplined revolutionary party to lead the proletariat. His principle of democratic centralism means in practice that all members of the party must adhere to central party policy. The Russian party, which successfully carried out the revolution in 1917, became the model for all Communist parties in both Communist and non-Communist systems.

In the Soviet Union the Communist party exercised control not only over the state and over industrial and agricultural production but also over all social organizations and all forms of communication. Under Stalin (1879–1953) this control was more complete than it was after his death.

For many years the Soviet Union controlled the policies of foreign Communist parties and the activities of regimes created in Eastern Europe after World War II. In the latter systems a Communist party based on Marxist-Leninist principles was the ruling group. All factories were nationalized and agriculture was largely under collective control. Communism was therefore regarded as a monolithic bloc with its center in Moscow.

Starting in the 1960s, the Communist movement began to fragment. The Communist parties in non-Communist systems such as Italy, Spain, and sometimes even France showed a degree of independence and were occasionally critical of the Soviet Union. Some of these parties—sometimes called *Eurocommunist*—declared that they believed in the democratic process and would allow free elections and abide by electoral decisions if they came to power.[12]

In 1948 Yugoslavia, under its Communist leader, Tito, refused to accept orders from the Soviet Union and was expelled from the international Communist movement. The most significant division in the Communist movement, however, was between the Soviet Union and China. In spite of their common claimed inheritance of Marxism-Leninism, the two countries were divided by ideological issues and rivalry for leadership of the international Communist movement, as well as by a dispute over their common border.

The last few years have seen dramatic changes in the former Soviet Union and the collapse of the Communist systems in Eastern Europe. These systems toppled when it became clear that the Soviet Union would no longer use force to maintain the monopoly of power and privileged position of their Communist rulers. The East European states have, at different speeds, introduced elements of a market economy, and some have moved to a more democratic regime.

The political and economic changes during the 1980s in the Soviet Union have stemmed from the policies of *glasnost* (openness) and *perestroika* (restructuring) of the Soviet leader, Mikhail Gorbachev. But the policies were accompanied by violence, internal turmoil, civil war in some parts of the country, and an attempt to overthrow the leader in a coup in August 1991. Gorbachev, who had tried to preserve the Union, resigned in December 1991.

The stagnation of the Soviet economy, marked by scarcity of goods and inefficient modes of production and distribution, led to a call for a move from the centralized command economy under state control to a more market-oriented economy, in which controls would be reduced and individual farming and private business would be encouraged. Total control of resources was regarded as incompatible with the process of modernization and with a modern economy that requires free flow of information and decentralized decision making.

During the glasnost period, one-party rule by the Communist party and democratic centralism gave way to looser political control, competition between different political groups and ideas, relaxation of censorship, open discussion and criticism of official policy, abandonment of Marxism-Leninism as the official creed, some contested elections, and the opening of borders to allow people to travel and emigrate. The Soviet Union has also disintegrated as a political structure, with the rise of nationalism in many of the republics—ethnic group assertion, and religious enthusiasm. The republics have become independent states and the Soviet Union was replaced in December 1991 by the Commonwealth of Independent States, a grouping of most of the former republics in a loose alliance. The Russian Federation took over many of the functions of the former Soviet Union.

The totalitarian system has thus, surprisingly, been transformed from within. It remains uncertain what the former Soviet Union will become, and what economic and political system the republics will adopt. They could become authoritarian states, dominated by a political leader or by the military, or more democratic, constitutional states.

There has always been a further problem in the classification of systems as Communist or non-Communist. It neglects the large number of nations, now the majority in the world, that are neither Communist states nor Western democracies. Since the Bandung Conference of 1955, when 29 African and Asian nations met to discuss their common interests, a group now known as third world countries—most of which achieved political independence since

---

Feature 1.3 Eight Classifications in Comparative Politics

Number and kind of rulers
Political culture
Political development
Economic systems
Constitutional democracies
Authoritarian systems
Totalitarianism
Communist, non-Communist, and third world

1945—has emerged, with some exceptions, as nonaligned in conflicts between the other two groups. Containing a majority of the world's population, these countries themselves vary considerably in wealth, ranging from oil-rich Saudi Arabia to impoverished Bangladesh, and in level of political development and importance. But all of them reject any form of colonialism, advocate political and economic independence, and stress the need for nation building.

The eight classifications of political systems that have been presented throw light on different aspects of political behavior or institutions in different nations (see Feature 1.3). Which one should the student use for analysis and comparison? The answer is twofold. Use the one that illuminates the largest number of features in a system: economic, social, and cultural as well as political. Or use that which is most helpful for understanding a particular issue: the claim to legitimacy of the rulers, the political culture, the relative power of institutions and their personnel, the degree of freedom, the stability or efficiency of the system, or the nature of domestic and foreign policies.

THE POLITICAL PROCESS

For comparative analysis it is useful to study the ways in which the electoral process works in different countries and the parties and groups that play a part in that process. Even nondemocratic countries hold elections, which supposedly demonstrate the solidarity of the people with the existing political leadership and are intended to promote consensus. But to be meaningful, elections must present voters with alternative candidates, parties, or issues from which to choose, and they must be fairly and honestly organized. Elections must also allow peaceful change of government, meaning that all will accept the electoral decision and that, at the same time, the minority will be permitted to oppose the policies of the successful majority.

Political development has meant that an increasing proportion of the population obtains the vote and that there is greater political equality. Gradually, disqualifications for representation based on religion, property, education, and sex are removed. Ownership of property and educational degrees are no longer necessary to vote, and in all but a few countries women are no longer excluded from suffrage. The minimum age limit of 21, once generally accepted, has recently been lowered in many countries.

People generally take part in political activities through membership in a party or interest group, and by voting. In a number of systems opportunities are provided for direct political participation of the people in deciding some issues. The chief forms of such participation are referendums or plebiscites, approval of constitutions, initiatives presenting petitions or bills, and recall of elected officials. In addition to these devices, governments and politicians may take account of the views of citizens expressed in public opinion polls and change their policies or attitudes accordingly. Nevertheless, in all systems the extent of direct participation by any considerable part of the people is limited.

Functional Representation

Earlier assemblies consisted of representatives from the legally defined and hierarchical groups of "estates" into which society was divided. Gradually, in most countries, assemblies began to represent citizens as individuals rather than as members of groups and occupations.

The case for some form of functional representation is still argued by part of the Left, especially guild societies and Socialists; by some pluralists who think representation should take account of occupational activity; and by those advocating a corporate system. (*Corporatism,* which has been prominent in Latin systems, is a system of interest representation in which certain occupational categories participate in official bodies.) The supporters of functional representation believe that geographically oriented parliaments and parties are not sufficiently representative of the economic interests of the community. In spite of the practical difficulty in selecting the functional groups to be represented and in deciding on the relative weight of the different occupations, a number of countries, including France and Germany, have set up various kinds of economic and social councils to represent interest groups. In most countries such councils have been limited to giving advice and possess no real power. Moreover, interest groups have found that they are better able to influence political decisions through direct contacts with governments or parliaments or through membership in official advisory committees than through economic and social councils.

Not surprisingly, functional representation existed in some Communist systems. In the Soviet Union the system of soviets, or councils, supposedly representative of the workers, was not very meaningful in reality. In Yugoslavia, however, the workers' councils in industry and the agricultural cooperatives were of some significance for a time. Yet, even there, the "workers' democracy," which was supposed to be responsive to the demands of workers in factories, was in fact controlled by the Communist party.

Territorial Representation

There are many different methods of territorial representation, whether in single-member or multimember constituencies.

Single-Member Constituencies These are relatively small geographic areas, often approximately equal in population, which elect one representative. The usual method, as in the United States, is that the candidate with the highest number of votes wins—the *plurality* system. This has the virtue of simplicity, tends to limit the number of parties that win seats, and generally fosters a two-party system. One party may gain an absolute majority of seats. Logically, this electoral method can lead to the formation of strong single-party governments and make coalitions unnecessary.

But it is also a system that is mathematically inequitable. A candidate may win with a minority of the total votes cast for the various parties in the constituency, as shown in the following table.

CONSTITUENCY: MANHATTAN, EAST SIDE

Silverman	25,463
Harper	23,185
Collins	14,694
Michel	8,247
Silverman is the winner with 35.5 percent of the votes	

A majority in the legislature may represent a minority of the population, thus distorting national opinion. Minor parties are usually underrepresented because they receive a smaller percentage of seats than of votes cast for their candidates.

Other methods include a second-ballot system, as in France when no candidate has won an overall majority at the first ballot, and the alternative-vote system, which allows for electors to rank the various candidates, and for their preferences to be transferred from the lowest candidates until one candidate obtains a majority.

Multimember Constituencies   There are areas in which a number of representatives are chosen by each voter. When this system is followed in its most extreme form, the whole country might be one constituency, as in Weimar Germany (1919–1933) and in Israel. The least extreme examples are constituencies that elect between two and five members, as in France during the Fourth Republic.

The most common electoral system in multimember areas is proportional representation (PR). Seats in the legislature are allocated to parties in proportion to their share of the electoral vote. A more accurate representation of electoral opinion is thus produced. But PR also produces or perpetuates a multiparty system, thereby usually making government coalitions of different parties necessary because it is extremely rare for one party to obtain an overall majority. Government is thus often less likely to be stable or effective than in the plurality system, though the Scandinavian countries are an exception in this regard. Italy, for example, has had 50 governments in 42 years. Every country using PR has at least four parties of some importance in its legislature. PR also allows small extremist parties to obtain representation.

What is the most desirable electoral system for a nation? The answer is that electoral systems are methods, not ends in themselves. Their value must be related to the political

system as a whole. A single-member plurality system, such as the U.S. system, tends to reduce the number of parties. In Britain it has, with some qualification, allowed a strong government to emerge with a coherent policy. The PR method tends to lead to a multiparty system which accurately reflects electoral divisions; but it also tends to preserve those divisions and to make strong government less probable.

INTEREST GROUPS

Students of comparative politics examine the different kinds of interest groups and the various ways that such groups formulate demands, express political views, and make claims on government.

Pressure on rulers has always taken a variety of forms, ranging from riots, acts of violence, and rebellions to social movements, political parties, and peaceful presentation of petitions. What is distinctive in modern times is the powerful, sustained role of groups in getting or preventing action and in influencing decisions and policy. Interest groups are now necessary for the running of the modern state.

Interest groups are very diverse in character.[13] Many have a formal structure and organization, but some are informal. Some are temporary bodies organized for one specific purpose and often disband when that is achieved. Others are permanent organizations concerned with a continuing problem or issue. Some are concerned primarily with the interests of one party of society, while others are concerned with a common interest or a general problem relevant to the whole society or even to the international community. Some, such as ecological, civil rights, or women's groups, can be regarded as social movements.

The impact of groups depends on a number of factors:

1. The demands of the group and the way those demands are seen by the politicians and officials handling the issue.

2. The functions performed or planned by the state and the degree to which groups are consulted about those functions or can supply information about them.
3. The size, reputation, and cohesiveness of the group and the amount of money and energy it is prepared to expend on the issue.
4. The degree of concern of the members of the group about some particular problem.

This is not a complete list of the relevant factors, but it is helpful to analyze some of these factors when comparing interest groups.

POLITICAL PARTIES

An interest group is concerned with influencing decisions on a limited number of issues; a political party, in addition to this function, is also concerned with running candidates, contesting elections, and holding office. But it is sometimes easier to distinguish between them in theory than in practice. In Weimar Germany the German Farmers' party was essentially an interest group. In the United States an antiabortion group became the Right-to-Life party. In Britain a close relationship exists between the Labour party and the trade unions, which provide over five-sixths of the membership and about 80 percent of the financing of the party.

How then can we define a party? A starting point is to see it as a group of people who hold certain political beliefs in common or who are prepared to support official candidates of the party. Members of a party work together to win elections in order to gain and maintain political power. Parties struggle for power as well as to achieve certain policies and goals.

Parties have been compared in different ways. One interesting method, proposed by an author of this book, is to see them as being of three types: traditional, representative, and mobilizing.[14] Traditional parties reflect the social and economic control of a hereditary or an oligarchic elite and last until that control is ended. Representative parties, such as those in the United States, put forward the views of followers of the parties at a particular time. Mobilizing parties, such as the parties of the third world and most Communist parties until the late 1980s, aim at converting the population to a particular point of view.

The reason for the creation of parties and their main base varies widely as Table 1.7 shows.

POLITICAL INSTITUTIONS

All political systems carry out certain basic functions. Although these functions have been defined in different ways, it is still most useful for beginning students of comparative politics to think of them in the traditional language of

Table 1.7 THE MAIN BASES OF WORLD POLITICAL PARTIES

Main basis	Party
Ideology	Communist, Nazi
Economic interest	U.S. Republican, Lok Dal (Indian farmers)
Religion	Muslim Brotherhood (Egypt), BJP (India)
Nationalism	Scottish National party, Parti Québecois
Ethnic	People's Progressive party (Guyana), Tamil Federal party (Sri Lanka)
Caste	Parts of the Indian Congress party, Janata Dal
Specific issue	Green Party (Germany)
Faction	Japanese Liberal Democratic party, Italian Christian Democratic party
Mobilization	TANU (Tanzania)

legislative, executive, and judicial functions or powers. The legislative function involves discussion of public affairs and enactment of general rules and laws. The executive function involves the application of those general rules to specific cases and the formulation of policy based on those rules. The judicial function involves resolution of disputes between individuals or between individuals and the state.

Constitutions usually determine what institutions are to carry out these functions as well as the extent and limit of their powers.[15] The interrelationship between functions and institutions depends on (1) whether the system is unitary or federal (see Figure 1.3), and (2) whether there is a separation or nonseparation of functions, or powers (which is the word usually used).

A *unitary* system is one in which a set of central institutions exercises authority as in Great Britain, China, or France. Local and regional authorities obtain their powers from the central authority, which can amend those powers if it desires.

A *federal* system is one in which powers are divided between a central government and state or provincial governments. Both levels of government have certain powers of their own derived from the constitution or interpretations of it. The states do not get their powers from the central government; power is shared between the central and state institutions. Federalism is thus more complex than a unitary system.

For comparison, the distinction between federal and unitary systems is useful, but modern trends in government have sometimes blurred the distinction. In many federal systems, such as that of the United States, the central institutions have grown stronger, while in some unitary states, such as Britain and France, some decentralization of power has occurred.

The concept of *separation of powers* originated in the seventeenth and eighteenth centuries as a method of controlling excessive use of power by one group or institution. It involves the establishment of three separate institutions—a legislature, an executive, and a judiciary—each almost exclusively responsible for the exercise of its separate function. It may also entail separation of personnel by forbidding any person to be a member of more than one branch of government at the same time. The United States is a model of this concept of separation of powers.

In systems that do not embody a separation of powers, such as the British, the members of one institution, the executive, are also members of the legislature. The executive usually controls a majority of the legislature and, because of party discipline, can control the legislative process as well as decision making in general. This concentration of power has often led to strong government.

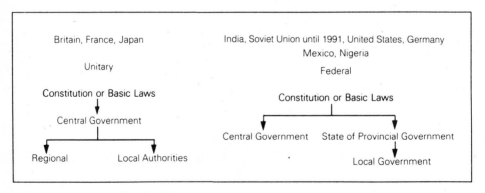

Figure 1.3 Unitary and Federal Systems

Again, it is important to remember that these are *types* of systems rather than exact reality. In all modern systems each institution exercises some functions associated with the other two institutions. Some degree of cooperation between the three institutions is necessary to perform the work of government. A separation of powers need not necessarily result in weak or stalemated government, which may result from a variety of other factors, such as political parties, a strong legislature, an active high court that declares legislation invalid, or the mores of political behavior.

THE POLITICAL EXECUTIVE

The executive branch of government is the major organ of modern political leadership. Its prominence reflects the increase in the activities of the state in domestic affairs and its special role in foreign policy.

The kind of executive branch found in a system is shaped by many factors. A useful beginning method of comparison is to examine the relationship between the executive and legislature. In nondemocratic systems the executive is likely to have almost complete control over the legislature. In democratic systems a more varied relationship exists. Four familiar types are the following:

1. *Cabinet government.* The classical model of this type is the British system, but in this book Germany, Japan, and India also illustrate it in different ways. Political leadership is provided by the cabinet ministers, a small group of leaders of the party or parties headed by a prime minister who control a majority in the legislature, of which they are also members. The link between the executive and the legislature is crucial. The cabinet is collectively responsible to the legislature for political decisions, government policies, and legislative programs. Individual ministers are responsible for the conduct of their administrative departments and for their political actions.

2. *Presidential systems.* The United States is the model for the presidential system, which has been imitated by many other countries. A single head of the executive, the popularly elected president, is both the political leader and the head of state, hence the major policy maker. The president appoints all the chief members of the government and executive agencies. The members of the cabinet are all subordinate and responsible to the president. Collective responsibility to the legislature does not exist. The present Fifth Republic of France is an interesting mixture of the presidential and cabinet systems.

3. *Assembly government.* In this type of system the legislature dominates the executive, which has little disciplined control over legislative and financial matters. The legislature is in many ways the real decision-making body in the system. The regimes most characteristic of this type were the French Third (1875–1940) and Fourth (1946–1958) Republics, with weak political executives, constant government instability—102 governments in the Third and 24 in the Fourth Republic—and few disciplined parties. The legislature saw itself, rather than the executive, as the true representative of the sovereignty of the people.

4. *Council government.* Systems of collective leadership are rare. The oldest example is the Federal Council of Switzerland. This political executive of seven, elected by the legislature, shares ministerial duties and administers the country. Communist systems have also experimented with this type. In the Soviet Union, after Stalin, collective leadership existed for short periods before an individual leader consolidated his political position.

LEGISLATURES AND ASSEMBLIES

All political systems have legislative bodies or parliamentary assemblies of some kind, with members either elected or appointed. Their significance varies over time in an individual system as well as comparatively between one system and another. Assemblies play different roles and exercise functions of different kinds.[16]

Assemblies have declined in power and prestige in most countries in recent years, the United States being the major exception. This decline has occurred for a number of reasons. Government functions and expenditures have greatly increased since World War II. The complexity of both internal and international affairs often prevents members of the legislature from fully understanding issues or having sufficient information about them because of the inadequate research facilities and staff available to them.

The executive can claim to be as representative of the people as is the legislature. The bureaucracy, or permanent administration, at the disposal of the executive has grown substantially in number and significance. The leaders of organized parties have dominated politics, and the mass media, especially television, have tended to concentrate on the personalities of the leaders. In the newer nations the executive is usually viewed as the instrument through which modernization can most rapidly occur (see Table 1.8).

Parliaments are therefore no longer the dominant bodies in political life. Rarely do they control the legislative program, act as a watchdog over government spending and the financial process, or control ministerial behavior in any continuous real way. Democratic governments are created and normally fall as a result of electoral decisions, and only rarely as the result of parliamentary debate. The power of party organizations in generating political leadership and creating disciplined political forces has reduced the possibility of independent behavior on the part of parliamentarians once a party decision on an issue has been made.

PUBLIC POLICY

Comparison of what different countries do—their public policy—is as significant as comparison of the political culture, processes, ideas, or institutions already discussed. Public policy is inevitably related to those other aspects of political systems and can only be explained in the context of the rest of the system. Only

Table 1.8   MAIN FUNCTIONS OF ASSEMBLIES

Activity	Example
Select head of state	Italy, Soviet Union
Approve head of government	Germany, Israel
Approve individual ministers of government	United States
Hold ministers accountable by motions of no confidence or censure	Britain, Italy
Impeach the executive	United States
Support the executive	Soviet Union
Pass legislation	Most systems
Debate	India, Switzerland
Question ministers	Canada, Netherlands
Hold committees of inquiry into government action	United States
Provide criticism as loyal opposition	Britain
Maintain financial control	United States
Act as ombudsman or parliamentary commissioner	Sweden, New Zealand

then can one attempt to answer such questions as why the United States does not have a national health insurance system while Germany has had one since 1883, or why it has traditionally been easier to get support for public housing in Western Europe than in the United States, or why the United States has been so far ahead of other countries in the development of a public education system extending to the whole population.[17]

Multiple Affairs of State

It is true of all countries that the role of government has grown in the twentieth century. The state is no longer limited, as in earlier times, largely to maintaining internal order and external defense, providing a minimum of basic services, and raising taxation to pay for these activities. Government has expanded for a wide variety of reasons: economic recession, war, social justice, help for the underprivileged, protection of minority rights, demands for the redistribution of income or wealth, and the ideas of social reformers.

States are now concerned with a mix of policies concerning social welfare, economic management, and protection of the environment. A substantial part of government budgets is spent on defense, either directly on the armed forces and weaponry or indirectly on research and the development of technology. But spending on social services is now the largest item in many budgets and continues to grow as people live longer and more is spent on pensions and hospitals.

In all states—liberal, socialist, conservative, or communist—there is some economic planning, though to considerably different degrees. Attempts are made to stimulate economic growth, to increase employment, to check inflation, to get a favorable balance of trade with foreign countries, and to regulate industry and other economic activities, from mining coal to making cigarettes. Governments have recently become increasingly aware of ecological and aesthetic issues and of

the need to improve the quality of life in their countries.

Governments are also faced with a variety of problems that may limit their capacity to act. In some countries a backlash has occurred against the rising cost of programs, which has necessitated both an increase of taxation to pay for them and a larger bureaucracy. U.S. government spending has risen faster than gross national product since 1960. A state may not be able to cope with all the demands made on it or with the increased expectations of citizens. Some observers have suggested that government may become "overloaded."[18] External factors, such as the very rapid increase in the price of oil in the 1970s, may accelerate the process of inflation and increase unemployment, causing further transfers of resources from a country.

Why Do Public Policies Differ?

Political scientists differ in the importance given to political and other variables in explaining the diversity of public policies. The following paragraphs look at some of the relevant factors without ranking them in order of importance.

Political Structure and Institutions   The likelihood and kind of actions taken by the state will be affected by some of the factors discussed previously: a unitary or federal system, separation or nonseparation of powers, national or locally based parties, democratic or nondemocratic politics, the nature of the elite political group(s), and the qualities and interests of the civil service.

The Political Process   Relevant here is whether political decisions are based on ideology or are more pragmatic and the result of bargaining, as in the United States. Public policies will also depend on the strength of interest groups and the nature of the party system.

The Prevailing Ideas in the Community   Public policy will differ depending on whether the dominant ideas are those of liberalism, democratic socialism, communism, conservatism, nationalism, fascism, or anticolonialism. It is probable, for example, that Americans more than most peoples want the state to play a limited role.[19] Ideas, in turn, are partly a response to current social problems and to the external concerns of the country and its international role.

The Basic Elements of the Social System   Factors such as the geography of a country, demographic and racial composition of the population, economic and occupational distribution, and the degree of literacy will affect policy. Some studies argue, for example, that factors like economic development, the age structure of the population, and the age of the social security system explain most of the differences in the social security expenditures in different countries.[20]

CONCLUSION

We have now reviewed the reasons why individual political systems should be studied and why comparisons are useful. We have looked at the various bases on which comparison may proceed, at some major differences among systems, and at some major categories in which different systems may be analyzed. The reader is now invited to begin the challenging and exciting task of understanding a number of the major countries in the world and to compare their political systems in a meaningful way.

Key Terms

assembly government
authoritarian
behavioralism
bureaucracy
cabinet government
charismatic
coercion

communist
constitutional democracy
developing countries
elite
Eurocommunism
federal system
functional representation
glasnost
Mikhail Gorbachev
gross domestic product (GDP)
gross national product (GNP)
human development
human freedom
interest groups
legislature
legitimacy
liberal
Marxism
modernization
multimember constituency
parliament
party system
perestroika
political culture
political development
political socialization
presidential system
proportional representation (PR)
separation of powers
single-member constituency
socialist
Stalin
third world
totalitarian
trade unions
unitary system

Notes

1. David Easton, *The Political System* (New York: Knopf, 1953), p. 55.
2. Albert O. Hirschman, *A Bias for Hope* (New Haven: Yale University Press, 1971), p. 27.
3. M. Kent Jennings and Richard G. Niemi, *The Political Character of Adolescence* (Princeton: Princeton University Press, 1974).

4. Gabriel A. Almond and Stephen J. Genco, "Clouds, Clocks, and the Study of Politics," *World Politics* 29, no. 4 (July 1977), p. 495.

5. Max Weber, *From Max Weber,* H. H. Gerth and C. W. Mills, eds. (New York: Oxford University Press, 1946).

6. Bernard E. Brown, in John Wahlke et al., eds. *Government and Politics* (New York: Random House, 1966), pp. 214–216.

7. Gino Germani, *Authoritarianism, Fascism and National Popularism* (New Brunswick, N.J.: Transaction, 1978).

8. David Collier, ed., *The New Authoritarianism in Latin America* (Princeton: Princeton University Press, 1979).

9. Carl Friedrich and Zbigniew Brzezinski, *Totalitarian Dictatorship and Autocracy* (New York: Praeger, 1961).

10. Michael Curtis, *Totalitarianism* (New Brunswick, N.J.: Transaction, 1979).

11. Jeane J. Kirkpatrick, *Dictatorships and Double Standards* (New York: Simon and Schuster, 1982).

12. Bernard E. Brown, *Eurocommunism and Eurosocialism* (New York: Cyrco Press, 1979).

13. David Truman, *The Governmental Process* (New York: Knopf, 1951); Samuel Finer, *Anonymous Empire* (London: Pall Mall, 1958).

14. Jean Blondel, *Political Parties: A Genuine Case for Discontent?* (London: Wildwood House, 1978).

15. K. C. Wheare, *Modern Constitutions* (New York: Oxford University Press, 1963).

16. Jean Blondel, *Comparative Legislatures* (Englewood Cliffs, N.J.: Prentice-Hall, 1973).

17. A. J. Heidenheimer, H. Heclo, and C. T. Adams, *Comparative Public Policy: The Politics of Social Choice in Europe and America* (New York: St. Martin's Press, 1975).

18. Michel Crozier, S. P. Huntington, and J. Watanuki, *The Crisis of Democracy: Report on the Governability of Democracies* (New York: New York University Press, 1975).

19. Anthony King, "Ideas, Institutions and the Policies of Governments: A Comparative Analysis," *British Journal of Political Science* 3, no. 3 (July 1973), pp. 291–313.

20. Harold Wilensky, *The Welfare State and Equality* (Berkeley: University of California Press, 1975), pp. 27–28.

Suggestions for Further Reading

Adrian, Charles F. *Politics and Economic Policy in Western Democracies* (North Scituate, Mass: Duxbury, 1980).

Ball, Alan R. *Pressure Politics in Industrial Societies* (Basingstoke: Macmillan, 1986).

Bill, James A., and Carl Leiden. *Politics in the Middle East,* 2nd ed. (Boston: Little, Brown, 1984).

Dye, Thomas R. *Understanding Public Policy,* 3d ed. (Englewood Cliffs: Prentice-Hall, 1978).

Eidlin, Fred. *Constitutional Democracy: Essays in Comparative Politics* (Boulder: Westview, 1983).

Hodder-Williams, Richard, and James Ceaser. *Politics in Britain and the United States: Comparative Perspectives* (Durham: Duke University Press, 1986).

Hollander, Paul. *The Many Faces of Socialism: Comparative Sociology and Politics* (New Brunswick: Transaction, 1983).

Kavanagh, Dennis, and Gillian Peele. *Comparative Government and Politics* (Boulder: Westview, 1984).

Lijphart, Arend. *Democracy in Plural Societies* (New Haven: Yale University Press, 1977).

Norris, Pippa. *Politics and Sexual Equality: The Comparative Position of Women in Western Democracies* (Boulder: Rienner, 1987).

Putnam, Robert D. *The Comparative Study of Political Elites* (Englewood Cliffs: Prentice Hall, 1976).

Runciman, W. G. *Social Science and Political Theory* (New York: Cambridge University Press, 1969).

Sartori, Giovanni, *Parties and Party Systems* (New York: Cambridge University Press, 1976).

Smith, Gordon R. *Politics in Western Europe: A Comparative Analysis,* 4th ed. (London: Heineman, 1983).

Weiner, Myron, and S. P. Huntington, eds. *Understanding Political Development: An Analytical Study* (Boston: Little, Brown, 1987).

Welch, Claude. *No Farewell to Arms? Military Disengagement from Politics in Africa and Latin America* (Boulder: Westview, 1987).

Welsh, William A. *Leaders and Elites* (New York: Holt, Rinehart and Winston, 1979).

Wiarda, Howard J. *New Directions in Comparative Politics* (Boulder: Westview, 1985).

Wilson, Graham K. *Business and Politics: A Comparative Introduction* (London: Macmillan, 1985).

ONE

Industrial Democracies

CHAPTER 2

The Government of Great Britain

Michael Curtis

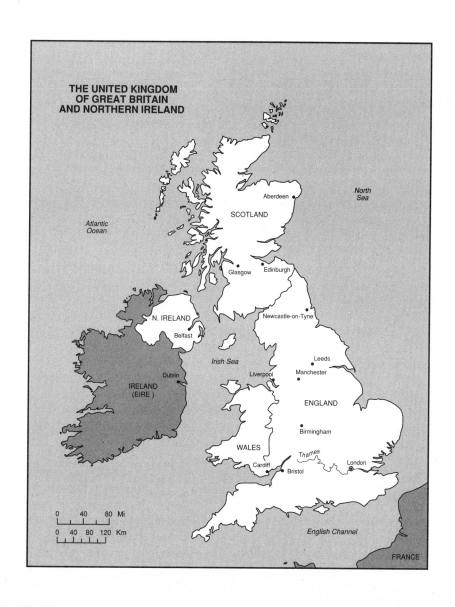

THE UNITED KINGDOM OF GREAT BRITAIN AND NORTHERN IRELAND

A. Political Development

Why study the British political system? There are a number of answers to this understandable question. Britain has the oldest operating political system in the world; some of its governmental institutions have been in continuous existence for nearly a thousand years. Symbolically this is illustrated by the memorials to many notable figures in public and cultural life in Westminster Abbey, the building of which was begun in the eleventh century. No one needs to be reminded of the intellectual and literary influence of Britain's writers, such as Chaucer, Shakespeare, Milton, Austen, Dickens, Shaw, Woolf, and Auden, and its philosophers, such as Hobbes, Locke, Hume, Mill, Bentham, and Russell. Its political influence, both directly and indirectly, has been equally important.

Through its former control of about one-quarter of the world's population on every continent, Britain has directly influenced many countries, including the United States. From Britain, the United States has absorbed a similar idea of the rule of law and a concern for personal freedoms. There are similar political institutions, such as a single-member-constituency electoral system for the lower house, a two-chamber legislature, a two-major-party system, a cabinet, and a civil service based on merit. Oscar Wilde once said that

Britain and the United States were two countries separated by a common language. Certainly there are great differences in the way that political power is exercised and institutions function in the two countries. Nevertheless, it was appropriate that the British memorial to President John F. Kennedy be placed at Runnymede, where King John was tamed by the feudal barons into signing the Magna Carta in 1215.

Today the British Empire, on which the sun never set, no longer exists. But most of the countries once ruled by Britain belong to the 50-member Commonwealth with its population of over 950 million. Though not a political power in itself, the Commonwealth is a unique organization and the largest multiracial association in the world.

Indirectly, Britain has influenced other countries by its political ideals and values, and by some of its political practices, such as a meaningful parliament which could control the excesses of executive power, an officially recognized loyal opposition, political moderation and tolerance, and a process of change by gradual and peaceful means.

The British system is also instructive for those interested in modernization and political development. Britain was the world's first industrialized country, a process which began at the end of the eighteenth century. For Karl Marx, Britain was the model of the capitalist system in the middle of the nineteenth century. The proportion of the working population employed in factories and manufacturing rose while that in agriculture declined. With the repeal of the Corn Laws in 1846, allowing the entry of cheap food, and the adoption of free trade principles, Britain lived by exporting its manufactured goods and by importing food and raw materials. As a result, the country has been very concerned with problems of foreign trade and international exchange. London became the financial center of the world in banking, insurance, and shipping, and the British currency, the pound sterling, became the medium for much of the world's trade.

A century ago Britain was the workshop of the world, producing two-thirds of the world's coal, half of its iron, over half of its steel, half of its cotton goods, and almost all of its machine tools. Britain's exports of capital goods—machines and technology—led to industrialization in other major countries, which soon became competitors and began to supplant Britain technologically and industrially. Yet with the industrial exports had also gone other exports such as ideas, institutions, and ways of life. Britain was the foremost example of the process of modernization and industrialization without a revolution from either above or below.

But Britain has also paid a heavy price for having the first mature industrial system and for being dependent on international trade. Its capital equipment became outmoded, and its relative economic position in the world weakened as other countries advanced industrially. Its dependence on imports of food and raw materials made it vulnerable to outside forces.

In the modern age Britain has become a postindustrial society with a mixed economy and a significant social welfare system, in which private enterprise coexists with a public sector and public expenditure now amounts to about 40 percent of the gross national product. In the 1980s Britain was acutely troubled by

problems such as inflation, less than full employment, and comparatively slow economic growth, which have plagued other advanced nations to differing degrees.

POLITICAL DEVELOPMENT

The British system illustrates the gradual evolution from internal chaos and divisions, which resulted in the Wars of the Roses between rival contenders for the throne in the fifteenth century and the Civil War between the king and Parliament in the seventeenth century, to a stable unitary system with a long process of development of political structures, institutions, and behavior.

Britain exemplifies political change from a strong monarchy with an important aristocratic class to a political democracy. A constitutional monarch reigns over a country in which the parliamentary cabinet system and political parties are the dominant political organizations representing the different political expressions of the power of the people. With the gradual expansion of rights and privileges and the removal of civil and religious disabilities, all can legally participate in politics without discrimination (see Table 2.1).

But all political systems retain certain traditional practices and institutions that seem to run counter to the logic of political development. In Britain these would include anomalies such as the continued existence of the House of Lords, now composed of over 1200 members, most of them hereditary peers; the rebuilding of the destroyed House of Commons after World War II so that it physically resembles the old chamber and can seat only half of its members; and the uses of eighteenth-century wigs and gowns by the Speaker of the House of Commons and by the judges and barristers in the High Courts of Law. Indeed, it is ironic that the leading political figure, the prime minister, was long paid for holding an office, First Lord of the Treasury, which no longer has a function, but was not paid for being prime minister, the func-

Table 2.1   REMOVAL OF POLITICAL AND CIVIL DISABILITIES

1656	Jews allowed back into the country
1689	Toleration Act—members of all religious orders except Catholics and Unitarians permitted freedom of worship
1774	Residency qualifications for members of Parliament declared unnecessary
1778	Some restrictions against Roman Catholic worship removed
1779	Dissenters relieved from subscribing to some of the 39 Articles
1807	Slave trade abolished
1828	Dissenters allowed to become members of Parliament
1829	Catholics permitted to become members of both Houses of Parliament
1858	Jews permitted to become members of both Houses of Parliament
	Property qualification for members of Parliament ended
1871	University religious tests abolished
1872	Secret ballot instituted
1888	Atheists allowed to be members of Parliament

tions of which are nowhere legally or precisely defined.

There is no end to political development in Britain. In recent years the British system has been responding to social and cultural changes as well as to economic difficulties and political problems. Innovations such as the referendum on the European Community in 1975, the proposal for devolution of power to Scotland and Wales in 1978, and the restoration of direct rule in Northern Ireland since 1972 have been just some of the responses. The Labour party exercised power between 1974 and 1979 even though it was supported by less than a majority in the House of Commons. New parties of the political center, such as the Social Democrats, were started and ended in the 1980s. Britain has been trying to find a new role in international affairs after its days of imperial glory and since becoming a member of the European Community in 1973. In public policy, British governments have tried to overcome the difficulties of slow economic growth, trade union power, and poor management by attempts at voluntary price and income controls and then by removal of those controls.

BRITAIN AS A MODEL IN POLITICS

For the student of politics, Britain has long been useful as an example in the comparison of different systems. Britain with its constitutional and civilian government, essentially two-party system, and representative democracy, has been instructive for this purpose.

Britain has adhered for three centuries to the subordination of the military to political power, and the military has been loyal to governments of all political complexions. Not since Oliver Cromwell's government (1653–1658) has Britain had a military dictator or been seriously threatened by fear of a military coup. Britain had also been an example of an essentially two-party system as distinct from regimes with one dominant party, a number of parties, or none at all. In Britain, as in the United States, only two parties have, in effect, been strong enough to share the bulk, though a declining proportion since the 1960s, of the electoral vote and exert political control while alternating in the exercise of executive power.

Britain is a *constitutional democracy*. All citizens, individually and through organizations, can participate and attempt to influence political decisions. For the most part this is done indirectly through the electoral system, by which the representatives of the people are sent to the House of Commons, the powerful chamber of Parliament, the supreme legal power in the country. The *representative* system based on the *majority principle*, by which a simple majority is sufficient to win, is also premised on the permitted existence of political minorities, which have the right to try to become the majority in their turn, and on basic freedoms of speech, meeting, and the press which allow political commentary of all kinds.

Britain is one of few countries which do not have a single formal document regarded as a constitution to define the political system and state the rights and duties of citizens. Unlike most other systems, all changes of a constitutional nature take place without any special legal provision for them; nor is there a supreme or constitutional court to decide on the constitutionality of legislation passed by Parliament. But Britain is the classical example of a system that is "constitutional" in the sense of adherence to rules and to accepted ways of political behavior as contrasted with countries that are nonconstitutional, or arbitrary, in their political practices.

The British constitutional framework results from the following different components (see Figure 2.1).

1. A number of legislative statutes and documents of outstanding importance have provided the foundations of a considerable number of political institutions. These include the Magna Carta, 1215; the Petition of Right, 1628; the Bill of Rights, 1689; the Habeas Corpus Act, 1679; the Act of Settlement, 1701; the Acts of Union with Scotland in 1707 and with Ireland in 1801; the Franchise Acts of 1832, 1867, 1884, 1918, 1928, 1948, 1958, 1963, and 1969; the Parliament Acts, 1911 and 1949; the Crown Proceedings Act, 1947; the Ministers of the Crown Act, 1937; the Nationalization Acts between 1947 and 1950; the European Communities Act, 1972; the British Nationalization Act, 1981; the European Communities (Amendment) Act, 1986. They differ from other statutes, not in a technical sense, but only in their political importance.

2. Certain principles have been established by common law, which is comprised of the decisions of judges and the courts in individual cases. Personal liberties of speech, press, and assembly are to a considerable degree the result of judicial decisions over the last two centuries.

The most important principle is the rule of law, which implies the certainty of legal rules rather than arbitrary judgments in determining the rights of individuals and in examining the behavior of authorities. There is no punishment unless a breach of the law has been established in a court of law. False imprisonment is prevented by a writ of habeas corpus, by which an individual obtains an explanation of the reason for detainment. The rule of law also implies that everyone, includes all officials, is subject to the law. No one can plead the orders of a superior official in defense of illegal actions or can claim the right to be tried in a special court under a different code for official actions.

In recent years some, such as the group Charter 88, have argued for a more formal bill of rights provided by a written code as in the United States. This demand has grown largely as a result of two of Britain's external agreements. Britain ratified the European Convention of Human Rights in 1951 and has

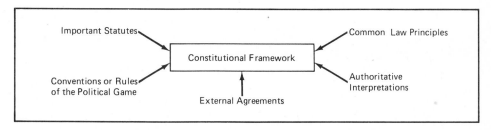

Figure 2.1 The Constitutional Framework of British Government

thus been subject to grievances taken before the European Commission on Human Rights, which has decided against Britain on several occasions. The British government must therefore decide whether to alter domestic law if it does not agree with the European convention. Furthermore, British membership in the European Community, the laws of which may take precedence over British law, has allowed judges to decide on conflicts between the two sets of law.

Yet, though the British judiciary in the 1970s occasionally ruled against the interpretation by ministers of the extent of their powers, it still cannot rule on the validity of statutes passed by Parliament. Britain does not have a court like the United States Supreme Court that can declare legislation unconstitutional.

3. Certain books written by constitutional experts are regarded as so authoritative that some of their views on constitutional issues are commonly accepted. They include such works as Walter Bagehot's *The English Constitution,* A. V. Dicey's *Introduction to the Study of the Law of the Constitution,* and Erskine May's *Parliamentary Practice.*

4. Numerous political rules and practices, known collectively as *conventions,* are observed by all participating in the system. Though they have never been passed in any formal or legal manner, they are usually observed as completely as any laws. Occasionally, however, there may be differences about the exact meaning of a convention. Among the most important of these conventions are the following:

a. The real heads of the government are the prime minister and the cabinet.
b. The government is formed from the party that can control a majority in the House of Commons.
c. Cabinet ministers will normally be chosen from the two Houses of Parliament, and the prime minister will come from the House of Commons.
d. The cabinet will operate on the basis of *collective responsibility* to ensure political unity.
e. The government will resign or ask for a dissolution of Parliament if defeated in the House of Commons on a motion of no confidence.
f. The monarch will ultimately accept the wishes of his or her government.
g. Only the government can propose votes on grants of money in the House of Commons.
h. Those affected by a proposed action will normally be consulted by the government before a final decision is made.

Without these conventions, regular and orderly government in its present form could not function. They create harmony between the executive and legislative branches of the government through various understandings about the workings of the parliamentary cabinet system. The conventions ensure that government is ultimately responsible to the will of the people because an election decides which party is to form the government and thus who is to be prime minister. In a society such as the British, in which traditional institutions have survived changing political circumstances, as the monarchy has done in a political democracy, conventions allow institutions to adjust to political reality.

Conventions are observed not because it is illegal to disregard them, but because they enable the political system to work in accordance with the agreed fundamental principles on which consensus exists.

THE IMPORTANCE OF CONSENSUS AND ITS LIMITS

Britain until very recently has been a model of political stability and consensus. This consensus on the nature of the regime and on the method of change has been the outcome of two factors: (1) "the quiet and orderly habits of the people,"[1] and its generally nonviolent behavior by comparison with other European countries, and (2) the avoidance of any serious political disruption, except in Ireland, arising from religious differences. British politics has depended on all participants abiding by "the rules of the political game" or understandings. These rules[2] include the pragmatic working and adaptation by gradual change of political institutions and organizations; tolerance of different political positions; the belief that government should govern, and with adequate powers; agreement on procedural matters, the validity of political dissent and of trade union organization, through which the working class has a stake in the system: the view that the people should be consulted about political action, through their representatives and groups to which they belong; and moderation in political behavior.

All parties accept the essence of the British political system: a stable democracy which provides for the exercise of strong power by the government, but which also allows substantial personal freedoms and rights. There has been an alternation of political power between the parties in a system characterized by a limited constitutional monarchy, a bicameral parliament, the supremacy of parliament, the linking of the executive and the legislature through the members of the government sitting in parliament, the responsibility of the government to parliament and indirectly to the people, an independent nuclear deterrent.

All accepted the existence of a welfare state, the need for full employment and adequate incomes, free collective bargaining, a mixed economy with both private and state enterprises, and a foreign policy based on membership in the Western alliance and on an independent nuclear deterrent.

However, that consensus on substantive issues has been qualified in two ways. Alternation of Labour and Conservative governments in the 1970s led to reversal of policies, sometimes called "adversary politics," in a number of areas including rent control, old age pensions, and comprehensive schools. Even more significant, Conservative governments under Margaret Thatcher and John Major since 1979 reduced and sold off a considerable part of the public sector in their efforts to obtain a more efficient and competitive economy and a more self-reliant society, and tried to reduce the influence of trade unions and curtail the spending of local authorities.

POLITICAL STABILITY

The last revolution was in 1688. How is this remarkable political stability to be explained? There are various explanations of why the British people accepted the political institutions and those classes which controlled them. Some of them are analyzed in the following paragraphs.

Political Culture

The acceptance by the population of political authority on the one hand, and the existence of individual rights on the other, has resulted in political moderation. The balance among the British people between limited political activity and general acquiescence in what government does has led to an attachment to the political system and to agreement on the rules of political behavior. Britain has been regarded as the model of a democratic political culture in which there is regular competition for the control of government (the existence of which is dependent on the electoral will of the people). Training in this civic culture takes place in many social institutions—for example, the family, peer group, school, and workplace—as well as in the political system itself.

Deference of the People

Since Bagehot introduced the idea,[3] some have stressed the deference of the population, including a significant part of the working class, to the social elite or members of the upper social classes, the well-born or the wealthy, who because of their social position are regarded as the natural or uniquely qualified political leaders by a people that accepts traditional values and authority. In practice, the Conservative party came to be regarded by many as the embodiment of the natural ruling class or as particularly gifted to govern. But whatever the significance of the deference of people in the past, the fact that the Conservative party did not win four of the nine elections since 1964 has suggested that deference is less important today and not the sole explanation of the political stability.

Pattern of Authority

Some analysts suggest that there is a correlation between the pattern of authority in government and administration and that in parties, interest groups, and nonofficial organizations and institutions.[4] In Britain the pattern is strong leadership, which is efficient and can make itself obeyed but which is limited by substantive and procedural restraints. There is minimal direct participation by the vast majority of the population. Voters choose between alternatives presented by party leaders. The parties themselves are not only disciplined but also dominated by the leadership.

Traditional values uphold leadership and authority in politics and society. They permeate the elite institutions such as the monarchy, the established Church, the "public" schools, Oxford and Cambridge, the military and administrative hierarchy, and the senior civil service.

Relative Deprivation

One hypothesis[5] suggests that the feeling of people that they are deprived economically or socially—and their consequent political behavior—depends on with which other people or group they compare themselves rather than on real social conditions. The British working class has usually not taken the nonmanual underprivileged classes as a comparative reference group. Therefore, the working class's feeling of deprivation has not been as strong as objective inequalities might have led them to believe. This, in turn, has produced a less disruptive and more passive political attitude.

Effect of Geography

Perhaps the most important single factor explaining British stability and the continuity of social and political life is that Britain is an island. Since 1066 the existing political institutions have not been disrupted by invasion. This happy fact permitted the creation of stable borders, a luxury not enjoyed by other European countries that were forced into wars to create or maintain national unity. Moreover, this island power developed both a navy (until 1939 the largest in the world) for its protection, as well as a shipping fleet that became the basis for its commercial expansion, capital accumulation, and the conquest of an empire, which at its height consisted of over 15 million square miles of territory on every continent of the world.

THE UNIFIED SYSTEM

The process of unification of the country took more than five centuries. The United Kingdom is now composed of four national units on two main islands and surrounding small islands. England constitutes 52 percent, Wales 9 percent, Scotland 33 percent, and Northern Ireland 6 percent of the total area. Northern Ireland, or Ulster, constitutes 16 percent of the area of the second island, the rest of which is occupied by the Republic of Ireland (see Table 2.2).

The British population is a heterogeneous mixture of people: Celts, Romans, Scots, Picts,

Table 2.2   THE UNITED KINGDOM

	Area (000 square miles)	Population (million)
England	50.3	47.2
Scotland	30.4	5.2
Wales	8.0	2.8
Northern Ireland	5.4	1.5
Total	94.1	56.7

Angles, Jutes, Danes, Norsemen, Normans, East Europeans, West Indians, and Asians. With the recent large increase in nonwhite[6] immigrants, who constitute 6 percent of the total population, Britain is now a multiracial society. But the prospect of much greater immigration from the Caribbean and Asian Commonwealth countries such as India, Pakistan, and Bangladesh, led to limitations on that immigration by statutes in 1962, 1968, and 1971, which were passed after there had been a certain amount of opposition in the country.

Though English is the standard language (the form spoken in the southeast is the most prestigious norm), other languages are also spoken. About 20 percent of the Welsh population speaks Welsh, a form of British Celtic which is of equal validity with English in the administration of justice and the conduct of government business in Wales. Some 2 percent of the population of Scotland, mainly in the Highlands and western coastal regions, speak Gaelic, and about 2 percent in Northern Ireland speak the Irish form of Gaelic. The newer Asian communities speak a variety of languages.

A NEW PLURALISTIC SYSTEM?

Although Britain is a pluralistic society in ethnic origin, language, religion, and race, the differences have rarely caused political problems affecting the unity and centralization of the system. But in recent years the issue of race and the emergence of nationalist senti-

ment have upset the stability of the political order.

The presence of the new nonwhite communities, with their different languages, religions, life-styles, and tendency to remain in certain inner-city areas, has caused friction and riots and led to statutes such as the 1976 Race Relations Act, which makes discrimination unlawful on grounds of color, race, or ethnic and national origins in employment, housing, education, and provision of goods and services (see Table 2.3). Some members of the Islamic community demonstrated in 1989 for the withdrawal of the book *Satanic Verses* by Salman Rushdie; the more extreme members called for the recognition by the state of Is-

Table 2.3   RACE AND SEX IN BRITAIN

Immigration and Nationality

1948	British Nationality Act: Commonwealth citizens able to enter Britain
1962	Commonwealth Immigration Act: restricted entry for overseas British subjects
1971	Immigration Act: entry restricted to those with at least one British grandparent, or who were naturalized, or who had lived in Britain for five years.
1981	Nationality Act: British citizenship restricted to those already legally in Britain, or one British parent and registered abroad

Civil Rights

1965	Racial discrimination in housing and jobs outlawed
1968	Racial discrimination in provision of goods and services outlawed
1970	Women to get same pay as men for similar work
1975	Discrimination on grounds of sex forbidden; Equal Opportunities Commission set up
1976	Criminal offense to incite racial hatred; Race Relations Board to assist conciliation among races; Commission for Racial Equality set up to investigate complaints of racial discrimination

lamic laws on marriage, divorce, and inheritance.

The centralized, unitary political system has been troubled in the last decades by the rise of nationalist sentiment in Scotland and Wales, and the constitutional framework has been disturbed by political problems in Northern Ireland.

In Northern Ireland the minority Catholic population, numbering about 500,000, has long objected to discrimination against it in political rights, employment, and housing by the Protestant majority of about 1 million. The Catholic civil rights campaign in 1969 resulted in greater tension between the two separate communities and an increasing level of violence, which led the British government to send army units to maintain order. Though concessions were made on civil rights, no agreement could be reached on Catholic political demands. As a result of the continuing violence and the terrorist activity by the Irish Republican Army (IRA), the powers of the Northern Irish government and Parliament were suspended, and direct rule by the British government began in March 1972. Attempts to restore devolution of power from London to Northern Ireland have so far failed, though Britain in 1978 shifted the responsibility for security back to the local police and a part-time civilian corps, both largely Protestant.

An assembly elected in Northern Ireland in 1982 charged with making proposals for devolution failed and was dissolved. By a 1985 agreement with Britain, the republic of Ireland was given a consultative role about the future of Ulster. But attempts in 1991 to foster talks among Britain, the main constitutional parties in Northern Ireland, and the Irish government on home rule for Ulster failed.

In Scotland, after the Act of Union of 1707, the continuation of separate educational, legal and religious institutions, and a local government system provided the country with a distinctive historical and cultural identity. But not until recently has there been a revival of the political nationalism that was strong in the eighteenth century. Economically, industrial production and commerce in Scotland has been tied to the rest of the British economy, which which it trades two-thirds of its imports and exports.

Politically, Scotland now sends 72 members to the House of Commons, which is 11 percent of the total members even though Scotland represents only 9.5 percent of Britain's electorate. The British system responded to Scottish concerns in 1927 by the establishment in London of the position of Secretary of State for Scotland, now a cabinet minister, who has responsibility for both the formulation and execution of a wide range of policies. Central administration is implemented by the Scottish Office, a group of Scottish departments in Edinburgh, the capital of Scotland. In general, Scottish affairs are discussed in parliamentary legislative committees only by those 72 members of Parliament (MPs) from Scottish constituencies and by the Scottish Grand Committee.

The argument that Scotland's problems, especially those of ailing heavy industry and shipbuilding, were due to the neglect or exploitation by London, the increased stress on national pride, and the discovery of large oil reserves in the North Sea off the Scottish coast stimulated the Scottish National party (SNP) to become the proponent of self-government in the 1960s. In 1966 the SNP obtained 5 percent of the Scottish vote in the general election and 4 percent in local elections. In the October 1974 election it won 11 seats and came second in 42 of the other constituencies. The SNP was supported by people of all social classes and geographic regions of the country, though most leaders came from middle-class backgrounds. However, it declined in recent elections, getting only 3 seats with 14 percent of the poll in 1987, and 3 seats with 21.5 percent of the poll in 1992.

In the sixteenth century, Wales was united with England and became part of the English system of administration. Since then, nationalist expression has been more literary and cultural than political. But for some years there have been demands for administrative arrangements similar to those of Scotland. Only in 1957 was a full-time Minister of State for Welsh Affairs appointed. In 1964 a Welsh Office was set up in Cardiff, the Welsh capital, and a Secretary of State for Wales with a seat in the British cabinet was appointed. In Parliament, to which Wales now sends 38 MPs, there is a Welsh Grand Committee, on which the Welsh MPs sit to discuss Welsh affairs in general, as well as all legislation pertaining to Wales. The Welsh nationalist party, Plaid Cymru, gained 3 seats and 7 percent of the votes in Wales in 1987, and 4 seats in 1992.

In 1969 a Royal Commission on the Constitution—the Kilbrandon Commission—was appointed to examine the problem of Scotland and Wales. Reporting in 1973, the commission rejected both the division of the United Kingdom into independent states (separatism) and the creation of states sharing sovereignty with Parliament (federalism). It recommended the *devolution* of political and administrative powers from London for both countries. The British Parliament in 1978 passed two statutes that would establish elected assemblies with responsibility for a wide range of internal affairs in Scotland and Wales.

Both statutes were submitted to referendums in March 1979 with the stipulation that they would only take effect if at least 40 percent of the electorate, as well as a simple majority, approved. The voters in Wales rejected the statute by nearly 4 to 1. Scottish voters approved their statute by 51.6 percent of the voters but only 32.5 percent of the total electorate. Both statutes were therefore repealed in June 1979. Devolution has not yet been implemented, though many in Scotland and Wales still favor it. Scots in particular want greater control over their affairs and their own elected assembly with real power.

POLITICAL PROBLEMS

Britain is now confronted by a number of complex political problems. The relationship of the four countries within the United Kingdom remains undecided. The impact of membership in the European Community on British sovereignty and on the rights and duties of citizens is uncertain. The growing numbers of nonwhite immigrants has led to greater racial tension. There are now six parliamentary constituencies in which nonwhites are a majority, and ten others in which they are prominent.

Three other problems have troubled the system. The first is the "adversary" politics of the 1970s, stemming from the considerable changes in public policies with their disturbing impact on the economy. These changes, resulting from electoral decisions and the alternations of parties in power, may be the outcome of only relatively slight shifts in voting. A second problem has been a greater tendency for some laws, especially in the area of trade union law, to be disregarded by important groups in society. The 1973 Conservative wage control act led to a conflict with the miners' union, a period of strikes and internal difficulties, and the ensuing general election of 1974, which the Conservative party lost. This resistance to government policy has been related to the third problem, the absence of strong government, on which Britain has traditionally depended, until the 1980s.

Why has British government appeared to be less strong since the 1960s, at least until 1979, than in earlier years? Part of the reason was the inability of any party to obtain a clear majority in the House of Commons between February and October 1974 and between 1976 and 1979. After the 1964 election the successful party had only a small majority. In addition, internal dissent increased among the members of both major parties in the House of Commons. All governments in this period were forced by events to make important concessions in their policies. However, the 1979 Conservative Government under Mrs. Thatcher asserted itself strongly in some areas, especially in the conduct of the war against Argentina in 1982, the program of privatization, reduction in the power of trade unions, insistence on a poll tax, and opposition to a single European currency.

THE NATURE OF BRITISH SOCIETY

Political systems inevitably reflect economic, social, and cultural forces in the country, though there is no inevitable or automatic link among them. The British system has reflected, among other forces, a prosperous industrialized economy; sharp differences between social classes; the aristocratic values such as obedience, fair play, and sportsmanship that lasted into the present era; the ideal of the gentleman; a working-class subculture; and religious differences.

Certain significant characteristics of contemporary British society that will be discussed in the following sections.

A Postindustrial Society

Britain is now a postindustrial society in which there has been a shift from the production of goods to a service economy, with a very prominent professional and technical class and with a sophisticated technology (see Table 2.4). Occupationally, services now account for 70 percent of the work force of the country, industry for 24 percent, and agriculture for 1.2 percent. There has been a dramatic increase in the service sector in the last two decades. Services now account for about 62 percent of the gross domestic product, manufacturing for about 30 percent, construction for 6 percent, and agriculture, fishing, and mining for about 1.4 percent

The public sector grew at a faster rate than the private sector until the late 1970s, after which private employment increased relative to public jobs. Of the total 27.7 million in the current work force, 17.5 million (71 percent)

Table 2.4 PROFILE OF BRITAIN 1991

Population—56.5 million; 6 percent nonwhite (two-fifths born in Britain); 27 million labor force (12 percent self-employed, 7 percent unemployed); 39 percent in upper and middle class; 20 percent of electorate belong to trade unions; 20 percent of age group in higher education; life expectancy, 73 for men and 78 for women.

Social life—66 percent own home premises; 27 percent rent council premises; average household 2.5 persons; 11 million (21 percent adults) shareholders; 95 percent households have TV and refrigerator, 80 percent telephone, 66 percent central heating, 60 percent at least one car; 80 percent telephone, 66 percent central heating, 60 percent at least one car; 8 percent have private medical insurance; 11 percent of household budget spent on food.

Economic factors—Gross Domestic Product £ 508 billion; government expenditure is 38 percent of GDP; 4th largest oil producer; inflation 9 percent; interest rate 13 percent; balance of payments deficit £ 20 billion; 10 percent of labor force in finance and business services; investment increased 67 percent and manufacturng productivity 51 percent between 1981 and 1989; about 70 percent of public expenditure spent on social security, health, education, and defense (largest item is welfare benefits largely because of demographic and economic changes).

Source: Central Office of Information, 1991. (£ = $1.65, 1991)

are employed in the private sector, 2.3 million (9 percent) in central government, 3 million (12 percent) in local government, and 750,000 (3 percent) in public corporations. The number of self-employed rose from 1.9 million in 1979 to 3.1 million in 1989, about 12 percent of the work force.

About 10.2 million belong to the 309 trade unions; of these, 8.4 million are affiliated with the Trades Union Congress (TUC). Union membership has declined 25 percent since 1979, especially among manual workers and particularly in southeast England. This decline can be attributed to the replacement of old industries, a base for strong unionization, by high technology firms; the increase of the self-employed to 3.1 million; and the pro-

Feature 2.1 **Working Women in Britain 1991**

Women form a larger percentage of the workforce in Britain than in any of the countries of the European Community except Demark. The earnings gap between the sexes is wide. Male predominance exists at almost all levels of management and in higher positions in both manual and nonmanual occupations. Women working full-time earn on average 77 percent of the wage of males. About 4.8 million women work part-time, mostly in service occupations. Women make up about 80 percent of employees in service occupations and the health service.

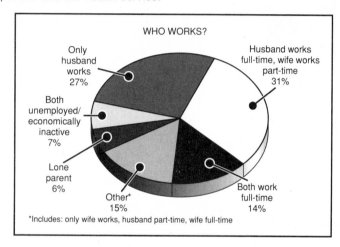

WHO WORKS?

Only husband works 27%

Husband works full-time, wife works part-time 31%

Both unemployed/ economically inactive 7%

Lone parent 6%

Other* 15%

Both work full-time 14%

*Includes: only wife works, husband part-time, wife full-time

Source: Family Expenditure Survey, U.K. Equal Opportunities Commission, 1991.

gram of privatization which has reduced the numbers working in the public sector, another union stronghold, by about 600,000 between 1979 and 1990.

Women, now 40 percent of the labor force, are also less unionized than men. With their consciousness raised by the women's liberation movement, women have been more eager to obtain a job than remain in the home (see Feature 2.1). Women in Britain now tend to marry younger, have children later, bear fewer children, and stay in a job at least until their first child is born. Increasingly they return to full- or part-time work after having children. The higher divorce rate has reinforced the trend for women to work.

Women have been protected by law in a number of ways. The 1970 Equal Pay Act states that women are entitled to the same pay as men when performing similar work. The 1975 Sex Discrimination Act makes sexual discrimination unlawful in employment, education, occupational training, and provisions of housing, goods, facilities, and services. With regard to both statutes the Equal Opportunities Commission exists to promote equal opportunities for women.

There has been a steady rise in the general standard of living and in the consumption of goods, especially of housing, cars, better-quality food and drink, and recreation, and more credit borrowing. At the beginning of the twentieth century only one in ten families owned their own home; in 1952 the proportion was less than one in three; and by 1988, 66 percent of the 21 million homes in Britain were owner occupied. In spite of occupational changes, Britain is still a highly urban as well as densely populated country. About 60 percent of the population lives in cities of over 50,000 people, though only 28 percent of the population of Wales does so, and only one-fifth of the total population lives in rural communities. In recent years there has been an increase in the population of the suburbs and a decline in those in the inner-city areas.

A Class Society

Britain has remained a divided, though changing, society in which people of different occupations, income levels, and education have different life-styles, modes of dress, speech patterns and accents, favorite games, ways of leisure, and mortality rates due to different standards of health. It has been dominated by an elite, albeit an open elite into which the successful could enter, that has occupied the key positions in the financial world, the professions, government administration, and the Conservative party. The principles of the elite have been moderation, fair play, loyalty, and its ideal of the gentleman and the cultivated amateur.

A class theory of politics would argue that class is the major factor influencing voting behavior and that the political parties are representative of the different social classes. In Britain this would mean that the working class would vote for the Labour party and the middle and upper classes for the Conservative party. But this broad generalization is only partly true. About one-third of the working class does not vote Labour, while one-fifth of the middle class does. Nor are the leaders and members of the parties recruited from one class. The programs of the parties do not reflect the interest of one class, as all of them have tried to broaden their appeal.

Britain is still a country with great inequality in the distribution of wealth. About 25 percent of total personal wealth is owned by 1 percent of the adult population and about 61 percent by 10 percent. In 1914 the bottom 90 percent of the population owned 8 percent of all personal wealth; by 1974 they owned 37 percent. The top tenth got 30 percent of pretax income in 1987, compared with the 22 percent obtained by the bottom 50 percent. Britain remains a society in which class differences, due to these inequalities in wealth and income, are strongly felt, and where barriers to social and economic mobility still exist. Yet dramatic changes in the last few years have reduced the old class consciousness, with the shrinkage of the manual working class and with the striking increase in shareholders to 11 million in 1991, compared with 3 million in 1979. This has resulted from three factors: the sale of public enterprises (privatization), employee share schemes, and personal equity plans making it more attractive for small savers to invest.

A Dominant but Pluralistic Religious Society

Britain is also a pluralistic society in its religious diversity after centuries of discrimination. There is now no religious disqualification for public office. (The only exception is the monarch, who must be a member of the established Church of England.)

Protestant Though few people go to any church on a regular basis, Protestantism is still the dominant religion, with the Anglican Church nominally accounting for 65 percent of the English and 45 percent of the Welsh population. The free or nonconformist churches account for 20 percent of the population in England and 45 percent in Wales.

The Church of England is the established church (the concept of "establishment" derives from this fact) and the monarch is its Supreme Head. The chief dignitaries of the Church—the two archbishops of Canterbury and York, the 43 bishops, and the deans—are formally appointed by the monarch, who accepts the recommendation of the prime minister, who is advised by ecclesiastical representatives. Politically, 26 of the higher clergy sit as members of the House of Lords, but no member of the Church of England can sit in the House of Commons. The Church is a large landowner and has considerable possessions in industrial shares and property; however, though many of the senior figures in the Church have come from elite backgrounds, the Church does not speak with a monolithic voice in political, social, and economic affairs. The present Archbishop of Canterbury, George Carey, comes from a working-class background. The monarch is also head of the Presbyterian Church of Scotland, which has been the established Church since 1707.

The free or nonconformist Protestant churches, strong in the west of England and in Wales, have historically been critical of or opposed to the establishment. In general, there has been a correlation between areas of religious nonconformity and those of political dissent, associated first with the Liberal and later with the Labour party. The largest of the free churches are the Methodist Church, with over one-half million adult members, and the Baptist Church with 180,000 members.

Catholicism   There are some 4.25 million adherents to Roman Catholicism. The religion is strongest in Northern Ireland, where it ac-

A place of worship: St. Paul's Cathedral.

counts for about one-third of the population, and in northwest England. Though some old aristocratic families are Catholic, as are some prominent converts and members of the upper class, most Catholics are members of the working class and the majority stem from Irish immigrants. Catholicism has not been the politically divisive issue that it has been in many other political systems, but the Labour party has sometimes nominated Catholic candidates in heavily Catholic constituencies.

Other Religions   The Jewish community dates from 1656, after being expelled from Britain in 1290. In the twentieth century it was increased by immigration from Eastern Europe after pogroms and anti-Semitic outbreaks and from Germany during the Nazi regime in the 1930s. It now consists of about 400,000 people. As a result of the recent immigration of Asians, there is now a considerable number of non-Christian adherents, primarily Muslims, of whom there are now over 1.5 million, Buddhists, Hindus, and Sikhs. Most live in large urban areas.

Since World War I, religion has not been a divisive political issue, except in Northern Ireland. In general, the correspondence between a particular religion and a particular party has remained—the Anglican Church with Conservatives, the Catholics with Labour, and the nonconformists with the Liberals and Labour—but the ties are much less strong, especially among Anglicans, than in previous generations. In the late 1980s, a small Islamic fundamentalist movement emerged, demanding separate status and insisting on Islamic law.

Another place of worship: The Regents Park Mosque.

A Welfare State

The British welfare system developed to deal with problems of poverty and unemployment; to provide for the aged, the sick, and the infirm; and to maintain minimum living standards. The main elements of the current welfare system are the national health service, personal social services, and social security, which now account for about 40 percent of total public expenditure.

The national health service provides almost free treatment for all who want to use it and allows free choice of medical practitioners and hospitals. Personal social services include services for the elderly, the physically disabled and mentally ill, home care, social clubs, and day care for children under age 5. Social security exists to provide a basic standard of living for people in need through unemployment benefits, retirement pensions, sickness benefit and invalidity pensions, child benefits, benefits to widows, and death grants.

A Mixed Economy

Britain was the first capitalist country in the world when, in the eighteenth and nineteenth centuries, the ownership and control of industry was in private hands. Today it is more appropriate to regard the economy as a mixture of private enterprise and various public controls.

Most manufacturing enterprises are privately owned except for the steel, aeroengine, and (since 1977) most of the aircraft and shipbuilding industries. Few, since 1945, argued a laissez-faire position and a minimal role for public control over the economy. Although only the left wing of the Labour party believes in the state ownership of the means of production, distribution, and exchange, most people in the different political parties accepted a substantial role for the state, the largest employer in the country. Only since 1979 has public policy, under the Thatcher and Major governments, emphasized the reduction of the state sector, the sale of public enterprises to private ownership, and a freer market economy.

THE SOCIALIZATION PROCESS

Education and Class

The educational system has reflected and helped to perpetuate the class structure. In 1944 the system was reorganized and students were streamed into separate modern secondary, technical, and grammar schools. Most students ended their education between 14 and 16 years of age to become manual workers. The occupational pattern and the working-class status of these youngsters who had left school was in most cases set for life. Those who left school at age 18 entered white-collar or minor managerial jobs and became part of the lower middle, sometimes middle, class. Only those who had further education beyond 18 years of age were likely to enter the professions or become managers and executives, the middle-class occupations.

In the 1970s comprehensive schools, which like high schools in the United States provide a wide range of education and educate students of different backgrounds together, replaced many of the selective secondary and grammar schools to help end the undesirable social effects and class stratification of educational streaming.

Outside the state system are parochial schools, independent grammar schools stressing academic achievement (many have impressive reputations), and the 260 "public" schools, which are expensive and socially significant. The most prominent of the public schools—such as Eton, Harrow, Winchester, and Rugby—are prestigious institutions, consciously training young men for leadership positions in politics and society by discipline, building of character, and inculcation of traditional values. They have been a unique means of recruiting members of elite groups, constituting an "old boy" network in prominent positions. Though they represent only 4 percent of the British student population, graduates of the public schools, like those of the older universities, have occupied a highly disproportionate number of positions in the cabinet, the House of Commons, the senior civil service, the upper ranks of the armed forces, the High Courts, and the Church of England, as well as in major banking and financial institutions. Perhaps more surprisingly, public school graduates also accounted for 42 percent of the Labour Cabinet in 1966–1970 and 18 percent of Labour MPs in 1978. About 75 percent of Conservative MPs in the House of Commons elected in 1987 attended a public school. Between 1900 and 1985 old Etonians alone accounted for almost one-fourth of government ministers and top ambassadors. It is interesting in light of this that none of the last five prime ministers, including three conservatives, attended a public school.

Traditionally, higher education has been dominated by Oxford and Cambridge, which have provided the political and social elite. In the last two decades there has been a considerable expansion of higher education for both social and educational reasons. The full-time student body has increased to over 500,000, about 13 percent of the 18-year-old population. There are now 46 universities attended by about 270,000 students. Another 250,000 take courses on a wide range of topics at the 30 polytechnics in England and Wales or attend other colleges providing further education in Britain. The most prestigious of the Universities remain Oxford, with its 39 individual colleges, and Cambridge, with 29. Graduates of "Oxbridge" still constitute a high proportion of the elite groups in the country, including the Cabinet and the House of Commons. Nevertheless, the Conservative government in 1991 called for abolishing the distinction between universities and polytechnics, which have increased in importance in recent years, thus removing barriers between academic and vocational education.

A CHANGING BRITAIN

Britain is confronted by social problems, of which the challenge to authority is one of the most difficult. Although these matters are difficult to measure statistically, most observers would agree that there has been a decline in discipline in the family, especially with the higher divorce rate, and in the school, and that there is less respect for authority in general.

Britain has long been a free and—despite unnecessary secrecy in government—open society. It has also generally been a peaceful society in which the police went unarmed. A sign of increased social problems has been the considerable rise in crime. The increasing violence and the terrorist acts, perpetrated mostly by the IRA in British cities, have meant that some of the police now carry weapons, though the majority still go unarmed. But it has been the economic problem that has been of most concern to British politicians.

Britain is still a significant industrial and economic power. It is the fifth largest trading nation, exporting nearly 9 percent of total exports of manufactured goods by the industrial countries of the world. These exports constitute about one-half of all British exports. Britain still accounts for nearly one-third of all international banking business. About 10 percent of "invisible" trade in the world (banking, insurance, shipping, tourism, and income from overseas investment) is handled by Britain.

As Britain became industrialized it also became a larger importer of foods and raw materials; today its imports also include a growing proportion of semimanufactured and manufactured goods. For almost 200 years the value of British imports of goods was usually larger than the value of exports. The deficit on this balance of "visible" trade was overcome in the total balance of payments by a surplus on invisible trade, the receipts, from which are about one-third of total receipts. But in recent years, as the deficit in visible trade increased partly due to the rise in raw materials prices, the dramatic rise in oil prices, the large contribution to the budget of the European Community, the lower exchange rate of sterling, foreign competition, and the loss of many Commonwealth markets to other industrialized countries, the earnings on invisible trade were often not enough to overcome the deficit.

Discovery of oil in the North Sea helped change the picture. Britain is currently the world's fourth largest producer of oil which now provides some 10 percent of total exports. Between 1979 and 1986, Britain had two deficits and six surpluses in its balance of payments. Since 1986, there have been only deficits.

The economic problems of recent years have preoccupied British politics. Britain has suffered the disadvantages, as well as having gotten the rewards, of being the first mature industrial nation in the world and of now having old capital equipment. Its older industries—coal, textiles, and shipbuilding—have contracted, and productivity per worker remained low compared with other advanced nations. It suffered from having exported capital abroad rather than using it internally and for being dependent on the international economy, which has made Britain vulnerable to external factors. The persistent balance of payments problem discouraged sustained investment and limited the rate of growth. Britain's economic and political problems were aggravated in the 1970s by the very high inflation rate, which in 1975 rose to over 26 percent, and by exchange rate difficulties. The unemployment rate rose to 13 percent in 1983; by 1991 it had fallen to 7 percent or 2 million people.

The postwar British performance in production, trade, and growth disappointed its political leaders. In the 1950s Britain was one of the ten richest countries in the world. From the mid-1960s to the mid 1970s the economy grew by only 2.7 percent per year. In 1976 Britain ranked twenty-fourth in per capita gross national product, which was about half that of the United States.

There have been differing explanations for the low level of productivity per worker and the relatively slow economic growth. Some criticize the overmanning of jobs and the restrictive practices and obstructions of the powerful trade unions, which they see as more interested in job security than in increases in production, as well as the immobility of the labor force. Other critics stress inadequate management that is slow to introduce innovations, insufficient research and development, low levels of replacement of capital goods, reluctance to adapt production to new needs, and poor sales drive. The ethos of the social system and the ideal of the cultivated amateur and gentleman have been blamed for the failure to attract well-educated people as industrial managers and for the view of industrial activity as distasteful. Britain's desire to remain an important world power has meant large expenditure on overseas bases, large military forces, and considerable expenditure on nuclear research and development and on expensive delivery vehicles in the attempt to become a nuclear power.

Government policies have been criticized for many reasons: the disincentive of high tax rates, the lack of effective economic planning, the slowness in retraining unemployed workers, the concentration on prestigious and wasteful items such as supersonic aircraft rather than on more profitable industries likely to grow, and the inability to control inflation. Though there is validity in all of these criticisms, much of the British economic problem has been caused by external factors: the inevitable growth of other countries, many of which are industrializing rapidly and some of which are technologically mature; the rising cost of imports of food and raw materials; the loss of protected markets for exports to the former colonies; the sacrifices made by Britain in the two world wars, which seriously depleted British capital and led to the sale of overseas investments; and large external debts.

All British governments tried to solve the economic problem by increasing productivity, growth, and exports; by reducing the rate of inflation; and by maintaining confidence in the British pound. In the decade since 1979 the Thatcher government encouraged growth by cutting taxes, controlling the money supply for a time, approving only those wage settlements connected with increases in productivity, and stressing the value of competition. The economy has grown faster, inflation fell, strikes declined, while trade unionism was weakened. But the level of unemployment has remained high, the share of manufacturing in the economy has declined, and deficits have occurred in some years.

Key Terms

Anglican church
Bill of Rights
class
consensus
constitutional democracy
conventions
deference
devolution
Magna Carta
majority principle

mixed economy
Northern Ireland (Ulster)
Oxbridge
pluralistic society
postindustrial society
privatization
public school
referendum
Reform Acts
representative system
rule of law
sovereignty
United Kingdom
welfare state

Suggestions for Further Reading

Bagehot, Walter, *The English Constitution* (Ithaca, N.Y.: Cornell University Press, 1966).

Banton, Michael. *Promoting Racial Harmony* (New York: Cambridge University Press, 1985).

Beer, S. H. *Modern British Politics*, 3rd. ed. (New York: Norton, 1980).

Johnson, Nevil. *In Search of the Constitution* (New York: Pergamon, 1977).

Jowell, Jeffrey, and Dawn Oliver, eds. *The Changing Constitution* (Oxford: Clarendon, 1985).

Kavanagh, Dennis, and A. Seldon, eds. *The Thatcher Effect* (Oxford: O.U.P., 1989).

Kavanagh, Dennis. *British Politics: Continuities and Change* (New York: Oxford University Press, 1985).

Marshall, Geoffrey. *Constitutional Conventions* (London: Clarendon, 1984).

Norton, Philip. *The Constitution in Flux* (Oxford: Robertson, 1982).

Rose, Richard. *The Territorial Dimension in Government: Understanding the United Kingdom* (Chatham: Chatham House, 1982).

Wilson, Tom. *Ulster: Conflict and Consent* (Oxford: Blackwell, 1989).

B. Political Processes and Institutions

VOTING

The electoral system for the House of Commons is a simple one, comprising single-member constituencies, plurality decision or top of the poll winner, and the principle of one person, one vote. Since the first Reform Act of 1832, which began the process of standardizing the qualifications for voting, the suffrage has gradually been extended to the whole citizenry over the age of 18. During the same period, factors such as the necessary ownership of property, double or triple voting based on ownership of a business or possession of an MA degree, residential qualification, and deliberately unequally sized constituencies have been eliminated (see Table 2.5).

Registration of voters is the responsibility of the local authorities, not of the individual, and an annual register of those eligible to vote in each constituency is issued every February. Since 1948, a postal vote has been possible for those who are incapable of voting in person, have moved from the constituency, or will be away on business. Middle-class voters are more likely to register for a postal vote than working-class voters, and the Conservative organization is better able to mobilize postal voters than other parties.

There are now 651 constituencies with boundaries that are a compromise between population and geographical size. In 1944, four boundary commissions—one each for England, Wales, Scotland, and Northern Ireland—were set up to ensure an equitable relationship between representation and population and to recommend, every five to seven years, alteration of constituency boundaries as population shifts. The changes in 1983 and 1992 increased constituencies to 524 in England, 72 in Scotland, 38 in Wales, and 17 in Northern Ireland. Wales and Scotland are deliberately overrepresented as a concession to nationalist sentiment.

Election is by plurality, or the highest vote obtained. This method has the virtue of clarity and simplicity. Politically it has helped to sustain the system of two major parties in which the Conservative and Labour parties have shared the bulk of the electoral vote and seats in the House of Commons. These two parties alternated in political power for almost the same number of years between 1945 and 1979, while until 1983 the third party, the Liberal, had not obtained more than 14 seats (see Figure 2.2). But the plurality system has also produced serious inequities and distortions of the will of the people at both the level of the individual single-member constituency and the national level.

At the individual constituency level, seats may be won by a minority vote where there

Table 2.5 EXTENSION OF THE FRANCHISE

Year	Main group enfranchised	Other features
1832	Industrial middle class	Redistribution of seats from small boroughs to the counties and towns
		Registration of voters necessary
		Increased suffrage by 217,000
1867		Increased suffrage by 1 million
1872	Urban workers	Secret ballot
1883		Bribery and corrupt electoral practices become criminal offenses
1884	Agricultural workers	Increased suffrage by 2 million
1885		Equal-sized constituencies
1918	Women over age 30	Increased suffrage by 12.5 million
		Redistribution of seats
		Limit to two votes (places of residence and business or university)
1928	Women over age 21	Increased suffrage by 7 million
		Universal suffrage over age 21
1948		One person, one vote
		Abolition of university vote and seats
		Abolition of business vote
		Redistribution of seats
1969	Persons over age 18	Increased suffrage by 3 million

are more than two parties and the successful candidate polls fewer votes than those of all the other candidates. In February 1974 there were 408 seats (64.3 percent of the total) won by less than a majority. Between 1945 and 1979, 30 percent of all seats were won by a minority vote.

At the national level the opinion of the people may be distorted and political parties may not be truly represented in proportion to the votes they receive in the country, as is shown in Table 2.6.

In October 1974 Labour won an absolute majority of the seats with less than 40 percent of the votes. There is no exact correlation between the votes obtained by a party in the country as a whole and the number of seats it wins in the House of Commons. Indeed, it may even happen, as in 1951 and February 1974, that the party with the smaller percentage of votes in the country may win more seats than the party with a larger percentage of votes. The Conservatives in 1987 got over 57 percent of the seats with 42.3 percent of the vote, whereas the Liberal-Social Democratic

Alliance got only 3.5 percent of the seats with 22.6 percent of the vote.

A second problem is that a relatively small change in electoral opinion may produce a much larger proportional change in the distribution of seats between the parties. This disproportionate result is produced by changes in voting in the "marginal seats," those that are normally won by small numbers of votes. In 1979 there were 74 seats held by the Labour or Conservative parties by margins of less than 2000 votes. 83 seats were won by majorities under 5 percent.

The main inequity in the system is that the Liberal party, in spite of considerable support all over the country, has not won more than a few seats in the postwar period. Unlike a regional party such as the SNP or the Plaid Cymru, whose votes are concentrated in a small number of constituencies, the Liberal and, in 1983 and 1987, the Social Democratic vote was spread throughout the country. The Liberal Democrats only got 20 seats in 1992.

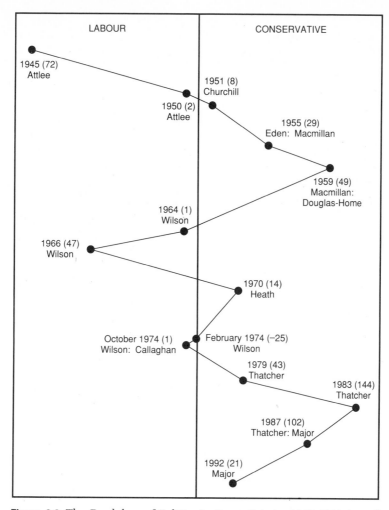

Figure 2.2 The Pendulum of Politics in Great Britain, 1945–1991 (overall majority in House of Commons)

The present system is unfortunate for the Liberals and other parties in two other respects. The first is that its candidates often lose a large number of their deposits (304 in 1979); elections are therefore expensive for the party. The second is that Liberal electoral support is very fluid. Persons who might vote Liberal if they thought a party candidate were likely to win are reluctant to do so if they feel the candidate is likely to lose and the party as a whole will do badly. They might prefer to influence the outcome of the election by voting for a candidate of one of the two major parties.

Not surprisingly, the Liberal party and the former Social Democratic party (SDP) advocated a change in the electoral system. But the two major parties are still unwilling to approve a change because they benefit from the present system. This method has helped perpetuate the two-party system in the postwar period by normally producing a majority of seats for one of the two major parties, which is then able to form a government. Not since 1935 has one party obtained 50 percent of the total poll, but parties have had comfortable majorities in 10 of the 14 postwar elections. A different electoral

Table 2.6   GENERAL ELECTIONS, 1974–1992

Election	Percentage of votes cast			Number of seats won			
	Con.	Lab.	Lib.	Con.	Lab.	Lib.	SDP
1974 (Feb.)	38.2	37.2	19.3	297	301	14	—
1974 (Oct.)	35.8	39.3	18.3	277	319	13	—
1979	43.9	36.9	13.8	339	269	11	—
1983	42.4	27.6	25.4[a]	397	209	17	6
1987	42.3	30.8	22.6[a]	376	229	17	5
1992	41.8	34.4	17.8[b]	336	271	20[b]	

[a] Combined vote of the Liberal and Social Democratic (SDP) parties (Alliance).

[b] Liberal Democratic party

system would result in a fairer distribution of seats in relation to the votes cast for the parties; but it would also lead to an increase in the number of parties represented in the House of Commons, make it difficult to obtain a majority, and therefore change the formation and functioning of government.

IS THE ELECTORAL SYSTEM WORKING?

The present electoral system has therefore been defended essentially on the grounds that it provides one of the two major parties with a comfortable majority in the House of Commons. The winning party can then form a strong government which is able to formulate a coherent policy that will be approved by Parliament. This has generally been true in the postwar period when the Conservative and Labour parties have obtained the bulk of the electoral vote and one of them has obtained a majority of seats. The peak was reached in 1951, when their combined vote was 96.8 percent of the poll and 77 percent of the total electorate.

But from 1951 there was a steady drop in their electoral support, as well as a decline in the proportion of those voting in general. The decline in strength of the two major parties resulted in February 1974 in a minority government, with Labour getting 25 seats less than an absolute majority, and in October 1974 in an overall majority of only 1 seat. The two major parties got only 76 percent of the poll in 1992. In 1959, parties other than Conservative or Labour gained only 9 seats, 6 of which were Liberal, whereas in 1987 they gained 45 seats, of which 22 went to the Alliance, 6 to the nationalist parties, and 17 to Northern Ireland.

The decline in recent electoral support for the two major parties is attributable to two main factors: the rise in nationalist sentiment and, perhaps temporarily, in Liberal-Social Democratic support, and the decrease in the strength of partisanship for the Conservative and Labour parties.

The cumulative rise in Scottish nationalist strength has been rapid in recent elections: from 11.5 percent in 1970 to 30.4 percent of the vote in Scotland in October 1974 (see Table 2.7). Not only did the SNP win 11 seats in October 1974, but it also came in second in 42 other constituencies, taking votes from both major parties. The party slogan "It's Scotland's oil" appealed to those who believe that Scotland should control the North Sea oil revenues. By 1974 the SNP had become a broad-based party drawing support from all social classes, geographical regions, and age groups, and from former voters, especially younger people, from other parties.[7] In Scotland it can be considered part of a three-party system, though its support declined in 1992 to 21.5 percent of the poll.

In October 1974 the Welsh Plaid Cymru won 3 seats, with 10.8 percent of the Welsh vote, and came in second in six constituencies, but its strength was largely confined to the rural, Welsh-speaking part of the country. Influenced by literary figures, the party has been more concerned about the extinction of the Welsh culture and language than about broader political issues. The Welsh protest vote against the major parties—unlike the

Table 2.7   VOTING IN SCOTLAND AND WALES: 1987 AND 1992

Scotland

Party	1987		1992	
	Votes (%)	Seats (%)	Votes (%)	Seats (%)
SNP	14.0	3	21.5	3
Labour	42.4	50	39.0	49
Conservative	24.0	10	25.7	11
Liberal Democrat	19.2	9	13.1	9

Wales

Party	1987		1992	
	Votes (%)	Seats (%)	Votes (%)	Seats (%)
PC	7.3	3	8.8	4
Labour	45.1	24	49.5	27
Conservative	29.5	8	28.6	6
Liberal Democrat	17.9	3	12.4	1

Scottish, which has increasingly gone to the nationalist party—has often gone to the Liberals. In 1992 it won 4 seats and 8.8 percent of the poll.

The Ulster Unionists, once automatically associated with the Conservative party, are now more independent. Elections in Northern Ireland had little reference to the rest of the United Kingdom and were primarily concerned with political affairs in Ulster since 1974.

In spite of the fact that many electors have a partisan self-image or psychological commitment to one of the two major parties, there has been a drop in support for them. The Conservative vote fell in October 1974 to 36 percent, the lowest in its history. The Labour party has lost considerable support among those who should be its firmest adherents: young, males, working-class trade unionists. A source of real

alarm for the party is that in 1979 it got the votes of less than half of the working-class voters. Partisan loyalties have declined in all age groups, not simply among the young.[8]

Both parties have experienced a decline in membership, a weakening of party allegiance, and expressions of dissatisfaction with their leadership. The perception has grown that neither major party is coping well with issues, both national and international. This view is made stronger by the evidence of important differences within each of the parties on issues such as the European Community, prices and incomes policy, and industrial relations.

Nevertheless, despite the decline in the major party vote of the electorate as a consequence of the rise of minor parties and the decline in partisanship, there has not been a similar decrease in the number of seats gained by the major parties. The working of the present electoral system still allowed Conservatives and Labour to obtain 93 percent of the seats while getting only 76 percent of the electoral vote in 1992, which was the fourth successive win for the Conservatives.

ELECTIONS

When are general elections held? The whole House of Commons is elected for a period of five years, but only one Parliament since 1945 has lasted the full allotted time. Most elections were called by the prime minister at a time thought best for the ruling party to win. Campaigns last less than a month, and in recent years, especially because of television coverage, have concentrated on the major party leaders.

By-elections in an individual constituency are held on the death or resignation of a member of Parliament (MP). The number of by-elections during the life of a Parliament thus depends on the duration of the Parliament and the age of MPs. During the 1987–1992 Parliament there were 23 by-elections in four years.

There are two interesting features of by-elections. The first is that the vote is always considerably lower than in the same constituency at general elections. The second is that the voters usually register a more antigovernment view than they did at the previous general election, thus decreasing the strength of the government party in the House of Commons. Between 1922 and 1979 the government party lost 126 seats and gained only 9 in by-elections. Labour governments have been affected most adversely. In the postwar period, from 1945 to 1978, Conservative governments lost 16 and won 4 seats, while Labour governments lost 25 and gained none. Between 1989 and 1991 Conservative candidates lost seven by-elections because of strong resentment by voters against the poll tax imposed by the Conservative government.

The Candidates

There are no primaries or nominating conventions in British politics. Primaries are virtually impossible in the British context because of the unpredictable timing of elections mentioned above.

By law a candidate for a constituency is simply nominated by 10 registered electors of the area; until 1970 no party affiliation was officially attached to the name of the candidate. In fact, almost all candidates are sponsored by a political party. It has been rare for a nonparty candidate to run or for a candidate not associated with a major party to win.

Until World War II a varying number of constituencies were uncontested. Since 1951 all constituencies have been contested. In 1987 there were 2325 candidates, including 633 Labour, 633 Conservative, 633 Liberal and Social Democratic, 71 SNP, 38 Plaid Cymru, 19 Communist, and 133 Greens. A record number of 327 were women. In 1992 the number of women candidates increased to 548, of whom 58 were elected. The total number of candidates increased to 2964.

Any person over age 21 can stand as a candidate with certain exceptions: those who are disqualified from voting; clergymen of the churches of England, Scotland, and Ireland, and of the Roman Catholic Church; and people holding certain offices, including judges, civil servants, members of the armed forces, policemen, and various public officials, except members of the government. Candidates need not reside in their constituencies, and there is no counterpart to the district qualification in the United States.

One requirement is that each candidate must deposit £500 with the registrar, which is returned if the candidate gets over 5 percent of the total vote in a constituency. The money is forfeited if the candidate receives less than that amount. This provision has been costly for the Liberal party and minor parties, which thus hesitate to sponsor more candidates.

Who Are the Candidates?

An implicit problem in representative democracies is that the candidates and the representatives elected are not a model of their constituents. The British system bears out this generalization. The percentage of male candidates is far greater than the percentage of men in the general population, and candidates are wealthier and better educated than the average constituent.

Among Conservative candidates it is noticeable that 57 percent attended a public school, 35 percent went to "Oxbridge" (Oxford or Cambridge), and 33 percent to some other university. What is perhaps more surprising in a party that gets most of its support from the working class is that 14 percent of the Labour candidates went to public school, 13 percent went to Oxbridge, and 45 percent to some other university.

In 1987 the two dominant occupations were business and the professions. Most Conservative professionals were lawyers, while most Labour professionals were teachers at some educational level. The Alliance also had a high proportion of teachers among its candidates. The Conservatives have become a less aristocratic group and Labour more professional.

In all parties there have been a limited number of women candidates; in only three elections have there been more than 100. The highest number was the 548, or 14 percent of the total, who ran in 1992. Of these women candidates, 134 were Labour, 139 were Liberal Democratic, and 46 Conservative; of these candidates, 41 were elected, less than half of the proportion of male candidates.[9]

The Nature of Voting

Though recent changes in voting behavior must be borne in mind, and despite the fluid political situation, certain general statements about voting in the post-World War II period can be made in the following paragraphs.

A High but Declining Poll Voting is not compulsory, but the vote in general elections in the postwar period has always been over 72 percent of the electorate, though smaller at by-elections, and reached a peak of 83.9 percent in 1950. (Compare this with the 52.3 percent of the electorate who voted in the 1980 U.S. presidential election.) There was a steady, though irregular, decline until October 1974, when it dropped to 72.8 percent, before increasing to 75.5 percent in 1979 and then declining to 72.7 percent in 1983. In 1992 it increased to 77 percent.

The abstention rate is higher among younger people, new residents of a constituency, the unmarried or divorced, blacks, the unemployed, and private rather than council tenants. These groups are less involved in political parties, less interested in politics, and less exposed to political information in general. In an electorate where the under 30s and the over 70s—the groups that vote least—have become an increasing proportion, demographic factors have reinforced an overall decline in political interest and the belief, perhaps temporary, that the outcome of elections is not important.[10] The decline in the poll may also be explained by the greater mobility of the population, the reduction of voting in safe seats in the inner cities, and abstentions by some potential Liberal supporters.

Class There has been a strong correlation between class and party voting. The Conservatives normally get 90 percent of the upper-middle-class vote and between two-thirds and three-quarters of the middle-class vote. Labour gets some two-thirds of the working-class vote, while the Liberals and Social Democrats draw from all social classes. The middle class as a whole is more strongly Conservative than the working class is Labour. In a society where class consciousness has been as strong as in Britain, this relationship is understandable.

Yet, the link between class and party voting has never been complete. About one-third of the electorate does not vote according to this premise. In addition, extremist class parties such as the Communist party have always done rather poorly. But the most serious qualification of class-party voting has always been the working-class Conservative vote, which has amounted to about one-third of the total working-class vote. There are a number of possible explanations for this contradiction of class voting. Those who, though objectively part of the working class, see themselves as middle class and adopt middle-class values and ways of life are more likely to vote Conservative than those who think of themselves as working class. Members of the working class who have had more than the minimum secondary and further education are more likely to vote Conservative than those who have not. Workers in agricultural areas who have close contacts with their employers, who do not belong to unions, who are religious, who belong to local organizations and are integrated into the local community are more likely to vote Conservative than the average worker. Above all, there is an explanation, discussed in Chapter 1 in connection with political stability, based on the deference of part of the working class. It used to be argued that this group preferred a socially superior political leadership, which it believed to be a natural ruling group. But it is more likely that this group believes that the Conservative party is more efficient than its rivals and that its wielding of power will ensure greater material benefits. Whatever the explanation, the Conservatives have done particularly well in the working class among older people, women (until 1979), those who own their own homes and those who own shares. The increase in home ownership—66 percent of voters now own homes—has meant greater Conservative support. About 44 percent of the home-owning working class voted Conservative compared with 32 percent voting Labour in 1987. By contrast, about 57 percent of working-class tenants in public housing voted Labour in the same election. In the same way, a majority of first-time shareholders voted Conservative, and only 17 percent voted Labour, in 1987.

The 1987 election suggests that the class basis of party choice that weakened. More skilled workers voted for the Conservatives than for Labour, and only 48 percent of all manual workers voted Labour, whose share of the vote of trade unionists dropped to 42 percent. The Labour vote remained largely working class, but the working class ceased to vote largely Labour and split among the three main party groups: Labour, Conservative, and the Liberal-Social Democratic Alliance.

The evidence is mixed at present, but there appears to be less subjective class identification, a weakening of class alignment, especially by young voters, and less acceptance of the basic principles of a party by its supporters.[11]

Party Identification The best guide to voting choice for most of the electorate has been identification with a party and psychological commitment to it. A majority of the voters determine their party allegiance at the first general election in which they vote and then retain it. This allegiance has been the basis for response to party programs, for evaluation of the competence of party leaders, and for voting and political behavior in general. Among Labour and Conservative voters in 1974, 9 out of 10 thought of themselves as Labour or Conservative. In contrast, only half of the Liberal voters felt a similar identification with the party.

Why do people identify with a party? The strongest single influence has been the party preference of parents, especially if both parents voted the same way. Identification also results from other factors, including the supposed link between the party and a class, and the image of what policies and principles the party represents. For the Conservatives the image has included such characteristics as capable leadership, skill in foreign policy, patriotism, and maintenance of the free enterprise system. For Labour it has been the pursuit of a more egalitarian society and concern for the underprivileged. Part of the dilemma of the Liberals is that their image is rather diffuse, devoid of specific policy content of general appeal.

In the early 1980s the Labour party moved to the left and alienated some traditional supporters. In the early 1990s it has moved to more centrist positions, renouncing extreme policies that lost votes.

In the recent past the party identification factor has given considerable stability and predictability to the voting pattern for the major parties. But in the 1970s and 1980s strength of party identification appears to have declined and the ties of voters to a particular party to have grown weaker. Voters are less prone to vote for the party of their parents. The changes in the social structure discussed in Chapter 1, a general criticism of the performance of governments of both parties, and the presence of new issues that cut across party lines have contributed to this decline in party identification, the rise of the Social Democrats, and perhaps also to a certain cynicism about parties. In particular, part of the decline since 1970 in the Labour and Conservative vote and in the turnout at the poll has been attributed to two factors: (1) less party identification in the young and newly enfranchised part of the electorate, and (2) a decline in the number of those who define themselves as "very strong identifiers" with a party.[12]

Partly due to these factors and partly to the appeal of the Liberal-Social Democratic Alliance for former Labour voters, the Labour party in 1983 obtained by only 28 percent of the vote, lost 119 deposits, and won the smallest number of seats in the House since 1935.

Sex   Until recently, men have been more politically active than women, with a particularly low political interest among working-class women. Women voted Conservative to a greater degree than did men. In 9 of the last 12 elections a majority of women voted Conservative. But, since 1979, women have tended to vote less Conservative. In 1983, for the first time, the Conservatives got less support from women than from men, but in 1987 they got 11 percent more support from women than did Labour.

Race   Nonwhite immigrants have overwhelmingly voted Labour, partly because the vast majority are members of the working class. In 1987 only about 7.5 percent of blacks and 20 percent of Asians voted conservative. But the presence of a significant number of immigrants in a constituency and the nonwhite immigration issue may also produce the opposite effect on voting. In the 1970 election the Conservatives were believed to have gained about six seats as a result of their being perceived—largely owing to the speeches made by the then-prominent Conservative Enoch Powell—as the more restrictive major party on allowing immigration. Some voters— 190,000, or 0.6 percent of the total—supported the anti-nonwhite-immigration National Front, which in 1979 ran 303 candidates, of whom all but one lost their deposits. The racial appeals of the National Front have drawn more support from working-class and poorly educated voters

than from other groups, but its 13 candidates in 1992 all did poorly in the election.

Religion   In contemporary times, religion has not been a politically divisive issue, except in Northern Ireland and, in the early part of the 1990s, among parts of the Islamic community. Because there is a link between class and membership in a particular religion, there are similar explanations for voting behavior as resulting from those two factors. In general, members of the Anglican Church vote more Conservative than do individuals of other religious denominations; members of the nonconformist churches are likely to support the Labour or Liberal parties; and Catholics, largely working class, vote strongly Labour.

Age   Younger people tend to vote Labour in greater proportions than their elders, especially those between 50 and 64. But the youngest people also have the lowest rates of turnout. On the whole it is true that the Conservatives are supported more by older than younger voters; yet in the 1960s the early-middle-aged group was less Conservative than their juniors. This has been explained in one analysis by the argument that it is the conservation of those political tendencies that were established when young that increases with age, not conservatism itself. Voting habits will therefore be influenced by those tendencies that were dominant when people first entered the electorate.[13] Older people became adults when Labour was still a minor party and therefore have less allegiance to it than younger people. Some recent changes in the voting patterns of young and old have appeared in recent elections; in 1983, though not in 1987, young voters supported the Conservatives more than Labour.

Regional Variations   For generations, certain areas have been strongholds of particular parties. Labour does well in south Wales, central Scotland, the industrial north of England, and in the inner cities. The Conservatives are strong in southern and eastern England, and in the suburbs and county areas, which have grown in population and economic prosperity. In 1987 Labour won only 3 of the 176 seats in Southern England, excluding London. In this part of the country, average earnings are much higher than in the rest of the country. Recent elections reinforced Labour control over urban areas and Conservative control over rural areas. The Liberals and Social Democrats do best in the west of England, Wales, and the Scottish islands. Labour has a plurality in Wales and Scotland, though the latter was challenged by the SNP in October 1974. The Conservatives usually have a plurality in England and, until recently, in Northern Ireland. In Scotland, the Conservatives in 1992 gained only 10 seats out of 72 compared with 22 seats in 1979. In the 1970s and 1980s, politics in Ulster were very fluid because of complex internal problems.

Occupation   Those employed in nationalized industries and public service organizations are more likely to vote Labour than those working in commercial organizations and the self-employed. People in both the working and middle class who have experienced unemployment are more likely than the average to vote Labour. Trade unionists vote Labour to a greater degree than do nonunionists. The strongest working-class support for Labour comes from predominantly working-class constituencies in large towns, industrial areas, and mining villages; union members; workers in large factories and offices with over 250 employees; those with working-class parents; those living in council apartments; and those who have been unemployed for a period of time. However, the number of manual workers and of those working in large factories, and the number of council tenants all have been declining.

Party and the Leader

Voting may depend on the images people have of the parties and their leaders, and on percep-tions of party positions on issues. The assumption that people were more likely to vote for a party than a leader may no longer be true in view of the prominence of the leaders on television and the time given to their speeches and personalities.

POLITICAL PARTIES

The British system has often been regarded as the classic example of a two-party system in which the Conservative and Labour parties—national, large, cohesive, disciplined, ideological but generally moderate—have alternated as the government and the opposition. The Liberals have not won more than 20 seats since 1945. A considerable number of minor parties have existed and run candidates in national and local elections. But none, except the nationalists in recent years, has had much success. Extremist parties have fared poorly. On the left, the Communist party, founded in 1920, has never gained more than two parliamentary seats and since 1950 has been unrepresented. On the right, the present National Front, a party opposing nonwhite immigration, has not been able to win either a parliamentary or a local council seat. The Green party emerged in 1985 out of an ecological group. In 1987 it received less than 1 percent of the vote, but in the 1989 election for the European Parliament it obtained 15 percent. In the 1992 election, its 258 candidates rarely got more than 1 percent of the vote.

A possible change to a multiparty system appeared with the formation of the Social Democratic party (SDP) in 1981 by some prominent Labour politicians who were disturbed by militant leftism in their party and by organizational changes allowing more influence to extraparliamentary forces, extremists in some of the constituency parties and the trade unions. The SDP argued that it was committed to parliamentary democracy, rejected the idea of class war, favored controls on trade unions, approved a mixed economy, and supported British membership of both the European Community and NATO.

The SDP and the Liberals agreed to form an Alliance to support each other electorally. This did well at some by-elections and in local elections. But the Alliance was less successful nationally, though it won 23 seats and came second in 311 constituencies and got 25 percent of the poll in 1983, and won 22 seats and came second in 260 constituencies and got 22 percent in 1987.

As a result of this disappointment, a majority in SDP agreed to merge with the Liberals and form a new party, the Social and Liberal Democrats (SLD) in 1988. A minority of the old SDP remained as a small separate group, transforming itself in 1990 into the Campaign for Social Democracy. In the 1992 election the Liberal Democrats got 17.8 percent of the vote and 20 seats. The future of the political center and of the party system remains uncertain.

PARTY ORGANIZATIONS

Local and Regional

All the major parties have the parliamentary constituency as the basic unit of party organization. The Conservative and Liberal constituency associations are composed of individual members who subscribe to the party and who manage the local organizations, elect their own officers, select parliamentary and local government candidates, raise funds, engage in educational work, and conduct the electoral campaign in their area. However, the constituency Labour parties are composed not only of individual members but also of affiliated organizations, such as trade unions, cooperative societies and branches of the Cooperative party, branches of Socialist societies and some professional organizations, and trade councils.

Total membership of all parties has declined in the last two decades. The Conservative party has declined from about 3 million in the late 1950s to less than 1 million members,

the SLD now have about 60,000 members and the Labour party has about 200,000 individual and 5.5 million affiliated members.

National Organization

Each party has a national organization that works through different committees, holds an annual conference in the autumn, and has a central headquarters to control the working of the party machinery and prepare publications.

The National Union of Conservative and Unionist Associations is a federation of constituency associations (see Figure 2.3). It is responsible for the organization and growth of these associations and acts as a link between the leader of the party and the associations. The Union is nominally governed by the Central Council, which meets once a year and which, in the postwar period, has chosen the officers of the Union. But because the Central Council is too large a body for effective action, the group that acts on its behalf and meets more frequently is the Executive Committee; this committee is composed of the party leader, chief officials, and representatives of the regional organizations.

The Conservatives hold an annual conference, attended by the Central Council and representatives of the constituencies, to discuss the reports of the Council and of the Executive Committee, and debate resolutions on party policy. It is understood that the conference is purely advisory; it is usually a platform for the main party leaders rather than a challenge to them. Most of the resolutions are congratulatory of the leadership, which has never been beaten by a vote on any serious issue. The resolutions in any case are not binding on the party leadership. It is characteristic of the Conservative conference that it is usually more right wing than the leadership.

The Conservative Central Office, the party headquarters, is concerned with the efficient organization of the party. It provides general guidance and technical assistance, helps the formulation of policy by supplying background

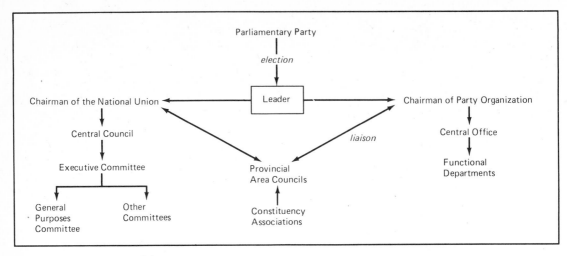

Figure 2.3 Organization of the Conservative Party

material through its research department, and offers advice on electioneering. It is headed by a chairman, appointed by the party leader, and officers who are responsible for the different departments concerned with specific functions.

The Central Office cannot coerce the constituency associations, which operate through local volunteer workers and obtain and spend their own funds. The local associations also, in the main, control the process of selection of parliamentary candidates, though the Central Office supplies a list of available candidates on request and may influence the final choice.

The Labour party has the most complex organizational structure. It began as, and has remained, a federal body composed of four main groups (see Figure 2.4):

1. The more than 600 constituency associations, which now have about 200,000 members. They are responsible for their own organization and selection of parliamentary candidates. The number of activists is relatively small, and they are usually more left wing than either the party leaders or their MPs. Most party members spend little or no time at party meetings or activities.

2. The 59 affiliated trade unions, which account for 5.5 million, or 95 percent, of the members. Not all unions are affiliated with the party—113 unions are now attached to the Trades Union Congress—and not all members of a union that is affiliated want to be members of the party. About one-third of the membership of the affiliated unions have "contracted out," or refused to have part of their union dues go to a political levy for the party. About three-quarters of the Labour party funds come from the unions.

The largest union affiliations are the Transport and General Workers (TGWU) with 1 million affiliated, the Amalgamated Union of Engineering Workers (AUEW) with 800,000, the General and Municipal Workers (GMWU) with 650,000, and the National Union of Public Employees (NUPE) with 500,000.

Since all organizations are represented at the annual conference in proportion to their membership, the four largest unions almost constitute a majority if they all vote the same way. The influence of the unions is made even

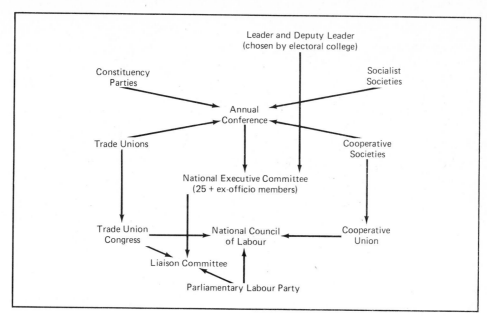

Figure 2.4 Organization of the Labour Party

more pronounced by the "card vote," by which the whole vote of a union is cast for the majority position regardless of how large the minority vote is among the union delegates on the resolution.

A number of unions sponsor parliamentary candidates, most of whose election expenses they pay. Because their constituencies are usually safe seats, those candidates are much more likely to win than nonsponsored candidates. In 1987, of the 633 Labour candidates, the unions sponsored 164, of whom 129 or 80 percent, were successful; 13 of the latter were women.

3. The cooperative organizations are linked to the Labour party in the same way as the unions are. One cooperative Society, the Royal Arsenal, has been affiliated since 1927 and another since 1979. There is a separate Cooperative party, founded in 1917, but it is now in reality an adjunct of the Labour party. Since 1922 all Cooperative party parliamentary candidates have been endorsed by the Labour party and have run as Labour and Cooperative.

4. A number of Socialist societies, small in size and composed largely of professionals or intellectuals. The most well known of these bodies is the Fabian Society, which was founded in 1884. The total membership of these societies and of the cooperative groups is about 54,000.

The nominal policy-making body in the Labour party is the annual party conference, which debates resolutions, changes the constitution of the party, and elects the major administrative organ, the National Executive Committee (NEC). The conference is attended by representatives from the four different elements making up the party and by the chief officials of the party, MPs, and parliamentary candidates.

The NEC consists of the leader of the party, the deputy leader, the treasurer, and 25 other members who are elected at the conference. Of these 25 people, 12 are chosen by the trade union delegates, 7 by those from the constituency parties, 1 by representatives of the cooperative and Socialist societies, and 5 women by the whole conference.

The NEC is the administrative authority of the party and is the body responsible between annual conferences for deciding policy matters and enforcing the rules of the party. It controls the central organization, supervises the work of the party outside Parliament, decides disputes between members or associations, and manages the party funds. Together with the Parliamentary Labour party (PLP), the NEC draws up the election manifesto based on conference proposals, but there is sometimes friction between them.

The NEC also plays a role in the selection of parliamentary candidates. Like the Conservative Central Office, it maintains a list of acceptable candidates that the local constituencies can request, but the final choice is made by the local parties.

The NEC can expel a member or disaffiliate an organization for activity contrary to party decisions. In the postwar period a number of organizations, described as Communist-front groups, were forbidden to members. Since the mid-1980s, a number of left wing members, belonging to the Militant group, have been expelled or suspended for challenging or defying party policy.

THE PARTIES IN PARLIAMENT

The major Conservative organ in Parliament is the 1922 Committee, which is composed of the nongovernmental Conservative MPs and expresses their opinions to the leadership of the party. When the party is in power, its leaders, now members of the government, do not attend the committee's weekly meetings. After the discussion of policy issues or political problems, the chairman of the committee expresses its views to the leadership.

The leader of the party is now chosen by the MPs. From 1881, after the death of Disraeli, until 1963 the Conservative leader

"emerged" after a series of informal "soundings" of the views of different sections of the party. Of the 11 leaders in this period, 5 were of aristocratic descent and the others came from business or professional politics.

The Conservative leader is now elected by the MPs in the House of Commons and is then presented for confirmation to a meeting composed of the Conservative MPs and peers, prospective candidates, and members of the Executive Committee of the National Union. In 1965, Edward Heath was first elected in this way, and in 1975, after the voting rules were revised, he was replaced by Margaret Thatcher, the first woman to lead a major British party. Her leadership was challenged in 1990 when she failed to win the necessary absolute majority and lead over her opponent. She decided not to run in a second ballot, which was won by John Major.

The Parliamentary Labour party (PLP) consists of Labour members in the House of Commons and those in the House of Lords. It is led, when the party is in opposition, by the Parliamentary Committee, or "shadow cabinet," which consists of the leader and deputy leader, 15 others elected by Labour MPs, and 1 elected representative of Labour peers. The leader and deputy leader of the PLP are the same people who have been elected as the leaders of the party by the electoral college. Table 2.8 shows a breakdown of MPs by gender, education, and profession.

In recent years most of the members of the shadow cabinet have become cabinet ministers if the party gains power. This custom was reinforced by a party rule in 1981 which states that all 18 members of the shadow cabinet will be given cabinet positions if the party wins the next election. When the party is in power, a liaison committee links the government and other Labour MPs, who thus have the opportunity to influence the policies of the government. Groups of Labour MPs based on territory and subject matter have also been formed for that purpose.

Table 2.8   MAIN PARTY CANDIDATES, 1992

	Conservative	Labour	Liberal Democrat
Men	584	508	494
Women	61	126	136
State school	167	451	n.a.
Private school	307	9	n.a.
University	515	516	320
Legal profession	51	22	27
Teacher	22	113	119
Business/director	181	24	98
Political officer/ trade union official	15	25	5

PARTY LEADERSHIP

In all the parties the parliamentary leader has until recently been regarded as leader of the whole party. Unlike the formal process of democratic decision making in the SLD and Labour parties, the Conservative party leader is responsible for deciding party policy and for the choice of the shadow cabinet, or consultative committee, when the party is in opposition. The leader controls the party headquarters and appoints the chief officials, who are responsible to him or her.

Paradoxically, the Labour party has been more loyal to its leaders than have the Conservatives, in spite of the latter's stress on unity and loyalty. In the twentieth century the Conservatives have had 12 leaders, 7 of whom were overthrown by a party revolt, while an eighth was almost overthrown twice. During the same period Labour had 7 leaders, one of whom (MacDonald) left his party, and another (Lansbury) resigned because of disagreements with party policy. All the others died in office or resigned voluntarily.

Until 1976 the Liberal leader was also elected by the MPs of the party. In that year the Liberals established a new procedure by which the leader was chosen by an electoral college composed of about 20,000 delegates from the constituencies. The new SLD party elects its leader by ballot of all members.

POWER WITHIN THE PARTIES

A complex relationship exists among the different sections of the parties, in which no one element has complete power over the others, and in which each section has some, if unequal, influence on decision making in the party. Differences over policy and personnel exist between the central party organizations and the constituency associations, especially the activists in them; between the organizations in the country and the parliamentary party; and between the leadership of the party, especially when it is in power, and the MPs of the party (see Table 2.9).

Important as the party organizations are, the real power in the formulation of policy has remained with the parliamentary elements of the parties. The Liberal and Conservative parliamentary parties, from which comes the prime minister and governmental leaders, existed before the mass organizations in the country were created. The dominance of the Conservative parliamentarians over the rest of the party is understandable in view of the fact that between 1886 and 1991 the Conservatives were in power for 73 years and the party leaders were also prime ministers and cabinet ministers.

Although the Labour party is different from the others in having begun as a mass organization, by the 1920s the Parliamentary

Table 2.9   POWER IN THE PARTIES, 1992

	Conservative	Labour	SLD
Leader	Elected by MPs (1990 John Major)	Elected since 1981 by electoral college (40 percent trade unions, 30 percent PLP, and 30 percent constituency parties) (1983 Neil Kinnock, resigned 1992)	Elected by party members (1988 Paddy Ashdown)
Shadow cabinet	Appointed by leader	Elected by MPs	Appointed by leader
Party headquarters	Under control of leader	Under NEC, which is elected by annual party conference	Under National Executive Committee, which is elected annually

Labour party had become the strongest element and the body that chose the political leaders. This has been partly due to the fact that the parliamentary leaders have generally been strongly supported in the past by the trade union leaders, who for the most part held similar political opinions.

Activists of the party, at both the national and local level, have rarely been able to challenge the parliamentary leadership successfully. The political reality is that the electoral decision and the parliamentary representatives, not the party as a whole, determine who is to be prime minister. The party organizations have been able to influence and sometimes limit the activity for the parliamentary leadership, but they rarely formulate policy.

Skillful manipulation by political and union officials controlled the agenda and the debates of the annual conference, and tended to exalt the parliamentary part of the Labour party over the mass movement. In recent years the Labour conference has asserted itself and changed the organization of the party. In 1979, when the left wing of the party controlled a majority, resolutions were approved for all Labour MPs to be automatically subject to a reselection process by their constituency parties in order to remain as candidates for the

next election and for the NEC to take, after appropriate consultation, the final decision on the contents of the general election manifesto. The other party conferences have also tried to play a more significant role. Even in the Conservative party the leader since 1966 has attended the whole conference rather than simply being present to speak at the end.

The constituency parties on a number of occasions have attempted, sometimes successfully, not to renominate MPs who differ politically from the activists controlling the local organization. Selection of candidates is now largely in the hands of the local organizations. Though the central offices keep a list of nationally approved candidates and can veto an undesirable local choice, they cannot force the local organization to accept a candidate, and only very rarely have they exercised a veto even when it involved an individual who had rebelled against party policy or leadership.

The internal struggle for power within the parties continues. This has recently been shown in a number of ways. All the parties have made the choice of the party leader open to wider participation: the Conservatives by election by the MPs; the Liberals by bringing the whole membership of the party into

---

Feature 2.2 Toward the Center: Party Proposals in 1991

CONSERVATIVE

As Prime Minister, Mrs. Thatcher attempted to change the British economy and society by her strong commitment to the free market, property-owning democracy, self-reliance, and the reduction of the power of trade unions. She attempted to change certain entrenched institutions, such as the higher civil services, universities, BBC, Church of England, the legal system, and local government. Her decision to impose a poll tax led to opposition. Mr. Major plans to replace the poll tax by a tax largely based on capital value of property. To deal with discontent about the public service, Major proposed a citizens charter addressed to raising the quality of services, increasing individual choice, and getting better value and accountability.

LABOUR

The party has changed or moderated its position on a number of issues. It has renounced unilateral disarmament and opposition to Polaris and Trident missiles, and any considerable renationalization of industry, though it would restore public ownership over a few services. It recognizes that trade union power should not be increased; calls for the maintenance of the National Health Service on present lines, increased child benefits and pensions, and adherence to the economic and financial arrangements of the European Community; and emphasizes the need for fiscal and monetary respectability.

LIBERAL AND SOCIAL DEMOCRATS

It calls for PR for all elections, a fixed term for the House of Commons, replacement of the House of Lords by an elected Senate, home rule for Scotland and Wales, more decentralization in England, a bill of rights, a supreme court, a free market, federal Europe, central European bank and currency, and an increase in the powers of the European Parliament.

---

the process; and Labour by establishing an electoral college in which the trade unions and other affiliated organizations would have 40 percent of the voting strength, and the PLP and the constituency parties would each have 30 percent. Within the Labour party, the extreme left—Militant Tendency, with about 7,000 members—has challenged the policies of the leadership, and ethnic minorities have demanded separate black sections. More than one hundred Militants have been expelled since 1983 by the more moderate Labour leadership.

INTEREST GROUPS

Interest groups have long existed in British politics and now play a significant role. They are usually differentiated from parties in that they do not hold or seek political office, though some groups sponsor parliamentary candidates. Interest group leaders now participate in consultative or even administrative functions and serve on government committees and advisory boards. In certain matters, they may even have a veto on government decisions.

There are numerous interest groups concerned with all aspects of life. For analytical purposes, a frequently used distinction is between sectional interest and promotional groups. Sectional interest groups defend and promote the interests of their members, whether individuals or enterprises. They include organizations concerned with the economic interests of labor, business, and agriculture, with social affairs such as automobile organizations, or with living arrangements such as tenants' groups. Promotional groups are concerned with a particular general cause, principle, or policy issue. They advocate a specific conception of the public interest. Examples of such groups are the Howard League for Penal Reform, the National Society for the Prevention of Cruelty to Children, and the Royal Society for the Prevention of Accidents. Recent years have seen the rise of a number of protest movements, of which the most vocal has been the Campaign for Nuclear Disarmament, and groups concerned with welfare and environmental issues. The most significant interest groups affecting the working of the political system are the business organizations and the trade unions.

Business

There are hundreds of business organizations concerned with a number of functions: providing common services, exchanging information, regulating trade practices, negotiating with trade unions on wages and conditions of work, and representing the business position to the government.

Most employers' groups are organized on an industry rather than the product basis. Some are local or deal with a part of an industry; others are national and deal with a part of an industry; others are national and deal with the whole of an industry. There are about 150 national employers' organizations, most of which belong to the Confederation of British Industry (CBI), formed in 1965 of a number of industrial groups. The CBI is the central body representing national business and industry. It acts as an advisory and consultative body for its members and presents their views publicly. Its representatives sit on many official bodies and advisory groups. the CBI has been called the voice of British business, but this is only partly true because of the widely varied interests of industrial and commercial organizations.

Industrial employers groups and labor groups are no longer in an approximate political and economic balance as they were 20 years ago. Organized labor is now much more important and is checked only by the power of financial groups in the City of London. The CBI has had little consistent direct influence over government policy as a whole, though it has had little consistent direct influence over government policy as a whole, though it has had an impact on some industrial and business issues.[14] On the other hand, the important financial institutions—usually referred to as the City—have been politically important.

This importance results from two factors. First, the City is still the world's most significant financial and credit center, including the Bank of England and the central offices of many British banks, the largest number of foreign banks, the stock exchange, the largest gold market and international insurance markets, and international commodity markets. Second, many public issues have been connected with regulation of money, credit, price levels, and currency relationships and balance of payments, all of which need the expertise of the City. The leading persons in the City are usually closely connected with the Conservative party in the same way that union leaders are with the Labour party.

Trade Unions

Trade unions began with the industrial revolution, but not until the mid-nineteenth century did unions of skilled and semiskilled workers become well organized in their demands for higher wages and better working conditions. In the latter part of the century, unions of unskilled workers that pursued a more active industrial policy were formed. The attacks on the unions by court decisions led to the establishment of a political lobby, the Trades Union Congress (TUC), and later to the Labour party.

The TUC is a loose confederation which does not direct individual unions and has little power over them, but acts on behalf of the whole union movement to achieve objectives that would be difficult for separate unions to obtain. Since World War II the TUC has sat on countless governmental committees, advisory bodies on economic issues, agricultural marketing boards, and consumer councils, and has given its views on questions of general economic and social policy. The leaders of the TUC have become members of numerous QUANGOs (Quasi Autonomous Non-Governmental Organizations).

The unions have been linked with the Labour party since their decision to establish a pressure group in Parliament. The unions still provide the bulk of party membership and financing. Of the 113 unions in the TUC, 59 are affiliated with the party. About 60 percent of the members of these affiliated unions have paid the political levy which automatically makes them party members, though many do not realize they are doing so. They represent about 5.5 million members, or over 95 percent of the total party. The large manual and industrial unions form the basis of Labour's main union strength. They supply not only most of the annual funds of the party but also the extra money needed for campaigns. The unions constitute 40 percent of the electoral college which chooses the leader and deputy leader of the party. The unions also sponsor parliamentary candidates.

But the alliance between the unions and the party has been an uneasy one. There was considerable cooperation between 1945 and 1951, when there was a voluntary restraint on wage demands, largely because of the close personal relations between the government and union leaders. Again, under the Labour government of 1964–1970, the unions generally supported the government, including its income policy, until 1969, when an attempt was made to introduce legislative controls over unions. Similarly, in the Labour government of 1974–1979, the unions abided by the social contract and restraint in wage increases, until 1978–1979, when they defied the government's income policy that sought to limit wage increases to 5 percent per year.

The significant influence of the unions on policy—especially in 1974, when a series of strikes led the Conservative government to call an election which resulted in its defeat—brought calls for limits on their power; the Conservatives after their return to power in 1979 imposed such limits. The most important of these are ending the legal case for the closed shop; allowing employers the right not to recognize unions; union contributions to political parties have to be approved by secret vote of members; forbidding political strikes; forbidding mass picketing; strikes must be approved, and union leaders must be elected by secret ballot. Working days lost through strikes have been substantially reduced. So has the membership of unions.

Tactics of Interest Groups

Interest groups have used a variety of different techniques to influence decision making.

1. An occasional method is to organize a public campaign or demonstration. This was done in the 1950s by the Campaign for Nuclear Disarmament and the movement to abolish capital punishment. Most groups see this as neither desirable nor effective.

2. Groups are more likely to try to influence the government and civil service. They keep in contact with the administration in those departments concerned with their problems. This enables them to provide information and advice, try to affect policy planning, and be consulted on the implementation of policy. This interaction with government takes place on several levels:

a. Governments need the advice and information of expert groups. Car manufacturers will be consulted on safety regulations for vehicles. Those groups with special authority or reputation, such as the Howard League, are likely to be heard when they wish.

b. Policy may be decided in collaboration between government and interest groups. The annual farm price review results from bargaining between officials of the Agriculture Department and the National Farmers' Union (NFU). The latter decides what share of government support will go to specific types of farmers and regions. A close relationship, more like a partnership than merely one of consultation, exists between the NFU and the government.[15]

c. The administration of policy may be dependent on cooperation of groups, for example, the National Health Service relies on the various branches of the medical profession. Administration may even be delegated to groups. The University Grants Committee, composed of university administrators, is to a large degree entrusted with the organization and financing of higher education. At the local government level the National Society for the Prevention of Cruelty to Children and the Women's Volunteer Service help implement welfare policy.

d. Groups participate in countless advisory committees or councils which make recommendations to ministers and officials. The bodies may be permanent [such as the National Economic Development Council (NEDC) or the Council for Scientific Policy] or ad hoc organizations. Most are national bodies, but some are regional (economic planning councils) and local (national insurance advisory councils).

3. Groups seek to persuade MPs or try to have them act on their behalf. Groups other than the unions, such as the veterans' organization and the farmers after World War I, sponsored parliamentary candidates, but this is now rare. But MPs, who sometimes accept an honorarium from a group, speak at party meetings, introduce bills, or move amendments to other bills on behalf of groups. About 100 all-party interest groups now exist in the House of Commons.

In Britain, with the government's considerable intervention in and expenditure on economic and social affairs stemming from the welfare state and the mixed economy, the role of groups whose information and participation in the policymaking process is essential has increased. This greater role has led some analysts to argue that decisions are taken on the basis of cooperation among politicians, officials, and leaders of the interest groups, and that the functional representation of corporate interests is more significant than the representation of voters. Some even suggest that business organizations and trade unions in practice have been able to exercise a veto over public policy.[16] Yet, in spite of the tripartite interaction and the strong influence of groups in executive actions, the role of government and the executive remains central in British politics.

THE EXECUTIVE

Over a century ago Bagehot in *The English Government* distinguished between the dignified and efficient parts of the political system. Some institutions were important for symbolic reasons, while others exercised real power.

The British executive can still be viewed in the same fashion. The head of the state is the monarch, who reigns but has virtually no political power and only limited influence. The real political power is centered in the prime minister and the cabinet, with the civil service assisting and influencing the exercise and administration of that power. The British system has been based on the existence or possibility of strong, effective government. Over the last three centuries the executive power of the king was first restrained by Parliament and then transferred to ministers.

THE MONARCHY

The present monarch, Queen Elizabeth II, can trace her descent back to at least the ninth century. The powers formerly exercised by the monarch are now in the hands of various individuals and institutions. By a series of arrangements beginning in 1760, the monarchy turned over to the government the hereditary revenues derived from the Crown Lands and other sources and has received in return an annual grant (Civil List) to cover the salaries and expenses of the royal household.

The functions of government are now exercised by political ministers who are collec-tively and individually responsible to Parliament, but the monarch still participates in a formal way in some executive and legislative activities. The monarchy survived in Britain because the sovereign became a constitutional monarch, neither exercising the wide powers of the crown nor being responsible for their exercise. According to constitutional procedure, the sovereign always ultimately accepts the will of the government, although the monarch may make known his or her opinion and can attempt to influence the decision made.

The most important single political power of the sovereign is the choice of a prime minister. When there is a clearly recognized leader of a party that is able to control a majority in the House of Commons, the choice of the individuals is obvious and immediate. But where one or both of these conditions are not

Queen Elizabeth II with the leaders of the seven major industrial democracies and the European Community, July 1991.

present, a real choice may exist for the sovereign.

The monarch today still has a symbolic and ceremonial role to play in the system, but the monarchy has been divested of its former political power.

THE GOVERNMENT

The real power is exercised by the government, composed of the political ministers and junior ministers, of whom the most politically important are the prime minister and the cabinet.

The government consists of about 100 members, all nominated by the prime minister and appointed by the monarch. It essentially consists of holders of administrative posts of a political character and the whips of the government party. It never meets as a whole to discuss policy or to take action. There is no fixed number of departments. These are established to deal with issues or to meet changing conditions or political and social crises. In the postwar period the number of major departments has been reduced from 30 in 1945 to 16 in 1989, and almost all of them are now in the present cabinet.

Concessions to nationalist sentiment have been made by the transfer of certain social services in Scotland to the Scottish Departments and the consequent strengthening of Scottish administration in the 1950s, and by the establishment in the cabinet of the Welsh Office, which was given responsibility for many functions in 1964.

Ministers are individually responsible to Parliament for the work of their departments. They introduce legislative proposals, press the concerns of their department, and argue its case and requests for money in cabinet and interdepartmental committees. They discuss departmental issues with interest groups and others affected by or interested in those issues and speak in defense of the department in Parliament. It is their task to see that decisions and policies are correctly implemented by the civil servants in the department.

THE CABINET

The most significant members of the government constitute the cabinet, those ministers who are chosen by the prime minister to attend cabinet meetings and are made privy councillors. The cabinet has replaced the privy council as the chief source of executive power since the eighteenth century, but the latter still exists as an executive organ, largely giving formal effect to policy decisions made by the cabinet and making orders-in-council. A significant heritage from the past is the Judicial Committee of the privy council, which is the final court of appeal on certain legal issues arising in the colonies and in those independent countries of the Commonwealth that have decided to retain the arrangement.

The cabinet, which is not a legal body, is based on political understandings or conventions. Its members are normally the leading figures of the party controlling a majority in the Commons. The cabinet is the chief single body concerned with the initiation, control, and implementation of political policy and the most important decision-making body. It initiates most legislation and controls the legislative process. It is responsible for the coordination of governmental activity; all ministers must implement cabinet decisions insofar as their departments are affected.

For politicians the cabinet is the top of the political ladder, except for the position of prime minister. It constitutes the core of the British political elite. A number of conventions underlie the existence and operation of cabinet government.

1. The cabinet is ultimately dependent on the support of the House of Commons which has come into existence as a result of the general election. A government that is defeated on a major issue or on a vote of censure or no confidence is expected to resign or to ask for a dissolution of Parliament. A government whose party has been clearly defeated at a general election will resign immediately, as did the Labour government the day after it lost the 1979 election.

2. Unlike the American cabinet, the members of which are drawn from a wide variety of sources and backgrounds, the British cabinet is drawn, with rare exceptions, from members of the two Houses of Parliament. This fusion of executive and legislative functions in the hands of the same people is a striking denial of the concept of the separation of powers. This convention also means that the members of the cabinet are selected from a relatively small pool of available people. Moreover, in recent years most of the members of both Labour and Conservative cabinets have come from the shadow cabinets of the two parties.

3. Except in wartime or in a serious political or economic crisis, the entire cabinet will be members of the same political party if that party can control a majority in the Commons. In this way, political coherence and unity can be obtained. Britain is the only country in Western Europe that has not had a coalition government in the postwar period.

4. The monarch is excluded from the discussions of the cabinet, though he or she is kept informed of its conclusions by the prime minister, who is the acknowledged head of the cabinet. The advice offered by the cabinet, even on personal issues (as in 1936 on the marital plans of King Edward VIII, who was eventually obliged to abdicate), must be accepted by the monarch or a constitutional crisis will result.

5. All members take the oath of privy councillors and are bound to secrecy by this and the Official Secrets Act. There is now a 30-year limitation on the publication of Cabinet documents, and secrecy is generally preserved.

6. The members of the cabinet are collectively responsible for all decisions and actions, as well as individually responsible for the performance of the particular department or unit each may head. There is free and frank discussion of issues in the cabinet.

Members may and do disagree about the desirability of a policy, but they must support and implement policy decisions once they have been made. The British system is based on the premise that a government that is publicly divided on a given subject cannot govern.

The principle of collective responsibility means that all ministers must support and defend government policy and not speak or act against it. The principle applies now not only to cabinet ministers but also to all members of the government. If ministers continue to oppose or cannot accept a decision made on an important issue, the principle suggests that they should resign. Since 1945 there have been only twelve important resignations over policy issues, mostly over financial and economic matters. But the resignation in October 1990 of Sir Geoffrey Howe, a prominent cabinet minister, in protest against the prime minister's policies, led to the downfall of Mrs. Thatcher herself three weeks later. In recent years cabinets have sometimes remained divided, but without resignations. In addition, the development of the system of cabinet committees and the dominant role of the prime minister has meant that cabinet members tend to feel less personally committed to every decision.

Collective responsibility also implies that an attack on a minister in regard to important policy, as distinct from criticism of the administration of that minister's department, will be taken as an attack on the whole government unless it disclaims responsibility. If the latter is the case, strong criticism of a minister may lead to resignation, but not to a vote on the government as a whole.

This concept of collective responsibility and decision making is to be distinguished from the principle of ministerial responsibility, which means that individual ministers are responsible for all the work and actions of the government departments that they head. Though it is most improbable that ministers will be familiar with all the work of the department, they must respond to parliamentary criticism of or inquiry about it.

Theoretically, if parliamentary criticism of a department or a minister's performance or neglect of duties is sufficiently great, the minister is obliged to resign. Resignation has also resulted from ministerial indiscretion, either inadvertent or more blatant, as in the sexual escapades of the minister of war in 1963 or the use of indiscreet language about Germans by the minister of trade in 1990. But there are many more examples of ministers not resigning in spite of considerable parliamentary criticism of their activity. Over the last century there have been only about 25 resignations on the principle of ministerial responsibility.

Cabinet Membership

The number and members of the cabinet depend on the prime minister, whose decisions result partly from the administrative needs and governmental functions to be performed and partly from political necessity to accommodate the ambitions of colleagues, to have different ideological sections of the party and territorial parts of the country represented, and to include some individuals loyal to himself or herself. The cabinet, which realistically contains the political rivals and possible successors of the prime minister, is thus the result of administrative, political, and personal factors.

Except during the two world wars, when the size of the cabinet was reduced to 8 or 9, it has numbered between 18 and 23 ministers. Usually, the important departments will be included in the cabinet, though no one becomes a member simply because of his or her office. The minister of a department has been included in one cabinet but excluded from the next, depending on the priority given it by the different cabinets or on the political weight of the minister.

Although members of the cabinet are drawn from both Houses, certain ministers, especially those with financial responsibilities, will almost always be chosen from the Commons. Only occasionally will someone outside Parliament be appointed. The average tenure of a departmental office between 1964 and 1991 was under $2\frac{1}{2}$ years. Ministers are not experts and rarely have executive experience, as they have spent much of their lives in politics.

In reality, the choice of the prime minister is constrained by the existence of the shadow cabinet, the group of opposition party leaders who criticize the government and formulate alternative proposals. Though there is no compulsion, prime ministers in recent years have appointed most of the members of the shadow cabinet to the cabinet itself. In 1979, for example, 17 of the 21-member shadow cabinet became members of the 22-member Conservative cabinet. In 1974, Prime Minister Wilson appointed all 12 members of the Labour shadow cabinet to his cabinet. This is now mandatory in the Labour party.

Procedure in the Cabinet

Cabinet meetings are called by the prime minister, usually once or twice a week. Members ask the cabinet secretariat to put items on the agenda and receive copies of it before each meeting. They are thus able to study the issues and to attend meetings with an informed opinion on them. Ministers who are not cabinet members are normally invited to attend when a subject affecting their department is on the agenda.

It has usually been assumed that the cabinet does not vote on issues, but that discussion takes place until a collective decision is reached when the prime minister sums up "the sense of the meeting." But some recent cabinet ministers have stated that voting did sometimes take place on substantive as well as procedural matters.[17]

There are two other qualifications of the principle of collective decision making by the cabinet.

First, in reality members do not always participate in discussion, especially as the range of subjects has increased. This is largely the result of the heavy burden of duties imposed on cabinet members, which includes the reading of official papers, attending and speaking in Parliament, supervising the work of their departments and giving directions to officials, attending official functions, maintaining contact with their parliamentary constituencies, and undertaking a round of speeches through-out the country, as well as attending cabinet meetings. Ministers tend to fight in cabinet for their departmental policies and budgets.

Second, not all issues are fully discussed by the cabinet as a whole. Various devices are used to reduce the burden on it. Decisions made by individual ministers have sometimes been accepted by the whole body. Agreement on issues has been reached by interdepartmental ministerial meetings or in private meetings between ministers, including the prime minister. Above all, cabinet committees, consisting of a small number of cabinet members, and occasionally nonmembers, have been established to relieve the burden on the cabinet as a whole and to speed up decision making now that there has been a great increase in governmental activity. Sometimes the real decisions are made by a small committee rather than by the cabinet as a whole. In crisis or wartime, a small cabinet of five or six members is usually set up to make major decisions. This was done during the 1990–1991 Gulf crisis and war.

The number and membership of cabinet committees were kept secret until 1992. There are about 25 standing and 130 ad hoc committees set up to discuss specific subjects or problems. Often the committee decision is allowed to stand, and thus the agenda of the cabinet as a whole can be reduced. The membership of the committees is usually paralleled by similar committees of civil servants.

THE PRIME MINISTER

The prime minister is the acknowledged head of the executive. Unlike the U.S. presidency, the office of the prime minister is largely based on conventions. Despite the office now being over 250 years old, there are still few statutes referring to it or to the functions to be performed. The prime minister was once regarded as primus inter pares (first among equals) in the cabinet, but this is an inadequate description for an individual who is preeminent in it and the dominant political personality.

As already mentioned, legally the prime minister is chosen by the monarch, who selects the person capable of forming a government. The choice is obvious if one political party possesses or controls an absolute majority of seats in the House of Commons and if that party has an acknowledged leader. This was the case with the appointment of Harold Wilson in October 1974 and Margaret Thatcher, the first woman to become prime minister, in 1979.

But there are other occasions when the monarch has a real choice between individuals. If the prime minister dies or resigns, the choice of a successor is not always obvious. The monarch had to choose between rival candidates in 1957 and 1963. If no party has an absolute majority in the Commons, as in February 1974, the monarch might have a choice between the leaders of the different parties. In those situations the monarch will not act without directly or indirectly consulting a number of political leaders.

A convention of the twentieth century has limited the monarch's choice to members of the House of Commons. Since 1923, when Baldwin rather than Lord Curzon was appointed, all prime ministers have been members of the lower chamber. When Lord Home was appointed in 1963, he immediately disclaimed his title, left the House of Lords, and won a seat in the Commons. This convention illustrates the predominance of the Commons over the Lords, the fact that governments can be defeated and forced to resign by vote of the Commons but not by the Lords, and the reality that the Labour party is stronger in the lower than in the upper House.

Prime ministers differ in personality, energy, political interests, and administrative abilities, but all are seasoned politicians with experience in Parliament and in the cabinet. All prime ministers have had considerable apprenticeships in Parliament before appointment. In the twentieth century as a whole, as in the postwar period, the prime minister's average tenure as an MP has been 28 years. Most

Prime Minister John Major on a soap box in the 1992 election campaign.

Table 2.10   THE RISE OF JOHN MAJOR (1943–)

1959	Left grammar school without diploma; worked as clerk and laborer
1965–79	Worked in a bank
1968–71	Conservative local councillor in London
1979	Elected M.P. at third attempt
1981–83	Parliamentary private secretary to ministers in Home Office
1983–85	Assistant to Conservative whip in House of Commons
1985	Junior minister in Ministry of Health
1986	Minister of state for Social Security and the Disabled
1987	Chief secretary to the Treasury
1989, July	Foreign Minister
1989, Oct.	Chancellor of the Exchequer
1990, Nov.	Elected party leader, and immediately became Prime Minister, the youngest P.M. in the twentieth century
1992, April	Led the Conservative party to election victory

of them have held a number of other cabinet positions. The average tenure in this century has been three different posts and eight years in the cabinet. Mrs. Thatcher had only one previous post and four years in cabinet, and John Major had only one year in a senior cabinet post before becoming prime minister.

In the twentieth century there have been 19 prime ministers. They have differed in social background: five came from the aristocracy, seven from the middle class, six from the lower middle class, and one from the working class. All the aristocrats and five of the seven middle class prime ministers went to a public school, five of them went to Eton and two to Harrow. Twelve attended university at Oxford or Cambridge. It is distinctive that the last five, including Margaret Thatcher and John Major (see Table 2.10), came from the lower middle class, attended state (nonpublic) schools, and can be regarded as examples of the principle of meritocracy.

Functions

The prime minister chooses and can dismiss members of the government. But, unlike the U.S. president, the prime minister's range of choice is restricted; rarely does he or she choose someone from outside Parliament and even more rarely from outside the government party. Many choices will be obvious because the leading members of the successful party, especially many of those who have been in the shadow cabinet, will be appointed; the most important of them may even be consulted by the prime minister in choosing the others. The P.M. must keep the confidence of senior colleagues. He or she can dismiss or demand the resignation of ministers, but may not always be able to get rid of those who have some independent political strength in the party or country.

The prime minister decides the size and composition of the cabinet. He or she forms a cabinet that is satisfactory from both a political and an administrative point of view. Thus, prime ministers will usually include not only people who reflect different elements or political opinions in the party but also some on whose loyalty they can rely or whose counsel they value.

The prime minister also establishes and appoints the members of Cabinet committees. He or she sets up task forces, working parties, and ad hoc meetings as may seem necessary to deal with issues.

The prime minister calls cabinet meetings, takes the chair, determines the items of business, and controls the agenda. The P.M. also chairs some cabinet committees. In the task of summing up the sense of the meeting, the prime minister is allowed to interpret to some extent the decision reached. The P.M. is also the ultimate decider and spokesperson of cabinet policy, controlling the flow of information about the government.

The prime minister reports the conclusions of the cabinet and is the chief channel of political communication to the monarch. By convention, no minister can see the monarch without first informing the prime minister. Many of the prerogatives of the Crown, such as declarations of war and peace and dissolution of Parliament, are in fact exercised by the prime minister.

The prime minister acts as an arbiter and tries to resolve disputes between departments. The degree of interest the prime minister today has in any particular department varies, but traditionally he or she is always in close touch with the Foreign Office.

The prime minister dispenses considerable patronage, and has a power of appointment that includes not only the members of the government but also the senior members of the civil service, the chief members of the judiciary, military leaders, and the archbishops of the Church of England. Twice yearly an official Honors List bestows some title or honor on individuals chosen by the prime minister for some contribution to public life.

The prime minister controls the major appointments in the Civil Service, especially those of the permanent secretary to the treasury, the secretary of the cabinet, and the prime minister's chief adviser on problems concerning the machinery of government.

The prime minister is also the leader of his or her party within Parliament and in the country. In Parliament he or she answers questions twice a week in the House of Commons and speaks on important occasions and in debates.

The P.M.'s task is to keep the party as united as possible; and his or her political survival depends on it. When the prime minister loses control of the party, as did Chamberlain in 1940, Eden in 1956–1957, and Thatcher in 1990, he or she is obliged to resign. But normally the prime minister can expect loyalty from his or her party, and he or she is aided in the maintenance of discipline by the whips, who since 1964 are paid and are regarded as part of the government team. Mrs. Thatcher served as P.M. for 11 years, the longest consecutive term in the twentieth century.

Is the Prime Minister a Quasi-President?

There is universal agreement that the prime minister is the most important political figure in Britain. This has led some to regard the office as similar in the extent and degree of its power to that of the U.S. president. Some argue that the country is governed by the prime minister, who leads, coordinates, and maintains a series of ministers who are advised and supported by the civil service.[18] Richard Crossman,[19] himself a former cabinet minister, thought that prime ministerial government had replaced cabinet government as a result of the increased role of political parties, the influence of the cabinet secretariat, which is close to the prime minister, the control of the prime minister, the control of the prime minister over major civil service appointments in the departments, and the influence of the mass media and television in particular, which normally focus attention on the leader. In addition, the prime minister has more time for thinking about general policy issues or current problems than do the ministers at the head of particular departments who are responsible for a heavy administrative load.

Certainly it is true that the prime minister has sometimes taken the initiative in foreign affairs and in emergencies and has been personally responsible for political decisions, of which in recent years the Falklands war in 1982 and the poll tax were the most striking. In addition, until recently, the cabinet did not discuss the annual budget and was only informed about it a few days before the budget was introduced in the House of Commons. However, there are examples of the prime minister's views not prevailing in cabinet.

Although the powers of the prime minister are strong, they are qualified in certain respects:

The prime minister can retain power only as long as he or she retains control over the party, and both the cabinet and Parliament. Unlike the U.S. president, he or she does not have a fixed term of office.

The range of the prime minister's choice of cabinet is very limited compared with that of the U.S. president; moreover, he or she is always aware of potential successors in the cabinet.

The prime minister relies more than the U.S. president on collective decision making. While he was prime minister, Harold Wilson thought the cabinet was supreme as the decision-making body. The relationship between the prime minister and the cabinet changes with the individuals and issues involved. Mrs. Thatcher often appeared to act in an authoritarian way. By contrast, John Ma-

jor is a more tactful and less abrasive person. But the place of the cabinet remains central in policy making, and the prime minister cannot really be regarded as a presidential figure.

THE CIVIL SERVICE

The British civil service has long been admired for its competence, political impartiality, and dedication, and only in recent years have mounting criticisms led to structural changes in its organization. In the nineteenth century the civil service was based on patronage and was sometimes corrupt and inefficient. The modern civil service was based on the 1854 Northcote-Trevelyan report, most of whose recommendations were implemented. The civil service became a single organization instead of a series of separate departmental staffs. Entry into the service was based on open competition, not on patronage. The successful candidate entered the service, rather than a particular department, and could be transferred from one department to another. All examinations were conducted by the Civil Service Commission, not the individual departments, and corresponded to both the level and academic content of those taken in the educational system at the same age of applicants. The exams were always general rather than specific.

The civil service has been organized into departments according to subject matter. Almost all departments have their headquarters in London in or near Whitehall, and branch offices throughout the country. The civil service, based on the distinction between intellectual and routine work, was divided into three service-wide classes: administrative, executive, and clerical. Outside these classifications were the professional, scientific, and technical officials, as well as the manual and manipulative workers, mostly in the postal and telegraph systems.

Criticism of various aspects of civil service organization and behavior mounted in the 1960s, based largely on the elitist nature of the senior civil service, their limited experience, their lack of initiative, the lack of scientists in top administrative positions, narrowness of outlook, and poor methods of training. As a result, the Fulton Committee on the civil service was established. Reporting in 1968, the committee was critical of the civil service's stress on the gifted amateur and generalist who was expected to be able to deal with any subject matter. It was also critical of the division of the civil service into general classes, the inferior status of scientists, the relative lack of specialized experts, and the frequent movement of senior civil servants between departments.

Only some of the changes recommended were introduced. A Civil Service Department was established, taking over the management of the service from the Treasury Department. A Civil Service College was set up to give courses in management techniques to new entrants. The three-class organization was ended, and part of the service was restructured along classless, unified lines. In the currently reduced (562,000 by 1990) civil service, the largest unit is the administrative group, composed of the former three classes. An important change was a new grade, administrative trainee, made to strengthen middle management. The Civil Service Department was abolished by Mrs. Thatcher in 1981, but the prime minister remains in charge of the machinery of government. In 1988, she proposed a plan for semiautonomous agencies to manage services now administered by departments. By 1991, 50 such agencies had been set up, employing 200,000 civil servants. The general idea behind these agencies is to introduce a more entrepreneurial and competitive spirit into administration.

A constant cause of criticism of the senior civil service—the 3,000 top positions in the home and foreign service—has been that its members come largely from the middle and upper class, with less than 5 percent coming from the working class, and that a high proportion of those in the elite group, the former administrative class, was educated at the public schools and at Oxford and Cambridge. The Fulton Report stated that 72 percent of the direct entrants into the administrative class came from "Oxbridge" and 48 percent from the public schools. The proportions were even higher for entrants into the senior foreign civil service, of which about 10 percent were educated at Eton.

The Role of the Civil Service

The senior civil servants advise ministers on formulating policy and decision making. Their role is based on impartiality and anonymity. All governments, irrespective of political persuasion, have been served loyally by the nonpolitical civil servants.

The work of the civil service is anonymous because of the principle of ministerial responsibility; the minister alone is responsible to Parliament for the operation of his or her department, even though in practice the minister may not always be aware of what has been done. Civil servants are free to give unbiased and frank advice to ministers without having to defend their views. On some occasions, however, the anonymity is shattered when civil servants appear before parliamentary committees to answer questions about their department's accounts or administrative procedures and occasionally to give evidence to a tribunal of inquiry.

The obverse of anonymity has been the secrecy behind the making of decisions, both in form and content. The shielding of the civil service from the glare of partisan politics has also meant that it is restricted in its political activities. No member of the senior administrative group, above the clerical staff, can participate in national political activity; a member can take part in local politics only with departmental permission.

The determination of policy is the responsibility of ministers; the task of the civil service is to carry out that policy with energy and goodwill. The minister is a politician, not an expert on the issues of his or her department, and he or she must decide policy not only on its own merits, but in light of the government program as a whole and of what is politically rather than administratively possible at a certain point.

But the reality of ministerial-civil service relations is often different from the theory. Departmental policy may often result from past administrative experience and the cumulative decisions made by the civil servants while dealing with individual cases. Moreover, civil servants do not merely implement policy; they also play a role in policy making, advising on options for new policies. The long experience and great knowledge of the senior administrators may often lead them to take the initiative in suggesting new policies. Ministers are not experts in the affairs of their departments and have time to pay attention to only a relatively small number of those affairs.

Ministers may often accept the advice or acquiesce in the views of their civil servants. The role of the civil service has grown with the vast increase in government business, owing to the expanded activity of government in internal affairs; the time pressures on ministers; the influence of the cabinet secretariat; the growth of interdepartmental committees, which tend to settle problems at an early stage; and the creation of high-level civil service committees to parallel and give advice to Cabinet committees.

But influential as the civil service may be, ministers are not its puppets, nor are civil servants "statesmen in disguise." Senior civil servants are mostly concerned with the administration of existing policies rather than policy planning, with immediate needs rather than long-term policy. The interaction between ministers and senior civil servants is complex, but the political ministers are still the dominant element in the policy-making process.

THE LEGISLATURE

Parliament—or strictly speaking the Queen-in-Parliament, since the monarch must assent to all legislation—is the supreme legislative body. It has the authority to pass, change, or repeal any law without being subject to restraint or veto by the courts of law or any other body; on the contrary, Parliament can reverse the decisions of the courts. No issues are outside the control of Parliament. It can pass retrospective legislation that legalizes past illegalities and punishes actions that were lawful when performed. By the 1911 Parliament Act, the term of Parliament is fixed at five years, though it can be dissolved at any time. But Parliament is able to prolong its own life as it did during both world wars. ·One Parliament cannot bind its successors.

In fact, Parliament uses self-restraint in the exercise of this legal supremacy. It is conscious of the common law tradition and of political conventions that foster moderation. The effective power of Parliament is limited in real ways. Parliament rarely passes legislation which is contrary to the views of the population or deprives individuals of rights. The principle of the *mandate* suggests that the electorate has given general approval of changes proposed by the electoral manifesto of the successful party. Though this does not mean that the electorate has approved of all proposals in the manifesto, it implies that a major change will only rarely be introduced in Parliament if it was not included in the party manifesto, except in a time of emergency or crisis.

Parliamentary action is also affected and influenced by the major interest groups in the country, which by convention are always consulted on legislation related to them. In the 1960s and 1970s some regarded the trade unions as having a virtual veto power on proposals concerning industrial relations and incomes policy. Perhaps most important of all, Parliament is dominated by the government, which, as the majority party, generally controls the time, procedure, and actions of Parliament and is responsible for the initiation of all financial and most legislative proposals.

In the 1970s a new factor, British membership in the European Community, affected parliamentary supremacy. Britain is now pledged to adhere to the rules and decisions of the Community, which signifies some qualification of Parliament's legal supremacy. The European Court of Justice ruled in 1990 that British courts could suspend a statute that was incompatible with law of the European Community. The Court ruled in 1991 that parts of a British law breached the law of the EC, and therefore had to be changed. Parliamentary supremacy has also been limited by the 1950 European Convention on Human Rights, by which Britain accepted the obligation to recognize certain fundamental rights.

Composition of Parliament

The two chambers of Parliament now at Westminister have existed for seven centuries. Though for some time the House of Commons has been the more significant political body, the House of Lords had an unlimited veto power over legislation until 1911. In that year the Parliament Act limited the veto of the Lords to two years over bills passed by the Commons in three successive sessions and abolished the veto over financial bills. In 1949 this delaying power of the Lords was reduced to one year.

House of Lords

The House of Lords today consists of about 1200 members. Its heterogeneous composition still reflects the nature of its origin with the greater noblemen and higher clergy. The main categories are the following:

1. Some 818 hereditary peers (since 1958 including women) who inherit or have been appointed to the peerage and who pass on the titles to their heirs. Since the Peerage Act of 1963 they can disclaim their titles for their lifetime.

2. About 330 life peers created under the Life Peerage Act of 1958. Their title expires at their death. Prime Minister Major announced in 1991 that a number of life peers belonging to all the major political parties would be appointed to be groomed for ministerial office.

3. Nine Lords of Appeal in Ordinary (law lords), who are appointed to act as judges when the House of Lords acts as a court of law. They must have been barristers for at least 15 years and have held high judicial office for at least 2 years.

4. Twenty-six senior dignitaries of the Church of England. They are the archbishops of Canterbury and York, the Bishops of London, Durham, and Winchester, and 21 other bishops in their order of seniority as bishops.

Although the House of Lords still has the function of considering and approving all legislation, its powers have been significantly limited by the Parliament Acts of 1911 and 1949. The Lords can propose amendments to bills and can delay them by voting against them, but they have no power of absolute veto. Since 1949, a bill passed by the Commons in two successive sessions does not need the consent of the House of Lords. In 1991 the War Crimes Bill became law in this way after having been voted down twice by the House of Lords in 1990 and 1991. The House of Lords has no power over finances. It can still reject, however, delegated legislation, which requires the approval of both Houses. By convention, it will not vote against the principles of a government bill if the bill was featured in the governing party's electoral manifesto. The House in 1991 did defeat parts of a government bill on life sentences for murder that was not in the 1987 Conservative manifesto.

Formerly a body consisting almost entirely of hereditary peers, relatively few of whom attended its sittings, the Lords since 1958 has included life peers (men and women), who are more likely to participate in its activity. Whereas the average daily attendance in 1955 was 92, there are now 300 who attend.

The Lords are unpaid; however, since 1957, attending members receive a daily allowance for expenses and lodging. Because of the experience in public affairs and the intellectual caliber of many of the new life peers—as well as the presence of past and present cabinet ministers, other public servants, and former MPs—debate on important topics in the House of Lords may often be on a high level.

On the whole, the House of Lords has exercised its functions with discretion. Only four bills—the 1949 Parliament Act, two statutes passed in 1914, and the 1991 War Crimes Act—have become law under the provisions of the 1911 Parliament Act. The subordination of the Lords to the Commons and to the executive has been accepted in general, but proposed legislation has sometimes been delayed.

It is this power of delay and the Conservative majority in the House of Lords that have been the main reasons for criticism. In a democratic system like the British, it seems paradoxical for a nonelected body to delay the legislation passed by the elected lower chamber and to claim it is acting in the best interests of the country. Because of the automatic Conservative plurality in the House of Lords, a Labour government has more to fear in this regard than a Conservative one. Because of the unrepresentative nature of the House of Lords, the Labour party is still theoretically pledged to its abolition.

The House of Lords still performs a useful role as an organ of review in the revision of legislation, the initiation of noncontroversial legislation, the discussion of important topics, and the examination of delegated legislation—which all save the time of the Commons. It performs an important judicial function as the final Court of Appeal and Court of Criminal Appeal. By convention only the law lords and the lord chancellor attend these sittings of the House as a court.

House of Commons

There are now 651 members (MPs) of the House of Commons elected from the territorial constituencies of the country. The number and distribution of the seats can be altered according to population changes after recommendations by the four boundary commissions. Currently, 524 represent English, 38 Welsh, 72 Scottish, and 17 Northern Ireland constituencies. Members are elected at a general election or at a by-election on the death or resignation of an MP.

There are no property, religious, sex, or education disqualifications. Any person over 21 can be elected, except members of the House of Lords, aliens, clergy of the established churches and the Catholic Church, felons, and holders of most official positions other than members of the government. Since 1963, an MP who has succeeded to the peerage can disclaim his title and remain in the Commons. MPs are paid less and have inadequate facilities compared with U.S. congressional members. Only in recent years have they obtained some secretarial assistance and office space. They now receive a salary of about £29,000 and another £25,000 for secretarial costs. Nevertheless, there is no shortage of candidates for the Commons. People are attracted to it for nonmaterial rewards, including public service, personal prestige, and the opportunity to exert influence on public affairs.[20]

The glory of Parliament may have dimmed somewhat in recent years, but the Commons still plays a significant role in the political system. Parliament not only possesses legislative supremacy and authorizes all expenditure and taxation; the Commons is politically important because its party composition is the basis for the formation of governments. It enables the leaders of one political party to rule and those of the opposition party to be considered as a possible alternative government. It is the major

political arena in which there is continuous interaction among the parties. Ministers explain
and defend their policies in it against the attacks of the opposition.

If it is not the real determinant of policy
or decisions, Parliament wields influence over
the executive which makes concessions to it.
For its members, Parliament is a forum for the
raising of complaints and grievances on behalf
of their constituents, for arguing political views
of their own, and for subjecting the executive
to criticism. It is also the main path to political
distinction and to membership in the government (see Table 2.11).

Who Becomes an MP?

The members of the different parliamentary
parties have become similar from the standpoint of social background and career. MPs
have become increasingly professional in their
background and life-style, and therefore less
characteristic of their constituents. This is
especially true in the Parliamentary Labour
party, where the proportion of manual workers has fallen and that of professionals has increased since 1945.[21] The average age of the
PLP has fallen to 49; recruiting younger MPs
generally means less opportunity for working-
class candidates, who tend to emerge later in
life.

The Conservative MPs, with 50 percent
from professional backgrounds and 37 percent
from business in 1989, illustrate the postwar
shift away from landowners, farmers, and people with an aristocratic background to business
people and industrial technocrats. A considerable number have been local councillors. Conservative MPs have rarely had working-class
backgrounds.

The number of women MPs in the postwar
period has remained approximately the same:
about 5 percent until 1987. It did decline
in 1979 when only 19 women were elected,
though one of them, Mrs. Thatcher, became
prime minister. Women have always been underrepresented in the Commons, which has

Table 2.11   THE POWERS AND LIMITS OF PARLIAMENT

Powers

Provides road to political success and to becoming a
    minister

Main forum for discussion of grievances of constituents
    Approves legislation and policy thus giving them
    greater legitimacy

Allows representation and expression of different views
    of citizens on policy

Recent activities

Greater independence of MPs in voting in 1970s and
    1980s; governments defeated in some standing
    committees, and in 1986 on a bill

Departmental select committees set up in 1979 in
    House of Commons to investigate administration
    and recommend policy; House televised since 1989

More attention paid to constituents

Some committees discuss issues of European
    Community

Limits

Power of executive

Increasing impact of interest groups outside
    of Parliament

Increasing burden of work

Little impact on decisions of European Community

been a male-dominated "club." Parliament is
thus a more middle-class, better educated
group of people than the average citizen, and
it contains a disproportionately greater ratio of
males to females than the general population.

There has also been a trend for MPs to
remain longer in Parliament and thus to be regarded as professional politicians. The House
of Commons has always been attractive to people in the professions, who in many cases combine their careers as lawyers, journalists, or
business people with afternoon and evening
attendance in the House.

MPs and Political Parties

About 80 of the 651 members of the House of Commons are in the 1992 government. All MPs are members of political parties, and the arrangements in the House reflect the fact that its working is interrelated with the party system and the operation of government.

The only exception to the partisan nature of MPs is the Speaker (with three deputies), who is the chief officer of the House of Commons. Unlike his U.S. counterpart, the British Speaker is an impartial, nonpartisan figure who gives up his party associations. The general rule is that the Speaker, who is elected at the beginning of a Parliament, will be re-elected in subsequent Parliaments irrespective of which party controls a majority. For the first time a woman was elected in 1992.

The chamber is small and rectangular. It is a political arena in which the opposing parties physically face each other, as shown in Figure 2.5. The Speaker sits at one end of the chamber. The benches to his or her right are used by the government party, while the official opposition party and other parties not supporting the government sit on his or her left. The members of the government and the shadow

British MP Betty Boothroyd gestures during her speech to fellow members at the House of Commons in London before they elected her first woman Speaker.

cabinet sit on the front benches, with their supporters behind them on the back benches. The physical separation reflects the political differences between the two sides.

The smallness of the chamber, which seats only 350 MPs, together with the fact that MPs speak from their places rather than from a rostrum, has led to a more intimate style of speech than is often the case in other countries. By tradition, MPs do not read speeches

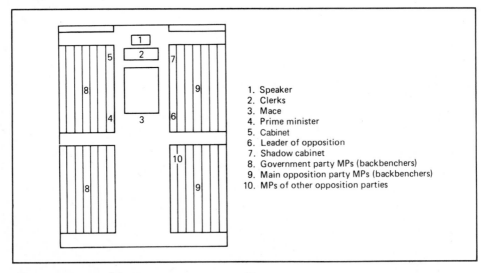

1. Speaker
2. Clerks
3. Mace
4. Prime minister
5. Cabinet
6. Leader of opposition
7. Shadow cabinet
8. Government party MPs (backbenchers)
9. Main opposition party MPs (backbenchers)
10. MPs of other opposition parties

Figure 2.5 House of Commons

or speak boisterously. They refer to colleagues in a dignified and polite way.

With rare exceptions the MPs are organized in parliamentary parties. The Parliamentary Labour party (PLP) is composed of Labour members of both Houses. The major organ of the Conservative party in Parliament is the 1922 Committee, composed of all Conservative backbenchers.

The Opposition

The official opposition, the largest nongovernmental party in Parliament, is a vital part of the British system. Its leaders are seen inside and outside Parliament, as an alternative government. Its function is both to subject government to criticism and to seek to replace it, as well as to participate in the working of the system.

The opposition acts as a responsible group in criticism of the government. It proposes alternative policies and tries to change government policies, get concessions on government bills, and defeat the government. By convention, governments resign or request dissolution of Parliament if defeated on a major question, though since 1867 only five governments have resigned for this reason. In 1979 the opposition successfully moved a vote of no confidence for the first time since 1892. In Parliament, the opposition is continually addressing itself to the electorate as a whole with its eyes on the next election.

The opposition also cooperates with the government party in formulating the business of the House. It chooses the subjects for debate on a number of occasions, currently on the 16 days available to it. It is given time at the committee stage of bills to move amendments and time in the House itself for both opposition leaders and backbenchers to question ministers. The government even provides the time for the opposition to move motions of censure against it. Since 1937 there has been an official, paid leader of the opposition who is consulted by the prime minister on political arrangements; by convention, the shadow cabinet receives information from cabinet ministers relevant to the conduct of affairs. There is consultation between the two sides on some questions concerning foreign affairs and defense.

The opposition is represented on standing and select committees in proportion to its membership in the Commons. An accepted rule is that the chairpersons of the Public Accounts Committee and the Select Committee on the Ombudsman, as well as other committees, are members of the opposition.

How Important Is the MP?

Important though MPs are, their prominence has declined for several reasons: the extension of the suffrage, the organization of constituency associations and the rise of disciplined political parties; the increase in the function and activity of government and the growth in power of the bureaucracy; and the nature of modern general elections, which are to a large degree about which party leader will become prime minister.

MPs are aware that the electorate is the ultimate political sovereign and that their reelection depends on their activity in Parliament. Attendance is not compulsory, and no financial loss is attached to nonattendance, but it is rare for MPs to neglect their parliamentary duties. MPs also frequently visit their constituencies, particularly on weekends, and hold "surgeries," at which they meet their constituents. They ask questions in the Commons and speak in debates on matters affecting their areas.

The crucial fact about MPs is that, with rare exceptions, they are members of parties that they are expected to support loyally and without which they could not have been elected. In the Commons, MPs are still subject to the persuasion, if not the discipline, of the whips and rarely engage in a conflict with the parliamentary leadership. Party cohesion exists partly because of agreement by party

MPs on policy issues, partly because of ambition for promotion, especially among those of the government party, and partly because of the probable political isolation experienced by those consistently opposing party policy. The ultimate threat by a prime minister, faced by revolt within his party, is to dissolve Parliament, but this is a theoretical rather than a real menace.

Nevertheless, some revolts against the leaders, when the party is in power and in opposition, have occurred. The 1970s witnessed a greater degree of dissent than in previous years, with MPs more prepared to vote against their party whether in or out of power[22].

This recent greater assertiveness and independence of MPs can be attributed to a number of factors. MPs found that they were seldom denied readoption as candidates or ministerial promotion because of their rebellious actions. Defeats of the government—65 times between 1972 and 1979—did not mean resignation or the dissolution of Parliament, which will occur only on a motion of confidence. The major parties have been internally divided on significant recent issues such as the European Community, devolution, and income policy, also, MPs have believed, correctly in a number of cases, that fear of defeat may make a government change its mind.

For some time the dominant body in the operation of the Commons has been the Government, which controls the timetable, the allocation of time, and the procedure of the Commons and is responsible for the initiation of most legislation. During the years from 1939 to 1948, backbenchers had no legislative initiative; they currently have 12 days to introduce bills as well as 10 days to move motions.

The great increase in the amount of legislation, and in its scope, variety, and technical nature, has meant both that few MPs are knowledgeable about much of the legislation and the wide range of problems with which it deals and that little time is available for the discussion of government legislation. Most amendments of that legislation are minor, and they are made or agreed to by the Government. Of those amendments proposed by ministers, almost all are accepted by the House; of those proposed by government backbenchers, 9.5 percent are successful as are 4.4 percent of those proposed by opposition MPs.[23]

In addition, many rules are now made by ministers in the form of delegated legislation. There are several reasons for this large development of ministerial power: the technical nature of the rules, the speed with which they can be made, the flexibility available to change them, and the opportunity of discretionary choice. Although some opportunity to discuss delegated legislation is available to MPs, there is little parliamentary scrutiny of it.

An Assenting Assembly

MPs participate in the work of the Commons in a variety of ways: through question time, participation in debates on legislation and on policy, membership on standing and select committees, and proposal of motions and initiation of some legislation.

In the parliamentary golden age of the mid-nineteenth century, the Commons regularly defeated governments without being dissolved. Since that period, few governments have been defeated and obliged to resign or have Parliament dissolved as a result of the actions of the House of Commons.

A number of criticisms can be made of the failings of contemporary parliaments. Parliamentary control over administration and finance is ineffective. Most MPs feel inadequately informed abut administration. The real initiative in the legislative process and policy making is in the hands of the executive. Procedure in the Commons is still poorly organized and archaic. The majority political party is the real strength underlying the operation of the political system. Nevertheless, recent experience has shown that MPs can exercise some control over governments. The assertiveness and dissent among MPs led to a surprising number of government defeats in the 1970s and 1980s.

JUDGES AND POLITICS

Unlike the United States, Britain does not have a system of judicial review, and courts cannot declare legislation void. As the legal sovereign, Parliament, not the courts, decides on the nature and extent of legislative power. The function of British judges is to apply the law to the particular cases before their courts rather than to decide on the desirability or correctness of the law itself. Some judges interpret the law in a way that upholds individual liberty or in accordance with social and personal justice. But most judges interpret statutes narrowly, holding that it is Parliament, not judicial interpretation, that should change a law that is unjust.

British judges have long had the reputation of being impartial and neutral. The judges' impartiality results partly from the common-law tradition and judgment based on precedent and partly from the method of their appointment. Judges are not political appointees; few of them have been MPs, and even fewer have been partisans of a political party, as they come from the ranks of barristers with long and successful careers. In the legal profession, there are now about 5,500 barristers, of whom 750 are women, and over 40,000 solicitors.

Judges are independent of the other branches of government and their salaries are not open to discussion by Parliament. Since 1701, judges have been appointed on "good behavior," meaning until retirement, which since 1959 has been at age 75. They can only be dismissed by resolutions of both Houses, an event that has not yet occurred. They are scrupulous about a fair hearing in court and impartial application of the law.

The qualities of impartiality and neutrality are always present in cases concerning disputes between private individuals. But there are also other cases in which decisions of judges may affect a wider group of people, or in which they can exercise some discretion. These cases have recently included subjects such as immigration, industrial relations, race relations, police powers, and human rights. It is on questions of this kind that the generally conservative view of judges may be felt. Judges form one of the prominent elite groups of the country. Over 75 percent of senior judges were educated at public schools and at Oxford and Cambridge; over 80 percent come from upper or upper-middle-class backgrounds. A conservative position is to be expected from individuals who not only come from these social backgrounds but also have had a successful career and adhere to the tradition of the common law and precedent.

Judges have been reluctant to limit the scope of ministerial powers and have habitually upheld the exercise of the discretionary power of ministers (who can take action under a statute if they think it necessary). Judges have approved executive action, provided it was not out of bounds or exercised unfairly, unreasonably, or in bad faith.

But in the last three decades some judges have tried to control administrative action and assert judicial discretion in cases on the scope of executive prerogative in war or on ministerial privilege.

The distinction between policy making by the politician and the application of law by the judges is not always easy to draw in practice. Judges, in reality, help to create criminal law by deciding what is criminal conduct. Judges have often been used by governments to chair tribunals of inquiry or Royal Commissions. In this role judges can influence public policy while maintaining their neutrality as judges.

Judges have a new function as a result of British membership in the European Community. This membership means that Britain is now bound by Common Market treaties and laws. The law of the European Community will be interpreted and applied by British courts, and if that law conflicts with parliamentary statute, courts may have to decide on its validity.

The increase in the scope of public activity has meant that the ordinary courts of law are inadequate to deal with many issues. To fulfill this function, administrative tribunals concerned with the justice or appropriateness of decisions have been established and judicial and quasi-judicial powers have been given to departments and administrative bodies. A series of administrative tribunals—the members of which are rarely lawyers—cover such issues as rent, immigration, pensions, family allowances, mental health, industrial injuries, and national health insurance.

The courts have played a historic role in restraining executive power to its legitimate function and in fostering the existence of individual rights. In this age of strong public or governmental action, some have voiced concern that the common law may not be able to protect these rights and that a bill of rights along American lines should be passed. In fact, Britain has ratified the European Convention on Human Rights, and any British subject can now appeal to the European Courts on these matters. But individual rights in Britain have been, and remain, dependent not simply on legal safeguards imposed by judges, but also on traditions of civility, self-restraint, and tolerance.

Key Terms

backbencher
by-election
cabinet
city
civil list
civil service
collective responsibility
common law
Confederation of British Industry
Conservative Party
constituency
crown
delegated legislation
electoral swing
frontbencher
House of Commons
House of Lords
ideology
individual responsibility
Labour party
mandate
marginal seat
Militant Tendency
minister
National Economic Development Council (NEDC)
National Executive Committee (NEC)
opposition
Parliament
Parliament Acts 1911 and 1949
Parliamentary Labour Party
party identification
permanent secretary
Plaid Cymru
prime minister
QUANGO
question hour
Scottish National Party (SNP)
Social and Liberal Democrats (SLD)
Social Democratic Party (SDP)
standing committee
Trades Union Congress (TUC)
Treasury
vote of censure
vote of no confidence
Westminster
whip
Whitehall

Suggestions for Further Reading

Blondel, Jean. *Voters, Parties and Leaders* (Baltimore: Penguin, 1963).

Bradley, Ian. *The Strange Rebirth of Liberal Britain* (London: Chatto and Windus, 1985).

Butler, David, and D. Kavanagh. *The British General Election of 1987* (London: Macmillan, 1988).

Butler, David, and Donald Stokes. *Political Change in Britain* (London: St. Martin's, 1974).

Conley, Frank. *General Elections Today* (Manchester: Manchester University Press, 1990).

Drucker, Henry, ed. *Multi-Party Britain* (London: Macmillan, 1979).

Finer, S. E. *Anonymous Empire*, 2nd ed. (London: Pall Mall, 1966).

Foote, Geoffrey. *The Labour Party's Political Thought*, 2nd ed. (Beckenham: Croom Helm, 1986).

Franklin, Mark N. *The Decline of Class Voting in Britain* (Oxford: Clarendon, 1985).

Harrop, Martin, and W. L. Miller. *Elections and Voters* (London: Macmillan, 1987).

Heath, Anthony, Roger Jowell, and John Curtice. *How Britain Votes* (New York: Pergamon, 1985).

McKenzie, Robert. *British Political Parties*, 2nd ed. (London: Heinemann, 1963).

Mughan, Anthony A. *Party and Participation in British Elections* (London: Pinter, 1986).

O'Gorman, Frank. *British Conservative Thought from Burke to Thatcher* (New York: Longman, 1986).

Pulzer, Peter. *Political Representation and Elections in Britain*, 3rd ed. (London: Allen and Unwin, 1975).

Rose, Richard, and Ian McAllister. *Voters Begin to Choose* (Beverly Hills: Sage, 1986).

Stanworth, Philip, and Anthony Giddens, eds. *Elites and Power in British Society* (New York: Cambridge University Press, 1974).

The Executive

Broadbent, Ewen. *The Military and Government* (New York: St. Martin's, 1988).

Bruce-Gardyne, Jock, and Nigel Lawson. *Ministers and Mandarins* (London: Sidgwick and Jackson, 1986).

Drewry, Gavin, and Tony Butcher. *The Civil Service Today* (Oxford: Blackwell, 1988).

Fry, Geoffrey K. *The Changing Civil Service* (Boston: Allen and Unwin, 1985).

Hennessy, Peter. *Cabinet* (New York: Blackwell, 1986).

Hennessy, Peter, and Anthony Seldon. *Ruling Performance: British Governments from Attlee to Thatcher* (New York: Blackwell, 1987).

Kavanagh, Dennis. *Thatcherism and British Politics*, 2nd ed. (Oxford: Oxford University Press, 1990).

King, Anthony, ed. *The British Prime Minister*, 2nd ed. (Durham: Duke University, 1985).

Mackintosh, John. *The British Cabinet*, 3rd ed. (London: Stevens, 1977).

Marsh, Ian. *Policy Making in a Three Party System: Committees, Coalitions and Parliament* (New York: Methuen, 1986).

Rose, Richard. *Understanding Big Government* (Beverly Hills: Sage, 1984).

The Legislature

Mellors, Colin. *The British MP* (London: Saxon House, 1978).

Norton, Philip, ed. *Parliament in the 1980s* (New York: Blackwell, 1985).

Norton, Philip. *The Commons in Perspective* (New York: Longman, 1981).

Richards, P. G. *The Backbenchers* (London: Faber, 1972).

Shell, Donald. *The House of Lords* (Ottawa: Barnes and Noble, 1988).

Walkland, S. A., ed. *The House of Commons in the Twentieth Century* (London: Oxford University Press, 1979).

Walkland, S. A., and M. Ryle, eds. *The Commons Today* (London: Fontana, 1981).

Judges and Politics

Abel-Smith, Brian, and R. Stevens. *Lawyers and the Courts* (London: Heinemann, 1970).

Berlins, Marcel, and C. Dyer. *The Law Machine*, 3rd ed. (Harmondsworth: Penguin, 1989).

Burney, Elizabeth. *Magistrate, Court and Community* (London: Hutchinson, 1979).

Devlin, Patrick. *The Judge* (London: Oxford University Press, 1979).

Jackson, R. M. *The Machinery of Justice in England*, 7th ed. (New York: Cambridge University Press, 1977).

Stevens, Robert. *Law and Politics* (London: Weidenfeld and Nicolson, 1979).

C. Public Policy

THE MIXED ECONOMY

Like other Western countries, Britain has a mixed economy. Part of it is owned and administered by public authorities; this public sector employs 5.5 million workers, including central and local government and public corporations. However, most of the economy is under private ownership and control. The private sector has increased since 1979 as the Conservative government cut the public sector and denationalized or "privatized" many enterprises.

Both Labour and Conservative governments intervened in economic affairs in the postwar period in differing degrees. This intervention stemmed partly from the desire to implement social principles such as the public ownership of resources, the welfare of citizens, and the reduction of unemployment, but also from the effort to solve economic problems by increasing production and trade. Governments therefore not only nationalized industries, but also promoted industrial development, supplied money and credits to both public and private enterprises, increased the level of investment, helped firms in trouble, proposed "targets" and planning agreements for industry and the restructuring of industry, and attempted to restrain wage increases.

The public sector today comprises three parts: central government, local government, and the nationalized industries.

Central government is responsible for all spending on social security benefits, health, defense, trade, industry, overseas payments and foreign aid, and central administration. It also partly finances housing, education, transport, and law and order programs. Most of the expenditure is paid for by taxation (see Figure 2.6).

Local government now accounts for about one-quarter of total public spending. The largest item is education, followed by housing, transport, law and order, and social services. This expenditure is paid for property taxes and by grants from the central government.

The nationalized industries in 1979 accounted for 10 percent of gross domestic group (GDP), employed almost 2 million (8 percent of the work force) and took 14 percent of fixed investment. The industries dominated areas such as coal, electricity, gas, broadcasting, public transport, communications, and iron and steel. Because they were producers of basic goods and services, as well as large consumers of raw materials, they significantly affected investment, employment, prices, and cost of living in the whole economy. By 1988, denationalization had reduced them to 6 percent of GDP, 750,000 workers, and 9 percent of investment.

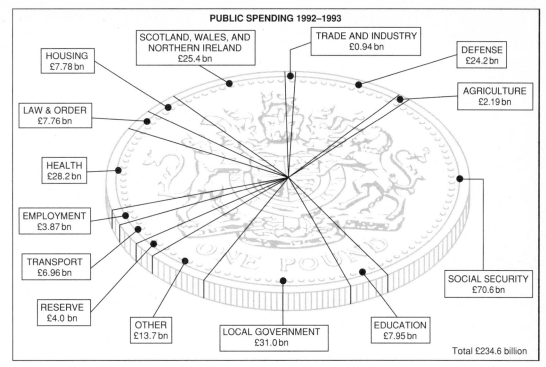

Figure 2.6 Public Spending, 1992–1993

THE DECLINE OF NATIONALIZED INDUSTRIES

The motives to nationalize industries were varied. They included public control over significant parts of the economic system; efficient organization and development of the economy; influencing the level of investment to achieve full employment; better industrial relations; preventing possible abuse of a monopoly situation; continuation of enterprises, even if unprofitable, to provide a social service or minimize unemployment; or assistance to failing firms. Added to these economic and social resons was the ideology of the Labour party, whose constitution (Clause IV) calls for "public ownership of the means of production, distribution and exchange."

The most prominent form of nationalization in the postar period was the public corporation. Each nationalized enterprise is administered not by a government department

but by the board of the corporation, which is free from political interference in its daily management and administration. The minister who appoints the boards does not have direct responsibility for the operation, but approves the general lines of capital development, research, and borrowing, and can give general directions.

In the main the nationalized industries, especially coal and railroads, suffered substantial deficits, and their overall performance was poor. In addition, two major issues lacked clarity: the objectives of nationalization and the relations between corporations and the ministers. Differences on the objectives are the result of mixed motives for nationalization. Should the enterprises be run primarily from the point of view of efficiency and along economic lines with balanced accounts, or should they be more concerned with low prices, convenience for customers (rail), and prevention of unemployment (coal mines), and thus act as a

Feature 2.3 **Thatcherism in Theory and Practice, 1979–1990**

THEORY

Personal Values

Traditional and moral values, individual self-reliance, personal responsibility, thrift, hard work, family, freedom under the law, free choice.

Social Attitudes

Consumer choice, capital punishment, reduced state role in economy, private property, property-owning democracy.

Political Ideas

Law and order, nationalism, strong defense including nuclear deterrent, maintenance of role in NATO, ally of United States, anti-terrorist, strong anticommunism, restoration of national confidence, caution on European integration, limited influence of trade unions, weakened left-wing local authorities.

Economic Approach

End postwar consensus on mixed economy, reduce public sector, free market, remove economic controls, limit government spending, strive for economic growth, control inflation, limit level of wage settlement, reduce budget deficit and monetary growth, reduce taxes, reduce money supply, stable currency.

PRACTICE

Individual Self-Reliance

Sale of council houses, rise in shareholders (11 million), increase in small business (10 percent of employed), personal pension schemes, private medical insurance, mortgage tax relief, private choice of schools for children.

Domestic Policy

Limits on trade unions (ballots needed for election of union members, before strikes, on political funds); limits on picketing, secondary actions, and closed shops; union funds now liable for damages; limits on local authorities (ceiling on rate increases); community (poll) tax (same rate for all in local area); national education core curriculum; more broadcasting competition.

Defense and Foreign Affairs

1982, Falklands War; 1983, broke relations with Libya, cruise missiles in Britain; 1984, Hong Kong agreement (becomes Chinese in 1997), concession for U.S. planes to fly to Libya, cut in British contribution to European Community, approval of end of trade barriers in EC by 1992, maintenance of nuclear deterrent (Trident); 1985, Anglo-Irish agreement; 1988, support of INF treaty; 1990–1991, support of U.S. policy in Gulf War, befriended Gorbachev.

Economic Policy

Decontrol of foreign exchange, prices, income, minimum wage, credit buying; privatization (sale of public enterprises); cuts in tax rates, inflation, government borrowing, numbers in civil service; rise in public expenditure as proportion of GDP; economic growth through increased productivity, but rise in unemployment, fall in manufactures' share in GDP; sale of council housing; increase in number of self-employed; growth in personal consumption; increased investment; balance of payments deficits; high mortgage rates; joined exchange rate mechanism of European Community 1990.

Thatcher Style

Highly personal; fewer meetings of full cabinet and more meetings of committees and ministers; ended Civil Service Department and Think Tank, No. 10 policy advisers; more active in choosing senior civil servants; rarely intervened in debates or major speeches in House of Commons; strong convictions; controlled direction of economic and foreign policy; changed political agenda of the country; won three successive national elections; longest-serving P.M. of twentieth century.

social service irrespective of deficits they may incur? Should they be used by the government to control parts of the economy and to help implement general economic, wage, and price policies? Should they help implement British technological inventions, or should they be regarded as possible experiments in workers' participation?

Some confusion also existed about the respective roles of ministers and the boards in decisions made by the corporations. Ministers have the general powers previously mentioned and particular powers over each industry. But ministers rarely gave directions in a formal way. Instead, to avoid political responsibility, they preferred to influence decisions by informal consultation or by "arm-twisting" or "persuading" the chairman of the industry to do their bidding.

A major change took place with the privatization policy of the Thatcher government that consisted of selling off the assets and shares of nationalized industries to private owners (see Feature 2.3). This policy also allowed some services previously administered by public authorities to be performed by private firms. Prime Minister Thatcher argued that privatization brought certain benefits: the industries would be more efficient and profitable in a more competitive market, away from interference of officials; their objectives would not be overridden by irrelevant political, social, and economic factors, thereby increasing business confidence; the government would raise large amounts by sales; Britain would become a property-owning democracy (now 11 million shareholders). By 1991 about 60 percent of state industry had been privatized (see Table 2.12). The government claimed that output, profits, investment, and industrial relations in those enterprises had all improved.

The Conservative government also sought to promote competition by ending the monopoly of a number of enterprises, such

Table 2.12   NATIONALIZATION AND PRIVATIZATION TO 1992

Nationalized industries	Major industries privatized since 1979
Coal Electricity Steel Post Office Girobank Railways Waterways Civil Aviation Authority Water London Regional Transport Shipbuilders (Merchant)	Telecom Gas National Oil British Airways British Airports Authority Aerospace Shipbuilders (Warships) Transport Docks National Freight Enterprise Oil National Bus British Petroleum Cable and Wireless Jaguar Rolls-Royce Rover British Steel National Power British Technology Group

as long distance buses and express delivery services, and of certain professional activity, such as some legal work.

ECONOMIC PLANNING

All postwar governments accepted the need for planning, which resulted from increased government activity and expenditure. They saw the need for creating nationalized industries and increasing productivity, economic growth, and exports. Governmental intervention took a variety of forms: financial aid and incentives to stimulate industrial investment; taxation changes and loans to strengthen development areas and transfer workers from services to manufacturing; physical controls to induce firms to move to less developed areas; subsidies to aid failing enterprises and controls on wages, prices, and foreign exchange. Bodies, such as the National Economic Development Council (NEDC) and the national Enterprise Board, were set up to assist the economy and to foster greater efficiency.

These governments sought, mainly through the annual budget, to maintain a high level of economic activity, and strove for full employment, economic growth, and a rising standard of living. They stressed expansion of demand rather than anti-inflationary measures, and relatively little attention was paid to restraint of money supply.

The Thatcher government broke with this approach. It sought, at first, to reduce infla-

Chancellor of the Exchequer Norman Lamont with the budget, March 1991, and his wife.

tion by restricting the money supply, hoping to increase output and employment. It tried to revitalize the private sector by lowering taxes and interest rates that would result from cuts in public expenditure and borrowing. It emphasized market forces by reducing the public sector, taming the trade unions, ending controls on prices and wages, and trying to curb the spending of local authorities. To do the last, and to attempt to make clear to citizens how much local authorities were spending, Thatcher imposed a poll tax on residents of an equal amount, to replace rates on property. This was seen by many as unfair, and was largely responsible for Conservative electoral defeats at by-elections in 1989 and 1990, and, to some extent, for her own downfall as party leader and Prime Minister in 1990. The poll tax was replaced by a new local tax, partly based on the value of residential property, in 1991–1992.

The government from 1979 on was particularly interested in limiting or controlling the power of the trade unions. Unions must now hold ballots for the election of union leaders, before a strike is called, and on their political funds. Limits have been set on picketing, secondary strike action, and closed shops. Union funds are now liable for damages in civil actions. Union membership declined substantially during the 1980s.

THE WELFARE STATE

Britain has long concerned itself with the poor. Before 1914, national insurance, old-age pensions, and unemployment insurance were adopted. But it was not until after World War II that the plans for a welfare state and for social improvement were implemented. The Beveridge Report in 1942 had proposed the extension of the process of insurance to provide adequate subsistence for all. Two years later Beveridge called for a system of full employment.

The Labour government of 1945–1950 introduced the basic elements of a welfare system which has been modified and extended during the ensuing 40 years. Three elements of this system have been particularly important: social security, the national health service, and personal social services. The last is the responsibility of local authorities and voluntary organizations, while the first two are the direct responsibility of central government.

Social Security

The social security system is a complex one with over 30 different benefits. The major postwar reform in this area has been the extension of national insurance to cover unemployment, sickness, maternity, retirement, industrial injuries, and death. A National Insurance Fund was established, to which insured persons and their employers contribute and from which they are paid when necessary. The contributions cover about 90 percent of the benefits paid, with the state paying the rest. The system is universal, applying to everyone, but individuals can have their own private insurance in addition to the national system.

Unemployment benefit is payable for one year in each case of unemployment. Sickness benefits of various kinds cover loss of earnings during absence from work. Maternity pay, normally for 18 weeks, is now usually paid by employers. A variety of different grants, depending on the individuals and relationships, are paid on death. The most significant of these grants go to widows who receive allowances for the first 26 weeks of widowhood, as well as other possible allowances.

Since 1946 pensions have been paid to men at age 65 and women at age 60; individuals may defer retirement for five years and qualify for a higher pension, however. Since 1959, the basic pension has been supplemented by an additional amount in return for larger contributions, an earning-related scheme. Pensions are also paid to disabled veterans. An injured worker receives benefits for a period depending on the disablement.

Family allowances have been given since 1945 to mothers who receive a sum for all children who are below the minimum school-leaving age or in full-time education (now up to the age of 19). In 1977, child benefits replaced family allowances and the income tax allowances, which have been phased out. Children also receive other benefits: medical examinations, free milk (which since 1971 has been limited to those under 7 years of age), and school meals. Benefits introduced in 1988 included an income support scheme for families whose income is under a certain level, a family credit for low income working families with children, and aid for rent and local rates.

The cost of these services has been high. Social security accounts for about 9 percent and retirement pensions alone for 6 percent of GNP. If health and education are included, the social services account for over 23 percent of GNP and 47 percent of total public expenditure. But, in spite of the cost, for political reasons Conservative governments did not reduce the services and benefits. Indeed, expenditure increased under Thatcher and Major, partly because of the larger numbers of elderly and unemployed people and single-parent families.

The National Health Service

Introduced in 1946, the National Health Service (NHS) was one of the towering achievements of the Labour Government. When the NHS was established, the state acquired all hospitals except teaching hospitals. Doctors could no longer sell their practices or set up practice in an area that already had too many doctors. But concessions included the right of doctors to private practice, maintenance of private paying beds in hospitals, the right of the patients to choose their doctor, and local rather than central administration of hospitals. Medical and dental services were free to all who used the service. Doctors in the service receive a basic salary plus a certain fee for each patient. Hospitals have been run by regional boards and committees. Over 90 per-

cent of doctors decided to enter the service. Residents in Britain can choose to join the system, as over 90 percent have done. They have free choice of an NHS doctor, dentist, optician, and pharmacist, and have access to specialists and hospital treatment through their doctor.

The creation of the NHS and the provision of free medicine resulted initially in higher costs than had been anticipated. Charges, covering only a small part of the cost, were therefore imposed for drug prescriptions, dental treatment, dentures, and spectacles. But over 80 percent of the cost is financed from the regular tax. The most costly item has been the hospitals, which now account for about three-fifths of the total cost; the teaching hospitals are particularly expensive. The NHS, employing 1 million people, including 30,000 doctors, now accounts for 10 percent of public expenditure and 6 percent of GDP. The NHS has faced some difficulties in recent years because of the demands on it. Problems have arisen over pay for medical personnel, industrial disputes, low morale, waiting lists in hospitals and for operations, a shortage of specialists, demands caused by the increasing proportion of older people, and the high cost of medical care and high technology equipment. The cost of the NHS, which treats 30 million patients a year, rose 50 percent in real terms between 1979 and 1990. The government has therefore recently tried to shift emphasis from the treatment of illness to the promotion of health and the prevention of disease, and to decentralize the system by allowing some hospitals to administer their own budgets and to become self-governing trusts with their own boards of directors.

HAS BRITAIN FOUND ITS ROLE IN FOREIGN POLICY?

At the end of World War II, Britain was still one of the three major powers; its empire and Commonwealth contained one-quarter of the world's population. It remained the major European economic and military power until the mid-1950s. By 1952 Britain had manufactured atomic bombs, and in 1957 it exploded a thermonuclear bomb. It was the dominant power in the Middle East and the second most important power in the Far East, and had a "special relationship" with the United States.

But in the postwar period Britain has become an important but middle-sized power. It declined economically, in both production and trade, as other nations developed industrially. British economic growth was lower than other major Western European countries. Britain increased its imports not only of raw materials but also of manufactured chemical and semi-manufactured products. Britain never fully recaptured its export markets, over half of which had been lost as a result of World War II. Britain has been technologically inventive— for example, television, radar, the jet engine, and the swing-line plane—but has been deficient in exploiting inventions.

The British Empire has been almost completely transformed into independent nations, most of them now members of the commonwealth. Unable to produce missiles to launch its bombs, Britain became dependent on the United States, which supplied it with the Polaris missile. Britain could not sustain the burden of supporting other countries, such as Greece and Turkey, or of protecting Palestine, from which it withdrew in 1948. It began withdrawing its forces from other areas: the Suez Canal zone in 1956, Jordan in 1957, Iraq in 1958, the Persian Gulf in 1969, and Singapore in 1971. In 1997 the colony of Hong Kong will come under Chinese rule.

Britain's relative economic decline, as well as the demand for independence of its former colonies, affected its foreign policy. Both major parties agreed that Britain should be a nuclear power and for a time sought to maintain its bases east of Suez. Both Labour and Conservatives intervened to help keep the peace, to safeguard oil, tin, and rubber supply lines, and to protect other countries, such as Malaya from 1948 on,

Kenya between 1952 and 1960, and Kenya and Tanganyika in 1964, as well as the Middle East. About 10 percent of central government's expenditure was for defense.

Britain had to adjust its foreign policy to three developments: the decline in its special relationship with the United States, the end of the empire and the increase in the Commonwealth, and the creation of the European Community.

From Special Relationship to Ally

The close British-American relationship during World War II was transformed by postwar events, the first of which was the quick termination of the U.S. lend-lease program in 1945; this forced Britain to borrow heavily in the immediate postwar period. The strategic strength and economic might of the United States and its emergence as the dominant world power meant that Britain was an ally, not an equal partner. The relationship is now one of consultation and exchange of information and opinions on issues of common interest.

Britain is one of four countries in the world with a military nuclear capacity, and it intends to maintain that capacity. The core of its defense effort is now based on its membership in the North Atlantic Treaty Organization (NATO). Britain is committed to the deterrent strategy of NATO and to consultations of the Nuclear Planning Group within it. It contributes forces to all three elements of NATO's strategy: strategic nuclear, theater nuclear, and conventional armaments.

Britain's contribution to the first is its force of four nuclear submarines, each equipped with 16 Polaris A3 missiles armed with nuclear warheads with a range of 2800 miles. This Polaris system is due to be phased out by the mid-1990s. To replace it, the Government decided to buy the U.S. Trident submarine-launched missiles and to construct four new submarines to carry them. The submarines will be assigned to NATO, but will be under British control.

The Royal Navy, the strongest European navy in NATO, contributes its wide variety of ships—the third largest number of surface combat ships in the world—including an aircraft carrier, nuclear-powered submarines, and guided-missile destroyers to the alliance. In addition to its NATO assignments in the Atlantic and the North Sea, the Navy sends task fores into the Indian Ocean, partly to help safeguard oil supplies.

Britain's main field army, the British Army of the Rhine (BAOR) is stationed in northern Germany. BAOR, recently reduced to 25,000 soldiers, has a full range of modern mobile weapons at its command, including tactical nuclear weapons, that can be dropped from aircraft or fired from artillery. It is supported by a tactical unit of the Royal Air Force (RAF). The RAF as a whole has some 500 combat aircraft at its disposal, including units in Britain that provide part of NATO's mobile force.

Out of the NATO area, Britain still stations troops or plays a role in a number of areas such as Hong Kong (until 1997), Cyprus, Gibraltar, the Falklands, and in the major oceans. Britain played a significant role in the Gulf War of 1991. With the end of the Warsaw Pact in 1991, Britain plans to make substantial cuts in all its armed forces. Its army will be reduced to a ceiling of about 116,000 troops.

From Empire to Commonwealth

Before World War II the British Commonwealth, as it was then called, consisted of Britain and six dominions, which (except for South Africa) were largely populated by individuals of British extraction, economically developed, with democratic systems and values (again except for South Africa) similar to the British. Preferential trading arrangements, adopted in Ottawa in 1932, were extended to all the dominions.

The rest of Britain's possessions throughout the world were colonies ruled by Britain. They began demanding independence soon after the end of the war, beginning in Asia and then throughout Africa and the rest of the world. Most nations on gaining independence have chosen to be members of the Commonwealth, which in 1992 numbers 50 countries with a population of 1.3 billion (see Table 2.13).

The Commonwealth, now consisting of diverse races, religions, and cultures, is a voluntary association with members all being equal in status. Some are republics which acknowledge the monarch as head of the Commonwealth, some are constitutional monarchies owing allegiance to the monarch, and four have their own monarchs. Some are political democracies in the British sense, but others have one-party systems or are under military control. Some are based on private ownership, while others regard themselves as Socialists. A few are wealthy, but most are poor countries with a low per capita income.

The Commonwealth is a loose association of independent nations, all once ruled by Britain, which have in no way chosen each other but are linked by accident. British law no longer extends to the Commonwealth. It does not reach collective decisions or take united political action. It is neither a trade bloc—although some economic privileges do exist—nor a military alliance, though its weapons, uniforms, and military training are similar to Britain's and there are combined exercises and joint research organizations. It has no center of sovereignty, no central lawmaking body or parliament, and no organ to speak for it; in 1965, a secretariat was established, but it does not make decisions that are binding on its members.

Tangible and intangible bonds have linked the Commonwealth. The latter result from the use of English by the professional classes, similar educational experiences, and common backgrounds in some cases. More tangible have been the regular meetings of heads of governments, political leaders, and professional people; collaborative functions in areas such as health, education, and agriculture; and representation of the members by High Commissioners in London. Some preferential trade

Table 2.13   INDEPENDENT COUNTRIES IN THE COMMONWEALTH

(in order of date of independence)

1. United Kingdom		27. Swaziland	1968
2. Canada	1867	28. Republic of Nauru	
3. Commonwealth of Australia	1901	(special member)	1968
4. New Zealand	1907	29. Tonga	1970
5. India	1947	30. Western Samoa	1970
6. Sri Lanka	1948	31. Bangladesh	1973
7. Ghana	1957	32. Commonwealth of the Bahamas	1973
8. Malaysia	1957	33. Grenada	1974
9. Federal Republic of Nigeria	1960	34. Papua New Guinea	1975
10. Republic of Cyprus	1961	35. Seychelles	1976
11. Sierra Leone	1961	36. Solomon Islands	1978
12. United Republic of Tanzania	1961	37. Tuvala (special member)	1978
13. Jamaica	1962	38. Dominica	1978
14. Trinidad and Tobago	1962	39. St. Lucia	1979
15. Uganda	1963	40. Kiribati	1979
16. Kenya	1963	41. St. Vincent and the Grenadines	
17. Malawi	1964	(special member)	1979
18. Republic of Malta	1964	42. Zimbabwe	1980
19. Zambia	1964	43. Vanuatu	1980
20. The Gambia	1965	44. Belize	1981
21. Singapore	1965	45. Antigua and Barbuda	1981
22. Guyana	1966	46. Maldives	1982
23. Botswana	1966	47. St. Christopher and Nevis	1983
24. Lesotho	1966	48. Brunei	1984
25. Barbados	1966	49. Pakistan	1989
26. Mauritius	1968	50. Namibia	1990

Note: The special status of Nauru, Tuvalu, and St. Vincent and the Grenadines provides for all the privileges of Commonwealth membership and attendance at all Commonwealth meetings with the exception of the meetings of Commonwealth heads of government. Eire left the Commonwealth in 1949, South Africa in 1961, and Pakistan in 1972. In 1965 Rhodesia unilaterally declared its independence, but in 1979 it again came under British administration and in 1980 became the independent republic of Zimbabwe. Fiji, which joined the Commonwealth in 1970, left it in 1987. Pakistan rejoined in 1989.

arrangements still exist. Most of Britain's bilateral and much of its multilateral foreign aid has gone to the Commonwealth.

But Britain's ties with the Commonwealth have weakened. The very diversity of its members means that no common ethnic or cultural bonds exist. Controls have been imposed on nonwhite immigration into Britain. Britain can no longer offer military protection to the members. Few of them retain the Judicial Committee of the Privy Council in London as the final court of appeal from their own courts.

The Commonwealth is a useful bridge among races, areas of the world, and richer and poorer nations. But it has declined in economic value and political importance for Britain. This is especially true in the changing pattern of trade as Britain has turned to Europe, and the Commonwealth countries have begun manufacturing their own products. British exports to the Commonwealth decreased from 37.3 percent of the total in 1958 to 8.5 percent in 1987. In the same period, exports to the European Community increased

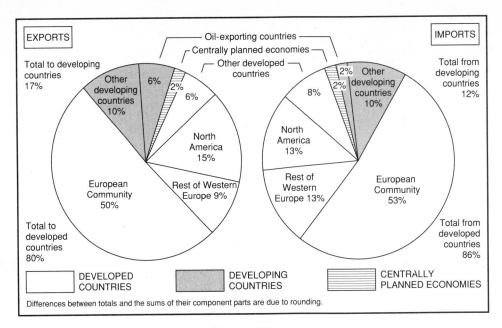

Figure 2.7 Geographical Distribution of Trade, 1989

from 13.9 to 42 percent, and imports from it rose from 9 to 52 percent. British trade has shifted from the Commonwealth to other industrial countries, especially those of Western Europe (see Figure 2.7).

In its negotiations with the Common Market in the 1960s, Britain was concerned with protecting Commonwealth interests, especially Caribbean sugar and dairy-producing areas such as New Zealand, and did in fact gain some advantages for Commonwealth countries. But the Commonwealth was not a real obstacle to closer economic and political relations with Western Europe.

Britain and Western Europe

In the immediate postwar period Britain was not interested in joining in the proposals for greater European unity. Its status as one of the "Big Three" powers, its worldwide role, its Commonwealth, its special relationship with the United States, its higher standard of living and trade pattern, and its insular political tradition and fear of European entanglement—all

led Britain to refuse to participate in the Economic Coal and Steel Community in 1951, the proposed European Defense Community in the 1950s, and in the formation of the European Economic Community (EEC) and European Atomic Energy Community (Euratom) in 1957.

Britain preferred to maintain a much looser free trade area and organized the European Free Trade Association in 1959 as an alternative. But the speedy success of the EEC, popularly known as the Common Market, the rapid recovery of Western Europe after the War—at first assisted by U.S. economic aid—the realization of the importance of a large single market, and weakening relations with the United States and the Commonwealth led Britain to apply for membership in the European Community (EC). After being vetoed twice by France, in 1963 and 1967, Britain was accepted and joined the Community in January 1973.

When the Labour party, split on the issue of the EC, formed the government in 1974, it decided to renegotiate the terms of Britain's membership and then put the issue to vote by the people. A number of changes were made, including the system of financing the EC budget, the reduction in the cost of the common agricultural program, and better access for certain Commonwealth produce. As a result, the government, though still divided, recommended that Britain remain in the EC. The referendum, the first in British history, was approved by 67 percent of the vote in 1975.

Britain accepted the EC's agricultural policy, which means higher prices for food and the gradual reduction of Commonwealth trade preferences. In return, it hoped that the larger market and progressive removal of European tariff barriers would induce a faster rate of economic growth, a restructuring of the British economy, and greater economies of scale in production.

Membership in the EC did not immediately revive British industry, but trade with it increased and not accounts for about half of Britain's imports and exports. However, Britain in the late 1980s had a trade deficit with the EC.

Britain was also concerned about the size of its net contribution to the EC budget, as it contributed considerably more than it received in return. This inequity resulted from two facts: the EC largely raises its revenue from customs duties, farm levies, and value-added taxation (VAT), which is costly to Britain, which imports most of its food; most EC expenditure goes to farmers, thus benefiting countries with a larger farming population than Britain's. As a result of vigorous protest by Prime Minister Thatcher, Britain's contribution was reduced in the 1980s.

Britain is now subject to EC's law, which has direct effect in the country, as it accepts and gives the force of law to the rules, principles, and procedures of the EC. The Court of Justice of the European Community has ultimate authority to rule on interpretation of the law. In the institutions of the EC, now composed of 12 states, Britain has 2 of the members of the European Commission, the execu-

tive of the EC, and 81 of the 518 members of the enlarged European Parliament, which was directly elected for the first time in 1979.

For Britain some new political problems exist. The historic concept of the supremacy of Parliament is now qualified by the right of EC institutions to make rules applying to Britain without parliamentary consent and by the ability of the EC Court of Justice to rule on whether British law is compatible with European Community law as it did in 1990. Though there has not as yet been any serious constitutional clash between Britain and the EC institutions, problems remain now that there is a level of government above that of Britain and now that Britain is for the first time bound to some extent by the written constitution of the European Community. Britain has welcomed the EC objective of a free internal market by 1992, and approves of a greater European role in world affairs, but it has been reluctant to become a member of the European Monetary System or to accept the idea of a European bank, let alone a United States of Europe.

It did, however, join the exchange rate mechanism of the European Monetary System in October 1990, though it remained opposed to rapid moves to an economic and monetary union, and to a single European currency. It also still insists that any such union must be based on free markets and price stability. Equally, the Conservative governments under Thatcher and Major have rejected the idea of a federal Europe, and have been concerned about any reduction of British sovereignty. Though the Conservatives agreed that some common European policies, such as a single market and a negotiating position on world trade, are necessary, and that Europe should have a more coordinated foreign policy and a stronger voice in world affairs, they did not accept the view that all European cooperation must take place through the institutions of the European Community.

In the field of defense, this view has led Britain to suggest that Western European Union (WEU) should be the bridge between

NATO and transatlantic security and defense on one hand and common political and security policies of the EC on the other. In this way WEU could be the basis for a European defense identity, without NATO being undermined.

Politically, Britain under the Thatcher and Major governments has been opposed to an extension of majority voting in the EC, to wider powers being exercised by the Commission or to the EC having larger taxing powers. It has called for the reform of the Common Agricultural Policy of the EC, which is costly for Britain, and for a single market that should be realized in all states, especially in the fields of financial services, transport, and public procurement. Britain has also been troubled by the diminution of its sovereignty, as in late 1991 when the Community threatened to take legal action to stop British Rail construction projects for environmental reasons.

CONCLUSION

Whether examined from an international, social, economic, or political point of view, the British system has changed in the postwar world. Internationally, Britain cannot be seen as a superpower, though it is still a significant world power with a capacity for independent action as was displayed in the 1982 Falklands war. It has drawn closer to Western Europe, which now accounts for half of British trade. Nevertheless, Britain still maintains a variety of important foreign ties, especially with the United States, with which it shares common political and democratic values as well as military and intelligence-gathering connections.

Socially, Britain is now a country with a mixture of peoples of different races and background, a less rigid class system, and for most individuals, a more affluent lifestyle. Economically, Britain has experienced mixed success. It is currently a self-sufficient oil-producing country. In the mid-1980s, real GDP grew at a faster rate than in the United States, the inflation rate was low, and the trade unions, with a declining membership, in general were less militant. The Thatcher government stressed individual responsibility, encouraged economic initiative, sold off many nationalized industries, and dismantled state controls over the economy. At the same time, unemployment remained relatively high, and the proportion of total GDP spent by government did not diminish significantly.

Britain has been regarded in the postwar world as a model of a successful and stable political system with two strong parties, which alternated in power, and with a general consensus that included approval of full employment, a welfare state, and free collective bargaining. That admired model has not, in recent years, fully corresponded to current reality. The Conservative party was elected to power for the fourth successive time in 1992, and the electoral base on which the Labour party depended for support has been shrinking. Other parties, especially the nationalist parties and the Social Democratic and Liberal parties at different elections, have registered considerable strength. In the major parties, ideological positions have been emphasized and, in the case of the Conservatives, implemented into legislation but have been less emphasized in the 1990s. Difficult issues such as the Irish question, the inequality of women, racial discrimination, environmental problems, and the role of Britain externally, remain to be adequately resolved. It is clear that in the 1990s there will be no shortage of difficult problems on the British political agenda.

Key Terms

commonwealth
devolution
economic planning
European Community (EC)
European Free Trade Association (EFTA)
family allowances
mixed economy

National Health Service
nationalized industries
North Atlantic Treaty Organization (NATO)
Polaris missiles
privatization
social security
Western European Union (WEU)

Suggestions for Further Reading

Adamson, David. *The Last Empire: Britain and the Commonwealth* (London: Tauris, 1989).

Ashford, Douglas. *Policy and Politics in Britain: The Limits of Consensus* (Philadelphia: Temple University Press, 1980).

Bartlett, C. J. *British Foreign Policy in the Twentieth Century* (New York: St. Martin's, 1989).

Bayliss, John. *British Defence Policy* (London: Macmillan, 1989).

Butler, David, and A. H. Halsey, eds. *Policy and Politics* (London: Macmillan, 1978).

Calvocorossi, Peter. *The British Experience, 1945–1975* (New York: Pantheon, 1978).

Fraser, Derek. *The Evolution of the British Welfare State* (New York: Barnes and Noble, 1973).

Gamble, Andrew, and S. A. Walkland. *The British Party System and Economic Policy, 1945–83* (Oxford: Clarendon, 1984).

Haas, Richard, and Oliver Knox. *Policies of Thatcherism* (Lanham: UPA, 1991).

Hall, Peter. *Governing the Economy: The Politics of State Intervention in Britain and France* (Oxford: Polity Press, 1986).

Hogwood, Brian. *From Crisis to Complacency* (Oxford: Oxford University Press, 1987).

Jones, Bill, ed. *Political Issues in Britain Today* (Dover: Manchester University Press, 1985).

Kay, John, Colin Mayer, and David Thompson, eds. *Privatisation and Regulation: The U.K. Experience* (Oxford: Oxford University Press, 1986).

Lodge, Juliet. *The European Community and the Challenge of the Future* (London: Pinter, 1989).

Louis, William R., and Hedley Bull, eds. *The Special Relationship: Anglo-American Relations Since 1945* (New York: Oxford University Press, 1986).

Savage, Stephen, and Lynton Robins. *Public Policy under Thatcher* (London: Macmillan, 1990).

Titmuss, Richard. *Essays on the Welfare State*, 3rd ed. (London: Allen and Unwin, 1976).

Wallace, William. *The Foreign Policy Process in Britain* (London: Allen and Unwin, 1977).

A. Notes

1. G. M. Trevelyan, *Illustrated English Social History*, vol. 2 (New York: McKay, 1951), p. 89.

2. James B. Christoph, "Consensus and Change in British Political Ideology," *American Political Science Review* 59, no. 3 (September 1965), pp. 629–642.

3. Walter Bagehot, *The English Constitution* (London: Oxford University Press, 1928).

4. Harry Eckstein, *Division and Cohesion in Democracy* (Princeton: Princeton University Press, 1966), pp. 241–248.

5. W. G. Runciman, *Relative Deprivation and Social Justice* (Berkeley: University of California Press, 1966).

6. The term *nonwhite* refers to blacks, mostly from the West Indies and Africa, and also to Asians, including Indians, Pakistanis, and Bangladeshis.

B. Notes

7. David Butler and Dennis Kavanagh, *The British General Election of October 1974* (London: Macmillan, 1975).

8. Ivor Crewe, Bo Särlvik, and James Alt, "Partisan De-Alignment in Britain, 1964–1974," *British Journal of Political Science* 7, no. 2 (April 1977), p. 182.

9. Anthony Mughan, *Party and Participation in British Elections* (New York: St. Martin's, 1986), pp. 84–85.

10. Ivor Crewe, Tony Fox, and Jim Alt, "Nonvoting in British General Elections, 1966–October 1974," in Colin Crouch, ed., *Participation in Politics* (London: Croom Helm, 1977), pp. 38–109.

11. Mark N. Franklin and Anthony Mughan, "The Decline of Class Voting in Britain:

Problems of Analysis and Interpretation," *American Political Science Review* 72, no. 2 (June 1978), pp. 523–534.

12. Ivor Crewe, *British Journal of Political Science* 7, no. 2 (April 1977),pp. 187–188.

13. S. E. Finer, *The Changing British Party System, 1945–1979* (Washington, D.C.: American Enterprise Institute, 1980).

14. Wynn Grant and David Marsh, *The Confederation of British Industry* (London: Hodder and Stoughton, 1977).

15. Peter Self and H. J. Storing, *The State and the Farmer* (London: Allen and Unwin, 1962), p. 230.

16. S. H. Beer, *Modern British Politics* (London: Faber, 1969), p. 407.

17. Patrick Gordon Walker, *The Cabinet* (London: Cape, 1970), pp. 27–28.

18. John P. Mackintosh, *The Government and Politics of Britain* (London: Hutchinson, 1974), pp. 36–38, 64–66.

19. R. H. S. Crossman, Introduction to Walter Bagehot, *The English Constitution* (London: Watts, 1964), pp. 51–53.

20. Henry Fairlie, *The Life of Politics* (London: Methuen, 1968) p. 37.

21. Colin Mellors, *The British M.P.* (London: Saxon House, 1978).

22. Philip Norton, *Dissension in the House of Commons, 1974–1979* (London: Allen and Unwin, 1974), p. 198.

23. J. A. G. Griffith, *Parliamentary Scrutiny of Government Bills* (London: Allen and Unwin, 1974), p. 198.

CHAPTER 3

The Government of France

Jean Blondel

A. Political Development

TRADITIONS AND CONTRADICTIONS IN FRENCH POLITICS

The Instability of French Politics Up to the 1960s

France is, without doubt, the most mysterious of the Western countries. It refuses, almost doggedly, to fit the framework of the rest of Western Europe and of the Atlantic world. Despite the fact that the Fifth Republic, set up by Charles de Gaulle in 1958, has proved to be a stable regime and made it possible for France to have her first Socialist government backed by a substantial majority in Parliament in 1981, it must be remembered that not even four decades ago, the country seemed on the verge of political catastrophe, with generals in Algiers threatening a military invasion. The previous regime, the Fourth Republic, ended after only 13 years of great political instability. Moreover, in the preceding 150 years, France had had about 20 constitutions, only one of which—that of 1875, which set up the Third Republic—lasted over two decades.

Indeed the Third Republic, like the Fourth, which took its place after World War II, was characterized by much greater instability than contemporary Italy; governments lasted little more than half a year and almost never had any real authority. Although not altogether

certain, it may be that, with the Fifth Republic, France has at last acquired real political stability. If so, it is the product of a political system that is somewhat different from those of other Western countries and poses problems, so far not fully resolved, about the respective positions of president and government.

Social and Economic Development

Explanations for the history of political instability in France are not easy to find. Economic performance does not provide the answer. France is a rich country, one of the richest in the world. Its per capita gross domestic product (GDP) of $17,100 in 1989 was somewhat higher than that of the Netherlands ($15,100), a little lower than that of West Germany ($18,200), and markedly higher than that of Britain ($14,500). If, as political scientists believe on the basis of considerable evidence, wealth and political stability are closely associated, France should be as stable as the Netherlands and more stable than Britain or Ireland.

The structure of the class system does not provide clues either. Incomes and wealth are somewhat more unevenly distributed in France than in northern Europe, but the large majority of the population has sizable incomes and a very substantial proportion are small property owners. Indeed, France has traditionally been a nation of small-business people, shopkeepers, artisans, and, above all, farmers. Land tenure is not a problem. Political unrest can be attributed to conflict over land reform in Latin America and the countries of southern Europe, but in France the land is owned by large numbers of smallholders, and agricultural workers and sharecroppers are a tiny minority.

France's contemporary difficulties are therefore not the direct consequence of social and economic characteristics common to Latin or other countries that experience instability. The problems are more deeply embedded in the culture of the country, in its history, and in many of its structures, especially the administrative structures the French have created. They appear to arise in large part from a number of contradictions that the French do not seem able to surmount. The result has been that, for a long period at least, the legitimacy of the regime has been relatively low; indeed, only recently has the political system been fully accepted by almost all the French citizens.

The Clash between Liberalism and Authoritarianism

One contradiction, perhaps the most obvious since the eighteenth century, is that between traditional authoritarianism and liberal democracy. This contradiction left its scars: the Revolution of 1789 introduced values of republicanism, liberalism, and egalitarianism, which a substantial segment of the French did not accept readily and at times combatted by force. France was the first country on the European continent to adopt constitutionalism and liberalism, but it was also the first country to experience modern authoritarian rule, under the two Napoleons at the beginning and in the middle of the nineteenth century. Because the experience was distasteful to so many and because the liberal tradition was strong, France escaped twentieth-century totalitarianism in peacetime. It did, however,

succumb to it under the impact of the German occupation between 1940 and 1944. Liberal democracy became truly legitimate only in very recent times.

Nationalism and Internationalism

There is also a contradiction between nationalism and internationalism. The French are internationally minded, but only to the extent that the world reflects and adopts their own values. Thus the Revolution of 1789 was the only time the contradiction was resolved, as the imperialism of the French was then associated with the desire to spread an idealistic gospel. The armies of the Republic invaded Europe to defeat the "tyrants" and liberate the people. Later, in the French colonies, slow assimilation was the official policy. In the eyes of the French, time was needed to "civilize" the native peoples. Opposition naturally grew in these colonies, but this opposition was misunderstood and was often held by the French to be wholly misguided as it did not recognize France's civilizing mission.

France's view of the outside world reveals a third contradiction. There is a belief in the greatness of the country that often scarcely corresponds to reality. Previously, when political power was based on the strength of armies and on cultural prestige, France did rather well. It was the most populous of European countries, and the French language and civilization spread all over Europe (see Feature 3.1). European aristocrats worshipped French culture, and French armies periodically fought to impose their will. But the industrial revolution gradually changed the basis of power; a small country like England could control the world by its exports of manufactured goods. The French were caught unprepared. There was a tradition of public works (roads and urban planning) but not of industrial enterprise. Indeed, to this day the French are more proud of grand projects of dubious commercial value, such as the Concorde, than of truly successful ventures in light engineering or consumer

---

Feature 3.1 French Culture and the French Language

In some ways, France remains a little outside the major social and cultural changes that have taken place in the second half of the twentieth century. The French have a degree of resistance to what they regard as forms of americanization. This accounts for the awkward way in which French governments, and also the French people, react to world developments. This situation stems in large part from the fact that the French continue to maintain a strong belief in their culture, which an important sector of the country's elites believe must be defended against all kinds of encroachments. One of the ways this battle is fought is in the use of the French language, which is felt in need of protection against the "invasion" of anglicisms and which must be continuously supported as a flagship helping to propagate French culture. Thus French governments sustain efforts to extol *francophonie*. Such a policy may have some advantages in keeping strong ties with certain countries, particularly Africa, but it also has disadvantages, as it tends to isolate the French from the rest of the world. The French do not see foreign language skills as essential and are, on the contrary, often officially told that they must use the French language in various circumstances.

---

goods. Hence a bitter resentment and jealousy persists to this day toward the Anglo-Saxon countries.

This also accounts for the curious attitude the French traditionally had toward the Soviet Union. Initially, the Communist party enjoyed substantial support in France between the 1930s and the 1980s. The party did decline in stages from its peak in 1946, and it was reduced from more than one-quarter of the electorate in the 1950s to under one-tenth in the late 1980s, but its influence has not wholly vanished. Meanwhile, the French Communist party was probably the most totalitarian of Western Communist parties. It faithfully followed the Soviet line before Gorbachev came to power. It allowed no dissent and has allowed only a little since the late 1980s. The attraction of the Soviet Union in a country that was the first to have a constitution and spread the gospel of freedom could be explained, in part, by the fact that France tended to want to be independent of the United States and the conglomerate of Western nations that has been embodied since World War II in the At-lantic alliance. In hard reality, by its values and way of life as well as its geographical position, France is part of the Western world, but there is perhaps also a lingering view that France could somehow regain its strength by not being entirely associated with the Atlantic camp.

The Role of the Bureaucracy

There remains in French society a final contradiction: the fact that the bureaucracy has been both a major instrument of change and a major hindrance to French development. Because civil servants and technocrats have been the originators of industrial strength, and because they have often believed that they had to build this strength in the midst of a population that was passive and often markedly antagonistic to it, the centralization of the French state was viewed by the authorities as a necessity. Further justifications were also added. Centralization meant a uniform structure, and surely there would be more quality if the country were more uniform. The view that differences meant allowing lower standards became a modern argument for centralization. Who would want education, for example, to be less developed in some parts of the country than in others? If the civil service did not intervene, there would be little progress and much patronage and graft. A centralized bureaucracy was thus morally justified.

These contradictions are at the root of the French predicament, but are becoming less acute as commercial and industrial France is slowly becoming more dominant. The cultural prestige of France has dwindled, and only industrial strength can give the country both prosperity and influence in the world. The growth of Germany and Japan have perhaps contributed to changing the attitudes of many of the French, who have clearly become concerned with being first and foremost an industrial nation, in which industry keeps abreast of the latest developments and the most modern techniques. But France is finding it difficult to achieve this goal "naturally." The impact of traditional structures is strong; we shall encounter them at almost every step of this rapid overview of French political and social life.

THE HISTORICAL PERSPECTIVE OF FRENCH POLITICS

A perceptive French observer once remarked that throughout history his motherland has been obliged to live dangerously; he saw France's perilous history as the consequence of an exposed geographical position. Others have claimed that the French lived dangerously because their Celtic origins made them combative. Still others have ascribed France's adventurous history to an inquiring and even aspiring national mentality, which some of the French turned into individual genius in art, literature, and philosophy while others were building both the most brilliant and the least exalted political traditions.

Perhaps the cause for the French fascination with the game of politics—even though they may be unwilling to cheer any of the players—is that France's political history is a

Bicentennial Celebration of the French Revolution at the Arc de Triomphe, 1989.

continuous current that can be seen as a maze of threads. To unravel this jumble one must begin with the great rent in French history, the Revolution of 1789. With great drama, and eventually with a missionary and military zeal that threatened *anciens régimes* throughout much of the rest of Europe, the French routed the monarchy, the aristocracy, and the privileged Roman Catholic Church in the name of liberty, equality, and the republican form of government. But the old order, though defeated, was not destroyed. Its defenders were able to revive the monarchy in the nineteenth century and delay for decades any definitive regulation of the Church's powers. Moreover, the antirepublican tradition resisted the passage of time; its supporters attempted to undermine all the republics from the First (1792) to the Fifth (1958), though they are now reconciled to the processes of popular sovereignty.

The Revolution of 1789 and Its Various Strands

The defenders of the Revolution and the Republic quickly divided over whether they should give priority to equality or liberty. In the early revolutionary period, great effort was made to destroy the political privileges of the titled and aristocratic classes. The Declaration of the Rights of Man and the Citizen, adopted tumultuously in the revolutionary Assembly of 1789, detailed the expectations of French citizens for basic freedoms and justice on the basis of the law. The Declaration was primarily political and represented the momentary ascendancy of the libertarians over the egalitarians.

There were, however, strong undercurrents in the Revolution that were bent on a leveling of all economic and social distinctions between men. The dictatorship of the *progressist* party of the time, known as the "Jacobins" (1793–1794) was a move toward the use of the State as an instrument of vigorous social change. The efforts of the Jacobins did not prevail and were in fact succeeded by the much more conservative (and stabilizing) regime that Napoleon installed after taking power in 1799. However, the Jacobins added to the matrix of French political development a new and powerful political strain that was to assert itself several times in the nineteenth century and most dynamically in the twentieth century.

Traditionalists and Liberals in the Nineteenth Century

For most of the nineteenth century the libertarians had only a shaky hold on France. This was a period of adaptation and experiment, as political strands became snarled by ideas borrowed from one another. The antirevolutionaries returned in 1814–1815, though the traditional monarchy that reappeared with

Louis XVIII had to agree to a considerable dose of liberalism, but the reactionary attempts of his brother and successor, Charles X, ended in revolution in 1830. Then the French, hoping to repeat seventeenth-century English history, put on the throne a cousin of the last king, Louis-Philippe d'Orléans (hence the name "Orleanist" given to the supporters of Louis-Philippe in contrast to the name "legitimist" given to the supporters of Charles X and his heirs). The new Orleanist monarchy started as a parliamentary regime, but ended after having made too many efforts to manipulate Parliament, instead of concentrating on the new political aspirations of the French. The Revolution of 1848, which swept over the rest of continental Europe as well, put an end to the liberal monarchy and indeed to the monarchy altogether.

The Napoleonic Tradition

The most curious intermixture of political strands flowing from the French Revolution was the imperial tradition, into which Napoleon Bonaparte (1799–1814) stumbled, which his nephew Louis Napoleon perfected in the Second Empire (1852–1870), and which some contemporary commentators felt was reincarnated in the Fifth Republic of General de Gaulle (see Table 3.1). The Bonapartes claimed that they were embodying the general will of the nation as a result of their plebiscitary appeals to the population. They could then pretend that they were followers of the revolutionary assemblies.

In fact, however, the imperial tradition, despite some trappings borrowed from the Revolution, was both antiliberal politically and rather conservative socially (it was not reactionary but aimed essentially at maintaining the rights of the newly enfranchised bourgeoisie). Indeed, in some ways the Second Empire can be said to have been more progressive than the First Empire: it was the period when France experienced her first great industrial boom and really began to move from a pre-

Table 3.1   CHRONOLOGY OF POLITICAL DEVELOPMENT IN FRANCE

To 1789	*Ancien régime* (dates of reign): Louis XIV, 1643–1715. Louis XV, 1715–1774; Louis XVI, 1774–1792
1789-1792	Constitutional Monarchy, Constituent Assembly, Constitution of 1791, First legislative Assembly
1792–1799	First Republic: Convention Constitution of 1793 (not applied), Directory Constitution of 1795
1799–1804	Consulate: Napoleon, first consul; Constitutions of 1799 and 1802
1804–1814 and 1815	First Empire. Napoleon I, emperor; Constitutions of 1804, 1814 (not applied), and 1815
1814–1815 and 1815–1830	Restoration. Louis XVIII, 1814–1824; Charter of 1814; Charles X, 1824–1830
1830–1848	Orleans monarchy: Louis Philippe I, 1830–1848; Charter of 1830
1848–1851	Second Republic: Napoleon Bonaparte (nephew of Napoleon I), president; Constitution of 1848
1852–1870	Second Empire: Napoleon III, emperor; Constitutions of 1852 and 1870
1870–1940	Third Republic: Constitution of 1875.
1940–1944	Vichy Regime: Pétain, "Head of State."
1945–1958	Fourth Republic: Constitution of 1946
From 1958	Fifth Republic: Constitution of 1958; Charles de Gaulle, president, 1958–1969; Georges Pompidou, president, 1969–1974; Valéry Giscard d'Estaing, president, 1974–1961; François Mitterrand, president, 1981–1988, and reelected, 1988 (mandate expires 1995).

dominantly agricultural economy to a modern, developed society.

The division between the organs of political will—the emperor—and the organs of state authority—the administration, the military establishment, and the judiciary—represented an entirely new and unexpected arrangement after the Revolution's stress on constitutional reform and on the problems of executive-legislative relations. The distinction between government and administration, never very clear until then, was established in part by accident, in part through the maintenance of the well-developed bureaucracy of the monarchy, and in part through the vigorous action of Napoleon I. Through him, France was given a well-functioning administration, codes of law, and a theory of the administrative process that were to be the envy of many countries for several generations. Much of the state machinery created by Napoleon I is still in existence. Many political battles have been fought, but they have been fought largely over govern-

ments and their policies, not over the administrative instruments of governments.

Republicanism and Its Strands

The republicanism that emerged during the nineteenth century was ultimately comprised of a few simple elements: insistence on the expression of the public will through a sovereign and directly elected assembly; a lay society, in which the Church would not play an official part; and distrust of executive authority as a threat to freedom, against which the people had an obligation to rise when and if tyranny appeared imminent. Several times the people did in fact take to the barricades. This particular form of civic violence came to have a mythical value; it symbolized the revolt of the people against tyrants (and after having indeed been used rather symbolically against the Germans leaving Paris in 1944, the technique was adopted again by students in the university district of Paris, the Latin Quarter, in the May

1968 uprising). An egalitarian strand has also existed, but has never succeeded for long. The 1792 terror eventually led to Napoleon; the 1848 revolution led to the Second Empire; and when this regime fell after its defeat by Prussia in 1870, the Paris Commune seized power in the capital, but it was smashed, ending in one of the bloodiest episodes of repression in French history.

At that point "moderate" republicanism was truly established. A national assembly composed mainly of monarchists started drafting constitutional laws, hoping that a monarchical restoration could take place between the rival claimants. The republic triumphed by default, and almost by accident, in 1875. Thus the Third (1871–1946) Republic was born, and the Constitution that was then grudgingly adopted lasted until 1940. It was destroyed by German arms after a series of attacks coming from both extremes and by the weakness and internal divisions of its supporters, who proved increasingly incapable of solving political problems.

The Second World War and Its Consequences: The Vichy Regime, The Resistance, and the Fourth and Fifth Republics

Modern French history spans the Third (1871–1946), Fourth (1946–1958), and Fifth Republics (since 1958); it was interrupted between 1940 and 1944 by the "corporate state" of Pétain, whose authority derived from the German victory over France and not, despite the appearances of a legal transfer, from the will of the French people. In many ways, the Vichy régime (so called because the seat of government was transferred to Vichy, in central France, while northern France was occupied) symbolized all that was antirepublican in French life, while the Resistance has often been described as a pure revival of the republican spirit.

The Resistance, which began organizing about a year after the French defeat contained elements from all shades of French republicanism, ranging from conservative nationalists to

tough communist leaders. At the Liberation in 1944, the Resistance was the main political force in the country, though de Gaulle had created a government in exile long before, first in London and later in Algiers. The new constitution adopted in 1946 reaffirmed republican principles, but also had strong left-wing overtones inherited from the Resistance. The left was not strong enough to overcome the other awkward historical legacies in French politics, however. As a result, the Fourth Republic markedly resembled the Third Republic with a powerful, sovereign, popular assembly; a weak executive; and an administrative apparatus that floated in an ambiguous limbo below the government.

The Weakness and Fall of the Fourth Republic

Being weak and transient, the governments of the Fourth Republic were unable to solve the major political problem of the time: decolonization. Indochina severely undermined the political system, especially when the French army had to endure an ignominious defeat at Dien Bien Phu in 1954, after eight years of war. Only then was a strong prime minister, Pierre Mendès-France, chosen. He did produce a settlement that effectively disengaged France from the conflict, but he remained in power for only six months afterward. Meanwhile, the war had begun in Algeria; by 1958, the conflict was so tense between the supporters of the status quo—backed by one million French settlers in Algeria—and those who, in one form or another, wanted to introduce reforms, that successive governments were unable to move. One million French conscripts were sent to the other side of the Mediterranean, thus increasing antiwar feelings among much of the youth and many other groups, but the war was not won. By May 1958, a frustrated army high command came to question the legitimacy of the regime. Pushed by civilian extremists, commanders in Algiers ceased to recognize the authority of the Paris government and even landed a small force in Corsica. Rumors of an impending army coup spread throughout France, creating a climate of tension, plots, and counterplots. De Gaulle was called by a large majority of the Assembly on June 1, 1958. Some hoped that he could keep Algeria French. Others thought that only he had the power to solve the problem. The Fifth Republic was born.

THE BACKGROUND OF THE SOCIAL ORDER

In the 1950s and 1960s, France moved fast socially and economically; indeed, for many, the tragedy of modern France has been that politics has not kept pace with socioeconomic change or has been very slow to respond to it. Yet, despite these changes, aspects of the traditional background of French society remain visible in many parts of the country. Four characteristics of this traditional social order have special prominence. First, the French population—long static at 40 million and now over 55 million—has peasant origins. Second, France is geographically and even linguistically divided. Third, the class system and particularly the division between bourgeois and worker (*ouvrier*) has long been important and has affected life-styles. Fourth, France is traditionally, at least nominally, Roman Catholic,

but it was also fiercely anticlerical in the nineteenth and early twentieth centuries. It was on such a social landscape that the kings first and Napoleon later built a centralized administrative machine and that the Republic imposed a centralized political culture.

Peasant Origins

France was long a peasant nation—indeed perhaps the only peasant nation: A substantial proportion of its population still worked as smallholders, not as farm laborers. By the outbreak of World War II, as much as one-third of the population worked on plots that inherited from their parents and to which they were passionately attached (see Table 3.2).

Though owners of the land, these farmers had a difficult life. Plots were small and often fragmented because the civil code of Napoleon required that estates be divided equally among all the children. This led to low productivity even in rich areas, low incomes, and a low birthrate, lower before 1945 than in all other developed nations—a state of affairs that fostered pessimism among large numbers of farmers.

The flight from the land was a means by which the lot of farmers' families could be alleviated. As a matter of fact, migrations from vil-

Table 3.2 OCCUPATIONS OF THE FRENCH POPULATION

	Percent of the active population			
	1954	1962	1975	1988
Farmers and farm laborers	26.5	24.0	9.4	7.0
Owners of businesses	12.0	10.0	7.8	7.9
Higher management and professions	3.0	4.0	6.7	10.7
Middle management	6.0	7.5	12.7	20.0
White-collar workers	16.0	17.0	22.3	26.0
Manual workers	33.5	35.0	37.6	27.0
Other (army, police, etc.)	3.0	2.5	3.5	1.4
	100.0	100.0	100.0	100.0
Total (millions)	19.3	20.1	21.7	21.5

lage to city were characteristic of Western Europe. In France they had less influence on the new city-dweller than in other countries, however, peasant origins remained very important. Urbanization often did not affect the newly arrived. On the contrary, residents of cities took on attitudes more characteristic of rural than of urban communities. Preconceptions, fears, worries, and a rather negative and anarchistic individualism came to dominate much of the middle and lower-middle levels of French society: shopkeepers, artisans, mechanics, and workers in commerce and even in industry, as well as the many civil servants.

The peasant complex, as this orientation might be called, is thus a strong element in that much-discussed French characteristic, individualism. But it is also combined in a strange association with other elements and thus quickly shows its limits. The peasant complex appears in the negative way in which the French react—or traditionally reacted—to voluntary groupings; they did not believe in them, scarcely supported them, and thus could demonstrate, as in a self-fulfilling prophecy, that they received few benefits from them. But the respect for negative criticism, the fear of appearing naive, and the suspicion of all men and institutions were all forms of conformity, and indeed of conformism. These characteristics had considerable drawbacks for the French economy, made experiments an object of ridicule, and were indeed the very cause of the outside imposition of rules, which the peasant community could not and would not establish.

Since World War II the characteristics of the farming community have altered markedly. The flight from the land took such proportions in the late 1950s and in the 1960s that the weight of the peasantry in society diminished notably. From 1954 to 1975 the farming population was more than halved, from 5.2 million to under 2 million, and there was a further decline to under 1.5 million in the 1970s and 1980s. Those who remained on the land acquired larger plots. Mechanization and the commercialization of farm products gave farmers a different outlook on their role in society. With about one person in twenty engaged in agriculture and with many of these having become farming businessmen, France has ceased to have a large body of citizens who alone can tilt the scales in elections and generally give the political culture a very special flavor. But attitudes do die hard; memories are long. The past political order on the land still plays a substantial part in the political life of the present.

Regional Sectionalism and the Influence of Paris

The second characteristic of the traditional French social structure is its sectionalism. This was maintained partly by the size of the peasantry, but more general historical and geographical characteristics are also involved. Mountains and plateaus separate the country into natural regions and isolate certain areas from the main communication axes. Brittany in the west, the southwest (sometimes known as Aquitaine), the Alpine area, and Provence (from the Latin Provincia) all constitute sharply differentiated regions that until fairly recently remained culturally isolated from one another. They were isolated and different from the more accessible northern and northeastern parts of the country, which have more plains and thus an easier agriculture, more industry, and more natural lines of communication. History was molded by these geographical constraints and added a further dimension to them; local particularism was widespread.

French sectionalism manifests itself in many ways. As everywhere, there are differences in accent, in turn often the product of the survival of local dialects, some of which, as in the South, have a Latin origin and are related to Italian (Provençal) or Spanish (Catalan), whereas others (Alsatian and Flemish) have Germanic roots and yet others (Breton and Basque) have little or nothing in common with the main European languages. Also, different forms of living are often the consequence of different climates, which vary sharply as one moves from humid but temperate Brittany to the cold Massif central or Alsace and to the pleasant, almost Californian, Mediterranean coast. The shape of traditional houses gives such a characteristic appearance to towns and villages in Alsace, Provence, or the Paris area that they seem to belong to different countries. But these variations are the symbols of other, more profound variations in modes of living; the outdoor life in the clement South and Southeast contrasts with the indoor life of the tougher North and East.

These differences naturally lead the French to be attached to their *petite patrie*, their home areas. Conversely, the "strangers" who establish themselves in a new area find real human relationships slow to develop, partly because they are not aware of local traditions and customs. Important consequences follow; for instance, for a long time, political candidates had little chance of being elected if they ran for office in areas where they had no local roots.

The peculiar position of Paris has to be considered in this context. The political, social, economic, and cultural preeminence of Paris is beyond doubt, but it is resented. Paris is much larger than any other French city or metropolitan area. Eight million people live in the Paris area (administratively, the city proper has a population of only about two million), while the next three largest metropolitan areas—Marseilles, Lyons, and Lille—barely reach one million, and the fifth largest town, Toulouse, has about one-half million. Provincial capitals are therefore not in a position to challenge the metropolis.

Changes are taking place, as the factors that work against sectionalism, such as the car and television, also bring Paris nearer to increasingly large numbers. The wider economic context of the European Common Market also tends to decrease the preeminence of Paris. But for another generation at least, Paris will remain an extraordinary pole of attraction, as well as a drain on the better resources of the provinces, to an extent not witnessed in any other European country.

Social Class

The third influence affecting most of the French, class consciousness, is a function of the cleavages that have torn the fabric of modern society. To a certain extent it is an outgrowth of the industrial revolution, which started in France in the late eighteenth century but acquired full momentum only at the end of the nineteenth. Social distinctions run sharp and deep, particularly in the large cities. Although these began to decrease in the 1950s, the bitterness that they caused unquestionably accounts in part for the large Communist vote.

Social mobility does occur, of course, and does so at about the same rate as in other developed societies. This development is not new. Moreover, through education in particular, large numbers of sons and daughters of peasants, of lower middle-class employees, and even of manual workers have entered the middle class. Some educational channels have indeed always been known to make social promotion possible. A number of prestigious graduate schools, in particular the *Ecole Polytechnique* and the *Ecole Normale Supérieure*, have been powerful instruments of social mobility open to the very talented. At lower levels, numerous other schools or examinations, particularly those leading to the middle ranks of the civil service, the armed forces, and the railways, have long enabled the brighter sons and daughters of poorer families to enter the rather large French lower middle class. Finally, thrifty working-class young people often set up small businesses that they hope slowly to expand, and thereby acquire a status (and a freedom) that their original jobs did not give them.

In France, social class is based to a large extent on occupation and on education, as well as on income. Though there is a tradition of respect for the crafts (the skills of artisans are often extolled), the esteem for industrial manual work is low. In recent years social tensions have decreased, in part for a different reason: large-scale immigration has enabled the French to avoid working in the mines, the building trades, and certain sections of the engineering industry in which workers from Poland, Italy, Spain, and, since the 1950s, North Africa, Portugal, or Turkey are numerous. This has to an extent enabled the French to move out of the less pleasant forms of work, but has also created the conditions for major ethnic tensions, particularly between North Africans and indigenous French. These tensions have erupted in violence and, especially from the 1980s, have provided a basis for a strong extreme-right movement; the National Front, which we shall consider later.

Meanwhile, the French working class has markedly changed since the 1950s. As middle-class gadgets and a middle-class life-style (from cars to holidays abroad) are increasingly spreading on the basis not of what people do but of what they earn, traditional class cleavages cease to be so sharp. Vast new high-rise projects, financed largely from public funds, house people who work in widely different types of jobs. They contribute to a social melting pot that contrasts with the kind of separation, almost segregation, that used to characterize working-class districts. But a cultural and political lag has outlived social transformations. The rejuvenation of the French economy since the late 1940s is only slowly having an effect on the behavior of the working-class leaders; only gradually are attitudes toward class and society in general being modified among both manual workers and professionals.

THE CHURCH

France is nominally a Catholic nation. One million Protestants (Calvinists in the South, Lutherans in Alsace) and about 700,000 Jews are the only other sizable "indigenous" religious groups; there are also now about one and a half million Muslims among immigrants, mainly from North Africa, many of whom have

settled permanently. But this Catholic nation is profoundly anticlerical, in parts wholly de-Christianized, and still affected by the great political battles that led to the separation of church and state in 1905. For the majority of the French, Roman Catholic practice is limited to baptism, marriage, and funeral. Weekly attendance at mass and general observance of religious prescriptions is limited to a minority of one-third or even less, though this minority is not uniformly spread throughout the nation. Brittany and Alsace are strong Catholic areas; the western part of the Massif central and the Southeast are antireligious or at best areligious. The historical origins of these variations are complex. Much seems to be due not to the priest but to the local gentry. Where, as in Brittany, the mass of the peasants were kept subservient, the authority of the gentry managed to buttress that of the Church. Where, as in the center west, the local gentry was discredited and had to leave during the Revolution, the Church suffered major damage.

As in most predominantly Roman Catholic countries of Western Europe, there is a traditional association in France between church and social order, between religious practice and political conservatism. Throughout the nineteenth century the Church hierarchy maintained close contacts with the leaders of the right; this triggered bitter attacks of the left, including the moderate left, against the Church. The situation gradually became tense in the last decades of the nineteenth century, as the Third Republic ceased to be led by conservative monarchists hoping for a restoration and came into the hands of the republicans. The climax was reached in the 1890s with the Dreyfus case, in which a Jewish military officer was accused and condemned to deportation in French Guiana for having betrayed secrets, a case that was only reopened after a long and bitter struggle despite numerous signs that a judicial error had been committed.

At the turn of the century, the military, the conservatives, and the Church appeared united in their opposition to the principles of the modern liberal state. Though separation between church and state would probably have eventually taken place, "the Affair," as the Dreyfus case was called precipitated the divorce. In 1905, the privileges the Church had enjoyed were abolished, priests lost their status of civil servants and were no longer paid (with the side effect that Protestant ministers and rabbis also lost their salaries), and various religious orders were disbanded or had to leave the country (among them the Jesuits, who were not to be tolerated again before 1918 and not formally allowed in the country before World War II). The "elder daughter of the Church," as France was known under the *ancien régime*, had completely broken with her past.

Most Roman Catholics became embittered against the Republic. However, some began to realize that a change of climate had to occur. This was helped in the 1890s by the pronouncements of Pope Leo XIII, though his successor, Pius X, seemed to return to more traditional views of the role of the Church in society (indeed, the first progressive catholic movement, *Le Sillon*, created in 1894 by Marc Sangnier, was condemned by the Pope). Progress remained slow in the interwar period, the main breakthrough occurring only in the 1940s and 1950s, when the Christian Democratic party was formed and was, for a while, one of the largest parties. Workers and peasant organizations were also founded and grew in strength, particularly among the young. The role of the workers' priests (condemned and disbanded in 1953 after the movement had appeared to the hierarchy of the Church to be dangerously secular in character) has been often mentioned, but though less spectacular, the part played by the Catholic youth movements has been more profound and has helped to alter significantly the image of French Roman Catholicism and has even been instrumental in the general transformation of French society.

Some antipathy against the Roman Catholic Church still exists. While the status of the Catholics and of the Church has improved acceptance and reconciliation are not yet complete. The main area of controversy has been subsidies to church schools, which were introduced first in a limited way in 1951 and expanded in 1959. The matter was reopened after the 1981 Socialist victory, when the government attempted to combine subsidies with greater control of the schools. This led to demonstrations on a vast scale, so large that the proposals had to be abandoned. There remains, therefore, a manifest sensitivity on the issue of the Church; the problem is not fully solved.

THE ADMINISTRATIVE AND CULTURAL CENTRALIZATION OF MODERN FRANCE

Divisions run deep in France. Not all are due to the Revolution, as we have seen; many date from an earlier period. They cut across each other and lead to a fragmentation of the basic social attitudes, which accounts for much of the ideological and political sectionalism of the country.

The very number and complexity of the social divisions account for state centralization, both administrative and cultural. If the French kings, and later the Empire, had not given the country a strong and unified administrative system, it would probably not have survived. If the Republic had not attempted to give the country a uniform political culture cutting across geographical and social barriers, the Republic would probably not have survived. Administrative centralization was thus practiced by all regimes and led to the construction of an impressive network of state agencies throughout the country; these have only recently begun to be dismantled.

The real contribution of the Republic, mostly since the 1890s, was the new political culture, which was spread uniformly through a centralized educational system. The state education system was to be liberal, lay, and egalitarian; it was not totalitarian, as it aimed at developing the critical faculties of children. It was nonetheless imparted to all, mainly at the primary-school level. It was largely based on the frame of mind of the writers of the eighteenth-century French Enlightenment, particularly Voltaire, who for about half a century had waged a war against the power of the church and of the state, which were viewed as opposed to rational thinking in order to reduce criticism of the social order.

This critical frame of mind was probably instilled too quickly to too many, through the village schoolteacher, the *instituteur,* who was to become the "priest" of the Republic and whose opposition to the *curé* became a classic joke in French local politics before World War II. This critical ideology clearly undermined the authority on which all states, even republic ones, have to be based; only the centralized administration was therefore able to maintain the state. This, of course, made France more difficult to govern, but one can understand why republican politicians thought it necessary to spread their somewhat negative ideology. By emphasizing the right to criticize, they created problems for their successors: the political system has been bedeviled in the twentieth century by the very success of the republicans of the 1880s and 1890s, who bequeathed their political culture to millions of their fellow citizens. But had the republicans not been so successful, France might not have been a republic for long.

Such is the background with which modern French governments have had to contend. Not surprisingly, the various traditions reduced the margin of maneuver of ministers and governments. The centralizing tendencies are of course the most visible, and the most overwhelmingly strong, of these traditions. But the weight of traditions can be seen also in the very large part played by the public sector, in its various facets, on the French economy. Centralization brought about a spirit of enlightened despotism and of *dirigisme* (administrative controls) that has always been important in the political, administrative, and economic life of the country. In recent decades, France has undergone major changes, but the impact of the past lies close to the surface. It would be as foolish for observers to forget these traditions as it would be fatal for politicians to disregard them.

Key Terms

administrative centralization
Church vs. State
class consciousness
The Declaration of the Rights of Man and the Citizen
The Dreyfus Affair
Jacobins
Napoleon Bonaparte
regional sectionalism
Republicanism
Revolution of 1848
Revolution of 1789/Revolutionary Assembly

Suggestions for Further Reading

Aron, R. *Histoire de Vichy* (Paris: Fayard, 1954).

Ardagh, J. *The New France* (Baltimore: Penguin Books, 1973).

Avril, P. *Politics in France* (Baltimore: Penguin Books, 1969).

Bodley, J. E. *France* (London: Macmillan, 1898).

Brogan, D. W. *The Development of Modern France* (London: Hamish Hamilton, 1940).

Chapsal, J., and A. Lancelot. *La vie politique en France depuis 1940,* 4th ed. (Paris: Pr. Univ. de France, 1975).

de Gaulle, C. *Memoirs* (New York: Simon & Schuster, 1968–1972).

Ehrman, H. *Politics in France,* 3rd ed. (Boston: Little, Brown, 1974).

Fauvet, J. *Histoire de la Quatrième République* (Paris: Fayard, 1959).

Frears, J. R. *France in the Giscard Presidency* (London: Allen and Unwin, 1981).

Giscard d'Estaing, V. *La démocratie française* (Paris: Fayard, 1976).

Hoffmann, S., G. Ross, and S. Malzacher, eds. *The Mitterrand Experiment* (Oxford: Polity Press, 1987).

Macridis, R. *French Politics in Transition* (Cambridge: Winthrop, 1975).

Peyrefitte, A. *Le mal français* (Paris: Plon, 1976).

Pickles, D. *The Government and Politics of France*, 2 vols. (London: Methuen, 1973).

Thompson, D. *Democracy in France* (New York: Oxford University Press, 1958).

Viansson-Ponte, P. *Histoire de la République gaullienne*, 2 vols. (Paris: Fayard, Paris, 1971).

Williams, P. M. *Crisis and Compromise* (New York: McKay, 1964).

Williams, P. M., and M. Harrison. *Politics and Society in De Gaulle's Republic* (New York: Doubleday, 1973).

Wylie, L. *Village in the Vaucluse* (Cambridge: Harvard University Press, 1964).

B. Political Processes and Institutions

The advent of the Fifth Republic in 1958 coincided, by and large, with the emergence of truly modern politics in France, although, as we already noted, elements of the past are still prominent. The constitution was changed, bringing about a deep transformation of the respective role of president, government, and parliament. At the same time, moreover, the strength and characteristics of groups and of parties were markedly affected, although these remain weaker and less well-organized than elsewhere in Western Europe.

Interest groups have long been weak and frowned upon; the Revolution of 1789 fought the "corporate state" of the *ancien régime,* in which each trade was organized in closed craft networks that were entered only after long periods of apprenticeship and which provided their members with monopoly privileges. In the name of liberty the Revolution abolished the ancient guilds and forbade individuals to coalesce to limit production or regulate the entry of others into a profession (with several important exceptions). Trade unions were, therefore, tolerated only three-quarters of a century after the Revolution and had to wait another 25 years to be fully recognized. Other groups also suffered, while parties were undermined by the conception that politicians should have direct contacts with electors and remain free from the bureaucratic influence of headquarters and leaders. Only since the 1950s did a major change of attitude occur, somewhat paradoxically, as de Gaulle continued to attack groups and parties, but needed a party to maintain his hold on the country.

INTEREST GROUPS

Thus, although more pluralistic than at any time since 1789, France still has fewer associations than other Western countries. Some groups still display a systematic form of opposition, at substantial variance with an associational model in which the main goal is to reconcile differences. Moreover, the main target of group attacks is the state; collective bargaining being recent and viewed with some suspicion, the typical approach is still to ask the state to make the provisions or to force (for instance, by law) private employers to make the provisions. The idea of partnership between economic actors is only slowly gaining ground.

Trade Unions

Workers' Unions   The French trade unions movement is very divided, largely for political reasons. Also, its membership is small, proportionately the smallest in Western Europe, and smaller than in the United States. However, many workers vote for union candidates at works councils organized by law in firms beyond a certain size. Late development and political divisions account for these weaknesses.

The early history was difficult; full recognition was achieved only in 1884. Trade unions quickly came to be controlled by militants who believed in direct action, and by the turn of the century they had displaced the more reformist or even Marxist elements from the leadership. The syndicalists were against employers; they also believed in an uncompromising attitude toward politicians. They did not wish to enter agreements with the Socialist party, which was expanding at the time. For the *Confédération Générale du Travail* (CGT), created in 1895 as a federation of all major trade unions, working-class victories would not be won piecemeal through parliamentary means but in one major push through the general strike. But the union was never powerful enough to launch any such action. In fact, when war broke out in 1914, trade unionists defended the "bourgeois" state.

After World War I, the majority of labor leaders adopted a more reformist stance, but the emergence of communism brought about a split and introduced party politics into the trade union movement. The CGT ideology followed that of the Socialist party, whereas the more militant elements entered the Communist-led *Confédération Générale du Travail Unitaire* (CGTU). But this body was not successful and was disbanded in 1936, when a "popular front" alliance came into being. Then, its members rejoined the CGT. Communist trade unionists gradually acquired more influence in the newly reunited body, and by 1945, thanks to the part they played in the Resistance against German occupation, they almost entirely dominated the CGT. Socialist trade unionists tried unsuccessfully to recover some of the lost ground, but in 1947, when the unions came to be openly used for political reasons in a wave of strikes launched by the Communists, they broke from the CGT and created a new CGT-*Force Ouvrière* (the

name of the newspaper of those who held these views).

Meanwhile, Catholic trade unions had gained considerable ground. Created in 1918, the *Confédération Française des Travailleurs Chrétiens* (CFTC) gradually increased its following among white-collar employees and among manual workers in strongly Christian parts of France (Alsace in particular) and slowly gathered followers throughout the country. By the 1950s it had become the second largest trade union. To widen its appeal, it decided in 1964 to drop the word *Chrétiens* (Christian) from its title and to rename itself *Confédération Française Démocratique du Travail* (CFDT). A small segment of the trade union refused to follow and continued under the old name of CFTC.

French trade unions are rather secretive about their (limited) membership numbers. However, *Force Ouvrière* and the CFDT have perhaps three-quarters of a million to one million members each and the CGT about twice as many, but membership is declining. In all, only 10 to 15 percent of the total work force is unionized, with considerable variations between occupational groups. This is the lowest proportion among highly industrialized countries.

Consequences of Divisions Among Workers' Unions   This division has been detrimental to the working class, as it has enabled employers and governments to pay less attention to workers' demands by playing one union against the other. Moreover, the unions' separation has at times led unions to get involved in demagogic proposals to avoid being overtaken, and it convinced many French workers that unionization was not necessary. Admittedly, the division is not always as clear-cut as it might appear on paper. In some cases (as in the printing trade) all the members of an occupational group belong to the same union; in many firms and offices, one or two unions tend to predominate. The CGT is strong mostly in the coal mines, on the docks, and in mechanical engineering (particularly around Paris); the CFDT's strength is in light industry and among white-collar workers; and *Force Ouvrière* leads among textile workers in the north and among civil servants everywhere, though it is not, as some claim, the main trade union among civil servants. Competition between two unions is common, and, at the national level, all three major unions take stands and are involved in consultations among themselves, with the government, and with employers.

The combination of this traditional weakness of unions and of legislative efforts to integrate the working-class representatives into the society led to a mixture of compulsory cooperation at the top and of semianarchistic, and often ineffective, outbursts at the bottom. These factors show at least one limit of the associational model of group involvement in the political system. Formally, unions are often involved. Particularly since 1945, laws have introduced working-class representation into a large number of bodies. The social security system is largely run by the trade unions; firms have a factory committee (*comité d'entreprise*) in charge of large sums devoted to leisure and cultural activities; and boards of nationalized industries have union representatives. Many advisory committees of the government in the planning field, for instance, include trade union members. In practice, however, unions often lack the power to press their demands at the level of the firm. Members often do not agree on a common stand, and unions cannot promise financial help in case of strikes; thus, workers often continue to work when a strike is called.

Changes in Workers' Unions Attitudes

This picture may be changing. Since the 1950s, the CFTC (now the CFDT) has campaigned for a new approach to the relationship between workers and society. In contrast to the CGT and the Communist party, which typically put forward a "cataclysmic" model and systematically opposed the capitalist system, the CFDT embarked on a process of educating workers toward new attitudes in the factory and in society at large. Instead of emphasizing the need for workers' organizations to prepare for an eventual onslaught on the state, as the CGT traditionally tended to do, the CFDT aimed at developing cooperation. Instead of basing its statements on ideology and slogans, it produced an economic analysis of society and of the firms and confronted employers with realistic requests. Overall, the CFDT played a large part in developing collective bargaining, which came about in France only at the end of the 1950s, although it was legalized in 1936. It was also the first union to place emphasis on the need to improve job conditions, in particular to reduce boredom and repetitiveness. This found considerable support, especially among younger workers. Before and since 1968, the CFDT has supported strikes of the semiskilled, women, and nonskilled workers, often forcing the CGT to follow suit.

The 1968 strikes were massive, but they showed the continued strength of an anomic undercurrent in the French working class. Moreover, many strikes that occurred in the 1970s also started as grassroots movements (especially among semiskilled automobile workers, most of whom are immigrants). However, attitudes have begun to change. Some of the more recent strikes have been tough and prolonged. They have also been more than occasionally successful; for instance, the successive strikes in 1982 against all the major automobile firms. Overall, strikes have become rare, perhaps partly because of the reforms of the Socialist government of the first half of the 1980s. The influence of the CGT has markedly declined, as was shown at elections for the Social Security Boards in the second half of the 1980s. The entrenched class antagonism of the past seems to be giving way to more realism and greater moderation.

Other Unions

The three major trade union organizations cover, in theory at least, all types of employees. But many white-collar workers, most lower and middle management (the *cadres*), the professions, and students have typically been organized in different unions, though a minority belong to the three major organizations. Sectional unions exist among professional people—doctors, dentists, and lawyers, for instance—who are typically self-employed. Special unions also exist for some other groups, such as school and university teachers. The primary schoolteachers' organization, the *Fédération de l'Education Nationale,* includes teachers of all ideological creeds, with Communists constituting about half the total, and is run almost on party lines. Other teachers' organizations, aside from the three main unions, are basically conservative. The *Société des Agrégés,* covering the most prestigious of the secondary-school teachers, has continuously opposed reforms designed to bring about a democratization and modernization of teaching and greater equality among teachers. For a while, in the 1950s and early 1960s, students succeeded in creating one of the best and most active French trade unions, the *Union Nationale des Etudiants de France*. With a large membership, it combined care for the welfare of individual students with an interest in the broader aspects of the life of the country. But the Algerian war and the events of 1968 led to a radicalization of the leadership that proved unacceptable to the mass of the students. The union split and lost its vigor.

Finally, much of the employed middle class—the various levels of management in commerce and industry—are organized in a general union, the *Confédération Générale des Cadres* (CGC), which aims at maintaining the differentials that *cadres* have acquired in the growing French economy. Together with the three major workers' unions it participates in general government-union discussions, but clashes between the CGC and workers' unions are frequent in view of basic ideological differences. On the whole, associationalism has markedly increased, but still neither workers and employers, or workers and government

recognize each other as full and equal components of the social fabric.

Business Organizations

The configuration of business organizations is somewhat simpler than that of manual and white-collar workers' organizations. But even there, some divisions exist owing to both the traditional influence of small business and the economic changes, which have benefited large firms. A new climate of business-government relations developed after 1945. Earlier, industrial pressure—mainly from industrialists—on government was frequent, but tended to occur in secret and outside the framework of organizations. The turning point occurred when the first French Socialist government, elected in 1936, initiated general negotiations among government, unions, and business. These negotiations led to an agreement which stressed, for the first time, the importance of business organizations. After World War II, however, the reconstituted *Conseil National du Patronat Français* (CNPF) started to operate in an unfriendly environment; 1945 and 1946 were years of left-wing dominance and strong antibusiness ideology. Employers seemed divided among themselves. Although the CNPF was a federation covering all types of firms, small and medium-sized enterprises were organized into a semi-independent confederation, the *Confédération Générale des Petites et Moyennes Entreprises* (CGPME), which because of the larger number and smaller incomes of its members and the prevailing cult of the *"petit"* in France could afford to be more militant. Employers of large firms were uncertain about their rights. Some members of the *patronat,* organized into a *Centre des Jeunes Patrons,* displayed a more progressive attitude and criticized their colleagues for their conservatism.

The division between the CNPF and the CGPME (now renamed CGPMI) has remained a feature of the contemporary French business scene. On the whole, the CNPF has cooperated with government, in part because governments have usually been of the right or center and because of many personal ties between leaders of large businesses and civil servants. Additionally, big business has been broadly sympathetic with the policy of growth and industrialization promoted by French governments since the 1950s. This policy still prevailed, albeit in a somewhat bruised manner, in the conditions of economic depression of the late 1970s and early 1980s. Relations have been relatively good even with Socialist governments of the 1980s, despite the large-scale nationalization program. State and business are engaged in a form of partnership.

Defensive Attitudes of Small Business Small businesses are in a different position. They came to be viewed with suspicion both by civil servants anxious to rationalize the economy and by the public, who found cheaper goods in supermarkets and discount stores. They lost some of the tax advantages granted to them earlier, when the cult of small business made good political capital. As a result, discontent was channeled not only through the CGPME, but also through more radical organizations, two of which temporarily acquired national political significance: the *Union de Défense des Commerçants et Artisans*, founded by Pierre Poujade in the mid-1950s, and the *Comité d'Information et de Défense-Union Nationale des Artisans et des Travailleurs Indépendants* (CID-UNATI), founded by Leon Nicoud in the late 1960s. Both leaders favored direct action. Nicoud was jailed several times for being involved in operations against government buildings. Although the success of these organizations was short-lived, the PME continued throughout the period to voice, in a more responsible manner, the basic grievances of shopkeepers and small businesses. Good results were occasionally obtained, such as restrictions on the development of large discount stores.

Outbursts of the "underdogs" of French business, then, occurred in the Fifth Republic, but more sporadically than before 1958.

The party system of the Fifth Republic has been better able to contain the activities of these groups. But the contrast between the "civilized" forms of pressure exercised by large businesses and the somewhat anomic, and occasionally violent, actions of small-business people indicate that traditionalism continues to play a part in contemporary France.

Farmers' Organizations

The evolution of agriculture has been more rapid than that of any other sector of French society. Flight from the land and development of mechanization have altered the conditions of the farmers in every part of the country by giving those who stayed more elbow room and some scope for expansion, though they have also been confronted with acute problems of capital and investment. The problems of the farming community differ widely from region to region. In the North and the Paris area, the wheat and beetroot growers had long constituted an aristocracy. As plots were larger, mechanization was widespread, and incomes were rather high; many agricultural workers were employed by industrial firms that had become involved in production on the land as a business venture. Elsewhere, small farms have been the norm. They are sometimes efficient, particularly in the cultivation of fruit, grapes, and vegetables (especially in the valleys), but are often quite small; indeed, land has often been divided into small strips, sometimes separated by long distances. Before the late 1950s there had not been a rearrangement (*remembrement*) of the parcels received by a family through accidents of inheritance.

The main pressure group of farmers, the *Fédération Nationale des Syndicats d'Exploitants Agricoles* (FNSEA), often found itself confronted with sudden demands from the rank and file, and it had great difficulty channeling them into a coherent program. But the creation of this body represented progress. It emerged from an abortive 1945 attempt to organize an all-embracing *Confédération Générale de l'Agriculture* (CGA), which would have included cooperatives as well as agricultural workers. But this comprehensive body proved unable to solve the conflicts arising among its various components, and only the organization of the farmers (*exploitants agricoles*) survived.

For most of the 1950s the FNSEA was led by the larger group of northern farmers. A challenge was to come as rapid change took place in the structure of agriculture and its relation to the rest of the community. At first, anomic protests of small farmers began to resemble those of shopkeepers, with roadblocks and the dumping of unsold vegetables being fairly common means of demonstrating anger. Though the government had made funds available through credit institutions (*Caisses Nationales de Crédit Agricole*) to enable farmers to improve and modernize their plants, buy tractors, and increase their use of fertilizers in agriculture (in most cases, French farmers used only one-third or one-fourth the fertilizers used by Belgian or Dutch farmers), discontent seemed to be rising as mechanization spread.

Attitudes then began to change from the late 1950s, in part through the influence of Catholic associations. The long-term benefits of the industrialization of farms began to be accepted. The *Jeunesse Agricole Chrétienne* and the *Centre National des Jeunes Agriculteurs* endeavored to educate the farming community to participate in the modernization process and to promote the spread of cooperative ideas in a sector of the population that had hitherto been highly individualistic. Gradually these ideas were adopted by the FNSEA itself. Some of the Catholic leaders, such as Michel Debatisse, became leaders of the FNSEA. The agricultural policy of the European Community also suggested immense opportunities. Despite recurring difficulties in some sectors, particularly in the wine-producing areas of the south (especially over imports from Italy, Spain, and other Mediterranean countries), agriculture can be said to be the sector of French economic activity in which the move away from tradition has been the most marked,

through a combination of internal education, government help, and expanding horizons.

Other Groups

Since the mid-1960s, interest groups have come to play a regular part in the panorama of French political life, although the development remains somewhat patchy. Until the late 1950s, promotional groups had not been influential (see Feature 3.2). The first upsurge of group activity occurred at the time on Algeria and on the question of institutions; the period 1959–1960 saw the development of a variety of clubs, primarily political in outlook, which were in some ways the heirs of the salons of the eighteenth century.

Environmental and Consumer Groups

The Algerian war was indeed instrumental in the development of the protest organizations, as the political parties seemed impotent and none of them, not even the Communist party, was able or willing to take a firm line against the war. Antiwar groups had to develop independently. The end of the Algerian war in 1962 made these bodies obsolete, but new groups gradually began to emerge. Consumer associations started to inquire into the quality of products, forms of marketing, and relative costs. Environmental societies campaigned against the pollution of the seaside and the development of private beaches, attacked the takeover of vast areas for army camps, and opposed plans for highways and lines for the "very rapid" trains over good agricultural land and in residential areas. Some groups were purely local and exclusively concerned with one issue, whereas others were national and fostered general aims. Meanwhile, by the mid-1970s, antinuclear groups had also become vocal and often violent, in part as a reaction to the French government's vast program of nuclear stations. Finally, women's groups also began to be active: in 1971 a convention called the Estates

---

Feature 3.2 **The Weakness of Protest Groups in France**

Groups are unquestionably still much weaker in France than in other Western democracies. What was true in the nineteenth century continues to be true, despite some changes, at the end of the twentieth. Not only are trade unions weaker and more divided than elsewhere, it is that the groups that flourish in other countries do not emerge, or scarcely emerge, in the French context. The huge protests of antibomb groups in Britain had no counterparts in France, despite the fact that France has nuclear weapons. The large-scale demonstrations against nuclear power stations in Germany are without equivalent in France, despite the fact that France has more nuclear power stations than other countries. Even feminist groups have been weak, although women have not made more advances in France than elsewhere. The low level of associationalism in France was mentioned by Tocqueville in his *Democracy in America* in the 1830s; it is remarkable that the same trend should still prevail. This is unquestionably one of the most important, albeit negative, characteristics of French political culture.

General of Women had taken place, rather symbolically, at Versailles (where the 1789 Estates General had convened) and showed that women's organizations were to be counted as a force in French political life.

Regionalist Groups

There have also been active interest groups aimed at promoting regionalism. Long limited to the Bretons and (though less so) the Basques, regionalist ideas extended to large parts of the country, particularly the southern half, where the militants of the *Mouvement Occitan* and even more the Corsican nationalists stated that the "colonization" of the country by the north and by Paris had to end. Gradually, some fusion seemed to occur between environmentalists and regionalists in the form of ecological movements, which grew in strength and became relatively successful at a number of elections.

In the 1980s, however, the strength of most of these movements declined, in part because the Socialist government of 1981–1986 introduced regionalist and decentralization measures and in part, generally, because of the

greater extent to which groups were being listened to by the government. Only in Corsica (and more recently in New Caledonia, a French possession in the Pacific) did radicalization, and even terrorist activities, occur on a substantial scale. Of course terrorism is not a new phenomenon in France or elsewhere in Western Europe; in the early 1960s, it took place widely as a result of the Algerian war. But the terrorism of the 1980s has not been exclusively associated with demands of autonomy or independence, as in Corsica. Although never comparable in scale to the development it had in Western Germany or in Italy, terrorism has given cause for concern, in part because of the effect it may have on forms of racism, which in turn have had a significant impact at the political level in the 1980s.

GROUPS AND THE POLITICAL SYSTEM

The Fifth Republic began with an anti-interest-group bias. De Gaulle was adamant to tame the lobbies, but he was immediately confronted with protest on two traditional lines:

the rights of veterans and the predominance of state schools. The government took little notice of the huge demonstrations that took place, and it won. The groups had shown their vitality, but de Gaulle seemed to have proven his point: when the state is strong, it can withstand the pressures of groups. Gradually, however, a change began to take place. Indeed, the "benign neglect" in which groups had been left led to an accumulation of grievances that resulted in the explosion of May and June 1968. Since then, leaders of the Fifth Republic have been more cautious.

The idea of consultation is not new in the French administrative process. Its origins can be traced to the *ancien régime* and to the Napoleonic system, when it was limited to narrow sectors of the population. Representativeness then gradually increased. When trade unions became more inclined to collaborate with the government after World War I, an economic council was instituted, which was given constitutional status in 1946 and in 1958. Composed of representatives of all sectors of the population, including consumers and intellectuals, the Economic and Social Council gives advice on bills and on the more important government regulations; it debates the five-year plans for the economy and has done so with increasing seriousness. Together with the many representative bodies on which trade unionists are present (boards of nationalized industries, social security boards, and others) and with the associations of farmers (*Chambres d'Agriculture*) or of business leaders (*Chambres de Commerce*), the Economic and Social Council helps to give a broad formal basis to the consultative process.

Increased Consultation

What had been lacking until recently, therefore, was not so much a formal machinery but a willingness to discuss or a climate of consultation. Previously there was little or no sense of partnership; only in one privileged sector, big business, did it exist. Personal ties between leaders of industry and higher civil servants made informal discussions possible and indeed frequent. For small business, agriculture, employees, and consumers, no similar relations existed. Admittedly, the uncooperative and unrealistic attitudes of many trade unions and other groups can be blamed, but these attitudes were also in part the product of an earlier lack of partnership.

A change occurred in the 1970s with Presidents Pompidou and Giscard d'Estaing. Pompidou's first prime minister, Jacques Chaban-Delmas, undertook to bring about a partnership between the various "live forces" (*forces vives*) of the nation. In the 1980s, having accused the Gaullists and their associates of not giving enough scope for consultation, the Socialists were therefore naturally inclined to open an era of real consultation. Efforts were made in this direction, but the program of reforms undertaken by the Socialist government was so large in the fields of local and regional government, public enterprise, and workers' participation that the government was anxious to act quickly. As a result, the effective extent of consultation in the early 1980s was not ostensibly much greater than in the previous decade.

The role of interest groups has increased. The administration can no longer decide on big projects without opposition; it has to engage in discussions with interested groups. Yet much still has to be done to reconcile the French with the basic need for and the real value of association. Because so few workers belong to unions, these remain weak. Their leaders feel ostracized and many resort to blanket opposition. Also, much still has to be done, despite recent changes, to bring government and civil service nearer to the nation; a centralizing spirit and centralized structures are major handicaps to a real partnership between groups and the state. Therein lies the major problem of French society, a problem that the 1981–1986 Socialist government did at least begin to tackle with a greater sense of urgency than had ever occurred in the past.

THE PARTY SYSTEM

Before 1958, French parties were weak, poorly organized, and undisciplined. This was largely the result of the traditions we examined earlier in this section, and in particular to the high degree of localism. With the advent of the Fifth Republic, the situation changed somewhat, but neither regularly nor continuously. In a first period, roughly during the 1960s, the Gaullist party established itself as the dominant party. It won an unprecedented victory in 1968, when it gained a large majority of seats (though only 45 percent of the votes); however, this was followed by a decline in the 1970s. It has scarcely polled above 20 percent in the 1980s, most of the votes going to groups of the center, which are only loosely held together.

Emergence of the Socialist Party as the Major Party

The election of 1981 changed the party configuration in more ways than one. The Socialist party, for the first time in French history, won an absolute majority of seats; it gained only 38 percent of the votes, but this too was a first, as never before had it obtained the support of more than a quarter of the electorate. This victory was won largely at the expense of the Communist party, which dropped from over 20 percent to 16 percent, and went into a major decline in the 1980s. The Right did win the election of 1986, but the Socialist party remained the largest party, with 32 percent of the votes cast, a small setback for which the May 1988 reelection of the Socialist President, François Mitterrand more than compensated. This was followed by a parliamentary election the following month at which the Socialist obtained 38 percent of the votes and a nearly-absolute majority of seats at the second ballot. The Socialist party thus became the dominant force in French politics, as the Right became further divided in the second half of the 1980s by the emergence of the National Front (at the extreme right), which obtained 10 percent or more of the votes at parliamentary elections.

Thus, the French party system remains complex, although it appears to be moving away from a very fractionalized traditional form of multipartyism to a situation more reminiscent of Scandinavia, where the largest party is Socialist and the Right is divided. But there is enough fluidity and there have been enough changes in the course of the last three decades to make it hazardous to assume that the current equilibrium will be maintained in the future.

THE ELECTORAL SYSTEM

The streamlining of the party system from the 1960s was manifestly helped by the electoral system that has been in force since 1958, except for the 1986 general election. The system is known as the *scrutin d'arrondissement à deux tours*, a two-ballot system within single-member constituencies taking place on two successive Sundays. This type of electoral system had been in use during most of the Third Republic, but it was replaced in 1945 by proportional representation (PR), which was advocated by the left because the two-ballot system traditionally favored center parties. PR was again introduced by the Socialist majority in 1985, but the Conservative coalition that replaced it in 1986 returned to the majority system. On the first ballot, only candidates receiving 50 percent or more of the votes cast in the constituency are elected. Between the first and the second ballot (on which the candidate who gets the most votes is elected irrespective of his or her percentage, but on which only candidates who obtained more than 10 percent of the votes on the first ballot may run), deals take place and candidates withdraw voluntarily, sometimes without further ado, sometimes in favor of other candidates better placed in the race.

The Two-Ballot System and Its Effect

It is worth examining the effect of the two-ballot system. Before 1939, this system tended to benefit center parties, as these could receive votes from the Right in left-wing areas and from the Left in right-wing areas. In the Fifth Republic, the impact has been very different: it has consolidated the strength of dominant parties, Gaullists in the 1960s and early 1970s, Socialists since 1981. But this electoral system does not result in two-party dominance, as agreements are struck between groups of parties based on trade-offs between one constituency and another; this did not occur before World War II because the parties within each camp were loosely organized (see Table 3.3).

For a short period in the late 1970s, parties again seemed to become looser; in the 1978 general election the French voters divided fairly evenly among four broad groups. On the Left, the Communists—by far the best-organized French party, with half a million card-carrying members—obtained about 20 percent of the votes. On the center-left, the Socialist party and its small ally, the Movement of the Left Radicals, obtained nearly 25 percent of the votes (see Figure 3.1). The *Union pour la Démocratie Française* (UDF), a coalition of loosely organized medium-sized and small parties closely connected with the president of the Republic, Giscard d'Estaing, gained 24 percent of the votes and markedly eroded the Gaullist party, which had hitherto dominated the center-right and the Right in the Fifth Republic, but obtained only 23 percent of the votes. These divisions have been overshadowed by the sensational result of the Socialist Party at the 1981 election. The coalition of the Right and Center won again at the 1986 election, but with a much smaller majority, partly because of the introduction of proportional representation by the Socialists (in turn abolished by the center-right coalition after it came to power), partly because of a slight decline of the Socialists (to 32 percent of the votes, still their second best result ever), and partly because of the emergence of the extreme-right National Front, which gained 10 percent of the votes.

The Right and Center

Ups and Downs of the Gaullist Party

Unlike Britain, France never had a Conservative party; yet, in two occasions at least, it seemed that the Gaullist party would be able to unite the large majority of the electors on the Right. The first time was in the late 1940s, when de Gaulle created the *Rassemblement du Peuple Français* (RPF) which was pointedly called a "rally" because its founder wanted to indicate that his organization was different from all other political movements. The RPF was, for a time, very successful. In the municipal elections of 1947, it swept most large towns, obtained nearly 40 percent of the votes cast, and seemed to be a major challenge to the government of the Fourth Republic, but traditional parties of the center proved resilient and gradually eroded Gaullist strength. In the 1951 General Election the Gaullists obtained only a little over one-fifth of the votes cast; a year later they split, and by 1956 Gaullism as a movement had all but disappeared.

The resurgence of Gaullism after de Gaulle's return to power in 1958 resulted from the inability of the Fourth Republic political leaders to deal with the Algerian problem. But this time the return of Gaullism seemed likely to be more than a passing phenomenon. The *Union pour la Nouvelle République* (UNR), as the Gaullist party then came to be named, obtained one-quarter of the votes in 1958, and achieved dominance at the 1962 election when it obtained over 40 percent of the votes. These successes were repeated at the elections of 1967 and 1968. By then, the Gaullist party seemed fully established; it was, indeed, also the closest to a mass party on the Right that France ever had, although it did not have a very large membership (unlike the old RPF of the late 1940s). From about 50,000 members in the early 1960s, the party reached about three times this figure in the early 1970s. Membership drives occurred from time to time, but they were not pushed hard and were not very successful.

Table 3.3   ELECTIONS TO THE NATIONAL ASSEMBLY SINCE WORLD WAR II
(A) PERCENTAGE OF VOTES CAST FOR EACH PARTY (METROPOLITAN FRANCE ONLY)

Year		Total votes million	Communist	Socialist	Radical and ass.	MRP	Ind. cons.	Gaullist	Others
1945		19.2	26.5	24	11	25	13	—	0.5
1946	(June)	19.9	26	21	11.5	28	13	—	0.5
1946	(Nov.)	19.2	28	18	11	26	16	—	1
1951		18.9	26	14.5	10.5	13	12	22.5	1.5
1956		21.5	26	15	15.5	11	15	4	13.5
1958	1st ballot	20.5	19	15.5	11.5	11.5	23	17.5	2
	2nd ballot	18.0	20.5	14	8	7.5	23.5	26.5	—
1962	1st ballot	18.3	22	15	8	9	15	32	—
	2nd ballot	15.2	21.5	16.5	7	5	9.5	40.5	—

Year		Total votes million	Communist	(Ext. Left)	Federation and other left	Democratic center		Gaullists and independent Gaullists		Others
1967	1st ballot	22.9	22.4		21.0	12.8		37.8		6.0
	2nd ballot	18.8	21.4		25.0	7.1		42.6		3.9
1968	1st ballot	22.5	20.0		21.2	10.3		43.6		4.9
	2nd ballot	14.6	20.1		22.3	7.8		46.4		3.4
1973	1st ballot	24.3	21.2		23.6	12.4		38.4		4.1
	2nd ballot	21.3	20.6		26.4	6.1		46.3		0.6
1978	1st ballot	29.1	20.6	3.3	24.7	23.8		22.6		4.9
	2nd ballot	25.5	18.6		30.8	26.1		23.1		1.4
1979	(European)	21.3	20.6	3.1	23.6	27.2		16.2		8.9
1981	1st ballot	25.0	16.2	1.3	37.6	19.1	Joint	20.9	National	4.9
	2nd ballot	18.5	6.9		49.5	18.7	Lists	22.4	Front	2.4
1986		29.1	9.7	1.5	32.8	8.3	21.5	11.0	9.7	5.6
1988	1st ballot	24.0	11.1	0.3	37.7			40.3	9.9	0.6
	2nd ballot	20.0	3.1	—	49.0			46.8	1.1	—

The policies were, on the whole, those of the authoritarian right. Admittedly, de Gaulle believed consistently in the idea of collaboration between capital and labor. A profit-sharing scheme was even put forward, but its details were not worked out in practice. The bulk of the thinking was nationalistic, strongly anti-Communist (support came to the RPF mainly for this reason), and somewhat reactionary on colonial matters (particularly on Indochina), though the position of the leader on this question was kept ambiguous. More apparent than its ideology was the physical presence of the movement. French political life, normally complex, individualistic, and tiresome, is not usually ugly, but with the emergence of the RPF, fighting started to break out, the local Communist party headquarters was burned, and even thugs appeared; however, the second Gaullist party, which emerged after 1958, acted responsibly.

In its heyday in the late 1960s, the Gaullist party seemed, therefore, able to attract the support of a large proportion of the electorate without having to build a massive organization. It had been successful in providing de

Table 3.3 (B) SEATS (FRANCE AND OVERSEAS)

		Total seats	Communist	Socialist	Radical and ass.	MRP	Ind. cons.	Gaullist	Others
1945		586	161	150	57	150	64	—	4
1946	(June)	586	153	129	53	169	67	—	15
1946	(Nov.)	618	183	105	70	167	71	—	22
1951		627	101	107	95	96	98	120	10
1956		596	150	99	94	84	97	22	50[a]
1958		578	10	47	40	64	129	206	81[b]
1962		480	41	67	45	38	51	234	4

	Total seats	Communist	Federation and other left	Democratic center		Gaullists and independent Gaullists	National Front	Others
1967	486	73	121	30		244	—	18
1968	487	34	57	27	64	296		9
1973	490	73	104	32		262	—	19
				UDF[c]				
1978	490	86	115	138		150	—	1
1981	491	45	289	73		84	—	—
1986	573	35	215	129		145	35 ·	12
1988	577	27	277	130		128	1	12

[a]Mainly Poujadists

[b]Mainly from Algeria

[c]Union for French Democracy

Gaulle and his government with a solid majority, although it was no longer as monolithic as it was once accused of being. Far from being Fascist or even really authoritarian as the first Gaullist party had been, the UNR was based on a strong discipline, which was naturally accepted; whips were not imposed in a ruthless fashion. In parliamentary debates, criticisms may not have been voiced on major matters, but they were often expressed on less important questions. This was in part because there was a "community of feeling," or common approach, between de Gaulle and his supporters in Parliament and elsewhere. Of course, many would have disagreed on tactics in foreign or home affairs, but most Gaullists agreed on the basic aims in both areas.

Decline of the Gaullist Party   This dominance of the Gaullist party in French politics seemed, for a while, to survive the departure and death of the founder of the Fifth Republic, in part because of the large parliamentary majority de Gaulle bequeathed to his successor, Pompidou. The beginnings of the decline, however, can be traced to one of the first decisions of the new president; he agreed to appoint to the government a number of members of small fringe parties who had hitherto been on the sidelines. Thus Pompidou, unlike Adenauer in West Germany in the 1950s, did not attempt to force non-Gaullist parliamentarians of the Right and Center to choose between joining the Gaullist party and abandoning effective political life. Pompidou

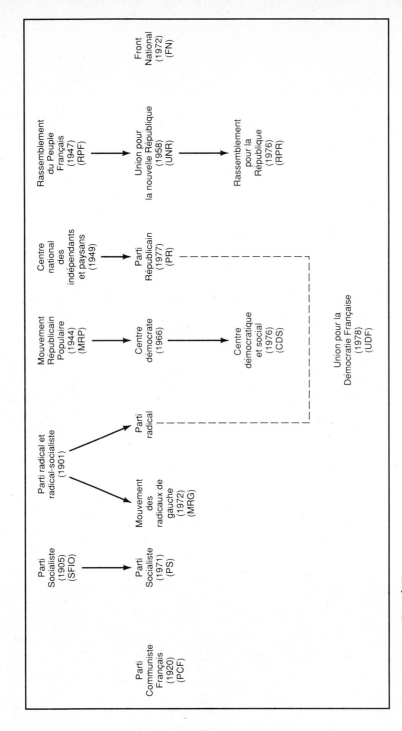

Figure 3.1 Main French Parties

undermined his own party by relying increasingly on non-Gaullist politicians—and in particular, on Giscard d'Estaing—to counterbalance the strength of the Gaullists. But the real blow to Gaullist supremacy was administered in 1974 by one of the younger leaders of the Gaullist party, Jacques Chirac, who led a substantial group of Gaullist members of Parliament to support the candidacy of Giscard d'Estaing for the presidency against the official Gaullist candidate, Chaban-Delmas. Giscard won, and he rewarded Chirac for a while by appointing him prime minister. But the Gaullist party had lost its dominant position, and was to lose the prime ministership in 1976. All subsequent efforts by Chirac, who became the Gaullist party leader, to strengthen the organization and to oppose, at times bitterly, the president whom he had so significantly helped to elect proved unsuccessful and even futile. The Gaullist party, which had by then been renamed *Rassemblement pour la République* (RPR), had ceased to embody the Fifth Republic. The electorate of the Right began to desert the party. By 1978, the Gaullist party obtained only one-quarter of the votes cast, a proportion that did not change markedly during the 1980s, despite the efforts of its leader, Jacques Chirac. The Right was once more divided.

The Resilience of the Center

By the late 1970s, France seemed to be reverting to some of its traditional divisions on the Right. Almost alone among the large Western democracies, and indeed alone among Western democracies outside Scandinavia (where the Right, though not united, is disciplined), France has been characterized traditionally by an undisciplined and loosely organized Center and Right which curiously seem to succeed in staying in power for very long periods. But this constant inability of the Right to be organized has been so commonly criticized that efforts have been made periodically to streamline its many groups and parties. In the late

1930s a new party, the *Parti Social Français,* seemed for a while poised to make considerable gains. But because of the war, the 1940 election, which would have provided the test, never took place.

In 1945, when prewar conservative groups were badly shaken by the fact that many of their members had collaborated with the Vichy regime of 1940–1944, a Christian party, the *Mouvement Républicain Populaire* (MRP) had a marked success, obtaining over one-quarter of the votes. But it was too progressive to satisfy the conservative electorate, and its alliance with the Communists made it somewhat suspect. The emergence of the RPF caused the vote for the MRP to drop to about 10 percent. Yet, as we have seen, the strength of the RPF was in turn quickly eroded. By 1956 the shopkeepers' party of Pierre Poujade seemed to be on the verge of constituting a new catalyst, but its policies were too crude to attract the bulk of the Right; it gained only 12 percent of the votes and was soon swept away by the second Gaullist tide.

Neither organization nor ideology can provide the real explanation for the resilience or recurrence of groupings of the Center and Right; the explanation can be found only by considering the social base. Before World War II, and to a large extent in the 1950s as well, the Right and Center groups consisted of prominent local politicians who had first established their influence at the municipal and county levels and had enough following to be elected to Parliament. These developments flourished in a context in which political behavior was highly sectional; this in turn, explains why parties remained organizationally very weak and undisciplined in Parliament. The village and small-town bases of politics thus echoed the rather static character of the society.

The socioeconomic changes that followed World War II seemed likely to end the dominance of these traditional politicians, especially since the war record of many of them had been weak or downright lamentable. The

Radical party, for instance, was discredited by having led France during the years that preceded the collapse of 1940. Yet, in the course of the late 1940s and early 1950s, the Radical party and other traditional groupings made a surprisingly rapid comeback. Their leaders showed considerable skill and strength in opposing the first Gaullist party; they became partners in government with the Christian Democrats and the Socialists, as those two parties alone could not command a parliamentary majority. They eventually provided most of the prime ministers of the last years of the Fourth Republic, only to show once more, in 1958, their inability to lead the country decisively in times of crisis.

The Two Major Center Groupings: The UDF and the CDS

The gradual return of these groups to the fore in the 1970s, after over a decade of Gaullist dominance, is therefore in the French political tradition; despite the economic and social changes, the appeal of the "independent" Right and Center is still strong. To be sure, but primarily to compete with the Gaullists, the independent Right and Center have had to be better organized than in the past. From the 1978 General Election, these groups federated under the label *Union pour la Démocratie Française* (UDF). But the various segments of the UDF have kept their identity, the two strongest elements being the Republican party founded by President Giscard d'Estaing and the *Centre démocratique et social* (CDS), which is the heir to the Christian party of the 1940s and 1950s. Overall, the UDF is more a coalition of somewhat autonomous chieftains joining forces to repulse a common enemy than a true federation, let alone a single party.

Thus, from the 1978 general election and throughout the 1980s, the Right and Center have been divided into two major forces of about equal strength: Gaullists and non-Gaullists. Moreover, since the early 1980s, a

challenge to the Gaullists and non-Gaullists has come from the extreme Right, with the National Front led by Jean-Marie Le Pen, an ex-Poujadist deputy of 1956. This party of somewhat Fascist undertones, whose main plank—and source of success—has been an attack against (mainly North African) immigrants, gained substantial successes in various urban areas; it obtained 10 percent of the votes at the 1986 election and even 14 percent at the 1988 presidential election (but only 10 percent of the votes at the subsequent parliamentary election). Thus, divisions have markedly characterized the Right since the 1980s and at a time when the Left seemed to be increasingly uniting within the Socialist party.

The Left

While the Right and Center were traditionally based on loose, personalized groupings, the Left has long been organized around political parties, but always around more than one. Before World War I, the Socialists competed with the Radicals; indeed, the Socialists themselves had been divided for a substantial period. After World War I, the Communist party (CP) quickly gained votes, reaching 12 percent in 1931 and 15 percent in 1936, and peaking at 28 percent in 1946. Although it lost votes when de Gaulle returned to power in 1958, it hovered around 20 percent for about two decades and was a force to be reckoned with, especially because the decline of the Socialist party was even more pronounced in the 1950s and 1960s. Only in 1981 did the CP's strength substantially diminish again, first to 15 percent, and later to about 10 percent. This means that the CP has been marginalized and that the Socialist party has truly become the dominant party of the Left and, indeed, of the French political scene in general. But the long hold of the CP on French politics needs to be looked at, as France has been one of the few European countries (along with Italy, Finland, and Portugal) in which Communist strength has been considerable for over a generation.

The Communist Party (CP) The success of the French CP has puzzled observers, both French and foreign. Simple economic explanations are obviously not sufficient. The standard of living is as high in France as in other Western European countries (indeed higher than in some), and development in France was just as fast, at least until the mid-1970s. Those who in the late 1940s had hoped that an improvement of living conditions would be accompanied by a substantial decrease in Communist party membership have been disappointed. The Communist vote was to be reduced, but not at that time and not for economic reasons.

One has to go back in history to account for the resilience of the CP, a history marked in large part by the discredit of the Socialist party and by that party's subsequent decline. The CP was born of the discontent felt by many socialists after World War I, as their party had firmly supported the war. The Resistance provided a second boost during World War II. Up to 1941, when the war was labeled bourgeois and imperialist by the Soviet Union, French Communists refused to participate in the defense of their country (their members of Parliament were dismissed in 1940) and even supported the Germans in the early period. But after the Nazi invasion of the Soviet Union, the Communist party took a leading part in the Resistance and gained considerable prestige as a result (nicknaming itself the *parti des fusillés,* the party of the shot). The party went into the government in 1944, probably hoping to remain in it for long periods. In May 1947, however, the Communist ministers were dismissed. With the intensification of the cold war, the Communist party used trade union strength to harass the government (the strikes of November 1947 were among the most difficult episodes of postwar French politics). But the government won, and the Communist challenge became less effective. By the end of the Fourth Republic, in 1958, the Communist party was a nuisance, not a menace; it could help any party to overthrow governments, but it could do little to achieve its own aims.

The CP thus occupied, from the 1950s at least, the comfortable position of being the only "real" defender of the workers against capitalism; yet, it was at the same time a very rigid and monolithic organization. Its detractors criticized the organization for its complacency, its total lack of intellectual life, and its internal dictatorial methods. Purges had taken place from time to time, enabling the secretary-general to remain at the helm of a large machine, but vitality was absent. While the Italian Communist party gave signs of independence and vigor, the French counterpart remained Stalinist long after the death of the Soviet dictator. Moreover, the CP felt no official concern for the invasion of Hungary in 1956 and did not urge any liberalization. It simply repeated the theory of the impoverishment of the proletariat in capitalist regimes. This did enable the party to weather its defeat in 1958 without much trouble, but it did not make for a very rosy future.

In the 1960s, however, signs of liberalization seemed to emerge. In August 1968, for the first time in its history, the French CP dared to voice a criticism of the Soviet Union and attacked, though in a somewhat lukewarm manner, the occupation of Czechoslovakia. But it did not touch the subject again until four years later, when some disquiet was voiced at the political trials taking place in the same country as a result of the "normalization" process. This latter criticism may have been prompted, in great part, by the need to placate the Socialist party, with which the CP had just formed an electoral alliance. A few years later, after the 1978 defeat at the polls, the French Communist party again retreated into its characteristic position of faithful and loyal supporter of the "Socialist Motherland."

Reasons for the Strength of the CP
Why, then, has the French Communist party been so strong electorally? What do Communist electors think when they vote for the party? One of the most potent attitudinal factors has been the communist leadership's ability to use to its advantage the disgruntlement

of the working class as well as antigovernment feelings among some of the peasantry and petty bourgeoisie. The palinodes of the Soviet Union notwithstanding, many manual workers felt that only by voting Communist could they protest against the government, the employers, and the bourgeois system in general. These feelings, on the other hand, are linked to the antiestablishment and egalitarian tendencies of other sections of the community. They are, naturally, more marked in those parts of the country that strongly oppose Paris and what it represents, such as the center of the country and the southeast (all along the Mediterranean coastline) than they are in the eastern and western regions. This accounts for the fact that the most individualistic of the French people can conceive of the Communist vote as a natural mode of expression.

The tightly knit character of the party organization also accounts for its longevity. The Communist party is the only French party that can be deemed to have created a "society," and a very disciplined and hierarchical one at that. Membership figures are very unreliable, but the party had about 300,000 to 400,000 paying members (about 8 to 10 percent of its voters and more than other parties had) in the 1960s and 1970s. For long periods in many cases, these members have been tied to the party through a network of cells (each consisting of a few members, mostly on the basis of residence, despite efforts of the party to create large numbers of factory cells), or "sections," in county and national organizations. Decisions are taken on the basis of "democratic centralism"; that is, in practice, the views of the secretariat and of the executive committee are virtually always adopted unanimously at congresses and opponents are quickly singled out and in most cases dismissed from the party.

Thus, the Communist party could be successful for a long period, given that it has more officials and a more elaborate structure than other parties. In the long run, however, it suffered from its bureaucratic tendencies. It began to decline in 1981 and continued to lose

support in the mid-1980s, but then remained stable despite the events taking place in the Soviet Union and Eastern Europe. Admittedly, substantial dissent did take place in the 1980s, culminating with the fielding of an "unofficial" Communist candidate, alongside the official one, at the presidential election of 1988. These dissensions have precipitated its decline.

In the wider context, it is difficult to measure the extent to which the working class has been helped as business and conservative governments have been induced to agree to concessions, for fear of the CP increasing its strength. But the debit side of the balance sheet is apparent. The French Left has been torn; it has devoted much energy to discussing problems of ideology, of "line" in relation to the Communists. Left-wing governments have been paralyzed, as in 1936, or more frequently prevented from coming into being after World War II by the presence of the Communist party, but never as markedly as in 1978 after the Communist party decided that the "Common Program of the Left," which it had drafted a few years earlier jointly with the Socialist party, had become obsolete. Here, perhaps, lies the reason why the French CP suffered its major setback of 1981. With the Socialist government of 1981–1986, it became apparent that the Left was able to act and form an effective government. From then on, the CP was no longer necessary, and it was abandoned by large numbers of its electors.

The Socialist Party   The major victories won by the Socialist party, in 1981 and afterward, make it difficult to realize how weak the party was in the 1960s. Born in 1905, and for over half a century called the French Section of the (Second) Working-Class International (SFIO), the Socialist party originated from two groups created in the 1890s: one, humanitarian and liberal, the other, Marxist. Until 1914, the party practiced "noncollaboration" with bourgeois governments, and it seemed to be moving gradually toward a commanding position. At the 1914 general election, the party had about 100 deputies, or one-sixth of the chamber. Jaurès, the great humanitarian leader of the party, tried with all his strength to rally the antiwar forces, but he was assassinated just before hostilities started, and French Socialists, like their German colleagues, were made to accept the *Union Sacrée;* some of its members joined the cabinet.

Earlier Setbacks of the Socialist Party

The Communist split of 1920 had little immediate effect on the Socialist organization, but it did hamper its electoral appeal. The party stagnated at the polls during the 1920s and 1930s, gaining votes on its right but losing about the same number on its left. At the 1936 general election, the party emerged as the great winner, having led to victory the Popular Front coalition, which included the Radicals on its right and the Communists on its left, as well as various Socialist splinter groups. For the first time a Socialist, Leon Blum, was called to head the government, and for a few tense spring days the dream of the Socialist party seemed realized.

But the victory was small (the Socialist party obtained only one-quarter of the votes) and hollow. Expectations of manual workers had been raised so high by the election result that sit-down strikes soon became the norm in large factories. The Communists pushed for takeovers while the Liberals were already backing out. Blum, a follower of Jaurès, a *grand bourgeois* who strongly believed in both equality and liberty, made a number of important reforms (the 40-hour week, paid holidays, and collective bargaining), but he did not succeed in retaining the confidence of the workers or, understandably, of the employers. Financial difficulties grew and the government, in difficulty with the Senate, resigned after a year in office. The Socialist party then entered a long period of decline. It was divided over the Vichy regime in 1940, and while it took an important part in the Resistance, it was far behind the Communists. It was central to many coalitions of the Fourth Republic after World War

II but, perhaps as a result, its support dwindled, falling from 25 percent of the votes in 1945 to 15 percent in 1958. It entered the era of the Fifth Republic as a losing and demoralized party.

Reorganization of the Socialist Party

From the mid-1960s, however, efforts were made to broaden the base of the Socialist party and to change its image. Hopes were entertained, in the first instance, for the creation of a federal organization that was expected to be substantially larger than the Communist party. The Radicals and the Center Democrats, as well as representatives of some of the political clubs, were to belong to the new organization, sometimes viewed as a potentially large umbrella for the Left. But minor Socialist groups opposed the move, and the Center Democrats, unsure of their conservative voters, rejected the proposals. Thus, the old anti-Catholic reflex grew in the Socialist party itself. A smaller and looser grouping comprising Socialists, Radicals, and some tiny organizations was to be a more modest but influential alternative. Its presidential candidate, Mitterrand, polled 45 percent of the votes in the presidential election of 1965, and it returned 121 members of Parliament in the 1967 general election; however, it did not survive the crushing electoral defeat of 1968.

Mitterrand, though, was to prove stubborn in his aim to unite and, indeed, lead the Left. Helped by the disarray caused by a further defeat of the Left at the polls in the presidential election of 1969, which followed de Gaulle's resignation, Mitterrand campaigned for the reconstruction of the Socialist party, now known simply as the *Parti Socialiste*. Having become leader of the new party, he entered a series of negotiations with the Communist party designed to expand the collaboration between the two organizations. The "Common Program of the Left" adopted in 1972 was markedly Socialist (and listed several nationalizations), but it was nonetheless more moderate than the Communists would have wanted. The result was the first upsurge in Socialist votes in 30 years in the 1973 general election.

The Socialist party continued to increase its strength after 1973, though Mitterrand was once more defeated by a small margin in the 1974 presidential election. Hopes were increasingly entertained, however, that the economic recession and the natural unpopularity of a majority coalition in power for 20 years would result in a Socialist victory. The "Common Program of the Left" was generally viewed as the natural alternative; in the municipal elections of 1977 the two opposition parties did particularly well, and the Socialist candidates were especially successful.

The "Common Program of the Left"

In late 1977, however, the Communist party decided to make strong demands for a redrafting of the "Common Program"; it made suggestions for major changes to sharpen the "radical" character of the program. It insisted on nearly all these demands, however, and negotiations broke down. The Communist party endeavored to undermine the Socialist party at its base, and though it failed to erode Socialist unity, it did damage the credibility of the Left in general and therefore bore considerable responsibility for its defeat in the 1978 general election. The 1978 result was, nevertheless, the best result achieved by the Socialist party since 1945. For the first time since World War II, it was the largest party in the country.

The breakdown of the Common Program led to a short period of stagnation, if not of decline, as indicated by the upsurge of Giscard's party and the ecologists in the 1979 European elections. Divisions within the Socialist party seemed to point to a further victory for Giscard. However, during the winter of 1980–1981, the tables were turned rapidly. Mitterrand declared himself a candidate and rallied the whole Socialist party behind him. The Communist party fielded their secretary-general, Georges Marchais, whose popularity was low and personal record unappealing. The scandals and arrogance associated with Gis-

card, coupled with the ever deepening economic recession, meant an upsurge in the fortunes of the Socialist party, whose slogan (*Une force tranquille*) and whose symbol (the rose) turned out to be clear winners.

The Socialist Victories of 1981 and 1988

At the first ballot of the presidential elections of April–May 1981, Mitterrand was still 2 percent behind Giscard, but the Communists had lost 5 percent of the votes. On the second ballot, two weeks later, when only the top two candidates could stand, Mitterrand edged out as the winner with 52 percent of the votes. Moreover, a Socialist bandwagon took form; the National Assembly was dissolved and on June 21, 1981, for the first time in French history, the Socialist party had an absolute majority of seats in Parliament. Communist representation had been halved; the CP could be given four seats in government between 1981 and 1984 without danger.

Five years of stable government of the Left then followed. At first reforms took place rapidly and on a large scale: nationalizations, industrial reforms, and administerial decentralization were among the main changes. By 1983, however, economic difficulties led to a major rethinking, as France could not push for growth alone in a world in which retrenchment and "monetarism" were dominant. The Socialist government became moderate, inducing the Communists to leave the government in 1984.

The Socialist party did lose votes at the subsequent general election of 1986, but it remained the largest party with 32 percent of the votes. It had gained a reputation for moderation and statesmanship; it had shown greater unity than the conservatives who, although pledged to rule together (as they did between 1986 and 1988), displayed a high level of dissension. This may explain in part the second victory of Mitterrand at the 1988 presidential election and of the Socialist party at the subsequent general election. This time, though, the party remained a few seats short of an absolute majority. The prime minister appointed by the president in 1988, Michel Rocard, practiced a policy of openness (*ouverture*) to the elements of the center parties and stressed sound management rather than ideological pronouncements. Rocard remained popular in the country, though perhaps not among the party activists, throughout his three years in office. Perhaps for this reason, he was suddenly replaced by Edith Cresson, the first woman French prime minister. Although this was regarded as a rather skillful move by Mitterrand, largely because the new incumbent was a woman, it should be noted that French presidents have customarily replaced prime ministers about halfway through their seven-year term. De Gaulle did so in 1962, Pompidou in 1972, Giscard in 1976, and Mitterrand himself during his first term in 1984. As a matter of fact, the Cresson government was so thoroughly defeated at regional elections in March 1992 that the prime minister was dismissed and replaced by Pierre Bérégovoy, hitherto minister of finance.

With the Socialist party being, since 1981, the dominant party, the French party system has once more been profoundly modified, at least temporarily. In more than one way, however, the turning point of 1981 and the subsequent election results have been the consequence of the presidential elections of 1981 and 1988. They have also been the consequence of the president's current position in the political system and, in general, of the character and institutions of the Fifth Republic.

THE SPIRIT OF THE CONSTITUTION OF 1958

The Constitution of 1958 was introduced primarily to strengthen the executive. From 1870 to 1958, French governments had been weak and unstable, except for about a decade at the turn of the century, when the campaign against the Catholic Church gave cohesion to the majority and some real strength to the leader of the government. De Gaulle was convinced that

chronic instability was one of the major causes of the decline of France. He felt that only by a change in the institutions could the man at the top be able to take a long-term view of the interests of the country. He therefore based his cure on constitutional remedies; but the medicine was somewhat unorthodox.

De Gaulle and the Constitution of 1958

De Gaulle did not adhere to any of the constitutional models devised in the eighteenth and nineteenth centuries and broadly adopted in the major democracies. He wanted to ensure governmental stability and executive authority, and was not anxious to give representatives of the people effective means of supervising the executive. Nor did he wish to devise an equilibrium between executive and legislature. He therefore proposed neither a revamped cabinet system nor a presidential system, but pushed for a hybrid system giving marked preponderance to the executive (see Feature 3.3). Yet, as the cabinet system and the presidential systems were the only two forms of constitutional arrangements (together with a streamlined party system) that seemed effective elsewhere in sustaining liberal democracy, the new French institutions were attacked from the start as both authoritarian and impractical. Few expected that they would last beyond de Gaulle; indeed, though they were kept alive under the subsequent presidents, there are still some doubts about the long-term future of the Constitution, because the hybrid character of the system appears to make it rather vulnerable.

The new organization divides executive authority between two sharply distinct segments. On the one hand, the president has the somewhat lofty and almost undefinable task of looking after the long-term interests of the nation. On the other, the government, headed by the prime minister, is in daily charge of the affairs of the country, both on detailed questions and over general matters. This raises two main difficulties. First, there is a large "gray

Feature 3.3 **de Gaulle and Mitterrand**

By far the two most important presidents of the Fifth Republic have been Charles de Gaulle, who founded the regime in 1958, and François Mitterrand, who reorganized the Left and gave it a new strength. Charles de Gaulle, born in 1890, had a military career during which he unsuccessfully attempted to give the French army a more modern outlook. Shocked by the defeat of June 1940, he rallied in London and created the Free French Movement, which was to become the embryo of the government of liberated France in 1944. Having led this government until January 1946, he resigned in disgust at what he considered to be party domination of the regime. He founded his movement, the Rally of the French People, in 1947, but remained in the wilderness of the opposition until 1958, when the events of Algeria led him to implement his ideas of a president-led and rather more nationalistic form of government. But he found himself in great difficulty as a result of the massive popular demonstrations of 1968. He sought to retake the initiative by proposing to the people in 1969 a reform of the Constitution which would have reduced further the role of the Second Chamber, but was defeated. He immediately resigned and retired to his home in the east of France where he died one year later, in 1970.

Charles de Gaulle.

François Mitterand, President of the Republic.

François Mitterrand can be regarded as having done for the Left what de Gaulle did for the nation. Born in 1916, he started as a young deputy and minister in the 1940s, at the time belonging to a small party of the Center. He opposed de Gaulle from 1958 and moved gradually to the Left, being a strong challenger to the founder of the Fifth Republic at the election of 1965, when he obtained 45 percent of the vote. He was instrumental in giving the Socialist party a new life in 1971 and boldly agreed to an alliance with the Communist party in 1972, being determined to overtake that party. His policy succeeded magnificently at the presidential and parliamentary elections of 1981 when, for the first time, the French Socialist party gained an absolute majority of seats in the National Assembly. He agreed to appoint a conservative government in 1986, after the Socialist party had lost its majority, but he was brilliantly reelected president in 1988. By the early 1990s, however, his popularity began to wane as his political flair, in both internal and foreign affairs, seemed to desert him.

area" of divided responsibility, particularly because the Constitution does not define precisely the respective sectors of president and prime minister. Hence clashes between the two will likely occur. Moreover, although the president has the power to appoint the prime minister, a second set of problems arises from the fact that this prime minister has to have the confidence of the legislature. If the majority parties in the legislature are different from the president's party, clashes may occur. Until 1986, this situation had not arisen. However, the 1986 election opened a new era and the strength of the institutions has now been put to the test, so far with success.

PRESIDENT AND GOVERNMENT

Despite what has happened in practice, it is important to note that, according to the letter of the Constitution, the powers of the president of the Republic are relatively limited. He is not much more than head of state, at least in normal times. The "cohabitation" period, between 1986 and 1988, showed clearly the constraints on the president's power. De Gaulle had to agree to compromises in 1958 with the Fourth Republic politicians who were anxious to retain most of the parliamentary arrangements and feared presidentialism. Whether de Gaulle wanted a presidency on American lines

was never clarified; he settled for a president who was to be concerned with the long-term interests of the country rather than with daily politics.

Formal Powers of the President

Thus, the president of the Republic, elected for seven years as under the previous Republic, has only a limited set of constitutional powers in normal times. Most of these powers existed in the Third and Fourth Republics. There is nothing unusual, by French republican standards, in the following eight powers being granted to the president:

1. Appointment of the prime minister or premier and of the ministers on the proposal of the prime minister (but not the power to dismiss the prime minister).
2. Promulgation of laws voted by Parliament (the president may ask Parliament to reconsider a law within two weeks of its having been voted, but he has no power of veto).
3. Signature of decrees, including those appointing some higher civil servants and officers of the armed forces (but the decrees must be approved by the Council of Ministers).
4. Chairmanship of the Council of Ministers.

5. Chairmanship of the high councils of the armed forces.
6. The right to send messages to the National Assembly.
7. Ratification of treaties, which are negotiated in his name.
8. The power of pardon.

In the Third, Fourth, and Fifth Republics, presidential decisions have had to be countersigned by the prime minister and, where appropriate, by some of the ministers. The countersignature process is basic to the operation of the parliamentary system. The State's seal of authority is given to a decision in the form of the presidential signature, but the only persons held responsible are the members of the government and not the head of state. No particular significance must, therefore, be attributed to the fact that the president of the Fifth Republic signs decrees or ratifies treaties; this is deemed simply to mean—in the tradition of French constitutional practice—that the president gives state authority to measures decided by others who have countersigned them.

Presidential Power of Dissolution

There are four powers that are new to the Fifth Republic and are the prerogative of the president alone. However, by their very nature and by the restrictions to which they are subjected, these powers can be exercised only at rare intervals or in emergencies. In these instances the president does not require the countersignature of the prime minister; they are truly and substantively presidential acts. Of these powers, only one, the right of dissolution, has been really effective and has markedly helped to modify the conditions of political life. Before 1958, dissolution has been used rarely (in fact, not at all between 1877 and 1955) because of the overwhelming power of the National Assembly. Indeed, as the 1955 dissolution was to prove, the ill-organized nature of the party system meant that dissolutions had little effect. Since 1958,

on the other hand, dissolutions have been used to great effect in 1962, 1968, 1981, and 1988, in the context of a more streamlined party system. Moreover, the threat of dissolution is clearly an important element, for instance, to oblige the conservative coalition of 1986–1988 to remain disciplined. To this extent, at least, a new presidential power has played a large part.

On the other hand, the other three new powers of the president have been rarely used and, when they are, have little effect. One of these gives the president the power to decide that a constitutional amendment proposed by the government to Parliament need not be approved by referendum after it has been adopted by Parliament (which is the normal procedure). In this event, the proposal is sent to a joint meeting of the two chambers separately. This provision is designed to accelerate the procedure in cases of technical amendments. It was used by de Gaulle in 1960 to loosen the links between France and her African ex-colonies and by Giscard in 1976 with respect to the duration of parliamentary sessions.

The President and Referendums

The president is also entitled, on the basis of Article 11 of the Constitution, to refer certain government bills to the electorate: bills dealing with the organization of public authorities, carrying approval of a (French) community agreement, or proposing to authorize the ratification of a treaty which, without being contrary to the Constitution, would affect the functioning of the institutions. This article led to the clearest cases of unconstitutional action by de Gaulle, both in spirit and in letter. Controversies arose at three levels. First, the article states that the president may, on the proposal of the government during parliamentary sessions or on the joint proposal of the two assemblies, use the referendum procedure. In all the cases in which the article has been used—it was used by de Gaulle in several instances on Algeria in 1961 and 1962, on the method of election of the president in 1962, and on regionalism in 1969—the initiative came from de Gaulle himself, not from the government. It was also used by Pompidou in 1972 to approve British membership in the Common Market. The proposal formally came from the government, but no one doubted who the originator was. A power meant to be one of "arbitration" (to use a favorite Gaullist expression) had been transformed into one of positive action.

In the cases in which the power was used, this was done in a somewhat unconstitutional manner, either because the bill was submitted to a referendum and was not discussed by Parliament or because, as in 1962, on the election of the president by universal suffrage, it was used as a substitute means to amend the constitution without parliamentary approval. This last proposal, which led to the referendum of October 1962 and created considerable stir (including the fall of the government and the dissolution of the National Assembly), was a clear case of unconstitutional action by de Gaulle. It was also the last time that the procedure led to an important reform. During the following seven years the procedure was not used at all. In 1969, de Gaulle used it again, on regionalism, but he lost and left power. His successor, Pompidou, used it only once, and Giscard did not use it at all. Mitterrand proposed to use it in 1984, but because its constitutional scope was previously broadened, the required constitutional change was blocked by the Senate. It was used again in 1988, but the issue (the future status of the Pacific island of New Caledonia) did not attract substantial interest and the turnout at the polls was only 33 percent.

Emergency Powers

The fourth new power of the president needs to be mentioned because it created a major controversy at the time of the drafting of the Constitution, though it has not been used since 1961. Article 16, allowing the president to assume full powers in certain emer-

gencies, was hailed by de Gaulle's supporters as the means by which constitutional catastrophes such as that of 1940 could be avoided. Opponents saw in it the means by which a legal dictatorship could be established. In fact, neither seems to be the case. The article bears the stamp of de Gaulle's initiative, but it is handicapped in two ways: first, Parliament is required to meet, which is somewhat ludicrous if one really thinks of emergencies of the kind mentioned in the first part of the article; second, powers of this type are no substitute for authority, as the fact that, according to the article, the president is mandated to act ("shall take the measures...") does not give him the effective power to command the armed forces, the civil service, or any other body.

De Gaulle seemed to have second thoughts about the article after he had the experience of its use in 1961, following an attempted coup by four generals in Algiers. The procedure was cumbersome; specifically, the scope of parliamentary action in the context of Article 16 was ill-defined. It was in fact a great relief for the government (more than for Parliament!) when at the end the summer of 1961, Article 16 ceased to be operative. Those who seemed to have benefited most from the emergency were the farmers, whose lobby was able to make itself more felt, thanks to the chamber being in permanent session.

Popular Election of the President

Such are the powers of the president. The new ones clearly point to de Gaulle's main preoccupation, namely, that the president should have authority to act in grave situations. This is probably why, after having accepted in the first instance, as a matter of compromise, that the president of the Republic be elected by a limited electoral college, de Gaulle later insisted on seeing through the amendment of 1962 aiming at the election of the president by universal suffrage (with a two-ballot, or runoff, system, the second ballot taking place two weeks after the first between the top two candidates if no one obtained an absolute majority

Feature 3.4 **The Popular Election of the President May Weaken Parties**

The election of the French president by universal suffrage may perhaps not have had only the effect of streamlining French politics: it has also seemingly tended to increase divisions between neighboring parties and even within parties. One of the main reasons why the Right of the political spectrum is not united is that both the Gaullists and the Centrists (the UDF) have their presidential hopefuls. The Socialist party has avoided major problems in the 1970s and 1980s because of the towering position of President Mitterrand: difficulties loom large for the future, as there are a number of Socialist hopefuls. The way the selection will take place in the party is not clear, as there are no mechanisms along the lines of American primaries. There is a danger that the party will find it difficult to unite behind one candidate if the nomination process is long and painful. The French Fifth Republic, therefore, still seems unable to develop the kind of discipline that is required if politics is to proceed smoothly and responsibly.

at the first ballot). Opposition to popular election of the president (the president was elected by the members of the two chambers of Parliament in the Third and Fourth Republics) was largely due to the fear of Bonapartism: as we noted, the only popularly elected president, Louis-Napoleon, made himself emperor after a *coup d'etat* in 1851.

In 1958, de Gaulle was forced to accept a compromise, which led to the creation of an electoral college of about 80,000 delegates, mainly representatives of local authorities. This had the effect of overrepresenting the rural areas. De Gaulle was first elected under this arrangement in December 1958 (obtaining 80 percent of the votes). But de Gaulle wanted to increase the authority of the president; he feared that after his term Parliament might want to return to the previous system of election of the president by Parliament and this would once more reduce the prestige of the president. He cunningly thought that if popular election was introduced it would probably be more difficult for Parliament to come back on the reform, particularly if it proved successful (see Feature 3.4). Not only did the

people approve the reform (though unconstitutionally presented) by a majority of over 3 to 2 (61.7 percent voted yes), but the first popular election of the president in December 1965 led to a very active campaign. De Gaulle's re-election was somewhat difficult (he received only 44 percent of the votes cast on the first ballot and 55 percent on the second), but this difficulty indicated the popularity of the contest.

Thus, when de Gaulle resigned in 1969 on having lost the referendum on regionalism, no one questioned the election of the president by universal suffrage. The parties presented candidates, and Georges Pompidou was the first to be chosen. The disunity of the Left led to the candidate of the center, Alain Poher, being in second place behind Pompidou on the first ballot and thus remaining the only competitor to Pompidou on the second. When Pompidou died in 1974, the tables were turned. The Left did not repeat its mistake of 1969; Mitterrand was its sole candidate, while Giscard d'Estaing stood against Chaban-Delmas. Mitterrand obtained 45 percent of the votes on the first ballot, but this was not sufficient to give him victory. Seven years later, in 1981, he did win by a small margin which was increased in 1988. In all three cases since 1974, the turnout was very high. Clearly the Fifth Republic has succeeded in one respect: it introduced a procedure that became very popular. The Left, which originally opposed it, abandoned its attacks and was indeed a marked beneficiary in 1981 and 1988. The presidency, regardless of party, has acquired an authority it did not have in the past, enabling the president to play the main part in French political life.

THE GOVERNMENT

The influence of the president on the government stems from his or her authority alone, as the Constitution clearly states that the government, headed by the prime minister, is in charge of policy. This was rediscovered, *a contrario*, after the 1986 election, when President Mitterrand had to appoint a government composed of Gaullists and members of the center parties. According to Article 20: "The Government shall determine and direct the policy of the nation. It shall have at its disposal the administration and the armed forces." And Article 21 continues: "The Premier shall direct the operation of the Government. He shall be responsible for national defense. He shall ensure the execution of the laws." It is difficult to be less ambiguous. Although the president of the Republic, according to customs dating back to the Third Republic, chairs the Council of Ministers, it is the government as a whole, headed by the prime minister, that is responsible for national policy.

Role of the Prime Minister

As in many other countries, the position of the prime minister (*premier*) grew gradually in the course of the last century. The Constitution of 1875 did not formally recognize the premier, but in practice all governments had a head, then known as president of the Council of Ministers (rather illogically, as the president of the Republic chaired the meetings of ministers). However, because French governments were often uneasy coalitions, premiers were often compromisers rather than leaders. The Constitution of 1946 sought to increase the authority of the premier and gave him specific powers. He alone was to be designated by the chamber, and he alone appointed the rest of the cabinet. But these provisions were to no avail: there was little difference between a premier of the 1930s and one of the 1950s. Yet the Constitution of 1958 did keep some of these powers of the premier (now named prime minister for the first time). He leads the government, has the power to implement the laws (*pouvoir réglementaire*), is responsible for national defense, and makes a number of important appointments. The Constitution stresses the leadership role of the premier as much as is compatible with the position of the president of the Republic and with the collective character of the government.

The government remains legally a collective organ. Important measures of the government are taken in the Council of Ministers (decrees are signed by the president after they have been approved by the council). It is the government that is empowered to "determine and direct the policy of the nation." Collective decision making is also associated with collective responsibility through the mechanism of the vote of censure, which entails, if adopted, the resignation of all the ministers. The conflict between the prime minister's leadership and collective decision making is as difficult to solve in France as elsewhere, and the matter is further complicated by the role of the president.

Structure and Composition of the Government

Formal arrangements have not markedly modified the internal structure of French governments. Names of ministries change from time to time, but the structure has followed a gradual evolution since the Third Republic. Typically, a government has about 20 ministers (slightly fewer than in the last years of the Fourth Republic); it includes about as many secretaries of state of lower status. But a number of changes have affected the decision-making processes, and even the nature of the cabinet. Three of these need to be mentioned. First, prime ministerial instability has sharply decreased. From 1958 to 1992, France has had only twelve prime ministers (see Table 3.4).

Second, there has been a marked influx of technicians in the government. De Gaulle first brought civil servants into the cabinet, in part on the grounds that the government should in some sense be (like himself?) above the daily turmoil of political life: the government should run the State, and de Gaulle conceived of politics as an activity divorced from State policy making, a view which probably stems from the part played by the civil service in the running of modern France. Thus Couve de Murville, successively foreign minister and prime minister, was from the career foreign service, and Pompidou, a teacher and a banker, had never been in politics before 1962 except as a personal adviser to de Gaulle. Since the early 1960s, cabinets have included between one-quarter and one-third civil servants. But

many of these subsequently became members of Parliament, like Pompidou and Couve de Murville, whereas successive presidents continued to draw their prime ministers (Barre in 1976) and ministers (e.g., Cheysson or Dumas by Mitterrand) from outside politics.

Third, in order to give the executive more independence, Article 23 of the Constitution, introduced at de Gaulle's specific request, forbids ministers to remain in Parliament once they are appointed to the government. The provision also exists in some parliamentary democracies (the Netherlands or Norway), but it does contravene the general principle that the executive stems from the majority of the National Assembly and aims at leading it. What de Gaulle wanted to achieve was to detach ministers from the legislature, because ministerial crises had occurred in the past to help personal careers of some ambitious men. Although they can come and speak (but not vote) in Parliament, ministers no longer belong to the legislature and, thus, can be expected to take a loftier view of daily politics. They are also nearer to the president and more likely to follow his leadership. Despite the fact that the procedure has clumsy consequences, such as the appointment of a substitute to avoid a cascade of by-elections at each ministerial reshuf-

Table 3.4   PRESIDENTS AND PRIME MINISTERS IN THE FIFTH REPUBLIC

Presidents		Prime Ministers	
C. de Gaulle	1958–1969	M. Debré	1959–1962
(reelected 1965 for		G. Pompidou	1962–1968
7 years; resigned 1969)		M. Couve de Murville	1968–1969
G. Pompidou	1969–1974	J. Chaban-Delmas	1969–1972
(died in office)			
		P. Messmer	1972–1974
V. Giscard d'Estaing	1974–1981	J. Chirac	1974–1976
		R. Barre	1976–1981
F. Mitterrand	1981–1985	P. Mauroy	1981–1984
(reelected 1988		L. Fabius	1984–1986
for 7 years)		J. Chirac	1986–1988
		M. Rocard	1988–1991
		Mme E. Cresson	1991–1992
		P. Bérégovoy	1992–

fle, it is no longer suggested that it should be abandoned.

PRESIDENT, PRIME MINISTER, AND GOVERNMENT IN THE FIFTH REPUBLIC

As we have seen, and as we shall see again in relation to the position of Parliament, institutional changes have brought about a new framework and introduced hurdles which have helped the Fifth Republic to give France a stable political system. But institutional changes alone are insufficient to account for the transformations of the structure of the French executive. The Constitution calls for collective government; yet, effective arrangements are more hierarchical. The president is not constitutionally entitled to determine policies; yet, from the very start, de Gaulle did intervene, and Pompidou, Giscard, and Mitterrand followed his lead. But the role of the president, always very much in question, has come seriously to be challenged after the 1986 election, with the advent of what has come to be known as *cohabitation*. As it turned out, Mitterrand did handle the situation very skillfully, but his real power during the period of the Chirac 1986–1988 conservative government was markedly reduced, especially in home affairs.

Extent of Presidential Intervention

Until 1986, the extent of presidential intervention had gradually tended to increase. In the early period, de Gaulle's involvement was seemingly due to the special problem of the Algerian war and was confined to some special sectors. It was suggested that the presidential sector was composed essentially of foreign affairs, defense, Algeria, overseas France, and some key institutional problems. The prime ministerial sector was to comprise all other matters, particularly economic and social matters, in which the government, led by the prime minister, was said to be the initiator.

This conception of sectors was never officially recognized by de Gaulle as marking the limits of his area of intervention; yet, it went beyond the letter and spirit of the Constitution. As a matter of fact, de Gaulle went further and intervened in many aspects of internal affairs, possibly because they touched problems of foreign policy indirectly or because they might have had an impact on the political system. In 1964, de Gaulle said:

> "Clearly, it is the president alone who holds and delegates the authority of the State. But the very nature, extent, and duration of his task imply that he be not absorbed without remission or limit by political, parliamentary, economic, and administrative contingencies."

The idea of a separation between sectors seemed to be replaced by a more hierarchical distinction, leaving the prime minister to deal with those contingencies which are "his lot, as complex and meritorious as it is essential."

Subsequent presidents came to view their role as one of steering many important matters that affect the well-being of the nation, directly or by implication. Hence, there are many instances of direct action by the president in financial matters. De Gaulle decided in 1968 not to devalue the franc; less than a year later Pompidou reversed the decision. Many aspects of regional or cultural policy, economic development, or social security reform can be ascribed to the president's steering.

Semipresidential Character of the Fifth Republic

Yet the system remained only half presidential in that, on many other issues, the president has tended to be an arbiter rather than an actor. On various important economic and social problems, especially under de Gaulle and Pompidou, prime ministers and individual ministers have initiated policies with the president of the Republic being seemingly neutral. Under Giscard, too, a certain aloofness also prevailed, although the president's commitment to the policies of his second prime minister, Barre, was clearer than that of the two previous presidents had been to the policies of their prime ministers. In this respect, the role of the third president was greater, partly because Giscard had more knowledge of and interest in economics and partly because economic difficulties made solutions more pressing.

Mitterrand embarked on the same path, keeping some distance from the daily turmoil and letting his prime minister deal with the major economic and social problems resulting from the government's efforts to counter economic depression. But Mitterrand was also very closely associated with government policy, and he was clearly instrumental in the change of economic policy after 1983.

Intervention on such a scale implied the development of a presidential staff. Indeed, in the early period, de Gaulle seemed to want to dismantle the Council of Ministers and replace it by a number of committees chaired by the president. This was not to occur, but the president did maintain a large personal staff of *chargés de mission* and *conseillers techniques,* which have constituted a parallel organization to that of the prime minister. They cover most important fields of government action and are the sign of the president's interest in a given problem, though they are not on the scale of the American presidential staff.

"Cohabitation" Period of 1986–1988

The 1986 general election brought about an entirely new situation, however, one which had long been expected to occur but did not materialize for a quarter of a century—namely, the arrival of a parliamentary majority different from that of the president's party. Since the mid-1970s, the possibility of such an occurrence had been canvassed and what presidents would do remained quite unclear, though Giscard had already promised in 1978 that he would abide by the decision of the people if the

Left were to win in Parliament. This did not happen and, in 1981, the newly elected president, Mitterrand, could dissolve the chamber and obtain a Socialist majority. But the 1986 election produced the converse result: with Gaullists and "Centrists" together having a small overall majority, Mitterrand was faced with the decision of whether to abide by the results of the polls.

Mitterrand's reaction was quick. He stated openly that he would choose the new prime minister from among the new parliamentary majority. He then soon appointed Chirac, the leader of the Gaullist party, who found himself for the second time in power, this time under a Socialist president. It was clear from the start that, temporarily perhaps the president's powers would be markedly curtailed. No longer would governmental policy would be the president's policy, at least in home affairs.

A *modus vivendi*—the "cohabitation" idea—was adopted by prime minister and president. The president would accept what the new majority proposed, provided it was within the limits of what might be called "fair" and "honest" government. Thus denationalization proposals or changes in the electoral system (in fact, the return to the two-ballot system) would be accepted by the president, on condition that parliamentary debates not be curtailed and the rights of citizens maintained. The arrangement functioned for two years with a remarkable degree of success, two elements playing a major part. First, the president retained the right of dissolution if there were conflict with the prime minister, a real threat as the popularity of the new conservative government tended quickly to decline. Second, as Chirac wished to be a presidential candidate in 1988 (he was, indeed, to stand and was defeated by Mitterrand in May of that year), the prime minister was clearly unwilling to reduce the role and status of the presidency. Thus, in both its presidential phase and its "dualist" phase after 1986, the system of the Fifth Republic did help France achieve a level of stability it had not known before, and it resulted in an increase in the legitimacy of the institutions of the country. With the victory of the Socialists at the polls in the 1988 general election, however, the president of the Republic recovered the opportunity to exercise considerable influence, despite the fact that (although one may say also, because) the Socialist party fell slightly short of an absolute majority of seats (278 when the majority is 289).

THE LEGISLATURE

To understand previous French instability, and in order also to grasp the *raison d'être* of many of the constitutional provisions that attempt to curb this instability by reducing what was justifiably considered to be the excesses of the *régime d'assemblée*, it is necessary to recall that before the installation of the regime in 1958 much of French political life swirled around the lobbies of the *Palais Bourbon*, the seat of the lower house of Parliament, known as the Chamber of Deputies during the Third Republic and renamed the National Assembly in 1946. The Chamber of Deputies came to symbolize the Republic and all its works; it finally became the focus of all criticism aimed at the shortcomings of French politics.

Traditional Dominance of the French Parliament

Perhaps because it was the arena where the rights of man were first enunciated and defended, the National Assembly came to be in time the repository of republican legitimacy. Inevitably, however, confusion over rights and privileges developed; members became more and more parochial and tended to regard their function as the defense of advantages that had accrued to their district by circumstance, natural good fortune, or government action. From protectors of civil liberties, the deputies in the National Assembly were slowly transformed into champions of vested and purely local interest, a not uncommon development in leg-

islatures, particularly in the U.S. Congress, whose mores resemble in many ways those of the French Parliament before 1958.

Consequential Traditional Weakness of the Government

In these circumstances, the mark of a promising premier was his ability to deflect or postpone the demands for the extension of special privileges that poured in on the government. At the same time, the premier who wished to survive was constantly forced to nurse along the coalition constituting the majority by pleading with his own ministers not to lead an attack against him, and compromising the integrity of his legislative program in order to maintain the cohesion of his cabinet. To compound difficulties, the premier had to submit the plans of his legislative action to the often hostile committees of the house, whose chairmen were usually more anxious to further their own careers (perhaps by replacing the relevant minister or with brilliant critiques of the legislation under discussion) than to contribute to the progress of public business.

In their actions, there was a supporting philosophy to which the parliamentarians of the Third and Fourth Republics clung doggedly. Since the revolution the enemies of republicanism were believed to be lodged in havens where they could exercise influence disproportionate to their numbers. These havens included the Church, the bureaucracy, and the armed forces. A kind of rampant anarchism prevailed among the French people in general and among the elected representatives in particular. This harassment of the government could be justified as a republican virtue.

Yet the system, despite its faults, gave France a long period of liberal government. Only the defeat and indeed the collapse of the French army led to its downfall in 1940, and only major colonial problems led to its downfall in 1958. It had, admittedly, been helped by the Napoleonic administration, and if the regime showed resilience, it did not go much further.

Proposed schemes to increase the stability of the government were never adopted, though they were often discussed. The personal stakes were too high; the life of parliamentarians was too often punctuated by the ritual of government crisis. Reform had to come from outside, as it did in 1958; but only because de Gaulle was there did this reform result in substantial curtailment of the rights of the Assembly.

General Principles of Parliamentary Organization in the Fifth Republic

The framers of the Constitution of 1958 decided to introduce a number of technical devices designed to enhance the position of the government and to give the chambers the possibility of controlling, but not of blocking, executive action. These devices come under five headings. First, there are general provisions aimed at reducing harassment and at diminishing the opportunities for conflict in the general organization of Parliament. Second, the scope of legislation is reduced and the governmental prerogative is correspondingly increased. Third, opportunities for "guerrilla" warfare during debates are reduced by the introduction of a number of restrictions. Fourth, the operation of censure motions is severely restricted. Fifth, an overall control of parliamentary activity is provided by the possible intervention of the Constitutional Council. To these five types of devices, one should add the extended power of dissolution given to the president of the Republic.

Parliament is composed of two chambers, the National Assembly and the Senate, the upper house having regained the title, but not all the powers, that it had under the Third Republic, whereas the lower house kept the name the Constitution of 1946 had given it. The National Assembly is elected for five years (if it is not dissolved before) by direct universal suffrage. The Senate, sometimes nicknamed the "Grand Council of French Communes," is elected for

nine years, with one-third of its members retiring every three years. The electoral college, composed of representatives of local authorities, is complex in detail; senators are elected on the basis of the *département* (county) and the number of senators per *département* varies according to the population. There are two ballots. Rural overrepresentation gives the Senate a markedly different complexion from the National Assembly. The big winners in the Senate have always been the center-right parties.

Increased Strength of the Government in the Fifth Republic

Several devices were introduced in the Constitution to give the government a strong hand. First, both houses of Parliament sit only for about six months in the year, in autumn and spring, unless the government decides to call for a special session or unless Article 16 is invoked. The provision for special sessions was interpreted very restrictively by de Gaulle when the question arose for the first time in 1960; it has been interpreted more liberally since, especially in 1981 and in 1986 when the legislative program was heavy.

Second, the president of the National Assembly is elected for the duration of the legislature, instead of once a year, as was the case before 1958, in order to avoid the repeated conflicts of the past. The president of the Senate is elected after each partial reelection of the Senate every three years. The president of each house is assisted by a *bureau* composed of vice-presidents and secretaries drawn from the various parties. The presidents of the National Assembly and of the Senate are among the top politicians, and they are consulted by the president of the Republic, according to the constitution, in various circumstances (such as the dissolution or the use of Article 16). They conceive of their role as being more like that of the speaker of the U.S. House of Representatives than that of the speaker of the

French National Assembly.

British House of Commons; they attempt to influence the conduct of business by informally talking to members. Before 1958, these offices were stepping stones toward the presidency of the Republic and were therefore strongly contested.

Third, the government has an enhanced role in the organization of Parliament, as its business has priority. Before 1958, the Conference of Presidents, a body that plays a similar role to the Rules Committee of the House of Representatives (and indeed resembled it in its behavior before 1958) and that includes chairmen of committees and of the parliamentary groups (the parties in the chamber), decided on the order of business, and the government had only a representative, with no vote. Since 1958, the government's power has been strengthened. According to Article 43 of the Constitution, "Government and Private Mem-

bers' bills shall, at the request of the Government or of the Assembly concerned, be sent for study to committees especially designated for this purpose," and Article 48 stipulates that "the discussion of the bills filed or agreed to by the Government shall have priority on the agenda of the Assemblies in the order set by the Government." Government bills are thus sent automatically to a committee and are then extracted from the committee and presented on the floor of the Assembly.

Scope of Legislation

Traditionally, as is logical in a country with a parliamentary system, the French Parliament could legislate on any matter. Constitutions merely regulated the principles of organization of the public powers; there was no Supreme Court. Laws (*lois*) were defined merely as texts adopted by Parliament. By contrast, decrees were adopted by the whole government and *arrêtés* were adopted by a minister or a local authority. These documents derived their legal power from each other; the government could not make decrees, and ministers or local authorities could not make *arrêtés* unless a law had given them the authority to do so.

This meant that Parliament was always free to invade, if it so desired, a field that had been previously handled by decree or *arrêté*. Parliamentary interference did increase, and the government's influence, correspondingly, decreased, with the result that Parliament often had little time to devote to major issues. Thus, delegations of powers (*décrets-loi*) had become rather common in order to remedy the situation.

A complex Article 34 of the Constitution of 1958 tried to provide a general solution to the problem. It states that "all laws shall be passed by Parliament". The Article then proceeds to define the laws; it says that "laws determine the rules" (*règles*) relating to a large number of listed matters. The article then adds that "laws shall determine the fundamental principles" relating to certain other matters. Finally, the article says that its provisions "may be elaborated and completed by an organic law." The list is fair; it includes all the important matters with which one would expect a parliament to be concerned. But there are difficulties: what is meant by rules is not clear, as the word *règle* has no precise meaning in French law. Also, no legal definition of "principle" is provided. Conflicts have arisen, the arbiter, on this point, being the Constitutional Council. Finally, the possibility of elaboration and completion by an organic law is also rather vague.

The drafters of the Constitution tried to buttress the system by introducing yet another distinction among the laws themselves. Whereas before 1958 there were only two types of laws, "ordinary" laws and constitutional laws, there are now also "organic" laws and "ordinances." Organic laws are passed by Parliament, by a somewhat more stringent procedure than that for ordinary laws; they must also be deemed to be constitutional by the Constitutional Council before they are promulgated, in the hope that Parliament will be prevented from overstepping its powers. On the other hand, if Parliament wishes to delegate its legislative powers, any amendment to legislation made by the government as a result of such a delegation must take the form of an ordinance, which has to be ratified by Parliament at the end of the delegation period. The procedure has proved of some value for governments anxious to rapidly pass controversial legislation; it was especially useful in 1986, when the government's majority was small. This was a point, however, on which Mitterrand used his presidential authority to ensure that the conservative majority of the time did not overstep its rights. Overall this complex machinery has worked relatively smoothly, contrary to expectations, though more than occasionally there have been complaints by the opposition, both of the Left, before 1981, and of the Right, from 1981 to 1986 and after 1988, and for the same reasons.

The Legislative Struggle

In a parliamentary system the two main activities of a parliament consist of voting on laws and controlling the government; but the two are intertwined. Before 1958 it was indeed through the development of the legislative struggle that the patience, wits, and skills of ministers were being tested, as governments needed laws to implement their program. Thus, the question of control of the executive over the legislative process had to be regulated if the government was to be stronger.

A bill debated in the French Parliament goes through the following sequence, not very different from that which bills go through in the U.S. Congress. After having been laid on the table of either chamber by a member of that chamber or by the government (with the exception of finance bills which must be presented first to the National Assembly), the bill is sent to a committee, which then reports to the house (each house has a *rapporteur* from the committee who is in charge of presenting this report). The house discusses the bill first in general, then article by article, and votes on each article. There is then a final vote. At this point, the bill goes to the other house, which follows the same procedure. If both houses agree on the same text, the bill is sent to the president for promulgation (he can ask for a second deliberation, but has no veto). If the houses disagree, the bill goes again to each house; if there is still disagreement, a joint committee comprised of an equal number of members of each house is set up with a view to drafting a common text. Only if the government intervenes, as we shall see, is there a possibility of breaking the deadlock between the two chambers.

Committees Before and Since the Advent of the Fifth Republic

Before 1958, parliamentary committees were very powerful. Organized, as in the United

States, on the basis of specialized subjects (finance, foreign affairs, etc.), the 20 or so committees of the pre-1958 Parliaments had great opportunities to make trouble for the government. They were composed of the members of the parliamentary groups (elected on the basis of proportional representation) who were most interested in the problems concerned or had electoral reasons, from their constituency's point of view, to appear interested. Their chairmen, elected every year together with vice-chairmen (the seniority system never took roots in France, though some chairmen did remain in office for long periods), were naturally persons of influence within their sphere of competence.

Committees made life difficult for governments because they were built as if oppositions were to be maximized, and because the procedure of the chambers gave the committees full responsibility in relation to bills. When a bill, whether from the government or from a private member, went to a committee, it became in effect the committee's bill: the committee could so alter the substance that it would emerge unrecognizable. The government constantly had to make sure that the economy of the bill was not upset by a series of changes from committee and might have to be opposed one by one. The outcome was always uncertain, especially when the debate on the floor went far into the night.

The Constitution of 1958 sought to reduce drastically the power of committees. First, Article 43 limits to six the number of permanent committees in each house. It was hoped that they would become so large that they would include more than experts, but despite various rulings from the Constitutional Council, the government could not avoid the setting up of informal subcommittees. Second, and more importantly, committees are no longer empowered to substitute their bills for those of the government: Article 42 states that the discussion on the floor must take place on the government's text.

The Power of the Government to Curb Debate

There used to be considerable harassment on the floor of the Assembly. For instance, amendments were withheld until the bill came to the floor in order to embarrass the government and its supporters at the last moment. This is now forbidden. There used to be no closure and no guillotine: now Article 44 allows the government to request the chamber to vote by a single vote (*vote bloqué*) on the text under discussion. The procedure is rather harsh, but it is also true that the opposition often presents hundreds of amendments that could not be reasonably dealt with and would otherwise block the progress of bills. Clearly, it is now the case that government bills take precedence (see Table 3.5).

The Constitution gives the government two further sets of powers relating to the legislative procedure. On finance bills, which were much delayed before 1958, the Constitution of 1958 limits to 70 the number of days during which Parliament can discuss and decide on the budget. If it has not settled matters by the end of that period, the government becomes entitled to promulgate the finance bill

Table 3.5 ACTIVITIES OF THE NATIONAL ASSEMBLY

	Hours of sitting (yearly)	Numbers of bills passed		
		Government bills	Private members' bills	Total
1968	425	53	11	64
1971	632	92	26	118
1974	543	64	14	78
1977	609	144	35	179
1980	709	74	20	94
1981	789	54	3	57
1985	793	122	3	125
1989	835	85	17	102

by ordinance, a stringent weapon that, in fact, has not had to be used in the first 34 years of the Fifth Republic.

Finally, the government, and the government alone, can end a deadlock between the two chambers by asking for yet another reading by each chamber of the text adopted by the National Assembly. If there is still disagreement between the two chambers, the National Assembly is called to vote again, and this decision is final. Thus the Senate is not in a position to block *governmental* legislation. This provision has been used frequently between 1981 and 1986, because much of the legislative program of the Socialist government—in particular, but not only, its nationalization program—has been strongly opposed in the Senate.

The legislative struggle, therefore, goes on with wholly different weapons in the hands of the protagonists. Many said that the 1958 Constitution went too far in tilting the balance in favor of the government. This is arguable in light of past experience of both Gaullist or Giscardian and Socialist governments. The executive had to be strengthened, but as all procedural means were used with great skill in the past by the chamber, very strong procedural checks had to be built in to prevent the game from following its traditional rules.

The Vote of Censure

Only comparatively recently has the question of the vote of censure, in France and in other parliamentary systems, appeared to constitute a major problem. Traditionally, as can be seen by the British practice, parliaments were entitled to censure governments at will. But in France and some other countries where party discipline is weak and parties numerous, the result may well be great instability. Yet, difficulties also exist in attempting to limit the right of the assembly to censure the government, largely because of the legislative implications. If the right to censure the government

is curtailed but a parliament can easily reject bills proposed by the government, and in particular reject or delay financial bills, governments may still fall frequently. The vote of censure, therefore, has to be linked to votes on legislation. It was because the Constitution of the Fourth Republic did not organize such a link that governments continued to fall so frequently between 1946 and 1958.

Hence a curious provision of the 1958 Constitution stipulates that an absolute majority is needed to defeat the government, but that only those voting for the censure motion (that is, against the government) will record their votes, and supporters of the government simply do not vote at all. This means that abstainers are counted on the government side. Furthermore, if the government wants to see a bill through, but encounters difficulties, it can "pledge its responsibility on the vote of (the) text." In this case, the bill becomes law without a vote unless a motion of censure is tabled. If the censure is not adopted (the procedure is the one just described), the government is safe and the bill is adopted.

Perhaps such drastic arrangements were needed for the system to be foolproof. Thus the government has the upper hand; governments cannot be suddenly overthrown. Deputies have only two means of curbing the executive. They have the question, which was introduced in the Constitution of 1958. It is allegedly based on the British model but has taken the form of short debates, not of a grilling; there is no vote at the end of these debates. The other curb is the motion of censure. These are the Assembly's only means of supervision and control of the government; the rest of its activities are legislative and budgetary. On this, the Constitution went too far. The governmental instability of the Third and Fourth Republics may have led to the introduction of a stringent procedure, but the restrictions are too strong. It is to be hoped that, gradually, the government will be more ready to make concessions (as was the case under Giscard, but not since, because of the controversial character of the programs), and that the chamber also recognizes the need for its own self-discipline.

THE CONSTITUTIONAL COUNCIL AND EXECUTIVE-LEGISLATIVE RELATIONS

Perhaps one of the most important new developments of the Fifth Republic will prove to be, in the long run, the part played by the Constitutional Council in controlling legislation. The Constitutional Council, which is composed of nine members appointed in equal numbers by the president of the Republic and the presidents of the two chambers (and which also includes the past presidents of the Republic), was set up in 1958 as a means of ensuring that Parliament did not overstep its powers; thus, it has to approve the standing orders of both houses (a matter that led to conflicts in the late 1950s). The council also has jurisdiction over referendums and national elections, both presidential and parliamentary, which it must officially declare and settle in cases of dispute.

The main power of the council, however, has turned out different from that intended. The council's power stems from its being entitled to assess whether laws are in conformity with the Constitution. Unlike the U.S. Supreme Court, it can only do so if the government or one of the houses asks for a ruling, and does so in the period immediately following the approval of the bill by Parliament. Over the years, this power has come to be by far the most important. After having sided with the Gaullist government rather frequently during the early period, it became increasingly independent, ruling that bills or parts of bills were not "in conformity with the Constitution." In 1982, for instance, it declared that, subject to a few minor amendments (which were subsequently introduced), the nationalization program of the government was in conformity with the Constitution. In 1986, it also adjudicated over the "privatization" legislation of the conservative coalition. These rulings can also have an important symbolic character. In 1991, for example, the Constitutional Council stated that it was not permissible to officially recognize in a law the existence of the "Corsican people," as this would undermine the unity of the nation.

The New Equilibrium of Powers in the Fifth Republic

The Constitution of 1958, thus, has radically changed the character of French political life. The strength of Parliament has been reduced—too much according to some—and governmental instability is a thing of the past. For a quarter of a century, the system has been dominated by the president, whose authority was enhanced by the legacy of de Gaulle and by the mechanism of the popular election. This domination has been put in question by the "cohabitation" period of 1986–1988, though the authority of the president did remain high during the period, and it was perhaps higher than ever after 1988. As a result, the political center of gravity, for a while, has shifted to the government, and the prime minister in particular. Thus, there have been two types of behavior in the Fifth Republic, and it has proved extraordinarily flexible as an institutional mechanism. Yet, the role of the president has remained and will probably always remain strong, regardless of the affiliations of the prime minister and government or of the majority in the Assembly. Because of the popular election, the president continues to have authority; he can both ensure continuity in foreign policy and broadly supervise the workings of the executive.

Parliament has also changed in the course of the last three decades. In the early period of the Fifth Republic, the pendulum swung too far against the Assembly (though not quite as far as critics and parliamentarians usually claim). There has since been a recognition that the legislature has the right to discuss, supervise, and suggest, while the government has the right to lead.

Table 3.6   OCCUPATIONAL BACKGROUND OF
FRENCH DEPUTIES AND MINISTERS,
1991 (PERCENTAGES)

	Deputies	Ministers
Business Proprietors	7.1	6.7
Liberal professions	17.8	13.3
Lawyers	4.7	10.0
Teachers	28.2	20.0
Civil servants	26.3	40.0
Managers (private sector)	12.3	16.7
White collar	5.2	3.3
Manual workers	1.9	0
None	1.2	0
Women	5.7	20.0
Total number	575	30

The nature of representation in Parliament has also somewhat altered. Manual and white-collar workers are still very underrepresented, while the law, liberal professions, the civil service, and especially teachers, (who were 28 percent of the deputies in 1988) are over-represented. Agriculture and business have substantial representation in center and right-wing parties (see Table 3.6).

Overall, it seems that the French Parliament has become engaged more actively in its function of scrutiny and information, both at the level of general policy and at the level of detailed constituency matters in which an effective part can be played. Thus, Parliament may have abandoned some of the irresponsible forms of behavior in which it had engaged in previous regimes. At present, the government's right to lead is recognized as well as Parliament's right to discuss and supervise. Thus, by and through its institutions and the effects these have had on the party system and on the behavior of the actors, the Fifth Republic can be said to have brought about a real and lasting transformation of French political life.

Key Terms

Algerian War
Arrêtés
Chambres d'Agriculture/Chambres de Commerce
Communist Party
Confédération démocratique du Travail (CFDT)
Confédération Français des Travailleurs Chrétiens (CFTC)
Confédération Générale de l'Agriculture (CGA)
Confédération Générale du Cadres (CGC)
Confédération Générale des Petites et Moyennes Enterprises (CGPME)
Confédération Générale du Travail (CGT)
Confédération Générale de Travail Unitaire (CGTU)
Conseil National du Patronat Français (CNPF)
Constitution of 1958
Council of Ministers
Decrees
Valéry Giscard d'Estaing
European Economic Community (EEC)
Fédération Nationale des Syndicats d'Exploitants Agricoles (FNSCA)
Gaullist Party
interest groups
François Mitterrand
National Assembly/Senate
Parliament
Georges Pompidou
Rassemblement pour la République (RPR)
Régime d'Assemblée
Socialist party
Socialist Party/Movement of the Left Radicals
Union pour la Démocratie Française (UDF)
Vote of Censure

Suggestions for Further Reading

Groups

Barjonet, A. *La CGT* (Paris: Seuil, 1968).

Barjonet, A. *La CFDT* (Paris: Seuil, 1968).

Bergougnioux, A. *Force Ouvrière* (Paris: Seuil, 1975).

Ehrman, H. *Organized Business in France* (Princeton: Princeton University Press, 1957).

Kesselman, M., ed. *The French Workers' Movement* (London: Allen and Unwin, 1984).

Klatzmann, J. *L'agriculture française* (Paris: Seuil 1978).

Mallet, S. *La nouvelle classe ouvrière* (Paris: Seuil, 1964).

Meynaud, J. *Les groupes de pression en France* (Paris: A. Colin, 1958).

Parties

Anderson, M. *Conservative Politics in France* (London: Allen and Unwin, 1973).

Bell, D. S. and B. Criddle. *The French Socialist Party* 2nd ed. (Oxford: Oxford University Press, 1988).

Borella, F. *Les partis politiques dans la France d'aujourd'hui,* 4th ed. (Paris: Seuil, 1981).

Charlot, J. *L'UNR* (Paris: A. Colin, 1967).

Charlot, J. *The Gaullist Phenomenon* (London: Allen and Unwin, 1971).

Converse, P. and R. Pierce. *Political Representation in France* (Cambridge: Harvard University Press, 1986).

de Tarr, F. *The French Radical Party from Herriot to Mendès-France* (New York: Oxford University Press, 1961).

Fauvet, J. *Histoire du parti communiste français,* 2 vols. (Paris: Fayard, 1965).

Frears, J. R. *Political Parties and Elections in the French Fifth Republic* (London: C. Hurst, 1977).

Goguel, F. *La politique des partis sous la Troisième République* (Paris: Seuil, 1946).

Irving, R. E. M. *Christian Democracy in France* (London: Allen and Unwin, 1973).

Kriegel, A. *The French Communists* (Chicago: University of Chicago Press, 1972).

Penniman, H. R., ed. *France at the Polls* (Washington, D.C.: American Enterprise, 1975).

Institutions

Avril, P. *Le régime politique de la Cinquième République* (Paris: Pichon, 1964).

Birnbaum, P. *Les élites socialistes au pouvoir* (Paris: Presses Universitaires de France, 1985).

Leites, N. *On the Game of Politics in France* (Stanford: Stanford University Press, 1959).

Parodi, J. L. *Les rapports entre le législatif and l'exécutif sous la Cinquième République* (Paris: A. Colin, 1972).

Williams, P. M. *The French Parliament* (London: Allen and Unwin, 1967).

C. Public Policy

It is commonplace to contrast the traditional weakness of the French political institutions with the strength of the French bureaucracy. It is also commonplace to stress the virtues of this bureaucracy. There is indeed much evidence to support this praise. The French civil service helped the monarchs to build the unity of the nation, actively implemented laws, and intervened in the life of the provinces. It ensured the continuity of the state—indeed embodied in the state—throughout the various regimes.

There is, however, a negative side to the role of the civil service in French society, one more commonly stressed in France than abroad. The strength of the bureaucracy had, and continues to have, the effect of stifling initiative, of breeding irresponsibility, and generally of preventing the development of participation and democracy. The bureaucracy's aim is to unify and develop, often against the wishes of the population. The "enlightened despotism" of the bureaucracy may have brought about change, but it led to paternalism because local political and social elites were not encouraged to be entrepreneurial. This is being redressed, but psychological barriers remain, of which two are particularly important: the belief in the need for uniformity and the overwhelming importance of rules and regulations. Paradoxically, as a result, citizens feel impotent and aggrieved, but often believe in the myths of the bureaucracy. Judgments on the role of the French state must therefore be mixed.

THE ORGANIZATION OF THE STATE

To understand the pervasive nature of the bureaucracy, one must first appreciate the nature and role of the State. In France, and indeed in many continental European countries, the State is much more than a number of institutions designed to initiate and implement public policies; it is the legal embodiment of the nation. It thus encompasses all the public organizations and corporations, both central and local. In the United States and in Britain many public bodies began, and some still are viewed, as groupings of like-minded persons wanting to run a service. Such an associational view of public bodies has never prevailed in France, where public services are run in the general context of a state organization—which can coerce or compel, but also protect citizens—so local authorities and other public corporations can be better controlled. In the French legal jargon, these are merely "decentralized" entities of the State. For the French, State and law go together because the organization of the State is the embodiment of the principles of the law, and no public authority, however large or small, can operate outside this framework.

The Mission of the State and the Bureaucracy

Attitudes regarding centralization are likely to persist, even if the law is changed, because of another aspect of the philosophy of French bureaucracy. The State is not only a legal entity; it is a legal entity with a purpose: the well-being of the citizens. From the seventeenth century, and even more so from the early nineteenth century, the tradition of the French State has been one of "social engineering." Born from the strong mark that the kings, and later Napoleon, wanted to make on the nation—an approach which can be described as *dirigisme*—French social engineering was given its intellectual stamp of acceptability by various writers, philosophers, and sociologists. The aims and the role of civil servants, specifically of higher civil servants, must be related to the influence of men such as Saint-Simon and Auguste Comte, who were, in particular the former, the promoters of social engineering in the early years of the nineteenth century. Society has to be molded; it is, in the true sense, a machine, which can be perfected by appropriate means. In this the *Ecole Polytechnique* is a key element, and, characteristically, Saint-Simon and Comte were associated with teaching at that school. And whereas Saint-Simonisme faded out as a doctrine, its influence on attitudes was profound, indeed determining, during most of the nineteenth century (Napoleon III was Saint-Simonian), particularly in those periods when economic development took place at a rapid rate.

French Traditional Centralization This tradition has a variety of consequences on the role of the bureaucracy in the nation. The most important is the centralization of the French State, which includes as its corollary the spreading of the services of the State over the whole nation. But another consequence, perhaps not sufficiently stressed, is the greater concern for economic than for social well-being, because the happiness of men is viewed as being clearly dependent on the better organization of society for the *production* of goods and services: the approach is expansionist. Ideas might change as the potential dangers of economic growth to the health of citizens are more widely recognized and the protection of the environment becomes more widespread, but the process will be slow.

THE CIVIL SERVICE AND ITS CHARACTERISTICS

This philosophy of engineering is implemented and, even to a large extent, initiated by a civil service that has high prestige and considerable competence and is widely dispersed throughout the nation, although some of the differences between France and other Western countries have narrowed.

The real strength of the French civil service comes not only from its size—over two million men and women are employed by the central government (see Table 3.7)—but also from the organization and the traditions of the service. First, the bureaucracy extends widely in the provinces in a pyramidal manner. Ministries are divided into a number of *Directions générales* and *Directions*, which have a large staff in the capital, but most of which also have offices (external services) in the regions and in the *départements* (counties) and sometimes even small towns. These offices are supervised by the prefect on behalf of the government as well as by their departmental superiors in

Table 3.7 DISTRIBUTION OF CIVIL SERVICE POSTS, 1988 (PERCENTAGE)

Education	48.8
Post office and telegraph	21.8
Economy and finance	9.1
Interior	7.1
Equipment	5.7
Justice	2.3
All other	5.2
Total (number)	2,158,000

Paris. There is thus a vast network able to intervene or supervise local government action.

The *Grands Corps*

Another element in the civil service tradition results from the existence of the corps. Indeed, until 1945, there scarcely was a French civil service. Admittedly, all the *fonctionnaires* (civil servants) had some common rights (as on pensions), but there was neither a general code for the civil service (this was passed in 1946 under the title of *Statut de la fonction publique*) nor a general set of arrangements, for instance for the grading of civil servants. These were appointed by the various ministries to fill certain jobs, and for the more technical or specialized jobs (not necessarily senior, but at least skilled) they were recruited on the basis of corps. These corps constituted the basic cells of the service and were supposed to have a spirit of their own (*esprit de corps*), which would distinguish them from other branches and divisions and would give each of them a desire to excel, a point Napoleon saw clearly.

Because these divisions were prejudicial to the unity of the service and fostered inequality, postwar reforms tried to abolish the corps and replace them by general grades. But the spirit dies hard, and perhaps more importantly the 1945 reform of the civil service did not abolish the most prestigious of the corps, the *grand corps*, which in the economic field (Inspectorate of Finance), the administrative judiciary (Council of State), the home and local government sector (Prefectoral Corps), and various technical branches (Corps of Mines, Corps of Roads and Bridges), have for generations attracted aspiring civil servants. With their prestige and power, they managed to survive. The reforms tried to link them to the rest of the service, but to no avail. Up to the present, the French civil service continues to be run, in most of the ministries, by members of the *grands corps*. Although each of them has barely a few hundred members, they run the civil service and give it its tone.

The *Grandes Ecoles*

The domination of the *grands corps* occurs through the special training given in a few elite schools. In order to recruit the best possible candidates, the civil service sets up difficult examinations. But in order to achieve a standard of technical excellence (as we noted earlier, some of the corps are technical or require training in law), it trains the new recruits in special schools of the corps, which are intended to train an intellectual and educated elite.

There are many *grandes écoles* of this type (see Feature 3.5), some of them old (School of Mines, for instance) and some of them recent (School of Taxes). Two are particularly important because of their general impact on the civil service. One is the *Ecole Polytechnique*, originally created in 1795 to provide officers for the artillery and engineering branches of the army; it gives the nation its best technical administrators. The other is the *Ecole Nationale d'Administration* (ENA) created in 1945 as part of the effort to unify the civil service and prepare candidates for higher management jobs in all government departments (including the foreign service). Moreover, a school of similar status, the *Ecole Normale Supérieure*, trains the most brilliant of the future secondary school and university teachers. Competition for entry is fierce.

The ENA is a postgraduate school providing students with one year of training in the field (usually in the provinces), a year of study in the school itself, and a further training period or *stage* (usually in a large firm), before the new administrator is posted where he has chosen to go (in fact, only top candidates can choose; the others are left with the remaining places). The final examination, which leads to the posting, decides in particular whether students are to become members of a *grands corps*. Typically, the first 20 can do so, and the rest become *administrateurs civils* and will not normally reach the very top posts of the civil service.

Feature 3.5 **Education: Still Strongly Elitist**

Although social security is as developed in France as elsewhere in Europe, the French, overall, tend to emphasize economic policy more than social policy. The one element of social policy that is given high priority, however, is education, in part because it is traditionally regarded as a ladder for upward mobility and in part because of the massive protests of students and schoolchildren that have taken place periodically. The best-known are those of 1968, but these have been followed by further waves of protests, for instance in the second half of the 1980s. The French education system, and in particular the higher education system, has traditionally been elitist. The *grandes écoles* are regarded as providing their alumni with good career prospects; hence the difficult competitive examinations in order to enter them. Meanwhile, the rest of the higher education system tends to be a Cinderella: universities are badly provided for and the teaching staff remains typically distant from the students. The matter is made worse by the high degree of centralization of the system and, specifically, by the fact that professors tend to want to reside in Paris (and indeed often live there even if they have a post in the provinces). So far there has not been any real reform of the system to make the universities more autonomous and more responsible.

The Role of the *Grands Corps* in the Nation

Except for the diplomatic corps, which is somewhat separate and whose members typically remain in the foreign service (the service still has some of its past aristocratic flavor), members of the *grands corps* do not stay in the original service for more than a few years. They have acquired such prestige that those who belong to them are transferred to head divisions throughout the service. After a period in their original organization, members of the *grands corps* are "detached" (the official expression) to be posted over a wide range of public bodies, including nationalized corporations. Inspectors of finance do not merely serve in the Inspectorate; they are in charge of practically the whole of the Treasury, and of numerous other divisions and branches in which financial or economic expertise is required. The situation is broadly similar on the technical side. Graduates of the *Ecole Polytechnique* who have achieved particular excel-

lence enter one of the two technical *grands corps*, the Corps of Mines and the Corps of Roads and Bridges, and are later detached to run, not merely mining or roads and bridges division of ministries, but other government departments and various nationalized industries.

Technical excellence and skill can thus be achieved, but at some cost. Selection is exclusively based on examination and competition; too rigid a distinction is created between the very successful elements and the bulk of the members of the higher civil service. This sometimes leads to disillusionment and to a waste of early efforts.

Finally, an important consequence of the excellence of these schools is that they also indirectly provide large numbers of managers to the private sector. The prestige of the training is such that graduates of the schools are attracted everywhere in industry and business. The *pantouflage* (as this type of transfer is known) thus enables the civil service, indirectly, to have a substantial influence on the whole economic life of the nation.

Civil Service Control

The quality of the *grands corps* does account for much of the excellence of the service, but it also leads to clashes among the various branches, which tend to make demands that go beyond what the nation can afford. Thus, the double problems of supervision of the bureaucracy and of coordination among agencies lead to difficulties and to suspicion, in particular among politicians. Not surprisingly, control has played a crucial—and often very frustrating—part in French administration.

There are many forms of control. Some are internal to the civil service and date back in part to Napoleon. There are many inspectorates, though these are often weak, in part because the inspectors-general are older men who stayed in the service while most of their colleagues in the same age group found in private business a more active life and a better remuneration; their status is therefore relatively low. As a matter of fact, their main role now is no longer inspection in the strict sense, but inquiry; they are often asked to examine long-term problems and thus act in a way similar to a royal commission in Britain or a presidential commission in the United States. A second type of control is by the administrative courts, headed by the Council of State. These courts started as internal organs of supervision on the model of inspectorates and, like inspectors, still conduct inquiries and have advisory functions (on bills and decrees, the Council of State advises the government about legality, opportunity, and effectiveness). But they are now real courts and are at some distance from the administrators.

Ministerial Staffs (Cabinets)   Internal controls seemed insufficient to liberal governments issued from Parliament and suspicious of administrators; hence, the development of a ministerial *cabinet* around each minister. Members of this *cabinet* (to be sharply distinguished from the "cabinet," or government) are appointed by the minister. They help him keep in touch with constituents and with Parliament, preparing plans for legislative and other reforms and seeing that, once adopted, they are implemented. Perhaps above all, at least traditionally, they inform the minister about the activities of administrators and see that these are not at variance with the minister's ideas. They are, then, a protection against civil servants anxious to have their way as well as a brain trust making suggestions to a harassed minister.

The character of ministerial *cabinets* has changed in recent years, however. Originally chosen by ministers among their loyal friends, they have also come to include technicians drawn from the civil service itself because ministers are increasingly in need of technical advice. A minister of transport will staff his or her *cabinet* with an engineer of roads and bridges, an inspector of finance (to examine costs), a member of the Council of State (to help draft legal documents), and others. Of course the *cabinet* staff, usually young, is loyal to the minister and likely to follow the minister if he or she goes to another post; their career depends in part on the help they give the minister. But they are civil servants and part of their loyalty is to the civil service, especially to the corps to which they belong. Like other civil servants, they are anxious to foster developments rather than control other civil servants on behalf of constituents or politicians. *Cabinets*, therefore, provide only a limited check on bureaucratic impulses.

LOCAL GOVERNMENT

In contrast to the civil service and central government agencies, French local government has been one of the casualties of the administrative system. Its organization was markedly affected by Napoleon, who, rejecting the early decentralizing schemes of the Revolution, adopted an authoritarian plan whereby local authorities were not only supervised but almost entirely run by agents of the central government. A slow process of liberalization took place in the nineteenth century, in the 1830s and the 1880s in particular, but reforms were never radical enough to break decisively with the origins. The maintenance of a large amount of central government control was due partly to political reasons: even liberals always felt that full devolution of power to local authorities was dangerous, as much of the opposition to the government was an opposition to the regime as well. Local government has thus been caught in a vicious circle which as yet has not been entirely broken, despite some changes in structure and a modification in attitudes, especially since the 1950s when local authorities have been struck with the idea of development and have become markedly more entrepreneurial.

The *Département* and the *Commune*

The current structure of French local government dates from the Revolution of 1789, as modified by Napoleon. The French territory is divided into *départements,* of which there are now 96. This was an entirely artificial creation designed to break the strength of the old provinces (such as Brittany or Provence) into new counties, whose names were drawn from mountains or rivers (Jura, Var, and the like); the *départements* are in turn divided into communes—usually corresponding to the old parishes—of which there are about 37,000. This division has helped centralization and prevented real local autonomy from being acquired since, despite a substantial amount of democratization in the appointment of decision makers, the small size of the average commune has rendered administration ineffective and increased the need for help from the technical and other services of the central government. Yet, there has scarcely been any reduction in the number of communes, in part because of local resistance and in part because the strength of the civil service is better maintained by the present structure. The only way reorganization has occurred since the 1960s has been through the setting up of joint

authorities (urban districts), linking towns to the suburban communes, and of the Paris district, which has a similar purpose for the Paris area.

Communes do maintain strong sentiments of local autonomy and their representatives play a large part in French local life. Elected every six years by universal suffrage, municipal councillors in turn elect a mayor and a number of assistants (*adjoints*). Mayors, in running the local authority, inherit some of the authority of the State. As the basic law of municipal government of 1884 states: "The mayor is in charge of the affairs of the commune." Mayors can pass bylaws relating to police or health matters; they register citizens; they supervise the maintenance of roads, street lighting, street cleaning, and the like. Aspects of education and housing come directly or indirectly under their control. The mayor is a focal point, particularly in large cities, because in practice mayors tend to stay in office for long, even very long periods (two or three terms of six years are very common). The stability of communal government has always contrasted with the instability of national politics. Communal government is also executive-centered: the municipal government is typically dominated by the mayor.

Decentralization Efforts   Yet, mayors and municipal councils also have been traditionally tightly supervised by agents of the central government, especially those at the level of the county (*département*). This is in part because counties have had, until recently, a peculiar organization, based on close ties among central government agents and locally elected councillors. The executive of the *département* in particular was, until 1982, the prefect, who is both an agent of the central government and the servant of the elected county council. There is no doubt that the existence of prefects perpetuated the dependence of local authorities on the central government and has in particular prevented the *département* from being a true local authority. Thus the reforms of the 1981 Socialist government constitute a major step. Whereas the government retains the prefects as agents of the central government, *départements* are now run by an elected representative, the president of the general council of the *département*. Meanwhile, communes have been given greater autonomy: they no longer need, on the whole, prior approval of the government representatives to undertake most activities. Since these reforms, French local government seems at last to be moving in the direction of other Western European countries.

Regionalism

Reform has also taken place at a higher level, that of the region. From an administrative point of view, the 96 *départements* had long become much too small; but, because the central government did not wish to divest itself from real power, regionalism developed very slowly from the 1950s to the 1980s. A number of units were set up in the same way as *départements*, but with even less democratic control, as there were no direct elections. Regional councils were composed of representatives of *départements*, communes, and economic and social groups. The first step in this direction occurred in the Paris area in 1959, when the district of the Paris region was set up, headed by a government-appointed delegate general. In 1964, regional economic development councils were created all over France.

Because participation was one of the main themes of the 1968 revolutionary outburst, it is not surprising that the government should have promised to meet some of the regionalists' demands. A scheme for regionalization was therefore presented to the French people in 1969, but it was limited. Moreover, because the proposed scheme was coupled with a reform of the Senate, it was rejected in the referendum—de Gaulle resigned as a result. In 1972, a new regional reform was drafted and presented to Parliament for approval. This time it was passed, and 22 ordinary regions were set up. Regional prefects were appointed alongside the regional presidents and councils, and these have administered a small portion of the matters hitherto handled centrally by the civil service, whereas the presidents of the regions, often important politicians in their own right, have had some influence and prestige. But the real reform had to wait another decade. Here, too, the measures put forward by the 1981–1986 Socialist government constitute a major step. For the first time in French history, regional councils were elected by universal suffrage in 1986; they in turn elected their executives. As a result, there is now, in each region, a truly independent political body.

Despite the reforms, however, the effective implementation of local and regional autonomy has still to be felt. Time has to pass before attitudes change; moreover, financial powers, at the level of the region at least, are rather limited. Yet a major step has been taken: the main institutional blockages of the past have been broken. The structures are different. Regions, *départements*, and communes (even the small ones) are involved in a process of autonomy which will gradually transform and indeed abolish many of the old habits of centralization.

ECONOMIC INTERVENTION AND PUBLIC ENTERPRISE

The weakness of French local government stems in large part from the widespread belief that France can be a modern industrial and commercial nation only if the civil service has the power to shake the inertia of the provinces. A parallel view has traditionally been adopted with respect to business. Thus, there has been a marked development of public and semipublic undertakings, which often take the form of mixed companies (*sociétés d'économie mixte*). Moreover, large-scale nationalizations took place in 1945–1946 and an attempt was made to supervise business generally by means of an economic plan. Indeed, in 1982, the Socialist government for a while increased markedly the size of the public sector. It seems, however, that the tide has now turned. The "privatization" program of the 1986–1988 conservative government has been undertaken in the more general context of an effort to reduce the traditional role of the civil service in the economy (see Table 3.8).

The Plan

French economic development from the 1940s to the 1980s has often been associated with the activities of the *Commissariat général au Plan*. Although its role is now nominal, its impact has been such that it deserves more than passing mention. It started under the leadership of Jean Monnet, a strong-willed ex-civil servant and ex-businessman, who was to be crucial to the psychological success of the idea and was later, much in the same vein, to foster European unity. From the start, the Plan was to be flexible; it was to be run by a team, not by a hierarchical and bureaucratic organization. Its strength came from the intellectual authority of the experts belonging to it who

Table 3.8 DISTRIBUTION OF BUDGETARY EXPENDITURE, 1989 (PERCENTAGE)

Economy and finance	45.9
Education (including universities)	16.7
Labor, health	9.3
Defense	7.4
Equipment and transport	7.0
Interior	3.9
Agriculture	2.9
Veterans	2.2
Foreign affairs	1.5
Industry and commerce	1.2
Justice	1.0
Culture, tourism	0.6
P.M. Office (including Planning Commissariat)	0.2
Overseas departments	0.1
Total budgetary expenditure	1,197,600 million francs

were to attract to their views business people and workers, farmers and industrialists, and private and public entrepreneurs.

The character of the Plan changed over the years. It was first essentially concerned with the reconstruction and development of basic industries. It then extended its role to the whole of the economy, to regional development (it did help decentralization to an extent), and even to social policies. Meanwhile, after having been originally drawn exclusively by officials and with little discussion, even in Parliament, large segments of the community became involved through numerous committees. Thus employers, leaders of nationalized industries, and trade unionists were then associated with the preparation of the Plan. There were also increasing discussions in the Economic and Social Council, in the regional economic committees, and among the public at large. However, in a climate of greater liberalization and free enterprise, the Plan could only suffer. With the advent of the Socialist government of 1981, its importance was revived somewhat, but because of the imperative of economic retrenchment, it never again held major place it once had. By the 1990s, in fact, it had effectively disappeared all but in name.

The Vast Size of the Public Sector

The downgrading of the Plan coincided with the first real attempt made by any French government after World War II to reduce the size of the public sector. Until 1986, the public sector in France was among the largest in Western Europe; this was already true before the large-scale nationalization measures of the 1981 Socialist government. From a base that included, already before World War II, the post office, the railways, some shipping lines, and miscellaneous undertakings, such as potash mines in Alsace, electricity production in the Rhône Valley, and luxury china in Sèvres, the public sector expanded in 1945–1956 to include the whole infrastructure of the economy. The coal mines, major banks, insurance companies, gas, electricity, and much of aircraft manufacturing were nationalized for reasons of principle. Renault, the largest car manufacturer, was nationalized as a penalty for the owner's collaboration with Nazi Germany during the war. Much of the air transport and more of the shipping lines came under direct control of the government.

Private ownership of radio stations was no longer allowed after the war, allowing the state to acquire a de facto monopoly of radio and television within France. Because radio stations at the periphery of the country were operated on a private basis, the State acquired majority capital in a number of them. The major French news agency, *Agence France-Presse*, replaced the private prewar *Agence Havas*. As the demand for oil increased (France has very little within its territory), the state created companies, typically as a major shareholder, which engaged in research, production, and distribution of oil and natural gas on a worldwide basis.

Despite an already large involvement of the state in the economy, a further major development occurred in 1982 when the government, following to the letter the Socialist party's pledge at the 1981 election, carried through Parliament the nationalization of practically all the banks (including old, established private banks such as Rothschild) and of five major industrial groups in the chemical and electronic fields. Additionally, the major steel companies, already heavily subsidized by the state, were taken over.

These developments were possible only because the French bureaucracy developed, after World War I, a panoply of juridical forms of participation. Originally the state acted directly, in its capacity as a central government—the formula adopted for the post office when the monarchy turned it into a state monopoly. But a second technique was quickly found—that of the *établissement public* in which the funds are public and control is tight, but a board makes decisions and contracts with third parties on behalf of the agency. This is the for-

mula adopted in local government as well. But the method was not flexible enough.

The civil service thus came to create, almost on the private model, companies and corporations with the same structure, the same rights, and the same obligations as private firms. In the case of the large undertakings nationalized in 1945–1946 and in 1982, special legislative arrangements gave the corporations a somewhat different organization; for instance, boards have to include representatives of the state, the users, and the employees. In many other cases there was simply no difference from private business. State corporations, thus, could combine with private bodies to create subsidiaries.

Moves Toward Privatization Between 1986 and 1988

There is, therefore, an almost infinite variety of forms adopted by the public sector. It includes an immense network of bodies whose ramifications extend well beyond what the ordinary French citizen knows to be public firms. This naturally led to a blurring of the difference between the private and public sectors. It seems, however, that this development has reached its limits. For the first time, a government came to power in 1986 committed to privatization and to the abandonment of the traditional practice of linking private and public bodies. For the first time, too, the Left has not truly wished to modify the new equilibrium by increasing again the public sector. Its return to power in 1988 has not been associated with new nationalization proposals. Indeed, the Socialist government of the late 1980s and early 1990s undertook at least some partial privatizations, such as that of Renault, which became associated with the Swedish firm Volvo. It is also interesting to note that the French government decided—alongside other European governments at the time—to foster formally and consciously forms of classical private enterprise at the expense of the more mixed forms of companies, which had been considered the way of the future for at least a generation.

FOREIGN POLICY

De Gaulle's Worldwide Policy

Foreign policy was the main interest of de Gaulle; even the institutional reforms were in some sense provoked by the bias of the founder of the Fifth Republic for foreign affairs, as he felt that the instability and impotence of previous regimes had been the cause both of defeat in 1940 and of the generally limited influence of the country in the world ever since. Although he was not entirely wrong in his appreciation of the external effects of internal political uncertainties, he clearly underestimated the extent to which France could still be a prime mover in the contemporary world. Thus, his efforts at pushing for a strong and independent foreign policy ended in failure. Indeed, he might have himself grudgingly realized that he could not go much beyond symbolic gestures, such as the effort to build closer links with the Soviet Union or to defend the rights of some countries or groups against Anglo-Saxon "imperialism" (as he tried to do in Quebec and Latin America). In practice, he kept France within NATO (despite some changes) and within the European Community (despite a continuous emphasis on the fact that Europe should be a "Europe of Nations" and despite the fact that he unquestionably retarded the development of European unity).

Pompidou's Greater Realism

De Gaulle's departure from the scene meant a slow, indeed very slow, return to the recognition of the reality of France's international position: France is a medium-sized power, with some influence resulting from her cultural and economic ties with parts of Africa and, to a more limited extent, with Latin America; but it cannot have a direct effect on the course of events outside Western Europe where, on the contrary, France has a significant part to play, albeit as a partner and not as a leader. This gradual recognition can be seen in the fact that Pompidou, de Gaulle's successor and heir, began to make some moves away from grand world involvement and toward the acceptance of France's limited European role. Pompidou's acceptance of British entry into the European Community (EC) was of course motivated by his hope that Britain, like France, would reduce the speed at which "supranationalism" would take place. In this he was proved right, though the entry of Britain into the European Community also meant that the Community became genuinely a community of all Western European nations.

The More Limited Ambitions of Giscard and Mitterrand

The third President of the Fifth Republic, Giscard d'Estaing, went one step further: his friendship and close working relationship with the German chancellor of the time, Helmut Schmidt, could be viewed as symbolizing the same *rapprochement* as that of de Gaulle and Adenauer a decade or more earlier; but the purpose was different. De Gaulle wanted in a sense to use Adenauer to assert his leadership over Europe; Giscard, more modestly, both recognized the economic superiority of Germany and was primarily concerned with economic association. A step was thus taken toward real collaboration and the abandonment of the (wholly unrealistic) idea that France could do more than partly influence the course of events in Western Europe.

Mitterrand's role has been markedly more positive. Not being associated, directly or indirectly, with de Gaulle and Gaullism, he was able to assert that France's position was in Europe and, effectively, only in Europe. The economic difficulties (and the consequential social problems of unemployment) made it impossible for Mitterrand to expect to move at a truly different pace from his European partners, as we saw. His European conviction, however, was not merely the result of the need to solve or diminish France's economic and social problems, but was part of a general recognition that the country is in Europe and, indeed, that if France was wholeheartedly in Europe, it could play an essential role in the development and shape of the Community. It is notable that, perhaps as a result of this policy, Mitterrand was able to appoint his ex-minister of finance, Jacques Delors, to the presidency of the European Commission from 1985. In this way, he clearly had some means of influencing Community affairs, in particular as Delors proved to be one of the ablest leaders to preside over the European Commission. This is not to say that Mitterrand is a full federalist; nor is it to say that he completely eschewed the idea that France should have a worldwide policy. However, the greater realism of the first French Socialist president is an important development in relation to what de Gaulle was proposing to achieve—and failed to achieve—three decades earlier. This twist is perhaps the greatest paradox of the Fifth Republic and a further sign of the marked flexibility of this regime.

Yet, French governmental attitudes toward foreign policy (and to some extent toward other larger Western European countries) remain somewhat ambiguous. Whereas French governments (even those led by Gaullists) have come to proclaim their belief in the European idea, they also remain intent to play a large part—a somewhat unrealistically large part—in worldwide developments, whether in the Middle East, in Africa, or in Latin America. Indeed, the commitment to Europe is somewhat ambiguous in that French governments have more than occasionally been concerned with defending their economic interests to the hilt, and have also been somewhat slow at applying, in practice, the principles they claim to support in theory. Nevertheless, this mode of behavior is perhaps inevitable in a period of transition, during which France—as well as the other Western European powers—has to recognize that its role in the world must be reduced and that only through a common Eu-

ropean policy can the voice of the whole area be of real moment. The dilemma between "going it alone" and further integration is one that has affected, almost daily, the actions of French governments over the last decades, and it is likely to continue affecting them for many years to come.

CONCLUSION

In the 1950s and 1960s, the French economy was transformed dramatically. The colonial problems that destroyed one regime and brought another, at times, near the precipice were solved and forgotten; the international status of the country was high. Yet social tensions, which seemed to diminish for a while in the 1960s, reemerged dramatically in 1968. This reinforced the feeling among many of the French that the regime remained provisional. But the departure of de Gaulle one year later, in 1969, did not shake the institutions, and the transition from de Gaulle to Pompidou was smooth. Nor was the regime shaken by the transition from Giscard to Mitterrand in 1981, despite many earlier predictions that the *alternance* from right to left would be very difficult, if not impossible; nor was it even shaken by the emergence of a "cohabitation" government—a president of one party and a government of another ideological stance—despite further gloomy predictions that major difficulties would emerge.

In 1981, a Socialist government then embarked on a program of reforms. This undertaking was possible only because of existing institutions, which ostensibly had been tailor-made for de Gaulle. In 1986, a conservative government undid many of these reforms, but the regime, then too, was flexible enough to make these movements possible. Also possible was a further movement toward the Left, though admittedly less pronounced, in 1988. What had been viewed as institutional ambiguity turned out to be a major asset of the Constitution of 1958.

Cynics had claimed that de Gaulle wanted to have it both ways—namely, to be able to run the executive and yet have considerable control over the legislature, to have the elbow room of a U.S. president but the hold over the chamber of a British premier, and in practical terms, to be immovable for seven years but still be able to dissolve Parliament and to appeal to the people. Others had claimed that de Gaulle was incapable of understanding and appreciating the importance of constitutional structures, a view which has some truth, though the attitudes of the first president of the Fifth Republic on this matter were complex. He seemed to consider that constitutional arrangements were matters for lawyers, who can always find solutions if they are firmly led, and at the same time he had a simple, naive, almost religious belief in the virtues of constitutional reform to redress the imperfections of a political system. His approach to political analysis was more institutional than behavioral, to use the common expression of modern political scientists. Yet he made a change that, however ambiguous—or perhaps because it was ambiguous—allowed for a transition to occur and turned out to be adapted to French patterns of political behavior.

De Gaulle was often criticized because he preferred constitutional change to the establishment of a streamlined and responsible party system, such as that Adenauer succeeded in achieving in West Germany. De Gaulle was indeed old-fashioned in this respect. He did not like parties, which he often called "factions"; he saw them as divisive and as the cause of the ineffectiveness of French political life in the past. But paradoxically, in his concentrating on institutional change and endeavoring to reduce the role of parties, he did streamline the party system: he built a party on the Right which his successors, Pompidou and Giscard D'Estaing, undermined, and he indirectly helped the Socialist party to rebuild itself.

The election of 1981 constituted an historic event in more than one way; indeed, in the broadest political sense, more than Pompidou and Giscard, Mitterrand is the heir and the continuator of de Gaulle's approach. Mitterrand, like de Gaulle, defeated the Communist party on coming to power; he, like de Gaulle, established a strong majority party. The election of 1981 had the same political effect—streamlining and strengthening the party system—as the election of 1962, and Mitterrand, like de Gaulle, came to power with a mission, albeit a different one. De Gaulle's mission was to solve the Algerian crisis and, beyond this crisis, to bring France back to political and psychological sanity. Mitterrand's mission is to reconcile the French among themselves, to make them no longer fear taking on their own destiny, reaching the grassroots, whether in the regions and the communes or in the firms.

Here the comparison stops. To achieve this tall order, Mitterrand needed to exorcise the twin specters of unemployment and inflation. He did reduce the latter, but the former probably contributed to the defeat of his party in 1986. As a matter of fact, Mitterrand could not hope to succeed without the collaboration of other countries in Western Europe, of the United States, and of Japan. These nations, however, practiced economic orthodoxy; Mitterrand could not win alone. He had to accept the need for retrenchment and with it the clipping of many of his ideals. Yet, while the French turned away from the Left in view of its relative failures, Mitterrand himself, and indeed the Socialist party in general, gained a position of respect and acceptability they had not had before. This explains more than in part the return of the Socialist party to power in 1988 and, indeed, its having become (temporarily, perhaps) the dominant force in French politics. In the process, France has become a country in which pluralism and alternation could become firmly established.

Observers around the world have tended to admire the British form of government, but they have been fascinated by the French political system. For a while, under the Fifth

Republic, it was fashionable to say that a new French political system, streamlined and dull, was emerging. This was scarcely true at the time of the Algerian war, when virulence added unpleasantness to the political fights of the French, and it has not become true with the end of the colonial wars. There is now a search for a more just equilibrium between the various forces in society, between Paris and the provinces, between employers and workers, and between the majority of the French and the many minority groups—immigrants, the young, and the deviants. No doubt the Socialist experiment of 1981 disappointed some and repelled others; but France also changed in that no longer will the central bureaucracy or the elite groups be able to maintain their traditional hold on the society.

By 1981 the Gaullist (and Giscardian) phase of the Fifth Republic seemed to have outlived its usefulness. The bickering among the various political groups of the old majority and the increasingly ineffective attempts by Giscard to bring about a modicum of change were sufficient pointers to the decline in the vitality of those groups that had governed France for over two decades. It is to de Gaulle's credit that he made it possible for France to seize the opportunity to bring about a change, not so much of direction as of intensity of action and of determination and purpose; and it is to the credit of the French people that they seized this opportunity, though, of course, many motivations, from unemployment to scandals, played a substantial part. Thus, France will perhaps overcome some of its social problems while it also overcomes the institutional problems from which it has suffered for almost two centuries. But the path is narrow and tortuous. Ingenuity and imagination will no more suffice than a competent bureaucracy. Patience and determination—not the qualities for which the French are best known—will have to be shown if the motto "Liberty, Equality, Fraternity" is to be brought closer to reality.

Key Terms

adjoints
bureaucracy
Civil Service Control
Commissaires de la République
Départements
Directions Générales/Directions
French Civil Service
"Grands Corps"
Grandes Ecoles
social engineering

Suggestions for Further Readings

Bauchet, P. *Economic Planning: The French Experience* (London: Heinemann, 1963).

Cerny, P., and M. Schain, eds. *French Politics and Public Policy* (New York: Methuen, 1980).

Chapman, B. *Introduction to French Local Government* (London: Allen and Unwin, 1953).

Crozier, M. *The Bureaucratic Phenomenon* (London: Tavistock, 1964).

Crozier, M. *The Stalled Society* (New York: Viking, 1973).

Dufay, F. and J. C. Thoenig. *L'administration en miettes* (Paris: Fayard, 1985).

Gregoire, R. *The French Civil Service* (Brussels: Institute of Administrative Science, 1964).

Gremino, P. *Le pouvoir périphérique* (Paris: Seuil, 1976).

Grosser, A. *La politique extérieure de la Cinquième République* (Paris: A. Colin, 1965).

Machin, H. and V. Wright, eds. *Economic Policy and Policy Making under the Mitterrand Presidency, 1981–1984* (London: F. Pinter, 1985)

Ridley, F., and J. Blondel. *Public Administration in France*, 2nd ed. (London: Routledge and Kegan Paul, 1968).

Suleiman, E. *Politics, Power, and Bureaucracy in France* (Princeton: Princeton University Press, 1974).

Suleiman, E. *Elites in French Society* (Princeton: Princeton University Press, 1978).

CHAPTER 4

The Government of Germany

Donald P. Kommers

A. Political Development

On 3 October 1990, after 45 years of painful separation, Germany was once again a united nation. After midnight on that day, East Germany ceased to exist. The territory formerly governed by the German Democratic Republic (GDR) and its hardline Communist leaders was now an integral part of the Federal Republic of Germany (FRG). *Accession* was the magical term used. Under Article 23 of West Germany's constitution, "other parts of Germany" outside the territory governed by the FRG could join or "accede to" the FRG. Accession meant that these "other parts" of Germany joining the FRG would henceforth be subject to its constitution, better known as the *Basic Law* or *Grundgesetz*. In this instance, accession took place under the terms of the German Unity Treaty signed by the FRG and the GDR.[1] In signing the treaty the GDR agreed to dissolve itself, to embrace the Basic Law, and to bring its entire social, political, and economic system into conformity with FRG law.

Unification did not restore to Germany all the territory lost as a result of World War II. In 1945 the Soviet Union annexed northern East Prussia, including Königsberg, while all German territory east of the Oder and Neisse Rivers (East Prussia, Silesia, and part of Pomerania and Brandenburg) was placed under Polish administration. The Allies divided the rest of Germany and Berlin into four zones of occupation: a Soviet zone in the east and three zones in the west occupied by France, Britain, and the United States, respectively. The western zones, united in 1949 to form the Federal Republic of Germany, constituted only 60 percent of the territory of the German nation that existed between 1871 and 1937. The Saarland, which France annexed after World War II, was returned to the FRG in 1957 after its residents voted in favor of union with the FRG. It too entered the Federal Republic by accession under Article 23, becoming the smallest of West Germany's territorial states. With the GDR's accession, Germany has finally managed to recover three-fourths of the territory it had contained within its 1937 borders.

The division of Germany after World War II recalls the tragic course of German history down through the centuries. This history has been marred not only by territorial dismemberment but also by political discontinuity, which has manifested itself in recurrent patterns of revolution and reaction, leaving the German nation with a diverse and fragmented political legacy of democratic, authoritarian, and even totalitarian systems of government.

HISTORICAL BACKGROUND: MOLDING THE GERMAN NATION

The First Reich (800–1806)

Centuries after Britain and France had been unified under strong national monarchs, Germany was still a dizzying patchwork of sovereign powers—over 300 feudal states and some 1300 smaller estates—each with its own political institutions, laws, and customs. No imperial institution was prestigious enough to unify these diversities, and no emperor was strong enough to merge them into a single national state. The shape of the Holy Roman Empire of the German Nation (the predominantly German parts of the Empire founded by Charlemagne and restored by Otto I— and which has rightly been described as "neither holy, nor Roman, nor an empire") itself changed repeatedly over its thousand-year history, stretching in and out like an accordion—a process facilitated by the absence of natural frontiers on the northern plains of Europe— depending on the fortunes of war or the outcome of princely rivalries.

Religious and political division matched the severity of Germany's territorial fragmentation. The Reformation (1517–1555) polarized Germans religiously, creating a legacy of intolerance and hatred that lasted well into the nineteenth century. The Thirty Years War (1618–1648) was equally devastating in longrange political impact. The most destructive war in the first millennium of German history, it decimated the population, wrecked agriculture and industry, and destroyed an emergent middle class that might have formed the nucleus of a nationalizing and moderating force in German politics. It restored power to the princes, reinvigorated feudalism, and set the stage for the nineteenth-century struggle between feudal and proletarian forces. Moreover, Protestant religious teaching and princely absolutism combined to emphasize the duty of obedience to the State, thus inhibiting popular participation in politics.[2]

Napoleon to Bismarck (1806–1871)

An invader laid the basis of German unity. Occupying Germany in 1806, Napoleon banished the ghost of the old Reich and forced hundreds of principalities into a confederation of some 30 states governed by a unified code of civil law. Like so much else in German history, this experience led to contradictory results. On the one hand, French rule stimulated the development of a liberal movement focused mainly in southwestern Germany and rooted in the eighteenth-century revival of classical humanism. On the other hand, it triggered an outburst of German nationalism built almost exclusively on antipathy toward the liberal reforms of the French Revolution—a reaction paralleled in the cultural domain by a literary backlash that glorified tradition over reason, heroism over compassion, and the folk community over cosmopolitanism.

France's defeat in 1815 led to the Congress of Vienna and the establishment of a new confederacy of 41 states that largely retained Napoleon's extensive remodeling of Germany. In its effort to strengthen Germany vis-à-vis France, the Congress ceded large possessions in the Rhineland and Westphalia to Prussia, a German state that had by then grown into a formidable power in central Europe. The Prussian-led conservative Hohenzollern monarchy and militaristic Junker caste were destined to finish, through "blood and iron," the work of national unification started by Napoleon. Economically, the Prussian-sponsored customs union (*Zollverein*), which resulted in the removal of most trade barriers among the German states, was an important tool of national integration.

A watershed year in this period was 1848, when revolutions against monarchical regimes broke out all over Europe. German liberals had gathered enough strength to persuade several princes to go along with the election of a National Assembly, which convened in Frankfurt am Main in May and proceeded to create a united Germany under a new federal constitution containing an impressive bill of rights, an independent judiciary, and parliamentary institutions. However, by the following spring this "revolution" had been put down as Germany reverted to its traditional pattern of authoritarian governance, increasingly under Prussian domination. In 1966, under the leadership of Otto von Bismarck, Prussia defeated Austria, its closest rival for hegemony in Germany. Austria's defeat led to the creation of the North German Confederation in 1867, also under Prussian domination. Five years later, after conquering France, Prussia proceeded to establish a truly national state in the form of a constitutional monarchy.

The Second Reich (1871–1918)

The constitutional order installed by Bismarck in 1871 was a semi-authoritarian system that (1) limited the franchise to the wealthier classes; (2) subordinated the popularly elected house of parliament (*Reichstag*) to the executive; (3) established a Prussian-dominated and non-elected upper parliamentary chamber (*Bundesrat*) composed largely of landed proprietors and members of reigning families; (4) divided executive authority between a chancellor and the emperor (*Kaiser*), with effective political power lodged in the latter; and (5) empowered the emperor (preeminently the king of Prussia) to appoint and dismiss the chancellor, dissolve the Reichstag, declare martial law, and serve as supreme commander of the armed forces. In the socioeconomic sphere, the imperial era was marked by (1) an economic revolution that transformed a backward and predominantly agrarian society into a powerful urban, industrialized nation; (2) the establishment of an alliance between agrarian and industrial interests in foreign policy; (3) the colonization of overseas territories; (4) the adoption of a comprehensive program of state social legislation designed to purchase the loyalty and support of the working masses; and (5) an arms race with Britain and France,

triggered in part by an increasingly chauvinistic nationalism as many Germans, including intellectuals, dreamed of a larger and even more powerful global order under German hegemony.

Ralf Dahrendorf has characterized imperial Germany as an "industrial feudal society,"[3] meaning that industrialism failed to produce a modern polity in Germany as it did in Britain and France. Whereas modernization brought about liberal traditions of civic equality and political participation in Britain and France, Germany remained a preindustrial class society based on rank and status. The state bureaucracy, professional army, landed aristocracy, and patriarchical family remained the central pillars of the social structure. Human rights or other fundamental guarantees were conspicuously absent in the imperial constitution. Social conflict was put down either by repression or state paternalism, thus encouraging the political passivity of the German people, inducing them to seek the satisfactions of life by turning inward, toward themselves (internal freedom) and to the fostering of private values associated with friendship and family, rather than by turning outward toward the cultivation of public virtues.

The Weimar Republic (1919–1933)

Germany's defeat in World War I and the abdication of the monarch led to the establishment at Weimar of its first constitutional democracy since the short-lived National Assembly of 1848. The Constitution of 1919 continued a long tradition of German federalism by requiring every state to establish a republican form of government. Provisions for popular referenda as well as the direct popular election of the national president reflected Weimar's commitment to the principle of popular sovereignty. The constitution, however, contained a number of structural deficiencies that undermined political stability and endangered civil liberties. First, the chancellor was subservient to parliament and subject to dismissal by a popularly elected president. In addition, the constitution authorized the president to dissolve the Reichstag (the powerful new lower chamber), control the armed forces, suspend constitutional rights, and exercise broad emergency powers. Second, whereas the constitution guaranteed various rights and liberties, it failed to provide for their judicial protection. Third, the system of proportional representation splintered the electorate, leading to a succession of weak coalition governments. Fourth, political parties lacked prestige and even legitimacy in the eyes of most Germans. Finally, the ease with which the constitution could be amended or vital parts of it suspended paved the way to its ultimate debasement.

It is doubtful whether any constitution, however artfully drawn, could have contained the social and political volatility unleashed in postwar Germany. To begin with, the harsh terms of the Treaty of Versailles—for example, the internationalization of Germany's main inland waterways, the cession of territory to six bordering countries, enforced reparations, and the allied occupation of the Rhineland—compounded by the 1923 invasion of the Ruhr by France and Belgium, generated an outburst of frenzied nationalism that found its most virulent expression in the views and personality of Adolf Hitler.

Additionally, Germany's largely unchanged social structure constituted a fragile foundation on which to build a democratic republic. Republican institutions—whose legitimacy was questioned by a large segment of the country's elite—were simply incapable of serving as effective instruments of social control when economic conditions, which had declined dramatically in 1922–23 and had improved only after most people's life savings had been wiped out, worsened again at the end of the 1920s. Violence erupted in the streets as right-wing extremists, often fighting left-wing extremists, gathered strength and influence. The political unrest led to Hitler's installation as chancellor on 30 January 1933; Nazi success in the election of 5 March 1933, following the February burning of the Reichstag, anchored his hold on power. The passage of the Enabling Act shortly thereafter, granting the government dictatorial powers, ended the life of the Weimar Republic.

The Third Reich (1933–1945)

With Hitler's rise to power, constitutional government succumbed to National Socialist totalitarianism. Popular assemblies of the various states were abolished; political parties banned; autonomous groups and associations suppressed; dissent crushed; anti-Nazi political figures imprisoned, tortured, or murdered; and ordinary citizens deprived of liberty and property without due process of law. Having consolidated his power, Hitler proceeded, in violation of the Treaty of Versailles, to remilitarize the Rhineland and to build a war machine that by 1941 would sweep across Europe, threatening the security of the entire world.

Although the German dictatorship met with the brave resistance of various religious and political groups—including several attempts on Hitler's life—it took the almost total destruction of Germany from the outside to topple the Nazis from power. World War II (1939–1945) resulted in yet another enforced dismemberment and foreign occupation of the German nation, plus the elimination of Prussia as a separate territorial unit. Hitler had inadvertently facilitated the long trek back to political democracy. In a twelve-year orgy of repression and violence, the Nazis succeeded in destroying the old order, including many traditional institutions and values. Thus, Hitler's "social revolution," combined with Germany's physical destruction, cleared the way for the rebuilding of a new society.

TOWARD A NEW FRAMEWORK OF GOVERNMENT

The Occupation (1945–1949)

In 1945, Germany lay smoldering in ruins. Its once powerful military machine was shattered, its industrial establishment incapacitated, its urban centers demolished, its transportation and communication networks disrupted, its government at all levels in a state of total collapse, and its people demoralized and starving. Politically, Germany's future seemed bleak. At the Yalta and Potsdam conferences the victorious powers had agreed (1) to eliminate every trace of Nazism and militarism in Germany, (2) to disarm the nation completely, (3) to punish those responsible for war crimes, (4) to force the payment of reparations to nations hurt by German aggression, and (5) to prevent the reemergence of industries capable of military production.

In each of their zones of occupation, the Allies embarked upon programs of *denazification* and *democratization* as the first steps toward the reconstruction of a new political order. By 1947–48, however, cooperation among the Allies had ceased. For France, Britain, and the United States, democratization meant parliamentary democracy, competitive elections, civil liberties, and a free enterprise economy; for the Soviet Union, it meant Communist party rule and state ownership of the means of production. Furthermore, the Soviet Union had embarked upon a policy of conquest and one-party rule in Eastern Europe, creating satellite states organized in accordance with Marxist-Leninist principles out of the countries it had liberated from the Nazis. The Cold War was gathering force with a vengeance, and Germany was its flash point.

Unable to reach an agreement with the Soviet Union over the future of Germany, the three western powers decided to combine their zones of occupation into a single economic unit. The Soviet Union responded with the Berlin blockade, but the famous airlift of 1948–49 foiled the Soviet attempt to drive the western powers out of Berlin.

Economic union in the western half of Germany was soon followed by political union. With the reestablishment of state and local governments and the licensing of political parties committed to democratic constitutional-

ism, the allied military governors laid the groundwork for a new all-West German political system. A constituent assembly dominated by Christian and Social Democrats, elected in turn by the state legislatures, convened with Allied approval to write a new constitution. They chose to call it the Basic Law (*Grundgesetz*) rather than the Constitution (*Verfassung*) in order to underscore the provisional character of the new polity pending national reunification. This Basic Law, which created the Federal Republic of Germany, entered into force on 23 May 1949, after its ratification by the legislatures of more than two-thirds of the participating states (*Länder*). The Soviet Union responded by founding the German Democratic Republic, whose constitution entered into force on 7 October 1949.

Two States—One Nation (1949–1990)

The constitutions of both East and West Germany looked toward eventual reunification. This goal remained the lodestar of the Basic Law, but in the course of time it vanished from the East German Constitution when the GDR locked itself into a Soviet-style system of political rule. In 1974, dropping all references to reunification, an amended version of the constitution described the GDR as a "socialist state of the German nation," the equivalent of a declaration of independence. Although some relaxation had taken place in the relations between the two German states in the aftermath of *Ostpolitik*,[4] they still viewed each other with mistrust and hostility. The Berlin Wall stood out as the chief symbol of their mutual antagonism. Like the armed fortifications along the 529-mile border separating the two Germanys, the Wall was designed to keep GDR residents disillusioned with Communist rule from joining the nearly four million of their fellow citizens who had left for or fled to West Germany since 1949.

The earth-shaking events leading to German unity in 1990 will be recounted in Section C, but for now it suffices to remark that with all escape routes to the West blocked, East Germans settled down to make the best of what their formidable skills and social discipline could produce. By the late 1990s, the GDR had developed the strongest economy in the Soviet bloc and had one of the world's most productive economies. Even though the GDR's standard of living remained substantially below that of the FRG, East Germans could count on cradle-to-grave security, including free medical care, low rents, generous maternal leave and child care policies, and a uniform system of polytechnical education geared to the needs of the economy. However, the cost in personal freedom was high. By 1973, the economy had been thoroughly collectivized while the state's secret police (*Stasi*) kept East Germans in line politically.

East Germans might have been fenced off from their cousins in West Germany, but they could look at them through the eye of television. What they saw was a land of comfort and freedom. When West Germany arose from the ashes of World War II, few would have predicted that in the span of one generation its citizens would be able to boast of having created the world's fourth largest industrial power, a standard of living matched only by a handful of nations, and a highly stable political democracy. By any measure of social and economic development, the FRG would stand out as one of the world's most modernized states.

The growth of the FRG's economy and the stability of its political system doubtless had much to do with the nature of its constitution. The Allied military government insisted that any future government of Germany must be federal, democratic, and constitutional. West Germans went a step further, making absolute the principles of democracy and federalism in their new constitution. Article 79, paragraph 3, of the Basic Law—the so-called eternity clause—declares inadmissible any amendment that would erode democracy or effect the division of the federation into states.

In addition, the Basic Law guarantees personal rights and liberties, including occupational rights, and establishes a constitutional court to enforce these rights against the state. The founding fathers sought to stabilize the new polity by establishing a party democracy and combining it with a constitutional ban on parties that "seek to impair or abolish the free democratic basic order" (Article 21). In contrast to the Weimar Constitution, the Basic Law strengthens the hand of the chancellor even while making him responsible to parliament and bars parliament from voting him out of office without simultaneously electing his successor. The FRG's founders were clearly distrustful of reintroducing the mechanisms of direct democracy. They reaffirmed the principle of popular sovereignty, but it would now take the form of representative rather than plebiscitary institutions, including the indirect election of the federal president.[5]

SOCIETY AND THE ECONOMY

An understanding of contemporary German politics requires some attention to the profound social and economic changes that have occurred, first in the FRG since 1945 and then in the *Länder* that acceded to the FRG upon the dissolution of the GDR. While these five reconstituted *Länder* come with a vastly different political and socioeconomic formation from that of the western *Länder*, both societies are committed to the process of raising the standards of living and of production in the eastern area to parity with those enjoyed in the western area. The overwhelming majority of Germans nationwide have indicated through the ballot box that they are determined to erase all vestiges of the former GDR's command economy and to replace it with the mixed economy of the *advanced social welfare state*—an ideal that the national governments have pursued, more often than not, since the days of Bismarck.

Despite this note of historical continuity, it is difficult to determine whether, in a general western "postindustrial" setting, it is the economy that is driven by the polity or the polity by the economy, or both (to some degree) by the given social organization. Two things are clear: First, in a modern industrial democracy like the FRG, the political system and the social market economy are inextricably interwoven. Second, both the political system and the social market economy are more dependent than ever before for their strength and, indeed, legitimacy, on international associations. The roots of the industrial democracies are as diverse as the nations themselves, yet their future is increasingly defined in common.

Territory and Population

On the night of 2–3 October 1990, when East and West Germans came together on the great lawn before the Reichstag, the *Platz der Republik*, to celebrate their reunification, many of them flew the black-red-gold flag of the FRG, which had been the tricolor of the two previous German democracies as well (1848 and 1918). Germany was felt to be reclaiming the best elements of its common past. At the same time, a good number of European Community flags were also in evidence, with the circle of 12 gold stars on a field of blue, seeming to reflect the oft-stated aim of the two societies to work together henceforth, not for a "German Europe," but for a "European Germany."

In territorial size, reunited Germany is the fifth largest nation in Europe, up from tenth place. Although now geographically the third largest nation in the EEC, behind France and Spain, Germany is still significantly smaller, as Table 4.1 shows, than most of the countries covered in this volume. Moreover, even if the Germany of today had the desire or the ability to return to its 1937 borders, it would nonetheless remain a medium-sized state on the global scale—although as an industrial power the FRG ranks fourth in the world.

Table 4.1 TERRITORY AND POPULATION: GERMANY'S RANKING AMONG SELECTED NATIONS, 1989

Nation	Territory (sq. mi.)	Nation	Population (in millions)
USSR	8,650,000	China	1,160.0
China	3,692,900	India	797.0
USA	3,615,122	USSR	281.7
India	1,269-419	USA	226.5
Mexico	756,066	Japan	121.9
Nigeria	356,669	NIgeria	105.5
France	212,742	Mexico	82.7
Spain	194,900	Germany	78.7
Japan	145,856	FRG	62.0
Germany	137,787	GDR	16.7
FRG	96,019	UK	57.1
GDR	41,768	France	55.9
UK	94,512	Spain	39.1

Source: The New Encyclopedia Britannica, 15th ed. (Chicago: Encyclopedia Britannica, 1988), compiled from each national entry, and *Whittaker's Almanack 1991,* 123 rev. ed. (London: J. Whitaker & Sons Ltd., 1990), pp. 620–3.

The more important figures for contemporary Germany, both in Europe and the world, are those concerning its population. Even before reunification, the FRG was the most populous state in western Europe and second on the continent only to the Soviet Union. The acquisition of some 16 million East Germans does not dramatically change this picture, although it augurs well for Germany's future economic potential. Along with expanding its borders and its population, the FRG has gained a new neighbor, Poland, and a new set of demographics. The overall population is now marginally younger, somewhat more East European in origin, and proportionately more Protestant.

The population figures in Table 4.1 contain a fascinating tale of human migration and dislocation. Between 1949 and 1989 the FRG's population increased by 13 million, while the GDR lost over 2 million of its inhabitants. These statistics were not substantially affected by the birthrate in the indigenous population. In fact, West Germany had experienced a measurable decline in its native population since 1970. The rapid increase in population recorded after 1949 resulted mainly from the influx of nearly 10 million German refugees from Poland, the Soviet Union, East Germany, and other eastern countries and from the arrival of 2.5 million foreign workers who migrated to Germany in the 1960s.

By 1989, there were 4.8 million foreign residents in the FRG, 70 percent of whom had been there for 10 years or more. With the addition of the GDR's 120,000 foreigners—mostly Polish—these residents made up 6.5 percent of the population.[6] Then, in two and a half years, 2.5 million immigrants poured into western Germany. Just over 1 million were *Ubersiedler*, that is, East Germans who moved west before reunification; slightly less than 1 million were *Aussiedler*, that is, ethnic Germans drawn mostly from Poland and Russia; this leaves about a half a million immigrants as true "foreigners."

What is impressive about these figures is that they represent a rate of entry relative to the national population that is not only twice the rate of mass immigration to the United States in the 1920s but, apart from Israel, several times more than that of any EC or OECD country today. By 1991, however, several hundred thousand asylum seekers from Turkey, Romania, Yugoslavia, and the Middle East were pushing these figures slightly upward, intensifying right-wing opposition to the foreign presence in Germany, all of which was taking place amidst predictions that by the mid-1990s as many as 2 million ethnic Germans from the Soviet Union, Poland, and Romania would resettle in Germany.

From Bonn to Berlin and in Between

Germany at last has a hub like London, Paris, or Rome and one around which the economic, cultural, and political life of the country is likely to swirl. Berlin is that hub, the new capi-

Breaching the Berlin Wall.

tal of united Germany. With a population of 3.4 million, it is Germany's largest city. (Hamburg and Munich follow, with 1.6 and 1.2 million, respectively.) A sprawling urban landscape still blighted at the very center (i.e., where the Wall stood) by 40 years of division and in the former eastern half by both the scars left from the war and a legacy of Soviet Socialist architecture that was characteristically oppressive in style and shoddy in execution, Berlin nonetheless promises to become in time the trading gateway between East and West if not "the *de facto* metropolis of the new free Central Europe."[7]

Despite a bruising parliamentary battle, the decision to move the capital from Bonn to Berlin seemed inevitable and was strongly supported by the Federal Chancellor and President. Bonn, the sleepy provincial town beside the Rhine, was bound to give way to the cosmopolitanism of Berlin and the electrifying beat of its international life.

Apart from Berlin, the economic and political life of the country is centered in a number of conurbations in the Rhine-Ruhr (Essen, Dortmund, Cologne, and Düsseldorf), Rhine-Main (Frankfurt), and Rhine-Neckar (Mannheim); in the business-industrial concentrations around the cities of Stuttgart, Hamburg, Hanover, and Munich; and now in the east around Dresden, Leipzig, and Chemnitz. Fourteen cities boast populations of more than 500,000. The eastern *Länder*, however, are less urbanized than those in the west. Thirty-five percent of the former FRG's population live in cities with more than 100,000 inhabitants, but only 10.2 percent of former GDR residents live in such areas. Similarly, only 6.1 percent of western Germans live in areas with fewer than 2000 inhabitants; the figure for eastern Germans is 23 percent.

The FRG Economy

At the behest of the western occupying powers (the United States, Great Britain, and France), Ludwig Erhard, Director of the Economic Administration for the three western zones, initiated a currency reform in June 1948. This created a solidly based and freely convertible *deutsche mark* (DM), the financial and economic prerequisite to the construction of a modern industrial society. Erhard also became known as the father of the *social market economy* (*Sozialmarktwirtschaft*), a system of free enterprise guided and supported by the strong hand of government and undergirded by a comprehensive scheme of social welfare (see Feature 4.1). In this way, Germany managed to avoid the extremes of a pure *laissez-faire* economy and centralized state control.

The social market economy was established at the insistence of the Christian Democrats who, along with their sister party in Bavaria, the Christian Social Union, would head every Bonn government (though some-

times in coalition with the Free Democrats) from 1949 through 1969. Konrad Adenauer, Germany's strongest and most popular chancellor since Bismarck, chose Erhard to head the economic and finance ministries. From these positions of power and influence, backed by a coordinated economic strategy supported by labor and industry, they planted the seed of the social market economy, and it took firm root in German soil. The Christian Democratic monopoly in the early years was made possible in part by the adherence of the opposition Social Democrats to the classic Marxist socioeconomic doctrine until 1959. The electorate consistently rejected Social Democratic appeals to "class warfare" in favor of the Erhard-Adenauer call to construct a social market economy.

German federalism made its own distinctive contribution to the growth of the social market economy. As Christopher Allen notes, *Land* governments encouraged banks to adjust "their investment and loan policies to improve the competitive position of key industries in various regions" and to "invest heavily in vocational education to provide the skills so necessary for high quality manufacturing goods" capable of competing in world markets.[8] *Land* (i.e., state) governments also worked closely with business and organized labor, not only to encourage the development of a modern, competitive economy, but also to shape the framework of cooperation between trade unions, corporations, banks, and educational institutions, a process of coordination matched at the national level by such initiatives as the Economic Stability Act of 1967 and the Codetermination Act of 1975.

By 1965, the success of the original Erhard-Adenauer prescription was apparent. The FRG had become a *Wirtschaftswunder*, or *economic miracle*. The combination of a solid currency, a market economy, and a democratic and social federal state had not only fostered the reconstruction of western Germany but also the creation and distribution of wealth on an unprecedented scale. The FRG had become at once the wealthiest and stablest econ-

---

Feature 4.1 **Social Market Economy**

An outgrowth of German neoliberal and Catholic social thought, the social market economy is predicated on the belief that a free market is compatible with a socially conscious state. It seeks to combine the principles of personal freedom and social responsibility in a unified political economy. The production of goods and services, according to the theory, is to be left to free choice in an open market, but the marketplace is to function within a social framework created by law. This framework includes general public policies designed to enhance competition, ensure honest trade practices, and protect consumers. It is also government's duty in neoliberal economic theory to stabilize the economy as a whole and to care for the needs of persons not served by the market.

---

omy in the European Community. Within two more decades, this *Wirtschaftswunder* would carry West Germany to fourth place among all the nations of the world in terms of its gross national product (GNP) (see Table 4.2), as well as fourth among the Group of Seven (G-7) western industrial democracies (behind the United States, Canada, and Japan). This accomplishment is all the more interesting given the ranking of the FRG in territory and population seen in Table 4.1 and the *zero base*—the total destruction of World War II—from which it emerged.

The GDR Economy

At about the same time as the FRG's *Wirtschaftswunder*, the limits of progress in the GDR were becoming apparent. The future was written in the past. Between 1945 and 1949 the Soviet occupiers closed all private banks; ordered the surrender of all currency, bullion, and deeds; confiscated all estates of more than 250 acres; and began a process of systematized looting by shipping transferable property—from machinery to trains and the very tracks they ran on—to the Soviet Union in the form of "reparations." The brutal implementation of Stalinist economics in the GDR did finally yield impressive results in areas such as heavy industry and chemical engineering yet availed little in other areas, such as technological innovation and worker productivity. For one thing, these areas were not as susceptible to Stalinist methods of "persuasion"; for another, these methods themselves were now increasingly abandoned. Yet nothing could be found to replace them in the

Table 4.2   GROSS NATIONAL PRODUCT: GERMANY'S RANKING AMONG SELECTED NATIONS, 1986

Nation	GNP[a]	Nation	GNP per capita[b]
USA	$4,235,000	USA	$17,600
USSR	2,356,700	Japan	12,850
Japan	1,559,720	FRG	12,080
FRG	735,940	GDR	11,180
France	595,180	France	10,740
UK	504,850	UK	8,920
China	314,800	USSR	8,410
India	213,440	Spain	4,840
Spain	188,030	Mexico	1,850
GDR	185,751	Nigeria	640
Mexico	149,110	China	300
Nigeria	66,210	India	270

[a] In billions of U.S. dollars (thus, the GNP of the USA reads four trillion, two hundred thirty-five billion).

[b] In hundreds of U.S. dollars (thus, the GNP per capita of the USA reads seventeen thousand, six hundred).

Source: D. Daume (ed.), *1989 Britannica Book of the Year* (Chicago: Encyclopaedia Britannica, Inc., 1989), *in passim.*

command economy. The GDR seemed to have reached an impassible plateau.

The construction of the Berlin Wall in 1961 was a confession of economic—and political—failure. By 1961, some 3 million people, including many of East Germany's best technicians, had fled to West Germany in search of a better life and more challenging opportunities. The erection of the Wall stopped the hemorrhage, but at the cost of advertising to all the world the fundamental illegitimacy of the East German regime and economy in the eyes of its own "citizens."

No longer able to flee, the remaining workers soon made the GDR into the most economically advanced and prosperous state in the Soviet bloc. According to its own figures, the GDR came to rank eleventh among the world's industrial economies—and there it came to rest. Neither its ranking nor its productivity would advance further. Claims about overtaking the FRG were dropped by the GDR government. National pride was to be rechanneled into a new field: international sports competition. Industrial and technological comparisons, however, to say nothing of comparing standards of living, were henceforth *verboten*.

Unfortunately for the GDR, most East Germans could receive West German television broadcasts (as well as an annual visit from western cousins) and therefore draw their own conclusions. If the East Germans could be proud of their accomplishments vis-à-vis the East, they could only be mortified by what they were missing in the West. One measure of the distance between the GDR and the FRG was the rate of automobile and telephone ownership. By 1988, 97 percent of all FRG families owned an automobile; 98 percent had a telephone. The corresponding GDR figures were 52 percent and 7 percent. East Germans were also disillusioned by the quality of their consumer goods. The qualitative distance between the Trabant and the Volkswagen, not to mention the Mercedes, was one measure of how far the GDR had yet to go to close the gap between itself and the FRG. To its own political illegitimacy, the GDR now added economic resentment.

By the late 1980s, as West Germany pushed toward the creation of the world's largest and wealthiest free-trade zone, East Germany found that even its economic bedrock, its major heavy industries, were becoming increasingly outmoded and noncompetitive in the new, "postindustrial" global market. Worse, rumors were rife that the state itself was on the verge of bankruptcy—rumors fed by the patent "massaging" of the official economic and financial figures. The reconstruction of the city center of East Berlin as the showcase of State Socialist success—which had become a virtual obsession with Erich Honecker, the Kremlin's chosen successor to Walter Ulbricht—was particularly resented by workers outside the capital, with their deplorable housing and even more deplorable automobiles.

Yet it was not until the annus mirabilis, the year of wonders, between the collapse of Honecker's dictatorship in October 1989 and the democratic accession of the (subsequently reconstituted) East German *Länder* into the FRG in October 1990, that it began to dawn on the East Germans (and on western economists) just how far their economic, industrial, and environmental situation had deteriorated. Indeed, by the time of reunification it was obvious that the East was destitute: Not only could it bring very little to the merger, but it could not survive without a tremendous transfer of resources and expertise from the West. A new *Wirtschaftswunder* was the order of the day.

The Cost of Unity

Before the two Germanys united, it was generally agreed by eastern and western economists that it would take years for the new eastern *Länder* to catch up to the standards of productivity and living prevalent in the West. The Christian Democratic–Free Democratic coalition campaigned just after reunification (in the first free all-German elections since the Nazi era began) on a platform predicting a low-cost and quick turnaround in the eastern economy (e.g., 1994 was often cited as the year in which East-West parity would begin to emerge). By mid-1991, however, it was apparent that the length of time and the cost of reconstruction in the eastern *Länder* would be much greater than Bonn had anticipated.

The GDR's industrial areas turned out to be one massive rustbelt and among the most polluted areas in Europe. Whole sectors of the economy were collapsing, while the cost entailed in rescuing—to say nothing of rebuilding—them escalated in the west. Factories, roads, railroads, airports, sea and inland ports, canals and waterways as well as schools and public housing were in need of reconstruction, in many instances from the ground up. Add to this the cost of cleaning up the environment, paying the GDR's debts, and overhauling and upgrading the civil service, the universities, the judicial system, the national health system, and the telephone system, and the price of German unity begins to hit home.

Just prior to reunification, the FRG's Federal Bank (the *Bundesbank*) predicted that it would cost up to $126 billion just to remodel eastern German roads and railways. Modernizing the telephone system would cost $34.7 billion, while the cost of social security payments and unemployment benefits in 1990 alone was expected to reach $27.7 billion. The ultimate cost of reunification, some were predicting, would be more than a trillion dollars over the next decade.

It soon began to sink in that if the Bonn government were to absorb these costs to bail out eastern Germany, the standard of living would go down in the West. By 1990, after eight years of conscientious government restraint, the public sector share of the GNP was already reduced to 45 percent. With the first costs of reunification at the end of the year, the public sector share had shot up to around 52 percent while the overall deficit reached DM 1330 billion, up substantially from the postwar record high of DM 300 billion that Helmut

Kohl inherited when he became Chancellor in October 1982. In July 1991, finally, unemployment in the former FRG rose to 5.7 percent and, even more alarming to most Germans, national inflation rose to 4.5 percent.

The Kohl government was thus forced to break its 1990 campaign pledge by raising taxes, notwithstanding an economy clipping along at full capacity (the GNP increased by 4 percent in 1989). These increases in inflation, unemployment, taxes, and deficit spending meant that Bonn would have a proportionately decreasing amount of funds with which to sustain and rebuild the east. At the same time, however, the figures emerging from the new *Länder* were worsening: For instance, unemployment rose from 9.5 percent in June to 12.1 percent in July 1991. In a population totaling less than 17 million, 8.5 million of them workers, one million were out of work, and the flow-through effects of a decrease in consumer spending and in savings were apparent. Equally ominous were the layoffs impending in the major industries of chemicals, textiles, steel, and shipyards.

The *Treuhandanstalt*

Bonn's solution to this problem was the creation of the *Treuhandanstalt* (Trust Fund), a super agency authorized to take over all state-owned enterprises, to modernize them, to restructure their work forces, to convert them into corporations under West German law, and then to sell them to private investors as soon as possible or, if necessary, to shut them down. With its huge staff of financial advisors, tax lawyers, management consultants, land surveyors, engineers, and other specialists—about 3800 employees—*Treuhand* was and is the key instrument for converting the former state-owned economy into a social market economy. Its mandate is not to sell to the highest bidder, but to ensure that investors have the wherewithal and competence to preserve and create jobs and to ensure the future contribution of the enterprise to the area's of industrial prosperity.

As the experience with the ship construction industry shows, Treuhand's decisions often caused human suffering as well as political opposition. Treuhand merged 24 shipbuilding firms in the ex-GDR into one company and brought in a western manager to run it. To build a competive industry he closed 2 shipyards and 9 suppliers, at the cost of 40,000 jobs. Oppostion was fierce; in fact, it created a crossfire. Western German shipbuilders objected to the massive subsidization of a new competitor, and the state parliament of Mecklenburg-West Pomerania objected to the massive reduction of its main industry. Treuhand went through four plans. The state parliament vetoed every shipyard closure it proposed. Union protests became rife in the yards. Worst of all, not a single western firm could be interested in buying the overmanned yards with their outdated equipment.

On the plus side of the equation, *Treuhand* looks to be discharging its mandate despite such formidable obstacles. The succeeding director, Detlev Rohwedder (assassinated by Red Army Faction terrorists in March 1991), had called for it "to privatize fast, to modernize resolutely, and to close down carefully." In less than 21 months, *Treuhand* sold 5500 of the 10,000 companies under its aegis, grossing DM 11.6 billion, getting pledges of investments with an additional DM 90 billion, and securing 1,000,000 jobs. Privatization was proceeding at a pace of 20 firms per day. (Meanwhile, some 600 plants had been forced to close down.) In addition, *Treuhand* had sold over 29,000 small businesses under its control, mainly to eastern Germans. By 1992, with well over 300,000 new business start-ups in the former GDR, notes of optimism were beginning to appear in an otherwise gloomy score.

The Social Welfare (and Planning) State

In 1986 the FRG spent almost 32 percent of its GNP on social services—among the highest in Western Europe. Drawing upon a long tradition of state-supported social insurance, the FRG's system includes generous programs of health and disability insurance, retirement pensions, industrial accident insurance, and unemployment compensation covering almost 95 percent of the population. Old-age pensions, the largest of these programs, are related to earnings and financed by contributions from the insured and their employers. Social security payments, adjusted to inflation and other economic indicators, have increased nearly every year since 1957. (In January 1987 the average monthly pension was $770.) The system of benefits also includes relief payments for the needy, child benefit allowances, rent subsidies for old- age pensioners and retired civil servants, vocational rehabilitation services, and special reparations for former prisoners of war, refugees from East Germany, and persons who suffered losses under Nazism because of their race, religion, or political beliefs. (On GDR social policy see "Security and Equality.")

Taken as a whole, the FRG's social economy is notably less centralized than that of the French or the British and notably more sensitive socially than the American. Government ownership of industry and intervention in the market determination of goods and services are still other features of the social market economy. State ownership and control have been retained in areas such as transportation and postal facilities, where the market is unable to produce efficient service at prices the public can afford. In addition, the government controls more than 25 percent of the stock in nearly 500 companies, although in recent years some of these firms have been denationalized. On the other hand, several state governments have subsidized certain industries either for the purpose of reviving them or to keep them from moving their plants to other states or countries.

German economic policy until the mid-1960s contained a strong antiplanning bias. With the adoption of the Economic Stabilization Act of 1967, however, long-term fiscal planning became a vital element of the FRG's economy. Influenced in part by Keynesian economic theory, the act authorized the federal government (1) to coordinate the budgetary policies of state and national governments, (2) to change temporarily rates of taxation on personal and corporate incomes without prior parliamentary approval, (3) to stimulate the economy during periods of recession by public expenditures up to specified amounts, and (4) to harmonize general fiscal policy with monetary policy.

Economic and Social Stratification

Germany's occupational structure shows a nation gradually transforming itself from an industrial into a post industrial society. As Table 4.3 indicates, the services and trades sector of the economy in the old FRG has grown the fastest, overtaking industry by far. Most jobs created in the 1980s were connected with banking, insurance, education, the health professions, and the civil service. The social transformation suggested by the tabular data has given way to a rising middle class composed of salaried employees associated with the worlds of finance, commerce, and innumerable trades. No longer is the holding of property the decisive factor in class distinc-

tion, but rather the nature of a person's job and the prestige and income that go with it. The traditional crafts are another declining sector of an increasingly technological society. Tailors, shoemakers, painters, typesetters, and carpenters have seen their numbers dwindle in the face of a far greater demand for the services of building cleaners, automobile mechanics, TV technicians, electricians, and hairdressers—underscoring the widespread availability of discretionary income among most occupational groups, including common laborers. Still, the craft trades employ 15 percent of the work force, train 37 percent of apprentices, and account for 9 percent of the FRG's economic output.

Table 4.3 also underscores the sharp differences between the economies of the old FRG and the ex-GDR. The dominance of manufacturing industries in the eastern *Länder,* combined with central planning and the lack of competition, inhibited the emergence of a modern diversified economy as well as the development of new technologies. In addition, 94.7 percent of all persons employed in the GDR in 1988 worked for state-owned enterprises. In industry, the figure was 99.9 percent; in construction 92.3 percent; and in agriculture and forestry 98.5 percent. Only the traditional crafts (excluding construction) re-

Table 4.3 WORKING POPULATION BY ENTERPRISE

Enterprise	Former FRG				ex-GDR
	1960	1970	1980	1989	1990
Agriculture	13.7%	8.5%	5.2%	3.7%	11.0%
Industry	40.0	40.2	36.0	33.2	41.0
Construction	8.2	8.7	7.9	6.6	7.0
Transportation & Communication	5.6	5.3	5.6	5.6	7.0
Services & Trades	32.8	37.6	45.7	51.1	10.0
Other	3.0	2.4	3.4	4.4	24.0

Sources: Statistisches Jahrbuch für das vereinte Deutschland, 1991 and *German Unification: Economic Issues* (Washington, D.C.: International Monetary Fund, December 1990).

mained largely privatized. Since reunification, however, all crafts, trades, and professions have been privatized. More importantly, they have seen their numbers increase dramatically. In the professions, for example, there were four times as many doctors and dentists by 1992 than before unity. The number of private lawyers has doubled and tax advisors have shot up from 350 to 2800, whereas veterinarians and engineers in private practice have gone from zero to 1520 and 3000 respectively. These numbers, together with the proliferation of the service trades, may help to lift the eastern *Länder* into the postindustrial age within two decades or so.

The major sign of postindustrialism in the old FRG is the emergence of a large technocratic and managerial elite. Jobs in highly skilled professional and technical areas are increasing at a much faster rate than unskilled or semiskilled jobs. In the 1970s the number of engineers, computer technicians, economists, teachers, accountants, lawyers, and social workers in the FRG almost doubled, while university admissions in the natural and social sciences nearly tripled. By 1985 the professional-technical-managerial class contained 6.2 million persons, representing 23.4 percent of the total work force.

The socioeconomic changes described here have affected the nature of political cleavage in the FRG. While the society may reveal residues of a traditional class structure, FRG politics in recent decades have not been determined by old class divisions. The ascendancy of a new professional-technical-managerial class, supported by a vast army of white-collar employees performing highly specified roles in the social economy, has blunted the class feeling of earlier generations. The old class structure has entirely disappeared in the eastern *Länder*, and the political pressure from this part of Germany is likely to be in the direction of greater egalitarianism.

Issues based on old economic divisions, while still important, are often lower on the political agenda than *quality-of-life* issues such as energy conservation, environmental protection, educational opportunity, life-style freedom, social equality, and women's rights. Here we find a large measure of convergence between the eastern and western *Länder*, for these quality-of-life issues are also high on the agenda of the eastern states.

Security and Equality

The portrait of German society sketched up to now is one of general affluence and economic opportunity. If industrial wages, home ownership, and possession of consumer goods are considered, then income and property are certainly widely distributed in the western *Länder*. Yet, as is true of any system based on private enterprise, the social *market* economy tolerates large disparities in income and economic power among certain classes of persons. As Table 4.4 indicates, a large gap separated the lowest and highest-paid persons in 1985. Yet the *social* market economy has resulted in a remarkable leveling of society. Sociologists no longer depict the social structure as a pyramid, with the elite at the top, broadening into the masses at the bottom. Instead, they invoke the image of an onion to describe the social strata, with the broad middle classes dominating the center, narrowing at the ends to the extremes of rich and poor.

High unemployment rates in the 1980s, however—reaching a postwar high of 10.2 percent (2,487,100) of the work force in 1983—tarnished this image of a well-run social market economy. Even in 1990, with the economy running at full capacity, unemployment persisted at around 6 percent of the work force. The hardcore of the unemployed among persons living in the old FRG includes: (1) persons without any vocational or technical training, (2) workers 55 years of age and older, (3) those limited in their capacities by bad health, and (4) those employed on a part-time basis. (In Germany, unlike the United States, part-time employees are counted among the unemployed.) Collectively, these groups

Table 4.4 ANNUAL INCOME DISTRIBUTION BY HOUSEHOLD, 1985

Income Class	Self-Employed (1.9 million)	Employees (13.2 million)	Pensioners (10.2 million)
Over $48,780	36.9	0.6	—
29,268–48,780	35.2	9.2	4.5
19,512–29,268	13.5	23.9	11.2
14,634–19,512	6.9	26.8	17.5
9756–14,634	6.3	29.0	24.9
4878–9756	1.1	9.6	38.0
Under 4878	0.1	0.9	3.9

Source: Facts About Germany (Gütersloh: Lexikon-Institut Bertelsmann, 1987), p. 247.
The original data are in DM, which have been converted into dollars at the 1985 average
exchange rate of 2.4613 per dollar. *International Financial Statistics* (March, 1991), p. 242.

account for approximately 2.5 percent of the working population.

The ex-GDR, on the other hand, emphasizing equality over liberty, had constructed a socialist state in which the right to work was guaranteed and welfare and care were assured in the event of an illness or emergency. In addition, there was little disparity in income among persons employed in various sectors of the economy, although the salaries earned bought less than 50 percent of an equivalent salary in the western *Länder.* The average monthly wage in the GDR in 1988 amounted to only a third of the average FRG wage when controlled at parity."[9]

Social welfare was universal in the GDR, but the system lacked the efficiency and quality, especially in the area of medical care, of social welfare planning in the FRG. Social insurance in the GDR was organized on a monolithic basis: One institution administered the pension scheme, health care, family-related benefits, and poverty assistance. (In the FRG, these programs are carried out by different institutions and largely on the basis of employee-employer contributions keyed to the cost of living.) In 1988, pensions and medical care accounted, respectively, for 47.4 and 43.6 percent of the system's social expenditures. The average old age pension in the GDR

covered about 45 percent of net wages as opposed to about 50 percent in the FRG,[10] but again the latter was of far greater value. The child care system and leave policy for childbearing women, however, were more generous in the GDR.

This picture changed drastically when the two Germany's united under the social and economic system of the western *Länder.* For the first time in many memories, thousands of eastern German workers found themselves without jobs and subject to the welfare policies of the FRG. The GDR's lack of competition, free enterprise, and (for many) occupational choice, had taken its toll. The productivity of labor in the east was about 30 percent of the level in western Germany.[11] It would take years before wages in eastern Germany's structurally weak economy would even begin to approach western German levels, and this meant substantial unemployment, certainly over the short term. In the meantime, the FRG's social welfare system would be burdened with relieving the agony of those eastern German workers out of work—a full quarter of the labor force in 1991.

The FRG's social security system remains one of the most generous in the world. (In 1987 approximately 14 million persons were drawing benefits from it.) Yet, based as it is on an income strategy tied to lifetime earnings, its redistributive effect is limited. Elderly persons, especially widows on pensions, are the hardest hit, in part because of a discriminatory policy that allows such persons only 60 percent of the pension to which a living husband would have been entitled. Table 4.4 shows that in terms of income pensioners are the least well off. In the mid-1970s approximately 35 percent of pensioners over 65 lived on or below the poverty line and in grossly inadequate housing.[12] Although Germany may not have as large an underclass of destitute persons as some other western nations, the pockets of poverty that do exist are a continuing challenge to the nation's social conscience.

Women and Minorities

The West German constitution guarantees equal rights to men and women. In reality, women have not shared equally in the opportunities offered by the social economy. Germany's legacy of male supremacy has been extremely difficult to overcome (even in the reputedly more egalitarian eastern *Länder*), especially in the domain of family affairs, where tradition and law have for generations confined women to hearth, children, and the guardianship of their husbands. Although the tradition persists, the legal structure of gender discrimination has been gradually torn down by numerous decisions of the Federal Constitutional Court, by the 1958 Law on the Equality of Men and Women (*Gleichberechtigungsgesetz*), and by a new family code enacted in 1977. The latter provides for no-fault divorce, spousal support arrangements keyed to economic status rather than gender, and an equal division of property.

Opportunities for women outside the home can be measured by comparing their participation rates in the work force, their earnings, and the kinds of jobs they perform to those of men. In 1989 women in the FRG constituted 38.9 percent of the work force, whereas in the GDR it was about 50 percent.

(Ninety percent of east German adult women were employed in 1989.) In the GDR system of state-mandated liberation, however, women were expected to lead a dual life of homemaker and working person; as in the west, they still did most of the household work. As some of the figures in Table 4.5 might suggest, social policy in the GDR was designed to make a dual career possible. Child care facilities, for example, were everywhere and free of charge, just as maternity leave with pay (up to 50 to 90 percent of wages) was available for up to 26 weeks.[13] These generous benefits are not available in the FRG and, as a result, many eastern German women accustomed to working may now be forced to withdraw from the labor market. The impact on single mothers is likely to be particularly devastating. On the other hand, precisely because the right and duty to work was state-decreed, "many [east German women] appear to link self-realization to a life in which homemaking is a preferred

TABLE 4.5   FEMALE OCCUPATIONAL REPRESENTATION

Selected Occupations	FRG		GDR
	1981	1989	1989
Engineers	2.3	4.7	—
Architects	3.4	8.5	—
Scientists	5.7	12.7	—
Lawyers	8.2	—	39.7
Judges	13.6	17.6	50.0
Public prosecutors	11.8	17.6	28.3
University professors	—	5.2	—
Public school teachers	48.8	48.3	78.7
Civil servants	17.6	21.1	—
Physicians	30.8	27.8	53.4
Social welfare workers	79.1	80.0	91.6
Health care workers	86.3	85.4	83.0
Top managers	17.0	16.7	—
Office workers	70.8	68.0	—
Sales clerks	61.4	62.0	—

Source: Statistisches Jahrbuch für die BRD 1981; Statistisches Jahrbuch für das Vereinte Deutschland; and Statistischen Jahrbuch der deutschen Demokratischen Republik 1990 (Berlin: Rudolf Haufe Verlag, 1990).

option, and employment limited or not necessary at all."[14]

Average female earnings in the FRG in the mid-1980s were about 75 percent of average male earnings, owing both to wage-rate discrimination and to the lack of promotional opportunities associated with less stable and less skilled jobs.[15] And, as Table 4.5 makes clear, men and women tend to have different occupations. Women are concentrated in clerical and service jobs, although highly skilled jobs in the service area were dominated by men. Even in the GDR women were heavily concentrated in occupations related to social work, health services, and child care. Segregation in the FRG job market is in large part attributable to employee recruitment mechanisms that, although not always overtly discriminatory, tend to channel women into traditional female roles.

In 1980 the West German Parliament sought to remedy these inequalities by imposing affirmative-action duties upon employers. The Equal Rights Act, passed by an overwhelming legislative majority, requires equal pay for equal work; bars gender discrimination in hiring, promotion, and dismissal; eliminates job descriptions based on sex; shifts the burden of proving nondiscrimination to the employer; and requires the latter to display prominently copies of equal rights legislation in the workplace. Additionally, there have been recent commitments in the FRG to greater and wider vocational training for women.

While grievances based on sex have been the object of the law's special solicitude, those based on ethnicity have been allowed to fester. Large-scale immigration in the postwar era has transformed the FRG's racially homogeneous society into a nation of ethnic minorities. Most of the older immigrants— that is, the postwar expellees (mainly ethnic Germans)—have been almost wholly integrated into the dominant culture. The newer immigrants consist mainly of foreign workers recruited by industry on a massive scale during the 1960s. These workers and their families—mainly Turks, Yugoslavs, Greeks, and Italians—number 5,037,072 or 6.4 percent of reunited Germany's total population. (They make up 7.7 percent of the population in the western *Länder.*) Despite governmental incentives that encouraged nearly a million of these *guestworkers* (*Gastarbeiter*), as they are called, to return to their homelands during the mid-1970s recession, higher wages and the promise of a better life prompted most of them to remain in the FRG.

For these guestworkers and their families, the FRG has been anything but a "melting pot." Their experience is not unlike that of black or Hispanic Americans in the United States. Occupying low-status jobs that Germans do not want, they live in culturally isolated urban ghettos marked by substandard housing.[16] In recent years, hundreds of thousands of persons seeking asylum in the FRG have been added to this mix, triggering not only acts of violence and terrorism against these "foreign elements" but also an explosive national debate over what to do about the increasing numbers of persons seeking freedom and opportunity in Germany. By 1992, after extreme right-wing parties entered two state parliaments on their anti-foreigner platforms, pressure was building to limit the right of asylum and to adopt a U.S.-style system of quotas on immigration to Germany.

CULTURE: SOCIAL AND CIVIC

Education and Media

Reunited Germany boasts high levels of literacy, cultural and educational diversity, and opportunities for personal development and leisure. As in Berlin, parks, sport clubs, museums, public libraries, theaters, choral societies, opera houses, and multimillion member bookclubs abound in the country at large. There is a high consumption rate of media output; book and magazine readership is one of the highest worldwide.

The wealth of cultural opportunities in the western *Länder* builds on their efficient and diverse educational system. A common four-year primary system splits at the secondary level into three tracks: the five-year continuation of primary school (*Hauptschule*), the six-year intermediate school (*Realschule*), and the nine-year senior grammar school (*Gymnasium*); the former two emphasize preparation for later vocational and technical skills respectively; the latter, university preparation. Originally based in the classics, the *Gymnasium* offers a tough modern curriculum of arts, languages, mathematics, and science, leading to the famous school-leaving certificate, the *Abitur.* This tripartite system of secondary education has been sharply criticized in recent years as tending to reinforce social inequalities in the pupils' class and social backgrounds (see Section C).

The GDR had long dispensed with the tripartite system, replacing it with a unitary system of ten-year polytechnical schools. These were highly centralized and heavily oriented toward Marxist-Leninist indoctrination and preparation for work in a state socialist economy. In 1988, their nearly 800,000 pupils participated in work-experience schemes in over 5000 industrial, construction, and agricultural firms. Leisure time was similarly regimented. From 1955 on, a youth confirmation ceremony (*Jugendweihe*) was mandated for the eighth grade: a "political-ideological formation" in pseudo-religious form, with the emphasis placed on allegiance to the GDR, friendship with the Soviet Union, and diligence in socialism and scholarship. Failure to acquiesce in this or to join the socialist youth movement (Free German Youth) meant encountering severe discrimination, often including denial of university admission.

With the accession of the eastern *Länder* into the FRG, communist ideological control has ended in the schools and universities (as have the jobs of the ideologues in law, the humanities, and social sciences) and the *Länder* themselves, as in the west, have taken charge.

Religious instructed is being reintroduced, western language education expanded, and the humanities and social sciences reconstituted on their own basis. Independent schools are reopening and the *Abitur* restored to its pride of place. Yet the eastern *Länder* wish to retain a more egalitarian organization and orientation than that of the western *Länder;* they are looking toward more social-democratic models.

Overall, in the academic year 1990-91 reunified Germany counted 97 universities, 7 general academies, 17 teachers colleges, 16 theological schools, 43 academies of art, 98 technical colleges, and 24 other professional schools. The western university system alone had seen a fourfold increase in students between 1960 and 1980 and, prompted by student protests at overcrowding, had embarked upon a large building program. Between 1950 and 1980, the percentage of western university students from blue-collar homes grew from 4 to 25 percent. By 1990–91, eastern Germans represented 116,297 of the 1.1 million university students nationwide, easily the largest and most diversified group in the postwar period. These were impressive gains; yet Germany still has one of the lower rates of youth matriculating into the university.

Religion and the Churches

The relatively equal numbers of Catholics and Protestants in the old FRG has been tilted in favor of the Evangelical Lutheran Church with the accession of the five new *Länder.* Thus, on the eve of reunification, the old FRG counted official religious affiliation among its permanent residents (German and foreign) as roughly 26 million Roman Catholics, 25.75 million Protestants (both Evangelical Lutheran and "Free Church"), 32,000 Jews, 1.5 million Muslims, 1 million members of other religions, and 4 million with no religious affiliation. Figures from the ex-GDR are more difficult to present, both because of the reluctance of the communist regime to admit any significant religious aspiration in a would-be atheist state and the concomitant reluctance of its citizens to make a declaration of official affiliation that would automatically reduce them to second-class status at work and in school and bar them from the upper reaches of all professions. Nonetheless, it is clear that what religious activity there was between 1945 and 1989 remained overwhelmingly Protestant. Catholic figures, which remained free of direct government intervention, showed the six bishoprics within the five eastern *Länder* as ministering to only 5 percent of the local population, approximately 800,000 out of 16,000,000 people.

The denominational strife that once buffeted Germany has virtually disappeared as new forms of political and social cooperation evolved out of the common struggle of the major churches against the Nazi regime. Even in the purely religious sphere the major denominations have been trying to reconcile their differences. An ecumenical high point was the November 1980 meeting of Pope John Paul II with German Protestant leaders in Osnabrück, the site of the signing of the Peace of Westphalia in 1648, which confirmed the sectarian division of the Germans lands.

It is difficult to assess the role of religion in contemporary Germany. Figures in the old FRG showed a long-term decline in official affiliation. Thus, between 1950 and 1989, the proportion of Catholics decreased slightly from 44.3 to 42.9 percent, while that of Protestants dropped from 51.5 to 42.2 percent. An Allensbach Opinion Research Institute poll conducted in the west on the eve of reunification suggested that this secularization affected not only practice but basic belief.

However, the rates of basic religious identification do remain high, both in paying the church tax and in choosing a marital partner from one's own confession. The 1989 figures for marrying within one's faith in the old FRG showed 68.7 percent for Catholics, 63 percent for Protestants, and 32.5 percent for Jews. The social impact of the churches likewise remains high. They operate and maintain hos-

pitals, facilities for the handicapped, nursing homes, schools, and large charitable organizations such as the Protestant Diaconal Works and the Catholic Caritas Association, as well as immense overseas programs—all made possible by the church tax.

Organized as corporate bodies under public law—a constitutional status carried over from the Weimar period—the organized churches are entitled to state financial support. All wage earners are subject to a church tax equal to about 10 percent of their net tax. An employee must formally resign from church membership—236,763 (147,753 Protestants and 93,010 Catholics) did so in 1985—or be subject to the tax. Collected by state revenue officers, these taxes amount to several billion dollars a year and are distributed to the major denominations in amounts proportionate to their total membership, to be divided between ecclesiastical salaries, construction and maintenance costs, and social functions on the one hand and social work at home and abroad on the other.

This modus vivendi between church and state is not without its critics, both secular and religious, each side feeling that the influence of the other (whether the State on the Church or religion on the public life of the nation) is excessive. Nonetheless, the biennial Catholic and Protestant national "Church Day" conferences remain well attended and the influence of each denomination within its own worldwide communion remains strong.

At the end of the Weimar Republic, there were an estimated 590,000 Jews in Germany, of which 160,000 lived in Berlin. This latter community had grown from less than 1000 in 1700 and could boast some of the showpieces of the capital's architecture (e.g., the New Synagogue on Oranienburger Strasse). By 1945, no more than 40,000 had survived the Nazi exterminations, with perhaps 6000 of these hidden in Berlin. This remnant was then subjected to the same divisions of the capital and country as other Germans, plus a special persecution in the east of all things the communist government deemed "Zionist." Only in 1988 did Honecker, in an attempt to curry favor with Washington, begin to relent. Israeli policy was no longer equated with Nazi policy and east Berlin was permitted its first rabbi in over two decades. Today, personal indemnification and property restoration proceed apace in the ex-GDR; the Jewish community in the east is reunited with the one in the west, and the two great synagogues are completing renovations.[17]

Political Attitudes and Participation

West Germans were characterized in the first 20 years of the FRG as voting in high numbers but with little feeling. Opinion polls showed that the older age groups retained some sympathy for monarchy or dictatorship and that most voters were prouder of their economic system than of its political corollary. By the 1980s, this had changed. The FRG was a proven success and an increasing percentage of the electorate had grown up in it and come to identify with its procedures and institutions. On the other hand, national pride remained well below the average for European Community member states. Reunification in 1990 thus posed two issues: Would the East Germans follow the pattern of quick adaption to democratic practices and slow internalization of democratic feelings? In the meantime, if unforeseen economic difficulties arose, would West German civic culture now prove to be well enough rooted to weather the storm?

One measure of political democracy is the level of participation in elections. The turn-out rate for federal elections in the FRG began at 78.5 percent in 1949, exceeded 90 percent by the 1970s, and fell to a record low of 77.8 percent in the first all-German election of 2 December 1990. This is a respectable rate for an industrial democracy—and consistently higher than for U.S. presidential elections. As Section B shows, the results of these elections have given the FRG a highly competitive and relatively stable multi-party system, another sign of political maturity.

The measure of the health of a civic culture, however, extends beyond formal electoral and institutional arrangements. Since the late 1960s, the FRG has witnessed massive demonstrations against the war in Vietnam, degradation of the environment, low figures for university entrance and accommodation, stationing of missiles on German soil, and so forth. These *Bürgerinitiativen* (*citizens' initiatives*) have also championed forms of direct democracy (e.g., referenda). Some commentators have asked whether this species of "politics of protest" bespeaks a widening gap between formal democratic institutions and actual grass-roots democratic sentiments. Some would respond that these protests represent a vital outlet for minority sentiments that is politically acceptable; others, that they represent an internalization and therefore a triumph of democratic values; and still others would note that both the CDU and the SPD have successfully remodeled their local party electoral activities on these same *Bürgerinitiativen*.

The participatory character of the FRG's civic culture seems reasonably related to changes that have taken place in family, school, and society under the impact of advanced industrialization and its accompanying patterns of social stratification. The entrance of housewives into the labor market, the separation of family and workplace, increased social mobility and income, and the enormous expansion of communications have loosened up old authoritarian structures such as the male-dominated family and the traditional school curriculum. As agents of political socialization, family and school appear increasingly to promote values more consistent than in the past with the regime's formal values of human dignity, mutual respect and cooperation, and the pragmatic adjustment of social conflict. Generational change has also been an important source of political socialization. By the 1980 election the postwar generation constituted 48.8 percent of the population and 25.5 percent of adult voters. Levels of political interest and participation have been found to increase significantly with the length of residence and accumulated experience under the democracy of the FRG. Whether reunification will hasten or deepen this process remains to be seen.

Portions of the university population and radical left still reject the "bourgeois state" and all its works; but their election appeal peaked in the mid-1980s and then fell below 5 percent in December 1990. Although a minuscule left-terrorist element still operates occasionally (e.g., assassinating the head of *Treuhandanstalt* in 1991), the more disruptive elements of the public peace and the democratic consensus has shifted to the radical right, especially in its racist attacks on non-Germans. But they are likely to fare no better in garnering general public support than the far left.

Politics and Literature: A Footnote

When unified in 1871, Germany had a humanist tradition characterized by the genius of Goethe and Schiller, renaissance men of letters and civic leadership. Yet the predominant cultural expression of the Wihelmine and Weimar years was one of flight from political affairs into an "inner freedom" or strictly private culture. Figures already in authority were left to conduct public affairs, to define the aims and bounds of state power, and to suggest, albeit broadly, the proper form and content of culture.

The works of Hermann Hesse (1877–1962), such as the novel *Siddhartha* (1922; still a U.S. collegiate favorite), continued the age-old inquiry into the Germanic conflict between Nature and Spirit but did so in the relatively new form of stressing the need for personal, rather than communal or authoritarian, responsibility in selecting values. Thomas Mann (1875–1955) cast this need against the backdrop of the violent currents sweeping Germanic society: the degeneration of the great nineteenth-century mercantile order in *Buddenbrooks* (1901), the quest for regeneration and personal understanding through flight from society and its conventions in *The Magic Mountain* (1924), and the descent of artistic creativity itself into the demonic in *Doctor Faustus* (1947). More than anyone else, Mann gave expression to the struggle between the power and the subtle pessimism of *Germanism*.

During the life of the FRG, the works of Günter Grass (e.g., *The Tin Drum*) were especially noteworthy for their inquiry into how German culture had fallen into National Socialism and what should be retrieved and replanted from the ashes it left in 1945. Grass opposed German reunification until the very end, claiming that Germany lacked a sense of responsibility before history and could have served as a beacon for spiritual renewal and the deflation of purely national aspirations.[19] Equally popular with Grass is the work of Heinrich Böll (1917–85), such as, *The Clown* (1963), with its sense of the intrinsic worth and redemptive possibilities in life.

Thus, where humanism temporarily failed, history may have retrieved the situation. In the wake of two world wars, Germans have abandoned the turn to "inner freedom" and its concomitant neglect of public cultural and civic responsibilities. They have taken Hesse's point that responsibility is personal and that it becomes communal in its effect. The Germans continue to question their values and to extend the breadth and depth of their pluralist democracy.

CONCLUSION

This chapter section has traced Germany's development from a feudal society into a modernized postindustrial state and the merger by accession of the eastern sector into the western FRG. The FRG's economy, even before the merger, was among the richest in the world, and its social system, notwithstanding pockets of poverty, measurable and increasing discrimination against ethnic minorities and, most daunting of all, the massive reconstruction and clean up of the east, is marked by extremely high levels of economic security and welfare benefits. The political system created under the 1949 Basic Law, together with its liberal values, is of course a congenial framework for the development of a social market economy; both its endurance in the west and its acceptance in the east augur well for the future.

Religious divisions are no longer readily apparent in either sector of the reunited country; traditional class and economic divisions also have given way to the rise in the west of an overwhelmingly predominant new middle class of white-collar employees and professionals generated by ever-expanding service industries and technological enterprises; western business managers, industrial trainers, and university professors hope to replicate their success in the east. Although youth and intellectuals reproach the society for sinking into materialism, there is no evidence to suggest that western Germans are willing to forego what the economy has wrought; on the contrary, their challenge will be to redistribute their wealth so as to rescue and then revive the east. Germany has put its political and religious divisions behind it; now it resolves to do the same socially and economically.

Key Terms

Abitur
Basic Law
Bürgerinitiativen
Church tax
Deutsche Mark
Guestworkers
Länder
North German Confederation
Parliamentary Council
Social market economy
Treaty of Versailles
Weimar Republic
Treuhandanstalt

Suggestions for Further Reading

Ardagh, John. *Germany and the Germans* (London: Penguin Books, 1991).

Barraclough, Geoffrey. *The Origins of Modern Germany* (New York: Capricorn Books, 1963).

Bork, Dennis L., and David R. Gress. *A History of West Germany*, Vols. 1 and 2 (Oxford: Basil Blackwell, Inc., 1989).

Bracher, Karl Dietrich. *The German Dictatorship* (New York: Praeger, 1970).

Craig, Gordon. *The Germans* (New York: Putnam, 1982).

Hertzl, Frederick. *The German Public Mind in the Nineteenth Century* (London: George Allen and Unwin Ltd., 1975).

Katzenstein, Peter. *Policy and Politics in West Germany* (Philadelphia: Temple University Press, 1988).

Koch, H.W. *A Constitutional History of Germany in the Nineteenth and Twentieth Centuries* (London and New York: Longman, 1984).

Kolinsky, Eva. *Women in West Germany* (Oxford: Berg Publishers, Inc., 1989).

Lipschitz, Leslie and Donogh McDonald, eds. *German Unification: Economic Issues* (Washington, D.C.: International Monetary Fund, 1990).

Markovits, Andre. *The Politics of the West German Trade Unions* (Cambridge: Cambridge University Press, 1986).

Pachter, Henry M. *Modern Germany: A Social, Cultural, and Political History* (Boulder, Colorado: Westview Press, 1978).

Pinson, Koppel S. *Modern Germany*, 2nd ed. (New York: Macmillan, 1966).

Rist, Ray C. *Guestworkers in Germany: The Prospects for Pluralism* (New York and London: Praeger, 1978).

Roskamp, Karl W. *Capital Formation in West Germany* (Detroit: Wayne State University Press, 1965).

Spotts, Frederic. *The Churches and Politics in Germany* (Middletown, Conn.: Wesleyan University Press, 1973).

B. Political Processes and Institutions

POLITICAL PARTIES

The FRG is often described as having a two and one-half party system. Social and political circumstances have combined to produce a competitive party system in the FRG that is marked by persisting political loyalties. In the first national election, held in 1949, the three most popular parties—the Christian Democratic Union (CDU) and its Bavarian affiliate, the Christian Social Union (CSU); the Social Democratic party (SPD); and the Free Democratic party (FDP)—captured 72.1 percent of the total votes. By the 1970s these same parties commanded the support of virtually the entire West German electorate. But this result was not wholly fortuitous. To avoid fragmentation of the electorate, the dominant party elites early on enacted a law denying parliamentary representation to parties failing to win 5 percent of the votes cast in a national election or at least three seats in single-member constituencies. In addition, the Basic Law provides for the banning of certain "undemocratic" parties. This handiwork seemed to show that given the right set of circumstances constitutional structure could effectively channel political activity in predetermined directions.

Christian Democrats

History The CDU (*Christlich Democratische Union*) was founded in 1945 by Catholics who had been members of the Center Party in the Weimar period, together with liberal and conservative Protestants who had been members of other pre-1933 political parties. Apart from a general commitment to reconstruct the political order on Christian social principles, the new party seemed more concerned with presenting a united front against the left than with advancing a coherent political program—a formula hardly calculated to maintain unity over the long haul. At length, however, and to the surprise of many, the CDU evolved into a broadly based "catch-all" party (*Volkspartei*) more pragmatic than Christian and commanding the support of nearly half the German electorate. As early as 1953 the party could legitimately claim to represent nearly every major occupational and class grouping in the country, including a substantial sector of the laboring masses. The CDU-CSU domination of West German politics during the FRG's first two decades was so complete that the new nation was coming to be known in some quarters as a CDU state (Table 4.6).

Table 4.6 BUNDESTAG SEATS OCCUPIED BY THE CDU-CSU AND SPD, 1949–1990

Year	CDU	CSU	Combined percent	Combined seats	SPD	Seats	Total seats
1949	25.2%	5.8%	31.0%	139	29.2%	131	402
1953	36.4	8.8	45.2	243	28.8	151	487
1957	39.7	10.5	50.2	270	31.8	169	497
1961	35.8	9.6	45.3	242	36.2	190	499
1965	38.0	9.6	47.6	245	39.8	202	496
1969	36.6	9.5	46.1	242	42.7	224	496
1972	35.2	9.7	44.9	225	45.8	230	496
1976	38.0	10.6	48.6	243	42.6	214	496
1980	34.0	10.3	44.5	226	42.9	218	497
1983	38.2	10.5	48.8	244	38.2	193	498
1987	34.5	9.8	44.3	223	37.0	186	497
1990	36.7	7.1	43.8	313	33.5	239	662

Sources: Peter Schindler, *Datenbuch zur Geschichte der Deutschen Bundestages 1949 bis 1982,* 4th edition (Baden-Baden: Nomos Verlag, 1984), pp. 34–48; *Statistisches Jahrbuch 1991 für das Vereinte Deutschland,* p. 101; Karl Cerny (ed.), *Germany at the Polls* (Durham, N.C.: Duke University Press, 1990), pp. 272–3; and Alf Minzel, *Geschichte der CSU* (Opladen: Westdeutscher Verlag, 1977), p. 349.

Policy CDU policies have ranged from the progressive to the very conservative, reflecting tensions with its partner, the CSU, and the necessity for compromise among its constituent groups. The CDU's early support of codetermination in the iron and steel industries, government-sponsored savings programs, subsidized housing, and public stock sales to workers resulted from Christian social pressures within the party. Its later support of fiscal policies favoring individual entrepreneurship, private property, large profits, and high rates of capital investment reflected the increasing prominence of its business, industrial, and middle-class constituency. The CDU-CSU's continued support of conservative economic policies along with codetermination and moderately redistributive tax policies simply underscores its conscious effort to maintain links with all social classes.

Outside the economic realm, party spokesmen have tended to emphasize traditional moral and social values with a heavy accent on law and order in times of civil stress. The influence of the CSU, which is committed to a strong German federalism, has also prompted many Christian Democrats to defend local cultures and interests against the centralizing influences of the national government. In foreign policy the CDU-CSU has been an ardent supporter of European political and economic integration, the Atlantic Alliance, a militarily strong Germany, and of course German reunification.

Leadership Konrad Adenauer, the pre-1933 mayor of Cologne, was Germany's most wily politician since Bismarck. Projecting the image of another "iron chancellor," he became a powerful, capable, and widely respected leader, as confident in himself as in the future of the FRG. As chancellor from 1949 to 1963, he not only held together a diversified party constituency but led his nation through its formative years, building a new domestic consensus while mapping strategy, in tandem with the United States, for a strong anti-Soviet foreign policy. Adenauer's popularity and performance were not to be matched by any other CDU leader. Ludwig Erhard, the well-known elder statesman and father of the social market economy, succeeded Adenauer in 1963, but domestic problems forced him to give way in 1966 to Kurt-Georg Kiesinger, who was driven by circumstances into leading a tenuous coalition between the two major parties at a time of declining Christian Democratic strength.

Throughout the 1970s the CDU-CSU labored in vain to find a leader with national appeal to win back the chancellorship. Franz Josef Strauss, the popular and dynamic leader of Bavaria's conservative CSU, was too controversial a figure to heal the party's internal wounds or to attract the support of marginal voters. The nomination of the CSU's long-time head was partly an expression of the CDU's lack of confidence in the uninspiring leadership of its national chairman, Helmut Kohl. Yet it was the "uninspiring" Kohl, a gruff and hearty south German from Ludwigshafen, who rallied his party to a stunning victory in the 1983 elections, just five months after the Bundestag named him chancellor when Schmidt was ousted in a no-confidence vote.

Since then, Kohl has grown in the office, surprising Germans and foreigners alike with his self-confidence and leadership ability. As the youngest chancellor in the FRG's history and an unpretentious representative of the new, more progressive generation of CDU party leaders, Kohl surprised everyone again in the January 1987 federal election, a victory that set the stage for his response to the extraordinary events of 1989. Despite misgivings in many quarters, he seized upon a virtual blank check from Washington to negotiate the quick and complete reunification of Germany, setting the stage yet again for his election in 1990 as the first freely chosen chancellor of *all* the German people since 1932.

Greens bloom in 1990 federal election campaign.

Membership Throughout the 1950s and 1960s the CDU enrolled between 200,000 and 300,000 members, significantly below its immediate postwar high of 450,000. During this time the overwhelming majority of CDU members were middle-class Catholic males over 45 years of age. Apart from its occupational structure—75 percent of CDU members are self-employed persons, white-collar employees, and civil servants—this profile changed dramatically after the CDU's membership drive in the 1970s. By 1985, the CDU had 719,000 members, about 40 percent of whom were Protestant. In addition, the party could now boast of measurably higher percentages of women and men under 45 years of age: occupationally, 76.11 percent of the CDU's members were self-employed persons (24.75 percent), white-collar workers (27.96 percent), civil servants (12.43 percent), and housewives (10.97 percent). (The CSU's still overwhelmingly Catholic membership stood at 183,000 in 1985.) The CDU was clearly transforming itself into a mass-membership party analogous to the SPD.

Social Democrats

History The SPD (*Sozialdemokratische Partei Deutschlands*) traces its parentage back to the General Workingmen's Association, founded in 1863 by the brilliant young radical Ferdinand Lassalle. The first party to organize the working masses on a large scale, the SPD of imperial Germany won the votes of the emerging industrial proletariat and moved on from that popular base to share power in 7 of the Weimar Republic's 21 governing coalitions. When the party reorganized after World War II, it failed to expand its influence significantly beyond the industrial working class, having received no more than 35 percent of the popular vote in the first three federal elections. But in 1959, with the passage of its famed *Godesberg platform,* the SPD sought to transform itself from a narrow ideological party into a pragmatic people's party by shedding its Marxist roots, accepting the social market economy, and embracing Adenauer's foreign policy. To attract Catholic workers, the party also cut itself free from its anticlerical past. The strategy worked, for in 1966 Social Democrats gained enough acceptability to become part of a governing coalition for the first time since 1930. The SPD (supported by the Free Democrats) went on to elect the chancellor in four successive national elections, and in 1972 it even surpassed the CDU-CSU in popular votes.

Policy The pre-1959 SPD avowedly embraced socialist economic principles, calling for nationalization of the basic industries and abolition of the privileges of class and property. Attaching greater importance to German reunification than to European union, the party opposed German rearmament, the Iron and Steel Community, and the Western Alliance. The post-1959 SPD, while joining the CDU-CSU in support of Adenauer's foreign policy, also pressed hard, particularly in the late 1960s, for the normalization of relations with East Germany and other Soviet bloc countries. By late 1983, in the midst of the Pershing II missile crisis and a growing neutralist movement inside the party, the SPD lurched abruptly to the left as many of its leaders began openly questioning aspects of western, especially American, defense policy. In 1989–90, the SPD supported German reunification but with far less enthusiasm than the CDU-CSU, in part because of the expected cost of unity. Domestically, the party has been identified with programs calling for full employment, redistributive tax policies, strong antitrust enforcement, expanded welfare services, and the equal participation of capital and labor in the management of industry (codetermination). In the 1970s, when traditional economic issues receded into the background, the SPD was in the forefront of efforts to reform the educational system, to conserve energy, to protect the environment, and to promote women's rights.

Leadership The stages of the SPD's postwar evolution are represented by the characters and personalities of the six persons who occupied the party's major leadership positions between 1945 and 1986: the ascetic and iron-willed Kurt Schumacher; the capable but unimaginative party functionary, Erich Ollenhauer; the daring adventurer and moral leader, Willy Brandt; the versatile technocrat-politician, Helmut Schmidt; the middle-class intellectual, Hans-Jochen Vogel; and the moderate and personable politician from North Rhine-Westphalia, Johannes Rau.

Despite significant platform changes and three switches in candidate for the chancellorship (Hans-Jochen Vogel, Johannes Rau, and Oskar Lafontaine), the SPD failed between 1982 and 1990 to shake its image as a faction-ridden, impractical party unfit for governing in Bonn. Björn Engholm, Premier of Schleswig-Holstein, was elected chairman of the SPD in June 1991, with a 97.5 percent majority at the party conference, on a promise to bring new leadership and a new image to the national party. He delivered swiftly. By September 1991, the party presidium saw 6 of its 13 seats given to the new generation and a new rule: no votes on controversial issues. At the same time, Engholm began to emphasize the problems in the eastern *Länder* and the need for cost-effective solutions thereto. The party also won three consecutive *Land* elections, demonstrating that the CDU no longer could turn the image of being "the party of German unity" to the reality of electoral support.

Membership Served by over 10,000 precinct functionaries, the highly organized SPD is one of the largest mass-membership parties in Europe, enrolling for most of the postwar period between 600,000 and 900,000 persons. By 1977, party membership had climbed to over 1 million before dropping back down to 921,000 in 1989. Like the CDU, the SPD's membership has changed over the years, particularly in its occupational profile. In 1952

nearly 45 percent of all SPD members were blue-collar workers; by 1981 this figure had dropped to 28 percent as the party attracted increasing numbers of civil servants and relatively well-educated, white-collar employees from the "new middle class." The party had also become less overwhelmingly Protestant. By 1981 about 28 percent of party members were Catholic while one out of four was under the age of 35. But as Gerard Braunthal notes, "[e]ven though these shifts took place in the membership, the party still could not expect automatic support from a similar proportion of young or Catholic voters."[18] In any event, these figures clearly qualify the traditional description of the SPD as a workingman's party. In the 1970s the SPD's membership was still more reflective of the social composition of the population at large than that of the CDU or FDP, but clearly the major parties were consciously building more heterogeneous social and occupational membership profiles.[19]

Free Democrats

The FDP (*Freie Demokratische Partei*), founded in 1945 by Theodor Heuss and Reinhold Maier, is the modern counterpart of the older German liberal parties. Standing for free enterprise and individual self-determination in all areas of social life, it is the only minor party to have survived the 5 *percent clause* in all federal elections. By drawing steady support throughout the postwar years from large numbers of business persons, self-employed professionals, civil servants, and the secular middle class, this party of some 70,000 members has been able to capture from 6 percent to 12 percent of the national vote. In the early 1980s, however, particularly at the *Land* level, the FDP's fortunes declined owing to the rising popularity of the *Greens*, a small combination of nontraditional political groups discussed later.

The FDP has determined the governing coalition in 8 out of 12 national elections. Before 1966, when the party leaned rightward, it was a coalition partner of the CDU-CSU. Later, after its leftward lurch under new leadership, it allied itself with the SPD, a coalition that lasted from 1969 to 1982, when the party again joined hands with the CDU-CSU. Most have been uneasy coalitions. Describing the FDP's role as one of combatting the "conservative torpor" of the CDU-CSU and the "socialist utopia" of the SPD, party leaders have fought with the CDU-CSU over foreign policy and with the SPD over spending programs and social reforms. The party has also taken independently strong stands, consistent with its secular liberal orientation, on such issues as educational reform, abortion, pornography, and church taxes.

The FDP's impact on German politics has been more than slight. FDP leaders were the first to press for a new Eastern policy, thus setting the stage for subsequent moves in both major parties toward détente and the normalization of relations with East Germany; they succeeded in forcing Adenauer from office in 1963; they precipitated the Grand Coalition by voting against CDU proposals for higher taxes in 1966; they brought down Schmidt's government in 1982; and they played a major role in the march toward German unity in 1989–90. In addition, they have managed to secure appointment or election to important ministerial posts, to several seats on the Federal Constitutional Court, and on two occasions even to the federal presidency.

Splinter Parties

Splinter parties rise and fall with predictable regularity in the FRG. Each national election witnesses the emergence of a dozen-odd parties organized around regional or single issues. Their public support has declined precipitously over the years, dropping from 27.9 percent of the popular vote in 1949 to 5.7 percent in 1961 to less than 1.5 percent between 1972 and 1987. Each of these parties, falling prey to the 5 percent clause, has failed to secure parliamentary seats. Extreme right and left parties have also fared poorly in the FRG's politico-legal environment. On two occasions such parties have been declared unconstitutional under the terms of Article 21: the neo-Nazi Socialist Reich Party (SRP or *Sozialistiche Reichspartei*) in 1952 and the Communist party (KPD or *Kommunistiche Partei Deutschlands*) in 1956. (See "Impact of Constitutional Court.")

In the 1960s both Communist and nationalist right-wing parties, benefiting from an economic recession and the absence of effective parliamentary opposition during the period of the Grand Coalition, reappeared under new forms. The focal point of the extreme right has been the National Democratic party (NPD or *Nationaldemokratische Partei Deutschlands*), which won seats in five state parliaments and almost entered the Bundestag in 1969 with 4.3 percent of the national vote. But the CDU-CSU, in the minority after 1969, managed to contain and limit the NPD by appealing to its conservative constituency. By the end of the 1970s, the NPD suffered such heavy and continuous losses, including all of its *Land* parliamentary seats, that it withdrew from most state, county, and municipal election contests. The new German Communist Party (slightly renamed as the *Deutsche Kommunistische Partei* or DKP) is headed for a similar fate. Despite its 40,000 members, it is only a shadow of the former party, receiving 0.3 percent or less of the popular vote in national elections in the late 1980s.

The Greens   In the 1970s ecological, antinuclear, and peace groups began springing up everywhere in the FRG. In 1980, after notable electoral success at state and local levels, these groups formed themselves into a loose alliance known as the National Green Party. (Interestingly, it was cofounded by the daughter of an American army colonel serving in Germany and a German mother.) A countercultural movement disillusioned with the established parties and politics as usual, the Greens (*die Grünen,* as they are popularly known, or *die Grün-Alternative Liste* [GAL], the electoral title that emphasizes their position as a radical alternative) sharpened into the cutting edge of political activism in the 1980s. Their leaders, many of them drawn from the student protest movement and citizen initiatives of the late 1960s and 1970s, envision nothing less than the total transformation of West German politics. Some groups within the party have declared "war" on the "bourgeois-democratic state," while others hope to revitalize parliamentary institutions by more grass-roots democracy (*Basisdemokratie*).

The Greens may be characterized as a radical left-libertarian party fully committed to nonviolent methods of protest and change. In foreign policy, they insist on the FRG's disengagement from all military alliances, unilateral disarmament, nonalignment in Europe, and a development strategy sensitive to the ecological needs of poor nations. On the domestic front their policies are oriented toward conserving energy and protecting the environment. They support the abandonment of nuclear power plants, stiff penalties for polluters, and severe restrictions on industrial growth and the use of chemicals in agricultural production. Finally, they favor the democratization of industry and the educational system as well as the decentralization of the political order, including the adoption of the referendum at the national level.[20]

Standing on this platform, the Greens enjoyed considerable success. They won 5.6 percent of the national vote in 1983, the first minor party apart from the FDP to enter the federal parliament since 1957. Their percentage of the national vote increased to 8.3 in 1987, but thereafter, owing to escalating tensions within the Green party itself—especially between the so-called realists (*Realos*) who wish to cooperate with the established parties in pursuit of their aims, and the fundamentalists (*Fundis*), who insist on following a strategy of outright resistance to established values and institutions—the Greens began to lose their appeal.

One indication that the Greens in particular and the Radical Left in general had lost some of their "alternative" allure was furnished by the December 1990 all-German election. The Greens in the east campaigned on the record of their valiant role in helping to trigger the collapse of the Honecker regime; but the Greens in the west, in addition to their incessant infighting, were the victims of a changing national political agenda. Their alliance with the Greens in the eastern *Länder*, who in turn were allied with other left-wing groups organized as the *Alliance 90* (Bündis-90), failed to clear together the nationwide 5 percent threshold requirement for entering parliament. Almost one-half of the West German Green votes of 1987, that is, just over 1.4 million votes, were lost. The eastern Greens, however, did enter the Bundestag with eight representatives on their own: the Bündis-90 benefited from a one-time-only relaxation of the threshold rule for parties formed exclusively in the five *Länder* of the former GDR.

The continued squabbling among western Greens, combined with the rising socioeconomic costs of reunification—an issue that usually overrides the quality-of-life appeals favored by the radical left in the perception of the general electorate and especially the working class—suggest that electoral support for the Greens in the old *Länder* has reached a period of downturn. The situation scarcely looks better for the Greens in the new *Länder*. By 1994 or whenever the next general election is held, the eastern section of the party may find that memories of their leadership in the autumn of 1989 are not strong enough to compensate for the loss of the 5 percent rule's relaxation. As socioeconomic concerns accumulate in their five *Länder*, they may well find their appeal, like that of the ex-communist party, rejected as anachronistic or utopian or both.[21]

The PDS The PDS is the successor to East Germany's Socialist Unity Party (SED). In the months preceding reunification, the disintegration of the old SED accelerated with the impending demolition of the GDR. With the loss of some 800,000 members amidst revelations of corruption in the party's leading eschelons, the SED decided to dissolve and reconstitute itself as the Party of Democratic Socialism. Gregor Gysi, who had recently replaced Egan Krenz as party chairman, led the PDS into the March 1990 election on a platform calling for a reformed socialism with a human face. It took 16.3 percent of the vote in the only free election in the history of the GDR. Despite efforts to improve its image—efforts bound to fail after 40 years of oppression— the PDS suffered a second crushing defeat in the December 1990 federal election. The PDS dropped to 9.9 percent in the eastern vote and drew only 0.3 percent of the western vote for an all-German total percentage of 2.4 percent. But for the one-time eastern elimination of the 5 percent nationwide threshold, the party would not have won a single seat in the Bundestag. For the once-totalitarian party of Ulbricht and Honecker and its pretensions to represent the way to "Germany, One Fatherland," this was more than a staggering pair of defeats—this was a consignment to the "dustbin of history" that it had so fervently envisioned for democracy.

The Republicans Not to be lightly dismissed, however, is the distinct rise during the eleventh Bundestag of the far-right Republicans (*Republikaner*). The new Republican party, identified most conspicuously with its campaign to rid Germany of its large foreign population, has been a gathering force in the wake of increasing unemployment and structural changes in the economy. In 1989, after exploiting ethnic tensions in Berlin, the Republicans shocked the established parties by surpassing the 5 percent hurdle in that city's parliamentary elections. The shock deepened when shortly thereafter the party polled 7.1 percent of the total vote in the European parliamentary election held in June 1989, putting

them behind the Greens with 8.4 percent, but substantially ahead of the FDP with 5.6 percent.

With these "victories" in hand, the new party, led by its charismatic leader, Franz Schoenhuber, stepped up its activities at the national level in anticipation of the 1990 federal election. Just as the Greens gained at the expense of the SPD among middle-class voters, the Republicans were gaining at the expense of the CDU-CSU among lower-class voters threatened by economic stagnation, unemployment, or competition from foreign workers. The party's local successes in 1989, however, were not followed up nationally in 1990. It received 2.1 percent of the overall national vote and only 2.3 percent in the west. Its eastern vote was 1.3 percent. It appeared as if reunification had taken the wind out of the party's nationalistic sails.

The Republicans turned the tide again, however, in early 1992. Exploiting the deepening economic and political problems caused by the influx of hundreds of thousands of foreigners asking for asylum, the party gained 10.9 percent of the total vote in Baden-Württemberg's state elections, compared with 9.5 percent for the Greens and 5.9 percent for the FDP. On the same day in Schleswig-Holstein, another right-wing party more extreme than the Republicans entered the state parliament with 6.3 percent of the vote, substantially ahead of the FDP with 5.6 percent and the Greens with 4.9 percent. Now the world started to take notice, as many foreign newspapers saw somber omens in these figures. More sober voices traced these "victories" to protest voters who were sending a message to the CDU and the SPD over the state of the economy as well as the government's seeming inability to resolve the asylum problem. Yet the number of neofascist and racist attacks in *Länder* both east and west in 1991 and the fascist-revisionist claims about the Third Reich being put forward in public suggest attitudes and actions long deemed to have been abjured not only do linger on but can tap into socioeconomic discontent, particularly among the unemployed and undereducated youth.

Party Organization

The major parties are formally organized at the federal, *Land,* and precinct levels. The CDU bears the imprint of the FRG's federalized structure, with organizational power residing in the party's 13 *Land* associations. Like the American Republican and Democratic Parties, the CDU is a loosely structured party held together by a coalition of interests with a common goal of winning elections. The SPD, on the other hand, is a mass-organized party under a centralized leadership served by a large and disciplined core of full-time professionals in charge of 22 district parties (*Bezirksparteien*). The relative power and autonomy of the party district associations have permitted the development of strong regional leaders whose views the national leadership cannot ignore with impunity.

The highest formal authority in each party is the national party convention held every two years—although the FDP meets annually—consisting of delegates elected mainly by *Land,* district, and county associations. The convention sets the general outlines of policy, votes on organizational matters, and elects a national executive committee consisting of the party chairperson, several deputy chairpersons, secretary-general, treasurer, and several other elected members. At the national level, the SPD's organizational chart also includes a large party council, consisting of *Land* and local party leaders, and a nine-member presidium to supervise the work of the party executive committee.

The Basic Law (Article 21) recognizes a privileged role for the democratic parties in the inculcation and articulation of democratic values. This role has been reaffirmed by the Political Parties Act of 1967. Apart from provisions on the disclosure of finances, the Act largely codifies existing party practices and procedures. To safeguard internal party

democracy the act provides, inter alia, for (1) the right of all members to vote for party convention delegates; (2) the right of such delegates to vote on party guidelines and programs; (3) a secret ballot for the election of party officers, who must be elected every two years; (4) a reasonable balance of ex officio and elected members on the party executive committee; and (5) a written arbitration procedure for the resolution of intraparty disputes.

Party Finance

The parties derive their funds from several sources, including public subsidies, private donations, receipts from party events and publications, and contributions from party members and members of parliament. As Table 4.7 shows, the parties draw their funds from their strongest constituencies: the SPD relies mainly on membership dues, whereas the CSU and the FDP rely heavily upon donations from corporations and other private groups. The CDU depended heavily on private contributions during the Adenauer years, but as a result of its membership drive in the 1970s, when it first experienced financial difficulties, it is beginning to catch up with the SPD in number of dues-paying members.

The state began to reimburse the parties for their election campaign costs in 1959. At that time the three major parties (CDU-CSU, SPD, and FDP) received DM 4 million

Table 4.7   PARTY FINANCES, 1980–1984 (IN DM MILLION)

Party	Total income	Public subsidies	Donations	Membership
SPD	343	137	37	129
CDU	321	140	71	85
CSU	91	35	36	16
FDP	83	44	23	11
Greens	60	20	11	11
PDS	—	28	1	30

Source: Das Parlament, March 20, 1992, p. 11.

($2 million). Over the years these figures have swelled from DM 20 million ($10 million) in 1965 to DM 186 million ($116 million) in 1987 to DM 404 million ($255 million) in the federal election of 1990. Originally, federal law granted state funds only to those parties receiving at least 2.5 percent of the national vote. In 1968, however, the Federal Constitutional Court ruled that any party receiving as little as 0.5 percent of the vote is constitutionally entitled to state support at the rate, per voter, established by federal law.[22] In the 1987 federal election the parties received DM 5 ($3.13) for each second ballot vote cast on their behalf. This meant that over a four-year period following the election the SPD would receive reimbursement checks totaling DM 70 million ($43 million); the CDU, DM 65 million $41 million), the CSU DM 18.5 million ($11.6 million); the FDP, DM 17 million ($10.7), and the Greens, DM 15.6 million ($9.7 million).[23] East German voters accounted for the huge increase in state reimbursements in 1990 (DM 404 million).

The original purpose behind state funding was to help the parties compete on a more equal basis and to liberate them from the excessive influence of interest groups. Yet in the late 1970s, as the cost of political campaigns sky-rocketed, numerous illegal campaign finance practices dominated the news. Over 100 business firms, including the giant Flick conglomerate, were accused of tax fraud for funneling contributions to the political parties through dummy charitable organizations. The scandal affected each of the established parties, with the FDP absorbing the most damage because its leaders—particularly Hans Friederichs and Otto Lambsdorff—controlled the Finance Ministry at the height of the affair. The Greens, untouched by the scandal, exploited it to their advantage (although the affair only flared up in May 1983, two months after the federal elections in which the Greens had squeezed into Parliament with 5.6 percent of the vote) as the other parties, in December 1983, enacted a legislative reform package

designed to put a stop to practices that "go around" the law (*Umwegfinanzierung*).[24]

INTEREST ASSOCIATIONS

German constitutional theory regards political parties as the chief agencies of political representation, providing the vital link between state and society that makes effective majority rule possible. In reality, public policy results from the complex interplay of political parties and private interests seeking special favors from the government. Hundreds of national associations, ranging from recreational and fraternal to economic and professional groups, maintain offices and highly skilled professional staffs in the capital on a year-round basis. Bonn is the site of most lobbying activity because of the central importance of federal executive agencies in making public policy.

Contact between interest group representatives and public officials in the FRG is much more direct and formal than in some other advanced democracies, which is partly a vestige of the German corporatist tradition. (Corporate representation is still the norm in the upper house of Bavaria's bicameral legislature.) Major social and economic interests are represented on ministerial advisory councils, agency consultative committees, regional planning councils, public broadcasting stations, and the parliamentary study groups of the political parties. Additionally, federal ministerial officials meet on a regular basis behind closed doors with the top representatives of industry, banking, agriculture, and labor for the purpose of coordinating national economic policy. (The quasi-official compulsory membership trade and professional associations empowered to regulate occupational standards and practices are still other examples of direct interest group influence on public policy.) In contrast to German thought, corporatism is not a valued method of representation in the United States.

The link between organized interests and the political parties is equally firm. Far more than in the United States, these interests are actually represented by their functionaries in the national as well as the parliamentary parties (*Fraktionen*). Representatives of business, religious, agricultural, and refugee organizations have been conspicuous among CDU-CSU members of parliament, whereas trade union officials are to be found in SPD leadership positions at all levels of party organization. Members of parliament associated with trade unions, business associations, and other organized interests actually dominate the membership of parliamentary committees such as labor, social policy, and food, agriculture, and forestry.[25]

This complex web of public and private interlocking directorates prompted Peter Katzenstein to characterize the FRG as a "semisovereign state."[26] The FRG is semisovereign because the State shares its sovereignty with private centers of power and influence. In Katzenstein's view, popular elections do not empower the victors to change policy in accordance with an electoral mandate. Public policy is the product of formalized cooperation between a decentralized government and highly centralized private interest associations. Policy develops largely by consensus and thus "incrementalism rather than large-scale policy change typifies West German politics,"[27] a reality that helps to explain the stability of the FRG's political system, as well as the frustration felt by citizens who feel the system is insulated and biased against change.

Citizen Initiatives (*Bürgerinitiativen*)

The sudden appearance of numerous urban and rural protest groups in the 1970s was one sign of the citizens' frustration with the political process. Tens of thousands of German citizens have staged protest rallies involving *quality-of-life* issues such as nuclear power plant construction, urban renewal, air and water pollution, land-use regulations, new highway construction, and the cost of inner-city transportation. Their grass-roots activism—

protest marches, letter-writing campaigns, petition gathering, sit-ins, home-drafted newsletters, and other forms of spontaneous action—expresses the disenchantment of many citizens with the unresponsiveness of political parties, private corporations, and official bureaucracies. Their efforts have been most effective at the local level, resulting in the rollback of some public transportation prices, delays in the building of some nuclear power plants, and the postponement of official decisions to cut new highways through certain residential and open areas. Both the CDU and the SPD have responded to these successes and to the disenchantment that fueled them by making *Bürgerinitiativen* models for their local party interelection activities.

Major Interest Aggregations

Business The three largest business associations in the FRG are the German Federation of Industry (BDI), the Federation of German Employers (BDA), and the German Chamber of Trade and Commerce (DIHT). By the late 1980s, approximately 90 percent of employers belonged to this kind of association, a far higher percentage than that of employees in trade unions. The German Federation of Industry, which is dominated by a few large firms, embraces 23 major industrial associations. Its financial resources, expertise, high-powered staff, and close links to the federal ministries make it one of the most effective lobbies in Bonn. The Federation of German Employers, whose economic experts engage in collective-bargaining negotiations on behalf of nearly 90 percent of all private firms in the FRG, consists of 44 trade associations and 13 *Länder* organizations representing some 740 regional associations. The DIHT, speaking for 81 chambers of commerce, is concerned with the legal and promotional interests of organized business. Collectively these groups have been heavy contributors to the CDU-CSU, though the BDI's leaders have also donated funds to the FDP, a strategy calculated to secure a measure of access to Bonn's ruling circles under SPD-FDP coalition governments.

Labor   West German workers are organized into four major unions: the German Salaried Employees Union (DAG), the German Federation of Civil Servants (DBB), the Christian Trade Union Federation of Germany (CGB), and the German Trade Union Federation (DGB). The four unions represent 46 percent of the FRG's potentially organized labor force. These are not strictly blue-collar organizations. The DGB, by far the largest of these, consists of 17 affiliated unions with a total membership of 7.5 million persons, only 70 percent of whom are blue-collar workers. Higher civil servants (794,000), middle-level white-collar employees (473,000), and many Catholic workers (245,000) are represented in the DBB, DAG, and CGB, respectively.

The unions serve their members with an extensive infrastructure of educational, social, and political activity, besides keeping them and the general public informed through a massive communication network that in 1973 included some 50 periodicals with a monthly circulation of 13 million.[28] The unions are also heavily represented· in parliament. In the eighth Bundestag (1976–1980), no fewer than 327 (or 63.1 percent) of the delegates were members of one or another of the aforementioned unions. Nonetheless, membership levels have fluctuated. For instance, between 1982 and 1990 the CGB grew from 297,000 members to 309,000 members, while between 1980 and 1990 the DBB dropped from 821,000 to 799,000.

The entry of eastern Germany's work force into the west's unions has not been smooth. As eastern workers demand wage settlements on a par with western levels, western employers become more disinclined to invest in the less productive and all too often antiquated eastern plants. Likewise, where western unions exercise "a sense of proportion in the national interest" by taking mere modest raises, such as the 6 percent settlement accepted by the

civil service union leaders in the spring of 1991, the grass-roots membership complains that it is being made to pay for the problems in the east. Calls for western union members to make direct contributions to their eastern fellow members have been particularly poorly received. Hence, the goal of achieving equality in eastern and western living standards is not susceptible to quick or easy attainment in employee terms.

Churches   The Basic Law recognizes the corporate rights of religious communities, just as *Länder* concordats and church covenants guarantee the autonomy of the major religious denominations. The Evangelical (or Protestant) Church in Germany (EKD) is an alliance of 17 Lutheran, Reformed, and United Land churches. Their 29 million include some 5 million in the east. (Most Lutheran churches are, in turn, organized in the United Evangelical Lutheran Church of Germany [UELKD].) Its top legislative organ, the Synod, addresses various social, cultural, and educational issues. The Roman Catholic Church was consolidated upon reunification into approximately two dozen dioceses and archdioceses. Its 28 million members include 800,000 in the east. Its top policy making organ, the German Bishops Conference, functions independently of the Central Committee of German Catholics, an influential lay organization.

The political influence of the churches is less today than it was in the earlier years of the FRG. Clergymen once openly exhorted their members to vote for the CDU-CSU, but their ability to deliver votes and influence elections is severely limited today, as the German Catholic Bishops Conference rapidly discovered in 1980 after its issuance, just two weeks prior to the October election, of a pastoral letter implicitly critical of the SPD. Likewise, Lutheran pastors, although leaders in the revolution of 1989 and in the democratically elected GDR government in 1990, minister to a one-third minority of the population in the eastern *Länder* and a slightly smaller percentage in the western *Länder.* In both the Catholic and Protestant communions, the percentage of regular communicants continues to decline gradually, which suggests that their power of persuasion in the state may also subtly decline.

ELECTORAL POLITICS

The Electoral System

The German electoral system combines single-member districts with proportional representation. Each voter receives two ballots: The first is cast for a specific candidate running in a district, the second for a party list. The second ballot, on which the various party lists appear, includes the names of those candidates nominated by the parties, and it is also possible for a district candidate to be on the list. The number of parliamentary seats allocated to a party is determined by second ballot votes, that is, by its total share of the nationwide vote. Under this system, which the *Länder* also use, the seats allocated to a party would consist of all the district seats it has won together with other seats until the total number of seats equals the percentage of its nationwide, second-ballot vote.

The functioning of the system can be illustrated by the election results of 1983. In winning 48.8 percent of second-ballot votes, the CDU-CSU also captured 180 districts; the figures for the SPD were 38.2 percent and 68 districts; and for the FDP and the Greens they were 7.0 percent and 5.6 percent, respectively, and no districts. These results meant that Christian Democrats were entitled to 244 Bundestag seats. Thus, under the formula, the CDU-CSU was awarded 64 list seats which, when added to its district seats, totaled 244 or 48.8 percent of all second-ballot votes. The SPD, having won 68 district seats, was awarded an additional 125 list seats, totaling 193, whereas the FDP received 34 and the Greens 27 list seats, representing their respective shares of the national (second-ballot) vote.

It is possible, however, for a party to win more district seats than it would normally be entitled to by its second-ballot vote. When this happens, such "overhang" seats are retained, thus increasing the total number of parliamentary seats by that much.

The voting system can also be skewed by the 5 percent clause, which often results in "wasted" votes. In 1990, for example, the western Greens won 4.7 percent of the votes in the old FRG, just missing the 5 percent requirement. Under "pure" proportional representation, the Greens would have been entitled to 23 seats in the Bundestag but, having failed to win 5 percent of the vote, they received none. But Germans generally regard their "modified" form of proportional representation as far more equitable than the straight district-plurality system followed in Britain and the United States.

The 5 percent clause was not regarded as equitable, however, with respect to the first all-German election in December 1990. The Federal Constitutional Court ruled that political parties in the eastern *Länder* would be severely handicapped if the rule were to apply nationwide, as it normally does. For this particular election, therefore, as Table 4.8 indicates, the 5 percent rule applied separately to Germany's eastern and western regions. If seats in the Bundestag had been allocated on a nationwide basis, as is usually the case, neither the Greens (east or west) nor the Party of Democratic Socialism (the old SED) would have achieved parliamentary representation. The two-constituency tabulation presented in Table 4.8 is a one-time exception to the 5 percent nationwide rule.

Split-Ticket Voting

The German system gives voters the opportunity to split their tickets, a method by which coalition partners can help each other. In 1972, for example, the SPD openly encouraged its voters to cast their second ballot in favor of the FDP, while 60 percent of second-ballot

Table 4.8   FEDERAL ELECTION RESULTS, 1990[a]

Party	Nationwide	Old FRG	Ex-GDR	Seats won
CDU	36.7%	35.0%	43.4%	262
SPD	33.5	35.9	23.6	239
FDP	11.0	10.6	13.4	79
CSU	7.1	9.1	—	51
Greens (West)	3.9	4.7	—	—
PDS	2.4	0.3	9.9	17
DSU	0.2	—	1.0	—
Greens (East)	1.2	—	5.9	8
Republicans	2.1	2.3	1.3	—

[a]The percentages do not include the election results in Berlin. The DSU (German Social Union) ran as the "sister" party of Bavaria's CSU. The Greens (east) were allied with Alliance '90.

Sources: Statistisches Jahrbuch 1991 für das Vereinte Deutschland, p. 101 and *The Week in Germany* (New York: The German Information Center, December 7, 1990).

FDP voters supported CDU and SPD candidates with their first ballot. Split-ticket voting was also prevalent in the 1987 election when many SPD voters, troubled by their party's military and ecological policies, cast their second ballot for the Greens, whereas many CDU voters cast their second ballot for the FDP. The FDP in turn appeared to convince voters that the best way to keep the CDU-CSU "honest" and on the right course was to ensure its presence in the new government. As Table 4.9 indicates, large numbers of German voters appear to be leery of one-party government. No fewer than 40.1 percent of CDU-CSU voters and 41.7 percent of SPD voters thought that it would "not be good" for their respective parties to win an absolute majority of seats in the Bundestag. The corresponding percentages for the 1983 election were 27.1 and 29.5. These figures point to an increasing tendency on the part of German voters to split their ballots. The German preference for governing coalitions contrasts sharply with the attitudes of British voters who tend to associate responsible parliamentary government with unified party leadership backed by electoral majorities. This split-ticket voting is one indicator of the Americanization of FRG elec-

toral behavior; another is the phenomenon of the "floating voter" who does not owe a deep and consistent attachment to any one party. (At the same time, the campaigns themselves have been highly Americanized.)

Candidate Selection

Political parties monopolize the candidate selection process. Candidates seeking district seats are nominated either directly by party members or by conventions of party delegates. (There is no system of primary elections as in the United States.) In the CDU and SPD party executive committees elected in biannual congresses at the *Land* level select candidates for the Bundestag. Naturally the party will seek to nominate the candidate with the broadest popular appeal. But invariably he or she is a well-known party loyalist with years of faithful service to the organization. "Independent" candidates who circumvent the party organization are rarely if ever nominated. Party control over *Land* list candidates is even tighter. These lists are determined by secret ballot in party conferences, but in truth delegates vote mainly to ratify lists already put together by district and *Land* party executive committees in coop-

Table 4.9   VOTERS PREFERRING ABSOLUTE MAJORITY FOR SPD OR
CDU-CSU IN 1987 ELECTION

Absolute majority	CDU-CSU	SDP	FDP	Greens	Total
Good for SPD	0.0%	57.7%	1.0%	14.3%	22.2%
Good for CDU-CSU	59.8	0.0	8.5	0.0	26.5
Not good	40.1	41.7	90.5	85.7	50.3

Source: *Bundestagswahl 1987; Eine Analyse der Wahl zum 11. Deutschen Bundestag am
25, Januar 1987* (Mannheim: Forschungsgruppe Wahlen E.V., 1987), p. 48.

eration with national party officials. These lists are usually headed by leading party officials to ensure their election to the Bundestag.

Campaign Styles and Techniques

West German elections have evolved into major media events and highly professionalized undertakings similar to American presidential campaigns. While both the CDU and the SPD continue to speak in terms of the traditional FRG mass party, the *Volkspartei* (People's Party), both have been highly Americanized and centralized in their campaigns, especially in the use of new communication technologies and new marketing approaches. (The German courts, however, put an end to U.S.-style direct phone canvassing as an illegal infringement of individual privacy.) Campaign advertisements fill newspapers and popular magazines, while election posters and richly colored life-style photographs of leading candidates dot the landscape. Lapel buttons, paper flags, T-shirts, imitation money, letter openers, and bumper stickers by the tens of thousands convey their partisan messages. In the 1970s, the art of selling candidates and creating political images reached new heights of sophistication and brilliance as public relations firms assumed a central role in mapping campaign strategy.

Each party seeks to establish a "brand image" with catching colors and slogans. For example, the SPD, in emphasizing the statesmanlike quality of its leader, sought to capitalize on Schmidt's popularity by turning the 1980 election into a referendum on his chancellorship. The CDU-CSU, emphasizing stability and prosperity, just as clearly sought to influence conservative and middle-of-the-road voters, an appeal reinforced in the 1976 campaign by the insinuating watchwords "freedom or socialism" aimed at the SPD—a slogan that prompted the latter to retort with its equally insinuating "vote for freedom." The FDP, on the other hand, has cultivated itself as a "creative minority" by emphasizing its independence and portraying its leaders as persons of reason and common sense and concerned about the problems of small businesspeople and the "besieged" middle class. The Greens, finally, have seen in their color a powerful symbol of their political goals respecting the environment.[29]

GERMAN POLITICS IN TRANSITION

Federal Elections, 1949–1990: An Overview

The year 1969 marked the turning point of West German politics in the postwar era. Prior to that year, the CDU-CSU had won five successive national elections, most of them by wide margins over the SPD. Yet the clearest observable trend seen in Table 4.10 is the clockwork regularity of SPD gains between 1953 and 1972. The SPD's chance to enter a governing coalition occurred in 1966 when Erhard, the CDU chancellor, resigned against a backdrop of discord within his own party and

Table 4.10   FEDERAL ELECTION RESULTS, 1949–1990 (AS PERCENTAGE OF VOTE CAST)

Year	Turnout	CDU-CSU	SPD	FDP	KPD[a]	NPD[b]	Others[c]
1949	78.5	31.0	29.2	11.9	5.7	1.8	20.3
1953	86.0	45.2	28.8	9.5	2.3	1.1	13.1
1957	87.8	50.2	31.8	7.7	—	1.0	10.3
1961	87.7	45.3	36.2	12.8	—	0.8	5.7
1965	86.8	47.6	39.3	9.5	—	2.0	3.6
1969	86.7	46.1	42.7	5.8	0.6	4.3	—
1972	91.1	44.9	45.8	8.4	0.3	0.6	—
1976	90.7	48.6	42.6	7.9	0.1	0.3	0.5
1980	88.7	44.5	42.9	10.6	0.2	0.2	1.5
1983	89.1	48.8	38.2	7.0	0.2	0.2	5.6
1987	84.4	44.3	37.0	9.1	—	0.6	8.3
1990	77.8	43.8	33.5	11.0	—	—	9.8

[a] The Communist party was banned in 1956. It reappeared in 1969 under the name of Campaign for Democratic Progress (ADF) and competed later under its new label, the DKP.

[b] Figures include votes for extreme right-wing parties before the organization of the National Democratic party (NPD).

[c] The figures for 1983 and 1987 represent the total vote of the Greens.

a widening rift between the CDU-CSU and its regular coalition partner, the FDP. There followed the three-year period (1966–1969) of the so-called Grand Coalition under the CDU's Kurt-Georg Kiesinger (chancellor) and the SPD's Willy Brandt (vice-chancellor). In 1969, when Social Democrats reached a new high of 42.7 percent of the popular vote, the FDP, with 5.8 percent of the vote, decided to join with Brandt in producing Bonn's first SPD-led government.

The new coalition ruled with a slim voting edge of 12 votes, which by 1972 had virtually disappeared in the wake of defections from Brandt's Eastern policy (*Ostpolitik*). Christian Democrats, smelling an opportunity to get back into office, moved for a vote of no confidence, the first time that the parliamentary opposition had tried to topple a ruling government between federal elections. On 27 April 1972, the coalition survived the CDU-CSU challenge by the razor-thin margin of two votes, but on the very next day the Bundestag rejected Brandt's budget, plunging the gov-

ernment into still another crisis. The failure of the budget to win parliamentary approval came at a time of economic downturn and bitter wrangling in the cabinet over fiscal policy. Yet Brandt's personal popularity was at an all-time high, prompting him late in 1972, when the economic news was much brighter, to call for new elections in the hope of increasing his margin of parliamentary support. Accordingly, the chancellor invoked Article 68 and lost his vote of confidence, as planned, whereupon the Federal President dissolved the Bundestag and scheduled new elections for 19 November.

The 1972 federal election campaign—a bitterly fought contest—resulted in a solid victory for Brandt, marking the first time Social Democrats had exceeded the CDU-CSU in popular votes. Shortly thereafter, however, the party's fortunes declined again as the SPD suffered severe losses in several state and local elections, only to be followed by Brandt's resignation in May 1974, setting the stage, after Helmut Schmidt's takeover, for the 1976 election.[30]

In 1976 the CDU-CSU not only recovered its 1972 losses, but narrowly missed securing the majority that would have toppled the SPD-FDP coalition—a popular victory without power, as many editorial writers characterized the election. The CDU's revival was widely attributed to the expansion of its grassroots membership campaign in the early 1970s under its able general secretary, Kurt Biedenkopf, and to a highly effective national advertising campaign. Yet many spectators saw the election as an issueless campaign, decided mainly by the styles and personalities of the leading candidates.[31]

The 1980 election was in large measure a replay of 1976, except that the Christian Democrats had made the fatal mistake of nominating Franz Josef Strauss as their candidate for chancellor—a nomination that seemed designed less for victory than to keep the sister parties from falling apart after the election. The polls clearly predicted and the CDU anticipated that the "incalculable" and "uncontrolled" Strauss, as one CDU politician was quoted as saying, would be defeated. Meanwhile Schmidt exuded confidence, acting like the winner he would be on 5 October 1980, when West Germans returned the SPD and a much stronger FDP to power in Bonn.

As noted earlier, the fortunes of the new government declined rapidly. The popular chancellor's days were numbered in the face of increasing opposition from the FDP over his economic policy and from his own party over his strong pro-American nuclear missile policy. With FDP support the CDU-CSU chose Helmut Kohl as chancellor on 1 October 1982, whereupon the latter pledged to call new elections in March 1983. The year 1983 turned out to be a banner one for Christian Democrats. Far ahead of the SPD in the polls, they obtained their highest percentage of the national vote since 1957 but fell just short of a majority. The FDP had lost the support of many of its voters, who expected the party to make good on its 1980 election pledge to continue its coalition with the SPD. Old party regulars were relieved, however, when the FDP crossed the 5 percent mark of the electoral vote, permitting the new CDU-CSU–FDP coalition to function with a substantially enlarged majority. The 1987 election was very much a replay of 1983 and it underscored the dilemma of the SPD. Johannes Rau, the moderate chancellor candidate, promised the electorate that he would not consider a coalition with the Greens. But as the SPD organization itself moved steadily leftward to draw votes away from the Greens, many other voters, particularly the swing vote in German politics, supported the existing coalition led by Chancellor Kohl.

With the FRG's economy booming in the summer of 1989, the SPD under Oskar Lafontaine planned a campaign focusing on "a policy of ecological and social renewal of industrialized society" for 1990. Intervening events in the GDR—specifically the massive demonstrations and exodus of eastern Germans, which brought on, in succession, the collapse of the communist regime and the socialist economy and finally the palpable desire of the people to effect reunion as soon as possible—afforded Chancellor Kohl the opportunity, with the very capable support of his FDP Foreign Minister, Hans-Dietrich Genscher, to obtain Allied support for negotiations with East Berlin and Moscow that would reunite the two German states on 3 October 1990 and thereby make Kohl the first chancellor of all Germany since the war. Kohl's extraordinary determination and enthusiasm overcame all obstacles and all cautionary notes, including those of the President of the Bundesbank as to the costs of reunification. Kohl's project was, of course, welcomed by tumultuous crowds wherever he went in the east. Meanwhile, the SPD was reduced to reacting to his initiatives and to warning, Cassandra-like, of their possible unpleasant side effects. Its support was popularly perceived in the east as two little, too late; Kohl had the diplomatic power and the deutsche mark to offer; Lafontaine, rather qualified consent.

The results were clear well in advance in as much as the election turned on either giving credit where credit was due for reunification or expressing confidence in the current politico-economic stewardship. Either way, the overall east-west vote for the CDU/CSU reached 43.8 percent, only a 0.5 percent drop from 1987, while the overall vote for the SPD fell 3.5 percent to 33.5 percent; the Greens (and their Alliance), together with the reformed communists (PDS), won a combined total of 25 Bundestag seats only by virtue of the one-time relaxation of the 5 percent threshold. Although only the FDP improved its previous performance, the mandate for Kohl was clear.

A CHANGING ELECTORATE

The short-term effects of issues and personalities are important in explaining the outcome of particular elections. But a closer analysis of the voting returns reveals long-term shifts in the basis of party support and attachment. Voting patterns in the 1950s could be explained largely in terms of class and religion. By the 1970s these variables, although still important indicators of voting, were no longer sure predictors of how Germans would vote. The SPD, having shed its Marxist roots in 1959, had been making slow but steady gains in three traditional strongholds of the opposition—namely Catholic industrial workers, the nominally religious members of the middle class, and the secular, status-conscious bourgeoisie. By 1972 the SPD's advance into urban Catholic, white-collar Protestant, and mixed (Catholic and Protestant) constituencies appeared to have halted entirely, to the advantage of the FDP rather than the CDU, whereas Christian Democrats, as the 1976 election showed, were beginning to broaden their appeal in urban white-collar districts previously weak in CDU affiliation. Yet, while continuing to gain among the FRG's trade union population, SPD support was also increasing among nonunion employees and manual workers in rural districts, although the CDU

remained predominant in the agricultural sector. On the whole, Catholicism and ruralism correlated positively with high CDU-CSU voting, whereas the SPD's success over the long term seemed to lie less with its working-class membership than with the broadening of its base in the middle class.[32]

Recent studies of German electoral behavior concluded that the most dramatic shift in postwar voting patterns has taken place as a consequence of the changing character of the German middle class. Whereas traditional middle-class voters—property owners and farmers—have seen their numbers dwindle, the new middle class of civil servants and white-collar employees connected with the FRG's mushrooming service trades has more than doubled since 1950. Highly urbanized, younger, and less attached to traditional values, these voters seem more responsive to newer issues centering on foreign policy, environmental matters, educational reform, and alternative life-styles than to older economic concerns, although these older concerns do remain important, especially at a time of high unemployment. The SPD's gains among these new voters—a constituency that is disproportionately Protestant and nonchurchgoing—is evident from the data in Table 4.11. The real battleground for voters is on this turf.

During the 1970s, the SPD appeared to do the better job of bridging the gap between the old politics and the new. The elections of 1983 and 1987, however, show that the CDU was more successful in appealing to

Table 4.11 SOCIAL CLASS AND PARTY SUPPORT, 1987 (IN PERCENT)

Social class	CDU-CSU	SPD	FDP	Greens
Working	39	53	2	6
New Middle	45	41	6	8
Old Middle	54	27	7	12

Source: Russell J. Dalton, *Citizen Politics in Western Democracies* (Chatham, N.J.: Chatham House Publishers, 1988), p. 155.

middle-class voters. Yet many of these voters—especially those in districts with high concentrations of students, salaried workers, and civil servants—cast their votes in favor of the Greens, seriously cutting into traditional FDP strongholds. First voters and younger voters (ages 18–44) cast their ballots disproportionately for the Greens. Religious preference, according to one study, was found "to have no special correlation with a Green vote." As for the working class, its shift to the right in recent elections could presage deeper CDU penetration into the SPD's traditional constituency.

POLICY-MAKING INSTITUTIONS

In this subsection we turn our attention to the FRG's major policy-making institutions, its federal system, and its scheme of separated and divided powers. Upon their accession to the FRG, the eastern *Länder* brought their governmental systems into conformity with the Basic Law. Thus, unless otherwise indicated, the institutions, structures, and policy making processes discussed here are applicable to all of Germany.

Germany's main legislative institutions are the popularly elected *Bundestag* (house of representatives) and the *Bundesrat,* the indirectly nonelected upper house, whose delegates represent the *Länder* governments. The leading executive institutions are the chancellor and cabinet, collectively known as the federal government. The president, once a powerful head of state directly elected by the people, has been reduced in the FRG to a figurehead akin to the British monarch. One of the unique features of Germany's federal system is that the states are entrusted under the Constitution with the administration of national law. This system, often dubbed *administrative federalism,* is a carryover from the past. Finally, empowered to enforce the provisions of the Basic Law, the judiciary, at the top of which is the Federal Constitutional Court, serves as a check on the activities of the other branches of government.

The Federal President

The Federal President is the FRG's highest ranking public official, but he functions mainly as a ceremonial head of state, a vestigial reminder of the once-thriving presidency under the emperor. Symbolically, he remains important as a spokesman for the nation. Although the presidency is perceived as a nonpartisan office, its occupant is elected for a five-year term—under Article 54 of the Basic Law he may be reelected only once—by a federal convention composed of party representatives from national and state parliaments. The president is chosen as a result of bargaining between the coalition parties forming the majority in the convention. Yet the office has been filled by respected public officials widely recognized for their fair-mindedness and ability to communicate across party lines. Up to now, the office has served as a capstone to a successful career in politics.

On 23 May 1984, Richard von Weizsäcker, a Christian Democrat, became the FRG's sixth president. He was preceded by Theodor Heuss (FDP; 1949–1959), Heinrich Lübke (CDU; 1959–1969); Gustav Heinemann (SPD; 1969–1974), Walter Scheel (FDP; 1974–1979), and Karl Carstens (CDU; 1979–1984). Until 1974, an incumbent president otherwise competent and prudent in the exercise of his authority could expect, if he wished, to be reelected to a second term. The 1979 election, however, was largely an exercise in partisan politics. Scheel withdrew as the SPD-FDP candidate when the CDU-CSU entered the federal convention resolved, with a slim majority of 26 votes, to elect its own candidate, Karl Carstens. The 1984 election, on the other hand, was unusual for its lack of partisan maneuvering. Supported by both the governing center-right coalition and the opposition SDP, the federal convention chose as president Richard von Weizsäcker, the once popular Christian Democratic mayor of West Berlin—traditionally a Social Democratic stronghold—and scion of a patrician line of statesmen, theologians, and scientists, highly respected for his elegance and intellectual prowess.

The president's powers include the appointment and dismissal of various public officials, including cabinet officials and military officers, and the pardoning of criminal offenders. His most common official duty, apart from receiving and visiting foreign heads of state, is to promulgate, with his signature, all federal laws. Whether he can reject a statute on substantive constitutional grounds is disputed, although presidents have done so on at least five occasions.[33] A president's refusal to sign a properly enacted bill could conceivably bring about a constitutional crisis resulting in demands for the president's resignation or his impeachment.

Whereas the president's political powers are limited, his position is potentially one of significant moral leadership. President Weizsäcker, noted for his integrity and credibility, has often used his office in this way. Recently, he opposed amending the Basic Law to curtail the right of asylum in Germany and, in a stinging rebuke to young "skinheads" attacking foreigners, he went out of his way to visit several hostels for foreign refugees and to reassure their residents of the government's concern for their protection and welfare. (Several German newspapers carried a photograph of the president with a smiling Indian boy on his lap.) Additionally, and contrary to the stated position of leaders within his own party, he came out in favor of a quota system that would allow non-German immigrants to resettle in Germany. On the other hand, he strongly supported, for "historic reasons," his government's refusal to send troops to fight in the Gulf war against Iraq.

The Federal Government

The Chancellor The Basic Law puts the chancellor in firm control of the federal government. He alone is responsible to parliament, whereas his ministers—that is, the members of his cabinet—whom he may hire and fire,

are responsible only to him. Constitutionally charged under Article 65 (see Feature 4.2) to lay down the guidelines for national policy, he is chosen by a majority of the Bundestag and is usually the leader of the largest party in the governing coalition. Parliament, however, is not empowered to dismiss the chancellor at will, as it was able to do in the Weimar Republic. Under the so-called constructive vote of no confidence, prescribed by Article 67 of the Basic Law, the Bundestag may dismiss a chancellor only when a majority of its members simultaneously elects his successor. The stabilizing effect of this provision has led many persons to label the FRG a "chancellor democracy."

The constructive vote of no confidence has succeeded only once, in 1982, when the Bundestag voted Helmut Schmidt out of office after the FDP's withdrawal from the coalition government. (In 1972, Willy Brandt survived a Christian Democratic challenge to his leadership, the only other occasion on which parliament invoked the procedure under Article 67.) A new alliance between the FDP and the CDU-CSU elected Helmut Kohl as chancellor by a vote of 256 to 235, the first time in the FRG's history that a government had been replaced without an election.

Article 68 allows the chancellor to initiate a vote of confidence, authorizing him, if he loses the vote, to request the president to dissolve parliament and call for new elections. Brandt used this procedure in 1972 and Kohl used it again in 1983. Both chancellors planned to lose in the expectation that new elections would increase their parliamentary majority and thus their hold on governmental power. In both instances the strategy worked, although some constitutional lawyers argued that these were cynical political moves designed to circumvent the intent and spirit of the Basic Law.

In an important constitutional case arising out of President Carsten's dissolution of parliament in 1983, the Federal Constitutional Court ruled that the dissolving power is limited. It cannot be exercised out of mere con-

---

Feature 4.2 Article 65

The Federal Chancellor shall determine, and be responsible for, the general policy guidelines. Within the limits set by these guidelines, each Federal Minister shall conduct the affairs of his department autonomously and on his own responsibility. The Federal Government shall decide on differences of opinion between Federal Ministers. The Federal Chancellor shall conduct the affairs of the Federal Government in accordance with rules of procedure adopted by it and approved by the Federal President.

Basic Law, Article 65

---

venience, especially when the chancellor commands a *working* parliamentary majority. In this case, however, where such a majority appeared not to exist, the chancellor, Bundestag, and president, said the court, could each exercise their discretion on whether to invoke the dissolving machinery of Article 68.

The chancellor's role as the centerpiece of West German democracy is manifest from national election campaigns. As the parties have converged in their general policy orientations, national elections have tended to focus on the experience, personality, and leadership capability of chancellor candidates. Many Germans speak of the *chancellor effect* in national elections. The party of the chancellor has the advantage of incumbency and election results are often interpreted as a personal victory for the chancellor as well as a vote of confidence in the existing governing coalition. Only once in the last 40 years has a governing coalition changed as the result of a national election.

The Chancellor's Office　The most powerful instrument of executive leadership in the FRG is the chancellor's office. Originally a small secretariat serving the chancellor's personal needs, it has evolved into an agency of major political importance, even overshadowing the cabinet. It contains departments corresponding to the various federal ministries as well as a planning bureau, created in 1969, to engage

in long-range social and economic planning. Its staff of about 500 persons keeps the chancellor informed on domestic and foreign affairs, assists him or her in setting policy guidelines, coordinates policy making among the federal ministries, and monitors the implementation of cabinet decisions.

The chancellor's office is headed by a chief of staff, usually an experienced public official and close personal advisor. The chief of staff is a person of immense power in Bonn, his influence often exceeding that of federal ministers. Other chancellery advisors have obtained national prominence in their policy-making role. Such a person was Egon Bahr, the principal architect of Brandt's *Ostpolitik*. Finally, the chancellor is served by a press secretary, who in turn heads the Federal Press and Information Office (staffed by over 800 persons), which is also under the chancellor's direct control.

The Cabinet　While prescribing a chancellor-led government, the Basic Law (Article 65) also envisions a high level of cabinet responsibility. In practice, however, the cabinet has not functioned as a true collegial body. First of all, the chancellor decides how much authority is to be accorded to each minister: Adenauer and Brandt, for example, virtually served as their own foreign ministers, as did Schmidt in certain areas of foreign policy. On the other hand, certain ministers achieve enormous prominence in their own right and occasionally overshadow the chancellor. Hans-Dietrich Genscher, the chief architect of German foreign policy in the 1980s, was often thought to have been the dominant figure in foreign affairs under Chancellor Kohl.

Furthermore, cabinet members are not all equal in rank. For example, the minister of finance—probably the cabinet's most powerful official in the field of domestic policy—has a qualified veto over proposals affecting public finances. His objection to such proposals can be overridden only by the vote of the chancellor, with whom he is ordinarily closely affiliated, and a majority of the cabinet. The ministers of justice and interior also have special powers of review over cabinet proposals impinging upon their jurisdiction.[34]

In creating the cabinet, a chancellor is constrained by the demands of coalition politics and the interests of groups allied to and rivalries within his party. Often he is required to negotiate at length over the nature and number of ministries to be awarded the minor party in his coalition government. The FDP, the perennial minor party in German coalition governments, has often threatened to withhold its votes for the chancellor (i.e., the head of the major party in the coalition) pending agreement on the cabinet posts to be allocated to its party as well as agreement on a wide variety of policy issues. Coalition talks after the 1990 election resulted in a 75-page coalition policy document.

The formation of Chancellor Kohl's cabinet after the 1990 election reflects the compromises worked out in several days of coalition talks between the CDU-CSU and FDP. The FDP initially bargained for six cabinet positions but ended up with five, one more than in the previous cabinet. It was a foregone conclusion that Hans-Dietrich Genscher, head of the FDP and Vice-Chancellor, would continue as Foreign Minister. Nor is it by chance that the FDP held on to the ministries of Education and Economics and picked up Justice; for these are areas in which Genscher's

party has long-standing and vital interests. Among ministers belonging to the CDU-CSU, we find almost perfect parity in religious identification (7 Catholics and 6 Protestants). The cabinet's geographic distribution, however, is concentrated in the western *Länder.* Three ministers were chosen from the east, all from Mecklenburg-West Pomerania.

Chancellors have a great deal of flexibility in reshaping their cabinets. Kohl, for example, engineered a number of changes in 1991. Jürgen Möllemann was transferred from Education to Economics, while the former Ministry of Health, Welfare, and Family Affairs was split into three separate ministries. The Ministry of East–West German Relations was, for obvious reasons, abolished. Seven new faces appeared in the cabinet, including three appointees, as mentioned, from eastern Germany. Their credentials are typical of cabinet appointees. Nearly all are high-ranking party officials with previous ministerial experience at the federal or state level. Ten incumbent ministers remained at their posts. Only one—Klaus Kinkel—was appointed from outside of parliament. A professional civil servant, the new Minister of Justice, was formerly director of the Federal Intelligence Service. By 1 May 1992, Kohl had made two changes in his cabinet. Rudolf Seiters, chief of staff in the chancellor's office, replaced Wolfgang Schäuble as Interior Minister. (Schäuble assumed the chairmanship of the CDU/CSU parliamentary party in the Bundestag amid speculation that he would eventually succeed Kohl as party leader.) Gerhard Stoltenberg, for decades a familiar face on the national political stage, was forced to resign as Defense Minister over the illegal delivery of tanks to Turkey. Kohl filled the post with Volker Rühe, a close personal confidant and general secretary to the CDU.

Parliamentary State Secretaries   The office of parliamentary state secretary—to be distinguished from the permanent state secretaries of the various ministerial bureaucracies—was introduced in 1967. Parliamentary state secretaries are selected from among the more junior members of the Bundestag to help the ministries run their departments, defend their records in parliament, and maintain contact with the public. A new element in the Schmidt cabinet was the high number of former parliamentary state secretaries who were elevated to cabinet post. The office is now widely recognized as a training ground for cabinet service by all the major parties.

The Bundestag: Legislative Branch

The Bundestag, the parliament of the FRG, is the successor to the old imperial (1871–1918) and republican (1919–1933) Reichstag (see Feature 4.3). In these earlier regimes the legislative branch was politically and in some respects constitutionally subordinate to the executive establishment, just as elected representatives played second fiddle to professional civil servants. In contrast, the Basic Law elevates parliament to first rank among the FRG's governing institutions. Though commentators agree that parliament has fallen short of the founders' vision of a vigorously self-confident body in control of the executive, they are also of the view that the Bundestag has evolved from the rather submissive body of the Adenauer era into an increasingly assertive and vital agency of the national policy-making process. Even in the event of a national emergency, which only it can declare, the Bundestag's authority remains largely intact, thus helping to ensure that ultimate power shall always reside in the hands of civilian leaders and the elected representatives of the people.

Power and Functions While playing a role similar to the U.S. Congress, the Bundestag is structurally a very different institution. First of all, it is "the parliament of a parliamentary system of government" in that "it [also] determine[s] the political composition and tenure in office of the government."[35]

Secondly, and by the same token, the highest officials in the executive branch—that is, the chancellor and his ministers—are among the most important and influential members of the Bundestag. This symbiotic relationship between executive and legislative power is wholly incompatible with the U.S. notion of separation of powers. In the FRG, separation of powers is embodied largely in the role of the opposition within parliament. Its task is to call the government or ruling coalition—and thus the executive—to account in the crucible of parliamentary inquiry and debate.

Parliament checks the executive by its power to review the national budget, to pass on all bills introduced by the government, to hold hearings and investigations, and to confront the chancellor and his ministers in the legislative question hour, a device borrowed from British parliamentary practice. Individual ministers or their deputies may be summoned before the Bundestag at any time to defend their actions or the performance of their departments. The chancellor is often present on those occasions when leaders of the opposition schedule major inquiries (*grosse Anfragen*) on general government policy, of which there were 145 in the Eleventh Bundestag (1987–1990). Individual members of the Bundestag addressed no fewer than 20,251 minor inquiries (*kleine Anfragen*) to the government in the same four-year period, compared with the 2997 questions asked during the first 12 years of the Adenauer era.[36]

The screening of proposed legislation absorbs most of the Bundestag's time. By far the largest number of bills screened are initiated by the government. Of the 1117 bills received by the Bundestag in the tenth and eleventh legislative periods (1983–90), 54 percent were government bills, 37 percent originated in the Bundestag itself, and 9 percent were sent over by the Bundesrat. In these two legislative periods the government managed to pass 77 percent of the bills it introduced, as compared with a 16 percent and 7 percent success rate, respectively, for the Bundestag and Bundesrat.

Feature 4.3 **Bundestag in Berlin**

On 4 October 1990, for the first time in 57 years, a democratically elected all-German parliament met in the Reichstag building in Berlin. In the presence of the two men who paved the way to reunification — Helmut Kohl and Willy Brandt — 144 members of the former GDR Volkskammer joined 519 members of the Bonn parliament in celebration of German unity. The eastern German delegates were chosen by the Volkskammer as a whole to represent the eastern *Länder* pending the new all-German elections of 2 December 1990. On 20 June 1991, after heated debate, the Bundestag voted, by the slim margin of 17 votes, to move the Bundestag to Berlin. (The United Treaty had already designated Berlin as the capital.) Relocation in Berlin is expected within ten years. The Bundesrat, however, by a vote of 30 to 30, decided to remain in Bonn.

All-German Bundestag meets in old Reichstag.

As these statistics show, the federal government dominates the law-making process.

The principal officers of the Bundestag are the president, ordinarily a member of the strongest parliamentary party, and three vice-presidents. Together they form the Presidium, which is entrusted with the chamber's general administration. The chamber's more powerful executive arm is the Council of Elders, consisting of the president, vice-presidents, 17 to 20 delegates chosen by the various parliamentary parties, and 2 cabinet representatives. The council is charged with scheduling debates, regulating the question period, making committee assignments, and otherwise shaping the Bundestag's agenda. Staffed by the senior and most experienced members of parliament, it usually manages to achieve broad interparty agreement on legislative procedures.

Fraktionen and Committees The most important groups in the Bundestag are the parliamentary parties, or *Fraktionen*. In practice, they control the Bundestag's organization and decision-making machinery. Although constitutionally regarded as "representatives of the whole people, not bound to instructions [from any group,]" deputies who plan on advancing their legislative careers will not lightly oppose the policy decisions of the party hierarchy, for party unity and discipline are strongly embedded in the parliamentary party system. Party discipline, however, is exercised in only a small number of cases. Most bills—over 85 percent—are the product of group negotiation in which representatives of the federal government, the Bundestag, and the Bundesrat participate, and they are passed unanimously.

Each *Fraktion* divides itself topically into working groups or councils, which parallel the Bundestag's committee structure and serve as instruments for crystallizing party policy and developing the expertise of deputies. The *Fraktionen* include large numbers of deputies who represent various organized interests. These interest group representatives, as noted later in this section, dominate several Bun-

destag committees. In any event, the deputy who does his homework in the party group to which he is assigned—showing leadership, skill, forensic ability, and mastery of subject matter—often winds up as an influential member of a corresponding legislative committee and eventually a parliamentary state secretary.

The Bundestag also has a differentiated committee system, including standing, investigating, and special committees. Of these, the 23 standing committees are the most important. Comparable to the committees of the U.S. Congress, they and their numerous subcommittees are the workhorses of parliament. In the Bundestag, however, committee chairs are shared by all the *Fraktionen* in proportion to their strength in the chamber as a whole and are allocated on the basis of expertise instead of seniority. "This expertise," writes Michael L. Mezy, "leads to a sense of cohesion and group identification among committee members that frequently transcend party lines."[37] Yet "their decisions are usually accepted by the party caucuses and then on the floor of the Bundestag."[38] It remains to be seen whether the 144 additional representatives from the eastern *Länder,* with their radically different political backgrounds, will change German legislative politics.

Members of Parliament Typically, having studied law, political science, or economics, members of parliament often begin their careers in the youth branch of a political party, frequently assisting established politicians. Successfully fulfilling an apprenticeship in the party apparatus or, as is often the case, in a trade, farm, or labor organization closely linked to their party, they are then, in their late thirties, elected to parliament. They remain there for about 16 years, only to resign in their mid-fifties to draw a comfortable pension and to enter the employment of an organized interest group. The careerism and security inherent in this system of political recruitment are not calculated to staff parliament with "movers and shakers" and often insulate deputies against new and evolving trends in society.

Not all groups are equally represented in parliament. Civil servants, teachers, trade association officials, lawyers, and labor union officials make up about 80 percent of the membership. Nearly two-thirds are university graduates. For most of the 1980s women have represented about 15 percent of the membership, more than double the number elected in the 1970s. In the eleventh Bundestag, as in previous legislative periods, the SPD led overwhelmingly in labor union officials and party functionaries, whereas the CDU-CSU was disproportionately represented by businessmen and merchants. Self-employed persons were almost equally divided between the FDP and CDU-CSU. All three parties claimed, as usual, a fairly equal number of persons in the various professions.

Civil servants are clearly the most important occupational group in the legislature, reflecting the overlapping of administrative and parliamentary careers that has always been possible in Germany. As David P. Conradt remarks, "the strong representation of state officials in parliament is . . . consistent with the expert administrative orientation to politics that characterizes German political culture."[39] Such dual careers are actually encouraged by regulations that permit state officials to return to their old jobs in government after their legislative service and to accumulate pension rights from parliament as well as from the civil service.

The Law-making Process   Bills may be introduced by any member of the Bundestag or by the Bundesrat. As indicated earlier, however, the overwhelming majority of legislative bills originate with the federal government. A bill sponsored by the latter is first submitted to the Bundesrat, which is required to act on the bill within six weeks. If there are any changes, the Bundesrat must return the bill to the cabinet for its approval or disapproval. (Bills originating in the Bundesrat are submitted to the Bundestag by the cabinet after the latter has expressed its opinion on the bill.) The bill is then submitted to the Bundestag, where it is given a first reading. From there it is assigned to the proper committee. If it survives this stage, together with a second and third reading, it is transmitted to the Bundesrat. If the Bundesrat amends the bill, it may be sent to a joint conference committee for mediation. Any changes by the committee require the Bundestag's approval, once again, of the entire bill. The Bundesrat, however, has a suspensive veto over ordinary legislation and an absolute veto over legislation involving the Länder (for a discussion of these vetoes, see "Bundesrat")—but any such veto can be overridden by the Bundestag. After final approval a bill is countersigned by the chancellor or appropriate federal minister and then signed by the federal president, whereupon it is promulgated as law in the *Federal Law Gazette*.

The chancellor, federal and *Land* ministries, and representatives of organized interest groups are the major actors in the lawmaking process. They work closely with the *Fraktionen* in hammering out legislative policy, though, as earlier noted, committees play a critical role in filtering legislation for final passage. So successful are the committees in the performance of this role that few bills, once reported out of committee, are the subject of amendment or even debate from the floor. The intense plenary debates of 1979 on energy policy and on the repeal of the statute of limitations on Nazi crimes—debates stretching over several days—are exceptions to the customary practice of securing broad interparty agreement on most bills that become law.

FEDERALISM AND BUREAUCRACY

Like the United States, Germany divides power constitutionally between national and state governments. Federalism is in fact one of the unamendable principles of the Basic Law. The 16 *Länder* consist of 13 territorial states and the three city states of Berlin, Bremen, and Hamburg. Each *Land*, like the national government, has its own constitution based on principles of republican and democratic government. Each has a parliamentary system. A minister-president—lord mayor in the city-states—responsible to a one-house popularly elected legislature is the head of government in the territorial states. Historically, however, German federalism differs from the U.S. brand. The crucial distinction is that in the United States both federal and state governments exercise a full range of separate legislative and administrative functions, whereas German federalism confers the bulk of legislative powers upon the national government, with the *Länder* being mainly responsible for the administration of both federal and state laws.

The boundaries of the *Länder* were drawn without much reference to their ancestral ties. Only Bavaria, Saxony, and Thuringia survived with their pre-1945 boundaries relatively intact. In 1952, however, the GDR abolished the *Länder* and replaced them with 14 administrative districts under the control of the central government. These *Länder* were reestablished in July 1990 as one of the conditions of reunification. The *Länder* now range in population from 650,000 in Bremen to 17 million in North-Rhine Westphalia. They also differ vastly in territorial size: excluding the small city states, they range from Saarland with 2570 sq. km. to Bavaria with 70,554. The largest and richest states, measured in terms of population and geography, are in the west. The eastern *Länder*, by contrast, are relatively smaller and much poorer.

This imbalance between the eastern and western *Länder* has revived proposals to redraw state lines for the purpose of creating larger and more integrated political and economic units. The Basic Law permits the restructuring of the *Länder* so long as the system as a whole remains federal in design. Under the terms of the Basic Law (Article 29) any federal law proposing a state boundary change must be approved by the

Bundesrat and subsequently ratified by referendum in the affected Länder. This procedure was first used in 1952 when the states of Baden, Württemberg, and Württemberg-Hohenzollern were consolidated into the single state of Baden-Württemberg. The next change is likely to be Berlin's incorporation into Brandenburg, a change that the all-German government is obligated to consider under the Unity Treaty.

The *Bundesrat*

The Bundesrat, as the mainstay of German federalism, was designed to safeguard the vital interests of the *Länder*. But it is not a second chamber like the U.S. Senate. First, its powers are not fully equal to those of the Bundestag; second, its 68 votes are cast by officials who serve at the pleasure of the *Länder*. Thus, each *Land* delegation votes as a unit and in accordance with the instructions of its government. How a delegation—or the person appointed to represent the state—votes often depends on the party composition of the *Land* cabinet. Nearly all seats in the Bundesrat are occupied by *Land* minister-presidents or their delegates.

To accommodate the interests of the eastern *Länder*, the Unity Treaty also amended Article 51 of the Basic Law, changing the allocation of seats in the Bundesrat. As before, each state is entitled to at least three votes, but now states with a population of more than 2 million are entitled to four votes, those with more than 6 million receive five votes, and those with more than 7 million receive six votes. (In the past, the largest states had five votes.) This system favors the smaller states. The five largest states, with 64.4 percent of the population, have 28 votes in the Bundesrat; the remaining states, with 35.6 percent of the population, have 40 votes.

The Bundesrat's consent is required for all federal legislation affecting the administrative, financial, and territorial interests of the *Länder*. With respect to other legislation, it has a suspensive veto, as noted earlier. If the Bundesrat objects to a bill by a majority vote, the Bundestag may override by a majority vote; if the former is by two-thirds, the vote to override must also be two-thirds. Additionally, the Bundesrat is authorized to approve all federal action enforcing national law in the *Länder*, to participate in major legislative decisions taken during a national emergency, and to elect half of the members of the Federal Constitutional Court. This last prerogative is important, for the Bundesrat has a record of electing judges with strong federalist leanings, thus giving to the upper house an indirect influence in constitutional cases involving the interpretation of federal laws and ordinances.[40]

An Emerging Instrument of Opposition

In spite of its considerable powers, the Bundesrat during its first 20 years functioned largely in the shadow of the Bundestag, ratifying the latter's policies and those of Bonn's ruling party or coalition. Its leaders have tended to view the Bundesrat as a nonpartisan chamber concerned exclusively with the merits of proposed legislation, an image reinforced by the dominant role of bureaucratic officials in its proceedings.

Since 1969, however, the Bundesrat has risen in political importance and popular awareness. Until then the parties dominating the "lower" house also controlled the "upper" chamber. Owing to the distribution of power among the parties within the states, however, the Christian Democrats—the party out of power in Bonn—enjoyed a 21-to-20 voting edge in the Bundesrat between 1969 and 1975, an advantage that swelled to 11 votes by 1979, leading to sharp confrontations with the governing parties in the Bundestag. In 1992, however, as Table 4.12 shows, the tables were turned. The ruling CDU-FDP coalition in the Bundestag confronted a Bundesrat overwhelmingly controlled by SPD-led coalitions.

The Bundesrat, however, has developed interests of its own that transcend party lines,

Table 4.12   THE BUNDESRAT, 1 MAY 1992

State	Votes	Ruling coalition	Population (million)
Baden-Württemberg	6	CDU-SPD	9.6
Bavaria	6	CSU	11.2
Berlin	4	CDU-SPD	3.4
Brandenburg	4	SPD-FDP-GR	2.6
Bremen	3	SPD-FDP-GR	.7
Hamburg	3	SPD-FDP	1.6
Hesse	4	SPD-GR	5.6
Mecklenburg-W. Pomerania	3	CDU-FDP	2.0
Lower-Saxony	6	SPD-GR	7.2
N. Rhine Westphalia	6	SPD	17.1
Rhineland-Palatinate	4	SPD-FDP	3.7
Saarland	3	SPD	1.1
Saxony	4	CDU	4.9
Saxony-Anhalt	4	CDU-FDP	3.0
Schleswig-Holstein	4	SPD	2.6
Thuringia	4	CDU-FDP	2.7

Source: Handbuch des Bundesrates 1991/92 (Munich: C.H. Beck'sche Verlagsbuchhandlung, 1991).

and in the course of time, the upper house has managed to expand its influence via broadening interpretations of its constitutional power to veto legislation. During the tenth Bundestag (1983–87), 60.9 percent of all bills passed by the Bundestag required the Bundesrat's consent. The Bundesrat retained a suspensive veto right over the remainder or 39.4 percent of all bills passed.[41]

The FRG follows the pattern of the 1871 Reich and the Weimar Republic by conferring exclusive legislative and administrative responsibility on the national government in such fields as foreign affairs, interstate commerce, postal services, and transportation. Most other major public policies and guidelines are also established by the national government. But these policies and guidelines, as noted earlier, are carried out by the *Länder* as a matter of their own concern, not to mention the exclusive power of the *Länder* over cultural and most educational matters, police activity, and municipal affairs. As a consequence, the federal bureaucracy is relatively small when compared with the number of persons employed by other levels of government. If the 870,000 federal railroad and post office workers are not counted, a mere 10 percent of all public employees are on the federal payroll, whereas 55 percent are employed by the *Länder* and 35 percent at the local level.

Whether responsibility so divided would meet the needs of a modern industrial welfare state was an issue pondered by many Germans after 1949. By the late 1960s a shift in power toward the central government was clearly underway. The Federation's concurrent powers had been constitutionally expanded to embrace the production and utilization of nuclear energy, the promotion of scientific research, energy conservation, and control of environmental pollution. Bonn had also been accorded a new and leading role in the fields of university education, regional economic improvement, agricultural organization, coastal preservation, and general educational planning, although its initiatives here must, as always, be coordinated and negotiated with *Länder* and local governments.

Public Administration: Decentralized Federalism

There are five levels of public administration in the FRG, organized mainly on a spatial or territorial basis.[42] The first, of course, is the national level. But here (except for those few functions administered directly by the national government) the various ministries are mainly engaged in formulating general policy. Under Article 65 of the Basic Law each federal minister is in complete control of his department, though he runs it within the limits of the chancellor's policy guidelines. The command hierarchy of the ministries follows a uniform pattern. The top aides to each federal minister are the parliamentary state secretary (the ministry's chief spokesman in the Bundestag) and the permanent state secretary, who is ordinarily a career civil service officer and the ministry's top administrative official. In recent years, however, the latter have increasingly been chosen on the basis of political criteria from outside the ministry, particularly with respect to those secretaries who as "professional experts" are expected to play a significant role in program or policy development.[43] Finally, undersecretaries head the major departments of each ministry, which in turn are divided into sections, offices, or bureaus.

The ministries work out their programs and policies in accordance with the general policy guidelines and political predispositions of their top executives. Most people now recognize the political basis of each minister's authority as well as the legitimacy of long-range planning. Yet the ministries do not shape policy by issuing central directives from on high any more than they shape it from the bottom up on the basis of purely professional considerations. The planning units of the various ministries, which were created in the late 1960s, weave their program recommendations out of clientele demands, the expertise of bureaucrats, and the political orientation of the top executives. In general, policy planning is more of an interactive process, following what Mayntz and Scharpf call a *dialogue model* of policy making,[44] involving a good deal of discussion and bargaining within and among bureaucracies.

Land governments are the next level of administration. In addition to administering federal law as a matter of their own concern, they enact laws in certain areas within the framework of national policy guidelines and in areas of their exclusive jurisdiction. *Land* administration of federal law is not closely supervised by the national government, so even here *Länder* have considerable leeway in setting administrative policy. Each *Land* has adopted its own system of unified public administration. Public policies at the *Land* level are carried out by *Land* ministries, various functional *Land* agencies, and several self-governing corporations.

The last three levels of administration are the administrative district, counties and county-free independent cities, and municipalities. The administrative district (*Regierungsbezirk*), found in the six larger *Länder,* "is a general purpose regional *Land* institution of administration."[45] Most *Land* administration is actually carried out at this and the county level. Analogous to the French *départment,* the administrative district is the level at which "the concept of unity of administration is applied most consistently, since the goal is to subsume for coordination under the authority of the district officer as many national and *Land* administrative tasks as possible."[46] The county, at the lowest level of *Land* administration, carries out functions delegated to it by state governments. Finally, municipalities or associations of local governments, whose independence is also guaranteed by the Basic Law, and which also operate under the principle of unity of administration, are responsible, within the framework of *Land* law, for the provision of local public services.

Cooperative Federalism and Finances

No field of federal-state relations in the FRG is as important as that of public finance. As a result of a series of 1969 amendments to the finance section of the constitution, the federal government received greater flexibility and control over national tax policy, although the looser approach of the new provisions still required, as a matter of practical necessity, a high degree of federal-state cooperation. Table 4.13 shows the major sources of income for each level of government. State officials in revenue offices located in the various *Länder* collect shared revenues representing about two-thirds of the total tax revenue. Under vertical equalization procedures, the *Länder* and the federal government are entitled to equal shares of the revenue from corporation taxes. Local governments receive 15 percent of revenue from the income tax, while the *Länder* and the federation each receive 42.5 percent. Together, shared revenue represents nearly 50 percent of all tax receipts. The general sales (that is, value-added) tax is also shared (on a per capita basis) by these governments in accordance with a formula worked out annually by the federal chancellor and *Land* heads of government and requiring the Bundesrat's approval. In 1988, federal and state governments shared these revenues at a ratio of 65 percent to 35 percent.[47] Local governments and their respective *Länder* also work out similar revenue-sharing agreements.

Horizontal equalization procedures also require the wealthier states to share their revenues with poorer *Länder.* Here, too, federal law establishes the formulas for the distribution of such funds, although the Basic Law authorizes the federation to make supplementary equalization payments to financially weak states. (In 1986 the Federal Constitutional Court ruled that the federal government was constitutionally obligated to assist the weaker states in meeting their financial obligations.) In 1989, the financially strong *Länder* transferred DM 3.5 billion to the weaker *Länder,* while

Table 4.13   MAIN SOURCES OF TAX REVENUE

Federation	Länder	Local government	Shared taxes
Customs	Property	Real estate	Income
Freight (road)	Inheritance	Business	Corporation
Bills of exchange	Motor vehicle		Capital gain
Income surtax	Beer		Sales
Corporation surtax	Gambling		

the federal government's supplemental allocation to the weaker states amounted to DM 2.7 billion.

The new eastern *Länder* will not participate in these revenue-sharing arrangements. The Unity Treaty exempts these states from the fiscal provisions of the Basic Law for five years, during which time German leaders hope to repair their deficient economies and to restore some balance between east and west. In the meantime, the Federation and *Länder* have agreed to establish an off-budget plan known as the *German Unity Fund*. Under this plan, DM 115 billion will be transferred to the eastern *Länder* in installments over five years, 80 percent of which is to be raised in the capital market and the rest supplied from the federal budget. Because of this added strain on the FRG's financial resources, the system of federal financial sharing is likely to be restructured in the coming years.

THE LEGAL SYSTEM AND THE JUDICIARY

Legal Tradition and the *Rechtsstaat*

The *Rechtsstaat* or *law state* is a key concept in the German legal order.[48] All just states are of course based on law, but in its original form the German *Rechtsstaat* placed extraordinary emphasis upon legality. Germans viewed the state as a neutral entity entrusted with the resolution of public issues in accordance with objective standards of law, unsullied by the play of selfish interests or the machinations of poli-

tical parties. The sovereign state, the axis of the law state, was the guarantor of freedom and equality, just as rights and obligations arose from membership in the state. Liberty did not precede law; rather, law defined it, and the judiciary, staffed by a professional class of impartial and apolitical civil servants loyal to the state, was to enforce the law as written.

Under the Basic Law, the *Rechtsstaat* remains a vital principle of German constitutionalism, but not in its earlier nineteenth-century sense. The *law state* would henceforth be limited by constitutionally guaranteed individual rights enforced by the judiciary, just as it would be moderated by the humanity implicit in the constitutional notion of *Sozialstaat* (freely translated, a *socially conscious state*). In legal theory the sovereign is no longer supreme. Article 20 reads: "All state authority emanates from the people," and further, "Legislation shall be subject to the constitutional order; the executive and the judiciary shall be bound by law *and justice*" (italics added). Finally, Article 20 contains this remarkable provision: "All Germans shall have the right to resist any person or persons seeking to abolish [the] constitutional order, should no other remedy be possible."

The Court System

Germany has a uniform and integrated judicial system. All lower and intermediate courts of appeal are state courts, whereas all courts of final appeal are federal tribunals. Federal law specifies the structure of state courts, but their administration and staffing, including the training of judges, is under the control of the *Länder*. The trademarks of the German judiciary are collegiality and specialization. Except for courts of minor jurisdiction, all tribunals are multi-judge courts. Most operate in panels of three. (In 1989, the regular trial courts of general jurisdiction consisted of 1242 civil and 1084 criminal panels.) In addition to the regular courts, which handle ordinary civil and criminal cases, there are separate judicial hierarchies consisting of labor, administrative, social, finance, and constitutional courts. The federal courts, as shown in Table 4.14 cap these hierarchies.

Justice in the western *Länder* is carried out by 17,627 judges (as of 1989), nearly 80 percent of whom serve on the regular courts of ordinary civil and criminal jurisdiction. Some 4237 judges sit on the courts of specialized jurisdiction. The high federal courts, listed in Table 4.14, consist of 467 judges. Other legal professionals associated with the courts are some 3759 public prosecutors. The 51,266—60,460 if notary publics are included—attorneys practicing law in 1989 are also regarded as officers of the courts, although their practice is by law limited to a certain level of the judiciary as well as to certain courts within a given geographical area.

In 1991, the eastern half of the country was still in the process of restructuring its judiciary along FRG lines. The old GDR had rejected the "capitalist" *Rechtsstaat* in favor of a system rooted in "socialist" legality. Socialist law, unlike the *Rechtsstaat*, celebrated the values of security and solidarity implicit in the socialist vision of society. More simply organized and less fastidious about procedure than the FRG judiciary, courts functioned to carry out this vision, not to question it. The political state, not the law state, governed the judiciary. In point of fact, many judges were mere functionaries, while others made a travesty out of any notion of "justice."

Most GDR judges were members of the SED—they had to be—and their legal education was heavily infused with Marxist-Leninist ideology. By 1991, as batteries of western German judges deluged the east to begin the process of restructuring, eastern German judges as well as prosecutors were being dismissed en masse, pending reviews of their credentials and inquiries into their backgrounds. For many of these judges, now required to fill out long questionnaires about their personal and public lives, this was a humiliating and saddening experience, causing enormous resentment among conscientious judges not implicated in the crimes of the old regime. Most of these judges had reconciled themselves to the permanent loss of their jobs, for they were unlikely to survive the tough screening procedures installed by the FRG.[49]

The Judges

The training and professional standing of German judges varies from their peers in the United States or Britain. In the United States, for example, judgeships are usually awarded to lawyers in their middle years following successful private practice or experience in public office. In Germany, by contrast, lateral mobility of this kind is rare among legal professionals. After six years of study, which includes practical training in various administrative and judicial capacities, law graduates must make their choice of a legal career. Those deciding to become judges go through still another three-year probationary period, upon the successful completion of which they receive a judgeship with lifetime tenure and security. Judges can expect to ascend slowly the hierarchy of the judicial establishment if they meet with the approval of the *Land* Justice Ministry—the *Länder* are in charge of the training, recruitment, and supervision of judges—and if they are lucky and know the right persons in Bonn, they may end their careers as judges of one of the high federal courts.

The civil service orientation of the judiciary tends to be reinforced by the narrow social base from which judges, particularly those

Table 4.14 FEDERAL COURTS 1988

Court	Location	Number of judges	Cases docketed
Federal Supreme Court	Karlsruhe	271	4048
Federal Administrative Court	Berlin	52	3287
Federal Social Court	Kassel	40	2259
Federal Labor Court	Kassel	28	658
Federal Finance Court	Munich	60	3394
Federal Constitutional Court	Karlsruhe	16	3702

Source: Statistisches Jahrbuch 1990 für die Bundesrepublik Deutschland (Stuttgart: Metzler-Poeschel Verlag, 1990), pp. 339–341.

appointed by the *Länder*, are recruited. Almost half are themselves the sons and daughters of parents who have spent their lives in the civil service. Federal judges tend to be more diversified in social background and occupational experience, largely because of the method by which they are selected. They are chosen by a committee of electors composed of 11 members of the Bundestag together with those *Land* and federal ministries whose authority is in the same area as the federal court to which a judge is to be named. This mechanism allows interest groups, political parties, state and federal agencies, and the public to participate in the selection process, producing a federal bench somewhat less characterized by professional inbreeding and political conservatism than the state judiciary.

THE FEDERAL CONSTITUTIONAL COURT

The Federal Constitutional Court with its sweeping powers of judicial review is only as old as the Basic Law. To the surprise of many observers, this tribunal has developed into an institution of major policy-making importance in the FRG. Judicial review was a relatively new departure in German constitutional history. Postwar German leaders were of the opinion that, in the light of Germany's authoritarian and totalitarian past, traditional parliamentary and judicial institutions were insufficient to safeguard the new liberal democratic order. So they created a national constitutional tribunal, as well as equivalents at the *Land* level, to supervise the judiciary's interpretation of constitutional norms, to enforce a consistent reading of the constitution on the other branches of government, to resolve conflicts between branches and levels of government, and to protect the basic liberties of German citizens. Thus, the old positivist belief separating the realm of law from the realm of politics was abandoned, together with the idea that justice could automatically be achieved through the mechanical application of general laws duly enacted by the legislature.

Structurally, the Federal Constitutional Court is divided into two chambers, called senates, each of which is composed of eight justices chosen for single 12-year terms. Half of the justices are chosen by the Bundestag's 12-member Judicial Selection Committee and the other half by the Bundesrat. A two-thirds vote is required in both electoral organs. This method of selection, together with the requirement that the Bundestag and Bundesrat alternate in the selection of the court's president and vice-president, usually means that judicial appointments are the subject of intensive bargaining both among the parliamentary parties and, occasionally, between the Bundesrat and Bundestag. No one party has been strong enough to make appointments over the objections of the other parties. Thus, the court's membership has reflected fairly well the balance of forces in parliament as a whole.

Judicial Review in Operation

The Constitutional Court's jurisdiction includes 16 categories of disputes, all of which the Basic Law itself prescribes. (Table 4.15 presents the most important of these categories.) The Basic Law authorizes both judges and legislative groups, as well as state governments, to petition the court directly. Judges may initiative a "concrete" judicial review proceeding by asking the court to rule on a constitutional question arising out of a pending case if in their view the law under which a case has arisen is of doubtful validity under the Basic Law. On the other hand, a state government or one-third of the members of the Bundestag may initiate an "abstract" proceeding by petitioning the court to review the constitutionality of a federal or a state statute. Cases on abstract review tend to draw the judges directly into the arena of political conflict, prompting its harshest critics to deplore what they perceive as the "judicialization" of politics.

Constitutional complaints account for about 95 percent—an average of 3145 per year between 1978 and 1990—of all cases coming to the court and for about 55 percent of its published opinions. These cases relate to fundamental rights and freedoms guaranteed by the Basic Law. To encourage Germans to view the constitution as the source of their rights and freedoms, the Basic Law (Article 93 [13]) authorizes ordinary citizens to file complaints with the Federal Constitutional Court in the event that their basic rights have been violated by the state. (Prior to 1969, this right was conferred by statute.) Such an action involves neither court costs nor even the participation of legal counsel, an ideal situation in which Hans Everyman can bring his woes to the attention of the country's highest tribunal.

The Constitutional Court's Impact

Public opinion polls continue to show the high regard German citizens have for the Constitutional Court. In this respect, it outranks all other institutions in the nation's public life, including the civil service and the churches.[50] When the court speaks, Germany's "attentive public" listens; what people hear is often an outspoken tribunal reminding them of their constitutional values, their political morality, and their ethical goals as a nation.

The Federal Constitutional Court's landmark cases include decisions (1) outlawing the neo-Nazi Socialist Reichs Party and the former Communist Party of Germany; (2) upholding a

TABLE 4.15 WORKLOAD OF FEDERAL CONSTITUTIONAL COURT, 1951–1991

Category	Cases docketed	Decided by full senate	Otherwise resolved
Election disputes	89	62	9
Disputes between federal organs	87	45	36
Federal-state disputes	24	13	10
Abstract judical review	112	62	33
Concrete judical review	2,619	897	1,563
Constitutional complaints	82,353	3,689	12,639

[a]Cases decided by the three-judge chambers. A constitutional complaint is decided on the merits by the full senate only if a three-judge chamber (three in each senate) fails unanimously to reject it.

Source: Statistisches Übersicht des Bundesverfassungsgerichts (mimeographed) (Karlsruhe: Das Bundesverfassungsgericht, 1992).

Land education statute over the Federal Government's objection that it violated an international treaty; (3) nullifying an attempt on the part of the Federal Government to establish a national television station; (4) invalidating a federal statute providing for the general public financing of political parties; (5) declaring unconstitutional a liberal abortion law on the ground of its interference with the right to life; (6) sustaining the validity of prayer in state schools; and (7) after striking down parts of a federal census statute, creating a new right of "informational self-determination."

Key Terms

Abstract judicial review
Bundesrat
Chancellor democracy
Citizen initiatives
Constructive vote of no confidence
Council of Elders
Federal Law Gazette
Fraktion
Godesberg platform
Grand Coalition
Greens
Iron chancellor
New middle class
Overhang votes
Parliamentary state secretary
PDS
Realos
Rechtsstaat
Republicans
Second ballot
Semisovereign state
Vertical equalization

Suggestions for Further Reading

Baker, Kendall, Russell J. Dalton, and Kai Hildebrand. *Germany Transformed: Political Culture and the New Politics* (Cambridge: Harvard University Press, 1981).

Blair, Philip M. *Federalism and Judicial Review in West Germany* (Oxford: Clarendon Press, 1981).

Braunthal, Gerard. *The West German Social Democrats, 1969–1982: Profile of a Party in Power* (Boulder, Colorado: Westview Press, 1982).

Burkett, Tony. *Parties and Elections in West Germany* (New York: St. Martin's Press, 1975).

Burkett, Tony, and S. Schuettemeyer. *The West German Parliament* (London: Butterworths, 1982).

Clemens, Clay. *Reluctant Realists: The Christian Democrats and West German Ostpolitik* (Durham: Duke University Press, 1989).

Cerny, Karl H. *Germany at the Polls: The Bundestag Elections of the 1980s* (Durham: Duke University Press, 1990).

Dalton, Russell J. *Germany Votes 1990: Reunification and the Creation of a New German Party System* (Oxford: Berg Publishers, 1993).

Deoring, Herbert, and Gordon Smith. *Party Government and Political Culture in Western Germany* (New York: St. Martin's Press, 1992).

Dyson, Kenneth H.F. *Party, State and Bureaucracy in Western Germany* (Beverly Hills, Calif.: Sage Publications, 1977).

"Federalism and Intergovernmental Relations in West Germany: A Fortieth Year Appraisal" (Symposium Issue), *Publius*, Vol. 19 (Fall 1989).

Gunlicks, Arthur. *Local Government in the German Federal System* (Durnham: Duke University Press, 1986).

Jesse, Eckhard. *Elections: The Federal Republic of Germany*, (Oxford: Berg Publishers Limited, 1990).

Johnson, Nevil. *State and Government in the Federal Republic of Germany*, 2nd ed. (Oxford and New York: Pergamon, 1983).

Kelly, Petra. *Fighting for Hope* (London: The Hogarth Press, 1984).

Kennedy, Ellen. *The Bundesbank* (New York: Council on Foreign Relations Press, 1991).

Kommers, Donald P. *Judicial Politics in West Germany: A Study of the Federal Constitutional Court* (Beverly Hills, Calif.: Sage Publications, 1976).

Langguth, Gerd. *The Green Factor in West German Politics* (Boulder, Colorado: Westview Press, 1986).

Loewenberg, Gerhard. *Parliament in the German Political System* (Ithaca: Cornell University Press, 1966).

Mayntz, Renate, and Fritz Scharpf. *Policy-making in the German Federal System* (Chapel Hill: University of North Carolina Press, 1963).

Merkl, Peter, ed. *Forty Years of West German Politics* (New York: New York University Press, 1989).

Patterson, William and David Southern *Governing Germany* (Oxford: Basil Blackwell, 1991).

Smith, Gordon, Gordon Patterson, and Peter Merkl, eds. *Developments in West German Politics* (London: Macmillan Education Ltd., 1989).

Thaysen, Uwe, et al. *The U.S. Congress and the German Bundestag* (Boulder, Colorado: Westview Press, 1990).

C. Public Policy

CIVIL LIBERTIES: AN ORDERING OF CONSTITUTIONAL VALUES

The first part of the Basic Law (Articles 1 to 19) is a charter of fundamental rights and an affirmation of human personhood rooted in the natural law thesis that certain liberties of the individual are antecedent to organized society and beyond the reach of governmental power. As interpreted by the Federal Constitutional Court, the Basic Law has established a value-oriented order based on human dignity. Article 1 is no idle declaration. As the Basic Law's "highest legal value," the concept of human dignity has been employed by the Constitutional Court, much as the U.S. Supreme Court has used the due process clauses of the fifth and fourteenth amendments as an independent standard of value by which to measure the legitimacy of state actions as well as the uses of individual liberty.

Apart from the freedoms guaranteed by Articles 1, 2, 3,and 5 (see Feature 4.4), the Basic Law's fundamental rights include the freedoms of religion (Article 4, assembly (Article 8), association (Article 9), privacy (Articles 10 and 13), and movement (Article 11), together with the right to property (Article 14), the right to choose a trade or occupation (Article 12), and the right to refuse military service for

reasons of conscience (Article 12a). (Additionally, criminal defendants are accorded most of the rights and privileges normally associated with the Anglo-American notion of due process of law.) The primacy of these rights in the FRG's constitutional order is underscored by Article 19, paragraph 2, which states that "in no case may the essential content of a basic right be encroached upon."

These rights, however, have been proclaimed with an important German twist—that is, they are to be exercised responsibly and used to foster the growth of human dignity within the framework of the political and moral order ordained by the Basic Law. Article 2 is a paradigm of the German approach to basic rights. While individual liberty and personal autonomy are jealously guarded values of the legal order, they are also constrained by the equally important values of political order and social morality (see Feature 4.5). Thus, the right to develop one's personality is limited by the moral code, just as the right to freedom of speech is limited by the inviolability of personal honor. As the Federal Constitutional Court noted in the Privacy of Communications Case: "The concept of man in the Basic Law is not that of an isolated, sovereign individual: rather, the Basic Law has decided in favor of a relationship between individual and commun-

Feature 4.4 **Selected Basic Rights**

ARTICLE 1

1. The dignity of man shall be inviolable. To respect and protect it shall be the duty of all state authority.
2. The German people therefore acknowledge inviolable and inalienable human rights as the basis of every community, of peace and of justice in the world.

ARTICLE 2

1. Everyone shall have the right to the free development of his personality insofar as he does not violate the rights of others or offend against the constitutional order or the moral code.
2. Everyone shall have the right to life and to the inviolability of his person. The liberty of the individual shall be inviolable. These rights may be encroached upon pursuant to a law.

ARTICLE 3

1. All persons shall be equal before the law.
2. Men and women shall have equal rights.
3. No one may be prejudiced or favored because of his sex, parentage, race, language, homeland and origin, faith, or religious or political opinions.

ARTICLE 5

1. Everyone shall have the right freely to express and disseminate his opinion by speech, writing, and pictures and freely to inform himself from generally accessible sources . . . There shall be no censorship.
2. These rights are limited by the provisions of the general laws, the provisions of law for the protection of youth, and by the right to inviolability of personal honor.

ity in the sense of a person's dependence on and commitment to the community, without infringing upon a person's individual value."[51]

With regard to the polity as a whole, the Basic Law creates what the Federal Constitutional Court refers to repeatedly as a *militant democracy.* This means that certain forms of speech and behavior described as anticonstitutional—activities that would probably be protected under prevailing U.S. constitutional doctrine—may legally be punished. The Basic Law itself predicates political free-

---

Feature 4.5 **Freedom and Order in German Constitutionalism**

The Basic Law ... reflects a conscious ordering of individual freedoms and public interests. It resounds with the language of human freedom, but a freedom restrained by certain political values, community norms, and ethical principles. Its image of man is of a person rooted in and defined by a certain kind of human community. Yet in the German constitutionalist view the person is also a transcendent being far more important than any collectivity. Thus, there is a sense in which the Basic Law is both contractarian and communitarian in its foundation: contractarian in that the Constitution carves out an area of human freedom that neither government, private groups, nor individuals may touch; communitarian in the sense that every German citizen is under obligation to abide, at least in his overt behavior, by the values and principles of the moral and political order.

Source: Donald P. Kommers, "The Jurisprudence of Free Speech in the United States and the Federal Republic of Germany," *Southern California Law Review* 53 (1980): 677.

---

dom on the acceptance of certain principles of political obligation. Freedom of association, for instance, is guaranteed, but associations "the purposes or activities of which ... are directed against the constitutional order" are prohibited (Article 9). Similarly, political parties "whose aims ... seek to impair or abolish the free democratic basic order" may be declared unconstitutional (Article 21). These provisions spring from the abiding conviction of the FRG founders, who drafted the Basic Law in the aftermath of Weimar's collapse and Hitler's totalitarianism, that a democracy is not an unarmed society, and that it has the right to dissolve organizations and prohibit activities aimed at the destruction of republican government so long as the rule of law is thereby preserved.

Public Servant Loyalty Decree:
A Case Study

The Loyalty Decree of 28 January 1972, commonly referred to as the *extremist resolution* (*Extremistenbeschluss*), serves as a useful device for illustrating the principle of *militant democracy*. It also helps to illustrate the problem

of policy implementation under the FRG's peculiar brand of federalism, as well as the complexity of constitutional argument that frequently arises under the speech, association, and political obligation clauses of the Basic Law.

Loyalty to the established political order has been a hallmark of the German civil service. Article 33 of the Basic Law carries on this historic tradition, providing that the "exercise of state authority as a permanent function shall as a rule be entrusted to members of the public service whose status, service, and loyalty are guaranteed by public law." Federal law lays down the general guidelines for the organization and conduct of civil servants. Supplemented and enforced by state regulations, these guidelines have long insisted upon the allegiance of civil servants to the constitution.[52] Chancellor Brandt and the Conference of State Governors issued the Loyalty Decree against a backdrop of political terrorism, violent student demonstrations, and the renewed determination of radical groups to "march through the institutions" of the FRG. They insisted that the decree was simply a restatement of existing policy and intended merely to ensure the uniform application of civil service guidelines.

One of the Loyalty Decree's main principles required civil servants (*Beamten*), public-sector workers (*Arbeiter*), and employees (*Angestellten*) "to defend the free democratic basic order as defined in the Basic Law during service and nonservice hours." It banned from the public service those persons engaged in anticonstitutional activities as well as persons who are members of organizations pursuing anticonstitutional goals. The decree's most controversial paragraph provided that any person belonging to an organization "that pursues goals hostile to the Constitution" was presumptively unfit for public service. Opponents of the decree, however, made the point that the loyalty provisions would effectively bar some persons from their chosen profession—for example, applicants for teaching positions—because certain jobs are held almost exclusively by state employees. In any event, as an effort to clarify standards of recruitment and dismissal from the public service and to ensure uniform and nondiscriminatory application by the *Länder* of national guidelines, it was a failure.

When compared to the laws of other democratic nations, the provisions of the Loyalty Decree were not extraordinary.[53] It was the manner of their enforcement that raised a storm of protest in Germany and abroad. Several *Länder*, mainly under CDU-CSU leadership, seized upon the decree's "membership" provision to deny public service jobs to persons in any way connected with communist or other "subversive" organizations. Other states, mainly under SPD leadership, followed the more liberal policy of not excluding persons from the public service in the absence of real evidence of anticonstitutional behavior on the part of the applicant. Meanwhile, the federal office for the protection of the constitution and its *Länder* equivalents stepped up their surveillance of subversive activity and initiated security checks of increasing numbers of public service applicants. Although

thousands of persons were swept up in the net of official inquiry, only a small number of applicants were actually denied public employment on the grounds of doubtful loyalty.[54]

However, a few of these denials became a *cause célèbre*, eliciting strong public outcries from literary figures, students, clergymen, and other intellectuals who attacked the decree as a pernicious attempt to stifle dissent and block social change. Some politicians and editorial writers responded by questioning the loyalty of these critics, thus seeming to confirm the critics' charge that fear and distrust were sweeping the land. Other commentators saw the whole enterprise as a cycle of overreaction: the government overreacting to the security threat in the first place, the critics responding with gross exaggerations of the decree's impact, and the critics of the critics retaliating in language far more robust than enlightening.

The public controversy came to a head in the Federal Constitutional Court's decision of 22 May 1975. The constitutional complaint before the court challenged Schleswig-Holstein's refusal to allow a recent law school graduate to embark upon his required in-service training with state agencies because of his participation in several meetings of an organization of radical law students engaged in "anticonstitutional" activities at Kiel University. The loyalty provisions used to justify the refusal were identical to those contained in the federal decree, so to this extent the validity of the federal decree itself was squarely before the court.

The constitutional analysis in this case was complex. Four articles of the Basic Law—Articles 5 (freedom of expression), 12 (right to choose a trade), 3 (equality under law), and 33 (equal eligibility for public service)—were in need of interpretation. The constitutional principles of *Rechsstaatlichkeit* (the rough equivalent of the U.S. notion of due process of law) and proportionality were also involved. The most important arguments rested on Articles 12 and 33. Article 12 guarantees to all West Germans the right "freely to choose their trade, occupation, or profession." Article

33, paragraph 2, proclaims that "every German shall be equally eligible for any public office according to his aptitude, qualifications, and professional achievements." But Article 33, paragraph 4, provides that the "status, service, and loyalty" of public servants is to be "governed by public law."

Several constitutional issues were before the court. Is employment in the public service a *trade* or *profession* within the meaning of Article 12? Does Article 33 imply a limitation on the reach of Article 12? Does the term *loyalty* used in Article 33 fall within a reasonable definition of the "aptitude" required under the same article? Does Article 33 confer an entitlement to public service employment or merely a privilege? Is the principle of proportionality violated if limitations upon the right to enter the public service cannot be shown to further a compelling state purpose? Should Article 33 be broadly construed—and thus supportive of the complainant—in the light of Article 3, paragraph 3, affirming that "no person may be prejudiced or favored because of his ... political opinions"? Or should Article 33 be narrowly construed—and thus damaging to the complainant—in the light of other constitutional doctrines requiring the protection and active support of the "free democratic basic order"?

After weighing and balancing these considerations, the court sustained the decree's validity but found fault with its administration.[55] The principle of *Rechsstaatlichkeit*, said the court, limits the discretion of appointing authorities. Procedural guarantees must be observed. These include the right of the applicant to be precisely informed of the damaging evidence in his file and to a fair hearing, including representation by counsel and the right to rebut evidence against him. The court also held that membership in an organization with anticonstitutional aims is a valid consideration in determining the loyalty of an applicant but cautioned that such membership alone would not be sufficient to exclude a person from the pub-

lic service. Other facts must also be present to substantiate a judgment of disloyalty. With the situation of the complainant in mind, the court rebuked state authorities for drawing inferences of disloyalty from statements made and activities carried out in the heat of emotion during the applicant's student days. Finally, three dissenting justices maintained that, as applied to the complainant, the decree did amount to a *Berufsverbot*, since lack of in-service training would effectively bar him from a career in the private practice of law. For this reason, they held, the legal educational requirement of in-service training with the State should not be regarded as public service within the meaning of Article 33, although they conceded that this training period could not be used to promote anticonstitutional goals.[56]

The political response to the court's decision was both supportive and swift. Over the opposition of the CDU-CSU, the Bundestag passed a resolution affirming the principles laid down in the decision. The *Länder*, however, continued to follow different policies. By the mid-1980s most states controlled by the SPD were no longer routinely screening applicants for their loyalty, while CDU-controlled states kept up their erstwhile vigilance with varying degrees of intensity. At the federal level politicians grew weary of the continuing controversy, and Willy Brandt publicly expressed his regret for originally supporting the Loyalty Decree. In 1979, the ruling coalition (SPD-FDP) rescinded the Decree and adopted new and less stringent guidelines applicable to federal civil servants. The restoration of the CDU-CSU-FDP coalition in 1982 led to a slight increase in the screening of applicants for federal positions, but by that time the public salience of the civil servant loyalty issue had declined. The letter of the law still demanded loyalty, on and off duty, from all public employees, but with the embers of the cold war beginning to expire in the late 1980s, the FRG's liberal democracy seemed far less endangered by extremists than it had been in the 1970s. Civil libertarians and the proponents of the FRG's *militant democracy* continued, of course, to disagree over the legitimacy of the original decree and its long-range impact upon freedom and democracy in the FRG.

THE POLITICS OF EDUCATION

In the 1960s older Germans were aware of the fundamental social, economic, and political changes that had taken place since the 1920s. But when they looked at the schools, they saw the same system through which they had passed some 40 years earlier. The four-year common elementary school, a Weimar Republic institution, was at the bottom of the pyramid. Then came the tripartite structure of secondary schools (briefly described in Section A). Each level offered a different curriculum and played a distinct educational role. The second-level primary school trained its pupils for vocational schools and handicrafts; the intermediate school channeled its students into technical schools and middle-level jobs; and the academic high school (*Gymnasium*) prepared its students for the university and the learned professions. The teaching profession was similarly stratified as the content and duration of training, together with examinations and certification procedures, were dependent on the particular level of school for which the teacher was preparing. General education was kept institutionally separate from vocational schools. Finally, at the top, was the university, still largely an elite research-oriented institution based on the traditional Humboldt model of the nineteenth century. This system was subjected to the fierce crossfire of several opposing groups in the late 1960s.

Secondary Education

When the SPD came to power in 1969, it placed educational reform at the top of the federal government's social agenda. The reforms proposed were advanced under the slogans of modernization and democratization. Essentially these reforms sought to loosen the tripartite structure by combining general and vocational education, by introducing a diversified curriculum of scientific and technical education around a common core of academically oriented studies in all schools, and by instituting courses of study that would keep professional options open for as long as possible. Systems of advancement were proposed to encourage many more students than in the past to qualify for admission to the university. The federal government also favored the eventual adoption of the integrated comprehensive school as the model of secondary education in the future. Its educational policy seemed clearly informed by an egalitarian vision of a "classless" common public school oriented toward personal growth and emancipation.[57]

At the elementary and secondary levels, the government's program achieved only token success. Federalism, interest groups, and sharply divided opinions about the nature and purpose of education conspired to block the implementation of any uniform system in the FRG. Under the Basic Law, educational policy is the primary responsibility of the *Länder*, an independence zealously guarded by local educational officials. *Länder* controlled by Social Democrats have been more sympathetic to basic structural reform than those controlled by Christian Democrats. By 1978, long-lasting SPD and CDU governments had created, respectively, 135 and 19 comprehensive schools, whereas other *Länder* (Baden-Württemberg and North Rhine-Westphalia) had created 65. Together, they enrolled a mere 2.09 percent of all students attending primary and secondary schools. But even these schools differed in their practices and approaches to education.

The lack of centralized control over educational planning in the FGR furnished the context for strong interest-group support of the status quo. Opposing teachers' organizations allied to trade unions or *Land* educational bureaucracies fought to a virtual stand-off; Catholic teachers in denominational schools resisted what they perceived as a threat to educational pluralism; parents themselves were mobilizing to oppose or to temper educational experimentation. Clearly, educational reformers had overestimated the public's desire for change. Even the SPD's ardor for reform cooled in the 1970s after several of the party's *Land* education ministers had failed to marshal adequate support for their proposals. The SPD could advance its reform proposals only at the "risk of alienating just those segments of the white-collar and professional classes which [it] needed most to expand [its basis of electoral support'."[58] And, as recently as 1978, civic pressure groups in North Rhine-Westphalia took advantage of a popular referendum to defeat a school proposal, forcing that *Land's* SPD-FDP government to shelve its master plan for comprehensive schools.

School reform also foundered on serious disagreement over the purpose of education and the locus of responsibility for the educational enterprise. Yet, for all the debate, considerable pioneering was going on within the system, and many partial reforms have been accomplished. While the future of the comprehensive school remains uncertain, the iron curtain that once separated the three schools in the tripartite system has been lifted. There is now the possibility of lateral movement between schools, and within each level curricula have been expanded to accommodate the different needs and abilities of students. Entry into the *Gymnasium* and intermediate school is now easier for socially and culturally deprived children. Several *Länder* have introduced compensatory education for these children. Several have established foreign-language training and a ninth compulsory year of learning in the second-level primary system. Baden-Württemberg has successfully experimented with vocational academies, whose combination of practical and theoretical training at a relatively advanced level makes it a genuine alternative to the university. Finally, the increasing permeability of the system has resulted in several routes of access to the university.

Higher Education

Problem The German system of higher education was hit by a major crisis in the 1960s. Traditionally an elite institution hierarchically organized around research institutes monopolized by full professors, the typical German university was designed to handle relatively small numbers of students. This structure was wholly unprepared to accommodate, or properly train, the rising number of students qualifying for university admission in the 1960s. The high postwar birth rate and reforms in secondary education drove the number of university students to a high of 253,000 in 1965, nearly double the 1955 total of 130,000. By 1980, the student population would surge to a staggering 1 million. The building of additional universities in the 1960s failed to relieve the pressure on higher education. Modeled after the old universities, they introduced few changes in academic governance, curriculum, or teaching methods. The result was to deepen the frustration of students, teaching assistants, and academic reformers.

Aggravating the crisis was the social discrimination reflected in the composition of the student body. As late as 1966, students from working-class families represented a mere 5.7 percent of all university students. By 1980 this figure would reach 20 percent. Yet, despite the increasing inflow of students from all social sectors, the FRG ranked substantially lower than some other industrial nations in the proportion of its youth enrolled in the universities.[59] Consequently, as the 1970s approached, many political, educational, and business leaders were beginning to ask whether the system would continue to meet the demands of an advanced and increasingly diversified political economy.

Reforms The need for reform in West German higher education has long been recognized, but the barriers to change have been high and formidable. One such barrier is the traditional autonomy of the German university. Another is state sovereignty in the field of education. Prior to 1969, reforms national in scope depended entirely on cooperation among the *Länder*. The Standing Conference of State Cultural Ministers (KMK), established in 1949, has been a dominant influence in setting higher education policy. But its conservative leadership, bound by instructions from *Länder* governments and working under a rule of unanimity, served mainly as a block to fundamental reform. Not until the founding of the Science Council (WR) in 1957—an independent national advisory board organized jointly by the states and the federal government—was serious planning for the future undertaken. The work of this group and the German Education Council (BR)—also a joint federal-state body set up in 1965—laid the basis of a larger federal role in educational planning.

The year 1969 was the turning point in the shift of power over educational matters to the Federation. Amendments to the Basic Law recognized a federal role in educational planning and the promotion of scientific research (Article 91b) and authorized the Federation to enact "skeleton provisions [framework law] concerning... the general principles governing higher education" (Article 75a). Shortly thereafter the Federal Ministry of Education and Science was created, followed in 1970 by the establishment of the Federal-State Commission for Educational Planning (BLK). Both agencies soon developed into cogent instruments of reform, generating studies and reports that would form the basis of the Higher Education Framework Act of 1976. Lastly, the Federal Constitutional Court assumed a critically important role in laying down uniform national rules over university governance and admission procedure.

As the policy changes described show, higher education since 1960 "has been transformed from an elite to a mass system."[60] This rather sudden transformation contrasts sharply with the slow pace of change that has occurred in other domestic policy areas. The decentralized character of the FRG's political system, together with the widespread representation of private interests in the councils of government, imposes severe limits upon the capacity of the parliamentary parties to bring about major change in domestic policy. However, as Peter Katzenstein argues, higher education proved to be more open to general societal pressures and partisan politics, in part because of the relative disinterest of "parapublic" institutions.[61] In addition, the political parties manifested a common interest in educational reform, the CDU-CSU because of its concern for economic growth and efficiency, the SPD because of its interest in promoting social equality.

At the same time, federalism and particular interests continued to exert their influence over the course of educational policy. The effective implementation of federal policy still depends on *Land*-enabling legislation, and much room remains for variation and experimentation at the local level. In addition, several nongovernmental interests with strong *Land* links are represented in the national educational policy-making process. On the academic side, the influential West German Rectors Conference (WRK) and various professorial organizations, especially the CDU- leaning Union for Academic Freedom, have resisted major changes in university governance. Outside of the academy, unions and employer groups have had a hand in drafting state-enabling legislation. Indeed, the pattern of interest-group representation prevalent in so many areas of German social and political life is duplicated in education. For example, the Permanent National Education Commission established by the Federal Framework Act of 1976 provides for a 26-member body consisting of 11 *Land* representatives; 11 university members, including professors, assistant professors, students, and staff; 2 federal delegates; and 1 representative each for labor and management.

Policy   Quantitatively, the reforms in higher education were most impressive. Student enrollment quadrupled between 1960 and 1985, and nearly one quarter of those students were the sons and daughters of working-class parents. Meanwhile, the *Länder* reorganized and expanded existing institutions of higher education. "Engineering schools revamped and broadened their curriculum and were accredited as universities. A new stratum of junior faculty was hired to restore student-teacher ratios to the levels of the 1950s. The number of university 'assistants' increased from 9000 in 1960 to 28,000 in 1971. State governments founded 18 new universities, among them Bochum and Regensburg."[62] Finally, federal and state policy makers agreed to create "comprehensive" universities for the purpose of "combin[ing] theoretical and applied work in new ways."[63]

Qualitative reforms were equally impressive. Reforms instituted most faithfully in the new universities included curriculum revisions, standardized programs of study, rationalized use of plant and equipment, accelerated degree programs, and the adoption of new administrative structures. At some older universities the compartmentalized structure of formerly autonomous institutes gave way to coordinated and cooperative programs of study. Even the definition of research was changing. An older notion identified exclusively with professional activity leading to the discovery of new knowledge was being supplemented by a more student-oriented emphasis on acquisition of knowledge that is new for the individual. Not surprisingly, reforms in university decision making have sought to define more precisely the roles of professors, assistant professors, research assistants, students, and staff as one means of more effectively integrating teaching and research. The power of these various groups, together with policies affecting university admissions, has been extremely controversial and the subject of considerable litigation.

University Governance and Admissions   The judicial determination of national education policy was even more pervasive in the area of admission standards and procedures. The flood of students into the universities in the 1960s led to the imposition of a numerus clausus on admission to overcrowded fields. In its unanimous decision of 18 July 1972, the Federal Constitutional Court held that a numerical limit on admission to given fields of study (in this case law and medicine) violated the right of West Germans under Article 12 (Basic Law) "freely to choose their trade, occupation, or profession."[64] In so ruling, the Court left the *Länder* with one of two choices: either expand facilities to accommodate qualified students or define more clearly the criteria and priorities of admission policy. In response to the court's decision the Standing Conference of State Cultural Ministers established the Central Office for University Admissions and negotiated a detailed interstate compact on admission criteria. In what many commentators regarded as another example of excessive judicial activism in the field of education, the Constitutional Court nullified some of these criteria, too, and made clear that it was prepared to order the admission of any qualified student who could prove that university facilities were not being fully utilized.[65]

These decisions prompted Parliament to pass the Federal Higher Education Framework Act of 1976 establishing uniform guidelines for, inter alia, academic administration, research and teaching, planning and development, and admission procedures. In the sensitive area of admissions the Central Admission Office, in cooperation with the states, formulated revised criteria pursuant to the act's guidelines, including specific quotas for hardship cases, veterans, foreign students, and persons willing to enter designated fields. The remaining students were to be selected on the basis of aptitude and achievement and according to their length of time on the Central Admission Office's waiting list. These experiments continued as the decade ended amid expectations that the pressure on universities would be substantially eased (owing to low birth rates in the 1960s) by the mid-1980s. Finally, in 1984, a new conservative coalition government sought to reorient educational reform in the direction of greater excellence and competition among institutions of higher learning as well as more emphasis upon the critical importance of research universities. In revising the Framework Act the new government strengthened the position of chaired professors and shifted, partly in response to limited funds and tighter budgets, the system of student aid from grants to loans.

CODETERMINATION

The issue of *codetermination* exemplifies the usual pattern of politics and policy in postwar Germany. This pattern is largely one of consultation and accommodation within and between state agencies, private groups, and political parties, particularly those in the governing coalition. The corporatist strain in German public life has institutionalized this process of consultation, in this case between interests representing labor and management within and without the political parties. The filtering of this process through the FRG's decentralized political system means that a large degree of consensus is necessary before any real movement in public policy can be achieved. This is why policy change in the FRG has been aptly described as *incremental* rather than *large scale*, even in the face of major shifts in electoral politics.

The politics of codetermination support the incrementalist thesis. First of all, the participation of workers in industrial decision making has a long history in Germany. In the early 1840s workers were already, even in the absence of unions, demanding a voice in shaping the conditions of their labor, a "right" that narrowly missed being incorporated into the Frankfurt Constitution of 1848. Thereafter,

however, some employers voluntarily accepted proposals to allow workers to establish factory committees to advise management on labor-related matters. These proposals were legally recognized in 1891 with the passage of the Labor Protection Act (*Arbeitsschutzgesetz*). However, the establishment of factory committees remained at the discretion of employers.

The Auxiliary Service Act of 1916 (*Hilfsdienstgesetz*), a wartime measure that set the stage for further developments in worker representation, was another example of labor-management cooperation. The act created committees of workers and salaried employees in all establishments that were vital to the war effort and that employed more than 50 persons. Yet, the committees were advisory in character and could be ignored by the employer. It was not until 1920, with the passage of the Work Council Act (*Betriebsrätegesetz*), that employers were required to listen to, even if they did not accept, the proposals or complaints of their employees. The act, now extended to all concerns, both public and private, with at least 20 employees, authorized workers and white-collar staff employees to elect councils empowered to lay their recommendations on social and financial matters before the employer. Employers could still reject the councils' advice, but workers at least had a voice in factory management. Finally, in 1922, with the passage of the Supervisory Board Act (*Aufsichtsratsgesetz*), the voice was upgraded to a vote. Now, for the first time in German history, employees were entitled to at least one representative on factory management boards. Supported by a large cross-section of the public—liberals, Catholics, trade unions, and the business community—the work councils became the main pillar of industrial democracy—and peace—in Germany.

Needless to say, with the coming of Hitler, the work councils, while continuing to exist, lost their vitality as Nazi legislation strengthened the hand of management. In 1945, right after the war, the work councils were revived. Under Allied Control Council supervision each *Land* was authorized to provide for the reestablishment of work councils modeled on the Work Council Act of 1920. The *Land* statutes differed significantly from one another. Some conferred on work councils only a right to economic information; others limited codetermination to social and personnel decisions; and others granted councils a substantial participatory role in determining basic company policies relating to production and operating methods.[66]

Current codetermination policy traces its origin to the pattern that developed in the iron and steel industry in the British zone of occupation. Trade union pressure combined with the Christian social outlook of the young CDU and the strong pro-labor orientation of the SPD to bring about the Codetermination Act of 1951. This act provided for the equal representation of workers on the supervisory boards of the mining, iron, and steel industries. The supervisory board was to consist of five employee representatives, five shareholder representatives, and an eleventh "neutral" person.[67]

Over the course of the next 25 years, labor struggled to achieve in other industries the kind of parity that the 1951 act established in iron and steel. In 1952, however, parliament enacted the Works Constitution Act (*Betriebsverfassungsgesetz*), establishing one-third employee representation on the management boards of all private industries employing between 500 and 2000 workers, a principle that a 1965 statute extended to the public sector. These work councils participate with management in determining wage structures, working hours, employment, transfer and dismissal policies, training and welfare programs, and grievance procedures.

Additional years of consultation between labor and management and mutual adjustments between the established parties resulted in the Works Constitution Act of 1972, which replaced the 1952 act. It authorizes every factory or business with more than five employees to elect a work council. Councillors are elected in a secret ballot by all employees of the firm, their main function being to bargain with plant managers over issues not dealt with within collective bargaining agreements.

Finally, in 1976, after four more years of struggle and compromise among the various parliamentary fractions, the Bundestag passed the Codetermination Act (*Mitbestimmungsgesetz*). The overwhelming parliamentary majority that voted for the act underscored the consensus achieved over several years of negotiation. The act extended the principle of numerical parity to all enterprises with more than 2000 employees, affecting about 7 million workers in more than 500 firms. It provides for 12- to 20-member supervisory boards, depending on the size of the plant, with an equal number of shareholder representatives and representatives from the work force, the latter to include delegations elected separately by blue-collar, white-collar, and managerial staff. Under the statute the board chairperson and vice-chairperson are elected by a two-thirds majority of the board membership. Barring a two-thirds vote, the vice-chairperson is elected by a majority of the employee members and the chairperson by a majority of the shareholder members. Decisions of the supervisory board are taken by a majority of votes cast. In case of a tie, the chairperson is authorized to cast the deciding vote. The unions were not entirely pleased with the allocation of seats on the board or with the provision that allows the chairperson—usually a shareholder—to break a tie vote, but it gives them a significant foothold in the industrial decision-making process.

Not long after the act's passage on 4 May 1976, several industrial firms and employer associations, together with the German Association for the Protection of Security Holdings, filed a constitutional complaint in the Federal Constitutional Court challenging the law's validity. They charged (1) that the equal representation of workers in company decision making violated the right to property under Article 14, (2) that enforced parity between stockholders and employees infringed both the right of association and the right to form associations under Article 9, and (3) that the act infringes the entrepreneurial freedom to choose a trade or profession under Article 12. The complainants also charged that the principle of parity in managerial decision making would be the first step to equal representation in the actual management of industrial firms.

In its landmark decision of 1 March 1979, the Federal Constitutional Court sustained the validity of the statute in a guarded opinion.[68] Reemphasizing its teaching in older decisions that the Basic Law does not prescribe a particular economic system, the court rejected the arguments of the business community on the ground that the act does not constitute "an inadmissible interference with the self-determination of companies in regard to their organization and decision-making processes." In short, the court suggested that the statutory scheme left intact the core of associational autonomy as guaranteed by the constitution. But the court did hedge a little, indicating that if the worse fears of the business community were to be realized in the future, a constitutional issue of critical importance could then clearly arise. This seemed to be the court's way of admonishing parliament against bolder initiatives that would extend the principle of codetermination into the actual organization and operation of private firms.

In its present form, however, the court has suggested that codetermination is a legitimate application of the constitutional ideal of a "social federal state" (Article 20) based on law. "The connection between the demand for codetermination and the principle of the state governed by the rule of law," writes one commentator, "may be made clear by reference to the fact that those employees in the Common Market who strive for the realization of economic democracy are also striving for greater freedom, equality and substantive justice." He concluded, as the court implied,

that "[c]odetermination may be considered as a means of the partial realization of this aim, although the 'economic democracy' is capable of different interpretations."[69]

FOREIGN POLICY AND THE ROAD TO UNITY

The "German Problem" and Ostpolitik

One aspect of the "German problem" was the simple yet age-old one of how to define Germany. This problem remained at the center of East-West conflict for two decades following World War II. It was a problem involving the FRG's relationship to the German Democratic Republic (GDR) and Eastern Europe. West German rearmament within the North Atlantic Treaty Organization (NATO), coupled with the refusal under a succession of Christian Democratic governments to recognize the Oder-Neisse line as a permanent boundary between Poland and Germany, was viewed by the Soviet Union as a dangerous threat to peace in Central Europe. The city of Berlin represented still another component of the German problem. Cleft by concrete and barbed wire, and later by the infamous Wall, the city had become the most poignant living symbol of German separation and East-West confrontation.

There clearly could be no resolution of the German problem without a relaxation of tension in Central Europe. Moscow was the key to any such resolution. It is significant that both Adenauer and Brandt journeyed to the Soviet Union—the former in 1955, the latter in 1970—in search of "normalized" relations between Bonn and Moscow. For Adenauer, however, normalization meant the reestablishment of diplomatic relations with the Soviet Union, which he accomplished, and the reunification of Germany, which he failed to achieve. In his Moscow talks he spoke of the "abnormality" of Germany's division, leaving his Soviet hosts with the message that "there can be no real security in Europe without the restoration of German unity." A decade and a half later, with

Germany still divided, Willy Brandt appeared before a Soviet television audience, redefining *normalization*. He announced that "it is now time to reconstitute our relationship to the East upon the basis of the unrestricted, reciprocal renunciation of force, proceeding from the existing political situation in Europe."

Brandt's Eastern policy was designed to achieve this result. The cornerstone of the new policy was the Soviet-West German Treaty on the renunciation of the use of force, signed in Moscow in August 1970. The Warsaw Treaty, signed in November of the same year, rounded out the foundation of détente. Essentially, these treaties recognized existing boundaries in Europe, including the Oder-Neisse line separating the GDR and Poland. Another stone in Brandt's rising edifice of détente was the 1971 Quadripartite Agreement on Berlin. In fact, Brandt conditioned Bonn's ratification of the Moscow and Warsaw treaties upon progress toward settlement of the Berlin question. Pledging to settle all their disputes by peaceful means, the four powers reaffirmed their individual and joint responsibility for Berlin. While the Soviet Union acknowledged the special ties between West Berlin and the FRG, the Western Allies deferred to the Soviet contention that West Berlin was not "a constituent part of the Federal Republic and not to be governed by it."

The capstone of détente was the Basic Treaty between East and West Germany, signed in December 1972. The FRG and GDR both agreed to develop normal relations with each other on the basis of equal rights. The concept of "two German states in one nation," which the FRG urged on the GDR, was conspicuously left out of the treaty. Instead, the right of both German states to "territorial integrity" and "self-determination" was affirmed, along with an agreement "to refrain from the threat or use of force." In addition, the two states agreed that "neither...can represent the other in the international spheres or act on its behalf." In supplementary protocols both states also agreed to settle their frontier problems, to improve trade relations, and to cooperate in scientific, technological, medical, cultural, athletic, and environmental fields.

Gorbachev and *Glasnost*

The advent of Gorbachev and the associated policies of *glasnost* (openness) and *perestroika* (reform) placed East-West relations in a new light and encouraged many Germans to think once again about the prospects of eventual reunification. GDR leaders, however, remained adamant in their view of the Basic Treaty as a step toward a fully sovereign and independent GDR—an interpretation the FRG has never accepted. Unlike Poland and Hungary and the Soviet Union itself, the GDR refused to move toward democracy or free markets. The hardliners in charge of the regime—most of them old men—brooked no opposition to the socialist system of their creation. By 1989, however, as thousands of young GDR citizens fled to the FRG by way of Hungary in search of freedom and employment, GDR leaders seemed to be standing alone, isolated in their own backyard. They accused Hungary of violating various legal treaties and denounced the FRG for encouraging the exodus, but these charges were seen for what they were: feeble attempts to hide the fragility of a regime deeply in trouble in the face of a "new order" emerging in Eastern Europe.

The GDR was impaled on the horns of an excruciating dilemma. It could either loosen up the regime and allow the free movement of its people in and out of the country or continue on its present course. The first option would lead to greater contact between east and west Germans and intensify the desire for reunification. The second option—keeping a tight grip on its people—would lead to another crisis of legitimacy and to the continued flight of its most productive citizens. With the collapse of the hardline Communist regime in October 1989 a hastily reassembled government under younger and more pragmatic leadership chose the first option. In the following weeks, events unfolded with dizzying speed, surprising and confounding even close observers of German affairs. By the end of the year the Communist party had disavowed its leading role, promised to hold free elections in the months ahead, and exposed the corruption of its long-time leaders as an increasingly angry and outspoken citizenry demanded their prosecution. In the meantime, the Brandenburg Gate flew open, GDR citizens waved FRG flags in the streets, and East and West German leaders began to talk about a new relationship against the backdrop of Chancellor Helmut Kohl's controversial ten-point plan for German reunification.

The Progress and Politics of German Unity

The path to German unity is a fascinating tale. On the one hand, the story seems to show that the forces of history, once unleashed, cannot be stopped. On the other hand, unity would not have come about without the cooperation of the Allied Powers, especially the United States and the Soviet Union, and the intense negotiations between the GDR and FRG. Although the FRG held most of the trump cards in these negotiations, the GDR managed to extract significant promises from the FRG, including some changes in the Basic Law. The negotiations between the GDR and FRG, on the one hand, and Britain, France, the Soviet Union, and the United States, on the other, did not proceed on separate tracks. They were conducted—in coordinated simultaneous fashion—over many months; hence, the common reference to the *two-plus-four* talks. This mix of international and domestic politics, with its interplay of constitutional law and public policy, made the new Germany possible.

Four landmarks pointed the way to reunification. These are the State Treaty on Monetary, Economic, and Social Union (18 May 1990), the All-German Election Treaty (3 August 1990), the Unity Treaty (31 August 1990), and the Treaty on the Final Settlement with

Respect to Germany (12 September 1990). The GDR and the FRG negotiated the first three treaties, but often in consultation with the Allies; the last was the product mainly of the two-plus-four negotiations. Many of the events leading up to these treaties, including the opening of the Berlin Wall on 9 November 1989 and the East German election of 18 March 1990, have already been recounted in this chapter. (See Feature 4.6 for other major events on the path to German unity.) What has not been discussed is the debate in Germany over the various methods by which unity might have been achieved. This debate is important because it is bound up with the question of when and under what circumstances a people should give to itself a new constitution. Whether a reunited Germany should have a new constitution was a hotly contested issue in the early stages of the reunification movement.

Reconstituting the German People

The Basic Law itself provided an authoritative basis for a new constitution. After all, it was originally framed as a transitional document pending Germany's reunification. Together with the Preamble, Articles 23 and 146 also emphasized the document's impermanence. Article 23, discussed briefly at the outset of this chapter, provides that the Basic Law shall apply to "other parts of Germany" upon "their accession." Unity, as already noted, was achieved by this quick and easy procedure. Article 146, however, declared that the Basic Law "shall cease to be in force on the day on which a constitution adopted by a free decision of the German people comes into force."

Reunification pursuant to Article 146 would have meant (1) the dissolution of both the GDR and FRG governments, (2) the framing of a new constitution, presumably by an elected constitutional convention, (3) ratification by the electorate or perhaps by the state legislatures, and (4) the election and for-

---

Feature 4.6 **Path to German Unity**

1989

July–September	GDR citizens flee to the FRG by way of Hungary.
October 9	100,000 persons demonstrate in Leipzig to the chant, "We are the people."
October 18	Honecker removed as head of GDR.
November 7	GDR government resigns after 1 million persons demonstrate in Berlin.
November 9	Berlin Wall is breached.
November 28	Chancellor Kohl announces a 10-point program for unity.
December 1	GDR Constitution amended to end the SED's monopoly of power.

1990

March 18	First free election in GDR. Overwhelming victory for parties allied with CDU.
April 12	GDR legislature elects first democratic government. Lothar de Maizière elected Prime Minister.
May 18	State treaty on monetary, social, and economic union.
July 22	GDR legislature reestablishes its five constituent states (Länder).
August 3	All-German election treaty.
August 31	Unity Treaty signed.
September 12	Two Plus Four Treaty signed.
October 3	Day of German unity. GDR ceases to exist.
October 4	First all-German legislature meets in the Berlin Reichstag building.
October 24	Five eastern states elect new parliaments.
December 2	First all-German Bundestag election.

---

mation of a new government under the terms of the new constitution. The process may not have occurred precisely in this sequence, but it would surely have been a long and cumbersome affair, not to mention the divisiveness that would have been caused by reopening constitutional issues resolved when the Basic Law was drafted in 1949.

One can understand why some Germans might have preferred this route to unity. After all, here was a chance for Germany to make a fresh start and, equally significant, what could be more democratic than for *all* the German people to give themselves a new constitution in free, self-determination. What a "free deci-

sion of the German people" would have meant, however, was never clear. Debate on this issue might also have resulted in another divisive battle over the method of selecting the constitution makers and of ratifying the constitution, matters on which the Basic Law is silent. Then, too, we need to recall that the organizations that started the revolution in the GDR—such as New Forum, Democracy Now, and the Initiative for Peace and Human Rights—did not set out to unify Germany. Rather, the Central Round Table to which these and other opposition groups belonged wanted to democratize the GDR and retain the humane values of socialism. The Round Table even drafted a

Brandenburg Gate after reunification.

new GDR constitution and, like the Basic Law, it looked toward eventual unity but saw it as a long-term objective.[70]

Chancellor Kohl also started slowly. In November 1989, following the tumbling of the Berlin Wall, he unveiled his famous Ten-Point Plan for Germany's eventual union. He envisioned the development of a *contractual community* in which the two Germanys would establish confederative structures leading first to social, monetary, and economic union and eventually, perhaps in a few years, to political union. Events, however, overtook him as well as the East German Round Table. The "bloodless coup" occurred on 18 March 1990, when East Germans voted in their first free election since Hitler was named chancellor in 1933. Unity *now* was their unmistakable message. Fired up, and with Chancellor Kohl

at the controls, the "unity train" roared toward its destination. Along the way, one could hear the voices of the Round Table in the GDR and those of the "unity skeptics" in the FRG, but they were scarcely audible over the noise of the speeding train.

The State Treaty

The State Treaty united the social, economic, and monetary systems of east and west.[71] (See Feature 4.7) It effectively extended the FRG's social market economy eastward, installing in all of Germany an economy based on private ownership, competition, and the free movement of goods and services. As of 2 July 1990, the West German D-Mark became the official currency of the GDR. Under the terms of the treaty, "[w]ages, salaries, grants, pensions,

---

Feature 4.7 **Selected Provisions of the State Treaty**

The law of the GDR will be modelled on the principles of a free, democratic federal and social order governed by the rule of law and be guided by the legal regime of the European Communities (General Guidelines, A.I.1).

Regulations which commit individuals or state institutions, including the legislature and the judiciary, to a socialist system of law, a socialist body politic, the aims and targets of centralized economic control and planning, a socialist sense of justice, socialist convictions, the convictions of individual groups or parties, socialist morality, or comparable notions, will no longer be applied (General Guidelines, A.I.2).

The issuance of coin shall be the exclusive right of the Federal Republic of Germany (Article 10 [13]).

The GDR shall harmonize the provisions governing the promotion of environmental protection with those of the FRG (Article 16 [5]).

The GDR shall introduce a system of unemployment insurance including employment promotion which shall be in line with the provisions of the Employment Promotion Act of the FRG (Article 19).

---

rents and leases as well as other recurring payments shall be converted at a rate of one [east German] to one [west German mark]." All other claims and assets were to be converted at a rate of two to one. One effect of the currency union was to increase the importance of Germany's central bank, already renowned for its control over monetary policy in the FRG.[72] The bank would now take responsibility for all of Germany and sorely test its capacity to fight inflation in the face of price rises that were surely to occur from the transfer of billions of D-Marks into the east.

The State Treaty covered other areas such as intra-German and foreign trade, agriculture, environmental protection, social and health insurance, pension plans, budgetary planning, revenue administration, and tax policy. For each of these areas, the treaty required the GDR to adopt laws consistent with policies prevailing in the FRG. In some instances, however, transitional arrangements were worked out to ease the pain of the legal and structural changes that the GDR would have to make. One of these temporary arrangements was

the establishment of an arbitration tribunal to resolve GDR-FRG disputes arising under the Treaty in the event that they could not be settled by negotiation.

The All-German Election Treaty

The GDR election of 18 March 1990 set the stage for the all-German election of 2 December 1990. As noted earlier, the election resulted in an impressive victory for the CDU-led Alliance for Germany and thus for German unity. The new People's Chamber went on to create a grand coalition consisting of the Alliance for Germany, the SPD, and the Federation of Free Democrats under the leadership of Lothar de Maizière (CDU). It was this coalition that negotiated the unity treaties with Bonn's CDU-FDP coalition government.

Before unity could be achieved, however, the contracting parties had to agree on holding a national election. The GDR's voting system differed from the FRG's. First, each voter had only one vote in a system of pure proportional representation, in contrast to the

Chancellor Helmut Kohl (left) and Prime Minister Lothar de Maizière (right).

FRG's two ballot system. Second, there was no 5 percent threshold; to gain one of the 400 seats in the People's Chamber, a party needed to win only 0.25 percent of the vote. Finally, political movements such as New Forum could put up candidates, whereas the FRG allowed only political parties to enter candidates in federal elections.

GDR–FRG negotiations sought to compromise these differences. Prime Minister de Maizière wanted to drop the national 5 percent rule so that organizations like Alliance 90, which received only 2.9 percent of the vote on 18 March would be included in the all-German Bundestag. He regarded the representation of such groups as a matter of political morality in the light of the crucial role they played in the GDR's peaceful revolution. Finally, with the support of the SPD in both governments, an agreement was reached. The GDR relented on the 5 percent rule, but the two sides worked out a so-called piggyback arrangement that would permit smaller parties or groups in the GDR to field candidates in alliance with other, larger parties in the west.[73] This plan, however, favored some small parties at the expense of others. For example, the strength of Bavaria's CSU would carry its sister party, the GDR's DSU (German Social Union)

into the Bundestag, whereas the old Communist SED—now dressed up as the PDS—was unlikely to find a willing partner in the FRG to help it win the needed 5 percent of the national vote.

Upon the initiative of the PDS, Greens, and far-right Republicans, however, the Federal Constitutional Court struck down the agreement, holding that it discriminated against these parties.[74] The unanimous decision also invalidated the 5 percent rule as applied to them, whereupon the court suggested a plan that in its view would be more consistent with the principle of electoral equality. It advised the Bundestag to apply the 5 percent clause separately in East and West Germany and to allow small groups in the GDR to form joint tickets to help them over the 5 percent hurdle. Without further ado, the Bundestag went along with the Court's suggestion. The amended statute allowed some of these groups to win seats in the Twelfth Bundestag.

The Unity Treaty

The Unity Treaty—a massive document consisting of 433 printed pages—is the historic agreement that provided for the GDR's accession to the FRG and the application of the Basic Law to all of Germany. Its 45 articles, annexes, and special provisions touch almost every aspect of German public policy. The Treaty's "Special Provisions on the Conversion to Federal Law" appear in 19 chapters that deal with the laws, procedures, and institutions subject to the jurisdiction of the various federal ministries. While extending FRG law immediately to numerous policy areas in the eastern *Länder*, these special provisions also contain transitional and interim measures that seek to accommodate the special interests of or conditions in the ex-GDR.

Constitutional Amendments The Unity Treaty amended several provisions of the Basic Law. First, the preamble was amended to delete all references to the goal of reunification, for "Germans in [the sixteen *Länder*] have [now] achieved the unity and freedom of Germany in free self-determination." This new language effectively freezes Germany's present borders, making it legally impossible for Germany to lay claim to other territories lost as a result of World War II. Second, and to the same end, the treaty repealed Article 23—the very provision under which the GDR acceded to the FRG. In short, no "other parts of Germany" are left to be incorporated by accession. Third, the treaty added the following italicized words to Article 146: "This Basic Law, *which is valid for the entire German people following the achievement of the unity and freedom of Germany,* shall cease to be in force on the day on which a constitution adopted by a free decision of the German people comes into force." Fourth, Article 135a was amended to relieve the FRG of certain liabilities incurred by the GDR or its legal entities. Finally, the treaty changed the number of votes allocated to the states in the Bundesrat under the terms of Article 51.

Amending the Basic Law by treaty was an unusual procedure and arguably in violation of Article 79 (1), which declares that "the Basic Law can be amended only by statutes. . . ." Despite the fact that the treaty was passed by a two-thirds vote of the Bundestag and Bundesrat, two-thirds being required for amendments to the Basic Law, several groups, backed by a former Justice of the Federal Constitutional Court, brought suit, claiming that each amendment in the Unity Treaty should have been the subject of a separate statute, allowing for extended debate on each proposal. (Certain refugee groups were particularly disturbed over amendments that sealed Germany's eastern borders.) The Constitutional Court, however, rejected the complaint. In the light of the Basic Law's overriding commitment to reunification, the court ruled, the government enjoyed broad procedural discretion in choosing the means to this goal.[75]

In addition to the above amendments, the Unity Treaty inserted a new article—Article 143—into the Basic Law (see Feature 4.8). The new article allowed the all-German government to deal flexibly with issues that might otherwise have slowed down or even stopped the unity train. Abortion, property rights, and inter-governmental relations were among these issues. The eastern *Länder*, for example, were unable to abide by the revenue-sharing provisions of the Basic Law or other obligations growing out of its scheme of federal-state relations. Allowing the east to deviate from these provisions was a practical necessity. Moreover, no constitutional obstacle threatened to block the deviation. In any event, the Basic Law's federal-state provisions, especially Sections VIIIa (Joint Tasks) and X (Revenue Sharing), will probably be amended in the light of fiscal and economic developments in the east. Indeed, the Unity Treaty commits German legislative bodies to consider changing the Basic Law's provisions on federal-state relations by 1994.

Abortion The deviation clause of Article 143 (1), however, is another matter. Its incorporation into the Unity Treaty represented a compromise between east and west over abortion. In 1975, as noted in Section B, the Federal Constitutional Court struck down the FRG's liberalized abortion law, holding that it violated the right to life within the meaning of Article 2 (1) as well as the principle of human dignity that the state is duty-bound "to respect and protect" under Article (1).[76] In so ruling, the Court obligated the state to make abortion a crime at all stages of pregnancy subject to exceptions specified by law. The GDR, on the other hand, permitted abortion on demand within the first three months of pregnancy. The effect of Article 143 is to allow eastern and western Germany to follow their respective policies on abortion. The FRG conceded this much to the GDR. But the treaty also requires the Bundestag to enact a common policy on abortion by the end of 1992 "to ensure better protection of unborn life and provide a better solution in conformity, with the Consti-

---

Feature 4.8 **Article 143**

---

(1) Law in the territory [of the eastern *Länder*] may deviate from provisions of this Basic Law for a period not extending beyond 31 December 1992 in so far as and as long as no complete adjustment to the order of the Basic Law can be achieved as a consequence of the different conditions. Deviations must not violate Article 19 (2) and must be compatible with the principles set out in Article 79 (3).

(2) Deviations from sections II, VIII, VIIIa, IX, X and XI are permissible for a period not extending beyond 31 December 1995.

---

tution, of conflict situations faced by pregnant women" (Article 31 [4]). This was the GDR's concession to the west.

These concessions, however, raised a difficult constitutional issue, for Article 143 bans deviations from the Basic Law in violation of Articles 19 (2) and 79 (3): The first flatly prohibits any encroachment on a basic right; the second bars any amendment to the Basic Law contravening principles laid down in Articles 1 (protecting "human dignity") and 20 (enshrining the rule of law). The constitutional issue is whether the deviation clause encroaches upon the principle of human dignity with respect to abortion. In addition, may a treaty suspend the application of a Constitutional Court ruling authoritatively defining the meaning of this principle? These questions remained unanswered in 1992 as the Bundestag heatedly debated a number of abortion reform proposals. Whatever the all-German policy turns out to be, the Constitutional Court will doubtless have the last word on its validity.

Property   The deviation clause of Article 143 (1) was also designed to deal with the problem of property rights. On 15 June 1992, the GDR and FRG governments signed a Joint Declaration on the Settlement of Open Property Issues. This agreement provided that all property taken by the GDR's Communist government between 1949 and 1989, including expropriated businesses and property placed

under state administration, was to be returned to their rightful owners. Compensation would be paid in the event that property could not be returned. The treaty contained one exception to this policy of restitution: Expropriated property would not be returned to their former owners if needed for investment purposes—a rule applied mainly to factories and large businesses—if innocently acquired by third parties, or if incapable of being returned in its original form. In each case, however, compensation would be forthcoming.

The most controversial of the Unity Treaty's property-settlement provisions was the exclusion from restitution of property expropriated by the Soviet Union in eastern Germany between 1945 and 1949. The Soviet Union had seized all land holdings over 250 acres and distributed most of them to small farmers. Prime Minister de Maizière refused to undo these takings. For one thing, any return of these millions of acres to their former owners would have caused enormous social unrest in the east. For another, the Soviet Union insisted on the exclusion. Yet the right to property, the rule of law, and equality under law are core values of the Basic Law. Accordingly, former owners of land in the east, invoking these values, challenged the 1945–49 exclusion in the Constitutional Court. In this instance, however, the achievement of unity—one of the Basic Law's highest values—trumped the right to property in the form of its restoration.

Furthermore, said the Court, the 1945–49 takings occurred before the Basic Law entered into force.[77]

Other Treaty Provisions   As already noted, the Unity Treaty provided for the creation of the *Treuhandanstalt*, set up the German Unity Fund, and revised the constitutional formula for intergovernmental revenue-sharing. In addition, all property and assets owned by the GDR, including the special funds of its railway and postal systems, would become the property of the FRG. Several provisions dealt with the status or continuing validity of GDR treaties, court decisions, and administrative rulings, most of which were to remain in effect unless incompatible with the Basic Law or federal law. GDR school certificates, university degrees, and titles were to retain their validity, although only in the eastern *Länder*, whereas judges and civil servants would be required to submit to recredentialing procedures. The treaty also required the former GDR to adopt EEC regulations, to maintain the church tax, and to decentralize cultural, educational, and athletic institutions. The German government would also be responsible for "rehabilitati[ng the] victims of the iniquitous SED regime" obliging it to sponsor "appropriate arrangements for compensation" (Article 17). In this connection, and at the insistence of the GDR, the six million files of the disbanded state security policy (*Stasi*) were to remain in the ex-GDR until an all-German parliament could enact a law regarding their storage and access. GDR officials were interested in keeping control of the files and to allow public access to them. The FRG, on the other hand, wanted them moved west and kept under the control of federal security police.

Finally, the contracting parties agreed that within two years further amendments to the Basic Law would be considered in the light of reunification. To wit: (1) a revision of federal-state fiscal relationships; (2) the incorporation of Berlin into Brandenburg; (3) the introduction of state objectives into the Basic Law;

and (4) holding a referendum within the context of Article 146. The last two proposals could lead to general constitutional reform. Eastern German leaders, drawing upon their socialist heritage, will try to incorporate more social and economic rights into the Basic Law, an endeavor likely to be supported by the western Greens and the SPD. Together, these groups are also likely to press for a popular referendum on a revised constitution or, what is more probable, on the Basic Law itself.

The Two-Plus-Four Treaty

After seven months of negotiation, the four war-time Allies and the two Germanys signed the treaty that finally closed the books on World War II.[78] The Allied Powers relinquished all their occupation rights and restored full sovereignty to a united Germany. Under the treaty, the new Germany (1) accepts its present boundaries and guarantees the border with Poland; (2) renounces aggressive warfare as well as the production and use of biological, chemical, and nuclear weapons; and (3) agrees to reduce its armed forces (ground, air, and naval forces) to 370,000, to allow Soviet troops to remain in the ex-GDR until 1995, and to finance their return to the Soviet Union. Germany also agreed to ban any NATO presence in the east while Soviet troops remain there. A major Soviet concession was to allow the FRG to choose its military alliance.

Finally, in a supplementary letter to the Allied foreign ministers, Foreign Minister Hans-Dietrich Genscher and Prime Minister Lothar de Maizière noted that Germany would abide by the 15 June 1990 Joint Resolution excluding property expropriated between 1945 and 1949 from the general terms of the Unity Treaty. They also pledged on behalf of Germany to preserve monuments to war victims erected on German soil and to maintain war graves. The two German leaders also declared that in united Germany "the free democratic basic order will be protected by the Constitution. It provides the basis," they continued, "for ensuring that parties which, by reason of their aims or the behavior of their adherents, seek to impair or abolish the free democratic basic order as well as associations which are directed against the constitutional order or the concept of international understanding can be prohibited." This language was taken directly from Article 21 of the Basic law, which authorizes the Federal Constitutional Court to pronounce antidemocratic parties unconstitutional. It thus appears that the new Germany will also be a "fighting democracy."

CONCLUSION

The portrait of Germany sketched in this chapter is one of a polity that up to now has worked and one that has brought about a high measure of stability and prosperity. The FRG also appears to have come of age politically. Its people are committed to democratic values, its party system is open and competitive, and its policymaking institutions are responsive to public opinion. Only time will tell whether the transition to democracy will be as smooth in the eastern *Länder*.

The FRG is a decentralized state marked by a system of administrative federalism, a fragmented bureaucracy, autonomous federal ministries, and a powerful Bundesrat capable of blocking parliamentary action. These institutions, like the political parties and parliament itself, are closely linked to various social and economic groups in the private sector. producing a politics largely of compromise and consensus. The Federal Constitutional Court, another independent center of power, watches over this system, keeping the major organs of government within their proper spheres of competence while helping to protect individual rights and liberties. Finally, having regained full sovereignty under the Two-Plus-Four Treaty of 1990, and increasingly confident of its power to influence events in Europe and the world, Germany can be expected to define its own foreign policy, preferably in harmony with American interests but against

them if necessary, but indubitably within the general framework of the Atlantic Alliance and an expanding European community.

Key Terms

Codetermination
Gymnasium
Loyalty Decree
Militant democracy
Numerus clausus
Ostpolitik
Socialist Unity Party (SED)
Works council
Two-Plus-Four Treaty
Lothar de Maizière
"Round Table" talks
Framework Act
Ten-Point Plan
Alliance 90
Stasi

Suggestions for Further Reading

Böckenförde, Ernst-Wolfgang, *State, Society and Liberty*. Translated by J. A. Underwood. (Oxford: Berg Publishers, 1991.)

Braunthal, Gerard. *Political Loyalty and Public Service in Germany* (Amherst: Massachusetts University Press, 1990.)

Bulmer, Simon, ed. *The Changing Agenda of West German Public Policy*. (Brookfield, Vt.: Gower Publishing Co., 1989.)

Bulmer, Simon, and William Patterson.*The Federal Republic of Germany and the European Community*. (London: Allen and Unwin, 1987).

Fritsch-Bournazel, Renata. *Confronting the German Division: Germans on the East-West Divide*. Translated by Caroline Bray. (Oxford: Berg Publishers, 1988).

Haftendorn, Helga. *Security and Détente*. (New York: Praeger, 1988).

Hanrieder, Wolfram P. *Germany, America, Europe: Forty Years of German Foreign Policy*. (New Haven: Yale University Press, 1989).

Katzenstein, Peter J, ed. *Industry and Politics in West Germany*. (Ithaca: Cornell University Press, 1989).

Katzenstein, Peter J. *Policy and Politics in West Germany.* (Philadelphia: Temple University Press, 1987).

Karpen, Ulrich, ed. *The Constitution of the Federal Republic of Germany.* (Baden-Baden: Nomos Verlagsgesellschaft, 1988).

Kommers, Donald P. *The Constitutional Jurisprudence of the Federal Republic of Germany.* (Durham: Duke University Press, 1989).

Menges, Constantine. *The Future of Germany and the Atlantic Alliance.* (Washington, D.C.: The AEI Press, 1991).

Swenson, Peter. *Fair Shares: Unions, Pay, and Politics in Sweden and West Germany.* (Ithaca: Cornell University Press, 1989).

Quint, Peter E. "The Constitutional Law of German Unification." *Maryland Law Review,* vol. 50 (1991): pp. 475–631.

The Unification of Germany in 1990: A Documentation. (Bonn: Press and Information Office, 1991).

Wellenreuther, Hermann, ed. *German and American Constitutional Thought.* (Oxford: Berg Publishers, Inc., 1990).

A. Notes

1. Treaty Between the Federal Republic of Germany and the German Democratic Republic on the Establishment of German Unity, August 31, 1990. *Bundesgesetzblatt* (Federal Law Gazette) II, p. 889.

2. This and the following historical subsections rely heavily on Geoffrey Barraclough, *The Origin of Modern Germany* (New York: Capricorn Books, 1963); Koppel S. Pinson, *Modern Germany,* 2nd ed. (New York: Macmillan, 1966); and H. W. Koch, *A Constitutional History of Germany in the Nineteenth and Twentieth Centuries* (London and New York: Longman, 1984).

3. Ralf Dahrendorf, *Society and Democracy in Germany* (Garden City, N.Y.: Doubleday, 1967), p. 62.

4. *Ostpolitik,* which means Eastern policy, is the term used to describe the efforts of West Germany, especially its chancellor Willy Brandt, to normalize relations with the eastern countries. The high point of these efforts, which took place between 1970 and 1973, was the Basic Treaty between the Federal Republic of Germany and the German Democratic Republic.

5. Dennis L. Bank and David R. Gness, *Democracy and its Discontents 1945–1963,* Vol. 1 (Oxford: Basil Blackwell, 1989), pp. 231–249.

6. Much of the statistical information supplied here and in subsequent sections of this chapter is derived from *Statistiches Jahrbuch 1991 für Vereinte Deutschland* (Wiesbaden: Matzler Poeschel, Sept. 1991).

7. John Ardagh, *Germany and the Germans* (London: Penguin Books, 1991), p. 63.

8. "Corporatism and Regional Economic Policies in the Federal Republic of Germany: The 'Meso' Politics of Industrial Adjustment," *Publius* 19 (Fall 1989), pp. 156–157.

9. Leslie Lipschitz and Donogh McDonald, *German Unification: Economic Issues* (Washington, D.C.: International Monetary Fund, December 1990), p. 53.

10. Gunther Thumann, "The System of Public Finance in the German Democratic Republic," in Lipschitz and McDonald, op. cit., p. 159.

11. Ibid., p. 78.

12. For a discussion of the West German social welfare system see Wolfgang Zapf, "Development, Structure, and Prospects of the German Social State" in Richard Rose and Rei Shiratori, *The Welfare State: East and West* (New York: Oxford University Press, 1986), pp. 126–155.

13. Sabine Hübner, "Women at the Turning Point: The Socio-Economic Situation and Prospects of Women in the Former German Democratic Republic," *Politics and Society in Germany, Austria, and Switzerland,* vol. 3 (1991), p. 26.

14. Ibid., p. 3.

15. Female labor statistics are drawn from "Women in the Labor Market," *The OECD Observer,* May 1980, pp. 4–7.

16. See Ray C. Rist, "Migration and Marginality: Guestworkers in Germany and France," *Daedalus* 108 (Spring 1979): 95–108.

17. See Richard L. Merritt, "Politics of Judaism in the GDR," *Studies in GDR Culture and Society*, vol. 9 (New York and London: University Press of America, 1989) pp. 163–187.

B. Notes

18. Gerard Braunthal, "The Social Democratic Party," in H. G. Peter Wallach and George K. Rosomer, eds., *West German Politics in the Mid-Eighties* (New York: Praeger, 1985), p. 90.

19. Party membership figures, including those of the SDP and FDP, have been drawn from Heino Kaack, *Geschichte und Struktur des deutschen Parteiensystems* (Opladen: Westdeutscher Verlag, 1971), pp. 483–495; Heino and Ursula Kaack, *Parteien-Jahrbuch 1973/74* (Meisenheim am Glan: Verlag Anton Hain, 1977), pp. 327–332; Ossip K. Flechtheim, *Die Parteien der Bundesrepublik Deutschland* (Hamburg: Hoffman und Campe Verlag, 1973), pp. 400–410; and from Wallach and Rosomer, *West German Politics* pp. 71, 89, and 90.

20. See Petra Kelly, *Fighting for Hope* (London: The Hogarth Press, 1984).

21. Some commentators feel that the Greens are here to stay. Others see the party as the product of a "transient protest vote, basically by the new educated classes not yet fully integrated into German society." In this view, "the Greens will decline drastically as soon as unemployment... eases and the Social Democratic party has redefined its role as spokesman of the less-integrated political Left." Wilhelm P. Buerklin, "Governing Left Parties Frustrating the Radical Non-Established Left: The Rise and Inevitable Decline of the Greens," *European Sociological Review* 3 (September 1987), p. 110.

22. The anomaly stems from a constitutional court decision which avoided an earlier statute confining state subsidies to parties represented in the Bundestag. The Court laid down the 0.5 percent rule as the minimum necessary to guarantee the equal protection of all political parties under the law.

23. For an excellent discussion of party finance, comparing the SPD and CDU, on the one hand, and the British Labor and Conservative Parties on the other, see Susan Edith Scarrow, *Organizing for Victory: Political Party Members and Party Organizing Strategies in Great Britain and West Germany, 1945–1989* (Ph.D. Dissertation, Yale University, 1991), pp. 304–318.

24. This section on party financing relies heavily on Arthur B. Gunlicks, "Campaigns and Party Finance in the West German 'Party State' " *The Review of Politics* 50 (Winter 1988), pp. 30–48.

25. Gerhard Loewenberg, *Parliament in the German Political System* (Ithaca, N.Y.: Cornell University Press, 1964), pp. 197–198.

26. See Peter J. Katzenstein, *Policy and Politics in West Germany* (Philadelphia: Temple University Press, 1987), p. 10.

27. Ibid., p. 362.

28. Richard J. Willey, "Trade Unions and Political Parties in the Federal Republic of Germany," *Industrial and Labor Relations Review* 28 (1974), p. 46.

29. For an excellent study of changing campaign styles in Germany see Scarrow, op. cit., chapters 5 and 10.

30. For a detailed discussion of the 1972 campaign see Arnold J. Heidenheimer and Donald P. Kommers, *The Governments of Germany*, 4th ed. (New York: Thomas Y. Crowell, 1975), chapter 5.

31. A fine treatment of the 1976 election is Karl H. Cerny, ed., *Germany at the Polls* (Washington, D.C., American Enterprise Institute, 1978).

32. Good treatments of the 1969, 1972, and 1976 federal elections are "The West German Elections of 1969," *Comparative Politics* 1 (July 1970); David P. Conradt and Dwight Lambert, "Party System, Social Structure, and Competitive Politics in West Germany: An Ecological Analysis of the 1972 Federal Election," *Comparative Politics* 7 (October 1974); and Cerny, *Germany at the Polls*.

33. See Klaus Schlaich, "Die Funktionen der Bundespräsidenten im Verfassungsgefüge," in 2 *Handbuch des Staatsrechts* 541 (1987): Rdnr. 88.

34. Frank Pilz, *Einführung in das politische System der Bundesrepublik Deutschland* (Munich : Verlag C.H. Beck, 1977), p. 99.

35. Winfried Steffani, "Parties (Parliamentary Groups) and Committees in the Bundestag" in Uwe Thaysen et al., *The U.S. Congress and the German Bundestag* (Boulder, Colorado: Westview Press, Inc. 199), p. 273.

36. Kurt Sontheimer and Hans H. Röhring, *Handbuch des politischen Systems der Bundesrepublik* (Munich: R. Piper & Co., 1977),p. 689.

37. *Comparative Legislatures* (Durham: N.C.: Duke University Press, 1979), p. 98.

38. Ibid. See also Gerhard Loewenberg, *Parliament in the German Political System* (Ithaca, N.Y.: Cornell University Press, 1964), pp. 334–352.

39. *The German Polity* (New York: Longman, 1978), p. 130.

40. See Donald P. Kommers, *Judicial Politics in West Germany* (Beverly Hills, Calif.: Sage, 1976), pp. 128–144.

41. See Hans-Georg Wehling, "The Bundesrat," *Publius* 19 (Fall 1989), p. 57.

42. Arthur B. Gunlicks, "Administrative Centralization in the Making and Remaking of Modern Germany," *Review of Politics* 46 (1984), pp. 336–340.

43. See Renate Mayntz and Fritz W. Scharpf, *Policy-Making in the German Federal Bureaucracy* (New York: Elsevier, 1975), pp. 88–89.

44. Ibid., p. 100.

45. Gunlicks, "Administrative Centralization," p. 336.

46. Ibid., p. 337.

47. See Rudiger Voigt, "Financing the German Federal System in the 1980s," *Publius* 19 (1989), p. 109.

48. This subsection on law and the courts draws heavily from Donald P. Kommers, *The Constitutional Jurisprudence of the Federal Republic of Germany* (Durham, N.C.: Duke University Press, 1989). See also Donald P. Kommers, *Judicial Politics in West Germany: A Study of the Federal Constitutional Court* (Beverly Hills, Calif.: Sage, 1976).

49. See Inge Markovits, "Last Days," *California Law Review* 80 (January 1992), pp. 55–129.

50. Klaus von Beyme, *Das Politische System der Bundesrepublik Deutchland nach der Vereinigung* (Munich: R. Piper & Co., 1991), p. 67.

C. Notes

51. Walter F. Murphy and Joseph Tanenhaus, *Comparative Constitutional Law* (New York: St. Martin's Press, 1977), p. 660.

52. See Peter Frisch, *Extremistenbeschluss* (Leverkusen: Heggen-Verlag, 1976), p. 140.

53. The United States Code, for example, bars a person from the civil service who "is a member of an organization that he knows advocates the overthrow of our constitutional form of government." 5 U.S.C. Sec. 7311 (1976).

54. See Gerard Braunthal *Political Loyalty and the Public Service in West Germany* (Amherst: The University of Massachusetts Press. 1990), p. 47.

55. Decision of 22 May 1975, *Entscheidungen des Bundesverfassungsgerichts*, Vol. 39 (1975): 334. (Hereafter cited as BVerfGE.)

56. Ibid., 361.

57. See generally *Bildungsbericht 1970* (Der Bundesminister fuer Bildung und Wissenschaft, 1970).

58. See Arnold Heidenheimer, Hugh Heclo, and Carolyn Teich Adams, *Comparative Public Policy* (New York: St. Martin's Press, 1975), p. 54.

59. In 1976, only 20 percent (compared with 6 percent in 1950) of West German youths entered the university. By contrast, the figures for the United States, Japan, and France were respectively 43, 37, and 29 percent. See Ladislav Cerych and Sarah Colton, *European Journal of Education* 15 (1980), p. 31.

60. Peter J. Katzenstein, *Policy and Politics in West Germany* (Philadelphia: Temple University Press, 1987), p. 296.

61. Ibid., pp. 323–324.

62. Ibid., p. 304.

63. Ibid., p. 306.

64. Decision of 18 July, 1972, 33 BVerfGE 303.

65. Decision of 9 April 1975, 39 BVerfGE 258.

66. Dietrich Hoffmann, *The German Co-Determination Act 1976* (Frankfurt am-Main: Alfred Metzner Verlag, 1976), p. 11.

67. *Co-determination in the Federal Republic of Germany* (Bonn: Federal Ministry of Labor and Social Affairs, 1980), p. 10.

68. Decision of 1 March 1979, 50 BVerfGE 290.

69. Clive M. Schmitthoff, ed., *The Harmonization of European Company Law* (London: The United Kingdom National Committee of Comparative Law, 1973).

70. "Verfassungsentwurf für die DDR" (Berlin: Arbeitsgruppe "Neue Verfassung der DDR" des Runden Tisches, April 1990).

71. Treaty Between the Federal Republic of Germany and the German Democratic Republic Establishing a Monetary, Economic, and Social Union (New York: German Information Center, 1990 [official translation]).

72. For an excellent study of the role of the Bundesbank in the FRG's political system, see Ellen Kennedy, *The Bundesbank* (New York: Council on Foreign Relations Press, 1991).

73. Vertrag zur Vorbereitung und Durchführung der ersten gesamt-deutschen Wahl des Deutschen Bundestages zwichen der Bundesrepublik Deutschland und der Deutschen Demokratischen Republik, *Bundesgesetzblatt* 1990, Teil II, p. 822.

74. Decision of 27 September 1990, 82 BVerfGE 322. See also *Frankfurter Allgemeine Zeitung*, August 2, 1990, p. 1.

75. Decision of 18 September 1990, 82 BVerfGE 316.

76. For a full translation of this decision see *John Marshall Journal of Practice and Procedure.*, Vol. 9 (Spring 1976): 551-684.

77. Decision of 11 December 1990, 83 BVerfGE 162.

78. The Treaty of the Final Settlement With Respect to Germany (New York: German Information Center, 1990 [official translation]).

CHAPTER 5

The Government of Japan

Theodore McNelly

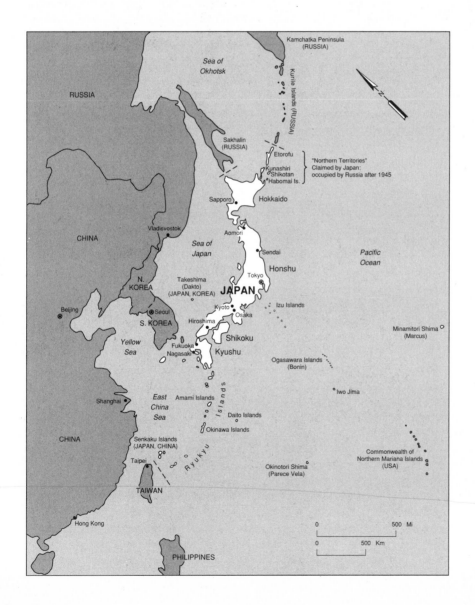

A: Political Development

In terms of area, Japan is a middle-sized country like Great Britain, France, and Germany, but its population (123.6 million in 1990[1]) is roughly twice that of any of those nations. Today Japan's gross national product (GNP) is the world's second largest, and the GNP per capita is one of the world's very highest. The quality of life, however, suffers from overcrowding, as one-fourth of the population is jammed into Tokyo and its immediate surroundings.

The Japanese are keenly aware that their country lacks the natural resources necessary for modern industry, such as iron ore, coal, and oil; these must all be imported and paid for by exports. If the present global trading system were to break down or if Japan were excluded from it, its now prosperous economy could be threatened with imminent collapse. Many Japanese recall the days before World War II when Japan possessed twice its present area. Korea and Taiwan were directly ruled by Japan, and Manchuria (*Manchukuo*) and much of China were controlled by Chinese collaborating with the Japanese. These areas provided Japanese industry with much of its raw material. Indeed the need for natural resources and agricultural land were often cited in the past as justification for Japan's imperialism, and some Asians remain fearful that Japan might some-

time again embark on a policy of aggression. However, it seems unlikely that the Japanese would engage in military adventures that could disrupt the global economy that has brought prosperity to their country.

THE LAND AND THE PEOPLE

Japan is an island nation. Although its total land area is about that of Montana, its four main islands and outlying smaller islands are dispersed over a huge area of the west Pacific Ocean. As the crow flies, the distance from the northern tip of Hokkaido to the southernmost of the Ryukyu Islands (just east of Taiwan) is about 1800 miles. Japanese territory extends as far south as Okinotori Shima (Parece Vela), between the Philippines and the Commonwealth of the Northern Mariana Islands (a U.S. possession), and as far east as Minamitori Shima (Marcus Island), midway between Wake Island (U.S.) and Japan's Izu Islands. The strategic importance of Japan's outlying possessions is substantial, because responsibility for their defense is increasingly being assumed by Japan's Maritime Self-Defense Force.

At their closest point, Japan's principal islands are separated from the Asian mainland by 100 miles of high seas. This location has helped, throughout history, to protect them from foreign invasion. Although at times foreign influence has been intense, the Japanese have usually been left alone to develop their culture and institutions in isolation. Therefore, many cultural characteristics of the Japanese, such as their language, the architecture of their homes, and their traditional food and clothing, are very different from those of their closest neighbors—so much so that they are often considered "unique."

Yet, Japan has much in common with other developed countries: modern science and industry, nearly universal literacy, a high material standard of living, a large investment in education at all levels, and a fondness for television and automobiles. A western tourist in Tokyo would find that city—with its noise, tall buildings, and traffic jams—disappointingly similar to big cities anywhere in the world. The principal exotic feature would be the Chinese characters on the fronts of stores, as the Japanese use Chinese characters rather than Roman letters to write their language, although the spoken Japanese language is fundamentally different from spoken Chinese.

Minorities

Ancient Chinese descriptions of Japan suggest that it was originally inhabited by warlike, nature-worshipping tribesmen. Archaeological and anthropological evidence indicates that these mongoloid people may have migrated in prehistoric times from northern Asia, and that there may also have been migrants from the South Seas to Japan. In Hokkaido, Japan's northernmost main island, there remain several thousand Ainu, a caucasoid people whose ancestors apparently lived in Japan before the arrival of the mongoloids. In the Ryukyu Islands reside well over one million Okinawans, who until a generation or so ago were as likely to speak Okinawan as they were to speak Japanese. Racially, they seem

to have been of southern origin, but since coming under Japanese rule over a century ago, they have intermarried with the Japanese. The natives were thoroughly Japanized, and while Okinawa was under American military government, from 1945 to 1972, they sought the return of their land to Japanese rule. Some Okinawans seek to prevent their distinctive language, art, and music from being erased completely by Japanese culture.

In addition to the Okinawans and the Ainu, there are two substantial minorities. There are over 650,000 Koreans, whose families have lived in Japan for several generations. They are not Japanese nationals and insist on the right to Korean-language schools and complain of discrimination, such as having to be fingerprinted (as are other aliens) by Japanese authorities. In addition, there are some 2 million burakumin (literally, "village people"), who are the descendants of eta, a caste of "untouchables" engaged in hereditary occupations related to the slaughtering of animals, such as the making of leather and leather goods. Communities of burakumin may be found concentrated in certain areas of large cities, and their occupations and diet as well as other cultural characteristics may distinguish them from majority Japanese. Racially, they are indistinguishable from majority Japanese, but employers and the families of potential marriage partners try hard to avoid people with buraku ancestries. Although discrimination against this minority is illegal, the Burakumin Emancipation League regularly makes political or judicial issues of apparent cases of flagrant discrimination.

In spite of what has just been said, fewer than 2 percent of Japan's population may be considered "minority." Except for the importation of 2 or 3 million Korean laborers into Japan during World War II, there has been no substantial immigration to the Japanese islands in recorded history. As a result, the Japanese have a strong consciousness and pride in their racial distinctiveness and homogeneity. Japan, as contrasted with India, the United States, and many other countries, is blessed with the absence of ethnic strife. The Japanese society is not pluralistic and does not seriously aspire to be. The Japanese government does not legally permit the immigration of unskilled workers in spite of labor shortages. In the past few years, however, the lure of high wages in Japan has attracted legal and illegal immigrants from other parts of Asia, as well as Brazilians and Peruvians of Japanese ancestry.

CHINESE INFLUENCE

Chinese historical accounts and ancient Japanese legends suggest that before 500 A.D. the Japanese were a race of tribes, sometimes at war with one another. By the sixth century A.D., one clan and its allies had consolidated their rule over the rest and established their chief as the "emperor." The imperial clan propagated the myth that the first emperor, Jimmu, was the grandchild of the sun-goddess, Amaterasu, who had commanded her descendants to rule the land. The sacred sword, jewel, and mirror, all of legendary origin, constitute the imperial regalia and are taken as evidence of the antiquity and legitimacy of the imperial dynasty.

Buddhism and Confucianism

The coming of Buddhism and Confucianism from Korea and China in the sixth century exacerbated clan rivalries as different groups sought either to sponsor the new ideas or rallied around traditional religious beliefs and ideologies. In order to distinguish the traditional nature worship from Buddhism, the old beliefs came to be referred to by the Chinese expression *Shinto*, or "way of the gods." Gradually, as often seems to be the case in Japan, foreign ideas gained widespread acceptance, but they were adapted to the needs of the Japanese and often improved. For example, the Buddhist pantheon came to be confused

in the minds of many with the gods of the traditional Shinto faith. One emperor is said to have dreamed that the Hindu deity Vairocana appeared in the form of a bright sun and declared itself to be none other than Amaterasu, the emperor's ancestress.

Later in the sixth century, Crown Prince Shotoku distinguished himself as a scholar of Confucianism. Acting as regent, in 604 he proclaimed his famous "Seventeen-Article Constitution," which was actually a collection of Confucian precepts calling for harmony, obedience, diligence, and honesty in the conduct of administration. Confucian ideology provided a convenient rationale for the establishment of a centralized bureaucratic monarchy in place of rule by clan chieftains. The Edict of Reform of 646 formally abolished hereditary guilds, set up a system of imperially appointed governors to rule the provinces, reformed the distribution of land among the people, and set up a system of taxation, usually in the form of rice, that would be paid to the central government. The centralizers cited the Chinese doctrine: "Under the heavens there is no land which is not the king's land. Among the holders of land there is none who is not the king's vassal."

The Taiho Code of 702 established a central administrative structure in imitation of the government of Tang China. The old custom of the Japanese court had been to maintain no fixed residence but to move from one place to another. In 710, following the Chinese example, a permanent Japanese capital city with straight streets and Chinese-style buildings was established in Nara. A university was set up where the sons of the nobility could learn the teachings of Confucius. A few years later, apparently to escape the overweening influence of the Buddhist clergy, the capital was moved to Kyoto, which remained the emperor's capital until 1868.

FEUDALISM

Although the imperial court in Kyoto was evidently committed to the ideal of a centralized, bureaucratic monarchy based on the Confucian notion of government by merit, the principle of hereditary rule tended to prevail. The Chinese theory that a wicked imperial dynasty could be overthrown was not adopted by the Japanese, who did not accept the idea that their divinity-descended monarch could be anything other than virtuous according to Confucian standards. The Fujiwara family of hereditary court nobles, who—like the emperor—traced their descent to mythological times, dominated the court and usually provided imperial consorts, regents, and civil dictators (*kanpaku*). The latter carried on the actual administration of state affairs.

The imperial court and capital became the center of intrigues and plots within and among the imperial family, the Fujiwara nobility, and rival Buddhist monasteries. The emperor, from time to time, made large grants of tax-exempt land to presumably deserving members of the imperial family, Fujiwara bureaucrats, Buddhist monasteries, and Shinto shrines. As less and less land provided revenue for the central government, the imperial court gradually became impoverished. Great tax-exempt manors grew into hereditary feudal baronies with their own armies. Unable to finance its own military forces and to maintain order in the provinces and even in the capital, the imperial government became dependent on the barons in order to enforce its rule.

In 1192, the emperor appointed a feudal baron, Minamoto Yoritomo, as "Barbarian-Subduing Generalissimo," or *shogun*. The title became hereditary in the Minamoto family. Minamoto Yoritomo established his own capital at Kamakura in eastern Japan, hundreds of miles from Kyoto. From 1192 until 1868, Japan was ruled not by the emperor or his court but by the military government of the shoguns. The emperor was kept powerless and isolated in Kyoto, and sometimes lived in poverty. The military government (*bakufu*) presided over a full-fledged feudal system, not unlike that of Europe in the Middle Ages, with a hierarchy of lords and vassals, and peasants at the bot-

tom. The code of the *samurai* (hereditary warriors) emphasized loyalty to one's overlord and military discipline. One of the most notable accomplishments of the Kamakura *bakufu* was the defeat of the Mongols, who twice tried to invade Japan by sea in the thirteenth century. The defenders of the nation were aided by the prayers of Buddhist and Shinto priests and great storms, the "winds of the Gods" (*kamikaze*). The tradition grew that Japan enjoyed supernatural protection and was invincible.

The Tokugawa Regime

Warfare among local feudal lords raged across the land in the sixteenth century, when the country was nominally under the control of the Ashikaga dynasty of shoguns. Finally, in 1603, after decades of civil war, Tokugawa Ieyasu, using guile as well as military strategy, brought the country under his rule. Ieyasu, the first of the Tokugawa shoguns, had remarkable political skills. After subduing or making alliances with the other feudal lords, he established a regime that endured over two and a half centuries. He set up his capital in a swampy town called Edo, in Eastern Japan. He required his defeated rivals to support the construction of a huge system of moats around his palace. He redistributed the fiefs of the feudal lords in such a way that his former enemies were kept separated from one another. The feudal lords (*daimyo*) were required to live alternatively in Edo and in their fiefs. When they left Edo they had to leave their families behind as hostages. When they returned to Edo they were forbidden to bring weapons with them. In order to prevent a possible conquest of the country by the European powers, Christianity was forbidden. Limits were placed on the size of ships so that the Japanese could not leave the country. Only the Chinese and the Dutch (who were confined to an island in Nagasaki harbor and who agreed not to propagate the teachings of Christ) were permitted to trade with the Japanese. Over a period of years, Edo, the capital of feudal Japan, with the costly and pala-tial residences of the daimyo and shogun, be-came possibly the world's largest city. The long period of peace enforced by the shoguns en-couraged the rise of a capitalist class, because money came to replace rice as the principal medium of exchange. The isolationist policy helped to prevent the conquest of Japan by European imperial powers.

THE IMPERIAL RESTORATION

Changes in the economy wrought hardship on many of the samurai and peasants. At the same time, there arose a nationalistic ideology, fostered by the study of "national literature," which was based on Shinto legends that em-phasized the divine origin of the state and the monarchy. Some nationalist scholars con-tended that the shogun had usurped the au-thority of the emperor and that the monarchy should be restored to its rightful position.

In 1853, Commodore Matthew Calbraith Perry came to Japan with a message from the American president demanding that the coun-try open its door to foreign trade. The refusal of the American fleet to leave Japanese wa-ters even in the face of military threats from the shogun forced a crisis. The nationalists and the hereditary feudal rivals of the shogun de-manded that the shogun "expel the barbarian and revere the emperor."

The shogun simply did not have the mili-tary and naval resources and political support needed to resist the American demands. The shogun's concessions to the foreigners pro-voked his enemies to intensify their demands that he abdicate. Efforts to work out a com-promise in which the emperor and shogun would rule jointly did not work out. Finally the shogun agreed to a restoration of the emperor, with the understanding that the shogun would be a principal councillor to the throne. When it became clear that the western daimyo, who leagued against him, were determined to ex-clude him from the new regime, some of the shogun's followers rebelled. A full-scale civil

war was averted, and the imperial regime was restored.

In 1868, the youthful Emperor Meiji es-tablished his capital at Edo, taking over the shogun's palace and moats, and renamed the city Tokyo, or Eastern Capital. At first, there was much confusion about what the new group of ruling clans wanted. Some of the architects of the restoration would have been happy to leave things as they had been under the Toku-gawa shoguns, but with themselves as the ef-fective rulers. Others felt that the times called for sweeping economic, political, and military changes. After considerable debate and out-breaks of violence (especially by samurai who were unhappy about the inadequacy of the pensions promised them by the new regime), the advocates of change won out. The feudal system was formally abolished with the return of the land and population from the daimyo to the emperor. The daimyo and the samurai were pensioned off, and their privileged status was abolished. The outcast *eta* were declared emancipated, and everyone was equally a sub-ject of the emperor.

The Imperial Constitution

During the struggle for power, some samurai leaders demanded that a representative assem-bly be established. After several false starts, in 1889 a new constitution was promulgated. The principal author of the Imperial Constitution (usually referred to as the Meiji Constitu-tion) was Count Ito Hirobumi, a leader of the Choshu clan. (Throughout this chapter, the family name precedes the given name of Japanese individuals, as is the custom in Japan.) Ito had gone to Europe to study con-stitutions and had been greatly impressed by the basic law of Prussia, which provided for a powerful executive. Ito hailed the new Japanese constitution as the "Emperor's gift to the Japanese people." The autocratic ide-ology of the document was explicitly declared in Article 1: "The Empire of Japan shall be reigned over and governed by a line of Emperors unbroken for ages eternal." The theory and interpretation of the document were further clarified in Ito's *Commentary on the Constitution of Japan*. Although the text of the Constitution was never altered until the entire document was replaced in 1947, the actual operation of the government, as we shall see, underwent significant changes during the 58 years that the Meiji Constitution was in existence.

Japan's new leadership was determined to make Japan a rich and powerful country and wanted to ensure that their influence in Tokyo would not be hobbled by the newly established Imperial Diet (Parliament). The Imperial Diet consisted of an aristocratic House of Peers and a House of Representatives composed of members chosen by a small electorate of high-paying taxpayers. The Constitution provided that if the Diet failed to approve the budget proposed by the government, the government could enforce the budget of the preceding year, thus preventing Parliament from using the power of the purse to control the executive branch. Prime ministers were appointed by the emperor on the recommendation of the *Genro,* or Elder Statesmen, a powerful institution not mentioned in the Constitution. Until 1918, all prime ministers were appointed from either the samurai class or, in one instance, the hereditary court nobility. The emperor had "supreme command of the army and navy." This provision largely removed the military from the control of the prime minister and the Diet. The prestige and power of the executive and the military were vastly enhanced during the victorious wars with China (1894–1895) and Russia (1904–1905).

TAISHO DEMOCRACY

Political parties emerged, and their influence in the Diet had to be dealt with by the oligarchy. In 1918, when rice riots throughout the country proved more than the old leadership could handle, they chose Hara Takeshi, a commoner and the leader of the Seiyukai party, to serve as prime minister. With the establishment of party government in 1918 and the agitation for people's rights in the years immediately following the First World War, party leaders began to talk of the coming of "normal parliamentary government," in which the prime minister would be the leader of the majority party or majority coalition in the House of Representatives. At the same time, the movement favoring universal manhood suffrage became irresistible. In 1925, the Diet passed the universal manhood suffrage law, which would make the lower house a truly democratic body. In the same year, however, the Diet also enacted a peace preservation law that made illegal any attack on the principle of the emperor's sovereignty. Intellectuals and party leaders hoped that Japan would become a parliamentary democracy like England. This tendency came to be known as Taisho democracy, referring to the reign of the Taisho emperor (1912–1925). Had it not been for the world depression in the 1930s, which had devastating consequences in Japan, democracy might have become more firmly established in that country.

THE RISE OF MILITARISM

Junior officers in the army, largely drawn from the impoverished peasantry, tended to blame capitalists and the politicians, believed to be controlled by the capitalists, for the plight of the people. Advocating a "Showa Restoration," or restoration of direct imperial rule, they aspired to a more just social order. Several coups d'etat were attempted and cabinet ministers were assassinated. Prime ministers lived in fear for their lives. Increasingly, cabinet posts were assigned to military men and the representation of parties in the cabinets was reduced. The ministers of war and navy (who had to be generals or admirals) would threaten to refuse serving in a cabinet or proposed cabinet whose chief or whose policies did not please them. Thus the military could exercise a veto over the policies and personnel of the government.

War in Asia and the Pacific

The civilian government in Tokyo was unable to restrain the Kwantung Army (the Japanese forces stationed in the southern tip of Manchuria, China) from carrying out its own policy. Japanese troops seized all of Manchuria and set up a puppet state (*Manchukuo*) headed by the former emperor of China. Under international condemnation, Japan resigned from the League of Nations, and in 1937 a full-scale war broke out between China and Japan. Japanese forces captured Nanking, the Chinese capital, and killed tens of thousands of civilians. Japan allied itself with Germany and Italy, and the three Axis powers announced their intention to establish "New Orders" in Europe and Asia.

War broke out in Europe in 1939, and on December 7, 1941 ("a date that will live in infamy," President Roosevelt called it), Japanese carrier-based aircraft made a surprise attack on Pearl Harbor, devastating the American navy and arousing the wrath of the American people, who regarded the attack as unprovoked. Within a few months, Japan conquered the Philippine Islands and the British and Dutch possessions in Southeast Asia. By the spring of 1945, the Americans had captured island bases close enough to mainland Japan to launch frightful air attacks on Japanese cities. In August, after two cities had been destroyed by American atomic bombs and the Soviet Union (with which Japan had a neutrality treaty) had declared war on Japan, the Japanese government accepted the terms set forth by the Allies in the Potsdam Declaration of July 26, 1945.

THE ALLIED OCCUPATION

The main purpose of the Allied occupations of Germany and Japan was to ensure that those nations never again threatened the security of peace-loving countries. Because of the common belief that the people, as distinguished from their leaders, were peace lov-

ing, it was thought that democratic regimes were less inclined to be warlike than autocratic governments. Thus, in addition to completely disarming Germany and Japan, the Allies set out to establish democratic institutions in the defeated countries. Moreover, it was widely thought that fundamental economic and social reforms were essential to provide a lasting basis for democratic political institutions. There was continuing controversy about the need, extent, and precise character of the social reforms that would have to be carried out. The unconditional surrender of the defeated states meant that there was virtually no limit to the authority of the occupying powers to intervene in the internal affairs of Germany and Japan.

The occupations of Germany and Japan differed in two essential respects:

1. Japan proper, unlike Germany, was not cut up into four zones, each administered by a different Allied power. Instead all of Japan (except Okinawa and Japan's former possessions, Korea and Taiwan) was placed under the unified control of the Supreme Commander for the Allied Powers (SCAP). General Douglas MacArthur was appointed supreme commander by President Truman with the concurrence of Joseph Stalin. The policies of the United States were in effect controlling.

2. In Germany, where no national German government existed following the surrender, the Allied authorities directly enacted legislation. In Japan, the emperor and imperial government remained in place, and SCAP issued directives to the Japanese government, which was required to enact laws or issue ordinances to carry out the Allies' (essentially American) policies. Thus the policies of military government in Japan were uniform for the whole country and were administered indirectly.

Democratization

From the beginning, there were complaints that the emperor should have been arrested and either tried as a war criminal, or made to abdicate, or both, and that the Japanese government, composed of reactionaries, could not be trusted to carry out the sweeping reforms required by the Allies. However, the system worked with a minimum of friction between the Allied (overwhelmingly American) forces and the Japanese, and as we shall see, substantial democratic reform was accomplished in Japan. By contrast, the occupation of Germany was the focus of continual bitter controversy within and among the Allied countries, and at the time of the Berlin blockade (1948–1949), there were fears that war might break out between the Soviet Union and the western powers. While Germany became the center of the Cold War confrontation, Japan seemed to represent the epitome of tranquility, and MacArthur enjoyed wide praise for the smoothness of his operation.

The policies of the Allied occupation of Japan were largely based on the Potsdam Declaration of July 26, 1945. Japanese military and naval forces were disarmed and repatriated. In addition to trials set up among the East Asian countries for the punishment of Japanese violations of the laws of war, an International Military Tribunal for the Far East was established for the trial of class A war criminals, those accused of crimes against peace (planning and carrying out aggressive war) and crimes against humanity, following the precedents of the Nuremberg trial. Officeholders or office seekers who had been military or naval officers or holders of positions in the Imperial Rule Assistance Association (a totalitarian organization) or in other militaristic or ultranationalistic organizations were declared ineligible for public office. This "purge," the administration of which was entrusted to the Japanese government, was intended to clear the way for new leadership in Japan.

Under SCAP guidance, a sweeping land reform was carried out which made virtually every peasant a landowner. Partly as a result, Japanese farmers became politically very conservative because they suspected that Communists might try to deprive them of their land. The great *zaibatsu* monopolies were partially broken up and their stock sold publicly. The unionization of labor was encouraged. For the first time, women were given the right to vote. Freedoms of speech and press were granted.

THE DEMOCRATIC CONSTITUTION

In MacArthur's view, the occupation's most notable accomplishment was the establishment of a thoroughly democratic constitution. The

General MacArthur poses with Emperor Hirohito at the general's official residence (the American Embassy in Tokyo) in September 1945. The effort of the Japanese government to prevent this photograph from being published was overruled by MacArthur's headquarters.

general first raised the issue of constitutional revision with Japanese officials in 1945, but Prime Minister Shidehara publicly stated that it was unnecessary to amend the Meiji Constitution, which, he said, had been abused by the militarists. In his view, all that was needed to democratize the country was the enactment of the appropriate legislation. But it became increasingly clear that the Allied Powers would require drastic reforms, and private groups and individuals as well as the government began to propose constitutional amendments.

In February 1946, when it had become clear that the Shidehara cabinet was unable to produce a sufficiently democratic constitution—the cabinet's proposals were more conservative than those of political parties and private groups—General MacArthur's Government Section secretly drew up a model constitution for the guidance of the cabinet. Faced with the possibility that the Far Eastern Commission might insist on a constitution that would abolish the monarchy, the possibility that the Allies might try the emperor as a war criminal, or the possibility that the cabinet might be forced to resign if MacArthur personally sponsored the Government Section draft, the Shidehara cabinet accepted the American proposal as the basis for a new constitution. The cabinet's constitution revision bill was submitted to the Diet as an "imperial project" in accordance with Article 73 of the Imperial Constitution concerning constitutional amendment. The new democratic constitution was passed by overwhelming majorities in both houses of the Imperial Diet, approved by the Privy Council, and promulgated by the emperor in November 1946. The new "Constitution of Japan" became effective on May 3, 1947.

Japan's new basic law proclaimed the sovereignty of the people, guaranteed basic human rights, and renounced war and the maintenance of military forces. The emperor was declared to be "the symbol of the State and of the unity of the people," and would have no "powers related to government." The House of Peers, the Privy Council, and titles of nobility (save for the imperial family) would no longer exist. A parliamentary-cabinet system of democratic government (in which the cabinet was responsible to the lower house of the Diet) was set up. The constitutionality of legislation and governmental acts would be subject to judicial review. Sexual and racial discrimination was forbidden.

The new constitution represented such a radical departure from the previously published conservative (some said "reactionary") view of the Japanese cabinet that the document was obviously the product of urging from occupation officers. Nonetheless, after several decades during which the provisions of the new constitution were taught in the public schools, it gained widespread popular acceptance. The antiwar provision enjoyed popularity from the very beginning, and women, students, intellectuals, journalists, laborers, indeed, just about everyone, became attached to their new constitutional rights.

Many Japanese conservatives, however, have been unhappy with the document. They object to the no-arms clause, which, they hold, makes it difficult or impossible to defend the country. The emperor, they say, should be made "head of the state" and be more respected. The family should enjoy more constitutional protection. The Constitution, they assert, overemphasizes the people's rights and neglects to set forth their duties. When the occupation ended, there appeared a spate of articles and books exposing real and purported facts about the occupation that had hitherto been suppressed by SCAP censors. The conservatives began to insist that the Constitution had been forcibly "imposed" on Japan and that an independent Japan should have an "autonomous" constitution.

Popular Acceptance of the Democratic Constitution

In 1954, the conservative-dominated Diet created a Commission on the Constitution that would examine the origins and operation of the document and make possible recommendations for its amendment. By the mid-1960s when the commission made its report, however, the conservatives were still unable to elect the two-thirds majorities needed in both houses of the Diet to amend the Constitution. Although several prime ministers have publicly declared that they favor the amendment of the Constitution as a matter of principle, they have made no serious effort to do so, given the extremely controversial nature of the issue. In the meantime, the government has been able to strengthen the Self-Defense Forces without amending the Constitution, thus reducing the urgency of the issue. It must be said that there has been widespread unhappiness with the manner in which the government had gradually rearmed the country in apparent violation of the disarmament clause of the Constitution, and with the reluctance of the Supreme Court to deal forthrightly with this issue.

The democratic constitution is now 46 years old. Despite the conservative drive to amend it, not a word of it has been altered. Much controversy has surrounded its interpretation and a number of famous constitutional debates have been dealt with by Japan's Supreme Court. On the whole, the document is popular and its principles have been adopted as accepted components of the political culture.

THE RETURN OF INDEPENDENCE

After the new constitution had gone into effect in 1947, MacArthur felt that there remained little else for the occupation to do aside from reviving the Japanese economy. He announced that it was time for a peace treaty. As the Cold War worsened, however, American policy makers became reluctant to withdraw their military forces from Japan given the growing Communist threat in China and North Korea. A formula was devised whereby the Allied occupation would formally end, Japan's sovereignty would be restored, and the Japanese government would invite the United States to station forces in Japan. The Soviet Union, however, would not consent to this arrangement. Such a treaty would favor the United States over the Soviet Union and compromise the neutrality of Japan. War broke out in Korea in 1950, and the American negotiators pushed ahead with their proposals in Japan. The Japanese government agreed with the American plan. Japanese socialists and pacifists strongly opposed the "one-sided" peace, asserting that it would alienate Japan's powerful neighbors, the Soviet Union and Communist China, and could drag Japan into a U.S.-Soviet war. The government asserted that a treaty acceptable to both superpowers was not a viable possibility. If Japan wished to end the occupation and regain its independence promptly, the best thing to do was to sign the treaty with the non-Communist powers.

The Japanese Peace Treaty was formally signed in San Francisco on September 8, 1951, to become effective on April 26, 1952. The Soviet Union sent a delegation to the conference but it refused to sign the treaty, the details of which had been worked out before the conference was convened. Neither the Nationalist nor the Communist government of China was represented. On the same day that the peace treaty was signed, Japan and the United States signed a mutual security treaty, which provided for the stationing of American forces in Japan. Urged by the United States, the Japanese government negotiated a peace treaty with the Nationalist government of China, based in Taiwan. In April 1952, SCAP headquarters in downtown Tokyo was closed, but American forces remained in Japan under the terms of the security treaty.

The peace settlement alienated Japan from both the Soviet Union and Communist China and in effect made Japan an ally of the United States. The Japanese sought to negotiate a peace treaty with the Soviet Union, but were unable to do so because of disagreements over the Japanese claims to northern islands under Soviet military occupation. In

1956, the two countries issued a "joint peace declaration" formally ending the state of war between them. The territorial dispute continued unabated and as of the spring of 1992 there was no formal peace treaty between Japan and the Soviet Union. Japan is an economic superpower and remains closely bound to the United States by trade, security ties, and a democratic, capitalist ideology.

THE EMPEROR SYSTEM TODAY

According to the 1889 Imperial Constitution, Japan was to "be reigned over and governed by a line of Emperors unbroken for ages eternal." The emperor was "sacred and inviolable." He was "the head of the Empire, combining in Himself the rights of sovereignty." The objective of the samurai who had engineered the imperial restoration was to establish an authoritarian regime in which they could rule the land in the name of the emperor. There was no hint in the Imperial Constitution that Japan could become a democracy; indeed, democracy would seem to be out of the question if the emperor was sovereign ruler. However, the practical difficulties of managing the Diet and administering the State forced the oligarchs very reluctantly to concede some voice to political parties in making policy.

In the 1930s, the emperor's prestige was exploited by militarists to mobilize public support for their empire-building efforts in Asia. After World War II, hoping to prevent the revival of Japanese militarism and imperialism, many people in the Allied countries strongly urged that both the system of emperor worship and the imperial throne be abolished once and for all. The incumbent emperor, they believed, should be tried as a war criminal. MacArthur feared that the indictment of the emperor would provoke a popular uprising in Japan and that the people's resentment of the occupiers would make it virtually impossible to educate the people in the ways of democracy and peace. So the emperor was not tried, and the imperial throne was preserved.

On New Year's Day, 1946, the emperor issued a rescript in which he renounced the notion that he was divine. This statement pleased General MacArthur and was apparently an important factor in the rehabilitation of the imperial institution. Under the postwar democratic Constitution, the emperor was deprived of all powers related to government, and war and the maintenance of armed forces were banned. The postwar emperor would be a powerless and harmless symbol.

Hirohito

On 7 January 1989, over 43 years after the end of World War II, Emperor Hirohito died at the age of 87. He had served as prince regent for 5 years during the mental illness of his father and in 1926 ascended to the imperial throne. He served as emperor for 20 years under the Meiji Constitution and for over 40 years under the democratic constitution. He survived several assassination attempts and lived through two world wars and 7 years of occupation by foreign military forces. Few of the world's statesmen have closely witnessed or participated in so many great events. With the accession of Emperor Akihito to the throne in 1989, the *Showa* (Enlightened Harmony) era ended and the *Heisei* (Peace Attained) era began. The new emperor pledged to uphold the Constitution and to strive for world peace.

The Imperial Family

The emperor's palace occupies a large park-like area in the very center of Tokyo, where real estate prices are the highest in the world. Enormous amounts of fuel are expended every day by automobiles, trucks, and buses that have to circle around it to get from one part of the capital city to another. It is customary in Japan frequently to use the imperial reign name rather than the western calendar in designating years. For example, 1992 is usually referred to as "Heisei 4," the fourth year of the

Emperor Akihito accompanied by his wife Empress Michiko in his first public statement pledges to uphold the democratic Constitution and strive for world peace, on January 9, 1989, two days after his father's death.

reign of the present emperor. When an emperor dies, his reign name is used to designate him, so that Emperor Hirohito was the Showa Emperor. Progressive critics say that the use of reign names unduly exalts the emperor.

The imperial family, whose popularity was greatly enhanced by the crown prince's marriage to a beautiful and intelligent commoner in 1959, is constantly in the news. The older of the present emperor's two sons is the crown prince (*kotaishi*), who is thirty-one years old and unmarried. In 1991, the crown prince's younger brother, Prince Akishino, married the daughter of a professor at a prestigious college, and in October of the same year they had a baby daughter, the present emperor's first grandchild. Popular weekly magazines often feature reports of efforts to find a bride for the crown prince. The crown prince, like his

uncle, Prince Mikasa, is a serious historian and has given lectures on Japanese history. Only males may inherit the throne. The new emperor's two sons, his brother, his uncle, and his uncle's three sons, in that order, are currently in the line of succession to the throne.

A Modern Monarchy In the nineteenth century with the rise of parliamentary democracy in western monarchies, the role of king was ultimately reduced to ceremonial and symbolic functions. His only political role was to select as prime minister a man who could command a majority in the parliament. World Wars I and II were very destructive of royal and imperial thrones, and the function of choosing a prime minister devolved upon the president in parliamentary democracies, following the precedent of the French Third Republic. In Japan, under the democratic constitution, the emperor "appoints" as prime minister the individual chosen by the Diet and "appoints" as chief judge of the Supreme Court the person chosen by the cabinet. The emperor presides over the openings of Diet sessions and his seal is necessary for important state documents.

Largely because the principle of popular sovereignty is explicitly proclaimed in the Japanese Constitution, some theorists plausibly argue that Japan is a republic. Although non-Japanese sometimes refer to the Japanese emperor as "head of state" (in contrast to the prime minister, who is "head of the government"), the Constitution describes him as "symbol of the state." Some Japanese conservatives would like to amend the Constitution to describe the emperor as the head of the state. In 1966, the celebration of *Kigensetsu* (February 11), the founding of the state by the mythical first emperor (presumably in 660 B.C.), was revived. This move and other conservative attempts to enhance the status of the imperial throne have been fervently resisted by progressives and pacifists in Japan and viewed with concern by foreign observers.

In 1988, the mayor of Nagasaki publicly blamed Emperor Hirohito for having needlessly prolonged World War II. This statement was made during the emperor's prolonged fatal illness and provoked a nationwide controversy. A year later, a rightist shot and gravely wounded the mayor in front of the city hall. The would-be assassin was tried and sentenced to 12 years of penal servitude. When he ran for reelection in 1991, the mayor was denied the support of the LDP, but was reelected by a narrow margin.

Many progressive Japanese were especially disturbed by the reactionary implications of the Shinto ceremonies connected with the formal accession to the throne by Akihito in 1990. At the same time, imperial court circles tend to be cautious about doing anything that would make the throne a focus of controversy.

The Throne and Japan's Political Culture

Emperor Hirohito played an important role in ending World War II and in the adoption of the democratic Constitution; indeed without his cooperation, it would have been difficult if not impossible to bring about the rapid democratization of Japan. The accession to the throne, the marriage, the illnesses, and the death of an emperor focus the attention of the entire country on the institution. It is not easy to assess the relative importance of the monarchy in contemporary Japan. A minority fears that it may someday be exploited to advance the agenda of political reactionaries or militarists. Another minority would like to enhance the role of the emperor, possibly by amending the Constitution.

Many Japanese think little about the imperial institution, but take it for granted or follow media reports of the activities of the members of the imperial family. The role of the throne in the Japanese polity is rather similar to that of the monarchy in Great Britain. The imperial throne represents Japan's historical continuity, national solidarity, and constitutional stability.

HISTORY AND THE POLITICAL PROCESS IN JAPAN

How is Japan's political history relevant to what is happening in Japan today? As we have seen, the occupation of Japan had as one of its principal aims the democratization of that country's political and social institutions. The ideals of peace and democracy have been subscribed to by an overwhelming majority of the Japanese. The quality of Japanese politics may be measured against the democratic ideals of the immediate postwar era and the provisions of the democratic Constitution. The sources of some contemporary political phenomena may be sought in the history of the country as well as in its present-day social system.

In 1987 Prime Minister Nakasone talked of "closing the books on the postwar [period]." The statement seemed to imply a repudiation of the postwar reforms. The prime minister formally visited the Yasukuni Shrine where Japan's war dead are deified. For some years, the Ministry of Education has been using its authority to review textbooks so that, it was charged, Japan's aggressions against China and Korea were glossed over. Official visits to Yasukuni and the textbook issue have provoked protests from China, Korea, and other of Japan's erstwhile victims as well as from religious groups, intellectuals, and others in Japan. Since 1985, two Japanese cabinet ministers have been forced to resign because of tactless statements that seemed to justify Japan's militaristic record. Intellectuals and politicians continue to debate the meaning of the prewar and wartime policies of their nation. The Japanese have problems in dealing with their history, and the memory of Japan's former aggressive policies continues to complicate its relations with its neighbors.

Key Terms

Ainu
Amaterasu
burakumin

Edo
eta
Fujiwara
Genro
Hirohito
Japanese Peace Treaty
Meiji
Okinawa
purge
Supreme Commander for the Allied Powers
  (SCAP)
Shinto
shogun
Taisho democracy

Suggestions for Further Reading

Brackman, Arnold C. *The Other Nuremberg: The Untold Story of the Tokyo War Crimes Trial* (New York: William Morrow, 1987).

Cohen, Theodore. *Remaking Japan: The American Occupation as New Deal* (New York: Free Press, 1987).

Dower, John W. *Empire and Aftermath: Yoshida Shigeru and the Japanese Experience, 1878–1954* (Cambridge: Harvard University Press, 1979).

Field, Norma. *In the Realm of the Dying Emperor* (New York: Pantheon, 1991).

Finn, Richard B. *Winners in Peace: MacArthur, Yoshida, and Postwar Japan* (Berkeley: University of California Press, 1992).

Hadley, Eleanor M. *Antitrust in Japan* (Princeton: Princeton University Press, 1969).

Hane, Mikiso. *Japan: A Historical Survey* (New York: Scribners, 1972).

Hardacre, Helen. *Shinto and the State, 1868–1989* (Princeton: Princeton University Press, 1989).

Ienaga, Saburo. *Pacific War, 1931–1945: A Critical Perspective on Japan's Role in World War II* (New York: Pantheon, 1979).

Inoue, Kyoko. *MacArthur's Democratic Constitution: A Linguistic and Cultural Study of Its Making* (Chicago: University of Chicago Press, 1991).

Ishii, Ryosuke. *A History of Political Institutions in Japan* (Tokyo: University of Tokyo Press, 1980).

Ito, Hirobumi. *Commentaries on the Constitution of the Empire of Japan*. Translated by Ito Miyoji. (Tokyo: Insetsu Kyoku, 1889).

Kades, Charles L. "The American Role in Revising Japan's Imperial Constitution," *Political Science Quarterly*, Summer 1989, pp. 215–248.

Kataoka, Tetsuya. *The Price of a Constitution: The Origin of Japan's Postwar Politics* (New York: Crane Russak, 1991).

Kawai, Kazuo. *Japan's American Interlude.* (Chicago: University of Chicago Press, 1960).

Maki, John M., transl. and ed. *Japan's Commission on the Constitution: The Final Report* (Seattle: University of Washington Press, 1980).

Nishi, Toshio. *Unconditional Democracy: Education and Politics in Occupied Japan, 1945–1952* (Stanford: Stanford University Press, 1982).

Reischauer, Edwin O. *The Japanese Today: Change and Continuity* (London: Cambridge University Press, 1988).

SCAP, Government Section. *The Political Reorientation of Japan*, 2 vols. (Washington, D.C.: U.S. Government Printing Office, n.d.).

Takeuchi, Tatsuji. *War and Diplomacy in the Japanese Empire* (Garden City, N.Y.: Doubleday, Doran, 1935).

Ward, Robert E., ed. *Political Development in Modern Japan* (Princeton: Princeton University Press, 1968).

Ward, Robert E., and Yoshikazu Sakamoto, eds. *Democratizing Japan: The Allied Occupation* (Honolulu: University of Hawaii Press, 1987).

Ward, Robert E., and Frank Joseph Shulman, eds. *The Allied Occupation of Japan, 1945–1952: An Annotated Bibliography of Western Language Materials* (Chicago: American Library Association, 1974).

Williams, Justin. *Japan's Political Revolution under MacArthur: A Participant's Account* (Athens: University of Georgia Press, 1979).

B. Political Processes and Institutions

POLITICAL PARTIES

Political parties arose in Japan among samurai who felt excluded from the new regime in the 1880s. By organizing and agitating they sought to pressure the government into establishing an assembly, and the government did so when it promulgated the Imperial Constitution in 1889. The Constitution, however, left the executive dominant over the legislative branch, the Diet. The existence of political parties was not recognized by the Constitution, and the oligarchs were reluctant to share their power with party politicians.

In 1898, the samurai leaders of the two principal political parties (Okuma of the Progressive party and Itagaki of the Liberal party) merged to form the Constitutional party. The new party's strength in the House of Representatives was sufficient to pressure the Genro to appoint Okuma as prime minister. In 1900 Prime Minister Ito, in order to organize a working coalition in the House of Representatives, accepted the leadership of the Seiyukai party. Thus political parties proved their usefulness in organizing lower house elections and in mobilizing support in the lower house for the passage of the government's legislation. In 1918, with the appointment of Hara, a commoner and leader of the Seiyukai, as prime

minister, it appeared that the power of the samurai oligarchy was greatly weakened and that political parties might come into their own as a dominant factor in politics.

As we have seen, the ascendance of political parties was checked in the 1930s with the rise of militarism and beginning in 1932, most of the prime ministers were either generals or admirals. In 1940, the major parties voted to dissolve themselves, and a quasi-totalitarian state, led by the Imperial Rule Assistance Association (IRAA), came into being. At the end of the war, the IRAA was abolished and the prewar political parties were revived with the strong encouragement of MacArthur's headquarters. Indeed, the Americans hoped that the promise of "normal constitutional government," advocated by the political parties in the 1920s, would be realized.

POLITICAL PARTIES IN MODERN JAPAN

Political parties seem to be a necessity in modern states, whether they be democratic or totalitarian. Political parties initiate and advocate political programs, sponsor candidates who will work for the adoption of these programs, raise money and campaign for their candidates, and provide blocs of votes in the legislature for enactment of their programs (or defeat of their rivals' programs). In a parliamentary-cabinet system of democracy, the leader of the party (or coalition of parties) that controls a majority in the parliament normally serves as the prime minister. Modern representative democracy would likely be an impossibility without political parties, despite all their much criticized faults.

Electoral campaigns, voting strategies in parliament, and choice of a prime minister and his or her cabinet ministers are all greatly affected by the number as well as the individual characteristics of political parties. From 1945 to 1955, Japan had a multiparty system. In 1955 the two wings of the Socialist Party reunited and the two conservative parties combined into one party, inaugurating an essentially two-party arrangement that later became known as "the 1955 system." In the mid-1960s multipartyism seemed to revive. Actually, since 1955, the "dominant party system" has prevailed in Japan. That is to say, until 1989 when the LDP lost its majority in the upper house, only one political party has consistently controlled majorities in both houses of the Diet and held the prime ministership. For over 30 years, without exception the prime ministers and nearly all their cabinet ministers have been members of the Liberal Democratic party (LDP). This is not because Japan is a party dictatorship like the Soviet Union before 1991. It is simply because the other political parties have been unable to muster enough votes among the electorate (who are perfectly free to choose whomever they want for public office) to elect majorities in either house of the Diet.

THE LIBERAL DEMOCRATIC PARTY

The Liberal Democratic party (LDP) was formed in 1955, largely in response to the reunification of the Socialist party earlier that year. The big businesses that had been financ-ing the two rival conservative parties, the Liberal and the Democratic, were concerned that these two parties would waste their funds fighting with each other and fail to protect business from the establishment of a Socialist government committed to the nationalization of privately owned companies, as had occurred in England. Some critics maintain that the Liberal Democratic party is misnamed—that it is neither liberal nor democratic. LDP politicians and their supporters are commonly referred to as conservatives.

The Liberal Democrats stand for private enterprise, protection of the interests of farmers, close economic and strategic ties with the United States, and the maintenance and strengthening of self-defense forces. The top leaders of the party usually are either former bureaucrats or professional politicians. Only a tiny percentage are lawyers by profession. The LDP has served for over 30 years as Japan's ruling party. In the early 1960s, the Japan Socialist party (JSP) was regarded as a serious rival of the LDP; some observers fancied that the JSP was bound to win a parliamentary majority within a few years. Both the LDP and the JSP began to lose their accustomed share of the people's votes when the minor parties—Democratic Socialist party (DSP), Komeito, and Japan Communist party (JCP)—began to attract favorable attention and a "multiparty system" began to emerge. Some observers used the term "one-and-a-half party system" to call attention to the fact that the LDP always held power while the JSP, the principal opposition party, could never win a majority in either house of the Diet.

Issues that have been used against the party have often been adopted by the LDP. One example was the Okinawan question in the 1960s. The opposition parties kept demanding the reversion of Okinawa to Japanese rule, implying that the pro-American LDP was not willing or able to remove Okinawa from American administration. As the issue became more salient in the late 1960s and there seemed to be a possibility that it could be exploited by the Socialists to drive the LDP from office, the prime minister, using his skill as a negotiator and his good relations with the United States, was able to bring about the reversion in 1972. Thus, an issue that had been used against the LDP redounded to its credit. The LDP is the one party that can get things done because it controls the legislative majority and maintains good relations with the United States, and the latter can make a difference.

FACTIONS IN THE LDP

Like the other political parties, the LDP is riddled with factionalism, Indeed the party is essentially a coalition of the party's factions in the two houses of the Diet. Some LDP factions have more seats in the Diet than do some of the other political parties. These factions are essentially alliances of politicians working together to raise money and gain political power and rarely do they stand for a particular policy distinct from the policies of the party as a whole. Each faction has a leader, ordinarily one of the faction's most senior members in terms of number of times elected to the Diet. No faction is headed by a woman. An important qualification for faction leader is the ability to raise funds for the faction.

Virtually every LDP Diet member belongs to a faction. A politician will affiliate with a faction (1) to use the faction's influence in obtaining sponsorship of the party in an election (sponsorship by the party means that one gets money and publicity from the party in a campaign), (2) to receive campaign funds from the faction, and (3) to get the faction leader's support for nomination to a position as cabinet minister or parliamentary vice-minister. The faction leader may hope that his faction and the leaders of several other factions will support him one day for the coveted post of president of the LDP. The LDP president usually is elected by the Diet (where the LDP enjoys a majority) to become prime minister. After the faction leader retires or dies, the faction normally continues in existence and one of the other senior faction members becomes the faction's leader.

For years the factions have borne the brunt of all kinds of criticism. On the face of it they seem feudalistic. Political idealism seems to be completely absent in the factions, which are only out for power and money for their members. Every few years, some party leader proclaims that the factions have been abolished, or that a leader's own faction has been abolished, but within a few weeks, one sees newspaper reports of meetings of the faction members. Factional rivalries occasionally threaten to tear the LDP apart, but at election time, the LDP leaders are usually able to bring the party together to make a solid stand against the opposition parties.

Until the Socialist landslide in the 1989 upper house election, the LDP never failed to win a majority, or at least a plurality, of seats in every election to the upper or lower house of the Diet. In this sense, Japanese politics have been boring, because one always knew in advance that the conservatives would win. Two unpredictable factors were the size of the LDP victory and the size of the victories or losses of each of the LDP factions. The relative strengths of the factions are of vital importance in the intraparty fights for the party presidency, seats in the cabinet, and other benefits for the party members. Thus, after each election, the newspapers report the new factional strengths (see Table 5.1).

Every two years, the LDP Diet elects the party president. A president may usually be reelected only once. Because the LDP president is normally destined to become the next prime minister, the rivalry for the party presidency is very intense. In the past, various procedures have been used to choose the president. Because no single faction leader has enough followers of his or her own to become elected, a leader must make alliances and deals with the leaders of other factions. In the course of the intrigues and maneuvers among the

Table 5.1   FACTIONAL STRENGTHS IN THE
LIBERAL DEMOCRATIC PARTY

In January 1991 the factional strengths were as follows
(each faction is identified by the name of its leader):

LDP faction	Representatives	Councillors	Total
Takeshita	70	36	106
Abe*	66	25	91
Miyazawa	62	21	83
Watanabe**	48	19	67
Komoto	25	7	32
Nikaido group	3	—	3
No faction	8	6	14

*Mr. Abe died in June 1991 and was succeeded as faction
leader by Mitsuzuka Hiroshi.

**This faction was formerly led by Nakasone

Source: Adapted from Asahi Nenkan, 1991, p. 98.

Note: On the eve of the 1991 LDP presidential election, the
LDP factional strengths in the Diet (both houses together) were:
Takeshita, 105; Miyazawa, 81; Mitsuzuka, 80; Kato group (se-
ceders from Mitsuzuka's faction), 8; Watanabe, 67; Komoto, 31.
(Asahi Shinbun, Satellite edition, October 25, 1991, p. 4.)

party leaders, substantial sums of money may
secretly change hands and promises may be
made that are not always kept. The system
is open to corruption and chicanery, and as
the stakes are money and power for individual
politicians rather than the public good, the in-
ternecine conflicts of the LDP often provoke
public disgust.

In the 1991 election for LDP president,
each of the 395 LDP Diet members could
cast one vote and 101 votes were cast by party
branches. Miyazawa Ki-ichi received 285 out of
the 496 votes, winning by a comfortable majority. The leaders of two rival factions, Watanabe and Mitsuzuka, won the remaining ballots. In addition to Miyazawa's own faction, the
largest faction, that of former prime minister
Takeshita, and the faction led by Komoto both
supported Miyazawa.

The Recruit Scandal

In the 1970s many politicians and bureaucrats
were implicated in the Lockheed bribery scandal, including former Prime Minister Tanaka,
who was found guilty and sentenced to hard
labor by the Tokyo court in 1983. (While he
appealed his sentence, he continued his political activities.)

In 1988, it was revealed that many politicians and bureaucrats had received lavish
gifts from the Recruit Company, including
shares of stock in the company. Prime Minister Takeshita and three members of his cabinet resigned because of their involvement.
As most of the principal leaders of the LDP
were implicated, it was almost impossible to
find a suitable successor to Takeshita. Finally,
Foreign Minister Uno Sosuke was offered the
LDP presidency, although he was not a faction
leader. (He was a member of the Nakasone
faction.) On 2 June 1989, he became prime
minister.

Almost immediately, Uno's past affair with
a talkative former geisha was exposed in the
press. The sex scandal, added to the unpopular new sales tax, helped bring about a Socialist landslide in the 1989 upper house election. Uno resigned the party presidency and
was succeeded by Kaifu Toshiki (Komoto faction). Kaifu became prime minister on 9 August 1989.

The matter of political reform became a
big issue. As part of a reform package Prime
Minister Kaifu in 1991 proposed a new electoral system that combined single-member
districts with proportional representation.
This was bitterly opposed not only by the opposition parties but by some LDP politicians
as well. The leaders of the major factions who
had been compromised in the Recruit affair
now decided that it was time to reenter the
race for the party presidency, and contrived to
defeat Kaifu's proposals. Although Kaifu was
more popular with the public than his powerful
rivals, he felt that he had no choice but to re-
nounce any effort to win a second term as party
president and with it the prime ministership.
Kaifu, who was not himself a faction leader (he
was a member of the Komoto faction) had been
like Uno before him—a stand-in until a return

to normalcy, that is, until the memories of the Recruit scandal had sufficiently faded so that the party's faction leaders could reclaim the party presidency for one of their own number.

Kaifu's successor, Miyazawa, had held cabinet positions of foreign minister, finance minister, and deputy prime minister. He had acquired a reputation as both a diplomat and an economist, and as a fluent speaker of English he was expected to conduct Japan's relations with the United States effectively.

THE SOCIAL DEMOCRATIC PARTY OF JAPAN

The Japan Socialist party (JSP) won a plurality of the seats in the lower house in the 1947 election. As a result, the JSP and the Democratic Party formed a coalition government under the leadership of Katayama Tetsu, the JSP leader. The ascension of Katayama, a labor lawyer and a Christian, as Japan's first Socialist prime minister was welcomed by MacArthur's staff, which had regarded Yoshida, the outgoing prime minister, as too conservative. The coalition cabinet, however, could not survive the defection of left-wing Socialists who differed with Katayama over the budget. The successor coalition cabinet included Socialists but was led by the Democrat Ashida Hitoshi. In 1948—when the Ashida cabinet, after a few troubled months, was forced to resign because of a major scandal—Mr. Yoshida formed a conservative cabinet and remained prime minister until 1954. Never since 1948 have Socialists served in the cabinet. The lack of governmental experience has been a substantial handicap to the image of the Socialists among the voters, who place a premium on competence. In 1950, the JSP split because of a dispute over the peace treaty.

When the left and right factions of the JSP reunited in 1955, it appeared that the party had a new lease on life. Alarmed by the Socialist threat, the Liberal and Democratic parties united to form the Liberal Democratic party (LDP). Japan's economic recovery, touched off by the Korean War boom in the early 1950s, deprived the Socialist ideology of its earlier appeal. The Socialists, however, were able to capitalize on the public suspicions of conservative efforts to amend the Constitution and the unpopularity of the new security treaty negotiated by Prime Minister Kishi with the United States in 1959. Popular demonstrations and factional rivalries in the LDP forced Kishi's resignation. Although the LDP won the subsequent general election, there were hopes that the JSP, the second largest party, would soon become the governing party. Instead, the economic boom of the 1960s made the LDP virtually invincible, and with the secession of Nishio's right-wing Socialists, the emergence of the Komeito (which we shall discuss later), and the revival of the Communists, the JSP was faced with rivals for the leadership of the opposition camp.

In the 1970s as the security treaty with the United States and the existence of the Self-Defense Forces became more widely accepted, the Socialists were no longer able to capitalize so successfully on these issues. Their advocacy of "unarmed neutrality" seemed increasingly irrelevant and had to be deemphasized to make electoral alliances with other opposition parties. In the 1969 election, the JSP won fewer seats (90) than the total seats won by the other three opposition parties (92), greatly weakening the viability of the JSP as the leader of the opposition. The 1986 general election was absolutely disastrous for the JSP, when it won only 85 seats, the fewest seats in any election since 1949.

The JSP, from its very beginning, has been torn by internal strife. An uncompromising doctrinaire left wing has long refused to adjust to pragmatic realities, and when moderates have seceded from the party, the Left is even less inclined to compromise. Unlike the Socialist parties of Western Europe, which have strongly supported NATO, the JSP has opposed the alignment with the United States, and instead has seemed to show a preference for the (former) Soviet Union, Communist China, and North Korea. When the Sino-Soviet dispute broke out in the 1960s, some of the JSP members praised the Chinese and blamed the Soviet Union. The external influences on the party have tended to discredit it. When the JSP leadership perennially proposes a left coalition, it is faced with the adamant refusal of the Communists to collaborate with the Democratic Socialists and with the latter's refusal to work with the Communists. After the 1986 electoral debacle, the JSP in an uncharacteristically imaginative stroke, elected a woman (Doi Takako, a law professor), as their leader.

A New Lease on Life

Making the unpopular new sales tax its principal issue, the JSP won a landslide victory in the 1989 upper house election. Ms. Doi announced plans to moderate JSP stands on the security treaty and defense in order to pave the way for a JSP-led coalition. However, in the 1990 lower house election, the poor showing of the JSP's potential coalition partners (DSP and Komeito) and their alienation from the JSP suggested that a JSP-led coalition cabinet was not a credible possibility. The Japan Socialists' poor showing in the 1991 local elections further eroded the party's prospects. The party formally moderated its opposition to the Self-Defense forces and changed its English (but not its Japanese) name to Social Democratic Party of Japan (SDPJ). Ms. Doi resigned the chairmanship of the party, whose members elected as her successor the moderate Tanabe Makoto. Tensions continued among the pacifist, leftist, and moderate factions.

THE COMMUNISTS

The oldest of the three minor parties is the Japan Communist party (JCP). It had a very troubled and usually illegal existence before World War II. At the end of the war, occupation officials obtained the release of the Communist leaders from jail, including Tokuda Kyuichi,

the prewar party leader. Nosaka Sanzo, who had communized Japanese prisoners of war in Yenan, returned from China. The Communists, who had been the prime targets of the discredited Japanese militarists and ultranationalists, were regarded by the Left as martyrs and heroes, but they made themselves unpopular with much of the public for demanding an end to the emperor system.

At the beginning of the occupation, the Communists proclaimed many of the same goals championed by the Allied occupation, such as the breakup of the monopolies and land reform. For a while they advocated the formation of a democratic front and aspired to join a coalition cabinet made up of the progressive and moderate parties. Communists won positions of leadership in labor unions, and in 1947 called for a general strike. MacArthur ordered that the strike be called off, and the Communist leaders lost much of their prestige in the labor movement.

In 1950, the Cominform (the Soviet-run organization that directed the policies of Communist parties worldwide) published a devastating criticism of the opportunism of the JCP, and the party became involved in violent revolutionary activities. This provoked MacArthur's headquarters to ban from political activity ("purge") the leaders of the JCP. The party lost most of its popularity and all of its seats in the Diet. In the 1960s, even as it was embroiled in internal controversies over the Sino-Soviet dispute, it attempted with some success to modify its image. During student uprisings of the late 1960s, the JCP occasionally assumed the role of moderator between the most radical students and the university authorities. Because of its opportunism and willingness to compromise matters of principle, the student radicals were alienated from the Communist party.

The JCP has softened its revolutionary rhetoric and adopted issues that immediately concern the voters, such as the environment, railroad fares, and education. Following the 1989 House of Councillors election, 6 of the 14

Communist councillors were women, while 4 of the 26 Communists in the lower house were women. Because the electoral system, which we will discuss later, has operated very much to the disadvantage of the JCP, the Communists have made a big issue of it. Increasingly the JCP has assumed an image of bourgeois respectability, and has asserted its independence from outside control by criticizing the Soviet occupation of Japan's northern territories and the bloody suppression of the student democracy movement in China in 1989. Largely because of revenue from their publications, the JCP is Japan's second richest party, and during electoral campaigns its loudspeaker trucks are a very common sight and sound.

At the same time, pragmatic progressives often find it difficult to cooperate with the Communists; they fear that in so doing they will weaken their own non-Communist parties. Moreover, in recent years the JCP has shunned united fronts and electoral alliances, thus dividing the forces opposing the conservatives. Some observers suspect that the Communist tactic of attacking other progressive parties as well as the conservatives may be part of a long-term strategy to weaken or destroy the non-Communist Left so that, at an opportune moment, the Communists rather than the Socialists or Komeito will be adopted by the electorate as the only viable alternative to the conservatives who have been ruling Japan for four decades.

The JCP still suffers from the suspicion (of both the Left and Right) that its primary goal is the seizure of power rather than the benefit of the Japanese people. Neither the Soviet nor the Chinese models of communism are today attractive to the electorate. In evaluating the political strategies of the JCP, one should take into account that this party may have different long-range goals from the other political parties. For example, during the 1960s, although the JCP did not enjoy spectacular electoral success, its policy positions (such as the defeat of the U.S.-Japan security treaty) were adopted by other political groups. The party's formal platform remains committed to revolution, and its image suffers from its past association with the Soviet and Chinese Communist Parties.

THE DEMOCRATIC SOCIALISTS

In 1960, some of the Socialists of the right wing quit the JSP in protest against its ties with the JCP, its use of extraparliamentary tactics in opposition to the U.S.-Japan security treaty, and its apparently pro-Soviet, anti-American posture. The seceding group formed the Democratic Socialist party (DSP) under the leadership of Nishio Suehiro, a former labor leader. Domei (the moderate labor union confederation) and anti-Communist intellectuals unhappy with both the JSP and LDP, have traditionally supplied the DSP with money and support. Since its founding in 1960, the DSP has become increasingly conservative, especially on defense issues.

Partly because the electoral system tends to work against the small parties, the DSP has had a tough row to hoe in electoral politics, and its existence has always seemed precarious. Part of its problem has to do with its ambiguous identity. A strong Socialist might want to cooperate more with the SDPJ or to work within that party to make it more effective. A committed anti-Communist might find the LDP more congenial than the DSP. In 1980, when it appeared that the LDP might fail to win a majority in the House of Representatives, the question of a possible coalition cabinet was widely discussed in the media. The JSP especially hoped to lead a coalition that would include the DSP and the Komeito. DSP leaders also liked the idea of a coalition and made it clear that they would be happy to enter a coalition led by the Liberal Democrats. When the LDP won a comfortable majority in the 1980 election, they had no need to include the DSP in their administration. The dissolution of the Domei labor union federation in 1989 and the absorption of its members into the new Rengo deprived the DSP of critical support. The loss of nearly half of its seats (from 26 to 14) in the 1990 election raised new questions about the party's viability.

THE KOMEITO

At the close of World War II, many Japanese were without food or shelter, unemployment was widespread, and people sought refuge in religion. Among the "new religions" that emerged at this time was the *Soka Gakkai,* or Value-Creating Society. This was a kind of lay educational organization that had sprung up before the war as an auxiliary to the old Nichiren Shoshu sect of Buddhism. The Soka Gakkai, in addition to emphasizing traditional forms of chanting and scripture study, practiced faith healing and stressed a wide variety of social and cultural activities. Evangelism was the duty of all the members, and high-pressure methods were used to recruit converts. The Soka Gakkai has become a global organization and has branches in many countries, including centers in major U.S. cities. (In the United States it is known as Nichiren Shoshu in America [NSA].)

The Soka Gakkai has claimed that faith in its doctrines has brought material prosperity to many believers. The worldly concerns of the Soka Gakkai have involved it in politics. In the 1960s it formed the *Komeito,* or Clean Government party. This party would be unlike either the LDP or JSP. It would not represent capitalistic interests nor would it propagate socialism. The formal ties between the Komeito and the Soka Gakkai were officially severed in the 1970s, but in the public mind, the Komeito remains closely associated with the Soka Gakkai. Because of the rapid growth of the Komeito in the 1960s some observers feared that it might become a mass-based authoritarian party that might use its influence to impose its religious beliefs on the rest of the society. In recent years, the party has focused its attention on peace, the environment, and other conventional issues, and it occasionally makes electoral alliances with the Socialists.

The Komeito generally sponsors candidates in districts where there is a high probability of victory. As a result, its ratio between number of seats won to number of votes is the highest among the parties. Where it does not sponsor a candidate, the candidates of other parties are most tactful in their treatment of the Soka Gakkai and Komeito. In terms of seats held in both the upper and lower houses of the Diet, the Komeito is the third largest party and plays a leading role in the opposition. It is also prominent in local politics.

WOMEN IN JAPANESE POLITICS

Women were given the right to vote by General MacArthur in 1946, a right confirmed by the democratic Constitution later that year. In the 1946 general election, 39 women were elected to the House of Representatives. In that election, large multimember districts were used, a factor which may have made it easier for women to be elected. Never since have women candidates for the lower house done so well. In the 1990 election for the lower house, 12 women, 7 of whom were Socialists and none of whom were Liberal Democrats, won seats.

In the 1989 upper house election, which the JSP under the leadership of a woman, Doi Takako, won by a landslide, 22 women were elected. When to these were added the 11 women members whose seats had not been at stake, the total number of women councillors came to 33, amounting to 13.1 percent of all of the seats in the upper house. One of every eight councillors was a woman. Male chauvinism in Japan (often said to be a major bastion of that persuasion among the industrialized states) had suffered a major defeat.

The bright and attractive middle-aged women candidates who emerged in the 1989 campaign were popularly dubbed "madonnas." They were especially sensitive to education, consumer, and environmental issues and had been especially aroused by the imposition of the consumption tax. It has been observed that many of these women had been active in PTAs and that after their children had grown up they now had the time to apply their leadership skills in the political arena.

Possibly in response to the political clout of "woman power," the new conservative prime minister, Kaifu, in 1989 appointed to the cabinet for the first time *two* women. But in the general election the following year, the LDP did not include a single woman among its 325 candidates and won that election handily. Because of her party's poor performance in local elections in 1991, Doi had to step down from the SDPJ chairpersonship.

THE ELECTORAL SYSTEM FOR THE LOWER HOUSE

The term of the members of the House of Representatives is four years, but normally the House is dissolved before the four years have elapsed, so that general elections are normally held once every two or three years.

The Constitution provides that the qualifications of both the voters and the members of the Diet shall be determined by law, but there can be no discrimination because of race, creed, sex, social status, family origin, education, property, or income. The law provides that to vote one must be 20 years of age or older.

The electoral system for the House of Representatives is different from that of any other major national legislative assembly. At the time of the 1986 and 1990 elections there were 130 electoral districts (see Table 5.2). One district elected 6 members, 43 districts each elected 5 members, 39 districts each elected 4 members, 42 districts each elected 3 members, 4 districts each elected 2 members, and 1 district elected 1 member. The 130 districts, therefore, altogether sent 512 members to the House of Representatives.

In Japanese lower house elections each voter is permitted to vote for only one candidate. The candidates receiving the most votes are declared elected. Thus, in a five-member district, each voter selects only one candidate and the five candidates receiving the most votes are declared the winners and will represent the district. This arrangement makes it possible for a minority party to win a seat in the district, and it reduces the possibility that a plurality party will win all the seats in a district. (In a single-member-district (SMD) system, with which the British and Americans are familiar, the plurality party wins the single seat for the district and the other parties are left with nothing to show for their pains.) The Japanese call their arrangement the "medium-sized district system" and it is known to political scientists as the single nontransferable vote (SNTV) system.

Electoral Reform

The Japanese SNTV system, however, often produces proportional representation (PR), which assigns a number of seats for each political party proportionate to the number of the party's votes. The system works best for the LDP and the SDPJ; they generally receive more seats than their respective proportions of the vote would justify under proportional representation. The system works badly for the small parties, which win fewer seats than their proportion of the votes would justify under PR. Another problem has been the failure of the government to redistribute seats when some districts lose population and others gain population. The LDP majority in the Diet has been reluctant to reduce the representation of rural areas, which have been loyally electing conservative candidates. Several years ago, the Japanese Supreme Court declared unconstitutional the apportionment plan then in force, and a new distribution of seats was used for the 1986 election. As things turned out, the reapportionment did no appreciable damage to the LDP, which won a landslide victory in that election.

From time to time the LDP has seriously considered eliminating multimember districts and replacing them with one- or two-member

Table 5.2 HOUSE OF REPRESENTATIVES ELECTIONS

Parties	1946	1947	1949	1952	1953	1955	1958	1960	1963	1967	1969	1972	1976	1979	1980	1983	1986	1990
Progressive (Democratic)	94	121	69	85	76	185												
Liberal (Democratic Liberal)	140	131	264	240	199	112												
Cooperative	14	29	14		35*													
Liberal Democratic							287	296	283	277	288	271	249	248	284	250	300	275
New Liberal Club													17	4	12	8	6	
Japan Socialist	92	143	48				166	145	144	140	90	118	123	107	107	112	85	136
Right-wing Socialist				57	66	67												
Left-wing Socialist				54	72	89												
Democratic Socialist								17	23	30	31	19	29	35	32	38	26	14
Labor Farmer			7	4	5	4												
Social Democratic Federation														2	3	3	4	4
Komeito										25	47	29	55	57	33	58	56	45
Japan Communist	5	4	35	0	1	2	1	3	5	5	14	38	17	39	29	26	26	16
Minor parties	38	25	17	7	1	2	1	1				2						1
Independent	81	13	12	19	11	6	12	5	12	9	16	14	21	19	11	16	9	21
Total	464	466	466	466	466	467	467	467	467	486	486	491	511	511	511	511	512	512

[a] Hatoyama Liberal

districts. Because the LDP would receive majorities (or pluralities) in nearly all districts, the results would be disastrous for the SDPJ and catastrophic for the smaller parties, which would have virtually no chance. The effort of the Hatoyama cabinet to change the system to small districts (called the "Hatomander") provoked street demonstrations and the cabinet withdrew its bill from consideration.

Campaigning in multimember districts involves LDP candidates competing with each other for votes, and the resulting expense is an incentive to corruption. In 1991, Prime Minister Kaifu proposed a system that combined single-member districts with PR as part of a political reform package. The opposition parties, as well as some Liberal Democrats, strongly opposed any change that would threaten them with disaster. When Kaifu's proposals were blocked by rivals in his own party (who had been looking for an issue with which to embarrass him), he gave up any thought of another term as LDP president and prime minister.

The ballot in Japan does not carry either the names of the candidates or the parties: the voter must write his or her favorite candidate's name on the ballot. The LDP usually endorses several candidates in each district; conservative voters thus must choose among the LDP candidates. These mechanical factors tend to emphasize the individual candidate over the party.

ELECTORAL STRATEGIES

A principal problem with the SNTV is that if a party endorses too many candidates in a district, the votes of the party's supporters will be spread too thin among too many candidates, and none (or fewer than would otherwise be the case) will get enough votes to win a seat. (Or it might even happen that a party endorses too few candidates, so that it does not get the full benefit of the party's strength in the electorate.) The pressure in the party to sponsor too many candidates is very great. In recent years, the LDP has managed to severely restrict the number of its endorsements to ensure the optimal result. The LDP usually endorses two or more candidates in each district, but fewer candidates than there are seats for the district.

Rarely does the SDPJ have enough supporters to elect more than one Socialist candidate in a district, so it usually endorses only one candidate. The Communists also endorse only one candidate per district. In most districts, the Communists always fail to win a

single seat, so many Communist votes are wasted. The DSP and Komeito each normally endorse one candidate only in those districts where a fair chance of success exists. The DSP, Komeito, and JSP occasionally make electoral alliances, by which they agree to support one another's candidates, thus making the most effective use of progressive votes. In 1980 and again in 1986, the government held the election for the upper and lower houses at the same time, making it difficult for the opposition parties to organize electoral alliances. In both cases, the LDP won by landslides.

The nature of the electoral system makes it possible to determine the outcome of the election in advance—in broad outline. For example, in the 1990 general election only the LDP endorsed enough candidates (the party endorsed 325) to have the possibility of winning a majority (257) of the 512 seats in the lower house. Even if every one of the 148 Socialist candidates had won seats, they still would not have captured a majority of the seats in the chamber. The same could be said of the other parties. Thus, even before the election was held, everyone knew that none of the opposition parties could possibly win a majority of seats. Because only the LDP had a mathematical potential to win a majority of seats, the LDP was the only party that would be able to establish a one-party cabinet, whereas a cabinet made up of the other parties probably would be an unpredictable and unstable combination. Voters desiring political stability would be inclined to vote conservative in order to produce a single-party cabinet with the stable majority in the House of Representatives necessary to govern effectively.

UPPER HOUSE ELECTIONS

The House of Councillors consists of 252 members, 100 of whom are elected using a system of proportional representation and 152 of whom represent electoral districts. The six-year terms of the members are staggered so that elections are held every three years to fill one-half of the seats.

At each election, 50 seats (of the 126 seats at stake) have to be filled by proportional representation. Each political party proposes a list of candidates and each voter indicates the list that he or she prefers. Parties are awarded seats roughly in proportion to the number of votes their lists have won. Thus, a party whose list wins 18 percent of the vote is awarded the

Table 5.3 HOUSE OF COUNCILLORS ELECTIONS

	1947	1950	1953	1956	1959	1962	1965	1968
Progressive (Democratic)	6 (22)	1 (8)	3 (5)					
Liberal (Democratic Liberal)	8 (30)	18 (34)	16 (30)					
Cooperative	3 (6)							
Liberal Democratic				19 (42)	22 (49)	21 (48)	25 (46)	21 (48)
New Liberal Club								
Ryokufukai		6 (3)	8 (8)	5	4 (2)			
Japan Socialist	17 (30)	15 (21)	11 (17)	21 (28)	17 (21)	15 (22)	12 (24)	12 (16)
Democratic Socialist						3 (1)	2 (1)	4 (3)
Labor-Farmer		1 (1)						
Social Democratic Federation								
Komeito						7 (2)	9 (2)	9 (4)
Japan Communist	3 (1)	2		1 (1)	1	2 (1)	2 (1)	3 (1)
Minor Parties	6 (7)	1 (2)	(1)	1	1	2[a]		
Independent	57 (54)	12 (7)	15 (14)	5 (4)	7 (3)	8 (4)	2 (1)	2 (3)
Total	100 (150)	56 (76)	53 (75)	52 (75)	52 (75)	58 (78)	52 (75)	51 (75)

	1971	1974	1977	1980	1983	1986	1989	Total Seats After 1989 Election[b]
Progressive (Democratic)								
Liberal (Democratic Liberal)								
Cooperative								
Liberal Democratic	21 (42)	19 (43)	18 (45)	21 (48)	19 (49)	22 (50)	15 (21)	109 (6)
New Liberal Club			1 (2)	0 (0)	1 (1)[c]			
Ryokufukai								
Japan Socialist	11 (28)	10 (18)	10 (17)	9 (13)	9 (13)	9 (11)	20 (26)	66 (14)
Democratic Socialist	4 (2)	4 (1)	4 (2)	3 (2)	4 (2)	3 (2)	2 (1)	8 (0)
Labor-Farmer								
Social Democratic Federation			1 (0)[d]	1 (0)				
Komeito	8 (2)	9 (5)	9 (3)	9 (3)	8 (6)	7 (3)	6 (4)	20 (3)
Japan Communist	5 (1)	8 (5)	3 (4)	3 (4)	5 (2)	5 (4)	4 (1)	14 (6)
Minor Parties		9 (1)	1 (1)	1 (1)	4	3	3 (13)[e]	20 (2)
Independent	1 (1)	4 (3)	3 (2)	3 (5)	(3)	(6)	(10)	15 (2)
Total	50 (76)	54 (76)	57 (76)	50 (76)	50 (76)	50 (76)	50 (76)	252 (33)

Note: Figures not in parentheses refer to the proportional representation constituency—which before 1983 had been preceded by the national constituency—those in parentheses refer to the prefectural constituencies.

[a] Doshikai.

[b] Total seats, including both proportional representation and prefectural constituencies. Seats held by women are shown in brackets.

[c] The alliance of the New Liberal Club and the Social Democratic Federation won 1 (1)?

[d] The Socialist Citizens League, which later became the Social Democratic Federation.

[e] Includes 11 seats won by Rengo in prefectural constituencies.

corresponding 18 percent (9) of the 50 seats. The top nine candidates on the party's list are then awarded the seats. Of course, in practice the details of the mathematics are more complicated than this. The list system was first used in Japan in the 1983 election and remains controversial. (In previous elections, the relevant 50 seats were filled by SNTV, using the country at large as a single district. Each voter chose one candidate and the 50 candidates winning the most votes won the seats.)

The principal objection to the list system of PR is that candidates at the top of the lists of the major parties are virtually assured election whether they campaign or not, whereas those at the bottom of the list have almost no chance. Voters are not given a voice in choosing the candidates for a party's list. The lists are composed by party bosses who tend to favor old-guard party regulars who have the support of their faction leaders.

Also, at each election 76 seats are filled by using the 47 prefectures as electoral districts. At each election each district is entitled to elect from one to four councillors depending on the size of the district. (see Table 5.3). The SNTV is used. Each voter chooses one candidate, and the candidates winning the most votes are declared elected.

The electoral systems for the two houses of the Diet seem complicated when they have to be described to non-Japanese. For the voters, however, elections are simple. The rules of the game have a lot to do with who wins and who loses, so that politicians are much preoccupied (as are the courts) with possible improvements in the system. But any change would affect each party differently. As it now works, the larger parties tend to win a share of seats slightly higher than the proportion of the number of votes won by their candidates. The smaller parties, which do not have the voting clout in the Diet to change the system, would fare somewhat better under a more precise version of proportional representation. In Japan, as elsewhere, theoretical justice does not always prevail over the realities of political power.

THE ELECTORAL SYSTEM AND THE PARTY SYSTEM

The tendency of American political scientists is to analyze elections in terms of a triad of variables: candidate, issue, and party. A fourth factor, a constant taken for granted and therefore not mentioned, is the electoral system. The Japanese party system would work very differently if the electoral system were different.

The present configuration, as has been said, is that of a "party dominant" system, in the sense that one party tends to virtually monopolize political power. The LDP has been the dominant party; the JSDP is the second major party, but from 1948 until 1989 has been too weak to challenge the dominant party seriously. The DSP, JCP, and Komeito are the minor parties in the system; also there are several almost inconsequential splinter parties. The SNTV allows minor parties to survive, whereas survival would be much more difficult for them in the American SMD system.

The electoral systems have been under attack on two grounds. First, it is alleged that the SNTV system itself is unfair: certain parties are underrepresented (a leftist complaint), and the size of the multimember districts requires excessive campaign expenditures, thus inviting corruption (a conservative complaint). Second, the seats have not been adequately reapportioned to compensate for the shift in population from rural to urban districts (see Feature 5.1).

THE JAPANESE PARTY SYSTEM AND DEMOCRACY

What are the implications of the Japanese party system for democratic politics? Does the lack of rotation in office and the apparently permanent domination of the system by the LDP mean that democracy is impossible in Japan as some observers believe? To answer this question, consider both the negative and

---

Feature 5.1 **Malapportionment**

Over the years, as more and more people have moved to the cities, the apportionment of seats in both houses of the Diet has failed to keep pace and some districts are grossly over- or underrepresented. In 1990, each lower house seat for the Chiba prefecture fourth district represented 464,108 inhabitants, whereas each member in the Tokyo eighth district represented 137,417 people. In effect this meant that in the Tokyo eighth district a vote carried over three times as much weight as a vote in the Chiba fourth district.

In the House of Councillors, the most extreme imbalance was between the Kanagawa prefectural constituency, where there were 1,995,105 people per councillor, and the Tottori prefectural constituency, where there were only 307,871 voters per councillor. Thus each Tottori prefecture inhabitant was over six times more represented in the upper house than a person living in the Kanagawa prefecture.[2]

On several occasions, the courts have condemned the apportionment in some districts as unconstitutional, but have not gone so far as to invalidate an election or redraw district lines. Recognizing differences between functions of the lower and upper houses, the courts have tolerated wider discrepancies in apportionment in the upper house than in the lower. The Diet has only reluctantly made minor changes in the allotment of seats for fear of depriving incumbents of their constituencies. We may expect the Diet to tinker with the apportionment under pressure from the judiciary at the same time that fundamental reforms in the structure of the electoral system are being debated. (Of course, the Japanese example pales in comparison with the apparent malapportionment in the U.S. Senate. In 1990, Alaska had as many senators as California, whose population was 54.1 times that of Alaska.)

---

positive factors in the equation. The negative elements are the following:

1. The Japanese people have a fondness for conformity.
2. Japan lacks large ethnic and religious minorities that would tend to challenge the dominant ruling group.
3. The overwhelming majority of the people believe that they belong to one class—the middle class—and that they do not need class-based political parties.
4. Politicians in the opposition parties never have a chance to govern at the national level and acquire credible resumes.

5. Money seems to be all powerful in the LDP, which seems excessively subservient to big business and unduly susceptible to outright bribery.
6. The opposition's political parties are unduly attached to unpopular or obsolete ideologies and are incapable of gaining the mass support needed to function effectively in the democratic system.
7. Candidates who are incumbents (or are relatives of retiring incumbents) are nearly always assured of election, thus discouraging the emergence of new personalities and ideas.

On the positive side we note the following:

1. The Constitution and electoral laws make it possible for politicians to be elected as individuals, as members of small parties, and as members of large parties.
2. The Constitution provides for the right to vote without sexual, racial, or other unfair discrimination.
3. Although there is little real competition between political parties for cabinet posts, there is competition among the factions of the LDP; rotation in office is provided for by the rivalry among semiautonomous LDP factions.
4. The multiplicity of political parties provides voters with real choices.
5. Local government provides opportunities for leaders of the opposition parties to acquire political experience and national reputations.
6. If mass media are a reliable indication, the highly literate general public is interested in and is fairly well informed about political matters.
7. The voting rate in Japan is fairly high, certainly higher than in the United States.

THE DIET

The Japanese call their parliament *Kokkai*, which literally means "national assembly," but the English word *Diet* is usually used to describe it. Under the Meiji Constitution, Japan's bicameral parliament was referred to as *Teikoku Gikai*, or, in the official English translation, *Imperial Diet*. The Japanese Diet, created in 1889, is the oldest parliament in Asia. Today's House of Representatives represents a continuation of the prewar lower house. But today's House of Councillors (the upper house), is a democratic institution, very different from the prewar House of Peers, an aristocratic body.

General MacArthur is known to have preferred that Japan's democratic parliament be unicameral, like the Nebraska legislature. Japan, MacArthur's staff pointed out to Japanese officials, did not have a federal system and therefore did not need an upper house to represent the states. The Japanese believed that a second chamber was needed to act as a check on the popularly elected chamber. They wanted an upper house based on functional (or vocational) representation. The Americans held that functional representation would violate the Constitution, which provided that qualifications of both Diet members and electors could not involve discrimination because of "race, creed, sex, social status, family origin, education, property, or income." As enacted, the democratic Constitution provided for a House of Councillors but failed to indicate the nature of its composition. Later, a law was passed prescribing the electoral system described earlier in this chapter.

From the beginning the function of the House of Councillors, the product of a compromise, was an enigma. If the House of Representatives were a truly democratic body that accurately represented the people's will, there was no need—from a democratic point of view—for a second chamber, which at best would only confirm the will of the democratic lower chamber and at worst would obstruct the democratic will.

The six-year staggered terms of the members of the House of Councillors and the relevant electoral laws were expected to make that body more conservative than the lower house, but in the 1989 election, the Socialist-led opposition parties captured a majority of the seats. As a result, the opposition has recently been in a position to veto key legislation, and the conservative administration in Japan (like the Bush administration in the United States) has had to deal with stubborn opposition in the legislative branch.

Because the prime minister is not constitutionally empowered to decide to dissolve the House of Councillors, he must deal with its obstruction as best he can. In this sense, government in Japan after the 1989 election may be said to be "divided," a contingency that is unusual in the parliamentary-cabinet system of government.

The Legislative Process

To become law, a bill must be debated in both chambers of the Diet. If the House of Councillors does not pass a bill within 60 days after its approval by the lower house, the bill is considered to have been rejected by the councillors. The councillors' veto may be overridden in the lower house by a two-thirds vote. If the councillors refuse to pass the budget or to approve a treaty, and their difference with the House of Representatives is not resolved in a joint committee, the will of the House of Representatives prevails. The amendment of the Constitution requires approval of two-thirds of the entire membership of each house and ratification by a majority of the voters. No party, not even the LDP, has captured the majorities in both houses of the Diet necessary to amend the Constitution, and it is very conceivable that the House of Councillors could veto a proposed amendment.

Most bills originate in a ministry of the government, which is sensitive to the demands of big business, agriculture, and the conservative voters that put it in office. After the ministry has approved the bill, it may be discussed with the relevant study group in the LDP's Policy Research Council. It is circulated among various concerned ministries, and is considered by the full Policy Research Council. After the cabinet's approval of a bill, arrangements must then be made to put the bill on the Diet's agenda.[3]

Ordinarily, bills are sponsored by the government and, in each house, they are referred to the appropriate standing committees. Because the LDP usually commands a majority in every committee, and often holds the chairmanship of every committee, committee approval is assured. If the bill is sufficiently repugnant to the sensibilities of the opposition, the opposition may use obstructive tactics (sometimes including physical force) in either the committee or the plenary session, or both, to prevent a vote from being taken. The use of obstructive measures is not purely the function of emotional outrage; by using boycotts and filibusters concessions may sometimes be extracted from the government. Delaying tactics may prevent a bill from coming to a vote before a Diet session is closed. Faced with enough opposition, which may include massive street demonstrations, the government might even give up trying to enact its bill. (This happened in 1959, when the government tried to enact its police duties bill.)

As earlier noted, the Councillors' terms of office is six years. The upper house is not subject to dissolution, so that the members may serve out their full terms. With longer terms of office and with the system of staggering terms, the composition of the upper house is much more stable than that of the lower house. This stability is enhanced by the fact that incumbents stand a very strong chance of being reelected.

In 1989, for the first time in decades, the upper house fell under the control of the political opposition. The LDP government does not have the two-thirds majority in the lower house needed to override an upper house veto, and finds it necessary to seek the support of other parties in order to enact its program.

THE CABINET

To use Bagehot's terminology,[4] since 1946, whereas Japan's imperial throne may be the "dignified part" of the Constitution, the cabinet is the "efficient part" of it. Under the Meiji Constitution, executive powers were dispersed among the *Genro*, the Privy Council, the cabinet, and the military Supreme Command. When needed, the residual power of the sovereign emperor to issue ordinances could be employed. Although executive authority overwhelmed the power of the weak Imperial Diet, the authority of the cabinet, which was not even mentioned as such in the Imperial Constitution, was subject to constant challenge from the *Genro*, the Privy Council, and the military. Under the postwar constitution, these rivals of the cabinet no longer exist, and "Executive power shall be vested in the Cabinet."

RESPONSIBLE GOVERNMENT

"Responsible government," insisted upon by the Allied Powers, required that the executive be answerable directly to the people or answerable to an assembly elected by the people. Either a congressional-presidential system after the American model or a parliamentary-cabinet system after the British model would have been acceptable to the Allied Powers, but given the existence of a monarch and the precedent of Taisho democracy, the British model would be much more compatible with Japanese tradition. At the time of the drafting of the postwar constitution, Japan had a multiparty system. It was apparently anticipated that the cabinet, unsupported by a stable majority, would be subservient to the Diet, which was declared to be the "highest organ of state power."

The first business of the Diet after a general election (i.e., a House of Representatives election) is to designate the prime minister from among its members. An election is held in each house, and if the two houses are unable to agree on a single individual, the decision of the House of Representatives becomes the decision of the Diet. Because the Liberal Democratic party normally occupies a majority of the seats in both houses (or at least in the House of Representatives), it is a foregone conclusion that the LDP president will be elected prime minister. This is why the factional struggle for the LDP presidency previously discussed is so important. The Constitution requires the emperor to "appoint the Prime Minister as designated by the Diet."

Following the victory of the JSP-led opposition parties in the 1989 House of Councillors election, the Socialist leader, Ms. Doi Takako, was elected by that house to become prime minister, but the lower house, which on this issue constitutionally prevails over the upper house, chose Kaifu, who was duly appointed prime minister by the emperor. (Ms. Doi was again proposed for prime minister after the 1990 general election, but was defeated in the upper as well as in the lower house because this year the other opposition parties refused to support her.)

The prime minister occupies a position in Japanese politics that is different from that of the president of the United States. The American president is elected by the people (via the electoral college) and therefore may claim a popular mandate for his program. His tie with the voters is virtually direct. The prime minister, on the other hand, is not directly chosen by the people but rather by the Diet, which serves as an electoral college for this purpose. Because of the vagaries of political intrigue in

Miyazawa Kiichi, the leader of a large faction in the Liberal Democratic party who became prime minister in November 1991.

the LDP involved in the choice of that party's president (who normally is chosen as prime minister by the Diet), the prime minister is ultimately chosen by the Liberal Democratic party. It is not necessary to be personally popular or a great orator in order to become prime minister, but it is normally necessary to be a faction leader in the LDP. (Of course if the prime minister is thoroughly unacceptable to the public, the public may choose to punish the LDP at the next election.)

Table 5.4   JAPAN'S PRIME MINISTERS, 1945–1991

April 7, 1945	Admiral Suzuki Kantaro
(August 15, 1945, Japan time, World War II ended.)	
August 17, 1945	Prince Higashikuni Naruhiko
October 9, 1945	Shidehara Kijuro (Progressive)
May 22, 1946	Yoshida Shigeru (Liberal)
(May 3, 1947, new Constitution became effective.)	
May 24, 1947	Katayama Tetsu (Socialist)
March 10, 1948	Ashida Hitoshi (Democrat)
October 19, 1948	Yoshida Shigeru (Democratic Liberal), 4 terms*
December 10, 1954	Hatoyama Ichiro (Democrat), 3 terms
(Since Hatoyama's term all of the prime ministers have been Liberal Democrats)	
December 23, 1956	Ishibashi Tanzan
February 25, 1957	Kishi Nobusuke, 2 terms
July 19, 1960	Ikeda Hayato, 3 terms
November 9, 1964	Sato Eisaku, 3 terms
July 7, 1972	Tanaka Kakuei, 2 terms
December 9, 1974	Miki Takeo
December 24, 1976	Fukuda Takeo
December 7, 1978	Ohira Masayoshi, 2 terms
July 17, 1980	Suzuki Zenko
November 27, 1982	Nakasone Yasuhiro, 3 terms
November 6, 1987	Takeshita Noboru
June 2, 1989	Uno Sosuke
August 9, 1989	Kaifu Toshiki, 2 terms
November 5, 1991	Miyazawa Kiichi

Note: The term of a prime minister formally begins with his appointment by the emperor following his designation by the Diet. The length of his term is not fixed by the Constitution or a statute, but depends on personal and political factors.

*Yoshida, having previously been prime minister, served a total of five terms.

Since the end of the second World War, as of early 1992 Japan has had 21 different prime ministers, while during the same period, the United States has had only 9 presidents. Their average tenure of office has been only two years, four months, as compared to the American chief executives' five years, one month. The relatively short tenures of the Japanese heads of government may be explained by interfactional rivalry in the LDP, the short term of office of LDP presidents, and ill health. Since 1945, prime ministers who have served the longest periods in office have been Sato, Yoshida, and Nakasone, in that order (see list of postwar prime ministers in Table 5.4.).

The relationship of the prime minister to the Diet is very different from that of the president to the Congress. Having been chosen as prime minister by the majority in the Diet—a majority consisting of his or her own political party—the prime minister may confidently expect party members in the Diet to ensure the passage of legislation that his or her government proposes. Although the Diet is described in the Constitution as the highest organ of state power, in practice it is the Liberal Democratic party that rules Japan, for that party dominates all three branches of the government: legislative, executive, and judicial. However, after the opposition parties led by the JSP won a majority of the seats in the House of Councillors in 1989, the LDP leaders have had to make compromises with one or more other parties or see their legislation defeated.

Cabinet Members

The prime minister must select a majority of his cabinet members from among the members of the Diet, and all cabinet ministers must be civilians. In practice, the cabinet members are selected primarily on the basis of political expediency. Posts are allocated to members of the different LDP factions in such a way as to ensure maximum stability. Diet members like to become cabinet ministers because the title is one that confers prestige on them for the rest of their lives. It is one of the duties of a faction leader to get as many cabinet posts for his followers as possible. The most prestigious posts are the ministries of finance and of foreign affairs. These are often stepping stones to the prime ministership.

Following the 1983 election, in which the LDP failed to win a majority of the seats, Nakasone appointed a member of the New Liberal Club to his cabinet. This was the first coalition cabinet in almost 30 years. Although the LDP had garnered a majority by accepting several independent MPs in its ranks, the coalition with the New Liberal Club facilitated the LDP's control over the Diet committees. After its landslide victory in 1986, the LDP did not need a coalition partner and held majorities and occupied chairmanships in all of the standing committees in the lower house and most of the standing committees in the upper house.

The cabinet lasts only as long as it is acceptable to the Diet. If the House of Representatives votes no confidence in the cabinet, the cabinet must either (1) resign, in which case a new prime minister must be designated or (2) ask the emperor to dissolve the House, in which case elections are held for the lower house. In practice, it is most unlikely that the members of the majority party, the LDP, will allow a no-confidence resolution to pass and possibly force an election which might imperil their seats. (But this did happen in 1980 when a bloc of LDP members temporarily deserted Prime Minister Ohira when the Socialists introduced a no-confidence resolution.) The LDP cabinets have usually had little to fear in the way of votes of no confidence or defeats of their major legislation.

The constitutional term of office of members of the House of Representatives is four years, but the cabinet normally does not like to wait that long and prefers to hold general elections at politically propitious times. The Constitution was formerly interpreted to mean that the prime minister may ask for a dissolution only after the House of Representatives has voted no confidence. After the occupation had ended, and MacArthur's staff could no longer enforce its interpretation, Yoshida without a prior no-confidence vote asked the emperor for a dissolution. This highly controversial act ("surprise dissolution") set a precedent, and the lower house is dissolved whenever the cabinet deems it politically advantageous to the LDP to hold an election. Only once (in 1976) have the lower house members been able to serve out their full four years.

The Constitution does not provide for the dissolution of the House of Councillors. In 1980 and 1986 "double elections" were held. That is, the lower house election was scheduled for the same day that the triennial election for the upper house was held. In both instances the opposition parties found it difficult to make electoral alliances and the LDP won resounding landslide victories. In the future, prime ministers may be tempted to have more double elections.

MONEY POLITICS

In 1972, Prime Minister Tanaka, who was a wealthy construction magnate as well as a politician, was forced to resign because his personal financial irregularities were exposed in a leading monthly magazine. (This scandal was unrelated to the Lockheed scandal which came later.) LDP elders engineered his replacement as party president (and prime minister) by Miki Takeo, a leader of a minor faction, but a man with a reputation of integrity. During Miki's administration, the Lockheed scandal came to light, and Miki's policy, not very popular in his party, was to get at the truth even though many LDP politicians seemed to be directly or indirectly implicated. The affair was thoroughly exposed in the media, Diet hearings, and the courts during the following years.

In 1976, former prime minister Tanaka was arrested on suspicion of violating currency regulations and taking a bribe from the American Lockheed Corporation, which had tried to sell aircraft to the All Nippon Airways and the Air Self-Defense Force. During his trial, Tanaka continued to be active in politics. When Nakasone Yasuhiro, whose faction was only the fourth largest in the LDP, sought the party presidency in 1982, he depended heavily on the support of Tanaka's faction, the party's largest faction. When Nakasone's first cabinet was formed it was dubbed the "Tanakasone Cabinet" because so many of its members belonged to the Tanaka group, whose support was indispensable if Nakasone was to govern. The scandal gave no appearance of weakening the dominance of the Tanaka faction in the party. Tanaka resigned from his party but continued as leader of the LDP's largest faction. When, after his conviction in 1983, he refused to resign his seat in the Diet, opposition members began a boycott of the lower house. Nakasone dissolved the house but in the ensuing election, which resulted in the loss of many seats by the LDP, Tanaka, a master of pork barrel tactics, was overwhelmingly reelected and his faction emerged almost as powerful as ever.

Tanaka appealed his conviction to a higher court and maintained control of his faction, which in January 1987 was still the LDP's largest. He apparently hoped that a higher court would find him innocent and he could again become LDP president and prime minister of Japan. After a stroke in 1985, his health worsened and a struggle ensued within his faction for leadership. In 1987, Takeshita Noboru won the intrafactional fight and most of the Tanaka faction became his. (Finally in 1990, Tanaka chose not to run for reelection.) Takeshita was favored by Nakasone as the latter's successor and was elected LDP president in October 1987. He became prime minister the following month.

The Lockheed scandal and Tanaka's enormous influence in the LDP even after his bribery conviction strengthened the view that money dominated Japanese politics and that the politicians cared more about power and money for themselves than about the people's well-being. The Recruit scandal was a princi-

pal factor in Takeshita's resignation and the JSP landslide victory in the 1989 upperhouse election. During the Kaifu administration, scandals in the banking and securities industries hurt the government's image and precipitated the resignation of the finance minister. Kaifu's political reform program ran into opposition in his own party and he renounced any ambition to be reelected to the LDP presidency.

Although the conservative politicians may be very much beholden to business interests for contributions, the spoils system as we know it in America is almost nonexistent in Japan. The bureaucracy is staffed entirely by career civil servants chosen and promoted on the basis of merit. The only jobs in the executive branch dependent on partisan sponsorship are the posts of cabinet ministers and parliamentary vice-ministers. These are held by LDP Diet members who owe their appointment in the administration to their respective faction leaders and the prime minister.

THE COURTS AND JUDICIAL REVIEW

There are several levels of courts: 1 Supreme Court, 8 high courts, 49 district courts (with 235 branches), and 570 summary courts. In addition, there are 49 family courts (with 235 branches). The courts all pertain to the national government. Supreme Court judges are appointed by the cabinet and are subject to the approval of the people at the time of the next general election and every ten years thereafter. No judge has ever been turned down as a result of the popular vote. The chief judge of the Supreme Court is "designated" by the cabinet and "appointed" by the emperor. The imperial appointment presumably places the chief judge on a plane of equality with the prime minister.

Japan's prewar legal system under the Meiji Constitution was heavily influenced by the French and German models, which represented the European civil law tradition. Under Japan's postwar Constitution, it is fair to say that while the legal principles introduced by the occupation are clearly evident, old attitudes still exist among the senior members of the judiciary, who are predominantly conservative.

Under the 1948 Code of Criminal Procedure the former inquisitorial procedure was replaced by the adversary procedure, believed to be more favorable to the interest of defendants. The right of trial by jury, such as prescribed in the Bill of Rights of the American Constitution, does not exist in Japan. Judges make decisions without the assistance of lay juries. The Japanese Supreme Court has held that capital punishment is not unconstitutional.

Probably the most notable power of the courts is their authority to review the constitutionality of governmental acts and of legislation. In Japan, as in America, it has become customary for the political opposition to challenge the constitutionality of legislation they especially dislike, so that the courts may serve political purposes. Although the Constitution explicitly grants the power of judicial review, the courts have been rather reluctant to strike down legislation, partly out of deference to tradition and to the Diet, which according to the Constitution is "the highest organ of state power," and partly because of concern about the political consequences of a highly controversial decision.

Article 9

The most controversial clause of the Constitution, Article 9, which renounces war and the maintenance of military forces, has been the focus of much judicial attention. In 1959 in the Sunakawa case, a district court declared that the security treaty with the United States was unconstitutional because it provided for the maintenance of military forces. If this decision had been allowed to stand, American forces in Japan would have had to go home. The Supreme Court, however, promptly overruled the district court, indicating that the

treaty was not *clearly* unconstitutional and that a political question was involved.

In the Naganuma Nike missile case, a district court declared that the laws creating the Self-Defense Force and the Defense Agency violated Article 9. A high court and finally the Supreme Court ruled in 1982 that the original plaintiffs lacked standing to sue. The Supreme Court left undecided the question of the constitutionality of the Self-Defense Forces, and to this day we do not have a definitive ruling on this issue.

For some years it was feared that the failure of the Supreme Court to come directly to grips with the interpretation of Article 9 would result in the ultimate disappearance of the review authority. But since 1970 the Supreme Court has found some statutes unconstitutional. The power of judicial review was a postwar innovation. In Japan, where a single political party seems to hold power permanently and dominate both the executive and the legislative branches of the government, it may be just as well that the judicial branch imposes some restraint on the power of the State.

LOCAL GOVERNMENT

The political relationship of the national government and the provincial and local governments, as we have seen, has been a frequently contended issue in Japanese politics. The establishment of feudalism in the twelfth century represented a victory over the Chinese theory of absolute centralized monarchy, and in 1868, the imperial restoration revived the power of the imperial capital.

Before World War II, the imperial government in Tokyo seemed all powerful. Prefectural governors were appointees of the Home Ministry, which controlled the national police. The Education Ministry controlled the country's system of public schools and universities. The prefectural governments were more like American county governments than like autonomous state governments. Like France and England, Japan's governmental system was unitary rather than federal.

Japan's relatively modest area (about the size of Montana) and the religious, linguistic, and cultural homogeneity of its population seem to argue against the need to establish a federal system. The postwar constitution did not create federalism or a panoply of "state's rights" in Japan, but it does provide that prefectural governors and other local officials, including mayors and assemblymen, will be elected. Prefectural governments do not have constitutions of their own (as American states do), but exercise powers delegated to them by the national government, and the laws they enact may not contradict laws passed by the national Diet.

Japan's 47 prefectures (*todofuken*) include one metropolis (*to*), namely, Tokyo-to, one circuit (*do*), namely, Hokkaido, two urban prefectures (*fu*), namely, Kyoto-fu and Osaka-fu, and 43 *ken,* once referred to as "rural prefectures." Actually, most Japanese live in or near the great urban complexes of Tokyo, the Osaka-Kyoto-Kobe area (in western Honshu), and the Kitakyushu and Fukuoka area in northern Kyushu. The urban buildup has largely wiped out the agricultural areas that separated many of the cities and towns from one another. In the 1950s and 1960s, many cities (*shi*), towns (*cho*), and villages (*son*) were politically merged, thus greatly reducing the number of local government entities (*shichoson*).

The main concerns of prefectural and local governments are education, roads, sewage, garbage collection, police, and protection of the ecology. The public continuously complains about the inadequate management of these concerns, but local governments do not have adequate financial resources to run them effectively. The dependence of the local governments on the national government for financial aid severely limits the scope of local authority.

In the 1970s a number of the mayors and governors of leading cities and prefectures were "progressives" (usually Socialists),

supported by progressive assemblies. By earning recognition as a local elective official, a progressive politician might aspire to a seat in the national Diet. Local government thus seemed to provide a base for the expansion of progressive power, which ultimately sought to take control of the national government. In the 1980s, as the result of losing critical local elections, the progressives lost their grip on principal local governments, and the LDP landslides in the elections for the national Diet have dampened their optimism.

Key Terms

Article 9
Democratic Socialist party (DSP)
dissolution
Doi Takako
factions
Heisei
"highest organ of state power"
House of Councillors
Imperial Rule Assistance Association (IRAA)
Japan Socialist party (JSP)
judicial review
Komeito
Kigensetsu
Liberal Democratic party (LDP)
Lockheed Scandal
Naganuma Nike Missile case
Nakasone Yasuhiro
no-confidence resolution
party dominant system
prefecture
Showa
Social Democratic Party of Japan (SDPJ)
Soka Gakkai
Tanaka Kakuei
"Tanakasone cabinet"
unitary government

Suggestions for Further Reading

Baerwald, Hans H. *Japan's Parliament: An Introduction* (London: Cambridge University Press, 1974).

Baerwald, Hans H. *Party Politics in Japan* (Boston: Allen and Unwin, 1986).

Beer, Lawrence W. *Freedom of Expression in Japan: A Study of Comparative Politics, Law, and Society* (New York: Kodansha International 1984).

Campbell, John. *Contemporary Japanese Budget Politics* (Berkeley: University of California Press, 1979).

Curtis, Gerald. *Election Campaigning: Japanese Style* (New York: Columbia University Press, 1971).

Curtis, Gerald. *The Japanese Way of Politics* (New York: Columbia University Press, 1988).

Flanagan, Scott C., Shinsaku Kohei, Ichiro Miyake, Bradley M. Richardson, and Joji Watanuki. *The Japanese Voter* (New Haven: Yale University Press, 1991).

Fukui, Haruhiro. *Party in Power: The Japanese Liberal Democrats and Policy Making* (Berkeley: University of California Press, 1970.)

Hrebenar, Ronald J. *The Japanese Party System: From One Party Rule to Coalition Government* (Boulder, Colo.: Westview Press, 1986).

Ishida, Takeshi, and Ellis S. Krauss, eds. *Democracy in Japan* (Pittsburgh: University of Pittsburgh Press, 1989).

Itoh, Hiroshi. *The Japanese Supreme Court; Constitutional Policies* (New York: Marcus Wiener, 1989).

Itoh, Hiroshi, and Lawrence Ward Beer, eds. *The Constitutional Case Law in Japan: Selected Supreme Court Decisions, 1961–1970* (Seattle: University of Washington Press, 1978).

Kishima, Takako. *Political Life in Japan: Democracy in a Reversible World* (Princeton: Princeton University Press, 1991).

Kishimoto, Koichi. *Politics in Modern Japan: Development and Organization*, 3rd ed. (Tokyo: Japan Echo, 1988).

Koh, B. C. *Japan's Administrative Elite* (Berkeley: University of California Press, 1991).

Luney, Percy R., Jr., ed. *The Constitution of Japan: The Fifth Decade* (an issue of *Law and Contemporary Problems*, Vol. 53, Nos. 1 and 2 [Winter/Spring, 1990], published by School of Law, Duke University).

McCormack, Gowan, and Yoshio Sugimoto, eds. *Democracy in Contemporary Japan* (Armonk, N.Y.: M. E. Sharpe, 1986).

Maki, John M., ed. *Court and Constitution in Japan: Selected Supreme Court Decisions, 1948–60* (Seattle: University of Washington Press, 1964).

Okimoto, Daniel I., and Thomas P. Rohlen, eds. *Inside the Japanese System: Readings on Contemporary Society and Political Economy* (Stanford: Stanford University Press, 1988).

Pharr, Susan. *Losing Face: Status Politics in Japan* (Berkeley: University of California Press, 1990).

Pharr, Susan J. *Political Women in Japan* (Berkeley: University of California Press, 1980).

Reed, Steven R. *Japanese Prefectures and Policymaking* (Pittsburgh: University of Pittsburgh Press, 1986).

Scalapino, Robert A. *The Japanese Communist Movement, 1920–1966* (Berkeley: University of California Press, 1962).

Steiner, Kurt, Ellis S. Krauss, and Scott C. Flanagan, eds. *Political Opposition and Local Politics in Japan* (Princeton: Princeton University Press, 1980).

Tanaka, Hideo, ed. *The Japanese Legal System: Introductory Case Studies and Materials* (Tokyo: Tokyo University Press, 1976).

Thayer, National. *How the Conservatives Rule Japan* (Princeton: Princeton University Press, 1969).

Totten, George O., Allan B. Cole, and Cecil H. Uyehara. *Socialist Parties in Postwar Japan* (New Haven: Yale University Press, 1966).

Upham, Frank K. *Law and Social Change in Postwar Japan* (Cambridge: Harvard University Press, 1987).

Von Mehren, Arthur Taylor, ed. *Law in Japan: The Legal Order in a Changing Society* (Cambridge: Harvard University Press, 1963).

C. Public Policy

Today Japan's gross national product (GNP)—which is $1.8 trillion—is the second largest in the world. Given the present rates of growth in America and Japan, it is conceivable that Japan may surpass the United States and have the world's most productive economy by the year 2010.[5] At the end of World War II, Japanese industry had been thoroughly devastated. What accounts for Japan's "economic miracle?" In a parallel development, Japan was completely disarmed at the end of the war but today has the world's fourth largest defense budget. In global politics, Japan has been reluctant to take initiatives and has been content with the role of America's junior partner. Urged to assume a greater responsibility for its own defense and that of the free world, will Japan assume a position of political leadership commensurate with its economic preeminence?

THE ECONOMIC MIRACLE

At the end of World War II, the Allied Powers did not regard the reconstruction of the Japanese economy as their responsibility: the Japanese were themselves to blame for the war that had brought disaster to their country and should be made to learn from the experience. Besides, it would be unjust to provide a more comfortable life for the Japanese aggressors than for their victims.

Moreover, industries that would facilitate Japanese rearmament (such as the manufacture of aircraft) should be banned, it was held.

This tough policy, however, proved impractical. In 1946 when there were severe food shortages in the cities and Communist agitators were capitalizing on the food crisis, General MacArthur imported food from America. If only to relieve the American taxpayer of the burden of feeding Japan, the Japanese economy would have to be rehabilitated. The United States opposed the policy of extracting reparations from Japan, as it was believed that the Americans would be indirectly footing the bill. To the dismay of the British, who did not want to see the Japanese become fierce competitors in world markets, the American occupiers belatedly began to foster the economic revival of Japan. Poor in natural resources and overpopulated, Japan would have to "trade or die." Since the labor unions fostered by Allied policies increasingly fell under the domination of Communists, MacArthur took action to check their influence. Notably, he ordered that the general strike scheduled for 1 February 1947 be called off, and its leftist leaders lost face. The labor relations law was modified to forbid strikes by government employees. The honeymoon between the political left and MacArthur's headquarters began to come to an end. In 1948, the program of breaking up

Japan's family monopolies, the *zaibatsu*, was halted in midstream.

THE KOREAN WAR BOOM

By 1950 the policies of neither the government of the Socialist Prime Minister Katayama nor of SCAP had been able to rescue Japan from unemployment, inflation, and every kind of shortage. When war broke out in Korea in June of that year, the American military hired Japanese firms to repair damaged equipment and manufacture uniforms, blankets, trucks, and other war material. "The Korean War boom" nudged the Japanese economy off dead center, and soon prewar levels of production were achieved. From 1950 to 1973, the average annual growth rate of Japan's GNP was over 10 percent, "probably the highest sustained rate of increase that the world has ever seen."[6]

The Japanese no longer had to maintain a costly military establishment, and—unlike the British, French, and Dutch—they were not encumbered with rebellious colonies; it thus became easier to raise funds for economic reconstruction. Most of the money needed for rebuilding Japanese enterprises was obtained as loans from banks, rather than from the sale of shares. The Japanese are remarkable for the very high percentage of their income that they save. In the 1950s Japanese and American entrepreneurs set up "joint ventures" in Japan, which facilitated the introduction of advanced American technology. Later the Japanese, rather than attempt to duplicate in their laboratories what had already been discovered elsewhere, purchased the most recent American technology. In the 1970s, the Japanese became the world's leaders in the application of modern technology to industrial production. The Japanese pioneered the development of fully automated assembly lines and now lead the world in the use and manufacture of robots.

Over the decades, the Japanese have gradually changed the mix of their manufactures. From textiles they moved to transistor radios and cameras. They then went to steel, ships, and automobiles. The Japanese lead the world in the manufacture and export of automobiles, musical instruments, photocopiers, cameras, and VCRs. By the mid-1980s, the production of supercomputers seemed to be one of the increasingly rare areas in which the Japanese had not caught up with or surpassed the Americans. With vast amounts of currency from exports and savings, Japanese banks have become the leaders in global finance. In 1987, Japan became the world's biggest holder of currency reserves, with a total of $81.1 billion. (The United States was in fifth place— behind Taiwan.)[7] Japan is now the world's leading donor of development assistance to third world countries.

COSTS OF THE MIRACLE

Japanese economic leadership has come at a cost. Pollution of the atmosphere and destruction of greenery by Japanese factories became leading political issues in Japan in the 1970s. The country's trading partners continually complain of unfair trading practices and the failure of Japan to buy from, as well as to sell to, foreign countries. Widespread plant closings and unemployment in America's Northeast and Midwest—America's "rust belt"—were blamed on Japanese imports. The Japanese were charged with "dumping," that is, the sale of goods abroad at a price higher than the price at home, or the sale of goods at a price lower than the cost of production. Demands for sanctions against dumping, for protective tariffs, and for the opening of the Japanese markets have become major political issues in the United States.

THE GLOBALIZATION OF THE ECONOMY

Japan is afflicted with many of the same economic and social problems that plague the other postindustrial countries in Europe and North America. Constant modernization of production processes requires that new jobs or retraining be provided to those who become unemployed because of technological advances. South Korea, Taiwan, Hong Kong, and Singapore are becoming "Little Japans" by their manufacturing and exporting many goods, including automobiles, TV sets, and computers, that compete with Japanese exports. In a decade or so, Japan may be faced with serious competition from industries in China, India, and Brazil, which have large populations and substantial natural resources. Because of the high cost of labor and land in Japan, Japanese entrepreneurs, like their American counterparts, are increasingly seeking overseas sites for their plants. The dramatic appreciation of the yen in relation to the dollar has accelerated Japanese acquisition of U.S. manufacturing plants.

The world's economy is rapidly ceasing to be divided along national frontiers and has become more globalized. Japanese firms are becoming increasingly multinational. The structure of the Japanese economy is undergoing rapid change. These changes may be expected to impose great stress not only on the Japanese people but also on the people of the world who do business with them. For example, Japan's trade imbalances and the appreciation of the yen may require that the Japanese—who are money rich but whose actual standard of living is modest—save and produce less but consume more. In the past ten years, the average Japanese household has been saving over 15 percent of its disposable income, as compared with American families, who save only 3 or 4 percent. The expansion of the Japanese market that would accompany an increase in Japanese consumption might reduce Japan's reliance on exports and increase imports.

THE HIGH QUALITY OF JAPANESE PRODUCTS

It seems unlikely, however, that there are any quick fixes for the trade imbalance between Japan and its principal trading partner, the United States. Before World War II, "Made in Japan" was a synonym for shoddy quality, but since 1960, Japanese products have earned the reputation for being the best. Although for a while Japanese goods enjoyed a price advantage over American products, increases in labor costs in Japan and the appreciation of the yen have made them less price-competitive. However, nowadays consumers are willing to pay considerably more for a quality product.

Although Japan's population is only one-half that of the United States, its colleges and universities train equally as many engineers.[8] Japanese manufacturers are not content merely to produce goods of superior quality. Although the Japanese used to be dismissed an "imitators," or even "good copiers," today they are masters of innovation and Japanese products often incorporate features that make competitive products obsolete. Their market research is excellent and they are willing to sacrifice profits in order to enhance their market share. Once the competitors are driven out of the market, the competitors find it difficult or impossible even to remain in business.

In Japan, the customer is sought after and respected. It is not uncommon in Tokyo to see clerks in the street in front of their stores earnestly imploring passers-by, "*Irasshaimase, irasshaimase!*" ("Please, do come in!").

GOVERNMENT INTERVENTION IN THE ECONOMY

In the Meiji era (1868–1912), the imperial government fostered the establishment of modern industries in Japan, often using funds borrowed from abroad and using Europeans as advisers. Once the industries were brought to a paying basis, they were sold to private companies. Thus, it was the government, not private entrepreneurs, who launched the industrial revolution in Japan. While England was preoccupied with World War I, the Japanese took over a large share of the British market in Asia and became a leading manufacturer and exporter of light industrial goods. The Japanese navy, the world's third largest, fostered the production of advanced communications and optical equipment.

After World War II, the nationally regulated banking system directed funds to companies for the construction of new factories, replacing those destroyed by the war. Thus Japan's postwar industrial plants were more up to date and efficient than those of other countries.

Although Japan is often said to be a capitalist country with a free market economy, there seems to be no ideological commitment to the notion that government should not involve itself in the economy. Quite the contrary, the government is expected to and is ready to intervene not only to correct economic imbalances but also to take the lead in directing national economic change.

The Ministry of International Trade and Industry (MITI, dubbed *meetee* by non-Japanese) has played a conspicuous role in fostering the development of Japanese industry and foreign trade since the 1960s. Government bureaucrats, who enjoy substantial prestige, are often longtime school friends of business and political leaders. It is not necessary for the Diet continuously to pass new laws to facilitate government's involvement in the economy. *Administrative guidance* is the term usually used to denote the great influence of the bureaucracy on business activity. Businesses are aware that the bureaucracy has at its disposal effective, albeit informal, rewards and punishments to ensure conformity to government policies.

In recent years members of the Diet have become increasingly involved in policy making. Groups of legislators belonging to Diet committees who are experts in the policies of particular government agencies are noticeably influencing policy. Known as *zoku* (literally, tribes), they act as lobbies at the highest level of government. The growing influence of the *zoku* suggest that the democratically elected Diet and the political parties are increasing their influence in relation to the bureaucracy.

Denationalization

Japan has long had a very extensive system of railroads. Much of their revenue comes from passenger traffic, as commuters in Japan's great metropolitan centers depend on them to get to work. Until the 1980s most, but by no means all, of the railroads were owned and operated by the national government. The *shinkansen* trains (known among foreigners as "bullet trains") were built beginning in the 1960s; they became world famous for their speed and convenience, linking many of the major cities and running at 10- and 15-minute intervals. In their frequency of operation, they resembled a city subway system but operated much faster and on a national scale. The bureaucratic structure and politicized national

Commuters squeeze into a train doorway during rush hour at Shinjuku Station, Tokyo.

railroad workers union, however, seem to have acted as dampers on efficiency and the system ran up enormous deficits. In 1987, the Japan National Railways was denationalized and divided into privately owned and operated regional segments which immediately improved service and stopped operating in the red. Thus, although the government may be strongly inclined to involve itself in the economy, it is no longer committed to the principle of directly owning and managing enterprises.

THE JAPANESE ECONOMY TODAY

The holding companies of the prewar *zaibatsu* (financial cliques) were partly broken up during the Allied occupation. However, many of the businesses formerly controlled by the family-owned holding companies are still affiliated in various ways and now are often referred to as *keiretsu* (economic groups). The names of some of the prewar *zaibatsu* (Mitsubishi, Mitsui, Yasuda, Sumitomo) may still be found attached to leading Japanese companies. There are, for example, the Mitsubishi Bank, Mitsubishi Chemical Industries, Mitsubishi Electric Corporation, Mitsubishi Heavy Industries, Mitsubishi Mining and Cement Company, Mitsubishi Motor Corporation, Mitsubishi Paper Mills, Mitsubishi Steel Manufacturing Company, and Mitsubishi Trust and Banking Corporation (not to be confused with the Mitsubishi Bank), to mention only some of Mitsubishi's affiliated companies.

Most major Japanese corporations are connected with one or another *keiretsu*. The name of a company may not necessarily indicate what its affiliations are. The directorships of the affiliated companies often interlock, and companies often own stock in affiliated companies. The varied enterprises (including banks) making up a *keiretsu* often prefer to do business with one another rather than with outsiders, without regard to cheaper prices or rates tendered by the outsiders. Sensitive to the hazards of cut-throat competition and economic instability and the need to compete in

global markets, the Japanese government has not always been zealous in trustbusting. Foreigners often find the system very difficult to penetrate.

Banks (usually with *keiretsu* affiliation) play a leading role in the growth of Japanese business. Interest rates in Japan have long been lower than elsewhere and the Japanese are great savers, so that companies are able to obtain money cheaply for the improvement and expansion of their facilities, or sometimes for stock or land speculation. In the late 1980s, the price of stock and of land had been driven to unprecedented heights, and these were used as collateral to obtain loans for more speculation. Nine of the world's ten wealthiest banks are Japanese.

Financial Scandals

In 1991, a series of financial scandals dominated the news. Tax evasion by land speculators and occasionally high government officials was exposed. Counterfeit certificates of deposit were used to obtain huge loans. Most serious was the practice of the four leading brokerage houses of reimbursing favored clients for their losses on the stock market. In some instances, it appeared that the brokers had deliberately manipulated the market to benefit favorite clients, in one case a gangster. The system seemed to be rigged in favor of insiders, and prices on the stock market were seriously depressed as a result.

Business associations such as the Keidanren (Federation of Business Organizations), Keizai Doyukai (Committee for Economic Development), and Nikkeiren (Japanese Federation of Employers Associations) effectively lobby both the Liberal Democratic Party and the bureaucracy on behalf of their interests. Japan's financial leaders, usually referred to as *zaikai*, are the nation's economic elite. The LDP and its factions get most of their funds from Japanese business. It is often said that Japan is run by a triumvirate of big business, the LDP, and the bureaucracy. But small business and agriculture are often able to use their electoral clout with the LDP to extract benefits from the state.

The Probusiness Climate

There is a national consensus in Japan that government, business, and labor must all collaborate in order to seize and hold shares of the global market for Japanese goods. The patriotic solidarity among Japanese in their national endeavor to compete effectively with other countries has led some observers to refer to the Japanese as "Japan, Inc." By contrast, the adversarial relationships among business, labor, and government that prevail in the United States put Americans at war with one another and no doubt weaken America's position as a competitor in world markets.

After World War II, although Japan lagged behind the other leading industrial states in the development of welfare programs, such programs were vastly expanded in the 1970s, and Japan has become a welfare state. Fortunately, even during what the Japanese media refer to as business slumps, there is a severe labor shortage and unemployment does not exceed 2.5 percent. There is no huge underclass of hereditary welfare recipients in Japan such as one finds in the United States. The LDP stresses the importance of a prosperous capitalist system in order to finance welfare programs and social security. With one of the world's most modern medical and hospital systems and national health insurance, the Japanese now have the longest average life span in the world.

As people live longer, a great strain is imposed on pension systems and the medical and hospital costs for the elderly rise. In the traditional farm villages common in prewar times, grandparents lived with their children and grandchildren, but in the modern urban environment, the expensive apartments are barely large enough to accommodate two generations, and separate living quarters must be provided for the elderly with or without

some measure of government subsidy. A principal issue in contemporary Japanese politics, as in the other industrialized countries, has been the question of how the needs of the growing numbers of elderly will be met.

The budget of the national government is heavily strained by the costs of education, welfare, agricultural subsidies, and the like. In the 1980s, administrative reorganization (to reduce the size and cost of government) and tax reform became hot political issues.

THE JAPANESE ECONOMY IN GLOBAL PERSPECTIVE

In the immediate postwar years, when industrial production was virtually at a standstill and unemployment and inflation were rampant, Socialist ideologies were especially popular among intellectuals (many had been Marxist before the war) and labor leaders. When the Left and Right Socialists reunited in 1955, there seemed to be a possibility that Socialists might soon gain control of the Diet and carry out a Socialist revolution in Japan. The dramatic expansion of the capitalist economy in the 1960s, however, brought unprecedented prosperity to virtually every sector of the population and prevented radical ideologies from attracting a popular following. By the 1970s the overwhelming majority of Japanese considered themselves members of the "middle class" and few seem to take Socialist doctrine seriously today.

Dependence on Global Trade

The nation's enormous economy is, as every Japanese person is keenly aware, extraordinarily dependent on world trade. Resource-poor Japan relies on other countries for iron ore and other essential raw materials. Japan has been trying to reduce its dependence on the Middle East for petroleum, but in 1988 petroleum supplied 57.3 percent of its energy, and most of this oil had to pass through the Strait of Hormuz (in the Persian Gulf). Economic self-sufficiency is not an option for Japan. The global trading system established largely under American leadership after World War II is largely based on the concept of free trade. The theory was that the free movement of goods across national frontiers is essential for global prosperity and world peace. Japan, a powerful competitor, has prospered under this system. A global war, or more likely than that the erection of national barriers against Japanese goods, would be disastrous for Japan. The concepts of "comprehensive security" and "resource diplomacy" connote Japan's consciousness of its dependence on global trade.

As Japan emerged as a leading international trader in the 1960s, its trading partners began to complain about the destruction of their own industries by Japanese competition. Indeed, by the 1990s, most of Japan's trading partners suffered from more or less severe trade deficits with Japan. For decades, the Americans complained that Japan enjoyed the right to sell automobiles, TVs, and electronic products in vast quantities to America but refused to buy from America. Actually, Japan is the world's leading importer of American agricultural goods and has accepted "voluntary" limits on auto exports to the United States, but the imbalance has remained huge. In 1990 the United States began negotiating with Japan concerning a structural impediments initiative (SII). The archaic distribution system in Japan, consisting of multiple layers of middlemen and many small-scale retailers, seemed closed to foreign imports. The small-business lobby in Japan had brought about the enactment of legislation seriously restricting the establishment of large discount stores that might distribute inexpensive imports. The SII negotiations were successful in obtaining Japanese agreement to modify the large-scale retailers law. At the same time, the Japanese agriculture ministry and the LDP leadership have insisted that no foreign rice be imported by Japan: Japan should preserve self-sufficiency in rice, closing this market completely to foreign, especially American, producers. The Japanese

were paying several times the going international price for rice, and Japanese rice production could be destroyed by imports of this food. There was much talk of the almost mystical relation between rice farming and the essence of Japanese culture, and about the need to be self-sufficient in food from the standpoint of national security.

While the Liberal Democrats pride themselves on their ability to manage relations with America, Japan's principal trading partner, LDP politicians are keenly aware of their traditional dependence on small-business people and farmers for their electoral support. The *zoku* Dietmen who watch after the interests of these businessmen and farmers are among the most important fundraisers for the party and exert corresponding clout in the Diet. While the Liberal Democratic cabinets may strongly favor trade liberalization, they are faced with the problem of resistance in party ranks and voter defections. In the 1989 upper house election, the liberalization of meat and fruit imports was an issue that won many farm votes for the Socialists. Some Japanese writers pointed out that a liberalization of imports would greatly reduce prices for the Japanese people and enhance their living standards, but the consumer movement in Japan has thus far shown itself no match for producers' lobbies. Many Japanese resent the idea that they must reorganize their society or distinctive culture—purely internal matters—in order to accommodate the demands of foreigners. It may take a number of years to bring about the kind of structural changes in the Japanese economy necessary to correct the trade imbalances that distress the country's trading partners. Japanese leaders are becoming increasingly aware that unless some changes are made, barriers may be erected against Japanese goods, and the trading system hitherto so profitable for the Japanese may be closed to them.

In 1991–1992, while Americans were suffering from a severe recession, the Japanese continued to prosper. The expansion of the

Japanese economy had slowed considerably following recent severe drops in stock and land prices (the collapse of the "bubble economy"), and growth continued at an enviable rate. Unemployment did not exceed 2.5 percent; indeed the principal brake on the economy continued to be the shortage of labor.

At the same time, American leaders have been complaining that some of their allies, especially the Japanese, have not been carrying their fair share of the burden of defending the free world. In 1991, after the Cold War had apparently ended and American and European forces were engaged in war in the Middle East, there were complaints that the Japanese were not making an adequate contribution to the effort. The Diet rejected the government's proposals for sending self-defense forces in a noncombatant capacity to the Middle East, but approved an appropriation of $13 billion to be used in the effort, in addition to sending a minesweeping mission. There were still complaints in the United States that the Japanese, unlike the Americans and Europeans, were not making an adequate contribution in terms of manpower and were slow in delivering the funds promised.

Japan's ambivalent, confused, and somewhat belated reaction to Desert Storm (the war against Iraq) evoked a much broader question that had been on the minds of many observers of Japan since the 1960s: Would Japan, an economic superpower, seek to become a military superpower? Does economic might inevitably become strategic might?

EDUCATION

Japan's leaders have long been keenly conscious of the importance of education in the development of their country's economic strength. During the Meiji period, the imperial government established a system of public education to indoctrinate the population in patriotism and to train a literate work force. By 1940, Japan had one of the world's highest literacy rates. The Allied occupation sought to democratize the content of education and reduce the role of the national government in its administration. Elected school boards and parent-teacher organizations were established. (Later, when members of the leftist National Teachers Union were being elected to the school boards, these institutions were made appointive.) The term of compulsory education was increased from six years to nine. Although the schools are locally administered, national standards must be maintained. About one-half of the cost of public education is borne by the national government and expenditures per pupil are essentially equal nationwide.

The Japanese regard their schools as the key to individual and national economic success. Although some foreign observers seem to regard the Japanese educational system as a model to be emulated, the Japanese are keenly aware of its shortcomings. Because entrance to a prestigious university is necessary for entrance into the best careers, parents are determined that from kindergarten on their children will pass the competitive examinations allowing them to move upward from one reputable school to the next. The first nine years of education are compulsory, and no tuition is charged for admission to public schools. After the ninth grade, nearly every child attends high school, although it is not legally required, and tuition is charged by public as well as private institutions.

School meets Saturday mornings as well as all day Monday through Friday, and summer vacation lasts only one month. Homework assignments begin in first grade, and helping the child with his or her schoolwork is a principal duty of every mother. To prepare for examinations to enter a good high school or a university, about one-half of the children attend *juku*, expensive privately operated schools, after regular school hours. The examination system tends to stress rote memory of information rather than creative thinking. It generates great stress on both children and parents. The "examination hell" is generally believed to interfere with the wholesome physical and moral development of children. Just as there have been efforts to reduce the working week for adults, there have been recent attempts to eliminate Saturday morning classes for the children, an idea resisted by some parents. There is a general agreement that the examination system must be radically reformed or replaced with something else, but there is no consensus as to what specific changes should be made.

In Japan, the children do not make it a practice to bring deadly weapons and drugs into the school, nor do junior high school girls expect the school to provide day-care for their babies, as in some American cities.

Higher Education

In Japan, about one-third of all college-age young people attend college. (Colleges in Japan are referred to as universities, or *daigaku*). The most prestigious is the University of Tokyo ("Todai"), followed by the other former "imperial universities." There is at least one national university in each prefecture, and some prefectures and municipalities support their own public universities. The most famous private universities are Keio and Waseda, in Tokyo, together with a number of reputable prewar private institutions. Many private universities were established during the 1960s when the national government encouraged their proliferation with substantial subsidies.

The academic demands on undergraduates in Japan are modest, and there is a tendency for the students to spend much of their time trying to enjoy life and recover from the rigors of the examination system that got them into the university. In the 1960s, Japanese universities, like those of other leading industrial nations, were seriously disrupted by mass student demonstrations. Students nowadays are apt to be politically conservative. One-third to one-half of all top positions in the government bureaucracy and in big business are occupied by products of Todai, and graduation from a

leading university is regarded as a sine qua non for success in life.

FOREIGN POLICY

Alignment with the United States

As earlier indicated, when Japan made a peace treaty with the United States and other non-Communist countries in 1951, it also entered into a mutual security treaty with the United States, which permitted American forces to remain at bases in Japan. Ever since then, the debate over Japan's foreign policy has revolved around the two poles of unarmed neutrality on the one hand and rearmament and the American alignment on the other. (The Japanese are usually reluctant to call the tie with America an alliance, partly because it does not require Japan to defend American territory from attack, although the United States is expected to defend Japan.)

Japan's position as America's "junior partner" in a world divided by the Cold War has largely determined Japan's orientation toward the rest of the world. In 1960, the U.S.-Japan security treaty was replaced by a "revised security treaty" more favorable to Japan, although there was widespread opposition to it in Japan. Demonstrations opposed to the new treaty and to President Eisenhower's scheduled visit to Japan resulted in the death of a coed (regarded as a martyr by activists), the "postponement" (in effect the cancellation) of Ike's visit, and the resignation of Prime Minister Kishi. The 1960 security treaty was approved by the House of Representatives after police were introduced to permit a vote to be taken (see Feature 5.2). It would remain in force for ten years, after which time it would remain effective unless one side or the other renounced it. In 1970, although there were popular demonstrations against the treaty, it had become less controversial and both governments have permitted it to continue in force. Japan has remained loyal to its commitments to the United States and did not recognize Communist China un-

---

Feature 5.2 Automatic Approval of Treaties

Where treaties are concerned, if the decision of the upper house differs from that of the lower and no agreement can be reached in a joint committee of the two houses, the decision of the lower house becomes that of the Diet. Or if the upper house fails to take action in 30 days after receiving the treaty from the lower house, the decision of the lower house becomes that of the Diet. The joint committee option has been neglected in recent decades, so the government may simply wait for the 30-day period to elapse. This procedure is known as "automatic approval" of a treaty. Thirteen treaties have been approved automatically without action by the upper house. Thus, unlike the U.S. Senate, the Japanese upper house cannot veto treaties.

Perhaps the most dramatic case of the "automatic approval" of a treaty occurred in 1960. The new U.S.-Japan security treaty had been approved at a riotous session of the House of Representatives that the Socialists refused to attend. The House of Councillors failed to deliberate on the treaty because of a boycott of that chamber by the Socialists. On 18 June 1960, the date of the expected automatic approval of the treaty, thousands of demonstrators surrounded the Diet building protesting against the treaty and the manner of its passage in the lower house. But the parades, speeches, shouts, and placards of the multitude were of no avail against the inexorable ticking of the clock, and the treaty was officially deemed approved by the Diet at the stroke of midnight.

---

til after Nixon made his famous trip to China in 1972. (But the United States did not extend completely formal recognition to the Beijing regime until 1979.) Japan, like the United States, has not formally recognized Communist North Korea.

Continuously in the 40 years since the end of the occupation, American military, naval, and air forces have been stationed in Japan. They have served as a deterrent against invasion or attack and in that sense have advanced the cause of Japan's security. Yet many Japanese have been concerned that the American forces are primarily intended to enforce American Cold War policy and therefore could embroil Japan in a world war of someone else's making. American air bases in Japan were used during the Korean War to launch raids against North Korea, provoking fears that the Communist powers might make retaliatory air attacks on the Japanese bases, which are uncomfort-

ably close to Japanese cities. Obviously American bases in Japan would be prime targets for preemptive attacks, and in that sense would be a danger rather than a protection for Japan.

It would be virtually impossible to defend Japan's great cities from air attack, especially from nearby Soviet air bases, and a war against a major country to defend Japan would likely be suicidal. The Japanese have long doubted that either the Soviet Union or Communist China has any serious desire to invade Japan unless it would be to deprive the Americans of Japanese bases and resources. At the same time, Japan's insular geographical position greatly reduces its vulnerability to a land invasion. And since the American retreat from Vietnam, there have been nagging doubts—reinforced by President Carter's talk of withdrawing American forces from Korea—that the United States would have the will or the perseverance to defend Japan if the need arose.

The rationale for the U.S.-Japan security treaty was not convincingly conveyed to many of the Japanese people, and it was often regarded as a concession to America in exchange for the end of the occupation.

The apparent end of the Cold War in 1990 probably reduced the importance of the strategic affiliation with America. During the 1991 war in the Persian Gulf, American requests for Japanese military and financial assistance provoked a revival of the peace movement in Japan. The SDPJ especially asserted that such involvement would violate the pacifist provision of the Japanese Constitution.

RELATIONS WITH THE SOVIET UNION

After the conclusion of the Hitler-Stalin nonaggression treaty of 1939 it was widely believed that the Soviet Union might join the Axis powers (Germany, Italy, and Japan). In April 1941, Japan entered into a Neutrality Treaty with the Soviets. Two months later, Japan's ally, Germany, invaded Russia, but Japan and the Soviet Union did not go to war, nor did the outbreak of war between Japan and the United States result in hostilities between Japan and the Soviet Union.

After the war in Europe had ended, the Japanese tried to induce Stalin to mediate a peace between Japan and the Allied Powers. Stalin replied to this request on August 8 (two days after the atomic bombing of Hiroshima) with the announcement that on the next day the Soviet Union would be at war with Japan. The treacherous attitude of the Soviet Union toward its commitment in the Soviet-Japanese Neutrality Treaty was regarded by Japanese diplomats as outrageous. After the war, tens of thousands of Japanese prisoners of war were detained for several years in the Soviet Union as laborers and indoctrinated with Leninism-Stalinism. When the prisoners finally returned to Japan, many of them told of the economic backwardness and low level of civilization of the Soviet Union. In 1956 the Soviet Union

and Japan issued a joint peace declaration, but because of the dispute over the Northern Territories, to be discussed later, the two countries have thus far failed to complete a peace treaty for the conclusion of World War II.

The arguments for unarmed neutrality after the dreadful war were very compelling to the Japanese. But the Soviet record of almost unrelieved hostility toward Japan provoked anti-Soviet suspicions and a popular reluctance to scuttle the tie with the United States. In any event, once the alignment with the Americans had been in place for several years, a Japanese withdrawal from it would appear pro-Soviet and anti-American rather than neutral. But more than appearances were involved. The security treaty has been a key factor in the balance of power in the Far East. The abandonment of the treaty might invite new problems in the Korean peninsula, the disputed Northern Territories, or elsewhere.

After the United States had returned Okinawa to Japanese administration in 1972, the pressure in Japan for the return of certain northern islands occupied by the Soviet Union intensified. Although in the Japanese Peace Treaty with the non-Communist countries, Japan gave up its claims to Karafuto (Southern Sakhalin) and to the Kurile Islands, the Japanese insist that the islands of Habomai, Shikotan, Kunashiri, and Etorofu (from which the attack on Pearl Harbor was launched) do not pertain to the Kuriles and are rightfully Japanese. These islands had been homes for several generations to thousands of Japanese and had served as important fishing bases. These "Northern Territories" are part of a chain of islands extending from Hokkaido to the Kamchatka Peninsula and limit the access from Siberia to the Pacific Ocean. They were heavily fortified by the Soviets.

The buildup of the Soviet fleet and air force in the Western Pacific in the 1980s and spy scandals involving Soviet agents and Japan Self-Defense Force personnel deepened Japanese distrust of the Soviet Union. Relations were not improved when in 1983 the

Soviet air force shot down a Korean airliner that had wandered over Soviet territory (near the disputed islands), with the loss of 269 passengers, including 28 Japanese. In spite of occasional hints that some of the disputed territory might be returned, the usual attitude of Soviet diplomats was that the islands were indisputable Soviet territory and they refused to engage in negotiations about it.

The End of the Cold War

In 1990, the Soviet government hinted that a negotiable solution might be found for the Northern Territories dispute, and the Japanese government spoke of extending economic aid to the Soviet Union. The Soviets did permit visits by Japanese to the disputed area and to Southern Sakhalin, but seemed to fear that a return of the territories to Japan would encourage secessionism in other parts of the Soviet Union. At the same time, it seemed that the Japanese would not seriously consider economic aid to the Soviets unless the latter made concessions on the territorial issues and negotiated a peace treaty (for World War II) with Japan. A complication is the presence of thousands of Soviet citizens in the disputed territory, who may have reservations about coming under Japanese rule or emigrating. The dissolution of the Soviet Union in 1991 and the apparent end of the Cold War inspired some hope that the Soviets would be more responsive to Japan's desires in the near future. In 1992 Russian diplomats showed a growing willingness to make a territorial settlement with Japan as a prerequisite for economic aid.

RELATIONS WITH THE TWO CHINAS

In the 1960s and 1970s, the security tie with the United States involved Japan in the American political and economic boycott of Communist China, although Japan, with a policy of "separation of politics and economics," engaged in limited trade with Communist China

through unofficial channels and informal cultural contacts encouraged by Beijing's policy of "people's diplomacy." The Japanese official boycott of the Beijing government ended in 1972 with Prime Minister Tanaka's visit to Communist China and the establishment of formal diplomatic relations between his country and the People's Republic of China (PRC).

After prolonged and difficult negotiations, a Sino-Japanese peace treaty was finally signed in 1978. It contained an "antihegemony" clause, insisted upon by the Chinese, which was regarded as provocative by the Soviet Union. China had been complaining of the Soviet military buildup on China's border, the invasion of pro-Chinese Kampuchea by Vietnam (a Soviet ally), and the Soviet invasion of Afghanistan. When the Carter administration recognized Communist China the following year, there was speculation that a U.S.-China-Japan alliance aimed against the Soviet Union was in the making.

Before Japan's rapprochement with Communist China, Japanese progressive intellectuals harbored romantic notions about the high ideals of the Communist revolution in China while many businessmen fondly expected a boom in exports to the PRC when trade restrictions were lifted. These attitudes were encouraged by a sense of guilt for Japan's past aggressions against China, the concept of cultural indebtedness to China, the idea that China's radicalism was an understandable response to America's hostility, the notion that, as Asians, the Japanese could understand the Chinese better than the Americans could, and the view that American Cold War diplomacy was to blame for the alienation between Japan and China.

After 1972, when the PRC was officially opened to the Japanese people, the excesses of Mao's cultural revolution and the trial of the "gang of four" in China disillusioned Japanese intellectuals. At the same time, China's poverty and backwardness seriously obstructed the growth of trade with that country. In 1989 the ruthless suppression of the prodemocracy demonstrators in Tiananmen Square (Beijing), shocked the Japanese and reminded them of the blessings of their own democratic system.

Taiwan

When Japan officially recognized the Beijing regime in 1972, it simultaneously withdrew its formal recognition of the government of the Republic of China (ROC) in Taiwan (formerly referred to in English as Formosa). Quasi-official relations, however, continue between Japan and the ROC, and the economic ties between the two countries are very important for both of them. (Taiwan is Japan's fourth largest trading partner, while mainland China ranks as the fifth.[9]) In Japan, as in the United States, political conservatives and some commercial interests have been unhappy with the treatment that has been meted out to the ROC by their government. The ROC is a major trader in the global economy.

Because Taiwan was a part of the Japanese Empire from 1895 to 1945, there are important economic and cultural ties between Japan and Taiwan. Many of the Chinese in Taiwan want to be ruled by neither the Chinese Nationalists nor the Communists, but would prefer independence from China. Recently the Chinese Nationalists have been democratizing their regime, bringing more native Taiwanese into the political system. Recent statements by spokesmen of the Beijing and Taipei governments portend a rapprochement between the two that could ultimately lead to the reunification of China and a political reconfiguration in the Western Pacific.

THE TWO KOREAS

Japan's relations with Korea are still poisoned by the memory of Japanese colonialism. The events leading to the annexation of the Korean kingdom in 1910 and the cruelty with which Japanese authorities suppressed the national independence movement are still fresh in the minds of Korean patriots. Although the country gained its independence in 1945 with Japan's defeat, it was immediately divided between U.S. and Soviet occupation zones, in South and North Korea respectively. When American and Soviet troops left the country, they left behind anti-Communist and pro-Communist governments in their former zones, and the Korean War broke out in 1950.

The Japanese were fearful that their own country might be engulfed in the war, but when it ended in 1953, the Japanese economy had been invigorated by the Korean War boom. American policy discouraged the Japanese government from establishing relations with Communist North Korea. The fact that both South Korea and Japan have security treaties with the United States did not seem to mitigate the distrust between the Japanese and the Koreans. In 1965, 20 years after the end of the war and the attainment of Korean independence, South Korea (the Republic of Korea, ROK) and Japan negotiated an agreement that normalized relations between the two countries. Although there was agreement that Japan should grant economic assistance to Korea (and it did), the Koreans made their claim on the basis of their right to reparations, a moral assertion that the Japanese were reluctant to accept. The treaty was bitterly attacked by neutralists and leftists in Japan on the ground that it was aimed against the Communist states in Asia, especially North Korea and Communist China, and would further alienate Japan from her Asian neighbors and involve Japan in American anti-Communist adventures.

Bad feelings between Japan and South Korea are perpetuated by reports of discrimination against the Korean minority in Japan, the apparent revival of Japanese nationalism, and the tendency of Japanese government to maintain informal relations with North Korea. The South Koreans feel that they bear a disproportionate share of the burden for the defense of the free world countries in the Far East and that the Japanese should recognize this. Trade friction has risen between the two countries, as the Koreans accuse the Japanese of refusing to buy from Korea while Korea is importing large amounts of Japanese goods. At the same time Korean automobiles, TVs, VCRs, computers, and power stations compete with Japanese products on the world market.

The end of the Cold War may be alleviating the frictions between Japan and the Koreas. Recently Japan has become involved in efforts to assist in Korean reunification and reduce tensions in Southeast as well as Northeast Asia.

NATIONAL DEFENSE

"Realists" tend to evaluate Japan's defense policies in terms of the global distribution of power and Japan's diplomatic and strategic position. Many Japanese, however, tend to begin their discussion of Japan's defense in terms of Article 9, the "pacifist clause" of their postwar Constitution, which they dub the "Peace Constitution."

Article 9 of the Japanese Constitution reads as follows:

> Aspiring sincerely to an international peace based on justice and order, the Japanese people forever renounce war as sovereign right of the nation and the threat or use of force as means of settling international disputes.
>
> In order to accomplish the aim of the preceding paragraph, land, sea, and air forces, as well as other war potential, will not be maintained. The right of the belligerency of the state will not be recognized.

(The *actual text* of the Constitution is cited here because it is often misquoted.)

When the Constitution was adopted in 1946, it was generally believed that Article 9 prohibited *defensive* as well as offensive wars and banned *defensive* as well as offensive arms. Most constitutional scholars insist on this strict interpretation, but the Japanese public has over time come to accept the existence of the Self-Defense Forces (SDF) as legitimate. However they interpret its technicalities, the majority of the Japanese people approve of and support the no-war no-arms clause of their Constitution. They do not want to repeat the horrors of the 1930s and 1940s and view Article 9 as a formidable obstacle to militarism and war.

THE SELF-DEFENSE FORCES

In 1950, shortly after the outbreak of war in Korea, General MacArthur directed the prime minister to create a 75,000-member "National Police Reserve," evidently to help maintain internal security in Japan while the American occupation forces were fighting in Korea. The Police Reserve was shortly renamed the Security Force. In 1954, the Land, Maritime, and Air Self-Defense Forces (incorporating the former Security Force) and the Defense Agency were brought into being by acts of the Diet.

In 1990, there were 156,000 men and 1,200 tanks in the Land SDF, there were 44,000 men and 165 ships (including 14 submarines), totalling 288,000 tons, in the Maritime SDF, and there were 46,000 men and 390 airplanes in the Air SDF.[10] In terms of size, Japan's Self-Defense Forces are very modest as compared with the military establishments of its Asian neighbors. But Japan's defense budget is among the world's largest even though it may account for only 1 percent of the gross national product.[11] In addition, some 50,000 American military men, representing the four services, are stationed in land, air, and sea bases in Japanese territory.

The Japanese government said that the Self-Defense Forces did not constitute "war potential" prohibited by the Constitution because they were not capable of fighting a modern war. In more recent years, the government has been saying that the defense of Japan is not forbidden by the Constitution and that although offensive weapons and the dispatch of the SDF overseas are banned, the minimum force needed for Japan's defense is permissible. During the national debate over Japan's participation in the UN military actions against Iraq in 1991, the public looked more favorably than before on sending SDF personnel overseas provided their purpose was to enforce UN-sponsored peacekeeping operations and they were not involved in combat. As pointed out in the discussion of Japan's Supreme Court, the court has avoided ruling directly on the constitutionality of the Self-Defense Forces and thus avoided saying that they are unconstitutional.

The prime minister has supreme control over the SDF and is advised by the National Defense Council, which includes the director of the Defense Agency (a cabinet minister), the foreign and finance ministers, and the director of the Economic Planning Agency. Because the prime minister is a civilian and is responsible to the Diet, this system, according to government sources, assures civilian control.

In 1970, Japan signed (and in 1976 ratified) the Nuclear Nonproliferation Treaty, committing the country not to make or acquire nuclear weapons. Japan maintains the three principles that the nation will (1) not produce nuclear weapons, (2) not acquire them and (3) not allow their introduction into Japanese territory. There have been reports over several decades that American vessels visiting Japanese ports carry nuclear weapons in contravention of the three principles. The U.S. government refuses as a general principle to confirm or deny the presence anywhere of its nuclear weapons. The Japanese government has not tried to publicly embarrass the United States by insisting on an unequivocal denial of the presence of American nuclear weapons on Japanese territory, as Japan is shielded by the American nuclear umbrella.

Military Technology

Beginning with the Korean War, Japan became involved with military production, and by manufacturing its own equipment has acquired important American technology. Japan manufactures fighter planes under American licenses. In the 1980s the point was reached when the American military began to ask for Japanese technology. In 1991 a prominent Japanese politician asserted that the sensational American victory over Iraq would not have been possible without Japanese technology.

If Japan develops its own fighter planes and other weapons systems, it may feel the need to export them to help defray development costs. The export of military technology and of weapons has become an extremely controversial issue in Japan, involving as it does very delicate diplomatic and economic questions as well as the spirit of the "Peace Constitution." Japan's rules for the export of military technology are (1) not to Communist countries, (2) not to countries where the U.N. prohibits exports, and (3) not to countries involved in international conflicts (except the United States). In 1991, the Japanese proposed that the United Nations oversee a program for making public all international weapons sales.

The Mission of the Self-Defense Forces

The Japanese government's position has long been that the SDF could be used only for defense. They could possess only defensive weapons and its personnel could not be sent overseas. The SDF is often mobilized to deal with earthquakes and other natural disasters, and in the minds of many Japanese such humanitarian projects represent their most appropriate use.

The mission of the SDF in the event of an invasion of Japan would be to fight for up to two weeks while the United States came to Japan's rescue. Japan would provide American forces with intelligence and protect shipping lanes. Because a modern war in Japan would be calamitous, it is hoped that the American commitment to defend Japan together with Japanese resistance would constitute a credible deterrent against a potential aggressor. With the breakup of the Soviet Union and the end of the Cold War, the possibility of a Russian attack on Japan seems very remote.

The issue in 1991 was the nature of Japan's participation in the UN-sponsored liberation of Kuwait. After bitter debate, Japan sent humanitarian aid and contributed $11 billion to the anti-Iraq coalition. After the fighting ended, the Japanese dispatched a minesweeping mission to the Persian Gulf. In June 1992, following much turmoil in the Diet, that body passed the government's bill allowing the SDF to participate in UN peacekeeping operations (PKO). (SDPJ Diet members claimed that the PKO bill violated the "Peace Constitution," boycotted the final vote on the measure, and submitted their resignations from the lower house.) It is now legal to send SDF units overseas under the auspices of the United Nations. Japan, an economic superpower, is becoming a military power.

Key Terms

antihegemony clause
dumping
Japan, Inc.
Keidanren
keiretsu
MITI
nontariff barriers
Northern Territories
PKO
Soviet-Japanese Neutrality Treaty
structural impediments initiative (SII)
Todai
U.S.-Japan Security Treaty
zaibatsu
zoku

Suggestions for Further Reading

Calder, Kent E. *Crisis and Compensation: Public Policy and Political Stability in Japan, 1949–1986* (Princeton: Princeton University Press, 1988).

Campbell, John. *Contemporary Japanese Budget Politics* (Berkeley: University of California Press, 1979).

Frost, Ellen. *For Richer, For Poorer: The New U.S.-Japan Relationship* (New York: Council on Foreign Relations, 1987).

Harries, Meirion, and Susie Harries. *Sheathing the Sword: The Demilitarization of Postwar Japan* (New York: Macmillan, 1987).

Ishida, Takeshi, and Ellis S. Krauss, eds. *Democracy in Japan* (Pittsburgh: University of Pittsburgh Press, 1989).

Johnson, Chalmers. *MITI and the Japanese Miracle* (Berkeley: University of California Press, 1982).

Lincoln, Edward J. *Japan's Unequal Trade* (Washington, D.C.: Brookings Institution, 1990).

McKean, Margaret A. *Environmental Protest and Citizen Politics in Japan* (Berkeley: University of California Press, 1981).

McNelly, Theodore. "General Douglas MacArthur and the Constitutional Disarmament of Japan," *Transactions of the Asiatic Society of Japan*, vol. 17 (1982), pp. 1–34.

Morley, James W., ed. *Security Interdependence in the Asia Pacific Region* (Lexington, Mass.: D. C. Heath, 1986).

Nishi, Osamu. *The Constitution and the National Defense Law System in Japan* (Tokyo: Seibundo, 1987).

Okimoto, Daniel I., and Thomas P. Rohlen, eds. *Inside the Japanese System: Readings on Contemporary Society and Political Economy* (Stanford: Stanford University Press, 1988).

Orr, Robert M. *The Emergence of Japan's Foreign Aid Power* (New York: Columbia University Press, 1991).

Packard, George R. III. *Protest in Tokyo: The Security Treaty Crisis of 1960* (Princeton: Princeton University Press, 1966).

Pempel, T. J. *Policy and Politics in Japan: Creative Conservatism* (Philadelphia: Temple University Press, 1982).

Prestowitz, Clyde V., Jr. *Trading Places: How We Allowed Japan to Take the Lead* (New York: Basic Books, 1988).

Schoppa, Leonard James. *Education Reform in Japan: A Case of Immobilist Politics* (New York: Routledge, 1991).

Van Wolferen, Karel. *The Enigma of Japanese Power; People and Politics in a Stateless Nation* (New York: Knopf, 1989).

Vogel, Ezra. *Japan as Number One; Lessons for America* (Cambridge: Harvard University Press, 1979).

Welfield, John. *An Empire in Eclipse: Japan in the Postwar American Alliance System* (London: Athlone Press, 1988).

Notes

1. *Jiji Nenkan, 1992*, p. 150.
2. *Asahi Nenkan, 1991*, p.96.
3. Hans H. Baerwald, *Party Politics in Japan* (Boston: Allen and Unwin, 1986), pp. 116–117.
4. Harry Eckstein and David E. Apter, eds., *Comparative Politics: A Reader* (New York: Free Press, 1963), p. 192.
5. Michael W. Chinworth, "Japan and the United States: Seeking Security," *The World and I*, 3, No. 1 (March 1988), p.22; Herman Kahn, *The Emerging Japanese Superstate: Challenge and Response* (Englewood Cliffs, N.J.: Prentice-Hall, 1970), p. 2.
6. Edward J. Lincoln, *Japan: Facing Economic Maturity* (Washington, D.C.: Brookings Institution, 1988), p. 14.
7. *Washington Post*, March 6, 1988, Washington Business Section, p. 6.
8. U.S. Department of Education, *Japanese Education Today* (Washington, D.C.: U.S. Government Printing Office, 1987), pp. 49–50.
9. In 1989. *Asahi Nenkan, 1991*, p. 486.
10. *Asahi Nenkan, 1991*, p. 474.
11. *Asahi Nenkan, 1991*, p. 688.

CHAPTER 6

A Changing Europe

Michael Curtis

A. The European Community

The diverse proposals since World War II for some kind of union of Western European countries reflect the complexity and richness of European history and politics. Europe is not a given entity with a single past or tradition. Eastern and Western Europe are both heirs to Roman and Christian traditions, but the Byzantine Empire, Orthodox religion, and Islamic Arabs have made Europe more than a predominantly Romanic and Germanic group of peoples.

After the fourteenth century, the word "Europe," until then rarely used, tended to be identified with "Christendom." But in fact there was never a single political organization for the whole of Christendom or a medieval international order, and Latin and Greek were not really universal languages. In the sixteenth century the influence of the humanists and of the new cartography, which emphasized political authority in territorial areas rather than ecclesiastical rule, began to challenge Europe's identification with Christendom.

European culture cannot be simply defined or described by a single formula. Rationalism, individualism, the devotion to economic activity, industrialism, and the preoccupation with ideals of democracy, communism, fascism, and socialism have all contributed to the pattern of European behav-ior. Political concepts such as the rule of law and constitutional government, social concerns such as care for the handicapped and the distressed, personal qualities of tolerance and a reliance on persuasion rather than coercion, and shared cultural values exemplify those characteristics still confined largely to European nations or their direct descendants.

The movement for European integration has a long lineage, going back to the Greeks and continuing in various ways throughout history and up to the present. Although the motives have always been complex, the essential reasons have remained largely the same: the preservation of peace, the need for a common defense, the ambition to act as a stronger power bloc, the conservation of a common European culture, the wish to create greater material well-being, and the easing of restrictions on trade.

The present movement to some form of European union has been influenced not only by these same motives, but also by significant external factors. The role of the United States as common friend, supplier of material aid in the immediate postwar years, defensive protector of the West, and now economic competitor, has given an Atlantic dimension to the European story. The fear of Soviet expansion and the threat of communism to western democracies after 1945 led Western Europe, in association with the United States, to common defense and security arrangements.

The new Europe has been impelled by both positive and negative factors. Europe needed to recover from the devastation and depletion of material resources caused by World War II, and economic growth and social improvements would be advanced by European cooperation. The small, separate European markets compared poorly with the size and economic strength of the United States, as individual countries were politically weaker than before the war, less significant internationally, and obliged to end their colonial empires.

Political factors also spurred the moves toward a more united Europe. Many thought that after two world wars in one generation, it was imperative to prevent the possibility of further intra-European conflict, especially between Germany and France. (The German problem seemed incapable of solution except within the framework of a larger community.) The economic and military dependence of Western Europe on the United States created a desire for protection against a possible American recession, and inspired awe of American strength. Europe recognized that it was no longer the political center of the world, that apart from Britain it did not possess nuclear weapons, and that it would be difficult for it to play an independent political role or act as a third force in world politics. In addition, there was a strong fear of expanding Soviet imperialism, which had reached to Berlin and Prague and had substantial ideological support in the West, where one-third of the Italian electorate and one-quarter of the French had voted Communist.

The interrelation of political, economic, and military factors explains the large spectrum of alternative proposals concerning the new Europe and the various institutions that have been constructed. Politically, the proposals ranged from regular meetings of heads of governments, to regional and functional conferences on specific problems, to a confederal and finally a federal political system. Economic

alternatives ran from a tariff and customs community to a full economic union. Possibilities for integration also existed in military alliances among individual sovereign states, collective alliances with common leadership, and integrated defense forces.

A UNITED STATES OF EUROPE?

These European proposals also took account of differing attitudes toward the United States. Some favored an Atlantic alliance, partnership, or community with the United States, whereas others called for an independent Western European political entity, economically sound and militarily strong, capable of acting as a third force without ties to the United States or anyone else.

At the core of the different views toward European integration have been attitudes toward the continued existence of sovereign nation-states. The European nation-state has been a constructive force in the creation of political unity, cultural homogeneity, patriotic feeling, and personal identity. But the destructive twentieth-century wars, partly resulting from militant nationalism, led Europeans to question whether the sovereign nation-state could provide the basis for a peaceful Europe. Some still argue that only the nation-state can be responsible for its own protection and welfare, and that nations should be associated only in some framework of intergovernmental cooperation, with unanimity as the procedure for decision making. This view that sovereign power should largely remain with nation-states was reflected in the policies of Charles de Gaulle and Margaret Thatcher. Others hold that limited cooperation of this kind, while useful, is inadequate for solving problems of peace, order, and economic well-being in modern life. They argue that the solutions will come not from the nation-states but from some form of European integration or unity, or a United States of Europe.

The movement toward European integration was created by intellectuals and political elites rather than by mass demand. The post-war attempt to influence the citizen body and make European integration a popular movement, in fact, hardly lasted after 1949 and the institution of the Council of Europe. All other European organizations have been formulated and organized by elite political groups or key political actors whose dedication to Europe is strong and whose idealism has been tempered by political reality. But even if the integration idea does not enflame millions as communism and nationalism have done, it nonetheless attracts increasing support by the success of these European organizations (see Feature 6.1).

The impetus to European integration began simultaneously in the political, economic, and military fields. In September 1946, Winston Churchill, then leader of the opposition in Britain, talked of "recreating the European family, or as much of it as we can" by building "a kind of United States of Europe." Representatives of a number of organizations aiming at such a result met in The Hague in May 1948 and agreed on the establishment of an assembly of representatives of European parliaments, a European charter of human rights, a European court, an economic union, and the inclusion of Germany into a European community.

During this time the United States, for a number of political and economic reasons, took a historic initiative. In June 1947, Secretary of State George Marshall, in a commencement speech at Harvard, proposed American aid for a Europe still suffering from physical destruction, economic dislocation, and lack of productivity, and suggested "a joint recovery program based on self-help and mutual cooperation." Moscow forced Poland and Czechoslovakia to withdraw their requests to be included among the Marshall Plan recipients, and none of the Eastern European countries, then under Soviet control, accepted the Anglo-French invitation in July of 1947 to join an organization of European economic recovery. The Iron Curtain had effectively divided Europe. In

April 1948, after 16 Western European governments agreed that cooperation would continue even after Marshall Plan aid had ended, the Organization for European Economic Cooperation (OEEC) was established, and a series of bilateral agreements was concluded between the United States and OEEC countries.

Western Europe, meanwhile, was concerning itself with its military defense. In March 1947, the Treaty of Dunkirk was signed by France and Great Britain for mutual protection against any renewed aggression by Germany. As a result of changing international relationships, this pact was extended to include the Benelux countries—Belgium, the Netherlands, and Luxembourg—in the Brussels Treaty Organization, set up in March 1948. The BTO was set up under Article 51 of the United Nations Charter as a regional organization able to undertake individual or collective self-defense if an armed attack occurred. The Organization was a 50-year alliance based primarily on the principle of collective defense; members agreed to take steps in the event of renewed German aggression, and pledged automatic mutual military assistance. The BTO was intended not as a supranational organization, but as an intergovernmental one in which the chief policy organ was the Consultative Council of the five foreign ministers.

The Communist capture of power in Prague raised the possibility of the whole of Western Europe being at the mercy of the Russian forces. With the advent of the Berlin blockade in April 1948, it rapidly became apparent that the BTO was not strong enough to resist the Communist threat. Already in March 1946 Winston Churchill, in a speech at Fulton, Missouri, talked of an "iron curtain" in Europe and called for a military alliance between the United States and the Commonwealth. In April 1948 the Canadian Foreign Minister, Louis St. Laurent, suggested an Atlantic defense system. After the Vandenberg Resolution in the U.S. Senate, which ended the historic American policy of no entangling alliances, the Truman Administration went ahead with

Feature 6.1 Key Events in European Integration

1947   Treaty of Dunkirk linked Britain and France

Secretary of State George Marshall proposed joint recovery program for Europe

General Agreement on Trade and Tariffs (GATT) ratified

1948   Benelux began to operate

Organization for European Economic Cooperation (OEEC) formed

Brussels Treaty Organization set up

1949   North Atlantic Treaty Organization (NATO) formed

Council of Europe established

1950   Robert Schuman proposed that coal and steel be put under a common European authority

1952   European Coal and Steel Community (ECSC) formed

1954   European Defense Community (EDC) defeated

Western European Union (WEU) formed

1958   European Economic Community (EEC) and European Atomic Energy Community (Euratom) established

1960   European Free Trade Association (EFTA) formed

Organization for Economic Cooperation and Development (OECD) replaced OEEC

1962   Common Agricultural Policy (CAP) adopted

1963   Yaoundé Convention between EEC and 18 African states

1967   Merger of Commissions of ECSC, EEC, and Euratom in European Community (EC)

1968   EEC customs union completed

1973   Britain, Denmark, and Ireland joined EC

1974   European Council met for first time

1975   Lomé Convention between EC and 46 African, Caribbean, and Pacific states

1979   Direct election of European Parliament

European Monetary System (EMS) became operative

1981   Greece joined EC

1986   Portugal and Spain joined EC

Single European Act signed, became operative in 1987

1989	EC countries endorsed a plan for European Monetary Union
	EC coordinated Western assistance to Poland and Hungary
1990	Five *Länder* of former East Germany joined EC as part of united Germany
	Two intergovernmental conferences, on economic and monetary union, and on political union, opened
1991	European Economic Area (EC and EFTA) proposed
	Maastricht agreement on economic and monetary union

negotiations throughout the summer of 1948. On 4 April 1949, the North Atlantic Treaty Organization (NATO), with twelve members—Belgium, Britain, Canada, Denmark, France, Iceland, Italy, Luxembourg, the Netherlands, Norway, Portugal, and the United States—was established.

From the beginning of the discussion on the new Europe, differences existed between the "federalist" and the "functionalist" point of view about the nature of a European political institution. The federalists believed that the best way to encourage collaboration among European nations and deal with the problem of sovereignty was to set up a constitutional convention and a European constitution. The functionalists argued that vested interests, multilingual nations, and diverse customs and traditions prevented such a radical step, and that any new organization must be based on the power of the states. At the same time, however, they recognized the need to subordinate the separate national interests to the common welfare.

The issue was decided with the establishment of the Council of Europe in August 1949. In the debate on the nature of the Council the federalists, who argued for an elected bicameral legislature and an executive federal council responsible to the legislature, were defeated. The Council has remained an intergovernmental organization.

EUROPEAN COAL AND STEEL COMMUNITY

The first step to a European community came in May of 1950 with a proposal for a common market for coal and steel. The proposal was made by French Foreign Minister Robert Schuman, on the suggestion of Jean Monnet, the French public servant often regarded as the inspiration of the European movement. From an economic standpoint, the plan could lead to joint Franco-German control over the Ruhr and assure French coke supply, and could end the struggle between the two countries over the Saar's coal and steel. It would also increase the internal market needed for economic expansion. But above all, the motivations were political. National antagonisms could be transcended, and the reconciliation of the two old enemies could lead to a closer European political association. The plan could thus be the first concrete step toward the goal of European unity. For Germany, the plan meant the removal of Allied controls over the German economy; for German Chancellor Konrad Adenauer, the Rhinelander, it meant the realization of an idea of friendship he had proposed 30 years earlier.

The plan was greeted enthusiastically in some European countries, but Britain refused to participate. After a year of negotiations, the governments of six countries—France, Germany, Italy, Belgium, the Netherlands, and Luxembourg—signed the Treaty of Paris in April 1951, and in July 1952 the European Coal and Steel Community (ECSC) came into existence, the first European body in which any institution had supranational powers. The six nations set up the ECSC High Authority, a unique institution to which member governments transferred part of their sovereign powers in the area of coal and steel. ECSC had a Council of Ministers, an Assembly (to be renamed a Parliament) and a Court of Justice, and could act directly on the citizens and businesses of the member states. ECSC achieved quick success with the increase of coal and steel trade among the six countries by 129 percent in the first five years.

Monnet regarded the ECSC as the first of several concrete achievements which would be the building blocks of the new Europe in military, political, and economic matters. Even before ECSC came into operation, another proposal was put forward for a European army, and in May 1952 a treaty for a European Defense Community (EDC) was signed by the six ECSC nations. The EDC would be supranational with common institutions, common armed forces, and a common budget. The six countries also began discussing proposals for an even more ambitious European Political Community which would include a European Executive Council, a council of ministers, a court, a bilateral assembly, and an economic and social council. But when the French Parliament refused to ratify the EDC treaty in August 1954, both plans failed.

At this point Anthony Eden, Foreign Minister of Britain—which had refused to participate in EDC or to put its forces under supranational control—proposed that the BTO be enlarged to include Germany and Italy in a new organization, the Western European Union. Britain pledged to keep some forces on the European mainland, and Germany would be admitted to NATO and supply troops to it. But with the defeat of EDC and EPC, the European integration process had been temporarily checked. Defense policy for the moment would remain a national responsibility. The advocates of European unification then decided that the best policy was to pursue economic integration.

THE ECONOMIC COMMUNITY

The proposed EPC had included provisions for a common market with free movement of goods, capital, and persons. Two organizations already existed to facilitate trade. On the international level, the General Agreement on Trade and Tariffs (GATT), concerned with reduction of tariffs and quantitative restrictions on goods and setting up a common set of trade rules, was signed by 23 nations in October 1947. A narrower agreement in 1944 by Belgium, the Netherlands, and Luxembourg created a customs union (Benelux), which actually came into operation in 1948. Benelux abolished tariff barriers among the three countries and imposed a common tariff on imports from nonmember countries.

In May 1955 the Benelux countries, aided by Monnet and others, proposed a wider common market and other steps toward integration. These proposals for organizations to deal with a common market and customs union, and with atomic energy, were discussed by the six ECSC countries, with Britain again refusing to participate. In March 1957 the Treaties of Rome were signed (see Feature 6.2), and on 1 January 1958 the European Economic Community (EEC) and the European Atomic Energy Community (Euratom) came into existence. The EEC would merge separate national markets into a single large market that would ensure the free movement of goods, people, capital, and services, and would draw up a wide range of common economic and social policies. Euratom was designed to further the use of nuclear energy for peaceful purposes. In 1965, the three executive bodies of ECSC, EEC, and Euratom were merged into the European Community (EC). (For a list of

Feature 6.2 **The European Communities**

There are three European communities governed by separate treaties: the European Coal and Steel Community (ECSC), by the Treaty of Paris, 1951; and the European Economic Community (EEC) and the European Atomic Energy Community (Euratom), by the Treaties of Rome, 1957. The term "European Communities" is used in legal documents to refer to the three bodies, but the generally accepted term is now "European Community" (EC).

Table 6.1   EUROPEAN AND REGIONAL ORGANIZATIONS

	EC	Council of Europe	NATO	OECD	EFTA	WEU
Belgium	X	X	X	X		X
Denmark	X	X	X	X		
Germany	X	X	X	X		X
Greece	X	X	X	X		
Spain	X	X	X	X		X
France	X	X	X	X		X
Ireland	X	X		X		
Italy	X	X	X	X		X
Luxembourg	X	X	X	X		X
The Netherlands	X	X	X	X		X
Portugal	X	X	X	X		X
UK	X	X	X	X		X
Austria		X		X	X	
Cyprus		X				
Iceland		X	X	X	X	
Liechtenstein		X			X	
Malta		X				
Norway		X	X	X	X	
San Marino		X				
Sweden		X		X	X	
Switzerland		X		X	X	
Turkey		X	X	X		
Finland		X		X	X	
USA			X	X		
Canada			X	X		
Japan				X		
Australia				X		
New Zealand				X		

organizations and their member nations, see Table 6.1)

THE SIX BECOME TWELVE

Attempts in 1957–1958 to create a wider free trade area to include the six ECSC nations and other European countries failed. Instead Britain, wanting an organization with no common external tariff or objective for economic or political unification, led the move toward the establishment in November 1959 of the European Free Trade Association (EFTA). This body, consisting of Austria, Britain, Denmark, Norway, Portugal, Sweden, and Switzerland, was to be concerned with liberalization of trade, not with political objectives.

Within two years, however, Britain changed its mind because of the obvious success of the EEC, and applied for membership in July 1961. After being rebuffed twice, Britain became a member of the European Community on 1 January 1973, together with Denmark and Ireland. The government of Norway had also agreed to join, but the Parliament refused ratification after the Norwegian electorate voted against accession. Greece joined the EC in 1981, and Spain and Portugal in 1986.

The Community in 1992 consists of 12 members. Other countries—Turkey, Austria, Sweden, Malta, Cyprus, and recently several Eastern European countries—have applied for membership. However, the admission of new members to the existing 12 will be delayed until the completion of the Community's current agenda: creation of a single market by 1992, economic and monetary union, and progress toward political unification. The last admission was the five *Länder* of the German Democratic Republic (East Germany), which joined the EC as part of united Germany in 1990 (see Table 6.2). Enlargement of the EC means that it will become more diverse economically, geographically, and culturally.

Table 6.2 WESTERN AND EASTERN EUROPE

		Population (millions)	GDP $billion (1989)
EC	Belgium	9.9	151
	Britain	56.9	827
	Denmark	5.1	104
	France	56.2	948
	Germany[a]	77.2	1403
	Greece	10.1	54
	Ireland	3.7	33
	Italy	57.3	866
	Holland	14.8	223
	Luxembourg	0.4	7
	Portugal	10.3	45
	Spain	39.3	377
EFTA	Austria	7.5	126
	Finland	5.0	116
	Iceland	0.3	5
	Norway	4.2	93
	Sweden	8.3	190
	Switzerland	6.5	175
	Liechtenstein		
E. Europe	Bulgaria	9.0	68*
	Czechoslovakia	15.7	154*
	Hungary	10.6	92*
	Poland	38.4	276*
	Romania	23.3	126*
	Soviet Union	288.0	2535*
	Yugoslavia	23.8	154*
EC associates	Cyprus	0.70	090*
	Malta	0.35	0.2*
	Turkey	55.6	82

Sources: UN; OECD; IMF; CIA.

*1988

[a]Germany is the unified two former states in 1990.

A UNIQUE ENTITY

The EC is not a federal political system, but it is considerably more than an intergovernmental agreement or commercial arrangement. Its objective is integration, not merely cooperation among states. The Single European Act (SEA), which was signed in 1986 and became

---

Feature 6.3 Law in the European Community

The foundation of the three communities rests on the Treaty of Paris, signed 1951, and the Treaties of Rome, signed 1957. The European Economic Community (EEC) provides a framework, to which legislation and policies have been added, calling for a customs union, ending cartels and monopolies in the EEC, free movement of people, services, and capital, and a common policy for agriculture and transport. The Treaty has been amended by the Single European Act, signed 1986. The Treaty has been amplified by case law resulting from determinations made on the basis of the Treaty, and by regulations, directives, decisions, recommendations, and opinions.

---

operative in 1987, speaks of transforming relations among the states "into a European Union." The EC is a unique society, and its institutional structure and procedural rules do not fit easily into any of the categories of political systems discussed in the introduction of this book.

The EC does not operate on the basis of a clear separation of powers. It is founded on international treaties (of Paris and Rome) among sovereign nations, not on a constitution (see Feature 6.3). Yet it is more than an international organization because it has power in certain fields to enact laws and regulations that are directly binding and applicable to citizens of the member states, and to adjudicate cases in certain topics in its court. The voting arrangements by ministers, allowing some decisions to be made by simple or weighted majority rather than by unanimity, means qualification of national sovereignty, as does the obligation of members to take specific common actions and decide on common policies. The legislative power of states is limited by their commitment to achieve coordination of economic and monetary policy, and harmonization of social legislation. The Community method is to seek communally devised solutions rather than individual or bilateral state action.

In recent years, the EC has said that it operates on the basis of "subsidiarity." This term, drawn from Catholic socioeconomic doctrine, means that the EC is granted jurisdiction and is responsible only for those policies that cannot be handled adequately at the state, national, regional, or local level.

Budget

The European communities have been financed in different ways. The ECSC is financed by a levy on the value of coal and steel production paid directly to the EC. The EEC and Euratom were originally financed by differing amounts from the member states, but in 1970 the EC decided to raise its own resources for additional revenue. Its income now comes from a number of sources (see Figure 6.1): levies on imports of agricultural produce, customs duties on other imports from non-EC countries, a small part of the Value-Added Tax (VAT) collected in member states, and a proportion of the GNP of the states.

THE INSTITUTIONS OF THE COMMUNITY

As in the original ECSC, there are four major institutions in the EC: the Commission, the Council of Ministers, the European Parliament, and the Court of Justice. Other bodies,

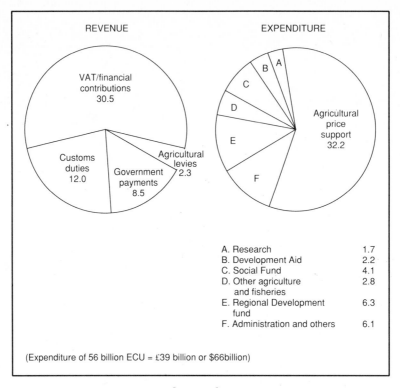

Figure 6.1 1991 EC Revenue and Expenditure

such as the European Council, the Committee of Permanent Representatives (Coreper), the Economic and Social Committee, and the Court of Auditors, also play roles of different kinds.

European Commission

The central institution is the Commission, which is both an executive and a civil service of the EC as well as the body that prepares and formulates policy proposals and legislation for approval. It is responsible for administering the Community and for ensuring that decisions are carried out. It has authority to bring legal action against persons, companies, or states that have violated EC rules. The Commission is the guardian of the Community treaties, seeing that the treaties and rules are

correctly applied and properly implemented. In addition, its task is to defend the interests of the Community (see Table 6.3).

There are now 17 commissioners—two each from Britain, France, Germany, Italy, and Spain, and one each from the other seven countries—who are nominated by their governments and approved by agreement of the 12 states for a renewable four-year term. The European Parliament has wanted to approve the nominations but has not yet been given authority to do so. The president is chosen from among the commissioners for a two-year term. All commissioners are expected to act in the interest of the EC rather than in defense of national interests, although they have not always followed this rule. The Commission acts in collegiate fashion with decisions made by majority, not unanimity. Each commissioner

Table 6.3 THE COMMISSION OF THE EUROPEAN COMMUNITIES

PRESIDENT
1

VICE-PRESIDENTS
6

MEMBERS
10

17 Members appointed
by common accord of
the governments of
the Member States for
a term of four years

Members			Members	
1	Belgium		Italy	2
1	Denmark		Luxembourg	1
2	France		The Netherlands	1
2	Germany		Portugal	1
1	Greece		Spain	2
1	Ireland		United Kingdom	2

Responsibilities

Proposing	Monitoring	Administering	Representing
measures for the further development of Community policy	observance and proper application of Community law	and implementing Community legislation	the Community in international organizations

is assigned a specific policy area or areas of main responsibility, and each has a "cabinet" or small staff of aides. The Commission as a whole has a staff, based mainly in Brussels, of about 13,000 people. Its current president, Jacques Delors, is widely regarded as the most effective head the EC has had.

The Commission's chief role as initiator is to propose new policies and regulations to the Council of Ministers; decisions in the EC can only be taken on the basis of these proposals, which are agreed on by the Commission as a whole at its weekly meetings. The Council of Ministers can accept or reject these proposals, or it can modify them by a unanimous vote. The Commission has often amended its own proposals to meet criticism by the Council, but Project 92 (the Single European Act) may strengthen the position of the Commission after 1992. Because the Council will be able to make more decisions by majority vote rather than by unanimity, the Commission is less likely to weaken its proposals to obtain agreement by all the states.

The Commission also has power to act on its own in some areas: competition policy, farming, trade policy, and customs duties. It does not have power over fiscal or monetary policies or over central banking, though it has been trying to extend its general authority.

The Council of Ministers

The main forum for decision making is the Council of Ministers. The Council consists of representatives of the 12 states and must approve proposals of the Commission before they can be implemented. The Council, unlike the Commission, is not a fixed group of people. Its membership changes according to the subject being discussed, such as finance, agriculture, transportation, or the environment; the ministers responsible for these activities in the states will make up the Council. But most often the Council consists of ministers responsible for foreign policy who meet once a month (see Table 6.4).

The Council differs from international organizations that require unanimity to make decisions. The logic of European integration was that the Council would increasingly decide by majority vote. This was stalled by the Luxembourg Compromise of 1966, a concession to the nationalism of President de Gaulle, which said that the other governments would not overrule a member state that opposed proposals it held to be contrary to its national interest. This veto power by a state has rarely been used since 1966, because the Council has generally acted by consensus. The Single European Act which took effect in 1987 provides for greater use of majority voting in the Council, though unanimity is still needed for certain matters such as taxation, company law, agreements with non-Community countries, workers' rights, and free movement of people.

In other matters, ministers, who are helped by working groups of national officials, can decide by majority vote. The Council has 76 votes that are weighted: Britain, France, Germany, and Italy have ten each; Spain has eight; Belgium, Greece, the Netherlands, and Portugal have five each; Denmark and Ireland have three each; and Luxembourg has two. Of the total, 54 votes are needed for a "qualified majority" to approve proposals. Coalitions of 23 or more votes can therefore still block decisions.

An essential part of the decision-making process has been the Committee of Permanent Representatives (Coreper)—the representatives of the member states who hold ambassadorial rank—which meets weekly to prepare meetings of the Council of Ministers. Coreper has played a significant role in coordinating the attitudes of the states with the proposals of the Commission. Most of those proposals go to Coreper before going to the Council, and decisions on some issues have been reached by the states at the Coreper level.

Other Executive Bodies

Although they have no formal status and were not created by the Treaties of Paris or Rome, two other significant bodies have been ac-

---

Table 6.4   THE COUNCIL OF MINISTERS

Representatives of the governments of the Member States 12
Permanent Representatives Committee (Coreper)

LEGISLATION

Weighting of votes		Weighting of votes	
10	France	Greece	5
10	Germany	The Netherlands	5
10	Italy	Belgium	5
10	United Kingdom	Denmark	3
8	Spain	Ireland	3
5	Portugal	Luxembourg	2

Qualified majority:
54 votes out of 76

knowledged by the Single European Act. One is the European Council (not to confused with the Council of Ministers), which consists of the 12 heads of state or government assisted by their foreign ministers and the president of the Commission. Sometimes referred to as the EC summit, this council has met two or three times a year since 1975, primarily to discuss foreign policy, defense, and important economic subjects. The European Council has made a number of important decisions and is an intergovernmental body, not one of the official institutions of the EC.

The second body is European Political Cooperation (EPC), which began in 1970 and is now acknowledged in the Single European Act, though it is also not a formal part of the EC itself. EPC is a forum in which the 12 foreign ministers meet regularly to discuss coordination of foreign policy and the political and economic aspects of security. Assisted since 1981 by a small secretariat in Brussels, EPC has coordinated the policy of the 12 countries at several meetings of the United Nations and on a number of international issues, beginning with the 1980 Venice Declaration on the Middle East.

The EPC, like the Council of Ministers and the European Council, is chaired by one of the states every six months. The overlap between the different executive groups, which are all trying to coordinate the opinions of the national foreign ministries, has sometimes made it difficult to differentiate the working of the EPC from that of the Council. The Single European Act suggests that EPC will play an even more important role in the future, a development which may help to resolve the question of who makes foreign policy in the EC. It could also decide whether nonmember states such as the United States should deal with officials from the Commission, the Council, or the individual 12 countries, a problem that is complicated by the fact that a different country assumes the presidency of the Council and the EPC every six months.

THE EUROPEAN PARLIAMENT

The Parliament, renamed from the Assembly established under ECSC, is composed of 518 members (now directly elected in the 12 states for a five-year term) in approximate proportion to the size of the different populations (see Figure 6.2). The largest countries have 81 seats; the smallest, Luxembourg, has six. The Parliament meets one week in each month in plenary sessions in Strasbourg, France, but its committees meet in Brussels and its secretariat of 3600 meets in Luxembourg. Its members come from over 60 political parties and almost always come together in political groups—ten in 1992 plus an eleventh, nonaffiliated group—not in national blocs. They can use any of the nine official languages of the EC.

The Parliament has been useful as an arena for the discussion of EC matters and as a representative of over 340 million people. But its powers are largely limited to giving its opinion on draft directives, proposals, and regulations coming from the Commission. The latter may decide to amend its proposals as a result of that opinion. The Parliament has power to dismiss the Commission on a vote of censure by a two-thirds majority, but this has never been done. It also must approve or reject the budget which is prepared by the Commission for decision by the Council of Ministers; it has rejected the draft budget on two occasions. Since 1975 the Parliament has helped the Commission draw up the budget, and can make amendments in limited areas. The Parliament has no formal powers of control over the Council or any influence on the appointment of members of the Commission.

The Single European Act has increased the Parliament's legislative role, allowing it to accept, reject, or amend some legislative proposals. The Act has also given it power to ratify new international agreements concluded by the Council and the admission of new members to the EC. In the complicated process of decision making, the Commission can ac-

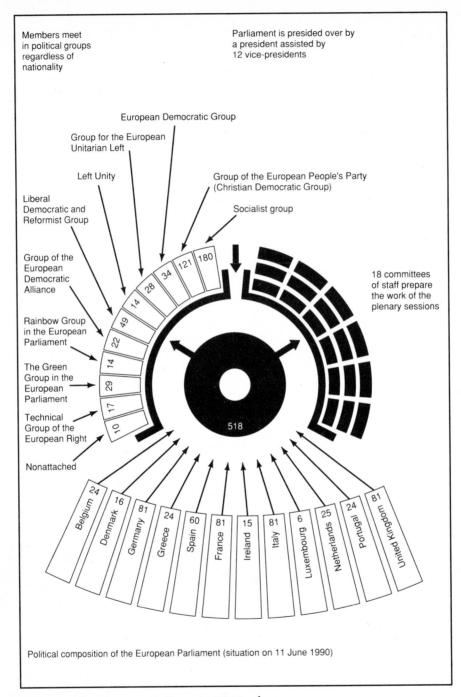

Members meet
in political groups
regardless of
nationality

Parliament is presided over by
a president assisted by
12 vice-presidents

European Democratic Group

Group for the European
Unitarian Left

Left Unity

Liberal
Democratic and
Reformist Group

Group of the European People's Party
(Christian Democratic Group)

Socialist group

Group of the
European
Democratic
Alliance

Rainbow Group
in the European
Parliament

The Green
Group in the
European
Parliament

Technical
Group of the
European Right

Nonattached

18 committees
of staff prepare
the work of the
plenary sessions

180
121
34
28
14
49
22
14
29
17
10

518

Belgium 24
Denmark 16
Germany 81
Greece 24
Spain 60
France 81
Ireland 15
Italy 81
Luxembourg 6
Netherlands 25
Portugal 24
United Kingdom 81

Political composition of the European Parliament (situation on 11 June 1990)

Figure 6.2 The European Parliament: 518 Members

European Parliament, Strasbourg.

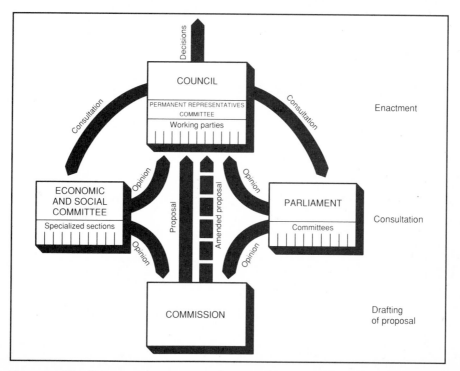

Figure 6.3 The Community's Decision-Making Process

cept or reject any amendment asked for by the Parliament, and the Council of Ministers can overturn the result only by unanimity (see Figure 6.3). Some members of the EC have argued that Parliament should be allowed to introduce proposals and to question or dismiss members of the Commission.

THE COURT OF JUSTICE

The Court, located in Luxembourg, consists of 13 judges—one from each state and the pres-ident of the Court—appointed for six years. By the Single European Act, a junior court of First Instance was set up in 1988 to assist the Court. The European Court of Justice (ECJ) differs from two other bodies: the International Court of Justice in The Hague (the World Court), and the European Court of Human Rights, which was established by the Council of Europe in Strasbourg. Member states of the EC must accept the final decisions and judgments of the ECJ but have no legal obligation to ac-cept those of the other two courts, which are not part of the EC (see Table 6.5).

Table 6.5 THE EUROPEAN COURT OF JUSTICE

Governments of the
Member States appoint
the 13 judges
and six Advocates-General
by common accord for
a term of six years

COURT OF JUSTICE

Full court of 13 judges

2 chambers with 5 judges

4 chambers with 3 judges

TYPES OF PROCEEDING

Actions for failure to fulfill obligations under the Treaties (Commission *vs.* Member State) Actions by one Member State against another	Actions on grounds of failure to act (against Council or Commission)	References from national courts for preliminary rulings to clarify the meaning and scope of Community law Claims for damages against the Community

COURT OF FIRST INSTANCE
12 judges

Staff cases
Actions in the field of competition law
Actions under anti-dumping law
Actions under the ECSC Treaty

The essential functions of the ECJ are to ensure that EC law is properly applied and to resolve disputes over that law. It works by unanimity and thus, unlike the U.S. Supreme Court, no public dissent is registered. All member states are obliged to accept its rulings and its powers which are stated in the Treaties of Paris and Rome. The states have accepted that EC law is now also national law in their countries, that EC law prevails over national law if there is a conflict between them, and that the ECJ's decisions overrule those of national courts. The ECJ has by now laid down a body of Community law that applies to the EC institutions, states, and citizens. In 1991 the Court upheld the power of the Commission to dismantle state-owned monopolies without the formal approval of the member states.

Other Agencies

The Economic and Social Committee consists of 189 persons representing employers, workers, and various interests such as consumer groups and professional associations. It meets once a month in Brussels to give its opinion on policies and legislative proposals in certain fields. It has the right to be consulted, but has no right of amendment.

The Court of Auditors, based in Luxembourg, consists of 12 members appointed by the Council of Ministers. It supervises expenditure, checking all EC revenue and spending, and has investigated cases of mismanagement and fraud.

The European Investment Bank provides loans in many economic sectors to help less-developed regions of the EC, to modernize enterprises, and to create employment.

THE COMMON MARKET

The original objectives of the EC stated in the Treaties of Rome were the development of economic activities, a balanced expansion, greater stability, a higher standard of living, and closer relations between the member states. The members were therefore supposed to establish a common market and to try for similar economic policies.

The first step was a customs union among the original six countries, which meant removing tariffs on internal trade and imposing a common external tariff against nonmember countries (see Feature 6.4). By 1968 the union had been completed, leading to a great increase in internal trade among the six, from $6.8 billion in 1958 to $60 billion in 1972.

But other barriers to trade continued, preventing the establishment of a real common market. In the late 1980s the EC proposed new measures to eliminate barriers to free trade and movement and create a single market by the end of 1992. These included ending customs checks and border controls within the EC, harmonization of technical standards, mutual acceptance of professional qualifications and diplomas, a Community market for financial services such as banking and insurance, and approximate taxation rates. The Single Eu-

---

Feature 6.4 **The Common Market**

The Common Market has ended all internal customs duties, and has replaced the individual national tariffs on imports from outside the European Community by one set of tariffs, the Common External Tariff. Goods entering the EC can then circulate within the EC without any further tariffs.

Feature 6.5 Single European Act, Signed in 1986, Operative 1987

Amended the Treaties of Rome
Qualified majority voting in Council of Ministers on certain subjects
Cooperation procedure to give Parliament more input into legislative process
Timetables set up
Implement a complete common market by 1992
Formal recognition of European Political Cooperation

---

ropean Act, with its important amendments to the Community treaties, has facilitated the implementation of most of these measures to complete the internal market (see Feature 6.5).

The SEA also provides for progress in economic and monetary policy, social policy, research, and environmental issues, and for cooperation in foreign policy. Above all, it calls for the movement toward a European Union.

The essential objective of the SEA is the creation of a common market in which goods, services, people, and capital can move without obstacles such as frontier delays, fiscal barriers (including Value-Added Tax (VAT) rates and excise taxes), or technical obstructions such as national health and safety regulations. Tariffs and direct trade barriers have been ended since the mid-1960s. The new plan is to end all indirect barriers that hinder commerce or prevent competition, and to allow a citizen of the 12 countries to be able to practice a trade or profession in any of the other countries. To that end, the EC has agreed on directives to harmonize the different industrial and technical standards, to end barriers to movement of money, to reduce protectionist regulations and subsidies, to abolish checks at EC borders, and to bring the different tax rates closer together.

The SEA, however, has even broader implications. The ambition of many proponents of the Act is a common European market not only without frontier barriers, but also with a political dynamic and will, cooperating closely in foreign policy and monetary affairs and being able to make decisions in many fields. The most ambitious proponents are aiming toward a political union or United States of Europe.

In 1950 Robert Schuman said that "Europe will not be made all at once or according to a single general plan. It will be built through concrete achievements, which first create a de facto solidarity." So far, attempts at creating common defense, foreign, and political policies have failed, but there have been significant achievements, such as the customs union, the common agricultural policy, and increasing monetary union.

Common Agricultural Policy (CAP)

The objectives of the CAP are to maintain food supplies at stable and reasonable prices, to improve agricultural productivity, and to ensure a fair standard of living for farmers. The CAP accounts for about 60 percent to 70 percent of total EC expenditure and covers about 90 percent of farm output in the 12 countries. A number of goals underlie the CAP: price guarantees for farmers, common prices for agricultural commodities, variable import levies to raise import prices to the EC level, and subsidies to EC farmers to enable them to export and sell at world prices, which are generally below the internal EC market. These export subsidies account for about one-half of the total CAP budget (see Table 6.6).

Table 6.6 EUROPEAN AGRICULTURE IN 1986

	Farm size (hectare)	Share of agriculture in gross domestic product (%)	Share of agriculture in working population (%)
Belgium	14.1	2.5	2.9
Denmark	30.7	5.0	6.8
F.R. of Germany	16.0	1.8	5.3
Greece	4.3	16.6	28.5
Spain	12.9	6.1	16.1
France	27.0	3.7	7.3
Ireland	22.7	10.2	15.8
Italy	5.6	5.0	10.9
Luxembourg	28.6	2.6	4.0
The Netherlands	14.9	4.2	4.8
Portugal	4.3	23.1	21.9
United Kingdom	65.1	1.8	2.6
EUR 12	8.9	3.5	8.3

The CAP has been successful and important for the farming community, now a much smaller part of the employed than 30 years ago, but it has also been severely criticized on several grounds. It is expensive, and some argue that it takes too large a part of the EC budget. The Community spent about $37 billion in 1991 in state subsidies to farmers. Prices of agricultural commodities are higher than world market prices; this means that the CAP adds about $1500 a year to the food bill of an average family. The high prices stimulate production, resulting in surpluses that are very costly to store. These "wine-lakes" and "butter mountains" distort competition and depress world prices. Many outside countries, especially the United States, have accused the CAP of being protectionist by preventing or reducing imports. They have called in particular for the elimination of EC subsidies which encourage excessive and inefficient production. In 1990–1991, the GATT negotiations (called the Uruguay Round) were deadlocked because of disagreement on this issue. The United States and other agricultural exporting countries called for the EC to cut farm support by 75 percent and export subsidies by 90 percent.

The EC proposed only a 30 percent cut over a ten-year period. Both France and Germany were unwilling to eliminate or cut the subsidies which, in effect, kept their small farmers in business.

ECONOMIC AND MONETARY UNION

Accompanying the creation of the single market are steps toward the objectives of an economic and monetary union (EMU) with a single European currency, a European central bank responsible for management of the monetary policies of the states, and greater convergence of economic policies.

Since 1979 the European Monetary System (EMS) has attempted to coordinate economic policies and to stabilize the currencies of the EC countries. The exchange rate mechanism of the EMS obliges member states to limit fluctuations in the value of their currency to small amounts. Central banks of the states ensure that these limits are kept by raising or lowering interest rates, buying and selling currencies, and adjusting fiscal policies. The EMS uses the European currency unit (ECU) to fix

---

Feature 6.6 **The ECU**

The ECU is a "basket" of specified amounts of each EC currency which are determined by reference to the economy of member states. The value of the ECU depends on the current market rate of each currency. The ECU is also the accounting unit of the EC, and is expected to become the new single currency in the EMU.

---

central rates for the member states (see Feature 6.6). The EMS has helped to keep inflation and interest rates low and rates of investment high.

Most, though not all, of the EC member states are prepared to go beyond the EMS to adopt a single currency and set up a central bank. The first stage of economic and monetary union started in July 1990 with the strengthening of policies on the issue among EC countries through existing institutions and with the participation of all the countries in the exchange rate mechanism of the EMS. All restrictions were lifted on capital movements between most countries. In December 1990 an intergovernmental conference of the states opened to work on the next stages of an EMU treaty. Agreement was reached at Maastricht in December 1991 (see page 331). The end of the process will be complete linking of exchange rates—central monetary control by the Community, a central bank, and one currency for the 12 countries.

The EC has been less successful in other areas. It has been unable to introduce a common transport policy called for by the Treaty of Rome because transportation has largely relied on national structures. Its competition policy, aimed at preventing favored treatment to certain businesses, the formation of cartels, and the abuse by firms of a dominant market position, has not yet become significant, nor have its social and regional policies.

EXTERNAL RELATIONS

The EC is the world's largest trading unit, accounting for about 20 percent of world trade. (The United States accounts for 15 percent and Japan 9 percent of world trade.) It therefore plays a significant role in GATT and its tariff negotiations. In the current Uruguay Round of multinational negotiations (which began in 1986 among 105 countries) the European Commission, the bargaining agent for the EC, has differed from other countries on the crucial issue of agricultural subsidies. There is no single authority in the EC to deal with third parties or define common interests. Different views persist concerning foreign and security policies and which EC institution should handle policy-making functions.

Complex Relations

The EC now has a complicated set of relations with nonmember states, varied trade agreements with countries throughout the world, and association agreements with Turkey, Malta, and Cyprus. Two of these external links are particularly interesting. One is the relationship between the EC and its main trading partner, the European Free Trade Association (EFTA), which now includes seven countries with a combined population of 32 million. Both the EC and EFTA have abolished customs duties and restrictions on trade in manufactured goods in a free trade area, and in 1991 the two bodies agreed on the creation of a European Economic Area. This involves a single market with free movement of goods, services, people, and capital, but without EFTA having any vote on EC laws. The fundamental difficulties so far have been that EFTA, as a much looser organization, does not have the sense of collective purpose or the institutional structure of the EC to enable it to reach an agreement. Moreover, a number of EFTA countries, especially Austria and Sweden, have either applied for membership in the EC or are expected to apply in the near future. Almost two-thirds of EFTA's trade is with the EC, but only one-quarter of the EC's trade is with EFTA, whose population has an average per capita income of $19,000, about double the EC average.

A second important link is with the countries of the third world. Since the Yaoundé Convention of 1963, the EC has extended special preferential trading arrangements to the ex-colonies of EC countries. The EC is now linked to 69 African, Caribbean, and Pacific (ACP) countries through a series of Lomé Conventions, the latest of which was renewed in 1989 for a ten-year period. The ACP countries are freed from customs duties on almost all their exports to the EC, and also receive financial aid from the EC.

In addition to EFTA, the third world Lomé conventions, and the association agreements, the EC has concluded cooperation arrangements with many other countries, including Eastern and Southern Mediterranean nations, which have been given duty-free access for their industrial exports and agricultural trade and have received financial grants and loans. The EC has also entered into a Euro-Arab dialogue, discussing agricultural, trade, and technical matters with Arab countries.

Since the decline of communism and the end of Soviet control in Eastern Europe, the EC has become involved in the affairs of the East in a number of ways. It coordinated the 1989 Phare program in which 24 countries sent aid to Poland, Hungary, and other Central and Eastern European countries. It entered into bilateral trade agreements with each of the Eastern countries, which the EC would like to see form a regional group, and assisted in their environmental problems. This has meant allowing these states a degree of free trade with the EC, granting them aid and loans, and providing for a number of joint projects. The EC does not regard these states as politically or economically ready for EC membership or association, to be considered in 1992.

THE COMMUNITY FUTURE

The three communities have as official objectives the creation of "an organized and vital Europe," laying "the foundations of an ever closer union among the peoples of Europe," and combining together to "contribute to the prosperity of the peoples." The EC has already become an important part of European politics. Many decisions have been made that affect the states and their citizens in important ways, and many more will directly affect citizens after 1992.

At the meeting in Maastricht, the Netherlands, in December 1991 the leaders of the 12 countries agreed on a treaty that commits the EC to monetary union, a single currency, and a central bank by 1999 (see Table 6.7). They also agreed to establish common foreign and security policies with a view to increasing their influence on the world stage, and to work toward "the eventual framing of a common defense policy." All the countries except Britain endorsed an agreement to seek a common system of social laws on matters such as minimum wages, vacation time, working conditions, and labor-management relations. Britain also reserved the right to make a decision on its acceptance of the monetary union until a later stage.

At this point the nature of the EC has not been clearly defined. It is still a confederation of independent states that have pooled some

Table 6.7 MAASTRICHT TREATIES ON
EUROPEAN UNION AND ECONOMIC
AND MONETARY UNION
DECEMBER 1991

Chief features of the treaties:

1. Single currency by 1999, but optional for Britain
   and Denmark, and an Economic and Monetary
   Union with a Central Bank
2. Eventual European defense, but in collaboration
   with NATO
3. Common foreign policy making, and implementation by majority vote
4. Some more legislative power given to the European Parliament with a veto on some items
5. Common citizenship of European Union
6. More majority voting in the Council of Ministers
7. European Social Community accepted by all states
   except Britain
8. Fund set up to help poorer EC countries

powers and some aspects of sovereignty in economic matters, but that retain their authority
to deal internally with law and order, foreign
policy, and defense. Strong differences exist
between those calling for more supranational
government and more EC impact on citizens
and those who think that active cooperation
between sovereign states is the best way to
build a successful European community, and
would be content with little more than an intergovernmental body.

Differences on two other matters are of
great concern to the United States The first
is the dispute about the Community's subsidies on agricultural exports and the degree of
European protectionism. The United States
claims that these subsidies are unfair and that
they distort markets in the rest of the world.
The dispute has already blocked progress on
the GATT negotiations. The second issue is
that of defense. Some in the Community believe that there should be a strong European
pillar in NATO on which Europe could rely for
its defense. Others argue that Europe should
be responsible for its own security and defense, and suggest that the Western European

Union would be the best organization for this
purpose. France and Germany proposed in
1991 a joint military brigade that would be the
basis for a European corps.

There are also important disagreements
over questions such as the relative merits of
free trade and protectionism; a complete market economy or one with the state intervening
to a considerable degree; the extent of welfare
systems and of social rights; the enlargement
of the Community to embrace new members,
including Eastern European states; and the
problem of democratic control over the work
of the Community institutions. Resolution of
these questions will not come easily to a group
of states that have had such a long and complex
history, and that now must reformulate their
attitudes toward the former Soviet Union and
Eastern Europe and toward policies on many
issues, such as arms control, nuclear proliferation, the Middle East, the United Nations, and
the United States.

Key Terms

Benelux
Brussels Treaty Organization
Committee of Permanent Representatives
  (Coreper)
Community Method
Common Market
Council of Europe
European Atomic Energy Community
  (Euratom)
European Coal and Steel Community (ECSC)
European Community (EC)
European Currency Unit (ECU)
European Economic Area
European Free Trade Association (EFTA)
European Parliament
General Agreement on Trade and Tariffs
  (GATT)
Jean Monnet
North Atlantic Treaty Organization (NATO)
Organization for Economic Cooperation and
  Development (OECD)
Robert Schuman

Single European Act
Treaty of Dunkirk
Treaty of Paris
Treaties of Rome
Western European Union (WEU)

Suggestions for Further Reading

George, Stephen. *An Awkward Partner: Britain in the European Community* (New York: Oxford University Press, 1990).

Gianaris, Nicolas. *The European Community and the United States: Economic Relations* (New York: Praeger, 1991).

Giavazzi, F. et al., eds. *The European Monetary System* (Cambridge: Cambridge University Press, 1988).

Harrop, J. *The Political Economy of European Integration* (Aldershot: Elgar, 1989).

Heywood, Robert W. *The European Community: Idea and Reality* (San Francisco: EM Text, 1990).

Lintner, Valerio. *The European Community: Economic and Political Aspects* (New York: McGraw-Hill, 1991).

Lodge, Juliet. *The European Community and the Challenge of the Future* (London: Pinter, 1989).

Nugent, Neill. *The Government and Politics of the European Community* (Basingstoke: Macmillan, 1990).

Pinder, John. *The European Community: The Building of a Union* (New York: OUP, 1991).

Pinder, John. *The European Community and East Europe* (London: Pinter, 1991).

Pryce, Roy, ed. *The Dynamics of European Union* (London: Croom Helm, 1987).

Urwin, Derek W. *The Community of Europe: A History of European Integration since 1945* (New York: Longman, 1991).

Williams, Allan M. *The European Community: the Contradictions of Integration* (Cambridge, Mass: Blackwell, 1991).

B. Political Change in Central and Eastern Europe

For over 40 years following World War II, Europe was divided into two blocs: a Democratic West, becoming more prosperous; and a Communist East, relatively poor with political systems modeled on that of the Soviet Union. The latter nations were ruled by a Communist party (the only legal party), a large secret police, a Marxist ideology, central planning and direction of the economy, strict censorship, control of information, and restrictions on travel. They were also dominated by the Soviet Union itself, and were members of Comecon and the Warsaw Pact.

At the end of the 1980s the changes in Eastern European systems were rapid and dramatic, and have transformed the European continent. Much of this was due not only to their own economic, social, and political problems, but also to the people of the Soviet Union and their differences over the proposals of Soviet leader Mikhail Gorbachev for *perestroika*, or restructuring. The Eastern Europeans were aware of the decline of communism as a force, of the lack of support for Communist party leadership, and of the fact that the Soviet Union under Gorbachev would no longer intervene in their internal affairs or use force to prevent change. Eastern Europe also appreciated that the Communist decline and the policy of *perestroika*, calling for economic and political reforms, was leading to moderation of the Cold War between the Soviet Union and the United States. The tension in the postwar period between the two countries was partly an ideological struggle between a liberal democracy with a market economy and a Communist system with a centrally planned economy, and partly a conflict over influence and competing interests in a world dominated by two superpowers. The tension was lessened in the 1980s with a growing mood of political cooperation with the West.

Internal dissension within the Eastern European system came to a head in 1989 (see Feature 6.7). Movements for an end to Communist rule and for change to a more prosperous and productive economy began in Poland and Hungary and rapidly spread to Czechoslovakia, East Germany, Bulgaria, and to a lesser extent, Romania. This revolution, almost entirely peaceful, was most dramatic in East Germany, the German Democratic Republic. On 9 November 1989 the Berlin Wall, a symbol of the Cold War dividing East and West, came down; in December 1989 and March 1990 two Communist governments collapsed; and in Oc-

Feature 6.7 **Political Change in Central and Eastern Europe in 1989**

April:	Poland	Solidarity became legal again, some political reforms enacted.
May:	Hungary	Fences along Austrian border dismantled; East Germans began crossing that border.
June:	Poland	Overwhelming victory by Solidarity in parliamentary elections; General Jaruzelski elected president (July).
August:	Poland	Tadeusz Mazowiecki of Solidarity became first non-Communist prime minister.
September:	Hungary	Restrictions ended on East Germans entering the country and escaping to West Germany via Austria.
	Poland	Solidarity dominated new government coalition.
October:	Hungary	Communists changed name to Socialist party; agreement on multiparty system.
	East Germany	Mass exodus and demonstrations led to downfall of Communist leader Erich Honecker.
November:	East Germany	Travel restrictions abolished; Berlin Wall opened; new coalition includes many non-Communists.
	Bulgaria	Communist leader Todor Zhivkov ousted.
	Czechoslovakia	Street demonstrations lead to downfall of Communist leader Milos Jakes; talks with Civic Forum; end of "leading role" of Communist party.
December:	East Germany	"Leading role" of Communists (Socialist Unity party) ended.
	Czechoslovakia	New coalition government with non-Communist majority; Vaclav Havel elected President; Alexander Dubcek became speaker of Parliament.
	Bulgaria	Communists renounce "leading role," and call for free elections.
	Romania	Massacre of demonstrators in Timisoara led to downfall and execution of Communist leader Nicolae Ceausescu; National Salvation Front took power.

East and West Germans meet as the Berlin Wall falls, November 1989.

tober 1990 the G.D.R. was united with the Federal Republic of Germany. The dramatic changes can be analyzed in the following way.

ALBANIA

The Socialist People's Republic set up in 1946 has not been overturned as have the other Eastern European countries. Although the government embarked on limited reforms in 1989, power in 1992 is still held by the Communist Party of Labor, the only legal party, which won the election held in March 1991.

BULGARIA

The People's Republic set up in 1946 was close politically and economically to the Soviet Union, which accounted for 75 percent of its trade. However, in 1989 the Communists took the lead in political change by removing Todor Zhivkov, leader since 1954, who opposed Gorbachev-style reforms and who was responsible for repression of ethnic Turks in the country, 300,000 of whom had fled the country in the summer of 1989. The Communists renounced the leading role of the party—which was renamed the Socialist party—and organized a free election. At this parliamentary election in 1990, the Communists won 47 percent of the votes and a majority of the seats, partly because opposition groups were poorly organized. Bulgaria was the first Eastern European country in which a reformed Communist party won power in a free election.

CZECHOSLOVAKIA

Czechoslovakia, which had the most significant pre-World War II democratic tradition, came

Table 6.8   CENTRAL AND EASTERN EUROPEAN PROFILE

	Soviet Union	Bulgaria	Czecho-slovakia	Hungary	Poland	Romania
Population (million, 1988)	286.4	9.0	15.6	10.6	38.0	23.0
GDP (billion US$, 1988)	1,590.0	50.7	118.6	68.8	207.2	94.7
GDP per capita (US$)	5,552.0	5,633.0	7,603.0	6,491.0	5,453.0	4,117.0
Annual growth of GDP (%) 1981–1985	1.7	0.8	1.2	0.7	0.6	−0.1
1986–1988	2.3	1.9	1.5	1.5	1.0	0.1
Living standards (1987):						
Cars per 1,000 inhabitants	50.0	127.0	182.0	153.0	74.0	11.0
Telephones per 1,000 inhabitants	124.0	248.0	246.0	152.0	122.0	111.0
Share of workforce in agriculture (%)	21.7	19.5	12.1	18.4	28.2	28.5
Gross domestic investment/GDP (%)	33.2	32.7	24.7	28.5	36.5	37.1
Share of private enterprise in GDP (%)	2.5	8.9	3.1	14.6	14.7	2.5
Exports of goods as % of GDP (1988)	6.8	23.0	19.7	14.7	6.4	11.2
Exports of manufactured goods as share of exports to non-Socialist countries	63.0	59.3	72.4	79.6	63.4	50.6

Source: OECD.

under Communist control in 1948. Attempts to liberalize the regime by the Communist leader Alexander Dubcek in the "Prague Spring" of 1968 were brutally suppressed by the Soviet Union and most Warsaw Pact countries. In 1989 street demonstrations calling for political change led to the resignation of the Communist leader and most of his colleagues. Opposition activists formed the Civic Forum consisting of 12 groups, including Charter 77, a human rights group set up after the 1968 repression. The most prominent figure was Vaclav Havel, a distinguished writer and human rights activist whose plays were banned and who had been imprisoned for five years. A new government with a non-Communist majority was formed. In December 1989, Havel was elected unanimously as interim president when all other candidates withdrew, and was reelected for two years in July 1990. Dubcek was chosen as the parliamentary speaker. Free multiparty elections in June 1990 led to victory for the groups that led the 1989 protests, as the Civic Forum won 47 percent of the vote and

a majority of parliamentary seats. Economic reforms were introduced in 1991. Most price controls were removed, the currency was made convertible, privatization was begun, and the economy was opened to foreign investors.

HUNGARY

The People's Republic proclaimed in 1949 became the Hungarian Republic in October 1989. Hungary was the Eastern European country most anxious to transform itself economically, especially after the brutal suppression by the Soviet Union of an attempted uprising in 1956. In that period Hungary was a unique laboratory for economic experimentation in the Communist world. As a result of reform efforts in the Communist Socialist Workers Party, the name of the party was changed to Socialist party; the party gave up its leading role in October 1989 and began discussions with opposition groups. In 1990, elections were held for a single-chamber parliament in which Democratic Forum, a center-right group with 25 percent of the votes, and Free Democrats, a center-liberal group with 21 percent of the votes, emerged as the leading parties, with the reformed Communists getting 11 percent and the unreformed Communists 4 percent of the votes. A coalition government was formed led by the Democratic Forum.

POLAND

The People's Republic set up in 1947 was replaced in December 1989 by the Polish Republic. Some political concessions had been made in 1980 by the Communist regime after shipyard and other strikes and the organization of a free trade union (Solidarity) led by Lech Walesa, a shipyard electrician in Gdansk. Those concessions were halted with the imposition of martial law. Growing difficulties and more strikes in late 1988 led Communist leaders to discuss economic and social problems with Solidarity and Walesa, who was awarded the Nobel Peace Prize in 1983. In 1989, Solidarity was again legalized and the Catholic Church was more officially recognized. In the parliamentary election in June, Solidarity won an overwhelming victory. In the Senate it won 99 out of 100 seats; in the lower house, where it was only allowed to contest 35 percent of the seats, it won all 161 allowed. General Jaruzelski, elected president in July, invited Solidarity into a coalition government. This, the first non-Communist government in postwar Eastern Europe, was headed as prime minister by Tadeusz Mazowiecki of Solidarity. Two major political groups emerged: the Center Alliance and the Civic Movement for Democratic Action. In December 1989 Walesa, backed by almost all political and social organizations and by the Catholic Church, won the presidential election in a second ballot by 74 percent of the vote. But the parliamentary election in October 1991 produced a deeply fragmented chamber, with 29 different parties gaining seats.

ROMANIA

The People's Republic set up in 1947 was replaced by the Republic of Romania in December 1989. Change occurred in 1989 partly as a result of spontaneous anti-Communist and pro-Western protests of the people, and partly by the action of some parts of the Communist party and the security police who were critical of the corruption, the economic mismanagement, and the brutal rule of Communist leader Nicolae Ceausescu. After the violent suppression and killing of several hundred demonstrators in Timisoara by the police, protestors took over Communist party headquarters and later executed Ceausescu, who had fled. A number of violently anti-Communist political groups emerged, but the new National Salvation Front, containing many past and present Communists, remained the dominant party. At the May 1990 parliamentary election, the Front got 66 percent of the vote. A month later, demonstrations by students and workers in Bucharest were repressed with considerable force by coal miners specially brought in to restore order.

UNEVEN CHANGE

The changes so far in Eastern Europe have been uneven. Three countries—Poland, Hungary, and Czechoslovakia—appear committed to democratic regimes and liberalized economies. But Communist elements retain some power in Romania and Bulgaria, and they retain considerable power in Albania. Yugoslavia is a separate case, with its federal system disintegrating because of civil war between rival ethnic and national republics and groups. But apart from Albania, the totalitarian systems and monopolies of power by the Communist party have ended. In their place, other groups and movements such as Solidarity and Civic Forum have emerged, and new political parties have competed in parliamentary elections.

The Eastern European states have been taking varied roads, and at different speeds, in search of pluralistic democratic systems, protection of political and human rights, and economies more oriented to the market and private ownership than to management by state-owned enterprises, price controls, and central planning. In this period of transition these states have experienced problems of economic hardship, inflation, high taxes, and unemployment. Many of the states also face complex internal problems because of the presence of ethnic minorities in their territories, territorial disputes with their neighbors, and mutually hostile national movements.

EASTERN EUROPE AND THE SOVIET UNION

Relations with the Soviet Union changed as it relinquished its hold on Eastern Europe. The countries are now making their own external economic and military decisions and their own security arrangements. In January 1949 Stalin created the Council for Mutual Economic Assistance (Comecon), consisting of 10 states, to coordinate the economies of Eastern Europe and other Soviet bloc countries such as Cuba and Vietnam. It was always dominated by the Soviet Union, the largest member, but began disintegrating in the late 1980s as some European members sought to make bilateral trade and investment arrangements with the EC. In 1991 it was agreed that it should be ended, but the implementation of the decision was delayed.

Similarly, the Warsaw Pact, founded in 1955 by the Soviet Union and seven Eastern European countries to counter the inclusion of the Federal Republic of Germany into NATO, was dissolved in March 1991, when all its military arrangements and structures were ended (see Feature 6.8). The Pact, which was superimposed on a number of bilateral agreements on military matters among the states, was always an instrument of Soviet power. The Soviet Union used the Pact to suppress demands for liberty in Hungary in 1956 and Czechoslovakia in 1968, and to coerce local leaders to impose martial law in Poland in 1981.

In October 1989 the Warsaw Pact countries renounced the Brezhnev doctrine, formulated by the former Soviet leader, which stated that the Soviet Union had the right to intervene militarily in other Pact countries if Socialist systems were in danger of being overturned. Instead, they adopted the "Sinatra doctrine:" each state would do things its way. The military part of the Pact came to an end when it was clear that the Soviet Union was no longer able or willing to be concerned about the other six members. These states are now responsible for their own security. Moreover, as the states began dismantling the internal Communist apparatus from 1989 on, they also called for the removal of Soviet troops from their countries. In some countries this has already been done; troops still remain in Poland and East Germany. As a result of agreements with the United States, Soviet nuclear arms were completely removed from the eastern part of Germany.

EASTERN AND WESTERN EUROPE

In the less threatening atmosphere of Europe today a larger role may be played by the Conference on Security and Cooperation in Europe (CSCE), a summit meeting of leaders from Eastern and Western Europe, the United States, and Canada which originated in the Helsinki Final Act of 1975. CSCE addresses itself to questions of European security, economic, scientific and technological cooperation, and to humanitarian principles. Now consisting of 35 countries including the United States, Canada, and all of Europe, CSCE is an important forum for wider political and military dialogue among the leaders of these countries. It has welcomed the end of confrontation and division in Europe and the new era of democracy and peace. In November 1990,

Feature 6.8 **Life and Death of Communist Pact**

May 14, 1955 Warsaw Treaty signed by Albania, Bulgaria, Hungary, East Germany, Poland, Romania, Soviet Union, and Czechoslovakia.

1956 Hungarian withdrawal canceled by Soviet invasion.

1961 Berlin Wall crisis. Albania pulls out after split with Moscow.

1968 Pact forces invade Czechoslovakia.

1969 Command structure changed after Romanian complaints of inequality.

1973 Pact begins 16 years' fruitless negotiations with NATO on mutual and balanced force reductions in central Europe.

1975 Pact renewed for another 10 years.

1985 Renewed for a further 20 years.

1988 Gorbachev announces he will withdraw 50,000 Soviet troops from Eastern Europe.

1989 Pact and NATO open CFE talks.

June Poland elections.

July Pact summit acknowledges right of each member to its own political line.

November–December Berlin Wall falls, Communist governments collapse in East Germany, Czechoslovakia, and Romania.

1990 February–March Czechoslovakia and Hungary agree on complete withdrawal of Soviet forces.

June 7 Pact summit turns alliance into "treaty of sovereign and equal states built upon democratic principles."

June 26 Hungary withdraws.

Sept 24 East Germany withdraws. Moscow agrees its 370,000 troops in East Germany will return home by 1994.

Nov 19 Pact and NATO sign CFE treaty and declare they no longer regard each other as enemies.

1991, Jan 16 Czechoslovak Parliament asks government to negotiate abolition of Pact.

Feb 1 Bulgaria says it will quit Pact.

Feb 12 Soviet Union agrees to dismantle Pact's military structures.

Feb 25 Military cooperation scrapped.

March 31 Soviet commanders surrender powers.

June 18 Czechoslovakia says Pact to be wound up.

June 19 and 27 Last Soviet troops leave Hungary and Czechoslovakia.

July 1 Pact dissolved.

CSCE adopted a "Charter of Paris for a New Europe," in which the then 34 states committed themselves to human rights, minority rights, self-determination, democracy, and economic freedom. At the same time the states signed an agreement on conventional armed forces in Europe, imposing a ceiling on nonnuclear weapons of East and West. Whether CSCE will evolve into a closer relationship and a solid framework for cooperation among the countries will depend on the evolution of the Eastern European states and the various Republics of the former Soviet Union.

Key Terms

Civic Forum
Comecon
Conference on Security and Cooperation in
   Europe (CSCE)
Democratic Forum
Lech Walesa
National Salvation Front
perestroika
Solidarity
Warsaw Pact

Suggestions for Further Reading

Chirot, Daniel, ed. *The Origins of Backwardness in Eastern Europe* (Berkeley: University of California Press, 1989).

Gerrits, Andre. *The Failure of Authoritarian Change: Reform, Opposition and Geo-Politics in Poland in the 1980s* (Aldershot: Brookfield, 1990).

Heinrich, H-G. *Hungary: Politics, Economics and Society* (London: Pinter, 1988).

Johnson, Paul M. *Redesigning the Communist Economy: the Politics of Economic Reform in Eastern Europe* (Boulder: East European Monographs, 1989).

Klein, George and Milan J. Reban, eds. *The Politics of Ethnicity in Easter Europe* (Boulder: East European Monographs, 1981).

Kolankiewicz and Paul G. Lewis. *Poland: Politics, and Society* (New York: Pinter, 1988).

Lewis, Paul G. *Political Authority and Party Secretaries in Poland, 1975–86* (Cambridge: Cambridge University Press, 1989).

Lovenduski, Joni and Jean Woodall. *Politics and Society in Eastern Europe* (Basingstoke: Macmillan Education, 1987).

Michel, Patrick. *Politics and Religion in Eastern Europe* (Oxford: Polity, 1991).

Ost, David. *Solidarity and the Politics of Anti-Politics: Opposition and Reform in Poland since 1968* (Philadelphia: Temple University Press, 1990).

Ramet, Pedro. *Cross and Communist: the Politics of Religion in Eastern Europe and the USSR* (Bloomington: Indiana University Press, 1987).

Volgyes, Ivan. *Politics in Eastern Europe* (Chicago: Dorsey Press, 1986).

PART
TWO

Communist and Post-Communist Systems

CHAPTER 7

The Government of the Former Soviet Union and the Successor States

John S. Reshetar, Jr.

FORMER SOVIET UNION

States of the Former Soviet Union

1. Russia	6. Azerbaijan	11. Kyrgyzstan
2. Belarus	7. Turkmenistan	12. Estonia
3. Moldova	8. Uzbekistan	13. Latvia
4. Ukraine	9. Kazakhstan	14. Lithuania
5. Armenia	10. Tajikistan	15. Georgia

A. Political Development

The Soviet political system that had represented revolutionary change and utopian promise in the second decade of the twentieth century found itself in a profound crisis as it entered the century's last decade. The failures of centralized economic planning and state ownership resulted in negative economic growth, empty store shelves, inflation, strikes, rising unemployment, and a declining living standard. The Communist party's (CPSU) General Secretary, Mikhail S. Gorbachev, used its Twenty-seventh Congress in February 1986 to characterize the rule of his predecessors as a period of stagnation and corruption. He warned then that "it is impossible to retreat and there is nowhere to retreat" and that "history has not given us much time."[1]

Subsequently, in July 1991, Gorbachev noted that in the early 1980s the country had been in a "state of depression" and "the previous theoretical and practical model of socialism [had] . . . proved to be insolvent." He lamented the fact that "old and new ailments of society were not exposed, let alone treated, but were suppressed, which further aggravated the situation and in the end led to a severe crisis."[2] This proved to be a crisis of political leadership and economic policy, social and ethnic conflict, and "spiritual" and moral degeneration. After six years of ineffective reform efforts, Gorbachev's Soviet government found itself in disarray, overwhelmed by events and demands as the non-Russian union republics and the Russian republic asserted their sovereignty and lack of confidence in the political center. In 1991 the very name of the Soviet Union became a matter of dispute as its disunity became increasingly apparent. Though often mistakenly referred to as a "nation," the Soviet Union was actually a collection of countries, a multinational empire. The Soviet crisis thus represented an extraordinary combination of the collapse of a system and the disintegration of an empire.

The Soviet political order had evolved from its beginnings in military defeat, revolutionary war, and utopianism into a cruel totalitarian dictatorship under Stalin, and subsequently into an oligarchy of aged and ineffective leaders. It had its origins in the Russian Revolution of 1917—one of the most significant events of the twentieth century—and emerged on the ruins of the Russian Empire, which failed to survive the dislocations and crises created by World War I. The Russian Revolution began in February 1917 with the abdication of Emperor Nicholas II and the collapse of the monarchy. Administrative breakdown, war weariness, and an inability to supply the army and feed the capital precipitated the empire's collapse. A weak and indecisive Provisional Government attempted to continue Russia's participation in the war on the side of the Allies (Britain, France, and the United States).

Feature 7.1 **What's in a Word? Political Semantics and Multiple Meaning**

The ordinary Russian word *sovet* (soviet), originally meaning simply "council" as well as "counsel" (advice), became synonymous with a distinctive political system and a form of dictatorship characterized by harsh repression and terror, endless propaganda, and massive military power with the state as the principal employer. It became a synonym for socialist and communist as well as for the *GULag*—the vast network of prisons and forced labor camps designed to enforce political compliance. It was also applied to individual republics and to the union of republics. It was used to identify republic parliaments and city and village councils.

Sovet was employed to define U.S.S.R. citizenship, if not nationality. It was used as a generic term to refer to U.S.S.R. citizens whose nationality was unknown, suppressed, or conveniently forgotten. It was said to represent a new type of person, devoid of nationality and created by the Soviet Communist party to serve the Communist cause.

The term was employed to replace the adjective "Russian" in the renamed successor to the Russian Empire, and provided a label with which Russians could conveniently claim to be "internationalists," while regarding the Soviet Union as an enlarged version of "Russia" that could also claim to be a different entity. It was used as an adjective of convenience to refer to unattractive aspects of the political system that the user, for whatever reasons, did not wish to attribute to the Russians. It provided the synthetic term "Soviet people" to propagate the myth that the Soviet Union was both a "normal" polity and a cohesive cultural and demographic entity.

This highly overworked and excessively politicized word was finally delivered from decades of semantic abuse in 1991.

As the war grew more unpopular and the army disintegrated, the Provisional Government was unable to defend itself from the growing discontent and the threat of a seizure of power.

The threat of a coup or takeover of the Russian capital, Petrograd (now St. Petersburg, formerly Leningrad), came from the most extreme Russian Marxists, known as the Bolsheviks, under the leadership of Vladimir Ilyich Ulianov, better known by his pen name V. I. Lenin. The Bolsheviks succeeded in gaining control of the soviets (or councils) of workers, peasants, and soldiers' deputies in Petrograd and Moscow. The soviets, which were revolutionary organs that arose spontaneously at the very beginning of the Revolution, were only

haphazardly representative and not popularly elected. Initially, the soviets were controlled by such non-Bolshevik parties as the agrarian Socialist Revolutionaries and the more moderate Marxists, known as the Mensheviks. The Russian word *sovet* means "council," but the takeover of the soviets in the principal cities by Lenin's Bolsheviks gave the word a distinct *political* meaning associated with Communist rule and a new type of system based on the dictatorship of a single party (see Feature 7.1).

Lenin succeeded in seizing power from the Provisional Government because it was never fully in command, as it had to share power with the Petrograd soviet from the very beginning of the Revolution. The Provisional

Government also lacked the intelligence-gathering ability and the security police of the previous imperial regime. It could not rely on the army because the troops stationed in the capital were not loyal and had come under the influence of Bolshevik agitators. In addition Lenin had the support of the so-called workers' red guard—a paramilitary force that could be armed and sent into the streets to intimidate those who opposed the Bolsheviks. Thus Lenin's takeover of the Russian capital on 7 November 1917 was a relatively easy undertaking, but there followed years of bloody civil conflict. In a very literal sense the Soviet system was spawned by war (World War I) and also succeeded in establishing itself by means of (civil) war.

Initially Lenin obtained control of the central portion of the country. He established a Russian Socialist Federated Soviet Republic in July 1918, but was confronted with several centers of resistance. Russians, who opposed the establishment of a Communist regime, including part of the military, waged a civil war that Lenin eventually won in 1920–1921 because of the fatigue brought on by Russia's demoralization and the absence of any unified military command or political center among the forces that opposed the Bolsheviks. Lenin had the advantage of having a divided opposition that could not develop an attractive and sufficiently powerful alternative to Bolshevik rule. Political moderates had little chance to succeed in a time of turmoil and simple propaganda slogans, though Lenin's principal Russian opponents were political conservatives or reactionaries who sought to restore the old order.

The more numerous non-Russian peoples who had been subjected to Russian rule within the empire seized the opportunity presented by Russia's collapse and proclaimed their independence in 1917–1918. The Finns, Ukrainians, Georgians, Armenians, Poles, Estonians, Latvians, Lithuanians, and others established independent states. Although Lenin was ultimately able to establish Soviet (and Russian) rule over most of the non-Russian peoples, the future form and name of the Russian state was changed. In December 1922 the Union of Soviet Socialist Republics (U.S.S.R.) was formed as a federation, at least in theory, consisting of separate Soviet republics for the various nationalities.

THE IMPERIAL LEGACY

Lenin's Bolshevik party and the Soviet political system that it created became the successors to the Russian Empire, though ironically Lenin had dedicated his political life to the overthrow of that empire and its monarchy. The monarchy was not overthrown, but collapsed in February 1917 with the abdication of the emperor, a lack of leadership, and a breakdown of the military and administrative systems which touched off bread riots and disorders in the capital. The overthrow of the Provisional Government gave Lenin the opportunity to extend Soviet rule from the center of the former empire. But he faced the same problem that the Russian autocrats had faced: how to rule a huge ethnically diverse empire from a single distant center. Although the Bolsheviks rejected many traditional Russian values and introduced significant changes in the Russian way of life, in the end they came to represent Russian dominance of the U.S.S.R. Thus many Russians who might have had doubts about the nature of Soviet rule came to accept it as the heir to the Russian Empire and as the only available means of preserving Russia's claim to greatness and satisfying its yearning to rule over neighboring peoples.

THE GEOGRAPHIC SETTING

The former Soviet Union could claim to be, in terms of area, the largest country under a single political regime. It covered one-sixth of the earth's land mass and extended a distance of more than 6000 miles over 150 degrees of longitude and 11 time zones.

Most of this vast land mass has an intemperate continental climate because it is remote from the oceans that would have a moderating effect, warming the land in winter and cooling it in the summer, and is exposed to the frigid climate of the Arctic. Temperature extremes vary greatly—parts of Siberia have a range of 150° F. Much of the land has limited rainfall, receiving less than 20 inches of precipitation annually.

The land is reasonably well endowed with natural resources, including petroleum and all important minerals, and can be largely self-sufficient. However, transportation costs are often high when oil, coal, natural gas, and raw materials are distant from users. There is heavy reliance on railways that are slow and not well maintained, and there is no modern highway system.

The area of the former Soviet Union has not been entirely self-sufficient in agriculture and has had to import grain. This has been due, at least in part, to natural conditions such as the limited rainfall and the short growing season, especially in the northern latitudes. Despite the area's vast size, the amount of land suitable for agriculture is limited. This has resulted in the costly cultivation of marginal lands and reliance on extensive agriculture, bringing more land under cultivation, instead of intensive agriculture which would increase crop yields.

Thus, in geographical terms the Soviet Union possessed both advantages and disadvantages. Its sheer size provided it with a measure of invulnerability, although the region has historically remained open to invaders over the steppe route from the east (the Mongols and Tatars) and the west (Poland, Sweden, France, and Germany). The Soviet Union claimed the world's longest coastline, and yet much of the region faces icebound Arctic waters and the north Pacific. Ice-free ports on the Baltic and Black seas have been vulnerable to closure by the countries that control access to them. Such apparent disadvantages have been compensated for in other ways. An excellent year-round ice-free port at Murmansk on the Barents Sea provides naval forces with ready access to the Atlantic Ocean and world sea lanes, and ports on the north Pacific Ocean could be kept open during the winter with icebreakers.

Although not landlocked, both the Russian Empire and the U.S.S.R. have historically sought to penetrate such neighboring lands as Poland, the Balkan countries, Turkey, Iran, Afghanistan, Mongolia, China (including Manchuria), and Korea in their bid to gain strategic advantage.

NATIONS AND SOCIAL CLASSES

The Soviet Union claimed the world's third largest population, exceeded in size only by China and India. Yet this population of more than 280 million is not homogeneous and must be viewed in terms of its ethnic and social composition. The principal nationalities (see Table 7.1) represent highly diverse peoples with distinctive ethnic, linguistic, religious, and cultural qualities. Although the Russians constituted approximately one-half of the population of the U.S.S.R., their relative weight declined from 58.4 percent in 1939 to 50.8 percent in 1989.

The eastern Slavic population consists of Russians, Ukrainians, and Belorussians. The Ukrainians are the second most numerous Slavic people and trace their origins to the Kievan Rus' of the ninth to thirteenth centuries. Subsequently the Ukrainians were part of the Lithuanian state, which united with Poland in 1569. The eastern Ukrainians, who rebelled against Polish rule in 1648, established an independent state that later came under the influence of the Muscovite state—after making a fatal decision to turn to the Muscovite tsar for military aid in 1654. The western Ukrainians did not come under Soviet Russian rule until World War II. The Belorussians, or White Ruthenians, are not Russians despite the similarity in name. They are known as *Belarusy*, whereas the Russians are *Russkie*. The Belarusy were also part of the Polish-Lithuanian state and did not come un-

Table 7.1 PRINCIPAL NATIONALITIES OF THE FORMER SOVIET UNION

Nationalities	1959 census (thousands)	1959 Percentage of total population	1970 census (thousands)	1979 census (thousands)	1979 Percentage of total population	1989 census (thousands)	Living within own republic in 1989 (thousands)	Living Outside own republic in 1989 (thousands)	Percentage declaring given language as native in 1989
Russians	114,114	54.6	129,015	137,397	52.4	145,155	119,886	25,289	99.8
Ukrainians	37,253	17.8	40,753	42,347	16.1	44,186	37,419	6,767	81.1
Uzbeks	6,015	2.9	9,195	12,456	4.7	16,698	14,142	2,556	98.3
Belarusy	7,913	3.8	9,052	9,463	3.6	10,036	7,905	2,131	70.9
Tatars	4,968	2.4	5,931	6,317	2.4	6,649			83.2
Kazakhs	3,622	1.7	5,299	6,556	2.5	8,136	6,535	1,601	97.0
Azerbaijanis	2,940	1.4	4,380	5,477	2.1	6,770	5,805	965	97.7
Armenians	2,787	1.3	3,559	4,151	1.6	4,623	3,084	1,539	91.7
Georgians	2,692	1.3	3,245	3,571	1.4	3,981	3,787	194	98.2
Moldovans	2,214	1.1	2,698	2,968	1.1	3,352	2,795	557	91.6
Lithuanians	2,326	1.1	2,665	2,851	1.1	3,067	2,924	143	97.7
Jews	2,268	1.1	2,151	1,811	0.7	1,378			11.1
Tajiks	1,397	0.7	2,136	2,898	1.1	4,215	3,172	1,043	97.7
Germans	1,620	0.8	1,846	1,936	0.7	2,039			48.8
Chuvash	1,470	0.7	1,694	1,751	0.7	1,842			76.5
Turkmens	1,002	0.5	1,525	2,028*	0.8	2,729	2,537	192	98.5
Kyrgyz	969	0.5	1,452	1,906	0.7	2,529	2,230	299	97.8
Latvians	1,400	0.7	1,430	1,439	0.5	1,459	1,388	71	94.8
Mordovians	1,285	0.6	1,263	1,192	0.5	1,154			67.1
Bashkirs	989	0.5	1,240	1,371	0.5	1,449			72.3
Poles	1,380	0.7	1,167	1,151	0.4	1,126			30.5
Estonians	989	0.5	1,007	1,020	0.4	1,027	963	64	95.5
Others	7,215	3.3	9,016	10,343	4.0	12,143			
Total	208,828	100.0	241,719	262,400	100.0	285,743			

Source: Tsentral'noe Statisticheskoe Upravlenie SSSR, *Itogi Vsesoiuznoi perepisi naseleniia 1970 goda*, vol. 4; *Natsional'nyi sostav naseleniia SSSR* (Moscow: "Statistika," 1973); *Naselenie SSSR, Po dannym Vsesoiuznoi perepisi naseleniia 1979 goda* (Moscow: Politizdat, 1980); *Soiuz*, No. 40, October, 1990, p. 6 (reproduced in *Current Digest of the Soviet Press*, Vol. XLII, No. 42, Nov. 21, 1990, p. 13); and *Narodnoe khoziaistvo SSSR v 1989 g. statisticheskii ezhegodnik* (Moscow: "Finansy i Statistika," 1990), p. 30.

der Russian rule until the end of the eighteenth century.

The various Turkic peoples constituted approximately 17 percent of the Soviet population. They are related to the Osmanli Turks of Turkey and extend from Iakutia in northeastern Siberia across Central Asia (Turkestan) to Azerbaijan. Their subjugation by the Russians began in the sixteenth century (in the case of the Kazan and Volga Tatars) and was not completed until the 1880s (Turkmenistan). The Uzbeks are the most numerous of the Soviet Turkic peoples, and Uzbekistan has served as a cotton-producing center. The Kyrgyz live to the east of the Uzbeks on the frontier with Chinese Turkestan (Xinjiang). The Kazakhs, formerly a nomadic people, have been subjected to large influxes of Russians and Ukrainians as a result of Moscow's decision to cultivate the vast, dry virgin lands. The Turkmens occupy a largely desert republic and mostly reside close to the border with Iran and Afghanistan. The Azerbaijanis inhabit the western shores of the Caspian Sea and are largely Shiite Muslims in contrast to the other Turkic peoples, who are Sunni Muslims.

The Turkic peoples include the Volga Tatars, who live along the mid-portion of the river and east of it, and the Siberian Tatars of western Siberia (the Tobol'sk area). The Crimean Tatars came to the Crimea in the thirteenth century, but were forcibly resettled during World War II and their return to their homeland was greatly delayed. Other Turkic peoples include the Bashkirs, Chuvash, Kara-Kalpaks, Tuvinians, Karachais, and Balkarians. Inhabiting a rugged mountainous land on the Afghan frontier, the Tajiks are linguistically an Iranian people and are also Muslims.

The Armenians represent an old culture that was flourishing long before the Russians emerged as a people. Armenia was also the first Christian state and has a unique national church. The Georgians, neighbors of the Armenians, also have a very distinctive language and accepted Christianity in the fourth century. The Armenians and Georgians came un-der Russian rule early in the nineteenth century as a result of pressure from their Muslim neighbors and Russian penetration of the area south of the Caucasus Mountains.

The Baltic peoples belong neither to the Slavic nor the Germanic worlds but constitute separate ethnic entities that came under Russian rule in the eighteenth century. They include the Estonians and Latvians, who are Lutherans, and the Lithuanians, who are Roman Catholics. Though the Baltic states obtained their independence after World War I as a result of the Russian Revolution, they were annexed by the Soviet Union in 1940. They seceded from the U.S.S.R. and regained their independence in 1991. Other non-Slavic peoples include the Moldovans (Moldavians), who are actually Romanians of the region of Bessarabia annexed by Russia in 1812 and were part of Romania from 1918 to 1940.

Among the nationalities that had no Soviet republic were the Jews, Germans, and Poles. The Jewish population came under Russian rule when Catherine II annexed Lithuania, part of Ukraine, and Belorussia. Although one-half of the world's Jewish population lived in the Russian Empire prior to World War I, subsequent events, such as the Nazi occupation of Ukraine and Belorussia, repressive practices on the part of Soviet authorities, and emigration caused their number to diminish. Germans in the former Soviet Union are largely descendants of colonists who settled in the Russian Empire during the eighteenth century; their Volga German Autonomous Republic was liquidated and its population deported to Central Asia in 1941. Among the other peoples who have been under extensive pressure from the Russians are the Finno-Ugrian peoples, including the Mordovians, the Udmurts, the Mari, and the Komi.

Although the Soviet Union claimed to be building a "classless Communist society"—according to the 1977 Constitution—social strata recognized officially included the "working class, the collectivized peasantry, and the people's intelligentsia." Social classes can be distinguished in terms of income levels, status, and prestige, and by the degree of their influence in society. Yet Soviet rulers, for ideological reasons, sought to minimize social differences. Thus "workers" were said to constitute 58.8 percent of the population in 1989, collective farmers 11.7 percent, and "salaried" persons 29.3 percent. The self-employed and others were only 0.2 percent of the population. Such broad categories blur real social distinction, as each contains numerous subgroups.

Soviet official social categories also omitted the political class—an elite that consisted of the leading *cadres* (officials) of the CPSU as well as government ministers and high-level bureaucrats, leading diplomats, military figures, and KGB personnel. This ruling class enjoyed superior housing, country homes, chauffeur-driven automobiles, servants, vacations and foreign travel, and access to special "closed stores" that sold scarce and imported items at discount prices or for "certificate rubles" worth more than ordinary rubles. There were also fringe benefits such as medical care in exclusive clinics and hospitals that were far superior to those serving ordinary Soviet citizens.[3] Leonid Brezhnev as general secretary of the Communist party could acquire a large private collection of expensive foreign automobiles. The elite could accumulate considerable wealth, often by corrupt means, and give their children academic diplomas and arrange prestigious and well-paid positions for them.

In the 1980s the term "mafia" gained currency and was used in several senses. It was applied to CPSU officials and to members who held key positions in nonparty organizations and participated in networks based on mutual advantage and self-enrichment. The "mafia" also referred to those engaged in large-scale black market activity. With the emergence of individual and private (nominally cooperative) enterprise as a result of changes in economic policy, another type of "mafia" appeared: racketeers engaged in extortion and theft at the expense of successful legitimate businesses.

Soviet society came to be characterized by significant inequalities of income, education, and educational opportunity. Yet the intelligentsia—which included professional, scientific, scholarly, educational, artistic, and literary persons—represented great differences in rewards. Thus Soviet physicians, two-thirds of whom are women, were poorly paid. Many Soviet citizens, including unskilled workers and pensioners, fell below the poverty level by the early 1990s. At the same time there emerged a new class of "ruble millionaires" as a result of increased corruption, severe goods shortages, and a developing market.

The Soviet population has long been characterized by a disparity in the sex ratio. Women have significantly outnumbered men as a result of famine, the Stalinist blood purges, and World War II, apart from longevity differences. There were 17.6 million more women than men in 1979 and 15.7 million more in 1990. The U.S.S.R. experienced a steadily declining birth rate that was especially evident in Russia and in Ukraine. The natural increase declined from 17.8 (per 1000 population) in 1960 to 7.6 in 1989. However, the increases in the Turkic republics and in Tajikistan have been four to eight times greater than in the Russian Republic.

RUSSIAN POLITICAL VALUES AND SOVIET POLITICAL CULTURE

If the Soviet Union and its political system were unique in certain respects, explanations must be sought in the pre-Soviet Russian political tradition and in the culture as a "way of life." A political culture reflects the ideals, beliefs, and values that a people hold in common. It defines a people's attitudes toward authority, relations between rulers and ruled, and the degree of trust accorded rulers and what they can or cannot do. The degree of loyalty that a political system elicits will depend on the extent to which it is in accord with the dominant political culture.

However, certain reservations must be kept in mind. There are various subcultures (regional, social, ethnic) that may be in conflict with the dominant political culture. St. Petersburg traditionally has represented somewhat different values from those accepted in Moscow. The numerous non-Russian nationalities have not shared the values and preferences of the Russians. It should also be noted that culture represents learned behavior; it is acquired, being transmitted from generation to generation, and is not biological or based on racial attributes. Originally, political culture was derived from the study of national character, which tended to regard cultural traits as fixed. As learned behavior, cultural patterns and values can be changed over time; the degree of such change will depend upon circumstances and a willingness to reappraise and modify values.

No people or political system can escape its past. Each people possesses a political tradition and fund of experience that influence its institutions, practices, values, and norms of political conduct. The Russian political experience reflects certain unique traits, issues, and problems.

KEY SYNDROMES

Centralized power and absolutist rule comprise one of Russia's most persistent traits. The Russian political tradition emerged from the Muscovite State, which developed an autocratic order originally headed by princes, one of whom, Ivan IV ("the Terrible"), adopted the title of tsar, a Russian version of *caesar*. The Muscovite State and its rulers gained an advantage over neighboring principalities by collaborating with the Mongol-Tatar conquerors who subjugated much of Eastern Europe in 1240. By serving as collectors of tribute and by being outwardly servile, the Muscovite princes succeeded in establishing a power base that enabled them to subjugate their neighbors, including Finnish peoples living to the east and north of Moscow. Muscovite princes learned

much from the Mongols and Tatars regarding taxation, intelligence gathering, military organization, census taking, and the importance of the postal system and communications.[4] Mongol rule gradually weakened, but it lasted nearly two and a half centuries until 1480.

The rulers of Muscovy were also influenced by the autocratic political system of the Eastern Roman (Byzantine) Empire, in which Orthodox Christianity was the state religion and the emperors posed as defenders of religious doctrine. Muscovy received Christianity from the Ukrainians, but Byzantium taught the Russians that the West (Rome) was "heretical" and not to be trusted. Orthodox Christianity also meant that Muscovy would develop in cultural isolation from the West. After Byzantium fell to the Turks in 1453, Muscovite rulers could depict themselves in the sixteenth century as being specially chosen, because Muscovy allegedly was the only Orthodox Christian state free from Ottoman Turkish and Muslim domination. This sense of exclusiveness and self-satisfaction helped to motivate Muscovite expansionism and the urge to acquire an empire.

Russian political development was fated to adopt an autocratic pattern when Muscovy annexed the principality of Novgorod in 1478. Novgorod had been the most prominent Russian center for three centuries prior to the emergence of Muscovy. It was an important commercial center, but it also had a unique political order. Novgorod developed as a republic with nonhereditary princes and with other elected officials. A popular assembly (*veche*) met in the marketplace, but actual power was exercised by a limited number of local magnates. If Novgorod had prevailed instead of Muscovy, Russian political culture might not have developed in the autocratic pattern of absolutist rulers, but would probably have assumed a republican form.

Absolutist rule in Muscovy was also made possible or even necessary by the steady territorial expansion of the Muscovite State. Muscovy is first referred to in the chronicles in 1147. By the fifteenth century it covered 15,000 square miles, but in the course of the subsequent four centuries it expanded approximately 570 times to an area of 8.5 million square miles. The Muscovite State was renamed the Russian Empire in 1721 by Peter I. Empire building meant the subjugation of other peoples. The Volga Tatars were conquered in 1552, and within a century Siberia, with its alien peoples, was acquired. Eastern Ukraine came under Muscovite influence in 1654 as a result of a treaty of alliance between the Ukrainian Cossack state and the Muscovite tsar—the terms of which were then systematically violated by the Russians. The Baltic peoples (Estonians, Latvians, and Lithuanians) were annexed during the eighteenth century, as were the Belarusy and the Crimean Tatars, along with the central Ukrainians. During the nineteenth century the Russian Empire annexed the Caucasus, Georgia, Armenia, Azerbaijan, Finland, part of Poland (including Warsaw), and Turkestan (Central Asia). The end of the nineteenth century saw the empire seeking gains at the expense of a weakened China, in Manchuria especially, and in Korea—an effort that was thwarted as a result of Russia's military defeat at the hands of Japan in 1905.

Russian territorial expansionism, pursued on an unparalleled scale, could hardly have been accomplished without an autocratic political order. The fact that the Russian emperors ruled large numbers of alien subjects—the Russians were a minority of 43 percent in their own empire—guaranteed the perpetuation of autocratic rule. The last emperor, Nicholas II, remained an autocrat even after the 1905 Revolution, when he was compelled to agree to the establishment of a weak legislative body, the Imperial Duma.

The notion of service to the ruler who personified the state was well established in the Russian political experience. Strong monarchs such as Ivan IV were able to keep the nobles (boyars) subordinate by making land ownership (of estates) conditional upon service to the state and unconditional obedience to the tsar. When the monarchs were weak personalities, the autocracy functioned through the bureaucracy, whose officials were just as arbitrary and demanding as the absolute monarch.

It is not surprising that the heavy weight of Russian autocratic rule doomed the brief experiment with democracy under the Provisional Government in 1917. Russians had failed to develop any effective restraints on autocratic power, and it was relatively easy for Lenin and his Bolsheviks to adapt the Russian tradition of centralism and absolutist rule to their own purposes. The Communist ruling class claimed the right to rule on the basis of its professed monopoly of philosophical truth, wisdom, justice, and moral good. The Communist party assumed the role of a collective counterpart or successor to the Russian tsars and emperors, who in their claim to total power ruled on the basis of divine right. The Russian autocrats were said to be responsible to God and to their own conscience, whereas the Communist rulers claimed to be responsible only to "history" as understood in the Communist philosophy.

Truth seeking and the claim to possess truth have characterized the Russian understanding of political values. In Russia, political power has traditionally been wedded to ideology based on total solutions, sweeping assertions, absolute values, and the notion of official truth. The claim to possess truth and to be pursuing maximal goals in its name promoted a brand of unyielding politics that tended to reject moderation and compromise.[5] It also favored the adoption of "devil" theories of politics emphasizing enemies and "dark" and "impure" forces seeking to destroy Russia. In imperial Russia the truth was embodied in the official Russian Orthodox Church, and it served as a major source of support for the autocratic political order, with the emperor serving as guardian of the faith.

The official "truth" of the Soviet political system—Marxism-Leninism—represented different values from those of the tsarist

The statue of the "Mother Birthland" (*Mat' rodina*) at Volgograd (Stalingrad) in Russia commemorates a decisive battle of World War II in early 1943. It is representative of costly and massive Soviet public monuments.

regime; however, the notion of official truth remained a basic attribute of both regimes. The Russian philosopher Nikolai Berdyaev contended that the Russians are an "apocalyptic people" concerned with ultimate ends and total solutions (maximalism) and with the prophetic element in life.[6] If this is the case, it is easier to understand why Marxism-Leninism could be accepted as the ideological basis of the Soviet system. Marxism-Leninism offered predictions in the guise of social science and depicted the ultimate triumph of good, as represented by the Communist party, over evil. Social justice would supposedly triumph, and the Russians would serve as interpreters and guardians of the doctrine and could claim to be carrying out the will of history. Marxism-Leninism and its vision of the future could claim to have universal application and to be internationalist in outlook. It had wider appeal abroad than the official truth of the Russian Empire and served to rationalize Russian imperial ambitions and expansionism in the Soviet period.

Resistance, sectarianism, and *anarchic tendencies* have represented a reaction by the Russians to the harsh absolute rule of political centralism. There is much evidence to indicate that Russians have not submitted totally or unquestioningly to their rulers. Historically there has been a wide and deep gulf separating the rulers and the ruled. Authority has been distrusted and resisted when circumstances have permitted. The *veche* (popular assembly) in the pluralistic eastern Slavic society of Rus' in the pre-Mongol period opposed princes, especially in Kiev and Novgorod. Russia witnessed the great peasant revolts of Bolotnikov and Stenka Razin in the seventeenth century and Pugachev in the eighteenth century.[7] In the nineteenth century, the fierceness of Russian revolt prompted the greatest of Russia's poets, Aleksandr Pushkin, to characterize it as "senseless and ruthless." The twentieth century saw the burning of the manor houses of estate owners and the bursting forth of peasant wrath in the 1917 Revolution.

Russian resistance is also evident in a rich tradition of religious sectarianism that flourished despite the existence of an official Russian Orthodox state church. The seventeenth century saw a great schism between the official church and the Old Ritualists (Old Believers), who refused to accept a revision of religious practices. Subsequently a variety of exotic sects emerged, including the *Dukhobory* (Spirit Fighters), who refused to accept political authority, perform military service, or pay taxes. In the Soviet period various Protestant sects made their appearance in opposition to the regime's official atheism and to the subordination of the Russian Orthodox Moscow Patriarchate to the Soviet rulers.

Russian interest in anarchism prompted the philosopher Berdyaev to observe that anarchism was largely a Russian creation and that Russians do not really like the state but either meekly submit to it or rebel against it as circumstances dictate or permit.[8] It is significant that such prominent Russians as Mikhail Bakunin, the novelist Leo Tolstoy, and Prince Peter Kropotkin contributed to the theory of anarchism. Bakunin's anarchism was violent and atheistic, based on "creative" destruction; Tolstoy's was nonviolent and religious; and Kropotkin's anarchic communism was based on mutual aid in place of the wage system. If Russians have had an inclination toward anarchism and resisting the state, as Berdyaev contends, the existence of harsh and repressive authoritarian systems in Russia becomes more understandable. The fear of anarchy may explain why Soviet rulers insisted on "moral political unity."

Alienation of the intelligentsia was a problem for both the tsarist imperial and Soviet Russian regimes. The term "intelligentsia" is one of the few Russian words to be adopted into foreign languages. It originally referred to the nineteenth-century "men of ideas" who criticized contemporary conditions on the basis of abstract ideas. In rejecting prevailing values, the intelligentsia became alienated from the Russian state, church, nation, and way of life, and instead often embraced foreign ideas, including Marxism. The Soviet rulers created a large intelligentsia of specialists, but alienation persisted among political dissidents and persons who sought to emigrate.[9] It is ironic that Svetlana Alliluyeva, the only daughter of the late Soviet dictator Joseph Stalin, defected in 1967, rejecting the Soviet system and its values and renouncing her membership in the Communist party as well as her Soviet citizenship.[10] The effort of Mikhail Gorbachev to co-opt the intelligentsia by allowing it greater freedom of expression was designed to obtain its support for his reforms and deal with its alienation.

Russia's identity and its appropriation of foreign ways have also contributed to its reliance on a severe and demanding political order. Russians have persistently debated the question of Russia's relationship to Europe and Asia, what Russia is, and whether or not it has some special historic mission to fulfill. The problem of Russia's identity was complicated by its efforts to subjugate and assimilate neighboring peoples and by the scale of its borrowing and appropriation of foreign technology beginning with the reign of Peter I. The Russian elite has contained many non-Russians or assimilated elements. Peter I recruited Baltic Germans to carry out his reforms and hired foreigners to develop a Russian navy. Many Russian explorers in the eighteenth and nineteenth centuries were actually Germans. The Russian ruling dynasty, known as the House of Romanov, became German after 1762 during the reign of Catherine II and her ill-fated husband, Peter III. Italians constructed much of the Kremlin, and foreigners erected most of the imposing structures in the new capital of St. Petersburg. The Muscovite State, in its expansion and transformation into the multinational Russian Empire, developed an imperial consciousness prior to the emergence of a Russian national consciousness and thus created a persistent identity problem.

Russia's heavy reliance on borrowing is reflected in the presence of large numbers of English, French, and German loan words in the Russian language as common nouns for household objects. All languages contain foreign loan words, but the degree of their presence in the Russian language is vivid testimony to the Russian ability to borrow and appropriate. Yet this practice and the Russian effort to dominate and assimilate non-Russian peoples have resulted in the need for an imposed identity (such as the notion of a "Soviet people"), and have posed the related threats of "contamination" and fragmentation. Russia's unity has been complex and synthetic, and its rulers have traditionally resorted to extreme measures in attempting to preserve it.

Pretense and mendacity have been employed to justify and maintain the political order and society. Fedor Dostoevsky, in an essay entitled "Something on Lying" (1873) published in his *Diary of a Writer,* posed the unusual question: "Why does everyone among us [in Russia] lie and without exception?" The writer contended that lying was engaged in "out of hospitality" and for effect, noting that the truth is "for us too boring and prosaic, insufficiently poetic, too commonplace."[11] The reliance on pretense, deception, and self-deception was evident in the claims of Soviet political leaders, who for decades claimed that Soviet society was "superior" and that its political system under a party dictatorship was "democratic." The Soviet Union, based on coercion and territorial aggrandizement, was said to be "voluntary." Concealment was evident in such matters as the denial of the famines of 1932–1933 and 1947, official statistics on Soviet fatalities in World War II, the size of the Soviet military budget, the radiation levels and fatalities resulting from the Chernobyl nuclear catastrophe, the claim that there were budget surpluses when there were actually large deficits, and the inflated official exchange rate for the ruble in the absence of convertibility.

The revelations made by Nikita Khrushchev in his campaign against Stalin's dictatorship and by Gorbachev regarding his predecessors served to confirm the role of mendacity and pretense in Soviet politics. The Communist party's reliance on resolutions and proclamations reflected a preference for verbal "solutions" and claims, with assertion being equated with achievement but actually reflecting problem avoidance. Aleksandr Yakovlev, who as an adviser to Gorbachev investigated the party's crimes and rehabilitated large numbers of victims, told the Twenty-eighth Party Congress, "Over the course of seventy years we have too frequently permitted ourselves to ignore everything that was not to our liking. Even today ... we sometimes continue to deceive ourselves and play the hypocrite."[12]

PSYCHOCULTURAL THEORIES

Theories of the Russian character have been based on various hypotheses and on a limited amount of clinical psychological evidence. Some observers have noted contradiction in the Russian character evidenced in "mood swings" and in sudden shifts in attitude and behavior—as from activity to passivity, from euphoria to melancholy, or from friendship to hostility. The philosopher Berdyaev saw the Russian character as a "combination of opposites" including such contradictory traits as individualism and collectivism, nationalism and universalism, God-seeking and militant atheism, humility and impudence, and slavery and rebellion.[13] Similarly, Russians have been both attracted to and repelled by the West.

Other observers have noted the presence of guilt, hostility, and fear in Russians. Preoccupation with enemies (internal and external) and "dark forces" has played an important role in Russian life. The Soviet media readily denounced such "enemies" as capitalists, fascists, Trotskyites, Maoists, imperialists, neocolonialists, bourgeois nationalists, monopolists, revisionists, and dogmatists. Guilt feelings persisted in the Soviet practice of "criticism and self-criticism" and in the inability of Soviet citizens to fulfill all of the demands made upon them by the authorities (including the numer-

ous obligations incorporated into the 1977 Soviet Constitution).[14]

LENINISM—THE RUSSIAN VERSION OF MARXISM

Marxism, a product of Western European thought and of the industrial revolution, found a receptive following among many Russian intellectuals. It provided a doctrine that claimed to explain all of history and human behavior and to be "scientific" as well. Russian intellectuals under Lenin's leadership appropriated Marxism and modified it to suit Russian needs. Thus, the Soviet Union acquired an official ideology that can be said to have replaced the Russian Empire's state religion of Orthodox Christianity.

Marxism-Leninism as an ideology is a system of thought, a "world outlook" that attempts to explain or rationalize all of reality. It is a method of political analysis that offers a plan of action and a vision of the future. It acquired some of the characteristics of a sectarian or quasi-religious movement despite its claim to be scientific and its advocacy of militant atheism. It promised humanity a form of secular salvation and claimed to be the sole source of truth and ultimate knowledge. It required converts to master the Marxist-Leninist "scriptural" writings, as understood in their current interpretation, and to accept Communist party discipline. In insisting upon ideological orthodoxy, party leaders employed the practice of condemning deviationist movements, which are the Communist counterpart of religious heresies. Leninists even made Lenin's embalmed body in the Red Square mausoleum an object of veneration comparable to a religious relic.[15]

Essentials of Marxism

Although Lenin reinterpreted and developed the thought of Karl Marx (1818–1883) and Friedrich Engels (1820–1895), Leninism reflected the basic tenets of Marxism and its view of capitalism. These tenets included the doctrine of historical materialism, which holds that social relationships are determined by the "mode of production"—the ways in which livelihood is obtained and the nature of the prevailing technology. The material base of society determines its social and class structure. When the social relations ("relations of production") come into conflict with the mode of production, revolution occurs. The concepts of *base* and *superstructure* reflect the doctrine of historical materialism. The base represents the economic structure of society, whereas the superstructure represents political institutions, legal systems, constitutions, religion, philosophy, the arts, and literature. The superstructure is fundamentally a reflection of the economic base, though noneconomic factors are conceded a limited role. Historical materialism thus teaches that economic necessity is the basic determinant in historical development.

Marxism provided a Communist analysis of capitalism rather than a clear blueprint for a Communist society. In the Communist version of capitalism and of precapitalist societies (feudalism and slaveholding societies), the class struggle is seen as the principal motive force. Such societies are supposedly divided into exploiters and exploited—the former constituting the ruling class, which owns the means of production and rules in its own interests by means of an appropriate superstructure. In bourgeois capitalist society the exploiter is said to be the bourgeoisie, which owns the means of production, and the exploited class is the industrial proletariat, which has only its labor to sell and is said to work for a subsistence wage.

Historical change and the developing class struggle are explained in terms of the dialectic, a concept that Marxism-Leninism appropriated from the German philosopher Georg W. F. Hegel (1770–1831). In its original Greek meaning, dialectics referred to the art of disputation by which truth is discovered through the clash of opposing arguments. Hegel, an idealist

(and not a materialist) philosopher, saw a concept (thesis) as inevitably generating its opposite (antithesis), and thus by means of mutual interaction a new concept (synthesis) would emerge. Marxism-Leninism gave Hegel's dialectic a materialist content, combining historical materialism with it to form dialectical materialism.

The dialectic is based on the notion of contradiction, conflict, and the struggle of opposites. It stresses the interdependence of all phenomena and objects and the need to avoid viewing them in isolation. The dialectic emphasizes constant movement and change. The "law" of the *interpenetration, unity, and strife of opposites* holds that each phenomenon is a changing unity of contradictory parts that are in conflict but must interact, as each part plays its predetermined role, until a new synthesis emerges. Dialectical materialism sees conflict as "progressive" and development occurring as a result of inner self-movement; that is, the source of movement or change lies in the internal contradictions that are said to characterize everything.

A second "law" is the *transformation of quantity into quality* and vice versa. It explains development as resulting from gradual and not readily noticeable *quantitative* changes that occur in every object and phenomenon and that lead to abrupt *qualitative* change once a sufficiently large quantitative buildup occurs. Political revolution (a qualitative change) in capitalist societies thus is said to occur as a result of quantitative changes such as the size and relationship of social classes, the growth of monopoly, inflation, changes in living standards, and agrarian unrest. Each new qualitative stage that emerges is, in turn, subjected to new processes of quantitative change.

A third "law" is the *negation of the negation*, which represents the notion of historical stages or epochs in which each new quality serves as the negation of the preceding quality and is itself, in its turn, negated by a new quality. Thus the negation of a new historical synthesis is reflected in the Communist view of history, which sees one epoch negating another. The slaveholding society is said to have negated primitive communism, but it, in turn, was negated by feudalism; feudalism, the negation of the slaveholding society, is itself negated by capitalism; and capitalism, the negation of feudalism, is supposed to be negated by communism.

In thinking dialectically, Marxist-Leninists hold that opposites cannot be separated or reconciled. Life and death, positive and negative, advance and retreat, action and reaction, offense and defense, war and peace, and conflicting social classes cannot be understood apart from each other. The dialectic teaches that anything can be transformed into its opposite. Friends or allies can become enemies; success can contain the seeds of failure or vice versa; and stability can abruptly be replaced by instability. It emphasizes the importance of conflict and struggle and promotes a brand of politics that is not conducive to moderation and compromise.

In stressing the interrelatedness of everything, Marxist-Leninists may see associations and relationships where none actually exist. As dialecticians they look for certain developments and for enemies that may not be readily perceptible. Even truth has a relative quality for them, as a statement that is inaccurate or false today may be true tomorrow. It is therefore acceptable to make a false statement that can be regarded as *potentially* true. Because contradiction is the essence of the dialectic, it is regarded as normal; this enabled Soviet political leaders to accept inconsistency in the form of contradictory policies and tactics. Soviet policy shifted abruptly, as when Lenin abandoned War Communism in 1921 and adopted the New Economic Policy (NEP), or when Stalin replaced the NEP with his policy of collectivization of agriculture. Soviet leaders were praised while in office and then condemned or treated with silence. The interaction and transformation of opposites was thus readily apparent in Soviet politics.

Tenets of Leninism

Marxism has assumed different forms in various countries. Marx and Engels provided a general appraisal of the capitalism of their time, but they did not offer any specific advice as to the political form that the Communist revolution would assume. Leninism provided not merely a Russian version of Marxism but a means by which Marxists could establish a Communist political order. The vehicle for this purpose was the party of professional revolutionaries established by Lenin. As early as 1902 Lenin, in his work *What Is to Be Done?*, advocated the formation of a unique type of elite political party composed of a limited number of dedicated, disciplined, tested, and trained Communists. The party was to be the vanguard of the working class and of the industrial proletariat. In practice, Lenin substituted his Communist (Bolshevik) party for the working class because he distrusted the "spontaneity" of the masses. He established a new type of highly centralized party that was trained in conspiratorial methods and capable of acting unquestioningly under the leadership's direction.

Priority of the political struggle was a basic tenet of Leninism, largely because its founder warned against the "dangers" of having the workers settle for mere economic benefits and reform through trade unions and strikes. Lenin noted that if the living conditions of workers improve they will neglect the political struggle and be "bought off" by their employers. Thus the purpose of Lenin's party was to seize power even though the ultimate success of communism as a movement was supposedly predetermined in Marx's view of history. Although revolutions supposedly resulted from objective conditions and the inevitable crises of capitalism, with its developing class struggle, Lenin believed that events could be accelerated if the party was capable of seizing the opportunity. Leninism emphasized *voluntarism,* or the ability of the party to act consciously, being aware of the role that it is playing and seizing the occasion to bring about or take advantage of a revolutionary situation.

Leninism was to give meaning to the term "dictatorship of the proletariat." The notion of the dictatorship of any ruling class is basic to Marxism-Leninism, whether it is the slave-holding class, the feudal lords, or bourgeois capitalists; each class is said to rule in its own interests. In Marxism-Leninism, the economic order determines the political order, and each ruling class is said to use the instrument of the state and its laws to oppress and exploit. Marx had used the term "revolutionary dictatorship of the proletariat" in 1875 (in his *Critique of the Gotha Program*); however, it was left to Lenin to establish the first one-party dicta-torship in the name of the industrial working class. Although Lenin in practice added the poorer part of the peasantry to the working class as an ally, he also distrusted it because of its desire for land and property-owning ten-dencies. The dictatorship of the proletariat was really to be the dictatorship of Lenin's Bolshe-viks for the purpose of fulfilling the revolution by crushing the bourgeoisie and establishing socialism. Lenin could promise the "withering away" of the State in 1917 (in his *State and Revolution*), but his successor, Stalin, could boast in June 1930 that the Soviet dictator-ship of the proletariat was "the strongest and most powerful of all existing state authorities." Stalin justified the Soviet dictatorship in di-alectical terms:

> We are for the withering away of the state. And at the same time we stand for the strength-ening of the dictatorship of the proletariat.... The higher development of state authority for the purpose of preparing the conditions *for* the withering away of state authority—there you have a Marxist formula. Is it "contradic-tory"? Yes, it is "contradictory." But contradic-tion is a part of life, and it fully reflects Marxist dialectics.[16]

Leninism, with its emphasis on the di-alectic, was also characterized by *tactical flex-ibility*, which accepted the notion of tempo-rary retreat. Examples were Lenin's conclud-ing peace with the Central Powers at any price in 1918 and his granting of limited concessions to small-scale capitalism in 1921 in order to re-vive the war-damaged economy.

Another characteristic of Leninism was the concept of *partiinost'* (party-mindedness or partisanship) in philosophy and in the social sciences that defined those disciplines in terms of their service to the Communist party. This doctrine was developed in Lenin's work *Ma-terialism and Empirio-Criticism* (1909), where he defined matter as "objective reality," which he saw the human sense perceptions "copying" with increasing accuracy. This was said to make possible the acquisition of "absolute truth" in the form of Marxism-Leninism. Lenin also rec-ognized the existence of relative truth, but at the same time condemned skepticism and ag-nosticism.

Lenin's *theory of imperialism* was devel-oped hastily in 1916 from the writings of oth-ers in an effort to explain why World War I had occurred and why most Socialists were supporting their country's war efforts. In *Impe-rialism, the Highest Stage of Capitalism*, Lenin argued that a new kind of "finance capital" (as opposed to industrial capital) had emerged as a result of the growth of monopoly. It was said to involve a merger and concentration of banking and industry and to export capital abroad to ar-eas having raw materials and abundant cheap labor. Capital was said to be exported because of the domestic stagnation that resulted from the growth of monopoly, declining profits, and shrinking markets at home. The export of cap-ital led to colonialism, and the competition for colonies and redivision of the spoils were said to lead to military alliances and wars.

Lenin's theory of imperialism was based on very limited historical evidence and did not fully explain the phenomenon of war. How-ever, Lenin used it to attempt to explain why proletarian revolutions were not occurring in the most industrially developed countries as they were supposed to occur, according to the teachings of Marx and Engels. According to Lenin, the increased profits from colonialism made it possible for the capitalist ruling class to "buy off" important parts of the working class with concessions, thereby creating "privileged sections" that became bourgeois in outlook (a "labor aristocracy"), and postponing or even preventing proletarian revolution led by Communists. Therefore, he had little choice but to conclude that Communist-led revolutions were more likely to occur in economically underdeveloped countries with no industrial proletariat. His theory of imperialism also offered an explanation as to how the first Communist regime could be established in Russia rather than in an economically more advanced country.

Leninism was subsequently modified by Lenin's successors—but always in the name of Leninism. For more than seven decades Marxism-Leninism was the official ideology of the Soviet Union, and dialectical materialism was the officially recognized philosophy. Marx and Engels were acknowledged in the Soviet Union, but their many statements critical of imperial Russia were suppressed by the Soviet rulers.

CRITICISM OF MARXISM-LENINISM

Critics of the Soviet ideology have raised many questions regarding the validity of Marxism-Leninism. In reducing all of human history to several stages (slaveholding, feudal, and capitalist), and in basing them on the doctrine of historical materialism, Marxism-Leninism has been said to oversimplify and to neglect the importance of nonmaterial motives. Such factors in human behavior as religion, nationalism, individual personality, sex, ethnic identity, and chance or accident are ignored or minimized. Critics have contended that the industrial proletariat of Communist ideology is only a political myth or symbol, for it does not possess the homogeneity, class consciousness, or common will attributed to it;

instead, the Communist party substitutes its own consciousness and will for that of the working class. Critics point out that Communist leaders—including Marx and Lenin—have often come from the alienated intelligentsia rather than from the ranks of factory workers. Thus the proletariat, supposedly the "gravedigger" of capitalism, does not succeed the bourgeoisie as the new ruling class but must be led by a political elite.

Critics have argued that Marxism-Leninism has been inconsistent in claiming to be a science while also making moral judgments and declaring one social class evil and another the source of virtue. The predictions offered by Marxism-Leninism have also been a source of controversy. In predicting the victory of one social class or of a Communist party, Communists have often failed to appreciate the fact that all predictions are conditional and can become self-denying prophecies if the victims of the prediction take steps to render it invalid. It can be asked why class warfare and Communist victory should be inevitable. Marxist-Leninists are said to confuse their "scientific" predictions with their wishes and actions; instead of waiting for the prediction to be borne out and validated by events, they act to bring it about—as if they had little confidence in its occurring without such action. Marxist-Leninist predictions have been inaccurate regarding the impoverishment of the industrial proletariat, which actually raised its living standard through trade unionism, cooperatives, and the ballot box. The middle class was not impoverished as predicted, and Communist revolutions did not occur in industrially advanced countries, but mostly in certain agrarian countries where conditions were far removed from the Marxist analysis. The predicted decline of nationalism failed to occur as the number of newly independent nations and active ethnic movements increased after World War II.

Marxist-Leninists also assumed that the dialectical process in history would be basically changed once Communist parties come to power. Communism is supposedly not to be negated by a new negation; the class struggle, the cause of all historical change, was supposed to cease under communism in a classless society. It was assumed that state ownership of the means of production and a monopoly of political power by a Communist party would bring about a transformation in human nature. The withering away of the state predicted by Lenin was conveniently forgotten in the Soviet Union. The Marxist-Leninist ideology did not provide credible explanations of the crimes and excesses of Stalin's dictatorship and of Mao's Cultural Revolution in China, or the bitterness of the Sino-Soviet dispute and armed conflict between Communist countries.[17] How "scientific" is the ideology if it fostered such leaders as Stalin, Khrushchev, and Brezhnev, who could be criticized by their successors for crimes or for incorrect policies?

RELEVANCE OF MARXISM-LENINISM

For the Soviet rulers Marxism-Leninism was not merely a philosophy or theory but a means of justifying and legitimizing their system of rule. For seven decades Soviet leaders sang the praises of their ideology as Gorbachev did at the Twenty-seventh Party Congress:

> Marxism-Leninism is the greatest revolutionary world view. It has substantiated the most humane objective that humankind has ever set for itself—the creation of a just social system on earth. It points the way to the scientific study of the development of society as a single, law-governed process in all of its vast many-sidedness and contradictoriness, and it teaches [us] to understand correctly the nature and interaction of economic and political forces, to select the correct directions, forms and methods of struggle, and to feel self-confident at the decisive turning points in history.[18]

So long as the Soviet system appeared to be functioning successfully, the adherents of Marxism-Leninism could claim that their ide-

ology was correct. They could also find confirmation of it in the competition for markets between capitalist countries, in the growth of corporate mergers and "monopolies," strike activity, bankruptcies, business failures, inflation, and unemployment in capitalist countries. Marxist-Leninists could derive comfort from the domestic critics of bourgeois society who have frequently found fault with any such society that is less than perfect.

The ideology was the source of much in Soviet political practice. The Communist party used it to justify its claim to a monopoly of political power and its role as the chosen instrument of "history" and the source of the official truth. Ideological requirements dictated many Soviet government policies: the nationalization of all land, state ownership of the economy, collectivization of agriculture, forced industrialization, and the refusal to permit even small private business enterprises based on hired labor (as distinct from cooperatives). The teaching of "scientific atheism" as an obligatory subject in all Soviet schools was based on Marxism-Leninism. Ideology prompted the Communist party to dictate standards in literature and in the arts and to influence the writing of historians and social scientists. Censorship was justified by the Marxist-Leninist view that ideas are important and have consequences.

LENINISM IN RETREAT

Although Mikhail Gorbachev, as party leader, continued to profess belief in Marxism-Leninism, he ceased quoting from Lenin's writings because they provided no prescriptions for the Soviet malaise and were incompatible with the market economy that Gorbachev claimed to be establishing. Marxism-Leninism came under attack in the intense discussion prompted by Gorbachev's reformist policies. The acknowledgment by Gorbachev of widespread failure on the part of his predecessors contributed to the discrediting of the ideology.

Statues of Lenin, regarded as the symbol of totalitarian dictatorship, were removed by democratically elected non-Communist officials, initially in the Baltic states, Georgia and Western Ukraine, but subsequently elsewhere. In some jurisdictions statues of Lenin were guarded by the police and military in a futile effort to defend an old and exhausted ideology that was incapable of providing solutions to the problems that it had created. Indeed, in an effort to solicit popular support, Communist leaders abandoned the blatant propagation of militant atheism as state policy, and sought to co-opt religious leaders and appear with them in public. The numerous paid professional propagators of Communist ideology in the Soviet educational establishment sought to "requalify" themselves and retain their positions as specialists in the "theory and history of culture."

Marxism-Leninism could claim credibility so long as the Soviet leadership was able to demonstrate some degree of competence in problem solving and claim that the ideology had a certain relationship to reality. As the Soviet economy deteriorated and the society became more fragmented, the claims made for the ideology proved to be vacuous and irrelevant. The abandonment of Marxism-Leninism by the Eastern European countries in 1989 as well as by Angola, Ethiopia, Nicaragua, and Yemen also served to discredit it.

Russians who desired to perpetuate the empire and their rule over other peoples had found Marxism-Leninism to be a convenient artifice for "justifying" their dominance and claiming to be adherents of "internationalism." However, the inadequacies of the ideology made it necessary for Gorbachev in 1991 to undertake another revision of the 1986 revised Communist party program "to include in our arsenal of ideas all of the wealth of the fatherland's and world Socialist and democratic thought."[19] But the swift pace of events nullified this effort. Russians, in their claim to an empire, have lacked a suitable replacement for Marxism-Leninism. Overt Russian nationalism could not serve as an appropriate substitute in a multinational empire in which Russian dominance was challenged. It can be said that Marxism-Leninism was negated by its own dialectic and its internal contradictions.

Key Terms

base
cadres
dialectic
historical materialism
intelligentsia
Marxism-Leninism
Muscovite State
negation of the negation
Novgorod
partiinost'
Russian Empire
soviet (*sovet*)
superstructure

Suggestions for Further Reading

Anderson, Thornton. *Russian Political Thought: An Introduction* (Ithaca, N.Y.: Cornell University Press, 1967).

Bennigsen, Alexandre, and S. Enders Wimbush. *Muslims of the Soviet Empire: A Guide* (Bloomington: Indiana University Press, 1986).

Buckley, Mary. *Women and Ideology in the Soviet Union* (Ann Arbor: University of Michigan Press, 1989).

DeGeorge, Richard T. *Patterns of Soviet Thought; The Origins and Development of Dialectical and Historical Materialism* (Ann Arbor: University of Michigan Press, 1970).

Dmytryshyn, Basil. *USSR: A Concise History.* 4th ed. (New York: Scribner, 1984).

Gregory, Paul R., and Robert C. Stuart. *Soviet Economic Structure and Performance*, 3rd ed. (New York: Harper and Row, 1986).

Hunczak, Taras, ed. *Russian Imperialism, From Ivan the Great to the Revolution* (New Brunswick, N.J.: Rutgers University Press, 1974).

Meyer, Alfred G. *Leninism* (Cambridge: Harvard University Press, 1957; reprint, 1986, Westview Press).

Millar, James R., ed. *Politics, Work, and Daily Life in the USSR: A Survey of Former Soviet Citizens* (New York: Cambridge University Press, 1987).

Nahaylo, Bohdan, and Victor Swoboda. *Soviet Disunion, A History of the Nationalities Problem in the USSR* (London: Hamish Hamilton, 1990).

Nove, Alec. *The Soviet Economic System*, 3rd ed. (Winchester, Mass.: Allen and Unwin, 1986).

Pipes, Richard. *The Formation of the Soviet Union: Communism and Nationalism, 1917–1923*, rev. ed. (Cambridge: Harvard University Press, 1964).

Rumer, Boris. *Soviet Central Asia: "A Tragic Experiment"* (Winchester, Mass.: Unwin Hyman, 1989).

Rywkin, Michael. *Moscow's Muslim Challenge*, 2nd ed. (Armonk, N.Y.: Sharpe, 1990).

Shatz, Marshall S. *Soviet Dissent in Historical Perspective* (New York: Cambridge University Press, 1980).

Szamuely, Tibor. *The Russian Tradition* (New York: McGraw-Hill; 1975).

Treadgold, Donald W., ed. *The Development of the USSR: An Exchange of Views* (Seattle: University of Washington Press, 1964).

Treadgold, Donald W., ed. *Twentieth-Century Russia*, 7th ed. (Boulder, Colo.: Westview Press, 1989).

White, Stephen. *Political Culture and Soviet Politics* (London: Macmillan, 1979).

B. Political Processes and Institutions

The Communist Party of the Soviet Union (CPSU) enjoyed a legal monopoly of political power from the establishment of the Soviet political system in 1917–1918 until it formally relinquished the monopoly in July 1990. In the aftermath of the unsuccessful coup of 19 to 21 August 1991 by part of the military and the security police, the CPSU experienced a precipitous collapse with the resignation of Mikhail Gorbachev as its general secretary, his dissolution of the Central Committee on August 24, and the suspension of all party activity. For over seven decades the CPSU had shaped the Soviet system's institutions and political practices and had provided the country's leadership. It also brought it to its deplorable condition in the 1980s and to its collapse.

The transformation from an absolutist dictatorial party to a beleaguered political dinosaur, stubbornly seeking to retain its leading role while steadily losing credibility, can be understood in terms of the CPSU's development and its methods of operation. The CPSU emerged from the small Bolshevik wing of the All-Russian Social Democratic Labor Party (RSDLP), which was the creation of Vladimir Ilyich Lenin. In the mid-1890s, as a young lawyer in the Russian capital of St. Petersburg, Lenin participated in a study group of Marxist intellectuals—the Union for the Struggle

for the Emancipation of the Working Class. Such activity led to Lenin's arrest and imprisonment in 1896 and subsequent exile to Siberia for three years. An attempt of several Marxist groups to hold a founding RSDLP congress in Minsk in March 1898 ended in failure when eight of the nine delegates were soon arrested. While in exile, Lenin developed a plan for organizing the new party more effectively, and after completing his sentence in 1900 he joined several émigrés in Western Europe in establishing a revolutionary newspaper, *Iskra* (The Spark).

Lenin's plan was to have the newspaper published abroad and smuggled into the Russian Empire, for the purpose of developing a readership that could be used to recruit members for his conspiratorial underground party of tested, dedicated, and disciplined professional revolutionaries. A Second Party Congress met in Brussels and London in August 1903, and *Iskra*, with Lenin as editor, was recognized as the party's official organ. However, a momentous division developed at the Second Congress between Lenin's Bolsheviks and the more moderate Mensheviks. The Bolsheviks claimed to have a majority as a result of the walkout of seven delegates who disagreed with Lenin's policies. The division between Bolsheviks and Mensheviks centered on such issues as the size of the party, membership requirements, and centralism in its organization. Lenin favored a smaller party and a more rigid definition of membership qualifications and demanded complete centralism and denial of local autonomy. The Jewish Marxists (the Bundists) called for ethnic recognition in party organization; they constituted a majority of the seven delegates who walked out of the Second Congress, enabling Lenin's minority to become the majority. Lenin rejected the notion of a party organized along ethnic lines and consisting of separate nationality groups.

Other issues that divided Bolsheviks and Mensheviks included whether or not to liquidate the illegal underground organization after the 1905 Revolution. Lenin opposed such action and favored the use of both legal and illegal means to achieve revolutionary goals. The Mensheviks advocated greater reliance upon legal and open forms of activity and condemned Lenin's use of armed robbery ("expropriations" by "combat units") for the purpose of financing the Bolshevik faction's clandestine revolutionary activities. In general, the Mensheviks were willing to let the bourgeois revolution and the development of capitalism in the Russian Empire run its course, whereas Lenin was very impatient and wished to accelerate the revolutionary process—as if to reveal his lack of faith in historical determinism. To a large extent the disagreement between Bolsheviks and Mensheviks was over methods and tactics rather than goals.

Although there were various efforts to heal the widening breach between Bolsheviks and Mensheviks (as at the Stockholm "Unity" Congress in 1906 and at the London Congress in 1907), all were doomed to fail. Lenin maintained his separate Bolshevik organization and factional treasury and heaped scorn upon his Menshevik fellow Marxists, denouncing them as "Liquidators" (for wanting to liquidate the underground party organization) and opportunists. The break between the two Marxist factions became complete in January 1912 when Lenin held a conference of his follow-

ers (with only 14 voting delegates) in Prague. Lenin formed a new central committee, declared his conference to be the "supreme party body," and designated himself leader of the "RSDLP (of Bolsheviks)."

However, Bolshevism was not a fully united faction, as Lenin had disagreements with his followers. A philosophical controversy began in 1908 when Lenin accused some of his closest followers of being idealists and of abandoning philosophical materialism. This quarrel prompted Lenin to publish his only philosophical work, *Materialism and Empirio-Criticism*. A related controversy was with the Marxist "God-builders," who wanted to give to socialism the emotional quality of the true religion of humanity, whereas Lenin, a confirmed atheist, wanted to do away with any thought of an analogy with religion. Bolsheviks who were dissatisfied with the performance of Marxist deputies in the Imperial Russian Duma (the tsarist legislature with limited powers) demanded that they be recalled or given an ultimatum (these dissident Bolsheviks were named Recallists and Ultimatists).

Disagreements and factionalism among the Bolsheviks persisted even after the establishment of the Soviet regime. Lenin was opposed by leftist Bolsheviks on the issue of concluding a peace treaty with the Central Powers in March 1918; the leftists wished to conduct a revolutionary war even though Russia lacked an effective army. Other opposition groups opposed Lenin's decision to hire bourgeois specialists, especially tsarist military officers. In 1919 the Military Opposition opposed the establishment of a standing army, favoring, instead a people's militia of the kind that Lenin himself had advocated earlier. The Democratic Centralist Opposition criticized the development of a party bureaucracy and the appointment (rather than the election) of party officials. The Workers' Opposition was dissatisfied over the influx of nonproletarian elements into the party—which in their view had ceased to be a workers' organization. In March 1921 at the Tenth Congress, Lenin took measures to outlaw all such oppositionist groups by adopting a formal ban on all factions. This action was followed by a purging of the party membership that resulted in the expulsion of 170,000 members.

PARTY LEADERSHIP

The Communist party of the Soviet Union had remarkably few leaders when compared with European democratic countries or the United States. During more than seven decades only seven men held the top leadership position. Lenin was unique as the party's founder; he never held the position of party secretary, but each of his successors headed the Secretariat. Originally the Secretariat was regarded as a service organization charged with keeping the party's records, but Stalin converted it into a powerful vehicle for his personal dictatorship and it eventually became the principal vehicle for achieving ultimate power in the Soviet political system. Stalin became general secretary in 1922 and ruled for more than a quarter century. He used the Secretariat and Central Committee administrative apparatus to reward followers and punish opponents. Lenin, during his final illness, called for Stalin's removal from the post in January 1923, but his "Testament" was suppressed in the Soviet Union for more than 30 years.

Lenin established the Soviet security police, originally known as the *Cheka*, in December 1917—an instrument that Stalin was to use arbitrarily as one of the pillars of his cruel and bloody dictatorship.[20] Lenin also provided Stalin with the organizational means of disposing of political opponents by outlawing factions and conducting purges of the party's membership. Nevertheless, Stalin also had to wage a fierce power struggle, first against the left opposition led by Lev Trotsky, and later against the right opposition led by Nikolai Bukharin. After ousting the Trotskyites, Stalin adopted their program by ending the New Economic Policy (NEP), but disagreed with them in insisting that socialism could be built by the Soviet Union alone without the aid of revolutions in other countries. Stalin first allied with the Right (which favored greater economic concessions to the peasantry and a slower rate of industrialization) and then turned against it after defeating the Left with its support. Stalin thus proved to be a master at dissimulation and at creating a party apparatus that became his personal machine.

Stalin's name is usually associated with full-blown totalitarian rule in the Soviet Union and the attempt to have the Soviet state equate itself with the totality of society and control all aspects of life. He employed terror and blood purges on a massive scale, established a huge network of forced-labor camps in which millions perished, and embarked on a program of forced industrialization and rapid collectivization of agriculture.[21] Rapid economic growth was based on deprivation and forced savings.

Apart from living in great fear and personal insecurity, Stalin's subjects were required to praise his wisdom and "genius." He proclaimed the establishment of socialism in the Soviet Union in 1936 and made himself the supreme authority in ideological matters, declaring that the Marxist superstructure could influence the economic base (and not simply be a reflection of the base); he also asserted that language (especially Russian language) exists apart from the superstructure and is not dependent upon the base. Stalin also restored the teaching of logic in the Soviet Union—after originally having banned it as being incompatible with the dialectic. Under Stalin the central party institutions ultimately declined in importance and were replaced by his personal secretariat and the secret police. In addition to being repressive, Stalin's rule was conservative in making divorce difficult and in banning abortions while coming to terms with the Russian Orthodox Church, and favoring Russian nationalism at the expense of the non-Russian nationalities.

Stalin's death in March 1953 ended his ruthless and arbitrary dictatorship. Following a period of collective leadership and the arrest and execution of secret police chief Lavrentii Beria, a power struggle ensued in which Nikita S. Khrushchev emerged as first secretary of the party. Following a crisis in June 1957, in which an attempt was made to oust Khrushchev, the first secretary also became head of the government. In February 1956, at the Twentieth Party Congress, Khrushchev launched an attack on Stalin's system of rule in a "secret speech" delivered at a dramatic late-night session, in which the dead dictator was depicted as an evil psychopath. The criticism of Stalinism (called the "cult of personality") was accomplished by a fresh political style, with Khrushchev traveling about the country, offering impromptu statements and advice, and permitting some relaxation of the rigid censorship. Khrushchev also revived the various central party bodies, including the Congress and the Central Committee. Instead of physically eliminating political rivals after executing Beria and his principal aides, Khrushchev had them forcibly retired with a pension paid for with silence. Khrushchev attempted a variety of reforms affecting economic policy and administrative reorganization and, unlike Stalin, traveled abroad extensively. Khrushchev's policies and his efforts to replace party officials resulted in considerable instability and led to his abrupt ouster on 14 October 1964 by his associates, most of whom he had elevated to high office.

The plotters who removed Khrushchev in a palace coup formed a collective leadership with Leonid I. Brezhnev as first secretary of the party. The new oligarchy repealed Khrushchev's administrative reforms and criticized him and his policies by innuendo. It called off his anti-Stalin campaign, ordering a substantial rehabilitation of Stalin's reign, and erected a monument over the dictator's grave (Khrushchev had removed Stalin's embalmed body from Lenin's Red Square mausoleum in October 1961). Khrushchev was treated as an "unperson" by his former associates and lieutenants. His numerous published speeches were withdrawn from circulation, and he was even denied a state funeral and burial near the Kremlin Wall when he died on 11 September 1971.

Brezhnev assumed Stalin's title of general secretary in 1976, though he could not acquire Stalin's powers. Brezhnev reaffirmed political centralism by restoring a large number of central government ministries, but he did not become head of government as Khrushchev had. The general secretary did become chief of state in June 1977 and also had a new constitution adopted in that year. As party leader, Brezhnev sought a consensus in the Soviet oligarchy and tried to obtain prior approval for his actions, thus avoiding Khrushchev's method of publicly advocating highly controversial policies prior to their adoption. As a result of the search for consensus, decision making under Brezhnev became slower and more cumbersome, and needed reforms were neglected.

Brezhnev died in November 1982, and was succeeded by Yuri Andropov, the first general secretary to come from the security police (KGB), which he headed for 15 years. The choice was unique in other respects: he acquired experience in Eastern European affairs as Soviet ambassador to Hungary (where he directed the suppression of the Hungarian rebellion in 1956) and as a CPSU Secretariat official responsible for relations with Eastern European Communist parties from 1957 to 1967; and he became general secretary at age 68, a much more advanced age than any of his predecessors. As KGB chief, Andropov demonstrated his resourcefulness in intensifying both overt and covert Soviet foreign intelligence operations and in employing repressive measures against political dissidents at home. His access to vital information obtained by the KGB probably contributed to his success in preventing the election of Konstantin Chernenko, whom Brezhnev had groomed as his successor and who had enjoyed great publicity in the last years of Brezhnev's leadership. As would befit a security police chief, Andropov emphasized discipline and order and attempted to launch an anticorruption campaign. Andropov's tenure of only 15 months as general secretary ended with his death on 9 February 1984, after having disappeared from public view for nearly six months because of illness, though pronouncements continued to be issued in his name along with false assurances that he would soon resume his duties.

Konstantin Chernenko, at the age of 72, succeeded Andropov. His election was probably due to the inability of two rivals, Mikhail S. Gorbachev and Grigorii Romanov, to obtain sufficient support. His election was the last collective act of the gerontocratic "old guard," and it provided a respite for officials who had felt threatened by Andropov's anticorruption campaign. Chernenko's poor health limited his tenure to 13 months—a period used to advantage by his successor, Mikhail Sergeievich Gorbachev.

The election of Mikhail Gorbachev as general secretary on 11 March 1985 represented an important leadership change. Relatively young at age 54, Gorbachev would initiate needed reforms, and was unique in being the first lawyer to head the party since Lenin, although he did not practice law. He became a party member while a student at the age of 21. From 1955 (when he graduated from the Moscow State University juridical faculty) until 1978, his career was confined entirely to his native Stavropol Territory (*krai*), north of the Caucasus Mountains. He first served in the local Communist youth organization and in 1963 assumed the first of several posts in the territory's Communist party organization. In 1970 at the age of 39 he became first secretary of the Stavropol Party Committee, a post that entitled him to Central Committee membership. Unlike his predecessors, Gorbachev had no experience in any of the non-Russian republics—a distinct disadvantage in dealing with troubling nationalities issues that would test his leadership abilities. He also had limited expe-

rience in Moscow, having served there for less than seven years before becoming general secretary. As a Secretariat member he acquired full membership in the Politburo in 1980.

Gorbachev proved to be an articulate, shrewd, and reasonably sophisticated leader. He also benefited from some fortunate circumstances. His predecessor as Stavropol Territory Party Committee first secretary, Fedor Kulakov, became the CPSU secretary for agriculture in 1970. This event enabled Stavropol to receive ample funding, which assured Gorbachev a good performance record in agriculture. When Kulakov died in 1978, Gorbachev became his successor as a CPSU Central Committee Secretariat member in Moscow. This appointment was made possible by Gorbachev's acquaintance with Andropov and the Soviet head of government Aleksei Kosygin, whom he had met while they vacationed at the Kislovodsk spa in Stavropol Territory.[22] Gorbachev became Andropov's protégé in part because both men were natives of Stavropol. He was also fortunate in being able to move away from agricultural responsibilities in the Secretariat. Despite his abilities, Gorbachev obtained the post of general secretary almost by default. He had the advantage of being able to remove his two principal rivals: Central Committee Secretary Grigorii Romanov and Moscow Secretary Viktor Grishin. Romanov was a weak contender because of various indiscretions, lack of polish, and inexperience and ineffectiveness in foreign policy. Grishin, who had arranged Chernenko's election as general secretary, was vulnerable because of his age and corruption in the large Moscow party organization that he headed.

Gorbachev had the advantage of organizing and presiding over the Twenty-seventh CPSU Congress in February 1986, asserting his leadership there and in summit meetings with President Ronald Reagan in Geneva, Reykjavik, Washington, D.C., and Moscow. His vigorous but controversial reform efforts prompted him to publish a work, *Perestroika*,

New Thinking for Our Country and the World (Harper and Row, 1987). Designed to appeal to foreign readers, the book was also available to the Soviet public. Although less candid than some of Gorbachev's speeches, the work reflected his determination to make the Soviet system more effective. Yet, Gorbachev's leadership style, policies, and reorganizational efforts also elicited uncertainty, skepticism, and resistance among critics who were alarmed by rapid change. The need for change and "new thinking" meant that the Soviet system confronted very serious difficulties. Gorbachev issued a revised version of the 1961 Party Program (a response to the many extravagant claims and unfulfilled promises made by Khrushchev), and enhanced his powers in October 1988 by assuming the chairmanship of the Supreme Soviet and establishing for himself the presidency of the U.S.S.R.

THE FAILED MODEL

The Soviet political and governmental system was based on the Leninist-Stalinist model that, according to the conventional wisdom of many observers, would be able to perpetuate itself. Its principal components were the mass membership CPSU and its auxiliary, the Leninist League of Communist Youth (*Komsomol*), which was to serve the party as a ready recruiting and training ground for young members. The CPSU apparatus (staffed by generalists, usually with specialized technical training and a narrow educational experience) operated through republic, province (*oblast'*), district (*raion*), and city party committees. The more than 3000 district party committees were directed by 122 province party committees. The district party committees supervised the more than 440,000 primary party organizations (p.p.o.) that were charged with carrying out party directives in factories, collective and state farms, educational institutions, government ministries, military units, embassies abroad, and housing developments. With each party member responsible to his or her p.p.o., discipline was supposedly ensured.

The p.p.o. was charged with attempting to promote productivity, reduce waste, and meet output quotas. It also organized campaigns, mass meetings, and public appeals in efforts to mobilize public opinion in accordance with party directives emanating from Moscow. The p.p.o. provided information for superior party bodies, serving as their eyes and ears. It enlisted new members and was responsible for supervising their training in Marxism-Leninism. It could expel members by a two-thirds vote of those present at a p.p.o. meeting, subject to the approval of the territorial (district or city) party committee to which it was subordinate.

Advancement was based on a partisan patronage system known as the *nomenklatura*, representing the lists of positions in all institutions and enterprises that could be filled only with the approval of the responsible CPSU (territorial) committee—each at its own level—from lists of approved prospective candidates. Promotion under this system generally depended more upon compliance and acceptability to party officials than on the competence of candidates. Acquaintance, connections, and being "politically correct" in expressing verbal support for party positions and policies frequently and vocally tended to determine advancement. Party dominance was also based on the administrative-command economy that established and enforced economic priorities and utilized scarcities to reward the faithful and bind them to the system.

The Partocracy

The Soviet political system was aptly termed a "partocracy"—a system of rule by and in the interests of a single political party that Lenin had immodestly deemed to be "the intelligence, honor, and conscience of our epoch."[23] The partocracy functioned either through an individual dictator, like Lenin or Stalin, or by means of an oligarchy (a collective dictatorship) consisting of a small group of men who comprised the Politburo and Secretariat of the CPSU Central Committee.

The Central Committee, as the parent body, was elected by the party congress held every five years. The Central Committee was authorized to "direct all party activities and local party bodies" in the lengthy intervals between party congresses, but would usually meet only twice a year because of its large size. In its place a politburo or "executive committee" was established to serve as the Soviet Union's supreme policy-making body; it held weekly meetings and usually consisted of 11 or 12 voting members and half as many (non-voting) candidate-members. The chief oligarch in this body was the CPSU General Secretary, who prior to 1990 was elected by the Central Committee. He headed its Secretariat, a collective body that varied in size and was responsible for the functioning of the various administrative departments of the central CPSU apparatus. These departments were concerned with the various sectors of the Soviet economy and with personnel matters *(cadres)*, as well as the supervision of science, education and culture, the media, the security police, the courts, prosecuting agencies and the legal profession, foreign policy, and relations with foreign Communist parties. The Secretariat administered the party's central fund, controlled its press organs and journals, and was responsible for the placement of personnel.

The Secretariat also supervised the party bureaucracies of the non-Russian union republics and the party committees in each *oblast'*, in the six territories *(kraia)*, and in the twenty autonomous republics. The *oblast'* or province was a key unit in the Soviet political and governmental system. The average *oblast'* is comparable in size to a smaller state in the United States, such as Connecticut or West Virginia. Less than half of the *oblasti* are in the Russian Republic and 25 are in Ukraine.

The *krai* is generally larger in size but more sparsely populated and more remotely located.

The partocracy was based largely on the first secretaries of the *oblast'* party committees *(obkom)*, who were usually the most influential officials at that level, serving as governors or satraps responsible to Moscow and dependent on it for their tenure. Most delegates to CPSU congresses were elected at *oblast'* party conferences, and the CPSU Secretariat generally treated union republic party organizations like *oblast'* organizations.

The CPSU had its own central bureaucracy with headquarters in a large older structure on the Old Square *(Staraia Ploshchad')* in the center of Moscow. The entire CPSU administrative apparatus had approximately 250,000 or more full-time officials and employees of 4625 territorial party committees at various levels. Prior to 1991 it also had the full-time services, at no cost, of secretaries and officials of 52,000 larger p.p.o.'s. These officials remained on the payrolls of enterprises but did no productive work, instead distributing Communist propaganda among the workers, holding endless meetings, and often interfering with management or colluding with it in various forms of corruption.

In its heyday the CPSU collected annually more than 1.34 billion rubles in dues, based on a scale of 0.5 percent to 3.0 percent of members' income. An additional 19 percent of the party's income was derived from its publishing and other enterprises.[24] The CPSU acquired in various ways (including confiscation) vast real estate holdings: office buildings, resorts, stores, hospitals and sanatoria, party schools, special hotels, and housing complexes. As the CPSU was placed in an increasingly defensive posture as a result of Gorbachev's reform efforts and revelations, demands were raised that its ill-gotten properties be nationalized or directed to better uses. With the party's collapse in August 1991, these properties were placed at the disposal of republic and local authorities.

The Reckoning

According to the conventional wisdom, the partocracy would attract the "best people" and its longevity would be assured by the self-perpetuating oligarchy. Marxism-Leninism would provide "adequate," if not the best, answers and solutions to its problems. The massive Soviet governmental and economic bureaucracy, backed by the security police and the military, would muddle through by means of its sheer weight and omnipresence. However, the agonizing and seemingly endless "moment of truth" that Gorbachev was compelled to initiate in 1985–1986 was a consequence of profound systemic failure.

In endeavoring to explain what "went wrong," it can be stated that Marxism-Leninism promoted closed minds and a form of rote learning that, combined with Russian self-satisfaction and complacency, produced a very debilitating condition. Under the superannuated Brezhnev oligarchy, many Soviet citizens could be deceived into believing that the Soviet Union was an advanced society representing "developed socialism" with a viable and advanced economic system. Under Gorbachev the elaborate, costly, and self-deluding notion that the Soviet leadership had been capable of solving problems could not be sustained. Indeed the CPSU was, for the most part, not attracting the best people but was actually attracting and rewarding some of the worst types: self-seekers, careerists, opportunists, blatherskites, and sycophants who could be counted upon to sustain the exercise in mass pretense. This was a long-standing problem noted by Nikita Khrushchev, who said that the CPSU had "many people without principle, lickspittle functionaries and petty careerists [who] seek to get much more out of our society than they put into it."[25] Thus the CPSU rewarded mediocre hangers-on and apparently had no place for honest persons of intellect with questioning and inquiring minds. As a result, it paid a high price in the end.

GORBACHEV: REFORMER IN SPITE OF HIMSELF

A fundamental contradiction in the reform effort was the fact that *perestroika* was undertaken in defense of Marxist-Leninist socialism when it was socialism in its Russian version that had brought the Soviet empire to economic, political, and moral bankruptcy. In almost any other country, a political party that had brought about such deplorable conditions would have resigned in disgrace, but the CPSU arrogantly entrusted itself with remedying all of the folly that had resulted from its own ideology, leadership, and policies.

This unenviable and even impossible task fell to Mikhail Gorbachev, who as CPSU general secretary developed a tripartite approach to reform based on *perestroika, glasnost'*, and "democratization." *Perestroika*, or "restructuring," was depicted as an effort to loosen the dead hand of the state's economic bureaucracy by giving plant managers greater authority regarding wages and hiring, placing greater reliance on sales and profits, and requiring self-financing (elimination of subsidies and interest-free investment capital) and economic accountability. Gorbachev sought to reduce (but not eliminate) centralism, especially as it impinged upon details of management and resulted in what was condemned as "petty tutelage." He permitted various producer cooperatives as well as "individual work activity" (self-employment) in the small-scale manufacturing and services sectors. Private housing was encouraged while social leveling (*uravnilovka*) in the form of consumption and wage egalitarianism was condemned. Joint economic ventures with foreign investors were authorized. Thus the aim of *perestroika* was to make Soviet socialism less inefficient and somewhat competitive.

The *glasnost'* (literally "vocality" but usually translated as "openness") component of Gorbachev's reform effort was intended to promote discussion of economic problems and to develop support for *perestroika*. Yet in admitting the corruption, mendacity, and failures of the Brezhnev era, Gorbachev could not confine the discussion to economic issues. Decades of repression, intolerance, and the "white (blank) spots" of historical censorship had created a tidal wave of frustration, resentment, and anger that led to demands that all of the ugly carbuncles and cancers on the Soviet body politic be confronted and revealed.

Gorbachev's "democratization" was *initially* more tactical in nature as it did not involve abandonment of the CPSU's political monopoly. The plan was to have party secretaries and even plant managers elected in an effort to introduce some accountability into the bureaucracy, get rid of the most odious Communist officials, and restore some modicum of public confidence. Gorbachev also sought to involve more non-Communists and women in the work of the local soviets (government councils). As with *glasnost'*, there could not be just a little democratization. Demands were made for religious freedom, for legalization of opposition parties, and for sovereignty and independence for the union republics.

The Dark Side: Contradiction and Reaction

Although Gorbachev was aware that perestroika was inevitable if the system was to be rescued from ultimate collapse, he was himself a product of that system and was thus limited by many of the inhibitions and taboos that had caused the malaise. He sought to reform the CPSU and the Soviet polity while remaining a loyal Marxist-Leninist and a committed centralist. His "new thinking" was often negated by "old thinking" and by his thin skin when facing criticism. Gorbachev's unattractive side was evident when he was disrespectful toward the Nobel laureate Andrei Sakharov before the Congress of Deputies and the entire country; he ordered the microphone turned off as the prominent physicist advocated an end to the

Communist Party's monopoly on the eve of his death.[26]

Probably the most sinister side of Gorbachev, and one that contributed to his undoing, was his strange relationship to and reliance upon the KGB. His role as the protégé of KGB chief Yuri Andropov was consummated with KGB sponsorship of him as CPSU General Secretary.[27] For Gorbachev the KGB was above all criticism; he simply ignored the numerous crimes perpetrated by its agents and maintained its privileged status, and promoted its chiefs Viktor Chebrikov and Vladimir Kriuchkov to full membership in the Politburo. He made it clear that the KGB was the mainstay of his regime along with the OMON—the interior ministry's special deployment forces under the command of Boris Pugo, a KGB general whom Gorbachev appointed to head the ministry.[28]

Gorbachev countenanced the use of armed force against civilians in Tbilisi in April 1989, in Baku in January 1990, and in Vilnius and Riga in January 1991, with considerable loss of life. *Glasnost'* and "democratization" did not eliminate KGB disinformation, calumny and provocations against opposition leaders and groups such as Boris Yeltsin, the democratic Ukrainian *Rukh* organization, and Lithuania's *Sajudis*. Police brutality was employed against peaceful demonstrators, and police provocation and violence were used against democratically elected deputies.[29]

GORBACHEV: HIS ERRORS AND FAILURES

The six years of Gorbachev's active leadership left a profound imprint on all of the republics and offered great opportunities for change. But Gorbachev made a series of errors that prevented him from fully utilizing these opportunities. These errors and failures had their source in Gorbachev's initial error: his gross underestimation of the malaise plaguing the Soviet system and what would be required to deal with it.[30] The very concept of "restructuring" implied that a mere reordering or rearrangement of Soviet management and administration and some concessions to small-scale entrepreneurship in the service sector would suffice to unbind the "flywheel" of the Soviet economy.[31] If the Soviet structure was fundamentally unsound and its structural integrity was in question, no amount of "restructuring" would suffice. The attempted overthrow of Gorbachev in August 1991 by a conspiracy representing the military, the police, and the central governmental bureaucracy testified to his failure to curb these forces.

A second error was Gorbachev's failure to establish clear priorities. Attempting to "accelerate" the economy, Gorbachev in 1988 undertook political reform which, in effect, turned Marxism on its head by attempting to re-order the Soviet political superstructure on a deteriorating economic base. Had he been able to concentrate on improving production of certain everyday household commodities—sectors of the economy in which improvements would have been readily evident—he would have been able to claim some credit as an economic reformer, at least in the short term. After establishing an ineffective presidential system, Gorbachev adopted a third priority: the preservation of the deteriorating union/empire. In the face of opposition from the union republics, he made an ill-advised attempt to force the signing of a "new union treaty." This move precipitated the August 1991 coup as the forces of reaction concluded that he had made too many concessions to the republics. Each of his priorities, then, was dissipated and led to diametrically (and dialectically) opposite results.

Gorbachev's third error was in his lack of appreciation for the utter failure of the CPSU's nationalities policies and for the seriousness of the non-Russian peoples' grievances against Moscow's centralist rule.[32] As a Russian Communist official whose entire career was limited to Russia—first the Stavropol territory and then his years in Moscow after 1978—Gorbachev was ill-prepared to deal with these crucial issues. His stubborn refusal to understand republics' demands for sovereignty and independence cast him in the reactionary role of guardian of an anachronistic empire, even as it was disintegrating. Indeed, his efforts to impose a new union treaty in 1991 directly contributed to his downfall.

Gorbachev's fourth failure was his indecisiveness and his attempt to placate hard-line Communists, neo-Stalinists, and Brezhnevites. Gorbachev's reform-minded economic advisers came and went as through a revolving door while he first embraced and then rejected new economic reform proposals put forth every few months. He attempted in vain to reconcile irreconcilable reform plans in the name of "market socialism." He could not adopt the "shock therapy" of rapidly introduced market conditions in April 1990 that he had been publicly advocating. This accelerated his loss of credibility, ironically at a time when he was acquiring greater "presidential powers." Gorbachev's temporizing and his toleration of the unreconstructed Communist Yegor Ligachev in the CPSU Secretariat and Politburo were indicative of his indecision. Ligachev was a lukewarm supporter of *perestroika* and an opponent of *glasnost'* and "democratization," but he remained in the leadership until the Twenty-eighth CPSU Congress in July 1990, when he openly criticized Gorbachev.[33] It is ironic that Gorbachev should have ignored the advice that he offered the doomed East German Communist leader Erich Honecker (on 7 October 1989, the fortieth anniversary of the German Democratic Republic, just prior to its collapse): "Life itself punishes those who delay."[34]

A fifth failure was Gorbachev's inability to abandon Marxism-Leninism and his ideological illusions regarding the CPSU. While conceding that "deformations" had occurred, he remained committed to "more socialism" and to an "improved socialism."[35] Whether this commitment was due to party ideological training or to the influence of his wife Raisa, a specialist in Soviet philosophy (Marxism-Leninism), cannot be ascertained.[36] Despite a pragmatic bent and a certain appreciation of realities, Gorbachev expressed this commitment in a visit to Minsk on 26 February 1991: "I adhere to the Communist idea, and with this I will leave for the other world."[37] This prevented him from rising above the post of CPSU general secretary and created a mental block that diluted every serious reform effort. Gorbachev remained bound by the CPSU and served as its head for too long, failing to develop his presidency.

Gorbachev's excessive reliance on verbal pronouncements, legal decrees, and Communist party resolutions was his sixth error. His prolixity and rambling style were often evident at press conferences and in speeches, and could be regarded as a rejection of the Bolshevik injunction against "the danger of merely talking"—a warning against what Lenin regarded as a vice of the Russian intelligentsia: its failure to move from talk to action.[38] The tendency to treat verbal pronouncements as a substitute for decision and to equate the written word with action may also have been a result of Gorbachev's legal training.

A seventh failure was both political and moral in nature. It resulted from Gorbachev's association with the KGB and its long-time chief, Andropov, and its sponsorship of the rise to power of both men. Gorbachev failed to condemn explicitly the horrendous crimes perpetrated by KGB personnel and did not bring responsible officers to justice. *Glasnost'* did not extend to the heinous activities of the KGB or its predecessors, the NKVD and MVD—except for the publicity given some of them by part of the media and by branches of "Memorial," a public, non-Communist organization. Gorbachev's poor judgment in casting his lot with the organs of repression in the autumn of 1990 and betraying his reform-minded supporters became evident in the abortive military and police *putsch* of 19–21 August 1991,

when he experienced the humiliation of house arrest.

A related error was Gorbachev's refusal to obtain a mandate based on popular election. His election as a member of the Soviet Parliament in 1989 was as a representative of the CPSU Central Committee, and proved to be a handicap. An electoral mandate that Gorbachev could have obtained in 1988 or 1989 as a popularly elected union president could have provided decisive support for a coherent program of radical reform—if he had developed such a program.

SUCCESS IN FAILURE

Critics of Gorbachev pointed out that he presided over a deteriorating economy in which ordinary citizens were driven to engage in "speculation" (reselling of goods at a higher price); standing in lines in front of stores became a form of "employment" as purchasers of goods in short supply could sell them at a profit. He was accused (by Boris Yeltsin and others) of pursuing contradictory policies and half-measures. However, Gorbachev had success in terms of the longer-range impact of his actions, whether they were intended or not. He was a qualitatively different Soviet leader and the first to acknowledge the symptoms of decay and degeneration. He could be criticized for treating symptoms rather than causes, but his admissions and policies had a profound effect on the Soviet ideology. In fact, Gorbachev may have been more successful as a debunker of the Soviet system than as its reformer. He failed to preserve the system, and made possible (often unintentionally) the many profound changes that led to its demise.

The reduced fear, especially among the youth, created a different political climate. It even resulted in the ouster of the prime minister of Ukraine, Vitali Masol, in October 1990 by hunger-striking students who demanded fulfillment of the 16 July 1990 Ukrainian declaration of sovereignty.[39] Gorbachev introduced a substantial degree of freedom of speech and press, which resulted in an outpouring of frustrations, grievances, and suppressed information and historical evidence. Yet many complained that free speech had little effect on KGB and police provocations or on local Communist party bosses who were reluctant to change their old ways. Although independent newspapers emerged, they often had difficulty obtaining newsprint and access to printing facilities. Despite the difficulties, however, the ferment of opinion and the questioning of old ways had a long-term salutary effect.

Soviet citizens were permitted to travel abroad, though usually with hard-currency restrictions, as part of Gorbachev's effort to make the Soviet Union a more normal or "civilized" country. Various taboos were abandoned or put into limbo; this included a truce in the Soviet war against political emigrés and especially against the politically active Ukrainian diaspora. The costly and only partially effective jamming of foreign radio broadcasts was suspended, including that against Radio Liberty, in November 1988. In addition, foreign tourists were permitted greater freedom of movement.

The holding of republic elections in March 1990 gave citizens a degree of choice between Communists and Democrats despite certain electoral irregularities and intimidation, especially in rural areas. This resulted in the election of anti-Communist governments in the Baltic states and in Western Ukraine and Georgia. Democratic oppositions emerged in various legislative councils (soviets) and parliaments. Former political prisoners were elected as parliamentary deputies in Ukraine: Viacheslav Chornovil, Levko Lukianenko, Mykhailo and Bohdan Horyn, Iryna Kalynets, and Dr. Stepan Khmara. They had been arrested as political dissidents and suffered years of imprisonment and internal exile for being unappreciated forerunners of *glasnost'* and democratization. While Gorbachev was serving the Brezhnev regime and promoting his career, these courageous and dedicated advocates of

reform were risking their lives for an even higher cause than the one that Gorbachev belatedly espoused.

The political dissidents were vindicated when Gorbachev acknowledged the need for "pluralism" and the right to establish unofficial "informal" organizations not controlled by the Communist party or the KGB. The recognition of a multiparty system in July 1990 (which had been stubbornly opposed by Gorbachev in late 1989) placed the CPSU increasingly on the defensive.[40] Yet the partocracy sought to delay change by requiring (and obstructing) the official registration of political parties and organizations by the ministry of justice.

The acknowledgment of "pluralism" made it necessary to recognize freedom of religion and to reduce the dependence of the Russian Orthodox Church (Moscow Patriarchate) on the Soviet government and its use by the KGB.[41] In 1989 the Ukrainian Greek Catholic Church emerged from more than four decades of underground existence, and conducted mass demonstrations demanding that it be legalized and regain control of its church properties. Gorbachev's visit to the Vatican in December 1989 resulted in a promise of religious freedom and recognition of all religious bodies.[42] The Ukrainian Autocephalous Orthodox Church, which had been banned by Stalin, reemerged in 1989 demanding legal recognition as its clergy and parishes rejected the Moscow Patriarchate; in 1990 it established its own Patriarchate of Kiev and All Ukraine.

These developments and reforms constituted the most substantial and pervasive legacy of Gorbachev's efforts. Yet while Gorbachev basked in his image abroad as a reformer, his ability to control the course of domestic events diminished. His declining popularity at home was a consequence of his failure to consummate radical economic and political reforms as well as reform of the legal system (see Feature 7.2.). This, in turn, was a consequence of his straddling the two highest political offices, the CPSU general secretaryship

The Search for a State Based on the "Rule of Law"

The Russian political tradition regarded law as an instrument of the autocracy and not as a means of constraining government and limiting the powers of rulers. This tradition obstructed the establishment of constitutional government in the Russian Empire and facilitated Stalin's dictatorship.

When Mikhail Gorbachev began to promote the concept of a state based on law (*pravovoe gosudarstvo*) in 1989, he did not envision the Communist party surrendering office to the opposition and accepting electoral defeat. In his view the problem of making the "bureaucratic command system" accountable could be solved by revitalizing the governmental councils (soviets). But each lower soviet was subordinate to the officials of the soviets that were superior to it in the chain of command; soviets elected in uncontested elections controlled by the Communist party could not restrain Communist government officials. Thus "socialist legality" came to mean arbitrariness and the belief that the state is supreme and should not be questioned.

A law-based Soviet state would have required a truly independent judiciary. Gorbachev sought to extend the terms of judges from five to ten years and abolished the practice of having the judges of the court of first instance (the "people's court") popularly elected. Instead, the judges of each court were elected by the soviet of the corresponding level of jurisdiction. Lay assessors (who participated with judges in hearing cases but not in deciding appeals) continued to be elected by citizens at workplaces and housing developments.

A major obstacle was the practice of requiring nearly all judges to be Communist party members. A judiciary selected by and dependent upon the Communist partocracy could not be independent. This led to a form of abuse known as "telephone justice" in which a judge would receive a call from a local party boss who would "suggest" to him or her how a particular case should be decided. The party even insisted that the chairman of the U.S.S.R. Supreme Court and the highest legal officer, the Procurator General, be members of its Central Committee.

A state based on law required the depoliticization of the procuracy — the system of state attorneys and prosecutors — to eliminate the possibility of political trials. It required that the security police (KGB) and the ordinary police (the "militia" under the interior ministry) not serve the Communist party and that the party organizations in them be eliminated. It required that the size and responsibilities of the KGB be greatly reduced and that the legal profession be emancipated from the dictates of the Communist party.

Essential criteria for establishing a rule-of-law state include the right to a speedy public trial with competent legal counsel (in contrast to the Soviet practice of holding persons up to nine months without bringing charges, and denying detained persons access to a lawyer until charges were formalized); the right of free movement within the country and the abolition of the internal passport system that required registration with the police; and the right to emigrate. A rule-of-law state acknowledges the right of aggrieved persons to sue public officials and permits the judiciary to rule against the government. Above all, there is need for a Bill of Rights that specifically denies to the state and its highest officers certain powers and forbids certain acts while making others highly conditional.

and the newly created U.S.S.R. presidency, and his inability to utilize either position to the fullest extent.

GORBACHEV'S LEADERSHIP

Gorbachev as Governmental Leader

Gorbachev as Communist party chief avoided any direct role in the Soviet government until he became chairman of the U.S.S.R. Supreme Soviet in October 1988. He then introduced a rather unusual presidential system that culminated in the new office of President of the U.S.S.R. established in March 1990.[43]

The new presidency was established by simple amendment of the 1977 Soviet Constitution, the fourth Soviet constitution. Previous constitutions were adopted in 1918 (for the Russian Republic), 1924 (for the newly established Soviet Union), and in 1936 (the Stalin constitution). Ease of amendment by legislative action and a tendency to treat the Constitution as a serial publication have promoted a lack of reverence toward constitutional documents. Gorbachev advocated adoption of yet another Soviet Constitution, but the proposal lost relevance with the collapse of the union in August 1991.

As a would-be political reformer, Gorbachev established an unusual and unwieldy legislative structure. In place of the bicameral Supreme Soviet established by Stalin in 1937, Gorbachev established a large Congress of People's Deputies that met briefly once or twice a year. It had 2250 members elected for five years. One-third of the deputies were elected from territorial constituencies based on population; one-third were elected from the republics and other national (ethnic) units, and one-third of the seats were allotted to various "public organizations" including the CPSU, the Komsomol (Communist Youth), and other organizations controlled by the CPSU. Thus the CPSU gave itself an additional 100 seats under this system of plural voting, and Gorbachev obtained his seat in the Congress as a member

of the CPSU contingent and not by popular election from a constituency.

Under this eccentric system the Congress of Deputies elected the two chambers of the U.S.S.R. Supreme Soviet, with 271 deputies serving in the Soviet of the Union and 271 in the Soviet of Nationalities. One-fifth of the membership of each chamber was to be replaced or reelected each year—an unusual feature that undoubtedly limited legislative prerogative and freedom of debate because it involved uncertain tenure. The Supreme Soviet held spring and autumn sessions, each of several months' duration, in contrast to the Supreme Soviet of 1937–1989, which met for only about one week of the entire year. The new Supreme Soviet was to be a "permanently functioning legislative, administrative, and monitoring ("control") organ of state authority." It appointed the head of government or premier (confirmed by the Congress), it confirmed all ministers (the Cabinet of Ministers), and it could create and abolish ministries. The Supreme Soviet elected the U.S.S.R. Supreme Court and appointed the Procurator General, the highest legal officer of the government. It also formed the Defense Council and could order mobilization and declare war. However, the Supreme Soviet was subordinate and accountable to the Congress of Deputies.

Gorbachev's legislative creation proved to be cumbersome despite the introduction of electronic voting, and much of its membership was of such a character as to cause the new parliament to lose legitimacy. Fewer than one-half (1101) of the deputies were popularly elected in contested elections; 399 were elected without opposition in accordance with the Stalinist-Brezhnevist practice of single-candidate elections. The electoral results could hardly be democratic when 87 percent of the deputies were CPSU members (party membership never exceeded 6.8 percent of the population and was declining) and 5.9 percent of the deputies were *Komsomol* members.[44] Such disproportion reflected Gorbachev's massive blindspot regarding the CPSU and its "leading role" as the "political vanguard." Thus the overwhelming mass of the population that was not Communist was, in effect, accorded 7.1 percent of the seats in the Congress. The 352 women deputies (15.6 percent) represented Gorbachev's pledge to give women an enhanced role in public life. The Congress also included 82 military officers.

The U.S.S.R. Congress of Deputies consisted largely of *nomenklatura* officials and was not a very representative body. Its members lacked legislative experience. Many deputies were reluctant to sit in the Supreme Soviet because it meant living in Moscow and neglecting one's livelihood, and was in many ways a frustrating experience. Yet clear divisions did appear in the Congress: a proreform Interregional Group, clearly defined nationality and republic groups, economic interests, and the backward-looking, antireform *Soiuz* (Union) group of hard-line Communists. Much criticism was expressed in the Congress and in the Supreme Soviet, and some ministerial appointments were rejected.

In March 1990 Gorbachev was elected by the Congress for a five-year presidential term over the objections of 41 percent of the deputies. On the surface this was a "strong" presidency with extensive decree-issuing and emergency powers, including introduction of "temporary presidential rule" in republics—revocation of their laws and removal of their governments. Gorbachev wanted his presidency to serve as a counterweight to the CPSU Politburo, but instead found that his broad—even quasi-dictatorial—powers were not sufficient either to solve the economic problems or to curb the rebellious republics and prevent the disintegration of the union/empire. In fact, the presidential powers were Gorbachev's undoing, as the plotters who sought to overthrow him invoked the same emergency powers of his office that they sought to usurp.

As the principal Soviet executive and head of state, Gorbachev was unable to gain adequate control over the central government. Although he often presided over parliamentary sessions and wagged his finger at critics, he failed to dismantle the centralized bureaucracy that obstructed his reform efforts in the economic ministries and in the military-industrial complex. He also lost any ability to control the activities of republic parliaments and *oblast'* and city governing councils. He was ineffective in attempting to abrogate laws and acts of republic authorities, and he found himself in the unusual position of issuing "legal" pronouncements regarding the alleged "unconstitutionality" of various acts of democratically elected republic and *oblast'* authorities, while at the same time being unable to prevent or rescind them.

Gorbachev as Party Leader: The Last Communist

Gorbachev's acquisition of presidential powers in March 1990 was accompanied by the abrogation of the CPSU legal monopoly on political power and the acknowledgment of a multiparty system. He had adamantly opposed such an abrogation of monopoly in December 1989 but relented two months later. This repudiation of political monopoly placed the surfeited, privileged, and corrupt CPSU apparatus on the defensive, as it was challenged by increasingly vocal democratic forces that were demanding accountability.

Gorbachev wanted to reform the CPSU in various ways because much of its bureaucracy sought to obstruct his attempted reforms. He reduced the size of the Central Committee apparatus, and especially its economic departments, in an effort to get party officials out of economic management. He sought to reduce the influence of the Politburo and Central Committee Secretariat even as he retained the post of general secretary. In April 1989 he removed 74 full (voting) members of the Central Committee on the grounds that they had become inactive because of age. His principal opponent on reform, the ideological chief Yegor Ligachev, was placed in charge of agriculture despite being unqualified for that responsibility; he opposed the leasing of land to collective farmers for individual cultivation and the introduction of a market economy. If this appointment was another of Gorbachev's concessions to Communist hard-liners, it also reflected an unfortunate tendency to temporize and improvise—attributes that in the end would lead to Gorbachev's downfall. Temporizing was also evident in Gorbachev's taking more than four years to rid himself of the Communist party first secretary in Ukraine, Volodymyr Shcherbyts'kyi, a holdover from the Brezhnev era. Shcherbyts'kyi was highly unpopular and totally incompatible with reform, but Gorbachev was prepared to ignore this on the mistaken assumption that a holdover from the Brezhnev era could keep Ukraine compliant. Such misperception and ignoring of political realities did not speak well of Gorbachev's ability to reshape the CPSU into an instrument of reform.

Increasingly, Gorbachev's political reform efforts were designed to circumvent if not supplant the party apparatus. This became evident at the Twenty-eighth CPSU Congress in July 1990, which saw much criticism from both advocates of rapid change and supporters of the old order. Gorbachev was reelected as general secretary by default in the absence of a serious opposing candidate, but dissatisfaction and division persisted.

Gorbachev was able to replace most of the Central Committee membership and reduce its size. He finally succeeded in retiring Yegor Ligachev, who unsuccessfully competed for the new post of deputy general secretary. He also succeeded in reducing the influence of the Politburo by doubling its membership (it now included the first secretaries of the fifteen union republic Communist parties) and having it meet monthly instead of weekly. Gorbachev was the sole holdover from the previous Politburo, as he excluded from it the head of the U.S.S.R. government (premier), the defense minister, the head of the KGB, and the foreign minister.

In a period of 18 months in 1990–1991 the CPSU lost at least 4.2 million members, and its membership was reported by Gorbachev to have declined to its 1973 level of 15 million. In addition, many of the remaining members had stopped paying dues without formally resigning from the party. Gorbachev noted that the party had "experienced an especially great loss in the republics where separatist movements have come to power."[45]

In 1990 Gorbachev had to acquiesce in the formation of a separate Communist Party of the Russian Republic with its own administrative structure. Gorbachev's greatest failure as CPSU leader was probably his inability to dislodge enough of the local officials of the partocracy—the party apparatus at the district (*raion*), city, and *oblast'* levels. There the entrenched bureaucrats and adherents of the "old thinking," fearing the loss of their positions and ill-gotten privileges, stubbornly obstructed reform in every way even while paying lip service to it.

The Yeltsin Phenomenon

The contradictory nature of Soviet reform was reflected in the tense relationship between Gorbachev and his nemesis and rescuer in 1991, Boris Nikolaevich Yeltsin. These two Communist officials clashed because of profound differences in personality and temperament, in their perceptions of events, and in the policies that they advocated.

The early careers of these two leaders were very different despite a common peasant background. While Gorbachev entered Communist party work as a bureaucrat at age 24, Yeltsin pursued a successful career as a construction engineer, becoming the head of a large housing construction firm in Yekaterinburg (Sverdlovsk). He did not join the CPSU until 1961 (at age 30) and did not enter party work as an official until 1968. He became a Central Committee member in 1981, ten years after Gorbachev. As a native of Siberia, Yeltsin was far closer to the Russian heartland than

Gorbachev, who came from the Russian periphery. Indeed Gorbachev's mastery of the Russian language was even questioned by the cognoscenti.

In 1986 Yeltsin was named head of the Communist party organization in Moscow, and was thus chosen to deal with the rampant corruption and economic woes of the municipal administration. When Yeltsin attacked these problems directly and forcefully, he encountered much opposition from entrenched venal interests. Yeltsin faulted Gorbachev for the slow pace of his reform efforts and criticized Politburo member Yegor Ligachev for obstructing reform. He did not endear himself at the Twenty-seventh Congress in 1986 when he attacked the "social injustice" of the benefits and material advantages that separated the party privileged from the Soviet public.[46]

In order to appease the corrupt ideologically orthodox in Moscow and rid himself of an outspoken critic, Gorbachev removed Yeltsin from his Moscow city post and as candidate-member of the Politburo in November 1987. Yeltsin accepted a junior ministerial post and appeared to be just another minor loser in the game of hardball Soviet politics. When he requested that the Nineteenth CPSU Conference "rehabilitate" him in July 1988 (while he was alive, rather than posthumously, as was usually the case in party practice), he was once again humiliated as Gorbachev rejected his request.

But Yeltsin achieved a dramatic comeback in August 1991 when, in a remarkable turn of events, Gorbachev was forced into the role of a hapless supplicant, depending upon Yeltsin to rescue him from house arrest and from the conspirators who sought to depose him. Yeltsin was able to acquire support as an outspoken populist while Gorbachev and the KGB sought to discredit him. Yeltsin's growing strength was derived from his advocacy of radical reform as Gorbachev maneuvered and meandered in his search for an unattainable "consensus." Yeltsin also acquired popularity as a defender of the interests of ethnic Russia and of the Russian

Republic against the union/center represented by Gorbachev, who stubbornly continued to advocate and personify a thoroughly compromised and ineffective centralism. Yeltsin's reputation for forthrightness won him favor among those who perceived Gorbachev as guileful and evasive.

Despite opposition from Gorbachev, Yeltsin was elected from Moscow to the U.S.S.R. Congress of People's Deputies and played a key role in the developing parliamentary opposition. In March 1990, Yeltsin was elected to the Russian Republic's Supreme Soviet (he was subsequently elected as its chairman) and in June 1990 Yeltsin demonstratively left the CPSU at the Twenty-eighth Congress.

Yeltsin called for Gorbachev's resignation in February 1991, but he subsequently sought an accommodation with the U.S.S.R. president on an ill-fated plan to reform and rescue the divided union. When Gorbachev sought to ban a pro-Yeltsin demonstration in March 1991 (to counter Communist efforts to unseat Yeltsin in the Russian Parliament) he was successfully defied, and the mass demonstration took place despite the presence of troops in the capital.[47]

When the Russian Republic opted for a popularly elected president, Gorbachev again sought covertly to prevent Yeltsin's election. However, Yeltsin easily won 57 percent of the vote against five opponents in June 1991, and became the first popularly elected president in the history of Russia. As president, Yeltsin began to express the long-repressed grievances of Russians against the union/center. On 19 November 1990 in Kiev, he signed a treaty with the government of Ukraine that acknowledged the sovereignty of Ukraine and Russia, and recognizing their existing borders.[48] Yeltsin insisted that the Russian Republic have its own KGB free of Union control and its own defense ministry and military forces; he claimed the republic's right to control all of its natural resources, which the union/center had used for its own purposes while flagrantly neglecting the republic's domestic needs.[49] Yeltsin called for an end to Soviet aid to Cuba, and enacted a ban on Communist party organizations in the workplace and their control of patronage, promotions, and various benefits. Earlier, in January 1991, when the Kremlin sought to employ violence against the seceding Baltic states, Yeltsin had directed an appeal to Soviet troops in Lithuania (delivered in Estonia) warning them not to be used by the forces of reaction and not to attack unarmed people. He asked them not to serve as "a pawn in a dirty game, a grain of sand in the Kremlin's building of an imperial sand-castle." He appealed to the troops not to believe the political officers and not to betray their own generation, warning that "dictatorship is arriving, and it is you who is bringing it, sitting with a submachine gun in a tank!"[50]

THE AUGUST 1991 COUP

The coup that sought to unseat Gorbachev and turn back the calendar was organized by a cabal representing the KGB (Vladimir Kriuchkov), the military (Marshal Yazov), the interior ministry or MVD (Boris Pugo), and the military-industrial complex. It included the premier, Valentin Pavlov, and had as its spokesman Vice-president Genadii Yanaev, whom Gorbachev had insisted be elected to that post after he was initially rejected by the Congress of Deputies. The "gang of eight" constituted a self-proclaimed State Committee for the State of Emergency in the U.S.S.R. It claimed mendaciously that Gorbachev was unable to exercise the duties of the presidency for unspecified reasons of "health" and announced that Yanaev would serve as acting president. It soon became clear that Gorbachev was being held under house arrest in his Crimean vacation retreat at Foros, near Yalta, and was cut off from all means of communication and had to obtain news of events from foreign radio broadcasts.

The putsch extended far beyond the self-proclaimed junta; it included numerous higher military officers and was supported by many CPSU apparatus officials at the republic and *oblast'* levels. The coup, a futile attempt to prevent the breakup of the empire, was precipitated by Gorbachev's plan to return to Moscow for the signing of his "new union treaty" on August 20—although it was not clear who else would sign this document. The putsch leaders claimed that Gorbachev's reform policies had reached a dead end but promised to pursue a "consistent policy of reform." In a vague and confusing statement the putschists condemned the turmoil and the "extremist forces" that allegedly sought to destroy the Soviet Union. They objected to the "war of laws" between the republics and the Union's president and the "destruction of the unified machinery of the national economy which has taken decades to evolve." The plotters contended that "the country has become ungovernable" and condemned the alleged use of power as "a means of unprincipled self-assertion" with the aim of establishing "an unbridled personal dictatorship"—although they did not specify whether this was the "sin" of Yeltsin or Gorbachev.[51] Although it promised to act against "the octopus of crime and scandalous immorality" as well as the "propagation of sex and violence" and the "tyranny of those who plunder the people's property," the junta had no specific program for rescuing either the economy or the empire. Its offer to conduct a public debate on Gorbachev's "new union treaty" reflected its misplaced suspicion of that instrument.

The 19–21 August 1991 coup proved to be poorly planned and the plotters ill-prepared. They apparently assumed that the removal of Gorbachev would be as easy as the 1964 ouster of Khrushchev, which was accomplished by hauling him before a Central Committee that was insistent on his removal. The putschists contented themselves with a televised press conference (from which the defense minister, the KGB chief, and the premier were absent) that revealed to viewers a motley assortment of undistinguished and unattractive bureaucratic types. The interior minister Pugo sat beside the principal spokesman, acting president Yanaev, whose hands shook visibly as he attempted to cope with the barbed and ironic questions of correspondents.

The putschists sent tanks and armored personnel carriers into the streets of Moscow and issued orders to all military forces and CPSU organizations in a vain effort to intimidate the opposition. But they miscalculated in relying on the divided and dispirited military establishment. They failed to obtain the acquiescence of Gorbachev and, more importantly, they failed to arrest or assassinate Boris Yeltsin. Although they were able to control the major media (as Gorbachev had done during the previous winter through censorship and closing several major newspapers), they could not control foreign radio broadcasts, the independent press, and recently developed nongovernmental information networks. In the end, the plotters experienced a failure of nerve.

Yeltsin defied the plotters and took refuge in the government house of the Russian Republic with aides and armed guards, as tens of thousands of supporters surrounded the building day and night and erected barricades for its defense. Military, KGB, and interior ministry forces loyal to Yeltsin refused to move against the government house and instead took up its defense. The conduct of the Soviet military in Moscow in August 1991 was thus very different from that in Prague in August 1968, where it had served as an instrument of repression. The plotters failed to cut off Yeltsin's communications and utilities, and he was able to communicate with world leaders such as President George Bush, British Prime Min-

Russian President Boris Yeltsin addressing supporters from a tank in front of the government house of the Russian Republic in Moscow during the August 1991 coup.

ister John Major, and President Mitterrand of France, who condemned the putsch and expressed their support for Gorbachev and Yeltsin. Although Yeltsin demanded the release of Gorbachev, he did so only because his adversary was being removed by unconstitutional means, giving him little choice under the circumstances but to make common cause as he was also a target of the conspirators.

The plotters failed largely because of their inability to rely on the military, their ineptitude and questionable reputations, and their inability to inspire public confidence in the unanticipated confrontation with the popularly elected Russian president, Boris Yeltsin. Their lack of character and stamina was evident when premier Pavlov suffered an attack of hypertension and Yanaev sought refuge in the bottle—and was later arrested in an inebriated state. The plot unravelled within seventy-two hours (despite the failure of Yeltsin's call for a general strike), and a shaken but not entirely chastened Gorbachev was able to return to Moscow to denounce the coup. Interior minister Pugo committed suicide, and the other plotters were arrested. Gorbachev's military adviser, the old-line Marshal Akhromeiev, also committed suicide.

An intriguing question prompted by the coup was that of Gorbachev's unwitting complicity in it. Gorbachev had repeated Khrushchev's careless error of vacationing away from Moscow at an inopportune time. Had he been less self-assured and more perceptive, he would have heeded the various warnings and ominous events that should have alerted him to the danger of a coup. His foreign minister Eduard Shevardnadze had warned of the threat of dictatorship when he resigned in December 1990. In June 1991 Premier Pavlov had sought unsuccessfully to have the Supreme Soviet grant him some of Gorbachev's presidential powers, and KGB chief Kriuchkov, defense minister Yazov, and interior minister Pugo had expressed profound dissatisfaction in a closed session of the Supreme Soviet.[52] There was also the mur-

der of six Lithuanian border guards on the Lithuanian-Belarus border that occurred on 31 July 1991 during the Bush-Gorbachev Moscow summit meeting. This dastardly act was probably the work of Pugo's OMON "black berets."[53] Apart from attempting to intimidate Lithuanians and other peoples in their struggle for national independence, the murders may also have been designed to embarrass and compromise Gorbachev in the eyes of President George Bush. Two days prior to the coup Gorbachev was warned by his former aide Aleksandr Yakovlev that a coup was imminent, but he chose to ignore the warning and even expressed the view that the plotters were incapable of mounting a coup.

Gorbachev cannot be viewed as an innocent victim of the coup. He appointed and promoted all of the plotters and had to know where they stood. Through his temporizing, Gorbachev had permitted the putschists to assume that they could persuade him to accept the coup and modify his policies accordingly. Yanaev, at the press conference, indicated that he was serving as acting president and that Gorbachev would assume his presidential duties as soon as his "health" would permit. The plotters sent a delegation to Gorbachev, apparently in order to come to an understanding. It can be argued that Gorbachev implicitly encouraged the plotters by his shift toward their position in the autumn of 1990, relying on coercive methods, police provocations, and intimidation. Gorbachev permitted Kriuchkov, Pugo, and the military a free hand in the Baltic states and reimposed media control and news blackouts. Thus Gorbachev, in casting his lot earlier with the KGB, the military, and the interior ministry, apparently led the plotters to believe that he relied upon them, condoned their methods, and would be prepared to join them when presented with a fait accompli.

In a sense, Gorbachev was an unwitting or silent accessory to the plotters if not an actual "co-conspirator."[54] He demonstrated poor judgment in selecting, promoting, and relying upon the plotters. He handpicked men of middling abilities and questionable character, possibly because he felt more compatible with them than with the various aides and advisers of superior intellect whom he had alienated. Several of his closest staff cooperated with the plotters. Gorbachev became a victim of his own guile and equivocation as well as his ego, his excessive self-confidence, and his carelessness. Some have speculated that Gorbachev cynically sought to utilize the very real threat from the antireform hard-line Communists as a means of extracting economic and financial aid from the West and Japan. In possibly seeking to use this threat as an undesirable alternative to his own leadership, Gorbachev became its victim.

THE AFTERMATH

The outcome of the failed coup was the very opposite of the plotters' intentions. It greatly accelerated the dissolution of the Soviet Union and once again demonstrated the endemic incompetence, mismanagement, and potentially dangerous nature of the center and of the CPSU. Yet the coup proved to be a remarkable turning point for Russia and the republics, paid for with the lives of three young men who died on the barricades. It was very literally a *coup d'état* in which part of the Communist state—indeed, some of the very highest officials who presumably enjoyed the unquestioned confidence of the U.S.S.R. president—struck a fatal blow at the entire fabric of the Soviet polity. It also created a vacuum in the center which gave Russia and the other republics a freedom of action they had not enjoyed since 1917–1918.

The coup and the resistance to it were essentially Russian phenomena; the plotters were all ethnic Russians (except for Boris Pugo, a Russified Latvian) and the immediate decisive resistance to the coup was largely Russian. The coup represented a conflict between Moscow and the Kremlin, between Russia and the Union. Boris Yeltsin emerged in a greatly strengthened position while Gorbachev re-turned to Moscow in a greatly weakened and isolated position. Initially, Gorbachev did not comprehend the profound changes caused by the failure of the coup. In a press conference on 22 August he praised socialism and defended the CPSU, failing to understand the full extent of his betrayal. It quickly became evident that the CPSU apparatus was either passively indifferent or actively supportive of the coup.[55] Indeed, the coup demonstrated the irrelevance of the CPSU as a constructive factor in the political system.

Yeltsin, as the leader of Russia, issued various decrees appointing new military commanders for Moscow and Leningrad (St. Petersburg) and placing troops of the army, KGB, and interior ministry in the Russian Republic under the jurisdiction of his office. The Russian Republic assumed ownership of all economic enterprises and properties in its territory, and Yeltsin restored the imperial Russian tricolor as the republic's flag, abandoning the red banner and the hammer and sickle.

Gorbachev was invited to address the Russian Parliament on 23 August 1991 and was received with skepticism and even outright hostility, being interrupted and heckled as he spoke. Such a response was prompted by Gorbachev's continued loyalty to the CPSU and his criticism of those who contended that it was a "criminal enterprise." Russian President Yeltsin, meanwhile, had suspended all activities of the Russian Communist Party. He insisted that Gorbachev read aloud the minutes of the U.S.S.R. Cabinet of Ministers meeting of August 19, which revealed lack of support for Gorbachev as nearly all ministers supported the coup. One member of the Russian Parliament summarized Gorbachev's status as U.S.S.R. President when he noted pointedly, "We don't need you but you need us."[56] Yeltsin insisted that Gorbachev approve all decisions taken by the Parliament and president of the Russian Republic during the coup, and Gorbachev had no choice but to give his assent.

The lack of support for Gorbachev within the central party apparatus during the coup

Demonstrators in Kiev protesting the CPSU, the August 1991 coup, and the OMON (the special assault forces of the interior ministry). They carry the Ukrainian national flag and the trident (a national symbol).

prompted him to dissolve the Central Committee and the central party organization on 24 August. The Central Committee building in Moscow was sealed, and officials and employees were denied entry because of alleged complicity in the coup. Similar bans were imposed throughout the former U.S.S.R. Although several republic Communist parties sought to change their names, many party leaders at the *oblast'* level, who were locked out of their party offices, continued to hold local or regional governmental posts and issue orders in an attempt to retain their powers and privileges. The U.S.S.R. Supreme Soviet, by a vote of 283 to 29 with 52 abstentions, suspended all CPSU activities on 29 August 1991.

Gorbachev's "new union treaty" could not be signed as a result of the coup, and the U.S.S.R. president was compelled to witness the adoption of declarations of national independence by nearly all of the former union republics. The process that had begun with Lithuania's abrogation of the communist monopoly of power on 7 December 1989, and its declaration of independence and secession from the U.S.S.R. on 11 March 1990, was largely consummated when Ukraine proclaimed its independence on 24 August 1991. But Russia, though insisting on its sovereignty, proclaimed on 12 June 1990, was reluctant to secede from the defunct union.

Gorbachev's union treaty draft was perceived by the coup plotters as surrendering too much to the republics in creating a supposedly new Union of Soviet Sovereign Republics. However, "sovereignty" in the Russian definition did not mean independence but only an enhanced autonomy. The projected new union was defined as the successor to the former U.S.S.R. and as a sovereign state with rights and obligations under international law despite its being comprised of "sovereign republics." The republics could enter into diplomatic and trade relations with foreign states, conclude treaties, and act as "full-fledged members of the international community" but could not infringe on the interests of the "Union state or their common interests."[57]

The contradictions in the new union treaty included dual citizenship (union and republic), and the union was to be the "protector" of the republics' sovereignity, although the extensive powers granted to it in Article 5 would have made it the usurper of their sovereignty. The treaty contained numerous legal traps including, in Article 6, a vague and lengthy category of "joint Union and Republic jurisdiction" that included military policy, "conditions governing the border zone," state security policy, and vast areas of economic and social policy. These broad powers would have once again subjected the republics to dictation from the center in the name of "uniformity." There was no list of enumerated powers granted exclusively to the "sovereign" republics. Legal traps included references to future unspecified "Union legislation" and to a future "Union consititution" that would have imposed additional restrictions on the republics but were not part of the treaty. Republics were not given any veto in drafting or amending the new constitution. The use of the Russian term *soiuz* to refer to the "union" raised serious questions because it is a word with multiple meaning, ranging from a loose and temporary alliance to the tightest bonds. Such an imprecise term is not appropriate for juridical usage—unless the purpose is to deceive and confuse. Nor did the draft treaty provide for the authenticity of its text in languages other than Russian—further proof of its discriminatory nature.

Gorbachev's "new union treaty" was actually not very new because it sought to reclaim much of the old centralism that had characterized the 1936 and 1977 U.S.S.R. Constitutions.

Gorbachev's claim that the treaty was based on the 17 March 1991 referendum was open to dispute because the referendum question, with its muddled wording, was deliberately crafted to confuse a variety of issues and produce a misleading result. The question was, "Do you consider necessary the preservation of the U.S.S.R. as a renewed federation of equal sovereign republics, in which the rights and freedoms of an individual of any nationality will be fully guaranteed?" The results were questionable because the referendum was boycotted by several republics and there were voting irregularities. In some republics there were alternative counterreferendum issues, as in Ukraine where a sovereignty question received more votes than the referendum question. Nearly 42 percent of the Soviet voters either did not vote or voted against the "renewed" union. The referendum also lacked support in the major cities.[58] Gorbachev's treaty resolved nothing and was a victim of the coup.

Gorbachev's role as guardian of the empire was evident in his precoup assurance that under the union treaty the "Soviet Union henceforth will continue to play the role of a great world power."[59] In his 23 August appearance before the Russian Parliament he expressed the Russocentric view that both the president and premier of the union should be Russians but the vice-president could come from the republics—"perhaps, best of all, from Central Asia."[60] Such attitudes cast Gorbachev in the role of another advocate of Russian empire and dominance, and they inevitably aroused suspicions in the other republics.

With the collapse of the coup and the treaty proposal, Gorbachev was compelled to employ other tactics in his tattered strategy of imperial revival. His dissolution of the U.S.S.R. cabinet of ministers because of its support of the coup meant that there was no longer a central union government. The Congress of People's Deputies was convened early in September 1991 in an effort to preserve some semblance of a political center.

Yeltsin told the Congress that "the collapse of the empire is final, but the republics have got to take its place."[61] The Congress balked at legislating itself out of existence but agreed to a new "transitional" center, only after Gorbachev pledged to retain the Supreme Soviet and pay the Congress deputies and permit them to retain their travel perquisites and immunity for the remainder of their terms.

The compromise, enacted at the insistence of Gorbachev and ten republic leaders, created a new interim executive body, the State Council, consisting of republic representatives and Gorbachev as chairman. The Supreme Soviet's Council of Nationalities was renamed the Council of the Republics, with each republic having but *one vote*. An Interrepublican Economic Committee was also established with its members chosen by the republics and its chairman selected by Gorbachev. The powers of the KGB and the interior ministry were also to be reduced.

The supposed "transitional" arrangement, was actually a "terminal" arrangement. Republics that had proclaimed their independence were suspicious of possible collusion between Gorbachev and Yeltsin and were apprehensive that the Russian Republic would usurp or seek to restore the role of the collapsed center. When the restructured Supreme Soviet met, four republics (Ukraine, Azerbaijan, Georgia, and Moldova) refused to participate.

The August 1991 coup was the denouement of Gorbachev's singular achievement: the introduction of significant democratic conditions and the partial dismantling and weakening of the centralized bureaucratic structures of the empire's metropol-center. Prior to this, the entire Soviet political system had been based on a triadic structure consisting of the following principal components: the CPSU oligarchy and its administrative apparatus that determined basic policy and conducted propaganda on its behalf, the governmental bureaucracy that managed the state-owned economy, and the organs of repression—military, police, and internal security organs (the MVD and the KGB). Gorbachev's reform efforts challenged and weakened an exhausted power structure but did not develop a viable substitute and the new personnel needed to give such an alternative life and substance. The ultimate source of this enormous failure must be sought in the policies pursued by the CPSU leadership for decades and the methods that it chose to employ.

Key Terms

Bolsheviks
Central Committee
Cheka
Congress of People's Deputies
CPSU (Communist Party of the Soviet Union)
Council of the Republics
"cult of personality"
General Secretary
glasnost'
KGB (*Komitet Gosudarstvennoi Bezopasnosti*)
Komsomol
krai
Mensheviks
nomenklatura
oblast'
oligarchy
partocracy
perestroika
Politburo
p.p.o. (primary party organization)
R.S.D.L.P. (Russian Social Democratic Labor Party)
Secretariat
Supreme Soviet
totalitarian rule
Workers' Opposition

Suggestions for Further Reading

Armstrong, John A. *The Politics of Totalitarianism* (New York: Random House, 1961).

Barry, Donald D., and Carol Barner-Barry. *Contemporary Soviet Politics*, 3rd ed. (Englewood Cliffs, N.J.: Prentice-Hall, 1987).

Bociurkiw, Bohdan R., and John W. Strong, eds. *Religion and Atheism in the USSR and Eastern Europe* (Toronto: University of Toronto Press, 1975).

Conquest, Robert. *The Harvest of Sorrow: Soviet Collectivization and the Terror Famine* (New York: Oxford University Press, 1986).

Conquest, Robert. *Power and Policy in the USSR* (New York: St. Martin's Press, 1961).

D'Encausse, Hélène Carrère, *Confiscated Power: How Soviet Russia Really Works* (New York: Harper and Row, 1982).

Doder, Dusko, and Louise Branson. *Gorbachev, Heretic in the Kremlin* (New York: Viking, 1990).

Dornberg, John. *Brezhnev: The Masks of Power* (New York: Basic Books, 1974).

Hill, Ronald J., and Peter Frank. *The Soviet Communist Party*, 3rd ed. (Winchester, Mass.: Allen and Unwin, 1986).

Hingley, Ronald. *The Russian Secret Police: Muscovite, Imperial Russian and Soviet Political Security Operations* (New York: Simon and Schuster, 1970).

Knight, Amy W. *The KGB: Police and Politics in the Soviet Union* (Boston: Unwin Hyman, 1988).

McCauley, Martin, ed. *Khrushchev and Khrushchevism* (Bloomington: Indiana University Press, 1988).

McNeal, Robert H. *Stalin: Man and Ruler* (New York: New York University Press, 1988).

Medvedev, Zhores A. *Andropov* (New York: Penguin Books, 1984).

Medvedev, Zhores A. *Gorbachev* (New York: Norton, 1986).

Morrison, John. *Boris Yeltsin, From Bolshevik to Democrat* (New York: Dutton, 1991).

Powell, David E. *Antireligious Propaganda in the Soviet Union* (Cambridge: M.I.T. Press, 1975).

Rigby, Thomas H., ed. *Stalin* (Englewood Cliffs, N.J.: Prentice Hall, 1966).

Schapiro, Leonard. *The Communist Party of the Soviet Union*, rev. ed. (New York: Random House, 1971).

Ulam, Adam B. *The Bolsheviks: The Intellectual and Political History of the Triumph of Communism in Russia* (New York: Macmillan, 1965).

Ulam, Adam B. *Stalin, The Man and His Era* (New York: Viking Press, 1973).

Unger, Aryeh L. *Constitutional Development in the USSR: A Guide to the Soviet Constitutions* (New York: Pica Press, 1981).

C. Public Policy

The Soviet Union acquired the status of a superpower not only by being on the victorious side in World War II, but also as a consequence of deliberate policies pursued by its leadership since 1945. These policies as well as the Soviet (Marxist-Leninist) view of international relations served to maximize Soviet power and caused many countries to be suspicious or fearful of Soviet intentions. The Soviet Union's human and material resources were mobilized and its military capabilities rapidly developed so that it could acquire nuclear parity, or better, as recognized in the SALT (Strategic Arms Limitations) Talks and agreements. The Soviet rulers were unashamedly power oriented, and the 1977 Soviet Constitution (Article 62) obligated all citizens to strengthen the "might and authority" of the Soviet State.

The policies and actions of other countries also contributed to the Soviet Union's emergence as a great power. The Soviet Union was sought as an ally by the French and Czechs in 1934 and by the British in 1939, but Stalin concluded a "nonaggression" pact with Nazi Germany in August 1939 and later joined in the German military campaign that led to the destruction of the Polish state and precipitated World War II. The Nazi-Soviet Pact enabled the U.S.S.R. to annex western Ukraine and western Belarus as well as Estonia, Latvia, Lithuania, and the region of Bessarabia (which had been part of Romania between 1918 and 1940)—territories with a non-Russian population of more than 22 million. Hitler's invasion of the Soviet Union in June 1941 involved Stalin's regime in World War II despite efforts to remain neutral.

The war was very costly to the Soviet Union (resulting in more than 20 million deaths) and initially involved a year and a half of military retreat. It was won, but not necessarily because of Soviet patriotism, Russian nationalism, or belief in Marxism-Leninism alone. The Soviet victory was also the result of other factors, including brutal German occupation policies that provided no attractive alternative to Stalin's rule, and $12 billion of U.S. Lend-Lease aid made available unconditionally to Stalin's dictatorship by the Roosevelt administration. In addition, the U.S.S.R. was spared having to fight a war on two fronts in Europe and in the Far East in 1941–1945—thanks to the decision of the Japanese militarists to attack the United States at Pearl Harbor and to seize Southeast Asia, Indonesia, and the Philippines in 1941–1942, instead of attacking Siberia at the time that the Soviet forces were retreating in the West.

The total defeat of Germany and Japan in 1945 and the weakened condition of France and Italy added to the Soviet Union's advantage, and resulted in a U.S.-Soviet bipolarity in place of the prewar multipolar international situation. The U.S. policy of demanding

Germany's unconditional surrender resulted in the postwar Soviet military presence in Central Europe.[62] The failure of Britain and the United States to prevent the establishment of Communist regimes in eight Eastern European countries and in North Korea (largely as a result of Soviet military occupation) led to the emergence of a Soviet bloc under Moscow's leadership. The wartime United Nations military alliance that defeated Nazi Germany and Japan deteriorated quickly as Stalin launched an intensive campaign to end the U.S. atomic weapons monopoly; the Soviets succeeded in detonating an atomic bomb in 1949 and acquired the hydrogen bomb in 1953. Soviet military power was deployed in Cuba, Angola, Ethiopia, Vietnam, South Yemen, and Afghanistan. The Soviet lead in the acquisition of the heaviest intercontinental ballistic missiles, the largest nuclear warheads, a limited antimissile defense capability, a hunter-killer satellite, the largest submarine fleet in naval history, and the first mobile intercontinental, ballistic missiles, did not prove the success or even the viability of the Soviet system.

THE SOVIET VIEW OF INTERNATIONAL RELATIONS

Soviet rulers viewed and understood international politics largely in terms of Marxism-Leninism, although traditional Russian expansionism and a sense of a special Russian role in history (Russian messianism) also affected the Soviet view of foreign countries. Marxism-Leninism emphasized conflict and the class struggle as the motive force in historical development. Class warfare was extended into the realm of international relations, and a certain level of tension and conflict was regarded as a normal condition in relations between states; however, tension was to be kept within limits in order to avoid high-risk military confrontations or "adventurist" undertakings. The conflict between capitalist and socialist ruling classes was seen as representing the "struggle of opposites" in dialectical materialism. The

1986 CPSU Program declared, "The dialectics of development are such that the very same means which capitalism puts to use with the aim of strengthening its positions inevitably lead to an aggravation of all its deep-seated contradictions. Imperialism is parasitical, decaying and moribund capitalism; it marks the eve of the socialist revolution."[63]

In the Soviet view of international politics, at least until the 1980s, quantitative changes were seen as leading to qualitative change that favored the Soviet Union. International developments were depicted and analyzed in terms of the "correlation of forces" concept, which reflected the relations between the great powers—actually, the strategic balance.

Foremost among the Soviet Union's objectives was the enhancement of its strategic power and its ability to influence the actions of other states and play a prominent, if not dominant, role in the world. The Soviet leadership's willingness to think in global terms was reflected in the official state seal of the U.S.S.R.: a globe with hammer and sickle superimposed upon all of Eurasia, Africa, the Near East, the Arctic, and Greenland, and intersecting in the Indian Ocean.

Soviet foreign policy makers sought to prevent the formation of alliances that could be directed against the Soviet Union and result in its isolation. Moscow attempted to divide its "capitalist" opponents by driving wedges between them and disrupting alliances, such as NATO, established to deter the possible threat of Soviet aggression. The Soviet Union always attempted to isolate the state that it regarded as its principal enemy: Great Britain was cast in this role in the 1920s, Nazi Germany in the 1930s, and the United States after World War II. Mikhail Gorbachev told the Twenty-seventh CPSU Congress that there were "three principal centers of contemporary imperialism—the U.S.A., Western Europe, and Japan [which] are full of obvious and concealed contradictions." He also conceded that "in the next few decades...new capitalist 'centers of power' may appear." He also identified "a new knot of contradictions *between transnational corporations and the national-state form of the political organization of society*" as well as a *"new, complicated and active complex of contradictions* [that] *has formed between imperialism and the developing countries and peoples."*[64] Soviet policy makers sought to utilize these various "contradictions" to their own advantage.

The Soviet Union also sought to retain some degree of primacy in the Communist world. This claim was first asserted in 1919 when Lenin founded the Third Communist International (Comintern). Although the Comintern was dissolved in 1943, the CPSU continued its practice of interfering in the affairs of foreign Communist parties. The U.S.S.R. intervened militarily in Hungary (1956), in Czechoslovakia (1968), and in Afghanistan (1979–1989) in order to overthrow Communist leaders and install or keep in power others deemed to be more loyal to Moscow. The CPSU rejected the Yugoslav Communist attitude that approved of polycentrism (the existence of several Communist centers), but had to acquiesce in the fragmentation of the international Communist movement while claiming a special role as the world's first Socialist state.

The accumulation of serious, even horrendous, domestic problems and a costly arms race may have prompted Gorbachev to offer to the Twenty-seventh CPSU Congress the following eloquent and sobering appraisal and warning:

> The present-day world is complex, diverse, dynamic, permeated with contending tendencies, [and] full of contradictions. It is a world of very complex alternatives, anxieties and hopes. Never before has our earthly home been subjected to such political and physical overloads. Never has man exacted so much tribute from nature, and never has he proved to be so vulnerable to the might that he himself has created.[65]

This was a harbinger of Gorbachev's "new thinking" which led to a general reappraisal

of Soviet foreign policy and had profound consequences.

THE STRATEGIC RETREAT: FROM SUPERPOWER TO SUPPLICANT

When Gorbachev assumed the Soviet leadership in 1985 he eased out of office the foreign minister, Andrei Gromyko, who had served in that post for 28 years. Gorbachev appointed an outsider—Edouard Shevardnadze, former head of the Communist Party of Georgia—for the purpose of undertaking a thorough reorganization of the foreign ministry and a reorientation of foreign policy.

As Gorbachev probed more deeply into the morass of the Soviet Union's internal affairs, he apparently concluded that the empire's foreign commitments greatly exceeded its capabilities. He sought to end the "isolation of socialist countries from the common stream of world civilization."[66] He undoubtedly understood that this anachronistic policy was setting the Soviet Union apart as an abnormal entity that lacked respect in the international community and fell farther behind the technologically advanced world.

The Soviet leadership's reappraisal of its foreign and domestic policies and its concern for its bad image may also have been precipitated by President Ronald Reagan's apt and cutting characterization of the Soviet Union as an "evil empire" and "the focus of evil in the modern world."[67] This statement, made on 8 March 1983, was undoubtedly effective in tactical terms as it touched a most sensitive nerve and, in the end, probably contributed to the effort to change the Soviet image.

The Reagan Administration's decision to pursue an antiballistic missile defense (Strategic Defense Initiative) posed the fundamental question of whether the Soviet Union could afford to compete in this new stage in the arms race. In the 1970s the Soviet Union had unwisely deployed the intermediate range SS-20 missile in Europe and had mistakenly thought that this would not elicit any response from NATO. When it did, it became necessary for the Kremlin to rethink its entire missile deployment strategy and much more. This led to the December 1987 and July 1991 agreements between Washington and Moscow which significantly reduced intermediate and strategic missiles.

Gorbachev's foreign policy also included abandonment of the so-called Brezhnev Doctrine, under which the Soviet Union engaged in armed intervention in foreign countries to prevent the overthrow of Communist rule. The Doctrine failed its most crucial test in Afghanistan, from which the Kremlin had to withdraw its forces in 1989 when the cost of occupation became too prohibitive. In 1986–1987 Gorbachev had attempted to crush the Afghan resistance by means of a punitive aerial offensive directed against the civilian population. This offensive failed because of the antiaircraft missiles provided to the resistance by Western and Moslem countries, but it did not prevent Gorbachev from being awarded the Nobel Peace Prize in 1990.[68]

The Soviet failure in Afghanistan demonstrated its vulnerability and fueled resistance to Communist rule in Eastern Europe. In 1989 thousands of East Germans sought refuge in the West via Czechoslovakia and Hungary, where officials proved to be indifferent or tolerant of the exodus. Gorbachev was thus confronted with widespread resistance in several Eastern European countries. When the East German Communist authorities suffered a failure of nerve and opened the Berlin Wall in the face of mass demonstrations, the 300,000 Soviet troops in East Germany could not be used (or relied on) to restore Communist rule. If Gorbachev had invoked the Brezhnev Doctrine, he would have faced a disruption in relations with the West which could have led to an economic embargo and general condemnation, and he would have destroyed his image as a reformer.

Instead, Gorbachev had to acquiesce in the dissolution of the German Democratic Republic, demolition of the Berlin Wall, and the unification of Germany. He agreed to the withdrawal, in stages, of Soviet troops from Germany and placed the remaining troops on German rations. The withdrawal of Soviet troops from Czechoslovakia and Hungary in 1990–1991 presaged the dissolution on 31 March 1991 of the Warsaw Pact, the Soviet Union's Eastern European military alliance. All of this was done while the Soviet Union accepted the continued existence of NATO as a defensive alliance.

The Council for Mutual Economic Aid (CMEA), Moscow's organization for integrating the Eastern European economies for four decades, unraveled as the Soviets were forced to cut those countries loose because of increasing difficulties in their own economy. CMEA had been based on unrealistic planned pricing which made it impossible to determine real costs. It also lacked viable terms of trade because of the inconvertibility (and uncertain value) of the ruble, resulting in a reliance on barter arrangements.[69] Another aspect of the retreat was the establishment of diplomatic relations between Moscow and the Vatican in March 1990.

The decision to retreat from the external Soviet empire in Eastern and Central Europe—despite objections from some in the military—was not accompanied by a comparable willingness to give up the internal empire that consisted of the fourteen non-Russian republics. This intransigence on the part of Gorbachev and his cohorts could only prolong the agony that would confront the Soviet Union as it sought to cope with its insoluble domestic problems.

FOREIGN AND DOMESTIC POLICIES

Soviet foreign and domestic policies were always closely related. Ambitious and costly foreign policies influenced domestic policies, and domestic conditions necessitated changes in foreign policy. Initially, in order to save the Soviet regime and his dictatorship in 1918, Lenin had to accept a peace treaty with the Central Powers. Following years of war that greatly damaged the economy, he had to improve relations with some of the capitalist countries, especially Germany, to promote economic recovery. The Soviet Union joined the League of Nations in 1934 at a time when Stalin was engaged in costly industrialization. When the Soviet Union needed to avoid or postpone a war for which it was not prepared (as a result of the purging of the military and domestic dislocations), Stalin signed a pact with Nazi Germany.

Although the Soviet Union was a victor in World War II, the wartime alliance was replaced by the Cold War; Stalin closed the country to foreigners and lowered the "iron curtain" because of the need to conceal the country's weakness and extensive wartime losses. When domestic conditions improved, the iron curtain was partly lifted in the mid-1950s. The détente of the 1970s was prompted, in part, by the need to import foreign technology and obtain financial credits. In the 1980s, Gorbachev advocated a "dialog" and reaffirmed the "peaceful coexistence of states with different social systems" because of the deplorable state of the Soviet economy. The Soviet need for more butter instead of more guns required a degree of international stability and a reduction of tensions.

The crisis that confronted the Soviet leadership in the late 1980s was, to a considerable extent, a consequence of its costly foreign policy and excessive preoccupation with military power. Such priorities resulted in the development of a "command economy" with all *basic* economic policy decisions made by political authorities and central economic planners. Wages and prices, capital investment, and consumption levels were centrally determined rather than left to market conditions. Nevertheless, consumer resistance developed as buyers refused to purchase goods of inferior quality. The "second economy" (termed by Gorbachev the "shadow economy") pro-

duced more expensive goods of better quality but with materials obtained in questionable ways through illegal diversions, embezzlement, and barter—apart from actual purchase (which could itself be illegal). The "command economy" reflected a fear and distrust of market forces associated with capitalism, whether they represented consumer choices, the money market competing for available investment capital, or the supply market that provides the raw materials and components needed by industry.

Such an economy could produce (and waste) large quantities of steel, coal, petroleum, and cement. It enabled the Soviet Union to engage in space exploration and to undertake costly large-scale projects such as the heavily subsidized Baikal-Amur Mainline (BAM), a new rail line 3200 km long, linking central and eastern Siberia along a route north of the Trans-Siberian Railroad farther removed from the Chinese frontier. It enabled the Soviet Union to acquire a large modern merchant fleet and to develop several cities within the Arctic Circle.

However, the imbalances, the system of administratively fixed prices that did not reflect real costs, and the heavy subsidization of rents, food, and public transportation, and other items led to a grossly distorted economy. In the absence of a money market (with capital investments often based on grants), capital was frequently wasted and not put to work quickly. Gorbachev criticized "laughable interest rates" that made efficient use of investment capital impossible and that resulted in the absence of a financial credit system.[70] Construction projects chronically lagged. A prominent factory director told the Nineteenth CPSU Conference: "With us it is regarded as normal to take 15 to 20 years to build a factory—and no one shoots himself, no one goes insane."[71]

Wages rose ahead of productivity, and workers were paid to produce goods of inferior quality ("for the warehouse") that consumers refused to buy. Savings bank deposits grew at a rapid rate from a total of 18.7 billion rubles in

1965 to 337.8 billion rubles in 1989. This economic factor reflected an oversupply of money in relation to goods and services available. It also testified to a large pent-up demand, inflationary pressures, and the ability of Soviet citizens to obtain additional income. Gorbachev revealed that in the 1971–1985 period the ratio between the growth in the money supply and the increase in consumer goods was 3.1 to 2.0.[72]

Soviet leaders had claimed for years that the governmental budget had annual surpluses. This claim proved false, and Gorbachev informed the Central Committee that revenues were able to cover expenditures by several means. These included the sale on the world market of petroleum and other energy and material resources, and the appropriation or transfer ("unfounded withdrawal") of funds belonging to enterprises and organizations (probably including tapping the reserves of *Gosstrakh*, the state insurance monopoly of the Ministry of Finance). The budget deficit was also dealt with by increasing the highly profitable production and sale of vodka and other spirits. Gorbachev revealed that the turnover tax (excise) revenues from the sale of alcohol during the Eleventh Five-Year Plan were 169 billion rubles.[73] He summarized the unsatisfactory financial condition of the Soviet Union when he told the Nineteenth CPSU Conference: "Over a period of many years expenditures of the state budget grew more rapidly than revenues. The budget deficit exerts pressure on the market, undermines the stability of the ruble and monetary circulation, [and] gives rise to inflationary processes."[74]

The priorities of the Soviet oligarchy resulted in serious dislocations in such areas as housing, public health and medical care, and ecology. In 1961, the CPSU Program promised that by 1980 every Soviet family would have its own apartment or dwelling. In 1986 the revised CPSU Program promised that by the year 2000 every Soviet family would have its own apartment or house. In 1988 Gorbachev stated that more than 35 million new apart-

ments and dwellings were needed to fulfill the goal.[75]

In the area of public health, Dr. Yevgenii Chazov (Minister of Public Health) revealed to the Nineteenth Conference that for years leading Soviet officials had acknowledged the "bitter truth" of inadequate expenditures for health care, and yet had stated that there were higher priorities. As a result, Dr. Chazov revealed that in terms of the portion of gross domestic product devoted to public health the U.S.S.R. ranked in the middle of the seventh decile among 126 countries. In infant mortality it ranked fiftieth in the world—after Mauritius and Barbados—and in average life expectancy it ranked thirty-second. Dr. Chazov noted that a hospital for handicapped war veterans in Moscow was under construction for 11 years. He complained of the shortage of pharmaceuticals. He pointed out that "as a result of poor water supply and a low sanitary-hygienic level in many dairies and meat-packing enterprises . . . annually in the country 1.7 million persons suffer from severe gastro-intestinal ailments."[76] Dr. Chazov resigned from the ministry because Gorbachev would not provide the resources needed to improve the health care system.

Under *perestroika* serious ecological problems were finally acknowledged, including soil depletion and loss of humus content, cutting of forests without reforestation, and air pollution in 102 cities—often exceeding safe levels by ten times. Major rivers have been badly polluted and the damming of the Volga and Dnieper (Dnipro) rivers to form large reservoirs has had deleterious ecological consequences. It was reported that the principal polluters of air, soil, and water were the enterprises of seven central economic ministries.[77] Such costly ecological disasters resulted from unsound planning and false priorities, as well as the Soviet leadership's neglect of domestic problems.

Seven decades of Communist rule exacted a horrendous toll in material, ecological, and human terms, and contributed to the degra-

A view of a portion of the Aral Sea reclaimed by the desert as a result of Soviet ecological negligence and mismanagement of water resources.

dation of Soviet society. The problems were exacerbated by the older population's willingness to accept an economy based on rations, low wages, dependency, and artificial egalitarianism; any wealth was suspect unless it was acquired under Communist party auspices. These conditions promoted cynicism, the stifling of initiative, and the decline of the work ethic and self-reliance.

If the Soviet system quite literally self-destructed, it was for a variety of reasons. State ownership of the economy had spawned a wasteful and inefficient central government bureaucracy staffed by surly, self-aggrandizing and only marginally competent officials. The system provided tragic examples of what happens when the center imposes its power-driven priorities at the expense of republics and cities (see Feature 7.3). The metropole's priorities ignored the development of the in-

frastructure and resulted in inadequate and crumbling utilities systems in the largest cities. In St. Petersburg—a city with a population of more than 4 million—the water system became a disgraceful source of infectious disease and toxicity.

Vast sums were expended on excessive military programs, and space technology was given priority (largely for military purposes) at the expense of civilian needs. The security police organs expanded beyond real needs, and their employees were overpaid in comparison with other occupations. The extension of financial credits to a variety of third world and Communist countries left the Soviet Union an unsatisfied creditor as recipients such as Cuba, North Korea, and Vietnam expressed ingratitude. Ironically, Lenin's denunciation of the capitalist "bureaucratic-military institutions which subordinate everything to

---

Feature 7.3 **The Decline of Empire**

The decline of several great continental empires has been a twentieth century phenomenon. The collapse of the Austro-Hungarian, Ottoman, and Russian empires was as remarkable and consequential as the collapse of the U.S.S.R. Attempts to reform and preserve empires have failed because of their essentially anomalous nature, and many were not acknowledged to be aberrational until the process of implosion was evident. Major characteristics of imperial decline include the following:

1. Widespread corruption, including theft and embezzlement; officials at all levels expect bribes for performing their duties.
2. The imperial bureaucracy not only proves incapable of initiating reforms, but actually obstructs and sabotages such efforts and seeks to preserve its privileges, opting for stagnation rather than innovation.
3. The military may suffer outright defeat or retreat and have serious morale problems, especially if it must rely on unwilling and unreliable conscripts from subject nationalities. In addition it often faces the dilemma of whether to serve as an instrument of repression against its own people.
4. Imperial rule proves to be excessively costly and ultimately exhausts revenue sources. Military power and economic bankruptcy provide an incongruous combination when the empire becomes dependent on foreign capital and technology.
5. Imperial decline is accompanied, and to a degree concealed by *hubris* — the arrogance, overweening pride, insolence, and self-deception on the part of the ethnic hegemon that the early Greeks recognized as preceding decline and fall. Hubris reflects the corrupting and perverse nature of imperial rule as the ethnic hegemon demonstrates loss of a sense of reality.
6. The quality of the empire's political leadership is crucial as its efforts at modernization, reform, and empire preservation fail.
7. The final stage in the collapse of empire is a failure of nerve and a crisis of confidence, as it finally becomes evident that the attempted solutions for crises and defeats are ineffective.

---

themselves and suppress everything" was actually applicable to the Soviet bureaucracy and the military and security establishments.[78]

THE PRICE OF EMPIRE

The peoples of the Soviet Union have had to bear the enormous costs of an assertive foreign policy. Maintaining the empire involved spending as much as 25 percent or more of the Soviet gross domestic product for military purposes. It meant reliance on conscription and the rejection of conscientious objection. Non-Russian conscripts were frequently abused while in military service, and homicide and suicide rates among them were excessively high. Service in the Soviet army was reduced from three to two years in 1967, and service in the navy was reduced from four to three years. At that time, compulsory military training with weapons practice for both sexes was introduced into the secondary schools.

Empire meant neglect of domestic problems. Its very size in territorial terms created large bureaucratic establishments that declined in competence and effectiveness. In addition to costly military forces, it required large police establishments to keep subject peoples intimidated and to impose internal order and an apparent unity. The attempt to govern diverse peoples from a single center (which was also the center of the dominant nationality—the internal hegemon) bred resentment and resistance. The imperial system was costly and wasteful because of its swollen bureaucracy and apparatus of coercion, and because of its efforts to retain conquests and great power status. Bigness led to the sacrifice of quality for quantity and to numerous forms of corruption and venality. The former Moscow city party committee's first secretary, Boris Yeltsin, observed at the Nineteenth Party Conference that "the decay (*zagnivanie*) is evidently deeper than some have assumed, and I know, on the basis of Moscow that a mafia definitely exists." He also noted that there were "millionaire bribetakers" among CPSU officials at the republic and *oblast'* levels who were not being punished by the Committee of Party Control.[79]

The unity of the imperial system, for all of its apparent power, had a synthetic quality and was unstable because it attempted to embrace too many and too much.[80] Because of its size and heterogeneous nature, the imperial system was difficult to identify with. Yet vast sums were squandered on grandiose public monuments and displays of military might in an attempt to sustain the myth of omnipotence and invincibility.

The Russians, as the dominant and core nationality, have paid a high price for empire. In denying non-Russian subject peoples the right of self-determination, Russians greatly limited their own freedom by having to sustain an authoritarian system designed to preserve the imperial patrimony and hold restive subject peoples within its grip. By creating and sustaining the synthetic entity known as the U.S.S.R., Russians experienced (and imposed upon themselves) a diminution or loss of original identity. Because of the multinational nature of the U.S.S.R., the adjective "Russian" was often supplanted by "Soviet" and even by the strange adjective "fatherland" (for example, with reference to machine building, medicine, and music). Russians were thus unable to acquire and develop genuine nationhood as part of the U.S.S.R. In professing a contrived "internationalism," Russia submerged itself in the union-empire. It is ironic that the Russian Republic in effect surrendered its membership in the United Nations to the union-empire while Ukraine and Belarus, as charter members of the United Nations, actually acquired greater international (legal) recognition than Russia.

The Russians paid a high price if, as Aleksandr Solzhenitsyn contends, the Russian "national way of life" and "national character" were disappearing and if Russian nationhood was being destroyed "without pity" by Soviet leaders who claimed to be of Russian nationality. Despite greater use of the Russian language, Solzhenitsyn argues that in its Soviet version it became "a sullied and bastardized form of the Russian language."[81] If so, this was a part of the price of empire as the Russian language ceased to be the possession of Russia and was corrupted by non-Russians and Russians alike.

An additional price of empire was the inundation of the metropole and imperial capital by subject peoples and alien elements. In the process, the dominant Russians cease to endear themselves to subject peoples. Fear of fragmentation of the empire promoted suspiciousness of "subversion" and obsession with security. It also engendered arrogance and blindness as Russians failed to understand the national ideals and aspirations of subject peoples. Solzhenitsyn, in his essay "Repentance and Self-Limitation in the Life of Nations," counseled his people to withdraw and engage in self-examination and divest themselves of the burdens of empire.[82] He also warned the Soviet leaders that "the aims of a great empire and the moral health of the people are incompatible" and that empire inflicts spiritual harm.[83]

NEW BEGINNINGS

The Soviet empire collapsed as a result of political and economic breakdown as well as moral failure. The August 1991 coup was followed by the collapse of the ruble in late 1991 as a result of enormous government deficits. Proposals to "save" the nearly worthless ruble with foreign aid and an international hard currency "stabilization fund" simply demonstrated the pathetic plight of the Soviet economy. For years Soviet officials had to rely on hard currencies to calculate foreign trade transactions as the convertibility of the ruble, like communism itself, remained an unattainable goal. Convertibility must be based not only on an economy's productive capacity but on the willingness of foreign citizens, businesses and governments to hold a country's currency and be able to use it for purchases and investments.

The collapse of the ruble was preceded by a secret depletion of the Soviet gold reserve and hard currency stocks. It was alleged that CPSU officials had converted their vast ruble holdings into gold and hard currencies and had made deposits in European banks. The deaths of two of the highest CPSU administrative officials by suicide or homicide tended to confirm the worst suspiciions regarding such transactions.[84] In Moscow rubles were being printed around the clock to finance the deficits of Gorbachev's shadowy "Union government."

The grievances of the non-Russian peoples had been systematically ignored by Moscow as a matter of course. Uzbekistan had been converted into a gigantic cotton plantation for the Russian textile industry, with Moscow setting the price of cotton. The irrigation required for cotton cultivation effectively dried up the Aral Sea to less than half its former size, with attendant loss of soil, and the careless use of pesticides created serious health problems. In Ukraine the metropole-center constructed 22 nuclear power plants without

the consent of the people; it also constructed gas and oil pipelines across Ukrainian territory without obtaining permission or paying any fees. In both cases electricity and fuel were exported to neighboring countries and the revenues were appropriated by Moscow. The horrendous after-effects of the Chernobyl catastrophe serve as a constant reminder of the costs of tolerating arbitrary rule from an external center.

Ukraine adopted an incremental approach in extricating itself from the toils of the Soviet Union. The process was spearheaded by the Ukrainian Parliament, the Supreme *Rada*, elected in March 1990. The Communist majority became divided and on many issues its members sided with the democratic bloc, which held nearly one-third of the seats. Following the proclamation of Ukraine's sovereignty on 16 July 1990, a number of measures were adopted. Ukrainian laws were declared to have primacy over Soviet laws, and Ukraine declared its neutrality and its commitment to being a nuclear-free country. The Rada's Presidium and the Ukrainian ambassador to the United Nations condemned Moscow's use of force against Lithuania in January 1991. Ukraine reduced its financial payments to the union by 80 percent in 1991, established its own National Bank of Ukraine, and concluded bilateral agreements with other republics. Following the August 1991 coup Ukraine established its own defense ministry and commenced formation of its own armed forces and national guard. It reorganized the KGB in Ukraine, renaming it the National Security Service (SNB). It also took steps to introduce its own currency, the *hryvnia*.

The death knell of the Soviet Union was sounded by the Ukrainian referendum of 1 December 1991, which approved the 24 August 1991 declaration of Ukraine's independence by a 90.32 percent majority. Leonid M. Kravchuk was also elected president of Ukraine by a 61 percent majority against five other candidates. President Kravchuk, armed with a clear mandate, asserted that Ukraine would not join any new union. Yeltsin stated that if Ukraine rejected Gorbachev's union, Russia would also refuse to join.

However, as Yeltsin was apparently relunctant to have Russia formally declare its independence from the U.S.S.R. as the other republics had done, Kravchuk seized the initiative by proposing the formal dissolution of the union and the formation, instead, of a Commonwealth of Independent States (CIS) that would not replace the defunct union but would serve as a consultative and coordinating forum for the former Soviet republics. The Soviet Union was dissolved by a declaratory act of the three remaining signatories of the December 1922 treaty that formally established the U.S.S.R. The three heads of state of Be-

larus, Russia, and Ukraine met at a government estate in the Belovezha Forest Reserve near Brest, Belarus and in Minsk on 7–8 December 1991 and declared that "the U.S.S.R. as a subject of international law and as a geopolitical reality ceases its existence."[85] The act and the formation of CIS were approved by the parliaments of the three countries. The commonwealth decision was a means of removing Gorbachev and eliminating his presidency in the disapperaing government of a disintegrated empire. It also negated Moscow's claim to be the imperial metropole.

Gorbachev's presidency came to a belated end on 25 December 1991 with his resignation. The red flag with its hammer and sickle

The dissolution of the U.S.S.R. and the announcement of the C.I.S. agreement are applauded in Minsk by (from the left): President Leonid Kravchuk of Ukraine, Belarus Parliament Chairman Stanislav Shushkevich, and President Boris Yeltsin of Russia.

was lowered over the Kremlin and replaced with the Russian tricolor.

The CIS was to facilitate cooperation among its members in the fields of foreign policy, economic relations, the environment, and immigration policy, and in combating organized crime. Coordinating bodies of CIS were to be located in the Belarus capital of Minsk. Yeltsin and Kravchuk asserted that CIS was not a state and its bodies would not constitute a government.

The CIS began in difficulties and distrust. Yeltsin's decision to administer "shock therapy" to Russia's economy by "freeing" prices on 2 January 1992 meant that the other member states had no choice but to comply, as their lower prices would result in massive outflows of food and goods to Russian purchasers. Relations became more strained when the higher prices required an increase in the supply of rubles and Russia failed to provide the needed currency. As an emergency measure, prior to the adoption of its own new currency, Ukraine introduced circulating coupons that quickly forced out the ruble. Yeltsin's higher prices provided little impetus for the development of a market economy in Russia in the absence of widescale privatization and competition, as the state remained the principal supplier and maintained a sellers' market. However, the price increases did reduce the Russian government's budget deficits.

Military issues were another source of tension. Ukraine had made it clear from the beginning that it would organize its owned armed forces, and it was joined by Azerbaijan and Moldova. Belarus and Uzbekistan expressed reservations concerning a common CIS military force. Yeltsin and the Russian-dominated military command in Moscow wanted to have the divided services of the the former union recognized as the armed forces of the CIS but under the old ethnic Russian command. Ukraine and other states saw this as a scheme to maintain what they regarded as occupation forces in their territories. In March 1992, Yeltsin announced that Russia would establish its own defense ministry—as Ukraine had done on 22 October 1991.

The nuclear weapons in the territories of Russia, Ukraine, Belarus, and Kazakhstan added to the disagreement as there was skepticism regarding Russia's ability and willingness to destroy nuclear weapons transferred to it by the other countries. President Kravchuk of Ukraine insisted that Russia not be given exclusive control of nuclear weapons but that they be under joint control of the four states.

Yeltsin's Russia also aroused suspicion by claiming to be the "legal successor" of the Soviet Union—a claim that contradicted the declaration establishing CIS, because it did not provide for any successor state. However, Yeltsin's claim was abetted by those NATO countries who gave to Russia the Soviet Union's permanent seat in the United Nations' Security Council (as an easy way of avoiding amendment of the UN Charter and the rival claims of Germany, India, and Japan to Security Council membership). The "succession" issue was also seen as a means of reaffirming the defunct Soviet Union's obligation to reduce nuclear weaponry by having Russia assume them. However, this rationale was based on the debatable assumption that Russia was a reliable guardian of the nuclear arsenal. Thus, the fact that Russia was the only one of the 15 republics that did not exercise its constitutional right to secede from the U.S.S.R. can be understood as a reflection of its desire to be the empire's "successor." However, in the matter of the repayment of the huge Soviet foreign debt (of more than $70 billion), Russia did not claim to be the sole "legal successor" but demanded that all of the former union republics pay a share of it.

Apart from the debt issue, disagreements arose in CIS over the assets of the defunct Soviet Union: banks owned in London, Paris, and elsewhere, embassy properties abroad, the four naval fleets, and various commercial enterprises and foreign investments, along with the "disappearing" gold reserves. Russia was reluctant to divulge and share these assets; it sequesterd them, took sole possession of embassy properties, and undertook to sell naval vessels—acts that prompted charges of Russian bad faith.

The tension between Russia and Ukraine had broader significance as Ukraine was the focus of the resistance to Russian attempts to dominate CIS. At times the strained relationship took the form of an economic cold war. Ukraine's resistance to any joint command of conventional military forces for CIS and its demand for a significant portion of the Black Sea fleet disrupted Russian plans. Chauvinistic Russian political figures, including Vicepresident Aleksandr Rutskoi, sought to exploit the issue of Crimea and demanded that it be ceded to Russia. The Russian mass media disseminated disinformation and false allegations regarding Ukraine, and Ukrainian authorities vigorously protested the Russian campaign to demean a neighboring state. Ukraine from the beginning sought to limit the role of CIS, regarding it as a means for liquidating the remnants of the Soviet Union; it ratified the CIS agreement only with numerous stipulations and conditions, and reserved the right to withdraw.

If the future of CIS was uncertain, that of Russia was no less so. Russians were bewildered by the breakdown of a Soviet system that they had been told was their crowning achievement. For many Russians it apparently came as a shock to learn that they were disliked in their role of ethnic hegemon and as bearers of russification and "sovietization." The defiance manifested by alienated subject peoples, who were finally asserting their separate identities and restoring collective historical memory, shattered the official myths that many Russians had so readily accepted.

The viability of the Russian Federation—which had been a federation in name only—increasingly came into question. Russia's political leadership aroused controversy as President Yeltsin was criticized by Vice-president Rutskoi, who sought to unseat him. Yeltsin professed democratic values but often acted arbitrarily and in an authoritarian manner, as when he also assumed the premiership. He appointed *oblast'* governors who were charged with shaking up local bureaucracies and affecting reforms with limited success. Critics charged that privatization of state economic enterprises was often to the advantage of Communist *nomenklatura* officials who were now becoming businessmen.

Moscow's record of incompetence as the center of the defunct union-empire inevitably brought into question its competence as the center of a far-flung and highly diverse "Russia." In a sense Russia suffered from many of the same problems, disparities, and contradictions that had plagued the Soviet Union. Russia was confronted by sovereignty claims of non-Russian regions such as Tatarstan (a modern successor to the Kazan Khanate), which demanded a share of the petroleum revenues that Moscow had appropriated. The great regions of Siberia (including Tiumen, Krasnoiarsk, and Iakutia) demanded cntrol over their resources and an end to their misappropriation and neglect of Siberia's infrastructure.

Having had to abandon both the Eastern European external empire and the Soviet internal empire, the Russians finally had to confront the problems of the core empire within "Russia" itself. The fact that 17 percent of the population of "Russia" is not ethnically Russian makes it necessary to seek new forms of relationship that respect the interests, concerns, and values of the non-Russian peoples. Russians also need to reexamine their own values, their entire historical record as an imperial people, and the nature of their political culture and what it has represented and brought them. Crucial to this self-examination is the question of whether Russians can divest themselves of the belief in a "single and indivisible" empire and become a conventional or "normal" national entity.[86] The Russians' ability to eschew a dominant role in their own republic or federation, despite their numerical superiority, will determine whether they will overcome their past or revert to old values and questionable practices.

Such attributes as arrogation, intimidation, and blaming others for Russia's woes cannot provide a sound basis for political relationships. Overcoming a people's past is an achievable goal. Russians had the opportunity to do so in 1917 and failed. The end of the Soviet Union gave the Russians their second opportunity in the twentieth century to scrutinize their past and reorder their future, thus gaining self-respect by respecting the rights of other peoples.

Key Terms

Brezhnev Doctrine
CMEA
Comintern
"correlation of forces"
hubris
imperial system
Lend-Lease
Warsaw Pact

Suggestions for Further Reading

Allworth, Edward, ed. *Ethnic Russia in the USSR: The Dilemma of Dominance* (New York: Pergamon Press, 1980).

Brzezinski, Zbigniew. *The Grand Failure, The Birth and Death of Communism in the Twentieth Century* (New York: Scribner, 1989).

Colton, Timothy and Thane Gustafson. *Soldiers and the Soviet State* (Princeton: Princeton University Press, 1990).

Conquest, Robert, ed. *The Last Empire: Nationality and the Soviet Future* (Stanford, Calif.: Hoover Institution Press, 1986).

Duncan, W. Raymond and Carolyn McGiffert Ekedahl. *Moscow and the Third World Under Gorbachev* (Boulder, Colorado: Westview Press, 1990).

D'Encausse, Hélène Carrère. *Decline of an Empire; The Soviet Socialist Republics in Revolt* (New York: Harper and Row, 1981).

Dibb, Paul. *The Soviet Union: The Incomplete Superpower* (Champaign: University of Illinois Press, 1986).

Hajda, Lubomyr and Mark Beissinger, eds. *The Nationalities Factor in Soviet Politics and Society* (Boulder, Colorado: Westview Press, 1990).

Hill, Ronald J. and Jan Ake Dellenbrant, eds. *Gorbachev and Perestroika: Towards a New Socialism?* (Brookfield, Vermont: Edward Elgar, 1989).

Marples, David R. *The Social Impact of the Chernobyl Disaster* (New York: St. Martin's Press, 1988).

Matthews, Mervyn, *Poverty in the Soviet Union* (New York: Cambridge University Press, 1987).

Nogee, Joseph L., and Robert H. Donaldson. *Soviet Foreign Policy Since World War II*, 3rd ed. (Elmsford, N.Y.: Pergamon Press, 1988).

Ra'anan, Uri, ed. *The Soviet Empire: The Challenge of National and Democratic Movements* (Lexington, Mass.: Lexington Books, 1990).

Rowen, Henry S., and Charles Wolf, Jr., eds. *The Future of the Soviet Empire* (New York: St. Martin's Press, 1988).

Rubinstein, Alvin Z. *Soviet Foreign Policy Since World War II: Imperial and Global*, 3rd ed. (Cambridge, Mass.: Winthrop Publishers, 1988).

Ulam, Adam B. *Expansion and Coexistence: The History of Soviet Foreign Policy, 1917–1973*, 2nd ed. (New York: Praeger, 1974).

Wesson, Robert G. *The Russian Dilemma*, rev. ed. (New York: Praeger, 1986).

Notes

1. *Pravda*, 28 January 1987. Gorbachev repeated this warning to the Central Committee on 18 February 1988. See *Izvestiia*, 19 February 1988 and *Pravda*, 26 June 1987.

2. *Izvestiia*, 26 July 1991.

3. See Mervyn Matthews, *Privilege in the Soviet Union, A Study of Elite Life-Style Under Communism* (London: Allen and Unwin, 1978), which is based on interviews with 58 former Soviet citizens. See also Michael Voslensky, *Nomenklatura: The So-*

viet *Ruling Class* (Garden City, N.Y.: Doubleday, 1984); Ilya Zemtsov, *The Private Life of the Soviet Elite* (New York: Crane Russack, 1985); and Vladimir Shlapentokh, *Public and Private Life of the Soviet People* (New York: Oxford University Press, 1989).

4. For a discussion of the Mongol-Tatar impact on Muscovy and the Russians see Charles J. Halperin, *Russia and the Golden Horde* (Bloomington: Indiana University Press, 1985) and Karl A. Wittfogel, *Oriental Despotism: A Comparative Study of Total Power* (New Haven: Yale University Press, 1957).

5. This can be illustrated with the complaint of Gorbachev that "we still lack the culture of discussion" and that some publicists "seek to settle personal scores or attach offensive labels." Mikhail Gorbachev, *Perestroika i novoe myshlenie, dlia nashei strany i dlia vsego mira* (Moscow: Politizdat, 1987), pp. 71–72. A highly revealing observation was offered to the Nineteenth Party Conference in June 1988 by the rector of Moscow State University, Dr. Anatolii A. Logunov, who noted that "we cannot change our psychology ... and stereotypes of the past remain with us. ... There is in us a strong desire to beat someone." *Izvestiia*, 1 July 1988.

6. See Nicolas Berdyaev, *The Russian Idea* (London: Geoffrey Bles, 1947), Chapter 9.

7. See Paul Avrich, *Russian Rebels, 1600–1800* (New York: Schocken Books, 1972).

8. Nicolas Berdyaev, *The Russian Idea*, pp. 142–144.

9. See Adam B. Ulam, *Russia's Failed Revolutions: From the Decembrists to the Dissidents* (New York: Basic Books, 1981).

10. See Svetlana Alliluyeva, *Only One Year* (New York: Harper and Row, 1969).

11. "Nechto o vran'ye," in Fedor M. Dostoevsky, *Polnoe sobranie sochinenii* (St. Petersburg: izd. A. F. Marksa, 1895), vol. 9, pp. 320–322 and 330. Dostoevsky noted that lying was largely a male phenomenon in Russia and that women were "more serious" and less likely to engage in it. See also Ronald Hingley, *The Russian Mind* (New York: Charles Scribner's Sons, 1977), pp. 90–104.

12. *Pravda*, 4 July 1990, p. 3.

13. Nicolas Berdyaev, *The Russian Idea*, p. 3.

14. These behavioral traits have been attributed originally to the traditional Russian patriarchal family, which is said to have bred tension between fathers and sons and to have produced a male personality type that was both domineering and servile in accordance with circumstances. Mood swings have also been seen as originating in the Russian child-rearing practice of swaddling, whereby infants experienced abrupt alternation of tight swaddling and complete restriction of movement with total absence of restraint. The swaddling hypothesis of Geoffrey Gorer emphasizes infant rage and destructive wishes due to swaddling that are said to result in diffuse guilt feelings, loneliness, and helplessness along with hostility. For a discussion of various theories of the Russian character, see J. S. Reshetar, Jr., *The Soviet Polity, Government and Politics in the USSR*, 3rd ed. (New York: Harper and Row, 1989), pp. 33–44.

15. On the usefulness of Lenin see Nina Tumarkin, *Lenin Lives: The Lenin Cult in Soviet Russia* (Cambridge: Harvard University Press, 1983).

16. I. V. Stalin, *Sochineniia*, vol. 12, pp. 369–370.

17. For an incisive discussion of the attractions and defects of Communist ideology, see Robert G. Wesson, *Why Marxism? The Continuing Success of a Failed Theory* (New York: Basic Books, 1976). See also Robert L. Heilbroner, *Marxism: For and Against* (New York: Norton, 1980).

18. *Pravda*, 26 February 1986.

B. Notes

19. *Izvestiia*, 26 July 1991, p. 2.

20. See Lennard D. Gerson, *The Secret Police in Lenin's Russia* (Philadelphia: Temple University Press, 1976) and George Leggett, *The Cheka: Lenin's Political Police* (Oxford: Clarendon Press, 1981).

21. See Robert Conquest, *The Great Terror; Stalin's Purges of the Thirties*, rev. ed. (New York: Macmillan, 1973).

22. For a concise account of Gorbachev's early career and rise to prominence see Zhores A. Medvedev, *Gorbachev* (Oxford: Basil Blackwell, 1986).

23. V. I. Lenin, *Polnoe sobranie sochinenii*, 5th ed. (Moscow: Gospolitizdat, 1962), vol. 34, p. 93. The term "partocracy" was apparently first applied to the Soviet polity by Abdurakhman Avtorkhanov. See his *Proiskhozhdenie partokratii* (Frankfurt am Main: Possev-Verlag, 1973), vol. 1, p. 21.

24. A. Petrushov, "Tainaia li kassa?" *Pravda*, 10 February 1989.

25. See Nikita S. Khrushchev, *Khrushchev Remembers* (Boston: Little Brown, 1970), pp. 17, 57, 182.

26. See reports by Francis X. Clines, *New York Times*, 13 and 18 December 1989.

27. See Christopher Andrew and Oleg Gordievsky, *The KGB: The Inside Story of Its Foreign Operations from Lenin to Gorbachev* (New York: Harper Collins, 1990), ch. 14.

28. The OMON (*otdely militsii osobogo naznacheniia*) militia units for special assignment were also known as the "black berets" and played a key role in the repressive operations of 1990–91.

29. The most flagrant case was that involving the Ukrainian parliamentary deputy Dr. Stepan Khmara, who was victimized in a police provocation in November 1990 and was not released until after the August 1991 coup. See *The Ukrainian Weekly*, 18 and 25 November 1990, 2 and 16 December 1990, 14 and 21 April 1991, and subsequent issues.

30. Gorbachev admitted that the leadership had underestimated the problems and had committed "miscalculations and errors" in undertaking *perestroika*, *Izvestiia*, 6 February 1990, p. 1.

31. In a visit to Vladivostok in 1986 he appealed for increased labor "discipline, responsibility, creativity, productivity" as the means of "unbinding our Soviet flywheel." *Pravda*, 27 July 1986, p. 1.

32. Gorbachev's and the Party's Russian "blind spots" on nationalities were evident in the Central Committee's platform adopted on 23 September 1989. It called for the "inter-national solidarity of the Soviet peoples," a "strong Union and strong republics," the "development of internationalist processes of mutual interaction of cultures," and "legal consolidation of the Russian language as the common state language." *Izvestiia*, 24 September 1989.

33. *Pravda*, 5 July 1990, p. 2. See also the interview with Ligachev in *U.S. News and World Report*, 22 October 1990, p. 50.

34. As reported to Serge Schmemann by an aide to Gorbachev, *New York Times*, 9 October 1989, p. A-6.

35. M. S. Gorbachev, *Perestroika i novoe myshlenie, dlia nashei strany i dlia vsego mira* (Moscow: Politizdat, 1987), pp. 32–33.

36. On the influence of Gorbachev's wife see the psychobiographical study by Gail Sheehy, *The Man Who Changed the World: The Lives of Mikhail S. Gorbachev* (New York: Harper Collins, 1990).

37. Serge Schmemann, "Gorbachev's Offensive: His Critics Are Denounced," *New York Times*, 28 February 1991.

38. Nathan Leites, *A Study of Bolshevism* (Glencoe, Ill.: The Free Press, 1953), pp. 215–225.

39. *New York Times*, 18 October 1990.

40. For Gorbachev's opposition to a multiparty system see his article in *Pravda*, 26 November 1989. Excerpts published in *New York Times*, 27 November 1989.

41. For evidence regarding the Russian Orthodox Moscow Patriarchate's dependence on Communist authorities and the role of the KGB in infiltrating the clergy see the open letter to Gorbachev signed by three priests and three deacons (dated 15 December 1988) in *Glasnost* (American edition), January–March 1990, pp. 25–27.

42. For the text of the new law on freedom of conscious and religious organizations, see *Izvestiia*, 9 October 1990, p. 3. Translated in *Current Digest of the Soviet Press*, vol. XLII, No. 40, 7 November 1990, pp. 6–8, 31.

43. It is revealing that Gorbachev administered to himself the presidential oath with his right hand on the constitution that he swore to uphold while having advocated its

replacement by a new document. See *New York Times,* 16 March 1990.

44. See the Credentials Commission report by B. V. Gidaspov, *Pravda,* 26 May 1989.

45. *Izvestiia,* 26 July 1991, p. 2.

46. *Pravda,* 27 February 1986, p. 3.

47. *New York Times,* 26 and 29 March 1991.

48. *Izvestiia,* 19 November 1990.

49. *New York Times,* 17 May 1990, report by Bill Keller on convoking of Russian Parliament.

50. "Don't Shoot," *Moscow News,* 27 January–3 February 1991, No. 4, p. 5.

51. "Obrashchenie k sovetskomu narodu," *Izvestiia,* No. 197, 20 August 1991. Another issue of *Izvestiia* (No. 198) of the same date was published by opponents of the coup as the regular evening edition and did not carry the plotters' appeal.

52. Serge Schmemann, "Soviet Hard-Liners Keep Up the Attack," *New York Times,* 25 June 1991.

53. See *Current Digest of the Soviet Press,* vol. XLIII, No. 31, 4 September 1991, pp. 19–20, 32.

54. See Melor Sturua, "The Coup's Ninth Man," *New York Times,* 22 August 1991. For Gorbachev's version, see his *The August Coup: The Truth and the Lessons* (New York: Harper Collins, 1991).

55. Gorbachev's law school classmate and long-time associate, Anatolii Lukianov was said to be implicated in the coup and did nothing to resist it; he allegedly signed papers, as chairman of the Supreme Soviet, supporting the coup. Anatolii Sobchak contended that Lukianov had manipulated the Supreme Soviet and its agenda in ways to mislead deputies and attempt to encourage their absence, especially in the six months prior to the coup, postponing voting until certain deputies were absent and ensuring a manipulated debate and a favorable vote. See *New York Times,* 27 August 1991.

56. As reported in the published transcript in the *New York Times,* 24 August 1991.

57. The text of the "new union treaty" was published in *Izvestiia,* 15 August 1991.

58. The results of the Soviet Union's first referendum are discussed in *Referendum in the Soviet Union, A Compendium of Reports on the March 17, 1991 Referendum on the Future of the U.S.S.R.,* compiled by the staff of the Commission on Security and Cooperation in Europe (Washington, D.C.: U.S. Government Printing Office, 1991).

59. "Soiuznyi dogovor otkryt k podpisaniiu," *Izvestiia,* 3 August 1991.

60. See transcript in *New York Times,* 24 August 1991.

61. See transcript excerpts in *New York Times,* 4 September 1991.

C. Notes

62. Charles E. Bohlen, U.S. ambassador to the Soviet Union (1953–1957), contended that President Franklin D. Roosevelt's "greatest single mistake . . . was his insistence on the doctrine of unconditional surrender which . . . probably lengthened the war by convincing the Germans they should fight on . . ." Charles E. Bohlen, *Witness to History, 1929–1969* (New York: Norton, 1973), p. 212.

63. *The Programme of the Communist Party of the Soviet Union, A New Edition* (Moscow: Novosti, 1986), p. 18.

64. *Pravda,* 26 February 1988 (italics in original).

65. *Pravda,* 26 February 1986.

66. Izvestiia, 6 February 1990.

67. Strobe Talbott, *The Russians and Reagan* (New York: Random House, 1984), pp. 116–117. The text of the speech delivered before the convention of the National Association of Evangelicals is reproduced on pp. 105–118.

68. Soviet foreign minister Shevardnadze conceded in October 1989 that Soviet intervention in Afghanistan had been a mistake and that "we had set ourselves against all of humanity, violated norms of behavior, ignored universal human values." He revealed that the crucial decision had not been discussed in the Politburo but was "made behind the back of the party and people." He also conceded that the Soviet leadership had lied regarding the Krasnoiarsk radar facility in claiming that this structure ("the size of an Egyptian pyramid") was for "space research" and not a

violation of the 1972 Anti-Ballistic Missile Treaty. *New York Times*, 25 October 1989.

69. See Jan Winiecki, *The Distorted World of Soviet-Type Economies* (Pittsburgh: University of Pittsburgh Press, 1988).

70. *Izvestiia*, 6 February 1990, p. 2.

71. *Izvestiia*, 1 July 1988.

72. *Pravda*, 26 June 1987.

73. *Ibid.* See also Vladimir G. Treml, *Alcohol in the USSR: A Statistical Study* (Durham, N.C.: Duke University Press, 1982).

74. *Izvestiia*, 29 June 1988. Evidence regarding Soviet budget deficits was first uncovered by the former Soviet economist and CPSU member Igor Birman in *Secret Incomes of the Soviet State Budget* (The Hague and Boston: Martinus Nijhoff, 1981).

75. *Izvestiia*, 29 June 1988.

76. *Izvestiia*, 30 June 1988.

77. *Izvestiia*, 2 July 1988, as reported by Fedor Morgun, chairman of the U.S.S.R. State Committee for Preservation of the Environment.

78. In Chapter 3, Section 1 of *State and Revolution*. See also Robert C. Tucker, ed., *The Lenin Anthology* (New York: W. W. Norton, 1975), p. 337.

79. *Izvestiia*, 2 July 1988.

80. The late Max Hayward of Oxford University characterized the U.S.S.R. as "a grotesque conglomerate for which the main raison d'être is a concept of imperial defense inherited from the Tsars." Foreword to *Ferment in the Ukraine*, ed. by Michael Browne (New York: Praeger, 1971), p. xi.

81. Aleksandr Solzhenitsyn, *The Mortal Danger: How Misconceptions About Russia Imperil America*, 2nd ed. (New York: Harper and Row, 1981), pp. 28 and 109.

82. Aleksandr Solzhenitsyn, ed., *From Under the Rubble* (Boston: Little, Brown, 1975).

83. Aleksandr Solzhenitsyn, *Letter to the Soviet Leaders* (New York: Harper and Row, 1974), p. 41.

84. Laurie Hays, "Soviets Tackle Mystery of Party's Hoard," *Wall Street Journal*, 15 October 1991, p. A-13.

85. Izvestiia, 9 December 1991, p. 1.

86. Gorbachev, even after the August coup, spoke of "Russia's unifying mission." *New York Times*, 24 August 1991.

CHAPTER 8

The Government of China

James D. Seymour

A. Political Development

China is the world's most populous nation-state, and the oldest surviving civilization. In 1912 the imperial system was replaced by a republic (which today survives only on Taiwan). In 1949 the People's Republic of China (PRC) came into existence, embracing almost all of the old empire.

At first glance, political organization in the PRC seems to resemble that which used to exist in the Soviet Union. On closer inspection, however, Chinese politics proves to be unique. Part of the explanation for why Soviet-style institutions were something of a misfit is found in China's cultural legacy.

HISTORY

Few of the world's peoples are as conscious of their history as the Chinese are. It is not uncommon for spokespersons for a particular political position to argue their case by writing historical exegeses that make no explicit reference to the issues at hand. There are several explanations for this curious practice. First, if a proponent's position is subsequently deemed heretical, the sanctions are apt to be lighter if one has refrained from naming names and discussing issues in a manner overt enough to excite public opinion. Perhaps Confucian bureaucrats had similar practicalities in mind when they engaged in the same

peculiar historicism. The effect then, as now, was to make a knowledge of Chinese history essential to anyone who would participate in or study Chinese politics. In China, as elsewhere, history has its unconscious legacy. Political traditions shape political behavior to a much greater extent than the participants are aware. Institutions can be modified or abandoned, but predispositions to behavior are not so easily changed. To understand the Chinese revolution of the mid-twentieth century, one must understand the legacy that the revolutionaries were trying to overthrow.

During the first millennium B.C., there emerged in China a kind of feudalism similar to the feudalism of Europe's Middle Ages. But a number of the small kingdoms that comprised the "China" of that era were remarkably modern. There were legal codes, sophisticated monetized economies with such institutions as ever-normal granaries, and impressive irrigation and flood-control systems. Some states—particularly the Qin (pronounced "Chin," from which the name China is derived)—emphasized militarism, and it was the Qin who subdued the other kingdoms in 221 B.C. and established the empire as a unitary state.

The short-lived Qin regime was probably as close to being totalitarian as any that the world would see until the twentieth century.

Chinese names and terms are generally spelled according to the *pin-yin* system. Though this system is fairly straightforward, there are a few pitfalls. The most notable of these are the following:

Chinese	English equivalent
q	ch
x	sh
c	ts

The first emperor was able to mobilize the population to build roads, canals, and the precursor of what might be considered the world's biggest monument—the Great Wall. To this day the Chinese debate whether the results justified the sacrifice and suffering, and the argument has important implications for contemporary policy makers. At the end of the third century B.C. there was a general consensus that the answer to this question was no. After a brief return to feudalism, China developed a new form of polity based loosely on the teachings of Confucius, a sage who had lived centuries earlier.

The Confucian order, especially if we separate it analytically from the Qin legacy and later alien influences, was notable for its civility (as opposed to militarism) and humanism (as opposed to both spiritualism and materialism). A milieu was created within which a vast land mass could retain its cultural integrity until modern times. The flourishing of the arts and letters has been, at least in longevity, unequaled elsewhere. It is difficult to imagine Tang poets, Sung artists, or even Mongol-era playwrights being so creative had there been a less ordered environment, and it is equally difficult to imagine the artistic continuity with the past exhibited during the later Ming and Manchu periods if social and political institutions had been less enduring.

Confucian civility and humanism were both the great strengths and the fatal weaknesses of the old order; and they were not the whole story of Chinese politics. The Qin authoritarian legacy never died, and Confucianism was further compromised by alien influences, which usually had a militarizing influence. It should also be pointed out that China was often torn by disunity and even civil war, which took a dreadful toll in human suffering. This was a problem for which Confucianism had only vague answers. The civil strife that occurred when Confucian institutions broke down has been an important part of the national memory and goes a long way toward explaining the Chinese people's fear of chaos and willingness to accept strong centralized government.

Despite occasional compromises, Confucianism remained the ideal by which, until this century, most politically aware Chinese preferred to be governed. We shall have more to say about Confucianism in our discussion of political culture. For now, let us simply note certain aspects of "traditional" Chinese politics that tended to differentiate the nation from other premodern polities. These aspects relate to the questions of personalization and equality.

The terms "personalized" and "depersonalized" refer to the extent to which politics is a function of the will of individual leaders. In a modern polity, leaders' actions are circumscribed by legal (constitutional) constraints and by the expectations and wishes of other people (ideally, we may say, by public opinion). If the ruler is deemed the personification of the state, or if he assumes a godlike aura, he is thereby detaching himself from such social constraints. In this sense, before the second century B.C. China was unmodern, for rulers generally claimed either to be divine or at least literally responsible to ancestral deities. But after the second century B.C., Chinese government tended to be secular. Furthermore, most political offices were filled by nonascriptive means; recruitment was on the basis of performance (in examinations) rather than birthright or other ascriptive considerations. This was not quite true of the emperor, but theoretically even the imperial family could lose the "mandate of heaven" if it failed to govern wisely. Thus, unlike Japan, China has been ruled by many different dynasties (see Table 8.1). A ruling house did not even have to be racially Chinese to be legitimate; the last dynasty, which reigned from 1644 to 1911, was Manchu.

Although no one would argue that this traditional system resulted in an egalitarian society, when it came to politics there was in theory (and to some extent in practice) equality of opportunity. The nation was administered by a class of scholars, and every farmer's son was supposed to have a fair opportunity to enter that class. In fact, although he could sit for the requisite examinations, a family usually needed to be relatively affluent before a boy could be spared from labor so that he could put in the many necessary years of study. Moreover, half of the population was excluded from the system by virtue of sex, and others because they belonged to one of the less respected professions (such as merchant, artisan, doctor, and monk). Nonetheless, the examination system weeded out many incompetents and provided for the entry of new blood into the elite.

The Confucian sociopolitical system functioned (with occasional interruptions) for two thousand years, but was found wanting when modern imperialism threatened the nation's integrity. From the mid-nineteenth century until the mid-twentieth century, China became a battleground for a bewildering array of forces—reactionaries, moderate reformers, liberal modernizers, Marxist revolutionaries, foreigners, and (most commonly) regional warlords. In the 1930s the imbroglio sorted itself out somewhat, with the conservative Nationalists (Kuomintang) and the Communists entering into an uneasy alliance against Japan, the most persistent and brutal of the imperialist nations. But immediately after World War II, the former allies embarked on a civil war which the corrupt Nationalists were morally and materially ill-equipped to fight. In 1949, they retreated to Taiwan.

When the Communists came to power, China became truly unified for the first time in decades. Now the state included colonial areas such as Tibet, and was called a people's republic. Its undisputed leader was the man who had led the Red Army to victory, Mao Zedong. A war-weary people were eager to accept almost any authority that could restore order. Some people, such as the poorer farmers, eagerly embraced Communist rule. Others, such as affluent farmers, business people, and intellectuals were often hesitant, though still unresisting. The new leaders moved slowly at first. Permanent governmental institutions were not established for some time, and initial economic reforms were usually moderate in scope (but not in the methods by which they were carried out). An umbrella organ, the Chinese People's Political Consultative Conference, was established to provide a forum in which various political and cultural groups could listen, though not necessarily be heard. The smaller nationalities occupying vast areas of the hinterland were promised autonomy, at least to the extent of retaining their own cultures. Overseas Chinese were urged to return and help build the new China, and many did. Thus, in reintegrating Chinese society, the Communists sought to embrace and

Table 8.1 MAJOR PERIODS IN CHINESE HISTORY

Zhou Dynasty	B.C. 1122–255
Qin Dynasty	255–206
Han Dynasty	B.C. 206–221 A.D.
Period of disunion	221–589
Tang Dynasty	618–907
Song Dynasty	951–1280
Period of Mongol rule	1280–1368
Ming Dynasty	1368–1644
Period of Manchu Rule	1644–1911
Republic	1912–1949
People's Republic	1949–

utilize a broad spectrum of the Chinese populace.

Soon, however, it was determined that some elements were unsuitable for integration into the new order because of their anachronistic political and social attitudes. The Chinese Communists had never been liberals (despite sounding so on occasion), and they were not about to permit any obstacles to stand in their way as they pressed forward with their revolution. So, in the early 1950s they began "reeducating" intellectuals; the recalcitrant were sometimes subjected to the sophisticated (and often ruthless) psychological techniques of brainwashing. Non-Communist organizations (churches, political parties, and the like) were reorganized and placed under the direct control of the Communist party's United Front Department. Farmers, notwithstanding widespread enthusiasm for the recent land reform program, gradually underwent obligatory collectivization—first with the formation of small mutual aid teams, then cooperatives, then larger collective farms, and eventually (in 1958) vast communes. In the cities, businesses and labor unions were placed under the supervision of the party, and a pervasive system of social controls was established in all neighborhoods. During the first half of the 1950s, the new regime obviously feared its opponents—both the bourgeoisie and "feudal" landlord elements at home and the foreign enemy, the United States, which seemed to be pressing on China militarily from the northeast (Korea), the east (Taiwan), and possibly the south (Vietnam).

By the middle of the decade, the Beijing (Peking) government became somewhat more relaxed. The Korean war had ended, the Vietnam question appeared settled, and it was clear that the United States would not participate in any effort by the Chinese Nationalists to invade the mainland. At home, the rocky road to a new order seemed to have been traversed successfully. In 1954 a national constitution was proclaimed and the structure of government was finally settled. In 1956 the Communist party held its Eighth Congress, declared that socialism had been basically achieved, and drew up new bylaws for the party itself. More and more, the People's Republic of China was appearing to emulate the Soviet Union, with a dual bureaucracy (party and government), centralized economy, and strict social controls.

But in 1956 Mao Zedong decided that the severe restrictions on intellectual and political life were excessive and counterproductive. He reasoned that the counterrevolutionaries had been safely eliminated from the political scene, and assumed that everyone else accepted the new order. Mao concluded that it would be healthy if people could more freely air their views and even criticize the Communist party. He thus called for a "blooming of the Hundred Flowers" (an allusion to a period of intellectual ferment in ancient times). People were initially reluctant to speak out, but in the spring of 1957 attacks on party policies came in torrents. Astounded, Mao called an end to the Hundred Flowers and ordered a rectification campaign against "bourgeois rightists"— the liberal professionals on whom he had been counting to modernize China. As a result, further serious modernization efforts would be almost impossible until after Mao's death in 1976.

Disillusioned with the experts, Mao turned to the men and women of solid political background (the "reds"). They were to lead the masses in a Great Leap Forward (1958–1960), in which human will was supposed to overcome harsh economic reality. Through such institutions as the communes, in which all the energies of the people would be mobilized in a diffuse fashion without the limitations of functional specialization, pure communism would be attained even sooner than had been projected. Unfortunately, it all collapsed because of inadequate planning, poor understanding of economics, and bad weather. (After Mao's death, the Great Leap would officially be declared a failure, owing to "smugness" on the part of the men who had then led China.)

China now underwent the Three Bad Years (1960–1962), during which perhaps 40 million starved to death. To save the situation, the communes were reorganized and decentralized, with greater reward allowed for individual initiative. Although the professional class remained repressed (largely in prison camps), the authority of the party hierarchy, which had been tarnished during the Leap Forward, was restored.

This reconstruction phase lasted through 1965 and was a period of notable successes in improved living standards. However, Mao Zedong and certain of his comrades (including his wife Jiang Qing and Defense Minister Lin Biao) sensed other dangers. These leaders did not want the new order to mean that people were simply comfortable and well fed. And they certainly did not want a situation in which the party elite only filled the roles of the former mandarins, which would mean that there had been no social revolution. Tension over this and other issues increased until the end of 1965, when China erupted in a Great Proletarian Cultural Revolution—Mao's answer to embourgeoisement, bureaucratism, and the decline of public spiritedness. Having reached the sad conclusion that the new institutions and modes of production were insufficient for achieving his larger purposes, he virtually reversed some basic Marxist principles regarding the relation between the *base* (class control of the means of production) and the *superstructure* (culture and institutions). Mao now believed that a successful revolution would have to attack the flaws of Chinese culture directly—both those deficiencies which had ancient roots and those which had emerged under the aegis of the party elite.

The politics of the Cultural Revolution were highly complex, with shifting alliances and a bewildering array of issues. To oversimplify a bit: By the mid-1960s, two of the various social groups had become highly competitive. The old-line civil war participants and their offspring were finding themselves severely challenged by middle-class elements, especially well-educated youths. There was also a third group of people who believed they spoke for the underprivileged. These "leftists" sought to destroy the influence of the other two groups, who were seen as enjoying undeserved privileges and lacking revolutionary spirit. Officially, the Cultural Revolution is said to have lasted a full decade—until the death of Mao in 1976—but its most intense phase lasted only until 1969. Between 1966 and 1968 most of the party regulars were removed from the political scene. As many as half a million people lost their lives, including chief of state Liu Shaoqi, who for two decades had been the number two figure in the Chinese Communist movement.

Even with Liu out of the way, the Cultural Revolution did not unfold exactly according to Mao's expectations. First, there was stiff resistance from party regulars; for a while in early 1967 it appeared that they might be gaining the upper hand. They did not, but soon a setback resulted from another development: the falling out between Mao and his most important supporter, Defense Minister Lin Biao. In 1971, Lin allegedly tried to assassinate Mao and stage a coup d'état. When these efforts failed, and Lin died in a plane crash trying to escape, there followed an astonishing series of campaigns against Mao's opponents. The People's Liberation Armed Services (PLA) were occasionally able to prevent developments from getting too far out of control, but only after Mao's death did Chinese politics return to anything resembling normal order. By this time, the old-line Communists and middle-class intellectuals had forgotten their old enmity in the face of a nearly devastating challenge from the Left. A new era was dawning, during which China would be dominated by two formerly-hostile groups: the old-line Communists and all but the most liberal intellectuals.

The net effect of the Ten Catastrophic Years (1966–1976) was twofold. First, it involved almost unimaginable human suffering. Although official Chinese statistics have been unreliable, they suggest that Lin Biao and the radicals were responsible for "torturing to death" 34,274 men and women and "persecuting" about 700,000 others. These figures only begin to tell the story of Chinese suffering and agony during those years. When it was all over, millions of outcasts had to have their citizenship restored; many could only be rehabilitated posthumously. Second, the Cultural Revolution meant a further setback for efforts to modernize China. During this period, most educated people were at the very least under a cloud, and what was left of the professional class (after the earlier Hundred Flowers debacle) was largely confined to prison camps or otherwise neutralized. The remainder of the population was either promoting revolution or trying to survive by avoiding involvement. As the economic situation grew increasingly desperate, party regulars and technocrats could only wait things out.

The world has rarely seen domestic politics played out in a more violent manner than during the Cultural Revolution in China. Many attribute this phenomenon to flaws in Chinese culture, for it was not the first instance of internal political violence. Others, however, argue that one need look no further than Mao's policies. The promotion of class struggle, the replacing of individualism with state-sponsored patronage, and the pattern of often hysterical political campaigns set the stage for tragic events.[1]

The demise of Lin Biao caused the nation to undergo much soul-searching. In many parts of the country small opposition groups formed, often comprised of urban youth who had been discarded to the countryside. They asked how there could have been such chaos in the nation's top leadership. Although these free thinkers were rooted out and often executed by the police in "class-cleansing" campaigns, this was the beginning of a disillusionment that would ultimately lead to a full-blown democracy movement.

By the beginning of 1974, events seemed to be turning in favor of party regulars. Former party secretary-general Deng Xiaoping, the number two target during the early years of the Cultural Revolution, was "rehabilitated" (his good name was restored) and regained much of his former authority. In 1975 he became chief of staff of the PLA. Because the armed services were the only institutions that remained intact, this appointment was notable—though it was not sufficient to protect Deng from leftist onslaughts. It was probably the skillful and relatively pragmatic premier Zhou Enlai who engineered the shift toward moderation. But Zhou was dying, and with his demise in January 1976 the political winds reverted. Deng Xiaoping was again stripped of all his party and government posts, and Hua Guofeng was named premier. Mao died on 10 September 1976, after allegedly saying to Hua, "With you in charge, my heart is at ease." Accordingly, Hua became chairman of the Chinese Communist party.

The question of who would run the country, however, could not be determined quite so easily. A power struggle ensued between leftists and moderates, and Hua, who had been a relatively junior member of the political hierarchy, lacked sufficient clout even to be an effective power broker. Deng and his followers, backed by the military, were able to arrest the leading leftists (Jiang Qing, Wang Hongwen, Yao Wenyuan, and Zhang Chunqiao), whom they now dubbed "The Gang of Four." Political power was back in the hands of the surviving moderates and party regulars, who used their regained monopoly over the media to vilify the leftists as the latter had so long done to them.

Deng Xiaoping undertook an ambitious plan to restore the damage wrought by the Cultural Revolution, and sought to make China a modernized nation by the turn of the century. His program is summed up in the expression "Four Modernizations," three of which were primarily economic: industrialization, improvements in agriculture, and scientific and technological advancement. (The fourth, military modernization, was not emphasized until the early 1990s.) This "modernization" sounded bourgeois and regressive to the conservatives (leftists), but by now they had been temporarily silenced. Most of the nation doubtless welcomed the change—as far as it went.

Some people, especially young intellectuals, hoped that the country's politics would become more open and democratic under Deng Xiaoping. During the late 1970s he seemed to promise this, for he tolerated (and sometimes encouraged) democratic activists' criticism of errant officials—at least if these officials happened to be Deng's enemies. During the winter of 1978–1979 there was a flourishing of activity by democratic activists in many cities. They pasted up posters in such places as Beijing's famous Xidan Democracy Wall, and published many crudely printed journals. Some of the activists were militant. One of the more brilliant, a young worker named Wei Jingsheng, published essays claiming that Deng's modernization scheme, being largely limited to the economic sphere, was lacking something essential. Wei insisted that the "new autocracy" that Deng Xiaoping was imposing on the nation was incompatible with true modernization. What China really needed, he wrote, was a *fifth* modernization, namely, political modernization, leading to democracy. Unfortunately, such democrats soon discovered that Deng would not tolerate this kind of dissent; the democratic movement was repressed, and its leaders were imprisoned. However, their ideas had a lasting impact, even on some people in the Communist Party.

Deng Xiaoping moved more cautiously against his opponents on the left. Although the Gang of Four and a few others were imprisoned, many leftists remained quietly in office, especially at the lower levels, where they continued to rule their communities and resist implementing reform. At the national level their influence was declining, but they remained a threat to the pragmatists. In 1987 they helped to oust party secretary-general Hu Yaobang, whom even many nonleftists considered too liberal; Hu had tolerated dissent on the part of intellectuals and failed to crack down on student demonstrations.

Hu Yaobang was succeeded by another pragmatic reformer, Zhao Ziyang. Zhao's rise to power had been the result of his earlier successful implementation of reforms in Sichuan province, a potentially productive area ravaged by the excesses of the Cultural Revolution. But not everyone wanted such reforms extended to the whole country, because they were based on free market economics. Therefore, conservatives pressed (successfully) for the selection of the Soviet-educated Li Peng as premier. Li was less enthusiastic than Zhao about any bold moves toward a decentralized or market-oriented economy. In 1988 Zhao was forced to largely abandon his economic liberalization, and instead began promoting *political* reforms, backed by a group of prominent intellectuals, that would have stripped the powerful gerontocracy of much of their power. There was also a reassessment of Mao, whose reign was now deemed "a historical tragedy."[2] But Zhao's reforms were too radical for the conservatives, and too timid to satisfy much of the public.

The spring of 1989 brought a dramatic series of developments. In early April Hu Yaobang attempted a comeback. He was able to attend a Politburo meeting on April 8, at which he reportedly got into a heated argument with one of the conservatives and was stricken by a fatal heart attack. Hu's death provided an excuse for large numbers of "mourners" to stage what were in reality a series of protest demonstrations against inflation, corruption, official profiteering, and the lack of political freedom. These protests were followed by similar demonstrations in many other cities. On May 14, about 2000 Beijing students began a hunger strike, and crowds grew to the millions. The outside world watched it all on television, and many Chinese followed events by listening to mysteriously unjammed foreign shortwave broadcasts. Reactionary editorials in the party newspaper *People's Daily*

failed to cow the people, and indeed only provoked them.

Meanwhile, the authorities were biding
their time. It took weeks for the hard-liners
to consolidate their position and find troops
who were willing to restore "order." Li Peng
even held a televised "dialogue" with student
leaders. But by May 19, Zhao, who was now
hopelessly outvoted in the Politburo, realized
that the cause of moderation was lost. The
next day an estimated 2 million people demonstrated in Beijing in support of the students
at Tiananmen (pronounced Tien ahn mun)

Square. That is a vast plaza surrounded by government buildings, Mao's mausoleum, and the
former imperial palace. (See photograph, page
468.) Perhaps it was only a desperate tactic to
improve his personal political fortunes, but
Zhao paid several sympathetic visits to hunger
strikers there, lamenting at one point that he
had come "too late." It was indeed too late for
him (he was abruptly dismissed by Deng Xiaoping), and it was also too late for the demonstrating students and workers, many hundreds
of whom were slaughtered in the early hours of
June 4 (virtually all well away from Tiananmen

During the 1989 crackdown on demonstrators, the world was captivated by the image of a young Beijing man
(identity still uncertain) bringing a column of tanks to a halt. The authorities claimed that this demonstrated
their restraint, but to most it reflected citizen bravery in the face of official violence.

Feature 8.1 **PRC International Relations**

1950	Sino-Soviet Alliance; China enters Korean War against United Nations forces.
1953	Korean War armistice.
1958	Shelling of Chinese Nationalists on Quemoy Island ends, after which relative peace in Taiwan Straits prevails.
1959	Tibetans revolt against Chinese rule; Dalai Lama flees to India.
1960	Open break with U.S.S.R.; Soviet advisors withdraw from China.
1962	Border war with India.
1964	China explodes atomic bomb.
1965	Outer Tibet declared "autonomous region" of China. U.S. CIA assistance to Tibetan resistance begins to wind down.
1966	Beginning of period of xenophobia and national isolation associated with Cultural Revolution, but support promised for North Vietnam in war.
1971	Bejing government gains UN seat.
1972	President Richard Nixon visits China, marking beginning of (informal) U.S.-PRC relations. Many countries subsequently establish diplomatic relations with Bejing.
1980s	Decade of economic and political opening to West and Japan.
1989	Soviet leader Gorbachev visits Bejing, marking improved relations. West/Japan impose economic sanctions on PRC in wake of June 4 Massacre.
1991	Anti-"peaceful evolution" campaign implies resistance to foreign influences on China.
1992	Most countries drop sanctions against China; Li Peng makes world tour, marking normalization of foreign relations.

Square, contrary to popular belief). There followed thousands of arrests and perhaps hundreds of executions, as well as a nationwide propaganda campaign to attempt to persuade the Chinese people that it had all been a "counterrevolutionary revolt." Many escaped the net by means of an "underground railroad," which enabled some democratic leaders to reach the West via Hong Kong.

The old guard had difficulty agreeing on the selection of a new secretary-general to replace Zhao. Finally, Deng put forward the name of a compromise candidate, a Soviet-educated engineer named Jiang Zemin. As

the mayor of China's largest city, Shanghai, Jiang had managed to suppress the democracy movement in a less bloody manner than had the leaders in Beijing. Although an advocate of economic reform, politically he proved to be the hardest of the hardliners. There was hardly a pretense of gaining popular support. In the ensuing years the leadership launched two campaigns to impress upon the public the folly of opposing the Communist party. One was a campaign against the "bourgeois liberalization," i.e., the values of Tiananmen-era demonstrators. The second was opposed to "peaceful evolution." (This term originated with John Foster Dulles, U.S. Secretary of State in the 1950s, who predicted that Communist societies would peacefully evolve into democratic ones with market economies.) Conservatives also attempted to "reverse the verdict" on the Cultural Revolution and improve the images of Mao Zedong and Lin Biao, but the idea did not sit well with those, including Deng Xiaoping, who had suffered during that period.

For a brief review of Chinese international relations, see Feature 8.1.

ECOLOGY

Probably the most serious problem facing China's rulers has to do with demographics. The issue is not so much that the country contains so many people (conservatively put at 1.13 billion in 1990) as that so little of the land will produce food. The population has been growing at a rate of 1.48 percent a year which, although low by third world standards, is high when translated into absolute numbers. Partly because much former farmland has been converted to residential or industrial uses, the amount of arable land per capita is now about one-half what it was in 1949. China, with almost one-quarter of the world's population, has only 5 percent of its arable land—a mere third of an acre per capita. This presents the nation with tremendous economic and ecological problems.

These difficulties have been exacerbated by the Mao-era policies. Following the 1949 revolution, the government adhered to the orthodox doctrine that a Socialist society (by definition) could not suffer from overpopulation, which was seen as a problem unique to capitalism. However, the census of 1953–1954 revealed that the country had a far greater population than had been assumed, and after much debate the pronatalist policies were reversed. Laws that had prohibited abortion and sterilization were repealed, and birth control was promoted by the media and by local organizations established for the purpose. Such programs have been promoted ever since, with the important exceptions of China's two most radical periods—the Great Leap Forward and the Cultural Revolution. During the Great Leap, the leadership accepted the claim of some Marxists that production could always be kept ahead of population growth. In 1962 a new birth control campaign was undertaken, only to be abandoned during the Cultural Revolution. Since then, however, family planning has been given a high priority in the nation's agenda, and in 1982 the practice of birth control even became a constitutional obligation.

To deal with overpopulation, major efforts have been made to persuade often skeptical couples to be satisfied with only one child, even a girl.

General population-control guidelines are laid down in Beijing, and each neighborhood is required to adhere to them. A group of families is required to decide among themselves who may have babies and whose turn it is to have one in any given year. Couples commonly find themselves limited to a single child. The authority of the state thus reaches into the most sensitive area of people's lives. Not only are birth-control devices free and widely available, but there is much political and social pressure on people to limit fertility. Single-child families are often encouraged by means of financial incentives and disincentives. In some cases women have been obliged (occasionally even forced) to have abortions, and there appears to be some discrimination in education and health care against children from large families. In the countryside, the population-control efforts have been much less successful than in the cities, and in 1988 the government modified the rural one-child policy in cases where the first-born is a girl.

As a result, although China's population growth is under better control than is the case in many third world countries, the average couple has more than double the "ideal" (and usually legal) limit of one child per family. Although hard-liners in the party favor drastic measures to check population growth, their implementation would only cause further political disaffection, especially in rural areas.

Overpopulation is related to a variety of environmental problems, including pollution, flooding, and resource exhaustion. Centuries ago China was largely covered with forests, but the timberlands have been disappearing at an accelerating rate. The authorities are rightly alarmed, but appear powerless to control the situation. Each year millions of cubic meters of lumber are taken illegally, wasting wood and soil and causing devastating floods.[3] There are sound ways of preventing such problems, but environmentalists have little influence in the higher political circles. As a result, environmental policies tend to deal with the symptoms rather than the causes.

SOCIETY

Despite some disagreement, Western scholars generally agree that traditional Chinese society was neither as rigid and exploitative as China's present leaders insist, nor as idyllic and opportunity-laden as exiled defenders of the old order claim. It was a society in which each person was born to a certain class and role. There was some social fluidity, but not much more than was required to maintain the overall social order. Without being replenished by new talent, the scholar gentry could not have survived as a class, and therefore it was possible for a tiny percentage of peasant boys to enter the gentry. In order to advance, however, a boy had to be the personification of traditional Confucian ideals; there could be no startling new ideas or obstreperous behavior toward elders. Still, Chinese society was not as illiberal as some traditional societies. There were escapes for the alienated, such as retreating to a Taoist monastery. Furthermore, gay people were well tolerated until relatively modern times.[4]

Thus, China had a fairly rigid class society. We will use the term "class" not in the Marxist sense, but in a somewhat loose sociological sense. Marxists traditionally consider that a person's class is defined by his or her relationship to the means of production. As we have noted, however, traditional China's gentry gained their status at least in part by virtue of their mastery of learning. The common people did not comprise a homogeneous group, and among them there was little cohesion. (Sun Yat-sen, the founder of the Chinese Republic in 1911, described Chinese society as a sheet of loose sand.) The same probably held true within each stratum. An analysis of Tianjin concludes that at least in that city, prerevolutionary society was extremely fragmented, which precluded not only transcendent civic consciousness but also class identities.[5] Thus, Marxist theory notwithstanding, as the Chinese Communists struggled for power they were not able to rely on the urban proletariat. Nor were the peasants particularly reliable as allies—they were as conservative in China as elsewhere. Indeed, after the Communists came to power (more by military than political means), they virtually had to create classes before they could wage the kind of class struggle deemed necessary. To some extent it was an artificial process, and by the 1990s "class struggle" had become essentially an empty term, used only by conservatives (leftists) as a tool for opposing reformers. But for many years, a person's class had important implications. If, before 1949, one's parents belonged to a "good" class (worker, poor peasant, or revolutionary) one's own class was "good." Likewise, "bad" class status (capitalists, rich peasants, landlords, dissidents) was hereditary.

Since the mid-1970s there has been an effort to deemphasize these class designations, especially for the second generation. No longer is upward mobility dependent upon political loyalty and "good" class background. Indeed, *People's Daily* declared that it is now proper to address as "comrade" former capitalists, industrialists, and intellectuals if they are now serving socialism. The paper urged that everyone be treated "equally and without discrimination." (After falling into disuse in the 1980s, the authorities have been trying to promote the use of "comrade." It is now commonly heard on television. However, many still eschew the term, which has a highly partisan and pseudo-egalitarian ring to it.)

Farmers

Of China's three social categories—workers, intellectuals, and peasants—the latter is the largest. Until recently, membership in one of these groups was usually determined at birth on the basis of inheritance from one's *mother.* It was possible for a young farmer to graduate to the "intellectual" category or to become a peasant soldier, but such steps were exceptional (almost unheard-of for women), and most young intellectuals have grown up in intellectual families. Transfer from peasant to worker status—or even moving out of one's *father's* village—was nearly impossible. Even if one engaged in nonagricultural labor, a "peasant" remained officially that. In short, until recently China had a rigid, legally enforced, status-based society.

There were problems with this system. For one thing, it was very unpopular, which mattered now that China was no longer totalitarian (as some argue was the case in the 1950s). Furthermore, although China had managed to avoid the overurbanization that afflicted so much of the third world, it had done so at the price of overpopulation in the countryside and widespread underemployment and poverty there. Thus, beginning in 1984 villagers were permitted to move to towns, where they enjoyed dual worker-peasant status. They still were not given ration coupons, so the arrangement was practical primarily for the more affluent farmers (who could bring food from their villages or buy it in the town's free market). Moreover, the immigrants were supposed to have skills and be able to hold a job (though by 1987 the richest could often simply purchase urban resident status). With these modest relaxations, the size of the towns grew phenomenally, often quickly doubling. Peasants also immigrated illegally into the larger cities, which had 80 million sojourners in 1990. Such people are often looked down upon by the more "sophisticated" urbanites, and are sometimes subjected to physical abuse by civilians and even by police. In only a few years China's urban-rural population ratio changed from 1:5 to roughly 1:2. As the number of country-to-city migrants grows, the economic, social, and political problems they present grow also. The huge "floating population," all living "outside the system," has exacerbated the already acute urban housing shortage. (In Shanghai, there are only four square meters of housing space per capita.) The authorities are therefore trying to manage China's urbanization by confining growth to the small and medium-sized cities. Still, China is seeing massive upward social mobility from peasant status to the much coveted worker status.

While the old static-residency system may seem unappealing to Westerners, it is possible that the Chinese, with their strong group affiliation, had less tendency to resist it. China historically has been a highly family-oriented society. Traditionally, "family" has meant the extended family rather than the nuclear family, and this is still somewhat true in rural China.[6] Confucianism raised the family to the status of a sacred institution. The ideal family was large—multigenerational and multibranch, housed together in a single compound. In practice, economics made such a family exceptional. The typical traditional Chinese family was probably much like the family today—that is, a three-generation "stem family," with an older couple living with one married child (probably a son) and grandchildren. At any rate, early fears that the Communists would destroy the family were unwarranted. Although steps were taken against the institution of lineage (clan), they never seriously contemplated abolishing the family. Around 1958 there was some talk about establishing homes for the aged, but these now generally house only people who have no relatives with whom they could live. Indeed, Article 13 of the 1950 marriage law makes it a duty for adults to support their parents. Thus, the most important change the Communists wrought is that the family's main external link is no longer to collateral branches (the lineage), but to the community (state).

Village society has undergone many changes since the revolution. Today we can say that a typical village has four status groups. First are the cadres and former cadres. (A "cadre" is a person who has authority over other citizens.) Although these men and women, who may or may not be party members, comprise a privileged group in Chinese society, we shall see later that their lot has not been an altogether easy one. Next are ordinary farmers—those who engage directly in dirt farming or some other kind of man-

ual labor related to agriculture. Third is a category known as the "Four Types," which includes relatives of cadres, nonagricultural workers, military officers, and teachers. Finally there are "bad elements," usually meaning the families of formerly well-to-do farmers or landlords. These families were subject to severe discrimination during the Mao years.

Workers

Until recent years, urban workers were the political backbone of the Communist party. They were treated as a privileged group, more "advanced" (and more politically reliable) than farmers, whose land had been taken from them. Although workers were not well paid, they usually enjoyed absolute economic security. By the late 1980s, however, workers found themselves victims of the economic reforms, which were slow to increase productivity (and therefore wages) and inevitably resulted in inflation. Workers thus had their own reasons for participating in the political protests of 1989. Student and worker leaders made some effort to unite the two groups, at least in Beijing, but these were not very successful, especially nationally. In the wake of Tiananmen, those workers who sought to establish genuine trade unions were treated more harshly than other errant citizens.[7] For the proletariat to turn against their own "vanguard" struck party leaders as the ultimate heresy.

Intellectuals

Although Communists consider worker status to be superior to peasant status, no such clear ranking exists between workers and "intellectuals" (meaning the middle-school educated). Indeed, how the intelligentsia should be viewed has been one of the hottest issues for the Chinese Communists since the 1940s. Numbering in the tens of millions, the intellectuals were viewed during the Cultural Revolution as "a stinking bad group," no better than counterrevolutionaries, former landlords, and "capitalist-roaders." This attitude was in part a reaction against the once-dominating role of the scholar gentry, but it also derived from the Marxist-Maoist idea that workers are superior to nonworking parasites. The logic of this suggested to some that "bourgeois intellectuals" should be eliminated as a class. However, this perceived need conflicted with the goal of modernizing the economy. For the latter to be accomplished, the intellectuals (which included the managerial class) needed to be accommodated and persuaded to serve the Socialist order.

Thus arose what the Chinese call a contradiction—in this case between "red" and "expert." Red refers to a person's political background and dedication; expert refers to one's ability to perform in a profession. There has been a tendency for the reds, who were often products of the guerrilla war or the Cultural Revolution, to be more interested in opposing class enemies than in modernizing (which they feared meant Westernizing) the nation. Many experts, on the other hand, saw Maoist ideology as being of little help in bringing the economy and culture of the country into the twentieth century, and they could point to many a disaster that ensued when institutions and enterprises were run by ideologues who did not believe in heeding the wisdom of the experts.

In theory, it should be possible to resolve this contradiction, and the official line has generally been that everyone should strive to be both red and expert. In practice, various leaders have tended to emphasize one or the other. Mao Zedong believed that if modernization proceeded without the proper ideological underpinnings, the broader social goals of the revolution would never be realized. He feared that the experts would come to comprise a privileged class, and one of the reasons that he finally launched the Cultural Revolution was to prevent this. The disaster that ensued only strengthened the conviction of people like Deng Xiaoping, who objected to empty sloganeering that diverted the national attention away from coping with China's pervasive poverty. After taking power from the leftists, Deng declared that the overwhelming majority of intellectuals had become a part of the working class itself. He undertook to improve their status and working conditions, and even ordered the rehabilitation of those who had been imprisoned or otherwise persecuted. As a result, nearly 3 million people had pejorative political and class labels removed.

There remained the question of how red the experts needed to be. How many hours a week should intellectuals participate in political study sessions? To what extent should scientists and other scholars be permitted to engage in research not clearly related to current party policies and goals? The old rule was that all scientific and technological work had to contribute to economic development, and there was only limited room for theoretical research or even such quality-of-life concerns as medicine or environmental studies. In short, researchers were required to subordinate their personal interests to the requirements of the state, although the strictness of the application of this rule has varied over time.

On the other hand, how much professional expertise should be required of the red cadres? Deng Xiaoping, the great modernizer, was on record as saying that it was more important for the reds to be expert than for the experts to be red. But conservatives have argued that this is improper—that if intellectuals are to serve the public, they need to be guided by those with a correct political viewpoint who by no means need to be professional in anything except politics. For Mao, part of the answer was to send cadres down to the grass roots for "rustication" (*xia xiang*—literally, "send down to the countryside"). This approach was revived in the early 1990s, when nearly one million were dispatched to "learn from the masses."

"New Class"

Such measures are designed to prevent cadres from becoming an elite divorced from the public. But China, like other Communist countries, spawned what the Yugoslav dissident Milovan Djilas termed a "new class" of people privileged by virtue of political or bureaucratic position. What is different about China in recent years is that the partial price reform created a new link between political power and money. People who have connections with government agencies or state enterprises have been ideally situated to sell cheap state-made products at high market prices, or buy materials on the free market and sell them to the state sector at inflated prices. These activities have taken place at all levels, but are most conspicuous at the highest echelons.[8]

Getihu

In the past decade, the partial demise of socialism has given rise to yet another social class, known as *getihu* (pronounced "gu-tee-hoo," and literally meaning "individual private household"). This term includes self-employed repair people, shopkeepers, street hawkers, taxi drivers who own their own cars, as well as owners of small factories, and businessmen who use connections to buy cheap and sell what the market will bear. Thus, *getihu* has various connotations. On the one hand, these people are seen as entrepreneurs who have demonstrated initiative and resourcefulness, qualities of special value in an overbureaucratized society. But there is also an implication that these people are opportunists, price-gougers, and social upstarts. They are therefore in the odd position of being held in disdain by both conservatives and democrats.

Getihu tend to travel a lot in order to take advantage of economic opportunities. In 1989 they were quick to appreciate the significance of the political developments in Beijing, and some became catalysts for protests in other parts of the country.

Ascriptive Groups

So far, we have been analyzing Chinese society in terms of formal occupational labels.

These are usually achievement or performance categories (though, as we have noted, there are many cases in which the labels are misleading). The society can also be broken down by ascriptive categories such as those based on age, sex, and race. We now turn to an examination of such groups.

Age: Youth The "liberation" of 1949 meant that things would be different for the young in two respects. First, most were now given a primary-school education. Second, the Communist party sought to politicize them. Beyond this, however, life for Chinese youths would be what it always was. When they were old enough they went to work. For most boys and girls, this meant working in agriculture, although opportunities for nonagricultural work (including small-scale industry in villages) have increased greatly in recent years.

Urban youth have constituted a special issue in Chinese society. Although they have a much better chance of attending middle school than their country cousins have, upon graduation there have not been enough jobs for them. Many would like to enter college, but openings are few and disaffection is widespread. In an attempt to mobilize potential leaders, the party has a junior branch, the Communist Youth League. This exists not only to indoctrinate young people, but also to enlist their support on behalf of state campaigns, including those against illegal economic activities, unsafe conditions, and the ubiquitous scourge of corruption.

The youth problem became particularly acute after the mid-1960s. The fate of the many who could not attend college or land a job (and even for many of those who did) was to be rusticated (exiled to the countryside). In some areas pressure to "volunteer" grew as the Cultural Revolution dawned. Although some public-spirited or adventurous youngsters did not mind the prospect, most preferred to avoid the physical labor and cultural void that rural life would mean for them. Youths of "good" class background were just as eager to avoid being transferred to the countryside as were the sons and daughters of middle-class intellectuals. However, the latter tended to do better on college admissions examinations and thus had a vested interest in maintaining the status quo. Most lower-class students, on the other hand, thought that admission to college should not be solely on the basis of academic achievement but should consider citizenship and class background as well—a view that was shared by those radical national leaders who came to power in 1966. Naturally, the young intellectuals did not give up their privileges without a fight. In the virtual civil war that engulfed China's cities between 1966 and 1968, the battle lines tended to be drawn over issues such as these.[9]

Many youngsters were unhappy about being rusticated. For their part, peasants generally had no interest in reeducating the newcomers and tended to find them a burden. Most villages suffered from a lack of land rather than labor, so an influx of hungry but not too robust youths who knew nothing about agriculture only exacerbated the locals' problems. The peasants were generally tolerant and kindly, but the fact remained that they did not need most of the skills that the young intellectuals offered. Even if their labor could be utilized, they could not do enough work to support themselves and usually had to have supplementary funds sent by their parents. In China, where there is no social security system, the young are expected to support their aging parents, so the new turn of events was humiliating to the young and threatening to the old.

In 1978, after China's new leadership declared that much of what had been counterrevolutionary was now revolutionary, China's unhappy urban-origin youth found some ground for hope; most were allowed to return home for a "vacation." The occasion coincided with the democracy movement, which many of these people joined with a vengeance. There were numerous demonstrations by youths determined not to return to the countryside.

However, the cities' economic problems were at least as serious as before the Cultural Revolution, and the youths could not be reintegrated into society. Unemployment and housing shortages were acute. A person's best hope was to live in one's parents' crowded quarters and eventually replace one of them at his or her place of employment. Those who could not work out such an arrangement often took to the streets, even though this risked arrest and a fate worse than rustication—incarceration. The demonstrations did not persuade the authorities to relent, and most of the youth had to choose between returning to the countryside or remaining in the cities illegally. A majority did the latter, and became a major source of disaffection between 1985 and 1989.

Opportunities for youth have increased considerably since the 1970s. In 1977 less than 5 percent of applicants were admitted to college; by 1987 the figure was up to over 27 percent. But that still left millions rejected and frustrated. Even among those who have matriculated, there has been a crisis of confidence. Polls reveal college students to be patriotic but increasingly Westernized,[10] and unwilling to blindly follow the often xenophobic Communist leadership. In the early 1990s, the authorities' response to this problem was to oblige youth to participate in military training and also to beef up the Communist Youth League, but such steps do not appear to have effected attitudinal changes.

China's leaders are fully aware of the younger generation's disaffection. Youth are chafing under China's closed system, in which they feel that they have no voice, and are creating serious problems for the regime. They have been unable to openly engage in political dissent, and many have adopted social behavior that violates official taboos in the area of personal relations. Nonmarital sexual relations, for example, are much more common than in Mao's time. T-shirts with subtle antisocial slogans like "Bored" or "Leave me alone" are popular. Some (usually soon banned) have borne the sayings of Mao Zedong, now cleverly turned against the regime: "Never forget class struggle," and "A single spark can start a prairie fire."

Age: The Elderly   In traditional China, most people did not survive until old age, but those who did were highly respected and enjoyed considerable influence—even power— over their juniors. Typically (or at least stereotypically), this often took the form of a matron lording over her daughter-in-law. The requirement that the young revere the old lay at the heart of Confucianism. When the Communists came to power, they were determined to end the influence of the past, and because older people tend to be more conservative, the new leaders placed their hopes in China's youth.

Gender   Like traditional societies in general, China's was largely male-dominated. This was certainly true within the family (though less so if the oldest member was a woman), and it was especially so in politics. On those rare occasions when a woman rose to prominence, she was usually considered to have played an unsavory role. We can attribute this only in part to the (male) historians' bias. The Chinese often assumed that female ascendancy in the power structure was a national disaster, and although this may have been a self-fulfilling prophecy, it had 3000 years of fairly consistent historical basis. As for lower-class women, most labored in the fields or were subjected to various degradations, such as being ornamentalized by practices like foot-binding. Girls were almost never taught to read, and not infrequently were obliged to become concubines or even prostitutes. Given the fate in store for so many females and the fact that they would be less productive than men, parents sometimes practiced female infanticide. (They still do. Although the practice also exists in some other third world countries, female infanticide appears to be especially prominent in China and India. In both countries, there are only about 93 females for every 100 males.[11])

When the Chinese Communists came to power, one of their first legislative acts was to assert the equality of women. The main effort, though, was not through law, but through propaganda. Mao Zedong declared that times had changed: "Women hold up half the sky," and are thus equal to men. "Whatever male comrades can do, female comrades can also." Unfortunately, many males came to resent "iron women" and "fake boys."

Mao's emphasis on *class* struggle meant that other social inequities, such as those based on gender, were given relatively short shrift. In 1966 he even abolished the Women's Federation (as irrelevant to the goals of the Cultural Revolution). So, while efforts have since been made to curb China's traditional sexism, problems remain. The best gains have been made in factories, where equal work receives equal pay. Even there, however, women have usually been relegated to lower-paid positions, and besides their factory work they have borne the main burden of housework. The problem has been similar in the countryside. Women often do most of the agricultural work, but men (who are generally stronger and more likely to get any locally available industrial jobs) tend to earn more, causing dissatisfaction among women.

As for upward mobility, however slight the chances may be for rural men, they are almost nonexistent for rural women. The party tries to guarantee substantial female representation on the people's congresses at all levels, but leadership continues to be predominantly male. Women have only slowly moved into positions of authority in enterprises, cultural institutions, and politics. Those determined to change their lives often end up as domestic workers in the homes of the more affluent city dwellers. In 1980 there were said to have been almost 5 million female cadres—a large figure, but still a small fraction of all cadres. The percentage of women in the National People's Congress did rise from 12 percent in 1959 to 21 percent in 1978. After the 1983 National

People's Congress no data on the subject were released, but less than 7 percent of the new State Council were female. Women who have risen to greater national prominence have invariably been the wives of powerful figures; when the latter have fallen from grace, the wives' political fortunes have taken similar nosedives.

In recent years, many urban women have sought to be more feminine in appearance, and like to be called by the cosmopolitan sounding "miss" (*xiaojie*). Conservatives take a dim view of all this, and promote the use of the genderless title "comrade."[12] When it comes to poor women, the niceties of titles have been irrelevant. Contrary to government policy, some women are abducted and sold to become wives (often virtual slaves),[13] and prostitution, unheard of for decades, is now common in some cities.[14]

Ethnic Groups   Unlike the former Soviet Union, the dominant nationality comprises the overwhelming majority of the population in China. The ethnic Chinese are about 92 percent of the population; others are often referred to as "minorities," a term not altogether pleasing to everyone. Tibetans consider themselves the majority in their nation, and refer to the ethnic Chinese simply as "Chinese," which implies that they are foreigners. However, Chinese authorities insist that everyone is "Chinese" and that their lands are properly a part of the PRC. Although only a small portion (8 percent) of China's population, the areas the minorities inhabit amount to about one-half of the PRC's territory. The nationalities often reside in sparsely populated, but not unimportant, regions, for much of China's presumed mineral resources are found there. More strategically significant is the proximity of the minority regions to neighboring countries, which are sometimes populated by nationalities kindred to China's.

Altogether, there are upwards of 50 ethnic groups, at least 8 having populations of over 3 million (see Table 8.2). Relations between these peoples and the ethnic Chinese have not always been tranquil. Except for those few that have been absorbed by Chinese civilization, minorities have traditionally been little integrated into the life of the nation (of which they have often been unwilling members). Communication among nationalities is a problem. The non-Chinese languages are usually unrelated to Chinese, and are generally written phonetically (like English, rather than ideographically, as Chinese is). Although

Table 8.2   DEMOGRAPHIC COMPOSITION OF THE PEOPLE'S REPUBLIC OF CHINA (TEN LARGEST ETHNIC GROUPS, 1990)

Ethnic group	Language group	Million	Primary location
Chinese (Han)	Chinese	1042	Eastern half of PRC
Zhuang	Thai	15	Guangxi
Manchu	Tungus	10	Liaoning, Hebei
Chinese Moslem (Hui)	Chinese	9	Widespread
Hmong (Miao)	Hmong-Yao	7	Guizhou
Uygur	Turkish	7	Xinjiang
Yi	Tibeto-Burman	7	Sichuan and Yunnan
Tujia	Tibeto-Burman	6	Hunan, Hebei
Mongol	Altaic	5	Inner Mongolia
Tibetan	Tibeto-Burman	5	Tibet

Source: Renkouxue xuangyue kan, 1990, no. 6, p. 99.

historically tolerant of (and even willing to be ruled by) races that adopted Chinese culture, the Chinese have considered unacculturated races barbaric and fit only to be subjugated. After the 1949 revolution the Communists took a somewhat conciliatory policy toward the various ethnic groups. The areas where these peoples lived were usually designated "autonomous," which during normal periods meant a degree of cultural autonomy and a cautious policy regarding social reforms. There was no intention of granting these regions *political* autonomy, and indeed a region was usually not declared "autonomous" until it was under full Chinese Communist control. Autonomy did not guarantee total submission to the Chinese, as the Turkic Uygurs of Eastern Turkestan (Xinjiang) have demonstrated on numerous occasions. Even among the more peaceful nationalities, dissatisfaction with Chinese rule has often been evident. For example, in Inner Mongolia during the Hundred Flowers thaw of 1957 one heard such slogans as "Mongolia for the Mongolians" and "Sons of Genghis Khan, Unite!" And when the former Soviet satellite of Mongolia became independent and democratic, China's Mongols eyed the situation there with relish.

The various nationalities' cultural development presents a mixed picture. Some have long had well-developed literary traditions, whereas others lacked written languages. Writing systems have been devised for the latter, but the role of non-Chinese languages has been a controversial issue among Communists. Tibetan literature, for example, has always epitomized Tibet's nationhood, and so use of the written language has not always been encouraged. The Uygurs and Kazakhs were not normally discouraged from using written languages, but for many years they were supposed to use the Latin alphabet, a practice which cut people off from the traditional literature in the Arabic alphabet. In a major concession, this policy was reversed in 1981 as part of a general liberalization in ethnic relations.

During the Cultural Revolution, the goal of ethnic homogeneity was defined as part of the "class struggle." Anyone who opposed Sinification was relegated to the category of class enemies, and there was considerable racist persecution and bloodshed. Efforts were made to end many of the distinctive features of the various cultures. For example, the Yao people of Yunnan were supposed to stop using their native language. The men, who were hunters, had their rifles confiscated, and the women were forced to cut their hair short and abandon traditional dress. To escape Chinese chauvinism, people reportedly fled into the forests, where some remained for years. Such abuses were curbed after the radicals were eliminated from power. The party platform of 1981 admitted, "We did not show due respect for minorities' right to autonomy. We must never forget that lesson." Although the government once again undertook to accommodate the special characteristics of the various ethnic groups, these peoples have still found themselves hurt by some government policies. It has been admitted that 30 percent of all minority school-age children were not in school, and that what education did exist needed upgrading. Because of language difficulties and lack of basic education, non-Chinese speakers have difficulty performing well enough on college entrance examinations to gain admission to universities.

Thus, whether ethnic policies are oppressive or permissive largely depends on what group has gained power in Beijing. But despite neglect and discrimination, population figures suggest that the story of China's minority peoples has not been altogether negative. These groups raise troubling questions concerning the overall integration of the nation-state. We will explore this problem later in connection with the question of national integration.

The complex mosaic of Chinese society has presented major challenges. Should the nation strive for a homogenized society in which all groups march toward communism in unison, as Mao Zedong apparently believed?

Or would the political and economic costs of eliminating the differences between social groups be unbearable, as his successors concluded?

POLITICAL CULTURE

The term "political culture" refers to the attitudes that influence people's political behavior and color the nature of a political system. Political culture, like all culture, is rarely static; but it is deeply embedded in people's personalities and not generally amenable to abrupt change. This poses a problem for revolutionaries, for it means that the assumption of political power merely marks the beginning of their work. For the student of politics, the fact that political cultures are never ephemeral eases the task somewhat, for it provides clues to understanding the problems faced by a new leadership—provided we are sensitive to history.

Although China has a vast literature relevant to traditional political culture, it must be read with caution because much of it is elitist in nature. It was written by the literati, who until this century almost unanimously subscribed to one school of thought (though a person could simultaneously believe in others as well). This belief system was considered so consummatory by its adherents that it did not even have a name. For convenience, in English we call this school Confucianism, after the man who compiled the earliest body of classical literature. Confucianism, which we shall examine shortly, embodied the political philosophy of the scholar-gentry class, which never comprised more than a tiny percentage of the population. There is a much smaller written legacy covering the culture of the populace at large, who were mostly illiterate farmers. We do know that they were less influenced by Confucianism than by Buddhism, Daoism (Taoism), and folk religion, none of which was as political as Confucianism.

Aside from religion, villagers' concerns were largely economic and social—sustaining life by growing crops, and maintaining family and lineage ties. Government was distant and largely irrelevant to daily concerns. Politics, such as there was, tended to be small in scale. Disputes among individuals were settled informally; resort to adjudication was rare. Local public works were performed by social groups, probably the lineages, not by government authorities. Popular philosophy was largely religious or mystical, but sometimes it had an indirect relevance to political and social issues, such as compensating for the shortcomings of Confucianism. Buddhism, for example, was egalitarian; it taught that salvation was available to all, though not in this world. But Buddhism made little positive contribution to political life in the country.

Thus, except as the recipient of their taxes, government had little meaning for the average man or woman. One's concern was largely for relatives, and there was little public spirit. Few moral limits existed beyond which people (other than relatives) could not be exploited. The socialization process instilled in people certain cultural imperatives, generally derived from or at least consistent with Confucianism. One was the requisite of harmony in human affairs. A premium was placed on avoiding conflict with known persons, though not necessarily with strangers. Violence was rarely legitimate. There was little in the way of competitive athletics (endangering one's body would be an unfilial act), and so this outlet for aggressive impulses was not available. Whether or not this made the individual prone to repressed hatred and gave rise to bickering and "indirect warfare" (as some scholars have maintained), it nonetheless did not provide for a psychocultural milieu in which fruitful competition took place. Only conventional, nonupsetting behavior was approved, and any loss of composure was shameful. There was inclination for conflict, but so much energy was devoted to repressing it that the conflict tended to come in great outbursts, which were (and still are) difficult for leaders to control and channel.

Of course, most cultures value harmony. However, inasmuch as Chinese seem to have a special phobia about chaos, rulers can take advantage of this in order to perpetuate their power. Many Chinese, especially those in the countryside, supported the crackdown in 1989 because what they feared most was disorder.

Another notable feature of traditional Chinese popular culture was group orientation (as opposed to individualism). A premium was placed on conforming to group pressures and values. Of course, this is true to some extent in all societies, but the rewards and penalties for individuality vary. In China, responsibilities were assumed by groups, which generally brooked no challenge from within. Usually the group was the family, within which work and resources were shared (as they still are), but there were other groups (neighborhood security groups, guilds, religious organizations, secret societies,[15] and the like), which operated much the same in principle and spirit. Making it difficult to assign responsibility tended to encourage irresponsibility. The task of, say, a county magistrate was simplified if he could hold a group responsible for the misdeeds of an individual, but this system meant that much of the group's energy was devoted to preventing or concealing nonconformity.

Within the collectivity there was a hierarchical ordering, and individuals tended to be passive in the face of authority. Relatives were invariably addressed not by their names but by titles indicating their relationship to the speaker. Siblings and cousins, for example, were identified in terms of seniority and sex. All this was complicated, but it presumably gave comfort by providing clear role definitions and aiding self-identity. Furthermore, the principle of familial hierarchical ordering was applied to nonkinship situations. There was a tendency to be highly rank-conscious, and though official ranks were based on merit, superior-subordinate relationships had an unprofessional, diffuse character. With no background of participatory decision making in the family training ground, it is not surprising that people would be passive if not obsequious.

In spite of the anti-individualist spirit of Chinese culture, people found various ways of coping with the more disagreeable features of authoritarianism. With personal prestige directly related to proper subordination to authority, many affected compliance. The Chinese concern for "face saving" was more than simply a manifestation of the basic human need for respect, and had profound implications for the operation of the political system. Institutional efficiency was unavoidably affected if, in the name of "face," men engaged in evasion and ostensible compliance; yet, these were considered perfectly appropriate means of dealing with awkward political situations. Indeed, saving face for a colleague was more important than correcting his errors.

A related psychocultural feature has been the tendency to show outward submission to the demands of authority while inwardly harboring reservations, and even sometimes secretly acting on them. A certain amount of circumlocution and courtesy is universal and quite functional; nevertheless, the candor and credibility that a modern political system requires have tended to be absent in China. (Nothing can be more debilitating than the subtle subversion of inward reservation and foot-dragging.) Confucianism tended to permit a certain amount of feigned norm compliance, and the Communists have found themselves plagued by what is termed "formalism"—the carrying out of orders in form but not in substance. Indeed, Mao Zedong once condemned "doubledealers who are outwardly compliant but inwardly unsubmissive, say one thing and mean another, speak in honeyed words to people's faces but play tricks behind their backs."[16] In calling for candor, Mao was demanding a fundamental change in China's political culture.

Although the Chinese have been disinclined to challenge authority, this does not mean that they never revolted. On the contrary, there were numerous agrarian revolts, and several major dynasties were at least in part founded on these. Still, one can hardly say that agrarian revolts provided the impetus for social change. In the first place, the vast majority of agrarian revolts failed—especially those with radical overtones. Movements that succeeded were either co-opted by upper-class elements or witnessed the transformation of their leadership into characteristic authoritarian and unegalitarian dynasties. Another factor that deters us from finding substantial revolutionary potential in traditional Chinese political culture is that most of the outstanding social rebellions were at the same time revolts against foreign domination.

Whereas the traditional culture of the common people was apolitical, elite political culture was *very* political. Indeed, during the imperial and republican periods, Chinese political culture was largely the political culture of the respective elites. This value system had its origins in the period roughly from the sixth to the third centuries B.C. That was a time when the educated people (unlike commoners) became less religious than their ancestors had been and adopted the secular philosophy. For example, the word *tian*, which had once referred to a god, now meant "heaven." At the hands of Mencius (ca. 372–289 B.C.) it came to be used even more figuratively. People had already understood that the kings' right to rule was bestowed by heaven as a mandate. In reinterpreting some of the ancient myths, Mencius fully secularized the political doctrine of the "mandate of heaven" and attempted to democratize it by reiterating, "Heaven sees as our people see; heaven hears as our people hear." True, few Chinese rulers took this seriously, and at the most "the people" included the scholar-gentry class. Still, the idea of legitimacy based on a revocable mandate, contingent on a dynasty's pleasing *tian* and *tian-xia* (all under heaven), has always been important.

Instead of being progressive and forward-looking, the scholar-gentry class was largely absorbed with the alleged "golden age" of the past. There is no little irony in the fact that history, which for Confucius and his disciples had been a tool for understanding the present, was warped and idealized by later generations of scholars, who often became obsessed with history for its own sake. Ancestors were honored in elaborate rites and were sometimes virtually worshiped. For all of this, Confucius bore some responsibility. He had, for example, rejected his disciple's suggestion that a particular sacrifice be eliminated, saying, "You love the lamb; I love the rite." Less often remembered was Confucius's exasperation over mindless exercises: "Rites, rites! Do they mean no more than jades and silks?"

We should bear in mind that the institutions that sprang from this ethos were the marvels of their time and the envy of much of the world. The idea that the political elite should be selected on the basis of ability demonstrated in examinations was revolutionary, even though we might now scoff at the kind of rigid "eight-legged essays" that contestants were obliged to write. At the same time, enough has probably been said here to suggest that there was much about traditional Chinese culture that posed problems for the modernization process. The culture of the populace was too apolitical, and the culture of the elite, though political, was insufficiently oriented toward problem solving and embodied counterproductive bureaucratic practices. When Confucianism died out in the early twentieth century, not all of these problems died with it.

Toward the end of the nineteenth century, Chinese intellectuals became increasingly aware of the shortcomings of the nation's institutions and culture. After Russia's Bolshevik Revolution some of them became interested in Marxism, and during the 1920s various Comintern advisors went to China to preach their radical doctrine. Why did these ideas strike such a responsive chord among Chinese intellectuals? Perhaps part of the explanation lies in the fact that certain aspects of Marxism have their analog in traditional Chinese elite culture. Like Marxists, Chinese intellectuals were usually atheistic materialists who nonetheless placed great stress on doctrine. Even the Hegelian dialectic corresponded with the Chinese tendency to think in terms of *ying-yang* opposites. But if this made Marxism more congenial for Chinese, the influence was subconscious. More to the point was the perceived modernity of Marxism-Leninism, which made the ideology seem like a viable alternative to Chinese ways. Suddenly, none of the shortcomings of Chinese culture mattered because culture was merely part of the "superstructure." Now, these intellectuals learned, the thing to do was transform the "base," then the culture would follow along. Here was a new "scientific" way to analyze history and society. It provided a vision of the future (communism) and outlined the way to get there (socialism).

Struck by China's backwardness, these intellectuals were impatient to catch up with the rest of the world. One of the appealing features of the Soviet brand of Marxism-Leninism was that it seemed to offer shortcuts. For example, Marxists need no longer be troubled by the fact that China had not passed through Marx's "inevitable" bourgeois-capitalist phase, for the Russians had shown that this was not necessary. Furthermore, Lenin and his colleagues had devised a new type of organization to hasten the transformation of a country: the elite, monolithic political party organized according to the principles of "democratic centralism." Although there was nothing particularly democratic about any of this, the new style of politics was rationalized on the grounds that the propertyless classes had to struggle against their exploiters—the owners of the means of production.

In China, class struggle has proven to be the most troublesome element of Marxism. It is not so much the idea is wrong (politics everywhere is often the struggle of the have-nots against the haves) but that it is so prone to abuse. It is terrifyingly easy for those in power to link their critics with "capitalist-roaders," which automatically makes them objects of class struggle to be repressed. Not only were genuine propertied elements persecuted after 1949, but so were liberal democrats and, astonishingly enough, genuine Communists who happened to be caught on the "wrong" side of political arguments. Even from a purely theoretical point of view, class struggle has been an awkward basis for politics. After all, the exploiting classes were eliminated in the early 1950s with the end of private ownership of the means of production. Thereafter, as *People's Daily* acknowledged early in the Deng Xiaoping era, "Some comrades have been puzzled, and ask: Now that the exploiting class has been eliminated, how is it possible that there is still class struggle? Who are the objects of class struggle? Who is waging class struggle against whom?"

In the face of the perplexity of these questions, the paper offered a "scientific" explanation to the effect that remnants of the exploiting class persisted. These are (1) unreformed survivors from the old exploiting class (for example, landlords); (2) "newly engendered exploiters of all descriptions and those who, though not exploiters, adopt a hostile attitude toward socialism and are thus partners of exploiters"; and (3) individuals whose minds are susceptible to the influence of exploiters. We can see, however, that the first category is largely meaningless today and that the others are catchalls for dissidents of all descriptions.[17] What is striking about this line of reasoning, which remained standard into the 1990s, is how far the Chinese have strayed from classical Marxism. According to Marx and Engels, one's class was determined by one's relationship to the means of production. Thus we might assume that class struggle must in some way relate to the conflict of interest between owners and laborers. But the Deng group here turns the issue around, saying in effect that one can infer from the "fact" of political error that the errant people are, by definition, associated with economic exploitation, and therefore are legitimate objects of class struggle.

During the brief period in 1978–1979 when advocates of democracy were permitted to express their views, it became clear that many people were not convinced by this rationale for repression. The most extreme dissidents argued that despotism was to be blamed not on fictitious exploiting classes, but on the despots themselves.[18] They saw class struggle not as a means for those exploited to gain control over their own destiny, but as a means by which "our officials—uneducated bureaucrats—have climbed to high posts." According to adherents of this view, the doctrine of class struggle was no longer applicable to China. As for society's many ills, these democrats attributed them to "feudalism," which is to say the cultural legacy of prerevolutionary China.

When such views were expressed by democratic activists, they were heretical, and those who expressed them paid dearly for their daring. However, China's leaders and media have, in their own manner, alluded to the same problem—the legacy of "feudalism." Under this rubric, criticism is aimed at such problems as lack of respect for law, the seeking of special privileges, and "patriarchy"—meaning the tendency of leaders at all levels to refuse to listen to their colleagues and subordinates. Other writers have complained at great length about such old problems of nepotism and autocracy. Attention has also been given to additional problems which demonstrate that the Chinese are products of their past. For example, the old practice of exchanging gifts between people whose relationship is purely business or political continues to be very much alive, to the distress of some. These practices interfere with the leadership's efforts to modernize the culture, and they die hard.

Closely related to feudalism is the question of factionalism.[19] In traditional China the highest value was placed on "harmony," but such Confucian values have now been repudiated. Nevertheless, the Chinese—or at any rate their leaders—still emphasize the importance of "unity" and consensus. Factionalism is seen as harmful, and its existence is usually (but not very convincingly) denied. Indeed, we can say that the factions China has are incompatible with a modern political order, which requires vehicles (parties) for interest aggregation and articulation.

In China, factions do not serve this purpose. They are not formed around policy concerns or social, geographic, or departmental interests. Instead, factions are groups seeking to protect and advance their careers. Party members and cadres are linked together by personal relationships that are hierarchical (rather than intimate) in nature: the important connections are those linking them to people at higher and lower levels. This system of invisible networks leaves little room to weigh openly the pros and cons of issues, as one's primary loyalty is to the people in one's faction. Although the phenomenon is largely hidden from outsiders, it would appear that China's cadres are engaged in factional warfare much of the time. Indirect confirmation of all this can occasionally be found in the documentary evidence. For example, the party journal once complained that party members were promoting "private interests" by assigning their own people to various lower posts and "attaching themselves to bigwigs."[20]

People do not refer to their own faction by any name because that would be an admission of impermissible behavior. If a faction gains a public identity, it does so on the basis of what its opponents say about it. This happens primarily when those opponents control the media, which can be mobilized to attack dissident factions. Such attacks are not easy for an outsider to understand; issues may be indicated, but these are usually secondary to the dispute and are stated in such abstract terms as to leave it unclear what the dissident faction really advocates. The one-sided debate is usually conducted in Aesopian language, with code names and slogans employed so that only those "in the know" will be aware of the true meaning of the struggle. Those in control of the media will thus deride their opponents by such opaque designations as revisionists, capitalist-roaders, whatever-ists, or leftists. No one will openly challenge the new line, but the silence of this official or that newspaper can be telling.

This style of politics permits the authorities to maintain the fiction that the consensus in general and their political position in particular remains unchallenged. However, everyone knows that when one of these campaigns is launched in the media, a struggle is brewing and the outcome is unsure. The battle lines begin to be drawn, and peripheral factions are forced by circumstances to join sides with a leading contender. If the struggle is national in scope, there is doubtless division among the top leaders in Beijing, and any fight that develops will probably touch the lives of virtually all Chinese—however poorly understood is the controversy that led to the changes. (The poisonous infighting that accompanies factionalism is not unique to the party leadership. It was also a conspicuous feature of the students and others at Tiananmen in 1989. Apparently, people lead the way they are led.[21])

The reason that the average Chinese knows so little about what is going on in the government is that such news is systematically kept from the public. Secrecy is a fact of life and colors the entire political process. Information that would be routinely disclosed as a matter of right in Western societies is classified in China. For example, one man was imprisoned for releasing the transcript of a trial. The law on secrecy is published and readily available to all, but it is sufficiently vague that one can get into trouble simply for discussing grapevine gossip. The secrecy rules apply to conversations with foreigners and with other Chinese, and are an important tool for the perpetuation of the elite's political power. Not only the party's politburo, but even the National People's Congress can meet without public knowledge. Secrecy does not, of course, guarantee that the present leaders will always retain their jobs, but it does mean that there will be little circulation of elites,

and that any power struggle will almost certainly be confined to a small group. The fate of those on the periphery of power—middle-level cadres—depends on their skill at reading the signals that come down to them, sensing the direction of the "wind" (to use a common Chinese term), and forging factional alliances accordingly.

Alien to China is the notion of a "loyal opposition" that supports the constitutional order while criticizing perceived shortcomings in the way the leadership conducts itself. Under Mao, and again in Deng Xiaoping's later years, the Chinese have had "class struggle" instead of political dialogue. Those who opposed "correct" politics and actions were deemed "counterrevolutionaries" and were subject to the heavy hand of the "organs of the dictatorship of the proletariat." Policies were "correct" because they were consistent with the prevailing ideology—as interpreted by those who monopolized the media. Perhaps there is no more important question facing the Chinese than that of the extent of a citizen's obligation to uphold and act according to official ideology. Many believe (along with the famous journalist, now exiled, Liu Binyan) that there is a higher form of loyalty, and people should be pragmatic and driven by their individual consciences. But the leadership rejects this approach to politics. As one spokesperson for the regime reportedly commented, "If you have mercy, you will fall into the opposition's trap. If you give an inch, they will take a mile, and this will lead to trouble and rebellion. One morning, in collaboration with some among us, they will attempt political change. Politics is a cruel, life-and-death struggle."[22]

By the mid-1980s, though dissidents could still go to jail as "counterrevolutionaries," the practice was much less common than it had been before 1982, and ideology was not quite the tool of repression that it had once been. Indeed, on 7 December 1984 (during a political thaw), *People's Daily* declared that it was "naive and stupid" to cling slavishly to Marxist principles. "Studying Marxism means the study of universal laws elaborated by general writings and opinions on how to solve problems. We can never rigidly adhere to the individual word and sentences or theories written with specific applications in mind." Much had changed, the editorial added, during the century following Marx's death. "Some of his ideas are no longer suited to today's situation, because Marx never experienced these times, nor did Engels or Lenin. . . . We cannot use Marxist and Leninist works to solve our present-day problems." If pragmatism actually came to replace traditional ideology in people's outlooks, it would signal a marked change in Chinese political culture. However, in 1989 the conservative leaders resorted to mindless Cultural Revolution-style polemics (such as party head Zhao being labeled "anti-Party"). The brutal nationwide crackdown on that year's huge democracy movement suggested that the leadership was far behind the public in terms of sophistication in conceiving political issues.

Ideology continues to be an essential underpinning of the regime. To a greater or lesser degree, political discussion is supposed to take place within the confines of Deng Xiaoping's "four cardinal principles," namely adherence to socialism, the dictatorship, party leadership, and the philosophy of Marx, Lenin, and Mao.

But this has not invariably been the case. An interesting phenomenon of the 1980s was a spate of articles, books, and even movies about the "defects" in China's political culture. One is tempted to recall Mao's inveighing against all the "old" ways of thought, but these new observers are far from being Maoists. The new genre was reflective and profound. For example, it was not uncommon to see articles about alleged "self-destructive" tendencies among Chinese.[23] The most famous negative exploration of the national character was "River Elegy," a popular and influential film in which the "stagnant" Yellow River was a metaphor for China's cultural shortcomings. The screenplay implied that the answers to the nation's problems were to be found by looking to the blue "ocean," which all Chinese understand to mean the West.[24] Regarding the political realm, favorable reference was made to such constitutional arrangements and separation of powers, particularly judicial independence, which were credited with helping the West to advance more quickly than China had. Such thinking affected the whole political climate, and helped to produce the Tiananmen demonstrations.

Key Terms

ascriptive
cadre
Confucianism
Chinese People's Political Consultative
    Conference
Communist Youth League
Democracy Wall
Deng Xiaoping
dynasties
fifth modernization
four cardinal principles
four modernizations
Gang of Four
Great Leap Forward
Great Proletarian Cultural Revolution
Lin Biao
mandate of heaven
Mao Zedong
Rehabilitation
Rightists
rustication
scholar-gentry class
Tiananmen
village status groups
Wei Jingsheng
Zhou Enlai

Suggestions for Further Reading

Andors, Phyllis. *The Unfinished Liberation of Chinese Women, 1949–1980* (Bloomington: Indiana University Press, 1983).

Asian Survey. Berkeley (monthly). (Each January issue contains a review of the previous year's political and economic developments.)

The Australian Journal of Chinese Affairs. Canberra (semi-annual).

Bibliography of Asian Studies. Ann Arbor (annual).

Chang, Jung. *Wild Swans: Three Daughters of China* (New York: Simon and Schuster, 1991).

China Information. Leiden (quarterly).

China Quarterly. London (quarterly).

China Review. (Hong Kong: Chinese University Press, 1991).

Davis, Deborah, and Ezra F. Vogel, eds. *Chinese Society on the Eve of Tiananmen* (Cambridge: Harvard University Press, 1990).

de Bary, Wm. Theodore, et al., compilers. *Sources of Chinese Tradition* (New York: Columbia University Press, 1960).

Dittmer, Lowell. *China's Continuous Revolution: The Post-Liberation Epoch, 1949–1981* (Berkeley: University of California Press, 1987).

Eastman, Lloyd E. *The Abortive Revolution: China under Nationalist Rule, 1927–1937* (Cambridge: Harvard University Press, 1974).

Fang Lizhi. *Bringing Down the Great Wall: Writings on Science, Culture, and Democracy in China* (New York: Knopf, 1991).

Gargan, Edward A. *China's Fate: A People's Turbulent Struggle with Reform and Repression, 1980–1990* (New York: Doubleday, 1991).

Grunfeld, A. Tom. *The Making of Modern Tibet* (Armonk, N.Y.: M. E. Sharpe, 1987).

Heberer, Thomas. *China and Its National Minorities: Autonomy or Assimilation* (Armonk, N.Y.: M. E. Sharpe, 1991).

Luo Zhufeng. *Religion under Socialism in China* (Armonk, N.Y.: M. E. Sharpe, 1991).

MacFarquhar, Roderick, and John K. Fairbank, eds. *The Cambridge History of China, vol. 14; The Emergence of Revolutionary China, 1949–1965* (Cambridge: Cambridge University Press, 1987).

Pye, Lucian W. *China: An Introduction, 4th ed.* (New York: HarperCollins, 1991).

Pye, Lucian W. *The Mandarin and the Cadre: China's Political Cultures* (Ann Arbor: Michigan Monographs in Chinese Studies, v. 52, 1988).

Smil, Vaclav. *China's Environmental Crisis: An Inquiry into the Limits of National Development* (Armonk, N.Y.: M. E. Sharp, 1992).

Smith, Christopher J. *China: People and Places in the Land of One Billion* (Boulder: Westview, 1990).

Spence, Jonathan D. *In Search for Modern China* (New York: Norton, 1990).

Teiwes, Frederick. *Politics at Mao's Court: Gao Gang and Party Factionalism in the Early 1950s* (Armonk, N.Y.: M. E. Sharpe, 1991).

Wang Ruowang. *Hunger Trilogy* (Armonk, N.Y.: M. E. Sharpe, 1991).

Zhang Xinxin, and Sang Ye. *Chinese Lives: An Oral History of Contemporary China* (New York: Pantheon Books, 1987).

B. Political Processes and Institutions

We turn now to a discussion of the prominent institutions of government. However, as we shall see later in this section, what distinguishes China from many other countries is that the political process is more personalized than institutionalized. The relative weight of the two factors is a matter of some debate among "China watchers," as is the reason that politics is so personalized. Some say this springs from Chinese culture; others say that the modernization process would have changed this if communism had not reinforced personalism in politics. At any rate, although it is important to understand the institutions, the student should bear in mind that they have often been a cover for (rather than the framework of) the real-life political process. (This may well change after Deng Xiaoping leaves the political scene and a new generation of leaders takes over.)

In Communist countries, there is probably no more important constitutional question than the relationship between the party and the state. In China, that relationship has undergone several drastic changes. It is not only a question of how much power the party has over the state; equally important is the manner in which the power is exercised. Often, the distinctions between state and party become blurred, and at the top the two are often collectively referred to as "the center."

In general, we can say that power has been monopolized by the men in control of the center (specifically, Mao Zedong and then Deng Xiaoping). One method at their disposal has been for the party to operate primarily by controlling the central government, which administers the country through the "branch" system. When this system is operative, the nation is dominated by powerful ministries. Alternatively, the leadership sometimes prefers to govern through the "area" system, whereby the party policies are carried out by regional party secretaries. Thus, enterprises, educational institutions, and all other organs of state listen more to the party secretaries in their area than to their superiors in the government.[25] Significantly, though to a somewhat lesser extent than was the case in the Soviet Union, Chinese leaders have maneuvered to strengthen their power base by emphasizing one or the other system. But by the mid-1980s China's reformers concluded that both the branch and area systems have their drawbacks, and have been seeking a less bureaucratic approach to government altogether. After Tiananmen, there was an attempt to shore up the power of the center by means of the "area" system. However, by this time much power had irretrievably devolved to the provinces.

THE STATE

The Central Government

The highest constitutional organ is the National People's Congress (NPC), an unwieldy body of over 2900 that only meets for about two weeks a year. In reality, it has usually been a handpicked congress functioning simply as a ratifying rather than deliberating body. In the mid-1950s and again in the 1980s, one occasionally heard some articulation of interests, and even dissenting votes. There was a movement to turn the institution into a real parliament.[26] In May 1989 nearly one-quarter of the NPC's 159-member standing committee unsuccessfully sought an emergency session to repeal martial law—a display of independence unknown before or since. The National People's Congress never came to have the features (such as effective committees) that make such bodies in other countries meaningful sources of legislation. A seat in the NPC has been aptly described as "an olive branch—offered less to ordinary citizens than to estranged social and political elites on the fringe of power."[27] That is, various groups are allowed representation, but are kept out of the inner circle of policy makers.

The president of the People's Republic (the chief of state) is elected by the National People's Congress, but his position is largely ceremonial. Indeed, the position was vacant for 14 years during and after the Cultural Revolution, a testament to Mao Zedong's contempt for constitutional trappings. Although a president can be more than a ceremonial figure, the incumbent's power derives either from some other office he holds or (more likely) from personal networks, or both. As we shall see in our discussion of the military, such was the case with Yang Shangkun.

The government is actually presided over by the State Council (cabinet), comprised of the prime minister, several deputy prime ministers, and many councillors and heads of ministries. The State Council represents a real concentration of power, although until the late 1980s it could not act independently of political (party) authority. Beginning in 1987, premiers had more clout (or at least staying power) than party chairmen like Hu Yaobang and Zhao Ziyang. (Before commencing his troubled party chairmanship, Zhao confided that he would rather have stayed on as premier.) During the 1980s there was much talk about the need for "separating party and government," but top people in the State Council (the premier and vice-premiers) have always been concurrently party luminaries. At the local level, party-government separation was never successfully implemented, and by 1990 the effort was abandoned.[28]

The Bureaucracy

For different reasons, both Maoists and their successors felt ambivalent about China's huge bureaucracy. Mao feared that China was becoming too elitist and wanted to cut the bureaucracy down to size, literally and figuratively. During the fondly remembered civil war days, the Chinese Communists had not been cemented together by a tightly centralized and disciplined organization; the movement had relied instead on a shared purpose and an elan that stemmed from popular esteem and sense of mission. Under these circumstances, the far-flung pockets of self-reliant revolutionaries were not dependent on a "center" for day-to-day directions.

Although this loose structure was very serviceable for waging guerrilla warfare, after victory the country could not be managed without a real bureaucracy. Nevertheless, many continued to look with favor on the looser and somewhat more democratic model of the early years, which was also a time when Communists had not been softened by desk jobs but were steeled in battle. Thus, beginning in 1968, officials were required to undergo the humbling experience of the training camps called "May Seventh schools," or other forms of rustication or humiliation.

All this ended with Mao's death. Unwilling to go too far in the direction of reliance on market mechanisms to modernize the nation, China's new leaders felt that they had no choice but to rely on the millions of bureaucrats to do the job. They acknowledged that this might engender some social stratification, but warned against a renewal of unbridled attacks on "bureaucratism." Nonetheless, even the new leadership found the bureaucracy a mixed blessing. There was concern that the bureaucracy was cumbersome and plagued by poor internal communications. According to the Leninist principle of democratic centralism, lower levels are expected to make recommendations to higher organs but are in turn bound by decisions made above. Even though centralism predominates over democracy, the center often has difficulty collecting reliable information from the lower levels on which to base sound decisions.[29]

Regions

Among the various lower levels of the Chinese administrative structure, the most immediate to the central government are the seven military regions. Not in the normal civilian administrative chain of command, they have been politically important primarily following periods of great upheaval, such as the civil war and the Great Leap Forward. The armed services (which will be discussed later) played an especially crucial role following the initial phase of the Cultural Revolution and again in 1989. The leadership guards against a return to warlordism by making sure that the military regions are not self-sufficient, but rather have to rely on each other for, say, spare parts.

Provincial-level Units

Next are the provincial-level units (including the three largest municipalities and the five autonomous regions for ethnic minorities), the leaders of which are appointed by the central authorities. Although the provinces are ancient administrative units, they had little political importance in the early years of the People's Republic, when the state was highly centralized. Around 1956, however, Mao realized that increased local autonomy would be advisable: "The center must not put local administration in a straitjacket." Such periods of decentralization (including the Cultural Revolution and the 1980s) typically last a few years, during which time provincial-level units may take some initiative in the planning process. Instead of every organ having to clear each step with a ministry in Beijing, it is guided by local considerations. At such times provincial newspapers take on a more local character and prices are administered locally. But central administrators, who often disapprove of decentralization, are apt to starve the localities for funds.

Trade patterns, often involving local protectionism, are another example of what can go "wrong" with decentralization.[30] Some provinces are efficient grain producers, whereas others need to import grain. From a macroeconomic point of view, the grain-surplus provinces should export to the grain-deficit ones, but they do not always do this; sometimes they prefer to retain a grain surplus in order to keep local prices down, forcing other provinces to import from abroad. On the other hand, a province may protect its own industry by banning various imports. Decentralization thus obviates some of the problems inherent in a command economy, but creates others.

Although the general policies by which the country is run have always been laid down in Beijing, China's provinces have usually had a remarkable degree of autonomy. This is especially true now that enterprises have autonomy, as Beijing learned early in the reform process that this required a degree of independence on the part of local government as well.[31] Over the years, different leaders have had various reasons for allowing various degrees of local autonomy. Mao opposed having an excessively powerful national bureaucracy in favor of self-sufficient localities. At other times, leaders concluded that a complex economy could not be orchestrated from the center. Therefore, China is not totalitarian in the usual sense; rather, one can apply the term "cellular totalitarianism."[32] Provincial leaders are powerful people to whom not only their subjects, but also Beijing, must listen.[33] They are now younger and better educated than their predecessors; they are less easy to push around and cannot be readily influenced by political nostrums.[34] Furthermore the vested interests that have resulted from the 1980s reforms (decentralization and marketization) have become so entrenched that it is unlikely the PRC will return to the kind of centralized politics that it once had. In his later years, Deng Xiaoping was barely able to cope with the situation. Faced with the threat of revolt among the provinces, in 1992 he found it necessary to tour the South to promote his economic reforms.

Local Government

Below the province is the *prefecture*, of which there are usually about 150 nationwide. Prefectures were originally supposed to assist the provinces in managing the subordinate counties and municipalities. In reality (though the situation varies greatly over time and from place to place), prefectures have had a tendency to grow into fully developed governments with a complete complement of the various administrative agencies. The party secretary of the prefecture is the lowest-level official appointed directly by the central authorities in Beijing.

The importance of the *counties* (below the prefecture) has fluctuated more or less inversely with the fate of the provincial government. In the 1950–1956 period, for example, when the provinces were eclipsed by the higher levels, the county was the point at which the centralized administrative functions converged. The county party secretary in particular became a powerful figure, responsible for integrating and transmitting the policies received from the center. Again during the first half of the 1960s, when Liu Shaoqi sought to recentralize government, the county was declared "the militant headquarters of the people."

Early in the Cultural Revolution the masses were called on by Mao Zedong and his loyalists to "bombard" these headquarters. At that time, however, his goal was not to strengthen the nation's central apparatus but to strengthen a still lower level—the *people's communes*. The latter were to be the key units for autarky. However, as we shall see, the communes were too small to be self-sufficient economic units; the county turned out to be the more appropriate level to administer local light industry, public works, and even enterprises such as mines and cement plants. So, notwithstanding Mao's goal of "self-reliant regeneration," the communes did not prosper when they tried to get along without integrating their economies with other areas.

The communes had actually been introduced in 1958, and were eventually set up throughout rural China. They were initially supposed to have about 2000 households, but after considerable experimentation a somewhat larger size was settled on. Eventually, the typical commune would have upwards of 10,000 people. It was originally intended that the communes would become the focal point for most social, cultural, political, and economic activities. The party Central Committee even declared that "the comprehensive management of agriculture, forestry, animal husbandry, side-occupations and fishery" would be followed by "the gradual transition to communism." This suggestion that the transition from socialism to communism was not far off caused concern in the Soviet Union, where no one relished the idea that utopia would arrive somewhere else first. When the Sino-Soviet split became public in 1960, the U.S.S.R. ridiculed the communes. Even within

China, many people realized that the communes were either too large or too small for many of their various intended functions. The experience of the Great Leap Forward demonstrated that the commune was no place for heavy industry; making steel simply could not be a backyard operation. It also soon became apparent that agriculture needed to be administered from a lower level, at least for accounting purposes. The communes proved most appropriate for the administration of what we might loosely term "services"—education (high schools), health care (clinics), finance (banks), and military security (the militia). By contrast, mass-production industry has generally been retained at the higher levels and the agricultural accounting has devolved to the villages or below.

As vehicles for forging revolution, the communes never lived up to their promise; and when it came to playing a role in the modernization of the country, they were a disaster. With the changes the reformers imposed on the agricultural system (which we will discuss below), the communes became irrelevant, and in the early 1980s they were dissolved. The local governments took over their administrative functions, leaving the country much less centralized than the more Leninist-minded would prefer. Indeed, their predictions of the dire consequences of administrative fragmentation proved to be on target. By the late 1980s local authorities and enterprises had embarked on such spending sprees (with borrowed money) that inflation became rampant.

There is, of course, no single perfect unit or level around which to build socialism or any other system. Stressing one level at the expense of the others means that government will not be properly attending to important matters inherent in other levels. The goal of the Maoists was to devolve authority on the smallest unit that could effectively undertake the activity in question, and their successors— though disagreeing on the specifics—take the same general approach. The main differences now are that the goal of local (or even national)

self-sufficiency has been abandoned and that there is less fear that devolution of economic authority will result in capitalism. Furthermore, when centralism is appropriate, current leaders are less hesitant to prescribe it than was Mao. It appears, however, that the debate between centralization and decentralization is unending.

We now look at how the leaders of the various levels of government are chosen, starting at the lowest level. The mayors of small *villages* (under 800 households, as are typical in the north) are now selected by means of direct election. In larger villages (more common in the south) mayors are chosen indirectly by delegates, each of whom is chosen by about ten households. When the party has a real presence in villages (which is not always the case), it often turns out that the mayors are the same party functionaries who had previously led the villages under collectivism, before "democracy." Although these "new class" people often do quite well for themselves financially, this is not invariably the case. When the reforms came many cadres found themselves without jobs, and the less industrious, educated, clever, and lucky among them were reduced to poverty.

At the next higher level, the *township*, there are popularly elected people's congresses. ("Council" might be a more appropriate term, but the Chinese use one term for these bodies at all levels.) There is at least a semblance of democracy in the way congress members are chosen: the party generally nominates about a half-dozen candidates, a couple more than there are seats to fill. The public can thus choose the ones they like, or at least reject the ones they dislike most.

The congresses choose the township heads, but do not have a completely free hand in such matters. Usually the Communist party nominates several candidates for the post, and although the congress can elect someone not nominated by the party, election results must be ratified by the county party committee. At any rate, once in office the township head does not have unlimited discretion. He or she is limited by the policies handed down by higher (nonelected) leaders. Equally important, such crucial positions as police chief and tax collector are essentially appointed. Otherwise, government leaders above the county level are nominally appointed by the people's congresses at each level.

Rural congresses are ephemeral bodies; when not in session (which is most of the time) there are no standing committees to carry on and thus the congresses virtually cease to exist.[35] The members of rural congresses at and above the county level are elected *indirectly,* that is, by the congresses at the lower level. For this reason, the system is democratic only to the extent that the township elections are fair. Until the 1980s voters had no choice, and had to vote by a show of hands. "Elections" invariably meant pro forma ratification of an official slate of candidates. Growing discontent with this election system was one of the issues that sparked the "democracy wall" movement of 1978–1979. After the election law of 1979, the process became marginally fairer, with secret ballots and more candidates than seats to be filled. The public can nominate candidates, but if there are too many the number must be reduced. Sometimes this is done through a sort of primary system, but often the process is "consultation"—one of the more obscure and apparently abused aspects of the electoral system.

When the election of local congress representatives is finally held, there is no campaign. Candidates' platforms must conform to what is officially acceptable. This makes elections much less meaningful than would otherwise be the case, especially in the cities. At the urban equivalent of the county level, congresses are elected directly by the citizenry, but these elections are much more tightly controlled by the authorities than are rural elections. Rural councillors have a certain closeness to their constituents that results in a degree of genuine representation, but urban voters generally consider the elections meaningless and

perfunctorily check off a few names on the ballot without any sense of political participation. They know that once the councillors are elected they will be obliged to abide by the dictates of the party, and will not represent the interests of their constituents.

Even when the voters are given real choices, the electoral system is still undemocratic. Not only are elections above the county level indirect and subject to party manipulation, but by law the rural majority is underrepresented at the higher levels. Because of the overrepresentation of cities in the congresses at all levels, a rural delegate to the National People's Congress represents about eight times as many people as an urban delegate. This is a problem so far unaddressed by either China's democratic movement or the reformers—both groups being essentially urban in their orientation.

THE PARTY

Nominally, China has a multiparty system,[36] but only one party has any political influence. The organizing of the Chinese Communist Party (CCP) began in 1920 with the emergence of six cells comprised of urban intellectuals in various cities. Although this particular event went largely unnoticed at the time, there was considerable pro-Bolshevik sentiment emerging among many intellectuals. The recent revolution in Russia seemed to be a development from which China could learn much. The Chinese were impressed when the foreign affairs commissar in Moscow renounced all rights in China that the previous tsarist regime had won, such as the Chinese Eastern Railroad across Manchuria. No other imperialist power appeared to be mending its ways, and so these new Russian leaders received a respectful hearing, as did their ideology. Still, by the time of China's first Communist party congress in 1921, the country probably had only about 50 people who considered themselves Communists. The congress had just 13 participants, plus two Russian delegates. The

Russians and their successors played a key role, helping to organize the party according to Leninist principles and manipulating the relations between the Communists and Nationalists (who had not yet come to power). In 1925, believing that the "bourgeois" revolution had to be consummated before there could be a meaningful Communist movement, the Russians insisted that the Communist party virtually dissolve and its members join the Kuomintang. This move proved to be a disaster for the Communists, who fell victim to the 1927 massacre known as the "White Terror."

Mao Zedong had attended the first party congress, but did not become the party leader until 14 years later. The White Terror persuaded him that China's revolution would not be truly proletarian, as it was impossible to organize workers in cities where right-wing authorities easily repressed such efforts. Mao and a few like-minded Communists decided to revert to the ancient Chinese practice of retreating to remote interprovincial borderlands, where they would try to organize the peasants not only politically but also militarily. Eventually the "official" Communists were forced to give up their underground existence in Shanghai and join Mao in Jiangxi Province. Throughout the 1930s and 1940s, the Red army was really the backbone of the Communist movement.

In the Soviet tradition, China's state constitution used to acknowledge the party's central role. The CCP was defined as the working class's "vanguard," and as such was to exercise leadership over the state and the entire population (Article 2). However, this clause was dropped from all but the preamble of the 1982 Constitution, apparently as part of Deng Xiaoping's efforts to check party interference in state operations.[37] The party also has its own constitution which sets forth the organizations' purposes, structure, and membership provisions,[38] which, once declared that any adult from the appropriate classes who was willing to accept party discipline and pay dues could become a member. But in the 1982 party constitution this was brought more into line with reality, and people are now only given the right to "apply" for membership. In practice, membership has always been by invitation and limited to an elite. It now numbers 50.3 million, or 7 percent of the adult population.

In most respects, the CCP is similar to the old Soviet Communist Party. It has a hierarchical structure, ranging from the half-dozen men who comprise the standing committee of the politburo down to the 3 million primary party organizations (cells). Under the politburo is the Central Committee, which in recent years has increasingly been dominated by provincial interests. The party's secretariat is in charge of the party's day-to-day party operations. (Once it was a major policy-making forum and overseer of government, but that is no longer the case.) National party congresses are large and meet infrequently, ratifying what the politburo has decided. The whole central party apparatus operates largely in secret, and parallels the government bureaucracy, which it tries to keep politically responsive. Lower-level units are functional, not territorial or ethnic. The party is dominated by old men from the largest nationality (ethnic Chinese); rank-and-file members enjoy social (but little political) influence—they are better off financially than most people, and must pay dues to the party. They are supposed to be true believers in Marxism-Leninism rather than religion.

During the 1980s at least token efforts were also made to democratize the internal operations of the party. At the Central Committee elections, held during Thirteenth Party Congress (1987), there were 5 percent more names than seats to be filled, and a few of the more disliked candidates lost. But meaningful democracy for the party would probably require permitting factions or blocs to form around contending policies. Some people advocated a "multifactional party system," but that idea has been shot down by the leadership.[39] The intraparty democratization efforts were therefore even less successful (or perhaps less sincere) than the efforts to democratize the state. As in government elections, party members continue to be given more choice of candidates, but nominees for internal party elections generally require the approval of the center before they can be voted on. Furthermore, as with the state elections, there is malapportionment. Not only is the country-side underrepresented, but party members in the central state apparatus are greatly overrepresented in, say, the national Party Congress. In the late 1980s, elections within the Party Congress were unusually democratic (judging by surprise defeats of some conservatives), but that has not been true in the 1990s.[40] Indeed, 79,000 members who had supported the democracy movement were eventually expelled from the party or (in the case of the more fortunate ones) given the rare right to resign. These obstreperous party members were often younger people, and especially in Beijing their dismissal exacerbated the "aging" problem of the party.

The leadership realizes that morale is low among party members generally. "The biggest danger is not attack by enemy forces domestically and abroad," commented a secret 1990 memorandum. "It is that the party ranks will abandon basic Marxist principles. Some comrades feel worried or doubtful, and ask whether China can hold out."[41] Some members, seeing what happened in the Soviet Union, decided that it was better to leave the party rather than die with it. Given such heretical thinking, the normal right of a party member to reserve opinion on policies with which they disagree appears to have been curbed. "If one insists on reserving different views from the party on questions of major political principle, one can hardly be described as a qualified party member."[42] In addition, it has been reemphasized that the CCP is the party of the working class; the notion that it should become an "all-people" party has been officially disavowed.

The leadership cannot function without the party, but it is well aware that the party, for good reason, is held in low public esteem. Al-though an effort has been made to at least get local party functionaries off the backs of economic administrators and enterprise managers ("separation of party and government"), even at the height of reforms, government functionaries at all levels have been constantly reminded to act in accordance with the line, principles, and policies of the party center. Zhao Ziyang even attempted to eliminate party cells from government agencies, but this failed and they are now stronger than ever, with cells established or reestablished in educational institutions, businesses, and rural administrative units.

LEADERSHIP

Given the cumbersome state and party apparatus, how do the leaders lead? It was the belief of Karl Marx that leadership is more a product of history than a positive determinant of events. Genuine revolutions were supposed to be leaderless. Although Engels modified this principle by saying that insurrections must be centralized, it is nonetheless fundamental to classical Marxism that leaders are at least replaceable, if not dispensable. A leader's main responsibility is to understand the times; events take care of themselves. Most of Marx's early disciples continued to deemphasize the role of leadership. However, the more realistic Lenin saw nothing but danger in spontaneous revolution promoted by the untutored masses. In Russia, at least, someone had to organize and educate the proletariat and ignite the revolution—not necessarily in that order. The key tools for Lenin were the elitist party and the skilled leadership. Only after the attainment of communism would there be no need to distinguish between the leaders and the led; then a truly leaderless society might be possible.

The Chinese Communists operate very much within this Leninist tradition. (For a list of PRC leaders, see Table 8.3.) For them the issue is not whether there should be leadership, but the relative importance of individual leaders compared to that of institutions and groups

Table 8.3 THE PRC'S PARAMOUNT LEADERS
AND THEIR CHIEF LIEUTENANTS

(Dates indicate periods of ascendancy; those in bold
print are dates of death.)

Mao Zedong (1935–**1976**)
    Liu Shaoqi (1945–**1966**)
    Zhou Enlai (1949–**1976**)
    Lin Biao (1966–**1971**)
    Deng Xiaoping (1954–1966, 1973–1976)

Hua Guofeng (1976–1981)

Deng Xiaoping (1977–)
    Hu Yaobang (1980–1987)
    Zhao Ziyang (1987–1989)
    Jiang Zemin (1989–)

of leaders. During Mao Zedong's chairmanship, the successful conduct of the affairs of the nation was officially attributed directly to his personal leadership. In reality, Mao's style of leadership varied considerably over the years. When he became the leader of the Chinese Communist party in 1935, his luck and skill combined to enable the party to enjoy success after success (in contrast to his hapless predecessors in that position). Inevitably, the leader became a legendary, almost worshipful figure. Even in the late 1950s, when Chinese communism encountered serious difficulties, Mao was able to overcome the challenges to his leadership and enjoyed absolute ascendancy. When party politburo members did not give him adequate support, Mao had an uncanny ability to go "under their heads" to the party's rank-and-file (and later to the public in general). In 1959, at the famous plenary session of the Central Committee at Lushan, Mao demonstrated what his would-be opponents were up against. At the meeting Mao was warned that if he insisted on purging popular figures like Marshal Peng Dehuai, the army might revolt. At that point in the debate, Mao tearfully declared that if the armed services turned against him, he would return to the villages and recruit another army. Mao carried the day, but his grip on the party and government continued

to slip, and he found himself treated "like a Buddha on a shelf"—respected but not followed.

The key to recovering political power and rekindling the revolution, Mao eventually concluded, was to regain and enhance his stature as China's omnipresent charismatic leader. In this process, the army and the general media would be the tools. By the late 1960s the nation was blanketed with every conceivable trapping of the cult of "The Great Teacher, Great Leader, Great Supreme Commander, and Great Helmsman." Not only portraits but badges, rituals, reports of near miracles, and the ever-read and -waved "little red book" of his quotations were the order of the day. In the book's introduction by Lin Biao (which Lin later regretted having written), Mao was described as a man of "genius" whose thought was "an inexhaustible source of strength and a spiritual atom bomb." Although such unabashedness had no appeal to intellectuals, the new approach was possible because Mao had long been the personification of Chinese communism. For the masses, to whom the party was largely an indigestible abstraction, the person of Mao seemed to be a more meaningful and promising rallying point.

As a vehicle for promoting the Cultural Revolution, the cult of personality served its purpose. But many were concerned about the implications of excessive reliance on one man's personality at the expense of institutions. Without legal restraints there was no way to control the overzealous, a problem which produced tremendous injustice and suffering. Indeed, Mao himself seems to have been aware of the contradiction between a personality cult and real revolutionary goals, and to have had grave reservations. To his wife, Jiang Qing, he reportedly wrote: "Now I have self-doubts. I know that when the tiger [in me] is absent from the mountain, the monkey professes himself king. I have become such a king. . . . The higher one is elevated, the harder one falls."

The fall did not come immediately, but there was a tapering off of the Mao cult during his last few years. When the end came, his posthumous charisma sufficed to install his follower Hua Guofeng as chairman of the party. Hua sought to preserve the image (and corpse) of Mao by building a mausoleum for the late leader in Beijing's Tiananmen, the great square so full of national symbolism for all Chinese. Hua began wearing his hair as Mao had, and tried to present himself as equally charismatic. But as we have seen, Mao's blessing was not enough to ensure that his chosen successor could retain power. Mao's contributions to history were being questioned, including his act of naming a political heir.

By the time of the Twelfth Party Congress (1982) the personality cult was completely rejected. Whereas the 1977 party constitution had hailed Mao Zedong as "the greatest Marxist-Leninist of our time," the new charter explicitly forbade personality cults. Reference was made to "Mao Zedong Thought," but this was interpreted as denoting the collective wisdom of the party's leaders and theorists. Since then, Mao's actual writings has hardly ever been read.

The 1980s saw the leaders groping for a new system to replace the old. They first tried "collective leadership," with Deng Xiaoping first among equals, but this system did not prove viable. His political conservatism clashed with more modern-minded party leaders, and Deng fell back on personalized one-man rule. He realized that this system, or at any rate he personally, would not last forever, and he gradually gave up his official positions. However, he could not bring himself to relinquish his power, which did not depend on those positions. Too old to actively manage the country, he became the great balancer, or arbiter of the factions he permitted to form at the top.

To oversimplify a bit, we can say that there were three factions. First, there were the reform-minded people originally led by Zhao Ziyang and later by Zhu Rongji. At the other extreme were the hard-liners such as Chen Yun and Peng Zhen, opposed to democracy of any sort and opposed to capitalist reforms. Between these factions was an amorphous group of middle-of-the roaders who wanted neither democracy nor brutal repression, neither capitalism nor highly centralized state socialism. These people often acted as power brokers between the two other factions. The only coherent, positive plan shared by the three factions was to retain power. Beyond this, there was no consensus.

There was one important change during the Deng era: the treatment of deposed leaders. Whereas Liu Shaoqi and Lin Biao had been made pariahs, this was not the case with Hua Guofeng, Hu Yaobang, and Zhao Ziyang. Conservatives wanted to punish Zhao, but Deng merely kept him out of sight and prosecuted his aides. Normally, the group at the top now stops short of purges; many of these would be destabilizing and might bring them all down. The survivors may seek legitimacy by means of ideological attacks on the fallen, but physical abuse in such instances is now rare.

How do leaders exercise their power? They are rarely able to rule by fiat, with one or a few people making unilateral decisions that are then carried out. The decision-making process is apt to be disjointed, protracted, and incremental. The processes of both policy formation and policy implementation are commonly characterized by negotiation among agencies of government and party, which are apt to have different points of view and different interests to protect. For the technocrats, ideology plays little role, and coercion by the central leaders, is unlikely to be productive except perhaps in times of political crisis.

As we have noted, Chinese leaders rely little on institutions. Real-life politics in China is played out not in formal organizations, but in personal networks and alliances. Although the Chinese can make a fetish of following bureaucratic procedures when they want to, they know that to really get things done one relies on *guanxi,* or personal relationships. More important than bureaucratic structures are personal connections based on patron-client relations, friendships, and family ties. The relative lack of importance of titles and offices is manifest even at the top level of the party. Thus, two successive secretaries-general, the slightly liberal Hu Yaobang and Zhao Ziyang, were dismissed (1987 and 1989, respectively) on the decision of Deng Xiaoping. Deng himself had little in the way of formal authority. (An avid card player, in his last years he bore no title other than Honorary President of the Chinese Bridge Association.) However, there were hundreds of thousands of bureaucrats whom he had rehabilitated after the Cultural Revolution who now happily did anything he asked. Furthermore, according to a secret 1987 agreement, no important decision could thereafter be made without Deng's approval. Other gerontocrats, like Deng, held power without responsibility; thus titled underlings had to "take the fall" when the old men, with little understanding of modern realities, made mistakes.

It is possible for a leader to succeed even without the kind of network Deng had at his command, but there must be compensating factors to rely on. Seniority is one such factor, although it is not essential; when Jiang Zemin became party secretary-general he was relatively junior. And although Jiang did not have personal ties with subordinates, he had two powerful patrons in Deng himself and Li Xiannian. He had few political friends, but he also had few enemies. Finally, the importance of his positions in institutions should not be discounted altogether. In the "politics of compromise" institutions may have little sanctity and offer the players little protection, but holding an office still means something. Being party head certainly meant that Jiang had better access than his rivals to valuable information, and the secretary-general's written approval was often required on party pronouncements and orders. And however tenuous Jiang's control of the military may have been, being chairman of the party's Central Military Commission gave him real power, for no military decree could take effect without his signature. Only time would tell whether such considerations would translate into ultimate authority

in a succession crisis; much would depend on whether Deng lived long enough to enable Jiang to build *guanxi* with his own new informal network of subordinates. In this he was handicapped, because Premier Li Peng, and not he, ran the state administration and was responsible for managing the economy.

On any given issue or policy question, once the bargaining process is complete and the policy has been laid down, everything depends upon the conduct of the cadres. Not only do those at the lower levels have their personal interests to consider, but they are also caught in the awkward position of having to impose orders from above on the reluctant people they see and lead on a day-to-day basis. Cadres are often confronted with the resentment of a public unhappy with the demands and prohibitions of the state. Thus, they often press for personal advantage or yield to the pressures from below, thereby seriously compromising state policies. This is especially true in China's cities, where people have had some education, tend to have their own ideas about politics, and do not blindly follow authority. In rural China, however, "leadership" is a more straightforward matter; few villagers openly question their obligation to accede to authority. As one farmer commented with regard to the 1989 demonstrations, "We didn't support the rioters. If Beijing is in chaos, then the whole country collapses. The leadership had to stop it. Besides, you have to obey the orders from your immediate superiors. That is a person's role in life."[43] Thus some Chinese are easily led, and some are not. For the latter, the leaders have certain tools at their disposal.

TOOLS OF CONTROL

The People's Liberation Armed Services (PLA)

China's military is more politicized than most—at the top level there is no clear distinction between military and party leadership. Still, it is only in times of crisis that the military looms large in the central political

Chairman Mao Zedong at Yanan in 1939, chatting with two of the youngest fighters in the forerunner of the People's Liberation Army.

process. Some of the most interesting periods in the political history of Chinese communism have been these crises. At such times, the Chinese army is the ultimate arbiter.

The "Red Army" was formed in 1927–1928, in the wake of the ruptured alliance between the CCP and the Kuomintang. The Communists first attempted to hold a few cities, but were forced to withdraw to mountain fastnesses in Jiangxi province. It was here that the army was really organized. Its military leader was German-educated Zhu De, and its chief political officer was Mao Zedong. From the beginning this was an army with "politics in command." By 1934 the Communist military forces could no longer resist Kuomintang pressure, and embarked on the dramatic Long March. One hundred thousand men and a handful of women undertook a 6000-mile trek which lasted a full year. Almost to the end,

when they arrived in northern China's Shaanxi province, they were pursued by the armies of Chiang Kai-shek. Only 10,000 or so completed the march, but the Chinese Communist soldier had nonetheless proven himself.

Soon the Communists were once again allied with the Kuomintang, this time against the Japanese. It was during the World War II period that they perfected their guerrilla warfare techniques. These were only marginally important in the war against Japan (the outcome of which was largely determined in other theaters) and in China's civil war which followed, but the PLA's guerrilla style, or "people's war," would influence military thinking for decades.

One tenet of people's war strategy was that "people are more important than weapons," from which it was concluded that it was not necessary to develop sophisticated hardware and state-of-the-art techniques. Even the navy was expected to plan for a type of guerrilla warfare which required few ships larger than coastal defense craft. The theory of "people's war" was abandoned after Mao's death. One of Deng Xiaoping's Four Modernizations was military. By reducing the size of the army and concentrating on elite forces, some improvements took place during the 1980s. However, little in the way of new funding for the PLA's modernization was forthcoming until after the 1989–1991 period, when the military's value to the regime was demonstrated and United Nations troops showed in Iraq how devastating ultramodern military technology could be.

Except toward Tibet, the Chinese Communists have not acted in an expansionist way. Although the army has fought some foreign wars, all have been indecisive and (save the Korean war) brief. Instead, the PLA has primarily served nonmilitary purposes relating to China's internal politics. During the early 1950s the PLA was instrumental in helping the Communists consolidate political control over the country. During the Great Leap Forward (1958–1960) Mao Zedong sought to integrate military and civilian life and to have troops spend two months a year engaged in productive work (farming, construction projects, and the like). But some in the army objected to the Great Leap in general and especially to the role assigned to the PLA. Critics included no less popular a figure than Defense Minister Peng Dehuai, who, as already noted, challenged Mao on these issues at the 1959 Lushan Plenum.

Lin Biao's appointment as defense minister that year proved crucial, for it meant that when Mao decided to launch the Cultural Revolution (essentially an attack on the government and party), the PLA was the only important institution that was in his camp. Indeed, the armed services had already established themselves as a revolutionary model from which others were to learn. Mao had spelled out his ideas on the subject in his famous May Seven (1966) Directive, in which he called for the PLA to be "a great school in which our soldiers learn politics, military affairs, and culture." The troops were also encouraged to engage in agriculture and industry, but most importantly, Mao called upon them to participate in the Cultural Revolution. To show civilians the way, the PLA made itself a paragon of egalitarianism and abolished ranks.[44] But after the Cultural Revolution broke out, the soldiers had to be more than models and social critics. With the party and government bureaucrats under siege, the military was often called on to take a direct managerial role in civilian factories, communes, and government bureaus. More often than not, they wound up supporting the "right" against the cultural revolutionaries. To the extent that the economy of the nation continued to function during these years, it was largely the PLA that was responsible. The institution also played an important political role, sometimes supporting the left and sometimes just trying to mediate disputes, according to the dictates of Mao Zedong and his wife, Jiang Qing. When Mao died, the PLA again played a crucial role in helping Deng Xiaoping to carry out a virtual coup d'état.

Since then, the civilian leadership has been trying to effect changes in the relationship between the armed services and the party. Under Mao, there had been an almost mystical link between the two, with the PLA directly under the party chairman's command. This institutional arrangement was supposedly eliminated from the 1982 Constitution, which made the army subordinate to the government. However, the government's defense ministry has been largely defunct since Defense Minister Lin Biao's 1971 coup attempt, and the PLA is in reality still directed by the Central Military Commission (CMC), a *party* organ. The senior soldiers have not objected to this arrangement; better that one's boss be one with real clout in the party than a government functionary with little influence or access to funds.

Still, tension persisted between the military and political policy makers. For example, in the mid-1980s the latter decided that egalitarianism in the PLA must be abandoned. Ranks, which had been abolished in 1965, were ordered restored. This simple but controversial move took four years to implement. In the meantime, the size of the army (especially the cadres) was reduced, with many civilian cadres brought in to help the modernization process. The government was quite frank in saying that "incompetent officers" must be discharged and replaced by people from "outside the establishment." This meant that officers would not be recruited from the ranks, as before, but from civilian agencies and the military academies. Not surprisingly, the PLA old guard is unenthusiastic about this "modernization." They want to preserve the prestige (though not necessarily the bloated size) of the force, and resent the downgrading or firing of veteran officers. If military modernization is one of the four modernizations, they wonder why the army must shrink so much, and why even as late as 1990 only 1.7 percent of the gross domestic product went for defense (one of the lowest percentages in Asia). "Reform cannot be implemented when there is no money on hand."[45]

Starved for funds, the PLA has increasingly gone into business. Military facilities that could be spared for nonmilitary purposes (and some that really could not) have been converted to profit-making hospitals, hostels, and campgrounds. Military facilities and equipment are often used for commercial transport. There is also much manufacturing by military-owned factories, as well as joint ventures with foreigners in such enterprises as luxury hotels. Ten percent of all soldiers, or 300,000 men, are said to be engaged in such nonmilitary work. Finally, the military-industrial complex has been involved in massive arms sales abroad, with no regard for the intentions of the buyers.[46]

By 1989, when Deng and Li Peng first tried to employ the army to revive the conservatives' flagging political fortunes, it appeared that Deng's previous attempt to retain personal control over an emasculated PLA had backfired. The PLA turned out to be depoliticized, commercialized, and often disgruntled. In May, some commanding officers refused to send troops to break up the demonstrations in Beijing. (They ended up in prison.) Others perfunctorily carried out orders, but the first soldiers sent toward Tiananmen were easily overwhelmed by the populace. The half-hearted effort seemed to collapse when highly articulate students reminded the troops of the traditional bond between the army and the people. That bond would soon be broken.

To understand how Deng was finally able to gain PLA support and overcome the peaceful rebellion in 1989, it is necessary to try to examine the real (informal) structure of the armed services, although this inevitably leads us into some speculation. The actual center of power in the PLA seems to have been the family of Yang Shangkun, who (aside from being state president) was general secretary of the powerful Central Military Commission, which sets military policy and appoints the seven regional commanders. The CMC's chairman (through 1989) was Deng Xiaoping, his last significant formal position. As usual in Chinese politics, there was much secrecy about the real power relations, but Yang apparently placed his relatives and supporters in strategic

military positions, most prominently a brother as head of the General Political Department. From the point of view of the political leadership, the wisdom of Mao's old axiom that "political power grows out of the barrel of a gun" had been confirmed. Once again they took the army seriously, and even increased funding for it. However, they were well aware of the tentative nature of rank-and-file support for the crackdown. Between 50 percent and 70 percent of each soldier's time was now spent in mandatory political study. The decade-long effort to depoliticize the PLA had collapsed and the military's main role was once again to support one political faction against the others.[47]

The Police

The importance of China's internal security apparatus has varied over time. It was crucial in consolidating Communist power in the 1950s, but in his later years Mao Zedong became disenchanted with the system, which was allowed to decay and become fragmented. In recent years, however, the reorganized security forces have become an essential element of the political order.

China has four security services. First is the Bureau of Public Security, which performs normal police functions (a sort of combination of the United States' local police and the Federal Bureau of Investigation). It is much feared, not very efficient, and essentially urban; it is only thinly represented in the countryside. The Bureau is a sprawling organization of 800,000 people which enforces order with the help of street committees. The latter consist typically of retired women who are often considered busybodies. They are concerned with domestic problems (impending divorces, unauthorized pregnancies, etc.), as well as being watchdogs against crime and political dissidence. They also promote public health campaigns, distribute food coupons, regulate bicycle traffic, and protect the environment.[48]

Second is the paramilitary People's Armed Police. The PAP guards government installations and the frontiers, including virtual colonies like Eastern Turkestan (Xinjiang) and Tibet. The People's Armed Police also swings into action whenever there is a civil disturbance such as a riot (of which dozens occur in the country annually). After the Tiananmen demonstrations, the PAP was expanded to a force of 600,000, and performs such functions as trying to prevent dissidents from leaving the country.

The best-known security agency is the huge Ministry of State Security (MSS), which has the main responsibility for preventing political dissidence. It has five academies of its own to train its personnel. Perhaps surprisingly, the ministry still has what are (by Chinese standards) liberal leanings, and is considered benign compared to the often brutal ordinary local police and the military.

The party has its own security machine, comprised of dual-purpose agencies such as the Discipline Inspection Commission (which investigates misdeeds by party members) and the United Front Department (concerned with non-Communist intellectuals, religious groups, and ethnic minorities). All of these agencies, including the three on the government side, regularly report to the party secretariat, which can mobilize this vast surveillance network to ensure political orthodoxy.

During the period of apparent liberalism in the late 1980s, there appeared to be greatly reduced surveillance of the public by the security apparatus, but this was something of an illusion. Actually, there was filming of dissident activities, tapping of telephones, photographing of unauthorized wall posters, and videotaping of private meetings. All of this resulted in a large volume of evidence that was produced at the victims' "trials." It is true, however, that both the MSS and the PAP had many sympathizers for the prodemocracy demonstrators, and the organs turned out to be unreliable props for the regime. They have since been reorganized and made to conform.[49] Although the lines of command among the four security agencies are murky, it is evident that they are under the de facto control of the Party's politburo; at this writing, the man in charge is Qiao Shi.

The Media

The main purpose of the press and broadcast media has usually been to glorify the party and its leaders. However, the media have not always been monolithic, and even when in power both Mao Zedong and Deng Xiaoping at various times found that they had difficulty getting the media to carry their messages. Once a disgusted Mao declared that he did not want to have anything to do with reporters. Gradually he came to perceive the entire press as hostile to the revolution, and in 1966 he instigated a massive purge. During most of the 1980s, China's 1600 newspapers and over 5000 magazines were actually "pluralistic" by Communist standards. Newspapers occasionally carried articles written by the party's most liberal thinkers. Of special interest was a genre of newspapers and journals concerned with legal issues. Because they included muckraking accounts, such as exposés of cadres' wrongdoing, they were informative and popular.[50] Also during this period, various worker-oriented papers championed the long-neglected rights of that class. But there were limits, and even Zhao Ziyang opposed press freedom. Journalists have always chafed under the restraints placed on them. During the demonstrations of May 1989 some of them marched with the students, shouting to crowds along the way, "Don't believe what we say. We tell lies."

That turned out to be a chilling foreboding of things to come. After the crackdown 80,000 people were convicted for involvement in "illegal publishing." Hundreds of publications were closed, and those that remained resumed speaking with one voice. The democracy movement had been a "counterrevolutionary plot" on the part of "a small number of bad elements" who had killed hundreds of soldiers; no students had been killed at Tiananmen. Clips of people who had allowed themselves to be interviewed for foreign television were now shown on local television as "rumor mongers." The interviewees were quickly arrested. Employees of international hotels were searched to make sure they were not carrying newspapers from Hong Kong or abroad, and foreign broadcasts were commonly jammed.

Cinema is an important medium in China. Although the artistic freedom of the 1980s resulted in the production of some fine films (such as "River Elegy"), little more than propaganda films have been seen since 1989. Workers are encouraged to view such movies during normal working hours.

Members of the political elite do not rely on the mass media for their information. Several dozen "internal" newspapers and journals give them more reliable accounts of domestic and international events. There are many types of these; the more bland are available to millions, but the most sensitive are only available to a handful. Writers who cannot be heard on the mass media can often have their articles printed in the internal press. This has been true of reformers in recent years, just as it had been of conservatives during the 1980s when they were out of power.

But the general public is limited to the normal media, whose writers are supposed to act as "the eyes, ears, and mouthpiece" of the party. Some believe it, and some are skeptical. When one Beijing college student was asked what she believes in the news media, she said, "sometimes the weather report."[51] For those who care, reading the press can be an exercise in deciphering. Often the surface words are not the real point, so one reads between the lines to figure out what is happening.

The Judiciary

In China, as elsewhere, there is tension between the need for internal security and the desire for freedom. In reality, "security" can mean two very different things—the security of the people from lawlessness, and the secu-

rity of the leadership from threats to its power. As for freedom, most people agree that too little of it has a stifling effect on a civilization, whereas too much can be chaotic and counterproductive.

Where do the Chinese stand on these issues? In the West it is generally assumed that freedom is only viable within a framework of law, and many Chinese would agree with this proposition. Unfortunately, there is also a common view of law in China that is quite different from the view in the West. In imperial times, the term "law" (fa) was co-opted by the so-called Legalists, who used law not so much for the protection of the citizenry as to assert the rulers' control. It was rare for a commoner to attempt to assert his (much less her) legal rights. During the republican period there was an attempt to fashion a more modern legal system, but the Nationalists did not control enough of the country for a sufficient length of time to put it into effect, and many elements within the Kuomintang (KMT) were of the old Legalist mold. (Legalism seemed to dovetail neatly with the fascism that was so popular in many parts of the world in the 1930s.)

Upon their accession to power, the Communists made some efforts to terminate past Chinese law. However, for many years they failed to draw up comprehensive replacement laws and were slow to establish new organs of judicial administration, and to this day the process is incomplete. Through the early 1950s many of the security organs and courts continued to exist much as they had before 1949. Not infrequently, these were staffed largely by former KMT officials, who continued to adhere to traditional practices and laws faute de mieux.

During these years the Communists continued to wage revolution against their opponents. But by 1954 the new government was prepared to wind down its extralegal campaign against former capitalists and landlords, and to regularize judicial practices. The shift seemed possible because the new regime had survived its first few years, eliminated its most serious opponents, and built up a corps of trained cadres who were supposed to understand the new laws and regulations and be able to administer the new judicial system. This turning toward a more formal mode of law was celebrated by the promulgation of a constitution in 1954, which mandated that "all personnel of organs of state must be loyal to the system of people's democracy, observe the Constitution and the law, and strive to serve the people." There ensued a three-year period which, in the Chinese Communist experience, was relatively close to constitutional government.

The constitutional experiment had widespread support at all levels. Although it is possible that Mao Zedong was not as enthusiastic about the Constitution as people like his deputy, Liu Shaoqi, there is no reason to assume that there were substantial disagreements. For his part, Liu praised the document, insisting that "Every person and every organ of state, without exception, must observe the Constitution." Years later, after his fall from grace, Liu's critics recalled that he had advocated the establishment of a comprehensive legal system which, they argued, had been tantamount to establishing bourgeois law and restoring capitalism. With due allowance for hyperbole, there is doubtless some truth to the charge that by 1954 Liu had sought to downgrade the state's role as a dictatorial instrument. The time had come, he believed, for regularization.

The practice of quasi-constitutional government and bureaucratic normalization was a success if measured by its stability and progress in modernizing the economy and political institutions. Viewed in terms of cultural and social revolution, however, this system of formal law was seen by some as constituting a serious roadblock. The constitutional experiment was thus brought to an abrupt end in June 1957, after many people, persuaded of their legal rights, had indulged in what the leadership considered an unacceptable orgy of liberalism and negativism. The Hundred Flowers period, therefore, had special mean-

ing for legal development. For those who advocated the formal model of law, it was a major test, and the result was a major setback. As a chief justice later delicately put it in 1964, the development of legal institutions "fell behind the development of the situation."[52]

Things would get worse before they got better. China was entering a *cultural* revolution, and law is an integral aspect of culture. At times the Maoist press went so far as to advocate the dissolution of law. *People's Daily* came out explicitly in favor of "lawlessness," proclaiming that only in such a spirit could revolutionaries control China's destiny. In an apparent reference to those desiring a return to law and order, the newspaper likened revolutionaries to "the Monkey King [in a traditional Chinese novel] who turns the heavenly palace upside down. We will destroy your 'law,' smash your 'world,' rebel against you, and seize your power."[53] In 1967 the chief procurator was publicly condemned, and the following year the president of the Supreme Court reportedly was driven to suicide. In this atmosphere, the courts ceased functioning.

During the 1980s considerable progress was made in effecting the rule of law, which came to play a greater role in people's lives. For example, it was not uncommon even for farmers to take legal action against errant cadres or people engaging in unfair business practices. In the late 1980s, when some local officials tried to recollectivize the land, farmers were occasionally able to resist this by resort to the courts. Such actions by citizens were unprecedented in China. Unfortunately, the tentative steps taken to insulate the courts from political interference were short-lived, and the 1989 crackdown inflicted great damage on the judiciary.[54] Furthermore, many problems had never been solved. The law codes leave much room for interpretation; judicial precedents often cannot guide jurists, as information about previous court rulings is generally secret. Indeed, even the laws themselves are sometimes secret, so the application of the law is often incomprehensible. One law that has finally been published is the criminal code. However, seemingly minor crimes are punished with erratic severity, especially "political crimes."[55] Indeed, to a large extent the judicial institutions exist less to protect the legal rights of citizens than to prevent anyone from threatening the power of the authorities .

In the past, cadres and businessmen saw little need to obey the center's laws that got in their way. As one mayor put it, "If laws are strictly enforced, the economy will be restricted; if laws are flexibly enforced, the economy will be invigorated."[56] Such attitudes are not surprising, given the absence of any tradition of legal accountability of bureaucrats. Still, two months before the Tiananmen crackdown an "Administrative Litigation Law" was adopted by the NPC.[57] This would give plaintiffs, including citizens, the right to bring lawsuits to challenge specific administrative acts. Also, the Civil Procedure Code was amended in 1991, and now promises to ensure consistency and enforceability of private (noncriminal) judgments. These two measures may well prove to be important steps toward the achievement of the rule of law in China, at least in the area of *civil* law.

However, the *criminal* law lags seriously behind. Trials for accused people are perfunctory, and there are undoubtedly many miscarriages of justice. This is especially true as the criminal law is applied to political dissidents, who are often under the vague concept of "counterrevolutionary" crime. According to the criminal code, counterrevolution encompasses "all actions that are aimed at overthrowing the dictatorship of the proletariat and the socialist order." Examples given are "organizing reactionary sects, perpetuating counterrevolutionary activities through the use of feudalistic superstitions" and "instigating [others] to oppose revolution." Whereas before 1989 it appeared that this pseudo-legal concept might be abandoned, it now appears that no such depoliticization of the law is likely in the foreseeable future. Indeed, in 1991 the Minister of Justice insisted that better use be made of

"the weapon of law" to combat domestic and foreign enemies and peaceful evolution. "Since our law is socialist law, it will without question serve the politics of the proletariat class, socialist construction, reform and the open door, as well as the consolidation of the dictatorship of the proletariat."[58]

The whole support system has been an integrated network. The media serve as the leadership's cheering section, making clear the official line and probably persuading most Chinese of its validity. Those unpersuaded are usually dealt with by the security apparatus and judiciary, but when skepticism becomes too widespread and vocal, the military can be summoned.

INTEREST GROUPS

In a polity where the state is powerful and the citizens are weak, there is likely to be little activity by interest groups, at least those of a private nature. Indeed, if the state is totalitarian (a theoretical possibility but usually infeasible as a practical matter), by definition there can be no political inputs from the society at all. On the other hand, when the *society* is strong (or "civic"), interest groups abound and the state must listen to them. After 1949 China was an unambiguous example of the strong state and weak society. Is this changing?

There are two different ways of examining interest groups in China. The first is to ask whether such groups are, from the rulers' point of view, legitimate or illegitimate. The party, the officially sanctioned minor parties, and labor organizations, all very tame, are examples of officially sanctioned interest groups. Such organizations are perhaps best thought of as part of the state rather than part of the society. This is not true of "illegitimate" pressure groups such as dissident intellectual organizations or unauthorized labor unions. There is also a gray area between legitimacy and illegitimacy. Here one speaks of the factions within the establishment (especially the party), which often vie to advance parochial group interests.

Even though there is a question as to the legitimacy of such groups, they are still more "state" than "society."

The second question is whether interest groups are organized, or whether they are simply individuals who have no connection other than sharing (perhaps unknowingly) certain views or wanting to advance parallel interests. If the latter is the case, we cannot speak of coalition or mobilization; there is no engaging in strategic interaction with the authorities. Everyone simply "does his own thing," but the state may nonetheless hear (and perhaps even heed) the message.

Farmers

Ironically, the least organized group in China's political economy is probably the one the center has had to listen to most attentively. One sometimes hears vague references to a "farmers' party." This is not literally a political party, but rather a collectivity of interests that are concerned with rural work—interests which have sometimes pressed the leadership of the Communist party to institute more rational and profarmer policies. Thus, although the farmers themselves are largely disenfranchised and unorganized, the Rural Work Department is sensitive to farmers' interests and the realities of the rural situation. Farmers also have their champions among journalists, academics, and members of the National People's Congress. Everyone knows that they can "vote" in their own way by dragging their feet. We shall explore this subject in greater detail later in the chapter.

Workers

A system of labor unions was set up in the 1950s following the Soviet example; these organizations have primarily performed welfare functions and do not otherwise represent workers. Locals were first organized around workers' representative congresses, which in turn reported to about 20 (now 30) national unions, together forming the National Federation of Trade Unions. This arrangement supposedly offered a means for workers to communicate with the regime, but more importantly it has provided a structure through which official policies are communicated to workers. To some extent unions have served as vehicles for promoting labor discipline, primarily by reserving nonmonetary benefits for the well behaved. Indeed, in the 1960s leftists charged that the unions were vehicles for "economism," meaning that they paid too much attention to workers' material needs and not enough to promoting discipline. Thus trade unions were actually disbanded in 1967, and only revived in 1974.

In the ensuing years there was much soul-searching about the impotence of workers in a putative workers' state. On 6 October 1980, *Workers' Daily* acknowledged that working people often "have little say about important issues in their own enterprises." Although workers' congresses were supposed to give voice to workers' sentiments, in reality they failed to do this. "A workers' congress has no decisive power over major issues of the enterprise, nor has it the right to appoint, replace, award or punish the enterprise's leading members." One newspaper urged that these congresses "be made into an organ of power," although the writer seemed dubious about the prospects for success: "In the process of popularizing workers' congresses, it is entirely possible that obstinate resistance will be encountered from those who always follow the beaten track and, in particular, from those who worship the notion that 'power is everything.'" The reformers insisted that enterprise directors be made more responsible for their management, including a degree of accountability to their employees. Thus, there have been experiments at having people compete for the position of manager, with the employees given some say. This new role for the workers comes at the cost of some reduction of party control.

Chinese workers have usually had at least one thing going for them: the "iron rice bowl."

Everyone had a permanent job, which usually could be inherited by a son or daughter. Beginning in the mid-1980s these guarantees began to fade, though efforts to introduce piecework in 1986 failed because of worker resistance. These issues, coupled with the problem that wages were not keeping up with inflation, prompted numerous strikes. Such job actions had apparently not been legal since 1982, when the right to strike was removed from the Constitution. By the late 1980s the trade union federation was taking the position that it would neither encourage nor prohibit strikes, which were occurring at the rate of about 100 per year. At the same time, the leaders of the federation were trying to turn it into an organ that would defend workers' rights. In May 1989, the executive committee of the labor federation gave much financial support to the Tiananmen demonstrators. It also voted to declare a nationwide strike in support of the students and workers then demonstrating for democracy, but by this time martial law had been declared in Beijing and the conservatives were able to prevent the strike.

Official unions were too tepid and ineffective to satisfy labor militants, who moved in 1989 to establish independent unions in a dozen cities. To old-line Communists, it is outrageous for workers to do an end run around the party of the proletariat. Probably the only dissidents arrested during the democracy demonstrations of May 1989 were the leaders of the new union, and when the real crackdown came the next month, workers who had participated in independent trade unions were treated with particular brutality. The head of the independent union in China's most industrialized city, Shanghai, was shown on television being held at gunpoint with his face badly swollen, apparently from beatings. Although since then it sometimes has been possible for workers to demonstrate against employment conditions without necessarily suffering reprisals, in general the official trade unions have reverted to their former role as agents of the party. The locals continue to serve a welfare role, but there have been reports of increasing corruption in these highly undemocratic organizations.[59]

Despite the ephemeral "farmers' party" and the occasional proworker sentiments of the labor federation, both farmers and workers usually have the problem that there is no one at the center to support. Workers, for example, have found the program of the reformers about as inimical to their interests as the old ways of the conservatives. The reality of China is that the only group whose interests are really represented is the "new class"—party members and well-positioned technocrats and intellectuals. Otherwise, China does not have autonomous interest groups as the term is understood in developed countries. Social strata such as farmers and workers have "interests," of course, both vis-à-vis the state (in which case passive resistance is their best ploy) and vis-à-vis other local groups (in which case they battle it out directly, perhaps without much involvement by the state[60]). The center is still subject to pressures from below, sometimes obliging the authorities to take certain actions, and often closing off options they might like to pursue.

Key Terms

the center
communes
counterrevolution
democratic centralism
guanxi
iron rice bowl
Jiang Zemin
internal press
little red book
Lushan Plenum
May Seven Directive
Ministry of State Security
National Federation of Trade Unions
National People's Congress
party congress
People's Armed Police

People's Liberation Armed Services (PLA)
Red Flag
State Council
United Front Department
Yang Shangkun

Suggestions for Further Reading

Chang, Parris. *Power and Policy in China* (Dubuque, Iowa: Kendal/Hung, 1990).

Ch'i, Hsi-sheng. *Politics of Disillusionment: The Chinese Communist Party under Deng Xiaoping, 1978–1989* (White Plains, New York: M. E. Sharp, 1991).

Jencks, Harlan W., "Civil-Military Relations in China: Tiananmen and After." *Problems of Communism*, May 1991, pp. 14–29.

Lee Chin-chuan. *Voices of China: The Interplay of Politics and Journals* (New York: Gilford Press, 1990).

Lee, Hong Yung. *From Revolutionary Cadres to Party Technocrats in Socialist China* (Berkeley: University of California Press, 1991).

Lee Lai To. *Trade Unions in China 1949 to the Present: The Organization and Leadership of the All-China Federation of Trade Unions* (Singapore: Singapore University Press, 1986).

Lieberthal, Kenneth. *Policy Making in China: Leaders, Structures, and Processes* (Princeton: Princeton University Press, 1988).

O'Brien, Kevin J. *Reform Without Liberalization: China's National People's Congress and the Politics of Institutional Change* (New York: Cambridge University Press, 1990).

Shue, Vivienne. *The Reach of the State: Sketches of the Chinese Body Politic* (Stanford: Stanford University Press, 1988).

Tang Boqiao. *Anthems of Defeat: Crackdown in Hunan Province, 1989–1992* (New York: Asia Watch, 1992).

Walder, Andrew G., *Communist Neo-Traditionalism: Work and Authority in Chinese Industry* (Berkeley: University of California Press, 1986).

C. Public Policy

POLITICAL ECONOMY

To the extent that a country has a market economy, politics and economics are more or less distinguishable. Economic decisions are made by economic means (through sales and purchases), and political decisions are made by political means (voting or otherwise influencing the government). On the other hand, to the extent that an economy is managed by the government rather than "self-run" by market forces, economics is simply an aspect of politics. In such an economy, a myriad of decisions (which in a market economy do not have to be made at all) must be made by someone in the government. Thus, although understanding the economic system is essential to the understanding of any nation, when it comes to understanding the politics of a nation, economics is more important in Socialist systems than in capitalist ones. China is an example of this.

A thousand years ago China had the world's most highly developed economy. Today, China is comparatively backward and is one of the two poorest countries studied in this book. In 1990 its per capita gross national product ($305) was higher than Nigeria's ($199), but slightly lower than India's ($320), and tiny compared to that of neighboring Hong Kong ($10,939), the British-administered territory

with its free-wheeling laissez-faire economy. China has by far the smallest percentage of the labor force engaged in industry and services. China's poverty may seem surprising in that the government has long defended the deprivation of political and cultural rights on the grounds that it emphasized economic rights instead. But over 40 years after "liberation," there was still only one telephone for each 134 people, one of the lowest ratios in the world (compared with 2 in Hong Kong, though better than India's 180 and Nigeria's 397). Most people probably do not have running water in their homes, and indeed a tap that serves a whole village is a luxury.

Some attribute the problem of China's poverty to the legacy of the past (particularly the devastation of warfare and exploitation by foreigners), whereas others emphasize the disadvantageous population-resource base ratio. Although many also see the problem as fundamentally political, few in authority have been willing to consider whether lack of democracy is part of the problem—a point often made by dissidents. There has been much soul-searching at all levels regarding whether a Socialist economic system can really be as productive as one based on free enterprise. This is still a very touchy issue.

At the 1987 party congress Zhao Ziyang, while insisting that the economy would continue to be dominated by the state-run sector, added that "heterogeneous economic elements" would be brought into play. He intended to expand the role of private (including foreign-owned) concerns, and even denationalize some government-owned enterprises. The state would regulate the market; the market would guide enterprises. He warned leftists that if the state "adopts the traditional method of direct control, enterprises will not have autonomy and markets can't be formed."[61] Not only would raw materials and products compete in the marketplace, but so, to a considerable extent, would money, labor, information, and real estate. Of course, he did not dare call this "capitalism," which the regime has always inveighed against. Instead, it was "commoditization"—a euphemism for a free market. But Zhao's program was premature.

China's leaders have a tendency to use riddles when they discuss economics. Deng Xiaoping insisted that "A market economy is not necessarily capitalist, and a planned economy is not necessarily socialist." Normally, "capitalism" means free markets and respect for private property; it is the latter aspect that worries conservatives. In an implicit criticism of the program of the now deposed Zhao, the unpopular spokesman for the government Yuan Mu declared in 1991, "Capitalist economists' notion of a market economy is one in which private property is sacrosanct...and where the role of economic planning is completely eliminated. This does not accord with China's national characteristics and is not a road that should be followed."[62] This seems to mean that a market economy should be allowed, but it must be kept under tight rein in order to exist alongside a planned, socialist economy. Tiananmen had shown that too much privatization "laid the ideological foundation for counterrevolutionary rebellion."[63] Thus, according to Jiang Zemin, "The private sector can be only a supplement to the state and collective sectors, and must never predominate."[64]

Actually, there is considerable fluidity in China's economic policies. Power struggles

within the leadership usually involve fundamental disagreements about the economic policies China should pursue. To be sure, all leaders have favored "socialism," but the term has meant different things to different people. Purists insist that private property and material incentives are precluded, whereas others have taken the more pragmatic view that anything that mitigates the people's poverty is compatible with socialism. It has been easy for new administrations to attribute the nation's ills to the previous leadership's erroneous notions about economics. Nonetheless, each successive leadership has found itself facing the same dilemma: how to modernize the economy without doing violence to the values of nationalism and Marxism. This often requires awkward theoretical gymnastics. Zhao justified his flirtations with capitalism by advancing the theory that China was still in the first half of a century-long "primary stage of socialism." This stage was to have three phases, with the economy first being dominated by agriculture, then industry, and leading finally to "the great rejuvenation of the Chinese nation" in the mid-twenty-first century. When Zhao was removed as secretary-general of the party, his economic policies were not fundamentally repudiated, but implementation was greatly slowed.

Agriculture

Putting his faith in industry and its working class, Karl Marx did not hold peasants in high regard. Likewise, though the Chinese Communists started out as agrarian revolutionaries, once in office they exploited the countryside in order to support industrialization. Between 1957 and 1987 the state expropriated over 6.7 trillion *yuan* by keeping the prices of agricultural produce low, and by inflating the prices farmers had to pay for industrial products. Farmers received so little benefit from their labor that they "rebelled" by keeping output low.

This shows that when farmers are mere government laborers they perform poorly, and state goals may not be realized. On the other hand, when they are free to allocate resources (including their own labor) as they see fit, and to freely dispose of their produce, then they perform well and there is enough food to feed the cities. The Communists finally accepted this reality, and since the early 1980s most farmers have prospered under an "agricultural responsibility system" that they in effect forced the authorities to institute. In the summer of 1989, when Beijing tried to promote the merger of small plots into larger farms of 5 to 200 acres, provincial leaders stopped the plan dead in its tracks. The reason: they knew that farmers would be furious.

So the land-holding system introduced between 1978 and 1985, the agricultural responsibility system, remains in place. In theory land is still the collective property of the village, but individual families have in fact become virtual owners of the plots, free even to "sublet" (sell) them at a price negotiated between seller and buyer. De facto private ownership is a matter of great importance. Over 60 percent of the work force is engaged in China's labor-intensive agriculture, and although that ratio is declining, farming is still China's major economic activity.

Whether or not there is enough food to feed China's 1.1 billion people depends on the *efficiency* of its agriculture. With so many farm hands available, efficiency does not mean labor efficiency; rather, what is important is maximizing the caloric return from the land. China has a smaller percentage of arable land (11 percent of the country's total area) than even Japan (15 percent) and much less than India (56 percent). In terms of productivity, the new responsibility system appears to have worked better than collectivized agriculture did. The benefits of the new system were immediately felt, and the early 1980s saw a sharp increase in production. However, since 1984 grain production has stagnated. Many of the gains from privatization were one-time, and could not be duplicated. Furthermore, the saving feature of China's agriculture had been the "green revo-

lution." Technological improvements between 1960 and 1984 benefited China enormously; the percentage increase in grain production was much greater than in India or the Soviet Union. But there is a limit to what technology can achieve, and grain production leveled off after 1984. China's population did not.

For almost a decade, the farmers did rather well financially. But a revolution of rising expectations was occurring. It became common for villages to have television, and suddenly people discovered how poor they were. Indeed, by the late 1980s farm family purchasing power was declining (especially in the case of grain growers), while urban workers' incomes were steady. Local officials are supposed to pressure farmers into selling grain to the state at low prices, but farmers are increasingly reluctant to do so. They feel little moral obligation in this regard, for state investment in agriculture has declined. Increasingly worldly, farmers are learning to resist cadre pressures. Cadres themselves commonly engage in improper activities or levy unauthorized "taxes," and farmers are thus in a position to employ a mild form of "blackmail" to prevent cadres from pushing them around. Failing that, they sometimes resort to violence against state institutions.

So by the early 1990s farmers sensed that they were slipping behind others in society. As we have noted, in the urban-oriented national leadership there was no one to represent their interests. The fact that the land is held under leases does not mean that farmers can use it as they please. The degree of government interference varies from year to year, but if national policy emphasizes grain to feed the cities, a farmer may have to grow at least some wheat or rice—even if the land is more suited to cash crops such as vegetables or fruit. Refusal to grow the required crop (and sell it cheaply to the state, perhaps for an IOU of dubious value) can result in farmers being deprived of their land. Those unable to make a profit on land designated for grain sometimes pay others to grow grain on it rather than lose the land. When farmers are allowed to grow what they want, on the other hand, there is simply not enough grain, and precious foreign reserves must be spent to import it. But dictates to farmers are difficult to reconcile with the spirit (and often the letter) of promises made by the reformers when they decollectivized agriculture. If land contracts are violable, farmers will not bother with the long-term inputs and sound cropping practices that are necessary for future productivity.

Such are the dilemmas facing Beijing's agricultural planners. Decollectivizing agriculture meant that the center had lost direct control of one-half of the nation's productive resources. Now they are torn between giving free rein to farmers so they will maximize produce, or trying to regain control and manipulating the situation so that farmers will grow mostly grain to feed the cities, thus avoiding the need for imports. A vague plan of the early 1990s for a two-tier farming system called for a layer of officialdom functioning over farmers, with the latter either encouraged or coerced into meeting heightened sales of grain quotas to the state, and perhaps to combine their fields into larger farms. Agriculture was still supposed to be basically private, but state-supplied services would have comprised a "collective tier" and used as a lever to press farmers to accommodate state demands. Although the plan was stalled because of near universal local opposition, the tug of war between the farmers and the center goes on.

Industry

Since 1949 great emphasis has been placed on China's industrial development. Most of the capital investment has gone into the 98,000 state enterprises. Although these are usually locally controlled, they are taxed by Beijing and function primarily in a plan-oriented, noncompetitive environment. Many firms cannot survive without subsidies, which consume 25 percent of the central government's budget. The 40 million workers in state enterprises are a privileged sector of society and enjoy the full benefits of the welfare state, including job security. Although they have always comprised a relatively small percentage of the work force, such workers used to account for nearly all of the state's industrial revenue (from taxes and a share of the profits). However, more than one-third of state firms were unprofitable in 1992, and the portion of the state's revenue derived from state enterprises had declined to barely half.

Although state enterprises have been at the cutting edge of economic development, each dollar of investment in them generates less output, profit, and taxes than in the far more numerous *nonstate* enterprises, such as local collectives. However, in terms of other inputs (such as materials) the latter are less productive, and they are less remunerative for the employees. In 1987, collectives accounted for only 35 percent of industrial output, compared with 61 percent for state firms. The ratio is gradually changing in favor of collectives and private enterprises (the latter still only 4 percent of output). The condition of workers in the collectives varies greatly. Enterprises that have established good relations with the state sector are in the best position. Some have over 1000 workers, making them large enough to be placed under the Ministry of Light Industry. (This itself does not make them state enterprises, and employees are still not eligible for state labor insurance benefits.) But many others are "street collectives," with only a few dozen employees. The pay in these is very low, and fringe benefits are meager. Few collective enterprises offer the kind of educational and medical services that state enterprises routinely provide. With some exceptions, the cooperatives in small villages are the poorest providers. Some of these pay only four dollars for a month's work (though this amount goes a long way in a village). Thus, a person's quality of life and even social status depend upon the type, profitability, and "level" of enterprise for which the person works.

Even by the standards of Communist countries, a worker in a Chinese state enterprise has generally been highly dependent on his employer. In the past, managers often completely controlled the supply of consumer goods available to the workers, who were also dependent on the enterprise for housing, credit, health care, and education. Today there is less worker dependence on the enterprise, owing to the wider availability of goods and services. But even Japan (where workers' lives are more entwined with their enterprise than in the United States) has a more limited employer-employee relationship than China. No Japanese employer would expect to intervene in the politics, travel, or family life of an employee—all common practice in China, where a state enterprise is a social organization, not merely an economic entity. It is the "unit" of these workers, and thus defines their existence.

In enterprises, as elsewhere in Chinese society, people are organized into small groups of a dozen or so members. This system was introduced in the 1950s in an effort to institute a more effective means for "mass mobilization" of workers. The group leader is a fellow worker (not a cadre) appointed by the shop director and party branch secretary, largely on the basis of personal loyalty and political reliability. Group leaders are expected to win the cooperation of the other members of the group in everything from quota filling to moral cultivation and politicization. In Mao's time, more days than not the group would hold a political study session, but today there are fewer such meetings (and none at all in the private, foreign-owned firms). Conflicts are usually contained within the group and must be mediated by the group leader, who is in effect a political broker. Workers used to be rewarded largely on the basis of "soft" criteria such as attitude and general industriousness. This is less true today, but it is not clear that the soft criteria have been replaced by "hard" (quantifiable) criteria—which, when applied, often lead to disputes. Any discontent toward authority must be absorbed by the group leader, who is expected to shield the superiors. Group leaders' power derives largely from their role as providers of information and opinions on workers to those who really make the decisions affecting the workers' lives.

During the iron rice bowl period job assignments were often arbitrary. Workers had little chance of changing to a better or more appropriate position, and almost no opportunity to transfer to another enterprise. One priority of the reformers was to increase worker mobility and job turnover, thereby rewarding individual initiative and matching jobs with workers according to their skills. In 1986, the State Council announced that all new workers in state enterprises would be hired for specific periods of time instead of permanently, as before. Since then, there have been slight gains in improving worker-job "fit." This improvement, however, may have been at the expense of "undisguising" the unemployed. Previously, factories were always assigned more workers than they needed; now millions of unneeded workers are in danger of losing their jobs—at least in theory. In the initial stage of socialism, we are told, all this is necessary. Unfortunately for the jobless, there is still little in the way of a labor market because the job assignment process remains basically bureaucratic. And theory aside, this is also true when it comes to firing workers from state enterprises. Dismissal requires the approval of both the trade union head and the Communist party secretary, which means that they almost never occur; losing a job in China is a devastating experience. China is a long way from establishing a full-fledged welfare system that would take care of unemployed workers. Thus, the idea that employment should benefit the workers (rather than maximize economic output) is still predominant, and firing underperforming workers is usually unthinkable, even though this fact reduces enterprise efficiency and profitability.

Chinese commerce has also undergone great change. In a society where people were accustomed to low prices and poor quality of goods (in short supply) in government stores, the new free-wheeling economics has come as something of a shock. Entrepreneurs can charge as much as they want, and the income of shop owners is about five times that of workers in state-run factories (though of course their housing is not subsidized).

Equality

Eliminating inequality was a major goal of Maoists, who sought (unsuccessfully) to reduce gaps between poor and more affluent farmers, between city and countryside, and between poor and better-off provinces. Their efforts were undermined by the priorities given to self-reliance and the growing of grain. With the principle of "comparative advantage" rejected, areas suitable to a particular crop could not specialize in it. The always poor western provinces, for example, actually suffered a decline in per capita agricultural output during the 1960s and 1970s. Restrictions on migration hurt farmers in poor areas the most, and the urban-rural gap widened. Since then, inequality has worsened. This should not be surprising, for it was a conscious party decision to allow "some to get rich before others."

What people notice most is how they are doing compared to their neighbors. Early in the reform era, inequality of income among households narrowed, but it now appears to be increasing. Rural society will likely become stratified in the near future. Some farmers will gain control over relatively large tracts of land, whereas others, having sold their rights to the land, will at best be able to work as hired hands (and at worse become vagrants). Some will slip into the cities, where the practice of affluent families hiring domestic servants from the countryside now goes unchallenged.

Perhaps most startling to us is the chronic gap between regions. Farmers in the wealthier eastern provinces have often gone into vegetable growing or industrial pursuits, and have prospered; the economy of the slowly industrializing West, on the other hand, has stagnated. The average Shanghai-area farm family makes nearly four times as much money as a family in Gansu Province. In the nine poorest provinces, almost half the children suffer from anemia due to malnutrition[65] (compared with 21 percent of all PRC children[66]). Most of China's reformers believe in investing and developing those parts of China with the greatest potential, namely, the coastal provinces. The assumption is that diverting capital and skilled workers to the poorer sections of the country would be throwing good money after bad, thus slowing the nation's development. This is a reversal of the Maoist developmental strategy, which considered the eastern urban centers overprivileged and the other parts of the country exploited. Thus, although the reforms have probably brought real benefit to all parts of China, they have also exacerbated the regional rich-poor gap, especially as it affects the ethnic minorities.

Another reason for Beijing to worry is that the economies of the newly affluent southeastern coastal provinces now operate almost entirely outside of the central government's economic plan and control. Even some reformers came to doubt the wisdom of putting all eggs in the coastal basket. They feared that these areas were becoming too integrated into the world economy, and were thus vulnerable to the whims of international economics and politics. Some worried about China getting into debt, while others predicted that Western capitalism was about to enter a protracted slump from which China had to insulate itself. This thinking was not altogether different from Mao's idea of national "self-reliant regeneration," though it was shorn of the helmsman's egalitarianism.

China's continuing poverty should not be allowed to obscure the fact that impressive economic development has occurred since the Communists came to power. The record of 5 percent real growth per capita during the first four decades is good both by third world and

Socialist standards. The economy grew little in the early 1990s because of the recession and after-effects of the 1989 crackdown, but the overall record is such that the leadership sees no need to rush headlong into free markets. Although these have emerged to some extent, resources (particularly capital and certainly urban labor) are still largely allocated rather than influenced by market mechanisms. Half of the economy is still centrally planned, and the experience of the Commonwealth of Independent States has not persuaded many in China that the economy would benefit by ending state planning. The massive subsidies may reduce the overall standard of living, but they prevent mass unemployment and the social and political instability that would result from laissez-faire economic policies. And from a purely political view, the prospect of a self-run economy terrifies China's leaders, much of whose power comes from control of the remaining levers of the economy.

NATIONAL INTEGRATION

We noted earlier that the PRC is a multinational state. Of the PRC's 1.1 billion people, 95 million are minority nationalities (1992 estimate). Some nationalities were assimilated or at least Sinified before the Communists came to power. For example, the Manchus (who actually ruled China during the last dynasty) hardly exist as a group. The Zhuang, China's largest minority, are still considered a nationality but have also lost much of their cultural distinctiveness. Although the Communists devised a new written Zhuang language, and published books in it, many Zhuang people can speak and read only Chinese. The written language still appears on the national currency, however, along with Chinese, Tibetan, Uygur, and Mongol. Other languages continue to be facilitated. In the early 1980s the government undertook to publish more books in non-Chinese languages and promote the teaching of these languages.

The minorities' economies have been troublesome for the Chinese Communists. Aside from animal husbandry, most of these peoples have been economically underdeveloped. With the exception of the PRC's ethnic Koreans (whose standard of living is actually higher than that of the ethnic Chinese) the incomes of most minority people lag far behind the country generally. Air and rail transportation have been extended to some areas, but roads are poor or nonexistent, and some regions (such as Outer Tibet) have no rail service. Efforts have been made to modernize the economies of many of the nationalities, but the better jobs often go to ethnic Chinese. Minorities have only benefited in those rare cases where affirmative action programs have been introduced to train them for these jobs. Many officials concerned with ethnic affairs feel that economic development among the minorities should be given high priority, not necessarily strictly on the basis of socialism; they consider it necessary to recognize the "special characteristics of the minorities."

This approach goes against much Chinese Communist tradition. Conservatives believe that minorities and ethnic Chinese should march toward socialism together. To these Maoist ideologues, the new line implies that large areas of the nation will remain politically and socially "backward." Their pressure was particularly acute during the late 1960s, when there was a drive to bring the socioeconomic institutions of at least some ethnic groups in line with those of the ethnic Chinese. The Mongol herders, for example, were required to form agricultural cooperatives. In some other areas, various nationalities living in proximity were integrated into a single commune, and were expected to exchange labor at different times of year according to the different needs of the dissimilar economies. They were also supposed to increase consumption of each other's produce—animal milk by the ethnic Chinese, grain by the others. But Chinese have a strong aversion to milk, and many nationalities prefer meat to grain. Thus, such experiments were highly unpopular. In those days, the outlook for the survival of distinctive national cultures within China appeared bleak, while the populations of the more Sinified nationalities were increasing.

This has not been the case since Mao's death; most of the minority peoples were temporarily exempted from birth-control requirements and nearly all groups grew in number at a much faster rate than the ethnic Chinese. They comprised only 6.1 percent of the total in 1953, but by the early 1990s that percentage had increased to 8.2.

Government insistence on the use of the Chinese language in schools once made it seem likely that the nation would achieve Mao Zedong's goal of having "neither Manchus, nor Mongols, nor Tibetans—they will all have become Chinese," but Mao's successors have not viewed integration in such terms. They have warned against "forcing backward nationalities to accept methods supposedly intended for their happiness."[67] The nationality question must not be treated as part of the class struggle; racial integration is a long-term process. This left open the possibility that the liberal approach was only a temporary expedient— although one newspaper declared that even in the distant future, when communism was attained, there would still be a nationality question. To keep "the question" under control, much of the minority training takes place far from home in China proper, in hopes that the students will begin thinking more like Chinese.

Administratively, the minorities have been organized into 159 autonomous areas, mostly county-level, but five are provincial-level. Although many of these "autonomous regions" are large enough to be countries, China's leaders have been adamant that there can be no thought of secession. The 1982 Constitution was explicit on this point. However, this flies in the face of international human rights conventions, which assert that peoples have the right to self-determination. It is also difficult to reconcile with East Asian history.

The Confucian system was not one of sovereign nation-states, but rather an international order in which civilization was divided into two or more concentric realms: the tightly controlled "middle kingdom" (*Zhongguo*—the Chinese name for China), and the more loosely (if at all) controlled outer realm(s). This system was one of which the Chinese can be justly proud. Unfortunately, the transformation of the old order into a new form of domination (a caricature of Western imperialism) has not proven particularly beneficial to the Chinese, pleasant for those in the "outer realm," or respectable to the rest of the world.

The Communists have not always been consistent in their attitude toward what are now the minorities. Although he later became more imperialistic, in 1936 Mao Zedong seemed to favor self-determination for areas that had not clearly and consistently been a part of China. Certainly he promised a far greater degree of autonomy than has generally existed.[68] The exception is Mongolia, which the Soviets insisted be granted "independence." Chinese acceptance of this shows that they can be flexible when they have to be. Indeed, where China is not affected, they do not seem to consider territorial integrity a moral issue. When the former Soviet republics gained independence, China quickly recognized them, even though some had at times been a more genuine part of the Russian empire than Tibet, say, had been with respect to China.

Tibet

In 1951, two years after they gained control of China, the PLA invaded Tibet. However, it took until 1959 for the Chinese to consolidate their control. By that time the Dalai Lama's theocracy, which had ruled the country, had gone into exile.

Beijing can put together a case that its claim to Tibet is sustained by history; the Tibetans can argue convincingly to the contrary. Although not all scholars are in agreement, the Tibetans would seem to have a much stronger argument. During the last nonforeign Chinese dynasty (the Ming, 1368–1644) what is now the Tibet Autonomous Region was not under Chinese control at all, nor was it during the Republican period. It is true that the pre-Ming Mongols, like the post-Ming Manchus, did control both China and (more loosely) Tibet, but because they were foreigners this is a weak basis for any *Chinese* claim. Today the Tibetan people strongly favor independence, and can cite international law concerning the right of such peoples to self-determination.[69] Morally, the Chinese claim to Tibet is weakened by the egregious manner in which they have treated the people there since taking control. Although Chinese propaganda has been infused with a sense of *noblesse oblige*, and there have been some economic gains, the general reality has been neglect at best and persecution at worst. This has been true even of the more "integrated" Tibetans of Inner Tibet (what in Chinese are called Qinghai, southern Gansu, and western Sichuan provinces). For example, between 1959 and 1961, 70,000 Tibetans were imprisoned in camps near the Chinese city of Lanzhou, where half of them died. The persecution continued during the Cultural Revolution, when there was near total destruction of temples and monasteries.

Today, Tibetans are in danger of being overwhelmed by an influx of Chinese just as the Mongolians were in Inner Mongolia. This is already beginning to happen in Inner Tibet. The arrival of so many Chinese, with their superior education level, trappings of modern civilization, and solid *guanxi*, has engendered an inferiority complex in many Tibetans,[70] 72 percent of whom are illiterate (compared with 27 percent for the PRC as a whole).

Although foreign governments do not officially consider Tibet a separate country, there is virtually no approval for the way the Chinese have treated "the roof of the world." In recent years, the exiled Dalai Lama has gained much international respect. In the United States, despite reluctance of the executive branch to become involved in the issue, Congress has been determined to make itself heard. Following the 1987 anti-Chinese demonstrations in the Tibetan capital of Lhasa, the Senate by a unanimous vote condemned the ensuing crackdown and attendant human rights violations. In the following years a number of resolutions were passed, some implying that Congress did not consider Tibet part of China. In 1991, the Tibetan cause even received an unintended boost from the executive branch when the Voice of America began broadcasting Tibetan-language programs.

Of course, Tibet will not become independent as long as the existing regime in China persists. But if China becomes democratic, will the situation change? There are more than a hundred Chinese for every Tibetan, and the Chinese people do not seem to have much more respect for Tibetans and their rights than do the leaders of the PRC. But there are signs that the attitudes of exiled Chinese dissidents are changing.

Will China "deconstruct" the way the Soviet Union did? What form will such disintegration take? Certainly centrifugal tendencies there are strong. To some extent this has always been true, especially when (as is now the case) there was dissatisfaction with the center. Thus, it would not be surprising to see China's provinces (both ethnic Chinese and minority) reaching for and attaining considerable autonomy. To a limited extent this is already happening, as in the case of Guangdong. For the ethnic minorities the picture is mixed. The largest, the Zhuang in Guangxi, are unlikely to behave differently than the ethnic Chinese. However, we have seen considerable independence-minded activities in such peoples as the Mongols and Xinjiang's minorities, both of whom have fellow nationals north of the international frontier.

We have lived in an era when the world's great intellectual controversies revolved around the merits of socialism and capitalism. Except in a few countries like the PRC, that issue seems to have been settled, and some say that there is little else left for debate. But the highly emotional issues of nationalism and ethnicity, which until recently seemed old-fashioned, actually have yet to be resolved. Should states be multi- or mononational? To much of the world this is still a burning issue. It even seems to eclipse the issue of human rights—no one being against these in principle. Ultimately, both the issues of nationalism and of ethnic rights present challenges to individual rights. Although the trend seems to be to favor individual over collective rights, the case of Tibet illustrates the importance of not abandoning the principle of collective rights altogether. The contradictions between collective and human rights, and between national and ethnic interests, will not be easy to resolve.

Taiwan

Once known to Westerners as Formosa, the island of Taiwan has been a major issue for Beijing. Although this was not their position before 1949, the Communists now consider the island to be properly a part of China. This view is shared by the Chinese Nationalists, who have ruled the island officially as the "Republic of China" since the Japanese lost it in World War II, but it is not shared by many of the Taiwanese people. The majority there favors de facto independence, and a growing minority (the "independence movement") favor the formal establishment of a new Republic of Taiwan. Although the United States has tried to avoid entanglement in the issue, it has insisted that any settlement must come about through peaceful means. Since 1979, when the United States normalized diplomatic relations with China, there have been no official U.S.-Taiwan ties, but Congress did pass a "Taiwan Relations Act" which implied some

obligations. The act commits the United States to "make available to Taiwan such defense articles and defense services in such quantity as may be necessary for Taiwan to maintain a sufficient self-defense capability."

By the late 1980s the situation became complicated by Taiwan's phenomenal economic success (which made the island less dependent upon United States support) and even more by the internal political liberalization. With the release from Taiwan prisons of the advocates of an independent, democratic Taiwan, China's leaders became increasingly worried that when it came to the Taiwan question, time was not on their side. Since then, the Chinese Nationalists have occasionally used Communists' threats as justification for imprisoning independence advocates (who actually threaten the power of the Nationalists more than they bother the Communists). Neither side is willing to establish government-to-government relations, as both deny the legitimacy of the other government. The PRC's goal is the establishment of "one country, two systems," which is supposed to provide a degree of autonomy for Taiwan (and for Hong Kong). In the meantime, it is willing to establish party-to-party relations, but the Nationalists are only willing to conduct relations through unofficial and "nonpolitical" organizations such as their Straits Exchange Foundation. China has a similarly-named semiofficial organization, and the two are in occasional contact. Under such arrangements, PRC-Taiwan economic and cultural relations have improved greatly, but settlement of the underlying political and constitutional questions seems far off. In the meantime, the Taiwanese may take their cues from the experience of Hong Kong after it reverts to Chinese sovereignty in 1997.

LIBERALISM

We noted earlier that much of traditional Chinese political culture survives. Some elements of the political culture (the habit of deference to and dependence on authority) inhibit

In May 1989, Beijing citizens "sat in" at Tiananmen Square. Art students sculpted the Goddess of Democracy. The tall monument in the background was the center of the demonstrators' activities; behind that is Mao Zedong's mausoleum.

democratization, whereas others at least promote pluralism. Even though the Communists turned out to be the most authoritarian rulers of all, many of the illiberal features of the Mao era were dropped after the Helmsman's death in 1976. Political intimidation, mass mobilization, and coercive indoctrination began to be downplayed. These were abandoned in part because they did not work and in part as a concession to Chinese culture. Thus China inched toward a system where citizens (at least the apolitical ones) were free to operate within a framework of law. Still, one cannot call the political system "liberal."

In a liberal democracy there can be no monopoly over the flow of ideas and information, which is an important reason why political power is broadly based. Although the China picture is very different, there has been

a growing appreciation of the price society pays when the flow of ideas and information is unduly hindered by those in possession of political power. Even the authorities realize that criticism on a few subjects is healthy, and it is thus acceptable to condemn bureaucratism and even criticize certain public works.[71] But democracy would require the ability of citizens to debate more sensitive and fundamental concerns. Although there cannot be open debate under present circumstances, new technology makes it increasingly difficult for the authorities to control ideas and information. The people are increasingly clever at utilizing fax machines and even computer viruses. (In 1991, there was one such virus that did no damage but caused "Remember June 4" to appear on the user's screen. Another less benign one asked the user to answer "yes" or "no" to the slogan "Down with [Premier] Li Peng." A negative response reportedly caused all of the system's files to be erased.)

Over the course of the past decade or so, much thought has been given to the question of why China is such an undemocratic nation. Although the answers have varied greatly, most of the democratic activists show at least some awareness of the link between political culture and political functioning. However, some give greater weight to culture than do others. Probably the best statement of the "culture" thesis is a literary tour de force by a Beijing University student named Hu Ping (today in exile in the United States).[72] Hu sees China's traditional political culture as essentially Legalist. (The term, it will be recalled, has little to do with the rule of law, but rather denotes unrestrained imperial power.) There was a veneer of Confucian humanism, but it was a situation of "Confucianism in form and Legalism in substance." According to Hu, the Legalist legacy is still dominant in Chinese political culture, and there can never be democracy so long as this is the case. The human rights that democracy requires will not be obtained as a gift from above, but only as a result of a change in the way the public thinks about politics: "Whether there is to be freedom of speech will depend not on rulers' wills, but on public demand."

On the contrary, there are those who blame not the culture but the system. Notable among these is the now-imprisoned Wang Xizhe, who wrote, "The bureaucratic cadre system, which bestows power from the higher levels to the lower levels, has caused many cadres to be concerned only with the struggle for power and profit, or with the protection of their own official position at all costs." Drawing heavily upon the writings of Marx, Engels, and Lenin, Wang undertook a lengthy analysis of "the division of labor in capitalist nations without capitalists."[73] Wang believes that China is "capitalistic" (and therefore undemocratic) because the workers have not been electing their managers, the managers are paid on a higher

scale than the workers, and the type of work performed by the managers is quite different from that of the workers. All of this Wang finds unavoidable for the time being.

In 1991, the leadership inadvertently lent some credibility to Wang Xizhe's interpretation. In a secret document denouncing recent democratization of the Soviet Union, it warned China's 50 million party members to look to their own interests, pointing out that democratic change in the former Soviet bloc has caused party members to be fired, reviled, and prosecuted.[74] This would suggest that if communism is to survive in China, it will be not so much because it resonates with the traditional culture as that the system has been established by powerful interest groups who believe that their welfare depends on perpetuating that system.

So different types of thinking (and degrees of disenchantment with Marxism) have underlain China's various democracy movements. The dissidents of the "democracy walls"[75] era have yet to be rehabilitated, and they have now been joined in prison by thousands of "June 4" (1989) dissidents—students, workers, and senior intellectuals. They and the millions who marched with them in the spring of 1989 in hundreds of cities and towns recognized that the country's political system is illiberal, undemocratic, and (to use the officially accepted term) "feudal." A growing number of Chinese equate openness with modernity, and see those who keep the system closed as doing so more to further their own interests than out of idealism. Indeed, the behind-the-scenes leaders of the Tiananmen movement, all intellectuals, tried to limit the issues to free speech and political dialogue with the authorities. Little thought was given to institutionalizing democracy. These men, like the students, referred to the public as "masses" or "commoners," not by the more respectful word *shimin*. Even that term, which literally means "city person," has a somewhat elitist ring in predominantly rural China. Thus, most dissidents do not appear to seek a society as open as most Western countries. Even the most liberal of Chinese intellectuals believe that China must be saved by the intellectuals; they are not particularly open to worker (much less farmer) participation. The call for a more broad-based political system, with central leaders directly elected by the people, came not from the great cities but from the smaller towns. *That* would be democracy.

Tiananmen and the subsequent crackdown had a profound effect on Chinese foreign relations. During the weeks leading up to the crackdown, the American public was captivated by the Beijing demonstrations, and almost everyone was aghast at the bloody aftermath. Still, the international community's efforts to impose sanctions against China were short-lived. The Bush administration opposed most sanctions and was generally mild in its reaction to the repression, mindful of what it considered larger strategic and trade interests. The hope was that American involvement in China's economy would have a liberalizing effect. Congress and public opinion were more inclined toward the view that long-term American interests would be best served by taking a strong stand with the Chinese people in their quest for political reform. To China's leaders, this all smacked of the sinister "peaceful evolution" plot, and they constantly warned of the danger of China becoming "totally Westernized." According to Jiang Zemin, Tiananmen had all been "an attempt by hostile international forces to subvert our socialist system." Just why a China governed by popularly elected leaders would be less Chinese than one ruled by Leninists is never made clear.

CONCLUSION:

China, then, presents a mixed picture. Improvements in the material standard of living have been episodic, but nonetheless impressive. Whether the pluses outweigh the minuses depends upon one's perspective. Older Chinese who remember the "bad old days"

are impressed by the progress that has been made. But many younger people, especially those who know something about the outside world, consider China backward.

Certainly great improvements have been made in the quality of life in recent decades, including notable advances in health care. Many communicable diseases have been virtually eliminated, and (if official statistics are accurate) China has a commendably low infant mortality rate.[76] The Chinese lead healthier, longer lives than do Indians, and on average probably have a higher material standard of living. Only when it comes to the life of the mind has liberal India outshone its northern neighbor. The subcontinent's freedoms contribute to the success of India's civil service system. That system was derived from European models, which ironically were inspired in part by the Middle Kingdom's meritocracy.

The public policy disputes we have discussed can be destabilizing, as the crisis of 1989 demonstrated. However, the people gained more from the reforms of the 1980s than they lost, so there must be more to the explanation of Tiananmen than disputes over public policy. The explanation lies in fundamental changes taking place in society. Ever since the 1950s China has been unsteadily inching away from totalitarianism and toward a civic society in which citizens and self-organized groups and institutions have an autonomous existence and are not beholden to the state or unduly influenced by national elites. In China's case, market reforms and the freer flow of information and ideas weakened the state and strengthened society. Whether society as a whole had actually reached the "civic" stage in 1989 is debatable, but certainly many people had tasted enough that they were willing to try flexing their political muscles.

When the Tiananmen demonstrations began, most of the participants favored saving socialism and reforming (rather than eliminating) the Communist party. The brutality of the crackdown changed that. Now, although the public seems to have lost faith in socialism[77] and to see little hope for the country as long as it is led by the Communist party, it lacks the means to effect political change. As the last major Communist country, China appears to be behind the times. It still has elements abandoned in many other countries—an awesome secret police, a monolithic news media, mandatory political study sessions, and mass loyalty meetings. Part of the explanation for China's failure to liberalize may lie in the fact that in terms of sociopolitical organization, the Communist party, though weakened, is still the only game in town. There are no powerful churches (as sometimes existed in Eastern European Communist countries), and there is no long tradition of a Soviet-style outspoken dissident community. The exception is Tibet, where Buddhism and the remnant lamist theocratic infrastructure represent a powerful challenge to communism, though not one that can stand up to China's armed force.

The lesson China's leaders learned from the demise of the Soviet Union and Eastern Europe was that democratic reforms in China would be suicidal for the leadership, and probably for the People's Republic of China. Thus, the PRC's political system remains probably the most backward aspect of the social order, with the average citizen allowed almost no input and very limited access to political information and ideas. There is a yearning for a more open and accountable political system, and by ignoring such sentiments those in control of the government incur major costs. This is the challenge Deng Xiaoping's successors face.

Key Terms

agricultural efficiency
collective enterprise
commoditization
green revolution
Hong Kong
Inner Tibet, Outer Tibet
June 4, 1989
Legalists
Lhasa

mass mobilization
one country, two systems
Republic of China
agricultural responsibility system
Taiwan independence
Taiwan Relations Act
Tibet Autonomous Region
two-tier farming
Zhao Ziyang
Zhuang people

Suggestions for Further Reading

Baum, Richard, ed. *Reform and Reaction in Post-Mao China* (Routledge, N.Y.: Routledge, 1991).

Hicks, George. *The Broken Mirror: China After Tiananmen* (Chicago: St. James Press, 1990).

Liu Binyan. *"Tell the World:" What Happened in China and Why* (New York: Random House, 1989).

Nathan, Andrew J. *Chinese Democracy* (New York: Knopf, 1985).

Ogden, Suzanne, et al., eds. *China's Search for Democracy: The Student and Mass Movement of 1989* (White Plains, New York: M. E. Sharp, 1991).

Riskin, Carl. *China's Quest for Development since 1949* (New York: Oxford University Press, 1987).

Saich, Tony, ed. *The Chinese People's Movement: Perspectives on Spring 1989* (Armonk, New York: M. E. Sharpe, 1990).

Seymour, James D. *China Rights Annals* (Armonk, N.Y.: M. E. Sharpe, 1985).

Shen Tong, *Almost a Revolution* (Boston: Houghton Mifflin, 1991).

Simmie, Scott, and Bob Nixon. *Tiananmen Square* (Vancouver: Douglas and McIntyre, 1989). (Concerning the 1989 democracy movement.)

Thurston, Anne F. *A Chinese Odyssey: The Life and Times of a Chinese Dissident* (New York: Scribner's, 1992).

—, *Enemies of the People: The Ordeal of Intellectuals in China's Great Cultural Revolution* (New York: Knopf, 1987).

Unger, Jonathan. *The Pro-Democracy Protests in China: Reports from the Provinces* (White Plains, New York: M. E. Sharp, 1991).

Wu, Harry Hongda. *Laogai—The Chinese Gulag* (Boulder: Westview, 1992).

Yi Mu and Mark V. Thompson. *Crisis at Tiananmen: Reform and Reality in Modern China* (San Francisco: China Books and Periodicals, 1989).

A. Notes

1. This second view is convincingly argued in Lynn T. White III, *Politics of Chaos: The Organizational Causes of Violence in China's Cultural Revolution* (Princeton: Princeton University Press, 1989).

2. A long article to this effect in *Guangming Daily*, 2 February 1989, is summarized in the *New York Times*, 7 February 1989, p. A-9.

3. See Lo Kangxiong and Wei Yunxiang, "Existing Problems in China's Law Enforcement," *Liaowang* (overseas ed.), 3 July 1989, pp. 16–18, translated in U.S. Joint Publications Research Service (hereafter: JPRS) CAR-89-103, 17 October 1989, pp. 51–54.

4. See Bret Hinsch, *Passions of the Cut Sleeve: The Male Homosexual Tradition in China* (Berkeley, CA: University of California Press, 1990).

5. Kenneth G. Lieberthal, *Revolution and Tradition in Tientsin, 1949–52* (Stanford: Stanford University Press, 1980).

6. See Huang Shu-min, "Re-examining the Extended Family in Chinese Peasant Society: Findings from a Fujian Village," *The Australian Journal of Chinese Affairs*, January 1992, pp. 25–38.

7. See forthcoming book by Robin Munro and George Black.

8. See Tianjian Shi, "The Democratic Movement in China in 1989: Dynamics and Failure," *Asian Survey*, December 1990, esp. pp. 1190–1192.

9. See A. Chan, S. Rosen, and J. Unger, "Students and Class Warfare: The Social Roots of the Red Guard Conflict in Guangzhou (Canton)," *China Quarterly*, September 1980. It should be cautioned that most of our remarks on this subject are based on this somewhat limited database of Guangzhou.

10. See Yang Huiru et al., "The Impact of Western Philosophy on Today's College Students," *Zhengming* (Nanchang), 15 January 1991, pp. 76–85, JPRS CAR-91-036, pp. 4–11.

11. *New York Times*, 17 June 1991, and 5 November 1991.

12. See Wei Ji, "From 'Miss' Back to 'Comrade,'" *People's Daily*, 17 May 1991, p. 8, translated in U.S. Foreign Broadcast Information Service, *Daily Report: China* (hereafter: FBIS), CHI-91-098, 21 May 1991, pp. 41 f., and Fang Zixing, "Discussing the Use of 'Miss' as a Title to Address Ladies," *People's Daily*, 20 November 1990, p. 8, FBIS CHI-90-248, 26 December 1990, pp. 30 f.

13. See "CPC Internal Document: Frantic Activities of Abducting and Selling People on Mainland," *Jiushi niandai*, 1 November 1991, pp. 29–31, FBIS CHI-91-230, pp. 29–32; Rong Lisheng, et al., "Causes of the Crime of Abducting Women," *Renmin gongan bao*, 16 August 1991, p. 3, JPRS CAR-91-055, pp. 68–69; John Kohut, "'Sources' Detail Extent of 'Slave Trade,'" *South China Morning Post*, 1 July 1991, p. 9, JPRS CAR-91-049, 30 August 1991; Sheryl WuDunn, "Feudal China's Evil Revived: Wives for Sale," *New York Times*, 4 August 1991, p. 11; "The Trafficking in Women," *Human Rights Tribune*, July 1990, pp. 8–13; Chen Rongsheng, "Rescuing Victimized Women, Protecting Innocent Children," *Shehui*, 20 August 1990, JPRS CAR-90-090, 7 December 1990, pp. 70–72; and Feng Yuan, "A Great Number of Abducted Women and China Saved in 1990," *People's Daily*, 30 December 1990, p. 3, FBIS CHI-91-008, 11 January 1991 pp. 25 f.

14. See New China News Agency dispatch, June 25, 1991, FBIS CHI-91-125, 28 June 1991, p. 30.

15. See Robin Munro, *Syncretic Sects and Secret Societies: Revival in the 1980s*, special issue of *Chinese Sociology and Anthropology*, summer 1989.

16. *Red Flag*, 1972, no. 3, FBIS, 29 March 1972.

17. Wang Guixiu and Zhang Xianyang, "What Are the Targets of Class Struggle at Present," *People's Daily*, 31 October 1979, FBIS, 9 November 1979. Deletions have not been indicated.

18. For example, Wei Jingsheng, "Which Is Wanted: Democracy or a New Despotism?" from *Exploration*, translated in James D. Seymour, ed., *The Fifth Modernization: China's Human Rights Movement, 1978–1979* (Crugers, N.Y.: Earl Coleman Enterprises, 1980), pp. 196–200.

19. The following discussion draws heavily on Lucian W. Pye, *The Dynamics of Factions and Consensus in Chinese Politics: A Model and Some Propositions* (Santa Monica, Calif.: Rand Corp., 1980).

20. *Red Flag*, no. 24, 16 December 1980, JPRS 77436, p. 18.

21. This problem is well told in a book by one of the student leaders: Shen Tong, *Almost a Revolution* (Boston: Houghton Mifflin, 1991).

22. Xiang Tiande, "The Leftists Are Again Becoming Active and Causing Trouble," *Zhengming*, March 1991, pp. 22–23, FBIS CHI-91-045, 7 March 1991, p. 10.

23. E.g., Wu Shishan, "Self-Destruction, a National Tragedy," *Shehui*, 20 November 1990, JPRS CAR-91-004, 25 January 1991, pp. 60–68; and Zhao Tiantang, "The Negative Factors of the Chinese Traditional Personality Type and Their Causes," *Shehui*, 20 February 1991, pp. 8–11, JPRS CAR-91-032, 13 June 1991, pp. 96–101.

24. Several articles exploring the significance of "River Elegy" appeared in *Bulletin of Concerned Asian Scholars*, July–September 1991.

B. Notes

25. On the "branch" (*tiao*) versus "area" (*kuai*) systems, see Jonathan Unger, "The Struggle to Dictate China's Administration," *Australian Journal of Chinese Affairs*, no. 18 (July 1987), pp. 17–83.

26. See, for example, Cao Siyuan, "A Thousand Li Journey is Started by Taking the First Step," *Shijie jingji daobao*, 28 November 1988, p. 7, FBIS CHI-88-241, December 15, 1988, pp. 15–18.

27. Kevin J. O'Brien, "China's National People's Congress: Reform and Its Limits," *Legislative Studies Quarterly* 13, no. 3 (August 1988), p. 368.

28. See Duan Zhiqiang, "The Question of Separation of Party and Government at Rural Grassroots," *Nongmin ribao*, 7 March 1990, p. 3, JPRS CAR-90-031, pp. 19–22.

29. For an official explanation, see Wang Piqu, "The Essence of Democratic Centralism," *Guangming Daily*, 7 October 1991, p. 3, FBIS CHI-91-205, 23 October 1991, pp. 28–30.

30. See Yan Wenguang, " 'Local Protectionism' Is the Social Basis of Extensive Management," *People's Daily*, 27 August 1990, p. 2, FBIS CHI-90-175, pp. 39–40.

31. Wu Minyi, "Some Thoughts on the Activities of Local Governments," *Jingji yanjiu*, 20 July 1990, pp. 56–60, FBIS CHI-90-174, pp. 28–33.

32. This term is suggested by Harry Harding in "The Evolution of Chinese Politics, 1949–1989," in Raymond H. Myers, ed., *The Republic of China and the People's Republic of China: Two Societies in Opposition* (Stanford: Hoover Institution Press, 1991), p. 338.

33. Robert Delfs, "Saying No to Peking: Centre's Hold Weakened by Provincial Autonomy," *Far Eastern Economic Review*, April 4, 1991, pp. 21–22.

34. Xiaowei Zang, "Provincial Elite in Post-Mao China," *Asian Survey*, June 1991, pp. 512–525.

35. On this problem, see article by Wang Kean in *Zhongguo xingzheng guanli*, 16 October 1988, pp. 37–39, JPRS CAR-89-035, pp. 18–20.

36. On the satellite "democratic parties," see James D. Seymour, *China's Satellite Parties* (Armonk, N.Y.: M. E. Sharpe, 1987). For an update, see Seymour, "A Half Century Later," in Roger Jeans, ed., *Roads Not Taken: The Struggle of Opposition Parties in Twentieth-Century China* (Boulder, Colo.: Westview Press, 1992).

37. For full text, see *Beijing Review*, 27 December 1982, pp. 10–29. (Compare *Beijing Review*, 17 March 1978, pp. 5–14.)

38. Text: *Beijing Review*, 20 September 1982, pp. 8–21. Compare *Peking Review*, 2 September 1977, pp. 16–22.

39. See Xi Guangqing, "Democracy, and Factions within the Party," *Qiushi*, 1 June 1991, pp. 12–15, 23 July 1991, pp. 35–38.

40. See J. Bruce Jacobs, "Elections in China," *Australian Journal of Chinese Affairs*, January 1991, p. 171–199.

41. Associated Press, 4 November 1991.

42. *Renmin ribao*, 21 October 1989, quoted in *Far Eastern Economic Review*, 9 November 1989, p. 15.

43. Nicholas D. Kristof, "Far from Tiananmen: TV and Contentment," *New York Times*, 7 October 1990, p. A-1.

44. Ranks had only been instituted in 1963; they were abolished in 1965.

45. Quoted in Zhang Zhongxian, "To Enhance One's Consciousness of Plunging into Army Reforms," *Jiefangjun Bao*, 7 April 1988, p. 3, FBIS, 29 April 1988.

46. See Gerald Segal, "Keeping a Grip on the Gun," *Index on Censorship*, October 1991, pp. 48–49; "PLA, Inc.?," *Kaifang yuekan*, September 1990, pp. 28–29, translated in *Inside Mainland China*, November 1990, pp. 26–28; Zheng Zuhua, "Arms Diplomacy of the CPC," 1 May 1991, pp. 52–53, FBIS CHI-91-089, 8 May 1991, pp. 29–31; and Nicholas D. Kristof, "Potent Office Weaves Web in China Arms," *New York Times*, 10 August 1991, p. A-16.

47. The Party journal sounded the death-knell of depoliticization in "An Analysis of 'De-politicization of the Military,'" *Qiushi banyue kan*, No. 2, 1991, pp. 18–25, translated in *Inside China Mainland*, May 1991, pp. 1–2. See also Zhang Shaosong, "Persist in the Party's Absolute Leadership Over the Army To Ensure That Our Army Is Always Politically Qualified," *Sichuan ribao*, 15 March 1991, p. 3, FBIS CHI-91-067, pp. 45–47.

48. Sheryl WuDunn, "In China's Cities, the Busybodies are Organized," *New York Times*, 13 March 1991.

49. On the PAP, see Ho Boshi, "Purge Within the Armed Police Force," *Dangdai*, 17 February 1990, p. 8, FBIS CHI-90-038, pp. 24–25.

50. An interesting collection of translations of examples of such articles can be found in the Fall 1988 issue of *Chinese Law and Government* (White Plains, N.Y.: M. E. Sharpe).

51. Quoted in Kathy Wilheim, "China Notebook," in Associated Press dispatch, 17 November 1991.

52. Xie Zhuecai, "Report on the Work of the Supreme People's Courts" (26 December 1964), *Main Documents of the First Session of the Third National People's Congress* (Beijing: Foreign Languages Press, 1965), p. 58.

53. Quoted in L. Schapiro and J. Lewis, "The Roles of the Monolithic Party . . . ," in John W. Lewis, ed., *Party Leadership and Revolutionary Power in China* (New York: Cambridge University Press, 1970), p. 138.

54. See Margaret Y. K. Woo, "Adjudication Supervision and Judicial Independence in the P.R.C.," *American Journal of Comparative Law*, Winter 1991, pp. 95–119; and Margaret Y. K. Woo, "Legal Reforms in the Aftermath of Tiananmen Square," *Review of Socialist Law*, 1991, no. 1, pp. 51–74.

55. Officially, it is claimed that there is supposed to be no such thing as political crime. However, hitherto secret documents reveal that there is indeed such a category of crime.

56. Quoted in Luo Kangxiong, *Liaowang* (overseas ed.), 3 July 1989, pp. 16–18, JPRS CAR-89-103, p. 51.

57. See special issue of *Chinese Law and Government*, Fall 1991.

58. *South China Morning Post*, 12 November 1991.

59. Lo Ping, "Workers: Frailty Is Not Your Name," *Zhengming*, 1 April 1991, pp. 25–28, FBIS CHI-91-072, 15 April 1991, pp. 47–51.

60. See Wu Shuqiang, "A Preliminary Analysis of Worker-Peasant Disputes Affecting Social Stability," *Renmin gongan bao*, 7 December 1990, p. 3, FBIS, CHI-91-005, 8 January 1991, p. 44.

C. Notes

61. *Asiaweek*, 6 November 1987, pp. 25 and 28.

62. *South China Morning Post*, 20 May 1991, p. 10.

63. Article in *Guangming Daily*, quoted in *New York Times*, 16 July 1989.

64. *New York Times*, 15 September 1991, p. 11.

65. *China Daily*, 15 January 1991.

66. *China Daily*, 15 January 1992.

67. Ye Yonghua, "Let Us Talk About the Marxist-Leninist View of Nationality," *Yunnan Daily*, 3 April 1981, JPRS 78312.

68. Mao said that Korea and Taiwan could be independent if they wished. "[Mongolia] will automatically become a part of the Chinese federation, at their own will. The Muslim and Tibetan peoples, likewise, will form autonomous republics attached to the China federation." Edgar Snow, *Red Star over China* (New York: Grove Press, 1961), p. 96.

69. The two covenants are the International Covenant on Economic, Social and Cultural Rights, and the International Covenant on Civil and Political Rights, both of which entered into force in 1976. They assert, "All peoples have the right of self-determination. By virtue of that right they freely determine their political status and freely pursue their economic, social, and cultural development."

70. See Nicholas D. Kristof, "China's Cultural Conquest: Tibetans Yield Meekly," *New York Times*, 23 September 1991.

71. See Yang Jisheng, "Bloated State Administrative Institutions," *Qunyan*, 7 August 1991, pp. 23–24, FBIS CHI-91-168, pp. 39–41.

72. "On Freedom of Speech," translated in *SPEAHRhead*, Winter 1980. Hu was a candidate for local people's assembly representative from Beijing University. This long essay was his "platform."

73. Translated in *Chinese Law and Government*, Summer 1981.

74. Associated Press, 4 November 1991.

75. Many of the relevant documents of this earlier democracy movement are contained in James D. Seymour, ed., *The Fifth Modernization: China's Human Rights Movement, 1978–1979* (Crugers, N.Y.: Earl M. Coleman Enterprises, 1980).

76. Infant mortality stands at 27 per 1000 (better than Nigeria's 96 and India's 88, but far from Hong Kong's 6).

77. Although there has been no recent public opinion polling on the subject, this is the impression of foreign journalists (*New York Times*, 4 June 1991), and implicitly confirmed by Lu Jining in "Reflections on Strengthening the Masses' Faith in Socialism," *Shehui kexue*, 15 February 1991, pp. 8–11, JPRS CAR-91-038, p. 8–11.

Third World Countries

CHAPTER 9

The Government of India

Bernard E. Brown

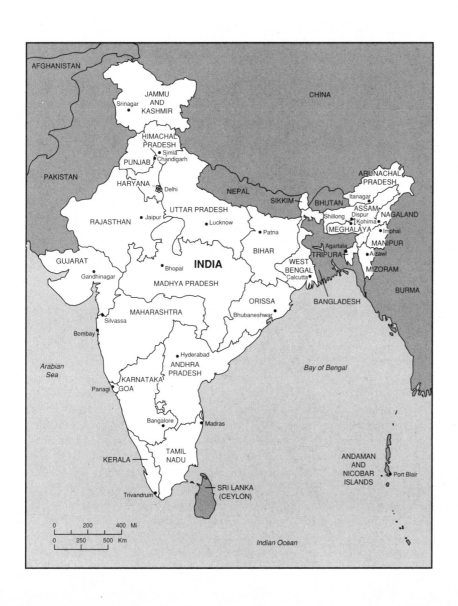

A. Political Development

India summons up for some in the West images from Rudyard Kipling—colorful bazaars, fabled palaces and temples, worshipers bathing in the waters of the sacred Ganges, snake charmers, cows wandering through streets, elephants as a means of transport, and red-coated English officers maintaining European customs in a completely alien land. Part of India's continuing fascination for outsiders is that aspects of the world described by Kipling may still be found. But alongside and more and more displacing the traditional culture are elements of a modern, industrial society. India now ranks among the ten largest industrial powers in the world, producing and exporting a wide range of products, including locomotives, diesel engines, and jet aircraft. In 1980, India entered the space age by becoming the sixth nation to launch a rocket and communication satellites. It is a major participant in research on telecommunications, space exploration, and nuclear energy. As of 1990 seven nuclear power reactors were in operation. Agricultural production has increased dramatically, spurred by a large research structure in universities and government. Life expectancy has gone up since independence from 32 to over 59 years, reflecting improvements in medical science and hospital care.

The contrast between the omnipresent bullock cart and the nuclear power plant makes India a compelling subject of study. The politics of modernization are spread out on a large canvas: the historical culture and society; the forces that penetrate and shatter that traditional synthesis; the dynamic tension between traditional and modern groups; the kinds of policies that facilitate modernization; and the problems thereby created. Students of politics are also drawn naturally to Indian affairs because they are concerned with power; and by virtue of its vast population, geographical location, industrial plants, and military strength, India is among the leading actors on the world stage.

The differences between Indian and European society are brought out in Table 1.2 of the introduction to this volume. The following observations may be drawn from this table: (1) Compared to European democracies, India is markedly poorer; the per capita income of Indians is about 3 percent of that of Western Europeans. (2) India remains an overwhelmingly agricultural country, with 63 percent of its population engaged in agriculture. By comparison, in the industrial societies of Western Europe only 2 to 7 percent of the people are still engaged in agriculture, and of course, the agricultural sectors of modern economies are far more productive than in preindustrial economies. (3) In cultural life and social structure, India is closer to the classic model of traditional societies—having a much lower literacy rate, a less developed educational system, and a lower life expectancy. To put it simply, India may boast of the same institutions that exist in Western Europe—parliament, prime minister, cabinet, president, supreme court, political parties, and the like—but these institutions serve and are responsible to a society that is still in the early stages of economic development.

Most political observers have assumed that there is a correlation between both education and high per capita income and democracy. Two reasons are suggested for this correlation: (1) Parliamentary democracy is based on competition among political parties and their leaders, with the electorate deciding among them after considering all arguments. If the governors are to be ultimately responsible to the people, there must be a widespread belief that the people are capable of making informed and rational choices. Such a political process presumably requires a high degree of literacy and of general education. (2) The delicate compromises worked out among interest groups and political parties in democracies reflect a social agreement on how the national income is to be divided. An expanding economy should make it easier to satisfy all claimants.

However, the correlation between democracy and both education and prosperity is not undisputable, as proven by the case of Germany. In the late nineteenth and early twentieth centuries Germany was in the forefront of the industrial and scientific revolutions—as advanced in literacy, education, and national wealth as Britain or France—and yet did not establish a parliamentary democracy until after World War I. Following the collapse of the Weimar Republic this same "advanced" European nation produced a Fascist regime. Clearly a high level of scientific and economic development is an insufficient condition for the emergence of democracy. The case of India is equally critical. Here is a society that after World War II was far less developed than those of Western Europe. Yet India—almost alone

among the nations of the third world—created a parliamentary democracy that has endured. No one interested in the theory of democracy can ignore the case of India.

As was pointed out in the introduction to this volume, the terms "traditional" and "modern" are generally used to help explain economic, social, and political differences. The typology of Max Weber (see Chapter 1) implies that transition between traditional and modern (or bureaucratic) systems is often facilitated by the rise of a charismatic political leader. We shall now survey the Indian experience of modernization, using roughly the Weberian categories of traditional, transitional, and modern. First, India will be considered as a traditional society (before the arrival of the British), then as a transitional society (under British rule), and finally as a modernizing society (since independence).

TRADITIONAL SOCIETY IN INDIA

When the British first arrived in India in the seventeenth century, they found a vast, sprawling congeries of peoples whose historical unity went back five millennia. Recent archaeological discoveries indicate that great cities developed in the Indus Valley from 4000 to 2500 B.C. that had a level of civilization equal to or exceeding that of Egypt, Mesopotamia, and China during the same era. Some elements of the Indus culture somehow managed to survive the catastrophe that brought about the destruction of this civilization, and later reappeared in Hinduism. Beginning at about 1500 B.C. the northern and central plains of India were invaded by waves of nomadic Indo-Aryans. The light-skinned Aryans gradually pushed the native Dravidian people, generally dark-skinned, farther and farther south. A fusion of culture took place, out of which emerged the Hindu way of life. It was during this time that the caste system developed, probably in order to maintain an appropriate distance between Aryan invaders and the native inhabitants. Our knowledge of this period comes largely from the epic literature of the ancient Vedas (religious hymns handed down by word of mouth) and the later Gita (a long poem on war and duty).

The early Hindu society resulting from the Aryan-Dravidian synthesis proved durable and resilient. Successive invaders, including the Greeks under Alexander the Great, were either ignored or absorbed into the national life. A serious challenge was posed, however, by Muslim incursions beginning about 1000 A.D. For 700 years the Muslims, with their militant ideology, were a formidable force. They succeeded in governing most of the country under the Mogul dynasty, founded in 1526 by a Turkish descendant of Genghis Khan. Some of the Mogul emperors, particularly Akbar, were men of considerable skill and talent. But by 1700 A.D. the Mogul empire was in an advanced state of decay. The stage was set for a new period—that of European or, more specifically, British domination.

The economy, social structure, ideology, culture, and politics of India in the seventeenth and eighteenth centuries, at the time of the British invasion and conquest, constituted in every respect a model of the traditional type of society. The masses of India lived in some 700,000 villages, each a virtually self-sufficient, self-governing entity with its own class and caste divisions. A few towns or cities developed as centers of royal authority, trade, or pilgrimage, but the overwhelming majority of the people lived in the villages. Royal authority might be concentrated in the hands of some mighty personage in Delhi or Lahore, but his power was barely felt in the villages except through the intermediary of the inevitable tax collector. In general, a committee of elders, or *Panchayat*, was responsible for order and justice within the village. Minor matters of a personal nature were usually settled by caste councils, whereas more serious crimes, such as cattle stealing and murder, went before the elders. Invaders, revolutions, monarchs, and empires came and went, but the Hindu village endured because of its self-sufficiency. In the face of a hostile army the villagers would arm and defend themselves; if attacked by superior force they fled, only to return later and take up cultivation again. The astonishing stability of this village system enabled the inhabitants of the Indus Valley to till their land and maintain their culture through 5000 years of turmoil and troubles.

The dominant activity was agriculture, although some handicraft industries developed, along with the manufacture of cloth, under the Moguls. Finished products of cotton and silk and handcrafted silver objects were exported to Europe, and a small merchant class came into being. Yet these activities probably did not involve more than 2 or 3 percent of the population, nor were the merchant and trader accorded much respect in Indian society, which was led by Brahmins (the priests) and noblemen. Indian farmers produced barely enough for subsistence, husbanding the rain water that fell during the four months of monsoon. In the event of drought, reduction of fertility, or desolation caused by invaders, famine was practically unavoidable. The lack of a more advanced technology made it impossible to expand the country's resources to feed a rapidly growing population, let alone improve its lot.

As in all traditional societies, Indian economic and social institutions were pervaded by family values. Individuals did not own the land; rather, the village families enjoyed rights of occupation as a consequence of clearing and cultivating their tracts. In the event that a family died out, all rights concerning their land reverted to the village. The male played the dominant role, and the household consisted of all his sons, grandsons, and their womenfolk, except insofar as the women married and entered other households or the sons left the village to strike out on their own. The villagers, in a sense, constituted one large or "joint" family, with the committee of elders playing a paternal role.

An element of cardinal importance in traditional Indian society was Hindu ideology.

Hinduism developed mainly during the period of fusion between Aryan and Dravidian cultures, but some of its elements can be traced as far back as the Indus Valley civilization. Like any traditional ideology, it affects and regulates all aspects of human behavior. It is more than a theology; it is a way of life, a code that determines how people shall live, eat, marry, cultivate land, share produce, and raise children. Much of the morality that informs Hindu ideology may be found in the Vedas and the Gita, and in the religious prose of the Upanishads (the main source of information on the formative period of Hinduism).

The central concept in Hindu ideology has been that of salvation, which is considered a release or deliverance of the soul from the endless cycle of birth and death. Life is miserable and evil. Material things are an illusion. The object of religion is to permit the individual to free himself of evil and illusion and to merge with the Absolute, or the World Soul. Until release is obtained, the soul is condemned to wander about the earth incarnated in one body after another—the kind of body depending upon the soul's record in its previous existence. There are many varieties of Hindu beliefs, some stressing the importance of ritual and others emphasizing the gods, such as Brahma, Vishnu, and Shiva (representing, respectively, creation, preservation, and destruction). But the theme is constant: life is a mystery; nature is to be accepted, not mastered; earthly existence is inherently evil; the true destiny of man is to escape from the melancholy cycle of birth and death through ultimate deliverance. Hinduism provided a scheme of thought that made life a little more tolerable in a society where the average individual could expect to live about 20 years, where famine was regular and catastrophic, and where hunger and unadulterated misery were the everyday lot of the great mass of people. But the striking drawback of Hindu thought, as of most traditional ideology, was that it offered no incentive to improve material conditions, to master and transform nature, to make more bearable the fate of men on earth. Hindu society was able to endure as a consequence of its stability and the widespread acceptance of its values, but it was not able to keep up with the rest of the world in technological development.

A distinctive feature of Hinduism as a way of life is the division of its Indian followers into over 3000 castes and subcastes, each with its own rules for eating, marriage, and general behavior. The institution probably derives from the efforts of learned Aryans to preserve their racial purity and culture from contamination by the Dravidians. In terms of the theory of birth, rebirth, and incarnation of the soul, caste marks the progression from a lowly to a higher state and, presumably, to total liberation from the cycle. There are four main classes or orders in the caste system, each containing numerous separate castes. In order of nobility or grace these groups are the Brahmins (the learned or priestly class); Kshatriyas (the warriors and rulers); Vaisyas (the traders and merchants); and Sudras (the serfs). In the past, certain wild tribes and people who performed menial tasks were considered outside this general scheme of things—even below the Sudras—and were called untouchables, or outcastes. (Over half a million people make their living, for example, by emptying latrines and chamber pots.) There were about 60 million of these unfortunate people in 1950, when untouchability was abolished by the new constitution, and their number has more than doubled since. Members of the scheduled castes—as they are officially designated—continue to suffer social discrimination in spite of the special legislation designed to protect them. Caste membership is not recorded by the national census, but social scientists believe that perhaps three-fourths of the population are Sudras or outcastes.

The caste system doubtless served a useful social purpose in a land subject to ceaseless invasion. Numerous races at different levels of development settled in India, and the caste system permitted each group to preserve its identity and yet somehow coexist with the others. Within a caste, no matter how lowly its general status, members found themselves accepted and helped. During periods of foreign occupation there was a natural tendency for the Hindus to defend themselves passively by withdrawing more and more deeply into their separate world of ritual and *dharma* (sacred law or duty that often involves minute regulations concerning food and relations among the castes). They were thus able to maintain their Hindu way of life against the foreigner. But the price paid for survival of the culture was high, as popular energies were devoted to theology and *dharma* rather than to the development of science and technology and the improvement of economic and social conditions. The caste system also created deep divisions within the society, and greatly reduced the effectiveness of central institutions in achieving national objectives in an increasingly competitive world.

THE IMPACT OF BRITISH RULE

By 1700, the Mogul power in India had virtually disintegrated. No native chiefs or groups at that time were capable of conquering or unifying the nation. The political vacuum was filled at first by European trading companies and then by the European nations themselves. After a period of economic and military rivalry among Britain, Portugal, France, and Holland, the British emerged as the paramount power in India. Their dominance, registered by Robert Clive's decisive victory over an Indian army at Plassey in 1757, was recognized by France in the Treaty of Paris of 1763. The British steadily extended their power into the interior, defeating one native ruler after another, sometimes permitting an Indian prince to retain his throne, sometimes assuming direct control themselves. The Mahrattas, the Gurkhas, the Sikhs, and the Burmese were all crushed in battle. By 1840 the whole Indian subcontinent was in British hands, with the exception of a few small enclaves retained by France and Portugal.

Thus, the inhabitants of a small island off the coast of Europe were able to extend their rule over a vast subcontinent in the other hemisphere of the globe, teeming with several hundred million people, and maintain their power there for almost two centuries. British supremacy was achieved by an amazingly small number of men. During the entire nineteenth century the British ruled India with about 500 administrators and 65,000 troops. The disparity in numbers—at the most 100,000 Britons ruling 200 or 300 million Indians—reflected the difference between these nations in military potential and economic power. The British had complete control of the sea, an immense superiority in military equipment and tactics, and above all, surplus wealth that could be used to recruit and pay large numbers of Indian troops. They also created a far more efficient administrative system than had existed previously. Divisions between the Muslims and Hindus and among the princely states also enabled the British to play one region or community against another—sometimes deliberately adding fuel to the fire of ethnic and religious rivalries—and to succeed eventually in subduing them all. Their successes were made possible in part by their advanced technology, which produced the necessary wealth, ships, and firearms.

India had managed to absorb all of its previous conquerors with the single notable exception of the Muslims. But even at the height of Muslim rule, the Hindu way of life in the villages was hardly affected by events at the imperial court, except insofar as hostile armies might march through the countryside. British rule, however, profoundly transformed India—economically, socially, and culturally. In the course of the century and a half leading up to independence in 1947, India had changed more than during the preceding five millennia. Large portions of Indian society had been wrenched out of the traditional mold, and an irreversible process of modernization had begun.

Some of the earliest British social reforms dealt with the custom of *suttee* (the burning of widows on the funeral pyres of their husbands), the institution of *thagi* (organized robbery and murder), and slavery. Gradually a system of English law was established that profoundly affected relations among the castes. But perhaps the most important of the early British measures were the creation of a new educational system and the introduction of English as a kind of national language. (Fifteen major languages and more than 800 dialects are spoken by the people of India.) The Indians were brought into contact with English literature and law and the whole new universe of Western science and technology. In the British scheme, as it was conceived originally, the educated Indians were to form a huge intermediary class between the governing elite and the masses and thus constitute a bulwark of the regime. In fact, this Indian middle class deliberately created by the British eventually led the movement to overthrow British rule. But in any case, English education became an abiding source of Western influence in India, upsetting old ideas, introducing modern knowledge, and helping to form a distinct new social class.

British rule also stimulated economic growth. A network of railroads covered the nation by the end of the nineteenth century, and for the first time in 5000 years the life of the village masses began to stir and change. The railroads opened regions to one another and India to the world. The mobility of the population was vastly increased; transport of agricultural products made it possible to avert or at least deal with famine; capital flowed into the country; and a few industries, including coal, iron, jute, and cotton, began to develop. The postal system and the telegraph likewise provided part of the framework for a more modern economy. Population drifted into the urban centers of Calcutta, Bombay, and Delhi. By 1940, there were 58 cities with more than 100,000 inhabitants, and there was a total urban population of over 16 million. Thus, although India remained overwhelmingly rural, urbanization had become a significant social phenomenon. In foreign commerce, by 1940 India ranked sixth in the world and had the eighth most important industrial economy,

employing over 2 million workers in large-scale industry. Nevertheless, agriculture was still the direct occupation of over 70 percent of the population, and 90 percent of the population continued to live in villages.

These changes—political, administrative, social, and cultural—shook Indian society to its roots. How did the Hindus react to the challenge thrown down by the West? Perhaps the first, instinctive reaction was to exalt traditional values and seek refuge in a revival of orthodoxy. Some Indians, however, sought to adapt the values of Hindu life to the new conditions. Still others, members of the educated elite, became completely Anglicized and lost touch with their ancient traditions. All these movements eventually merged into a nationwide drive for independence.

One of the early strongholds of Hindu orthodoxy was, curiously enough, the Indian troops in the pay of the British. These troops were mercenaries and had great pride in their military prowess, but no identification with the British regime as such. Their discipline took the form of a fanatic devotion to religious ritual. When British administrators began to reform Indian society, however, the reliability of the native troops was subjected to great strain. All the irritations and frustrations of the traditional groups burst into the open in the Sepoy Mutiny of 1857. Its immediate cause was the introduction of the new Enfield rifle, the cartridges of which were smeared with animal fat—said by outraged Hindus and offended Muslims to come from the cow, sacred to the one group, or the unclean pig, abhorred by the other. Native troops refused to accept the new cartridges, killed their officers, and seized control of large areas of the country. It took a year of bitter fighting to restore order, and the British thereafter were far more cautious in enacting reform measures. Other manifestations of the retreat into orthodoxy were the denunciation of everything European and the glorification of traditional Hindu or Muslim values and society. Among the new middle classes and intellectuals the view became widespread that the West was materialistic, in-human, and crass, while the East was spiritual and humane.

But a number of keen Indian observers realized that traditional India could not resist the new invaders and that the only way to preserve the old values was by reform and purification. Most notable of the early Indian reformers was Ram Mohan Roy, who discerned in the Upanishads a central theme of reason with which practices like suttee, polygamy, and infanticide were declared incompatible; that is, Roy urged social reforms for Hindu reasons, not Western reasons. He contended that the role of the West was to supplement, not to supplant, the values of the East. Roy gave Indian intellectuals a new measure of self-respect and pride. Religious and theosophical movements mushroomed, all advocating a return to the essential values of Hinduism or Islam purged of irrational customs.

The various groups within Indian society were initially divided over the questions of Hindu orthodoxy, reform, and the extent of imitation of the West. But they were united in their desire for self-government. In shattering traditional Indian society, the British had let loose the forces that inevitably would turn against them. Members of the new Indian middle and professional classes were humiliated by social slights and discrimination, and angered by policies that favored British over Indian economic interests. Resentment evolved into defiance.

At first, the demand for dignity and self-government took the form of requests that more Indians be recruited into the civil service. The Indian National Congress, founded in 1885, was essentially a middle-class reformist organization during its early years. At annual meetings it respectfully petitioned for increased Indian representation in the civil service and legislatures, all the while affirming loyalty to the British Empire. The negative British response to these entreaties strengthened the hand of militants who turned against the empire, calling instead for self-rule (*swaraj*). In 1906 the Congress officially endorsed the goal of *swaraj*, and many "extremists" urged a resort to violence in order to achieve that goal. Nationalism in India remained largely a middle-class movement until the emergence of Mohandas Gandhi as its undisputed leader around 1920. Gandhi's contribution was to reach out to and arouse the great masses of the people. He understood the Hindu mind and with a sure instinct always formulated political demands in a manner the people easily understood. Gandhi built up national pride by exalting native Indian languages and religious values, and by defending the spirituality of Indian village life in contrast to the materialism of Western civilization.

The technique Gandhi developed for advancing the cause of independence represented a masterly compromise between the policies of the liberal reformers, who wanted simply to register protests and sign petitions, and those of the extremists, who sought to oust the British by force and violence. Gandhi's supreme achievement was to involve the masses in the struggle against British rule while avoiding a direct challenge to British arms—that is, to keep the protest nonviolent. Although his preference for nonviolence was couched in religious and ethical terms, it probably did not escape Gandhi's attention that British superiority in military technology made a successful uprising an exceedingly doubtful prospect.

His technique of political action was far from passive, however, and indeed the term "nonviolence" is not an accurate translation of *Satyagraha*—a combination of two Sanskrit words meaning "truth-force." Elements of his doctrine were derived from Hindu practices; however, they also fitted quite nicely the particular needs of the Indian nationalists. The object was to win over the enemy by sympathy, patience, and suffering—by "putting one's whole soul" against the evil-doer.[1] The essence of the technique was *noncooperation*. Under British rule in this century, 400 million Indians were governed by about 1000 British civil servants and 50,000 British troops. It would have been utterly impossible for the British to deliver the mail, run the railroads, police the streets, suppress crime, educate the children, or administer the economy without the cooperation of Indian civil servants, troops, teachers, nurses, and so on. Hence in political terms Gandhi's insight was correct: foreign rule could maintain itself against violence but would founder if the Indian people simply refused to cooperate.

Gandhi's first call for nonviolent noncooperation, immediately after World War I, led to large-scale rioting which was stopped by the Mahatma himself. During World War II the British were increasingly reliant on Indian cooperation and thus vulnerable to the threat of noncooperation. Indian support for the war effort came to depend on a British commitment to independence—which was conveyed as early as 1942 by a special emissary of the British government, Sir Stafford Cripps, though at that time the discord between Muslims and Hindus made it impossible to work out an agreement. To understand the reasons for partition of the subcontinent between India and Pakistan, and the subsequent conflicts between the two nations, it is necessary to dwell upon the circumstances under which the British terminated their rule.

TOWARD INDEPENDENCE

The proposal by Sir Stafford Cripps, on behalf of the British cabinet, was to create a dominion of India with the power to choose independence at any time. Under his proposal the British were to be responsible for India's defense for the remainder of the war, but otherwise the Indians were to govern themselves. Plebiscites were to be held in certain princely states and in Muslim areas to determine what role these regions would have in the future dominion. It was specifically provided that any province could choose not to enter the new Indian Union and instead create its own independent government. In his discussions with representatives of the Muslim League and the Congress, as well as associations of untouchables, Sikhs, and Anglo-Indians, Cripps came up against the bitter divisions that were to plague relations among all these groups in the future.

Congress rejected the Cripps proposal out of hand, demanding instead immediate creation of an independent national government; it termed the principle of nonaccession for provinces a blow to Indian unity. The Muslim League also rejected the Cripps proposal, but because nonaccession did not go far enough. The League insisted on a partition of India into two zones, stating that it would be unfair to Muslims if they were under any constraint at all to negotiate their status within, or their exit out of, an Indian Union. The leader of the Muslim League, Mohammed Ali Jinnah, declared soon after the outbreak of war that the Muslims were a nation, not a minority within a Hindu nation. Said Jinnah, "We are a nation of a hundred million, and what is more we are a nation with our own distinctive culture and civilization, language and literature, art and architecture, . . . customs and calendar, history and tradition, aptitudes and ambitions. In short we have our own distinctive outlook on life and of life."[2]

To further complicate matters, the untouchables (or depressed classes) expressed the fear that the Cripps proposal would place them at the mercy of Hindu militants, and the Sikhs of the Punjab vowed that they would never permit themselves to be separated from the Indian motherland by the secession of Muslim provinces. After the failure of the Cripps mission, political debate in India became even more rancorous, ruling out any possibility that the British could extricate themselves gracefully from the subcontinent. Gandhi came to the conclusion that Japan was on the way to winning the war in Asia; the best course for India, he decided, was to invite the Allied forces to leave and then negotiate peace with Japan. As an ultimate weapon, he proposed using nonviolence if the Japanese insisted on invading and occupying India—a tactic that inspired little confidence among those familiar with the ruthless behavior of Japan's victorious army elsewhere. Under Gandhi's prodding, the Congress adopted a "Quit India" resolution; when the British thereupon arrested Gandhi, Jawaharlal Nehru, and other Congress leaders, the Indians responded with widespread civil disobedience.

The Muslim League and Jinnah spurned the Quit India movement, supported the Allied war effort, and insisted at every turn on the need for a separate Muslim state. As Jinnah put it in a speech in 1941: "It is as clear as daylight that we are not a minority. We are a nation. And a nation must have territory.... A nation does not live in the air. It lives on the land, it must govern land, and it must have a territorial state and that is what you want to get."[3]

After the war, the new Labour government in Britain discovered, to its shock, that the Indian problem could not be resolved simply by proclaiming independence. Elections held for the central and provincial legislatures immediately after the war revealed a dangerous polarization of communal groups. The Muslim League won almost all the seats in Muslim areas, and the Congress almost all the seats in Hindu areas; and the League and the Congress became increasingly irreconcilable. Jinnah vowed after these elections that the Congress flag would fly in the North "only over the dead bodies of Muslims."[4] The statement was prophetic. Independence for India was to be achieved only at the price of one of the greatest bloodbaths of modern times.

Physically unable to reinstitute imperial rule and politically unwilling to do so in any case, the British Labour government was intent upon granting independence to the squabbling groups somehow, and as rapidly as possible. In March 1946, Prime Minister Clement Attlee dispatched a cabinet mission to India with the task of finding a constitutional solution. Immediately the cabinet mission was confronted with the incompatible demands of the Muslims, who wanted the British to divide India and then quit, and the Hindus, who wanted the British to quit and leave it up to the Indians (and their Hindu majority, of course) to decide on a division. Unable to secure agreement, the cabinet mission made its own proposals. Pointing out that partition would leave huge minorities in each new nation and was therefore unworkable, the mission recommended that India not be divided, but that predominantly Muslim and Hindu areas should enjoy extensive autonomy within a very complex political structure with weak central power. A constituent assembly was to be elected, with representation from all areas, to assume responsibility for government and draft a constitution. The Muslim League and the Congress party both agreed, reluctantly and all the while laying down stringent conditions, to participate in the elections to this constituent assembly; in these elections, once again the League swept almost all seats in Muslim provinces and the Congress almost all seats in Hindu provinces. Amid much confusion the League and the Congress continued to stake out incompatible political claims; Jinnah called for a "Direct Action Day" to protest "Hindu treachery." That day—August 16, 1946—saw one of the most murderous communal uprisings of the twentieth century: almost 5000 people killed in Calcutta alone, many more thousands hurt, and 150,000 people in flight; at least another 7000 people were killed in the following months as communal rioting spread from Calcutta to nearby regions.

In despair, Clement Attlee announced in February 1947 that the British government intended to transfer power to Indian hands no later than June 1948, urging Indians to settle their differences before then. He sent Lord Louis Mountbatten to India as the new viceroy, with the mission of finding a way out. After fruitless consultation with League and Congress party leaders, Mountbatten concluded that there was no alternative to partition; with misgivings, the Congress party finally accepted the principle of partition. But now began a race against the clock—a thoroughly scrambled government of India had to be dissected, separated, and reconstituted over a territory in which most Muslims and Hindus were concentrated in separate areas but mixed together in some. In July 1947 the British Parliament finally passed the India Independence Bill, providing that power should be transferred to the two new nations on 15 August 1947. That day in New Delhi, Lord Mountbatten became governor-general of India and Nehru prime minister; the previous day, in Karachi, Jinnah took office as governor-general, and Liaquat Ali Khan as prime minister.

Both new states were immediately confronted with enormous problems. At the moment of independence, Pakistan consisted of two geographically separated areas. West Pakistan had some 34 million people living in a dry climate, while East Pakistan had 46 million people living in a wet, tropical climate—in an area only one-fifth as large as the western province. The peoples of West and East Pakistan spoke different languages and reflected wholly different cultural traditions. On top of the exceedingly difficult political and administrative problem of coordinating these two geographically separated areas there was a formidable challenge. Only three-quarters of the population of the new state was Muslim—that is, some 20 million Hindus were now ruled by their traditional Muslim rivals. Conversely, at least 40 million Muslims found themselves in the new state of India, subject to the rule of over 300 million Hindus.

The question immediately posed was, what would be the fate of 20 million Hindus at the hands of 60 million Muslims in Pakistan and of the 40 million Muslims confronted by 300 million Hindus in India? Would toleration and good sense prevail? Unfortunately, communal hatreds exploded immediately after independence. Violence was especially widespread and murderous in the Punjab, where whole villages were decimated and their inhabitants slaughtered or dispersed. Hundreds of thousands and then millions of terrified Muslims and Hindus fled for their lives—toward the sanctuary of either Pakistan for the former or India for the latter. But as those millions moved across hostile territory, they were fair game for thieves and killers. Almost 12 million people (slightly more Muslims than Hindus) fled from one state to the other—almost entirely to and from the Punjab. The situation remained relatively quiet in Bengal and East Pakistan. As many as one million people were killed in this holocaust.

In this climate of mutual hatred and killing, a territorial dispute pushed the new states of Pakistan and India into hostilities. The Muslim ruler of one princely state, Junagadh, disregarded the wishes of the overwhelmingly Hindu population and acceded to Pakistan. After the population rebelled, the ruler took refuge in Pakistan and Indian troops occupied the state. A similar situation existed in Hyderabad, a princely state in the middle of India where a small Muslim elite ruled over a largely Hindu population. India refused to accept the Nizam of Hyderabad's demand for independence, and took control of foreign affairs and defense as a first step toward complete annexation. The sticking point was Kashmir, where this time 80 percent of the population was Muslim, ruled over by a small Sikh and Hindu minority. When rioting broke out in Kashmir, New Delhi declared that the area would be taken over by India to restore order and hold a plebiscite on the state's future. An uprising by Muslims, supported by neighboring tribesmen, was countered by the Hindu ruler's own troops; to quell the revolt, New Delhi dispatched Indian troops to join the fighting. At the height of the tension created by communal rioting and armed conflict in Kashmir, the apostle of nonviolence and tolerance, Mahatma Gandhi, was struck down by an ultramilitant Hindu assassin. In announcing the news,

Nehru declared, "The light has gone out of our lives and there is darkness everywhere."[5] The first year of independence was a terrible ordeal for all the inhabitants of the subcontinent, Muslims and Hindus alike.

An enormous task confronted Jawaharlal Nehru and the Congress party as they set about creating order out of chaos. Consider briefly the dimensions of that task in August 1947. First, they had to provide for the safety of Muslims on Indian territory (of whom perhaps half a million were killed in a few months), assist and protect the millions of Muslims fleeing to Pakistan, and receive and care for the millions of Hindus who in turn were escaping to India. Second, they had to create a viable constitutional system out of the crazy quilt of princely states and provinces. In 1947 there were some 600 princely states, containing one-fourth of the population of India. Somehow this incoherent mass of governmental units had to be restructured, and something had to be done about the pretensions of Hyderabad to autonomy if not independence. Eventually Hyderabad was forcibly occupied by the Indian army.

The new political system had to be designed for a society far more heterogeneous than any in Europe. Although Britain, France, and Germany contain minorities (linguistic, religious, ethnic, and so on), each country has only one dominant, official language. The dimensions of the language problem in India are staggering (see Table 9.1). About 38 percent of the population speaks Hindi, and another 10 percent either Urdu or Punjabi (which are similar to Hindi), whereas Telegu, Bengali, Marathi, and Tamil are *each* spoken by 7 percent to 8 percent of the population and Gujarati, Malayalam, Kannada, and Oriya *each* by 3 percent to 5 percent. In all there are some 800 languages or dialects in India, of which over 60 are non-Indian languages. Most of these linguistic groups are fairly small, but about 100 of these languages or dialects are spoken by more than 100,000 people *each*.

Table 9.1 MAJOR LANGUAGES OF INDIA

	Millions	Percentage
Indo-Aryan Languages		
Hindi	331.0	38.8
Bengali	64.5	7.6
Marathi	62.2	7.3
Gujarati	41.6	4.9
Oriya	28.7	3.4
Punjabi	23.2	2.7
Assamese	14.0	1.6
Dravidian Languages		
Telegu	67.9	8.0
Tamil	56.0	6.6
Kannada	33.7	4.0
Malayalam	32.5	3.8
Other		
Urdu	44.2	5.2
English (mother tongue)	0.3	< 0.1
English (lingua franca)	21.0	2.5

Source: World Data, *1991 Britannica Book of the Year,* pp. 620, 759.

The Constitution provided that Hindi would become the official language of India after a transition period of 15 years. When that provision took effect in 1965, widespread rioting was triggered in the South. The government then amended the Official Languages Act to permit the continued use of English as an alternative language. In practice, instruction in schools is mainly in regional languages. Drawing the lines of states to take into account linguistic patterns, while maintaining national unity, is a formidable and delicate task.

In other respects, at the time of independence India presented a social profile typical of any Asian developing country: an extremely low per capita income; an overwhelming mass of the people engaged in subsistence agriculture and mired in poverty; an average life expectancy of about 32 years; and a literacy rate of only 16 percent. However, by 1947 India also had created at least the rudiments of an industrial base, especially in textiles, with an earnest start in chemicals, iron and steel, and engineering. Through the educational system, opportunities were afforded for the training of an economic, scientific, and political elite.

The independent India that emerged in 1947 was thus vastly different from the nation first ruled by the British a century earlier. In spite of Gandhi's idealization of village life and Hinduism (perhaps necessary for political purposes), the economy and social structure had undergone profound transformations. Industries and cities had sprung up among India's 700,000 villages, and a new middle class had come into existence. Independence did not mean restoration of the society that had existed in 1757; it was rather the signal for a new departure.

Political energies in India now had to be redirected. Instead of overthrowing authority, the problem was to create it; instead of glorifying the village and denouncing material goods, the goal now was rapid industrialization; instead of opposing power, the need now was to rally popular support behind the government. The construction of a national authority was undertaken by the Constituent Assembly (chosen indirectly by provincial legislators), which first met in December 1946. A constitution was promulgated in November 1949 and took effect formally on 26 January 1950 (the date now celebrated annually as Republic Day). The political institutions outlined by the Constitution are inspired directly by the British parliamentary system. The Indian president, House of the People (Lok Sabha), Council of States (Rajya Sabha), Council of Ministers, cabinet, and prime minister were intended to be the counterparts, respectively, of the British monarch, House of Commons, House of Lords, ministry, cabinet, and prime minister. The major departure from the British model is the provision for a federal system dividing power between the central government and the states. The main powers, however, are held by the center, so that India has many of the characteristics of a unitary system.

Democratic institutions were created by the Constituent Assembly; then the structure had to be given its democratic content through the electoral process, with the full participation of competing political parties. The first national elections were held over a period of

Table 9.2 CHRONOLOGY OF IMPORTANT EVENTS IN INDIA

1500 B.C.	Invasion of Indus Valley by Vedic Aryans.
327–325 B.C.	Incursion into Northwest India by Alexander the Great.
300–600 A.D.	Golden age of Hindu culture under Gupta dynasty.
1192	Establishment of first Muslim kingdom, the Delhi Sultanate.
1510	Portuguese conquer Goa.
1526	Babur founds a Mogul empire, later consolidated by Akbar.
1612–1690	British East India Company establishes trading stations at Surat, Bombay, and Calcutta.
1757	Victory of Robert Clive over the Nawab of Bengal at Plassey. Beginning of British Empire in India.
1857	Sepoy Rebellion (or Mutiny), leading to abolition of East India Company and establishment of Crown rule through a Viceroy.
1877	Queen Victoria crowned Empress of India.
1885	Creation of the Indian National Congress.
1919	First passive-resistance campaign organized by Mohandas Gandhi.
1942	Sir Stafford Cripps offers a British commitment to independence.
1947	British Parliament passes India Independence Bill. Power is transferred to India and Pakistan. Assassination of Mohandas Gandhi (January 1948) by a Hindu militant.
1949	Promulgation of the Constitution of India.
1950	Constitution goes into effect on 26 January (Republic Day).

four months in the winter of 1951–1952. The largest electorate in the world was mobilized in order to choose its first elected government under the new constitution.

See Table 9.2 for a summary of the important events in India up to 1950.

Key Terms

Brahmins
caste system
Gandhi, Mohandas
Hindus
Lok Sabha
Muslims
Nehru, Jawaharlal
Rajya Sabha
Satyagraha
Sikhs
Untouchables

Suggestions for Further Reading

Brecher, M. *Nehru: A Political Biography* (New York: Oxford University Press, 1961).

Brown, J. M. *Modern India: The Origins of an Asian Democracy* (New York: Oxford University Press, 1984).

Lamb, B. P. *India, A World in Transition*, 4th ed. (New York: Praeger, 1975).

Moore, R. J. *Escape from Empire: The Attlee Government and the Indian Problem* (Oxford: Clarendon Press, 1983).

Nanda, B. R. *Mahatma Gandhi: A Biography* (New York: Oxford University Press, 1981).

Nehru, J. *The Discovery of India* (Garden City, N.Y.: Doubleday, 1959).

Sarker, Sumit. *Modern India, 1885–1947* (London: Macmillan, 1983).

Wallbank, T. W. *A Short History of India and Pakistan* (New York: Mentor, 1958).

Wolpert, S. *A New History of India*, 2nd ed. (New York: Oxford University Press, 1982).

B. Political Processes and Institutions

In India, as in the other parliamentary democracies treated in this volume, the people express their interests and convey them to government through a network of professional associations (or interest groups) and through political parties. In organizing themselves for elections, the Indians have adopted an electoral procedure very similar to that of the British. But the context in which groups and parties function in India is radically different from that in Britain. A segment of the Indian community, inspired mainly by orthodox Hindu values, repudiates the secular state and views its institutions with suspicion if not contempt. Another element in the community identifies itself with the Communist movement and questions these institutions—for other reasons, of course. Thus, the consensus about political institutions and values on which the British system is based does not exist in India, or in most other developing nations.

Furthermore, the cleavages and contrasts in Indian society are far deeper and more intense than in Britain or any other industrial society. A tiny elite, Western in education and taste, is set off sharply from a largely illiterate mass attached to a traditional way of life. The gaps tend to be greater all along the line: between the rich and the poor, between urban life and village life, and between language groups and religious groups. There is also a stronger tradition of violence and impulse to resort to violence, in spite of Gandhi and perhaps because of the effort required to overthrow British rule. Above all, India is still largely a traditional society which has only started on its way to modernization, with all the social, economic, cultural, and political characteristics of such a society.

INTEREST GROUPS

There are trade unions, agricultural groups, business associations, and numerous professional societies in India, as in any democracy. But most Indians continue to gain a livelihood in the traditional sectors of the economy; for example, of the 222 million Indians in the work force as of the census of 1981 93 million were classified as cultivators, and 56 million as agricultural laborers. On the other hand, 7.4 million were engaged in manufacturing, 11 million in social, community, and personal services, 1.5 million in construction, 3.5 million in transport and communication, and the rest in other services.

From this rough social profile it is evident that the highly organized interest groups of business and labor so characteristic of Western democracies cannot draw upon similarly massive social forces in India. Nonetheless, workers and business people, as well as peasants, have organized in order to promote their interests. In structure, Indian interest groups resemble more the French than the British or German, inasmuch as working class and peasant groups are divided along political and ideological lines. The Indian National Trade Union Congress (INTUC) is a creation of the Congress party; the Bharatiya Mazdoor Sanga (BMS) is linked to the Bharatiya Janata party; and the All-India Trade Union Congress (AITUC) is affiliated with the Communist party of India. Similarly, each of these parties has created peasant groups and student associations.

Trade unions together have a claimed membership of some 10 million, which is a small percentage of the total work force of 222 million. Ten million unionized workers, nevertheless, could play an important role in the political process if they were disciplined, united, well organized, and well led. But such is not the case. Few union members pay dues regularly, and inadequate financing makes it difficult for unions to recruit, train, and pay competent leaders from within their own ranks. Leadership positions therefore tend to be assumed by intellectuals and politicians who are primarily interested in using the unions for personal or political ends rather than creating efficient structures through which the interests of workers might be defended.

Hence unions are not properly organized for the task of collective bargaining with employers; militancy takes the form of short, sometimes violent strikes. Because each union is either the creation of or is affiliated with a political party, most demands for higher wages and improved working conditions are conveyed directly to the government. When the Congress party has been in power, it has been in the government's interest to make INTUC a "transmission belt" of its own economic plan, putting pressure on the workers to accept discipline in order to contribute to economic growth and higher productivity. Similarly, it is important for the Communist party to utilize AITUC for its own political purposes—either to embarrass, subvert, or cooperate with the government, depending upon the Communist party's relations with the Congress party.

Business groups in India are organized for political purposes mainly through a great number of local associations and chambers of commerce, which are linked together loosely in national federations. The most important of these business groups is the Federation of Indian Chambers of Commerce and Industry, whose members include some 40,000 enterprises. Unlike the trade unions, the federation is not affiliated directly with any political party, but the business community as a whole tends to offer financial and other support to the more conservative wings of the Congress and opposition parties. The business community in India labors under several severe handicaps in its attempts to influence public opinion and the government. First, there is historic distrust of and disdain for commercial and business activity, characteristic of any traditional society. Aristocratic Brahmins have always looked down upon business people as particularly unworthy, interested only in profits and accumulation of material objects (as opposed to more noble and uplifting spiritual activity). The lower classes and castes have generally believed that they are exploited by business people and resent their opulent life-style. In addition, the founding fathers of modern India adopted socialism as an official policy and were openly contemptuous of the business or capitalist class.

Some business leaders created or supported a Forum for Free Enterprise, later affiliated with Swatantra, in an attempt to shape a more favorable public attitude toward the private sector and market economy. Business groups also regularly protest against expansion of the bureaucracy and of the nationalized sector. But the business associations tend to devote most of their efforts to consulting with administrative agencies and trying to stay out of the public limelight. Lobbying is not a well-developed institutional practice. Individual business leaders, however, contribute large sums to political parties, thereby ensuring access to the state. In the mid-1970s the climate of opinion became somewhat more favorable to business. Under Rajiv Gandhi and V. P. Singh (since 1984) there has been greater recognition of the need for entrepreneurial ability and professional management.

By far the largest single occupational group in India are the peasants, as is natural in any developing nation. But the peasant organizations of India are a far cry from comparable groups in Britain, France, and Germany. They have practically no structure and are little more than "outreach" agencies created by the major political parties to mobilize electoral support. The weakness of peasant groups and the absence of professional leadership among them reflects the lack of education and income of the peasants themselves. Both wings of the Communist party have made a major effort to exploit peasant unrest, especially among landless agricultural workers and poor Muslims. The All-India Kisan Sabha, an adjunct of the Communist party of India, has had considerable success in West Bengal; the more extreme Communist party of India (Marxist) has been even more adroit in appealing to the landless and poor peasants. In some areas, Naxalite revolutionaries (almost entirely middle-class intellectuals) have managed to gain peasant support for their program of violent insurrection.

An unusual feature of Indian politics is the proliferation of community associations that defend and further the interests of a caste or of a linguistic or religious group. Among the most important are the associations of Sikhs (the Akali Dal), Dravidians, Nagas, and assorted linguistic groups. These community associations have succeeded in bringing about a redrawing of state boundaries in order to accommodate linguistic groups and are sometimes powerful forces in regional politics. In principle, the secular political parties have sought to avoid creating any associations that would strengthen the caste system; but they are frequently compelled to acknowledge the popularity and power of the existing community associations.

In short, the Indian interest groups are rarely as well organized, well led, well financed, or effective as their European counterparts. Although the Indian interest groups offer some opportunity for political action, more often than not they serve the purposes of political parties rather than of their members. The functions of the interest groups have thus been largely absorbed by the major actors within the political system—the political parties.

VOTING

Popular interest and participation in elections are unusually high in India. Turnout in the first two general elections was over 45 percent of the eligible voters. Since 1967 between 56 and 63 percent of eligible voters went to the polls, though in 1991 turnout declined to about 53 percent. The level of participation is all the more remarkable considering that almost half of the Indian electorate, according to official statistics, is illiterate; and it may be assumed that many of those classified technically as literate are not able to read campaign literature with ease. Candidates must therefore reach the overwhelming majority of their supporters directly—through personal canvassing and mass meetings—or by radio; they cannot rely on the press. In order to permit illiterates to choose among candidates, the ballot lists not only the names of the candidates in each constituency but also the symbols of their parties (or, in the case of nonparty candidates, personal symbols). Voters then secretly mark one of the symbols with a rubber stamp, fold the ballot, and drop it in a box. Most observers agree that the system works reasonably well.

The electoral procedure is otherwise quite simple and straightforward, inspired largely by British practice. The size of the Lok Sabha (House of the People) is now fixed at 542, so that each member represents approximately 1.5 million people. The country is divided up into single-member districts; the candidate who wins the largest number of votes wins the seat. Some districts are reserved for members of the scheduled castes (outcastes or untouchables) or tribals. Candidates are required to file nomination papers and also put up a deposit, which is returned if the candidate garners over one-sixth of the vote. Campaign finances are scrutinized by the Election Commission, but many contributions and expenditures go unreported.

The percentage of women voting in elections has increased dramatically, going from perhaps only one-half the rate for men in 1952 to two-thirds in 1962, to three-fourths in 1967, and to about the same rate today. Women are also participating in greater numbers as candidates for office. Congress generally reserves a small number of nominations for women to make sure that there is some representation of, and appeal to, female voters. In 1989 there were 198 women candidates for the Lok Sabha (up from 173 in 1984), but only 27 were elected (down from 43 in 1984). A number of women have been ministers, most notably Prime Minister Indira Gandhi.

ELECTION RESULTS AND PARTY SYSTEM

The single-member district system always works to the advantage of large parties. In the first five general elections (1952, 1957, 1962, 1967, and 1971) that advantage was enjoyed by the Congress party—associated in the popular mind with the national independence struggle through the person of its leader, Jawaharlal Nehru. Its opponents were scattered among a number of smaller parties, representing conservatives, Socialists, Communists, orthodox Hindus, and ethnic and linguistic groups. In the first five general elections the Congress party won a clear majority of the seats in Parliament, but it was *not* at any time a majority in the country as a whole. Its popular

vote ranged from a high of 48 percent in 1957 to a low of 41 percent in 1967. The Janata party, which won 55 percent of the seats in the Lok Sabha in 1977, was also a minority party (with only 43 percent of the popular vote). In the election of January 1980, Indira Gandhi's Congress party won almost 70 percent of the seats with only 42 percent of the total vote. Under Rajiv, the same party swept a record 79 percent of the seats in 1984 with just under 50 percent of the vote. The rise of the Bharatiya Janata Party (BJP)—now the major opposition formation—has further splintered the party system. Congress scored 39.5 percent of the vote in 1989, but the opposition parties were fairly united; Congress won only 197 seats (out of 543) and was blocked from power. In 1991 the split between the Janata Dal and the BJP enabled Congress, with only 37.3 percent of the vote, to gain 225 seats, so that it could form a government with external support.

In the first 30 years of independence the Congress party dominated the political arena and furnished the prime ministers of the nation, an era interrupted in the election of 1977 when a coalition of opposition forces, coming together as the Janata party, succeeded in ousting the Congress party and Indira Gandhi from power. The victory of the Janata party followed upon, and was a reaction against, the imposition of emergency rule by Prime Minister Gandhi in June 1975. The 19 months of emergency rule that followed were a watershed in the political evolution of India.

Emergency rule was proclaimed following a decision by the Allahabad High Court in June 1975 that Indira Gandhi had violated several provisions of the electoral law during the preceding campaign. The prime minister headed off opposition demands that she resign by declaring an emergency. When a portion of the Congress party defected, Mrs. Gandhi succeeded in securing the support of the Communist party of India, thereby maintaining her majority in Parliament. The government silenced the opposition by imposing press censorship, banning political demonstrations, and jailing critics. When Mrs. Gandhi decided to permit elections to take place in 1977, it was generally expected that the Congress party would go on to an easy victory because the rate of inflation had been reduced and other economic gains were registered. But the opposition leaders came out of their prison cells, exploited deep popular dissatisfaction with censorship and other authoritarian features of the emergency, coordinated efforts through the newly formed Janata party, and won an astounding victory.

The contrast between the pre- and post-emergency party systems was striking. In 1971 the Congress party won 43.7 percent of the popular vote but 67.7 percent of the seats in the Lok Sabha, because it could exploit divisions within the opposition. The 1977 election was contested by only four "All-India" parties: the Congress party; the Janata party—a coalition of the former opposition groups, united in their hostility to Indira Gandhi and emergency rule; the Communist party of India, which supported the emergency; and the (Marxist) Communist party of India, which opposed the emergency. This time the Janata party, with about 43 percent of the popular vote, was able to benefit from the winner-take-all electoral system as the Congress party went down to about 35 percent of the vote.

One of the leaders of the Janata party, 81-year-old Morarji Desai, became prime minister. However, the contradictions within the Janata soon came to the fore, and the government began to drift. There was a sudden increase in inflation, communal violence, labor and student unrest, and—ominously—strikes by the police. Personality rivalries within the Janata led to unbearable tensions only a year after its landslide electoral triumph.

It was hardly possible for the public to follow the fortunes of the Janata party, so confused and rapid were the expulsions and defections. In the summer of 1979 the Janata party fell apart. Morarji Desai, anticipating a no-confidence vote, resigned as prime minister.

After a week of parliamentary maneuvering, President Sanjiva Reddy asked Charan Singh (now head of a Janata splinter party) to form a government. Singh had the support of his own party, anti-Gandhi Congress members, and Socialists. But the new government, opposed by Janata and unable to negotiate a working alliance with Indira Gandhi, lacked a majority in the Lok Sabha, and Charan Singh resigned after only three weeks in office.

Rather than ask Janata leaders to make another try at forming a government, President Reddy two days later dissolved Parliament and called for new elections, with Singh staying on as head of a caretaker government. The election was a resounding victory for Congress (I)—pro-Indira Gandhi—and Mrs. Gandhi, who won 351 out of the 525 seats at stake (elections having been canceled in 17 districts because of violence). The squabbling Janata and Lok Dal went down to separate and ignominious defeats, reduced respectively to 31 and 41 seats.

The party system apparently had reverted to normal: a dominant Congress party, approaching one-half the popular vote, could win a comfortable majority of seats because of the inability of a deeply divided opposition to act in concert.

Only a few months after taking office, Mrs. Gandhi's 33-year-old son and obvious successor, Sanjay, was killed senselessly in the crash of a stunt plane he was flying. Shortly thereafter Mrs. Gandhi prevailed upon her elder son, Rajiv, to enter into politics and take on responsibility for reorganizing the Congress party. Her government was being buffeted by charges of corruption and an increasingly unmanageable situation in the Punjab, where militant Sikhs were demanding autonomy. On 31 October 1984, two Sikh members of Indira Gandhi's personal bodyguard assassinated her, triggering a wave of violence in New Delhi.

India was in a state of shock. Rajiv Gandhi, designated immediately as the new prime minister by President Zail Singh, benefited from an outpouring of popular sympathy and support. He called for parliamentary elections in December 1984 (about the time they were due in any case). The result was a great personal victory for Rajiv, and a new lease on life for Congress (I). Out of 508 seats at stake in the Lok Sabha (elections were postponed in Assam and the Punjab because of continuing violence), Congress won 401 seats, more than in any previous election, with almost 50 percent of the vote.

The 1984 election seemed to mark a return of the Indian party system to its historically dominant model: a Congress party able to govern, despite its lack of a popular majority, because of the fragmentation of the opposition. But the party system continued to evolve. Rajiv Gandhi's government was rocked by charges (and evidence) of corruption, by mounting communal violence sparked by unrest in the Punjab, and by a surge of Hindu fundamentalism. In the election of November 1989, a reconstituted Janata Dal under the leadership of V. P. Singh won 17.8 percent of the popular votes and 143 seats, compared with 39.5 percent of the popular vote and 197 seats for Congress (I). Although Congress (I) had the largest block of seats, it could not command a working majority. President Venkataraman asked V. P. Singh to form a government after receiving assurance of "outside" support for Singh from the BJP (the militant Hindu party), which had won 85 seats, and the Left Front (mainly Communist parties) with 51 seats.

V. P. Singh's government lasted barely one year. It foundered on its internal contradictions—liberals versus Socialists, Communists, and Populists; secular forces versus Hindu militants and fundamentalists; and lower castes and outcastes versus higher castes. The BJP withdrew its support in November 1990 because the government ordered the arrest of its leader (who was demonstrating in favor of the building of a Hindu shrine on the site of a mosque), and the government fell.

Rajiv Gandhi declined to form a government, but expressed his willingness to support the leader of an anti-Singh faction within the Janata Dal, Chandra Shekhar, from the "outside." President Venkataraman therefore asked Shekhar to form a government, which won a vote of confidence by 280 in favor, 214 against, and 28 either abstaining or absent. Shekhar's majority came from about 60 members of his own newly formed Janata Dal (Socialist), along with the members of Congress (I) and allied parties. The BJP, Left Front, and Janata Dal loyalists all voted against. Shekhar was an interim solution; the major parties wanted time to organize for the inevitable new elections.

Shekhar's government, India's least representative, was completely dependent upon Congress (I), and lasted only four months. The break between Shekhar and Rajiv came over a relatively minor issue: Rajiv demanded punishment of all those involved in alleged police surveillance of his political activities. Congress (I) boycotted Parliament and was backed by the BJP, which was protesting on its own against wiretaps. Shekhar believed that Rajiv was maneuvering to form his own government, and recommended new elections instead. Rajiv joined in this recommendation, and the president then dissolved Parliament.

THE HORROR AND DRAMA OF THE 1991 ELECTION

As India prepared for its tenth general election, Congress (I) was still the dominant party and its leader, Rajiv Gandhi, the center of public attention. The opposition was neither united nor fragmented. Instead, it had evolved as two well organized, mutually hostile parties—the Janata Dal, still led by V. P. Singh, and the Bharatiya Janata Party, whose best known leader and potential prime minister was Lal Kishan Advani. India's party system entered into a new phase, that of tripolarity, modified by the existence of some locally dominant regional parties (the Communist parties in West Bengal, the Telugu Desam in Andrha Pradesh, and the AIADMK in Tamil Nadu). Of the three leading parties that squared off in 1991, the Congress (I) was present almost everywhere; the BJP was its leading opponent in the "cowbelt" of Northern India, and the Janata Dal its main adversary in Uttar Pradesh, Bihar, and Orissa. Thus, in every state there was usually a two-way contest, but nationwide there were *three* major parties.

The distinctive feature of this modified three-party system is that only the Congress (I) has sufficient popular strength to gain or come close to a majority. Neither the Janata Dal nor the BJP, former members of the same National Front coalition, could possibly govern by themselves. They could only come to power if they rejoined forces—unlikely in view of their incompatible programs—or if one received the outside support of Congress (I).

The voting was scheduled to take place over three days (May 20, 23, and 26) in order to permit security forces to move from region to region. The day after the first round of voting, Rajiv Gandhi made a campaign appearance in Sriperumbudur, a town in Tamil Nadu, near Madras. Horror once again struck the heart of India as Rajiv was assassinated by a bomb, which also killed over a dozen other people, including the terrorist carrying the concealed device. This was the culminating act of violence in an election that had already left over 100 killed during the campaign and another 50 on the first day of balloting. Rajiv's assassination was carried out by a Tamil nationalist suicide squad, seeking revenge for the Indian army's attack against Tamil rebels in Sri Lanka.

Voting was postponed to allow for burial of Rajiv and a respite from campaigning, then resumed on 12 and 15 June. Violence continued unabated, and an additional 200 people were killed. Elections were postponed in the Punjab (later canceled), and canceled in the state of Jammu and Kashmir.

When the votes were counted, Congress (I) did better than expected, winning 37.3 percent of the vote and clearly outpolling its two major rivals. A wave of sympathy benefited the party after Rajiv's assassination. In the first round of voting on 20 May there had been a swing away from Congress of almost 6 percent;

Rajiv Gandhi, Prime Minister of India, 1984-1989. Assassinated May 21, 1991 during an election campaign to win back the prime ministership.

in the second round, in June, there was a swing in favor of some 2 percent. With fewer votes than in 1989, Congress (I) won 28 additional seats—because the major opposition force was now split into two separate parties. The big surprise was the increase in popular vote by the BJP, which almost doubled its share, going from 11.4 to 19.9 percent. The Janata Dal went down dramatically to 10.8 percent of the vote, compared to 17.8 percent in 1989. The results of the 1989 and 1991 elections for the three major parties are shown in Table 9.3.

The two Communist parties, now firmly entrenched in West Bengal, won 45 seats in 1989 and 48 seats in 1991 (the CPI 12 and 13 seats, the CPI(M) 33 and 35 seats, respectively), maintaining their popular vote of about

Table 9.3 MAJOR PARTY ELECTION RESULTS

	1989		1991	
	Percentage of popular vote	Seats	Percentage of popular vote	Seats
Congress (I)	39.5	197	37.3	225
BJP	11.4	85	19.9	119
Janata Dal	17.8	143	10.8	55

Note: BJP-Bharatiya Janata Party. From *India Today,* 15 July 1991, pp. 40–55.

2 percent to 3 percent for the CPI and 6 percent for the CPI(M). In addition, the AIDMK, an ally of Congress, won 11 seats in 1991; the Shiv Sena, an ally of the BJP, won 4 seats; the Telegu Desam, a member of the National Front (led by Janata) gained 13 seats; and small revolutionary parties, members of the Left Front, took 6 seats.

Out of the 503 members of the Lok Sabha elected in May–June 1991 (the other seats remained vacant because of postponed or canceled elections), the Congress (I) had swept 225. With the support of the AIDMK and other small parties, Congress (I) could count on a grand total of 244 members—about a dozen short of an absolute or working majority. Some members of the Janata Dal were tempted to join in a coalition with Congress, but V. P. Singh held firm for remaining in opposition. The leaders of the major opposition parties—National Front and Left Front—announced that they would make no attempt to topple a Congress government, but would rather seek to work out a "consensual" approach on specific issues. The political class was exhausted by the campaign and its ensuing violence; no one was ready for new elections.

Let us now take a closer look at the major parties—Congress, Janata, Bharatiya Janata, Communist parties, and regional parties—that contested the 1991 elections.

THE CONGRESS PARTY

Founded in 1885, the Congress party was the spearhead of the national independence movement, sharing in the glory and triumph of Indian nationalism. It was supported during the preindependence period by a broad coalition of interests, including the rising intellectual elite and business class, and enjoyed genuine popularity. Under Nehru's leadership, the Congress party after independence pursued a policy of "democratic socialism" in the domestic arena and of nonalignment in foreign affairs. A key element of the party's democratic socialism has been reliance upon a series of national five-year plans, so that economic development and capital investment will proceed in a rational or, at any rate, deliberate manner. Despite the verbal emphasis on socialism, a planned economy, and nationalization of key sectors of the economy (especially the banks), after 30 years of Congress rule a large private sector continued to exist and even flourish. The Congress is also a party of social reform, seeking to eliminate patterns of caste discrimination and increasing opportunities for self-advancement by the disadvantaged. As a mildly left-of-center party, the Congress was able to retain broad support from peasants, workers, and members of the lower castes without alienating the business class as a whole. Given the deep divisions among the opposition parties—Socialist, conservative, Communist, and orthodox Hindu—the Congress appeared during the postindependence period to be the only party capable of governing.

In 1969, internal divisions and factionalism became a characteristic of the Congress party as well as of the opposition; it was the beginning of the end of the first period of Congress domination. The split within the Congress party began as a dispute between Prime Minister Indira Gandhi and the established party leaders over a candidate for the presidency. Mrs. Gandhi and the leadership supported different candidates. The leadership (known popularly as "the Syndicate") denounced Mrs. Gandhi for breaking party discipline; in turn, Mrs. Gandhi called a special meeting of the All-India Congress Committee, which vindicated her own position. Each group then expelled the other, with the courts finally deciding that neither faction had the right to use the symbol of the former Congress party. The break was clean and complete; the Syndicate called itself the Congress (O)—for organizational or opposition, while the Gandhi faction called itself Congress (R)—for ruling. Defection of the Congress (O) members of the Lok Sabha left Mrs. Gandhi short of an absolute majority. She was compelled to seek allies, mainly the Communist party of India. Mrs. Gandhi turned sharply to the left, advocating nationalization of banks and—a popular measure—elimination of allowances to former rulers of the princely states.

In the fifth general election in 1971 Congress (R) scored a clear victory over Congress (O), winning 352 seats in Lok Sabha compared to only 16 seats for the Syndicate. But the popularity of Congress (R) was fleeting, reflecting largely national pride in the performance of the Indian army in "liberating" Bangladesh and defeating the historic enemy, Pakistan. Mrs. Gandhi's political position became tenuous in the early 1970s, owing to runaway inflation, inability to avert a famine, and increasing cooperation among the opposition parties. The defeat of Congress (R) in 1977 was followed by another split between the faithful supporters of Indira Gandhi and those in the party who now condemned her authoritarian policies during the emergency. Mrs. Gandhi then created a new party, Congress (I)—for Indira—which went on to victory in 1980 while the anti-Gandhi Congress won only 13 seats.

The very name of the new party signaled the predominance of its powerful leader. Decisions were made at the top by Indira Gandhi and her immediate advisers. Mrs. Gandhi relied increasingly on her younger son, Sanjay, who had created a mass Youth Congress and played a key role in selecting candidates and organizing the 1980 election campaign. In recognition of Sanjay's power, and to designate him as the intended successor, he was appointed general secretary of Congress (I).

Mrs. Gandhi suffered a political as well as personal loss when Sanjay was killed in June 1980. Her other son, Rajiv, then started a political career. In a by-election he won the Lok Sabha seat left vacant by his brother's death, and was appointed as one of the secretaries of Congress (I). When supporters of Sanjay found themselves out of favor, political and family intrigues crisscrossed. Sanjay's young widow, Maneka, attended and spoke at a convention of Sanjay's followers in defiance of her mother-

in-law's wishes. After being ordered out of the prime minister's house, Maneka continued her political activities, inveighing against the corruption of her mother-in-law's party and government. She helped found a rival political party, the National Sanjay Organization, and eventually joined with Janata.

The assassination of Indira Gandhi in October 1984 left the party without a head. The party's executive committee immediately nominated Rajiv as prime minister, and its decision was accepted by the president. Rajiv took control of Congress (I), tried to soothe the nation, dissolved Parliament, and led his party to an unprecedented victory. Considering himself a spokesman for a new generation, Rajiv sought to introduce a more pragmatic style in Indian politics, emphasizing the importance of modern management techniques and results. He declared war on corruption, demanding instead professional devotion to the public interest. Rajiv vowed also to free business of bothersome government regulations, which would eliminate the need or temptation to bribe officials.

The anticorruption campaign was led by the finance minister, Vishwanath Pratap Singh, a poet and painter who was a loyal follower of Rajiv. V. P. Singh took his mandate seriously. To make tax reductions acceptable to the public, he insisted on vigorous enforcement of existing rules. Frequent raids by revenue agents at the homes and offices of India's richest families aroused both wonder and hostility. One major concern was the ability of wealthy Indians to smuggle money out of the country and into foreign bank accounts. Without informing the prime minister, V. P. Singh hired an American private detective agency, the Fairfax Group, to conduct an investigation. Among those targeted were powerful business leaders with close connections to Congress (I), including personal friends of Rajiv.

In January 1987, at a time of heightened tension with Pakistan, V. P. Singh was moved from finance to defense; this change also had the effect of stopping those controversial investigations. But as defense minister, Singh continued his anticorruption drive with renewed vigor. He discovered evidence that a large bribe (some $25 million) had been paid in 1981 by a German arms manufacturer in order to secure a contract to build two submarines. Singh's by now numerous enemies accused him of revealing information that might weaken India's defense; allegations were also aired that the Fairfax Group was linked to the CIA, and that the anticorruption drive was an attempt by an unnamed foreign power (by implication, the United States) to destabilize Indian democracy. V. P. Singh was forced to resign.

Immediately thereafter the government was rocked by another kickback story. A Swedish radio station announced that a bribe had been paid by the Bofors arms manufacturer to sell artillery to the Indian army. When the Swedish government confirmed the report, Rajiv responded lamely by creating a committee to investigate the affair. Congress (I) was losing momentum as the elections of November 1989 approached. Rajiv's bold new initiatives, announced with much fanfare at the beginning of his term, were not always followed up. He was accused by critics within the party of suppressing dissent and weakening state and local party structures. After his defeat in 1989, Rajiv bided his time, awaiting the collapse of the Janata Dal government under the weight of its own contradictions. In the 1991 campaign he seemed confident of regaining power, if only because the split of the National Front into two rival independent parties—Janata Dal and BJP—condemned both to minority status. Rajiv spoke of the need for vision, promised a more assertive Indian role in South Asia and the world, and defended Nehru's legacy of secularism. But his economic policy remained hesitant; he called for more deregulation of the economy and reduction of government expenditures, but also pledged to roll back prices on essential goods and build housing for the poor (requiring regulation of the economy and an increase in expenditures).

Narasimha Rao, Prime Minister of India, took office June 20, 1991.

Immediately after Rajiv's assassination, the seventy-year-old Narasimha Rao was elected hastily as the provisional leader. (Rajiv's widow, Sonia, firmly refused to be considered for the post.) After Congress won a near majority of the seats, Rao was challenged by the powerful party boss in Bombay, Sharad Pawar. The younger Pawar eventually stepped aside, and on 20 June the party's members in Parliament unanimously chose Rao as leader; he was immediately asked by President Venkataraman to form a government. For the first time since independence, no member of the Nehru-Gandhi dynasty was at the helm or in the wings of the Congress party.

THE JANATA PARTY

Although the Janata (or People's) party was only founded in 1977, shortly after the sixth general election, most of its component members long had an independent existence, particularly the Socialist party (itself a merger of parties dating from 1947 and later), the Jana Sangh (founded in 1951), and the Swatantra (founded in 1959). Diversity was at once the strength and the vulnerable point of the Janata. What kind of program could possibly unite advocates of socialism and defenders of free enterprise, proponents of secularism and orthodox Hindus? The Janata party was able to promulgate a credible program in 1977 that—at least for the period of the electoral campaign—satisfied all its constituent groups. Most important was the common opposition to emergency rule and a determination to undo Mrs. Gandhi's authoritarian measures (limitations on the judiciary, suspension of civil rights, press censorship, and forcible sterilization). The Janata program was critical of planning and called for self-reliance (satisfying the Swatantra and Jana Sangh), but also promised to alleviate poverty and redistribute wealth (thereby pleasing the Socialists). There was also an emphasis on development of small industry and agriculture, which was more in line with Mahatma Gandhi's legacy.

In all, six major groups made up the Janata party in 1977. The most important was the Congress (O), from whose ranks came Morarji Desai, the new prime minister, and 6 of the 20 members of his cabinet. Another splinter group from the former Congress was the Congress for Democracy, whose founder was one of Mrs. Gandhi's ministers right up to the announcement of the election. When Jagjivan Ram resigned, formed the Congress for Democracy, and joined forces with the Janata, he brought with him the precious political and moral strength (and votes) of millions of outcastes, of whom he was the most influential spokesman. Jagjivan Ram succeeded Desai as leader of the Janata in 1979.

The other four member groups of Janata had a prior existence as independent parties. The Swatantra is basically a conservative party, sympathetic to free enterprise (though some members reject Western materialism altogether) and favoring closer relations with the West. The Jana Sangh was dedicated to preservation of the Hindu way of life, focusing mainly on defense of the Hindi language (in opposition to English), hostility toward Pakistan, and legislation protecting religious practices of the Hindu majority (such as the ban on slaughter of cattle). The Jana Sangh polled a respectable 9 percent of the vote in 1967, but went down a bit in 1971. It had special appeal in those areas of northern India with a large population of Hindu refugees from Pakistan.

The Socialists included two closely linked groups: the Praja Socialist party and the Samyukta Socialist party. The Praja Socialists had previously supported the Congress party when it pursued Socialist policies; the Samyukta Socialists were more militantly opposed to the Congress party and took the lead in forming anti-Congress electoral alliances even with Swatantra and the Jana Sangh. Finally, the Bharatiya Kranti Dal was a centrist, regional party in Uttar Pradesh that had considerable success in appealing to the middle class and wealthier farmers.

The Janata's fragile unity collapsed when the party assumed the responsibilities of office. Personality rivalries reflected the internal contradictions of the Janata coalition. Some leaders wanted to press forward toward rapid economic development; others considered modernity the ultimate expression of spiritual corruption, and sought instead to favor home industries and agriculture. One group wished to assimilate the science and technology of the West; another group rejected Western materialism and resolved instead to revive and fortify Hindu culture. Some defended the outcastes, poor, and oppressed; others spoke out for wealthy business leaders and farmers. Opposition to the emergency rule turned out to be an inadequate program for a governing party. After its rout in January 1980, the Janata party split—and then split again—reducing itself within a few months to little more than a legal fiction.

Each fragment of the former Janata campaigned separately in 1984, and all went down separately to crushing defeat. The party name was continued by the rump that remained after the others had defected. After pondering their loss, opposition leaders rallied and began to cooperate. Dissatisfaction increased with the government's handling of ethnic conflict in the Punjab and Assam. Rajiv's credibility as a crusader against corruption also suffered from the foreign "kickbacks" scandals. The opposition got a big boost when Rajiv's former finance and defense minister, V. P. Singh, created a new party, the Jan Morkha (people's platform). In June 1988, V. P. Singh won handily in a by-election for a parliamentary seat in the city of Allahabad (Uttar Pradesh).

In August 1988, four opposition parties—Jan Morkha, Janata, Lok Dal, and Congress (S)—decided to fuse, calling themselves first the Samajwadi Janata Dal (Popular Socialist party) and later simply the Janata Dal (People's party). This party in turn took the lead in forming, along with some powerful regional parties (including Telegu Desam and Dravida Munnetra Kazhagam), a National Front. With V. P. Singh as general secretary and Rama Rao (Chief Minister of Andrha Pradesh and a former movie star) as chairman, the National Front went on to win the 1989 election.

V. P. Singh formed a Janata Dal government, with the support of the BJP and the Communist parties. But the prime minister had to perform an impossible balancing act. Committed to a secular and pragmatic program, V. P. Singh favored liberalization of the economy, opposed concessions to religious militants, and also sought to advance the interests of the lower castes and the outcastes. He thereby aroused the opposition of key elements in the coalition on whose support his government depended. Communists and small farmers were suspicious of liberalization and privatization; militant Hindus resented Singh's defense of secularism and of the rights of Muslims; and members of the higher castes were outraged by his affirmative action policy.

By the summer of 1990, Singh's government was on the ropes. The deputy prime minister and minister of agriculture, Devi Lal, publicly criticized the prime minister for being "weak." Lal was promptly dismissed, and joined forces with a long-time Singh opponent, Chandra Shekhar, to head up a strong dissident faction within the Janata Dal. In October, communal violence exploded over the issue of building a Hindu shrine on the site of a Muslim temple in Ayodhya. L. K. Advani, leader of the BJP, decided to place himself at the head of a religious pilgrimage to Ayodhya, which resulted in violence and fierce fighting between Hindus and Muslims. When Singh ordered the arrest of Advani, along with several hundred thousand demonstrators, the BJP withdrew its "outside" support for the government. Singh could no longer command a working majority. Rather than order new elections, the president summoned a special session of Parliament. Just before that session, the Janata Dal split apart. Lal and Shekhar created a new Janata Dal (Socialist). V. P. Singh entered the debate in Parliament having suffered the defection of some 60 members of his own party, and faced the opposition of both Congress (I) and the BJP. He lost a vote of confidence by an overwhelming margin: 346 to 142, with eight abstentions.

When Shekhar's minority government collapsed after only four months, V. P. Singh rallied the remnants of Janata Dal around his call for a social revolution. Himself the descendant of a princely family and a high-caste Rajput, Singh argued that India could only enter the modern world through transformation of the caste system, which he wanted to bring about not by violence but by affirmative action in hiring for government jobs. "Our independence will remain hollow," declaimed Singh, "if the power and authority of the state is not deployed in the pursuit of equity." Considering that perhaps three-fourths of Indian society is made up of members of the lower and scheduled castes, Singh's arguments would appear to be both sensible and politically astute. But his attack on the caste system provoked a reaction by higher-caste Hindus, who were supported by large numbers of the very people Singh wished to liberate. The major beneficiary of the call for caste system reform turned out to be the party of Hindu identity, the Bharatiya Janata party, whose emergence as the second political formation of India was the striking feature of the 1991 election.

THE BHARATIYA JANATA PARTY (BJP)

The meteoric rise of the BJP—going from 11.4 percent to about 20 percent of the vote between 1989 and 1991—has called into question India's status as a secular society. The BJP has moderate and militant wings. Hinduism by its nature is an all-encompassing and nondogmatic religion. The militant Hindu sects, especially the Shiv Sena, are more anti-Muslim than fundamentalist; but their hostility toward "special privileges" for Muslims, when pushed to an extreme, is expressed through devotion to Hindu ritual or culture. During the 1991 campaign, the leader of the Shiv Sena, Bal Thackeray, hailed the Hindu terrorist who had assassinated Mohandas Gandhi because "he saved the country from a second partition." A fiery female tribune of the "Hindu Awakening," Uma Bharti, saw the issue before the voters in simple terms: "whether this country belongs to Rama or to Babur!" (Rama is the incarnation of the Hindu deity, Vishnu; Babur is the founder of the Mogul Empire in India.)

The moderate leaders of the BJP—in particular the parliamentarian Lal Kishan Advani, and former foreign minister and amateur poet, Atal Behari Vajpayee—deny that the BJP is a religious party. But they believe it is important to assert the Hindu identity of India and, as Vajpayee has put it, "to take note of the changing Hindu psyche." A principal support of the BJP, perhaps surprisingly, is the upwardly mobile middle class, including successful small shopkeepers and artisans seeking to improve their social status through emulation of the behavior of higher castes. The BJP moderates are in favor of deregulation of the economy, privatization, and an infusion of foreign capital—all of which appeals to the progressive middle class. Another attractive feature of the BJP is that it seems to present a healthy or "clean" alternative—rooted in religion—to the perceived corruption of mainstream parties. The BJP's devoted volunteers present a sharp contrast to the hired toughs and rented crowds associated in the public mind with some of its competitors.

The episode that most clearly defined the character of the BJP was the pilgrimage it sponsored to the town of Ayodhya, the presumed birthplace of the Hindu deity Rama, the mythical character who is the central figure of the Ramayana. According to Hindu militants, a mosque (the Babri Masjid) was built on the precise spot where Rama was born. The shrine to Rama they have in mind can be constructed only if the mosque is destroyed or moved; and they have a long list of other mosques destined for a similar fate. L. K. Advani, usually thought of as a moderate, launched a *Rath Yatra* (march of Rama's chariot), making its way through the solidly Hindu areas of North India to the town of Ayodhya. Mounted on a chariot made up to look like that of Rama, Advani was surrounded by men dressed as the monkeys of Hanuman's army. (Hanuman was the head of an army of monkeys who helped Rama rescue his wife, Sita, from the clutches of the demon, Ravana.) The *Rath Yatra*, portrayed as a means of reuniting Hindus and making them proud of their culture, led to communal rioting between Hindus and Muslims wherever it went. Advani had organized it in response to V. P. Singh's proposal to reserve almost one-half of government jobs for the lower castes, which the BJP denounced as an attack on the integrity of Hindu society and a recipe for civil war.

Reaffirmation of Hindu identity, according to BJP leaders, will cleanse and strengthen Indian society. But it also leads to increased

Table 9.4 MAJOR RELIGIONS IN INDIA

	Millions	Percentage
Hindu	684.7	82.6
Muslim	94.0	11.4
Christian	20.1	2.4
Sikh	16.3	1.9
Buddhist	5.9	0.7
Jain	4.0	0.5
Other	3.6	0.4

Source: World Data, *1991 Britannica Book of the Year,* p. 762.

demands for autonomy and even separation by Muslims and other ethnic minorities, adding to the already formidable strains on the political system. Table 9.4 shows India's various major religious groups.

The Communist Parties of India

The Communist movement of India is split between an orthodox party—the CPI; a rival party originally sympathetic to the Chinese—the CPI (M), for Marxist; and several militant and even terrorist groups inspired by Trotskyism, Maoism, and peasant violence—mainly the CPI (M.-L.), for Marxist-Leninist, and the Naxalites. The Communist movement has deep roots in Indian society and considerable success in appealing to intellectuals, workers, and poor and landless peasants. Since the election of 1952 the combined Communist vote has averaged about 10 percent of the total, falling slightly in 1977 to a little over 7 percent, returning to almost 10 percent in 1980, dipping again to 8.6 percent in 1984, and remaining steady since.

The Communist party of India (CPI), founded in 1928, was always closely linked to the Soviet Union. The CPI cooperated with the Congress party during the struggle for independence in the 1930s, but relations between the two parties became strained with the outbreak of World War II. After the Ger-man invasion of the Soviet Union in 1941, the CPI and the Congress went separate ways: the Communists supported the war effort and the nationalists opted for noncooperation. Immediately after independence the CPI pursued a militant policy of organizing the workers for revolution, but Communist tactics were moderated as relations between India and the Soviet Union improved. In the 1950s, the CPI endorsed aspects of Nehru's foreign policy and pledged to achieve socialism by peaceful means.

However, the revolutionary elements in the party were restive. Pro-Chinese leftists withdrew from the secretariat in 1962; two years later they broke away completely and formed the Communist party of India (Marxist). The CPI (M) hailed the Chinese as opposed to the Soviet model of communism, and sought to use elections as a means of mobilizing workers and peasants for revolutionary action. In 1969 another fission took place. The extreme left created the Communist party of India (Marxist-Leninist), committed to a Maoist tactic of immediate armed struggle and terrorism. Indian Maoists called themselves "Naxalites" in honor of the tenant peasants of Naxalbari (a hill town in West Bengal), who were then forcibly seizing and occupying their land.

After the secession of the Marxists, the policy of the orthodox CPI remained the pursuit of its objectives through the electoral process, seeking alliances with all progressive forces. It collaborated with Indira Gandhi and her Congress (R) in 1969, providing the government the margin of support needed to stay in power. The Congress subsequently refrained from running candidates in about one-third of the districts where the CPI had a reasonable chance of winning. Cooperation with the Congress paid off for the CPI in 1971, enabling it to win 23 seats; but in 1977 the tactic backfired and the CPI was reduced to under 3 percent of the popular vote, retaining only 7 seats in the Lok Sabha. In 1980 the CPI did not collaborate with Indira Gandhi's Congress

(I) but still managed to win 11 seats. It went down to 6 seats with 2.6 percent of the vote in 1984.

Far from supporting Indira Gandhi during the emergency, the CPI (M) cooperated with the Janata, winning 4.3 percent of the vote in the 1977 election and 22 seats in the Lok Sabha—thus forging ahead of the orthodox party. The Marxists gradually toned down and finally abandoned Maoist policies. In 1980 they upped their vote to 6.1 percent, winning 35 seats. In 1984 they retained 22 seats with 6 percent of the vote, going up to 33 seats in 1989 and 35 seats in 1991, and seemed to be on the road to integration within the parliamentary system. The two Communist parties remained distinct, however. The CPI continued to acclaim the international leadership role of the Soviet Union, denouncing both Maoism and Eurocommunism. The CPI (M) refused to align itself with the Soviet Union, but became increasingly critical of China.

Despite the crisis of communism elsewhere in the world, both Indian Communist parties have maintained their strength, mainly because of their grip on local governments. They are functioning more and more like Social Democratic parties—accepting a mixed economy and devoting their energies to defense of their constituents, rather than making a revolution. Both Communist parties announced after the 1991 election that they would not vote to bring down the Congress government formed by Narasimha Rao.

Regional Parties

In addition to the All-India parties just described, there are several locally important regional parties, especially in the Punjab, West Bengal, and Tamil Nadu. These parties focus on ethnic, religious, or linguistic identity and occasionally enter into alliance with national parties for mutually profitable reasons. Many regional parties disappear once immediate demands are met, but a few have become firmly established.

Here is a rundown of the regional parties that have fared well in recent elections.

1. The Dravida Munnetra Kazhagam (DMK) and its rival secessionist All-India Anna DMK (AIADMK) both agitate in favor of the Tamil language and greater autonomy for Tamil Nadu. The popular film star, M. G. Ramachandran, broke away from the DMK in 1972, and founded the AIADMK to protest policies of the party after the death of its creator, C. N. Annaduri ("Anna"). The AIADMK was allied with the Congress in 1984, while M. Karunanidhi, head of the DMK, joined the National Front in 1988. After the death of M. G. Ramachandran in 1987, the AIADMK was rent by factionalism but remained allied to the Congress.

2. The Telegu Desam, created by film star T. N. Rama Rao in 1982, urges a stronger role for states. It has continued to ally itself with Janata.

3. The National Conference has long been the ruling party of Jammu and Kashmir. In 1984 the new leader, Farooq Abdullah, was removed as chief minister by the governor, and the National Conference split into pro- and anti-Congress factions.

4. The Akali Dal—defender of the Sikh faith—is a major force in the Punjab, usually winning about 25 percent of the vote in that region. The Akali Dal has generally allied itself with opponents of the Congress, including Janata and even the Communists.

The Indian party system is hardly distinctive because of the number of major parties or because of the importance of the Communist movements. After all, there are four major parties in France, and the Communist party is even stronger in France than in India. But there is a distinct "style" of politics in a country in which over two-thirds of the electorate is illiterate, the per capita income is just over $200 a year, and most people are still attached to traditional culture. That is, the Indian parties reflect not only the "modern" conflict among advocates of capitalism, liberalism, socialism, and communism, but also the still lively clash between a preindustrial and in many instances primitive society and the rapidly evolving, highly sophisticated industrial and scientific society. The conflict between secular forces and ethnic and religious movements has intensified with the rise of the BJP. Crosscutting currents of the primitive, traditional, and modern merge into a "mix" potentially more explosive than in the parliamentary democracy of any Western society.

POLITICAL INSTITUTIONS AND POLICY MAKING

The political institutions through which Indians govern themselves were created by the 1949 Constitution of India—the product of almost three years' deliberation by the Constituent Assembly (whose members were originally elected by provincial legislatures). One reason for the long delay in promulgating the Constitution is that the Assembly also functioned as the Provisional Parliament immediately following independence, and therefore members had to conduct the business of the nation at the same time that they were drafting a basic law. The leaders of the Congress party—especially Nehru, Rajenda Prasad, Sardar Vallabhbhai Patel, and M. A. K. Azad (a Muslim)—dominated debates and presided over the drafting of the document.

THE CONSTITUTION OF INDIA

The new Constitution went into effect on 26 January 1950. It incorporates much of the Government of India Act of 1935, adding considerable detail on civil liberties and the federal system. With its 395 articles and 8 schedules, the Constitution of India holds the distinction of being one of the longest in the world. The Indians essentially adopted the British parliamentary system, but modified it to suit their own circumstances. They could hardly replicate an English Constitution that had evolved over several centuries, and is expressed in unique medieval and early modern statutes and documents such as the Magna Carta (1215), the Bill of Rights (1689), and the Act of Settlement (1701). Instead, they followed the practice of all other democratic governments in the world by enacting a basic law. The preamble of the Indian Constitution reflects the philosophy of the movement for national liberation and is reminiscent as well of the Declaration of Independence and preamble to the Constitution of the United States.

> WE, THE PEOPLE OF INDIA, having solemnly resolved to constitute India into a SOVEREIGN, DEMOCRATIC REPUBLIC and to secure to all its citizens:
>
> JUSTICE, social, economic and political;
>
> LIBERTY of thought, expression, belief, faith and worship;
>
> EQUALITY of status and opportunity; and to promote among them all
>
> FRATERNITY assuring the dignity of the individual and the unity of the Nation;
>
> IN OUR CONSTITUENT ASSEMBLY...DO HEREBY ADOPT, ENACT AND GIVE TO OURSELVES THIS CONSTITUTION

The basic commitment of the Constituent Assembly was to a parliamentary system (that is, a cabinet responsible to the lower house); a republic (hence, an elected president would play the role of head of state); a federation with a strong center (striking a balance between national authority and provincial assemblies); and a secular system (not a state divided between Hindus and Muslims). Republican institutions and commonwealth membership were made compatible when India agreed to recognize the British monarch as the symbol of free association and as such the head of the Commonwealth, without otherwise acknowledging any allegiance to the Crown.

One respect in which the Indians departed from British practice and reflected American tradition was in guaranteeing civil liberties (called Fundamental Rights) and making them enforceable through courts. The rights thus protected under the Constitution make up an impressive catalog: equality, "freedom," freedom of religion, and the right to property, as well as some not specifically set forth in the American Bill of Rights—for example, freedom from exploitation, and cultural and educational rights. Especially important in Indian society are the abolition of untouchability, guarantees of equal opportunity in public employment, and prohibition of discrimination on grounds of religion, race, caste, or sex.

Balancing off the declaration of fundamental rights of citizens against the state are the "directive principles" that set forth the duty of the state toward the citizens. The Constitution enjoins the state to promote the welfare of the people by creating social, economic, and political justice. These principles are difficult to carry out because all political parties proclaim the promotion of the public welfare as their goal—but disagree on how to go about doing it. Similarly, abolition of untouchability and guarantees of full employment do not depend exclusively on constitutional provisions. Such measures become effective only under appropriate political, economic, and social conditions.

The Constitution of India goes further than most similar documents in stipulating that freedoms may be suspended or abrogated during an emergency. Part XVIII (Emergency Provisions) of the Constitution specifically gives the president the power to suspend the right to freedom in a national emergency, though the president may act only on the advice of the prime minister. After the Chinese incursion in 1962 a national emergency was declared—and lasted officially for six years. During this emergency, Parliament passed a Defense of India Act (modeled on the Defense of the Realm Acts in Britain), which empowered the government to detain any person it suspected on reasonable grounds to be "of hostile origin" or to be "likely to act" in a manner harmful to Indian defense, state security, maintenance of public order, India's relations with foreign states, or the efficient conduct of military operations.

The balance between individual rights and national unity or law and order swings decidedly toward the latter in an emergency. After the emergency relating to the conflict with China was finally lifted, Parliament passed an Unlawful Activities Prevention Act which continued many of the restrictions of the previous period. The power of the executive to override individual rights was further strengthened by the Maintenance of Internal Security Act of 1971. The most spectacular use of emergency power since the founding of the Indian Republic was the emergency rule invoked by Mrs. Indira Gandhi in 1975–1977.

After the decision of the Allahabad High Court in June 1975 that Mrs. Gandhi had violated the electoral law, the opposition parties began a mass campaign of civil disobedience to force the prime minister to resign. One of India's most colorful political leaders, Jaya Prakash Narayan, pointedly urged the army and police to refuse to obey "unjust orders." The prime minister thereupon advised the president to proclaim, by virtue of the power vested in him by Article 352 of the Constitution, that "a grave emergency exists whereby the security of India is threatened by internal disturbance." The police arrested almost 700 opposition leaders and about 30,000 people all told. Newspapers were forbidden to publish reports affecting India's relations with foreign countries, denigrating the office of the prime minister, causing disaffection among members of the armed forces or government employees, or bringing the government into hatred or contempt. These regulations were strictly enforced. The government also banned several militant Hindu organizations and the CPI (M).

Through the amending process the Constitution was changed so drastically that it became virtually a different system of government. Amendments can be added to the Constitution by a majority vote of both houses with at least two-thirds of the members of each house present and voting; in addition, amendments relating to the political institutions must be ratified by the legislatures of a majority of the states. Three amendments (the 39th, 40th, and 41st) were passed in rapid succession by Parliament and ratified soon after the emergency was declared. These amendments provided that the president's reasons for proclaiming an emergency could not be challenged in any court; also that all matters relating to the election of the president, vice-president, speaker of the Lok Sabha, or the prime minister should be referred to a new authority to be created by Parliament and not be judged by the regular courts; that this authority not be questioned by any court; and that all pending proceedings against the president, vice-president, speaker, and prime minister were null and void.

In addition, a Maintenance of Internal Security (Amendment) Bill was passed in 1976. It provided that the grounds on which a person had been detained should not be disclosed to the detainee or any other person. President Ahmed ordered the suspension for the period of the emergency of any person's right to apply to the courts for enforcement of Article 19 of the Constitution—that is, the rights to freedom of speech and expression, and peaceable assembly. The Supreme Court also held that the government could suspend habeas corpus. One justice declared that the public safety was the highest law in time of crisis.

The most sweeping change of all was instituted by the Constitution (42nd Amendment) Bill, known as A42. This amendment was passed by Parliament on 11 November 1976 (by a vote of 366 to 4 in the Lok Sabha and 191 to 0 in the Rajya Sabha); it was ratified by the legislatures of more than half the states within a month, received the assent of President Ahmed on 18 December 1976, and took effect a few weeks later. A42 amended

37 articles, repealed 4, and introduced 13 new articles. Among the most important provisions were the following:

Preamble. India was now described as a "sovereign socialist secular democratic republic.

Fundamental rights. No law giving effect to the "directive principles" might be declared unconstitutional on the ground that it infringed on the fundamental rights guaranteed by the Constitution. No law prohibiting antinational activities should be nullified on grounds of violating individual liberties. Antinational activities were broadly defined to embrace advocacy of secession; threatening the sovereignty or integrity of India or "the security of the state or the unity of the nation"; overthrowing the government by force; creating internal disruptions; and fomenting communal and caste hatred.

Fundamental duties. A new article was inserted into the Constitution, stating that every citizen has the duty to abide by the Constitution, cherish the ideals of the national struggle for freedom, defend the country, promote social harmony, and strive toward excellence.

The executive. The article stating that the Council of Ministers would "aid and advise the President in the exercise of his functions" was amended to read that the Council of Ministers would aid and advise the President, "who shall, in the exercise of his functions, act in accordance with such advice."

Amendments. It was stated that no amendment to the Constitution can be called into question "in any court on any ground."

Most of the provisions of A42 were reversed by two constitutional amendments adopted under the Desai government in 1977. Specifically, the provision empowering Parliament to legislate against antinational activity was repealed; and the president was given the right to ask the Council of Ministers to reconsider its decisions. Restrictions were also imposed on the use of emergency powers. A proclamation of emergency can now be issued only when the security of India is threatened by external aggression or armed rebellion. Internal disturbances not amounting to armed rebellion are an insufficient ground. The Council of Ministers must forward its request for an emergency to the president in writing; the proclamation must be approved by Parliament within a month by a two-thirds majority, can remain in force for only six months, and can be extended only after another vote by a two-thirds majority. Even though the main structures of the 1949 Constitution were restored, the emergency is a reminder of the fragility of civil liberties in India.

THE PRESIDENT AND VICE-PRESIDENT

The Constitution vests the executive power in a president, who is elected for a five-year term by an electoral college consisting of members of Parliament and state legislative assemblies. The voting procedure is complex in order to maintain a rough parity among the states based on population, with electors casting a preferential ballot. The vice-president is elected for a five-year term by both houses of Parliament in a joint session. As in the United States, the vice-president presides over the upper house of Parliament (the Rajya Sabha). The vice-president's main function, of course, is to take the place of the president in case of death or incapacity; in that event a presidential election must be held within six months.

In theory, the president is given vast powers under the Constitution. The president may dissolve Parliament, declare an emergency in a state, and rule that state by decree. The president may refuse to assent to a bill, although the veto may be overridden if the bill is repassed by both houses. Also, the president is commander-in-chief of the armed forces and appoints state governors and Supreme Court justices. It was understood by the framers of the Constitution that the president would act only on the advice of the prime minister, and this understanding has been respected in practice. The vast powers of the president have in fact devolved upon the prime minister. Perhaps the most important function of the president, consequently, is to appoint the prime minister. So far the president has had little discretion, because the leader of the majority party in the Lok Sabha is the only person who would have the confidence of Parliament. In 1979, however, the disintegration of the governing Janata party created a power vacuum that was partly filled by President Sanjiva Reddy.

The formal powers of the office give the president considerable influence within the political system, especially during periods of party instability. The president is entitled to be informed and consulted by the prime minister, has recently been accorded the power to ask the Council of Ministers to reconsider a decision, and must sign all legislation. The president is also the major symbol of national unity; hence the election of a president has always been a matter of great concern to the political parties and arouses the interest of the public. When President Reddy resigned in 1980, the candidate of the Congress party, Zail Singh, won election for the unfilled term easily, receiving almost three-fourths of the votes of the electoral college. He was a political ally of Prime Minister Indira Gandhi, and the first Sikh to hold that office. President Singh, however, did not get along well with Gandhi's successor, Rajiv, complaining bitterly that he was continually bypassed. He chose not to run for reelection. In July 1987 R. Venkataraman, candidate of Rajiv and Congress (I), was elected with over 70 percent of the vote. He did not even bother to campaign. Because no single party received a majority in the elections of

Table 9.5 PRESIDENTS OF INDIA

President	Election
Rajendra Prasad	1950
Rajendra Prasad	1952
Rajendra Prasad	1957
Dr. S. Radhakrishnan	1962
Dr. Zakir Hussain	1967 (died 1969)
V. V. Giri	1969
Fakhruddin Ali Ahmed	1974 (died 1977)
Neelam Sanjiva Reddy	1977
Zail Singh	1980
R. Venkataraman	1987

1989 and 1991, President Venkataraman has played a larger than usual role in the political process—particularly in deciding who should be invited to form governments and under what circumstances.

For a list of India's presidents since 1950, see Table 9.5.

THE PARLIAMENT

There are two chambers of Parliament: the lower house, Lok Sabha (House of the People), which now has 542 members, and an upper house, Rajya Sabha (Council of States), whose membership is limited to 250. The president appoints 12 members to the Rajya Sabha as representatives of the arts and professions, and all the other members are elected by the state legislatures; hence the upper house serves as a direct link between the state and national governments.

The Lok Sabha members are elected on the basis of single-member constituencies. Its normal term is five years, although it may be dissolved at any time by the president (on advice of the prime minister). According to the Constitution, the Lok Sabha must meet at least twice a year, with no more than six months between sessions. Most members speak in either English or Hindi but may use other languages if they wish. As in the British House of Commons, the Speaker is elected from among the

members and is supposed to be nonpartisan once in office. Unlike the House of Commons, the Lok Sabha has a system of standing committees that covers the whole range of government operations—including a Rules Committee and others that oversee the budget, exercise of delegated power, and general performance of the ministries. In recent years, up to half of the members of each new Parliament have never before served in that body. Inexperience and lack of office space and staff have contributed to the relative weakness of Parliament in its dealings with the cabinet and the civil service.

Legislative procedure in the Indian Parliament is similar to that in the British Parliament—though the Rajya Sabha has a more important role than the House of Lords. Legislation is drafted and introduced by the government; a severely limited amount of time is reserved each week for bills presented by private members (those who are not members of ministries). As in Britain, there are three readings. The first reading is of the title only and with no debate. The Speaker then assigns the bill to a select (or ad hoc) committee, made up with the advice of party leaders, just to consider that bill. The second reading is based on the report of the select committee; it is at this stage that debate and voting on each clause take place. The third reading is merely on the formal motion that the bill be passed. Money bills can only be introduced in the Lok Sabha; other legislation can originate in either house, although in practice most bills are presented first in the Lok Sabha.

If the two houses do not agree, the bill may be sent back and forth until all differences have been resolved. If there is still no agreement, the president may call a joint session of Parliament, where the matter is settled by a majority vote, thus giving the more numerous Lok Sabha members the upper hand. Joint sessions are rarely necessary, however. If the Rajya Sabha rejects a money bill, it can be enacted into law simply by having the Lok Sabha repass it.

Another feature of Indian legislative procedure based directly on British practice is the question period, which begins each daily session of Parliament. Members are permitted to ask questions of ministers concerning most matters of public policy; replies are generally of interest to the press. Members may ask follow-up questions that test the minister's ability to think under pressure. Occasionally, ministers have been forced to resign because of incompetence or scandal brought out during the question period.

The central notion in parliamentary government is that the cabinet is responsible to Parliament and must resign when it loses the confidence of that body. The Lok Sabha possesses one important weapon in its relations with the cabinet: any 50 members may introduce a motion of censure; if it carries, the cabinet must resign. The cabinet is not responsible to the Rajya Sabha, which has no power to censure the government. The opposition in the Lok Sabha has been so fragmented in the past that motions of censure were rare because no single opposition party had as many as 50 members. As in Britain, it is expected that the governing party will "manage" the deliberations of Parliament and in so doing will be supported by its members. Parliament plays an important role, not so much as policymaker, but as the forum in which declarations of government policy are made and government and opposition engage in structured debate.

THE PRIME MINISTER AND COUNCIL OF MINISTERS

The effective executive in India—prime minister, Council of Ministers, and cabinet—is based squarely on the British model. Exactly the same distinctions are made in India as in Britain among all three groups; they have the same relationship to Parliament, but the dominance of the executive over Parliament is perhaps even greater in India. The prime minister is chosen by the president; but in general the president has no choice. He or she must nominate the leader of the majority party in the Lok Sabha—otherwise the government would not have the confidence of that body.

The prime minister chooses ministers, who are then officially appointed by the president. Ministers must be members of Parliament; nonmembers may be appointed if within six months they become members of Parliament through a by-election. The Council of Ministers is collectively responsible to Parliament for all decisions of the government; as in Britain, however, this collective responsibility does not mean that each minister is fully aware of decisions made by colleagues, for the good reason that the Council of Ministers never meets as a collective entity. The ministry is a large group that includes heads and deputy heads of all the departments. By tradition, the most important ministers (usually from 12 to 18 in number) are invited by the prime minister to join the cabinet, which is not mentioned in the Constitution. The cabinet meets regularly once a week and is responsible for formulation and coordination of all government policy. By invitation, other ministers or experts can attend cabinet sessions for discussion of matters in which they have special interest or expertise.

Even the cabinet is too unwieldy for policy making, so all prime ministers have created specialized committees consisting of a few ministers responsible for a specific area or problem. The prime minister, who usually chairs these committees, is in a position to dominate their deliberations. Nehru formed an emergency committee of the cabinet with six members as the equivalent of the "inner cabinet" in Britain; it virtually replaced the larger cabinet as a decision-making body for important policy. Since then each prime minister has continued the practice of consulting regularly with some sort of inner cabinet.

As in Britain, a special agency of the civil service is assigned to the prime minister and cabinet to furnish secretarial and administrative assistance in preparing agendas, recording decisions, following up on implementation, and coordinating the various special committees of the cabinet. The central secretariat, headed by a cabinet secretary, thus provides an indispensable element of professionalism and continuity in cabinet deliberations. In view of the secretariat's reputation for irreproachable professionalism, it came as a shock when it was revealed in 1985 that one of its trusted and most important members had long been a spy in the service of a foreign power.

The prime minister is the "buckle that binds" the president, Council of Ministers, cabinet, and Parliament. The dominance of the prime minister within the system was especially evident during the tenure of the first occupant of the office, Jawaharlal Nehru. As

An Indian dynasty. Prime minister Jawaharlal Nehru, together with his daughter and future prime minister, Indira Gandhi, and her two sons Sanjay and Rajiv (who became prime minister after his mother's assassination in 1984). This photo was taken in 1956 during Nehru's state visit to West Germany. Chancellor Konrad Adenauer is directly behind Nehru.

leader of the national independence movement and the Congress party, Nehru was the towering figure of Indian politics in the years following independence. Many feared that his departure would usher in a period of chaos, but no succession struggle took place immediately after Nehru's death in May 1964. The Congress party unanimously chose one of Nehru's close collaborators, Lal Bahadur Shastri, as prime minister. Shastri did not possess the charismatic qualities of his predecessor but proved to be a reasonably effective leader. When he died suddenly in January 1966, the Congress party turned to Nehru's daughter, Indira Gandhi (no relation to Mohandas Gandhi), a former president of the party. Thereafter she was at the center of the political stage, except for the period between the defeat of the Congress party in 1977 and its triumphant comeback in 1980. The two prime ministers who served from 1977 to 1979—Morarji Desai and Charan Singh—were forceful personalities but were not able to fashion a solid majority. Indira Gandhi's elder son, Rajiv, continued the tradition of leadership by a member of the Nehru family after his mother's assassination. The successors to Rajiv—V. P. Singh (1989–1990) and Chandra Shekhar (1990–1991)—were at the mercy of their outside supporters and could not fully wield their power. Narasimha Rao came close to a working majority after the election of 1991, but still depended on outside support from other parties to carry out his program.

Table 9.6 PRIME MINISTERS OF INDIA

Jawaharlal Nehru	1947–1964	Congress
Lal Bahadur Shastri	1964–1966	Congress
Indira Gandhi	1966–1977	Congress
Morarji Desai	1977–1979	Janata
Charan Singh	1979–1980	Janata
Indira Gandhi	1980–1984	Congress
Rajiv Gandhi	1984–1989	Congress
V. P. Singh	1989–1990	Janata
Chandra Shekhar	1990–1991	Janata (Socialist)
Narasimha Rao	1991–	Congress

Nonetheless, the office of the prime minister has remained the major source of policy making and the chief political prize sought by all contenders. For a list of India's prime ministers since independence, see Table 9.6.

THE SUPREME COURT

The Constitution creates a Supreme Court, consisting of a chief justice and 17 associates, appointed by the president after consultation with sitting members of the court and of state courts. The Indian Supreme Court, unlike its British counterpart, may declare an act of Parliament unconstitutional. It is relatively easy, however, for Parliament to reverse decisions by the Supreme Court through the amending process. Several court decisions invalidating land reform legislation were overridden.

During the 1975–1977 emergency, the Supreme Court pointedly sided with the government, damaging its reputation as a judicial guardian of civil liberties. In 1976 the Forty-second Amendment prohibited the Supreme Court from reviewing changes introduced by constitutional amendment. But in 1980 the Court reaffirmed its power to safeguard the "basic structure" of the Constitution, even in amendments. The modern judiciary has gained widespread acceptance in India. But the experience during the emergency raises serious questions about the ability of the Supreme Court to withstand strong political pressures. For a summary of the structure of Indian government, see Feature 9.1.

THE BUREAUCRACY

Indians have long believed that their political system is more effective than those of other developing countries because of the bureaucratic structures inherited from the British; the belief may be at least partly correct. After independence, the old Indian civil service of the British period was refashioned as the Indian Administrative Services (IAS). The membership of the IAS is only about 4000 people—a

---

Feature 9.1 **Structure of Government In India**

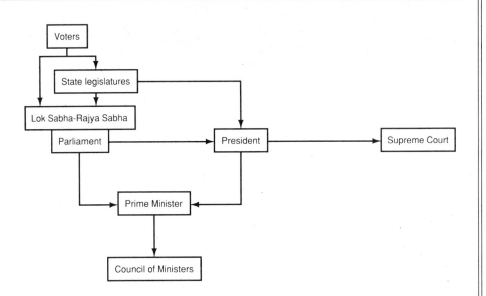

The above chart shows the channels of political responsibility within the Government of India. The voters directly elect the Lok Sabha and the state legislatures; the state legislatures select the members of the upper chamber, the Rajya Sabha (except for 12 members selected by the president, not indicated on the chart). The president is elected by an electoral college, consisting of elected members of both houses of Parliament, and of the legislatures in all the states, with the vote weighted on the basis of population. The president selects a prime minister, who is normally the leader of the majority party in the Lok Sabha, or enjoys the support of a majority. The prime minister selects the ministers. The president, after consulting with existing judges of the Supreme Court and of high courts of the states, appoints the judges of the Supreme Court.

---

minuscule fraction of the 13 million civil servants in India—but they are the "steel frame" of the whole edifice.

Recruitment into the IAS (approximately 140 annually) and into a few central services of individual ministries, such as the foreign service, is supervised by a Union Public Service Commission. As in Britain, an attempt is made through examinations and interviews to select young people of exceptional intelligence and talent, who are then given special training and form a policy-making stratum within the huge civil service establishment. One advantage of this system is to guarantee the competence of the higher civil service. However, the middle and lower levels of the civil service are generally far below the standard set by the top stratum.

In sum, the Indians have gradually adapted British-style institutions to their own circumstances. These institutions have become familiar to all Indians and are increasingly considered an appropriate mechanism for resolving political conflicts and working out compromises. The greatest crisis of the democratic system probably was the emergency; had it endured, the character of the Constitution as originally conceived would have been altered. But the Indian public brought the emergency to an end, and its verdict was accepted by Mrs. Gandhi and her supporters. Some observers have expressed concern that the personalization of power under both Indira and Rajiv Gandhi has led to an "erosion of institutions"— including the Congress party as well as Parliament and state governments. Atul Kohli has attributed institutional decay to "the destructive and self-serving acts of leaders who find institutions a constraint on personal power," as well as to mounting social pressures.[6] Without strong institutions as intermediaries between state and society, he contends, policy making has become arbitrary and ineffective.

Certainly we should not underestimate the difficulty of maintaining viable democratic government in any third world society. Yet the Constitution held firm in the first 40 years of its existence and acquired genuine legitimacy. Every year that passes increases the chances that the system will be able to meet critical new challenges in the future, despite the heterogeneity of Indian society and the intensity of its political divisions.

Key Terms

Advani, L. K.
Bharatiya Janata Party (BJP)
Communist Party of India—CPI
Communist Party of India (Marxist)—CPI (M)
Congress Party
Congress (I)
Council of Ministers
emergency rule
Gandhi, Indira
Gandhi, Rajv
Indian Administrative Services
Janata Party
Lok Sabha
Naxalites
President
President's rule
Prime Minister
Rajya Sabha
Rao, Narasimha
Singh, V. P.
Supreme Court

Suggestions for Further Reading

Eldersveld, S., and Ahmed Bashiruddin. *Citizens and Parties: Mass Political Behavior in India* (Chicago: University of Chicago Press, 1978).

Hardgrave, R. L., and S. A. Kochanek. *India: Government and Politics in a Developing Nation*, 4th ed. (New York: Harcourt Brace Jovanovich, 1986).

Hart, H. C., ed. *Indira Gandhi's India: A Political System Reappraised* (Boulder, Colo.: Westview Press, 1976).

Hartmann, H. *Political Parties in India* (New Delhi: Meenakshi Prakashan, 1982).

Kochanek, S. A. *The Congress Party of India* (Princeton: Princeton University Press, 1968).

Kochanek, S. A. *Business and Politics in India* (Berkeley: University of California Press, 1974).

Kohli, Atul. *Democracy and Discontent: India's Growing Crisis of Governability* (New York: Cambridge University Press, 1990).

Kohli, Atul, ed. *India's Democracy: An Analysis of Changing State-Society Relations* (Princeton: Princeton University Press, 1990).

Morris-Jones, W. H. *Government and Politics of India*, 3rd ed. (London: Hutchinson University Library, 1971).

Palmer, N. D. *Elections and Political Development: The South Asian Experience* (Durham, N.C.: Duke University Press, 1975).

Palmer, N. D. *The Indian Political System*, 2nd ed. (Englewood Cliffs, N.J.: Prentice-Hall, 1979).

Pyle, M. V. *Constitutional Government in India,* 4th ed. (Bombay: Asia Publishing House, 1984).

Sankdher, M. M., ed. *Framework of Indian Politics* (New Delhi: Gitanjali Publishing House, 1984).

Sen Gupta, B. *Communism in Indian Politics* (New York: Columbia University Press, 1972).

Venkateswaran, R. J. *Cabinet Government in India* (London: Allen and Unwin, 1967).

Weiner, M. *The Politics of Scarcity: Public Pressure and Political Response in India* (Chicago: University of Chicago Press, 1962).

Weiner, M. *India at the Polls: The Parliamentary Elections of 1977* (Washington, D.C.: American Enterprise Institute, 1978).

Weiner, M. *India at the Polls, 1980: A Study of the Parliamentary Elections* (Washington, D.C.: American Enterprise Institute, 1983).

C. Public Policy

Political institutions are not ends in themselves; they are designed to formulate policy. The ultimate test of a political system is its effectiveness in permitting a people to attain collective goals. The leaders of the independence movement in India were determined to modernize their nation and conquer poverty through democratic means. An appraisal of the political system they created, then, calls for a review of the effort by Indians to fashion a modern state, society, and economy.

MODERNIZATION: A BALANCE SHEET

In the first decade after independence was won in 1947, Indians succeeded beyond the expectations of most observers in endowing themselves with a rational and workable structure. Their Constitution was drafted, promulgated, and implemented. The key position within this structure was occupied by a charismatic leader who had led the struggle of national independence, a struggle which was shared by a political party that stood ready to shoulder the burden and responsibility of power. Buttressing the system was a civil service of considerable competence, inherited from the days of British rule.

Almost immediately those bothersome remnants of feudalism, the princes, were cast aside, and the vast territory of the subcontinent was at last integrated under one authority. Almost 600 territorial units were consolidated into 27 states. Further reorganization took place in 1956 when the government of India created 14 states out of the earlier 27, mainly along linguistic lines. Agitation by linguistic groups in Bombay, the Punjab, and Nagaland subsequently resulted in the creation of more states, and there are now 25 states and 7 union territories in the Indian Union. By and large the delicate technical task of reconstructing the polity along linguistic lines was fairly well done, but ethnic tensions continue to plague the nation. In 1948, Nehru expressed the fear that basing regional units on language would let loose the forces of "disruption and disintegration." In some measure his somber prediction came true. Strong regional parties have come to power or assumed important positions in key states—notably the CPI(M) in West Bengal, the DMK and AIADMK in Tamil Nadu, the Telegu Desam in Andrha, and the Akali Dal in the Punjab. Demands for state autonomy have often been accompanied by violent demonstrations, calling forth counter-demonstrations and police action that further embitter feelings. A particularly difficult problem developed in Assam in the 1970s, when the influx of Bengali refugees from Bangladesh was viewed by Assamese as a threat to the integrity of tribal cultures. A state election in 1983, boycotted by most Assamese voters to protest the participation of Bengali immigrants, led to rioting in which several thousand people were killed. Tribal unrest, punctuated by armed uprisings, has continued in the Northeast. The United Liberation Front of Assam killed almost 100 people in the last months of 1991 alone, including a number of Congress (I) politicians.

An even more serious challenge to national unity came in the 1980s from the Sikh population of the Punjab. The Sikh religion, which emerged in the fifteenth century, was an attempt to reconcile Islam and Hinduism. A series of gurus (or "teachers") fashioned a monotheistic creed, holding that all religions are fundamentally alike; the gurus opposed idolatry, priesthood, and the caste system. Persecuted by Mogul emperors, Sikhs became bitter enemies of Muslims, despite their many religious similarities, and created a warrior society to defend themselves. After combating the British in the early nineteenth century, Sikhs served in large numbers in the British army in India, and subsequently in the Indian army. In 1947, Sikhs joined with militant Hindus in fighting Muslims. Since then, however, they have sought to maintain their distinctive identity in opposition to Hindus.

In 1966 the Akali Dal—or Sikh political party—attained its major demand for the creation of a Punjabi language state with a Sikh majority. But conflict persisted regarding the status of the capital city, Chandigarh (on the border between the Punjab and Haryana), and control of river waters. The Akali began to demand autonomy for the Punjab; some extremists, notably Sant Jarnail Singh Bhindranwale (leader of the outlawed Dal Khalsa) called for an independent Sikh state. However, Sikhs constitute a bare majority of the population in the Punjab, which was ruled by Sikh Congress leaders, except for the brief period of an Akali-Janata coalition from 1977 to 1980. The movement in favor of Sikh revival and independence gathered strength, especially among young people. Sikh militants resorted to acts of terrorism (shooting Hindus at random, for example); and the Center declared an emergency, imposing president's rule. But this only inflamed Sikh extremists, who stepped up agitation and acts of violence. The deadly cycle of terrorism and police repression continued, and hundreds of people were killed in the first months of 1983 alone.

Bhindranwale directed activities from his headquarters in Amritsar's Golden Temple. The Indian army finally moved in, triggering a three-day battle in which almost 1000 people were killed, including Bhindranwale himself and over 80 Indian soldiers. Dozens of Sikh religious institutions were raided by the Indian army in their search for extremists. Several thousand Sikh soldiers mutinied, in some cases setting off armed confrontations with the regular army, and there was a surge of support among Sikhs for an independent Khalistan. On 31 October 1984, the horror reached a climax when Indira Gandhi was struck down by two Sikh members of her personal bodyguard. Mobs in the capital went on a rampage, killing almost 3000 Sikhs.

After calling for an end to the violence, Rajiv Gandhi sought a political solution. Assuming that the Akali Dal had been seeking participation in power rather than autonomy, much less independence, he gambled on state elections permitting the Sikh party to win and govern. But the political concessions may have come too late. In May 1987 the Center imposed President's rule on the Punjab once again, on the ground that the Akali Dal ministry had permitted terrorists and advocates of independence to take over. V. P. Singh vowed to heal ethnic and regional conflicts without giving in to separatism—no easy task. He visited the Punjab twice, and met a number of Sikh demands (for example, taking action against those accused of killing Sikhs in the aftermath of Indira's assassination). Chandra Shekhar also took part in talks with an Akali Dal leader. But violence continued unabated. Sikh militants went on robbing banks, killing Hindus at

Sikh demonstrators shouting anti-government slogans after the Indian army takeover of the Golden Temple in Amritsar, June 1984.

random, and assassinating politicians. On the final day of balloting in 1991 Sikhs attacked a train in the Punjab, killing 68 Hindu passengers.

Ethnic conflict also flared in Jammu and Kashmir, the only state with a Muslim majority. India and Pakistan had gone to war over Kashmir at the time of partition, when its Hindu ruler acceded to the Indian Union over the opposition of the Muslim population. Many Muslims in Kashmir remained receptive to cultural and political influences from Pakistan, and a special effort was needed to se-

cure their participation in Indian parties and government. In 1987 Rajiv compelled the National Conference to enter into a coalition with Congress (I), then used police extensively to win the state elections. Local opinion was inflamed by this open intervention from the Center, and an armed rebellion broke out which continued after Rajiv's defeat in 1989. The government, led by the National Conference, was dismissed in January 1990. Virtual martial law took effect in early 1991, and elections were canceled. It is probable that Kashmir can now be kept within the Indian Union only by force. The effort required to maintain a proper and workable balance between national unity and state autonomy is taxing the governing ability of the political class.

Remaking the map of India has gone hand in hand with an attempt to reorganize Indian society. The Constitution abolished untouchability and asserted the equality of women. This amounted in practice to a declaration of intent, because the status of 60 million untouchables and of women could not be changed overnight. Nonetheless, an act of Parliament unified marriage laws for the entire nation, permitting marriages between members of different castes and providing for divorce. The Untouchability Offences Act of 1955 made it illegal and punishable to discriminate against members of the untouchable class. But here, too, the enforceability of a statute was limited. More important are other developments that have the effect of undermining the traditional caste system. The design of new industrial towns does not take caste differences into account. The growing urbanization and industrialization of the nation are creating new patterns of life that weaken the millennia-old social structures. In addition, the Community Development Program is a positive force in furthering social change.

Despite undeniable progress in the past 40 years, caste remains a central fact of Indian life. Outcastes are still the victims of discrimination, beatings, and even killings if they enter high-caste neighborhoods, use Brahmin temples, or violate any of the numerous rituals consigning them to inferior status. In the 1991 election V. P. Singh made reform of the caste system a major campaign issue. Indian democracy cannot advance, nor can modernization be achieved, he argued, so long as three-fourths of the population (outcastes and Sudras) are kept down. But his specific remedy— reserving almost half of government jobs for the lower castes—provoked a virulent reaction by higher-caste Hindus. The backlash helped the militant Hindu BJP to virtually double its

vote and become the second party of India in 1991.

As part of the Community Development Program the Indian government has revived a tradition of village rule by elders that had existed before the advent of the British— the *Panchayat* (or "council of five"). Mohandas Gandhi praised the *Panchayats* as agencies of local democracy, but his plea to reinstitute them was turned down by the Constituent Assembly. In 1958 the government asked each state to create a system of *Panchayati Raj* as a way of involving village residents in democratic decision making; most areas in India are now covered. Basically, each village elects a council of about a dozen members; the heads of these councils within a large area, together with other members, form a second-level group; and the heads of all the councils within a district, along with elected legislators in that district and others, constitute the highest-level group. The *Panchayati Raj* have brought about impressive popular participation in local political life; but instead of the consensus dreamed of by Gandhi, local elections reflect national party conflict. Nor have the *Panchayats* assumed increasing responsibility for economic development and planning, as originally hoped.

It is in the economic domain that the heritage from the past has weighed most heavily. Modernization of the social structure is ultimately possible only with simultaneous modernization of the economy—each process being indispensable to the other. The great leader of the national independence movement, however, was unalterably opposed to industrialization. Gandhi once said

India's salvation consists in unlearning what she has learned during the last fifty years. The railways, telegraphs, hospitals, lawyers, doctors and such-like have all to go; and the so-called upper classes have to learn consciously, religiously, and deliberately the simple peasant life.... Every time I get into a railway car or use a motor bus I know that I am doing violence to my sense of what is right.[7]

This attitude may have been sound political tactics during the period when British rulers, in the eyes of the nationalists, were exploiting the Indian economy. It also represented a concession to Hindu culture, which seeks salvation in liberation from earthly existence, not in improvement thereof. After independence, however, Gandhi's successors had to face the problem of India's mass poverty. Some continued to exalt the virtues of village life and of a poor but spiritual existence, but the leadership of the Congress party, particularly the group around Prime Minister Nehru, broke completely with the Gandhian tradition. They set about deliberately to create a modern economy through a series of five-year plans. A noted Indian journalist observed, in this connection: "Posterity will probably rate Gandhi as one of history's magnificent failures."[8] A five-year plan in India covers a multitude of activities, both governmental and private. A planning commission in Delhi establishes certain targets and goals, measures progress, and calls attention to shortcomings. The process is relatively relaxed, involving little discipline over the economy. The goal is to launch India into a "take-off" period so that the economy will gain momentum and expand on all fronts.

The First Plan (1951–1956) emphasized expansion of agricultural production and public works. Considerable progress was made in agriculture through irrigation projects, reform of landholding, and construction of fertilizer plants. The Community Development Program and the National Extension Services introduced cooperative techniques in the villages. Throughout this period, agricultural and industrial production and per capita income rose. The Second Plan (1956–1960) was only a partial success. Some progress was made in creating the infrastructure of a modern economy; by 1959 industrial production had increased by more than 50 percent over 1951.

Among the bright spots was striking growth in such industries as iron ore and steel (63 percent increase), chemicals (114 percent), and machine tools (324 percent). The productivity of labor in some steel mills and locomotive works approached European standards. Modern forms of business enterprise began to spread in the private sector, displacing the older artisans and speculator-capitalists. But agricultural production faltered during this period, and severe food shortages materialized in some parts of the country. The overall rate of increase in the gross national product slowed down.

The Third Plan (1961–1965) reestablished a priority for agriculture, but the results were again disappointing. Land reforms were planned but not implemented, and agriculture stagnated. In 1964 and 1965 poor harvests caused hoarding, looting of granaries, and widespread hunger riots. In 1965, the United States shipped one-sixth of its total wheat crop to India as an emergency measure in order to alleviate hardship. Defense spending after the military clashes with China in 1962 and Pakistan in 1965 diverted badly needed funds and foreign exchange away from capital investment and economic development.

Since then, the plans have been primarily attempts to set goals that will stimulate national effort, and have not served as realistic guides to economic development. The Fourth Plan (1966–1971) placed renewed emphasis on agriculture and industry, but inflation and the cost of supporting millions of refugees from Bangladesh made it impossible to realize goals. The Fifth Plan (1974–1979), which was not even approved until 1976, also called for substantial increases in agricultural and industrial production, along with redistribution of income in order to bridge the gap between rich and poor.

During the emergency the government sought above all to reinforce social discipline, now identified as the key element in making possible genuine increases in productivity.

When the Janata party came to power in 1977, Prime Minister Desai called into question the previous grandiose schemes for rapid industrialization, advocating instead reliance on village and cottage industries. The Congress party after returning to office also emphasized the need for self-sufficiency and for making slower but steadier economic progress. The Sixth Plan (1980–1985) and Seventh Plan (1985–1990), adopted under Rajiv, both concentrated on antipoverty programs. The Eighth Plan (1990–1995) continued the emphasis on social services.

The five-year plans originally reflected Nehru's belief that the Soviet model of centralized planning offered the best hope for rapid industrialization and social justice. He distrusted capitalism, equating it with speculation, greed, and economic stagnation. Indian business leaders resisted Nehru's brand of socialism, demanding instead encouragement of private enterprise. Their spokesperson within the Congress party was the powerful S. V. Patel. The conflict between socialism and capitalism, which is fought out in Europe generally by separate political parties, took place in India within the Congress party. By the mid-1950s a compromise was reached. A mixed economy would exist in which the state would have direct control of some key sectors (armaments, nuclear energy, railroads), and the exclusive right to start new ventures in such sectors as iron and steel, shipbuilding, aircraft production, and telecommunications; the state would closely regulate most other key industries but would otherwise recognize and protect a large private sector; and—a concession to the heritage of Mohandas Gandhi—village industry would also be encouraged.

But within this mixed economy, where would the line be drawn between public and private? Under Nehru, the emphasis was on state control and Socialist values. But in the mid-1960s, there was growing dissatisfaction with the Nehru model and a widespread desire to better serve consumer interests. The Swatantra party, expressing the views of business, attacked the very concept of central planning and demanded the relaxation of government controls. Reflecting changes in public opinion, some measures to liberalize the economy were adopted by Nehru's successor, Lal Bahadur Shastri (1964–1966), and continued by Mrs. Gandhi.

In 1969 a split took place between Indira Gandhi and her more traditional rivals within the Congress. Mrs. Gandhi then swung to the left, sought allies among Socialists and Communists, and revived the Socialist policies of her father. Her government nationalized banks and insurance companies, the coal industry, textile mills, railroad car manufacture, and iron and steel production. Government control over the private sector was extended and strengthened. But the results of this sudden swing toward state ownership and control were disappointing: inflation, shortages and black markets, corruption and bribery, and economic stagnation. Mrs. Gandhi changed direction, loosening some controls. During emergency rule from 1975 to 1977, economic liberalization was given a boost by Sanjay Gandhi, who criticized the bureaucracy and lauded private enterprise.

After her return to office in 1980, Mrs. Gandhi resumed a policy of gradual deregulation of the economy. Her successor and son, Rajiv, determined to cut down the size of the public sector. The challenge was formidable. To take one example, the nationalized Steel Authority of India employed 250,000 people in producing 8 million tons of steel a year, at double the international price. In South Korea, the private Pohang steelworks produced 9 million tons of steel with 14,000 workers. Air India, to take another example, employed 17,000 people in 1987 to run 20 aircraft while racking up a loss of $40 million. In contrast, Singapore Airlines (admittedly an exceptionally efficient enterprise) ran twice as many aircraft with half as many workers, and at a profit. Rajiv became the apostle of professional management and deregulation—all the while proclaiming his devotion to the goal of social justice.

The trend toward liberalization of the economy continued under V. P. Singh, but his short-lived government was too enmeshed in controversy over ethnic violence and secularism to bring about much economic reform. His successor, Chandra Shekhar, pledged to stop liberalization, contending that the ills of India were caused by multinationals. But as the head of a caretaker government, he was in no position to take an independent line. When Congress (I) returned to power in June 1991, it swung sharply in favor of expansion of the private sector, as suggested by the International Monetary Fund (from which India had requested a loan to meet a severe shortage of foreign exchange). India is thus increasingly involved in, and exposed to pressures from, the world economy. Out of a Gross National Product in 1989 of about $287 billion, imports came to $20.5 billion and exports to $15.8 billion— so that foreign trade now amounts to over 12 percent of domestic production.

In its first months in office the Rao government devalued the rupee, cut the budget deficit, abolished many licensing requirements, reduced subsidies to farmers, adopted sweeping measures to open India to foreign investment, and proposed fundamental tax reform. Foreign Minister Manmohan Singh declared that 90 of India's 244 huge state-owned enterprises are "patently unviable" and should be shut down. These 90 enterprises have about 800,000 employees, and cost the taxpayers $750 million annually in subsidies. Economic restructuring, in India as in Eastern Europe, causes difficulties for a large part of the population. Trade unions and left-wing parties have organized public demonstrations, some turning violent, to protest the move toward a market economy. L. K. Advani, leader of the BJP, agreed that the reforms would have long-term advantages, but warned that the disadvantages had to be "bearable." Some within the Congress were wary of a policy that they saw as a betrayal of Mohandas Gandhi's goals of village industry and planning for human development. The Rao government, dependent for its existence on the support of other parties in Parliament, ran the risk of being forced from office if economic reforms were to create too much pain.

The Indian political class has come a long way from the heady days just after independence, when many Congress party leaders hoped that socialism would create a highly productive, classless society with equal opportunity and a "good life" (as Nehru put it) for all. Modest improvement has been made in the standard of living of the masses. GNP in the first 40 years increased by about one-third, and agricultural production tripled. The middle and professional classes have expanded, and now number well over 100 million. But unemployment increased dramatically, and most people continue to live in poverty. It is increasingly accepted that there is no easy way to industrialize an overwhelmingly traditional society, that social discipline is an essential ingredient in any policy of modernization, and that economic progress often produces heightened social strains and pressures.

MODERNIZATION AND DEMOCRACY

In any democracy, social and economic groups make claims upon the state; these claims constitute the raw material of the political process. Peasants, landlords, workers, managers, capitalists, merchants, and professionals, as well as ethnic, religious, and linguistic groups, press for satisfaction of their demands and participate in the process of working out compromises embodied in legislation. This continuing "crisis of participation" is a difficult challenge to political leaders even in long established and prosperous democracies. When political systems are "overloaded" with claims and counterclaims, they become ineffective and unstable.

The "load" on Indian democracy by any standard is enormous. A large part of the electorate is opposed to modernization as such because it threatens traditional religious beliefs; others are primarily concerned with promotion of their caste, linguistic, or regional interests; and still others call for the revolutionary transformation of society. Many Indians have wondered whether democracy is not a luxury for their nation—in any event, to be subordinated to other considerations. In a deeply divided society, democracy may permit so much criticism and obstruction that government can no longer function. This classic issue of democratic theory—the point at which the right of minorities to express themselves subverts the right of the majority to rule—was posed with special force by Prime Minister Gandhi during the emergency.

Mrs. Gandhi at first justified her policy of suppressing the opposition as necessary to assure the nation's security. "The actions of a few," she declared in a radio broadcast to the nation, "are undermining the rights of the vast majority." India's enemies were rejoicing, she warned, at the sight of a nation tearing itself apart. In the following months Mrs. Gandhi presented a more fully developed explanation of her resort to coercive means in order to attain democratic ends. The real challenge facing India, she said, is not how to maintain the right of an opposition to oppose anything and everything, but how to eliminate poverty, backwardness, and social abuses. She declared in a radio and television broadcast on 10 November 1975: "We want to fight and eliminate the poverty in our country prevailing since time immemorial. We want to remove backwardness. We can do so only if there is stability in the nation. And stability is impossible to achieve if unity gets weakened.... That was the problem before us." What was needed, above all, were "simple measures" to stamp out social abuses and anarchy.

Democracy is desirable, Mrs. Gandhi assured the nation, on one condition—that opposition be constructive. "But no one could claim that in the name of democracy anyone could do what he pleased and that such license was more important than India's progress, more important than the good of the Indian people." What was to be done? "There is only one magic which can remove poverty, and that is hard work sustained by clear vision, iron will, and the strictest discipline." To hammer home her point, Mrs. Gandhi frequently cited the problem of student agitation in universities. In a speech to the Rajya Sabha on 22 July 1975, for example, she recounted the tale of a train forced to stop over 30 times by students playfully pulling the emergency cord. When the engineer removed the cord, the students beat him up, put out the fire in the engine's boiler, and immobilized the train. Yet, concluded Mrs. Gandhi, no one would say that this was a "wrong thing" done by the students; by constantly challenging all authority, she claimed, the opposition made this kind of anarchy inevitable.

Many Indians agreed that poverty could never be alleviated in a climate of permissiveness and indiscipline. On the other hand, there was widespread dissatisfaction with authoritarian rule during the emergency—in particular, the arrest of opposition leaders and censorship of the press. Ample opportunities were afforded to members of the ruling party to suppress legitimate criticism, make arbitrary decisions, and even profit personally from their expanded political power. Public prosecutors under the Desai government claimed that the prime minister's son, Sanjay Gandhi, took advantage of his position to forward his career and finances. Democracy without consensus and social discipline may be ineffective (as seemed to be shown when the Janata party proved incapable of governing after its victory in 1977), but authoritarianism invites the abuse of power evident during the emergency. It is in India, perhaps more than any other nation, that the ability of democracies to cope with the problems of modernization in the third world is on trial.

FOREIGN AFFAIRS

Mohandas Gandhi's advocacy of nonviolence and passive resistance has not been accepted as a guiding principle of Indian foreign policy. The lack of support from other countries, especially those in the third world, when India suffered a military defeat at the hands of the Chinese in 1962 was a sobering experience. The manufacture and explosion of an atom bomb in May 1974, making India the sixth nation to become a nuclear power, dramatically illustrated India's resolve to safeguard its interests through a combination of diplomacy and strong military forces. There is also widespread agreement that keeping up with advances in military technology requires a solid industrial and scientific base. Hence the drive to modernize the Indian economy and society is intimately linked to the overall objectives of Indian foreign policy.

Independent India's first prime minister, Jawaharlal Nehru, formulated the major principle of Indian foreign policy, to which all of his successors have subscribed—nonalignment. For Nehru nonalignment meant a refusal to become part of the military alliance structures of either superpower, but it did not mean isolation or withdrawal from the international scene. On the contrary, the independence of India would enable it to intervene even more forcefully on specific issues in the cause of world peace. By avoiding alliances with either the United States or the Soviet Union, Indian leaders explained, they retained freedom of maneuver to defend their own national interests. Also, any alliance inevitably would cause divisions within Indian public opinion, create political instability, and divert attention from the pressing problem of dealing with poverty at home. For some Indians, moreover, each superpower represented a perceived evil— either greedy capitalism or oppressive communism—and India represented a "third way" in which concern for humanity and social justice is combined with freedom. Critics of Indian foreign policy may express skepticism

concerning Indian aspirations to (or illusions about) a higher idealism, but the ideals are nonetheless constantly invoked.

India has been confronted with serious challenges to its territorial integrity from two immediate neighbors: Pakistan and China. Since independence, and despite a verbal commitment to peace and nonalignment, India has been at war four times, not counting such minor actions as the occupation of Goa. In 1947 partition was accompanied by communal violence and the forced movement of millions of refugees. A war with Pakistan ensued in the winter of 1947 over Jammu and Kashmir; both sides accepted a cease-fire arranged by the United Nations in January 1948. In 1962 Indian and Chinese forces engaged in a sharply fought conflict in disputed territory, with the Chinese prevailing. In 1965 another war broke out with Pakistan in the Punjab, and in 1971 India seized the opportunity presented by a popular uprising in Bangladesh to inflict a devastating defeat upon the Pakistani army. The secession of Bangladesh has virtually assured India of dominance over Pakistan in the foreseeable future.

India's continuing conflict with both Pakistan and China has been a fundamental determinant of its foreign policy. As the Chinese became embroiled with the Russians in a territorial as well as an ideological dispute, India was drawn closer to the Soviet Union. Russians and Indians saw in each other allies of a kind against a common foe—China. Similarly, India became less friendly to the United States as the Americans joined the Chinese in offering military and economic aid to Pakistan (which, in turn, was a valuable military asset in the Sino-American confrontation with the Soviet Union). In 1971 India signed a treaty of peace, friendship, and cooperation with the Soviet Union that reflected also Indira Gandhi's growing collaboration with the Communist party of India. The friendship treaty, it was emphasized by Indian leaders, did not represent a departure from nonalignment because no military alliance was involved. The "tilt" toward the Soviet Union did not prevent India from seeking and receiving massive aid from the United States to avert famine and help develop its economy. With the virtual elimination of Pakistan as a military threat, India became less sensitive over the U.S. program of aid to Pakistan, and relations between India and the United States improved markedly after the Janata party's victory in 1977. The Russian invasion of Afghanistan in 1979 confronted Prime Minister Gandhi with an exceedingly delicate problem: how to prevent the United States from reinforcing and rearming Pakistan without at the same time endorsing Russian military intervention in an area of concern to India.

India was drawn into an ethnic conflict in Sri Lanka (formerly Ceylon) supposedly to protect the Tamil minority, but also to ensure that no foreign powers would exploit the situation and establish their influence in the region. Tamils, who make up one-fifth of the population of Sri Lanka, receive sympathetic support as well as material aid and arms from the Tamils of India, just across the strait. When the ethnic conflict worsened in 1987, Rajiv Gandhi took the lead in negotiating a peace agreement that in principle put an end to the turmoil. Nevertheless, some 50,000 Indian troops, dispatched to Sri Lanka to establish law and order, soon became involved in hostilities with the very Tamil militants whose interests they were originally supposed to safeguard. A suicide squad of Tamil terrorists (the Liberation Tigers) took revenge four years later by assassinating Rajiv.

In drawing up a balance sheet of independent India's foreign policy, the record of achievement is impressive. After a long period of stalemate, India emerged victorious from its historical rivalry with Pakistan and is now the dominant power in South Asia. However, India remains concerned that Pakistan is a wedge of American and Chinese influence in its region, and has accused Pakistan of supporting Sikh nationalists in the Punjab. Also, the northern frontier is still vulnerable to Chinese pressure,

and memories of India's defeat by the Chinese in 1962 still rankle. India has adhered to its policy of nonalignment, avoiding alliances with either the United States or the former Soviet Union, receiving economic and military aid from both, and reserving the right to disagree with both. In practice, India tended to be more free in its condemnation of the United States than of the Soviet Union (for example, defending Russia's intervention in Hungary in 1956).

Despite a continuing confrontation with its great neighbor to the north, it can be concluded that the Indian political class since independence has been fairly successful in defending the territorial integrity and basic interests of the nation. The ultimate test of a foreign policy is survival. Pakistan in its original form has failed that test; India—except for relatively minor incursions by the Chinese in the northern territories—has passed it. Given the deep social divisions and severe economic problems that existed when independence was proclaimed, foreign policy accomplishments attested to the vitality and effectiveness of the Indian political system.

With the growing crisis of communism in the 1980s, and the weakening of central authority in the Soviet Union after the failed coup of August 1991, a pillar of Indian foreign policy crumbled. Nonalignment can no longer have the same meaning in a world with one dominant superpower, and an ascendant Western economic model. A fundamental review of foreign policy is one of the major challenges facing Indian government in the post-Gandhi era.

Key Terms

Akali Dal
Bhindranwale, Sant Jarnail Singh
The Emergency (1975–1977)
Five Year Plans
nonalignment
Panchayat
Punjab

Suggestions for Further Reading

Bardhan, P. *The Political Economy of Development in India* (Oxford: Basil Blackwell, 1984).

Cohen, S. P., and R. L. Park. *India: Emergent Power?* (New York: Crane, Russak & Co., 1978).

Frankel, F. *India's Political Economy, 1944–1977* (Princeton: Princeton University Press, 1978).

Frankel, F., and M. S. Rao, eds. *Dominance and State Power in India: Decline of a Social Order,* 2 vols. (New York: Oxford University Press, 1990).

Kohli, Atul. *The State and Poverty in India: The Politics of Reform* (New York: Cambridge University Press, 1987).

Palmer, N. D. *The United States and India: The Dimensions of Influence* (New York: Praeger, 1984).

Rosen, G. *Democracy and Economic Change in India,* rev. ed. (Berkeley: University of California Press, 1967).

Rudolph, L. I., and S. H. Rudolph. *In Pursuit of Lakshmi: The Political Economy of the Indian State* (Chicago: University of Chicago Press, 1987).

Sen Gupta, B. *The Fulcrum of Asia: Relations Among China, India, Pakistan and the USSR* (New York: Pegasus, 1970).

Sen Gupta, B. *The Afghan Syndrome: How to Live with Soviet Power* (New Delhi: Vikas, 1982).

Weiner, M. *Sons of the Soil: Migration and Ethnic Conflict in India* (Princeton: Princeton University Press, 1978).

Weiner, M. *The Child and the State in India* (Princeton: Princeton University Press, 1991).

Ziring, L., ed. *The Subcontinent in World Politics: India, Its Neighbors, and the Great Powers,* rev. ed. (New York: Praeger, 1982).

Notes

1. From Gandhi's article, "The Doctrine of the Sword," written in 1920, cited in *Toward Freedom, The Autobiography of Jawaharlal Nehru* (Boston: Beacon Press, 1958), p. 82.
2. Cited in T. Walter Wallbank, *A Short History of India and Pakistan* (New York: Mentor, 1958), p. 196.
3. *Ibid.,* p. 213.
4. *Ibid.,* p. 217.
5. cf. Michael Brecher, *Nehru: A Political Biography* (New York: Oxford University Press, 1961), p. 149.
6. Atul Kohli, ed. *India's Democracy: An Analysis of Changing State-Society Relations* (Princeton: Princeton University Press, 1990), p. 309.
7. Cited in T. Walker Wallbank, *A Short History of India and Pakistan* (New York: Mentor, 1958), p. 157.
8. Frank Moraes, *India Today* (New York: Macmillan, 1964), p. 89.

CHAPTER 10

The Government of Mexico

Martin C. Needler

A. Political Development

Mexico is a distinctive country in many ways. When the astonished Spaniards first laid their eyes on the capital city, Tenochtitlán, at the beginning of the sixteenth century, they were looking at a city probably greater in population than any in Europe at the time. Counting methods vary depending on how much of the metropolitan region is included, but by some modes of reckoning Mexico City is today, with over 20 million people, again the largest city in the world.

The ancient Aztecs had one of the distinctive civilizations of the ancient world, and some of that distinctiveness is apparent today in the way of life of their descendants. To its Spanish conquerors, Mexico offered a deluge of products which have since made their way into the diets of people all over the world; today Mexico may be known abroad for its cuisine, its twentieth century school of mural painting, or its considerable petroleum production. Politically, as we shall see, Mexico is significant in having pioneered the political system now found throughout Africa and Asia, that of the dominant single party, sometimes known as the hegemonic party or the "democratic single-party system."

Mexico City has all the ills of a metropolis in the third world—impossible traffic jams, overcrowded buses, slums, and pollution. It contains about one-quarter of the national population, currently estimated at 90 million. Although the metropolis is the country's preeminent city in commerce, culture, and communications, as well as in politics, five other Mexican cities have over one million inhabitants and about two-thirds of the national population is considered urban. But that also means that a third of the population continues to live in the country's villages, of which there are more than fifty thousand distributed over the 761,000 square miles of the national territory.

The rural population is not spread evenly over the country, however. Much of Mexico is arid; perhaps 10 percent of the land surface receives rainfall adequate for unirrigated agriculture. Nevertheless, vast irrigation schemes have made possible the development of farming in these arid zones (especially in the Northern region of the country, which has emerged as a center for the export of fruit and vegetables to the United States), along with cattle raising, light industry, and tourism in the coastal resorts. Moving south, as the breadth of North America narrows toward the Central American isthmus, one encounters the mountainous, semiarid Center-North region, whose principal economic activity has always been mining; copper has overtaken silver as the leading product of this industry.

The Central region, focused on the national capital and the Federal District, has always had the densest concentration of population. In the rural areas there is dense settlement throughout the mountain valleys and the soils have been continuously worked for centuries, deteriorating in quality and providing no more than a bare subsistence for those who try to eke out a living on their tiny plots of land. A more productive agriculture is found in the Western region of the country, centering on the country's second largest city, Guadalajara. Its interconnected river valleys draining toward the Pacific provide rich soils and a long growing season. This rich area is a focus of Spanish colonial tradition and a stronghold of the Catholic church. The Eastern region, on the coast of the Gulf of Mexico, resembles areas of the Caribbean; it has plantations growing tropical products such as rice and sugar cane, and in the past African slaves were brought to the region, which today has a large mulatto population.

What the Mexicans call the South, the mountains lying south and west of the capital city, is a region of small cultivators and only slowly growing population. Its principal state, Oaxaca, is the most Indian state of Mexico; it is only recently that a majority of the population of the state has come to use Spanish and not one of the Indian languages by preference. The Yucatán peninsula, the "Southeast," which juts out into the Caribbean, is also firmly Indian in culture, although the Indians there are Maya—akin to the people of Guatemala rather than those of central Mexico—and still hold to a distinctive way of life.

It should be noted that in Mexico, as in the rest of Latin America, "Indian" is a cultural rather than a physical or genetic category.

A Mexican family on the beach at Mazatlán, building a sand castle in the form of an ancient pre-Colombian pyramid.

Physically, most Mexicans are Indian or mixed Spanish and Indian, that is, *mestizo*. A person ceases to be an Indian by acculturating to dominant national norms and abandoning specifically Indian characteristics, such as going barefoot, sleeping in a hammock or on the floor, and especially speaking an Indian language rather than Spanish. Clearly, it is difficult to remain culturally Indian in a city, but many Mexicans in rural areas are in transition from one way of life to another, changing their style of dress, using Spanish predominantly, and modifying their diet to include bread and canned goods.

Interestingly, however, although the national culture and way of life are predominantly modern and European, with only an admixture of Indian elements, psychologically Mexicans identify with their Indian past and not with the Spanish conquerors. There are statues in Mexico of Moctezuma and Cuauhtémoc, the last Aztec emperors, but not one of Hernando Cortés, the Spaniard who conquered them. In fact, the tale of how heroic but doomed Indians were conquered by ignoble but technologically superior Spaniards has provided some interesting paradigms by which Mexicans understand their national history. As one Mexican psychologist has put it, "The history of Mexico is full of stories which endure in it more because of their psychological value than because of the authenticity of their testimony."[1]

HISTORICAL SUMMARY TO 1910

When most Mexicans think about the country's history they see it as a pattern, repeated over and over. The pattern is that of heroic Mexicans trying to defend themselves against more powerful foreigners and being defeated, partly because of betrayal by some Mexicans who have sided with the foreigners. The conquest itself was made possible because Cortés had the assistance of some of the indigenous tribes and of his mistress and interpreter, Malinche. The original movement for independence, led at the beginning of the nineteenth century by Father Miguel Hidalgo and Father José María Morelos, who were themselves defeated and killed by the Spaniards, was finally successful when the upper classes, afraid that their privileges would be taken away by a liberal Spanish government, joined the cause of independence. Their leadership, however, nullified the original populist impulse of the independence movement, and their military leader, Agustín Iturbide, proclaimed himself emperor.

During the chaotic period of revolts, rigged elections, and foreign interventions that constituted the first half century of Mexican independence, law and order broke down, the economy decayed, and the country's finances were looted. The United States, under President James K. Polk, took advantage of the situation to provoke a war in which U.S. troops occupied Mexico City. The war was concluded in 1848 by the Treaty of Guadalupe-Hidalgo which led, together with the subsequent Gadsden Purchase, to the annexation by the United States of present-day Texas, New Mexico, Arizona, and California, approximately half of what had been the territorial area of Mexico.[2]

A few years later Napoleon III of France used the Mexicans' suspension of payments on their foreign debt as a pretext to send an army to Mexico whose real purpose was to create a French-dependent Mexican empire with Archduke Maximilian of Austria as Emperor. Maximilian and his bride, Carlotta, apparently believed in all innocence that the opportunistic reactionaries who came to his palace outside Trieste to offer him the crown represented the popular will of the people of Mexico.

In fact, they were simply looking for a way out of the anticlerical and antielite program, known as *La Reforma*, being put into effect by a Liberal government under Benito Juárez. Juárez led the military resistance against Maximilian, who was finally executed after his May 1867 surrender. Juárez, regarded by Mexicans as their greatest president, only survived his triumph by five years, and his successor as president was overthrown in a successful revolt in 1876. The new *caudillo*—the dominant personalist leader—who took power and dominated the politics of Mexico for 35 years, was Porfirio Díaz. Díaz was to serve as president for all but one term of the period until he was overthrown in 1910. Díaz began in politics as a Liberal and follower of Juárez, but his regime reinterpreted the idea of progress embodied in Liberalism to mean social and economic development brought about by the encouragement of foreign investment, and the suppression of Mexico's Indian character. Díaz imposed a "law and order" that involved intimidating the lower classes, especially Indian peasants. He promoted economic development—railroad building, mining, communications, and power generation—on the basis of special concessions for foreign investors. Large estates were built up, sometimes in foreign hands, and traditional Liberal anticlericalism was abandoned.

The Díaz regime was a great success, at least in the eyes of foreigners. But Díaz's fatal mistake was maintaining control with the same closed group that had come to power with him and leaving no openings for new middle- and upper-class elements. There were sectors of the population with legitimate grievances against the Díaz regime—Indians who were discriminated against, peasants who had lost their land to cronies of the president, workers in the new industries who were not allowed to organize and seek better conditions, business people whose competitors had better government connections. But just as a hydrogen bomb can only be set off by the explosion of an atom bomb that acts as its trigger, the great social movement that was the Mexican Revolution of 1910 needed a smaller revolution to get it going, the initial uprising against Díaz. This was an upper-class movement led by Francisco Madero, who came from a landholding family in the northern state of Coahuila.

Madero's original political goals had been limited to getting Díaz to open his regime to some new blood, but it was treated by Díaz as subversion and Madero's movement became an open revolt. Taken by surprise by the support garnered by the uprising, Díaz resigned. An interim government held elections, which were won by Madero. However, Madero made the mistake of not being revolutionary enough, leaving in office the officials and generals who had served under Díaz; subsequently, some of them conspired with the ambassador of the Taft administration to overthrow Madero's government. Madero was removed, and then shot, by the military commander, General Victoriano Huerta, known for his brutality, corruption, and drunkenness. A revolution against the Huerta government was not long in coming. It did not have a single leader, however, and the division among the revolutionary forces led to fighting among them after Huerta was defeated and overthrown.

THE MEXICAN REVOLUTION: THE EARLY YEARS

The principal revolutionary forces were led by figures that have become legendary in Mexican history. Emiliano Zapata, from the state of Morelos, continued to fight, as he had since the Díaz administration, on behalf of small landholders whose land had been taken from them by force or fraud; he had opposed Madero once it became clear that Madero was not serious about land reform. In the northern border state of Chihuahua, an army was raised by Francisco "Pancho" Villa (Doroteo Arango). Villa was a former soldier in the federal army who had escaped from the military prison where he had been placed for disobeying orders. Vaguely populist in ideological terms, Villa attracted followers—including intellectuals who wrote his political material—by his colorful and forceful personality, but he repelled others by his cruelty and opportunism. Villa's historical reputation has never been secure, and only recently, and after much discussion, did the Mexican Congress agree to include him in the pantheon of Revolutionary heroes whose names are inscribed in its hall. Zapata, on the other hand, is regarded in Mexican history as a man of noble and unselfish ideals.

Venustiano Carranza was the leader closest, historically and politically, to Madero. As senator and acting governor of Madero's home state of Coahuila under Porfirio Díaz, Carranza's support of Madero was important in giving credibility and impetus to the original revolution. Moderate and quite unrevolutionary in his aims, Carranza always regarded himself as the authentic heir to Madero and his logical successor. Carranza's claims were finally vindicated; he was recognized in October 1915 as de facto president by the United States and was formally elected constitutional president in March 1917 under terms of a new constitution.

The Revolutionary hero Emiliano Zapata depicted in a mural by Diego Rivera at the old viceregal palace in Cuernavaca.

This result was only achieved after much fighting, however. After the defeat of Huerta's forces, an interim national government representing all of the revolutionary factions was dominated by a coalition between Villa and Zapata. Carranza refused to accept the authority of this government; his armies, commanded by the best military strategist the revolution produced, Alvaro Obregón, defeated Villa's forces in a series of battles. Villa finally made peace and was allowed to retire. He was later assassinated, presumably with Obregón's complicity, when he was preparing to resume political activity. Zapata—like all the leaders of the first phase of the Mexican Revolution—was also assassinated.

Carranza's election took place under the terms of the new revolutionary constitution. This document had been drafted by the radical majority of the constituent convention and represented a progressive social democratic perspective. Ownership of mineral resources was vested in the national government, not in the owner of the surface of the land; labor's rights to organize and strike were guaranteed; and religious bodies were forbidden to own property. Carranza himself ran a moderate administration, and the social provisions of the constitution were only implemented by the succeeding presidency of Obregón. For a list of Mexican presidents since 1917, see Table 10.1.

Obregón announced his presidential candidacy with criticisms of the moderation of the Carranza government, making it impossible for Carranza to support him. Given traditional Mexican political practices, under which the candidate favored by the incumbent administration always won the election, there was plausibility to Obregón's charge that Carranza was planning to rig the elections to impose his own choice of successor, and Obregón led a revolt. Against Obregón's instructions, Carranza—again, like the other major revolutionary figures—was assassinated. An interim government under Obregón's fellow-Sonoran,

Table 10.1 PRESIDENTS OF MEXICO, 1917–1992

Years in Office	Name
1917–1920	Venustiano Carranza
1920	Adolfo de la Huerta
1920–1924	Alvaro Obregón
1924–1928	Plutarco Elías Calles
1928–1930	Emilio Portes Gil
1930–1932	Pascual Ortiz Rubio
1932–1934	Abelardo Rodríguez
1934–1940	Lázaro Cárdenas
1940–1946	Manuel Avila Camacho
1946–1952	Miguel Alemán
1952–1958	Adolfo Ruiz Cortines
1958–1964	Adolfo López Mateos
1964–1970	Gustavo Díaz Ordaz
1970–1976	Luis Echeverría
1976–1982	José López Portillo
1982–1988	Miguel de la Madrid
1988–	Carlos Salinas de Gortari

Adolfo de la Huerta, organized elections which were duly won by Obregón.

The administration of Alvaro Obregón (1920–1924) was especially significant. The revolt that made it possible was the last successful revolt in Mexican history, as Obregón himself foresaw. Of an unsuccessful revolt against his government in 1923, he wrote "a progressive evolution has been slowly taking place; ... it is no longer possible to start a revolution in Mexico and immediately thereafter find popular support... I feel strongly that this will be the last military rebellion in Mexico."[3] This was so in part because Obregón reorganized the guerrilla armies of the revolution—which had consisted of bands haphazardly recruited, trained, and organized, and owing loyalty to specific individuals—into a regular army based on discipline, hierarchy, and loyalty to the constitutional authorities. More important, he pursued policies that won broad popular support so that in a future crisis the great majority of the population would actively support the government, rather than remain passive bystanders or support armed insurrection. The Obregón administration took a clear position in favor of the efforts of labor unions to or-

ganize, establish a national trade union confederation, raise wages, and improve working conditions. Moreover, Obregón began to implement land reform legislation passed under Carranza, thus winning over the former supporters of Zapata.

The payoff came in the rebellion of 1923. Obregón chose as his successor General Plutarco Elías Calles. This was resented by the former interim president, de la Huerta, who thought the nomination should rightfully have gone to him, and in the traditional fashion he began a revolt. The army, not yet thoroughly reorganized, split about evenly, but one of the major factors that tipped the balance of power in favor of Obregón was the participation on his side of volunteer battalions and irregular forces of workers and peasants. Something new had occurred in Mexican history: workers and peasants fought on behalf of an incumbent government instead of against it.

The coalition that Obregón had put together degenerated somewhat under Calles. Although Calles started from a radical revolutionary position, this was soon modified by his growing conservatism and connivance in financial irregularities. A strong prolabor position became in fact acquiescence in labor racketeering and allowing companies to buy their way out of labor difficulties. The threatened resumption by the Mexican state, under the terms of the new constitution, of mineral rights ceded to foreign oil companies was somehow negotiated through the good offices of the U.S. ambassador to allow companies active before 1917 to retain their oil concessions. Calles became disillusioned with the land reform program, coming to believe that land was more productive when privately owned than when collectively owned by Indian communities, which was the mode in which most of the expropriated land had been redistributed.

Calles, a former school teacher, nevertheless continued Obregón's program of expansion of the educational system and the building of schools. He also followed up the program of the professionalization of the military; purging of the officers who had supported de la Huerta's rebellion made it possible to reduce the size of the military budget, the officers corps, and the army as a whole. Moreover, Calles went further than Obregón in enforcing the anticlerical provisions of the Constitution. Catholic resistance to the harsh measures taken by Calles included the suspension of religious services, and indeed a guerrilla war broke out against the government, centered in the devout Bajío region of western Mexico. The government conducted a ruthless counterinsurgency campaign against these "warriors of Christ the King" or *cristeros,* which was not called off until the end of Calles's term.

The country was in fact ready for a return to the more conciliatory and proagrarian policies of Obregón, and the former president indicated that he was ready to return for a new term. For this to happen, the Constitution had to be amended because it had enshrined the principle of no presidential reelection that had been the banner of Madero's revolution against Porfirio Díaz. Accordingly, Congress passed an amendment making the prohibition of reelection apply only to consecutive reelection;[4] thus Obregón would be eligible for the term that began in 1928. Moreover, another amendment extended the presidential term from four to six years. Elections were held and the popular Obregón was reelected, although not before a revolt by three frustrated would-be candidates had been put down. The Cristero War, however, was to claim its last victim. A group of religious fanatics, under the mistaken impression that Obregón was responsible for the anticlerical policies of Calles, organized the assassination of the president-elect, and Obregón joined the long line of revolutionary heroes brought to an untimely end.

At this point Calles rose to the occasion with an act of statesmanship. It was generally expected that he would use the pretext of Obregón's assassination to extend his own term; in fact, some disgruntled proagrarian supporters of Obregón went so far as to claim that Calles himself was behind the assassination. Calles, however, made clear that constitutional procedures, which called for the Congress to elect a provisional president until new popular elections could be organized, would be followed. Moreover, he took the assassination as a lesson that the political system of the Revolution should not have to depend on individual personalities, arguing that the time had come to place the regime on a more stable institutional footing by organizing a political party that would embody the aspirations of the revolution in permanent form. Up to that point, different leaders had organized ad hoc parties of their followers, while other parties represented major interest groups. Following the end of his term, accordingly, Calles organized the National Revolutionary Party, *Partido Nacional Revolucionario* (PNR), the precursor of the party that rules Mexico today.

For the provisional presidency, Congress elected Emilio Portes Gil, a young proagrarian former state governor acceptable to both Obregón and Calles supporters. The president elected to serve out Obregón's term was Pascual Ortiz Rubio, who turned out to be conservative, weak, and inconsistent. He referred all major decisions to Calles, who came to be regarded as Mexico's strong man and the real ruler of the country. Finally, the country's leading political figures refused to serve in Ortiz Rubio's cabinet, so he followed Calles's last piece of advice: he resigned. The remaining two years of the first six-year presidential term were filled by a moderate former general and associate of Calles, Abelardo Rodríguez, who had developed extensive business interests, especially in the North.

THE CÁRDENAS ERA

The first president to serve out the full six-year term (1934–1940) was General Lázaro Cárdenas, regarded by most Mexicans as the greatest president produced by the Revolution. He was also its most leftist president. Land reform proceeded at a pace that was probably the maximum technically feasible, and was no longer merely a question of restoring land wrongfully taken from Indian communities. Land could be expropriated from a landholder owning more than a certain amount and then assigned to any group of landless agricultural workers living in the vicinity. As with the Indian communities, however, ownership was vested in the group rather than in the individual, although—under an amendment to the law passed during the Calles administration—the right to farm specific plots of land could be inherited within a family. Under Cárdenas, however, some lands that were producing hemp (for rope) and cotton were set up as collective farms after expropriation, rather than being subdivided for individual family farming.

The Cárdenas administration was strongly prolabor, promoting labor organization and consistently favoring workers in industrial disputes. The racketeering head of the principal labor federation, Luis Morones, who had been a major political figure under Calles but was cut off from government favor by Portes Gil, was now overshadowed as the dominant figure in organized labor by a leftist intellectual named Vicente Lombardo Toledano.

Although generally pragmatic on economic questions, Cárdenas inclined to nationalism and socialism and was responsible for setting up some state corporations. The railroads were nationalized, as was the oil industry, after an industrial dispute in which most of the foreign-owned oil companies had made themselves thoroughly unpleasant and unpopular. The oil nationalization in 1938 and the setting up of a state oil corporation, today called *Petróleos Mexicanos*, or PEMEX, is generally regarded as one of the high points in Mexican nationalism. After the expropriation the foreign companies, which were vertically integrated—that is, they controlled the industry from exploration and development through processing and retailing—organized an international boycott of Mexican oil; the role of the state company was thus limited to supplying Mexico's own domestic needs.

Cárdenas also followed a left-wing line in foreign policy. He was president from 1934 to 1940, a highly emotional era in which the coming battle between democracy and the Fascist powers was taking shape. Cárdenas took a strong pro-Republican position in the Spanish Civil War and refused to recognize the Franco government at the war's conclusion. Mexico became the home of the Republican government-in-exile, and diplomatic relations with the government of Spain were not resumed until after Franco's death many years later.

Cárdenas also reorganized the ruling party to fit his leftist and nationalist principles. The party was renamed the Mexican Revolutionary Party, *Partido Revolucionario Mexicano* (PRM); it was reorganized explicitly as an alliance of classes, with separate "sectors" representing organized labor, collective peasant landholders, and progressive elements of the middle class. This last sector, called "popular," consisted primarily of unions of teachers and government white-collar workers, along with smaller associations of professionals, small private farmers, and small-business people. Cárdenas also included the armed forces as a full sector of the party, but this was not popular within the military itself, and the military sector was abolished by Cárdenas's successor after two or three years of existence.

THE ERA OF "STABLE DEVELOPMENT"

The moderate Manuel Avila Camacho, who served from 1940 to 1946, was the last general to be elected president of Mexico. He continued the work of his predecessors in reducing the political role of the army. A staff officer rather than a heroic leader in battle, Avila Camacho was little known before his nomination for the presidency; in fact, some called him "the unknown soldier." In the presidential elections he was opposed by an extremely popular general, the highest-ranking officer on active duty before he resigned to enter politics,

Juan Andreu Almazán. With support gathered from the interests alienated either by Calles or by Cárdenas—devout Catholics, business interests, disgruntled elements in the military, and even labor factions opposed to Lombardo Toledano—there seemed to be a chance that Almazán might get a majority of the vote. Unwilling to accept a victory for what looked like a coalition of the forces defeated by the revolution, Cárdenas agreed to the announcement of a fraudulent result. Apparently, Almazán won a majority in the Federal District, although not in the country at large, but in any case those were not the results announced.

Avila Camacho showed that the Mexican rule of no presidential reelection allows for the kind of flexibility that has enabled the system to survive; it is the tree that is able to bend with the wind that does not break. Another popular analogy has it that a presidential succession resembles a pendulum: incoming presidents usually swing away from the unpopular or unviable policies of their predecessors, making concessions to the groups most dissatisfied with their predecessors' policies.

What this meant for the president who followed Cárdenas was a position of greater moderation. The pace of land reform was slowed down, and no other industries were nationalized. Avila Camacho did begin a social security system for workers, but its coverage is still limited to employees of government and larger modern firms and does not extend to all Mexican workers. Hostilities against the church were called off, and good relations were fostered with the United States. Mexico participated in its first war on the same side as the United States when an air squadron was sent to fight the Japanese in the Pacific. Arrangements were worked out for the *bracero* program, under which Mexican laborers were contracted to work in the United States for fixed periods. Lombardo Toledano was eased out of his leadership position in the CTM, the Mexican Confederation of Labor, and replaced by the more moderate Fidel Velázquez, still the secretary-general of the CTM over 50 years later.

Avila Camacho capped his policies of national reconciliation and government from the center of the political spectrum by again reorganizing the ruling party, this time renaming it the *Partido Revolucionario Institucional* (PRI), the Institutional Revolutionary party, symbolizing the final coming to maturity of the revolution. Indeed, since Avila Camacho the country has been run by civilian presidents on the basis of centrist economic policy and a modus vivendi with the Church and with the United States. Stimulated first by the wartime lack of consumer goods to import, and then by the boom that followed World War II, the Mexican economy entered a long and sustained period of stable economic growth that ended only with the economic collapse that followed the fall in oil prices at the beginning of the 1980s.

The following president, Miguel Alemán (1946–1952), carried the pendulum further away from the Cárdenas years. Strongly probusiness, he presided over a threefold increase in Mexico's exports, a doubling of the value of agricultural production, and a 42 percent increase in industrial activity. At the same time, the state sector of the economy expanded and Mexico enjoyed a substantial increase in tourism. The increase in agricultural production resulted from the irrigation of vast expanses of dry land, especially in the North. This newly productive land was sold to private agribusiness interests, not distributed to landless peasants, who in any case live mostly in the center of the country. But the land reform program dwindled and some categories of large landholding were made exempt from expropriation. These were golden years for private business interests, including the personal interests of the president and his associates. Lombardo Toledano quit the PRI in disgust and founded his own *Partido Popular*, later to become the *Partido Popular Socialista* (PPS) or Popular Socialist party. It must be said that then, as in future years, Lombardo's tactics responded not only to Mexican realities but also to the international position being taken by Moscow-line Communists and fellow travelers, which at this time was to break up wartime popular front coalitions.

If the three presidents—Carranza, Obregón, and Calles—who presided over the initial period under the new constitution were responsible for the establishment of the country's basic institutional framework, then the three presidents who were the first to serve six-year terms—Cárdenas, Avila Camacho, and Alemán—established policies that set the parameters for their successors. On the left, Cárdenas's policies favored labor and promoted land reform; in the center, Avila Camacho's policies advanced pacification, political reconciliation, and cooperation with the United States; and on the right Alemán's policies fostered economic growth through favoring export-oriented industry, agribusiness, and tourism. These policies provided the basic mix their successors have followed, with differences of emphasis, to be sure.

These differences in emphasis are what gave rise to the concept of a pendular swing between one president and the next. Sometimes, in fact, a candidate was chosen because his reputation made it politically plausible that he would move in the required direction.

This was the case with the president who succeeded Alemán, Adolfo Ruiz Cortines. Alemán was becoming notorious for enriching himself illegally, in those years of economic boom, and former president Cárdenas, who was still the most popular political figure in the country, made it clear that he would find unacceptable any continuation of the situation, either in the form of a constitutional amendment and the reelection of Alemán (which a presidential emissary suggested to him) or in the succession of one of Alemán's close associates. Ruiz Cortines, the candidate who was picked, had a reputation for honesty that went back to his early days in politics handling payrolls for revolutionary armies. His presidency was conservative and unimaginative, however, and he left office the oldest man

to have served as Mexican president since Porfirio Díaz.

The succeeding president, Adolfo López Mateos, again provided a contrast with his predecessor. He was relatively young, and indeed was the first president to have been born after Madero first raised the standard of rebellion. He was politically on the left, and had been secretary of labor in the cabinet. Tactically, a more left-wing orientation was called for; Fidel Castro's coming to power in Cuba aroused enthusiastic support in Mexico, and Lázaro Cárdenas had come out of retirement to head a movement supporting the Cuban revolution.

In the tradition of Cárdenas, López Mateos stepped up the pace of land distribution. Electricity generation and motion-picture production were nationalized; significantly, however, López Mateos showed that his leftism was within the system and served to support it. His actions with respect to the labor movement showed that his service as secretary of labor had prepared him not merely to represent labor, but to manage the labor movement in the interest of the maintenance of the political system. A worker's profit-sharing program was legislated, but López Mateos showed no sympathy with unauthorized or politically motivated strikes and invoked the antisubversion laws to jail the leader of the railroad workers' union. Similarly, López Mateos continued Mexico's policy of being the only member of the Organization of American States to refuse, despite U.S. pressure, to break off diplomatic relations with Cuba, but he cooperated amicably with the United States in the resolution of various border problems. In addition, the electoral system was modified to guarantee the opposition parties a few seats in the Chamber of Deputies.

After López Mateos, the pendulum swung again. The unauthorized railroad strike and growing support for Fidel Castro suggested that law and order issues and the control of "political subversion" might be the key issues of the succeeding presidential term, so López

Mateos chose his minister of government, Gustavo Díaz Ordaz, as his successor. Although the economy continued to grow, helped by Mexico's membership in the new Latin American free trade area, the Díaz Ordaz administration became a spectacular failure precisely with respect to the law and order issue. The late 1960s was the time of worldwide student protest movements sparked by the war in Vietnam. Díaz Ordaz was particularly nervous because Mexico would be hosting the Olympic Games in 1968; the focus of world attention would be on Mexico and political disruption would be a possibility. In this atmosphere, a trivial student dispute escalated until the government was facing huge demonstrations of students and sympathizers demanding political liberalization. In a stunning overreaction, participants in a massive demonstration taking place in a large public square in the Tlatelolco

district were attacked by soldiers with tanks and automatic weapons, resulting in hundreds of deaths and universal repudiation of the Díaz Ordaz government.

After this incident the pendulum clearly needed to swing to the left, and the new nominee for the presidency was Luis Echeverría, a career administrator who had been born in the Federal District and had never been a candidate for elected office before. Echeverría attempted to model himself on Cárdenas and run a prolabor, proland reform, leftist government. He particularly tried to reconcile students to the regime by appointing ambassadors and other high officials who were barely out of the university. Despite his good intentions, Echeverría's hyperactive leftism proved counterproductive and self-defeating. The president had to back down on neutralist and pro-third world foreign policy positions when

The Plaza of the Three Cultures in the Tlatelolco district of Mexico City, site of the massacre of 1968.

these earned the disfavor of the United States and foreign tourists and investors. Speeches against foreign capitalism simply led to the flight of foreign investments, forcing Mexico to borrow heavily abroad and become more dependent on the world capitalist system. The resulting weakness of the peso forced its first devaluation in almost 25 years. The attempt to liberalize the regime met with opposition from entrenched party bosses and labor leaders, who organized gangs in universities that attacked the left-wing student groups thought to be the biggest agitators in favor of liberalization.

THE SYSTEM ENTERS PERMANENT CRISIS

For the next presidential term, the pendulum swung to José López Portillo, the moderate minister of finance and a well-regarded author of books on administrative law, and even of novels.

The increase in world oil prices forced by the Organization of Petroleum Exporting Countries (OPEC) made it worthwhile for Mexico to undertake the considerable costs of exploration in order to become an oil exporter. Exploration proved fabulously successful: Mexico surpassed Venezuela to become the world's fifth largest oil producer. Oil wealth gave Mexico the resources and self-confidence to follow a strong foreign policy independent of the United States; López Portillo backed Panama's efforts to renegotiate the Panama Canal Treaty and favored popular liberation movements in Central America. In the end, however, oil proved a curse as well as a blessing. Reckless spending of oil income provoked an inflation that hurt the poorer sectors of society; the flood of foreign exchange made it easy to import everything, and Mexico's own industries withered; and the temptations of easy money led to vast corruption, including that of the president himself. Meanwhile, consumer nations responded to higher oil prices by cut-

ting back consumption, and prices began to drop. Instead of adjusting to the reduced levels of income, the López Portillo government assumed that the price drop was only temporary and maintained its high level of spending, then borrowed abroad to cover the difference. But the price drop continued, and Mexico's debts became astronomical before the government appreciated the seriousness of the situation. People with money read the signs correctly before López Portillo did, however; they converted their pesos to dollars and sent them out of the country before the government gave up defending the value of the peso. Eventually the peso was devalued, and Mexico witnessed runaway inflation that rapidly dropped the living standards of the poor.

In an attempt to recuperate politically what he had lost economically, López Portillo decreed the nationalization of the banking system. The subsequent burst of leftist and nationalist euphoria soon wore off, however, leaving Mexicans still burdened with unemployment, inflation, and debt. The feeling of despair that settled on the country was made complete in September 1985 when Mexico City was rocked by a devastating earthquake, which was not only disastrous in itself but also revealed that legal construction standards had not been followed. Poor construction was especially evident in government buildings, implying once again corruption and kickbacks. Although the banks remained nationalized, under López Portillo's successor various financial services they had provided, along with industrial interests they had controlled, were split off and privatized.

This successor was Miguel de la Madrid, whose nomination took control of the system by career bureaucrats one step further. Like his two immediate predecessors, de la Madrid had never held elective office before being nominated for the presidency. A technician in administration, programming, and budgeting, de la Madrid had a Harvard M.P.A. and had served as Minister of Programming and Budget in the López Portillo cabinet. Inheriting a collapsed economy, a demoralized population, and a regime that had forfeited much of the prestige of its earlier achievements, de la Madrid had little room for political maneuver. His government's weakness was demonstrated by its failure to follow up on pledges to fight corruption after initially managing to make examples of the notoriously corrupt head of PEMEX and the Mexico City police chief. Mexico's opposition to Ronald Reagan's counterrevolutionary policies in Central America died away, and the government cut back living standards even more in an attempt to reduce inflation and pay off the foreign debt. It seemed bitterly ironic that the bill for the spending spree of the oil-boom years was being paid by those Mexicans who had benefited least from it. Foreign exchange became scarce and Mexican wages became cheap in international terms, leading to steady growth in export industry, especially the in-bond assembly plants located in the northern border area. Inflation eased somewhat and oil consumption crept up once more in the industrialized societies of the world, thus providing some faint rays of hope for improvement in the economic situation.

The president who stood to benefit from any economic improvement was Carlos Salinas de Gortari, who was elected in 1988. He was an example of the presidential nominee who could now be expected: a career administrator from the Federal District specializing in administrative and financial questions, with a foreign degree but without previous service in electoral office. Like his sponsor, de la Madrid, Salinas had an M.P.A. from Harvard but had carried the process a step further by earning a Ph.D. in political economy. Characteristically, again, he came from a family committed to the public sector; in fact, at the time of his nomination his father was serving as senator from the state of Nuevo León.

Key Terms

mestizo
La Reforma
Petróleos Mexicanos, or PEMEX
Partido Revolucionario Institucional (PRI)
Sonora
the pendulum
caudillo

B. Political Processes and Institutions

In addition to the obvious economic problems, Salinas faced difficult political problems as he took office on 1 December 1988. These related primarily to the character of the regime. How much should its democratic façade be allowed to erode its underlying authoritarian reality? As Mexico developed economically and socially, with a rise in general political sophistication and will to participate, sustained especially by a growth in the business and professional middle classes and the numbers of university students, the PRI's monopoly of power could be expected to erode. Previous governments had handled the problem by yielding political space to the opposition, but always managing to maintain not only the substance of power but also the PRI's dominant position at the center of the political spectrum and some appearance of openness and democratic procedure.

During the 1920s and 1930s, the dissenting tendencies both inside and outside the ruling party had been genuine, lively, and intermittently violent. With the great pacification operation of Avila Camacho and the onset of the boom years of stable development, the regime's management of politics had become smooth and largely efficient. The opposition party to the right, the National Action party, *Partido de Acción Nacional* (PAN), had at first been of the old vituperative type, vaguely threatening violence on occasion, but the small left and center-left parties had generally been well-behaved satellites of the PRI; their moderate opposition activities were genteel and regularly scripted beforehand, and their façade-strengthening merit was recognized with covert subsidies. During the 1970s the PAN was taken over by a more modern, more moderate leadership and began to win some local elections.

As opposition grew stronger and more autonomous, the regime's overall strategy became to build up the importance of the opposition to the right, which it then identified in its electoral propaganda with the elements that had ruled Mexico before the revolution, thus enabling the PRI to campaign as the defender of revolutionary principles and obscure how far it had actually departed from those principles. Tame and cooperative microparties of the left and center-left were used to draw support away from uncontrollable opposition groups on the left, and again they served to validate the PRI's claim of being the authentic representative of the revolutionary tradition.

These political strategies were implemented by giving opposition parties seats in the Chamber of Deputies; originally this was done in a rather fraudulent manner, by disqualifying or withdrawing PRI candidates in selected seats to allow candidates of the cooperative minor parties on the left to win by default. López Mateos put this practice on a constitutional basis by introducing a proportional-representation feature into the electoral law, which gave the minor parties some representation in the Chamber in proportion to their total percentage of the national vote. This provision was amplified under López Portillo and again under Miguel de la Madrid, so that finally 200 of the 500 seats in the Chamber were awarded on a regional-list rather than an individual-district basis so as to give each party a share of the 500 total chamber seats proportionate to its popular vote.

Opposition candidates regularly compete in presidential elections, and the regime was particularly disappointed when the PAN was unable to agree on a candidate and did not contest the presidential election of 1976. By the time of the presidential candidacy of Carlos Salinas, however, such tolerated and even encouraged opposition activities, which lent credibility to the system's democratic façade, had actually become threatening to continued national control by the PRI. Salinas's own victory in the presidential election had to be carefully managed so that his victory was convincing in two ways: his majority had to be large enough to make his mandate to rule seem clear, yet small enough to make it plausible that all of the opposition's votes had indeed been counted. The officially announced margin of his victory—50.36 percent—was not really convincing in either way. Most people assumed Salinas had won less than a majority—perhaps less than a plurality—and the numbers had then been "adjusted" upward.[5] In the legislative elections of that year, the opposition parties did well enough to capture 240 out of the 500 seats in the Chamber of Deputies. (For a look at the current members of the Deputies, see Table 10.2).

Table 10.2 MEMBERSHIP OF THE CHAMBER OF DEPUTIES, 1991–1994

Party	Seats won in single-member districts	Seats won by proportional representation	Total
PRI	290	30	320
PAN	10	79	89
PRD	0	41	41
PPS	0	12	12
PFCRN	0	23	23
PARM	0	15	15
Total	300	200	500

Note: PRI = Instituitutional Revolutionary party; PAN = National Action party; PPS = Popular Socialist party; PRD = Democratic Revolutionary party; PFCRN = Party of the Cardenista Front for National Reconstruction; PARM = Authentic party of the Mexican Revolution

Source: Press and Public Information Office, Embassy of Mexico, Washington, D.C.

A delicate question for the future was whether to recognize opposition victories in subsequent gubernatorial elections. One faction of the party argued that such recognition was necessary for credibility, and that opposition control of a state government did not necessarily threaten control at the center; the contrary faction argued that opposition control of the state government was merely the thin end of the wedge, which would not only give them a base from which to mount a more effective campaign but would also give them credibility and contribute to a bandwagon effect that could cause a threatening quantum jump in their support. The more democratic approach won out in July 1989 when the government recognized the victory of the PAN in gubernatorial elections in Baja California Norte.

THE ESTABLISHED SYSTEM

In the half century that has elapsed since the Cárdenas presidency, none of the country's leaders has acquired the historic proportions of Cárdenas himself. The system became stabilized and was brought under tight control.

The outgoing president essentially picked the party's nominee as his successor, taking into account not only the skills of the different possible candidates but also their ability to carry on his own work and to handle problems that seemed to be emerging. However, each president, while representing continuity, was also concerned with distinguishing himself from his predecessor and making his own mark on history, with the result that change was as much a feature of the system as continuity. Looking over this half century as a whole, several tendencies can be discerned.

1. A politically stable system was achieved. Although revolts or military interventions in politics are talked of from time to time, governments have in fact served out their allotted terms with a regularity unmatched not only elsewhere in the third world but also, when the effects of World War II and its aftermath are considered, unmatched in most of Europe. On the whole, military men have been subordinated to civilians.

2. The system has become institutionalized, as Calles wanted. The president is virtually an all-powerful figure until his successor is chosen. It is the formal office that confers authority, not "charisma" or deeds of daring.

3. Although different presidential administrations varied in their policies, the variation took place within the generally accepted framework of a mixed economy that resembles the economies of Western Europe. There are some nationalized industries and a framework of government regulation, but most economic activity is in private hands. The Salinas administration—in keeping with world trends generally—moved the balance decisively in the "capitalist" direction with the dismantling of part of the state sector and the revision of trade laws to open Mexico to foreign products and capital.

4. Mexico has experienced the social changes typical of developing countries. That is, mortality has been reduced and life expectancy lengthened; illiteracy has declined and the number enrolled in universities has increased strikingly; a massive movement to cities has shifted the balance so that a majority of the population is now urban; rates of population growth at first increased dramatically, but have more recently started to level off as a result of urbanization and attitudinal changes (Table 10.3).

5. The mix of economic policies arrived at by Mexican governments was particularly productive, and between 1940 and the early 1980s the country achieved a record of sustained economic growth whose duration was unmatched elsewhere in the world. This record was brought to an end by the collapse of oil prices in 1981, but after a painful period of decline, retrenchment, and readjustment, growth resumed in the 1990s. This was made possible by a new policy mix that stressed exports and openness to the world economic system, particularly to trade with and investment from the United States.

6. As the country has developed economically and urbanized, its class structure has changed. The benefits of economic growth have gone disproportionately to a new urban bourgeoisie, with a standard of living and pattern of consumption resembling those of the middle class in the United States. Alongside this new bourgeoisie in the modern sector of the urban economy is a growing lower middle class of sales clerks and office workers, and an industrial working class holding down factory jobs. More significant and much more

Table 10.3   CHANGE IN SOCIAL INDICATORS, 1965–1989

	1965	1988 or 1989
Life expectancy (years at birth)	59	69
Crude birth rate (annual, per 1000)	45	28
Enrollment in higher education (% of age group)	4	15
Urban population (% of total)	55	72

Source: The World Bank, *World Development Report 1991* (New York: Oxford University Press, 1991), various pages.

numerous, however, is the mushrooming urban underclass, the great number of people under-employed and self-employed in what has been called the "informal economy"—people who live in substandard housing; work in small establishments that evade the tax and minimum wage laws; peddle merchandise in the streets; and work as maids, shoeshine boys, or prostitutes. In this respect also, Mexico presents a classic third world profile.

7. As educational standards have risen and the social makeup of the population has changed, and as the economy has experienced new difficulties, political opposition has grown and the ruling party has been faced with difficult questions of what direction to take in containing opposition and retaining its monopoly of power.

THE RULING GROUP

Today, Mexico is essentially ruled by a "new class," similar to what Milovan Djilas described when writing of the bureaucratic elites that had arisen in Communist Eastern Europe.[6] This is a postrevolutionary ruling group of career administrators recruited primarily on the basis of merit, that is, by academic standing at the university. To some extent a hereditary element has developed, as public service has become a tradition in many leading families. Interestingly enough, the breeding ground for Mexico's national political leadership is the national university, the *Universidad Nacional Autónoma de México*, or UNAM. This has resulted in an almost complete segmentation of elite career patterns: the public sector elite trains in the national university just as members of the Roman Catholic church hierarchy train only in seminaries and military officers only in service academies; the leadership of the private business sector is educated in the technological institutes and schools of business, which are also privately owned and managed. Prior to the Salinas administration, it was unheard of in Mexico for a political leader to be a graduate of a private

institute of technology or school of business; a military academy background would be extremely rare, and a religious seminary out of the question.

This kind of leadership has developed only in the last 30 or 40 years. In the early days after the revolution, much of the political leadership emerged from the revolutionary army, in those days still an amateur political army and not the professionalized, academy-trained service it has since become. As the political system stabilized during the 1920s and 1930s, and as the fighting of the revolutionary era receded into memory, the military gradually withdrew from the political sphere. The ruling party had established its legitimacy, the political forces favoring the regime had become united, there was no power vacuum, and fighting was no longer a real possibility. The last military man to serve as president left office in 1946; the last military officer to hold a cabinet post not dealing with military affairs left office in 1970. As the generals and colonels retired from the political scene, their place was taken by the professional politicians, many of them lawyers, who had been active in organizing and operating the ruling party. Typically, they had come up through the ranks of state politics, sometimes in staff positions but often in elective posts.

With the final consolidation of the regime in its "institutional" phase, the central tasks of statecraft were no longer to foil uprisings or to weld a set of disparate regional politicians into a coherent national party, but became instead those of managing an expanding economy in the interest of maintaining economic growth; then the character of the country's leadership underwent another mutation, and the politicians yielded ground to the technocrats. The field has not been surrendered without a struggle, and one of the constant themes of current political commentary, especially around the time when a new party candidate for the presidency has to be picked, is the conflict between politicians and technocrats, or *políticos* and *técnicos*. This contest is always won by the technocrats, and Mexico has been presented with the extraordinary spectacle of a series of presidents, beginning in 1970 with Luis Echeverría, who never held elective office before being nominated for the presidency. In their careers, service in the higher reaches of the policy-making bureaucracy was relieved by occasional spells of teaching at the national university.

Until the inflation of the late 1980s shrank the value of the peso, service of this kind was generously compensated in salary, and additional stipends are given for service on the boards of national companies. A tradition of laxity in the handling of public funds and an absence of effective policing of conflicts of interest have contributed to illegal and semi-illegal self-enrichment, especially in the lower reaches of the bureaucracy, but sometimes touching the highest levels as well. During the easy-money years of the petroleum boom of the late 1970s and early 1980s, the defalcations of President José López Portillo were notorious. His successor, Miguel de la Madrid, attempted briefly to mount an anticorruption campaign, but indicted only two major offenders before his efforts ground to a halt in the face of massive resistance, especially from corrupt labor leaders, whose cooperation the president needed if he was to put through a much needed program of economic austerity without facing crippling strikes. However, Carlos Salinas actually had the most notoriously corrupt labor leader, Joaquín Hernández of the petroleum workers, arrested in January 1989, although it took a well-planned military operation to do so.

TECHNIQUES OF CONTROL

The political system has several means of maintaining itself. Toward potential leadership elements in its own natural constituency, such as university students, the regime follows a strategy of co-optation. Toward the population as a whole, the regime strives to maintain its legitimacy by means of public relations, pro-

paganda, and indoctrination. Toward the country's economic sectors and interest groups, the regime follows a strategy of reconciliation, attempting to spread around specific benefits to the extent that resources are available. To irreconcilable hard-core critics, exemplary punitive strategies are used as a last resort. We now consider these strategies in more detail.

The leadership elements in the party's natural constituency are, in effect, the politicians and the technocrats we spoke of earlier. The technocratic leadership comes directly from the public universities, especially the national university in the capital city. The politicians emerge from local and state party organizations and from functional organizations affiliated with the PRI: labor unions, the peasants' syndicates (federated into the *Confederación Nacional Campesina*), neighborhood associations, and leagues of professionals. Co-optation occurs primarily through the concession of benefits that are personal in nature, that is, a job for the leader rather than a change in the legislation that will benefit the group he represents. Jobs are available for the politicians in the party itself and in elective government positions.

Disappointment of one's ambitions need only be temporary, because when the presidency changes hands every six years there is tremendous turnover as individuals are promoted, retire, or lose favor. University graduates generally go straight into federal bureaucratic jobs in some specialty; some professional graduates may set themselves up in private practice, with a sideline as consultant to a ministry or public corporation, or with a part-time teaching position at the university or one of its preparatory schools. A striking demonstration of this kind of co-optation was the appointment of young university graduates to government positions by incoming President Luis Echeverría while they were still in jail cells for having taken part in the 1968 Tlatelolco demonstration.

The politician and technocrat career tracks converge in the cabinet and subcabinet, in positions in public corporations and nationalized industries, and sometimes in state governorships, when the holder of a subcabinet or minor cabinet position may be assigned the governorship nomination by the central party authorities. This might occur for various reasons: the national government may not want to side with either of the local factions contending for the nomination, it may wish to remove from the national power center a figure proving awkward or inconvenient for some reason, or it may be acceding to an insider's desire to go home to his native state or change career direction. The co-optation of group representatives and regional political leaders includes an averted gaze with respect to money-making activities which may not be altogether legal. This is especially true for labor leaders, who are usually pressed not to push their constituents' demands too strongly in order not to accelerate inflation or raise the costs of nationalized industries, and need to be bought off. It is also true of local and regional political bosses, many of whom build up powerful political machines that could be challenged only with a great deal of difficulty.

The legitimacy of the Mexican regime has two bases. First, the regime claims legitimacy as a constitutional democracy that functions in accordance with the norms generally accepted throughout the Western world: elections are held, laws are passed by the legally constituted legislature, an opposition press functions, and so on. It is true that the regime's claim to legitimacy on these grounds does not go unquestioned. Although elections are taken very seriously and opposition parties win a share of the seats in the Chamber of Deputies and of municipal offices, it is generally believed that the regime loses only those elections it wants to lose, and that from time to time results are manipulated to ensure that opposition parties do not win a state governorship or that the president can have a comfortable margin of victory. Election results, however, are taken seriously enough that an opposition boycott on the grounds that their cause is hopeless is extremely rare.

Second, the regime claims legitimacy as the heir to the great Mexican Revolution and the sacred values it embodied: nationalism, universal free public education, the restoration of the land to those who work it, and protection of the rights of the poor and humble—what is thought of in Mexico, at a subconscious level, as a vindication of Indian Mexico, the true Mexican nation, against foreign interests and the selfish and opportunistic Mexicans who join with them in exploiting the country.

The presidential succession has taken place in a constitutional manner since Obregón himself. The party that rules today is the same one that distributed the land, built the school, and nationalized the oil industry. In its liberation of the Indian and its defense of national interests, the regime has identified itself with the forces regarded generally in Mexico as the truly patriotic ones in the country's history. Of course, the government controls the content of education, specifying which approved history texts are to be used, so it is no wonder that school children in Mexico identify patriotism and the country's major achievements with the tradition of which the ruling party claims to be the current incarnation. The party appreciates this source of strength; it is no accident that the party's colors are the same as those of the national flag. Moreover, the dominant television network, TELEVISA, although privately owned and conservative in political orientation, always presents government and PRI in a favorable light—as well it may, in view of its very advantageous tax situation.

More sophisticated Mexicans are skeptical of the party's claim to incarnate the values of the Revolution. As a long-entrenched regime, the PRI government has spawned a distinctive class, or caste, with unrevolutionary privileges. For what it sees as reasons of sound economic policy, as well as because of pressure from "the north," its policies are often favorable to business interests, including foreign interests, and acceptable to international bankers. Because of evasion of the law and corruption, the land re-

---

Feature 10.1 **Abuse of Police Power in Mexico**

The international human rights organization, Amnesty International, has verified many reported cases of abuse of power by the various police forces in Mexico, including beatings, torture, and murder. Such reports, which previous governments often denied or swept under the rug, have been taken very seriously by the Salinas government, which has made the establishment of the rule of law part of its model for the modernized Mexico of the future. Because the mistreatment of prisoners occurs frequently in the attempt to extract confessions, the government introduced a law, passed by the Congress in August 1990, under which confessions are only valid if they are made in the presence of the suspect's lawyer or a judge. One year after the passage of the new law, however, the human rights organization Americas Watch concluded that it had negligible effect in ending police brutality.

Campaigns have been mounted by each recent president to try to reduce corruption, including police corruption, with mixed results. President Miguel de la Madrid had the police chief of Mexico City, whose luxurious style of life was notorious, arrested and brought to trial; this seemed to have some deterrent effect on corruption for a limited time, but today extortion of bribes by the police is still commonplace.

---

form has been compromised. Well-connected individuals, many of them former government and party officials, hold large estates in violation of the land reform laws.

In addition to positive methods of attracting support, the regime also resorts to intimidation and repression. It is not clear how generalized and frequent such acts are, and to what extent they are committed by low-level officials without the knowledge or consent of top national leaders (see Feature 10.1). According to persistent reports, agrarian dissidents and suspected urban subversives have even been assassinated by army and police units. Several journalists met with foul play during the de la Madrid years, although the president himself was not implicated.

Normally, it is unnecessary to resort to such extreme measures. The discretion that is involved in the implementation of the laws is adequate to coopt individuals and organizations, or to penalize those who prove uncooperative. For example, until 1988 there was a government monopoly on the production and

importation of newsprint, the paper used by newspapers, and the government sold it at prices considerably below the world market rates. A periodical might be punished by experiencing difficulties in its newsprint supplies, being then forced to buy paper at much higher prices on the free market; a favored publication might be supplied in excess of its needs and be able to sell the surplus at a profit. Mexico's joining the General Agreement on Tariffs and Trade (GATT) under Miguel de la Madrid, however, meant the end of the import monopoly, and thus of this technique of control.

Uncooperative businesses may experience labor difficulties. But repression falls most heavily on potentially radical elements of lower-status groups that are ostensibly the regime's own constituency: labor, peasants, and students, and it is against them that the most spectacular instances of repression have been directed. Just as they are the sources of mass support, they may also be the sources of insurrection.

A demonstration in the Zócalo, the main square in Mexico City, in front of the cathedral.

The military, too, is one of the basic supports of the regime. The major arena for political struggle during the early years after the revolution, the army was gradually depoliticized during the 1920s and 1930s. Nevertheless, its primary mission, which is the maintenance of internal order rather than border defense, has political implications, and presidents are always careful to give the military special treatment in pay increases and fringe benefits. Like civilian administrators, military officers are able to increase their incomes in ways not excessively troubled by provisions against conflict of interest. In addition, retired military officers are in demand as candidates for lesser elective offices. Yet it is worthy of note that, despite relatively favorable budgetary treatment, the lack of a serious international defense assignment has made it possible to limit the size of the armed forces and to limit military expenditures to levels that, on a per cap-

ita basis, are much lower than those common in Europe and elsewhere in Latin America.

INTEREST GROUPS

In classic Latin American fashion, economic interest groups are organized in an almost corporatist manner. Two organizations, the Confederation of Chambers of Industry, known as CONCAMIN, and the Confederation of Chambers of Commerce, or CONCANACO, group together local chambers of commerce or industry. Membership in one or the other organization is compulsory for manufacturing or commercial businesses, respectively, which have assets in excess of a rather low threshold. There are several other significant business associations, in which membership is voluntary: The Entrepreneurs' Coordinating Council, or CCE; the National Chamber of Manufacturing Industry, or CANACINTRA; and the Mexican

Employers' Confederation, or COPARMEX. The CCE tries to speak for the private sector as a whole, which makes its voice very strong when the private sector is united on an issue. Many questions, however, create splits in the business community, which weakens the position of the CCE and throws into relief the views of the more homogeneous organizations, especially CANACINTRA and COPARMEX. CANACINTRA primarily represents manufacturers producing consumer goods, and thus has an interest in the expansion of the domestic market and tariff protection against competing imported goods. It is willing to accept a higher general level of wages and salaries, as this increases its customers' purchasing power. COPARMEX has in recent years taken an active political role in favor of free enterprise and against government control of the economy, which put it in tune with the revival of neoclassical economic thinking in the United States and Western Europe, and in 1988 the conservative opposition party, the PAN, nominated a former president of COPARMEX, Manuel Clouthier, as its presidential candidate.[7]

Most of Mexico's labor unions are affiliated with the ruling party through membership in confederations that belong to the party's "labor sector," although the government workers' and the teachers' unions are affiliated with the "popular" sector. Some unions, however, especially those with leftist political views, remain independent of the party. But whether unions belong to the PRI or not, labor organization is highly regulated, as is the case with most Latin American countries. In order to enjoy the protections of the country's labor code, unions must be registered with the Ministry of Labor, which can control them in various ways. For example, the law stipulates that a strike may only be called after certain procedures have been followed, such as a membership vote; only if the strike is declared legal are strikers eligible for benefits during the period of the strike. Moreover, if stipulated conciliation procedures have not reached a mutually satisfactory result, the government may set-

tle the dispute by decree. The government, through the Ministry of Labor, thus has great discretion in handling labor cases. Nevertheless, at a time of economic distress such as the one Mexico experienced during the de la Madrid years, any interruption in production through a strike is to be avoided, even if the strike could eventually be settled on terms acceptable to the government, so labor's power is increased. Of course, labor leaders can use their influence for their own personal advantage rather than that of the membership, and it seems clear that the rank and file have not benefited as much as labor's potential bargaining power should have made possible. Ultimately, the loyalty of most workers to the ruling party means that labor's freedom of action is necessarily limited.

POLITICAL PARTIES

Although the PRI continues as the dominant party in the political system, the minor parties perform important functions. A former interior minister, Jesús Reyes Héroles, once said "Opposition is a form of support." He meant that by competing in elections the opposition parties signified their acceptance of the system as legitimate. In a sense, the dominant party has the best of both worlds. Unlike the single party in a dictatorship, it does not have to operate in a police regime that stamps out any sign of opposition, ruling by force over a sullen and resentful population. On the other hand, it does not run the risk, as it would in a completely competitive system, of losing office—with the attendant loss of jobs, contracts, and the whole structure of policy that embodies its values and aspirations. Thus, paradoxically, although the regime is believed to manipulate the results of elections—especially those that might threaten its monopoly of power—it used to encourage the opposition parties, and probably subsidized some of the minor ones secretly in the days before public financing for parties was legislated.

The major party on the right of the political spectrum is PAN, the National Action party. Founded in 1939 as a party opposing the fundamental principles of the revolution, that is, proclerical and probusiness, its tactical line has fluctuated, but since the 1960s it has played the role of loyal opposition. It competes in elections, abides by the rules of the game, and has stated that it "accepts" the revolution. In religious policy, it would like the anticlerical laws changed to remove provisions that the Church cannot hold property and cannot operate schools—provisions that are in any case ignored in practice. It would like the communal landholding units, or *ejidos* (discussed in Section C), broken up and converted into private landholdings. It supports various changes in the law in favor of private business, especially small-business interests. As an opposition party that has had success primarily at the municipal level, PAN criticizes electoral fraud and supports greater autonomy for local government. The party's vote has increased fairly steadily, reaching a little over 17 percent in the 1988 elections. Its support comes especially from religiously inclined members of the middle class. It is strongest in the Federal District and in the northern border states, where it has won several mayoralties and a governorship. The party claims that it has actually won a majority in gubernatorial elections in several northern states, but has been denied its victory because of electoral manipulation.

The PAN's support comes from business elements and Catholic intellectuals. A smaller party on the right, the PDM, *Partido Democrático Mexicano,* or Mexican Democratic party, which wins only 1 or 2 percent of the vote nationally, is strongest among Catholic peasants in the western states. Despite its name, there are antidemocratic and pro-fascist elements in its ideology.

The principal party on the left is now the PRD, the *Partido Revolucionario Democrático,* or Democratic Revolutionary Party, formed by Cuauhtémoc Cárdenas after the 1988 elections, using as his base the *Partido Socialista Mexicano,* (PSM) or Mexican Socialist Party. The PSM itself was formed by the unification of several smaller groups with the PSUM, *Partido Socialista Unificado Mexicano,* or Unified Mexican Socialist party, which had in its turn been formed by the merging of some minor parties with the old Mexican Communist party. The Mexican Communist party took a line independent of Moscow as far back as 1968, when it condemned the sending of Soviet troops into Czechoslovakia to put down the liberalization movement known as "Prague Spring." It then developed a line similar to that of the Italian Communist party, favorable to democratic institutions—the so-called Eurocommunist position. In 1980, the party condemned the Soviet invasion of Afghanistan and supported the independent Solidarity trade union movement in Poland. There seemed, in fact, little left of the characteristic defining features of a Communist party, and in 1982 the party voted to dissolve itself and form the new Unified Mexican Socialist party. The long-term prospects of the PRD are dubious; it did well (better than the official figures showed, no doubt) in local elections in 1989 but performed badly in the 1991 midterm legislative elections. It was likely, however, that tactical disagreements on the left and the PRI's power to coopt opportunists would return PAN to the position of principal opposition party that it had lost, only briefly, in the 1988 presidential elections.

An interesting small party on the left is the PPS, or Popular Socialist party. The party was founded in 1946 by Vicente Lombardo Toledano, the intellectual head of the labor confederation during the Cárdenas presidency who had been eased out as too radical by Cárdenas's successor. Lombardo left the ruling party to found the Partido Popular at an interesting time. The regime had taken a turn to the right with the selection of Miguel Alemán as the party's presidential candidate, and Stalin had abandoned his wartime policy of collaboration with bourgeois democratic forces, ordering Communist parties loyal to Moscow to break off any coalition arrangements with other parties. From then until his death in 1969, Lombardo managed the sometimes difficult task of collaborating with the PRI while also following the lead of Moscow. For the PRI, he performed the invaluable service of channeling left-wing opinion, especially student opinion, in a harmless direction. The PPS always endorsed presidential candidates of the PRI—except in one election, that of 1952, when Lombardo himself was a candidate. Not entirely coincidentally, perhaps, that was the year in which a strong left-wing candidate, Miguel Henríquez Guzmán, who had split off from the PRI, might have cut substantially into the vote of the ruling party had Lombardo's candidacy not divided the leftist vote. After Lombardo's death, the party dwindled somewhat in support, and has been kept alive only by benign electoral laws. Its loyal participation in the system has been rewarded by seats in the Chamber of Deputies, and until 1988 it held the distinction of being the only opposition group since the founding of the official party in 1929 to have held a seat in the federal senate. This was made possible by the withdrawal of the PRI candidate in what insiders believed was a deal to compensate the PPS for its not having made a fuss over the outcome of a gubernatorial election rigged against the party's candidate. The party finally broke its tradition of endorsing PRI presidential candidates to endorse the candidacy of Cuauhtémoc Cárdenas in 1988.

Cárdenas chose as his primary vehicle for that election another very minor party of the center-left, the PARM, or Authentic party of the Mexican Revolution, which split from the ruling party in the 1940s over the question of corruption, and had been kept alive by the PRI in part out of respect for the honorable revolutionary career of the party's leading figures. The Trotskyite PST (*Partido Socialista de los Trabajadores*, or Workers' Socialist party) also previously a fellow traveling party with the PRI, became so enthusiastic for the Cárdenas

candidacy that it renamed itself the "party of the Cardenista Front of National Reconstruction." When it retained that name in 1989 after abandoning Cárdenas and resuming its collaboration with the PRI, it performed a valuable service to the PRI by confusing less sophisticated pro-Cárdenas voters.

As previously noted, the ruling group continues to hold power in Mexico in part because it follows a policy of reconciliation of diverse interests, attempting to give important interest groups at least part of what they want and at the same time trying to co-opt their leaders. In a sense the same procedure is followed with opposition parties. However, changes in the nature of Mexican society have increased the potential appeal of opposition parties.

The PRI is strongest among the less sophisticated elements of the population, the rural and urban masses that accept the image the party tries to project of itself as altruistic, the source of progress and material benefits, the embodiment of revolutionary ideals, and the bearer of legitimacy, democracy, and patriotism. As studies of early political socialization have shown, the child in the elementary grades conceives of political authority as caring and benign, and it is the segments with least education that accept the PRI, the regime, and the president on these terms.

As Mexico has developed a more literate, better educated urban society, however, the constituency for opposition parties has grown. That is, the PAN draws votes from the middle class in the private and business sectors, and the left-wing parties draw from the intellectual and professional members of the middle class, together with some support from lower-class elements. The PRD appears to have succeeded in establishing itself as the leading opposition party on the left. In the face of these changes, the PRI has modified its tactics. Until 1988 and the breakaway of Cárdenas to form the PRD, its line of policy was to treat the PAN as the principal opposition, identifying it with the forces that were defeated in the Revolution and implying that it had United States support. This reinforced the PRI's revolutionary and nationalist credentials, and induced some people to vote for the PRI as the strongest bastion against counterrevolution and imperialism. However, after the rise of the PRD, and the decline of PRI strength in the Chamber of Deputies to below two-thirds of the membership, it became necessary to form an implicit alliance with the PAN in order to pass any of President Salinas's procapitalist economic reforms that required amendment of the constitution.

In fact, today the PRI fears PRD more than PAN. PAN has attracted votes from those who are, for religious or historical reasons, not predisposed to vote for the PRI anyway, but the PRD had, at least at its origin, the potential of replacing the PRI altogether by taking away its core constituency. The PRD leaders are particularly resented by the PRI as "traitors."

Accordingly, the PRI draws on its traditional repertoire of political tactics, providing monetary and other incentives to co-opt sectoral leaders who might be drawn to the PRD, and encouraging minor left-wing parties that might cut into its vote. At the local level, the PRI tries to maintain flexibility so that it can shift its position toward left or right depending on the nature of the challenge in a specific locality. Thus in the northern states the PRI has presented itself as favorable to the interests of the business sector and has nominated local business leaders as its candidates for mayoralties.

As opposition support among voters has grown, the regime has modified the electoral law several times to increase opposition representation in the federal legislature. This gives the opposition parties the illusion that they are gaining actual political power, and gives them an incentive to play the electoral game instead of rejecting the existing political system.

VOTING AND ELECTIONS

The formal institutions of Mexican government present no difficulties of understanding to North Americans, as they are clearly based on those of the United States. This is a system of separation of powers; the president is popularly elected separately from the two houses of the legislature, the Senate and the Chamber of Deputies. The Senate has two members elected by each state, or as the Mexicans say, by each "federal entity," as there are also senators elected by the Federal District (in the United States Senate the District of Columbia is not represented) and there used to be senators from territories, which have by now all become states.

Voting in Mexico is legally compulsory. This means that for various dealings with government agencies a voting credential, stamped to indicate that one has complied with his civic duty, is among the various papers and forms required—for example, to secure a passport or enroll children in school. If in fact the credential has not been stamped and the official cannot be persuaded to overlook it, then a bribe is called for, either to the official himself or to a doctor to certify that illness on election day made voting impossible. Partly because it is compulsory, but also partly because there is a strong feeling—reinforced by government public relations campaigns—that voting is an important civic duty, electoral turnout is high, generally over 80 percent in presidential elections (see Table 10.4).

In a speech early in his campaign, Carlos Salinas acknowledged implicitly the existence of manipulation in previous elections, saying that the credibility of electoral democracy had suffered significant blows in northern Mexico. "I want to win and I want also for people to believe in our victory, even if we suffer some defeats." In keeping with those sentiments, in the 1988 elections the PRI accepted the unprecedented loss of four senatorial seats, although that did not prevent the opposi-

Table 10.4   PRESIDENTIAL ELECTION RESULTS, 1988

Party	Candidate	Number of voters	Percentage
PRI	Carlos Salinas de Gortari	9,641,329	50.36
PFCRN	Cuauhtémoc Cárdenas	5,956,988	31.12
PARM, PPS			
PAN	Manuel Clouthier	3,627,159	17.07
PDM	Gumersindo Magaña	199,484	1.04
PRT	Rosario Ibarra	80,052	0.42

Source: Press Release, Embassy of Mexico, Washington, D.C., 14 July 1988.

tion's charging that the presidential elections were rigged nevertheless. In 1991 the president went further and forced the resignation of the governors-elect of Guanajuato [see Feature 10.2] and San Luis Potosí after obviously rigged elections were held.

The electoral law for the Chamber of Deputies is extremely interesting; it reveals the intention to build up the opposition parties to a significant level but still maintain the PRI as the dominant party. Until the 1950s, the electoral system had been that of the single-member district, familiar to Americans as the method for electing members of the House of Representatives. The country is divided into districts, each of which elects one person. This method has traditionally been regarded by political scientists as one that fosters the growth of a two-party system, because parties that have no chance of coming in first or second in a district become discouraged and their followers opt for one of the two principal parties as the lesser evil. At the same time, the theoretical models suggest, one party cannot rule forever because it cannot satisfy all interests equally. Nor does it want to: why should it spread the benefits of office thinner by including other interests once it has reached the bare majority it needs to win? Accordingly, where elections are conducted in single-member districts, the dynamics of the situation should eventually result in the emergence of a two-party system.

Like all predictive models, this one works if its assumptions hold, and if other things

remain equal. Indeed, in several of the northern states the situation has developed as the model suggests, and there is in effect two-party competition between the PRI and the PAN. If the parties do not alternate in power at the state level in the North, it has been primarily because of electoral manipulation on the part of the government party. Elsewhere, it could be argued, sufficient time has not yet elapsed for the dynamics to work themselves out fully; that is, for an informed electorate to develop consciousness of its group interests and acquire reliable information about where the various political parties stand in relation to those interests, and for potential supporters of the opposition to believe that it is worth participating in the political process. Presumably, after these factors have had time to work themselves out, a genuinely competitive party system will emerge in which the PRI would have to leave office from time to time, or else maintain power only by virtue of electoral manipulation. There are indeed cases, such as those of Turkey during the 1940s and India during the 1970s, of dominant-party systems in which the ruling party left office peacefully after sustaining an electoral defeat.

In any event, years before opposition parties posed any kind of threat to the hegemony of the PRI, more progressive elements in the ruling party, believing that the maintenance of the system was better served by flexibility than by rigidity, convinced President Adolfo López Mateos to introduce legislation adding a proportional representation feature to the elec-

---

Feature 10.2 The 1991 Gubernatorial Elections in Guanajuato

The 1991 midterm elections witnessed a triumph for the PRI, or rather a personal triumph for Carlos Salinas. A turnout of over 60 percent of those registered — exceeding all expectations — showed that there was general popular support for the president's policies, as the PRI recovered from its low point during the 1988 elections and made a strong showing. The PAN more or less retained its strength, but the leftist PRD suffered a drastic decline from the 1988 high point of the presidential candidacy of Cuauhtémoc Cárdenas.

In the state of Guanajuato, however, the PRI won *too* big. The votes in some precincts were cast unanimously for the PRI; in some precincts more votes were recorded than there were registered voters. But Salinas showed that he was serious in not wanting to return to the "bad old days" of blatantly rigged elections. In response to pressure from the president, the PRI governor-elect, Ramón Aguirre, resigned; the state legislature, which had a PRI majority, chose the PAN mayor of the city of León as interim governor until new elections could be held. Then the legislature initiated a change in the state's constitution to require the governor to be a native of the state. This new requirement would eliminate both Vicente Fox, the PAN candidate, and Porfirio Muñoz Ledo, the candidate of the PRD.

This outcome was typically Mexican. The president was punishing the state party, which had not followed his instructions about clean elections; and it was arranged by a deal behind the scenes. But even though the deal had made a concession to the opposition by letting them have the interim governorship, it had not involved any gratuitous yielding by the PRI of permanent control of the governorship; and if the PRI had to sacrifice their governorship candidate, the PAN's candidate had to be sacrificed, too. The outcome showed that Carlos Salinas wanted to be seen as a strong president, and that he was determined that elections not be rigged . . . or was it only that they not be crudely and obviously rigged?

---

toral law for the Chamber of Deputies, which gave opposition parties seats in the Chamber reflecting their percentage of the national vote. Electors vote twice in Chamber elections, once on each half of a divided ballot. On one side they vote for candidates in their individual districts, and on the other side they vote for a party to share seats in the proportional distribution.

This provision has been changed several times to increase the proportional seats. In the electoral law used for the 1988 and 1991 elections, they constituted 200 of the available Chamber of Deputies seats, while 300 members were to be elected in single-member districts. As in the German Federal Republic, the additional 200 seats are distributed so that the *total* representation of a party, including the seats won in districts, will reflect its percentage of the total vote. But another provision, justified as preventing a deadlocked parliament, stipulates that so long as "any party" (i.e. the PRI) wins a plurality of the proportional votes, it retains its majority in the Chamber. Moreover, since the opposition seats are divided among parties to the left and right of the PRI, the ruling party maintains a dominant position. In any case, the role of the Chamber of Deputies is still a limited one in the Mexican system.

When they were established, it seemed unlikely that the proportional provisions for opposition representation could ever get out of hand and threaten PRI control. The system was based on the premise of a single dominant party that wins a majority of the seats, with a minority of the seats earmarked as a concession to smaller parties, which remain in permanent opposition.

What the changes in the electoral law signified was the PRI's intention to exercise its hegemony in subtler ways, requiring a more delicate touch. The democratic façade was to be given greater plausibility; the opposition was to be encouraged through its small victories, thus guiding dissidence into safe channels. However, changes have a way of outrunning the intentions of those who introduced them, a possibility which cannot be excluded in Mexico.

Federal elections in Mexico are on three- and six-year cycles. Deputies are elected every three years, along with half of the Senate. Senators, like the president, have six-year terms.

CONSTITUTIONAL STRUCTURE AND NORMS

The Constitution of 1917 addresses itself to three substantive areas. It establishes the structure of national government, including the federal system and separation of powers; it provides for the defense of individual rights; and it establishes various principles and goals for public policy. Individual rights are guaranteed by the first 29 articles, which specify the rights and immunities of citizens with respect to government power, of the states and localities as well as of the federal government.

The president is prohibited reelection. Members of Congress may be elected only after skipping terms—that is, consecutive reelection to the same office is not possible. Some members of the legislature have actually alternated for several periods between the Senate and the Chamber of Deputies. The "no reelection" rules were established in their present form through congressional amendment in the aftermath of the assassination of Obregón; the Constitution had previously been amended to allow Obregón to run for reelection. The prohibition of presidential reelection is one of the most significant features of the system. It avoids personal dictatorship and forces a policy review and change of direction every six years. It secures the loyalty of those whose immediate careers do not seem promising but who know they will shortly get another chance. The Revolution of 1910 broke out, after all, over the issue of the perennial reelection of Porfirio Díaz. The Bolivian Revolution, similar in many ways to the Mexican, finally came to grief when President Víctor Paz Estenssoro had the constitution amended to permit consecutive reelection. The "no reelection" rule allows for continuing renewal, adjustment, and hope.

Amendments to the Constitution must be voted by two-thirds of the Congress meeting in joint session, and must then be approved by a majority of the state legislatures. When the Congress is not in session, a commission, composed of 29 members drawn from both houses, may act on behalf of Congress on matters too urgent to be left over for the next session.

Partly because of constitutional disposition and partly because of legislation, the president has considerable legislative power of his own. Constitutionally, as head of the executive branch, he has authority to issue decrees regulating the manner in which legislation passed by Congress is to be enforced. In addition, Congress has voted him the power to issue decrees in other matters—for example, the authority to transfer funds among different budgetary categories and to incur expenses beyond the amounts appropriated by the original budget.

The judiciary in Mexico normally does not play a significant political role. Most of the time, the judiciary stays away from political questions. Of course judges are appointed by the president, and if the executive is interested in the outcome of a particular case, it can normally expect judges to be responsive to its wishes. However, there are cases on record in which a court has rendered decisions against the executive branch. This has occurred by means of the granting of a writ of *amparo,* a judicial order forbidding acts of administrative officers that violate a specific guaranteed right of an individual, or ordering an official to take an affirmative action called for by the exercise of such a right. *Amparo* has no exact equivalent in Anglo-Saxon common law; it combines features of the injunction with those of specific writs such as *habeas corpus* or *mandamus.* One accustomed to the subtleties of politics in Mexico, however, may be inclined to suspect that on some occasions when a court has ruled against the executive branch, its decision may in fact have been requested by the executive, attempting to get itself out of a situation that had been politically untenable, or wishing to take a position for the record that contravened the results it hoped to achieve.

Below the Supreme Court are 6 circuit courts and 46 district courts in the federal system. The Federal District and the states have their own judiciaries.

STATE AND LOCAL GOVERNMENT

The state governments have their own distinctive constitutions; however, they all have elected governors and single-chamber legislatures, the number of members of which varies from state to state. Each state is on its own electoral cycle, and only one governor happens to be elected at the same time as the president. Hence, although it is the national party—in effect, the president—which decides who the candidates for governor will be, presidents inherit governors nominated by their predecessors, and it is only in their last two years of office, when they are already about to become lame ducks, that presidents have a complete set of governors of their own choice. Each state party has a convention to choose its candidate for governor, but in effect, just as at

the national level, the party chooses the candidate who has the president's approval. The governor of the Federal District is not elected, but is an appointee of the president and a member of his cabinet.

There are 33 states and one Federal District. Because the national government is supreme over the states, politically if not always legally, commentators often refer to the Mexican federal system as fraudulent. That is not altogether the case. Because the federal government is engaged in a continuous balancing act, trying to proceed with its objectives while conciliating a variety of entrenched interests with a minimum of open dissension, a well-managed local political machine may normally run a state pretty much as it likes. On the average of once or twice in a presidential term, however, the behavior of a specific state governor may reach such publicly scandalous proportions—because of either monumental embezzlement of public funds, use of state power to promote private business interests, or the assassination of dissidents—that he is removed by the federal government. This can be done in various ways. Impeachment by the state legislature is legally possible, but is a long, drawn-out operation that is likely to be unedifying. Accordingly, pressure may be brought on a governor to resign; if he is reluctant, the federal Senate may make a finding that the constitutional authorities of the state have ceased to exist, whereupon the president designates a new governor. Under Salinas, four governors have been removed.

The basic unit of local government is the *municipio,* which resembles a North American township or consolidated city-county government. That is, it consists of a town plus the surrounding rural area. The *municipio* elects a mayor and council, who are not eligible for immediate reelection.

Opposition parties have been most successful at the municipal level. In June 1988, 60 mayors were from opposition parties. The PAN in particular has captured the mayoralties of several large northern cities, where a genuinely competitive political system exists. Politics at the local level is fairly fluid; an upcoming election will see new alignments and factional shifts, leading individuals crossing party lines, and parties trying to recruit prominent local editors or business leaders as candidates.

The funding of local government is very flexible. Municipalities receive subsidies from state governments but can also raise their own funds by charging fees for municipal services and licenses; for some purposes, federal funds are available. Some economic development expenditures are financed by partnerships between the municipality and the private sector.

Authorities at all three levels of Mexican government have concurrent jurisdiction in several subject areas. Coordination of their activities is effected by a federal delegate; there is normally one such delegate per federal ministry per state capital. State governments are financed partly by federal subsidies and partly by their own taxing powers; typical state taxes are those on property, sales, inheritance, and income.

The position of state governor (there are no lieutenant governors, just as there is no federal vice-president) is an important one, not only administratively but also politically. Conflicts frequently occur between local interests supporting a popular local candidate and a national party wanting to place its own candidate in the position. Generally the national party is successful in imposing its choice in such situations; its candidate is usually a nationally well-connected figure for whom the state governorship is an important stepping stone, perhaps between a subcabinet and a cabinet position. Such imposed candidates are often people who were born in the state but have made their careers entirely in the Federal District. Some aspirants for governor intend to carve out local empires for themselves and become rich and powerful on the local scene, but for most career politicians the major league is the president's cabinet, which is the pool from which future presidents are drawn.

The president's cabinet currently has 23 ministries. The key ministry until 1992 was that of Programming and Budget, which replaced the previously most important Ministry of Government or Interior (*Gobernación*), which had in its turn replaced the Ministry of Defense—as fiscal management has replaced politics, which replaced combat as the principal source of power in the Mexican system. Early in 1992, the Ministry of Programming and Budget was absorbed by the Ministry of Finance, presumably as a result of a political victory of the Finance Minister, Pedro Aspe, for control of fiscal policy. The Finance Minister's rival for preeminence in the cabinet is the head of another ministry created in 1992, Social Development.

Outside the cabinet departments are many independent agencies and public corporations, which seem to run their own affairs with a minimum of presidential supervision. In some cases, most notoriously in the case of the petroleum monopoly, PEMEX, the agency officials become involved in racketeering and embezzlement on a large scale.

Corruption has always been a problem in Mexican public administration. In the early years after the revolution, allowing graft was a deliberate policy of President Obregón to co-opt possible military rebels into the political system. "No one can withstand a cannonade of 200,000 pesos," he is reported to have said. But as the danger of military insurrection receded, corruption was no longer functional for the maintenance of the system and became a nuisance. "Moralization" campaigns are waged periodically, especially after graft has become particularly notorious, as during the administrations of Miguel Alemán and José López Portillo. Sometimes a new governor of the Federal District will launch such an anticorruption campaign.

There has been some success in reducing the widespread petty corruption among the various police forces of the Republic, but the problem continues. When the economy is in crisis, presidents are too weak to act effectively against corruption. For example, Miguel de la Madrid's tentative moves against corruption in the petroleum workers' union were brought to a halt by intimations that if he proceeded he would face a long, crippling strike. Carlos Salinas was able to crack down on the union when he inherited a stronger economic position and had military units prepared to seize the oilfields and maintain production.

THE EVOLUTION OF PRESIDENTIAL TYPES

The characteristics of Mexican presidents, like the characteristics of the leadership group in general, have undergone striking modification over the years. The most noticeable differences are in family background, geographic origin, training, and career pattern.

As was noted before, the institutionalization of the revolution has brought about the development of a distinctive ruling group. The castelike features of this group have become especially apparent over time, and it is common to find people in political leadership positions who are the sons and grandsons of government officials and politicians in the dominant party. In fact, all three leading contenders for the PRI presidential nomination in 1988—Carlos Salinas, Manuel Bartlett, and Alfredo del Mazo—were the sons of important regime political figures, as was the leading opposition candidate, Cuauhtémoc Cárdenas.

Another symptom of the shrinking of the pool from which the ruling group is drawn is its dominant Mexico City flavor. In the early postrevolutionary years Mexico was ruled by generals, who were usually from the provinces and usually from the North; the politicians who followed had made their careers in state and local politics. But the technocrats who rule today are overwhelmingly products of the capital. Echeverría, López Portillo, and Carlos Salinas were all born in Mexico City, and de la Madrid was raised there, although born elsewhere.

The shift in academic training is also intriguing. The generals of the early revolutionary years, and their colleagues in government,

frequently lacked higher education; the politicians who succeeded them were typically lawyers. In the technocratic era, there has been an increase in cabinet members trained in a technical specialty other than law, such as engineering or architecture, or in administration and fiscal management. This shift in skill and training among cabinet members was reflected, with a slight time lag, at the presidential level. From 1920 to 1946, all elected presidents were generals (although two civilians, Adolfo de la Huerta and Emilio Portes Gil, served as provisional presidents). From 1946 to 1976, with the exception of Adolfo Ruiz Cortines, presidents were all lawyers by training; the three presidents since 1976 have been specialists in public administration and finance.

In terms of career immediately prior to the presidency, between 1920 and 1940 the incoming president had served as Secretary of War or Defense, except for the three presidents who shared the term Obregón was unable to serve, from 1928 to 1934. With the exception of Adolfo López Mateos, who had been Minister of Labor, from 1946 to 1976 the position held by each candidate prior to his election had been Minister of Government (*Secretario de Gobernación*, sometimes translated as Minister of the Interior). This department, among other things, is in charge of organizing elections and managing relations between federation and states, so it is the key ministry for handling political questions—just as the Ministry of War or Defense was the most important during the preceding era, when the possibility of an armed revolt was always present. José López Portillo, who served from 1976 to 1982, was selected while serving as Minister of Finance, and the two succeeding candidates were chosen from the Ministry of Programming and Budget, which only became a cabinet department during the López Portillo administration.

This shift in skills and career backgrounds clearly indicates the evolution of the character of the regime as the Revolution has become institutionalized. We take the presidents in chronological sequence: Obregón, Calles, and Cárdenas were revolutionary generals, heroic leaders in war; Avila Camacho was a desk general, a military administrator. Alemán was a politician rather than a career administrator; Ruiz Cortines, López Mateos, and Díaz Ordaz combined bureaucratic careers with periods of elective office. Echeverría was a career administrator born in the Federal District who never held an elective office before the presidency. López Portillo, de la Madrid, and Salinas combined administrative with academic careers, teaching at the national university concurrently or intermittently while holding their administrative jobs. All three had gone abroad for advanced degrees after completing a first degree at UNAM—López Portillo to the London School of Economics, de la Madrid and Salinas to Harvard. The skills required thus evolved from combat to elective politics, to general administration, to fiscal management.

Each time a new president comes to office in Mexico, there is an extensive turnover in government jobs. The fact that the ruling party does not change does not make much difference in this, nor does the fact that the incoming president was picked by the outgoing one. Indeed, the fact that new presidents are picked by their predecessors seems to impose a particular psychological obligation on them to demonstrate that they are independent and not simply puppets. Moreover, they want to demonstrate that they will avoid the errors of their predecessors, and so a great deal of ostentatious change in personnel and policy orientation is mixed in with the inevitable continuity from incumbent to incumbent.

In filling the major positions in their administrations, new presidents usually choose notable figures who are popular with specific interests they want to conciliate—including the international banking community—and they will retain or promote individuals of particular competence. They also surround themselves with people they have worked with during their careers, sometimes going back to their school days. This set of a politician's associates, colleagues, and cronies is called in Mexico a *camarilla;* they are people who think like he (or she) does, whom he can trust, who share similar backgrounds, and who have been loyal supporters. Carlos Salinas, for example, was a member of the *camarilla* of Miguel de la Madrid, their acquaintance going back to when Salinas was a student in a class taught by de la Madrid at the university. Luis Echeverría picked as his replacement José López Portillo, a lifelong friend since their days as students together.

THE PRESIDENT AND THE RULING PARTY

The keystone of the political system is the presidency. As in other presidential systems, the president is the dominant figure, prime mover, inspirer, motivator, and tone setter for all government activity. Of course the president cannot do everything himself, but everything is done in his name and, on the whole, within the guidelines he has laid down and by the personnel he has selected. The president is also the leader of the dominant party, which is fairly well disciplined, so that normally a PRI member of one of the legislative bodies can be expected to vote with the party.

The president's power is wielded in various forms: the appointment of cabinet members, and the supervision of their work and that of the ministries they head; control of the party's nominations for the Senate, the Chamber of Deputies, and state governorships; control of the work of Congress and the passage of legislation; and the issuance of presidential decrees. These decrees are legally supposed to be limited to the matters within the president's own competence, as specified by the Constitution, or to provide for the implementation of legislation passed by Congress. Given the extent of legal presidential powers, there is generally no reason for the president to act illegally. However, on occasion the president exceeds his legal powers, and the situation is brought into conformance with the law only retroactively. For example, President López Portillo nationalized the banks by decree, a procedure that seemed to have no legal warrant. Legislation was then hastily prepared and passed by Congress subsequently to regularize the situation from a legal point of view.

The centralization of power in the president and ruling party belongs to the "institutional" era of the last half century. In the 1920s, the president was the dominant *caudillo*, but there were other strong figures, regional bosses, and leaders of major interest groups. Prorevolutionary forces were represented in several political parties, and competition among parties for legislative seats and governorships was lively and sometimes violent. This competition, although it was now competition for the nomination of the ruling party, continued after Calles founded the National Revolutionary party in 1929, and preexisting organizations continued their separate identities within the PNR. Cárdenas reorganized the affiliated groups into four sectors when he transformed the party into the PRM, or Mexican Revolutionary party, in 1938.

Since Avila Camacho's term, toward the end of which the party's name was changed to the Institutional Revolutionary party, the system has been consolidated and conflict reduced to a minimum. The presidential candidate who ran against Avila Camacho in 1940, General Juan Andreu Almazán, was the last to threaten a revolt. The electoral law, which had previously stipulated that the first citizens to arrive at a polling station to vote would be sworn in as electoral officials, and had thus led to battles between supporters of rival candidates over who was to be first in line when the polls opened, was changed to provide for a different method of choosing electoral officials. After 1940, genuine competition within the party over nominations was restricted mainly to local offices, with party headquarters in Mexico City deciding on the party's candidates for the federal congress and governorships.

Nominations for congressional seats and municipal presidencies (mayoralties) are traditionally supposed to go to that sector of the party—labor, agrarian, or popular—which is strongest in the district. In sectoral terms, it is the popular sector—which, after all, includes such political powerhouses as the bureaucrats' union, the neighborhood associations, and the lawyers' association—that garners the lion's share of congressional seats.

CHOOSING THE PRESIDENT

As already mentioned, the nomination of the presidential candidate is in the hands of the outgoing president. The president is supposed to consult over the nominations, although how much he consults and how much attention he pays to the advice he is given is up to him. Nevertheless, in keeping with the apparent democratization and gestures toward openness of recent years, an attempt has been made to make it appear as though a quasi-democratic method of choosing the ruling party's presidential nominee is being followed. The process of picking a president during 1987 and 1988 thus went through nine stages.

1. By the two-thirds' mark in the presidential term (that is, by two years from its end) the president has replaced any cabinet members who are not performing satisfactorily. The existing cabinet lineup is the group from which the nominee will be chosen. At this point, the president has probably decided who his successor will be but gives no indication for another year, because as soon as the identity of his successor is known an incumbent becomes a "lame duck," and power begins to flow to the designated successor.

2. Twelve or 15 months before the election, the president may replace the party chairman to make sure the person in this role is competent, sympathetic to his choice of successor, and able to handle any discontent that may arise.

3. About a year before the election (in the 1988 succession, it took place in August

1987) the president gives the party chairman a list of "precandidates" from among whom a nominee will be picked. The party chairman releases this list to the press as representing the consensus of the party, and invites public discussion of the relative merits of each of the precandidates. This is largely a cosmetic exercise to give the impression of public consultation. It is possible, however, that a very strong adverse reaction or some especially derogatory information about the president's choice of successor might cause him to change his mind.

4. The actual candidate is unveiled (*destapado*) in October or November of the year preceding the election. The leader of one of the party's sectors announces that sector's choice; other sectors, party organizations, and individuals hasten to announce that the individual named is also their choice, and a general rush to get on the bandwagon occurs. Typically, the sector whose leader is picked by the president to make the announcement is the one likely to be unhappy with the choice, that is, which favored one of the other precandidates. Having that sector announce the choice first thus preempts the expression of any dissatisfaction. The last two presidents, Salinas and de la Madrid, were candidates particularly uncongenial to the labor sector, so labor was chosen to make the original announcement of support.

5. A party convention is held, which serves to ratify the choice already made by the president and to designate the presidential candidate officially.

6. The candidate then conducts a national campaign designed not so much to win votes as to familiarize the public with his name and features; to enable him (it has always been a "him") to make contact with local party leaders across the country, size them up, and learn of their concerns; and to create the impression, through extensive media coverage, that his assuming the presidency is inevitable and right.

7. The election takes place on a Sunday during the first week of July; the percentage of voters turning out is regarded as a significant indicator of support for the system.

8. After the election the president-elect assembles a new cabinet team. Prominent figures not included in the cabinet are given positions in the nationalized segment of the economy or in autonomous agencies, such as the social security institute, or are designated ambassadors.

9. The inauguration of the new president takes place on December 1.

The 1988 presidential elections presented particular problems. The government position was especially weak because of the difficult times the economy had been experiencing and the unpopularity of the austerity policy believed necessary to deal with the situation. The secession of Cuauhtémoc Cárdenas from the PRI and the move to support him of three center and center-left parties—PARM, PST, and PPS—that had hitherto always endorsed the PRI candidate created a difficult situation. However, the PAN was itself fielding a strong candidate in Manuel Clouthier, so the opposition forces were divided. Where an opposition force has succeeded in defeating a long-entrenched dominant party, it has been because that party does not occupy the center of the political spectrum; thus in the Philippines, for example, the incumbent, Ferdinand Marcos, was located politically on the right, so that the opposition could build a majority coalition out of the Center and the Left; unless—as in the defeat of Indira Gandhi in India—leftist and rightist oppositions are able to form an opportunistic coalition. But a divided opposition poses much less electoral threat.

In the event, the results announced gave Salinas 50.36 percent of the vote to 31.12 percent for Cuauhtémoc Cárdenas and 17.07 percent for Manuel Clouthier, the balance going to minor candidates. The fact that Salinas barely gained an absolute majority suggested strongly that the number had been "adjusted" after the fact, especially since pre-election opinion polls had suggested a weaker, though still possibly a plurality, performance for the PRI.

For the regime, then, the crisis continued in both its political and its economic aspects. Could the viability of the system be maintained in the face of such a powerful opposition? Could the Cárdenas forces be partly reabsorbed into the PRI and partly satisfied with legislative seats? Would letting the opposition win governorships appease them until the PRI could regain its strength, or would it encourage them to mount a total challenge to the system? Had the time finally come for the PRI to accept defeat in a presidential election?

The answers to these political questions would be determined in large part by how the economic questions were answered. Could the Salinas regime restore the nation's economic health, revive production, control inflation, create jobs? By the midpoint of Salinas's term, it appeared that that question had been answered in the affirmative. The runaway inflation of the de la Madrid years was ended, production revived, and flight capital began returning to the country. The national product started to grow again, and the president's pop-

ularity remained high. It seemed likely that the PRI had dodged the bullet and won itself a new lease on power. This impression was confirmed by the party's strong showing in the 1991 midterm congressional elections, which reflected both favorable popular opinion and the revival of the party's self-confidence, shaken by the economic downturn and the Cuauhtémoc Cárdenas campaign.

Key Terms

Partido de Acción Nacional (PAN)
Partido Revolucionario Democrático (PRD)
Co-optation
The "new class"
Chamber of Deputies
amparo
Ministry of Government (*Gobernación*)
Ministry of Programming and Budget
Constitution of 1917
municipio
Federal District
camarilla

C. Public Policy

AGRICULTURE AND LAND REFORM

Land reform policy has traditionally been regarded as the litmus test of the revolutionary character of Mexican governments. A government genuinely committed to alleviating the plight of the poorest Mexicans was one most wholeheartedly committed to land reform; conversely, a government that diminished the pace of reform, provided for limits, exceptions, or exemptions from the program, or placed maximum agricultural production ahead of social justice was a government that had betrayed revolutionary principles. Thus the government of Lázaro Cárdenas has been regarded as the most revolutionary for maximizing the rate of land distribution, and that of Miguel Alemán as the least revolutionary for promoting agribusiness rather than *ejido* communities. The leader of the early phase of the revolution who remains with most honor in Mexican history books is probably Emiliano Zapata, the agrarian leader from Morelos who never sold out, who never compromised, who never deviated from his goal of restoring land to those who worked it.

Nevertheless, the drafters of the Constitution and of the statutes of the PNR, the earliest incarnation of the present ruling party, seem to have intended a mixed policy for agriculture.

Such a policy would promote land reform for the benefit of Indian communities and poor landless subsistence farmers, but bearing in mind the consumption needs of city populations and the country's requirements for foreign exchange, it would at the same time promote efficient production for the market. Thus a modern commercial sector would exist alongside a subsistence sector. In the early days, when land was relatively plentiful, this kind of mixed policy presented no difficulties.

The laws governing land reform have been modified over the years, but the basic premise had until 1991 remained that if a single landowner held land above a specific size, then the surplus could be expropriated by the state. This land was then given to what may have been an actual village, but was more likely to be a fictitious community, the members of which had to be adults whose primary economic activity was farming but who did not own land. The community, real or fictitious, which then became the owner of the land was called the *ejido,* and its members were known as *ejidatarios.* The land was then divided up among the *ejidatarios,* who farmed it as though they owned it outright—since the Calles administration, the right to farm a specific plot can be inherited—except that until the Salinas reforms of 1991–1992 the land could not be sold or mortgaged. In the event that it was abandoned or even improperly farmed by the *ejidatario*, the plot reverted to the *ejido*, whose elected management committee might then assign it to someone else.

The rule that the land could not be sold or mortgaged guaranteed that the *ejidatario* could not lose the land, and avoided reconcentration. In a situation of absolute private ownership, the vagaries of agricultural production often mean, in third world countries, that over time land steadily passes into the ownership of banks, moneylenders, or simply more efficient farmers, thus creating a situation in which a small landed elite coexists with a great number of landless laborers. The purpose of land reform, then, is economic, because it ensures at least the means for subsistence to those engaged in agriculture; moral and social, in the sense that landless laborers previously wholly dependent on the goodwill of landowners for whom they worked would now be independent and able to make their own decisions; and political, because the peasants who had received land would become supporters of the government and agitation would not threaten government stability.

At present, almost 50 percent of the nation's land area planted in crops consists of *ejidos*, which enroll between 2 and 3 million members affiliated with the ruling party through their membership in the National Peasants' Federation, the *Confederación Nacional Campesina*. However, a greater number, probably over 4 million people, work in agriculture without owning land either privately or as members of *ejidos*.

In the early days, there seemed to be no contradiction between the goals of land reform and those of maximum economic production; Mexico was regarded as an underpopulated country with an unlimited supply of available land, adequate for all purposes. Population, however, has grown to the point where the supply of land available for distribution under the land reform program has been exhausted—especially in the areas of central Mexico that contain the bulk of the popula-

tion qualified and eager to receive land. New land has been brought into production by large irrigation projects, but primarily in the North of the country where desert land and usable water supplies have been available. This land made fertile by irrigation has been sold to larger-scale farmers able to invest in mechanization, who produce crops such as winter vegetables for export to the United States and thus provide the country with one of its major sources of foreign exchange.

In fact, wholesale violations of the land reform laws have occurred. Large properties have been exempted from expropriation by the simple device of subdividing them on paper, so that legally the situation is that of a series of properties owned by different individuals, perhaps members of the same family, each below the maximum amount allowed and thus safe from expropriation. Actually, all these properties are still owned by a single individual and continue to be farmed as a unit. Where land is expropriated, the law provides for compensation, but in fact compensation has been given only in a few cases in which the former owner has had good political connections; otherwise, claims for compensation gather dust in the files. Until recently the law provided that *ejidal* property could not be rented, but that provision was generally violated and has now been repealed.

Controversy has been continuous in Mexico over the merits of the *ejido* system. Those further to the right in the political spectrum, who support private property on principle, have argued that the *ejidos* should be broken up so that the plots are held as absolute private property by the members, thereby enabling them to raise money by mortgaging properties, giving them incentives to improve the land, and in general bringing the benefits of capitalism to that sector of agriculture. Some left-wing critics, on the other hand, have argued that the *ejidos* should not only be held collectively, but should also be farmed collectively by large-scale mechanized methods, like a Soviet *kolkhoz*. All across the political scale criticism have been made of how the *ejido* system works in practice, and *ejido* management committees are often guilty of abuse of power, extortion, and diversion of funds.

What merits do the various criticisms have? Arguments in favor of a Soviet-style collective farm management system seem ignorant of the actual drawbacks of Soviet collective farms; in the former Soviet Union collective farms are generally regarded as failures that need to be replaced by individual farming units, for reasons of both productivity and morale. Arguments that individual ownership would be more productive than *ejidos*, on the other hand, typically make comparisons that ignore differences of scale, of land quality, and amount of capitalization of private as opposed to *ejidal* farms. It does seem to be true, however, that when these factors are held constant, privately owned land units, even very small ones on land of similar poor quality to that of most *ejidos*, do have somewhat higher productivity.

Moreover, attempts by proagrarian governments to make capital available to *ejidatarios* have been unsuccessful. The difficulty is that *ejidatarios* have not been able to mortgage their land as security for payment of the loan, and the special banks set up to serve *ejidos* have the authority to write off a loan that is not repaid. The temptation is then very great for officials of such banks to loan the funds to their friends and relatives and take kickbacks when the loan is written off. There thus seems to be no foolproof way of trying to provide capital to the *ejidos*, even though there is no reason to expect that the bulk of such loans would not in fact be repaid if they could be made.

In November 1991, as part of his program of "modernizing" the economy, President Salinas announced that he would introduce legislation making it possible for *ejidatarios* to sell their plots of land. He had clearly accepted the argument that outright private ownership would be more productive despite the risk of negative political effects arising from any resulting tendency to reconcentration of land. Salinas's

speeches on the topic suggested that he believed the agrarian problem no longer had significant weight in Mexican politics, now that the country's urban population had passed 60 percent of the total and might reach 80 percent by the year 2000. Alleviating the plight of the poor now meant dealing with the problems of urban slums, not maintaining unproductive structures in the countryside.

To some extent, the government acts to maintain the level of food prices through a commodities purchasing program. After minimal processing, foodstuffs and other articles of prime necessity are retailed by the government through a network of stores and mobile outlets operated as CONASUPO, the National Commission on Popular Subsistence.

As Mexico's population has grown, so has demand for food products. And as the country has developed, its living standards have risen along with per capita food consumption. During the 1970s demand grew to exceed the supply of domestically grown food, and Mexico had to expend valuable foreign exchange on importing food. However, the Salinas administration raised the subsidized price of Mexico's staples, corn and beans, encouraging an increase in production to a level that met domestic demand and eliminated the need for imports. Moreover, the agricultural sector as a whole is a net producer of foreign exchange because of the high volume of exports, predominantly from irrigated private farm holdings in the North.

GENERAL ECONOMIC POLICY

Like most governments in the modern world, the Mexican government attempts to fix the general parameters of economic activity by fiscal and monetary means; it aims for sustained economic growth through planning and investment strategies; it attempts through welfare programs to mitigate the effect of inequality in income distribution; and it tries to maintain the autonomy of national decision-making processes by the regulation of foreign investment and international trade. Until the beginning of the 1970s, these objectives were achieved rather well. Except for a burst of inflation under Alemán, the peso remained fairly stable while, in one of the world's best economic performances, the economy grew fairly steadily at a high and sustained rate. Industry expanded on the basis of import substitution and production for the domestic market, protected by a system of tariffs and controls, while adequate amounts of foreign exchange were earned through agricultural exports and tourism. The rate of foreign investment, primarily from the United States, was high.

Although (with the exception of the crisis period during the 1980s) there were no restrictions on foreign exchange 'or on the repatriation of profits, there were controls on the types of activity in which foreigners could invest. Some industries were reserved for public enterprise, such as power generation, railroads, telephones and telegraphs, and petroleum. In 1982 banking was added to the list of industries from which foreign capital was excluded.

In addition, the general rule applied that individual firms had to have majority Mexican ownership; that is, foreign participation was limited to 49 percent of ownership in most economic areas, and 34 percent in areas thought to be politically sensitive, such as mining. In practice, there was a great deal of administrative discretion in how the rule was applied, and there were ways of evading its intent, if not its letter. As part of Echeverría's more nationalist and socialist program, legislation was passed regulating the payments that could be made to foreign entities for imported technology and the use of brand names, and limiting patent rights. Although this legislation caused grumbling on the part of foreign businessmen, who regarded it simply as providing a framework for the extortion of bribes, it by no means prevented them from doing business in Mexico.

One of the areas of investment that has particularly flourished is that of the so-called *maquiladoras*, the assembly plants built in a special customs zone along the border with the United States, in which materials can be imported free of duty if the finished product is then reexported. Essentially, this is a method of exporting Mexican labor without its having to cross national borders, and has attracted European and Japanese investment as well as American. The decision of the Salinas administration to seek a "free trade area" with the United States promised to extend this system to all of Mexico.

Even during the years of rapid growth, however, the number of jobs in the modern sector has never kept up with population growth and migration to the cities; and Mexico has long faced the problems of unemployment and disguised unemployment—that is, the proliferation of self-created forms of economic activity such as guarding parked cars, shining shoes, and selling lottery tickets—so characteristic of third world countries, which produce very small incomes and add nothing to the nation's production.

Even before the boom and bust in petroleum that began in the middle 1970s, it was becoming clear that there were serious limitations to the country's strategy of development based on import substitution. Apart from the irrationalities, inefficiency, and excessive costs that such a policy entails, employment was not expanding fast enough to cope with the number of new job seekers each year, let alone absorb the backlog of unemployed.[9] The López Portillo administration tried to expand Mexico's exports by placing more emphasis on agriculture and the processing of Mexico's own raw materials, as well as promoting manufactured exports. This meant removing tariff protection and subsidies to internationalize Mexican manufacturing, a change of orientation which made it possible under de la Madrid for Mexico to join the General Agreement on Tariffs and Trade, the international association of states promoting greater international trade by eliminating tariff barriers. Mexico had previously resisted U.S. pressure to join GATT.

With the oil boom, however, many of these policy problems were overtaken by events. The very rapid increase of petroleum production and export multiplied many times over the foreign exchange available, and thus led to an overvaluation of the peso. This made Mexican goods too expensive to export and foreign goods very cheap to import, which in turn led to a decline in Mexican manufacturing because everything the country needed could be imported more cheaply. Wealthy Mexicans took advantage of the relative cheapness of the dollar to buy property in the United States and build up dollar bank accounts. The size of the national government bureaucracy, and official corruption, increased greatly. When petroleum prices dropped later in López Portillo's term, the president gambled that the decline was only temporary and continued the same high levels of government spending with borrowed money. More capital left Mexico as it became clear to everyone except the president that a devaluation of the peso would have to come. Subsequent governments had very little freedom in managing the economy once the decision not to repudiate the foreign debt had been made.

FOREIGN DEBT AND INCOME DISTRIBUTION

Attempts are continuously under way to renegotiate and refinance the foreign debt—to reduce interest rates, stretch out payment periods, and discount the outstanding debt itself—because Mexican governments have felt that in order to maintain the credit necessary for continued international trade, it is not possible to contemplate repudiating the debt altogether. Given orthodox economic assumptions, this has meant a policy of deflation, reduction in rates of economic activity, cutbacks in government spending, wage freezes, and the channeling of any surplus to foreign debt payment—a policy, in effect, of redistributing the income of poor and middle-class Mexicans to foreign bankers. One of the planks in the 1988 election platform of Cuauhtémoc Cárdenas was repudiation of the foreign debt.

Mexico has not always followed policies of this type. The capitalist system, however, has a tendency to distribute income increasingly in the form of returns on capital—that is, as rent, profits, dividends, and interest—rather than in the form of wages and salaries. In other words, left to itself, the tendency of the capitalist system is to make the rich richer. To moderate this tendency efforts can be made by labor unions in the form of wage demands, or by government through a variety of tax and welfare measures that redistribute income from the more to the less affluent members of society. Some programs of this character are permanent features of policy in Mexico, such as the system of distributing basic goods through government retail outlets, and probably all Mexican administrations take some redistributive measures. Some governments, however, have been especially notable for this "left-wing" character of their policies—that of Cárdenas, of course, and those of López Mateos and Echeverría. Among other measures, the government of López Mateos introduced legislation providing for companies over a certain size to distribute a percentage of their profits to their employees.

Given the parameters of the world economic system, however, it is extremely difficult to pursue left-wing policies successfully. Capital can go on strike just as much as labor, as the history of the López Mateos and Echeverría administrations shows. Within a week of the inaugural speech of López Mateos, in which he identified his government as on the left, $250 million in funds were transferred out of the country. Echeverría achieved the same results in more contradictory form. Attempting to reduce Mexico's foreign debt, he made anticapitalist remarks that resulted in capital flight and forced him, paradoxically, to borrow more money abroad.

In fact, the course of economic development in Mexico had left the country with a very unequal distribution of wealth and income even before the economic crisis of the early

1980s. Generally, it could be said that the long period of stable economic growth created a small, comfortably well-off urban middle class, who benefited disproportionately, and a small super-rich elite; urban workers also benefited, but much less. Workers in agriculture and the "marginal" unemployed and underemployed people in the cities benefited little, if at all. The economic crisis of the 1980s hit particularly hard at those social elements least able to afford it, wiping out 10 to 20 years of moderate economic improvement.

THE SALINAS ECONOMIC POLICIES

The de la Madrid administration then embarked on an austerity program in the attempt to eliminate inflation, bring foreign trade back into balance, and make payments on the foreign debt. But the situation did not improve appreciably, and even more severe measures were applied toward the end of de la Madrid's term, which helped to contribute to the collapse of the Mexican stock market in October 1987. When Carlos Salinas became president he continued the line of policy he had begun as planning minister under de la Madrid. His objectives were to reduce the debt by negotiation and creative financing; and to bring inflation under control and revive production by a combination of free-market economics and agreements with major economic sectors. The economic pacts signed with business and labor representatives committed them not to exceed specified limits in price and wage increases. In addition, the president began the "National Solidarity Program" to involve state and local governments and organizations in making social welfare expenditures that would minimize the harsher effects of the crisis and the stabilization programs.

The main thrust of Salinas's neoliberal economic policies was to restore as much of a free market as possible to the economy. This approach was in line with the ideology and rhetoric, if not always the practice, of the Reagan and Thatcher administrations. It involved the following shifts in policy:

1. A great deal of government regulation, controls, licensing, and tariffs were abolished.
2. Many activities traditionally carried on by government were transferred to the private sector. This included the privatization of a substantial sector of the banking system, which had been nationalized during the last days of the administration of López Portillo.
3. A rigorous, and ultimately successful, effort was made to reduce inflation to a tolerable level of 25 percent per annum or less, especially by cutting the public sector deficit.
4. An attempt was made to open up the Mexican economy to the outside world by stepping up exports, ending controls on imports, and eliminating the obstacles to foreign investment. This liberation of trade reached the point of Salinas's supporting a North American free trade area, under which American, Mexican, and Canadian goods and capital would circulate freely in all three countries. The United States had long pressured Mexico to move in this direction; ironically now that Mexico had made a U-turn in economic policy and was prepared to open up its economy, opposition to a North American free trade area was stronger in the United States than in Mexico (see Feature 10.3).

This reversal of traditional Mexican economic policies by the Salinas administration entailed the abandonment of many revolutionary policies that had seemed sacred: state ownership of basic industry; insistence that foreign capital come into the country only with majority Mexican partnership; and controls that restricted certain lines of economic activity to Mexican nationals. As was to be expected, the

---

Feature 10.3 A North American Free Trade Area?

Traditionally, Mexico's economic development was based on protection and import substitution. After the economic downturn of the 1980s, drastic remedies were clearly needed. The international climate favored free-market ideas, and Mexico elected a president who believed in the promotion of free trade and close relations with the United States. As a result, a free trade area embracing Mexico, the United States, and Canada became a realistic possibility. Two principal arguments were made in the U.S. Congress by those opposing such an agreement, however. One was that particularly polluting industries would relocate in Mexico to avoid United States environmental legislation. To counter that argument, Mexican authorities undertook to bring their environmental legislation into line with that of the United States, and have indeed largely done so. Enforcement of the legislation needs to be tightened, however.

The second argument is that a free trade agreement would result in the loss of jobs in the United States. While this is certainly true, it is a necessary consequence of the working of a free-market economy. The whole nature of the capitalist system is to continuously replace labor with capital — that is, to introduce labor-saving machinery; moreover, a competitive market situation requires a continuous process of adjustment, one aspect of which is the loss of jobs by less efficient producers. A dynamic and growing economy, such as would be created by a free trade system, however, creates more jobs than it destroys, while it contributes to the development of the poorer regions within the system and lowers prices to consumers. American business, after all, is always trying to produce at lower cost, including lower wage costs. Under free North American trade, some American businesses will move to Mexico. Without the new system, they would move anyway, to Thailand or Malaysia or China. Meanwhile, American consumers need lower prices, and Mexico needs all the jobs it can get.

PAN welcomed the president's new policy direction. But even the leftist PRD withdrew its initial opposition to the North American common market, insisting only that the rights of Mexican labor be protected in any such arrangement. The economic crisis had been so severe that people generally welcomed any change of policy that held out hope of an improved situation.

The president's policies did indeed seem to be effective. Inflation was brought down, capital returned to the country, and Mexico's exports began to climb. At the midpoint of Salinas's term, two-thirds of respondents to a public opinion poll answered that they had a favorable attitude to his government.

THE MEXICAN OIL INDUSTRY

Petroleum is a particularly sensitive subject in Mexico. The expropriation of foreign oil companies by Lázaro Cárdenas was a great symbolic act of national self-assertion, and the national oil company became a special object of patriotic pride. In fact, the symbolism goes back further than that; one of the policies of Porfirio Díaz that earned his government the charge that it was *entreguista* — that is, that it had sold out to foreigners — was allowing foreign companies to own subsurface minerals, contravening the traditional Hispanic doctrine that ownership of land meant only ownership of the surface, while rights to the products of the subsoil remained with the sovereign. It was thus the traditional Hispanic law on this point, abrogated by Díaz, that was restored by the Constitution of 1917. In fact, under Díaz the oil companies operating in Mexico, like other mineral companies, were predominantly British; with the Revolution, favoritism to British companies ended, and American companies maneuvered themselves into a leading position.

The oil business has some characteristics that make it distinctive. The exploration phase requires large expenditures, which may all be lost if no oil is found. The production phase requires minimal expenditures but produces colossal revenues. Government concession to an oil company of a specific territory to operate in is necessary, but in the absence of competitive bidding for blocks of territory the award to one company or another is arbitrary. Once production has started, the revenues that are rolling in are a tempting target for government; the immobility of the production facilities means that the company is in effect a hostage to government demands.

The combination of these factors meant that oilmen in the early years were strong-willed, adventurer types who became hugely wealthy if successful. Their absolute dependence on essentially arbitrary government favor inevitably meant that they would try to reduce their risks through bribery, in one form or another, which meant that some politician would gain wealth for himself or his cause at the cost of the country's foregoing much larger amounts of wealth. It could hardly have been coincidental that the son of Porfirio Díaz served as a member of the board of directors of the major British oil company in Mexico, or that the U.S. Standard Oil Company contributed funds to the Madero revolution, after which the lawyer who represented Standard's interests in Mexico became Madero's attorney general. With one or two exceptions, the oil barons were too arrogant and cynical to know how to deal with a sincere revolutionary like Cárdenas, and their expropriation in 1938

owes much to their mishandling of relations with him. Their previous difficulties with a revolutionary government, that of Calles, had been satisfactorily resolved, presumably by the usual methods.

After the expropriation, the companies organized an international boycott of the purchase of Mexican oil, so that the state corporation limited its role to supplying the domestic market from established producing wells. The world's growing need for petroleum was met from production in the Middle East, Venezuela, Romania, and the United States. With no competition, and with established sources of production in a guaranteed and growing domestic market, PEMEX became mismanaged, wasteful, and vastly corrupt. During the 1960s, PEMEX had three or four times as many employees, in terms of the size of its operations, as comparable companies. Corporation executives took kickbacks from suppliers, sometimes on quite unnecessary purchases; union leaders took kickbacks from the wages of people hired through their influence; both executives and union officials were actually part owners of favored supplying firms.

Until the early 1970s, domestic oil prices were deliberately kept low to encourage the development of the economy, even lower than retail prices in other countries, based as they then were on a wholesale price of $3 or $4 a barrel. In the early 1970s OPEC, the Organization of Petroleum Exporting Countries, was able to get its act together to limit oil supply and thus force world prices up—with the implicit prior approval of the U.S. Secretary of State at the time, Henry Kissinger, in a typical example of that myopic "statesmanship" that inexplicably never deflated Kissinger's overblown reputation. Kissinger apparently believed that this would enable the Shah of Iran, a U.S. protégé, to buy vast numbers of weapons that would make him a bulwark of anti-Communist stability in the Middle East.

The rise in oil prices, which eventually approached $40 a barrel before dropping back to under $10—at the time of writing, they fluctuated around $20—made it worthwhile for Mexico to incur the considerable expense involved in exploration. These efforts were fabulously successful, as they could hardly fail to be: it transpired that as much as 70 percent of the entire territory of Mexico consists of the sedimentary basins in which hydrocarbon deposits are found. Exploration of less than 10 percent of the national territory showed that Mexico had the potential to become a producer on the scale of Saudi Arabia.

OIL POLICY

Because of the sensitive character of petroleum from the point of view of national pride, various policies have been adopted to make sure that Mexico's oil remains in Mexican hands. PEMEX has developed the technical capabilities to handle most phases of the industry, except for some specialized tasks involved in offshore drilling. On occasion, PEMEX has even given technical assistance to foreign state oil corporations. Prior to the Salinas administration, the law provided that all oil exploration and development on Mexican national territory was the responsibility of PEMEX; offshore drilling had to be conducted by Mexican companies. In fact, however, the so-called Mexican companies involved in offshore drilling were actually mere legal and financial shells for what were, in their technical aspects, essentially foreign operations. This arrangement provided lucrative possibilities for some Mexicans who served as "fronts" and provided legal cover—many of them, curiously enough, relatives and associates of PEMEX executives. In keeping with its general economic policy line, the Salinas administration began to change the rules so as to allow some development activity by foreign oil companies.

Logically, Mexican oil that is exported should find its principal market in the United States, which it can reach by pipeline. However, in defense of national autonomy, Mexican policy makers have been concerned to limit the dependence of the United States on Mexican oil supplies, fearing that such dependence would give the United States a major reason for interfering in Mexican affairs and even, in the event of an interruption of supply, for occupying the oilfields. Accordingly, policies were adopted under López Portillo to limit "any country" to no more than 50 percent of Mexico's oil exports, which should constitute no more than 20 percent of that country's oil imports. Given fluctuating conditions of supply and demand in the world market, it has not been possible to keep consistently within these guidelines. Mexico has diversified its export markets fairly successfully, however, with purchasers in Japan, Western and Eastern Europe, and the Caribbean region.

There have been two general perspectives on oil policy in Mexico. The more procapitalist view is that oil is a commodity like any other. So long as profit is to be made, Mexico should supply as much of the market as possible and maximize revenues, which will contribute to the development of the country. This view was represented especially by the head of PEMEX during the López Portillo years, Jorge Díaz Serrano. The more pro-Socialist line, whose most prominent exponent has been the leader of the Mexican Workers' party (PMT), Heberto Castillo, is that Mexico should restrict its exports of petroleum. It should instead conserve the fuel for future generations, use it domestically to develop industry, and use it principally not as fuel but as raw material for a Mexican petrochemical industry.

There are problems with both arguments. As the López Portillo years demonstrated, a high rate of production and export leads to excessive dependence on a single product and the overvaluation of the national currency unit, which results in increased importation of goods and the dwindling of national industry. The more Socialist position may overestimate world demand for petrochemicals, and ignores the possibility that foregoing current sales in the interest of conservation will seem foolish if the development of alternative cheaper power sources, perhaps nuclear fusion, eventually makes petroleum uncompetitive.

The more nationalist and Socialist view gained ground within de la Madrid's government in the wake of the discrediting of López Portillo, and Díaz Serrano was actually indicted and later convicted on corruption charges. The country's weakened financial state, however, made it impossible to follow a Socialist and nationalist position that would limit the country's foreign earnings, so long as the decision was maintained to pay off the outstanding foreign debt. As in other areas of the country's economic policy, Socialist and nationalist sentiments were overridden by the exigencies of the world capitalist economic system, and were finally abandoned altogether in the Salinas years.

FOREIGN POLICY

In its foreign policy, Mexico finds itself in a difficult and delicate position. Placed by fate next to the strongest country on earth, its economic well-being is heavily dependent on its relations with the United States. Yet because of its unhappy history, and because of the revolutionary principles that its government claims to represent, Mexico even more than other countries must assert its independence from its powerful northern neighbor. Approximately two-thirds of Mexico's exports go to the United States, and almost two-thirds of its imports come from the United States. Moreover, apart from oil, Mexico's largest foreign-exchange earner, by far, is tourism and border transactions, which are extremely sensitive to the quality of relations with the United States. Yet the United States is the country, let us remember, that has repeatedly intervened in Mexican affairs; its representative conspired in the overthrow of Francisco Madero; it waged aggressive war against Mexico, and annexed half of Mexico's national territory.

Mexican governments thus find themselves under the dual necessity of maintaining good relations with the United States while making clear the distinctiveness of their values and objectives in foreign policy, and maintaining their independence of action. These contradictory elements form yet another of the three great ambiguities that characterize Mexican politics. We have seen that (1) from some angles of vision Mexico is a democracy, but from others it has an authoritarian regime; (2) its economic policies can seem both capitalist and Socialist; and (3) in foreign policy matters, Mexico seems sometimes to be standing out against United States policies, proudly defending its autonomy and its revolutionary principles, whereas at others it seems to be meekly falling in line with U.S. dictates. Which tendency appears strongest depends partly on the relative strength of the two governments. When Mexico felt economically strong during the oil boom, López Portillo staked out a policy clearly opposed to that of the United States with respect to Central America; in the waning days of the Reagan administration, de la Madrid also made his opposition to U.S. policies clear. But between those times, when Reagan was at his peak and the Mexican economy at its weakest, Mexican governments kept a low profile in Central American policy. Nevertheless, given Mexico's economic dependence on the United States, it is surprising how independent of American wishes Mexican foreign policy has been. Mexico refused to sign the "Declaration of Caracas," pushed through the Organization of American States (OAS) by U.S. pressure, which provided the ideological basis for the U.S.-backed exile invasion that helped to overthrow the leftist government of Guatemala in 1954. Mexico also refused to go along with the other members of the OAS in breaking relations with Cuba, and declined to support the sending of an "Inter-American peace force" into the Dominican Republic in 1965. Mexico also resisted pressure from the Reagan administration to join in its crusade against the Sandinista government of Nicaragua, which resembled early postrevolutionary Mexican governments in many respects. It joined with other Latin American countries in trying to bring peace to Nicaragua and also to El Salvador, where the United States supported the conservative government side in a long, drawn-out civil war that neither side seemed capable of winning.

U.S. administrations have usually shown understanding for the Mexican government's need to demonstrate autonomy from the United States, and have not gone to the most extreme lengths to secure Mexican adherence to purely symbolic measures, such as votes in OAS meetings. When U.S. governments have felt very strongly about specific questions, however, they have usually been able to secure Mexican compliance. For example, at one point President Nixon secured Mexican cooperation with U.S. drug policies by ordering a tightening of customs inspections at the border which, in effect, brought border traffic to a standstill and forced a change in Mexican policy. For a long time, Mexico held out against U.S. pressure to join the tariff-cutting GATT, but the weak government of de la Madrid, which was in any case less opposed ideologically to GATT than previous governments of Mexico, finally agreed to join the organization.

In general, Mexican governments handle the conflicting requirements of national autonomy and pressure from the United States by resorting to the same calculated policies of deliberate ambiguity that they apply to domestic policy areas. Thus the Mexicans refused to break diplomatic relations with Cuba, but their secret services cooperated with the CIA in keeping track of travelers to and from Cuba through Mexico. Conversely, Mexico has respected U.S. wishes that it not join OPEC, the Organization of Petroleum Exporting Countries, but it has followed OPEC policies with respect to pricing without being a member.

There are a series of problems in Mexican-U.S. relations that grow out of the common border. Indeed, for some time the demarcation of the border was itself in doubt after the Rio Grande changed course. A final solution to that problem was reached during the late 1960s. The two countries have various cooperative mechanisms for attempting to solve other border problems, some of which have proved capable of solution, while others are perennial sources of difficulty. Some principal problems in recent years have been the division of the waters of the Colorado River, which both countries share; problems connected with Mexican migration to the United States; air pollution by industries on one side of the border which drifts across into the other country; the negative impact of U.S. food regulations on imports of vegetables from Mexico; the allocation of airline routes between the airlines of the two countries; fishing problems; and drug trafficking. From time to time, the U.S. government and U.S. public opinion fix on one of these issues and blow it up into a "crisis." For several of these issues, such as illegal immigration and drug trafficking, no satisfactory permanent solution appears possible, although intelligent joint management of policy may reduce the damage the situations create.

It is true that the long border, which is after all, as President López Portillo once said, the border between the first world and the third world, should give rise to a range of problems. It also gives rise to benefits and opportunities for both countries. The volume of tourism and retail sales to nationals of the other country is considerable on both sides; it constitutes a significant item in Mexico's balance of payments, about 25 percent of Mexico's total foreign income in an average year. At the same time, Mexicans contribute about one-fourth of all the income the United States derives from tourism. Mexican immigrants, legal or not, contribute their labor to the U.S. economy, and pay taxes greater than the value of public services they receive. At the same time, the money they bring back to Mexico from jobs in the United States is a significant source of capital for the founding of small businesses. In recent years, a significant and growing part of the Mexican economy has been the in-bond assembly plants, or *maquiladoras,* located in the border region.

CONCLUSION

Mexico has had one of the most stable political systems in the world. The constitutional succession has been unbroken since 1934; each president has served the full term for which he was elected and yielded his office to an elected successor. There are no more than a handful of other countries in the world about which a similar statement can be made. And yet this is a country that has been in a state of continual change. Mexico's population has increased enormously; it has gone from a predominantly rural to a predominantly urban society; a vast land reform program has been carried out; illiteracy has decreased almost to the vanishing point; the role of the military in politics has shrunk dramatically; and the role of opposition parties has grown.

Prediction in the social sciences increases in accuracy the fewer the number of variables in play and the more their effect can be fully grasped and measured. A great many factors will influence the future political evolution of Mexico; their interactions cannot be foreseen, nor their impact precisely assessed. The key question about Mexico's political future is the extent to which the ruling party can retain a dominant role and the extent to which changing circumstances will cause it to yield power, perhaps even the ultimate power of the presidency itself.

At this time one cannot say with certainty which of the alternative scenarios will come to pass—whether the opposition will grow to surpass its 1988 performance, attracting dissident elements from the PRI until its eventual victory can no longer be denied; or whether 1988 represents a high water mark from which the opposition tide will recede as the economy recovers, as Cuauhtémoc Cárdenas, the strongest opposition figure, passes from the scene, and as PRI tactics become more resourceful and effective. To be sure, a sincere reformer and democrat may emerge in the PRI leadership who ends the PRI monopoly of power. But any attempt to do so would face powerful resistance from forces within the ruling party that are prepared to move to a more authoritarian and repressive system rather than yield power.

Predictions are based on the experience of the past, and therefore tend to underestimate the likelihood of novel outcomes. But based on that experience—which shows the resilience and resourcefulness of the PRI's political managers, the party's capacity to co-opt dissidents, and its powerful will to remain in power—it would be rash to predict anything other than that Mexico will retain its distinctive dominant single-party regime for the foreseeable future.

Key Terms

ejido
maquiladora
CONASUPO
Organization of American States (OAS)
Disguised unemployment
General Agreement on Tariffs and Trade (GATT)

Suggestions for Further Reading

Brand, Donald D. *Mexico: Land of Sunshine and Shadow* (Princeton: Van Nostrand, 1966).

Cline, Howard F. *The United States and Mexico* (Cambridge: Harvard University Press, 1953).

Gentleman, Judith. *Mexican Politics in Transition* (Boulder: Westview Press, 1987).

Hansen, Roger D. *The Politics of Mexican Development* (Baltimore: Johns Hopkins University Press, 1971).

Hellman, Judith Adler. *Mexico in Crisis*, 2nd ed. (New York: Holmes and Meier, 1988).

Levy, Daniel, and Gabriel Székely. *Mexico: Paradoxes of Stability and Change*, 2nd ed. (Boulder: Westview Press, 1987).

Needler, Martin C. *Mexican Politics: the Containment of Conflict*, 2nd ed. (New York: Praeger, 1990).

Needler, Martin C. *Politics and Society in Mexico* (Albuquerque: University of New Mexico Press, 1971).

Paz, Octavio. *The Labyrinth of Solitude,* translated by Lysander Kemp (New York: Grove Press, 1961).

Paz, Octavio. *The Other Mexico: Critique of the Pyramid,* translated by Lysander Kemp (New York: Grove Press, 1972).

A. Notes

1. Jorge Carrión, *Mito y magia del mexicano* (México, D.F.: Porrúa Obregón, 1952), p. 7.
2. Texas (and, for a few days, California) had a period of existence as an independent republic before joining the United States. Mexico had been willing to tolerate the secession of Texas as an independent republic, but its refusal to accept the annexation of Texas to the United States was one of the causes of the war.
3. Obregón to Frank Bohn, 12 February 1924.
4. This was subsequently reamended so that anyone who has served as president can never be elected again.

B. Notes

5. According to a poll reported by the Los Angeles Times on 20 August 1989, 68 percent of Mexican respondents believed that Salinas had not actually won the election.
6. Milovan Djilas, *The New Class,* New York: Harcourt, Brace, 1957.
7. A good discussion of the organization can be found in Luis Felipe Bravo Mena, "COPARMEX and Mexican Politics," in Sylvia Maxfield and Ricardo Anzaldúa Montoya, *Government and Private Sector in Contemporary Mexico,* Center for U.S.-Mexican Studies, University of California, San Diego, 1987.

C. Notes

8. The PST became so enthusiastic, or opportunistic, that it changed its name from Socialist Workers' Party to "Party of the Cardenista Front for National Reconstruction."
9. Only one-third of those entering the labor force each year find regular jobs in the "formal" sector of the economy, according to the *New York Times* of 25 July 1989.

CHAPTER 11

The Government of Nigeria

Stephen Wright

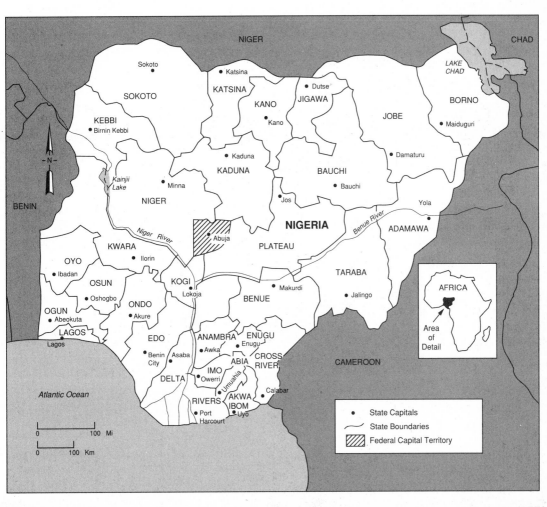

A. Political Development

Nigeria is Africa's most populous country, and also one of its most unpredictable. Since its independence from British colonial rule on 1 October 1960, Nigeria has struggled to survive through numerous political crises, including a bitter civil war between 1967 and 1970. The country has been ruled by military governments for all but four years since 1966 (see Table 11.1). Three heads of state have been assassinated in office, and the country has witnessed six coups d'etat. With such instability and rapid change, the development of the country's political process and institutions has been seriously affected; hence, the continuity and "rhythm" of government found in more developed countries is not present.

Nigeria's experience, however, is typical within an African context. Most countries on the continent face severe economic and political challenges, and many remain ruled by military regimes despite the burst of democratization in Africa over the last three years.[1] Such instability is a product of many factors, for which Nigerians are only partially responsible. Instability also has the positive aspect of allowing Nigeria to experiment with different styles of government to find one suited to its needs.

Despite the problems of governing and the prevalence of military regimes, Nigeria has remained one of the more open African societies, where press freedom and civil liberties have generally been respected, though not always maintained. Nigerians perceive their country to be both a leader and a model to other African states. The country's apparent economic strength, derived primarily from oil revenues, has at times given Nigeria leverage over neighboring states, and so its political and developmental programs are often mirrored in other countries of the continent.

Political intrigue has prevented an accurate census from being taken since independence (see Table 11.2), although the military government scheduled one to be concluded in 1992. Estimates of the population suggest a figure of 115 million in 1991, with a steep rise to 162 million expected by the year 2000, and an even steeper rise to 501 million predicted by 2030.

Electoral registers have always been inflated to promote illicit regional gains, and a recent register drawn up in 1987 had 72 million electors; using this number the country's population is suggested to be 150 million, a figure disbelieved by everyone, including the government itself. A register used for the 1990 local government elections contained only 56 million names, but a new register drawn up in late 1991 contained almost 65 million names. Whatever the precise figure, Nigeria accounts for approximately 20 percent of Africa's total

Table 11.1   NIGERIAN GOVERNMENTS, 1960-1991

Period	Head of state	Ethnicity	Type of government	How ended
1960-1966	Tafawa Balewa	Hausa-Fulani	Civilian	Attempted coup/ assassination
1966	Ironsi	Ibo	Military	Coup/assassination
1966-1975	Gowon	Middle Belt	Military	Coup
1975-1976	Muhammed	Hausa-Fulani	Military	Attempted coup/ assassination
1976-1979	Obasanjo	Yoruba	Military	Elections
1979-1983	Shagari	Hausa-Fulani	Civilian	Coup
1984-1985	Buhari	Hausa-Fulani	Military	Coup
1985-	Babangida	Middle Belt	Military	

population of 600 million, even though it is only one of some 50 states on the continent.

The political problems already mentioned reflect the strong undercurrent of diversity and division within contemporary Nigeria. The country is comprised of about 250 ethnic and linguistic groups, but the three largest groups have predominated: the Hausa-Fulani in the North, the Yoruba in the West (though geographically this is the southwest of the country), and the Ibo in the East (geographically the southeast). Much of Nigeria's independent life has been dominated by the mutual suspicions and cut-and-thrust politics between (and sometimes within) these groups, who account for some 60 to 65 percent of the total population. The smaller groups, including the Nupe and Tiv clustered in the country's "Middle Belt" region as well as the Edo, Ijaw, and Kanuri, have increasingly striven to resist the domination of the larger groups and exert influence upon the shape of political life.

This complex picture of sociocultural cleavages and diversity is compounded by crucial religious differences within the country. While actual figures are again a source of controversy, most observers agree that the country can be divided roughly equally: the North is predominantly Muslim, and the South is predominantly Christian (although a number of traditional religions have also survived).

The historical reasons for this division will be discussed later, but these religious differences, superimposed upon ethnic cleavages, have provided a most difficult issue for the Nigerian state to resolve.

Again, it is important to point out that these ethnic tensions are not wholly a Nigerian creation or responsibility, as British colonial administrators deliberately sought to divide these various groups and mobilize them against each other. Moreover, the British model of parliamentary government inherited by Nigerians at independence soon proved to be a poor framework for local political conditions, and only served to heighten competition and rivalry. Climatic, linguistic, and cultural differences were also responsible for sowing the seeds of discord that have weakened the country. Nigeria, then, developed not with any real internal logic, but as a "conglomerate" of rival ethnic and religious groups.

Unlike the British and American political systems, which have evolved gradually, the Nigerian system has been forced to make several significant readjustments in an attempt to resolve the internal tensions and create a style and structure of government suitable for its needs. To some extent, Nigeria provides a case study to fulfill a political scientist's dream (or nightmare) because several distinct types of political structure have been utilized within

Table 11.2　THE NIGERIAN POPULATION:
CENSUS RESULTS, 1952–1973
(IN MILLIONS)

	1952–1953	1963	1973[a]
Lagos	0.50	1.44	2.47
Western	4.36	9.49	8.92
Midwestern	1.49	2.54	3.24
Rivers	0.75	1.54	2.23
East-Central	4.57	7.23	8.06
Southeastern	1.90	3.62	3.46
Benue-Plateau	2.30	4.01	5.17
Kwara	1.19	2.40	4.64
Northwestern	3.40	5.73	8.50
North-Central	2.35	4.10	6.79
Kano	3.40	5.77	10.90
Northeastern	4.20	7.79	15.38
Total	30.41	55.66	79.76

[a]The 1973 results were canceled by the incoming Murtala government in 1975 because of allegations of massive corruption. None of the successive governments since 1973 undertook the politically hazardous task of a census, until the Babangida administration attempted one in 1991–1992.

Source: Adapted from Anthony Kirk-Greene and Douglas Rimmer, *Nigeria since 1970. A Political and Economic Outline* (London: Hodder and Stoughton, 1981).

its borders since independence. The First Republic (1960–1966) operated on a parliamentary system modeled after Britain's, whereas the Second Republic (1979–1983) adopted an American-style presidential constitution, complete with Senate and House of Representatives. Military regimes have also varied considerably, from the crude, somewhat politically unaware rule of Gen. J. Aguiyi-Ironsi (1966) to the benign, developmental approach of Yakubu Gowon (1966–1975), and from the crusading ideological mood of Murtala Muhammed (1975–1976) to the harsh, repressive regime of Muhammadu Buhari (1984–1985). The other military heads of state, Olusegun Obasanjo (1976–1979) and Ibrahim Babangida (1985–1992), have been more "moderate" in policy style.

If the Nigerian panorama already appears to be complex, then it is further complicated by two fundamental factors. First, although the country is federal in structure, there has been a constant political struggle between federal and state centers. At independence, the three regional governments (North, West, and East) were powerful enough to disrupt the effectiveness of the federal government, contributing to the downfall of the First Republic in 1966. Sociopolitical cleavages and political necessity forced a devolution of regional power to four regions in 1964, then to 12 states in 1967, 19 states in 1976, 21 states in 1987, and 30 states in 1991.

Second, the influence of the federal government over the states has been dramatically increased by its control of the country's oil wealth. During the 1970s Nigerian oil production rapidly increased, making the country the sixth largest producer in the world and Africa's preeminent member of the Organization of Petroleum Exporting Countries (OPEC). At the end of the decade, Nigeria was the wealthiest country in sub-Saharan Africa, with a strong voice on the world stage, but the subsequent oil glut, economic depression, and failure to diversify in the 1980s caused serious political and economic problems for the country. In addition, this oil wealth was seized upon by military and civilian leaders, and greed and corruption were predominant features of Nigerian political life. The military planned to transfer control of the national government back to civilians in January 1993, and in an attempt to create a new political culture it banned most civilian and military officeholders since 1960 from standing for election. This sudden, shock approach is not untypical of Nigerian politics, but many are hopeful that, unlike other attempts, this will be successful.

HISTORICAL INFLUENCES ON POLITICAL DEVELOPMENT

Nigeria in its contemporary geographical form was created only in the early part of the twentieth century, following the amalgamation of northern and southern colonial provinces for the convenience of British colonial administrators. The name "Nigeria" was in fact coined in Britain in 1897 in a letter to *The Times* of London; it was not decided upon by indigenes of the "new" country. The earlier historical development in western Africa concerns empires and competing kingdoms or principalities that no longer exist today, but whose former territories now comprise Nigeria as well as neighboring states such as Cameroon, Niger, and Benin. These kingdoms traded and competed with each other for many centuries prior to European colonization; they had reached advanced stages of technical, political, and cultural development—achievements overlooked in the arrogance and plunder of the colonial powers. The Benin empire, to take one case, was a classic example of a society developing from the twelfth century; its internal political system had pattern, legitimacy, and stability, while its bronze statues and sculptures are still widely recognized for their high artistic merit. The Oyo empire, which dates from the thirteenth century, has a similarly strong cultural history.

Cultural differences between these kingdoms were reinforced by geographical factors. In the southern areas, the tropical rain forest influenced the style of farming and living patterns and led to the development of what has been described as a "gun" society, a feature common after 1600 with the expansion of the slave trade in these areas. In the North, in contrast, the drier, open savanna lands led to the development of a "horse" society; the global slave system made less inroads here.[2]

For the last thousand years, Islam has influenced the northern savanna lands as trade by camel across the Sahara desert, to and from the Middle East and North Africa, made these people look inward toward the desert, in contrast to the southern kingdoms which looked outward toward the Atlantic Ocean. Islam has a much longer presence in Nigeria than has Christianity, and its influence in the North was reinforced and expanded in the early nineteenth century by the radical zeal of Usman Dan Fodio. Christianity first appeared with the Portuguese influence and missionaries along the coast some 300 or so years ago. Lagos (a Portuguese name) became a major port and later capital, and along with Calabar was used heavily in the slave trade, which was the dominant economic activity at that time. The British presence grew steadily through the nineteenth century, with Lagos annexed in 1861, and following the 1884 Berlin conference—which carved up Africa indiscriminately among the European powers—the British consolidated their grip on the disparate regions of what was to be the artificially created nation of Nigeria. At no time were the interests of "Nigerians" themselves considered.

British Colonial Rule

Although Nigerians were exposed to European and Middle Eastern influences for many centuries, the period of direct British colonial control lasted for less than 70 years. Nigerian resistance to British expansion was fierce, and the whole country did not come under British administration until the early 1900s. The British, like other colonizers elsewhere in Africa, had little idea of whom they had conquered or of the complexity of those societies. For some colonizers there was a sense of mission—the "white man's burden"—to improve the standard of living among Africans, but in reality the colonial period became more concerned with exploitation than development. The impact of British colonialism on the economic and political fabric of the country was immense, and the repercussions have had serious implications for contemporary Nigeria.

Although slavery was officially outlawed, the British showed little hesitation in reorganizing the Nigerian economy to suit their own requirements. The three nascent regions became identified with individual cash crops: the North was dominated by groundnut (peanut) production, the West by cocoa, and the East by palm oil. Possessing distinct economic bases, the regions were further separated from each other by the policy referred to as "indirect rule." Although British colonial administrators retained the controlling influence, this policy allowed chiefs and emirs to control local affairs within their own areas of jurisdiction. Distinct regional identities began to develop, with each looking inward for support and increasingly competing with the others for favors from the central colonial administration. Cultural differences were also reinforced in education, where southerners became deeply influenced and motivated by Western Christian, missionary, or "secular" education and values, while northern children (or the minority who received any formal education) were educated in a more traditional and perhaps "conservative" environment of Islam.[3] Prior to independence, this uneven educational pattern left many northerners feeling threatened that they would be unable to compete successfully for jobs with southerners, a valid fear which has still not been fully resolved, although quotas and federal initiatives (similar in some ways to "affirmative action" in the United States) have helped to restore the balance to some extent.

By 1939 three regions had been formally established by the colonial authorities, with commodity boards also at regional levels to purchase produce from within the region. Following World War II, nationalist agitation increased by building upon the prewar activity of groups such as Herbert Macauley's Nigerian National Democratic Party and the Nigerian Youth Movement. Such agitation became more successful as Britain's ability and willingness to maintain its colonial possession diminished. Nationalist movements formed nominally at the national level, but their activities were heavily influenced by regional and ethnic factors. Political parties that were established in the 1940s and 1950s displayed significantly monoethnic compositions, and elections in the 1950s reinforced regional rather than national orientations. Politicians were forced to compete for control of the regional commodity

boards because these held the key to finances and future political success.

A series of constitutional amendments during the 1940s and 1950s paved the way for independence. In 1946, the governor of Nigeria, Sir Arthur Richards, consolidated the process of regionalism by establishing three assemblies in the North, West, and East. In 1951, the MacPherson Constitution (named after another governor) allowed these regions to make their own laws and to elect their own representatives and ministers, and the three regions were given equal status in the central legislature. By 1954, problems had emerged that required a further readjustment of the political structure by the Lyttleton Constitution. Under this, a federal structure was organized dividing power between the federal government and the three regional governments. Direct elections were used to provide equal numbers of representatives for each region in the federal legislature. Regional orientations, however, were strengthened by giving taxation powers to each region, as well as by restricting administrators and bureaucrats to work only in their "region of origin."

This constitutional framework totally ignored the wishes of minority groups (approximately 40 percent of the population) a problem which was not addressed for more than a decade. The Eastern and Western regions gained self-government in 1957, but the North delayed this until 1959 in an attempt to buy more time to prepare itself for the competition and rivalry set to take place after independence was declared on 1 October 1960. At this time the North, which accounted for two-thirds of the territory of Nigeria and 40 percent to 45 percent of the population, had benefited from the alteration of electoral provisions from one that had seats shared equally among the three regions to one that awarded seats on the basis of population. The North managed to emerge at independence as the dominant partner within the federation, as well as have its own representative, Sir Alhaji Abubakar Tafawa Balewa, as prime minister. For an overview of

---

Feature 11.1 The Nigerian Development Model

Nigeria's political and economic development since independence in 1960 provides a confusing picture to those unaccustomed to African or third world politics. In the political arena, experimentation with a British parliamentary model between 1960 and 1966, and an American presidential model from 1979 to 1983 and again after 1992, indicates an attempt to find a pattern of government that "fits" the Nigerian scene. Military governments, which have been in office for two-thirds of the postindependence era, have arisen primarily because of failed civilian governments, although there have been certain positive qualities about some of the military administrations. On the economic side, Nigeria has kept relatively close to a capitalist model, officially scorning socialism and in the process allowing glaring inequalities to exist within society.

Is there a Nigerian development model? To a certain extent Nigeria's political and military elites have sketched out a path to follow. However, the general corruption of many of those leaders tends to make us conclude that the Nigerian model has developed to benefit those in power, rather than the vast majority of Nigerian citizens. Evidence from the 1991–1992 elections indicates clearly that the "newbreed" politicians possess many of the negative characteristics of their predecessors, and so there is little to suggest any improvement in the manner in which the country's polity and economy will be run in the Third Republic.

Nigerian politics since independence, see Feature 11.1.

THE FIRST REPUBLIC 1960–1966

Nigeria emerged in October 1960 as a fragile amalgam of distrusting partners. Ethnic divisions which had become accentuated during the colonial period were now magnified as groups vied with each other for patronage from and control over the federal center. Single political parties dominated the regional governments—the Northern People's Congress (NPC) in the North, composed essentially of Hausa-Fulani; the Action Group (AG) in the West, made up of Yoruba supporters; and the National Convention of Nigerian Citizens (NCNC) in the East, comprised almost exclusively of Ibo people.[4] Clashes over policy between federal and regional governments were exacerbated by divisions within the federal government itself, where the inherited parliamentary system promoted a confrontational attitude toward political debate. Minorities such as the Tiv, Nupe, Kanuri, and Ibibio could not get their voices heard. Within three or four years, the federal government had lost its control over the West, where political chaos became prevalent. Elections were rigged, thuggery and intimidation became widespread, and opposition leaders, notably the Yoruba spokesperson Chief Obafemi Awolowo, were imprisoned. The fragile political machinery of the country failed.

Against this political backdrop, other important developments were taking shape. The armed forces were becoming Africanized—at independence, only 10 percent of the officers were African, but by 1965 only 10 percent remained expatriate. Rapid promotion within the ranks had brought many southern, and specifically Ibo, officers to positions of leadership. These officers were predominantly trained in Britain, and were supposedly incul-

Sir Alhaji Ahmadu Bello (top, center) and, on his immediate right, Sultan Abubakar III of Sokoto accept self-government for the Northern Region from British colonial officers in 1959. This was a year prior to complete independence for Nigeria.

cated with the philosophy of nonintervention in politics. However, their skills of organization and discipline combined with their increasing concern over the political chaos in the country, helped to draw the military nearer to political involvement. The Ibo officer corps was also unhappy at what it considered to be northern ethnic control over Nigeria, and the failure by Ibos to get a fair slice of the Nigerian pie.

These tensions came to a head on 15 January 1966 when the country's first military coup d'etat took place, installing a government perceived by many to be Ibo-dominated and assassinating the North's two most powerful leaders, Tafawa Balewa and Sir Alhaji Ahmadu Bello, the Sardauna of Sokoto and premier of

the North. In recent years, some scholars have interpreted the coup as having been nationalist in origin, striving to rid the country of ethnic (northern) domination. Evidence for this view is inconclusive, but there was no hesitation within northern Nigeria in perceiving this to be an outright assault upon its people. The collapse and overthrow of the First Republic led, within 15 months, to a bitter civil war and an unbroken 13 years of military rule.

MILITARY GOVERNMENT 1966–1979

The seizure of power by the military on 15–16 January 1966 was an indication of the failure of the political system to provide satisfactory government. The military, however, fared little better than the civilians, and the social fabric of the country rapidly deteriorated. The junior officers who perpetrated the coup proved to be badly organized, and so leadership reverted to the Army Chief of Staff, Maj. Gen. J. Aguiyi-Ironsi. Although he was already in a precarious position, his decision in May 1966 to abolish the regions in favor of a unitary system of government inflamed northern opinion, and provided the grounds for a countercoup on 29 July 1966 in which Ibo officers were removed from power. Lt. Col. (later General) Yakubu Gowon, a 32-year-old, was chosen as a compromise candidate for leadership, both because he was from a minority ethnic group and because he was a Christian northerner.

Gowon attempted to defuse the tensions within the country by calling a Constitutional Conference in August–September 1966 to resolve regional differences. The North initially sought secession from the Republic because of its hostility to other regions, but in the end its leaders were persuaded against this. The East, however, came to favor secession, a desire strengthened by the massacre of many thousands of innocent Ibos in northern Nigeria during May and September–October 1966, causing millions to flee the North to the relative safety of the East. The East was also the center of the developing oil industry and thus had considerable economic potential; moreover, Ibos were renowned for their economic resourcefulness and expertise. On 26 May 1967, Gowon attempted to preempt secession by splitting the regions into 12 states, but four days later the Eastern Region declared its independence as "Biafra," and the civil war, or the "war of national unity," was begun. The war claimed the lives of untold millions of Nigerians and proved to be the ultimate test of unity and loyalty for the nascent state. The complex problem of national integration was one faced by nearly all African states, and so the war in Nigeria was watched closely by the rest of the continent. Only four African countries

formally recognized Biafra, and many Western states would only provide humanitarian assistance to the secessionists. The rest of the Nigerian federation united against this challenge and, with large military assistance from the Soviet Union and other Eastern European countries, finally crushed the rebellion in January 1970. Although Nigerian unity has not been seriously questioned since the war, the scars of that war are still evident in society today.

Gowon, to his credit and Nigeria's benefit, proved to be magnanimous in victory, and sought the reconciliation of all the factions in the war. Although Biafran soldiers were excluded from further military service, many officers were reintegrated into the Nigerian army, which had grown to over 250,000 troops by 1972—a significant social and political problem in itself. Economic reconstruction was facilitated by the rapid increase in oil production and revenues, which were themselves further boosted by the OPEC "revolution" of October 1973. Such was the confidence of the country by the mid-1970s that Nigeria cultivated its image as a continental leader, and the country appeared to be awash with oil money and large development projects. Across-the-board pay raises fueled inflation, but nobody seemed to worry. Indeed, the military leaders were at the front of the line helping themselves to Nigeria's wealth.

The vast corruption of the military leaders, the inefficiency and apparent lack of direction of development goals, the squandering of the oil wealth, and the failure to provide a program for return to civilian rule all helped to stir up divisions within the military, and Gowon was overthrown by fellow officers on 29 July 1975, exactly nine years after he had come to power. Murtala Muhammed set out to tackle the worst excesses of corruption, and fixed a timetable to return to civilian rule by October 1979. Murtala's radical and crusading zeal led to the dismissal of 10,000 government officials and 150 officers, and naturally upset many Nigerians who had gained illicitly from the previous regime. Hence, Murtala was himself assassinated on 13 February 1976 by disgruntled officers, many of whom were found to be from Gowon's home area.

Returning to Civilian Rule

Lt. Gen. Olusegun Obasanjo, the first (and only to date) head of state of Yoruba ethnicity, continued to implement the political transition program. A Constituent Assembly met in 1976 to draw up a new constitution and political framework for the country that would allow for potentially greater stability. Differences emerged between delegates, especially concerning the status of Shari'a, or Islamic, courts within the federation, but the Constitution when implemented in 1979 proved to be a balanced document, and it was generally welcomed by Nigerians.

Nigerians accepted that a federal system had to be maintained, and the discredited parliamentary system of the First Republic was replaced by an executive presidential system, balanced by a National Assembly of two federal houses, namely, the Senate and House of Representatives. Like their American counterparts, the Senate gave equal representation to the states of the federation (increased to 19 in 1976 following the report of the Irikefe Commission), and the lower House had its members distributed and elected on the basis of population. Government at the state level was to be under a governor and a single assembly. Following elections held in mid-1979, a fresh set of politicians was elected, and the Second Republic was born on 1 October 1979.

THE SECOND REPUBLIC 1979–1983

Only five political parties had been allowed to register under strict guidelines for the 1979 elections, and of these the National Party of Nigeria (NPN) emerged as the dominant one. The new president, Alhaji Shehu Shagari, was elected on the NPN ticket, and the party was able to secure a majority in both houses of the National Assembly. At the state level the picture was more complex, as the smaller parties were able to gain control of nine state governments. Although the military had forced all five parties to be of "national" rather than "ethnic" origin, the election results confirmed fears that ethnicity had not been suppressed. The Unity Party of Nigeria (UPN) was backed predominantly by Yoruba supporters, and won the states of the Southwest, whereas the Nigeria People's Party (NPP), closely linked to Ibo support, won the three states in the Southeast.

The NPN did succeed to some extent in cutting across ethnic barriers and striking bargains with southern elements, although it found it difficult to completely shed its image as the party representing northern interests. The electoral process was not as violent or combustible as it had been some 15 years earlier, but tensions grew in the early 1980s between a number of states and the federal government, and within a few states where the governor was not a member of the majority party. Pressure for the creation of more states rose dramatically as political elites around the country attempted to control their own futures. The power of patronage that the NPN possessed helped it to maintain its grip on the country, but opposition to the government grew substantially. Such antagonism was exacerbated by the chronic condition of the economy following the collapse in oil prices, as well as by the rampant and blatant corruption associated with the NPN.

Elections held in mid-1983 returned the NPN to office, but allegations of widespread ballot rigging cast serious doubts upon the results. Riots broke out in areas supported by opposition parties, particularly in the southwestern states, and the federal government appeared to be losing control and direction. Against this background, and with the fear of further bloodshed in the local government elections slated for January 1984, the military intervened on New Year's Eve 1983 and started its second period in government.

MILITARY GOVERNMENT AND POLITICAL TRANSITION 1984–1992

The first year of military government under Muhammadu Buhari proved to be a bitter experience for most Nigerians. Top civilian leaders, including the former president and vice-president, were jailed, and tribunals were organized for those suspected of corrupt practices. A severe clampdown on press freedom was instituted and a "War Against Indiscipline" (WAI) started to instill better behavior and moral values in the population. Set against the acute economic hardship faced by most Nigerians, the initial euphoria that had greeted the overthrow of the civilians was soon displaced by a similar distaste for the military leaders. Such unease was felt within the military itself, and in August 1985 Buhari was removed by his colleagues in a "palace coup," and Gen. Ibrahim Babangida took over the reins of office.

Babangida's government relaxed some of the harsher policies of its predecessor, and also introduced radical economic measures in an attempt to alleviate the severe hardship faced by the majority in the country. Although Babangida did not accept direct assistance from the International Monetary Fund (IMF) for this reconstruction, the policies implemented followed programs "suggested" by the fund. The most significant of these included an initial 60 percent devaluation of the national currency, the naira, the abolition of commodity boards and the privatization of many inefficient government-owned corporations (or parastatals), the relaxation of import-export regulations, and the gradual reduction of government subsidies. These were difficult and unpopular reforms to institute, and it is still too early to say whether they have been successful.

On political reforms, Babangida (after surviving a coup attempt in December 1985) also took a bold initiative and announced in January 1986 his determination to return the country to civilian rule by 1990. In July 1987 the complete program was detailed, with the transfer date pushed back to 1992. The program strongly resembles the plan of the late 1970s. Significantly, the presidential system of government has been retained in 1992, but only two political parties, the National Republican Convention (NRC) and the Social Democratic Party (SDP), were registered by the military to compete. The ban on political activity was raised in May 1989, but the military government refused to approve any of the groups that applied for registration. The government thus created the machinery and manifestos of the two parties. All politicians and military personnel who served in federal or state governments or assemblies from 1960 to 1991 were barred from contesting for office in 1992 in an attempt to recruit a more honest "newbreed" political elite. During 1992, state governments were under civilian control but were monitored by the military federal government, an interesting experiment in civilian-military "diarchy."

SOCIETAL AGENDAS

It should be evident already that Nigeria is a volatile and unpredictable country. Despite the setbacks and failures over the last 32 years, many Nigerians retain confidence that they are progressing and will eventually find the correct political structure for their country. It is certainly true that the "average" Nigerian is highly politicized and never seems reluctant to offer an opinion on events inside or outside the country. As a dominant economic and political force in sub-Saharan Africa, Nigeria provides a natural focus of attention to help us understand the dynamics of the continent.

The fluidity of Nigeria's political structure, and the experimentation with different styles of government, is indicative of numerous social and political problems to which the country is striving to find solutions. Some of these issues can be examined here.

Nation Building

Probably the most serious and difficult task facing the country since independence has been making people loyal to the concept of Nigeria, rather than allowing diverse ethnic sympathies to predominate over a national orientation. This task of nation building is common to almost all African countries, where artificial state boundaries often force people of differing cultural backgrounds to live together within shared borders. Since 1960, Nigeria has provided an arena for the struggle between ethnic identities and national identity as defined by the federal center, where the former has often won to the detriment of the common good. This transference of loyalties is difficult to achieve (as Europeans have found with the European Community), and can take place only when sufficient gains are perceived from the larger grouping.

Ethnicity in Nigeria is perhaps not as serious a problem in the early 1990s; efforts by successive governments to control it have had some impact. "Federal character" is a term widely used in employment and political circles (and in the Constitution) to denote fair and equitable opportunities for all ethnic groups within the federation, so that discrimination is actively discouraged. Military recruitment also follows this guideline. Political parties can no longer legally be regionally or ethnically biased, and must open offices in and recruit candidates from regions all over the federation. As we have seen, this did not prevent ethnic sentiment from surfacing in the Second Republic, but by allowing only two parties to contest in 1992 the military has forced some degree of consultation between diverse groups.

The role within Nigeria of traditional rulers, chiefs, and emirs has been a focus of bitterness as their powers have gradually diminished. The newness of the country and the rapid changes taking place within it mean that there is little continuity in government, or precedent by which to act. Unlike Britain, for example, where the system operates in a certain way perhaps only because it has been done that way for a century or more, there is no tradition or common set of values in the Nigerian context. The longest any civilian government has survived to try to develop these traditions is six years (1960–1966).

The dynamics of growth and change have generated pressures from a variety of sources to increase the number of states in the federation from 3 to 30 (see Table 11.3). In many ways the creation of new states has alleviated some sociocultural tensions, and has allowed minority groups greater control over how their affairs are run. Unfortunately, it has not automatically led to any more efficient control over resources or their use, and it could be argued that this multiplicity of government is a major drain on the country's limited finances. These new states have also not provided any better government, and the lack of honest and capable leadership in the country has seriously hindered the development of a true national consciousness. Despite the adding of nine new states in August 1991 and the resulting political confusion this action had on the transition program, it is quite possible that more states will be created in the future, as political pressures challenge the maintenance of the status quo.

Religious Tolerance

Nigeria contains almost equal numbers of Christians and Muslims, who together account for 60 percent to 70 percent of the national population. Christianity provides the major religion of the South, with Protestants concentrated in the Southwest, and Catholics in the Southeast. Islam is the predominant religious force in the North, and Nigeria's Muslim pilgrims to Mecca in the 1980s formed the largest single group from any country. There have been periods of extreme tension between Muslims and Christians, but the general tolerance between these groups has helped to minimize the impact of differences on Nigerian political development. Religion has cer-

Table 11.3 NIGERIA'S REGIONS AND STATES, 1963–1991

1963	1967	1976	1987	1991
Northern Region	Northwestern	Sokoto	Sokoto	Sokoto
		Niger	Niger	Kebbi
				Niger
	Northeastern	Borno	Borno	Borno
				Yobe
		Bauchi	Bauchi	Bauchi
		Gongola	Gongola	Adamawa
				Taraba
	North-Central	Kaduna	Kaduna	Kaduna
			Katsina	Katsina
	Benue-Plateau	Benue	.Benue	Benue
		Plateau	Plateau	Plateau
	West-Central	Kwara	Kwara	Kwara
				Kogi
		Kano	Kano	Kano
				Jigawa
Eastern Region	East-Central	Anambra	Anambra	Enugu
				Anambra
		Imo	Imo	Imo
				Abia
	Southeastern	Cross River	Cross River	Cross River
			Akwa Ibom	Akwa Ibom
	Rivers	Rivers	Rivers	Rivers
Western Region	Western	Oyo	Oyo	Oyo
				Oshun
		Ogun	Ogun	Ogun
		Ondo	Ondo	Ondo
Midwest Region	Midwestern	Bendel	Bendel	Edo
				Delta
Federal Capital Territory	Lagos	Lagos	Lagos	Lagos
			Abuja	Abuja

The Federal Capital Territory was transferred from Lagos to Abuja under the 1979 Constitution.

Source: Adapted from Anthony Kirk-Greene and Douglas Rimmer, *Nigeria Since 1970. A Political and Economic Outline* (London: Hodder and Stoughton, 1981).

tainly been used to reinforce divisions between competing political groups, but it has rarely been the sole or even fundamental issue of division. In this respect, Nigerian leaders have displayed both tolerance and maturity—or fear of the consequences to national unity should religious intolerance develop.

With such relative success in minimizing religious differences in the 1960s and 1970s,

it was perhaps surprising that intolerance and conflict should have increased in the 1980s and 1990s, although this was partly influenced by the surge of Islamic fundamentalism. In December 1980, the first violent fundamentalist outbreak claimed at least 4000 lives in the northern city of Kano, and continued outbreaks of fundamentalist agitation in other cities show that there are differences within

Islam and challenges to the established order. The establishment was itself in disarray by 1987 when the domestic leader of the Islamic faith, Sultan Abubakar III, began to fail in health after some 50 years in office, and bitter rivalries emerged over the issue of succession when the sultan died at the end of 1988.

In 1987, violent clashes between Christians and Muslims flared up in northern Nigeria, with many lives lost and hundreds of churches burned to the ground. Similar riots in 1991 and May 1992 resulted in hundreds more dead, and threatened to disrupt the political transition process. Relations between communities had been sensitive after Nigeria joined of the Organization of Islamic Conference (OIC) in 1986, as some Christians feared the creeping Islamicization of national affairs. Partly because of this debate, Nigeria's membership in the OIC was temporarily suspended in 1991. This issue by itself seemed an insufficient cause, however, and it is believed that religion is being deliberately used to inflame passions and destabilize the military government. Whatever the case, religion continued to be a potentially explosive issue in the 1991–1992 transition period.

Economic Management and Ideology

Nigeria is a capitalist society. Drawing from colonial experiences, successive Nigerian governments have supported capitalist economic strategies, and have refused to countenance Socialist alternatives. Although there are minimum wage policies in force—raised to 250 naira ($30) per month in 1991—and health and education schemes provide some assistance for the needy, there are few constraints on the market economy. Initially at independence, British influence over the economy was paramount, but gradual indigenization and Africanization policies have placed more influence in Nigerian hands, although certainly only in the hands of an elite and still with very strong influence by overseas companies. During the last six years,

as part of structural adjustment of the economy, renewed emphasis has been placed on foreign investment and participation in enterprises, while the federal and state governments have sold off most parastatals to the domestic and foreign business elites.

This overtly capitalistic strategy has concentrated wealth in the hands of the few, and has consequently drawn widespread, though ineffectual, criticism. The universities provide the major source of radical opposition, with academics and students alike pushing for socialistic and egalitarian alternatives, but scant regard is paid to them. The Nigeria Labor Congress (NLC) has also been outspoken in support of workers' rights, but successive governments have ignored it or, worse still, detained its leaders. The Babangida government expressly refused to adopt socialism as the national ideology to be followed after 1992, but the government did not recommend any strategy, stating that it would "eventually evolve with time and political maturity."[5] In essence, successive elites have prevented a more egalitarian economic and development strategy from emerging.

The prevailing economic structure of Nigeria provides other societal strain's that affect the political process. Agriculture has traditionally provided the backbone of economic wealth, but the oil boom led to the neglect of the agricultural sector. Investment was poured into expensive prestige projects, often industrial (and often with large "kickbacks" for business and government elites), and these did not bring much real benefit to the majority. In contrast, the rural areas received little investment and were allowed to decay. In the late 1980s the government desperately tried to rectify these policies, revitalize rural areas, and prevent the rural-urban population drift that has placed increasing strains on the urban areas. However, these policies recorded minimal success.

Despite (or perhaps because of) the considerable national earnings from oil, Nigeria remains a society of great inequalities—a factor which successive governments have failed

---

The Environment

Worldwide concern over environmental damage has grown dramatically in recent years, although little concrete action has been taken to date by industrialized powers. In Nigeria, the problems of merely making a living in a severely depressed economy leave little time for concern or action on the environment. The government, however, took some action in 1989 by setting up the Federal Environmental Protection Agency (FEPA). The greatest concerns in Nigeria focus upon pollution from oil spills, the storage of hazardous and toxic waste, the encroachment of the Sahara desert, and the rapid deforestation linked to overpopulation in the country. Ironically for a global oil power, wood still remains the primary source of energy for most Nigerians, and efforts at reforestation have not kept up with destruction of existing woodland.

Structural adjustment has put even greater strains on the government, and has left less money available for a thorough conservation program. Consequently, with the Nigerian population expected to rise by 400 million over the next 50 years, prospects are grim for the ecological balance of the country.

---

to tackle. Class divisions are pronounced, but they have not been the basis of political divisions to date. Although there have been political parties in both Republics that claimed to provide for working class concerns and espoused class-conscious ideologies, none have been truly class based, and they have all tended to rely upon residual ethnic support for their votes. Indeed, party leaders could be said to have deliberately exploited ethnic sentiments in order to reduce the possibility that a true national working-class solidarity would develop.

The urbanized middle class, which was emerging strongly during the oil boom years of the late 1970s, was badly hit by austerity in the 1980s. The wealthy business and political elites, however, have been able to maintain their own economic positions, and society has become even more divided on the basis of social and economic inequality. Class perspectives were vaguely worded into the constitutions of the NRC and SDP, but not sufficiently to provide for class-based politics and elections. One of the big questions concerning the Third Republic is whether the "newbreed" will alter the ideological orientation that has prevailed in Nigeria since independence. While it is still too early to answer this question with confidence, a preliminary assessment would conclude no.

Socialization

Socialization, the process by which people learn the values and beliefs of their society, is influenced by many factors within the Nigerian context. The newness of national identity contrasts with the pressures from long-standing traditions, while competing socialization processes take place to promote potentially mutually exclusive allegiances at ethnic and federal-national levels. The first language of most Nigerians is their own ethnic tongue, with English used as the only "national" language. Great emphasis in schools is placed on developing a national consciousness with loyalty pledges and instruction of national values, but this can run into conflict with learning experiences within the home or local community, where the belief that the state or federal apparatus has been discriminatory may prevail.

Military governments have attempted to instill greater self-discipline and national awareness among Nigerians, but with varied results. They have also stressed the need for greater honesty in society, and have attempted to stamp out the corruption that plagues all levels of Nigerian life. Unfortunately, the armed forces themselves have been guilty of the very things they are attempting to erase in the civilian population, and so the values of society have been slow to change.

The status of women within the domestic power structure is also shaped by the traditions and norms of society. Generally, women suffer discrimination by males in access to positions of authority, as well as in opportunities for economic development. But the scale of this discrimination is not uniform across the country. In many southern areas, for example, women have controlled market enterprises for many years and have significant input into the economy; in the North, Islam tends to prevent women's active participation in social and economic life because purdah tends to keep them confined to the home. Women were also denied the vote in northern states until 1979. Family planning, seemingly crucial in a country where women on average have six children each, tends to be given low priority by male administrators. In Islamic circles, many males are openly opposed to any form of family planning, charging it is a Christian conspiracy to hold down Islamic population growth.

Against the background of these and other agendas, The Third Republic is attempting to develop a collective conscience in society, a Nigerian "psyche," and is striving to develop political processes and institutions that will be able to withstand the pressures that have brought down all the previous governments of Nigeria.

Key Terms

Biafra
civil war
colonialism
coup d'etat
ethnicity
federal character
Hausa-Fulani
Ibo
Middle Belt
nation building
regionalism
religious tolerance
secession
socialization
Yoruba

Suggestions for Further Reading

Arnold, Guy. *Modern Nigeria* (London: Longman, 1977).

Dudley, B. J. *Instability and Political Order. Politics and Crisis in Nigeria* (Ibadan: Ibadan University Press, 1973).

Graf, William D. *The Nigerian State. Political Economy, State Class and Political System in the Post-Colonial Era* (London: James Currey and Portsmouth: Heinemann, 1988).

Hatch, John. *Nigeria: A History* (London: Secker and Warburg, 1971).

Kirk-Greene, Anthony, and Douglas Rimmer. *Nigeria since 1970: A Political and Economic Outline* (London: Hodder and Stoughton, 1981).

B. Political Processes and Institutions

The political process in Nigeria is complex, and attempts to study and comprehend it are made difficult by several factors. Accurate information concerning actors and decision making is often not present, so it can be difficult to isolate the forces at work within the process. Severe problems such as ethnicity, religion, the civil war, economic inequalities, and military coups d'etat impinge directly upon the political process and can often cause severe fluctuations in its functioning. There has been no direct or official continuity between political parties within the country; parties were banned in 1966 after the collapse of the First Republic, and new parties formed for the Second Republic in 1979. Likewise in 1983, these parties were proscribed, and two new parties were created for the Third Republic. Naturally, some of the leading political figures and policy bases have remained constant throughout, but these can only be understood on closer inspection.

To a considerable extent, the Nigerian political process has been dominated by personalities rather than by parties or policies. Admittedly, vague promises and programs have been enunciated by parties, particularly on education, health, and the economy, but voters have been far more interested in who the leaders of each party are and, more crucially, what their ethnic identifications are. In many elections, ballot rigging has occurred on such a grand scale that it has been difficult to gauge real winners and losers. As a general rule, it has been assumed that each party cheats in roughly equal ratios to the others, so election results do provide a justifiable winner of sorts.

An important issue to consider is whether the regular military intrusion into politics has had a positive or negative impact upon the political process, or whether in fact military rule should be seen as an integral part of the process itself. Indeed, a favorite comment is that the Nigerian system contains only two parties, the civilians and the military, and that both must be considered integral to the political process.

Since independence was gained in October 1960, Nigeria has also struggled to find a stable framework of political institutions through which to govern. The country has experimented with parliamentary (1960–1966), presidential (1979–1983), and military (1966–1979 and 1984–1992) structures of government, which have all operated within a federal system encompassing initially three regions and now 30 states, but no system or set of institutions has brought the degree of stability required. Many commentators, both in Nigeria and abroad, argue that it is not the political institutions themselves that have been at fault—particularly during the Second Republic—but the politicians who have been at the helm.

Before turning to the active political parties and institutions in the Nigerian polity, we need to consider the composition of both the civilian and the military leadership groups.

CIVILIAN ELITE

Politicians around the world do not always have the best of reputations, but Nigerian politicians, in the past at least, have been considered especially poor representatives and guardians of the state. The failure of the first two Republics (and certain military regimes also) can be blamed largely upon poor leadership, selfish interests, and gross corruption. Obviously not all Nigerian politicians can be so blamed, but Nigerian citizens are rarely complimentary about the politicians who have represented them.

Such an unequivocal condemnation raises the question as to who these politicians are, and how they get themselves elected. Most politicians are drawn from the wealthy business communities, professional groups, schools and universities, and government administration, and some hold religious or traditional positions of authority. Ethnic considerations have also been of paramount importance in climbing the political ladder within any given party, and have often proven to be more important than educational ability or qualifications. The desire to assist people from one's own community provides a very strong impulse for all Nigerians, and Western values concerning impartiality and nepotism do not command much respect, or are never properly implemented. It has been virtually impossible for politicians to be recruited—and certainly advance—without having the requisite ethnic identification, or at least promising to attract large numbers of his or her own ethnic constituency.

A major weakness of this elite has been the failure to apply a nationalist orientation to policy, with sectionalist or personal interest usually taking priority. In the First Republic, the ruling Northern People's Congress (NPC) was exclusively a mouthpiece of the Northern Region and the majority of federal spending inevitably went to that region. Its "successor," the National Party of Nigeria (NPN), although it attempted to be more national in outlook, still displayed a significant bias toward the northern states and sectarian interests. This apparent inability of civilian politicians to encompass a truly national orientation is a trait found in many African states, but it has been of considerable concern in Nigeria.

Perhaps the critical problem concerning the civilian elite is that its ethical and normative values have proved totally insubstantial. Civilians have unashamedly entered politics to make money. This has been called "extractive" politics, in which politicians merely seek their own personal gain rather than promote societal advancement. Frantz Fanon explicitly condemned such practices in African states, considering it just another form of exploitation under which the African masses have to suffer.[6] It may be unfair to paint all Nigerian politicians with such a broad brush, but they have tended to stick tightly to their stereotypes. Respected scholars of Nigerian politics appear to be in agreement. Billy Dudley wrote:

> For the Nigerian political elite, politics involves not the conciliation of competing demands arising from an examination of the various alternatives entailed by any course of political action, but the extraction of resources which can be used to satisfy elite demands and to buy support.[7]

Terisa Turner and Gavin Williams share a similar view that in Nigeria, "Politics thus comes to be the process of gaining control of public resources for the pursuit of private ends."[8] Chief Obafemi Awolowo, one of Nigeria's foremost politicians until his death in 1987, summed up his feelings by saying that, "Since independence our governments have been a matter of a few holding the cow for the strongest and most cunning to milk."[9]

The 1979 Constitution laid down very clear guidelines against corruption, and politicians at least pay lip service to the need for probity in office. But the record of civilians between 1979 and 1983 was a poor one, with an estimated $5 billion to $7 billion embezzled in just over four years, and arson resorted to in order to prevent official inquiries from finding evidence of such acts. By 1983, a number of important buildings had been burned, including two telecommunications centers in Lagos, as well as the Federal Ministry of Education and the Foreign Affairs Ministry. The behavior of the civilian elite in the 1980s was little or no better than that in the 1960s. So what can we expect of the "newbreed" after 1992? The answer to that question is difficult to assess at this time, but preliminary data of political activities in 1991–1992 indicate little improvement among the political class.

MILITARY LEADERSHIP

Since 1966, the military has controlled the government for all but for years (1979–1983). The most important justification normally put forward by the military for its intrusion into politics (both in Nigeria and in Africa as a whole) is the failure by civilians to maintain the political structure and to act in accordance with societal norms.[10] The military itself, particularly but certainly not exclusively in the early 1970s, displayed evident corruption, especially among its leadership, and "millionaire generals" flaunted their wealth without hesitation or fear. This wealth was generated by the rapid increase (and unaccountability) in national revenues accruing from oil. A glaring symbol of this corruption was the "cement scandal" of 1974. Owing to various illegal deals and contracts, the government found itself contracted for 20 million tons of cement. This was far beyond the ports' handling capacity, and at one time some 450 ships laden with cement were waiting outside Lagos harbor. This scandal, though one of the largest, was only one of many. The overthrow of General Yakubu Gowon in 1975 was defended by his successors as necessary to stem this corruption, but they merely made it less conspicuous. Many believe that the outgoing military leadership in 1979 only handed over power to elected civilians when the latter agreed not to probe into the financial affairs of retiring officers. This seems to have been the case again in 1992.

The armed forces do help to play a nation-building role, however, in the sense that recruitment and appointments are molded by considerations of federal character, and postings to various parts of Nigeria provide soldiers with greater awareness (and, it is hoped, empathy) of people with different social and cultural backgrounds. National rather than sectional interest is stressed through education and training, and officer recruitment is monitored carefully for equality. Such a balance, however, is a goal rather than a reality, and imbalance has been a focus of bitter controversy in previous years.

At independence in 1960, only 10 percent of the officer corps of the Royal West Africa Frontier Force (RWAFF) was African, as British expatriate officers retained control. This was both for political reasons, because of the pro-Western and pro-British leanings of the federal government, and for practical reasons, in that very few Nigerians had been trained as officers. Africanization took place rapidly, so that by 1965 all but 10 percent of officers were Nigerian. This pace of promotion had obvious military significance; young officers rose in the ranks at great speed, leading to what has been termed "professional disorientation." But the political problems were equally severe because the appointments and promotions gave a disproportionate influence to officers from the Eastern Region.[11] The growing frustration with the northern bias of the ruling NPC, combined with the inability of Eastern Region politicians to influence the political process, provided these officers with a justification to use their military muscle to bring an end to the First Republic in 1966.

Few people foresaw such a military intervention, believing that British influence and military training would be sufficient to inspire a nonpolitical stance by military officers and to prevent their interference in the political process. But the political awareness of officers had been awakened in 1964, when they were asked by both antagonists to intervene in the constitutional crisis between the president and prime minister, even though this crisis was finally settled by the civilians themselves. The 1966 coup dramatically and irreversibly changed the nature of the political process, and set off a chain of events within the military that continues to trouble it. The civil war divided the military into two factions, and although the Biafran secession was eventually defeated, only some officers of eastern origin were allowed to rejoin the federal armed forces. Even in the early 1990s, officers from southeastern states were unable to regain positions of influence within the senior ranks.

A significant shift in the profile of the military leadership took place in the 1970s, with "Middle Belt" officers from the smaller ethnic groups becoming more prominent. This influence has helped to balance competing forces within the military, and has brought greater stability to the military government since 1985. Those who have taken a place in military governments are career soldiers, although this does not preclude them from accumulating wealth. However, the record of the Babangida government in terms of promoting honest government and probity is a little better than any previous military or civilian regime, and this reflects favorably upon the military elite.

The question as to whether military rule has a positive impact on the Nigerian political process is value laden and ambiguous, and is one that induces significant debate. Military force certainly has been useful in suppressing political violence, but the military has never used excessive force in the control of soci-

ety. Coups have been relatively bloodless, and overthrown leaders (except in 1966 and 1976) are generally treated with respect. The military acted in apparent good faith in its attempts to draw up a constitutional program to return power to civilians in the Second Republic, as well as in the Third Republic. Nevertheless, the military's intervention has not solved the problems inherent in the Nigerian polity, and its relative lack of political awareness and skill has not made it well suited to probe into deep-seated difficulties in the political system. The military has also tended to favor the status quo, representing solid bourgeois interests and shoring up corrupt elites rather than working toward ridding the country of socioeconomic inequalities. Some have said, perhaps unfairly, that the failure of the Second Republic showed that 13 years of military rule did not affect or improve the political system, attitudes, or institutions, although the civilians must ultimately take the blame for failing to make the system work.[12]

The longer the military stays in office, the more disunity and divisions appear within its ranks. Some factions believe in the importance of military rule, whereas others support recivilianization and argue that military personnel have no place in politics. The military's training, discipline, and command structure do not really suit it for political office, and military governments have placed a heavy reliance upon co-opted civilians to administer the country. The option to share national leadership with civilians after 1992 was raised and rejected by the military, and President Babangida repeatedly stated that the military has no rightful place in government. This raises the intriguing question of why the military does not consider itself to be the "rightful" government in Nigeria. This is difficult to answer. There are probably numerous factors at work, based not only upon the military's own nervousness at remaining in power for long periods, but also upon of very strong sentiments within the Nigerian populace to continue with experimentation in civilian government.

THE FIRST REPUBLIC 1960–1966

Political Parties

The political parties of the First Republic all developed in preindependent Nigeria and thus began their operations within the context of colonial control. Although the first "protoparty" was formed in the 1920s, it was not until after World War II that parties really began to take the shape and form that made them active players in the political game. All the parties were led by an elite, and the financing was provided by wealthy individuals or banks within the party's geographical area of operations.

As we have already seen in the previous section, the regionalist philosophy of the colonial administrators served both to create and to reinforce divisions between groups within the country, and pushed political parties to seek support largely at an ethnic-regional level. Parties attempted to extend their influence outside their home bases, but this effort was not very successful, and where it was, success depended more upon forging alliances with minor parties representing smaller sectarian interests than upon actually breaking directly into another party's support base. By far the most dominant party of the era was the Northern People's Congress (NPC), and it is to that party that we will turn first.

The Northern People's Congress (NPC)
The NPC, established in 1951, controlled the federal assembly in Lagos and had its deputy leader, Sir Alhaji Abubakar Tafawa Balewa, as federal premier. The party's leader, Sir Alhaji Ahmadu Bello, decided to remain as northern premier, giving an indication by his preference as to which was the more powerful institution. The NPC dominated the Northern Region, and made it a "closed" system because of the very tight association of personnel at legislative, executive, and judicial levels. Because seats in the federal lower house were allocated on the basis of population, the NPC won the 1959 general election comfortably.

The NPC was blatantly northern rather than national in outlook, and restricted membership of the party to people of northern origin. Its policies both at home and abroad reflected the Islamic conservatism of its leadership, promoting steady capitalist growth and no change in Nigeria's external orientation. This philosophy antagonized progressive and non-Islamic factions in the other regions.

The NPC maintained an electoral alliance from 1959 with the major party of the Eastern Region—the National Convention of Nigerian Citizens (NCNC)—but this did little to broaden the base of its policies, nor did it help the NCNC to win concessions for itself from the NPC. Such dominance of the federal apparatus led the smaller parties to seek alliances in order to challenge NPC dominance. Rivalry in the South between the NCNC and Action Group over issues and alliances led to bitter electoral contests, the subsequent breakdown of law and order in the Western Region, and eventually to the military intervention of January 1966.

The National Convention of Nigerian Citizens (NCNC)
The NCNC, established in 1944, was the oldest party to operate in the First Republic, and centered itself upon the personality of Dr. Nnamdi Azikiwe, a leading nationalist in the independence struggle who became the first (ceremonial) president of Nigeria in 1963. The party originally also encompassed the English-speaking areas of Cameroon, and its preindependence name reflected that fact—the National Council of Nigeria and the Cameroons. At independence the party was almost exclusively based in the Eastern Region, relying largely upon Ibo support, but it was more progressive in its economic and social policies than the NPC. The NCNC was also ambitious to expand its influence into the West and Middle Belt, and by doing so it hoped to wrestle greater concessions from its federal partner, the NPC. The NCNC's pressure and activism in the neighboring Western Region provoked many vio-

lent clashes, but also helped to bring about the creation of the Midwest Region in 1964, over which the NCNC was able to win control. Frustration over its failure to make a greater impact on the Nigerian political process resulted following the 1966 military coups, in the NCNC becoming the primary caucus of the Biafran secessionary movement, although Azikiwe remained loyal to the federal camp.

The Action Group (AG)

The Action Group, established in 1948, was founded by and organized around the personality of Chief Obafemi Awolowo, a lawyer, and symbolized the cultural and political goals of the Yoruba. Its power center was the Western Region. Awolowo's belief was that the federation could only be kept together by the regions maintaining their own cultural identities and consulting as equal partners at the federal level. The AG strove hard to maintain control over its own region and to expand its influence beyond the West, but in both tasks it was less successful than the other parties.

The AG promoted policies of "welfarism," but as the party moved toward adopting democratic socialism, splits appeared within its ranks. These divisions were deepened in 1962 when Awolowo gave up his position as premier of the West to become leader of the federal opposition in Lagos. His successor, Chief S. L. Akintola, was opposed by Awolowo, but was able to hold sufficient support in the region to maintain his position. Differences within the Yoruba cultural entity, which have always been strong (and remained strong during the Second Republic and in the 1991–1992 transition), were exacerbated by these tensions, especially when Awolowo was imprisoned by the federal authorities for treason, a charge he always denied. With Awolowo conveniently out of the way until his release by the military in 1966— he favored an alliance in the South against the NPC—the AG faction led by Akintola sought an alliance with the NPC in order to maintain authority and control over the West. His creation of the Nigerian National Democratic

Party (NNDP) formalized the linkage with the NPC, but did little to improve the stability of the region. By 1966, law and order in the West had all but disappeared.

Smaller Parties

The NPC, NCNC, and AG represented, to some degree or other, the primary ethnic groups of Hausa-Fulani, Ibo, and Yoruba, respectively. The smaller groups in the country did not perceive their interests to be considered or promoted by these parties or within the regional governments, and so many of them formed their own parties to seek alliances and to improve their negotiating position. One such party was the United Middle Belt Congress, which attempted to bring together groups within the country's central areas. Some of these parties held radical perspectives, particularly the Northern Elements Progressive Union (NEPU). NEPU was launched in 1951 under the leadership of Mallam Aminu Kano as a breakaway group and challenger to the NPC. Aminu Kano's radical challenge to the northern establishment continued until his death in 1983, but the effects of NEPU, like those of other smaller parties, were at best localized and at worst ineffectual. At elections in the First Republic, these smaller parties together never polled more than 15 percent of the vote, whereas the three larger parties consistently held their own power bases and were the dominant actors at the federal level.

Elections

Elections provide a process by which governments are legitimized. In many African countries, where only a single political party is allowed or where there is quasi-military rule, elections still play an important role in legitimizing the government. In those few countries where open, competitive elections are allowed, these are fiercely fought because the spoils of victory—control over the governmental machinery—are great. In Western democracies, strict controls are placed on the use of party finances and the electoral machinery in order to ensure as fair a process as possible. Such regulations existed in Nigeria during the First Republic, but the willingness to abide by them did not. Furthermore, once the NPC controlled the federation and exerted its influence, there was no independent power center capable of maintaining a free, open, and fair electoral process. The fairest elections within the country, then, have been those held under the auspices of groups capable of holding such control—the British colonial authorities in preindependence elections, and military governments in 1979 and 1991–1992.

The concern displayed by parties of the First Republic in manipulating the electoral process was partly inspired by negative perceptions of opponents. All parties were perceived as likely to exaggerate their voting support within their own region, and so each reinforced its own intention to do the same. Electoral registers and the census results from 1962 and 1963 were inflated for similar reasons; population was the factor determining seat allocations in the federal lower house (as well as federal revenue paid to the regions). This gave the North a built-in majority, and added to the frustration of the other regions. With each party effectively controlling the electoral process in its own region, sweeping successes were usually recorded (except in the West for specific reasons), as opponents were unable to campaign and ballot boxes were stuffed with false votes. The result of this was that elections served to entrench parties within their own regions, increased sectarianism as a political force, prevented an accurate judgment on party policy, and caused increasing strain and tension in a country already fraught with problems. The elections, then, did not help to defuse tensions or redirect policy as they often do in Western democracies; instead, they helped to fuel a crisis.

The first ever popular, direct elections in Nigeria were held in 1959, a year prior to independence, and based on these results the government was established. The North received a greater allocation of seats than other regions on the basis of population, even though one-half that population—the female population—was disfranchised by religious custom (and only received the vote in 1979). The NPC was able to win 134 of the 312 seats in the federal lower house, but within a year sufficient numbers had switched allegiances to the NPC so that the party, in an alliance with the NCNC, was able to control a majority.

For the 1964 general elections, the NPC stood in coalition with Akintola's AG faction, the NNDP, and together they took 200 seats, with the NPC taking 162 of those. The rump AG had joined in an alliance with the NCNC in the United Progressive Grand Alliance (UPGA), and together they accounted for some 100 seats. The level of violence and intimidation during this campaign led the UPGA to call a boycott of the elections, but this only occurred in the East, which held fresh elections in March 1965. The absence of what could be termed "electoral morality" was evident, and showed that, "for the political elite, power was an end in itself and not a means to the realization of some greater good for the community . . . and that any talk about the rules of the game must be irrelevant."[13]

INSTITUTIONS OF THE FIRST REPUBLIC

The parliamentary system of government which operated throughout the First Republic was a legacy of British colonialism. The British government believed that what was good for Britain was good for its colonies, and that what worked in Britain would also work in Nigeria. This proved not to be the case. We have already explained how, during the last decade of colonial rule, very strong regionalist tendencies developed in Nigeria, notably with the development of regional governments and parties, and a deep-seated distrust was displayed by ethnic groups of each other. These factors were not conducive to the maintenance of political stability, nor did they foster respect for the institutions of government at independence.[14]

The President

To be accurate, Nigeria did not become a Republic until 1963, when Dr. Nnamdi Azikiwe became its first president after having served as leader of the Senate (until 1962) and as governor-general (in 1963). For the first three years after independence, Queen Elizabeth II (of England) technically remained the country's head of state, and she was represented in Nigeria by her governor-general. Although more than a dozen Commonwealth countries still retain the Queen as head of state, Britain's former African colonies have chosen to sever these linkages and become republics.

Azikiwe became the country's first ceremonial president after independence, more out of recognition for his leadership of the nationalist movement than from any real political influence he possessed. He was the dominant spokesperson of the East, the Ibo people, and the National Convention of Nigerian Citizens (NCNC), which formed a coalition with the ruling Northern People's Congress (NPC). The NPC would certainly not have allowed Azikiwe to become president if that position had carried any real political clout. The president's role was almost purely ceremonial, patterned to some extent on the role of the Queen of England but without any of her royal prerog-

Dr. Nnamdi Azikiwe gained his reputation as a prominent leader of the nationalist movement. After Nigeria's independence in 1960, Azikiwe went on to become the country's first president (1963–1966), and was an active political leader and presidential aspirant during the Second Republic.

atives, which have been maintained over the centuries. Azikiwe was officially able to call on the largest party in the Federal House of Representatives to form a government, but he had no effective power to influence that process. In a major constitutional crisis during 1964, Azikiwe refused to accept the federal election results because of blatant malpractices that were detrimental to his own party, and thus would not call on the NPC leader, Sir Alhaji Abubakar Tafawa Balewa, to be premier. Azikiwe called on the army to support him, as did Tafawa Balewa, but in the end it was the president who was forced to back down.

In addition to these weaknesses, Azikiwe was not given authority to conduct foreign policy, even though he was nominally commander-in-chief of the armed forces. His authority also did not extend to influencing policy in federal or state houses, and he had little ability to prevent any of the conflicts afflicting the Western Region during the latter years of the First Republic.

The Prime Minister

Patterned closely on the British model, the position of prime minister, or premier, was the most important in the federal parliament, and was occupied throughout the First Republic by Tafawa Balewa. There was no direct election for the position of prime minister, but Balewa took it on the basis of his position as parliamentary leader of the federal majority party. The premier, along with ministers selected by him, had ultimate responsibility for initiation and implementation of policy; the premier also used his strength within the federal lower house to ensure that policies were approved. Ultimately, the prime minister held responsibility for both domestic and international policy, including law and order and fiscal policy, but his failure to act decisively in the political problems of the West showed that he was not always willing, or able, to use these powers. It is also worth remembering that Balewa

was only the deputy leader of the NPC and that the real power broker, Sir Alhaji Ahmadu Bello, chose to remain as Northern premier.

The Federal House of Representatives

The House of Representatives was the central forum of political debate and controversy during the First Republic, and was modeled very much upon the British House of Commons. The 312 seats were allocated on a population basis, with the North's 174 seats being the largest share. This gave the NPC control of the House, and the Action Group (AG) became the "official opposition," with Obafemi Awolowo as leader. The parliamentary system requires a toleration of opposition groups, but this was not present in Nigeria. Awolowo was considered a threat to the government, and he and 20 colleagues were imprisoned in 1962 on a spurious charge of "treason." When the NCNC broke its partnership with the NPC, there was a chance for the two southern parties to coordinate their opposition to the NPC. But the AG and NCNC remained divided, and never effectively challenged the NPC.

The House held the responsibility for approving all major legislation in the federation. This duty specifically included the budget and other financial matters, as well as aspects of foreign policy. Strict party discipline, at least within the ruling NPC, made votes and victory a certainty for the government. Indeed, during the six years that the House was in existence, the government did not lose a single vote. As in the British system, policy decisions tended to be hammered out in private before being made public on the floor of the House. The presence of ministers and assistant ministers in the House also served to strengthen party unity. The significance of the House is perhaps lessened further when one realizes that it never met for more than 30 days in any one year between 1960 and 1966. Its independent governing role was certainly circumscribed, and it became essentially a "rubber stamp" institution.

The Federal Senate

The Senate was a nonelected body containing 48 chiefs and elders, who were nominated in equal numbers by the federal and regional governments. This upper house had few if any powers of action or initiation, but attempted to serve the symbolic purpose of bringing together traditional leaders into the modern political structure. It possessed the ability to delay fiscal bills for 30 days and other bills for six months, but was unable to overturn policy. On balance, we can conclude that very little interest was taken in the Senate, because it lacked political capability to influence decision making.

Regional Houses of Assembly

Each region—North, East, and West (and Midwest after 1964)—possessed its own single assembly with members elected in districts organized according to population. Only the West's assembly was not dominated by a single local party, and it was the scene of violent political controversy and turmoil. The regional government, each with its own premier nominated by the majority party, determined policy within its own jurisdiction, much like state governments do in the United States. These roles extended to areas such as education, the police, and economic planning and fiscal directives for that region. To this extent, they were powerful institutions within their own regions, and in the South this led to clashes with the NPC-dominated federal government over issues of policy implementation. Ideally, these assemblies were considered ways to improve the internal unity and freedom of action for regions within the federation, but in practice they came to be competing units, and such diversity served to increase tensions and undermine the First Republic.

MILITARY GOVERNMENT 1966–1979

The intervention of the military clearly had a serious impact upon the political process. Po-

litical parties were banned, elections became unnecessary, civilian elites were relegated to the sidelines, and the military ruled by decree rather than by consensus. The military's claim to be both protector and cleanser of the political system was a dubious one, especially when the country was plunged into civil war in 1967 (see Feature 11.3). Following the war, however, the military did help to heal some of the wounds between the warring factions, and can reasonably claim some responsibility for maintaining Nigeria as one country. In May 1973, General Gowon established the National Youth Service Corps (NYSC) in a further effort to promote integration within Nigeria, and to assist with development schemes. Under this program, new university graduates were asked to undertake a year's "national service" away from their home areas with the hope that this service would provide a greater national awareness and orientation. Unfortunately, the military leadership itself did not lead by example, and the military-technocratic alliance responsible for running the country often accumulated personal wealth at the expense of other concerns.

Gowon had promised in 1970 that the country would revert to civilian rule in 1976. In 1974, however, this program was postponed without explanation or an alternative date offered. This decision upset many in the country, especially the powerful northern interest groups who were unhappy with the perceived southern influence around Gowon. Dissatisfaction with Gowon's handling of affairs led to his overthrow in 1975 by a group of officers, who selected Murtala Muhammed as the head of state. Murtala acted against part of the corruption in society by discharging 10,000 civil servants and 150 military officers, and he laid down a timetable to return to civilian rule by 1979. Murtala also established a National Security Organization (NSO) to maintain a network of information and communication within the country, which unfortunately was unable to prevent Murtala's assassination in 1976.

The government of Lt. Gen. Olusegun Obasanjo, Murtala's successor, recognized one

---

Feature 11.3 **The Civil War**

The civil war fought between 1967 and 1970 was one of the worst on the African continent. With more than one million people killed and many more homeless and destitute, the war severely tested the unity of the country. The aim of the Biafrans had been to set up their own independent state in southeastern Nigeria, financed by oil revenues, and their claim received significant support in West Africa and in France. The federal side could not afford to relinquish such an economically important area of the country, nor could it allow secession for fear of sparking claims by other dissatisfied ethnic groups.

The internationalization of the war, drawing in the superpowers and other European countries, was also a tragedy, but the end of the war brought an era of reconciliation that few thought possible. The painful memory of the war makes any future secession less likely, and also provides an incentive to find a viable system of government to bring the whole nation together.

---

of its greatest responsibilities to be the creation of a constitution and political process that would solve the disharmonies of the First Republic. A priority of the military government was to ensure that the political parties of the 1960s were not recreated, and that the new parties would be national in organization, membership, and outlook. The military considered applications by 19 associations, but under its strict guidelines allowed only five parties to be registered and to contest the 1979 elections. None of these parties was truly Socialist, and this reflected the military's own political orientation. It was also assumed that the military would only disengage after passing over power to a government that shared similar perceptions and interests. Although these five parties were superficially more nationalistic in composition and policy, many of the dominant personalities of the 1960s returned, and parties quickly became identified with the predecessors of the First Republic.

Institutions of Military Governments

We are not so much interested here in the actual structure of the military, but rather in the institutions that the military has established

to rule. Obviously, military rule is different from civilian rule: there is no attempt made to be "democratic," as decisions are issued by decree; there are no elections; there are no political parties; and there is expected to be less debate and criticism, as the military operates by command and obedience.[15]

When Maj. Gen. Aguiyi-Ironsi came to power after the coup d'etat of January 1966, he established a Supreme Military Council (SMC) of top officers to be the main decision-making forum. In addition, he set up a Federal Executive Council (FEC), which included the top federal permanent secretaries and acted as the bureaucratic arm of the government. Ironsi's decision to scrap federalism and institute a unitary form of government sealed his fate and led to his overthrow in July 1966. The new head of state, General Yakubu Gowon, continued to use the existing institutions, but strengthened the SMC by having it ratify decisions made by the FEC. Gowon resuscitated the federal structure, and broke up the four regions into 12 states in May 1967. In the early 1970s, following the civil war, Gowon broadened marginally the base of his government by enlisting civilians to take control of various ministries (though they were still under ultimate control by the military). This infusion of important skills—which the military lacked—did not detract from the negative aspects of Gowon's rule, and he was overthrown in 1975.

Murtala Muhammed (1975–1976) and Olusegun Obasanjo (1976–1979) refined the military institutions of government. Murtala established in 1975 a National Security Organization (NSO) to control opponents of the state, and Obasanjo had a significant impact on government by establishing a third institutional tier, the Council of State. The Council was composed of the military governors of all the states (19 after 1976) who were no longer able to sit on the SMC. This enabled a clear distinction to be drawn between state and federal governing bodies, and was the pattern adopted by military governments after the demise of civilian rule in December 1983.

THE SECOND REPUBLIC 1979–1983

The Political Parties

To prevent regional identification, each party was required by law to have its headquarters in Lagos and an office in all the 19 states of the federation. This regulation ensured some form of national orientation, if not necessarily national support. Membership of the parties was open to all Nigerians and could not be restricted, as had been the case in the First Republic. Similarly, candidates could not be selected on any regionalist, ethnic, or religious grounds, and there had to be regular internal elections for leadership positions. The 1979 Constitution provided all the necessary safeguards and provisions for the maintenance of an equitable system, but political realities strained the system badly and prompted the military's return to political life on 31 December 1983.

The ban on political activity was raised in September 1978, and the parties had nine months to prepare themselves for the elections. Parties received some funding from the government to minimize chances of corruption. Each party was given the equivalent of 7 cents per voter, one-half before and the other half after the elections. The elections were monitored and controlled by the military government working through a Federal Electoral Commission (Fedeco), and although protests were raised in some quarters, the results were generally received without reservation. In contrast, the elections held in 1983 after the first term of office were conducted under the control of the incumbent civilian administration, and were regarded by many as suspicious and influenced by electoral malpractices. Again, as in the 1960s, no competent authority existed that could redress these grievances.

A fundamental difference in the political process in 1979, however, was the presence of a total of 19 states in the federation, as the large regional units of the First Republic had been subdivided in 1967 and 1976 to assist democracy and representativeness in the political process. The old Northern Region was now broken up into 10 states, for example, and the other regions were also divided to give greater expression to minority groups. As such, the political structure had become more open, more complex, and even more unpredictable after 13 years of military rule.

The National Party of Nigeria (NPN) The NPN drew its strength and support from the states of the North, and bore some resemblance to the old NPC. Its leader, Alhaji Shehu Shagari from the Sokoto state, became president of the Second Republic, and the party came to hold a majority in the Federal House of Representatives. The party was able to secure victory throughout the North, except in Borno and Kano states, and was able to build alliances in other areas of the country. This was most evident with the selection of the vice-president, Dr. Alex Ekwueme, who was an Ibo from Anambra state in the Southeast, and the chairman of the party, Chief Akinloye, who was a Yoruba from the Southwest. The party instituted a system of "zoning" by which senior offices would be rotated among the various zones or clusters of states, thus allowing the party to maintain a national image and balance. Some commentators have suggested that this was a ploy to allow a northern elite to rule under a national guise while never losing control over the party or the federation. We will never know the answer to that question, because the military intervention occurred before the issue arose.

The NPN's outreach from its northern base to areas around the country made it the most nationally oriented of the five parties, as well as the most successful in electoral terms. Its success, however, was determined to a large extent by the personalities the party contained and not by the policies it offered. Unlike the former NPC, in which birth and social connections were of crucial significance, the NPN

contained a majority of members present on the basis of education or wealth. The party included several senior retired military leaders, as well as many of the bureaucrats who had served in the military administrations.

The party's program was bourgeois in promoting capitalist development, increasing foreign participation in the economy, and preserving the mixed economy developed under the military administration. Unfortunately for the NPN and the country as a whole, the massive oil revenues of the 1970s disappeared rapidly in the early 1980s as the oil price fell and production and revenue targets were revised downward. Prestige development projects instigated by the NPN became white elephants, and disillusionment set in in protest against such wasteful expenditure. Despite the downward economic spiral and the increased

A typical local headquarters of the National Party of Nigeria (NPN), this one located in Zaria, Kaduna State. During the Second Republic, Kaduna State became a political battleground between the NPN and the People's Redemption Party.

hardship faced by the majority, the party's representatives continued their conspicuous consumption of the nation's wealth, with billions of dollars redirected from national to personal coffers. Such corrupt practices were not the sole preserve of the NPN; other party leaders strove to make fortunes, but the NPN's was on a grander scale because of its control of the federal machinery.

The United Party of Nigeria (UPN) The UPN formed under the leadership of Obafemi Awolowo, who had kept the Action Group going as a "social" group during the military era, and was therefore assured of support from the majority of those living in the southwestern states of Ogun, Ondo, Oyo, and Lagos. Awolowo was the party's presidential candidate in 1979 and 1983, running Shagari very close in the 1979 election. The UPN's platform was more radical than that of the NPN, with free schooling, better health-care facilities, and greater assistance for low-paid labor as its priorities. The party was able to capture the assemblies of the southwestern states, but was unable in the federal elections to make inroads into other parts of the country. Personality and political differences began to eat into UPN support as certain prominent leaders switched loyalty to the NPN, and history appeared to be repeating itself. The 1983 elections showed the NPN allegedly making substantial gains over the UPN, but widespread rioting drew attention to the dubious validity of the result, and new governments had little impact at all prior to the December coup.

The Nigeria People's Party (NPP) The NPP was originally formed by Alhaji Waziri Ibrahim, a wealthy businessman from the northeastern state of Borno. He attempted to pull together a national coalition, but divisions within the party soon made this impossible. Dr. Nnamdi Azikiwe originally stated his desire to remain outside of politics as the "father of the nation," but in December 1978 he agreed to join the NPP and became its pres-

idential candidate, leaving Waziri to form a second party. Most of the NPP's support came from former NCNC members of the old Eastern Region. The fact that the vice-president in 1979, Dr. Alex Ekwueme, was himself from this region did little to sway grassroots support toward the NPN. Another Ibo leader, Chukwuemeka Ojukwu, who led the Biafran secession, was pardoned by the federal government in 1982 and returned from exile in Côte d'Ivoire to join the NPN. Even this did little to draw people away from the NPP, with which they had a strong cultural identification. Ojukwu was elected to the Federal Senate in 1983 for Anambra state, although this result was bitterly contested.

The NPP's policies differed little from other parties; they promoted vague ideas of growth and economic development. The party made few inroads into other areas of the country, and gained little from its alliance with the NPN. This alliance was broken in mid-1981, and Azikiwe and Awolowo made attempts to forge a coalition to tackle the NPN, but personality and political differences did not allow this to occur; divided, the parties had little chance of stopping the NPN.

The People's Redemption Party (PRP) The city of Kano has had a tradition of political radicalism, and the PRP's support was concentrated in that city and in neighboring Kaduna state. Formed under the leadership of Mallam ("teacher") Aminu Kano, the PRP had its roots back in NEPU. The party promoted a Socialist, progressive platform, particularly on land rights, and thus offered a threat to privilege and established Islamic interests. The NPN was threatened to some extent by the PRP and worked to undermine its position. In Kaduna state, the PRP Governor, Alhaji Balarabe Musa, was balked and eventually impeached by the NPN-dominated Assembly, while in Kano clashes were manipulated between the governor and the emir in order to pressure the PRP. The NPN eventually managed to draw the PRP into an alliance, and following the death of Aminu Kano in 1983, factionalism weakened its vitality. Despite these problems, the PRP held its ground in the 1983 elections, but was never perceived as a likely contender in other regions.

The Great Nigeria People's Party (GNPP)

The party was formed following the split in the NPP, and the "Great" was added to distinguish between the two. The GNPP was centered upon one man, Alhaji Waziri Ibrahim. Waziri was a former NPC minister in the First Republic who had then made his fortune as an arms supplier to the federal government during the civil war. Although the party was registered by the military in 1979, it had little support outside the Northeast. Dialogue between the GNPP and other opposition parties took place in the early 1980s, but the GNPP's likely role in the country was small. In the 1983 elections, the party lost much ground and seemed destined to disappear completely.

The Nigerian Advance Party (NAP)

The NAP had attempted to become a registered party in 1979, but its application was rejected by the military because the party was not nationally organized. The association, under the leadership of Mr. Tunji Braithwaite, a Lagos lawyer, set out to establish its organization efficiently, and was allowed to contest the 1983 elections as the sixth party.

The NAP offered a nonethnic, Socialist platform, and its supporters were largely young professionals and students. Although its base was mostly in the Lagos area, it tried to elicit support all over Nigeria, with little success. By failing to attract much support for its policies, and by refusing to play on ethnic sentiment, the party foundered and was unable to win an election at any level or for any candidate.

The 1979 Elections

The elections in 1979 and 1983 were fought along the lines of the American and British models, with first-past-the-post, single-member constituencies. Both sets of elections were under the control of Fedeco, but the military's presence in 1979 made sure that these elections were fairer than those in 1983. Fedeco, established in 1977, was responsible the following year for drawing up electoral registers throughout Nigeria. These were hotly disputed, with fictitious names appearing, and many Nigerians found themselves disfranchised. The total number of registered voters was initially put at 47,433,757 in March 1978, but six months later additional registration pushed the figure above 48 million. This was considered to be very high, and in some areas contained 120 percent of those eligible to vote. This also partly explains the low turnout at the elections of, on average, 33 percent—that is, based on realistic numbers of eligible voters, this percentage was probably higher. Voting age in 1979 was lowered from 21 to 18 years, and women in northern states were allowed to vote for the first time.

Elections took place over five Saturdays in July and August. The first election on 7 July was for the Senate, and subsequent elections were for the House of Representatives, state assemblies, and state governors. A two-week period was allowed before the election for president on 11 August. With five election days to organize and control, the chances of problems increased, although teething troubles with the first election, such as insufficient ballot boxes or incomplete election officials, could most likely be corrected for later elections. This electoral system, unique in Africa, attempted to simplify the process by asking the electorate to make one choice each week.

The ballot papers contained symbols of all the parties, and voters were expressly informed of which symbol to look for. These symbols included a key (to prosperity) for the PRP, a house and maize (for stability and food) for the NPN, a candle on a Nigeria map (to light the way) for the UPN, and a family for the NPP. Unfortunately, even ballot papers were open to fraud, and some appeared to have deliberate smudges over "opposition" symbols to make them unrecognizable.

The NPN emerged as the leading party in the elections, taking 38 percent of the votes for the Senate, 37 percent for the House of Representatives, and 36 percent for state assemblies. Shagari polled 5,688,857 votes in the presidential election, over half a million more than his closest rival, Obafemi Awolowo (see Table 11.4). Despite the appearance of these new parties and competing manifestos, voters still went with old allegiances: "ethnic, regional, religious, and personality-leadership parochialisms"[16] were maximized, and besides the presidential election, "in no election whatsoever did any of the parties present candidates who were not indigenous to the state in which such candidates were contesting."[17] Many of the old guard politicians of the First Republic were returned to office, although the presence of 19 states certainly provided a different political map, especially in terms of the old North.

The results of the presidential election were challenged by Obafemi Awolowo, and the appeal went from an electoral tribunal to the Supreme Court. The Constitutions called on the presidential victor to win the highest vote as well as score at least 25 percent of the vote in two-thirds of the states. The appeal centered upon the question of what was two-thirds of 19. Shagari and the NPN argued successfully that it was twelve and two-thirds states, so he only needed one-sixth of the vote in the thirteenth state. The military government clearly supported Shagari, and "Papa Awo" was again left a defeated man.

The 1983 Elections

These were the first elections to be under full civilian control in almost 20 years. The election process cost an estimated $1 billion, and involved about 1 million officials. Fedeco drew up a new electoral register of 65.3 million voters, a staggering increase of 34 percent since 1978. Manipulation of these lists had been so great in some states that increases of 100 percent had been recorded. The NPN acted in its own interests by having the electoral timetable switched to place the presidential election first. The philosophy of this was simple: get Shagari reelected, and then gain from a bandwagon effect in the subsequent elections. The NPN's manipulation seemed to be no different from that of Mrs. Thatcher in setting the date for the British general election in 1983, but many opponents in Nigeria were unhappy.

Their displeasure was increased when election results came in for the weekly elections and showed that the NPN had increased its majorities at all levels and had taken two-thirds control of the National Assembly. The loosely organized Progressive People's Alliance (UPN, NPP, and GNPP) had made little or no

Table 11.4   PRESIDENTIAL ELECTION RESULTS, 1979 AND 1983

Candidate	Party	Votes cast 1979	1979 (%)	1983 (%)
Alh, Shehu Shagari	NPN	5,688,857	33.8	47.5
Chief Obafemi Awolowo	UPN	4,916,651	29.2	31.1
Dr. Nnamdi Azikiwe	NPP	2,822,523	16.7	14.0
Mallam Aminu Kano	PRP	1,732,113	10.3	—
Alh, Hassan Yusuf	PRP	—	—	3.8
Alh, Waziri Ibrahim	GNPP	1,686,489	10.0	2.5
Mr. Tunji Braithwaite	NAP	—	—	1.1

advances in NPN territory, but the NPN appeared to make considerable gains across the South. Allegations of electoral abuse brought chaos to the Southwest, where many considered the NPN to have blatantly cheated. This frustration and protest, combined with poor governmental performance and gross corruption, persuaded the military to oust the politicians from power on 31 December 1983, just three months after Shagari had been sworn into office for his second term.

INSTITUTIONS OF THE SECOND REPUBLIC 1979–1983

After four years of consultation and intense debate, Nigerians adopted a new set of institutions for the Second Republic, modeled on the American presidential system. There had been little satisfaction with the parliamentary system of government used in the First Republic, and many believed that the adoption of a new political structure could prove to be more successful. These institutions and respective powers, combined with a redefinition of national values and mores, were enshrined in the 1979 Constitution which, although suspended after 1983, continued to form the basis of constitutional life in Nigeria until the promulgation of the 1989 Constitution.

The 1979 Constitution

The importance of any constitution lies not only in what is written, but also in how it is implemented. In Nigeria, as we have already mentioned, the 1979 Constitution appeared to be an excellent document which addressed very carefully the fundamental rights of citizens, the organization and structure of the institutions of government, and the role of the judiciary at state and federal levels. Unfortunately, the provisions of the Constitution were not fully respected by the politicians.

The Constitution took three years to draw up. In October 1975, a Constitution Drafting Committee (CDC) was established by the military government to supply an initial draft of the constitution that would provide viable institutions of government, consensual politics, and an end to violence and malpractices. This committee was composed mainly of academics, lawyers, and business persons (without a single female representative), and presented its draft in September 1976 for government consideration. A Constituent Assembly (CA) was indirectly elected by local government areas in August 1977, and the 203 members (including only one woman) began to deliberate on the draft in October 1977. These people were again mainly business and academic elites, but also included a number of old guard politicians. Following their deliberations, the military government announced a finalized version of the Constitution in October 1978. Although the government accepted virtually all of the CA's provisions, it decreed a total of 17 changes, including a decision not to allow quotas (ethnic or "federal") in armed forces' recruitment.

Symbolically, the second section of the Constitution attempted to deter any future military incursion into political life:

> Federal Republic of Nigeria shall not be governed, nor shall any person or group of persons take control of the Government of Nigeria or any part thereof, except in accordance with the provisions of this Constitution.[18]

National integration and nation building were stressed as primary political objectives; these goals were to be promoted by encouraging "intermarriage among persons from different places of origin or of different religious, ethnic, or linguistic associations or ties," and by promoting "the formation of associations that cut across ethnic, linguistic, religious or other sectional barriers." Most significantly, the aim was "that loyalty to the nation shall override sectional loyalties."[19] The Constitution also guaranteed freedom of speech, information, and association, and provided specific guidelines on the functions and duties of the respective political institutions of the Second Republic.[20]

The President

Unlike in the First Republic, where the president was a ceremonial figure, the Constitution gave executive powers to the president, similar in range to those of the president of the United States. Some observers expressed fear that it was dangerous to centralize political power in the hands of a president in this way, but the majority considered it to be worth a try, and thought that it could help to promote unity in the country. The president was directly elected by a popular vote throughout the whole country, and would hold office for a maximum of two four-year terms. No electoral college was provided; to ascertain that the president was popular nationally, that person had to win not only the highest number of votes cast, but also one-quarter of the vote in at least two-thirds of the states. Failing that, a second election was to be held within a week with voting restricted to members of the National Assembly and State Houses of Assembly, and the candidate with the highest vote would become president. This was not necessary in 1979 and 1983, because Alhaji Shehu Shagari emerged as winner of the popular ballot.

The president, who had to be a Nigerian citizen of at least 35 years of age, was officially Head of State, Chief Executive of the Federation, and Commander-in-Chief of the Armed Forces. The president could not be a member of the National Assembly, nor could he or she vote in the Assembly. However, the president was allowed under the Constitution to address both houses on fiscal and other matters of national importance. The vice-president, who was elected on the same party ticket as the president (although some Nigerians had tried unsuccessfully to have the vice-president be the runner-up in the presidential contest), was to succeed the president if the latter became incapacitated or died in office.

The president was able to select his or her own group of ministers, who were not to be members of the National Assembly. In ad-dition, he or she could select the heads of the civil service, ambassadors, members of the Federal Electoral Commission, and the Federal Public Service Commission. The president's nominations for the National Defense Council and National Security Council required Senate approval. The president was also responsible for initiating both national and international policies, and held a veto over the legislation passed by the National Assembly, although this veto could be overridden by a two-thirds vote of the Assembly. The process of impeachment against the president could be started by a petition signed by one-third of Senate members, but both a full investigation and final impeachment needed two-thirds support of both houses. This issue never arose in the short life of the Second Republic.

Shehu Shagari was the only president to serve under the 1979 Constitution. Shagari was an experienced politician and wealthy business leader, having initially founded the old Northern People's Congress in his home area in northwestern Nigeria, and then going on to hold three federal ministerial positions between 1960 and 1965. Shagari served as Federal Minister of Finance in the military era between 1971 and 1975, and was also a member of the Constituent Assembly. His government started out in 1979 with some intent on ruling fairly. His first cabinet of 42 members reflected "federal character" (although with only two women), with 23 members from the North (10 states), four members from the East (two states), eight from the West (four states), and seven from the Middle Belt (three states). Gradually, the evenhandedness of the government evaporated as it became dominated by the selfish desires and policies of the National Party of Nigeria and discredited by rampant corruption. Shagari attempted to remain aloof from the pressures and maintain some semblance of national leadership, but his failure to act decisively against the excesses taking place around him made the president equally guilty.

The National Assembly

Unlike in the First Republic, the National Assembly comprised two houses of equal importance, the Senate and the House of Representatives. The Senate contained 95 members, with five representatives from each of the 19 states, irrespective of size or population. The Senate elected its own president and vice-president to control the affairs of the chamber, and elections for the Senate were to be held every four years. Membership was restricted to Nigerians over 30 years of age. The House of Representatives was composed of 449 members whose electoral districts were based on areas of roughly equal population size. No district was allowed to cross a state's borders. Elections for the House were to take place every four years at the same time as the Senate elections, the House also elected its own speaker and deputy speaker. Membership was restricted to Nigerians over 21 years of age.

Both houses of the National Assembly were responsible for approving legislation before it could be passed on to President Shagari for his signature. Each house had equal influence in this task, and each was able to initiate legislation. Most policy decisions emanating from the president and his ministers, including fiscal matters and treaties with foreign governments, required the approval of both houses before they could become law, although on many day-to-day decisions the president was able to use his prerogatives. Senate ratification was necessary for presidential nominations to the Supreme Court, the National Defense Council, and the National Security Council.

The Assembly also possessed important influence over the process of creating new states in the federation. To begin the process, two-thirds of delegates in the National Assembly from a particular area had to approve a plan for the creation of a new state. This plan then needed two-thirds support in the State Houses of Assembly in question, as well as the support of the population of that area, expressed in a referendum. The new state then required only simple majority support in all the states in the federation, but a two-thirds majority in both the Senate and the House of Representatives. Needless to say, despite calls by residents for the creation of up to 50 new states, none was able to gain legal recognition in the short tenure of office of the Second Republic.

Despite the immense effort expended to establish the National Assembly, its operation left much to be desired. In its early days, the Assembly was based in temporary accommodation. and much was heard of problems with transport and feeding of members rather than with the task of governing. The NPN held a majority of seats in both houses (see Table 11.5) through its alliance with the Nigeria People's Party (although this was broken off in 1981), and after the 1983 elections the NPN held this majority by itself. It was never able to control a clear two-thirds majority necessary for constitutional amendments. At times debate was instructive and informed, but the Assembly did not give the leadership people wanted and needed. The failure to implement the Code of Conduct left many Senators and Representatives actively pursuing their business interests from within the Assembly. The fact that the Assembly was only in existence for just over four years also did not provide an opportunity for consolidation of traditions and conventions. The structure itself perhaps allowed for success, but the politicians thwarted it.

State Governments

Each of the 19 states of the federation possessed a governor, deputy governor, and a single House of Assembly. Elections for each assembly were based on districts of roughly equal population size, with the stipulation that there should be three times as many seats per state as in the Federal House of Representatives. These state elections were to be held during the same period as federal elections. Relations between the branches of government

Table 11.5   PARTY CONTROL OF POLITICAL INSTITUTIONS 1979–1983 – BASED ON 1979 ELECTIONS

Institutions	Total	GNPP	UPN	NPN	PRP	NPP
Senate	95	8	28	36	7	16
Percentage	100	8.4	29.5	37.9	7.3	16.9
House of Reps.	449	43	111	168	49	78
Percentage	100	9.6	24.7	37.4	10.9	17.4
State Assemblies	1347	157	333	487	144	226
Percentage	100	11.7	24.7	36.1	10.7	16.8
States controlled by Parties		Borno Gongola	Bendel Lagos Ogun Ondo Oyo	Bauchi Benue Cross River Kaduna Kwara Niger Rivers Sokoto	Kano	Anambra Imo Plateau

Source: Adapted from tables in Billy Dudley, *An Introduction to Nigerian Government and Politics* (London: Macmillan, 1982).

within the states operated similarly to those at the federal level, with corresponding powers of initiation, implementation, and impeachment. Naturally, the limits of these powers were circumscribed to areas within the state.

This constitutional structure operated fairly smoothly in the majority of states, which were dominated by a single political party, but serious divisions emerged in Kaduna state, where intense rivalries left an NPN assembly facing a People's Redemption Party governor. After a series of clashes, the assembly forced through a politically inspired impeachment of the governor, in some ways adapting the presidential system of government to the rules and norms of the former parliamentary system.

MILITARY GOVERNMENTS 1984–1992

The military's intervention was initially well received by Nigerians who had suffered severe economic hardship under the Shagari government. The military could not offer a quick end to that, but at least promised a halt to the excessive corruption and abuse of power by the NPN. All political parties were proscribed by the military, the 1979 Constitution was suspended, and political activity in the country was officially banned.

The government of Muhammadu Buhari (1984–1985) used the structures of the previous military era but allowed the NSO to run rampant, victimizing many innocent people. When General Ibrahim Babangida came to office in August 1985, he tried to distance himself from Buhari by reshaping the institutions, although some of these changes were cosmetic. He changed the name of the SMC to the Armed Forces Ruling Council (AFRC), but its 29 members (reduced to 19 members in February 1989 in preparation for civilian rule) still remained the central decision makers of the state. President Babangida continued to have the military governors of the states in a separate body, but expanded the role played by the National Council of Ministers, whose 23 members (in 1989) included four officers from the AFRC and 12 civilians, although major decisions were still ultimately the preserve of the AFRC. Babangida also reorganized the NSO in June 1986 into three bodies: (1) the Defense Intelligence Agency, to oversee defense; (2) the National Intelligence Agency, for intelligence gathering overseas; and (3) the State Security Services, for internal monitoring. In addition, Babangida established two new institutions: the National Defense and Security Council (to provide public security), and the National Defense Council (to ensure territorial integrity).

By integrating a number of civilians into government—though rarely, if ever, leading political personalities—the AFRC gained valuable expertise and presented a "softer" image of its rule to the general population. The ministers, of course, were responsible to the AFRC and not to the people, but the appearance of civilian involvement perhaps gave greater credibility to the military. Nevertheless, the absence of dialogue and the inability to force the AFRC to justify its policies make military governments unacceptable in the long term to most Nigerians.

The military introduced the War Against Indiscipline (WAI) in March 1984 in an attempt to improve national behavior and moral values with a "dose of military discipline." When this program did not have the desired effect, the government revamped WAI in July 1986 to become the National Orientation Movement (NOM). This, in turn, was superseded by the Mass Mobilization for Self-reliance and Economic Recovery (MAMSER) in 1987. All these programs stressed discipline, national consciousness, patriotism, and honesty, but the prevailing social and economic conditions in the country made these goals difficult to achieve, and the military's own example was a poor one.

Austerity and hardship for the majority has increased under military rule, although not necessarily because of it. President Babangida's government instituted far-reaching economic reforms, but these were not too successful and even less popular. The military's commitment to return to barracks in 1992 led it to organize elections for local government areas in December 1987 as the first part of this timetable. Candidates were "nonpolitical" in that they had no attachment to any party or policy. A new electoral register was drawn up in November 1987, but as in previous years the figures appeared to be hopelessly exaggerated. The total of 72 million electors was 40 percent higher than the commission's own prediction, and showed that the military was unable to prevent the customary problems of electoral malpractice.

The local government elections in December 1987 involved 13,000 candidates and proved chaotic in many areas. Results in some states were canceled and fresh elections held in March 1988. Other nonpolitical elections took place in May 1988 for members of the Constituent Assembly who were entrusted with the task of considering the Constitution, modifying it where necessary, and acting upon the recommendations of a Constitutional Review Commission which had deliberated since September 1987. The assembly representatives were elected by the local government officers, but only one day's notice of the elections and candidates was given in order to minimize the chances of electoral malpractice. One-fifth of the 567 members of this assembly were government nominees, and their report was submitted to the government in April 1989.

It is evident that the military had problems organizing the elections in 1987 and 1988, even when political parties were not involved and where expression of political views was forbidden. Such difficulties did not augur well for the politicized elections of 1991–1992, when bitter competition between the NRC and SDP would be evident.

THE THIRD REPUBLIC 1993–

The Third Republic, due to begin in January 1993, has been carefully organized by the Babangida administration. The government's White Paper, issued on 1 July 1987, followed recommendations made after exhaustive discussions and investigations by a National Political Bureau (see Table 11.6). The 17-person

Table 11.6 ORIGINAL TRANSITION PROGRAM FOR THE RETURN TO CIVILIAN RULE (1987)

	1989	1990	1991	1992
1st Quarter	Promulgation of a new constitution	State elections	Census	Federal elections
2nd Quarter	Lift on ban on political activity	State elections	Census	Federal elections
3rd Quarter	Announcement of two political parties	Convening of state legislatures	Census	Presidential elections
4th Quarter	Local government elections on party basis	Swearing in of state executives	Local government elections	Third Republic

Source: The Guardian (London), September 3, 1987. Political problems led to a delay of this program. State executives were sworn in at the end of 1991, federal elections were pushed back to mid-1992, and the final transfer is expected in January 1993.

bureau (including one woman), under the chair of Prof. J. S. Cookey, had been established in January 1986 to consider the failures of previous systems and to make recommendations on a successful political framework for the country. Its final report was filed in March 1987, after receiving some 27,000 submissions.

Almost every type of political structure was reviewed over the year. Influential commentators favored the breakup of the federation into a confederation, while others recommended the "zoning" of the country into distinct political units so that each could provide the national leaders in strict rotation. The idea of joint leadership or "diarchy" of military and civilian elites received noticeable support, even though it had originally been mooted in 1972 by Dr. Nnamdi Azikiwe. This "mixed grill" government, however, did not gain majority support, nor did the idea of "triarchy," somehow bringing traditional leaders—such as chiefs, emirs, and so on—into the institutional framework.

The July 1987 White Paper confirmed that the Third Republic was to inherit many of the institutional features of the Second Republic,[21] including an executive presidential system and two houses of the National Assembly. In deciding upon the retention of this framework, the military rejected the Cookey bureau's majority recommendation that there should be

a unicameral legislature. It also rejected the proposal that 10 percent of the seats in the Assembly should be reserved for women and labor unionists. The military did decide, however, that elected representatives should receive small allowances, rather than salaries, to increase their national awareness and responsibilities. Another major difference with the new framework is that only two political parties were to be registered by the military (and "acceptable" to it) to fight the elections. This novel feature aimed to dissipate ethnic differences by forcing new political alliances.

The ban on political activity was raised on 3 May 1989 along with the promulgation of the new constitution. Within weeks, 49 associations were vying for official registration. With only two parties to be registered, these groups were forced into potential alliances and coalitions. The National Electoral Commission (NEC) was to monitor the rigorous registration procedures: a 50,000 naira registration fee, names and photographs of all members, and a detailed account of how the parties would tackle Nigeria's social, political, and economic problems. Only 13 associations managed to file applications prior to the July 1989 deadline, and after some deliberations the NEC sent a report to the president recommending the following associations: People's Solidarity Party, Nigerian National Congress, Peoples Front of

Nigeria, Liberal Convention, Nigerian Labour Party, and the Republican Party of Nigeria.

Babangida's dislike of politicians was common knowledge, and he was quoted as saying that political parties were "natural grounds for the idle and illiterate who have over the years failed to qualify for any reputable profession."[22] It was also known that Babangida wanted to screen out radicals and those who threatened to expose the military's corruption after the civilians regained control of gov-

ernment. Nevertheless, most observers were surprised in October 1989 when Babangida refused to register any of the parties, claiming that they were residual ethnic parties from previous republics, and announced that the military would organize two new parties and prepare their manifestos. When these were released in December 1989, they followed identical frameworks, except that the Social Democratic Party (SDP) favored somewhat progressive policies, and the National Re-

Table 11.7   CLAIMED PARTY MEMBERSHIP AND LOCAL GOVERNMENT ELECTION RESULTS IN THE 21 STATES AND FEDERAL CAPITAL TERRITORY, 1990

| State | Claimed party membership, August 1990 | | Local government election results, December 1990 | | | |
| | | | N.R.C. | | S.D.P. | |
	N.R.C.	S.D.P.	Chairs	Councillors	Chairs	Councillors
Akwa Ibom	148,669	99,257	16	152	4	96
Anambra	472,140	472,862	13	261	16	286
Bauchi	243,772	141,189	18	177	2	32
Bendel	234,345	215,644	8	95	10	115
Benue	185,052	179,639	4	98	15	119
Borno	184,603	217,358	12	132	11	170
Cross River	96,088	80,624	4	60	3	52
Gongola	199,387	207,517	11	115	7	115
Imo	461,786	454,404	13	167	15	187
Kaduna	186,701	196,672	7	67	6	78
Kano	220,073	282,133	15	156	31	304
Katsina	163,400	159,336	5	72	14	125
Kwara	100,146	122,044	2	59	11	152
Lagos	274,539	285,744	2	43	9	138
Niger	111,073	98,938	6	64	3	47
Ogun	169,229	179,947	4	39	8	105
Ondo	274,870	297,302	6	85	15	164
Oyo	368,947	411,247	10	150	32	347
Plateau	205,011	210,319	4	88	10	154
Rivers	133,678	136,000	7	104	7	80
Sokoto	501,308	232,344	37	349	—	52
F.C.T., Abuja	22,002	15,535	2	29	2	16
Total	4,956,819	4,696,056	206	2,562	231	2,934

Source: Reprinted from Oyeleye Oyediran and Adigun Agbaje "Two Partyism and Democratic Transition in Nigeria," *The Journal of Modern African Studies,* 29(2), June 1991, p. 215.

Table 11.8   GUBERNATORIAL AND STATE ASSEMBLY ELECTION
RESULTS, DECEMBER 1991

| States | Governors | Party | State assemblies | |
			NRC	SDP
Abia	C.O. Onu	NRC	25	9
Abamawa	Alh. Michika	NRC	18	14
Akwa Ibom	Obong Isemin	NRC	32	16
Anambra	Dr C. Ezeife	SDP	14	18
Bauchi	Alh. Dahiru Muhammed	NRC	38	6
Benue	Rev. M. O. Adasu	SDP	14	22
Borno	Alh. Lawan	SDP	15	27
Cross River	Mr David Ebri	NRC	13	15
Delta	Chief Alex Ibru	SDP	14	22
Edo	Chief Oyegun	SDP	10	17
Enugu	Mr O. Nwodo	NRC	19	19
Imo	Chief E. Enwerem	NRC	27	15
Jigawa	Alh. Birninkudu	SDP	—	—
Kaduna	Dr D. Tafida	NRC	20	16
Kano	Alh. Kabiru Gaya	NRC	68	33
Katsina	Alh S. Barde	NRC	18	30
Kebbi	Alh A. Musa	NRC	22	10
Kogi	Alh. A. Audu	NRC	22	10
Kwara	Alh. Lafiagi	SDP	2	22
Lagos	Sir M. Otedola	NRC	4	26
Niger	Alh. Inuwa	NRC	26	12
Ogun	Chief Osoba	SDP	1	29
Ondo	Mr Olumilua	SDP	6	45
Oshun	Isiaka Adeleke	SDP	4	42
Oyo	Kolapo Ishola	SDP	13	37
Plateau	Tapgun Fidelis	SDP	11	35
Rivers	Rufus George	NRC	29	19
Sokoto	Alh. Abdulkareem	NRC	28	—
Taraba	No Election	—	—	—
Yobe	Alh. Abubakir Ibrahim	SDP	8	18

Source: *West Africa*, 23 December 1991–5 January 1992.

publican Convention (NRC) supported more conservative, laissez-faire programs. Despite some bitterness about the controlled process, politicians quickly organized to occupy these artificial party shells. The transition program was modified to hold local government elections in December 1990 (see Table 11.7), and gubernatorial elections in December 1991 (see Table 11.8), but national and presidential elections remained fixed for mid-1992.

The local government elections, held by open ballot (see Feature 11.4) in December 1990, were relatively peaceful but had a low turnout. The SDP fared marginally better than the NRC in the country as a whole, and managed to win in healthy majorities, in Kano, Kwara, Lagos, and Oyo states. The NRC, seen by many observers as the natural descendant of the NPC and NPN of the First and Second Republics respectively, won strongly in Akwa

---

Feature 11.4 **Open Ballot Elections**

Beginning in 1990, elections in Nigeria have been undertaken by open, rather than secret, ballot. This entails Nigerian voters arriving at the polling booth at a predetermined hour. In a public head count, tallies are recorded and then sent on to a central recording office. A similar electoral procedure has also been tried in Kenya.

The open ballot has proven to be controversial, as one might expect, but a questionnaire undertaken by the National Electoral Commission in 1991 found a substantial majority of voters to be in favor of it, largely because this system was less likely to be rigged. By voting out in public, everyone could see the result, unlike a secret ballot, where the very secrecy of it enabled people to falsify results.

The open ballot has been able to work in Nigeria because of a strong (neutral) military presence. People are not sure about its future after 1992, when one party will control government and the police, and many feel that because of potential intimidation of voters, Nigeria will have to revert back to a secret ballot electoral system.

Ibom, Bauchi, and Sokoto states. Political tensions began to rise in 1991 as each party strove to compromise on the allocation of senior positions among different ethnic constituencies. Both parties adopted "zoning" policies, and it appeared that for presidential candidates, the SDP would put up a "southern" candidate, and the NRC a "northerner." But the bitter divisions within the parties, and the difficulties in resolving regional and ethnic issues, were most notable in the 1991 gubernatorial primaries, when these fierce intraparty conflicts led the government to postpone the elections twice. Elections for governors and state assemblies were finally held in December 1991, and results showed a fairly even balance between the two parties. More than 40 candidates were aspiring for the 1992 presidential election, so the transition would be tense.

The military's ability to control the transition period was questionable. Four attempts in three years to draw up an accurate voter register had brought four different figures. An abortive coup attempt in April 1990 unsettled the military leadership and showed deep divisions within the ranks. The austerity and hardship under the structural adjustment program

continued to "sap" the economy and promote bitterness and anguish among the populace, especially as stories of high-level corruption multiplied. Workers' strikes increased in intensity during 1991, and religious riots combined with political tensions to provide a volatile atmosphere. The creation of nine new states in August 1991 added further impetus to the political race to control the Third Republic, and also complicated further the task of factional balancing.

JUDICIARY AND LEGAL RIGHTS

Nigeria's legal system has been heavily influenced by norms, traditions, and practices inherited from Britain, but unlike Britain, Nigeria continues to have significant numbers of judicial executions. The country's legal practitioners have retained a fairly high profile and reputation in the country even through long periods of military rule. The judiciary gained credibility during the 1979 and 1983 elections when courts used their constitutional right to amend contested election results. The Nigerian Bar Association (NBA), established as long ago as 1886, attempted to maintain its independence from political pressures by boycotting military tribunals established after the 1983 coup d'etat to try politicians suspected of corruption. Since 1985, the AFRC has at times allowed the legal process to be maintained without excessive pressure. However, the widespread use of military tribunals has come under fire for providing poor means of defense for those on trial, and the Civil Liberties Organization (CLO) of Nigeria has been hounded by the military government. In a damning report published by the CLO in March 1991, the Babangida government was criticized for "executive lawlessness" in its disrespect for court orders, for imposing retroactive legislation, and for taking numerous illegal actions.[23]

President Babangida has resorted to judicial panels to investigate matters of national importance. These panels included the Justice Uwaifo and Justice Bello Panels in 1986, to consider the issue of political detainees; the Justice Mostafa Akanbi Panel, to consider problems of student unrest in 1986; and the Justice Karibi-Whyte Commission in 1987, to consider factors surrounding the religious disturbances in the country.

The 1979 and 1989 Constitutions provided legal structures at both state and federal levels. At the individual state level, three courts were established: a State High Court, a State Customary Court of Appeal, and a State Shari'a Court. A new Federal Court of Appeal was inaugurated to handle appeals from these three sets of courts. Pressure from Islamic groups to have a Federal Shari'a Court was unsuccessful, as only northern states instituted the State Shari'a Courts. Also at the federal level was a Federal High Court and a Federal Supreme Court. The Supreme Court was given the power of constitutional review, and used it immediately in 1979 to consider the disputed presidential election result and to confirm, in a split ruling, Shehu Shagari as the victor. This power was also used in October 1981 when the Court declared the government's Revenue

Act to be null and void, but overall it was not extensively used, although it has been retained in the 1989 Constitution.

LOCAL GOVERNMENT

The structures and role of local governments have varied considerably since independence in 1960. During the First Republic, each region had its own system of local government. In the East and West, local governments were loosely organized and relatively weak, whereas in the North they remained strong and influential, particularly when used by emirs as their channel of rule. In the early 1970s, local government structures began to change as the western states instituted a council-manager system of administration and the northern states strove to weaken the powers of traditional rulers. In 1976, the military government introduced the Local Government Edicts, which forced all local governments in Nigeria to adopt similar structural and operating procedures. Decisions of all local governments were now to be based on majority voting, and all governments were to be single-tiered, secular authorities. These changes helped to make local governments the natural third level of government in the country after the federal and state levels.

The trends of weakening the role of traditional rulers and increasing the efficiency of these local governments continued in the 1980s. The number of local governments increased during the Second Republic, but the military after 1984 cut back the number to 301. The situation was dramatically altered in May 1989, when 148 new local government areas were created, bringing the total to 449. This action was taken to increase the responsiveness of local governments to the needs of the people. More local government areas were created in August 1991 as a result of the creation of 9 new states, bringing the total to 589 local government areas. Although their powers are often undermined by state governments, local governments remain a primary level of participatory democracy, and it is only at the ward level that party membership is organized in the Third Republic. In 1978, 1988, and 1990, local government areas provided the initial elections and political candidates as the first step on the road back from military to civilian rule.

INTEREST GROUPS

The distinction between interest groups and political parties is blurred within the Nigerian context, both because of the strong sectional interests, which parties have promoted, and because parties have been banned for 22 of the 32 years since independence. During military rule, politicians became involved with various interest groups to maintain their contacts and political alliances. Most parties of the Second Republic developed from "social" organizations that were active prior to the raising of the ban on political activity. These groups generally comprised business leaders, high-ranking administrators, professionals, and former politicians. But these are by no means the only type of interest group, and it is useful to consider the most important ones here.

Business Groups

One of the most influential interest groups over the last decade has been the so-called Kaduna mafia. Kaduna is the former capital of the old Northern Region, and remains an important locus of northern Islamic influence in the country. Members of this loosely organized group are prominent business people, retired senior military officers, and others of equivalent stature. Nobody outside of the "mafia" really knows who belongs to this group, or whether it even exists, but it is a group about whom many have commented in recent years. These influential people are believed to have been inspirational in planning the December 1983 coup by giving back-

ing to the coup leader, Muhammadu Buhari, and by wanting to push aside Shehu Shagari, whose economic mismanagement (despite his "northernness") was damaging the infrastructure and business environment of the country. The "mafia" received a setback when General Babangida came to office in 1985, but still casts a shadow over governmental affairs, and will continue to do so in the coming years.

There are, naturally, other groups of business people, including retired senior military officers, throughout the country who have been able to influence state and federal policy. Given the lack of constraints on political leaders seeking economic fortunes while in office, the business community in general, and contractors in particular, have had a considerable impact upon government business by ensuring policies to suit their interests. Although not uncommon elsewhere, the open and blatant business group involvement in the Nigerian political process has been, and will continue to be, of major significance, as witnessed in the transition to the Third Republic.

Labor Unions

In contrast to the successful interaction of business and political elites, the Nigeria Laor Congress (NLC) has had little success in influencing the policies of civilian or military governments, or in promoting a more socialistic orientation in the country. Divisive internal battles within the labor movement caused the Obasanjo government to intervene and restructure the labor movement in 1978 into a total of 42 unions, all under the umbrella of the NLC. This has not prevented further internal squabbles, and in February 1988 the NLC Executive Council was dissolved by the government. Membership declined considerably in the late 1980s because economic hardship led to unemployment and a growing desperation to cling to a job, whether unionized or not.

The NLC has aligned itself with radical political forces in the past, but has been unsuccessful in attempting to make class issues the basis of political conflict, rather than ethnicity. The unions organized their only general strike in 1964, when 800,000 workers gained higher wages and the action by unions was considered a "strike against politicians" to protest the chaotic condition of the country. Strikes were made illegal by the military government after 1966, but numerous strikes nevertheless occurred in the 1970s. These strikes provided the stimulus for private and public salaries to rise by 30 percent after the Abedo Commission reported in 1971, and then helped provide even larger raises (up to 100 percent for the lowest paid) following the Udoji Commission in 1975.

Generally speaking, however, unions have not been a dominant force within society. As Douglas Rimmer concluded, labor "has been a fitfully active force, lacking sustained political influence and usually inexpert and ineffective in negotiation."[24] The NLC has vehemently protested the economic reforms implemented since 1986, but with little success. NLC leaders were arrested in June 1986, at the end of 1987, and in the middle of 1988, and President Babangida has regarded the NLC with suspicion, but with little concern. The NLC Executive was dismissed by the government in February 1988, and a new structure was organized. The NLC actively supported the creation of a true Socialist party and the development of a Socialist ideology for the country, but was warned repeatedly by the military to stay out of any political affiliations.

Media

The media in Nigeria is undoubtedly the most active and independent in sub-Saharan Africa. There are more than 20 daily newspapers in circulation, as well as weekly magazines, and several television and radio stations. The media has retained its outspokenness since independence, despite periodic threats and intimidation by various governments. The media has not always been impartial, however, as many newspapers or state-controlled radio stations have favored a political party or regional interest, but there has remained a willingness to take firm positions on issues of national importance, particularly corruption.

The present military government, like its predecessors, has attempted to control the media's coverage of events. Under Decree 19, it is an offense to comment "negatively" on the government's handling of the political transition program, although discussion and positive suggestions are still acceptable. Despite active protests by the National Union of Journalists (which has been in existence since 1955), jail sentences have been handed out over the last three years to journalists who have gone ahead and published articles embarrassing to the government. One prominent journalist, Dele Giwa, was assassinated in mysterious circumstances in November 1986. Giwa had written several scathing articles on government policy, and fell victim to a parcel bomb which appeared to have arrived in a package carrying the government seal. There was intense speculation that the government's security forces were responsible, but no firm evidence was uncovered.

Educated Nigerians are generally avid readers, and will read several newspapers daily. In this way, the media has some role in influencing opinions of the populace, but there is less to show that it has a role in influencing government decision making. The two leading dailies, the *New Nigerian* and *Daily Times*, are both government owned, and although this limits the level of criticism, it is perhaps surprising the extent to which these papers (and others) maintain their independence.

Book authors have also been major critics of Nigerian development, and their attacks have been much more difficult to contain. There are many excellent Nigerian authors helping to promote political development in this way, most notably Chinua Achebe and Wole Soyinka, the winner of the 1986 Nobel Prize for Literature.

Religious Groups

It is easier to comment that religious groups have an impact upon the political process than to pinpoint the groups involved and the policies influenced. During the First Republic, the Sultan of Sokoto and the Islamic establishment had obvious influence on policy through the sultan's brother, Alhaji Ahmadu Bello, the Sardauna of Sokoto, the Northern Premier, and the leader of the NPC. This influence was less evident in the Second Republic, but Shehu Shagari was from Sokoto state and had close connections to the sultan. An indication of the declining influence of the Islamic establishment has been noticed in recent years, as emissaries have had to be dispatched to Lagos to pressure the military government to modify policies. This was perhaps not the case with Buhari, who was more sympathetic to these pressures and who was himself considered at one time to be an outside candidate to succeed the sultan.

The overall purpose of this lobbying pressure is to maintain the influence and cohesion of Islam, particularly in the North (and especially since the North is no longer a monolithic bloc), to keep the Shari'a system of courts and justice, and to attempt to maintain Nigeria's foreign policy on pro-Islamic-Arab lines. Nigeria's decision to become a member of the Organization of Islamic Conference (OIC) in 1986 was considered to be a concession by Babangida to the powerful northern lobby, both religious and business. At a more popular, domestic level, the Islamic League maintains the loyalty of many Muslims and is outspoken against any policy that threatens the status of Muslims. In recent years, pressure has been exerted over issues such as state creation, education, and family planning. Fundamentalism has been of obvious concern since 1980, with the challenge of its ideology and with the riots that have taken place, but its impact on policy has been minimal.

The Christian Association of Nigeria (CAN) helps to bring together the opinions of a diverse range of Christian churches and groups, and exerts influence on their behalf. The CAN stands to protect Christian interests against what it considers to be aggressive and expansionist Islam. The organization is also working to maintain the secular disposition of the country and prevent the attachment of Nigeria to Islamic organizations overseas, such as the OIC and the Islamic Bank. Over the last two or three years, the CAN has been at its most active, and for both Islamic and Christian groups the intensity of lobbying increased during the transition of 1991–1992. The death of more than 500 people in religious riots in April and October 1991, and subsequent deaths in riots in May 1992, reminded everyone of the political potency of religion.

Universities

Universities provide the base for intellectual challenge to the status quo. By 1986, there were 17 federal universities, 6 state universities, and some 60 polytechnics and colleges in the country. Although individual academics such as Yusufu Bala Usman[25] and Patrick Wilmot (expelled from Nigeria in March 1988) have been renowned for their outspoken attacks on political leaders, the Academic Staff Union of Nigerian Universities (ASUU) has organized numerous actions in the past to attempt to influence a more radical appraisal of Nigerian development, and these actions contributed to a government ban on ASUU in July 1988 (removed in 1990). The students themselves have also been highly critical of government policy, notably the SAP and the increasing hardship faced by students on university campuses, and the military and paramilitary police have been involved in many campus clashes with students; the most recent skirmishes in 1990, 1991, and 1992 led to many student deaths. For all these challenges, little political headway has really been gained, and the universities have been unable to link up with labor unions to make their views and actions more effective.

Key Terms

Action Group (AG)
Armed Forces Ruling Council (AFRC)
ceremonial president
civilian elite
Constituent Assembly
diarchy
electoral systems
executive president
extractive politics
Federal Electoral Commission (Fedeco)
federalism
Kaduna mafia
military elite
National Assembly
National Convention of Nigerian Citizens (NCNC)
National Party of Nigeria (NPN)
Nigeria Labor Congress (NLC)
Nigeria People's Party (NPP)
Northern People's Congress (NPC)
parliamentary and presidential systems
recivilianization
religious groups
Republics; First, Second, and Third
sectarianism
Supreme Military Council (SMC)
triarchy
zoning

Suggestions for Further Reading

The Constitution of the Federal Republic of Nigeria, 1989 (Lagos: Federal Ministry of Information, 1989).

Diamond, Larry. *Class, Ethnicity and Democracy in Nigeria. The Failure of the First Republic* (Syracuse: Syracuse University Press, 1988).

Dudley, Billy. *An Introduction to Nigerian Government and Politics* (London: Macmillan, 1982).

Falola, Toyin, and Julius Ihonvbere. *The Rise and Fall of Nigeria's Second Republic* (London: Zed, 1985).

Kumo, Suleiman, and Abubakar Aliyu, eds. *Issues in the Nigerian Draft Constitution* (Zaria: Baraka Press, 1978).

Odetola, Theophilius O. *Military Politics in Nigeria: Economic Development and Political Stability* (New Brunswick: Transaction, 1978).

Olorunsola, Victor A. *Soldiers and Power: The Development Performance of the Nigerian Military Regime* (Stanford: Hoover Institution Press, 1977).

Oyediran, Oyeleye, ed. *Nigerian Government and Politics under Military Rule 1966–1979* (London: Macmillan, 1979).

Oyediran, Oyeleye, ed. *The Nigerian 1979 Elections* (London: Macmillan, 1981).

Panter-Brick, Keith, ed. *Soldiers and Oil: The Political Transformation of Nigeria* (London: Frank Cass, 1978).

Post, K. W. J., and Michael Vickers. *Structure and Conflict in Nigeria, 1960–1966* (London: Heinemann, 1973).

C. Public Policy

Nigeria's economy is dominated by oil. The export of this single commodity accounts for some 90 percent of the country's total foreign exchange earnings. Given oil's critical position in the economy, the commodity has also had a strong influence in shaping the country's foreign policy, especially during the oil boom years of the late 1970s, when Nigeria flexed its nascent muscles on the world stage. The relative demise of the oil market in the 1980s has added serious economic difficulties, and has limited Nigeria's willingness and ability to strike a bolder profile in world politics. The failure to diversify economic output into high-tech, capital-intensive industry has stifled Nigeria's aspirations to move into the ranks of the Newly Industrializing Countries (NICs). Major debates have ensued, both on the suitable national objectives of economic planning and development, and on the goals Nigeria should be pursuing in its foreign policy.

THE ECONOMY

Nigeria's traditional pattern of agriculture prior to colonial occupation had been one of subsistence farming, but British intervention radically altered the nature of production. Cash crop agriculture was developed, with crops grown not for domestic consumption but for export overseas. After the early part of this century, Nigeria's agriculture had been forged into the classic colonial, export-oriented structure, with groundnuts produced in the North, cocoa in the Southwest, and palm oil in the Southeast. The British built a rail system to freight these commodities (and minerals) to the ports, but not to provide a means of passenger transportation. This rail framework is still used today, although it is in urgent need of repair and modernization.

At independence in 1960, these three commodities together contributed the majority of Nigeria's export earnings. The major trading partner was Britain, which retained a controlling hand in many sectors of the Nigerian economy. Minimal "horizontal" trade was developed with neighboring African states, which had also been geared to cash crop production and "vertical" integration with the European colonial powers. During the First Republic, little in the way of structural economic change occurred. Political independence may well have been won, but Nigeria's economic profile remained unchanged; British involvement, investment, and areas of control were still being maintained. The impact of European and North American economic forces on the economy altered marginally in the 1970s, but many political economists argue that it remains of great significance today in Nigeria, especially with the privatization of state enterprises, the increasing emphasis on foreign investment, and the strong role of the International Monetary Fund (IMF) and the World Bank.[26]

Oil Boom

Through geological good fortune, oil has been the single most important factor in Nigeria's economic development over the last 20 years, although it has provided both positive and negative effects. Oil had been produced in the early 1960s, but the growth of the industry was hampered by the civil war. Once the war was over in 1970, oil production increased rapidly. From a level around the time of independence of 5000 barrels a day (b/d), production had risen to 1.4 million b/d in 1970, and reached a peak of 2.3 million b/d in 1979. Throughout the 1970s, oil revenues increased by 30 percent a year, and in 1980 reached a peak of $24.94 billion. By early 1989, production had fallen to 1.2 million b/d, and estimated income for 1989 was only $4.22 billion, but the slight boom during the Gulf crisis of 1990–1991 helped income quite substantially.

The government's expenditure levels had risen dramatically in the 1970s as a result of the financial bonanza. By 1980, the government was spending more money in one day than its predecessor in 1960 had spent in two months. The tremendous financial gains from oil led, in contrast, to rapid stagnation of other sectors, because Nigerians believed that oil could provide everything. By the mid-1970s, the contribution to exports of the staple agricultural commodities of groundnuts, cocoa, and palm oil had fallen to zero. Oil ruled.

Nigeria joined the Organization of Petroleum Exporting Countries (OPEC) in 1971 to promote its economic (and political) objectives, and also established the Nigeria National Oil Corporation (NNOC) to monitor oil production. The NNOC was merged with the Ministry of Petroleum in 1977 to form the Nigeria National Petroleum Corporation (NNPC), which has controlled the oil sector to the present. The government introduced in 1972 an Indigenization Decree, which prohibited foreigners from certain economic sectors and limited participation to 40 percent in others. The major overseas oil corporations, such as Shell, Gulf, Mobil, and Texaco-Chevron were all limited to a 40 percent stake in the oil sector. Superficially, this appeared to shift economic control into Nigerian hands, but overseas interests remained extremely influential. In addition, leading Nigerian entrepreneurs—both inside and outside government—did not operate with the national interest at heart, and many simply set out to decimate national wealth. These "lootocrats," as they have been termed, operated within a system of "pirate capitalism" that effectively wasted a golden opportunity to provide real economic development for the country.[27]

Admittedly, the "petro-naira" life-style and economy brought dramatic changes to the country, as money in the 1970s appeared to be no problem. Lavish prestige-enhancing projects were undertaken, such as the construction of a new federal capital at Abuja (on the model of Brasilia and Canberra). A worldwide black arts festival (FESTAC) was hosted in Lagos in 1977 at great expense, and it was held up as a symbol of Nigeria's growing status in the world. By the end of the 1970s, President Shehu Shagari was actively threatening to use the "oil weapon" against Western countries to promote foreign policy goals, and indeed used it in 1979 in nationalizing British Petroleum to pressure the British government to grant Zimbabwe its independence. During this era, there was "skewed development" or "growth without development" in the country; money was often diverted to unnecessary projects, and pockets, while deserving schemes, primarily agricultural ones, suffered badly. Urban migration gathered pace while investment in rural areas dwindled. Overall, efforts to improve the living conditions of the majority of Nigerians were minimal. The opportunities offered by oil were squandered by

General Ibrahim Babangida, seen here with Prince Charles of Britain, has imposed harsh structural adjustment programs to rescue the Nigerian economy. The programs, however, have been unsuccessful, and have created severe social and political tensions.

successive governments, and when the oil glut emerged and prices collapsed in the early 1980s, the economy reeled.

Oil Bust: Rethinking Development Priorities

The rapid shrinkage of the economy in the 1980s was a painful process to watch. In 1990, Nigeria's national earnings were only 20 percent of the 1980 figure. Industries, which had grown in the 1970s, were generally dependent upon imported spare parts, so they ground to a halt as the supplies were cut. Many development projects remained unfinished as funds ran out. The population's desire for fancy Western imported foodstuffs had to be curbed, but

Nigeria found that its agricultural production had declined to such a level that the country could not feed itself. The rural areas, already depressed, suffered even greater hardship. Formerly in a position of handing out loans to African neighbors, Nigeria now had to look around for loans itself. As with the majority of third world states, Nigeria's debt situation became alarming, and in 1992 stood at $32 billion, the second highest in Africa after Egypt.

Development implies that there should be a reduction in both the absolute level of poverty and the economic inequalities between segments of the population. During the oil boom years, the government appeared to lose sight of this fact, as growth became synonymous with development. Some significant developments were obviously recorded, most notably the provision of education in the country. At the primary school level (grades 1 through 6), the number of students increased from 2.9 million in 1960 to 11.5 million in 1980. Universities also expanded in number from six in 1962 to 16 by 1980. But even some of this progress was politically motivated, and the quality of educational services did not necessarily improve. And in the early 1990s, with over 2 million students leaving school and hitting the saturated job market annually, the underlying economic problems and weaknesses remain just as obvious.

Per capital income figures have declined in recent years, as have other economic indicators. These problems are accentuated by the rapid growth of the population at over 3 percent a year, which means that the total population figure will probably double in the next 20 to 25 years. Half of the national population is below 16 years of age, and the average fertility rate is six children per female. The seriousness of this problem is such that in February 1988 a new national policy for population control was introduced. The plan hoped to introduce sex education in secondary schools, and to lower the average number of children per mother from six to four. In the Islamic North, however, men generally have four wives, and this scheme would still allow 16 children per family. In response to this, the policy emphasis in 1989 shifted to "one man: four children." But this plan faced considerable opposition from various groups, and from Nigerian men in general.

It is important not to be overcritical and to stress that Nigeria made some significant developmental gains in a number of sectors, although not enough to bring the country close to standards in the first world: the lowering of infant mortality levels; the improvement of health care and educational facilities; the raising of life expectancy figures; the improvement of transport infrastructure; all these and others were examples of beneficial development. Un-

fortunately, the country has struggled to maintain them in the austere conditions of structural adjustment in the 1980s and early 1990s. In 1991, Nigeria was ranked by the United Nations as the 24th poorest country in the world on the human development index, based on infant mortality, literacy levels, and real GDP per capita. As Tables 1.2 and 1.4 in the introductory chapter show, Nigeria is the poorest of all the countries compared in this volume.

Since 1985, a structural adjustment program (SAP) has been implemented to attempt to restructure and diversify the economy. This program includes the privatization of many state-owned corporations—including the NNPC—as well as the massive devaluation of the naira (the naira fell in value from roughly $1 to 10 cents) and the restructuring of the agricultural sector. Although these have proven to be marginally beneficial in an economic sense, their social impact on the population has been devastating. Inequality has deepened, as has general poverty and hardship.

The International Monetary Fund and World Bank, as well as numerous Western donors, have supported the government's commitment to SAP, resulting in increasing bitterness among the Nigerian populace. Such serious economic problems complicate the political process by generating tensions and anxieties that can be exploited. These problems clearly affected the political transition program, which in itself has been a serious economic drain—elections cost hundreds of millions of dollars to run. The transfer of power to civilians was delayed from 1990 to 1992, and then to early 1993, partly to allow the economy more time to be repaired and to become buoyant, but many economists concluded correctly that 1993 was still too early to see any significant change.

Perennial Problems

Several issues have continued to trouble Nigerian governments, two of which require brief discussion here: the question of revenue allocation from the federal center to the states, and the problems generated by the repeated failures of census exercises.

Revenue allocation has been a divisive question in the past; it set states clashing against one another over their rights and needs and caused conflict between federal and state governments over respective allocations. The main issue at stake is how the income generated from economic production around the country is collected by the federal government and then how, and on what basis, it is redistributed to the states. During the 1950s, there were several changes in revenue allocations given by the colonial administration to the regions. Initially, the North pressed for allocations based on population size, the West on derivation of revenue, and the East on need. As their respective economic profiles changed, and as oil exploration grew in the East, the Western Region based its claims on uniformity, whereas the East began to favor derivation.

After independence the debate on revenue allocation intensified, but successive governments tended to favor derivation of income as a primary factor in assessing federal allocations. In 1970, a Distributable Pool was inaugurated. Using this pool, the federal government shared out payments to states, with half of the amount paid equally to all the states, and the other half paid on the basis of state population size. In 1975, this pool system was modified to receive 80 percent of revenue allocated to states, with the remaining 20 percent paid directly to the state of derivation. Income tax, now under federal control, was also paid back directly to the states. The civilian government of the Second Republic established the Okigbo Commission in 1980—the eighth such commission since 1946 to consider the allocation issue.

The new revenue act, initiated in 1982, decreased the influence of derivation (the NPN-controlled states were essentially nonproducers of oil) and stressed relative need and population size in allocations to states. The act consolidated the strength of the federal government, which kept 60 percent of all revenue generated nationally, with the remaining 30 percent and 10 percent allocated to states and local governments, respectively. Military governments since 1984 have maintained similar policies, although the Babangida administration changed these figures to 50 percent for the federal government, 35 percent to the states, and 15 percent to local governments, and at the same time allowed local governments more control over their spending.

A second basic economic problem centers upon the difficulty of accurate development planning when there is no firm evidence of the exact size or location of the population. Political considerations of electoral district size and revenue allocation have hampered attempts to undertake a valid census, and the country still operates from population estimates based on the (also controversial) 1963 census figures. These problems have added to the hazardous task of drawing up national development plans, which have been of little relevance in any case during the 1980s, when rapidly declining revenues have made a mockery of estimates and plans. It is difficult to be confident that an accurate head count in the country is possible, especially because the military's numerous attempts to register voters accurately since 1987 have been failures. President Babangida's decision to hold a census in December 1991 despite the volatile political environment made the census task appear to be even more hazardous (see Feature 11.5). History appears to stand against Babangida's attempt at an accurate census, and until revenue allocation and political representation can be divorced from considerations of population size, success in this task may well elude future leaders.

FOREIGN POLICY

The 1979 Constitution contained only one section that related directly to the country's foreign policy objectives:

Feature 11.5 **The 1991–1992 Census**

The inability of Nigeria to count accurately its population indicates a relative immaturity in its polity, and presents great difficulties in drawing up development plans to adequately meet the needs of the people. The fact that numbers influence both electoral district and revenue allocations has led to incessant intrigue between rival factions, making accurate head counts impossible.

Since 1863, there have been 12 attempts at a census, but none has brought results to inspire confidence. Since independence, three censuses have been attempted with mixed success. The 1991–1992 census was attempted in the most difficult of circumstances—in the middle of a fierce electoral contest—and so hopes were not high for its success. Organization was a logistical nightmare. In order to minimize corrupt activities, millions of dollars were spent on computers and transport, and the country was divided into 250,000 enumeration areas, with close to 600,000 enumerators employed. Precensus trials were undertaken in selected areas to smooth out administrative difficulties. The census itself was taken over a three-day period in December 1991, but results were not to be published until later in 1992. Perhaps then there will be a more accurate sense of how large Africa's most populous state actually is—or perhaps not.

The State shall promote African Unity, as well as total political, economic, social and cultural liberation of Africa and all other forms of international cooperation conducive to the consolidation of universal peace and mutual respect and friendship among all peoples and States, and shall combat racial discrimination in all its manifestations.[28]

Although a somewhat vague statement, it stresses that relations with African states, particularly in western and southern Africa, are considered to be priority areas of policy. Nigeria does have extensive diplomatic contacts with Western countries, however, and works through these both to bring improved trade relations for itself and to call on the West to continue to pressure the minority regime in South Africa. On the basis of its economic and demographic strength, Nigeria has always considered itself to be one of the leading countries in Africa, and its foreign policy

has been geared—in recent years, at least—to reflect this perception. Although there are numerous linkages with many African countries, particularly the neighboring countries in West Africa, the level of trade and general economic contacts with them remains low; relations can thus appear to lack a degree of depth and substance.

During the 1960s, the governing elite was content to play a quiet, conservative role in African and world affairs, and during the civil war (1967–1970) policy was geared toward securing a military victory against the secessionists. With the advent of the oil boom in the 1970s, Nigeria pursued an increasingly forceful and active role in world politics, spurred on by its oil wealth, and quickly found "friends" in the West, but this did not automatically lead to any greater successes. Such an active role was in marked contrast to Nigeria's foreign policy orientation immediately after independence.

While accepting a degree of generalization, it is possible and constructive to consider foreign policy through three decades to illuminate the fluctuations of style, emphasis, and content.

THE 1960s

From the time of independence in 1960 until the outbreak of civil war in 1967, Nigeria's foreign policy emphasized caution and a low profile, with a strong reliance placed on close relations with the West, and Britain in particular. Indeed, so cautious and quiet were Nigerian diplomats that it was at times difficult to know where the government stood on certain issues. This orientation was influenced by the conservative nature of the governing elite, with its strong Islamic roots, but it was also a consciously pursued policy that sought to distance the country from the provocative radicalism of its Anglophone rival in the region, Ghana. The Ghanaian leader, Kwame Nkrumah, advocated a single continental government for Africa, but Nigeria and the majority of African states resisted this and would only support closer international cooperation. These moderate states were successful in 1963 in having the new continental association, the Organization of African Unity (OAU), established within a loose, intergovernmental framework. Ghana's rhetoric, though not its actual policy, was also hard on the "neocolonial" links with Western countries, whereas Nigeria seemed content to continue with these economic linkages. Such conservatism in Nigeria also led to the refusal (upon British advice) to allow the Soviet Union to establish an embassy in the country until 1962.

It would be wrong to see Nigerian policy in a completely negative and passive manner, as it contained forceful stands on a number of issues. Its relations with Britain were strained in 1961 after its successful pressure to force South Africa out of the Commonwealth. In the following year, the Anglo-Nigerian De-

fense Pact, which gave Britain military training rights in Nigeria, was abrogated by the federal government following student protests and active condemnation of this quasi-colonial arrangement by Obafemi Awolowo and the Action Group. This protest contributed to Awolowo's later treason trial (following alleged subversive links with Ghana) and his subsequent imprisonment, but it did little to affect the dominant economic linkages that Britain retained with Nigeria. British military instructors also continued to train Nigerian troops. Nigeria's almost instinctive suspicion of French motivations in Francophone West Africa—all of its neighbors are former French colonies and remain French-speaking today—were intensified in 1961 following France's unscrupulous action in holding atomic tests in the southern desert of its then colonial possession, Algeria. This action outraged Nigerians and led to a break in diplomatic relations with France which lasted for several years.

The civil war, which broke out in mid-1967, forced a reconsideration of both domestic and foreign policy. Western countries, hampered by their own internal pressure groups sympathetic to Biafra's suffering (and oil reserves), were reluctant to sell the large quantities of military supplies requested by the federal government. The French were openly pro-Biafra, hoping to see Nigeria split into weaker territorial units. Consequently, in its time of greatest need, the government perceived it had little option but to turn to the Eastern bloc. The Soviet Union and other Eastern European countries provided considerable assistance to the federal forces, and this military program to Nigeria remained significant during the 1980s. Today, Britain, the United States, and France are the major suppliers, as assistance from Russia and Eastern Europe has diminished.

Following the end of the civil war in 1970, Nigerian policy makers gradually returned to a more sympathetic Western orientation, although this had been undermined to some extent by the experience of the war. The burgeoning economic strength emanating from oil revenues also provided fresh impetus for a more vigorous and independent foreign policy outlook.

THE 1970s

The 1970s witnessed an increasingly active and committed role for Nigeria in African and world affairs, and this was evident at several levels. Within the African continent, Nigerian diplomats were instrumental in bringing together the majority of countries to negotiate for better terms of trade with their dominant partners in the European Community. Nigeria's economic size, strength, and potential—and the country's willingness to use these in the bargaining process—enabled these third world countries, as well as others in the Caribbean and Pacific Ocean areas, to be more influential in the negotiations; thus, favorable trade arrangements for these states were agreed upon at the Lomé Convention in 1975, as well as in subsequent agreements in 1980, 1985, and 1990.

Nigeria was also taking the lead in organizing West African states in an economic grouping to assist the growth of intraregional trade and to increase industrial and development opportunities through cooperation within the region. These states formed the Economic Community of West African States (ECOWAS) in 1975, a 16-member organization, of which Nigeria is by far the strongest economically. Unfortunately, there have been problems in increasing the level of cooperation among the poorer states of the region, and Nigeria did not help matters by its expulsion of "aliens"—some 2 million unwanted West Africans in 1983 and another 750,000 in 1985. These events, combined with the smaller states' suspicions of the disproportionately stronger Nigeria, as well as residual linguistic and cultural divisions within the community, have slowed the pace of progress, but have not necessarily weakened the organization's viability.

Following the removal of General Yakubu Gowon from office in 1975, Nigerian foreign policy took on a sharper focus and was more precise in its orientation. The watershed event occurred in 1975 when the government decisively backed the Popular Movement for the Liberation of Angola (MPLA), a Communist movement struggling to gain control of Angola, despite the opposition of many African states and Western powers, particularly the United States. Nigerian support for the liberation movements in Mozambique, Namibia, Zimbabwe, and South Africa also flourished at this time, and the "oil weapon"—the threat to cut supplies to Western countries to persuade them to support liberation movements—was at the forefront of policy. This was apparently used by President Shehu Shagari in 1979 when, in an attempt to pressure Britain to allow Zimbabwe its independence, British Petroleum's operations in Nigeria were nationalized (significantly, BP was allowed back into the market in 1991). Although Zimbabwe quickly gained its independence, Nigeria's action was not as crucial as some believed, and the country's dependence upon oil revenues made it very unlikely that supplies would have been cut to major consumers.

South Africa proved to be a much tougher nut to crack, and Nigeria's attempts to pressure that country both directly and indirectly brought little success. Nigeria was a principal agitator behind the boycotts of the Olympic Games in 1976 and the Commonwealth Games in 1978 (and again in 1986), to maintain the international isolation of the South African regime. But it lacked the capability to bring dramatic results in South Africa, and partly out of frustration Nigerian policy makers and public talked openly of acquiring nuclear weapons—both to provide stiffer support of black African claims in South Africa, and to increase Nigeria's own status and bargaining position over this and other issues. Given the fact that South Africa is 80 percent black, it appeared unlikely that

Nigeria could credibly plan to use nuclear weapons against the country, as its aim was to protect rather than destroy the African majority. Nigeria's economic problems added to this strategic puzzle. With the rapid evolution of South Africa toward a postapartheid society, the nuclear option has been shelved, but the prospect of pursuing "peaceful" nuclear energy remains a topic of conversation.[29]

THE 1980s

Nigeria's rapid rise in economic fortunes and concomitant external influence in the 1970s proved transitory, and was quickly countered by the country's subsequent demise in the 1980s. The economic strength, which provided the basis for a surge of activity overseas, was replaced by a host of problems that diminished Nigeria's external interventions and muted its antagonism toward Western powers. The government maintained a high commitment to solving the problems of southern Africa, and played a leading role in the United Nations and the Commonwealth, but the AFRC was increasingly preoccupied with trying to solve national debt problems and seeking international financial assistance and investment. With an increased dependence upon Western countries such as Britain and the United States, and faced by a global oil glut, it was impossible for Nigeria to talk of the oil weapon or to pursue provocative policies toward the West, as it had done in the 1970s. Nigeria remained a leading mobilizer in Africa, however, even though its level of aid was lower than in previous years.[30]

The Soviet Union maintained cordial relations and still sent military advisors to Nigeria, and was expected to complete a major iron and steel complex at Ajaokuta in 1992. Nigeria's military leaders, however, believed that greater benefits could accrue from seeking aid and investment from the West, although they remained critical of the West's manipulation of the international economic system. Their policies in no way resembled the docile, pro-Western approach of the 1960s. Relations with France improved significantly after the mid-1980s, as both countries' agreed on the importance of preventing the expansion of Libyan interests in Chad (and further afield), and political and military cooperation greatly increased. The French were anxious to maintain their friendly contacts and position in this large Anglophone market, which remained France's most important trading partner in Africa. Soon the growing strength of French and West German interests in Nigeria threatened the position of the traditional dominant trading partner, Britain. Antipathy toward Britain in general, and Prime Minister Margaret Thatcher in particular, over British support for South Africa caused a stormy relationship, but Thatcher's visits to Nigeria in January 1988 and January 1989 seemed sufficient to secure Britain's position as Nigeria's largest supplier of goods.

Nigeria's relations with the United States have similarly ebbed and flowed, reaching their greatest heights in the late 1970s, when President Jimmy Carter paid the only visit to the country ever made by a U.S. president. This was as much an indication of the style and preferences of Carter's foreign policy as of the economic strength of Nigeria, which was then the United States' second largest supplier of oil. The subsequent economic downturn in Nigeria, combined with President Ronald Reagan's downplaying of regional arenas and reemphasis of global politics and neocontainment, relegated the African "giant" to a lesser role.

THE EARLY 1990s

The early 1990s have been a period of mixed fortunes for Nigeria. On the positive side, the Gulf War boosted, at least temporarily, oil revenues and gave some relief to the beleaguered economy. The rise in the country's OPEC oil quota to 1.85 million barrels a day in June 1991 gave encouragement that the windfall could be maintained through 1992.

Feature 11.6 **Nigeria and ECOWAS**

The West African region has traditionally received the highest priority in Nigerian foreign policy. Surrounded by French-speaking countries, Nigeria has had uneasy relations with them from time to time, and partly because of this has sought to bring the region closer together within the Economic Community of West African States (ECOWAS). Founded in 1975 following diplomatic work by Nigeria and Togo, ECOWAS has developed some cooperative economic linkages, but has not brought the region together as hoped. Nigeria dominates West Africa in terms of its economic and military strength, but as yet has not developed large-scale trade relations within the region, although smuggling and unofficial trade continue to be high.

Economic hardship facing all the ECOWAS countries has led them to promote national rather than regional solutions, and cooperation between members seems even more difficult than before. Success of ECOWAS is integral to the wider plans for a continentwide African Economic Community, which is planned to develop in stages until complete integration and an African common market is achieved in 2025—a goal that appears to be unattainable at this time.

Nigeria's hosting in 1991 of both the annual Organization of African Unity summit and the ECOWAS summit reinforced Nigerian perceptions of the country as the "center" of Africa (see Feature 11.6). Babangida's position as chair of the OAU for 1991–1992, combined with Chief Emeka Anyaoku's promotion to the position of secretary-general of the Commonwealth in 1991, enhanced this perception, and U. S. Vice-president Dan Quayle's visit to Nigeria in mid-1991, and his copious praise for the democratization process, helped to bolster Nigeria's international status. Nigeria's leadership of the ECOWAS peacekeeping force in Liberia (Ecomog), and its strong role in helping to maintain peace in Sierra Leone in 1991, showed that the country continued to be the dominant force in the West African region.

On the negative side, however, a number of problems, both old and new, afflicted foreign policy. Despite the miniature oil boom, the economy remained in dire straits, with negligible improvement in diversification. The national debt of $32 billion was a continual drain on the economy, and the turmoil of the transition program proved to be an equally draining political issue. But other serious fears developed because of events in Europe and the Soviet Union. The integration of the European Community market in 1992, and the vast economic opportunities opening up for Western business in the "new" markets of Eastern Europe and a newly configurated Commonwealth of Independent States (Soviet Union) appeared to leave Nigeria very much on the sidelines for potential investment and trade from overseas. The post-Cold War new world order gave little or no importance to sub-Saharan Africa, except perhaps for a postapartheid South Africa, which threatened Nigeria in both economic and political terms as a potential future "champion" of Africa.

CONCLUSION

Nigeria has experienced dramatic changes in its political, social, and economic life since independence was gained from Britain in October 1960. Although it is correct to conclude that instability is a constant theme underpinning Nigerian politics, it is perhaps more useful to perceive this as a result of the transition, via experimentation, from a country dominated by a colonial power to one searching for a system of government best suited to its needs and those of its people. The long periods of military rule, then, should not necessarily be seen in a totally negative light, but more as a product of this trial-and-error experimentation. Babangida's government could possibly prove to be one of the more positive and productive eras if a stable and legitimate political system is maintained by the civilian government after 1992. The key question is whether the "newbreed" politicians are more nationalistic, more honest, and less corrupt than previous political classes, improvements that allow the Third Republic to survive and work in order to provide the basis for future stability.

Against this political backcloth, an agenda of crucial social and economic issues also has to be resolved, both in terms of minimizing inequalities and providing the basic human needs of the majority of Nigerians, and of restructuring the economy to put the country on a more secure footing for the rest of the decade. Given the current economic insecurity combined with the volatile period of political transition, these next few years appear to be even more potentially troubling to Nigeria than anything faced in the recent past.

Key Terms

Anglophone
cash crops
census
devaluation
development
Economic Community of West African States (ECOWAS)
Francophone
human development index

Indigenization Decree
national debt
nuclear power
Organization of Petroleum Exporting Countries (OPEC)
population growth
privatization
revenue allocation
rural-urban migration
structural adjustment program (SAP)

Suggestions for Further Reading

Aluko, Olajide. *Essays in Nigerian Foreign Policy* (London: Allen and Unwin, 1981).

Gambari, I. A. *Party Politics and Foreign Policy: Nigeria under the First Republic* (Zaria: Ahmadu Bello University Press, 1980).

Gambari, I. A. *Theory and Reality in Foreign Policy Making. Nigeria After the Second Republic* (Atlantic Highlands: Humanities Press International, 1989).

Ihonvbere, Julius O., and Timothy M. Shaw. *Towards a Political Economy of Nigeria. Petroleum and Politics at the (Semi-) Periphery* (Aldershot: Avebury, 1988).

Okolo, Julius Emeka, and Stephen Wright, eds. *West African Regional Cooperation and Development* (Boulder: Westview Press, 1990).

Olaloku, F. A., et al. *Structure of the Nigerian Economy* (London: Macmillan, 1979).

Shaw, Timothy M., and Olajide Aluko, eds. *Nigerian Foreign Policy: Alternative Perceptions and Projections* (London: Macmillan, 1983).

Shepard, Robert B. *Nigeria, Africa and the United States. From Kennedy to Reagan* (Bloomington: Indiana University Press, 1991).

Stevens, Christopher. *The Political Economy of Nigeria* (London: Economist Publications, 1984).

Wayas, Joseph. *Nigeria's Leadership Role in Africa* (London: Macmillan, 1979).

Williams, Gavin, ed. *Nigeria: Economy and Society* (London: Rex Collings, 1976).

Zartman, I. William, ed. *The Political Economy of Nigeria* (New York: Praeger, 1983).

A. Notes

1. For books that provide a general introduction to African government and politics, see Richard Hodder-Williams, *An Introduction to the Politics of Tropical Africa* (London: Allen and Unwin, 1984); William Tordoff, *Government and Politics in Africa* (London: Macmillan, 1984); and Naomi Chazan, Robert Mortimer, John Ravenhill, and Donald Rothchild, *Politics and Society in Contemporary Africa* (Boulder: Lynne Rienner, 1988).
2. For a detailed discussion of Nigerian history, see John Hatch, *Nigeria. A History* (London: Secker and Warburg, 1971).
3. See Robert Heussler, *The British in Northern Nigeria* (London: Oxford University Press, 1968).
4. The National "Convention" was also known as the National "Congress." The NCNC was also known before independence as the National Council of Nigeria and the Cameroons.
5. *Government's Views and Comments on the Findings and Recommendations of the Political Bureau* (Abuja: Mamser, undated), Section 53.

B. Notes

6. Frantz Fanon, *The Wretched of the Earth* (London: MacGibbon and Kee, 1965).
7. Billy Dudley, *An Introduction to Nigerian Government and Politics* (London: Macmillan, 1982), pp. 62–63.
8. Gavin Williams and Terisa Turner, "Nigeria," in John Dunn, ed., *West African States: Failure and Promise* (Cambridge: Cambridge University Press, 1978), p. 133.
9. Quoted in Dudley, *Nigerian Government and Politics*, p. 225.
10. See William Gutteridge, *Military Regimes in Africa* (London: Methuen, 1975); and Morris Janowitz, *Civil-Military Relations—Regional Perspectives* (Beverly Hills: Sage, 1981).
11. For a discussion of the military in this period, see N.J. Miners, *The Nigerian Army 1956–66* (London: Methuen, 1971); and Robin Luckham, *The Nigerian Military: A Sociological Analysis of Authority and Revolt 1960–61* (London: Cambridge University Press, 1971).
12. Stephen Wright, "State-Consolidation and Social Integration in Nigeria: The Military's Search for the Elusive," in Henry Dietz and Jerold Elkin, eds., *Ethnicity, Integration and the Military* (Boulder: Westview Press, 1991).
13. Dudley, *Nigerian Government and Politics*, p. 70.
14. For excellent surveys of the First Republic, see K. W. J. Post and Michael Vickers, *Structure and Conflict in Nigeria 1960–1966* (London: Heinemann, 1973); and Larry Diamond, *Class, Ethnicity and Democracy in Nigeria. The Failure of the First Republic* (Syracuse: Syracuse University Press, 1988).
15. A comprehensive survey of the military between 1966 and 1979 is contained in Oyeleye Oyediran, ed., *Nigerian Government and Politics under Military Rule 1966–1979* (London: Macmillan, 1979).
16. Ladun Anise, "Political Parties and Election Manifestos," in Oyeleye Oyediran, ed., *The Nigerian 1979 Elections* (London: Macmillan, 1981), p. 89.
17. Dudley, *Nigerian Government and Politics*, p. 223.
18. *The Constitution of the Federal Republic of Nigeria, 1979* (Lagos: Federal Ministry of Information, 1979), Part 1, Section 1(2).
19. Ibid., Section 15.
20. For an excellent discussion of the institutions of the Second Republic, see Dudley, *Nigerian Government and Politics*.
21. *Government's Views and Comments on the Findings and Recommendations of the Political Bureau* (Abuja: Mamser, undated).
22. Quoted in *West Africa*, 7–13 August 1989, p. 1282.
23. Civil Liberties Organization of Nigeria, *Executive Lawlessness in the Babangida Regime* (Lagos, 1991).
24. Anthony Kirk-Greene and Douglas Rimmer, *Nigeria since 1970: A Political and Economic Outline* (London: Hodder and Stoughton, 1981), p. 106.

25. Yusufu Bala Usman, *For the Liberation of Nigeria* (London: New Beacon Books, 1979).

C. Notes

26. For a discussion of issues in the Nigerian economy, see Kirk-Greene and Rimmer, *Nigeria since 1970;* Gavin Williams, ed., *Nigeria: Economy and Society* (London: Rex Collings, 1976); and Julius O. Ihonvbere and Timothy M. Shaw, *Towards a Political Economy of Nigeria* (Aldershot: Avebury, 1988).
27. Sayre P. Schatz, "Pirate Capitalism and the Inert Economy of Nigeria," *Journal of Modern African Studies* 22, no. 1 (1984), pp. 45–57.
28. *The Constitution of the Federal Republic of Nigeria, 1979,* Section 19.
29. Julius Emeka Okolo, "Nuclearization of Nigeria," *Comparative Strategy* 5, no. 2 (1985), pp. 135–157; also see Oye Ogunbadejo, "Africa's Nuclear Capability," *Journal of Modern African Studies* 22, no. 1 (1984), pp. 19–43.
30. Ibrahim A. Gambari, *Theory and Reality in Foreign Policy Making. Nigeria After the Second Republic* (Atlantic Highlands, Humanities Press, 1989).

CHAPTER 12

Conclusion

FOR STUDENTS OF COMPARATIVE POLITICS AND GOVERNMENT: THE LARGER QUESTIONS ON THE AGENDA OF HUMANITY

The preceding chapters introduce students to a number of major foreign powers in different parts of the world and thus to the history, cultures, and politics of much of humanity. Students will soon realize there is no royal road to knowledge or an easy shortcut to the understanding of other countries. Such understanding requires long and careful study. But the student must avoid the peril of being overwhelmed by details and facts, important though they are, of foreign systems and must not lose sight of the larger questions with which this study is concerned. Two major themes that the student should keep in mind are the politics and problems of modernization, and the reconciliation of power and freedom.

In all of the countries presented in this book there has been an inexorable, if uneven, march away from traditionalism and toward "modernity." In Europe the traditionalism with which we begin is the feudal society that existed up to the late eighteenth century, elements of which continued to exist through the nineteenth century and even up to the present. Feudal society was undermined by complex developments. The technology of warfare, especially the invention of gunpowder, deprived the feudal aristocracy of its military dominance; increased trade and commerce brought about a massive expansion of the middle classes, who could not be fitted easily into the two-way relationship between lords and serfs; and the cultural climate throughout Europe was transformed by the coming of a scientific revolution. In an age of experimentation and scientific advance, the essential notions of feudalism—particularly that basing the right to rule on heredity—began to crumble. Whether one believes that science, technology, and industry represent progress or degradation is a separate question; the French Revolution and the industrial revolution were major facts of life that condemned feudal regimes and led to the creation of new political systems—the substance of our study.

In China and India, the traditional societies that preceded the creation of the present political systems were even less developed than the European feudal societies. By "less developed" we do not imply that there was an inferior civilization or culture in Asia (demonstrably false), but merely that the scientific, technological, and political movements that characterize twentieth-century societies were delayed in Asia. One measure of the distance between Europe and Asia was the relative ease with which Europeans were able to conquer and colonize the more traditional peoples of the world; and one indicator of the modernization of Asia was the ability of formerly subject peoples to overthrow European rule.

Our country studies reveal the march from the feudal to the modern condition in Britain, France, Germany, and Russia, and from the traditional to the modern in Japan, Mexico, Nigeria, China, and India. Modern political study is largely an attempt to understand why and how this march took place, why peoples have chosen different political systems to attain their objectives, and what price is paid for development as well as for stagnation.

At every stage of the modernizing process, all peoples confront the challenge of reconciling power and freedom. Power is necessary in order to orchestrate the activities of millions of individuals, to avoid anarchy, and to enable a people to achieve their collective goals. But the coercive state that is needed for defense, domestic tranquility, and the general welfare may also deprive people of the fruits of their labor, their freedom, and their very lives. This is the permanent dilemma of all government—whether in primitive, feudal, or industrial societies. Is it possible to reconcile power and freedom, and under what condition? It is not enough merely to speculate in the abstract or to dream up ideal solutions. We must review the historical development of the major societies to be able to convert speculation into theory and theory into testable propositions. After reading this volume it will be up to you, the reader and student, to make your own contribution to the understanding of the central problems on the agenda of humanity.

PHOTO CREDITS

Unless otherwise acknowledged, all photographs are the property of Scott, Foresman. Abbreviations indicate position of photos (R) right, (L) left.

Chapter 2

Pages 43, 44, and 69: AP/Wide World; page 74: Simon Townsley; page 82: AP/Wide World; page 92: Reuters/UPI/Bettmann.

Chapter 3

Page 107: J. Lagenvin/Sygma; page 138 (L): AP/Wide World; page 138 (R): Reunion Photo/Vidot/SIPA-Press; page 149: Fourmy/Rea/Picture Group.

Chapter 4

Page 177 (all): German Information Center; page 195: Regis Bossu/Sygma; pages 216, 244, and 246: German Information Center.

Chapter 5

Page 263: AP/Wide World; page 267: The Bettmann Archive; page 286: Koichi Sakamoto Oshihara/SIPA-Press; page 296: AP/Wide World.

Chapter 6

Page 325: R. Gaillarde/Gamma-Liaison; page 336: Jacques Witt/SIPA-Press.

Chapter 7

Page 355: Novosti/SOVFOTO; page 384: AP/Wide World; page 387: Lee Malis/Picture Group; page 397: Edward Igor/SIPA-Press; page 401: Novosti/SOVFOTO.

Chapter 8

Page 417: Charlie Cole/SIPA-Press; page 419: Rosenblum/Picture Group; page 448: AP/Wide World; page 468: Chip Hires/Gamma-Liaison.

Chapter 9

Page 499: Stefan Andrew-Ellis/Picture Group; page 502: Tom Haley/SIPA-Press; page 514: Monkmeyer Press Photo Service; page 521: AP/Wide World.

Chapter 10

Pages 532, 535, 541, and 551: Courtesy of Jan Knippers Black.

Chapter 11

Pages 586 and 602: AP/Wide World; page 607: Campbell/Sygma; page 627: T. Graham/Sygma.

Index

Note: t following the page number indicates a table.